Use these study tools to your advantage and explore the world outside of your classroom.

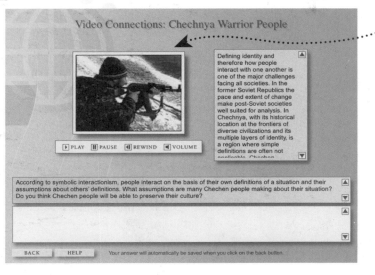

Video Connections

Great video for every chapter from around the world that connects sociology to real-world topics. Explore other cultures or consider problems in our own country as you view these videos and answer study questions related to the video.

Flashcards

All terms from the textbook are available for review in our innovative flashcard feature. Discard terms as you learn them, study from term or definition, or hear the more difficult terms pronounced.

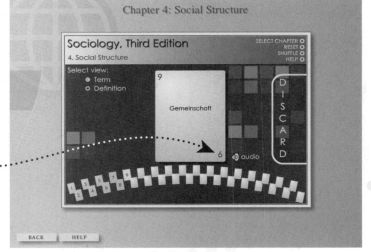

Diversity Data Animations

Every Diversity Data graph in the textbook becomes interactive on the CD-ROM. Rollover graphics allow students to focus on the variables included in these graphs that pull their data from the General Social Survey.

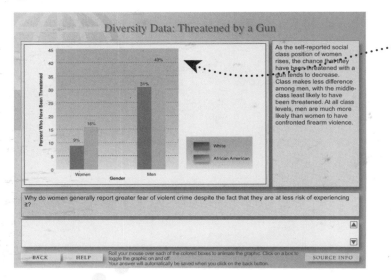

SOCIOLOGY

THIRD EDITION

LINDA L. LINDSEY

MARYVILLE UNIVERSITY OF ST. LOUIS

STEPHEN BEACH

KENTUCKY WESLEYAN COLLEGE

PEARSON
Prentice
Hall

Upper Saddle River, New Jersey 07458

Library of Congress Cataloging-in-Publication Data

Lindsey, Linda L.
    Sociology / Linda L. Lindsey, Stephen Beach.—3rd ed.
      p. cm.
    Includes bibliographical references and index.
    ISBN 0-13-111156-6
      1. Sociology.   I. Beach, Stephen.   II. Title

HM585.L56 2004
301—dc21   200256414

AVP, Publisher: Nancy Roberts
Executive editor: Christopher DeJohn
Developmental editor: Karen Trost
Editor in chief of development: Rochelle Diogenes
VP/Director of production and manufacturing:
    Barbara Kittle
Executive managing editor: Ann Marie McCarthy
Production liaison: Fran Russello
Editorial/production supervision: Bruce Hobart,
    Pine Tree Composition
Buyer: Mary Ann Gloriande
Prepress and manufacturing manager: Nick Sklitsis
Line art manager: Guy Ruggiero
Cover and interior border images: © DigitalVision Ltd,
    Royalty Free.
Creative design director: Leslie Osher

Designer: Anne DeMaranis
Electronic illustrations: Mirella Signoretto
Director of Marketing: Beth Mejia
Editorial assistant: Veronica D'Amico
Interior image specialist: Beth Brenzel
Manager, rights and permissions: Zina Arabia
Director, image resource center: Melinda Reo
Photo researcher: Julie Tesser
Image permission coordinator: Charles Morris
Text permission researcher: Lisa Black
Marketing manager: Amy Speckman
Marketing assistant: Adam Laitman
Media editor: Kate Ramunda
Media production manager: Michael Henry
Media project manager: Carol Abolafia

This book was set in 10/12 Janson Text by Pine Tree Composition
and was printed and bound by Von Hoffman Press, Inc.
The cover was printed by The Lehigh Press, Inc.

In memoriam—Marie Haug, 1914–2001

Linda L. Lindsey

To Corky, Paul, Joann, and Paula the Kansas City crew.

Stephen Beach

ISBN 0-13-111156-6

Pearson Education LTD., London
Pearson Education Australia PTY, Limited, Sydney
Pearson Education Singapore, Pte. Ltd
Pearson Education North Asia Ltd, Hong Kong
Pearson Education Canada, Ltd., Toronto
Pearson Educación de Mexico, S.A. de C.V.
Pearson Education—Japan, Tokyo
Pearson Education Malaysia, Pte. Ltd
Pearson Education, Upper Saddle River, New Jersey

BRIEF CONTENTS

CONTENTS

 **iNTERSECTIONS**   392

BOX FEATURES

GLOBAL CONNECTIONS

SOCIOLOGY OF EVERYDAY LIFE

DIVERSITY IN FOCUS

THEN AND NOW

PREFACE

Sociology is all about connections. The social groups in which we live our lives—families, friends, communities, and whole societies—connect us to one another in numerous and profound ways. We are also connected to others by the new information technologies, especially the Internet, currently transforming the globe, as well as by events such as the terrorist attacks of September 11, 2001 that held our world together in our collective grief. At the same time, our membership in these groups creates diversity. Sociology helps us explore and celebrate the many ways we are different from one another as well as our similarities and connections. We are diverse because we are female or male, African American or Native American, rich or poor, young or old, gay or straight. We are also diverse because we are Catholic or Muslim, urban or rural, and born in the developed or the developing world. Diversity is what's happening globally as well as in the United States. Both groups and individuals are more diverse yet more strongly connected to one another than at any other time in human history.

The third edition of *Sociology* emphasizes this blend of diversity and interconnectedness by stressing the **intersections of critical social variables, especially race, class, and gender.** To understand group life we must understand how people occupy these and other statuses simultaneously and how they intersect to form our social identities.

It also emphasizes the **intersection of sociological theory and application** as it reinforces that all application is *informed* by theory. Whether you will be using sociology throughout your life or only through this semester, this book will show how the key theoretical points will inform your life travel. Another point being drawn by the book is **the intersection of the student and the discipline** as you will always find examples and writing that are timely and relevant.

Thus the major goal of our text is to take students on a sociological journey through the United States and across the globe that demonstrates the threads of diversity and connectedness as intersections in their own lives. The authors hope that you find the trip both enjoyable and thought-provoking.

TEXT FEATURES

Students become excited about sociology through the introductory course. We have developed a text that forges a partnership between professors who teach the course and their students, who are its ultimate beneficiaries. Through its distinctive approach to the field, its readability and its relevance to student's lives, the third edition of *Sociology* assists professors in developing the sociological imagination in their students by encouraging them to see all dimensions of sociology. Material is presented in ways that allow students to become active learners and help professors translate the sociological perspective to the classroom.

In telling sociology's story to students, each author brings over 20 years of teaching the introductory sociology course to a variety of students, in large and small classes, and at a variety of institutions. The text, therefore, is grounded in teaching. The following text features demonstrate this foundation.

NEW FEATURES *Sociology, Third Edition,* updates data in all content areas and reflects the most important trends currently affecting society.

- **NEW—Intersections features** delve into the impact of diversity on a wide range of issues by offering students CHIP data exercises at 5 points throughout the textbook. Easily tied to the Website, this innovative feature illustrates the impact of race, class, gender, and age on various GSS questions.
- **NEW—September 11th** coverage is integrated throughout the textbook to demonstrate its profound impact on virtually all social institutions. Sociological analysis of this extraordinary event is found in a re-organized chapter on the Political Economy as well as an expansion of the chapters on Culture, Religion, and Social Change with discussions related to global terrorism, social coping, religious fundamentalism and countermodernization.
- **NEW—Sociology of Everyday Life features** demonstrate how the topics and events of everyday life come alive with new meaning when viewed from a sociological perspective, and offer students another bridge between sociological theory and its application to the lives they live.
- **NEW—Diversity in Focus features** highlight the already strong emphasis on diversity found throughout the book.
- **NEW—ContentSelect™ feature** ends each chapter with search terms provided to students to make easier use of the new Research Navigator™ site.

- **NEW—Census 2000 Updates**—text is completely updated with the data and analysis from the last full Census as well as the Census Briefs through 2002.
- **NEW—United Nations and World Bank Updates**—Data sets from 2001–2002 provide the most current material on global health, economic, and demographic issues provided from 2001.

THEORETICAL APPLICATIONS Theory is the core of sociology. The major sociological perspectives are introduced in Chapter 1 and are applied throughout the text. This edition reflects an expanded discussion of the feminist theoretical perspective and includes it throughout the text to extend coverage and explanations of diversity. Most chapters feature separate theory sections integrated with many research examples. Theoretical perspectives are applied repeatedly throughout the text. This approach helps students make connections between theory and their own lives, as reflected in the text's discussion of human sexuality (Chapter 7) and deviant behavior (Chapter 8). This text is thus both student friendly and sociologically rigorous.

LIFE CONNECTIONS Focusing on diversity, all chapters have a "Life Connections" section highlighting the relevance of the sociological material to a student's life. This material was carefully chosen to reflect the latest trends in the various social institutions that will help college students see their place in our society. Topics include American socialization through family, peers, and media; how gender, race, and class affect socialization (Chapters 5, 11, and 12); college life as an exploration of sexuality (Chapter 7); the identity of the offenders and the victims of crime in our society (Chapter 9); considering who goes to college (Chapter 16); and the training of social movement activists (Chapter 23).

SOCIETY CONNECTIONS Students are shown the relevance of the sociological perspective by seeing sociological theory connect with real, everyday social issues, as found in the "Society Connections" sections in all chapters. Issues such as sexual harassment (Chapter 6), welfare reform (Chapter 10), the continuing crisis in health care (Chapter 19), and smart growth and development in cities (Chapter 22) are discussed. These sections remind students that they are connected to one another through social groups— whether members of the groups or not—and that groups often clash when they have different visions of diversity and social change.

EMERGING INSTITUTIONS Social change is transforming the globe. *Sociology, Third Edition,* highlights important trends that are engines for change through the creation of new social institutions. Chapter 18 shows government and the economy converging into a new and powerful social institution, the political economy. In Chapter 20, we witness the evolution of new institutions based on sports and media that serve leisure needs. Social change is also occurring on a social psychological level; examples include how girls and boys are socialized differently (Chapter 5) and how children interact with peers from the other gender (Chapter 6).

FOCUS ON THE DEVELOPING WORLD The spotlight of global interdependence is now on the developing world. This text offers current information on social change and development derived from a variety of sources, including the World Bank, the United Nations, and non-governmental organizations throughout the world. This material provides insights into a host of issues, such as why crime rates vary cross-culturally (Chapter 9), how women are affected by economic development programs (Chapter 13), how population growth and urbanization affect the environment (Chapter 22), and why some nations choose to actively resist modernization (Chapter 24).

TEACHING TOOLS

Sociology, Third Edition, offers a variety of innovative teaching tools located throughout the text to help students see the relevance of course material to their own lives.

BOXED FEATURES Every chapter includes features that provide in-depth views of relevant topics based on recent research. These features end with critical thinking questions that serve as springboards for class discussion. There are five types of features in this edition.

- *Diversity in Focus* features provide data and issues relevant to diversity issues in the United States. Examples include: "A Generation Behind Bars," "Modern Slavery," "The Debate over Reparations," "Getting Off Welfare."
- *Sociology of Everyday Life* features show how sociological knowledge can be applied to a variety of settings, including the workplace. Examples include: "What Can I Do with a Degree in Sociology?," "Men's Images in the Media," and "Magic and Religion in America."
- *Then and Now* features highlight historical facts to show students connections between social change and modern life. For example, the effect of time on our living patterns is discussed in "African Americans Move Back South," and class issues are brought up in "Lifestyles of the Robber Barons." Other features that college students will

find especially interesting are "Changing Views on Capital Punishment" and "Women's Basketball: Before and After Title IX."

- *Global Connections* features offer comparative perspectives on important issues that may affect us differently depending on our culture, such as euthanasia, "Planning for Death in the Netherlands"; and the pressure to achieve, "Examination Hell in Japan." Global Connections boxes also allow students to use other cultures as mirrors to discover what they take for granted in their own cultures. Examples include genocide, "The Structural Roots of Genocide in Rwanda"; minorities in other cultures, "Minorities in Japan"; and polygamy, "The Second Wives of Hong Kong."

- **Diversity Data.** All chapters include graphs illustrating current data from the National Opinion Research Center (NORC) General Social Survey. These graphs are strategically placed to complement and extend chapter material, as well to illustrate for students the intersections within our society. Each graph is summarized and includes critical thinking questions allowing students to explore various sociological interpretations of the data. The diversity data feature emphasizes the ways in which race, class, and gender affect a person's attitudes. Graphs also show the interactive effects of multiple types of diversity.

- **Internet Connections.** In every chapter, students are offered creative Internet-based exercises placed to coincide with chapter content. The Internet offers an amazing array of sociological material that both student and professor will find exciting.

- **Key Terms.** Key terms are highlighted in each chapter, reviewed in other chapters, and defined in a glossary at the end of the book. The book also introduces a number of newer concepts and theories that are emerging in the sociological literature, such as end-point fallacy, classism, non-governmental organizations, gender schema theory, and rational choice theory.

- **Critical Thinking Questions.** Found at the end of each chapter and in all features, these thought-provoking questions move beyond description and allow students to apply their sociological imaginations in a variety of ways. For example, students may be asked to demonstrate how the same research can be explained by different theories. These questions can be easily adapted as the basis for class discussion and debating points for an entire chapter.

SUPPLEMENTS

The ancillary materials that accompany *Sociology, Third Edition*, have been carefully created to enhance the topics being discussed. Please contact your school's Prentice Hall representative for more information or to order copies for your classroom use upon adoption.

FOR THE INSTRUCTOR

INSTRUCTOR'S RESOURCE MANUAL For each chapter in the text, this resource provides a detailed outline, list of objectives, discussion questions, and additional activities.

TEST ITEM FILE This carefully prepared resource, available in both print and computerized form, includes 2,400 questions—100 per chapter—in multiple choice, true/false, and essay formats. The answers to all questions are page-referenced to the text. Prentice Hall Test Manager is a computerized test generator designed to allow the creation of personalized exams. It is available in a dual-platform format that works in Windows and Macintosh formats.

PRENTICE HALL FILM AND VIDEO GUIDE: INTRODUCTORY SOCIOLOGY, SIXTH EDITION This helpful guide describes films and videos appropriate for classroom viewing for each of the chapters in the text (more than 200 suggestions in all). The Guide also provides summaries, discussion questions, and rental sources for each film and video.

PRENTICE HALL COLOR TRANSPARENCIES: INTRODUCTORY SOCIOLOGY, SERIES VII Full color illustrations, charts, other visual materials, including all of the Diversity Data graphs, from the text as well as outside sources have been selected to make up this useful in-class tool.

PRENTICE HALL INSTRUCTOR'S GUIDE TO TRANSPARENCIES, SERIES VII This guide offers suggestions for using each transparency effectively in the classroom.

PRENTICE HALL INTRODUCTORY SOCIOLOGY POWERPOINT SLIDES These PowerPoint slides combine graphics and text in a colorful format to help convey sociological principles in a new and exciting way. Created in PowerPoint, an easy-to-use widely available software program, this set contains over 300 content slides keyed to each chapter in the text.

ABCNEWS Prentice Hall and ABC News are working together to bring you the best and most comprehensive video ancillaries available for your introductory course. Selected video segments from award-winning ABC News programs such as *Nightline, ABC World News Tonight*, and *20/20* accompany topics featured in each chapter. In addition, an instructor's guide to the videos includes a synopsis of video and discussion questions to help students focus on how concepts and theories apply to real-life situations.

> Volume I: Social Stratification I (0-13-466228-8)
> Volume II: Marriage/Families I (0-13-209537-8)
> Volume III: Race/Ethnic Relations (0-13-458506-2)
> Volume IV: Criminology (0-13-375163-5)
> Volume V: Social Problems I (0-13-437823-7)
> Volume VI: Intro to Sociology I (0-13-095066-1)
> Volume VII: Intro to Sociology II (0-13-095060-2)
> Volume VIII: Intro to Sociology III (0-13-095773-9)
> Volume IX: Social Problems II (0-13-095774-7)
> Volume X: Marriage/Families II (0-13-095775-5)
> Volume XI: Social Stratification II (0-13-021134-6)
> Volume XII: Institutions (0-13-021133-8)
> Volume XIII: Introductory Sociology IV
>   (0-13-018507-8)
> Volume XIV: Introductory Sociology V
>   (0-13-018509-4)

MEDIA SUPPLEMENTS

COMPANION WEBSITE™ In tandem with the text, students and professors can take full advantage of the World Wide Web to enrich the learning process in sociology. Features of the Website include chapter objectives, multiple-choice and true/false quizzes, flash cards, interactive CHIP exercises, as well as hundreds of links to interesting material and information from other sites on the Web that can reinforce and enhance the content of each chapter. The address is www.prenhall.com/lindsey and the site is free and open to all users of *Sociology, Third Edition.*

DISTANCE LEARNING SOLUTIONS Prentice Hall is committed to providing our leading content to the growing number of courses being delivered over the Internet by developing relationships with the leading platforms—Blackboard™ and Web CT™, as well as CourseCompass, Prentice Hall's own easy-to-use course management system powered by Blackboard™. Please visit our technology solutions Website at http://www.prenhall.com/demo for more information or contact your local Prentice Hall representative.

A PRENTICE HALL GUIDE TO EVALUATING ONLINE RESOURCES: SOCIOLOGY This short guide encourages students to be critical consumers of online resources. It provides students with a strong, basic understanding of what can be trusted and what cannot when researching on the Internet. This supplementary book is free to students when packaged with *Sociology, Third Edition.*

RESEARCH NAVIGATOR™ The goal of Research Navigator™ is to help students understand the steps in the research process so they can more confidently and efficiently complete research assignments. In addition, Research Navigator™ offers students three exclusive databases of credible and reliable source content to help students focus their research efforts and get the research process started.

Student and faculty access to Research Navigator™ is gained through an access code found in the front of the Evaluating Online Resources guide. The Evaluating Online Resources guide can be wrapped with the *Sociology, Third Edition*, at no additional cost.

Research Navigator™ includes three databases of credible and reliable source material:

- **EBSCO's ContentSelect™ Academic Journal Database,** organized by subject, contains 50–100 of the leading academic journals for that discipline. Instructors and students can search the online journals by keyword, topic, or multiple topics. Articles include abstract and citation information and can be cut, pasted, emailed, or saved for later use.
- *The New York Times* **Search-by-Subject™ Archive**—specific to Sociology—is searchable by keyword or multiple keywords. Instructors and students can view full-text articles from the world's leading journalists from *The New York Times.*
- **Link Library** offers editorially selected "best of the web" sites for Sociology. Link Libraries are continually scanned and kept up to date providing the most relevant and accurate links for research assignments.

CENSUS2000 INTERACTIVE CD-ROM Capturing the rich picture of our nation drawn by Census2000, this CD-ROM brings related Census data into your classroom in a rich, multimedia format. It pulls files directly from the Census Bureau Website, organizes them around your course, and offers pedagogy to support student learning. It is free when packaged with the Third Edition.

FOR THE STUDENT

STUDY GUIDE. This complete guide helps students review the material presented in the text. Each of the chapters in the study guide provides an overview of the corresponding chapter in the student text, summarizes its major topics and concepts, offers relevant multiple-choice and true/false practice quizzes with end-of-the-chapter solutions.

The New York Times and Prentice Hall are sponsoring *Themes of the Times*, a program designed to enhance student access to current information relevant to the classroom. Through this program, the core subject matter provided in this text is supplemented by a collection of timely articles from one of the world's most distinguished newspapers, *The New York Times*. These articles demonstrate the vital, ongoing connection between what is learned in the classroom and what is happening in the world around us.

To enjoy the wealth of information of *The New York Times* daily, a reduced subscription rate is available. For information, call toll-free: 1-800-631-1222. Prentice Hall and *The New York Times* are proud to co-sponsor *Themes of the Times*. We hope it will make the reading of both textbooks and newspapers a more dynamic, involving process.

10 WAYS TO FIGHT HATE This Brochure is produced by the Southern Poverty Law Center, the leading hate-crime and crime-watch organization in the United States and walks students through 10 steps that they can take on their own campus or within their own communities to fight hate on an everyday basis. It can be packaged for free with *Sociology, Third Edition*.

ACKNOWLEDGMENTS

Because of the monumental effort by the editors and staff of Prentice Hall, this edition was completed on time and continues to reflect the highest standards for textbook publishing in all its phases. Prentice Hall provided us with the peer reviews, editorial comments, and suggestions for reorganizing and updating material that nurtured our writing skills and creativity. We would particularly like to thank Chris DeJohn for overseeing the Third Edition from start to finish. Chris's continued support and enthusiasm for our work on this edition are sincerely appreciated. Publisher Nancy Roberts was always available to patiently listen and to offer encouraging words when time was short and deadlines loomed. Developmental editor Karen Trost provided insightful chapter reviews, recommendations for chapter organization, and suggestions for innovative content areas that certainly increased the quality of *Sociology, Third Edition*. Editor-in-Chief of Development Rochelle Diogenes ensured that all the pieces fit together and that authors, editors, and staff remained partners in the production process. Editorial Assistant Veronica D'Amico juggled a myriad of production tasks, yet assured that material was sent and questions were promptly answered. Fran Russello, of Prentice Hall, and Bruce Hobart, of Pine Tree Composition, expertly managed an extremely tight production schedule. Mirella Signoretto brought to life the Diversity Data graphs throughout the book. Anne DeMarinis created a design that reinforces and enhances the strengths of this book. The media program that enhances the book was deftly managed by Carol Abolafia, Michael Henry, and Jennifer Collins. We would also very much like to thank Amy Speckman for her hard work in managing the marketing of the book. Finally, we would also like to thank the Prentice Hall folks who represent the book so well to our colleagues.

Linda Lindsey would like to thank colleagues who reviewed portions of the manuscript for all editions, suggested research examples and bibliography from their specialty areas, offered innovative ideas for revisions, and provided feedback for new boxes and vignettes, including Larry Grieshaber, Kent Bausman, and Judith McGee (Maryville University), Sarah Boggs (University of Missouri-St. Louis—retired), Walter Brumm (California University of Pennsylvania), Glenn Walker (Bethany College), Michael Fonge (Houston Community College), Joe Overton (Kapiolani Community College), Brenda Hoke (Agnes Scott College), Michael Feener (University of California at Riverside), and Gerry James Jobes. Maryville's administration also provided encouragement for the project and I would like to thank Ed Palm and Keith Lovin in this regard. Other Maryville staff provided both assistance as well as much appreciated understanding for the demanding schedule at various stages of the project, including Juanita Aycock, Betty Bockhorst, and Sandy Reeder. Priya Dua, a recent Maryville graduate in social sciences, did an outstanding job in updating bibliography to review and I wish to sincerely thank her for a summer of her time and effort. A special thanks to friends and family who gave me needed and much appreciated ongoing emotional support for many months, including my mom, Ruth, Marsha Balluff, Betty Buck, Cheryl Hazel, Nancy Hume, Joe Overton, Phil Loughlin, Jim Massey, Morris Levin, and Bill Nagel. The St. Louis Bread Company in Kirkwood continues as my place of refuge to reflect and re-energize, and I thank their staff, especially Mary Klein, Berlinda McNeal, and Fran Suedmeyer for the wonderful setting they provide and the warmth they bring to all of us who inhabit it during our busy lives.

Steve Beach would like to thank a number of people who have contributed over the years to his professional and personal development. In particular, the following individuals played an important role in his evolution as a sociologist: Sanford Dornbusch, Gordon Craig, Edward A. Tiryakian, John Wilson, Joel Smith, Kurt Back, Alan Kerckhoff, John McKinney,

Marian Kilson, Audie Blevins, Saul Feinman, Garth Massey, Marilyn and Tom Carroll, Margaret Britton, Linda Lindsey, and Bill Conroy. He would also like to acknowledge the personal support of the following true friends; Jim Beach, Mike Stavlo, Laura Anderson, Mike Stoller, Larry and Ann Byler, John Forester, John and Eva Bacon, Nancy Meyer, Elaine Bodurtha, Jeff and Jenny Skinner, Dorothy Ann Lynch, Joann Spillman, Corky Carrel, Paula Thirlkel, Cheryl Daniels, Paul and Jeannie McCarthy, Bob Powell, Paul Leonard, Dianne Echohawk, Gail Woodruff, Ken Ayers, Mike Fagan, Billy Long, Matt Schoenbachler, Jim Welch, Bernie Bettinelli, Lynette Taylor, and all of the members of Stanford-in-Germany Group XIII.

We would also like to extend our thanks to our colleagues who have offered their opinions about this book through its development:

William Aho	Rhode Island College
Robert Anwyl	Miami-Dade Community College
John Arthur	University of Minnesota
Robert Bausch	Cameron University
Sampson Lee Blair	SUNY-Buffalo
Jane Bock	University of Wisconsin, Green Bay
Jane A. Brown	Case Western Reserve University
Daniel Cervi	West Virginia University
Glenna Colclough	University of Alabama at Huntsville
Yvonne Downs	State University of New York at Fredonia
Lois Easterly	Onondaga Community College
Lynn England	Brigham Young University
Nicole T. Flynn	University of South Alabama
Norman Goodman	State University of New York at Stony Brook
Sandra Goodwin	Onondaga Community College
Allen Haney	University of Houston
Alexander Hicks	Emory University
Patricia Johnson	Houston Community College
Professor J. Koch	Texas Tech
Dwight Landua	Southeastern Oklahoma State University
Stephen Light	SUNY Plattsburgh
Ken Muir	Appalachian State University
Meyl Nason	University of Texas-Dallas
Richard Paulman	Frostburg State University
Harland Prechel	Texas A&M University
Ferris Ritchey	University of Alabama, Birmingham
Mary Romero	Arizona State University
Luis Salinas	Houston Community College
Michael Schneider	Midland College
Gregory D. Squires,	University of Wisconsin at Milwaukee
Eric Swank	Morehead State University
Dianne Sykes	Marion College
Gail A. Thoen	University of Minnesota
Javier Trevino	Wheaton College
Tami Videon	Rutgers University
Dr. Margaret Walsh	Keene State College
Allen Williams, Jr.	University of Nebraska, Lincoln
Ronald Wohlstein	Eastern Illinois University
Richard E. Yinger	Palm Beach Community College
John Zipp	University of Akron

L.L.L.
St. Louis, Missouri

S.B.
Owensboro, Kentucky

ABOUT THE AUTHORS

Professor Linda L. Lindsey received her B.A. from the University of Missouri, St. Louis in sociology and education, and her M.A. and Ph.D. in sociology from Case Western Reserve University. She also holds an M.A. in education from St. Louis University. She is the author of *Gender Roles: Sociological Perspectives, Third Edition* (Prentice Hall) and has also written various articles and conference papers on women in development, health and healthcare issues, refugees, internationalizing the sociology curriculum, and minority women in Asia, especially in China. (This picture is taken from Victoria Peak in Hong Kong.) Her major interest, both personally and professionally, is the developing world. She has traveled extensively in pursuing her research and teaching interests, especially in conjunction with the Asian Studies Development Program, a joint program of the East-West Center and University of Hawaii. While home in St. Louis she enjoys swimming and hiking and is active in community service groups focusing on advocacy concerning women and children. Dr. Lindsey is currently Professor of Sociology at Maryville University of St. Louis. Dr. Lindsey encourages students and faculty to communicate their experiences with the text to her at lindsey@maryville.edu.

Professor Stephen Beach grew up in southern Wisconsin and suburban Chicago and earned an A.B. in history from Stanford University with minors in sociology and the humanities. He received an M.A. and a Ph.D. in sociology from Duke University after spending a year in Belfast, Northern Ireland, researching social movement dynamics. Dr. Beach's primary sociological specialities include the sociology of religion, popular culture, and collective behavior/social movements. He has taught at Duke University, Simmons College, the University of Wyoming, and Avila College; he is currently an Associate Professor of Sociology in the Department of Behavioral Sciences at Kentucky Wesleyan College in Owensboro, Kentucky. His personal interests include film, rock and alt-country music, college basketball, and progressive politics. He shares his home with a large gray and white Republican cat named Murgatroyd. Dr. Beach would be delighted to hear comments or answer questions from readers of this text; he can be reached at SteveBe@kwc.edu.

1

THE SOCIOLOGICAL PERSPECTIVE

Sociologists are men and women who are endlessly fascinated by human social life and who actively strive to understand why people behave as they do. The topics they study vary from the routines of everyday life to the great transformations that remake our world. Here are three recent news stories that any sociologist would find interesting:

Manhattan, New York

Where were you when it happened? The tourist photos from a disposable camera taken from "Windows of the World" atop the World Trade Center on a beautiful summer day are now among my most cherished possessions. Less than two months after my visit, the terrorist attacks in New York, Washington D.C., and Pennsylvania which killed over 3,000 people deeply influenced life in the United States and in other parts of the world. The haunting videos of planes crashing into the twin towers are indelibly etched in memories of people across the globe. A global economy still reverberating from the events of 9/11 and other terrorist attacks worldwide, such as the bombing of an Indonesian nightclub in Bali by Islamic fundamentalists that killed over 190 people, or the raid on a Moscow movie theatre that killed 115 hostages held by Chechen rebels, demonstrate the connections between the personal, the social, and the global. Understanding these connections is at the heart of what sociologists refer to as the sociological imagination. In introducing this concept over a half century ago, C. Wright Mills stated that the history affecting us all is world history. The events of September 11 connected people in the United States with people across the globe in an unprecedented manner. Social resiliency—the ability to bounce back after tragedy and anguish—is a hallmark of social life. We will see that social change and social stability go hand in hand. The sociological imagination will help you understand why this connection is such a vitally important one, especially in dealing with the turmoil of events such as the terrorist attacks of 9/11/01 that continue to march across our memories.

Tokyo, Japan

In most ways, Japan is a model post-industrial society, but it lags behind virtually every other modern nation in providing equal rights to women. Gender inequality is especially evident in the workplace. Only 1 out of every 1,000 corporate executives in Japan is female, and more than 95 percent of business managers are male. The average salary earned by women in Japan was precisely half of that earned by men in 1990, far below the ratio for any other developed country. The comparable figure for the United States was 74 percent. Ninety-seven percent of the workers on career tracks in Japanese businesses are men.

Discrimination against Japanese women is so pervasive that it has even affected the divorce rate, which is the lowest in the developed world. Women in Japan tend to stay married, even if their family life is deeply unsatisfying, because of a lack of decent employment opportunities for women, because very few men are willing to marry divorced women, and because welfare benefits for female-headed single parent families are extremely low (Kerbo & McKinstry, 1998:66–68).

3

Sociologists wonder why Japanese society has been so slow to offer equal rights to women. Will the wage gap narrow in coming decades? What are the prospects for the growth of a strong feminist movement in Japan?

Springfield, Illinois

Just two days before Anthony Porter was scheduled to die by lethal injection for a double homicide committed 16 years earlier, the Illinois Supreme Court issued a stay of execution on the grounds that Porter, an African American man with an IQ of 51, might not have been mentally competent to stand trial. He was still on death row, awaiting retrial, when another man confessed to shooting the victims over a drug dispute. A joyful Porter exclaimed, "Nobody but God did this!"

Porter had been helped by a group of college students at Northwestern University. As a classroom assignment, several of them had analyzed the records of the case, reenacted the crime, and concluded that the evidence just didn't add up. With the aid of a private detective, they located witnesses who said the police had pressured them to give false testimony. Faced with the new evidence, the real murderer made a videotaped confession to the detective. Porter was the tenth man to have been removed from death row since 1976 in Illinois alone (McCormick, 1999).

Sociologists wonder whether the death penalty is an effective deterrent. Is its application racially biased? How many innocent people have been executed? Will the United States eventually follow the lead of most European nations and abandon capital punishment?

As these accounts suggest, sociology is strongly oriented toward the study of social issues such as terrorism, the gender gap in wages, and capital punishment. It pays special attention to how women, ethnic and racial minorities, the elderly, and the poor are treated in society. And it is increasingly global in its scope, recognizing the escalating interdependence of people throughout the world.

WHAT IS SOCIOLOGY?

Some disciplines are best defined by their subject matter: Botanists study plants; political scientists study governments. But sociology is quite different. As a glance at the table of contents of this text will readily illustrate, sociologists study a very broad range of topics. What makes the field distinctive is primarily its *perspective*, the way in which it interprets human behavior, rather than its specific subject matter. Sociology is, in this view, less a body of research findings than a form of consciousness (Berger, 1963).

Formally defined, **sociology** is the scientific study of human social behavior. Sociology begins with the observation that social life displays certain basic regularities. Further, it assumes that social factors—rather than biological or psychological ones—are especially useful in explaining these regularities. Sociologists focus on how our behavior is shaped by factors such as the influence of the groups to which we belong (families, juvenile gangs, or protest movements), the social categories in which we are located (including race, gender, age, and social class), and how we are taught to behave by those with whom we interact. Sociologists also study how people actively create groups; collectively define the meaning of being Latino or white, old or young, rich or poor, male or female; and establish and communicate rules for behavior. In other words, sociology views individuals and society as mutually influencing each other. People create the society in which they live, and at the same time, they are shaped by it.

The sociological perspective does not focus on individuals in isolation, but rather on the impact of social forces on human behavior. Sociologists study *collectivities* such as groups, organizations, and whole societies. It is a fundamental theme of the sociological perspective that the characteristics of a social group cannot be directly predicted from the qualities of its members (Lemert, 2002). For example, people often become frustrated with bureaucracies and criticize individual employees for seeming cold and uninterested. In fact, on their own time these workers may well be warm and caring people, but they must act impersonally at work because they are part of an organization whose basic rules and structure require them to behave in a very formal fashion.

Many people tend to lose track of the importance of social forces and come to believe that they alone shape their lives (Bellah et al., 1985; Babbie, 1994). Such individuals would benefit by developing a *sociological imagination*, a term coined by C. Wright Mills (1959), which refers to a deep understanding of the relationship between larger social factors and people's personal lives. Without employing the sociological imagination, we may fail to recognize the true origins and character of the problems we face, and we may be unable to respond to them effectively.

Mills differentiates between *personal troubles*, which result from individual failings, and *social issues*, which are caused by larger social factors. For example, many years ago when divorce was quite uncommon, it was generally understood as a personal trouble caused by individualistic factors such as adultery; its remedy required that the particular people involved in a marriage change, perhaps through some form of counseling or therapy. Today divorce is widespread, and although personal factors and individualistic solutions remain relevant in specific cases, divorce in this country has become a social issue, influenced by social trends such as the increasing availability of jobs that pay well enough to allow women to support themselves if they choose to leave bad marriages and the greater acceptance of divorced individuals by society in general. Significantly, these two trends are less evident in Japan, which is characterized by a very low divorce rate, than they are in the United States. From this perspective, it does not make sense to assume that the best way to lower the divorce rate is to concentrate on individuals' failings. If we wish to respond to such social issues as divorce, hate crimes, terrorism, or poverty, we must use the sociological imagination in order to identify and change their collective as well as individual causes.

THE SOCIOLOGICAL PERSPECTIVE

The sociological perspective—the way sociologists view social life—has several important qualities: It employs the scientific method, it encourages people to *debunk* or be skeptical of many conventional explanations of social life, it directs our attention to social diversity with a special emphasis on race and gender, and it displays a strong global orientation.

Sociology as a Science

When we say that sociology is a science, we mean that sociologists collect information about social reality following a rather specific set of research procedures (to be discussed in detail in Chapter 2) that are designed to ensure that their conclusions are as accurate as possible (Salkind, 2000). This does not mean that sociologists are always right, but it does mean that, for example, if your roommate tells you that capital punishment is an effective deterrent to crime and you hear the opposite from your sociology professor, you would be wiser to believe your professor, because in most cases sociologists base their claims on systematic, scientific research, not on casual observation, stereotypes, hearsay, or tradition (Berrick, 1995).

Science is a way of seeking knowledge that relies on the careful, systematic, and repeated collection and analysis of **empirical evidence**—data that derive directly from observation and experience, not from conjecture, intuition, or hearsay. Thus, as scientists, sociol-

Sociologists are interested in identifying the social factors that help explain why minority athletes such as tennis champion Venus Williams have been exceptionally successful in college and professional sports.

ogists do not study phenomena that cannot be empirically observed, such as angels or demons. Sociologists also do not address questions such as "What is the best form of government?" because such questions involve personal value judgments: It would be impossible for everyone to agree on what "the best" means. Instead, they concentrate on topics such as why so many African Americans have been successful in professional sports or whether the wage gap between Japanese men and women is declining, because questions like these can be answered through empirical research.

Sociologists normally study a number of cases so that their findings can be applied fairly broadly. This process of *generalization* allows researchers to apply the same fundamental explanations to many different specific cases. Thus they would start an investigation of a topic such as minority involvement in professional sport by studying many different examples of minority participation in athletics—if possible, in different places and at different times. Such studies do in fact demonstrate that minority athletes, especially African Americans, have been greatly overrepresented at the professional level in recent decades (Coakley, 2001).

However, as is always the case in science, sociologists' ultimate goal in conducting research is not just to find out the facts, but to go further and uncover the causes of the regular patterns of behavior that have been identified. Sociologists are never content with just describing social life, and they are never satisfied with the claim that things just happen. They always assume that some causal factors, normally social ones, can be found to explain why things are as they are (Bourdeau et al., 1991).

This means that after careful empirical research has identified a pattern or regularity in social life, sociologists must develop a theory to explain the pattern (Collins, 1989; Cuzzort & King, 2002). In sociology, as in all science, a **theory** is an explanation of the relationship among specific facts.

Regarding the involvement of African Americans in professional sports, sociologists might start constructing a theory by noting that performance in sports is subject to very precise measurement. If a baseball player hits .350, he or she is obviously successful. This is true regardless of the individual's race. Measures of success in other fields, like business or medicine, are much less objective. Even prejudiced people must acknowledge the talent of a .350 hitter, whereas their biased perceptions might lead them to ignore and devalue the skills of persons of color in more subjective activities such as music or medicine.

A sociologist might theorize further that African Americans or other minorities may put extra effort into sports because they know that their athletic talents are likely to be recognized. In addition, there are many successful minority role models in professional athletics, whereas until recently there were relatively few successful businesspeople or doctors who were not white. These factors encourage blacks and other minorities to participate in sport as a means of obtaining upward social mobility.

In addition to being based on empirical research and designed to identify the underlying causes of social behavior, sociological theories must always be testable and subject to possible refutation. The ultimate aim of any sociological theory is to allow us to make accurate predictions about people's future behavior.

The classic example of the interplay of research and theory in sociology is a study of the causes of suicide conducted by the late-19th-century French scholar Émile Durkheim (Durkheim, 1966). Writing in an era when sociology was just beginning to establish itself as a science, Durkheim chose to research suicide precisely because it was widely believed at the time that this act was caused entirely by nonsocial factors, especially psychological ones.

Durkheim did not deny that *individuals* who commit suicide may be suffering from psychological problems, but as a sociologist he directed his attention to seeking an explanation of why *collective* suicide rate varied from group to group. He started by carefully obtaining empirical data on the subject. These data showed, among other things, that there were markedly higher suicide rates in geographical areas that were primarily Protestant rather than Catholic; that the incidence of suicide was higher among single people than among those who were married; and that city dwellers took their own lives more frequently than did people who lived in small towns.

Focusing initially on the religious factor, he asked what it was about being Catholic that might tend to lower the suicide rate or about being Protestant than might encourage suicide; in other words, he sought to develop a theory.

Both religions overtly discourage suicide. But Durkheim observed that, on the average, Catholics interacted more frequently with other Catholics than Protestants interacted with other Protestants. In part this pattern resulted from the stronger emphasis within Catholicism on regular church attendance; in part it resulted from the larger number of church-related voluntary associations (like youth groups or the Knights of Columbus) that were available in his era to Catholics, and in part it simply reflected the typically larger size of the Catholic family. Together, these factors meant that, compared with Protestants, Catholics tended to display higher levels of sustained involvement with other people—a quality that Durkheim called *social integration*. He concluded that more frequent interaction with like-minded others— with people who can continually remind us that suicide is bad—provided a sociological explanation for the observed differences in suicide rates between Catholics and Protestants.

Durkheim and other researchers tested and extended his initial theory by comparing the suicide rates among other groups of Catholics and Protestants and by comparing rates among other highly socially integrated groups, like married people and those who live in small towns, with the rates that are typical of less well-integrated people, such as those who are single and live in large cities. The findings of such research have quite consistently supported the original theory. Suicide rates tend to vary with the level of social integration. (Refer to Figure 1.1 for a look at how the factors of race and gender influence the suicide rate in today's world.)

Note carefully that these findings refer to collective rather than individual behavior patterns.

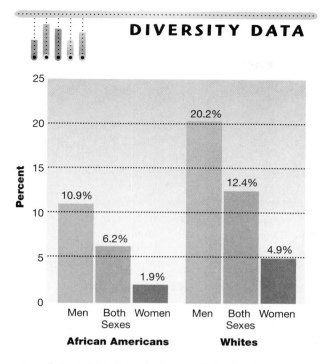

DIVERSITY DATA

FIGURE 1.1 Suicide Rates by Race and Gender for the United States. Fewer women than men and fewer African Americans than whites take their own lives.

Source: U.S. National Center for Health Statistics (1999).

> *To view an interactive version of each Diversity Data graph in this textbook, please visit the companion Website for this book at http://www.prenhall.com/lindsey and select the appropriate chapter.*

Durkheim's work shows that some groups are likely to have higher suicide rates than others, all other factors being equal, but we must not mechanically apply group-level findings to particular individuals—a logical error known as the **ecological fallacy.** The fact that Joan is a Protestant does have some effect on her chances of killing herself, but at the individual level this effect is limited. After all, most people, whatever their religion, do not commit suicide. If we commit the ecological fallacy—if we say that because, as a group, Asian Americans tend to do well in school, then Kevin, a Chinese American, will necessarily have high grades—we are simply stereotyping, not doing sociology.

What about free will? The logic of scientific sociology does suggest that human behavior is caused, or at least influenced, by social factors such as the level of social integration, but the effects are often indirect. Although being Protestant or unmarried does increase the likelihood of suicide, each individual still makes a choice. For this reason, all sociological theories are *probabilistic* or conditional: They predict future behavior, but they are always phrased in terms such as "given certain specified social conditions, a particular outcome is likely" rather than saying that "given certain specified social conditions, a particular outcome will occur." Human beings are not robots—but they are also not unaffected by those around them (Wrong, 1961).

Scientific, research-based theories are not the only way to explain why people act as they do. We can also derive useful insights into human behavior from poetry and drama, from philosophy and theology. But because sociological theories are based in careful empirical research, they are generally more precise and more useful than nonscientific paths to knowledge. We hear that "birds of a feather flock together" but also that "opposites attract." Both adages are sometimes accurate, but only scientific inquiry can tell us under exactly what circumstances one or the other is more correct.

Debunking

The term **debunking** refers to a habit of looking at both the obvious or surface-level explanations for social behavior and the less obvious and deeper explanations (Berger, 1963). Durkheim was debunking when he showed that suicide stems not only from psychological problems but also from low levels of social integration. Debunking is a theme in all the social sciences—but sociologists put a particularly strong emphasis on it.

Debunking is a state of mind that is undeniably a little cynical. When sociologists debunk, they assume that "official" explanations are incomplete and often self-serving. They see old realities in new ways. They refuse to ignore inconvenient facts. Sociologists who have studied how the death penalty is being used have convincingly debunked the myths that it is applied without racial bias and that innocent people are never condemned to die.

As sociology has become more popular, debunking has become increasingly common among the general public. For example, when the United States becomes politically or militarily involved in the Middle East, most people recognize that part of its motive is to keep cheap oil flowing to fuel our SUVs, although government spokespersons may attempt to justify the intervention in a more idealistic fashion. Similarly, when neighborhood residents band together to fight the establishment of a halfway house for recovering

These protestors against the Gulf War were skeptical of official explanations for American participation. Their mindest is similar in a sense to that of sociologists who make use of the debunking theme of the discipline.

drug addicts on their block, claiming that they are worried about the safety of their children, most people realize that while the residents may indeed be genuinely concerned about their children, they are also motivated by fear that property values might decline if a rehab facility is built in the neighborhood.

The sociological theme of debunking helps explain why the discipline thrives during times of social turmoil, when many conventional truths seem unconvincing, and is less popular in quiet eras (Mills, 1959). This is one of the reasons why sociology grew rapidly in the United States during the turbulent 1920s, the Great Depression, and the social upheaval of the 1960s, but was less widely accepted in more conformist decades like the 1950s and the 1980s. The challenge of global terrorism in the current era seems likely to remind people once again of the importance of developing their sociological imaginations.

The individuals who are most likely to question the established truths and thus to be naturally most inclined to debunk are those who are not members of the more powerful groups in society. Such people display the quality of **social marginality:** They are to some extent excluded, through no fault of their own, from the mainstream of society. It is no coincidence that most of the European founders of the discipline of sociology were Jewish, or that a great deal of the most important work now being conducted in sociology is being done by racial and ethnic minorities and

women. As partial outsiders, marginalized people are especially well situated to realize that the emperor may indeed be wearing no clothes.

Diversity

When sociologists debunk, they frequently find that the common-sense understandings many people embrace concerning social reality are systematically biased or distorted in ways that promote the interests of the more powerful members of society. These powerful people have the ability to strongly influence what we learn in school, from the media, and even in church. They often use their collective social power to more or less subtly encourage everyone to see society as they do, and this way of looking at life tends to legitimate their privileged positions.

As is documented throughout this text, sociological research often reveals that widespread beliefs about the poor, racial and ethnic minorities, women, the young and the elderly, the physically and mentally disabled, and gays and lesbians are inaccurate, sometimes wildly so. As a result, many sociologists have chosen to focus their research on such groups.

When sociology first developed in Europe, some early scholars made a point of studying economic diversity with special reference to the problems of the poor. When the field became established in the United States early in the 20th century, sociologists

One consequence of the globalization process is that sociological investigation, once largely confined to the more highly developed nations, is now conducted virtually everywhere in the world. Here a researcher interviews agricultural workers in Malaysia.

directed considerable attention to the problems of racial minorities; in fact, sociological research played an important role in the struggle for civil rights. Over the past 30 years, the discipline has closely studied the place of women in society (Smith, 1992). Note that two of the three accounts that opened this chapter reflect the sociological emphasis on diversity.

More recently, sociologists have begun to emphasize the combined effects of factors such as race, class, age, and gender. This line of thought, which is developed throughout the text, acknowledges the linkages or *intersections* between these social identities and reminds us that the experiences of multiply disadvantaged people—for example, elderly African American women—cannot be fully understood by studying the effects of each social factor separately.

Modern sociology also acknowledges that many societies are moving toward **multiculturalism,** the idea that different groups of people should be able to live side by side without one dominating the others or any group having to abandon its heritage. This concept is developed more fully in Chapter 3.

Globalization

A final important theme in modern sociology is its emphasis on the extent to which the world's societies are increasingly linked together into a single global system (Wallerstein, 1990; Greider, 1997; Friedman, 1999). This world-system has been growing since the 16th century, but the pace of globalization has accelerated tremendously in recent decades.

In the economic sector, the wealth of the multinational corporations has come to exceed that of many small and medium-sized nations (Barnet & Cavanagh, 1994). Transnational trade agreements such as NAFTA and groups like the World Trade Organization are shaping many aspects of our daily lives. New technologies are diffused around the world almost instantaneously, and more and more products are being constructed on a "global assembly line." Your new "Japanese" Toyota was probably assembled in the United States and contains raw materials or finished parts that originated in dozens of countries all around the world.

Similarly, as environmental awareness increases, we are gradually recognizing that only a regional or global perspective can allow us to reduce pollution and respond effectively to problems like global warming and resource depletion (Houghton, 1997).

More generally, a global culture is beginning to emerge. Despite resistance, English is becoming a universal language. Music, films, and television shows created in the United States are enjoyed worldwide. At the same time, however, U.S. popular culture is being more and more heavily influenced by developments in other nations. All of these changes have been greatly facilitated by modern means of transportation and by the new instantaneous media of communication, especially fax machines and the Internet.

This text consistently emphasizes this trend toward globalization. In particular, it stresses an important theme in modern sociology: the contrasts—and the interconnections—between the wealthy nations of the *developed world* (North America, Europe, Australia, and Japan) and those in the much poorer *developing world*, which contain over three-quarters of the human population. It is especially critical that we develop a strong global consciousness in an era in which international terrorism has come to dominate the political agenda of the United States and other developed nations. Terrorism is discussed at some length in Chapter 18.

MAJOR TOPICS OF SOCIOLOGICAL INTEREST

Although the field of sociology is extremely broad, most sociological research may be categorized into one of four very general areas: socialization, social stratification, social institutions, and social change. This text explores each of these topics in a separate section after first discussing critical issues concerning research methods, culture, and social structure that are relevant to all sociological inquiry (Chapters 2, 3, and 4). A brief overview of the four major areas of sociological interest will expand your understanding of the sociological perspective as well as provide an introduction to some of the subjects that are covered later in this book.

Socialization

Recall that sociologists consistently emphasize the extent to which powerful social forces guide, limit, or constrain human behavior. In fact, some go so far as to describe society as a system in which people in effect agree to abandon much of their freedom in return for the advantages that result from joining with others in cooperative activities (Babbie, 1994). This implicit social contract requires that we learn and accept the rules that govern social behavior. The principal mechanism by which this learning is accomplished is called **socialization,** which is defined in Chapter 5 as the lifelong process by which we learn our culture, develop our sense of self, and become functioning members of society. Most socialization takes place through an ongoing process of *social interaction*—the topic of Chapter 6. When socialization efforts fail, or when people are socialized to act in ways that the authorities or other powerful figures in society regard as wrong, the result is *deviant behavior*, some of which takes the form of crime—issues addressed in Chapters 8 and 9.

Social Stratification

In virtually every society in the world, people are divided into distinct social categories, including socio-economic classes, ethnic and racial groups, the male and female genders, and age grades such as teenagers and the elderly. Membership in these categories gives some people greater opportunities than others to obtain valued resources, including money, nice homes, attractive mates, prestige, power, and the ability to pass on many of these advantages to their children.

Of course, how well *particular* people do is affected by both their individual abilities and by their category memberships, but sociologists concentrate primarily on the latter factor. Because the advantages and disadvantages enjoyed by members of different social categories are *built into* daily life, sociologists use the term *structured social inequality* or, somewhat more narrowly, **social stratification,** to refer to this characteristic of societies.

Social stratification is not maintained principally by force or coercion. It is much easier and more reliable if the more advantaged people socialize everyone to accept a belief system or **ideology** that legitimates existing patterns of structured social inequality—that is, one that defines them as just and proper. Racism, sexism, and ageism are examples. Uncovering the way these ideologies function is an excellent example of the debunking theme in sociology. Social stratification is discussed further in Chapters 10 through 14.

Social Institutions

People in every society must accomplish certain basic tasks. Among other things, they must produce and distribute goods and services, care for and socialize their children, protect themselves against invaders and criminals, make decisions to which the society as a whole is committed, heal the sick, and respond to the sacred.

A **social institution** is a predictable, established way to provide for one or more of society's basic needs. Chapters 9 and 15 through 21 present sociological analyses of several important institutions: the family, education, religion, the economy, the political institution, health, the media, sport, and the criminal justice system.

Every society must fulfill all of these major needs, but each does so in a somewhat different fashion. Over time, the existing institutional arrangements come to be seen by the people of a given society as the right and proper way to behave. As a result, institutions like the family or government tend to be quite stable, and institutional change is often viewed as institutional collapse, as exemplified by widespread concerns over the supposed decline of the family. The sociological perspective often, but not always, suggests that changing institutional patterns are better understood as adaptations to new realities rather than as examples of degeneration.

GLOBAL CONNECTIONS

The United States Through Foreign Eyes

Travel, they say, is broadening—even if you stay out of the pastry shops! In this context, "broadening" means that when we see people acting differently from the way our friends and neighbors behave at home, we can use these observations to enhance our understanding of and appreciation for the tremendous diversity of human behavior. Travelers often return home enlightened as a result of their experiences, able to understand and empathize more effectively with people—not just with those from other parts of the world, but also with individuals in their own communities who differ from them with regard to racial or ethnic identity, gender, age, or economic status.

By the same logic, we can learn a lot about our own society from the observations of visitors from other countries. Here are three short, generally critical accounts that illustrate how some aspects of daily life in the United States struck recently arrived foreign scholars. First, some observations from a Thai professor about U.S. dining customs:

> Individualism is even reflected in the way Americans prepare, serve, and consume food. In a typical American meal, each person has a separate plate and is not supposed to share or taste food from other people's plates. My Thai friends and I are used to eating Thai style, in which you share food from a big serving dish in the middle of the table . . . One time my American host . . . invited a Thai girlfriend and myself to an American dinner at her home. When we were reaching out and eating a small portion of

one thing at a time in Thai style, we were told to dish everything we wanted onto our plates at one time and that it was not considered polite to reach across the table . . . If we were to eat in the [American] manner in Thailand . . . we would have been considered to be eating like pigs, greedy and inconsiderate of others who shared the meal at the table. (Natadecha-Sponsel, 1998:70–71)

Next, a poet from India observes how U.S. individualism seems to erode community ties, at least in contrast to the village life he had experienced back home:

> Neighborliness as a concept has all but been erased from what used to be understood as community life. There is only mild concern or interest in who lives next door; there is hardly any at all in who lives down the block. . . . Many properties have no fences—an attractive feature . . . but appearance belies the reality: The walls between neighbors are impenetrable, unscalable. Sometimes I think Americans have succeeded only too well in realizing their dream of living in private paradises that resemble solitary confinement cells. (Peerandina, 1998:23)

Other visitors to the United States are struck by what they regard as an informality so extreme that it amounts to rudeness. Consider the following reflection by a Philippine anthropologist:

> American children, I observe, are allowed to call older people by their first names. . . . [One] incident took place in the university cafeteria. To foster collegiality among the faculty and graduate students, professors and students usually

ate lunch together. During one of these occasions, I heard a student greet a teacher, "Hey, Bob! That was a tough exam! You really gave us a hard time, buddy!" I was stunned. I couldn't believe what I heard. All I could say to myself was "My God! How bold and disrespectful!" (Ojeda, 1998:52)

Comments like these remind us that whenever we view social reality, we do so through a kind of lens or filter that is the result of our own unique experiences. In other words, we each have our own distinctive perspective on life. This is very natural, very human—but it can also be limiting. We can greatly benefit by learning to view the world through multiple perspectives. This broadening of perspective, much like that resulting from extensive travel, is precisely the promise and the appeal of sociology.

1. If you have traveled abroad or to other parts of the United States, what are some of the different patterns of social life that caught your attention during your travels? How did you interpret and respond to these differences?

2. All of the examples cited in this box concern aspects of life in the United States that evoked negative reactions from foreign observers. What do you think people from other countries might like about this country?

3. How does the concept of social marginality help you to understand why outsiders are often able to see things that people who have grown up in a society may not perceive?

Sources: Natadecha-Sponsel, 1998; Ojeda, 1998; Peerandina, 1998.

Social Change

Sociology is centrally concerned with the analysis of social change. As we shall see shortly, the discipline initially emerged as a way of understanding and responding to the great transformations that created the modern world. The accounts that opened this chapter all implicitly or explicitly concern efforts to promote or oppose some sort of social change. Sociologists studying socialization, structured social inequality, and social institutions often explore how and why these phenomena change. However, several specialties have also developed within sociology to explore some of the dynamics of change in today's world. Chapter 21 introduces the concept of bureaucracy and explains how it has radically transformed the workplace. Chapter 22 investigates population growth, urbanization, and the rapidly changing relationship between people and the physical environment. Chapter 23 discusses collective behavior with a special emphasis on social movements—among the most effective means by which ordinary people can work for change. The final chapter (Chapter 24) combines a general discussion of social change at the theoretical level with a detailed analysis of global change and its impact on the developing world.

THE DEVELOPMENT OF SOCIOLOGY

Sociology is among the newest of the sciences, having arisen in Europe during the latter half of the 19th century. However, it grew out of a long tradition of social philosophy that stretches all the way back to the ancient world. Thinkers as diverse as Plato, Aristotle, Saint Augustine, Thomas Aquinas, Niccolo Machiavelli, Thomas Hobbes, John Locke, Jean-Jacques Rousseau, Edmund Burke, and John Stuart Mill all wrote extensively about social issues. However, their approaches differ from that of modern sociologists because they did not base their work on scientific research and because their primary concern tended to be identifying the character of the ideal society rather than describing social life as it really was and explaining why it took the forms that it did. Most scholars believe that sociology as we know it began around 1850 in an effort to understand and respond to a series of dramatic changes that had swept over Europe during the preceding 200 years.

The Sociohistorical Context

For many centuries after the fall of the Roman Empire, almost all Europeans lived in small farming villages in which life changed very little from century to century. Most people were serfs, subject to the everyday control of a small group of feudal lords and to the ultimate, although rather abstract, power of a monarch whose authority was believed to stem directly from God. The Roman Catholic Church controlled many aspects of daily life, literacy was extremely uncommon, tradition was rarely challenged, and the family was enormously powerful. Most people were born, lived, and died without ever traveling more than a few dozen miles from their homes. No doubt they assumed that their children and their

Wealth and poverty are not just the consequences of individual people's ability and efforts. They are actually built into the structure of society.

Contact with non-European people helped spur the development of sociology. Today, sociologists celebrate the richness and diversity in the world's many cultures.

children's children would live almost exactly the same way they did (Volti, 1988).

Four key developments shattered this traditional way of life, leading ultimately to the birth of sociology. First, growing out of the Renaissance and the work of thinkers such as Galileo, Newton, and Copernicus, scientific ways of investigating the natural world began to gain greater acceptance despite the hostility of the Church. The development of the scientific method and the gradual spread of early inventions like the printing press quickened the pace of social change.

Second, the thinkers of the Enlightenment, including Hobbes, Locke, and Rousseau, popularized radically new political ideas such as individual rights, liberty, equality, and democracy. These notions in turn inspired widespread demands for political reform culminating in the French and American revolutions. In both politics and science, the notion spread that the human condition could and should be improved through the application of reason (Nisbet, 1969; Adams & Sydie, 2001).

Third, during the early 19th century, the spread of the steam engine led to the Industrial Revolution in the nations of northern Europe. Millions of peasants abandoned traditional village life and flooded into the rapidly growing cities in search of factory jobs (Ritzer, 1994). A host of new social problems emerged, especially in the industrial slums where workers, including young children, routinely toiled for 12 hours or more each day, only to return at night to crowded, disease-ridden tenements. Poverty and crime increased massively. Appalled by these conditions, the earliest sociologists began to use scientific logic to understand their causes and attempted to develop rational solutions to social problems, which were now viewed as violations of basic human rights. In the process, the early sociologists thoroughly debunked traditional ways of understanding social life.

A final factor that influenced the early sociologists was the rapid expansion of colonialism, especially in the decades following 1880. By the time of World War I, most of Africa and Asia had been absorbed into the colonial empires of the major powers. Contact with non-European peoples increased sociologists' awareness of diversity, sensitized them to globalization, and provided them with alternate models of social life (Nisbet & Perrin, 1977; Lemert, 1997).

European Origins of Sociology

The founders of sociology attempted to use the logic and methods of science to identify what had gone wrong in European society and to explore how contemporary social problems might be successfully addressed. They thus combined an interest in objective analysis with a desire for social reform (Lazarsfeld & Reitz, 1989). Sociology first developed in France, Germany, and England.

FRANCE It should come as no surprise that academic sociology began in France. Paris was the undisputed intellectual center of Europe during the 17th and 18th centuries. In addition, the French Revolution of 1789 initiated truly radical changes in that society that dramatically altered relationships among different groups of people that had endured for centuries. The old aristocracy and monarchy were swept away, in some cases by the guillotine, only to be followed by successive waves of revolutionary governments, culminating in the military dictatorship of Napoleon.

Auguste Comte Best known among the first generation of French sociologists was Auguste Comte (1798–1857), who actually named the field (although he initially wanted to call it social physics). Comte took a generally negative view of post-revolutionary France. He favored responding to the fragmentation of society by rebuilding it along feudal lines but replacing the Church with a "priesthood" of sociologists who would use science to identify the proper way for people to live. Comte strongly advocated taking a scientific (he used the term *positivistic*) approach to the study of society, but in practice he did not conduct research, and his work is rarely read today.

Émile Durkheim In contrast, the other great 19th century French sociologist, Émile Durkheim (1858–1917), did do empirical research (recall his study of suicide rates), and his work is still widely viewed as relevant. Durkheim was more optimistic than Comte regarding the direction in which society was moving. However, he did note with concern a tendency, especially in the new industrial cities, toward the growth of what he called *anomie*, a general decline in the strength of the rules that guided people in deciding how they should behave in society. Durkheim linked anomie to low levels of social integration and regulation, and established that it was a source of numerous social problems, including deviance and suicide. Most of his writings focus on the causes of this decline in moral solidarity and on the institutions of religion and education, which he believed had the potential to lessen anomie.

GERMANY Sociology spread rapidly to Germany, where two important 19th-century thinkers, Karl Marx and Max Weber, developed analyses of the crisis of early industrial society that remain relevant today.

Karl Marx Marx (1818–1883) is, of course, best known for his radical political philosophy. His work inspired the state socialist systems that controlled the Soviet Union and Eastern Europe until the late 1980s and that continue to rule China, North Korea, and Cuba today (although none of these societies closely resembles the economic and political system Marx advocated). He saw himself as an economist, a political scientist, and a historian as well as a sociologist. He identified the chief problem facing modern society as the oppression of the workers by the capitalist factory owners. His primary contributions to sociology include the idea that social life can be fruitfully viewed as an arena of conflict between different groups, an emphasis on the importance of economics in shaping social life, and an orientation toward the study of structured social inequality, especially social class. His work is discussed at greater length in Chapter 10.

Max Weber Weber (pronounced *Vay-ber*) (1864–1920) ranks with Durkheim and Marx as a founding figure of sociology. His concerns centered on the increasing *rationalization* of the modern world, by which he meant that virtually all human activities were becoming more and more oriented toward the deliberate selection of the most efficient possible means to accomplish any particular task. Weber recognized that rationalization made society more productive, but he feared that it could eventually create a world full of people who acted like machines and who had lost much of the sometimes quirky individuality that made them fully human. He was less optimistic than Durkheim or Marx about the possibility that the negative aspects of modern life could be overcome. Weber's work continues to be relevant to many areas of sociology; it is discussed at some length as part of the analysis of bureaucracy in Chapter 21.

Chapter 24 will return to the notions of anomie, oppression, and rationalization and explore some ways in which these concepts continue to be useful in interpreting social life in the 21st century.

ENGLAND If your sociological imagination is functioning properly, you will probably have noticed that all of the figures discussed to this point have been male. Until the 1960s, women met great resistance when they attempted to enter academic careers, and even when they overcame this opposition, their work was rarely taken very seriously (Kandal, 1988; Deegan, 1991; Orlins & Wallace, 1994). Only in recent decades have sociologists begun to acknowledge the contributions of early female sociologists to the development of the field.

Harriet Martineau One such figure was Harriet Martineau (1802–1876), a British author who is best known for having translated Comte's works into English. A strong supporter of feminism and a passionate opponent of slavery, Martineau toured America in 1834 and, three years later, published a perceptive book called *Society in America* that was based on fieldwork at a time when empirical sociological research was uncommon. She also wrote *How to Observe Manners and Morals*, one of the earliest books to address the issue of sociological methodology (Hoecker-

Drysdale, 1992; Lengermann & Niebrugge-Brantley, 1998).

Herbert Spencer Far better known in the 19th century, though rarely read today, was Herbert Spencer (1820–1903). In his era, Spencer's work was given more attention than that of Durkheim, Marx, or Weber. He was strongly influenced by the writings of Charles Darwin, and his sociology is principally intended to explain how human societies evolve through a series of stages from simple to ever-more-complex forms. Today he is probably best remembered for staunchly opposing aid to the poor on the grounds that such assistance interferes with natural selection or "the survival of the fittest," a phrase Spencer originated. This philosophy, which has enjoyed something of a revival in recent years, is called *Social Darwinism*.

Sociology in the United States

Academic courses in sociology were offered in the United States as early as the 1880s, but the first U.S. department of sociology was not founded until 1892, when Albion Small established a program at the University of Chicago. The "Chicago School," as it was called, virtually dominated sociology in the United States until the late 1930s (Faris, 1979; Collins & Makowsky, 1998; Adams & Sydie, 2001).

Most early sociologists in this country shared the reformist concerns of the discipline's European founders. In fact, the Chicago School was probably more strongly oriented than the Europeans (aside from Marx) toward trying to improve society, perhaps as a legacy of the fact that many of its members were raised as liberal, reform-oriented Protestants (Lewis & Smith, 1980; Turner & Turner, 1990). U.S. sociologists were also more highly committed than most Europeans to empirical research.

In the early 20th century, the city of Chicago was growing very rapidly and displayed all of the ills of the industrial era. The Chicago sociologists viewed their city as a kind of vast social laboratory. They undertook major research projects to study such topics as poverty, crime, and immigration, interpreting these problems in the context of the physical growth of the metropolis in an approach called *urban ecology* (see Chapter 22).

While most Chicago sociologists, virtually all of whom were male, favored reform, they still saw their primary task as uncovering the fundamental principles that guide social life. They left the job of actually trying to improve society largely to the emerging, female-dominated discipline of social work. Some members of the Chicago School worked closely with Jane Addams (1860–1935), who founded a famous social agency called Hull House where she and her followers worked with Chicago slum-dwellers to

Jane Addams was the founder of Hull House, a famous social agency that worked with Chicago's poor. She used her sociological expertise to improve others' lives in an era when women were largely excluded from the academic world.

INTERNET CONNECTIONS

In the text there is a discussion of the background and contributions of past sociologists. Go to the Dead Sociologists' Index:

http://www2.pfeiffer.edu/~lridener/DSS/INDEX.HTML

a site that contains biographical information and a summary of some of the contributions of dead sociologists. Click the picture of each sociologist; it will then take you to more information on their contributions. Do you think their contributions are as valid today as they were in the past (dead but still alive)?

improve their lives. Addams won the Nobel Peace Prize in 1931 for her efforts.

Like women, racial minorities were largely excluded from prestigious positions in academics until the last few decades. For example, W. E. B. Du Bois (1868–1963), the first African American to earn a doctorate at Harvard, taught at the then predominantly black Atlanta University (Zamir, 1995). He wrote extensively on minority-related issues, and his activist orientation led him to become a founder of the National Association for the Advancement of Colored People (NAACP), a key organization in the civil rights struggle (Deegan, 1988). The careers of Addams and Du Bois are discussed further in the box entitled "Rediscovering Sociology's Diverse Roots."

During the 1940s and 1950s, sociology in the United States turned away from its reformist orientation and concentrated heavily on empirical research, often on topics unconnected to social problems, with the intent of validating sociology's status as an objective empirical science (Laslett, 1990; Lemert, 2002). The line dividing sociology from social work became sharper. The dominant figure in sociological theory in this era was Talcott Parsons (1902–1979), based at Harvard, whose work was highly abstract and largely removed from the real-world concerns of most earlier sociologists. The best-known activist of this era was C. Wright Mills (1916–1962), discussed earlier, whose writings concentrated mostly on the distribution of power in U.S. society.

The 1960s and 1970s brought tremendous changes. In the context of the war on poverty, the civil rights and feminist movements, the opposition to the war in Vietnam, and the substantial cultural changes initiated by the baby boom generation, sociology's ori-

entation to debunking contributed to a massive increase in the discipline's popularity. The number of sociologists in the United States rose from 3,000 to 25,000, and sociology became the largest single academic major in many colleges and universities. It was also during this era that the work of women and minorities began to have a major impact on the discipline.

A return to social conservatism in the 1980s, symbolized by the election of Ronald Reagan as president and the growth of post-Watergate skepticism about the possibility of meaningful social reform, led to a decline in interest in sociology. However, this trend began to reverse in the 1990s, in part because sociology is so well equipped to explore the increasing globalization of social life. The discipline today is probably as balanced as it has ever been between activist and pure science orientations, with most sociologists drawing on an eclectic mix of theoretical and empirical traditions (Huber, 1995). In addition to more emphasis on globalization, modern sociology has been greatly influenced by the continuing development of feminist scholarship. Also new is the fact that an increasing number of sociologists are working outside of academic settings.

THEORETICAL PERSPECTIVES IN SOCIOLOGY

Up to this point, we have been talking about *the* sociological perspective, but in fact there are several distinct theoretical orientations within the discipline. While virtually all sociologists agree on the scientific nature of the field and on the importance of social factors in explaining human behavior, there is less consensus regarding which theoretical perspectives are most useful.

Historically, most sociologists have tended to make use of one or more of three broad **theoretical perspectives** or general ways of understanding social reality: functionalism, conflict theory, and symbolic interactionism. Recent decades have witnessed the emergence of a fourth perspective—feminism—which is beginning to rival the other three in popularity. Each of these theoretical orientations makes different assumptions about the fundamental character of social life, and each directs its adherents to ask certain kinds of questions about the topics they are studying (Kuhn, 1970; Suppe, 1974; Wallace & Wolf, 1999). None of the major perspectives is better than the others in any absolute sense, although one may be more appropriate than another for the analysis of a given topic.

One important way in which theoretical perspectives vary concerns the level of analysis at which they operate. Functionalism and conflict theory are

macrosociological perspectives because they direct attention to large-scale social phenomena: large groups, organizations, institutions, and whole societies. In contrast, symbolic interactionism is **microsociological** because it concentrates on the details of interaction among people, mostly in small group settings (Adams & Sydie, 2001).

In the following discussion we outline the assumptions of each theoretical perspective and apply each to a sociological analysis of the prison, a topic that is also considered in Chapter 9. The different issues addressed by each perspective will constitute a continuing theme throughout this text.

Functionalism

Functionalism, or as it is sometimes called, structural-functionalism, is a macrosociological theoretical perspective that grew out of the work of Émile Durkheim, Herbert Spencer, the Italian sociologist Vilfredo Pareto, and Talcott Parsons. It was very popular in the United States around the middle of the 20th century and it remains important today.

Functionalism interprets all social groups regardless of size, from a family to a whole society, as systems whose parts are interdependent so that a change in one element necessarily leads to changes in every other element. For example, note how every player on a basketball team must constantly change position in response to his or her teammates' actions. Similarly, consider how a change in one aspect of prison life—

for example, a strike by the guards or the establishment of a new treatment program—will have some effect on the operation of virtually every other part of the organization.

Using the functionalist perspective, social groups can be compared to the interdependent organs in a body, with each organ carrying out a particular function necessary for the continued smooth operation of the whole system (Turner & Maryanski, 1979). This logic is termed the *organic analogy*. Just as the heart pumps blood, the intestines digest food, and the kidneys filter out wastes, in a prison the guards try to maintain order, the cooks prepare meals, and the parole board decides who will be released. Each part exists for a reason, and if it fails to perform its appropriate function, the whole system works less effectively, much as the whole body is harmed if one organ fails. Similarly, if a part of a social system serves no function, then it is likely to eventually fade away—which is why you will have a great deal of trouble finding a store that can repair an eight-track cassette player or a mechanic who is qualified to work on a Model T.

Note that the *function* actually provided by a social system, or by one of its parts, is not necessarily the same as its *purpose*—what we intend for it to do. Most people want prisons to reduce crime, but the very high rate of recidivism (repeat offending) strongly suggests that they frequently fail to perform this function effectively.

In this context, Robert Merton has suggested that we need to distinguish between the **manifest**

Thirty-nine people were killed by authorities during a major riot at the Attica State Prison in upstate New York in September of 1971. Functionalists analyze the activities of control agents as intended to maintain or restore a state of equilibrium.

THEN AND NOW

Rediscovering Sociology's Diverse Roots

Prior to the 1960s, virtually all senior academic positions in sociology in the United States were held by white males, except for some at traditionally female or black institutions. It is more than ironic that the discipline of sociology, which has extensively documented the consequences of discrimination against women and minorities, has a long history of ignoring the contributions of women and persons of color to its own development.

As our understandings have changed over the past 40 years, historians of the discipline have made a conscious effort to seek out early figures who made strong contributions to sociology despite having been excluded from the inner circles of academe. Jane Addams and W. E. B. Du Bois are two of the most important of these rediscovered sociologists.

Addams was born in 1860 to a wealthy family in Massachusetts. She attended the Women's Medical College of Philadelphia but dropped out due to illness. While traveling in England she observed social workers struggling to improve the lives of the residents of

Despite the pervasive racism of his era, W. E. B. Du Bois was one of the outstanding pioneers of early American sociology.

London's Victorian slums and resolved to carry their message home. In 1899, Addams founded Hull House, a "settlement house" located on Chicago's West Side, and for the next 20 years she and her followers worked with the city's poor, sick, and elderly.

Jane Addams was a charter member of the American Sociological Association and published 11 books and hundreds of articles, many in prestigious sociological journals. In 1931, she was honored with a Nobel Peace Prize for her work at Hull House.

William Edward Burghardt Du Bois was also a native of Massachusetts, born in modest circumstances eight years after Addams. His father was a Haitian of African and French ancestry; his mother's background was African and Dutch. Despite being poor and a minority, Du Bois became one of the leading scholars of his era, earning an undergraduate degree at Fisk University and becoming the first African American person to earn a doctorate at Harvard. His dissertation was in history, but while working on his degree he attended sociological lectures by Max Weber at the University of Berlin, and as the new field began to emerge he became an early convert, founding the department of sociology at Atlanta University.

Du Bois published a book on race every year between 1886 and 1914,

---

functions of a social system—the obvious functions we openly intend it to perform—and the **latent functions,** or the unintended and often unrecognized functions it also provides (Merton, 1968). Thus, a prison has the manifest function of crime reduction. It also performs several latent functions, some of which (such as providing employment to prison guards) do not interfere with its ability to perform its manifest function. Others definitely weaken its ability to function as intended (such as the fact that inmates often learn how to be better criminals from their fellow prisoners). The identification of such latent functions is an important part of the process of sociological debunking.

Classic functionalism also assumes that social systems tend to remain largely unchanged so long as all of their parts are functioning properly. This condition of stability is referred to as **equilibrium** or balance. It can be disrupted when elements of the system fail to perform their functions properly, often due to the intrusion of outside forces. These disruptions are referred to as **dysfunctions** because they keep the system from operating smoothly and efficiently (Merton, 1968). In the human body, diseases or accidents can be seen as dysfunctional; in the family, incest is highly dysfunctional; in a prison, a sharp cut in funding or the introduction of large numbers of poorly trained guards or exceptionally violent prisoners will undermine the system's ability to function properly.

Since social systems inherently resist change, if dysfunctions arise, internal mechanisms will activate to restore equilibrium, much as a thermostat turns on the air conditioning when the temperature rises and turns it off once the air has cooled off enough. The human body has similar mechanisms that try to main-

receiving the most attention for *The Philadelphia Negro,* an important contribution to the social survey tradition, and *The Souls of Black Folk,* in which he proposed the notion of *double consciousness.* No doubt influenced by the fact that both of his parents shared African and European heritages, Du Bois observed that every African American maintained a dual identity, simultaneously American and black.

Like Addams, Du Bois was largely ignored by the sociologists of his day; *The Philadelphia Negro* was not even reviewed in major sociological journals. In part, this was because both Addams and Du Bois were proponents of applied sociology: Addams founded Hull House and Du Bois was a central figure in the Niagara Movement, which grew into the National Association for the Advancement of Colored People, a group Addams also joined.

For many years, Du Bois worked as a leader within the black elite to improve the conditions of his people, but eventually he became disgusted with the slow pace of racial progress and veered sharply to the left, embracing revolutionary socialism and emigrating at the age of 93 to the African nation of Ghana, where he died two years later in 1963.

Despite the contributions of pioneers such as Addams and Du Bois, U.S. sociology remained overwhelmingly white and male far into the 20th century. Today, however, the demographics of the field are changing. In 1999, the most recent year for which information is available, 48 percent of the overall membership and 64 percent of the student members of the American Sociological Association (ASA) were women. Two-thirds of ASA members were white, 5 percent African American, 5 percent Asian or Pacific Islander, 2 percent Hispanic, and 3 percent Native American or "other." In addition, two caucuses have emerged within the ASA—Sociologists for Women in Society and the Association for Black Sociologists—that actively promote gender and racial-ethnic diversity in the discipline.

Reflecting their relatively recent entry into sociology, women made up just 22 percent of full professors, 51 percent of assistant professors, and 58 percent of students in departments that granted graduate degrees in 1997–1998. The movement of women and persons of color into sociology has already contributed to its growing emphasis on the intersection of race, class, and gender; to its support of multiculturalism; and to the emergence of the feminist theoretical perspective. As women and minorities continue to grow in numbers and to assume positions of greater influence within sociology, they will massively impact the directions in which the discipline moves in the 21st century.

1. How does being a female or a minority contribute to the development of an individual's sociological imagination?

2. Should sociologists follow the lead of Addams and Du Bois and become more involved in applying sociological findings in order to improve people's lives?

Sources: Du Bois, 1968; Addams, 1910/1981; Aptheker, 1990; Lewis, 1993; Spalter-Roth & Lee, 2000.

---

tain a steady temperature and blood pressure despite the disequilibrating influences of diseases and other dysfunctional factors. If the social system of a prison is thrown out of balance by dysfunctional changes that lead to resistance or rioting on the part of the inmates, then the authorities may institute a 24-hour lockdown or fire incompetent guards—steps intended to restore proper functioning.

Finally, the functional perspective suggests that people in a normally functioning social system will share a number of *values*—understandings of what is good and desirable—that help hold the society together and maintain a state of equilibrium (Turner & Maryanski, 1979). A primary purpose of the socialization process is to ensure that there is a fairly high degree of consensus concerning values. When such consensus does not exist, systems are likely not to function very effectively—precisely the reason there is so much conflict in prisons, where inmates and staff tend to have very different values.

CRITIQUE Functionalism correctly points out that changes in one part of society often lead to changes in other parts. In addition, we can all think of social situations in which stability has been maintained despite potentially disruptive or disequilibrating intrusions. However, some critics charge that the functional perspective overemphasizes the extent to which harmony and stability actually exist in society. By implying that order is more basic than change, and by maintaining that change is frequently dysfunctional, functionalists seem to be saying that the status quo is almost always desirable; yet we all know that sometimes (as in the desperate need to reduce the size of the prison population) change is badly needed in order to create a new and ultimately more effectively functioning sys-

Conflict theorists view prison life, with its clear-cut distinction between powerless inmates and powerful guards, as fundamentally similar to many other aspects of everyday social life.

tem. In short, classic functionalism tended to overlook the positive consequences that can result from conflict and struggle (Coser, 1956; Merton, 1967).

Conflict Theory

Conflict theory is a macrosociological theoretical perspective that is in many ways the mirror image of functionalism. It is heavily based in the work of Karl Marx, but it also reflects insights developed in the 20th century, most notably by Ralf Dahrendorf (b. 1929), Pierre Bourdieu (b. 1930), and Randall Collins (b. 1941). It dominated European sociology throughout most of the last century and has been increasingly popular in the United States since the mid-1960s.

Instead of interpreting social life as normally cooperative and harmonious, conflict theorists view society as an arena in which different individuals and groups struggle with each other in order to obtain scarce and valued resources, especially property, prestige, and power. Thus, in a prison, inmates and staff are continually in conflict in order to get what each group wants—in the case of the prisoners, privileges that will allow them to do "easy time"; in the case of the staff, higher wages and enough control to make their jobs safe. Similarly, the ethnic gangs into which inmates in many prisons are divided—African American, Hispanic, and white—compete with one other for power. Shifting to a larger frame of reference, the prison system is constantly struggling with other governmental functions, such as education or highway construction, for limited tax dollars.

Sometimes these struggles can be more or less equitably resolved for all parties, but conflict theory tends to argue that many social struggles are zero-sum games in which, if one party wins, the other(s) lose.

Conflict theorists do not deny that certain types of social arrangements are functional for particular individuals or groups, but they insist that we must always ask *for whom* they are functional. They view with great skepticism the functionalist assumption that many existing social arrangements can be interpreted as generally positive for an entire social system. For instance, new tax codes will be generally defended as "reforms" by their proponents, with at least the implication that they will benefit everyone, but in reality they generally help some people (usually the rich) far more than others. In the prison setting, strict rules often are functional for the guards but may work against the interests of the inmates. Note that what is dysfunctional for one person or group may be highly functional for another (Tumin, 1964). Cutbacks in prison funding, identified in the previous section as generally dysfunctional, may be very functional from the standpoint of the inmates because they weaken the ability of the warden and guards to control them.

The conflict perspective suggests that change, not stability, is normal. When a given social system—such as a prison—is stable, conflict theorists tend to interpret this not as a sign of harmony and shared values, but rather as evidence that one group—in this case, the prison staff—has enough power to force its preferences on everyone else (Dahrendorf, 1959; Gramsci, 1971; Collins, 1975; Duke, 1976). In other words, social order is more commonly the result of the exercise of elite power rather than a reflection of true consensus.

CRITIQUE Conflict theory counterbalances the optimism of functionalism by emphasizing the significance of power and struggle in social life; issues such as child abuse, terrorism, sexism, and revolution seem naturally suited for a conflict analysis. However, the conflict approach tends to ignore the many areas of social life in which most people really do arrive at an uncoerced consensus about important values such as the desirability of staying to the right when walking down a hallway. Struggles occur, but so does harmony.

Sociologists who favor conflict theory tend, in contrast to most functionalists, to believe that they should become actively involved in society, usually on the side of people who lack substantial social power (Fay, 1987). Critics believe that such activism violates the principle of scientific objectivity and charge that the work of conflict theorists will be disregarded by those who disagree with their values. Conflict theorists respond that functionalists whose research uncovers what appear to be unfair social arrangements but who do not try to change them are no more moral than bystanders who do not try to help people who have been hurt in a traffic accident.

Symbolic Interactionism

The third major sociological theoretical perspective, symbolic interactionism, originated in the United States. It is based on the work of George Herbert Mead (1863–1931) and Charles Horton Cooley (1864–1929), although it was first formally developed and named by Herbert Blumer (1969a).

The most critical difference between symbolic interactionism and the other major theoretical perspectives is its microsociological orientation. Instead of focusing on groups, organizations, institutions, and societies, symbolic interactionists study specific cases of how individual people behave in particular face-to-face social settings (Stryker, 1990; Denzin, 1992).

Both functionalists and conflict theorists regard groups, organizations, institutions, and societies as objectively real and as exerting a strong, even coercive power over human behavior. In contrast, symbolic interactionists emphasize that all these larger structures are ultimately nothing more than the creations of interacting people and that they can therefore be changed. While social structures may indeed appear to constrain our options, if we employ our sociological imagination and debunk them, we will discover that we have more freedom than we thought we did.

For symbolic interactionists, then, society is simply people interacting (Rock, 1985). The meaning of various aspects of social reality is not predetermined but is established through human action. People do not respond directly to the world around them, but rather to the meanings they collectively apply to it (Blumer, 1969b). For example, until recently, many Americans accepted stereotyped notions about racial minorities. But over the past few decades, activists have challenged these biased and inaccurate *definitions of the situation* (Thomas, 1923), and more and more people, whites and minorities alike, are adopting less restrictive understandings of what it means to be a member of a minority group. Furthermore, as socially accepted definitions change, so does people's behavior, which is an important reason minorities are now enjoying greater opportunities.

This point of view was eloquently summed up early in the last century by W. I. Thomas in what has come to be known as the **Thomas Theorem:** "If men [sic] define situations as real, they are real in their consequences" (Thomas & Thomas, 1928). In other words, if prison authorities are convinced that an inmate is a lost cause and therefore do not see any point in providing him with educational or other rehabilita-

We do have the ability to change the meanings we apply to people and their actions, and that can make a great difference in a person's life. The man shown here in a wheelchair taking part in the New York Marathon may have a physical handicap, but that is not limiting his ability to participate in a physical sport such as running a marathon.

tive services, then he will almost certainly leave the institution without a changed outlook or enhanced job skills and will be very likely to commit more crimes; on the other hand, if they see him as capable of being reformed and provide him with therapy and job training, it is much more likely that he will be able to avoid crime in the future.

Obviously, there are some practical limitations to our ability to alter social life by changing the meanings we apply to people and their actions—a physically handicapped athlete will never be a world champion runner—but symbolic interactionists maintain that much of reality is indeed *socially constructed*, a topic discussed at some length in Chapter 6 (Berger & Luckmann, 1966). Whether we view someone as a hopeless cripple or as a successful Special Olympian can make a tremendous difference in his or her life.

Since symbolic interactionists place so much emphasis on identifying the meanings people apply to social phenomena, they consider it especially important to research how individuals subjectively interpret reality. This is an approach that Max Weber termed *verstehen*, which may be translated as "to understand." Symbolic interactionists usually spend a great deal of time simply observing and listening to people with the objective of gaining an understanding of precisely how their subjects perceive the social world in which they live.

CRITIQUE Symbolic interactionism draws our attention to the importance of the way people define the social situations in which they find themselves, and it reminds us that social reality is, in the final analysis, a human construct. It liberates us by emphasizing that we can often change undesirable aspects of our lives. But macrosociologists, especially conflict theorists, argue that symbolic interactionists fail to acknowledge how difficult it is to change long-established social arrangements. The fact that a prison is ultimately a human creation is of very little relevance or comfort to an inmate serving a life term.

The Feminist Perspective

The feminist perspective directs our attention to the androcentric bias of both traditional sociology and contemporary culture (Lindsey, 1997). As we discuss in Chapter 13, an *androcentric* approach assumes that research conducted on males can explain patterns of social behavior for all people. For example, virtually all of the major theories of crime are based on research conducted on men and reflecting the distinctive realities of men's lives, yet they have historically been presented as explanations of crime in general rather than as theories of men's crime (Belknap, 1996; Naffine, 1996; Pollock, 1999). Feminist sociologists

address this problem by explicitly focusing on gender and by emphasizing the importance of the links among gender, class, and race. For example, when looking at women's experiences in prison, they would take into account how race, ethnicity, socioeconomic status, sexual orientation, and age might all influence that experience.

Consistent with conflict theory, feminist sociologists argue that structured social inequality is justified by ideologies that are frequently accepted by both the privileged and the oppressed. These ideologies are challenged only when oppressed groups gain the resources necessary to do so. As more women become sociologists, they are able to question traditional male-dominated sociological research and theories. Thus, the feminist perspective makes use of insights that occur naturally to people who have been personally disadvantaged by subordination (Handel, 1993; Lengermann & Niebrugge-Brantley, 2000). This is consistent with our earlier observation that individuals who are socially marginalized, in this case women, are often especially well prepared to embrace the sociological imagination.

Symbolic interactionism is also useful in building feminist theory, especially when it is linked to the conflict perspective. One promising direction is to focus on the unequal power relations between men and women from the point of view of the women who are "ruled." For example, corporate women who are continually passed over for promotion must manage their behavior in gender-appropriate ways that help them fight for promotion but also allow them to maintain a sense of personal integrity. Symbolic interactionists thus focus on how the label of "feminine" is important in how these women are judged by their peers and by themselves.

With regard to prison, feminists have noted that juvenile females typically serve longer terms in institutions than male juveniles despite that they generally have committed less serious crimes. In part this is because the most common reason young women are brought to the attention of the courts is precocious sexuality, which the male-dominated legal system finds much more problematic in girls than in boys. It also results from the sexist image that women are weaker and thus more easily changed or reformed than men. Thus, sexually active young women are locked away in the paternalistic hope of reforming them, while sexually active young men are often seen as simply "sowing their wild oats" (Chesney-Lind & Shelden, 1998).

CRITIQUE The feminist perspective has had a tremendous impact on sociology over the past three decades, greatly enhancing our ability to understand society as a structure of domination. Criticisms of this

TABLE 1.1

Three Theoretical Perspectives in Sociology

	Functionalism	Conflict Theory	Symbolic Interactionism
Level of Analysis	macrosociological	macrosociological	microsociological
Image of Society	objectively real social structure	objectively real social structure	subjective, a product of human interaction
How Order Is Maintained	voluntarily, through shared values	involuntarily, through exercise of power	through common definitions of reality
View of Change	usually disruptive	normal and often positive	results from alterations in subjective views of reality
Key Figures	Émile Durkheim Herbert Spencer Talcott Parsons Robert Merton	Karl Marx C. Wright Mills Ralf Dahrendorf Randall Collins	George Herbert Mead Charles Horton Cooley Herbert Blumer
Major Criticisms	too conservative; implies that which is must be	too radical; ignores cooperative aspects of social life	ignores effects of social structure

perspective center around the issue of bias. Can feminist sociology uphold the discipline's tradition of scientific objectivity? Some feminists respond by charging that the demand for objectivity is often a smokescreen hiding male bias: Androcentric research is frequently described as objective, while feminist work is decried as lacking objectivity.

Table 1.1 summarizes some of the most important characteristics of the major theoretical perspectives in sociology. Each of these ways of interpreting social reality has its own strengths and weaknesses, and we can gain the most insight by using more than one of them simultaneously (Emimbeyer & Goodwin, 1994). Reflecting the current trend in sociology toward the synthesis of theoretical perspectives (Levine, 1991; Lieberson, 1992), most of the chapters in this text employ multiple perspectives.

THE USES OF SOCIOLOGY

At this point, you may well be asking, Why should I study sociology? What's in it for me other than a few hours of college credit and a warm, dry classroom in which to sit when it's cold and wet outside? Sociologists believe that their discipline provides us with three general benefits: It can help us respond more effectively to major social problems, it can improve our ability to make a living, and it can assist us in making more intelligent decisions about the course of our lives.

Responding to Social Problems

We must have accurate information about troubling social conditions before we can develop practical plans to improve them. If, for example, we desire to create a more effective welfare system, we must find out how many people are currently receiving public assistance, what their social characteristics are, and how they came to be on welfare. We must also study both the strengths and the failings of the current system. If we want people to leave the welfare rolls as quickly as possible and earn a living on their own, we must explore what kinds of jobs are currently available, which skills they require, and how welfare recipients can most effectively be trained in these skills. As we will see in Chapter 11, there are many widely held myths about welfare; if we do not debunk these misunderstandings, then any effort to build a better system will fail because it will be based on a false foundation.

Sociology is well equipped to uncover the truth about social problems such as poverty, crime, terrorism, and discrimination precisely because of its emphasis on careful, reliable empirical research. In addition, the discipline's global orientation can familiarize us with how other societies have responded to these problems. This is one of the reasons why sociologists have a particularly important role to play in the struggle against global terrorism to which the United States is currently committed.

Some sociologists believe that the discipline's efforts to address social problems should be limited to researching the facts and developing theories to explain them. These advocates of **pure sociology** believe that it is the responsibility of other disciplines—especially social work, urban planning, and public administration—to actually use sociological data in the effort to improve social life.

Others, and their numbers are increasing, believe that sociologists should put their knowledge and skills to work in the real world. This orientation is called **applied sociology** (Sullivan, 1992; Larson, 1995). Applied sociologists have been particularly active as advisors and consultants in evaluation research in which they assess the effectiveness of programs designed to remedy various social problems. Others have gone further, actively developing and implementing plans to accomplish goals such as reducing racial and gender discrimination in the business world, fighting hate crimes, or helping neighborhood residents organize to demand needed changes from local governments. Today, over one-quarter of all sociology Ph.D.s are employed in applied roles in nonacademic settings (Lyson & Squires, 1993).

Each of the following chapters ends with a "Society Connections" section that explores how sociological research may help our efforts to solve major social problems.

Making a Living

Some students choose to major in sociology as a way to prepare themselves to enter the field as academics or high-level applied sociologists. If you make this decision, you will need to plan on earning at least a master's degree and probably a doctorate. However, an

INTERNET CONNECTIONS

The text discusses four key theoretical perspectives: functionalism, conflict theory, symbolic interactionism, and the feminist approach. Your understanding of sociological theory will be enhanced by accessing the *Map of Sociological Theory*:

http://www.hewett.norfolk.sch.uk/curric/soc/Theory.htm

From the opening page, click on "Brief Introduction to the Sociological Perspectives on Society." After doing this, you will note that the "map" is "clickable." Try clicking on "conflict/consensus," "functionalism," and "symbolic interactionism."

1. Compare and contrast the different theoretical perspectives. What are the strong and weak points of each?

undergraduate degree in sociology is also a useful job credential. The box on page 25 entitled "What Can I Do with a Degree in Sociology?" presents more information about this option.

Most students who take an introductory course in sociology will not become sociology majors. However, everyone who completes college will find some preparation in sociology valuable because sooner or later almost all college graduates end up working closely with people. You will need an accurate understanding of why people behave as they do so that you

A few decades ago, many businesses restricted the opportunities of women and minorities, but sociological debunking has encouraged millions of people to break through traditional barriers.

SOCIOLOGY OF EVERYDAY LIFE

What Can I Do with a Degree in Sociology?

A liberal arts degree in sociology (or in any other area) is a different sort of job credential than a pre-professional degree in a field like business, nursing, or education. Students who major in these areas are relatively narrowly prepared for specific jobs, whereas liberal arts majors obtain a broader education with special emphasis on the development of such skills as critical thinking, oral and written communication, and quantitative reasoning.

What sorts of jobs are available to someone with an undergraduate major in sociology? According to the American Sociological Association,

a well-educated sociology BA graduate acquires a sense of history, other cultures and times; the interconnectedness of social life; and different frameworks of thought. He or she is proficient at gathering information and putting it into perspective. Sociological training helps students bring a breadth and depth of understanding to the workplace. A sociology graduate learns to think abstractly, formulate problems, ask appropriate questions, search for answers, analyze situations and data, organize material, write well, and make oral presentations that help others develop insight and

make decisions. (American Sociological Association, 1999:7)

In the short run, students with pre-professional degrees sometimes find the job search easier, but over the long haul liberal arts graduates are better prepared for career employment.

Some undergraduate sociology majors do find employment in the discipline, generally in support roles in research, policy analysis, and program evaluation. They find that their courses in research, methods, statistics, and computer applications provide them with their most important technical skills. Many eventually return to school to earn advanced degrees in sociology that open the doors to higher level employment.

However, most people who complete an undergraduate education in sociology begin working in entry-level positions such as these:

social services—in rehabilitation, case management, group work with youth or the elderly, recreation, or administration.
community work—in fund-raising for social service organizations, nonprofit groups, child-care or community development agencies, or environmental groups.

corrections—in probation, parole, or other criminal justice work.
business—in advertising, marketing and consumer research, insurance, real estate, personnel work, training, or sales.
college settings—in admissions, alumni relations, or placement offices.
health services—in family planning, substance abuse, rehabilitation counseling, health planning, hospital admissions, and insurance companies.
publishing, journalism, and public relations—in writing, research, and editing.
government service—in federal, state, and local government jobs in such areas as transportation, housing, agriculture, and labor.
teaching—in elementary and secondary schools, in conjunction with appropriate teacher certification. (American Sociological Association, 1999:10)

1. How do the four key qualities of the sociological imagination—scientific orientation, debunking, diversity, and global focus—help prepare students for today's job world?

2. How would undergraduate preparation in sociology benefit students who seek graduate degrees in fields such as law, medicine, and social work?

---

can interact with them smoothly and inspire them to work collectively toward the accomplishment of shared objectives.

Sociology can also provide students with skills in applying scientific research methods, which can be helpful in careers as varied as education, marketing, law enforcement, and government service. These methods are discussed in Chapter 2.

Making Life Choices

Beyond the world of work, we all face many important life decisions: whether and when and whom to marry; whether to divorce or to remarry; how to vote;

where to live; how to relate to our parents as they age; how to raise our children; when and where to retire. Society provides us with "scripts" that guide us in these decisions, but in many cases, the standard scripts do not include all of the options that are really open to us.

The study of sociology has a unique capacity to make us aware of the full range of alternatives from which we may choose as well as to provide information that can help us make the decisions that are right for us. The remaining chapters in this book each include a "Life Connections" section, which demonstrates some of the ways in which sociology can help you to better understand different aspects of your everyday life. In the end, the authors of this text believe that sociology's greatest promise is simply this: It can help you to debunk your own life—to see that you have more freedom than you may have thought.

For example, some years ago, one of the authors had as a student a woman in her thirties who had recently been released from prison for killing her boyfriend, a man who had subjected her to severe mental and physical abuse. During a class discussion of family violence, she commented that she had grown up in an environment in which virtually every woman she knew had been beaten by a father, boyfriend, or husband. She had seen nonabusive families depicted on television, but never believed that people like that really existed. Through studying sociology, she began to realize that life held more options than she had thought possible. She learned that many people really do establish the kind of caring relationships that she had always believed to be nothing more

than fantasies. She learned that she had the right to expect to be treated with respect.

By the time this student reached her senior year, she had also begun to debunk her career options. She had been socialized to believe that women ideally should not work or that, if they must, they should limit themselves to traditionally female "pink collar" jobs like nurses, librarians, and social workers. Again, her knowledge of sociology broadened her horizons: She realized that women today have the freedom to enter virtually any occupation that interests them. Gifted with considerable artistic talent, she chose to pursue a fulfilling career as a sculptor.

In both of these ways, this student was able to greatly improve her life by using the sociological imagination to debunk the narrow scripts that she had once thought she had to follow. The authors hope that you too may find sociology to be useful in helping you to live as fulfilling a life as possible.

SUMMARY

1. Sociology is a perspective or way of thinking that systematically addresses the impact of social forces on human behavior.

2. Sociologists employ scientific research procedures in order to collect empirical data and construct theories that explain social reality as accurately as possible.

3. Sociologists try to identify the hidden as well as the more obvious explanations for social behavior, a process called debunking.

4. The discipline of sociology emphasizes diversity and the globalization process in explaining contemporary patterns of social life.

5. Sociologists pay particular attention to four general aspects of social life: socialization, structured social inequality, social institutions, and social change.

6. Sociology arose in Europe during the mid-19th century; its development was encouraged by the expansion of science, the ideas of the Enlightenment, the Industrial Revolution, and the spread of colonialism.

7. Women and minorities, largely excluded from the discipline until recently, are now making substantial contributions.

8. The functionalist theoretical perspective analyzes how the various components of social systems work to keep them operating smoothly and efficiently and to avoid dramatic changes.

9. Conflict theory maintains that social life is best understood as a struggle between competing individuals and groups for scarce and valued resources and that change in social life is constant.

10. The symbolic interactionist perspective focuses at the microsociological level on how the meanings that people construct through interaction shape human social behavior.

11. Feminism is an emerging perspective in sociology that draws heavily on the understandings of women and members of other groups that have experienced subordination.

12. Sociology may be useful in helping people solve social problems, earn a living, and make major life decisions.

KEY TERMS

applied sociology 24
debunking 7
dysfunction 18
ecological fallacy 7
empirical evidence 5
equilibrium 18
ideology 10

latent functions 18
macrosociology 17
manifest functions 17
microsociology 17
multiculturalism 9
pure sociology 24
social institution 10

social marginality 8
social stratification 10
socialization 10
sociology 4
theoretical perspective 16
theory 6
Thomas Theorem 21

CRITICAL THINKING QUESTIONS

1. Do you think that sociology can be as scientific in its approach to its subject matter as biology or chemistry are, or are there inherent limitations to the extent to which sociologists can be truly scientific?

2. Both sociology and psychology try to understand the causes of human social behavior. Why do you think some people tend to find one of these disciplines more useful or valid than the other?

3. Why do you think that sociology, and in particular its orientation to debunking, is more popular in some eras than in others? Do you think that the appeal of debunking is currently growing? Why?

4. What are some of the sorts of questions that sociologists using the four major theoretical perspectives might ask concerning terrorism?

INVESTIGATE WITH CONTENT SELECT

Journal Research Collections from Content Select This feature at the end of each chapter of this textbook will provide you with access to a great resource to begin your research—ContentSelect—part of Prentice Hall's Research Navigator Website. It is an online journal database that provides you with a gateway to over one hundred quality, peer-reviewed journals and many more current popular publications.

To access ContentSelect, use the Access Code found inside the front cover of your copy of the Prentice Hall Guide to Evaluating Online Resources for Sociology that may have been wrapped with your new textbook. Visit http://www.researchnavigator.com and click on the New User button. Enter your access code and your other pertinent information and create your own personal Userid and Password.

Upon returning to this site in the future, simply click on Returning Users and enter your personal Userid and Password. Select the Sociology-specific journal collection and you may or may not want to include the General Interest popular publications or any of the other journal collections.

Once in the Sociology database, enter the following search words into the search field:

Feminism
Max Weber
Globalization
Sociological perspective

2
THE RESEARCH PROCESS

Class and Race in an Urban Neighborhood

Elijah Anderson, an African American sociologist, began his 14-year study of an urban neighborhood in an eastern U.S. city when he and his wife moved into the neighborhood, and he continued it after he moved away. He spent many hours on the street—talking, listening, interviewing, and getting to know all kinds of people, from small-time drug dealers to police officers, middle-class whites, and African American community activists. By day, according to his description of the neighborhood, it is a pleasant community of close friends and civil people. It has a reputation for being the most diverse and socially tolerant area of the city. But at night things change. People Anderson interviewed see the same streets as a jungle after dark—places of uncertainty at best and hostility at worst. Strangers are monitored, especially African American males who cross the invisible class boundary when they wander into the neighborhood. The research reveals the intersection of class and race. Residents socialize with others they feel most comfortable with—people who are superficially similar to themselves in both social class and color. Class and race pieces fit together only because of the researcher's deep familiarity and personal experience with the neighborhood. (Adapted from Anderson, 1990)

How Is the United States Doing? Assessing a Nation's Social Health

Picking up the business section of a daily newspaper may tell us that the United States is doing quite well. The economy is steadily rebounding since 9/11; stocks are up, unemployment is down, interest rates are stable, and the number of first-time home buyers hit an all time high. Turning to the sections on health and welfare may provide a different view. Reports show that the gap between the richest Americans and everyone else is growing, suicide among young people has tripled since 1950, a large percent of people of color have no health insurance, and HIV infection rates for African American women continue to increase. Interviews with homeless people, who are growing in number, indicate that many believe they will remain on the street for the rest of their lives. Turning to the education section, a survey of middle-class parents finds them deeply concerned about how they can manage the cost of a college education for their children. The nation's portrait can be painted a number of different ways depending on which data are selected, combined, and presented to the public. Can people be optimistic about economic progress but pessimistic about social progress at the same time? Democratic societies must always provide accurate data on social progress to deepen the connection between society and citizen. (Miringoff & Miringoff, 1999; Stille, 2001; Centers for Disease Control, 2002; U.S. Bureau of the Census, 2002)

These vignettes illustrate several important ways social scientists conduct research. Elijah Anderson did *field research*, collecting data in the natural setting of his neighborhood that allowed for a great deal of in-depth understanding of the neighborhood. Social scientists who gauge economic and social progress may rely on *secondary research*, accessing available data such as stock market prices, unemployment rates, and statistics on health and welfare. To assess level of optimism, they also conduct *survey research*, through questionnaires people fill out themselves or through personal interviews where interviewers ask the questions and record the responses. Both middle-class and homeless people may be selected to participate in survey research. In addition to field research, survey research, and secondary research, social scientists may conduct *experiments* under conditions that they control. Using the stages in the research process as a framework, this chapter describes some important ways that social scientists collect and analyze data and demonstrates how all these stages are guided by sociological theory. It overviews those pioneering studies that have served as standards for research in sociology today. Finally, the chapter highlights some of the ethical issues that are raised when any research is conducted.

RESEARCH AND THE SCIENCE OF SOCIOLOGY

Research is a central element of modern life. The research reported to us—especially through the media—impacts our everyday lives in many ways. Research is used to determine how much we pay for car insurance, what kinds of TV programs we watch, and whether our tax dollars should be spent on a new jail or a new park. The latest research studies related to health and lifestyle aid in our choices of the foods we eat, the amount of exercise we get, and the medicines we take. Businesses rely heavily on consumer behavior research to determine the array of products and services they offer. Sociologists play key roles in both gathering and explaining research data. They are interested in *social* research—research regarding people and their interactions with one another. Their main focus is on social *scientific* research—studying people for the purposes of testing and building theories to explain social behavior. The quest for these explanations is the most important reason to do scientific research.

As a science, sociology is guided in its quest for knowledge by a set of standards designed to ensure that what we know is both accurate and useful. These standards are part of the **scientific method,** a systematic procedure for acquiring knowledge that relies on *empirical evidence*, defined in the first chapter as data derived from observation and experience. The scientific method is the basic blueprint for the work of sociologists.

In sociology, theory and research are always intertwined. Chapter 1 discussed how sociologists describe and explain human social behavior through a variety of theoretical perspectives, particularly functionalism, conflict theory, symbolic interactionism, and the feminist perspective. Sociological research tests, modifies, and develops specific theories based on these and other broad perspectives. The completion of any research project sets the stage for the next one, which builds on what has been learned so far to reach the next level of understanding. It is useful to think of the research process as the research *cycle*. Scientific knowledge is continually broadened, corrected, and refined.

Scientific research is expected to be *objective*—carried out in a neutral, unbiased way. Scientists try not to let personal beliefs or feelings interfere with the conduct of their research. Recognizing that sociology would be in peril if values or personal opinions biased research, Max Weber (1925/1946), one of the founders of sociology, called for sociologists to be *value-free* in their work. Weber also believed that sociology would be well served by using methods that provide the researcher with an understanding of the people being studied, yet in gaining such understanding, researchers often become personally connected to their research participants. Can researchers ever be totally value-free? Contemporary sociologists think

Sociological research uncovers patterns of behavior. This scene at a job fair held for the hundreds of people—from white collar and professional workers to semi-skilled—who lost their jobs as a result of the terrorist attacks, can be a field laboratory to determine how race, gender, ethnicity, and social class may be linked.

not. As scientists, sociologists must make decisions based on ethical principles, which by definition are based on values; otherwise, the people they study might be put at risk.

The scientific method helps protect science from errors in human judgment in two important ways. First, the scientific method, including the knowledge generated by using the method, is basically self-correcting. If the scientific method is used properly, different researchers investigating similar questions should arrive at similar conclusions. If they do not, then flaws in the original research were likely discovered by later research. Actual changes over time in the topic under investigation may also have occurred that are uncovered in the later research. In either case, new knowledge is gained. The second way science deals with errors in judgment is that research is carried out under fairly strict ethical guidelines, especially important to sociologists who use human subjects in research.

STEPS IN THE RESEARCH PROCESS

The scientific method provides a roadmap for the research process. This map designates different routes depending on whether the researcher's purpose is to start with a testable **hypothesis** (an expectation or prediction derived from a theory) or to *explore* a topic and end with a hypothesis. The route that starts with a hypothesis to be tested is the most common one in sociology. It is useful to refer to Figure 2.1 as you move through the process. We examine the major steps using the topic of "romantic love"—a topic that has been of interest to sociologists for many decades.

Formulating the Problem

There are always gaps in knowledge. The key role of scientific research is to help bridge these gaps. As Figure 2.1 shows, the vast body of knowledge includes theories and scientific laws as well as people's ideas and personal experiences about the social world. The first step in the research process is to formulate a problem designed to fill in some of these gaps, but in doing so, other gaps may be discovered. This stage of research begins with identifying a general topic to study and ends with forming a specific hypothesis or prediction about it. In between these beginning and end points in the problem-formulation stage come two other steps: reviewing the literature and specifying the research question.

The problem-formulation stage is often the most difficult because many different options are usually examined before a final hypothesis is developed. In addition, some exploration of past research must

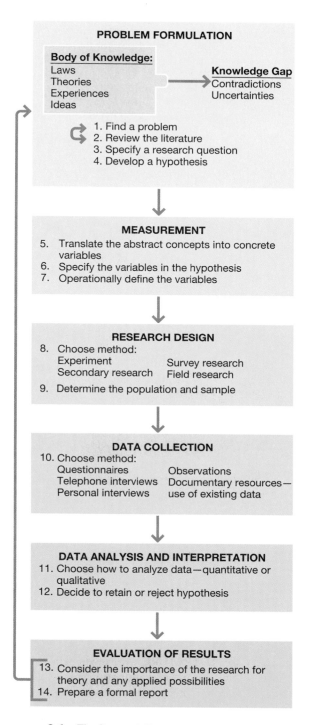

FIGURE 2.1 The Research Process.

occur even before a detailed literature review, as shown by the arrow loop linking steps 1 and 2 in Figure 2.1. This makes problem formulation very creative but also very time consuming. Students frequently report putting in many "wasted" hours on this stage. It is not wasted time, however, since familiarity with a topic is gained. Without this effort, a meaningful research question and hypothesis rarely material-

Sociologists may study media influences on behavior by examining the violent content of music. Teens who listen to music containing violent messages related to suicide, crime, drugs, and sex—such as in the lyrics and videos of rock star and rapper Eminem—may be more antisocial or violence prone than those who listen to other types of music.

ize. Of all the steps in the process, problem formulation often takes the most time, but when done accurately, it can yield large research payoffs.

REVIEWING THE LITERATURE Reviewing the literature involves a thorough examination of scientific journals and other reputable sources to yield information about the past research and theories related to the topic of interest. The researcher compares this information, drawing conclusions from many separate studies that address similar questions. The literature review allows the researcher to build a *conceptual framework* that summarizes information about the research and integrates important concepts. A well-integrated conceptual framework will expose gaps in the body of knowledge, an essential ingredient in scientific research; it is here that the theory on which the entire study is based is explored. The arrows in Figure 2.1 show that the research process is circular, suggest-

ing that when the conclusions are evaluated, they must be related back to the body of knowledge (theories) from which they originated.

A literature review on the concept of romantic love shows that it includes many components, such as altruism, sexual intimacy, compassion, sacrifice, and trust. The review also provides strong empirical evidence that these components are likely to be expressed differently by women and men. When the research on the components of romantic love is brought together with the research on how women and men express them, a conceptual framework is built. With a literature review showing that the concepts of gender and romantic love are linked by empirical evidence, the path to new research on the topic begins.

SPECIFYING THE RESEARCH QUESTION Since the literature review builds a conceptual framework that exposes gaps in the body of knowledge, the next step is to determine a research question that will help fill in the gaps. The research question usually asks about a relationship between concepts. For example, the researcher may notice that there is a gap in knowledge about the influence of gender on expression of romantic love. The researcher might then ask, What is the relationship between gender and the expression of romantic love?

DEVELOPING A HYPOTHESIS The researcher forms a hypothesis by predicting an answer to the research question. The concepts in a hypothesis are stated as **variables**—characteristics or traits that can be measured. Age is one example of a variable; it is a factor that differs from one person to the next. Age varies along a continuum, such as categorizing people under or over a certain age, or whether they see themselves as young, middle aged, or elderly. The variable age then is divided into categories called *attributes*. Researchers focus on those attributes that are relevant to their study. In research on gender and romantic love, gender is a variable, and its attributes are male and female.

In forming a hypothesis, a researcher relates an independent variable to a dependent variable. An **independent variable** is one that is presumed to cause change in the dependent variable. It follows, then, that a **dependent variable** is one that is presumed to be changed or caused by the independent variable. In other words, changes in the dependent variable at least partially depend on changes in the independent variable. Through the literature review the researcher forms the following hypothesis: *Men are likely to express romantic love sooner in a relationship than are women.* Here *gender* is the independent variable and *expression of romantic love* is the dependent variable. As gender varies (that is, as the researcher looks at men

In studying social interaction, research is often conducted in settings that are set up to be as natural as possible, but with some control over how the observations are recorded.

compared to women), the expression of love is predicted to change—gender is hypothesized to be a *cause* of the timing of when love is expressed. The research is being conducted to explain the change in the dependent variable, in this case the timing of the expression of romantic love.

Hypotheses may also account for other variables. The most important of these, **control variables,** are those that are held constant to clarify the influence of the independent variable on the dependent variable. For example, since the literature review determined that women in the lower social classes express love sooner than women in the middle or upper social classes, researchers would have to make sure that social class (the control variable) was held constant in any study of how gender affects expression of love. If not, they would have trouble explaining why one person is declaring love sooner than another: Is it because of gender or because of social class? When the control variable is added, the hypothesis can be refined: Regardless of social class, men express love earlier than women.

Measurement

In order to test our hypothesis, the concepts of gender and love need to be translated into variables that can be measured. **Measurement** is the process of assigning values, such as numbers, to variables. Measurement moves research from the abstract, conceptual level to the concrete, empirical level.

An **operational definition,** a key requirement for measuring any variable, specifies how concepts and variables are empirically measured. Gender is a given and needs only to be classified according to its two attributes, male and female. Love, on the other hand, is a very complex concept that needs to be narrowed

considerably for research purposes. The following example on the formation of an operational definition of romantic love illustrates this important measurement procedure.

What Is Romantic Love?

Conceptual level: Love is the attraction to another person that is associated with intense feelings of joy, passion, and sexual attraction.

Empirical level: Love is a state of emotional well-being and physiological changes when thinking about or being with the target of one's affection.

Operational definition: Love is determined by the number of times one calls and thinks about the love target and shows certain psychological, behavioral, and physiological changes in his or her presence, such as heart pounding, pupil dilation, smiling, laughing, and forgetfulness.

Notice how the definition becomes more specific as it approaches the operational level.

Operational definitions are necessary to measure variables, but can sometimes seem far removed from the original concept. This raises the issue of measurement quality. To condense the complexity of love into three simple indicators of joy, passion, and sexual attraction might not accurately represent what love is all about. If only one indicator, such as pupil dilation, is used (a person's pupil becomes larger when he or she is in the presence of a liked person), love may be reduced even more. This brings up the issue of **validity**—are you measuring what you think you are measuring? The greater the distance from the conceptual level to the operational level, the greater the concern about validity. The gender variable poses no

Romantic love can be studied many different ways. One way is to observe couples in public settings to determine if different couples show similar kinds of behaviors, such as kissing and hugging.

real validity problem, but the love variable does. Is our operational definition of love accurate?

A second issue of measurement quality involves **reliability**—would you get the same results if you repeated the measurement? The key concern about reliability is the *consistency* of the measurement. Again, gender presents no problem. But it may be more difficult to construct a reliable tool to measure love.

As for validity, researchers can never be completely certain that measurements are accurate. However, if they choose measurements that have been used successfully in past studies, they have reason to believe that those measurements have some validity. Sociologists have studied romantic love extensively, and a number of sound measurement tools have been developed.

Fortunately, science and the research process itself help deal with these measurement quality issues. As noted earlier, science is self-correcting because the research on which it is based is continually improved upon. Although it is not foolproof, continual refinements in measurement quality help in the self-correction process.

Now that we have our hypothesis, it is time to move on to research design and data collection.

Choosing a Research Design

The research process is guided by a **research design,** an organized plan for collecting data. There are four major types of research design—experiments, surveys, secondary research, and field research—which will be discussed more fully later in the chapter. The re-

INTERNET CONNECTIONS

After reading the section about analyzing data with the use of statistical measures go to the Website simulations/demonstrations:

http://www.ruf.rice.edu/~lane/stat_sim/

to learn more about different statistical measures. Click on one of the bubbles on the left then click on the highlighted statement and read about the measure and do the practice exercise.

Observational research techniques, including participant observation have many advantages. Go to "Collecting Data Through Observation":

http://trochim.human.cornell.edu/tutorial/brown/Laura TP.htm

What are the major advantages of observational field research? What are this method's weaknesses? What are the two most commonly used types of *direct observation*? What are the main concerns in using this method?

search question and its hypothesis help determine which plan to select. The selection of a research design is also determined by the **population,** the entire group of people who are the focus of the research and to whom the research results will be generalized. Since populations are usually too large to study as a whole, a **sample**—a subset or part of the larger popu-

GLOBAL CONNECTIONS

Doing Cross-Cultural Research

All research is influenced by culture, and problems arise when these influences are taken for granted. These problems are magnified in cross-cultural research when data from several different cultures are collected and compared. Often, a goal of cross-cultural research is to produce ethnographies of the various cultures being studied. This form of research requires good political conditions and open access to the gathering of data inside a culture. If these conditions are not met, data may be unavailable, or available data may be suspect. Another potential problem is translation. The same questionnaire items are often asked in different languages in order to compare responses across cultures, but it is sometimes impossible to translate items literally into another language. The following examples of printed signs translated into English illustrate the translation hazard:

On a Swiss menu: Our wines leave you nothing to hope for.

In an Acapulco hotel: The manager has personally passed all the water served here.

In a laundromat in Rome: Ladies, leave your clothes here and spend the afternoon having a good time.

In a Copenhagen airlines office: We take your bags and send them in all directions.

In a Greek tailor shop: Order your summer suits. Because is big rush we will execute customers in strict rotation.

In a Hong Kong dentist's office: Teeth extracted by the latest Methodists.

Detour sign in Japan: Stop! Drive sideways.

Researchers working in other cultures will do a better job when they take the following suggestions seriously:

1. Take a crash course in the language of the culture where you will be doing the research. You will probably never become bilingual, but understanding at least some of the language helps you better understand the culture.

2. Get as comprehensive a demographic and social picture as possible from all subjects in all cultures. Go beyond the usual age, gender, race, and occupation variables and seek out religion, ethnicity, sexual orientation, birth order, education, and family practices, to name a few. These key variables enhance understanding of cultural diversity. The intersection of these variables in the lives of your subjects are also revealed.

3. Prior to your research, take a few days to "tour" the culture. Start with an Internet tour, then tailor a brief onsite tour to familiarize yourself with the social institutions that you will be studying. If religion is your topic, visit the culture's places of worship and cemeteries. If economic development is your topic, visit stores, outdoor markets, banks, and charitable agencies. If gender relations is your topic, note the places where gender segregation occurs and where it doesn't. If sports is your topic, go to a soccer match or baseball game.

4. Work as closely as possible with people from the cultures to be compared, both as research participants and as research partners. If you don't have a partner in the host culture, get one.

5. Develop research tools that are appropriate to the cultures in question. Do not assume that a method that succeeds in Southeast Asia will also succeed in East Africa. Researchers in Vietnam and Thailand, for example, face a "courtesy bias" in which all household guests are treated with honor and politeness. Often the courtesy bias generates a cross-cultural Hawthorne effect. Subjects will give researchers any information they think the researcher—the household guest—desires, regardless of what they really believe about the topic under study. On the other hand, the Nuer of East Africa are suspicious of outsiders and expert at sabotaging inquiry at any level; they either refuse to answer questions or they give circular answers or meaningless responses to the simplest questions.

6. Collect the same data on yourself as you get from your subjects. This is not only a good way for the researcher to gain some insight on how subjects may be impacted by the topic, but it can reveal what the researcher takes for granted culturally. For instance, if you are from a secular state and want to compare religiosity in your culture with that of people living in a culture where the state and religion are one and the same, you will quickly discover the degree to which religion influences your own life.

Sociology as a discipline has much to gain from cross-cultural research and access to comparative data. This type of research is one of the best ways to enhance knowledge about the variety of human social diversity. Most important, cross-cultural research allows the formation of theories that explain how cultures are both alike and different, a necessary ingredient for global sociology.

1. What opportunities and challenges are offered by doing research on people from different cultures who happen to live in the same city? Demonstrate how the principles of doing cross-cultural research apply.

2. How would you deal with language and other cultural barriers when doing research on sexuality with couples in cultures in which women are restricted from interacting with strangers?

Sources: Triandis, 1994:82; Sjoberg & Nett, 1997; Martin & Beittel, 1998; Grant & May, 1999; Ember & Ember, 2001; Gille, 2001.

lation that is being studied—is drawn. The sample is supposed to represent the larger population. Survey research would be a good research design to use in our study of gender and expression of romantic love. A survey could be done on a sample of students in selected colleges who are believed to represent the larger population of all college students. Once the sample is selected, data collection can begin.

Collecting Data

Armed with operational definitions of variables and a research design, we are ready for data collection. Sociologists rely on four major methods of data collection: questionnaires filled out by respondents, interviews conducted by the researcher or trained interviewers, observations of behavior, and documentary resources, such as the economic indicators mentioned in the chapter opening. Each method can be used individually, but when they are used in combination, the quality of measurement, especially validity, is enhanced. *Triangulation* is the use of multiple data collection methods. A questionnaire may assess attitudes on a topic, but when questionnaire responses are found to be consistent with interviews and observed behavior, validity increases. For example, in a questionnaire about attitudes toward romance people may indicate they are not romantic, but when interviewed about this topic or observed holding hands or showing affection in public, they may reveal romantic behavior on a number of occasions. What people say and what they actually do may be different. As triangulation demonstrates, more valid data are obtained when questionnaires are supplemented by interviews

and observed behavior. Of these three methods of data collection, questionnaires and interviews are the techniques that are widely used in survey research design.

Analyzing and Interpreting Data

Carefully collected data are now in hand and ready to be analyzed. At this stage researchers summarize and interpret their findings, drawing conclusions about whether the findings support their hypothesis. In doing this, they answer four major questions (Bouma, 1993:178):

1. What did they ask?
2. What did they find?
3. What is concluded from the findings?
4. To whom do the conclusions apply?

Answering "What did they ask?" forces researchers back to the theoretical roots of their research question. They must address not only what they asked but also how they asked it, confronting the validity issue again. Did they measure concepts appropriately to link theory to data? In our study of romantic love, for example, is it valid to assess love by giving people questionnaires that ask how they respond to a loved one? If so, the study got off to a good start.

The second question ("What did they find?") involves coding and summarizing the data. *Coding* means transforming the raw data into numbers to make it suitable for analysis. There are many statistical tools available for data analysis. Students often fear this stage of the research process because they are

Face-to-face interviews are the best way to get answers to complex questions. Prearranged interviews in the home have much higher response rates and are enjoyed more by the respondents than interviews when respondents may feel intruded upon by the interviewer.

faced with a torrent of numbers that seems to demand a great deal of quantitative sophistication. The good news is that computers help process data efficiently. Once the researcher decides on the appropriate statistics, computers can do the calculations and generate tables quickly. The hard part is not actually "doing" the statistics, but understanding how to interpret them when they are presented. Some of the statistics most commonly used in sociology are shown in Figure 2.2. Courses in research and statistics can teach you many other data analysis techniques. Such courses are beneficial because research and its interpretation are done in almost any work setting.

Good statistical analysis of data makes answering the third question easier: "What is concluded from the findings?" Was the hypothesis supported, partially supported, or not supported at all, and under what circumstances? The degree of support for the hypothesis is critical for later evaluation of the results.

Finally, researchers must determine to whom the results apply. Do they apply only to the people in the sample, to a broader population these people represent, or to others who may have been studied previously on the same topic? Can the college students who provided data on their attitudes about romantic love represent all college students? Again, appropriate statistics and sampling techniques can answer this question.

Evaluating the Results

Creativity is a hallmark of the last stage of research, evaluation of the research results. This is the stage in which the researcher must consider two important issues: one theoretical and one applied. If the hypothesis is partially supported or is not supported at all, the theory from which the hypothesis was derived may be in doubt. Researchers refine the theory to explain discrepancies, offering potential for future research. New gaps are created that should be explored further. The arrows in Figure 2.1 extending from the evaluation stage to the problem-formulation stage account for this possibility. Even in studies in which hypotheses are supported, theories are usually refined. For scientific knowledge on social behavior to advance, theories need to be modified and conclusions applied to wider and wider groups of people. The process of science, therefore, "continues continually."

The applied issue involves the use of the study results in various settings. For example, if there are important differences between college men and women in expression of romantic love, do these differences impact their college lives? Chances are they do. Student service personnel may apply the results to better understand cycles of elation or depression that may interfere with study habits, academic performance, and interpersonal relationships. Researchers often provide reports of results to people who participated in the study as well as others who may find the results useful. Because research benefits science, it must ultimately benefit people in general (Sjoberg & Nett, 1997).

Measures of Central Tendency—Statistics that summarize data by describing the typical or average score in a distribution of scores. These statisitics can be demonstrated with a distribution of scores on a sociology exam, where seven students received the following scores:

55   68   73   79   88   88   95

1. *Mean*—The arithmetic average of a distribution. Add up the scores, then divide by the number of scores. The mean is 78 (546/7).
2. *Median*—The middle score in a distribution. List the scores from low to high (as shown above) and find the middle one. The median is 79.
3. *Mode*—The most frequently occurring score in a distribution. The mode is 88, the only score occurring more than once.

Measures of Variation

1. *Range*—The distance from the lowest score to the highest score in a distribution. The *range* can be stated as either 55 to 95, or as 40, found by subtracting the lowest from the highest score.
2. *Standard deviation*—Summarizes the distribution's spread around the mean. The standard deviation can be used to compare test scores over a semester. Tests with larger standard deviations, thus larger variability, may be redesigned since instructors may want student scores less spread out from the average score.

Correlation Coefficient—Measures the strength of a relationship between two variables. Pearson's product–moment correlation (r) is the most widely used statistic for correlation. The higher the correlation between two variables, the stronger the relationship. If data on test scores in college are highly correlated with income after graduation, we can say that test scores in college are good predictors of later income.

FIGURE 2.2 *Commonly Used Measures in Sociological Research.*

RESEARCH DESIGN

Some questions are better answered with one type of research design than another. Scientists can select from a variety of standard designs, as well as modify or combine aspects of different designs to facilitate answering the particular research question selected. We will concentrate on those most commonly used in sociological investigation, with special emphasis on survey research. One specific type of research design—the experiment—is the foundation for all science, regardless of discipline.

Experimental Design

The goal of science is to build sound theories for explaining topics important to the specific discipline. This goal is achieved through devising research that determines the effect one variable has on another. It is only through a well-controlled experiment, usually in a laboratory setting, that scientists can legitimately use the word *cause* in explaining the connection between variables.

Experiments rely on the essential condition that the researcher can manipulate, and thus control, the independent variable in certain ways. This need to control the independent variable makes a laboratory setting the logical site for conducting experiments, since the researcher oversees the setting and can better deal with anything that may intrude on the research. "Classic" experimental design involves four steps:

1. The researcher divides subjects into two equivalent groups: an **experimental group** that is exposed to the independent variable and a **control group** that is not.
2. Division into these groups is accomplished according to *random assignment*—by flipping a coin, for example—so subjects do not self-select either group. Subjects are not told to which group they are assigned. This precaution ensures that the two groups are as much alike as possible except for the exposure of the experimental group to the independent variable. Random assignment of subjects to experimental and control groups is the principal way to rule out other variables that may affect the results. If some subjects are more hungry, fatigued, bored, or more knowledgeable about the topic under study than other subjects—factors that may compromise the experiment—random assignment assumes that an equal number of hungry or knowledgeable subjects will be in each group. The researcher can therefore rule out potential influence of these factors on the dependent variable.
3. Before the experiment, the researcher measures the dependent variable in both groups by means of a *pretest*. After the experimental group is exposed to the independent variable, the researcher measures the dependent variable in both groups again by means of a *posttest*.
4. The researcher compares the pretest and posttest measurements for the two groups. Any difference in the dependent variable between the two groups can be attributed to the influence of the independent variable. If the experiment was conducted properly, and all conditions met, it can be concluded that the independent variable caused the change in the dependent variable.

WHAT IS A CAUSE? Determining causality is the most important goal in doing research, but it is also the most difficult. Four conditions must be met before a researcher can say that an independent variable or variables caused the change in the dependent variable. We will look at the research question "What is the relationship between education and income?" to show how these conditions can be applied. Education is the independent variable, and income is the dependent variable. The hypothesis—the probable answer to the research question—is that education "influences" income. To substitute the word *cause* for the word *influence*, however, all four of the following conditions must be met.

1. *Time order.* The cause must come before the effect. Something in the future cannot cause something in the present or the past. A person will complete some schooling before getting a job. Education precedes income.
2. *Correlation.* The independent and dependent variables are linked in a patterned way so that a change in one variable corresponds to a change in the other. There is a systematic statistical link between them. This systematic relationship is called a **correlation.** As education increases, income increases.
3. *Elimination of spuriousness.* The observed correlation or relationship between the independent and dependent variables cannot be explained by a third variable. Thus, research must eliminate the possibility of a false or **spurious relationship** that is not a relationship at all because another variable is the true explanation for it. In our example, education must be the sole reason for any variation in income. However, since more than one cause can produce an effect, if researchers can identify all the independent variables (or causes), it is possible to rule out spuriousness. Education in combination with gender and job specialty, for example, may be all the likely independent variables needed to explain differences in income. The "Life Connections" section explores these links further.
4. *Theory.* If one variable causes another, there must be some logical link between them that explains the relationship between the two. There is a logical fit between education (independent variable) and income (dependent variable). Higher-paying

jobs require more education and expertise that goes along with it, so education produces a corresponding rise in income. Research must always be framed in a theory that explains empirical findings.

Meeting all four conditions is difficult for researchers. Even when a logical correlation exists, there may be no clear indication of which variable comes first. Education may precede higher income, but the reverse could also be true. As education increases, income increases. But those with higher income can afford more education in the first place. So

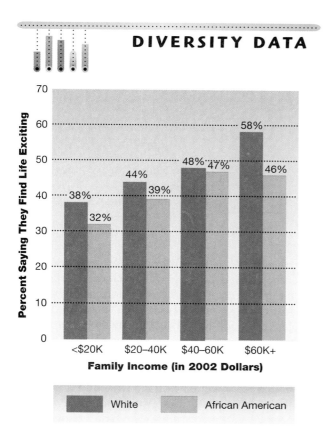

DIVERSITY DATA

FIGURE 2.3   Do Income and Race Relate to Who Finds Life Exciting? As family income increases, the percent of people who find life exciting also increases, for both whites and African Americans. Although income level is one of the strongest variables in predicting quality of life overall, race also appears to make a difference at the highest and lowest income levels for this relationship. What other variables might also predict it? Would any additional variables make the relationship between income and quality of life a spurious one?

Source: NORC. General Social Surveys, 1972–2000. Chicago: National Opinion Research Center, 2000. Reprinted by permission of NORC, Chicago, IL.

education causes an increase in income and income causes an increase in education.

The problem is even more difficult when studying correlations between variables on attitudes and behavior that are not as easily measured as are demographic variables like income or education. For example, sociologists have found that fans of "heavy metal" music, with its frequent themes of social chaos, hopelessness, despair, and depression, have more thoughts of suicide, belief in the acceptability of suicide, and an overall higher risk of taking their own lives than those who seldom listen to heavy metal music. (Lester & Whipple, 1996; Stack, 1998; Ryan 1999; Burge & Lester, 2001). Some teenage suicide victims had reportedly listened to Ozzy Osbourne's popular "Suicide Solution." Which comes first? Are depressed teens drawn to heavy metal music, or do they become depressed after listening to the music? Plausible theories might explain either time order.

Of all the criteria for causality, eliminating spuriousness is the most difficult to accomplish in sociological research. The heavy metal music example is an excellent illustration of this. Although the relationship between preference for heavy metal music and increased risk for suicide is documented, data also show that heavy metal fans have lower levels of religiosity and higher levels of drug use and family disorganization than nonfans (Scheel & Westefeld, 1999; Stack, 2000). When controlling for these variables, the original relationship becomes spurious. Other factors that are correlated to suicide risk among heavy metal fans are gender (boys are at higher risk than girls), race (whites are at higher risk than African Americans), and personality (introverts are at higher risk than extraverts) (Lester & Whipple, 1996; Stack, 2000; LaCourse et al., 2001). These are only a few of the many possible variables that still need to be studied. Thus, it is impossible to say that listening to too much heavy metal music causes suicide.

As discussed above, psychologists in controlled laboratory settings can use the technique of random assignment to rule out factors that may affect the dependent variable, thus eliminating spuriousness. But controlled laboratory settings are less suitable for large groups of people, the main concern of sociology. However, sociologists who do research on small groups of people may design experiments in natural settings that build in some control, even though spuriousness cannot be entirely eliminated.

ILLUSTRATING A FIELD EXPERIMENT   A field experiment is carried out in a setting typical to the lives of people being studied. An important set of field experiments conducted more than 60 years ago inadvertently encountered the problem of spuriousness. These experiments took place at the Western Electric

Can you spot the spurious relationship here? What is the independent variable? What is the dependent variable?

Source: DILBERT reprinted by permission of United Feature Syndicate, Inc.

Company's Hawthorne plant near Chicago, using as subjects employees who made telephone equipment (Mayo, 1933; Homans, 1951). The company had always been concerned about good working conditions and employee welfare. Managers wanted to learn how they could raise both worker productivity (the speed and efficiency of output) and worker satisfaction, the dependent variables. The independent variables included different working conditions, such as lighting changes, the number and duration of rests, total hours of work each day, degree of supervision, and type of equipment used. Although the researchers did not use a control group in these studies, they did take pretests of productivity and satisfaction before introducing each change in an independent variable. Then, after the change in that variable, they took posttests to gauge what, if any, effects had occurred. "Average" workers were chosen to participate in the research. These workers knew they were involved in important experiments and that the eyes of management were upon them. The experiments clearly showed that better working conditions improved productivity as well as employee satisfaction.

As the experiment continued, productivity increased. But something was puzzling. Productivity rose regardless of how the experimental conditions were changed. If lighting was dimmer, breaks were shorter, and there was less supervision, output still increased. Changes taking place in productivity had no simple correlation to the experimental changes in the working conditions. If the working conditions did not cause the changes in productivity, what did?

The answer turned out to be the experiment itself. The workers were being influenced simply by the knowledge that they were part of an important study—a phenomenon now called the **Hawthorne effect.** Workers wanted to please the researchers and look good in the eyes of management. As a result, they worked harder no matter what conditions they encountered. Simply by conducting the experiment, the researchers caused spuriousness—the presumed relationship between the independent variables and the dependent variable was false because the experiment itself and not the changes in working conditions caused the increase in worker productivity.

The Hawthorne effect is most likely to occur in a field experiment like this one in which the subjects come to the study highly motivated to "shine" in their performance. The researchers could not eliminate the desire to please the employer that was so widespread at the Hawthorne plant. Difficulty in controlling such influences is one of the limitations of doing experiments in natural settings. If the Western Electric researchers had used an appropriate control group, they would have detected the Hawthorne effect sooner. Given your knowledge of control groups, you can probably explain why.

For experiments to be successful, the trade-off between naturalness and control of setting must be resolved. Too much naturalness hurts control, and too much control hurts naturalness. If subjects act unnaturally because they are in an experiment, because they are being observed, or because the setting is too artificial, then results cannot be generalized to a wider population—even if causality can be inferred. Field experiments can only approximate the experimental ideal.

Surveys

In sociology, surveys are conducted far more often than experiments. Well suited to studying large numbers of people, **survey research** uses questionnaires and interviews for data collection. Studying people's attitudes is particularly suitable for surveys. Survey data can reveal what people think about almost anything—from their assessment of the president of the United States, to their confidence in the economy, to their concerns about global warming, to their degree of marital satisfaction, happiness during old age, or feelings of loneliness during adolescence. The increasing reliance on surveys makes knowledge of this tool a requirement for almost any career. Survey research typically provides information useful for **quantitative analysis**—assessment of data that are readily translated into numbers.

Like experiments, surveys can be used to test hypotheses, but correlations rather than causes are drawn from the data. It is impossible for surveys to build in all the potential variables that could eliminate

INTERNET CONNECTIONS

Go to Gallup Organization:
http://www.gallup.com/

and take a look at how public opinion polling (surveys) are done. Click on how polls are conducted and then click on take a quiz to test your knowledge of public opinion. After browsing the Website list some survey features used in polling.

spuriousness. A literature review may reveal that education explains a great deal of the income variation between people, but the same review may also suggest numerous other explanations. Three of the four conditions of causality can usually be met through survey research, but it is almost impossible to eliminate spuriousness.

SAMPLING Surveys do have one major advantage over experiments: Their results can be generalized to a much larger population. To understand why requires a knowledge of sampling, particularly random sampling. A **random sample** is one in which subjects are selected so that every member of the population has an equal chance of being chosen. If a sample of people surveyed is randomly selected and sufficiently large, the results based on that sample can be generalized to the broader population from which the sample is drawn. A random sample of students from a particular college represents the population of all students at the college, so in studying gender and love, for example, we can generalize the results and legitimately say that male students express love sooner than female students at "Midwest University."

To say that a sample must be sufficiently large does not mean the larger the better. This was shown in 1936 when *Literary Digest* magazine predicted that Republican Alf Landon would win the presidential election by a landslide over Democrat Franklin Roosevelt. The researchers used telephone directories and automobile registration lists to draw the sample. They sent out an astounding 10 million ballots, and over 2 million people returned the ballot. Yet this huge sample failed to predict Roosevelt's victory, even though he won by the largest margin in the nation's history. What went wrong?

Faulty sampling was the culprit. In the midst of the Great Depression, telephones and cars were luxuries that many could not afford, so the sample overrepresented higher income people, who were also more likely to be Republican. The sample virtually excluded poor and lower income people, who made up the majority of the population at the time. Without random sampling techniques, survey results cannot be generalized to the total population even if the number of survey respondents is huge. But with careful sampling, a random sample of no larger than 2,000 people can be used to accurately predict the outcome of a national election.

This is not to say that the findings of surveys from nonrandom samples are not useful. Frequently, survey researchers use *convenience samples* of people who are readily available to them. For instance, sociologists know a lot about college students—what they eat, what they wear, where they go for spring break, how they spend their money, whom they prefer to

SOCIOLOGY OF EVERYDAY LIFE

The Business of Consumer Behavior in Latino Communities

From a business point of view, the Latino market is hot. The Latino population is the fastest growing segment in the U.S. population, and businesses are scrambling to learn how best to tap the market.

San Antonio, Texas, has one of the largest Latino communities in the United States. A few years ago, recognizing that many Latinos are first- and second-generation immigrants, a telephone company designed a major campaign to sign up Latinos for special packages of long-distance services to cities outside of the United States. Spanish language newspaper and radio station advertising focused on the ease and low cost of calls between the United States, Mexico, and Central America. The ad campaign was successful—there was a major increase in numbers of new long-distance subscribers, and international calls among these subscribers skyrocketed. Unfortunately, the highest usage was from the poorest customers. In addition, not enough Spanish-speaking operators were hired to deal with the problems that arose because existing phone lines could not handle the call volume. Results: Many poorer customers who could not afford

to pay for the long-distance calls had their phone service cut off. Many middle-class customers abandoned this phone company because services were severely disrupted. The ad campaign was "successful" but the company lost money and customers.

In their quest to better understand Latino consumer behavior as well as the buying habits of America's increasing diverse population, managers in the global economy are today much more mindful of two fundamental business principles. The first principle is that they must have the best information available to control the destinies of their businesses. The second principle is that their businesses must be able to adjust to a rapidly changing competitive marketplace. Any business not accounting for these two principles is doomed, because it will be unable to compete in an information-driven, rapidly changing global economy. Sociology offers business important tools to deal with these two principles.

Information

Although research on consumer behavior is guided by the same principles as sociological research in general, consumer research is much more likely to be ex-

ploratory and qualitative. For business, the end product of consumer research is often the development of specific research questions that are then turned over to marketing departments. Marketing begins with the idea of a product or service and ends only when the consumer buys the product or service. Marketing research gathers and analyzes information about the market for decision making. This information is usually obtained through survey research and analyzed quantitatively. It fits the typical research model in Figure 2.1. In the San Antonio case, the company knew about the increased Latino immigration but failed to recognize other socioeconomic characteristics of the targeted consumers, such as lack of resources. Although sociologists do both consumer research and marketing research, sociological expertise is particularly relevant to the consumer behavior side in three major areas:

1. *Secondary research.* Businesses rely heavily on secondary resources, especially census data and economic indicators. Sociologists are also informed about many other rich sources of secondary data, such as national and international databases

---

date, and their attitudes and behavior on topics including politics, sexuality, family life, and race relations—all because college students are so readily available to researchers teaching at universities. Even though college students share some important characteristics with their peers throughout the country, caution is necessary in how the data are interpreted and generalized, because such samples are usually not random.

After the sample is determined, survey researchers generally select one of the three most common techniques for data collection: self-administered questionnaires, personal interviews, and telephone interviews.

QUESTIONNAIRES **Questionnaires** are data-collection devices that are filled out by the respondent and returned directly or by mail. They contain items based on operational definitions of all the variables of interest to the researcher—independent, dependent, and control. In our gender and love example, social class is a control variable and can be operationally defined as a combination of education, income, and occupation. Questionnaire items may ask respondents to check boxes on years of schooling, gross annual household income (in $10,000 increments), and whether they work in a white-collar or blue-collar job. These are called *closed-ended questions* because they offer fixed choices to issues the researcher al-on public opinion that tap changes in cultural values. Details of consumer culture valuable to businesses may be uncovered when these and other sources are viewed sociologically. Secondary research has identified a mushrooming youth market—that targets the lifestyles of 12–16 year olds with money to spend.

2. *Social variables.* Sociologists focus on three key social variables in consumer behavior that help people form ideas about what they want to buy: their culture, providing values and customs; their social class, giving them the resources for buying; and their reference groups, the people they want to be like. Distinctive "lifestyle" groupings of consumers emerge from combinations of these three variables. For example, research related to television and commercial preferences on middle-class Latino teens finds that that English is their language of choice outside the home, Spanish is spoken in the home, and teens often watch television with their extended family. Teens consider Spanish language ads outdated, want to see more ethnic diversity on television, and enjoy programs and ads where humor and music are spotlighted. This information can be used to target

ads and commercial programming to this significant lifestyle niche.

3. *Diversity links.* Businesses that link social variables have the edge in understanding their customers and marketing to them. Sociologists know that diversity in all its forms must be accounted for in research. Consumer research is no exception. If the San Antonio phone company had explored the links between ethnicity and social class, a disastrous marketing campaign could have been avoided.

Social Change

Business managers are under constant pressure to predict changes in consumer behavior. Those managers will gain maximum benefit from consumer research if they understand how the research corresponds to shifting social trends. Social change may be rapid and relentless, but there are patterns that can be uncovered and explained. Although the phone company in San Antonio had data indicating a large increase in Latinos, it neglected to monitor·broader social trends of immigration and income. The surge in this population was from new arrivals with fewer resources who immigrated at a time

when available jobs required higher level skills and education than the immigrants had. Business managers and consumer researchers who are also sociologists can readily show benefits to their companies or their clients when research on consumer behavior is explained according to principles of social change. These benefits translate to company profit. Savvy businesses know that social change related to sophisticated technology is a hallmark of the mushrooming youth market. The consuming youth of the global economy are identified by their habits and interests What are they called? "Teenage mutant cyborg vampire couch potatoes."

1. What research questions should have been asked before the phone company began its advertising campaign? What research techniques would best answer these questions?

2. How would you design a consumer research study exploring television viewing preferences of the Latino teen market that account for social class, ethnicity, and language? What other variables must be accounted for in your exploration?

Sources: Donohue, 1999; Wartzman, 1999; Porter, 2000; Reaching Teens of Color, 2000; Handwerker, 2001; Luther, 2001; Latham, 2002; Reed, 2002.

ready knows are important. Closed-ended items increase questionnaire return rate because they are easy to answer. The answers to these questions are also easy to summarize for analysis, and they tend to be reliable measures—people would give similar answers if asked the same questions again.

However, the same limited choices that increase return rate can make it hard for researchers to learn everything that respondents think about a subject. Sometimes the choices seem so limited that people refuse to answer the question, especially if it addresses an emotionally charged or controversial issue, such as support for capital punishment, gun control or abortion rights. Asking the respondent

whether she or he supports or does not support an issue, or even asking to designate degree of support on a predetermined scale, may not allow enough options to satisfy the respondent's desire for more elaboration. The more knowledge researchers have about a topic, the better the closed-ended questions they can construct.

The most important rule in constructing closed-ended items for questionnaires is that the list of possible responses must be both *mutually exclusive* (there should be no overlap in the alternatives) and *exhaustive* (all possible alternatives should be listed). Each respondent should be able to mark only one appropriate item. A multiple-choice question and its choices on an exam is a good example of this rule. When asked about religious preference, most Americans could comfortably respond to the categories of Protestant, Catholic, Jewish, and Muslim, since they represent the country's major religious groups. These categories are mutually exclusive, but not exhaustive, because there are also Hindus, Buddhists, and many other religious groups. And what about people who have no religious preference? Adding the categories of "other" and "none" makes the religious preference item both mutually exclusive and exhaustive.

Open-ended questions ask respondents to provide their own answers to a question rather than choose from a list of answers. This makes them more flexible than closed-ended questions and allows the researcher to ask for a more or less complete response. In assessing marital satisfaction, for example, commonly asked open-ended questions include, "What do you believe is the major strength of your marriage?" and "What is the one issue about which you and your spouse disagree most strongly?" A more extensive response is called for when follow-up questions are asked, such as "Provide a specific example of how the issue you identified has affected your marriage." Because respondents bring their own understanding to such questions and are free to answer as they see fit, validity is enhanced. But it is more difficult to code and summarize data from open-ended questions, decreasing the reliability of the results. In addition, people may not want to take the time to write out long or detailed responses, so too many open-ended questions may lower the return rate.

The mail questionnaire is an excellent and effective way to survey a wide distribution of people. It can offer anonymity, efficiency, and low cost. A short questionnaire that contains a mixed format of open- and closed-ended questions serves both researcher and respondent needs fairly well. The major disadvantage is that response rate—the percentage of people who return the completed questionnaire—is usually relatively low. A low response rate can compromise validity and bias a study. Follow-up letters to respondents offering them incentives, such as money or small gifts, increase response rates, but may bias results, since people who must be enticed to finally answer a questionnaire may be different from those who respond early without any tangible incentives. Although researchers disagree on what constitutes an "acceptable" response rate, a general rule of thumb is that 50 percent is adequate, 60 percent is good, and 70 percent is very good (Babbie, 2001:256). For survey researchers, however, the issue of return rate centers on whether there are any differences in those who return the survey and those who do not, which can bias the study.

PERSONAL INTERVIEWS The same general principles used in constructing questionnaires apply to constructing guides for personal interviews, which are conducted face-to-face. However, interviews eliminate some of the problems associated with self-administered questionnaires and are more flexible, for a number of reasons. First, some people, such as the visually impaired, may be able to respond verbally but not in written form. Second, if the respondent misunderstands a question, an interviewer can repeat and clarify it. An interviewer can also use probes to get respondents to expand on incomplete answers or to clarify answers that are inconsistent with the question.

Third, an interviewer can note any factors in the interview setting that may affect responses, such as noise or interference from another person. Ideally, the interviewer can maintain some control over the interview situation, scheduling the interview in the home or at another site where privacy can be assured. Fourth, by carefully matching the interviewer with the interviewees, researchers can obtain better quality results. For example, using an interviewer from the same culture as the interviewee makes the interview more comfortable for both parties and provides insights that may be lost to outsiders. But the chief advantage of a personal interview compared with a self-administered questionnaire is even simpler: People would rather talk than write. If the interview is set up in advance, this method produces response rates approaching 95 percent.

Interviews also have disadvantages. First, interviews cost more than questionnaires. The longer the interview and the more open-ended questions asked, the higher the cost, both in interviewer time and in summarizing the data later. Second, interviewers are expected to record all responses verbatim. Open-ended questions require fast and continuous writing, often resulting in inaccuracies even by the most competent interviewer. Third, interviewer bias can creep in, especially when respondents need questions clarified. Interviewers may inadvertently steer the respondent toward an answer.

The most difficult obstacle to resolve in personal interviews is that of anonymity. While confidentiality can be assured in interviews, anonymity is impossible, because the interviewer is face to face with the interviewee. The interviewer may not know the interviewee's name or address, but some type of relationship is established between them during the interview. Because of the lack of anonymity, interviewees may be reluctant to answer truthfully, especially when sensitive information is requested. If an adolescent is interviewed about unacceptable or illegal behavior, for instance, lack of anonymity could compromise the validity of the data.

TELEPHONE INTERVIEWS   When speed of data collection over a wide geographical area is essential, the best method is the telephone interview. Through *random digit dialing*, telephone numbers in desired exchanges can be randomly accessed, a procedure that permits calls to unlisted numbers, new numbers, and numbers for those who live in institutions, such as college dorms. Government agencies, nonprofit groups, and polling organizations routinely use telephone interviews in surveying public opinion (Tickamyer & Wood, 1998). Telephone research has become so efficient that within a few hours of any important event, researchers can survey public opinion worldwide, with results aired on the evening news or put on the Internet.

Certain procedures help ensure the success of a telephone interview. Length is one important factor. The best telephone interviews consist of a limited number of well-defined, usually closed-ended questions that can be answered in 20 minutes or less. However, successful 30-minute to 1-hour telephone interviews are possible when the topic is of particular interest to respondents. Conducting phone interviews from a single site also increases reliability. Supervisors are available to address any problems that arise and to oversee quality control. Identifying the sponsoring organization is important in surveys, but perhaps more so in telephone surveys, since sales gimmicks frequently come in the guise of research. When respondents are assured that a survey is legitimate and confidential, they are more likely to answer all questions.

Telephone interviews have several advantages in addition to efficiency. One is cost. Telephone interviews are more economical than personal interviews and mail-in questionnaires, which helps explain their growing popularity. Telephone interviews are two to three times cheaper than personal interviews. When low cost is linked to high measurement quality, the advantages of telephone interviews increase. Telephone interviews also offer interviewer safety when access to respondents from potentially dangerous locations is desired.

There are also disadvantages to telephone interviews. One is that respondents can become impatient if interviewers ask too much. As a general rule, interviews by phone should be kept as simple as possible. Benefits taper off quickly as interview complexity and length increase. Two other disadvantages are that visual aids such as graphs or maps cannot be used over the phone and that the interviewer has no knowledge of or control over factors that could be distracting a respondent, such as an interesting television program or a demanding child.

COMPARING SURVEY DATA COLLECTION METHODS   In an ideal research world in which time and money are of no concern, personal interviews would often provide more meaningful data than phone interviews. But in the real research world, time and money are dominant concerns. Researchers conducting surveys must weigh these factors against potential gains. They inevitably make decisions that stray from the ideal research process. These decisions should be made not as compromises but to ensure that the research is of high quality.

Secondary Research

In research designs using **secondary analysis,** data and information compiled for other purposes are accessed and reanalyzed. Secondary analysis relies heavily on the wealth of information available from documentary resources, including archives, newspapers, diaries, government and private records, public opinion polls, and other materials that may be tapped for research purposes, and it is the least expensive means of data collection. For example, studies linking music to violence do secondary analysis on variables such as existing data on air time devoted to different types of music, poverty and divorce rates, and records of gun ownership.

Sociology has a long and prestigious heritage of secondary research using documentary resources. The best known is Émile Durkheim's (1897/1964) classic work *Suicide*, in which he used official records on suicide in some European countries to generate a theory of social cohesion, or social connectedness (see Chapter 1). Durkheim found a consistent pattern of higher suicide rates in Protestant areas than in Catholic ones. He also found lower suicide rates for women, for married people, and for those with children. Suicide rates that vary by religion, gender, and marital and family status became key determinants for building his theory. Durkheim suggested that the greater a person's degree of social connectedness, the lower the suicide rate. Despite more than a century of massive social change since Durkheim's study, essentially the same correlation between suicide and social connectedness exists today (Simpson, 1998; Lester, 2000).

Secondary analysis is responsible for some of the most important theoretical work in sociology. For example, Karl Marx (1867/1975) used documentary resources—current economic indicators—to demonstrate his link between capitalism and class struggle. Max Weber (1905/1977) also used documentary resources to analyze capitalism, using historical documents to argue that religion is a dominant factor in determining its progression (the theoretical perspectives of Marx and Weber are discussed in Chapter 10). Durkheim, Marx, and Weber all analyzed available documentary resources to support their own

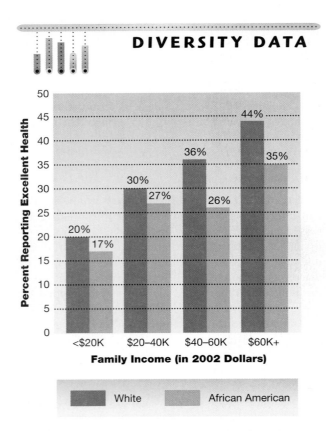

DIVERSITY DATA

Family Income (in 2002 Dollars)

Legend: White, African American

FIGURE 2.4 **Percent Reporting Own Health as Excellent, by Family Income and Race.** For both African Americans and whites, as income increases people who report their own health as excellent also increases. The correlation between income and health, or conversely, poverty and illness, is found globally. However, in the U.S. income does not appear to improve health for African Americans as it does whites, especially for those in the *upper* income categories. What other sources of data might be collected to determine if race or income is more important in explaining health?

Source: NORC. General Social Surveys, 1972–2000. Chicago: National Opinion Research Center, 2000. Reprinted by permission of NORC, Chicago, IL.

theoretical approaches, generating a wealth of potential hypotheses for later study. Taking the lead from Weber, Robert Bellah (1957) used original texts and documents from Japan to document the religious and philosophical roots of the development of a Japanese system of capitalism.

Contemporary research on social change continues to rely heavily on documentary resources, especially economic and social indicators generated by such organizations as the United Nations, the World Bank, and the World Health Organization. Another very valuable documentary resource is the General Social Survey, produced by the National Opinion Research Center. It is a collection of annual (biannual since 2000) national surveys on a variety of topics conducted by personal interview on a random sample of the U.S. population. The General Social Survey (GSS) contains hundreds of items of interest to sociologists and is relied on extensively as a source of documentary data. The Diversity Data graphs in this text are based on data from the General Social Survey.

Government data collected on a wide array of topics at particular points in time also offer valuable research materials. Sociologists routinely use government data to study changes in the rates of divorce, illness, unemployment, immigration, and crime. The demographic or population characteristics included in these data—such as gender, age, race, birth and death rates, and marital status—provide necessary background information for almost any research. The census in particular offers a vital demographic database for secondary analysis. When linked with other available data used as dependent variables, demographic information can suggest many plausible independent variables. For instance, what is the relationship between poverty and illness? Documentary resources can help answer this question using government statistics on income and employment as operational measures of poverty, and disease and disability rates as measures of illness.

Documentary resources available through the Internet offer research opportunities limited only by a researcher's ingenuity and patience. Cross-cultural research is fueled by secondary analysis, especially when Internet sources are easily accessed. It usually begins with a comparative approach, allowing data to be collected and analyzed according to the similarities and differences between cultures or countries, making extensive use of large, national data archives (Ember & Ember, 2001).

CONTENT ANALYSIS Researchers can examine documentary resources in a variety of ways. **Content analysis** is a technique in which researchers systematically examine and code the content of documents, such as magazines or newspapers, noting what they consider important to the research question. A researcher interested in political campaigns, for example, might look through newspapers and record the amount and depth of coverage given to different aspects of political candidates, from their demographic characteristics and personal backgrounds to their views on education or the economy. For example, content analysis has revealed differences in the media portrayal of male and female candidates (Bystron et al., 2001; Miller, 2001). With media reinforcement, voters often apply gender stereotypes that may put

Social change related to gender in politics, such as Hillary Rodham Clinton's successful campaign for the U.S. Senate, can be gauged using a variety of secondary research techniques, including how female candidates are portrayed in the mass media and through public opinion polls comparing female to male candidates.

females at a disadvantage. Female candidates are viewed as more sensitive than male candidates to social issues, but males are seen as more competent overall (Koch, 1999; Sanbonmatsu, 2002).

Progress for racial minorities and women has also been charted using content analysis. For example, content analysis has documented a long history of stereotyped portrayals of racial minorities in the movies and on television. Content analysis of roles for racial minorities—the number of roles, the amount of air time allotted to such roles, and whether the roles are leading or supporting, positive or negative—show that the number of roles has increased and portrayals

of African Americans, Latinos, and Asian Americans have become more positive over the last 30 years (see Chapter 6). However, content analysis reveals that stereotypes still persist, especially for Asian Americans. In films and television programs with themes dominated by violence and death, Asian American men are likely to be portrayed as detectives or martial arts experts and Asian American women as prostitutes, concubines, sexual goddesses, and passive homemakers. And despite growing numbers in the U.S. population, Asian American representation has actually declined (Hagedorn, 2000; Tamborini et al., 2000; Moy, 2000; Fong, 2002). Betty Friedan's (1963)

Content analysis of the global mass media before, during and after major events, such as the terrorist attacks on September 11, 2001 is a good technique to determine level of interest by the public and reaction by the media to the event over time.

pioneering work, *The Feminine Mystique*, used content analysis to trace women's images in popular magazines. Friedan showed that fictional portrayals of women changed over time but that "happy housewife" themes dominated. Content analysis of magazines over the next 30 years showed new themes emerging, such as educational opportunities, paid employment, and legal concerns. However, the themes of beauty and relationships with men still dominate (see Chapter 13). As these examples demonstrate, content analysis is an excellent technique for analyzing the media as both a reflection and an influence on society.

UNOBTRUSIVE MEASURES Documentary resources are categorized as **unobtrusive measures** because the researcher who uses them is removed from what is being studied and so can have no influence on the data. Another unobtrusive measure is a *physical trace*—evidence left from people's past behavior that can be examined for information about what those people valued, thought, or felt. An example is graffiti in public places, which can be analyzed for clues to social issues and social concerns. In repressive societies, where open protest is impossible, graffiti may function as a type of underground newspaper. Urban graffiti in the United States is a significant factor in the spread of gang violence and one that police monitor carefully (Phillips, 1999; Knox, 2001).

Many kinds of physical traces are available for sociological study. A researcher interested in assessing the degree of tension among fans at a baseball game can inspect the litter at the game's end and compare the number of beer containers with the number of popcorn or peanut bags. In a tense game with a close score, people crunch away their anxiety on popcorn or peanuts, but in a relaxed game with a foregone conclusion, fans sit back and drink beer. Physical traces are not necessarily tangible objects; selective wear on the floor of a museum, for instance, may indicate preferences in exhibits. It is even possible to count the fingerprints and nose prints on display cases for information; the cleaner the glass, the less popular the display (Webb et al., 1966). And to assess young children's interest in an exhibit, pay attention to the fingerprints and nose prints that are less than about three feet high!

Think of studying physical traces as investigating a crime. What evidence does the criminal leave behind that will lead to an arrest? For sociologists, what material is left behind as people carry out their daily activities that can be used as evidence to test a hypothesis? Criminology, which makes extensive use of unobtrusive measures, is a major specialty area for sociologists. Careers in the criminal justice system provide excellent opportunities for students of sociology, enabling them to transfer the principles of research methods to investigation of crime and criminal behavior.

ASSESSING DOCUMENTARY METHODS For documentary resources to be used successfully in research, two major hurdles must be overcome. First, the researcher must gain access. This is no problem with government sources, but many other documents—such as a company's sales records or a person's letters and diaries—are private. Second, even if access to private documents is granted, rarely will documentary data be perfect for a researcher's needs. For example, official records of household income may be broken down by larger increments than a researcher would like. Or a researcher may find it hard to compare crime statistics in different states because a felony in Texas is defined differently from a felony in New York. There is even the problem of whether the accuracy of the document can be trusted. Famous people write letters and keep diaries with the knowledge that these documents may be published after their deaths, so they tend to present themselves in the most favorable light possible. For all these reasons, documentary resources should be triangulated—combined with data collected in other ways—to ensure validity and reliability.

Field Research

Creativity is the hallmark of **field research,** a research design aimed at directly, in natural settings, collecting data on what people say and do. As mentioned at the beginning of the chapter, Elijah Anderson used field research to study an urban neighborhood. Field researchers collect data about the social behavior of people in natural settings. Sociologists conducting field research routinely triangulate data collection methods, especially observations and personal interviews. Often they do not begin with specific research questions, but rather do an exploratory study that ends with questions or hypotheses to be tested later. In this way, field research is sometimes just the first phase of an ongoing research project.

Do not confuse field experiments with field research. The Hawthorne experiments, for example, were done in the "field"—the natural setting of a workplace rather than an artificially created environment—but their purpose was to study the effects of specific factors on worker productivity. The researchers tested hypotheses and analyzed results quantitatively. In contrast, field research typically uses **qualitative analysis,** summarizing data in nonnumerical ways in order to discover underlying meanings and build theory. Rather than *testing* hypotheses, qualitative analysis is commonly used to *develop* hypotheses.

Sometimes the goal of field research is to produce an **ethnography,** a description of customs, beliefs, and values of a particular culture compiled by researchers who spend prolonged periods actually living with the people they are studying. These researchers rely heavily on data collection methods that allow them to get an "insider" view, a quality anthropologists often refer to as "being there." For field research to be effective, fairly close involvement between observer and those being observed is needed. Field researchers should open themselves up to the society being studied so that they feel as comfortable with it as they do with their own (Grills, 1998; Watson, 1999).

PARTICIPANT OBSERVATION   The best way to gain an insider's view is to actually become an insider through **participant observation,** in which the researcher witnesses, experiences, and engages firsthand in the activities of the group being studied. This requires that the researcher take on some accepted status (position) within the group.

COMPLETE PARTICIPANT ROLE   There are two typical roles for participant observers in field research. In the role of *complete participant,* the researcher becomes a member of the group being studied, interacting with subjects as naturally as possible, but does not inform them of the research being done. Maria Fernandez-Kelly (2001) chose the complete participant role when she took a job at a *maquiladora*—an apparel assembling plant in Mexico near the U.S. border that employs large numbers of women. Her intent was to explore the impact of working conditions, production quotas, and wages from the perspective of the women workers themselves. Their 60 cents-per-hour wage could be increased for higher production, but bonuses were dependent on everyone in the line producing at a rapid pace. The livelihood of the women depended on the amount of the bonus. As a worker, not as a researcher, Fernandez-Kelly realized that she *had* to do her best and could not fall short of the production goal, because everyone suffered as a result. The complete participant role offers extraordinary opportunities for research, but is often emotionally draining for the researcher. She gave in to the "subtle mechanisms that dominate will" and the shame attached to letting everyone else down. As she states:

> . . . as the days passed it became increasingly difficult to think of factory work as a stage in a research project. My identity became that of the worker. . . . Academic research became an ethereal fiction. Reality was work, as much for me as for the others who labored under the same roof. (Fernandez-Kelly, 2001:286)

PARTICIPANT-AS-OBSERVER ROLE   If it is not practical to become a complete participant, a researcher may choose the role of *participant-as-observer.* In this role, researchers inform subjects of the study being done and try to participate in the group as much as possible. Most field researchers prefer this role, largely because it is less deceptive. An example of participant-as-observer research is Elijah Anderson's study of a neighborhood in transition, highlighted in this chapter's opening vignette.

Another example of this research role is William Foote Whyte's *Street Corner Society,* a classic study of Italian American working-class men living in a slum area of Boston (Whyte, 1943/1981). Whyte's study hinged on his being accepted into the lives of these men. Realizing that gaining the support of a few key people was the best approach, he became friends with one of the group's leaders, "Doc," who introduced him to others until he gradually was accepted. Doc and a few other group members served as informants, becoming partners in his research and giving him information about what the men said and did in his absence. He could never be a bona fide member of the group, because he was a sociologist doing research, but he established a degree of intimacy and rapport that provided the insider status necessary to obtain valuable data. Whyte's research showed that the city "slum" is an organized community of kinship, friendships, neighborhood associations, and distinctive values that serve as anchors to those who live there. This slum neighborhood was not the chaotic place most outsiders imagined it to be.

Whyte's field research established both a theoretical framework and a research model that many other sociologists have since used in studying urban areas. For instance, Herbert Gans's (1962/1982) research in another Italian American community in Boston found patterns similar to those Whyte discovered. Gans focused on how some neighborhoods disrupted by urban change manage to maintain a sense of community. In another urban field study, *Tally's Corner,* Elliot Liebow (1967) entered the lives of African American men who congregated in front of a laundromat in Washington, D.C. He informed them about his research, and like Whyte, he gradually became accepted. He visited their homes, participated in their activities, and gave them financial and legal advice. Again, contrary to the stereotype of the urban ghetto, underlying stability was uncovered in a seemingly chaotic environment.

These pioneering studies offered insights into participant observation, especially related to access and degree of involvement with subjects, and have been capitalized on by contemporary field researchers. Feminist researchers are particularly interested in using participant observation to uncover information on social patterns that may be of benefit to the people being studied. Nicole Constable's (1997) interest in studying Filipina domestic workers in Hong Kong took an unexpected leap forward when she discovered that her rented apartment came with the part-time services of Acosta—just such a worker. Her discomfort at even indirectly hiring a domestic worker was put aside after rapport was established, and Acosta offered her entrée into a world that she would have been unable to realistically access on her own. With Acosta's help she began to visit domestic worker unions, organizations, and shelters, eventually becoming a volunteer at the Mission for Filipino Migrant Workers. Constable's general acceptance into their community allowed her to document the stigma, oppression, and often times the abuse many of these workers experienced, but also how they resisted the oppression and attempted to control their working conditions. As do women in similar situations throughout the world, these Filipina domestic workers obey their employers because they need the work to support their families, who remain in their home country. These workers can be described as neither completely passive pawns of exploitation nor active subjects who can successfully resist control (Constable, 1997:203). Constable's research contributes to the growing body of theory related to strategies domestic workers use to maintain dignity when their

roles are demeaned or scorned. She also considered the applied aspects of her research, since her findings could help others understand the lives of these women and would perhaps benefit them in some way. Research documenting the plight of migrant workers in Asia has helped improve their working conditions and bargaining power (Komai, 2001; Milly, 2000; Moon, 2002).

The key point in all these studies is the research design used. The participant-as-observer role provided opportunities for ethically acceptable research on otherwise inaccessible people and places.

PARTICIPANT-OBSERVER AS GROUP MEMBER

Another role for field researchers combines aspects of the complete participant and participant-as-observer roles. In this role the researcher does not have to become a member of the group under study because she or he *already* is a member. The people being studied may or may not be told that research is being conducted on them by another member of their group. Group membership allows for an easier transition from outsider to insider. Elijah Anderson initially lived in the neighborhood he studied and told people in his neighborhood about the research he was conducting. Sociologists are creative in using their everyday roles and experiences to do research, and special access by way of membership provides extraordinary opportunities for research.

When Julius Roth (1963) found himself confined to a hospital as a long-term tuberculosis patient, he turned adversity into advantage and saw his hospital bed as a "good observation post" to learn about the social structure of the hospital. But unlike Anderson,

Some of the thousands of Filipina domestic workers, who congregate every Sunday in the Central district of Hong Kong where traffic is closed off so they can relax, socialize, and exchange news. This setting allows a vital social network to be developed and nurtured and contributes to the empowerment of these women.

his subjects—staff and fellow patients—were unaware of his study. Although his patient status made him a "legitimate" group member, since subjects did not know about the research, he took on the complete participant role. Tuberculosis patients at that time were often quarantined for up to several years. Roth's first impression was the concern with time; almost as in a prison, the question on everyone's mind was "How long are you in for?" Roth showed how "timetables" were socially constructed using a symbolic interactionist framework. TB patients played "games" with hospital staff and with each other to discover their timetables and chart their progress. TB ran in unpredictable cycles; timetables served as a way for patients to symbolically control their destiny. As his own "time" progressed, Roth's insider status permitted in-depth observations that gradually led to a theory about how patients and staff socially constructed time according to norms, or informal rules. His participant-observation study is a good example of both the theory and the method of field research. Qualitative research through participant observation allows for developing hypotheses that can be tested later with quantitative research.

ON LEAVING THE FIELD Because their work involves establishing relationships with subjects, which can become intensely emotional, field researchers confront two important questions. The investigator must first ask, "How much of an impact has this investigation had on the people being studied?"

In a famous study of a doomsday cult, conducted by Leon Festinger and his colleagues (1956), Festinger and his coworkers acted as complete participants, pretending to be converts to a cult predicting that the end of the world was near. The members of the cult believed that aliens would save them from destruction by taking them to another world in a spaceship. Festinger wondered how the cult members would react when the appointed time for the end of the world came and went. Festinger and his colleagues tried not to influence the cult members' thinking, but the cover stories they devised to explain why they joined the group backfired on them. The cult members concluded that the researchers were really messengers from the alien rescuers! Since the world did not end as scheduled, the cult members reduced their dissonance by deciding that the end was still near, just later than they thought. The researchers had influenced the group in a way that might not have occurred otherwise and were there to observe it. Festinger's study led to the development of a major social psychological theory known as *cognitive dissonance*. This theory explains how people reconcile what they believe to be true with their real-life observations, such as those the cult members experienced.

In Festinger's study, the researchers' influence on the group being studied was outside the awareness of group members. In contrast, Elliot Liebow influenced his subjects in ways they were well aware of because he gave them various kinds of support. When Liebow ended his study and left "Tally's Corner," his availability for support and advice—which some of the men had come to rely on—came to an end. Even when a researcher maintains contact with subjects after a study is over, it is impossible to continue in the same capacity. Lives change and people move on. The difficulty in making this break with subjects is an important ethical issue in doing field research.

The second question the researcher must ask on leaving the field is, "How much of an impact have the people being studied had on me?" Too much distance between researcher and subjects hinders relationship building, but too much closeness hurts objectivity. Field researchers have the difficult task of simultaneously being objective observers and involved, concerned participants. Sometimes fieldworkers are accused of romanticizing subjects and selecting data that paint positive portraits while ignoring the negative parts of their subjects' lives. At other times, they may feel disdain and disgust toward their subjects but attempt to transform these emotions into more favorable ones. Researchers also report being haunted by decisions made during the course of their research that may have inadvertently put themselves and their subjects at risk (Lee-Treweek & Linkogle, 2000). In studying police and military subcultures where violence commonly occurs, fieldworkers witnessing excessive violence by the subjects of a study must decide on whether to report the violence, which is probably the ethical course of action. However, by reporting the violence, they know that their research is probably doomed (Robben, 1995; Westmarland, 2001). Fieldwork inevitably presents dilemmas from ambiguous situations that must be resolved by researchers. The ways they are resolved may impact the researcher for years to come.

Finally, fieldworkers can become so immersed in the lives of their subjects that they shed the researcher role and "go native," becoming converts to whatever group they are studying. This happens most often to the lone ethnographer in an isolated setting who has minimal contact with colleagues for long periods of time. But it is a risk all social scientists face when they begin to identify intensely with their subjects. Passion replaces sociological understanding and, unfortunately, the research story they intended to tell is lost. Sociological training for fieldwork is increasingly accounting for the critical impact that emotions have on participant observation—both during and after the

Source: © 1999 by Nicole Hollander. Distributed by Los Angeles Times Syndicate.

research (Kleinman & Copp, 1993; DeWalt & De-Walt, 2002).

FEMINIST RESEARCH METHODS AND LINKS TO DIVERSITY. Until fairly recently, sociologists routinely used white, male, middle-class samples in conducting research, particularly samples of college students. Entire theories were developed based on the attitudes and behavior of these subjects. But the world is not comprised of white, male, and middle-class people. As in many nations, the already strong multicultural heritage of the United States is fueled by immigration and the globalization of business. It is essential to consider race and ethnicity as variables in research. The variables of social class and gender must also be considered in order to avoid a distorted view of society and social behavior.

Recent research on women is an excellent example of how sociological research has broadened its horizons. Feminists have challenged the lack of diversity in research, and their efforts have led to an explosion of feminist research methods. Although these methods single out *androcentrism*, the male-centered bias in research, and call attention to the oppression of women, feminist methods can be applied to any group that may be disadvantaged, whether by race, ethnicity, social class, sexual orientation, or health status. These methods are guided by feminist theory, which issues a challenge to the status quo that subordinates women and other minorities (Chapter 1). With women as their focus, feminist research uses a variety of techniques to hear the voices of formerly silenced people (DeVault, 1999; Tolman, 2001).

Medical research in particular has shown an androcentric bias. Some studies that use males as the medical norm are rather infamous, such as a major federally funded study examining the effects of diet on breast cancer. Only men were used as subjects (Tavris, 1996). Or, consider the widely publicized study on the effect of aspirin on heart attacks using a sample of over 20,000 men. The reduced heart attack risk was so spectacular that results were made public even before the study ended. But since the sample was made up only of men, results could not be generalized to women despite the fact that heart disease is the number one killer of both genders. Lung cancer is also considered more of a man's health problem even though the death rate for lung cancer has increased 100 percent in the last two decades because of the increased smoking rates of women. But with few research studies done of women and lung cancer, the drugs and treatment techniques that work for men may not work for women (Stevens, 1999). In challenging the male-as-norm bias, feminist research is helping close the gap that excludes women as research subjects.

Since feminist methods typically lead to studies in which special relationships are developed between researchers and subjects, field research, ethnographies, participant observation, and in-depth interviews are favored techniques (DeVault, 1999; Gardner, 1999). The voices of victims of rape and domestic violence are better portrayed using these methods. Feminist approaches have allowed new research topics to evolve and old ones to be viewed from a different angle. For example, using feminist methods of data analysis to reanalyze qualitative data on childbearing among lower-SES African American adolescents reveals that these teens occupy a far different world than that revealed through other methods for qualitative data analysis (Merrick, 1999). Feminist researchers also readily take their findings beyond academic circles and show how research can be used to bring about social reform (Spalter-Roth & Hartmann, 1999). Research on the dismal working conditions and sexual harassment of the *maquiladoras* discussed above has helped spur cross-border union organizing and education of women workers about their legal rights in multinational plants (Mohanty, 1999; Louie, 2000). Feminist research not only furthers sociology's goal of more accurately representing human diversity in research, its social action agenda demonstrates the importance in applying sociological solutions for a more humane and just world (Babbie, 1998).

TABLE 2.1

Median Weekly Earnings in Dollars by Gender

	1985	1990	1995	2000
Males	406	481	538	646
Females	277	346	406	491

Source: U.S. Bureau of the Census, 2001, Table 621.

LIFE CONNECTIONS

Gender and the Wage Gap

Americans put a strong emphasis on achievement and talent, expecting these attributes to pay off in the workplace. Sociological research into the earnings gap between men and women in the United States has provided some fascinating data that may contradict this strongly held conviction. Table 2.1 shows a statistical relationship between gender and earnings. Gender is the independent variable and is divided into its two attributes, male and female. Weekly earnings in dollars is the dependent variable and is divided according to four time periods.

The table reveals that while income increased for both males and females, the increase for males was consistently higher. Only between 1990 and 1995 was the increase for women ($60) higher than for men ($57). This slight increase was not enough to enable women to catch up with men. In 2000 men earned $155 more per week on the average than women.

In order to determine whether gender is indeed a key variable in understanding the wage gap, other variables must also be taken into account. Sociological research shows that Americans strongly believe that education is the critical ingredient for economic success. Measuring the earnings of men and women at different educational levels can determine whether the original

relationship between gender and earnings holds true. Table 2.2 shows what happens when education is added as a third variable. This table reveals that at all educational levels, males still outearn females and that the wage gap generally increases at the higher educational levels. Male college graduates on the average earn $25,855 more than female college graduates.

Are these figures convincing enough to say that a wage gap in gender exists? What about other variables that might also explain the gender differences in earnings? Overall, the gender gap in earnings holds true even when race, age, occupation, seniority, and region are added to the picture (CPS, 2001; SBA, 2001; Spraggins, 2001; U.S. Bureau of the Census 2001; Hicks, 2002). For example, while white women earn slightly more on the average than women of color, regardless of race men outearn women (Center for Policy Alternatives, 2002; Hicks, 2002; U.S. Bureau of the Census). From all available records, the wage gap has been a persistent economic fact in the United States over time (Kemp, 1994; Freeman, 2000; Wage Gap, 2001; Reskin, 2000; Loutfi, 2001). The original relationship between gender and income is not spurious.

However, the gender wage gap has narrowed. In 1980 a women employed full time earned about 65 cents for every dollar a man employed full time earned; for women today that figure is about 73 cents. Although the narrowing of the wage gap by 8 cents in over two decades may be a sign of progress, the bad

TABLE 2.2

Annual Earnings in Dollars of Full-Time Workers by Gender and Educational Level

	Some High School	High School Graduate	Some College	BA degree+
Males	25,168	32,647	39,820	69,665
Females	17,218	23,841	27,610	43,810

Source: U.S. Bureau of the Census, 2000, Table 752.

news is that women's relative gains came largely because men are earning less (Boushey, 2001; Nussbaum, 2002; UAW, 2002). While we cannot say that gender is *the* cause of income differences between Americans, we can safely conclude that it is *a* cause—and a significant one. The data are certainly clear. But the reason for scientific research is to explain data. Why do men earn more money than women? As discussed further in Chapter 13, different theoretical perspectives provide different answers. Functionalists suggest that women act as a reserve labor force to be called on when needed by their families or by society. Conflict theorists suggest that men make the rules that will maintain their economic advantage over women; hence, gender discrimination in the workplace remains a reality. Symbolic interactionists suggest that since the workplace is largely gender segregated, powerful social definitions assign a lesser value to the work women do compared with the work men do. Each of the three perspectives explains the same data on gender and the wage gap differently. The best explanations account for most of the data and for changes in the data over time.

SOCIETY CONNECTIONS

The Ethics of Research

Like all scientists, sociologists routinely confront ethical issues in conducting their research. These ethical issues are more apparent in some studies than in others. As demonstrated by the infamous Tuskegee study

THEN AND NOW

The Tuskegee Experiment

At the beginning of the 20th century syphilis was a ravaging and incurable disease. Little was known about its progression in the human body. To learn more about the disease, in 1932 the U.S. Public Health Service (USPHS) worked with prestigious Tuskegee University to recruit as research subjects 399 African American men from Macon County, Alabama, one of the state's poorest rural areas. All of the men had syphilis, but were told they were being treated for "bad blood." On clinic days they ate, had a place to stay, and received free medical care—luxuries for poor people during the Depression. What they were told was a sham. What they were not told was the true research question: "What are the long-term effects of untreated syphilis on Negro males?" The study continued for the next three decades, even after penicillin became the standard remedy for syphilis. During World War II the subjects were screened out of the armed forces for fear they would leave the study because their disease would be discovered. But the disease was left untreated. Some men became incapacitated, blind, and impotent. Others died. In 1972, when the study became public, the American Medical Association charged the USPHS with conducting genocide against the poor. The race factor in the experiment could not be denied. In 1997 President Bill Clinton apologized to those who survived the Tuskegee Experiment. Attitudes about research experiments were examined in a focus group bringing together 60 African Americans who watched a television movie about the Tuskegee experiment. Although participants believed that research was important, they readily distinguished between the type of research they would be willing to participate in and why they would do so. As dramatized in the movie, the Tuskegee study clearly aroused suspicion about research that has not been erased among African Americans.

Today many legal, institutional, and professional pressures ensure that scientific investigations are carried out ethically. Ethical guidelines require an answer to the question, How has respect for the rights and welfare of the participants been demonstrated? Informed consent (see page 57) is one way to demonstrate this respect. Because there will always be research that cannot provide complete information to subjects and accomplish its purpose, the strategy of "reasonably informed consent" has been accepted as a model. If people are told what they can "reasonably" expect in terms of risk or discomfort, as well as potential benefits, and are given answers to their questions, then they should be able to make an informed decision about whether to participate as research subjects.

1. How could the Tuskegee experiment be redesigned so that it could be carried out ethically yet still provide important answers to the question of the impact of syphilis? What changes in the study question would have to be made?

2. Can the Tuskegee study legitimately be described as an experiment? Why or why not?

Sources: Reynolds, 1982:4; Jones, 1993; Harter et al., 2000; Reverby, 2000; Freimuth et al., 2001; Van Den Hoonaard, 2001.

(see *Then & Now*), research has sometimes been conducted under ethically deplorable conditions.

Research Subjects at Risk

Stanley Milgram's (1963, 1974) famous series of psychological experiments determined how far people will go in obeying orders. His research subjects thought they were being randomly assigned to one of two roles in the experiment, purported to be a study of how punishment affects learning, but in reality they were all made "teachers," and the "learners" were Milgram's confederates. The experimenter ordered "teachers" to give "learners" an electric shock in increasing intensity with each wrong answer. No real shocks were given, but the "teachers" did not know this. If they hesitated in delivering the shock, the experimenter firmly told them to continue. Although many trembled with distress, the majority still obeyed the experimenter. Many even administered shocks up to the highest level—even after a "learner," who was tied to a chair in the next room, stopped pounding on the wall and fell ominously silent. If a shock this strong had actually been given, the teacher would have killed the learner! Milgram's study caused the subjects severe anxiety as they struggled with the choice of whether to follow orders and administer shocks. Milgram's findings certainly gave important insights into human behavior, but at what price to his subjects? The challenge in studying human beings is to conduct research that is both sociologically relevant and ethically acceptable. We can explore the difficulty of meeting this challenge by looking at several other studies in which ethical compromises were made.

LOSING SELF-IDENTITY Philip Zimbardo (1972) was interested in the degree to which certain environments, such as prisons, could alter a person's sense of self-identity. This was (and is) an important question, given the reality that for many convicts, prison life does not "rehabilitate" but instead stabilizes a prison identity that is difficult to dislodge once the prisoner is released. Do prisons brainwash people so that thenonprisoner identity is abolished? Since Zimbardo could not study this question in a real prison, he decided to construct a mock prison in the basement of a building on the Stanford University campus over summer break. He recruited and paid male college students to participate in his research and randomly assigned them to "play" the role of prisoners or guards.

In only a few days, both groups shed their college identities and "became" prisoners and guards. Guards progressively became more threatening and brutal; prisoners reacted with submissiveness and fear, becoming servile, dehumanized robots. Zimbardo decided to end the experiment prematurely because of the real danger that the guards could do physical harm to the prisoners, some of whom became emotionally impaired after the first few days of the experiment. In less than a week the experience of imprisonment undid a lifetime of learning. As Zimbardo concluded, these abnormal personal and social reactions are best seen as products of an environment that created, and then reinforced, behavior that would be pathological in other settings.

Feminist research methods focus on how women are different and how they are alike. The viewpoints of women from diverse backgrounds are highlighted through these methods.

OBSERVING VERY PRIVATE BEHAVIOR In exploring deviant behavior, sociologist Laud Humphreys (1970) raised different ethical concerns about research than did Zimbardo. Humphreys was interested in studying "tearooms"—public restrooms frequented by men in search of "instant sex" from other men. The sex was quick, impersonal, and silent. Since this behavior was not only deviant but illegal, covert observation was the research method selected. It was actually participant observation because Humphreys served in the role of lookout for the tearoom, situating himself at the door or window and warning the men by a cough or nod if someone was approaching.

Humphreys discovered that more than half his subjects were married and living with their wives. Some of these men were heterosexual, except for the tearoom encounters. Others were active in a homosexual subculture and exhibited a strong gay identity. But how did Humphreys learn about the backgrounds of these men from only covert observations? He recorded license plate numbers, tracked down the owners' addresses, and six months later, with enough change in appearance to avoid recognition, he visited their homes as a survey researcher. His subjects never suspected the true purpose of his survey.

At a time when knowledge about homosexual activities and lifestyles was limited, Humphreys' research was extremely valuable. But the deceit to gain access to this group violated the privacy of people engaged in extremely private acts.

ACCESS THROUGH DECEIT Like Humphreys, Leslie Irvine (1998) could not disclose her identity as a researcher; otherwise, her ethnographic study of Codependents Anonymous (CoDA), a 12-step program similar to Alcoholics Anonymous, would have been impossible. As its name suggests, CoDA has rules about anonymity—meetings are open to anyone, but there is no membership roster, no last names are exchanged, and although there are regular attendees, the group continually shifts in composition. To obtain permission to attend meetings for the purposes of research would have been impossible, since there is no leader. Irvine originally believed she could attend a meeting, state her research purpose, leave flyers, and ask for volunteers to be interviewed. She sat through the first meeting in stunned silence, however, seeing her plans dissolve. It was quickly apparent that the spontaneity and open sharing expected at the meetings were incompatible with the detached observation supposedly called for in sociological research. But in figuring out what to do next in her research, Irvine found that the research began to evolve. She could not remain a silent observer for long and found herself "sharing" with the group, stepping into the role of *participant*-observer. Her loss of identity as a detached observer was easier to accept than the anguish she felt in interacting with people she deceived about why she was at the meetings. She cringed whenever she was reminded of her benefits from the group. She was there to get a dissertation written, not to help others deal with their perceived codependency.

Unlike Humphreys, Irvine's research purposes became clear to some CoDA participants. They believed her research would be valuable to those who "had" codependency and that her desire to help people, and even become a professor of sociology, were "symptoms" of her own codependency. They saw what they were prepared to see. In terms of the symbolic interactionism that framed her research, her subjects filtered the information she gave them through their own presuppositions; she did not have the power to change their understanding of her presence in the group (Irvine, 1998:175). Deceit may be deplorable in most situations, but without it, meaningful ethnological research in sociology might not be conducted (Herrara, 1999).

Informed Consent and the Need to Know

All the studies discussed here provided valuable data on social behavior, but each also raises ethical concerns. Milgram's and Zimbardo's subjects were not the same after the experiment. They had undergone a very emotionally stressful experience, and many were ashamed of their behavior. In the Humphreys case, although subject confidentiality was maintained, the lives of his subjects could have been ruined if their identities were divulged. On the other hand, Milgram and Humphreys could not have carried out their research if their subjects had been told its true purpose. Irvine's research clearly did not put her subjects at risk and in fact was probably helpful to them. It is also unlikely that Irvine would have been accepted into the group if she told them she was there merely to observe.

INTERNET CONNECTIONS

In the text there is a discussion of the ethical implications of social research. The American Sociological Association has assembled a code of standards and ethics for Sociologists. You may review these ethical standards at:

http://www.asanet.org/ecoderev.htm

What are some ethical issues involved in sociological research? What are the researcher's responsibilities?

Today, ethical codes are designed to protect subjects from harm or risk that may result from participating in scientific research. It is doubtful that Milgram, Zimbardo, and Humphreys could have conducted their experiments in the same manner today. Irvine's research proceeded in ways she never intended, but she was guided by institutional regulations and ethical guidelines that are much more rigorous. The American Sociological Association (ASA) sets ethical standards that underlie the professional conduct of sociologists. The guidelines on issues that sociologists may encounter are contained in the ASA Code of Ethics. The code has as its primary goal the welfare and protection of the individuals and groups with whom sociologists work. The basic principles established by the code call for sociologists to

1. Maintain the highest competence in their work.
2. Be honest, fair, and respectful of others in all professional activities.
3. Adhere to the highest scientific and professional standards.
4. Accept social responsibility for their work.
5. Respect the rights, dignity, and worth of all people.

With **informed consent,** a basic tenet of all scientific research found in the code of ethics of every professional association that uses human subjects, potential research subjects have enough knowledge about the research to make an informed decision about participation. The well-being of research participants must be safeguarded at all times (Sales & Folkman, 2000).

Sociologists see to it that confidentiality is protected. They do so to ensure the integrity of the research and to maintain open communication with research participants. The ASA Code of Ethics specifically calls for sociologists not to allow information gained in confidence to be used in ways that would unfairly compromise these participants (American Sociological Association, 1997).

Codes of ethics are general guidelines only and are always subject to interpretation. There are no easy answers to many ethical questions raised in doing scientific research. Ethical guidelines can be viewed not as constraints on research, but rather as enhancements to it. Science thrives in an atmosphere of free and open discussions, including discussions about ethical issues. A fundamental principle of science is that it gains headway not *despite* but *because* the research it is based on is carried out ethically and humanely. The future of all sociological research and the benefits that it provides depend on this principle.

SUMMARY

1. Sociologists use the scientific method as a blueprint for research. Key objectives for scientific research are to test, modify, and develop theories.
2. The first step in the research process is to find a problem to investigate. After reviewing the literature on work that has already been done on a topic, the researcher poses a research question and formulates a prediction or potential answer, called a hypothesis.
3. A hypothesis also predicts a relationship between two variables: the independent (causal) variable and the dependent variable. Both variables must be operationally defined in such a way that they can be measured.

4. Besides summarizing the results of their research and drawing conclusions, sociologists must deal with issues of measurement quality—validity (accuracy) and reliability (consistency) of data. They must also decide whether results from a sample of people can apply legitimately to a broader population.
5. There are four major types of research design (a plan for collecting data): experiments, surveys, secondary research, and field research.
6. The research design for an experiment typically has four steps: (1) Establish two separate groups, an experimental group and a control group; (2) randomly assign subjects to the two groups; (3)

measure the dependent variable both before and after the experiment; and (4) compare the two sets of measurements.

7. To establish a causal relationship between two variables, experimenters must satisfy four conditions: (1) The cause must precede the effect; (2) the two variables must be correlated, or linked systematically; (3) the relationship between the two variables must not be explained by another variable; and (4) there must be a logical explanation for the relationship.

8. Sociological experiments may be conducted in the field (the natural settings where people live and work). Because experimental conditions cannot be controlled in this type of setting, field experiments cannot usually determine causality.

9. Survey research is commonly used in sociology. Surveys report correlations rather than causality. Random sampling allows survey results to be applied to a wider population.

10. Sociologists collect survey data using questionnaires, personal interviews, and telephone interviews. Although personal interviews are the best for response rate and validity, they are more costly and time consuming compared with questionnaires and telephone interviews.

11. Secondary research involves analyzing data drawn from existing sources—such as archives, newspapers, diaries, government records, and public opinion polls. Since secondary research has problems with validity, it is often triangulated (used in combination with other methods).

12. Field research involves in-depth study of groups of people in their natural environments by sociologists who may choose to participate in the groups. This method is suited to qualitative—nonnumerical—analysis of data and is generally used to explore a topic or develop a hypothesis about a topic.

13. Past sociological research tended to focus on white, middle-class males. Feminist research strategies focus on more diverse samples of people, especially women and racial minorities.

14. Sociologists must take care to follow ethical guidelines in their research to protect the rights and dignity of those they study. Confidentiality and informed consent are imperative.

KEY TERMS

content analysis 47
control group 38
control variable 33
correlation 38
dependent variable 32
ethnography 49
experimental group 38
field research 48
Hawthorne effect 40
hypothesis 31

independent variable 32
informed consent 57
measurement 33
operational definition 33
participant observation 49
population 36
qualitative analysis 48
quantitative analysis 41
questionnaire 42
random sample 41

reliability 34
research design 34
sample 36
scientific method 30
secondary analysis 45
spurious relationship 38
survey research 41
unobtrusive measures 48
validity 33
variable 32

CRITICAL THINKING QUESTIONS

1. Demonstrate how theory and research are linked in a cycle and why this linkage is necessary for the objectives of science.

2. Explain why identifying the causes for human social behavior is the most difficult task sociologists face in doing research. How can they design research to overcome this difficulty?

3. You have been assigned to do field research on the aged. Because you are much younger than the group you are to study and do not feel comfortable joining them in their activities, you decide to remain an outsider. Is your choice an ethical one? How might it affect the results of your study? What might be a better solution to your problem?

4. Explain why informed consent is necessary to conduct research but can also compromise research goals.

INVESTIGATE WITH CONTENT SELECT

 Begin your research using Content-Select for this chapter by following the directions found on page 27 of this text to visit Prentice Hall's Research Navigator Website. Enter these search terms into the search field:

Ethnography
Qualitative Analysis
Wage gap

iNTERSECTIONS

EXERCISE 1. DO YOU FIND YOUR LIFE EXCITING?

In exercises at the end of the major sections of this book, readers can venture into survey research using high-quality data called the General Social Surveys, or GSS, which has been used by professional sociologists in hundreds of books and articles. With the GSS, we can probe into differences in American society based on race, class, age, and gender. The GSS is the source for nearly all of the "Diversity Data" sprinkled throughout the book.

Almost every year since 1972, those who run the GSS have drawn a random sample of about 1,500 adult Americans and sent interviewers to ask them standard questions about attitudes, behaviors, and family background. Some questions are asked yearly, some less often. Combining all respondents in all years, the GSS provides information on the views of the U.S. population over the past three decades. For example, nearly every year respondents were asked, "In general, do you find life exciting, pretty routine, or dull?" Overall, 46 percent of respondents said their lives were "exciting," 49 percent said "routine," and 5 percent said "dull."

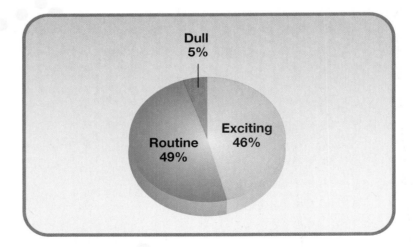

Now we'll use some of the principles from the chapter on Research Methods and investigate four research questions: (1) Who finds their lives more exciting, men or women? (2) Do whites or blacks find life more exciting? (3) Is life more exciting for people of higher or lower social class? (4) Do older or younger people report that life is more exciting?

To answer these, you need a computer program called CHIP, which can sort and count GSS respondents. You'll find it on our Companion Website™ at http://www.prenhall.com/lindsey. Click on the cover of this book, and select the appropriate INTERSECTIONS exercise from the drop-down menu at the top. (Make sure CHIP is set for % down, and its Row Variable is Life).

Each research question asks how life's excitement differs across some intersection of GSS respondents: across the sexes, races, classes, or ages. CHIP calls these intersections "Column Variables." To see which gender finds life more exciting, select Gender as CHIP's Column Variable. Then, click the Crosstab button.

Your computer screen will show a column of numbers for men and a column for women. Each column shows the percentages *of that gender* reporting that life is exciting, routine, or dull. (Percentages in each column necessarily add to 100 percent.) You will also find in parentheses the actual numbers of GSS respondents from which the percentages are calculated, but usually these are not as informative as the percentages. (Why not?)

1. Now that you have the percentages, you must use your head to properly interpret them.
2. What percentage of men find their lives exciting?
3. What percentage of women do?
4. What is the difference between these percentages?
5. What do you conclude?

Since the GSS is a sample of Americans rather than the entire population, its percentages only approximate the views of American men and women. Therefore we should regard men and women as having importantly different views only if they differ by a sizable amount. A good guideline is the "10 percent rule": *A difference less than 10 percent is too small to be important, while a difference of 10 percent or larger should be taken seriously.* Here the gender difference is 6.4 percent—less than 10 percent—so we might say that gender makes little difference in views about life's excitement.

Use CHIP to see how life's excitement varies by race, and by age. (Respondents are sorted into three age categories: 18 to 35 years old, 36 to 59 years old, and 60+.) Finally, what is the effect of respondents' class identification on excitement of life? Here class is based on the respondent's own perception of his or her social class.

Write a brief summary of your findings. Try to explain the differences you found.

3
CULTURE

62

Initiating a Masai Warrior

"Circumcision will have to take place even if it means holding you down," my father explained to the teenage initiates. "The pain you feel is symbolic. There is deeper meaning because circumcision means a break between childhood and adulthood. For the first time you will be regarded as a grown-up. You will be expected to give and not just receive and no family affairs will be discussed without your being consulted. Coming into manhood is a heavy load. If you are ready for these responsibilities tell us now." After a prolonged silence, one of my half-brothers said awkwardly. "Face it . . . it's painful. I won't lie about it. We all went through it. Only blood will flow, not milk." There was laughter and my father left. Among the Masai of East Africa, the rite of circumcision swiftly transforms an adolescent boy to an adult man. (Adapted from Saitoti, 1994:159)

Americana

The Festival of American Folklife is a summer event held on the Mall in Washington, D.C. Moving among the booths, one encounters midwestern farmers, rhythm-and-blues musicians, North and South American Indians, and Indonesians—all drumming, threshing, carving, singing, dancing, cooking, explaining, costuming, building, and generally going through the yearly ritual that showcases the United States as a nation of nations. *E pluribus unum*, hands across the water, black and white and brown together. Up and down the Mall, real Indians are carving and real Indonesians are sitting cross-legged under thatched roofs making ornaments, although a folk purist would be shocked to learn that the Indonesian uses a stapler to fasten the ornaments. One Delta bluesman wore a New York Mets cap and was making weathervanes in the shape of Tweety Bird and

Sylvester the Cat. Who is to say what is an "authentic" part of American culture? Everything at the festival is "authentic." One of the pleasures of the festival is that it turns everybody there into your own kind. Everybody is American. (Adapted from Allen, 1994:201–203)

The immense variations in human behavior are fundamentally determined by culture. **Culture** is a human society's total way of life; it is learned and shared and includes the society's values, customs, material objects, and symbols. Our culture provides our social heritage and tells us which behaviors are appropriate and which are not. Unlike the Masai, most Americans would regard circumcision at adolescence as cruel. The Festival of American Folklife highlights the fact that the cultural heritage of the United States is diverse, yet also binding—turning everybody into "your own kind" and fostering an American cultural identity. As these vignettes suggest, culture both unites and divides people—a theme we explore in this chapter as we examine its powerful role in determining human social behavior.

CULTURE AND SOCIETY

Culture encompasses all that we have developed and acquired as human beings. Culture guides our choices of food and clothing, our reading material and art, and our dating partners and friends. Stop reading for a moment and quickly survey the area around you. If you are in your dorm, the library, sitting on a bench in the quad, or reading at the beach, everything that encircles you is culturally produced. Culture can be subdivided into two major segments: **material culture,** which includes tangible artifacts, physical objects, and items that are found in a society; and **nonmaterial culture,** which includes a society's intangible and abstract components, such as values, beliefs, and traditions. The two are inextricably bound.

INTERNET CONNECTIONS

There is a discussion in the text on American values. Go to the Institute for American values:

http://www.americanvalues.org/

click on an article and select a topic or two in the bar on the right of the screen to browse through. After reading two or three articles what American values did you find being discussed in the articles? Write a short essay on the values you discovered in the articles.

Each person is a unique individual with his or her own hopes and dreams, likes and dislikes, attitudes and opinions, habits and routines. Yet many of our feelings, beliefs, and customs are reflections of our culture (Matsumoto, 2000). Customs about selecting a marriage partner, for example, are strongly influenced by culture. In the United States marriage partners are selected on the basis of romantic love. In most of the world's cultures, however, selection of a spouse is in the hands of marriage brokers, parents, other relatives, or matchmakers. Beliefs surrounding the care of newborns are also culturally based. Parents in India smudge a newborn's forehead with charcoal to hold back harmful spirits that could take the baby from the world. A Guyanan Wayapi father rests for several days after the birth of his child, believing he can divert the evil eye from the baby to himself until the baby is strong enough to do so on its own (United Nations, 2001). In both Western and non-Western cultures *couvade* is common, where a man experiences the symptoms, physical pains, and fatigue of pregnancy. Often his stress during his wife's delivery is so exhausting, she must care for him during his lengthy recuperation period (Munroe, 1999; Enoch et al., 2001). In some Gulf Arab cultures there is a strong culturally sanctioned belief that sick people should be completely dependent on others during their sickness to the extent that patients may be spoon fed or carried even if they are physically capable of taking care of themselves (Gallagher, 1995). In the United States and most of Western Europe, where such dependence is embarrassing, disdained, and to be avoided as much as physically possible, there is much less toleration for a long sick role, even in the face of serous illnesses.

Culture is so much taken for granted that we rarely consider alternatives to what we usually think and do. Only when we compare our cultural beliefs and customs with those of other cultures do we discover what we take for granted in our own culture.

Ethnocentrism and Cultural Relativism

In the study of culture, the essential element that sociology shares with all other sciences is a neutral and unbiased approach to the subject. The scientific method gives some protection against inaccurate reporting, but it does not tell us how to remain emotionally aloof from attitudes and behavior that we may find personally disturbing. Culture exerts such a powerful influence that most people exhibit **ethnocentrism,** the tendency to evaluate one's own culture as superior to others. Being a citizen of a particular culture instills a sense of group loyalty and pride that is useful when cultural unity is necessary, such as when facing a common enemy in war. But for social scientists or those who simply want to study or understand another culture, ethnocentrism is inappropriate.

An alternative to ethnocentrism is **cultural relativism,** the view that all cultures have intrinsic worth and that each culture must be evaluated and understood according to its own standards. On one level, cultural relativism is an ethical principle: You should not judge another people's customs until you understand them. On another level, it is pragmatic: You cannot do business with members of a different culture if you unknowingly behave in ways that offend them and if you misinterpret their polite behavior for stubbornness or backwardness. Equally important, cultural relativism is a scientific principle. In studying other cultures, as in all scientific endeavors, anthropologists and sociologists strive to be objective (Chapter 2).

Applying cultural relativism is easier said than done. Scientists, tourists, students, and businesspeople who first encounter cultures vastly different from their own will likely experience a feeling of **culture shock**—they will tend to experience feelings of alienation, depression, and loneliness until they become acclimated to the new culture. Anthropologist Conrad Kottak describes his own culture shock on his first visit to the Bahia region of Brazil:

> I could not know just how naked I would feel without the cloak of my own language and culture. . . . My first impressions of Bahia were of smells—alien odors of ripe and decaying mangoes . . . and of swatting ubiquitous fruit flies. . . . There were strange concoctions of rice, black beans, and gelatinous globs of meats and floating pieces of skin. I remember . . . a slimy stew of beef tongue in tomatoes. At one meal a disintegrating fish head, eyes still attached, but barely, stared up at me as the rest of its body floated in a bowl of bright orange palm oil. (Kottak, 1987:4)

Kottak eventually grew accustomed to this world. He not only learned to accept what he saw, he began to

SOCIOLOGY OF EVERYDAY LIFE

Laughing Through the Darkness

The Saudi Arabian ambassador to the U.S. said that bin Laden had an unhappy childhood growing up with 52 brothers and sisters. You think his childhood was unhappy, wait 'til we deliver his mid-life crisis.

(Jay Leno)

The Taliban is on the run and don't know where to go. Pakistan doesn't want them. Iran doesn't want them. Of course, they'll have no problem getting into the U.S.

(David Letterman)

The Defense Department found more tapes of bin Laden speaking to his followers. If you order the whole set right now, they'll throw in "The Taliban's Wet 'n' Wild Spring Break."

(Conan O'Brien)

Within days after the attack on the World Trade Center, Osama bin Laden jokes exploded in the media. Bin Laden, Taliban, and even terrorism jokes continue as staples of late-night comedy, prime-time television, political commentaries, and the Internet. Bin Laden has been mimicked by rapper Eminem in an ultrapoofy beard hip-hopping in a cave, as an Elmer Fudd type buffoon on a *South Park* cartoon episode, as a bulbous nosed clown with missing teeth in comic strips, and on the Internet in "morphing osama"—you can mess with his face any way you want—and "Osama yo' mama" as a chimpanzee. Some of the "50 ways to annoy bin Laden" when you are visiting his cave are to check to see if Saddam is on his speed-dial list; warn him you're "in a New York state of mind"; and when you leave, wave and say "Shalom." What do you do to bin Laden when he's caught? Perform a complete sex change operation and send him back to Afghanistan to live as a woman under the Taliban.

The cultural divide between the Muslim and Western world that widened after September 11 may have narrowed slightly because of humor. "Kader & Co." are Arab American and Muslim American comedians with roots in Palestine, Iran, Jordan, and Armenia who believe that the growing demand for humor can help bridge this divide. While hate crimes against Muslims and Arabs in the Untied States have increased sharply, interest in "their" brand of comedy has also increased. Thinking that Arab American comedy was doomed after September 11, Iranian American comic Maz Jobrani says, "I thought I'd never be funny again." But Arab American comics are in demand, and they are playing the hottest comedy clubs and night spots in Chicago, Los Angeles, and yes, New York. Palestinian American Aron Kader says, "All of a sudden, we're topical. Before, nobody cared (about Arabs). Now everyone's listening." What are they listening to?

- From Arab American comic Ray Hanania: "I'm married to a Jew. Until another Palestinian comic with a Jewish wife surfaces, I pretty much got the market cornered."
- From Egyptian American comic Ahmed Ahmed: "Any Arabs in the audience? Raise your hand, throw a rock, burn a flag."
- From Iranian American comic Maz Jobrani: "Since September 11, when people ask about my ancestry, I look them straight in the eyes and say, 'I'm Italian. We're all named Tony now.'"

Like generations of comedians before them, Arab American comics poke fun at themselves using ethnic humor and stereotypes that also send messages about the danger of stereotyping. Comic Ray Hanania bills himself as "just off the FBI's 10 most wanted list" and "the man you hope isn't sitting next to you on your next vacation flight." These comics are forging new paths for Muslims and Arabs in the ways that Dick Gregory and Richard Pryor did for African Americans, Margaret Cho for Asians, and John Leguizamo for Latinos.

Culture change is fueled by the media. In the already multicultural United States, the language of laughter heightens sensitivity to diversity but also transcends it. Jewish rabbi and stand-up comic Dr. Robert Alper has teamed with Ahmed Ahmed in a show billed "Arabs, Jews, Lighten Up." They have played to audiences in synagogues and other places of worship, and on stages throughout the United States. They both say that humor is what is needed in the time of tragedy, especially if supposed adversaries are brought together under a united banner. Multiculturalism continues to be recognized and respected, but the "American" at the end of the hyphen, whether it is Jewish, Arab, Muslim, African, Asian, Chinese, or European American—is the prevailing identity in times of national crisis.

Certainly, humor is culturally binding and can be used in support of better citizenship, altruism, responsibility, and tolerance. But in the face of cultural trauma, it is also offensive for many people and may be labeled as inappropriate, unworthy, sick, or racist. Critics charge that after September 11, television has not adjusted to the cultural change the United States has undergone and that programming seems inane and offensive. However, sociologists note that such labels themselves are the catalysts of cultural change and will inevitably spur further "rebellious" humor. In free societies, dissent is not stifled but is encouraged through humor.

1. How does humor reflect cultural change? Consider this in light of past and present views of various ethnic groups.

2. Taking your own cultural beliefs into account, how do you react to the humor and joking that surrounds the events of September 11 and since? How do your views represent functionalism, conflict theory, and symbolic interactionism?

Sources: Boskin, 1997; Hanania, 2002; Ali, 2002; Alper, 2002; ComedyLab, 2002; Lefcourt, 2002; Lipman, 2002; Martin, 2001; Meiss, 2002; Melendez, 2002; Political Humor, 2002; U.S. Politics, 2002; www.osamayomama.com

appreciate and enjoy its new wonders. Culture shock and ethnocentrism gave way to cultural relativism.

Values and Beliefs

Values are cultural ideals about what is considered moral and immoral, good and bad, or proper and improper. Since values offer viewpoints about ideal goals and behavior, they serve as standards for social life. Values also serve as criteria for assessing your own behavior as well as that of others. **Beliefs** are more specific than values; they are ideas and attitudes shared by a culture about what is considered true or false. An example of a value is "democracy is good." An example of a belief associated with this value is "nations with democratic governments offer a better quality of life to citizens than nations with authoritarian governments."

In small, traditional, relatively isolated societies, agreement on values may be close to universal. However, even larger, ethnically diverse cultures that experience ongoing and rapid social change have identifiable core values. These core values are embraced by most members of the culture and help distinguish it from other cultures. Over 60 years of research continues to document a consistently held core value set that defines the national character of the United States (Mead, 1942; Williams, 1951; Harris, 1981; Lipset, 1996).The following list, although not inclusive, identifies some of the most important American values. Some of these values, taken for granted in the United States, may be viewed negatively by people from other cultures.

1. *Individualism*. The United States is a highly individualistic nation, emphasizing personal independence and self-reliance. Individual self-interest rather than group goals is an acceptable guide to behavior.

2. *Achievement*. Talent, motivation, and work are the ingredients for success. Rewards are based on merit. Individuals whose hard work transforms their rags to riches are idealized models. A related value is competition, which maximizes both the merit and the reward. May the best person win.

3. *Material comfort*. The fruits of hard work and achievement are the financial rewards that can buy a desired lifestyle—what is wanted as well as what is needed.

4. *Democracy and equality of opportunity*. These values can be accomplished only in a political, educational, and economic climate that maximizes freedom of choice and equality of opportunity at all institutional levels. If the playing fields are equal—in school, the political system, and the economy—then the best person should succeed.

5. *Nationalism*. The United States is the world's role model for democracy, and Americans are proud of their political system and economic accomplishments. Regardless of their ethnic background, most people see themselves as Americans first.

6. *Group superiority*. Americans believe that their culture is superior to other cultures. Beliefs about superiority also extend to how other groups are ranked within the culture. Although Americans believe that all individuals are equal, some are viewed as "more equal"—more deserving of respect—than others because of their race, ethnicity, gender, age, wealth, achievements, or other social markers.

A college education in the United States represents an important cultural value related to achievement. Women and racial minorities now attend college in the highest numbers since the founding of the United States.

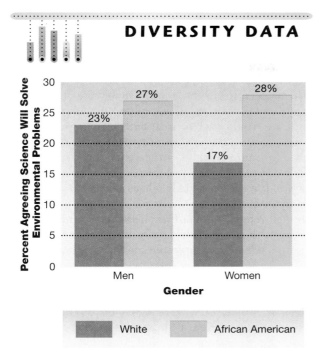

DIVERSITY DATA

FIGURE 3.1 Will Science Solve Environmental Problems?
For both men and women, and for whites and African Americans, only about one-fourth tend to agree science will solve environmental problems. However, Americans also highly value science as a basis of action. What explains this apparent cultural contradiction? Why is the largest difference in level of agreement between African American and white women?

Source: NORC General Social Surveys. 1972–2000. Chicago: National Opinion Research Center, 2000. Reprinted by permission of NORC, Chicago, IL.

7. *Science and efficiency.* Scientific principles are used as a basis for action. Logical ways of doing things that save time and money are favored. Emotion and intuition are out; practicality and rationality are in.
8. *Humanitarianism.* Despite a strongly individualistic culture, concern for the welfare of others is valued. Americans believe assistance should be offered to people who both need it and deserve it.

Some of these core values (for example, individualism and achievement) are functionally integrated: They support and reinforce one another. But the list also contains obvious contradictions. For example, belief in the superiority of certain groups is at odds with values relating to democracy, freedom, and equality of opportunity. To include group superiority on a list of core values is offensive to many Americans, since it may suggest that racism and sexism, for instance, are intrinsic to American culture (Bobo, 2001; Kennelly, 2001). Humanitarianism may also conflict

with individualism. When people believe they are individually responsible for their own fate, compassion for the poor may be reduced (Lane, 2001). The core values are not disappearing, but their rank shifts, or emphasis on one or the other changes over time.

At the same time, other values are emerging that may eventually become part of this core set. For example, the pursuit of material comfort and financial success has increased sharply. People expect to work hard to succeed, but they want to work less, retire earlier, and have more leisure time (Robinson, 1999; Kiyosaki, 2002). Leisure itself is becoming so important that it is emerging as another core value. In other cultures, such as Germany, leisure has long been a priority (Glouchevitch, 1992; *Economist*, 2000). Americans "take" vacations; Germans feel entitled to time off for recreation.

In some cases, contradictions in values are so obvious that public debate is open and contentious. Often these debates revolve around moral dilemmas created by the contradictions. For example, people in the United States generally disdain public expressions about the superiority of certain groups, especially regarding race and ethnicity (Crandall, 2002). In fact, condemnations of racism are routine. However, many are also uncomfortable with programs that mandate equal opportunity for people of color, such as affirmative action. Ethnocentrism is a fact of group life, and one that can translate into feelings of superiority, both between and within cultures. The value of maintaining cultural identity in a diverse society is rapidly increasing, and as we shall see, has produced much social tension.

Another example is the reliance on science as the key to social progress. Science is, by definition, secular; it operates on principles that are based on facts and evidence, not on assumptions and faith. Science demands that assertions be questioned, tested, and proved or disproved. But Americans also express very high degrees of faith, as indicated by religious affiliation, beliefs, and practices. Regardless of the particular religion with which they may identify, almost everyone in the United States believes in the existence of God or a universal spirit, and the majority attend religious services on a regular basis (Chapter 17). Faith and science often represent opposing viewpoints in debates related to issues such as teaching evolution in the schools, scientific experimentation on animals and humans, euthanasia, prolonging life, and research on fertility and cloning.

Norms and Sanctions

Values help define the character of a culture, but they do not provide specific courses of action. Values generally tell us what we should do, but not how to actually do it. They express *ideal culture* in guidelines and

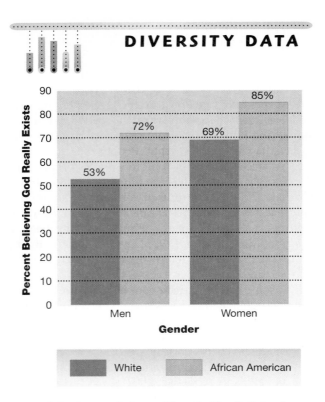

DIVERSITY DATA

Percent Believing God Really Exists (y-axis)

Men: White 53%, African American 72%
Women: White 69%, African American 85%

Gender (x-axis)

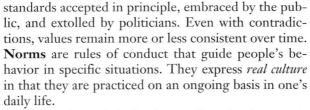

White | African American

FIGURE 3.2 Percent Believing That God Really Exists, by Gender and Race. The majority of white and African Americans as well as both genders firmly believe in God. The largest majority of belief is for African American and the slightest majority is for white men. How can American cultural values help explain this difference?

Source: NORC General Social Surveys. 1972–2000. Chicago: National Opinion Research Center, 2000. Reprinted by permission of NORC, Chicago, IL.

standards accepted in principle, embraced by the public, and extolled by politicians. Even with contradictions, values remain more or less consistent over time. **Norms** are rules of conduct that guide people's behavior in specific situations. They express *real culture* in that they are practiced on an ongoing basis in one's daily life.

The values of ideal culture tell us that honesty is the best policy. The norms of real culture tell us when it is permissible to tell "white lies" (to explain why we are late for work or a date, to reject an invitation politely, to save face, to embellish a story we're telling to friends, and so on). Norms also help us to decide which value takes precedence in a given situation. Unlike values, norms change much more rapidly and are modified or discarded as conditions change.

There are two categories of norms, based on the degree of importance we attach to a norm as well as the degree to which we are penalized when we violate

it. The first category is made up of norms called **folkways,** informal norms regulating customary ways of behaving. Our daily lives are organized around folkways that tell us how to act in a classroom, on a bus, or in a restaurant. They consist of thousands of conventional forms of behavior taught by our culture that allow us to move freely within it. Without folkways, we would have to treat each social encounter as a unique event. For the most part, we conform to folkways automatically. In diverse cultures we are likely to encounter groups that practice different folkways, but we learn quickly what is expected of us. For example, students who transfer from one college to another generally adapt their behavior to the different folkways they encounter, such as forms of dress and customs related to acceptable study and party times.

There are so many folkways that help guide our interaction, it is impossible to behave "properly" according to all of them all the time. Therefore, it is likely that some folkways will be violated; people will generally accept these as unintentional and forgivable lapses of proper human conduct.

Violations of mores, the second category of norms, are not as easily forgiven. **Mores** are norms that members of a society or culture consider vitally important, necessary, and inviolable. Violation incurs strong disapproval and often severe sanctions, ranging from expulsion to execution. A college transfer student may find tattered jeans and music after midnight acceptable in the new school (folkways), but neither the old nor the new school will tolerate cheating, plagiarism, or sexual violence (mores).

Norms—whether folkways or mores—are maintained through **sanctions**, penalties for violating norms as well as approval or reward for adhering to norms. As children, we learn our culture's norms not only through explicit instruction by our parents and others, but also by observing how other people react to our behavior. Without verbalizing specific rules, we learn what makes our parents smile or scold us, our playmates seek or shun us. As adults, abiding by norms becomes almost second nature. Most of the time, we play by the rules. We know that deliberate and even unintentional violations have consequences. Agreement on norms helps smooth social interaction. Hence we try both to abide by norms ourselves and to correct other people who violate them—whether by avoiding these people, reasoning with them, or bringing a lawsuit.

The American cultural value of achievement is demonstrated in sanctions when mores against plagiarizing another person's work are violated. The careers of historians as popular and famous as Stephen Ambrose and Doris Kearns Goodwin have been seriously damaged because of accusations of plagiarism, includ-

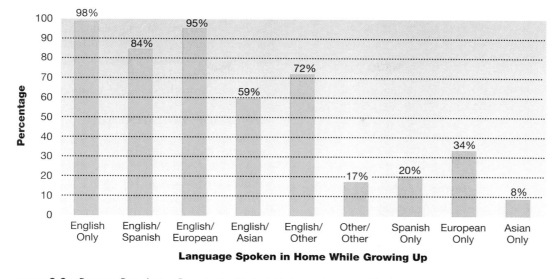

FIGURE 3.3 Percent Population Born in the United States by Language Spoken in Home While Growing Up.

Source: Greenberg et al., 2001 (National Center for Education Statistics)

ing quoting verbatim with no quotation marks, failing to cite sources, and generally passing off parts of another person's work as their own (DeWan, 2002; Lewis, 2002). In college the sanctions against plagiarizing are failing the course or expulsion. Outside of college, laws punish individuals and corporations for copyright violations, theft of company secrets and property, and insider trading of stocks. Because cultural components, especially values, are so interdependent, if deceit replaces merit as a measure of success, the entire social fabric is weakened. For this reason, violations of mores rarely go unsanctioned. Mores usually provide the basis for **laws**, formal norms codified and enforced by the legal power of the state.

CULTURE AS A SYMBOL SYSTEM

In any society, guidelines for behavior can be transmitted only if people share a common symbol system. A **symbol** is something that stands for or represents something else and is given meaning by those who use it. Agreed-upon meanings shared by a culture are, in essence, what distinguishes one culture from another. As mentioned in Chapter 1, the major principle of symbolic interactionism is that society (or culture) is "socially constructed." This principle suggests that every time we interact, we interpret the interaction according to the subjective meaning we bring to it. Although the cultural symbols we have in common allow us to interact more smoothly, each of us may bring to any encounter differing interpretations of the

symbols, affecting our perception of the "reality" of social interaction.

The Emotional Impact of Symbols

A flag is a symbol of a nation and both expresses and evokes powerful emotional reactions in its people, as shown by the dramatic increase in the display of American flags immediately following the terrorist attacks of September 11, 2001. Wars have started because an enemy desecrated a flag. Flag burning during the anti–Vietnam War movement of the 1960s and 1970s was severely sanctioned, both informally and legally. The American flag as a national symbol is so powerful that Congress regularly debates passing a federal law that would make flag desecration a crime. This debate reflects a conflict between the cultural values of nationalism and democracy: Is the flag sacred? Or will freedom of expression in a democracy be compromised if there are legal restrictions on how the flag is displayed or used, even as a form of artistic expression?

The flag of the Southern Confederacy also remains a powerful symbol. Some people associate it with a heritage of southern pride and tradition that should be preserved and respected. Others find it a reminder of an appalling era in U.S. history during which slavery flourished and a civil war tore the nation apart. To them, flying the Confederate flag today evokes images of bigotry and racism.

Both between and within cultures, groups may use different symbols to represent themselves. Symbols

A nation's flag is such a powerful symbol of cultural identity that its display is usually associated with a strong emotional reaction. When displayed with the flags of other nations, such as in front of the United Nations, flags become symbols for both national identity and international cooperation.

that evoke nationalistic, religious, political, and regional sentiments are usually invested with a great deal of emotion, both positive and negative. A symbol of an enemy elicits as much hostility from you as your symbol does from the enemy.

Language

All cultures are represented through language. A **language** is a shared symbol system of rules and meanings that govern the production and interpretation of speech. Language exerts such a strong influence on culture that it is often used as a key marker for determining the number of world cultures. If a major criterion for culture is a distinct language, the speakers of which cannot understand the speakers of another language, then there are about 4,000 to 6,000 cultures in the world (Scupin, 1998; Silverstein, 1998). Although social scientists use a combination of factors to distinguish between cultures, most consider language the marker of a distinct culture and identity. Research supports this popular view, indicating that when a language is "lost," the culture loses its most important survival mechanism (Pathay, 1998; Crystal, 2000). As we will see, language and all it represents is

a highly controversial issue. A small ethnic group existing in a larger, diverse culture may have a greater chance to maintain its cultural heritage only because its language is formally taught in school (Chapter 16). If language is a key cultural marker, then learning a language means learning the culture.

LANGUAGE AND THOUGHT One of the most important views of language and culture was put forward by the linguists Edward Sapir (1949) and Benjamin Lee Whorf (1956). According to the **Sapir-Whorf hypothesis**, language determines thought. Different languages have different grammars and vocabulary, and these in turn affect what people notice, label, and think about as well as how they organize and categorize what they perceive. Language tells us to notice some things and to ignore others, and thus shapes the ways in which its speakers habitually think about and actually "see" the world. For example, throughout desert regions in the Arab-speaking Middle East, where people depend on camels for their livelihood, there are 3,000 words for "camel" (Jandt, 2001). Another example is from the Inuit of the northwest coast of Canada, who have many different words for snow because snow is a major influence in their everyday lives. Speakers of English have only one word and hence see only "snow." If snow becomes important to English speakers—skiers, for example—then they develop new words for what they need to see.

Whorf used Hopi, a Pueblo Indian language still spoken in the Southwest United States, to support his case. The English language separates the concept of time into many distinct categories and words, such as duration (hours, seconds), cycles (mid-morning, late afternoon), phases (Monday, weekend, summer), past time (yesterday, last year), and future (tomorrow, next week). These terms also suggest that time in English is linear based. Hopi does not view time as linear, in part because there are no tenses in the language. There are no grammatical forms or expressions that refer to time. According to Whorf, the Hopi view of time is the perpetual "getting later of it" (Jandt, 2001). By focusing attention on specifics, the English language leads speakers to think about "this" or "that" storm and how it differs from other storms. In contrast, Hopi uses words that flow together into whole experiences. By merging past and present, wind and rain, cause and consequences, the Hopi language leads speakers to think about storms as a single phenomenon, wherever and whenever they occur. As a result, speakers of Hopi and speakers of English are said to have different perceptions of time and reality.

Subsequent research has shown, however, that although language and culture are intertwined, there is little evidence that language actually *determines* thought. Research clearly documents that concepts can and do exist independently of language (Bloch, 1994; Levinson, 1997). Prelinguistic children have concepts such as "house" before they learn the word house. Research with color shows that even when people do not have a word to name a color, they can readily identify the color or shade itself (Kay et al., 1997; Lucy, 1997). In English, a woman might describe a certain color as "ecru" or "ivory," whereas a man might describe it as "tan." They both see the same color, but cultural conditioning related to gender makes women more likely to have names for a wider range of color gradations. Speakers of other languages, who may have no words for the colors, also see the same shades, but may name them differently or add modifiers to existing color designations of their language.

Although the Sapir-Whorf hypothesis is generally not supported, it alerted researchers to important ways of viewing language and culture that hold true today (Holtgraves, 2002). Research shows that language can bias cognition; when we hear certain words, we conjure up images related to the words (Lipton & Hershaft, 1984; Flaherty, 1999, 2001). A good example for speakers of English is using the words *he* or *him* to refer to both males and females. When engineers as a group are routinely referred to as "he," people tend to categorize engineers as a group made up of males. The designation of engineer as "he" provides the taken-for-granted message that males naturally belong in the category. When language is changed to be more inclusive, our images about who belongs to appropriate categories also become more inclusive (Silverstein, 2001; Hellinger & Bussmann, 2002). Language may not be the sole determinant of thought, but it certainly provides directions for our perception, and thus for our attention (Bloom & Keil, 2001).

In the United States, people are becoming more sensitized to the power of words, especially when the words are associated with negative labeling. Yet when alternative word options are offered, people often express annoyance that they are being forced into "political correctness." This term represents a backlash against language changes that are thought to be unnecessary and artificial. However, according to symbolic interactionism, labels can change behavior. For example, labeling children as retarded, slow learners, or underachievers may become a self-fulfilling prophecy because teachers and parents offer them less challenging activities and pay more attention to their failures than to their achievements (see Chapter 16). A frequent result is that the children do not fulfill their potential and may come to see themselves as unintelligent. Children previously labeled "retarded" are now identified as "special needs children" in school settings. People feel more comfortable in seeking psychiatric therapy when they are referred to as "clients" rather than as "patients." For this reason, derogatory labels are being replaced by neutral, less stigmatizing terms or words of the groups' own choosing. Homosexuals who have endured labels of contempt such as "fag" or "fruit," especially in media portrayals, are now routinely referred to as "gay" and "lesbian." In the last decade, the homosexual and academic communities have resurrected the term "queer," and changed it from a pejorative, derogatory term to one that now designates new trends in research. The terms "queer theory" and "queer linguistics" are rapidly emerging as acceptable usages in the social

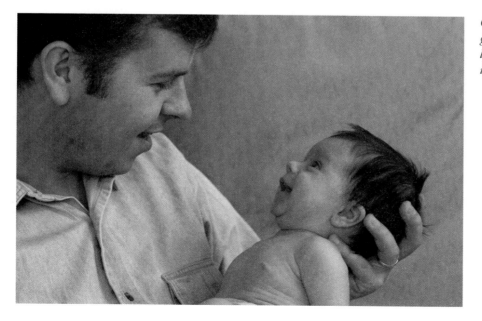

Children learn culture through language. Even at infancy they are learning appropriate behaviors during social interaction.

sciences (Barrett, 2002; Kulick, 2000, 2002). Not all the negative connotations that are culturally associated with such groups are removed by changing the labels, but the effort is a step in the right direction. The Sapir-Whorf hypothesis has not been completely abandoned (Rapport & Overing, 2000). Consistent with symbolic interactionism, language influences interpretations of social reality.

NONVERBAL COMMUNICATION Less obvious than sounds or words, but equally significant sociologically, is the nonverbal dimension of language, such as how people use space in their social interaction (Levinson, 1996; Keating, 2001). Cultures collide when such variations are misunderstood. In his classic work on the cultural differences in physical distance and space, Edward Hall (1959, 1966) states that how we distance ourselves from each other sends subtle nonverbal messages. In American culture, *intimate* distance, which extends to about 18 inches, is reserved for loved ones. *Personal* distance extends from about 1 1/2 to 4 feet and is reserved for friends and acquaintances. In other words, standing within touching distance symbolizes intimacy, and standing farther apart symbolizes familiarity but with a degree of formality. Most Latinos in the United States and Latin America, and most Arab cultures use closer personal spaces for interaction. An American conversing with a Brazilian might be uncomfortable when the Brazilian "invades" his or her personal space, so might unconsciously retreat a step—in turn causing the Brazilian to close the distance by moving forward a step. Arabs tend to interact at closer distances, but

also to talk louder and touch each other more than do Americans. What an American interprets as pushy or aggressive, a Brazilian or Saudi Arabian interprets as cold or unfriendly. In Middle Eastern cultures, it is easy to spot Americans in crowded rooms. They are the ones backed into walls and corners by their friendly hosts.

Germans and Japanese have wider personal space zones than do Americans, as shown in their architecture. Traditional German homes have lockable solid doors separating most rooms, in contrast to homes in the United States, where rooms are connected by halls and open doorways. Japan is a geographically small country with a relatively large population. Space is limited, so people must deal with privacy in a different way. Although small by U.S. standards, the rooms in Japanese homes can be divided with thin paper and bamboo sliding doors. A paper door cannot provide silence or invisibility, but it offers symbolic privacy. Use of physical space is one of many areas of nonverbal communication or as Hall (1959) called it, the "silent language" of any culture. Nonverbal communication is explored in Chapter 6.

LANGUAGE AND GENDER Although the distinction between men's and women's places in society has somewhat decreased, traditional gender roles are still embedded in language. Beginning with the pioneering work of Robin Lakoff (1975), research has shown that women and men from the same society who speak the same language have different styles of communicating—a pattern found in all cultures (Payne, 2001). Some of these differences for speakers of English include the following:

1. Women use more modifiers and tag questions than men. Rather than describing a person as "shy," a woman is apt to add a modifier, such as "kind of" or "somewhat." Adjectives provide other modifiers, so that a woman may describe a party as "divine" and a croissant as "absolutely wonderful." She may end a sentence with a tag question, as if she were asking the other person's permission to express her opinion: "It's a beautiful day, isn't it?" "I really liked the movie, didn't you?" (Lakoff, 1975, 1991; LaFrance, 2001).

2. In specialized role areas, women's vocabulary is more complex and descriptive than men's. Women use a greater range of words for colors, textures, food, clothing, cooking, and parenting. They describe themselves and others in terms of complex interpersonal characteristics, using a greater variety of words and communication styles. When talking to their children, mothers show both high involvement and high consideration (Flannagan et al., 1995; Beaumont et al., 2001).

INTERNET CONNECTIONS

The text discusses the relationship between language and *gender*. Deborah Tannen is a well-known authority on communication differences between men and women and her "genderlect styles" have become widely quoted in the gender studies literature. You may review these "genderlect styles" at:

http://www.usm.maine.edu/com/genderlect/index.htm

Describe the male and female patterns of communication illustrated in the presentations. Explain how the film "When Harry Met Sally" is an illustration of gender communication differences? What differences or similarities did you find?

This American couple may not be conversing verbally but their nonverval communication is quite strong. Consistent with American nonverbal styles of interaction regarding use of space and touching, they are openly, but silently, expressing care and concern for one another, most likely in a romantic sense.

3. Men use speech that is less polite and more direct than women. Men issue commands (the imperative form): "Close the door"; women make more polite requests: "Please close the door." Both genders use slang and expletives, but women do so less frequently and less explicitly: "Hell," and "shit" become "heck," and "shoot" (Selnow, 1985; de Klerk, 1990; Macaulay, 2001).

4. When discussing sexuality, young girls offer more detailed, serious reflections; young boys make fewer comments, joke about it, and make greater use of sexual slang. Males in all age groups use sexually degrading language much more frequently than females. Males direct derogatory sexual slang to females ("bitch," "slut") and gay men ("fag," "prick") (Burn, 2000; Murnen, 2000; Halstead, 2001; Niemi, 2001).

5. Women converse in open, free-flowing ways and appreciate self-disclosure, whereas men feel uncomfortable in this regard. Women tend to like both men and women who confide information about their private lives and inner feelings, but men do not. Men converse on "safe" topics, such as sports and politics, that do not require them to reveal personal details to each other. When men want to encourage or cement friendships with other men, they engage in activities like poker, sports, and watching television, which allow time together but discourage lengthy conversations. Male locker-room talk often involves joking, bragging, and competition. In the "ladies' room" at a theater or restaurant, women share experiences and seek common ground (Inman, 1996; Handler, 2001; Weatherall, 2002).

6. At the beginning of a male–female relationship, men talk more than women, but once the relationship "takes hold," communication decreases. Women would like to talk more, men would like to talk less. As she attempts to draw him out, he silently resists. Wives are more likely than their husbands to identify communication as a problem (Bruess & Pearson, 1996; Tannen, 2001).

Cultural norms and the roles that men and women play explain these patterns. Just as language reflects what is culturally important, specialized language patterns emerge with specialized roles. For example, men are more likely than women to be in workplace roles associated with giving orders, making speedy decisions, maintaining emotional distance between themselves and coworkers, and communicating by phone and email rather than in person. Men are therefore encouraged to talk less, use imperatives more, and refrain from emotional displays. On the other hand, women are more likely than men to be in domestic, home-based roles that are associated with nurturing, resolving conflicts between family members, and relationship issues (Carli, 2001; Ridgeway, 2001; Thomson et al., 2001). The tag questions and modifiers women use may not suggest that women are equivocal or tentative but rather that their nurturing roles make them more attuned to the feelings of other people.

Men and women are rewarded for the speech patterns that are culturally prescribed. As gender roles change, language changes accordingly. Gender differences in conversation topics, levels of self-disclosure, and types of emotions expressed are decreasing over time (Anderson, 1999; Hannah & Murachver, 1999; Alexander & Wood, 2000). Feminist researchers are now focusing less on differences between the language of men and women, and more on the context and place of talk and how talk may be intentionally structured according to gender to accomplish specific tasks, such as gaining support of coworkers or cementing a relationship (Bucholtz, 1999; Vogel et al., 1999; Crawford, 2001). As more women enter the boardroom as executives and more men enter the classroom as elementary school teachers or assume more equal parenting responsibilities in the home, language choice and style will change.

THE LANGUAGE OF LAUGHTER A Saudi, a Russian, a North Korean, and a New Yorker are walking

down the street. A pollster stops them and asks, "Excuse me, what is your opinion of the meat shortage?"
The Saudi replies, "Excuse me, what's a shortage?"
The Russian replies, "Excuse me, what's meat?"
The North Korean replies, "Excuse me, what's an opinion?"
Finally, the New Yorker replies, "What's excuse me?"
(Meat Shortage, 2002)

Laughter is social glue. People are significantly more likely to laugh when in groups than when alone, with chuckling also positively associated with level of pleasure in social interaction (Devereux & Ginsburg, 2001; Nezlek & Derks, 2001). Studying laughter and the jokes that elicit it are excellent ways to demonstrate the taken-for-granted influence of culture on our behavior. Strangers can exchange and enjoy jokes because they share common cultural symbols, stereotypes, habits, and assumptions about who jokes about whom, when, and where, and what subjects are joked about (Lefcourt, 2000; Roeckelein, 2002).

As the "humor columnist" for *Scientific American*, suggests, if you're telling the world's funniest joke about detective Sherlock Holmes and his gruff assistant Dr. Watson to someone who doesn't know who they are, you're like the lousy cook at the culinary institute who was just wasting thyme (Mirsky, 2002). If a joke must be explained, it loses its spontaneity and is therefore not funny. To understand the culture's humor requires an understanding of its stereotypes. To appreciate the meat shortage joke, knowledge and stereotypes about all four cultures is necessary, from wealthy Saudis, the economic woes of Russia, the political repression in North Korea, and the gruffness of New Yorkers. The following examples (ComedyLab, 2002) demonstrate, the need to know the American cultural context to understand the humor.

List of short books:
The Amish Phone Book
Spotted Owl Recipes by the EPA
Bob Dole: The Wild Years

State slogans:
Kentucky: Five million people, seven last names
North Carolina: Tobacco is a vegetable
New York: You have the right to remain silent, you have the right to an attorney

Government:
How many Republicans (or Democrats) does it take to change a light bulb? Three. One to change the bulb, one to call the media to publicize it, and one to blame the electric bill on the Democrats (Republicans).

What's the difference between the government and the mafia? One of them is organized.

Studying what a culture regards as funny also provides insight into the major theoretical perspectives in sociology. At the macro level, symbolic interactionism emphasizes that humor is relative and is socially constructed according to the values of a specific culture or subculture (Berger, 1997). At the interpersonal level, jokes also allow us to present a version of "self" in the way we would most like to be thought of, both as the joke giver and as the listener (Goffman, 1959). Both levels are indicated in the following joke, where a man presents himself as "one of the boys," even though he's about to marry: "I'm getting married, but it's not going to work out. My wife expects to move in with me."

Functionalism emphasizes that joking can bind a culture together. The act of laughing together can strengthen a sense of community and social identity (Lefcourt, 2000; Terrion & Ashforth, 2002). Humor and laugher can raise morale and confidence among soldiers who must depend on one another for their very survival. (Le Naour, 2001). Group cohesion is strengthened through the subtleties of a common language that allow for wordplay and puns that are mysterious to linguistic outsiders. Knowledge of American English and its culture can elicit a chuckle at the following puns:

Why would the vote count if only part of the chad is dislodged? We were suppose to count punch wholes.

My Quaker neighbor is very poor. I guess a Friend in need is a Friend indeed. (Politics, 2002; Religion, 2002)

Conflict theory emphasizes the use of humor as a political tool. Commenting on football during the protest movement of the 1970s, African American comedian Dick Gregory noted: "It's the only sport in the world where a black man can chase a white man and forty thousand people stand up and cheer." In situations where minorities may be powerless to respond in other ways, jokes can be effective responses against oppression (Boskin, 1997; Mahony & Lippman, 2001).

Racial and ethnic jokes have long been a mainstay of American humor. From a conflict perspective, such jokes reinforce the tellers' feelings of superiority ("we" are smarter, braver, and more honorable than "they"). At the same time, they serve to divert attention from the true sources of inequality and also to quell fears that the group in question might become serious competitors in the struggle for wealth and power. For this reason, many jokes contain a great deal of masked aggression (Roeckelein, 2002). What is most relevant for sociology is that the general script for these jokes remains constant over time, but the target of the jokes changes. The following jokes about mythical Lobodomians (from the word lobodomy— get it?) are benign examples:

How did Lobodomia get conquered so fast? The enemy marched in backwards and the Lobodomians thought they were leaving.
Lobodomian firing squads stand in circles.
How do you sink a Lobodomian battleship? Put it in water.
How do you know if a Lobodomian has been using your computer? Check for the whiteout on the screen.

Over time, Scandinavians, Germans, Italians, Irish, Chinese, Japanese, Jews, Catholics, African Americans, and Native Americans have been plugged into the same basic formula, with slight variations as to their supposed deficiencies. This suggests that when a racial or ethnic group mobilizes the resources to challenge how they are portrayed, the "old style" humor is no longer humorous. Stereotypes about the group are abandoned, at least in "polite" company, and new scapegoats found (Boskin, 1997). As eminent sociologist Peter Berger (1963:165) observes, important insights about cultures can often be gained "only while laughing" (Berger, 1963:165). Insight into the subculture of conflict theorists might come with the following:

How many sociologists does it take to change a light bulb?
It isn't the light bulb that needs changing, it's the system.

Culturally Speaking: What Separates Humans from Other Animals?

In 1960, the famed British scientist Jane Goodall was just beginning her research in the Gombe National Park in Tanzania, East Africa, observing and documenting the behavior of chimpanzees in their natural environment. The Gombe chimps, she discovered, used blades of grass and sticks to fish out termites from their hills. Even more significant, they reshaped these objects to conform to the particular termite hill to make them more efficient for enticing the tasty insects. Making and using tools, however rudimentary, had long been considered one of the distinguishing traits of humankind. Goodall wired the news to her mentor, the late anthropologist Louis Leakey, who wired back: "Either we will have to change our definition of mankind, or admit chimpanzees into the human family" (Goodall, 1986).

Most nonhuman animals communicate. Chimps and dolphins in particular have complex forms of communication that combine instinctive and learned behavior (Savage-Rumbaugh et al., 1998; Brown & Boysen, 2000; Herman et al., 2001; Tschudin et al., 2001). Innate communication occurs through signs with unvarying meanings. The vast majority of animal communication is based on these signs. However, chimps and gorillas that have been taught hand gestures can eventually learn to put them together to form simple sentences, often to convey what they want. They can even teach many of the gestures to their offspring (Fouts, 1994; Boyd & Richardson, 1996; Tomasello, & Call, 1997; Jensvold & Gardner, 2000).

A wealth of evidence from research in both natural and laboratory environments suggests that animals—in particular chimps and the higher primates—have many characteristics associated with culture. Some anthropologists suggest that the difference between human culture and chimpanzee culture is only a matter of degree, even if that degree is a vast one (McGrew, 1998; Boesch, 1999; Brumann, 2002). But to say that animals possess culture requires a giant leap that is hard to defend for three important reasons. First, there are biological differences, especially in the capacity to develop language, that separate people from the higher primates. Only the human brain has the potential for learning any cultural tradition to which it is exposed. Second, primates are social animals and may be able to learn some behaviors quicker through emulation, such as infant chimps seeing their mother roll a log over and eat the insects underneath. But they would have eventually learned the same behavior on their own if the wind rather than the mother caused the log to roll over. In addition, once a behavior is learned or a tool is invented, humans continually modify and "upgrade" it over time, whereas chimps do not (Tomasello, 1999; Bodley, 2000).

The third and most important reason animals do not have culture is because humanity's outstanding feature is its symbolic basis (Tuttle, 2001; Tomasello, 2002). Instincts or other unlearned patterns of behavior are not cultural precisely because they have no symbolic referent. Humans live according to meanings that they create, accept, or discard at will. No other animal has Tuesdays, for example. Nonhuman animals fully depend on their physical environment and live in the here and now, not in the symbolic world of Tuesdays and Sundays. "Ducks and beavers cannot even recognize Tuesdays, let alone organize their lives around them" (Barrett, 1991:55). Although many animals can vocalize and even socialize, they cannot meaningfully symbolize. Culture is the sole possession of humanity.

Some elements of culture may be identified in studying the behavior of chimps, but using symbols to convey ideas is not one of them.

CULTURAL CHANGE

Culture is not a random assortment of beliefs, practices, and symbols; to serve as a way of life, the different elements of culture must reinforce one another to some extent. At the same time, culture is never fixed or static. Culture is always changing, always "on the move"—whether because of innovations within a cultural group, changes in the physical environment, or contact with other cultures. **Cultural integration** describes the process by which cultural elements become closely connected and interdependent. Inevitably, a change in one part of the culture will produce change in other areas. When new cultural elements fit with existing beliefs and practices, cultural integration is strengthened and cohesiveness and harmony maintained. When too many conflicting elements are introduced, cultural integration is threatened.

Both cultural change and cultural integration are influenced by two very important elements, which serve as bridges between material and nonmaterial culture. The first is **technology,** tools and the body of knowledge pertaining to their use that help accomplish social tasks. The second is **popular culture,** cultural patterns that are produced and spread through the mass media, especially television. The American popular culture industry dominates the world and, as we shall see, has fueled the emergence of a global culture. Clearly, technology and popular culture are major ingredients for cultural change, but also major impediments to cultural integration.

Even what we might see as a trivial element of technology can have a major impact on a culture.

When the Mekranoti Indians of central Brazil were introduced to metal pots in the 1950s, they switched from roasting to boiling their food. This allowed nursing mothers to feed supplemental food to their infants earlier and in turn steadily decreased the average nursing period by almost three months (Milton, 1994). Because nursing provides a form of natural birth control, a metal cooking pot led to an increase in fertility, and this in turn impacted the entire social and economic life of the village. A simple cooking pot created major cultural upheaval for a tiny, relatively isolated society. In Malaysia and Indonesia, where government-controlled news lacks credibility in the eyes of the public, Internet access allows citizens to study alternative views of their own country (Wong, 2001). Think what one personal computer connected to a modem could do in another culture that was artificially isolated because of political repression

As you might expect, material culture changes faster than nonmaterial culture. **Cultural lag** is the gap that often exists between the time an artifact is introduced and the time it is integrated into a culture's value system. Scientific technology related to health and medicine provides numerous examples of cultural lag. Technology is available to create and prolong life as well as end it through euthanasia. Successful animal cloning has generated research related to human cloning. There have been remarkable advances in organ transplants from human to human and from animal to human. Research has allowed the egg and sperm of a formerly infertile couple to be incubated outside the womb and later implanted safely in the woman or in another woman who carries the fetus to term. In the latter case a woman literally "rents" her womb to the couple. Sperm banks now provide options for infertile couples as well as for those women who desire children but do not want to be married. Although these procedures are subject to rigorous guidelines, the ethical implications cannot be dismissed. The new technology raises essential questions concerning cultural values: What is life? When does life end? Who is a parent? Do children have the right to know their biological (or genetic) parents? and Who "owns" a child? Technological change is often the force that prompts cultures to reexamine fundamental values related to its moral and ethical views.

Each culture must decide how to answer these questions. But clearly, technological change—whether in the form of animal cloning, sperm banks, or a cooking pot—will continue to outpace value change in any society. In these examples cultural lag works against cultural integration.

Processes of Cultural Change

The spread of cultural elements, both material and nonmaterial, from one society to another is called cultural **diffusion.** It can be *direct*, such as when two cultures intermarry or wage war against one another and seize territory and prisoners, or when missionaries or tourists from one culture "invade" another. It can be *indirect*, when cultural patterns and products move into a culture without firsthand contact with members of the culture that originated them. The first trading centers and ports became the havens for indirect cultural exchange. Traders, sailors, and entrepreneurs met at these ports, then met at other ports, and eventually took back with them not only new products but different attitudes and behaviors. Today, indirect cultural diffusion occurs daily via the Internet. Any time you forward an email message that was forwarded to you from someone in a different society, indirect cultural diffusion occurs.

Cultural integration is enhanced when both direct and indirect diffusion allow the changing elements to be modified to suit the norms and material culture of the receiving culture. Through email and the Internet, this author has received over 50 variations of chocolate cookie recipes that evolved from recipes unique to cultural conditions—use of cocoa when cold storage is a problem, from metric to nonmetric instructions, from gas to propane to cow dung as fuel. Recipes have made the rounds from a tiny village in the West African nation of Mali, to Calcutta, India, to Sydney, Australia, and to Omaha, Nebraska. This form of indirect cultural diffusion is functional for satisfying a global sweet tooth.

Cultural change also occurs through *invention*, when existing cultural elements are combined to form new ones (the light bulb, the microchip), and *discovery*, the creation of new cultural elements or the reinterpretation of existing ones (the Internet, animal communication, the Bible). The innovations that result from both invention and discovery illustrate the power of cultural suggestibility. Scientists operate according to traditions and share a common framework or outlook for research (Kuhn, 1970). Thus, scientists who share the same traditions are likely to make parallel innovations (inventions and discoveries). This explains why so many important innovations of Western civilization were discovered by several people at the same time. Examples include the discovery of oxygen, the principles of genetics, the cellular basis of life, elements of calculus, rocketry, and the invention of the steamboat, telegraph, television, and telephone (Barrett, 1991).

THEORETICAL PERSPECTIVES ON CULTURE AND CULTURAL CHANGE

In explaining human social behavior, sociologists must always take into account the processes of change. Indeed, the strength of all sociological theories rests on how well they can explain changes in culture and society.

Functionalism

The functionalist theoretical perspective stresses that every society must meet basic needs, such as food and shelter, in order to survive. We will see in the next chapter how all societies develop basic social structures organized around these requirements. All known prehistoric and historic societies are thought to have common features, called **cultural universals,** that aided in their survival. More than a half century ago, anthropologist George Murdock (1945) compiled a list of more than 70 cultural universals, including family patterns, food taboos, religious rituals, adornment and decorative arts, ethics, folklore, food habits, and healing techniques. One of the most important cultural universals is the *incest taboo*, which restricts sexual relations or marriage between people who are closely related to one another. Although this taboo is universal, precisely whom it applies to—parents and siblings, first and second cousins, or an entire clan—varies. So it is with other cultural universals.

Cultural universals are shared by all societies, but the way they are acted out varies considerably from society to society, as illustrated by cultural habits surrounding food. Roast dog is a culinary delight in some

Cultural contact and, therefore, cultural diffusion are fueled by the media. When superstar Britney Spears first appeared in concert with an outfit exposing much of her torso, it was rapidly picked up in the dress of teens and young females throughout the globe. With Western popular culture dominating the global media, the hair styles, clothing, and jewelry worn by celebrities usually appear first in a celebrity's own culture but are quickly adopted in other parts of the world.

but Americans prefer oysters and clams. Jews and Muslims share a taboo against eating pork. Catholics eat pork and other meat, but on specified religious holidays consume only fish. Hindus do not eat meat, but their Muslim neighbors in India do—often a cause for violent clashes. Beef is widely consumed throughout the world, but the preferred parts of the cow vary from culture to culture. In the United States, people prefer filet mignon and prime rib, and almost everyone eats hamburgers. Americans generally do not like animal organs, but tripe (beef stomach) and sweetbreads (the thymus or pancreas) are considered delicacies in continental Europe, and kidney pie is a favorite in Great Britain. Lungs, tonsils, and thyroids are consumed readily in many African cultures. Many East African pastoralists, including the Masai, butcher cattle only on ceremonial occasions; their everyday staple is cattle blood (taken from live animals) mixed with milk (Kiple & Omelas, 2000).

According to the functionalist perspective, unique customs develop and persist because they are adaptive: They improve a people's chances of survival and reproduction. **Adaptation** is the process enabling a culture to maintain equilibrium despite fluctuations and change. Customs that reduce the survival chances of a culture are unlikely to persist.

The sacred cows of India are a good example. They remain a functional necessity for much of the culture. They give milk, pull plows, and provide dung for fuel and fertilizer for crops, and when they die a natural death, every inch of the animal is used in some product, from its hide for leather sandals to its bone for polished jewelry. Tanning leather is the job of the

provinces in China, Korea, Vietnam, and in many other parts of Asia. Grubs, beetles, iguanas, and lizards are relished throughout South America and in Australia. In Colombia, toasted ants are consumed daily. The French consume snails in great quantity,

lowest caste people, those at the very bottom of the social hierarchy, who depend on the job, hence the cow, to survive. In the midst of starvation a naive outsider might look at a healthy cow and ask why the cow is not eaten to survive. However, cows are more valuable and contribute more to human survival if they are alive than if they were butchered, cooked, and consumed. Religious values and mythology develop or are adapted in support of such cultural practices. The relationship between people and cows enhances adaptation and cultural integration (Harris, 1994). Functionalism suggests that such culturally variable habits emerged because they filled a purpose and may persist even if the original usefulness becomes obsolete.

Conflict Theory

Conflict theory holds that whichever group controls a culture's *ideology*, the value system defining social inequality as just and proper, also determines how power and resources are allocated. According to Karl Marx, the dominant ideology eventually becomes part of the value system of an oppressed group. The group may view its own culture as inferior and attempt to improve its position by adopting the ways of the dominant culture. One way in which an elite controls subordinate groups is through language, a fundamental element of culture.

During the 19th and early 20th centuries, the Pacific islands (Polynesia, Micronesia, and Melanesia) were colonized by Europeans. One of the expected benefits of colonization was education: Indigenous people were given the opportunity to go to school and learn to read, not in their own language but in that of their colonizers. In fact, schools and literacy were tools for implanting the dominant colonial ideology in local children; they eroded the values and the leadership of the traditional, orally transmitted culture (Topping, 1992). Literacy brings power but at the expense of vital aspects of traditional culture (Graff, 1995; UNESCO, 1999). When young people see the world through "literate culture" eyes, their elders often see them as betraying traditional, oral culture values. Youth think and act differently from their oral culture counterparts, a scenario being played out with indigenous peoples worldwide. Oral culture and its traditional values struggle to survive in a literate culture environment (Pablo, 2001; Zepada, 1995; Napora, 2001; Oyler, 2002). It is estimated that of the world's 6,000 languages, 1,500 have fewer than 1,000 speakers. About 300 languages account for 96 percent of the people of the world. There is little doubt that a large number of languages face extinction in the next few decades (Crystal, 2000).

The conflict perspective shows that language and literacy also can be tools for reclaiming autonomy and fighting against cultural subordination. Such is the case with the Aborigines in Australia's Northern Territory. Until the 20th century, Aborigines were denied all but a minimal education. They wanted their children to gain access to all English—not just to the selected types and topics they learned in the first missionary schools or in the later government-supported schools. This "secret" English helped the Aborigines gain control over their community's education program, which in turn helped them fight racism. Once they mastered the language, they could interpret government documents that impact them and write books consistent with their own ideology. Today bilingual education for Aboriginal children is emphasized. They study the history and traditions of the culture associated with their mother tongue as well as that of wider Australia (Special Protection Measures, 1995; RSJ, 2000; Malsen, 2002). The ability to use both traditional language and English provides Aborigines with a stronger resource base to ensure fair treatment and cultural protection as Australia continues to globalize and is itself engulfed in massive cultural change. For indigenous peoples, literacy allows access to an entire system of documents and history that had formerly been denied to them (Kelder, 1996; Graff et al., 1997; Bancroft, 2001; Malsen, 2002).

Similarly, native Hawaiians are working toward cultural revitalization, specifically aimed at preserving their language and the cultural traditions associated with it. The Hawaiian language revitalization program is the most developed of any such effort on the United States (Wilson, 1998:325). The flourishing of hula schools since the early 1970s, for example, is associated with the "Hawaiian renaissance." The dance and chants in all their different and subtle forms are imbued with powerful religious symbolism and speak to ancient traditions. Today both haoles (whites) and native Hawaiians recognize that the thriving interest in hula also symbolizes an increase in the power of Hawaii's indigenous peoples. In line with a democratic value system, they can more readily reinstate native languages in schools, teach children about their own cultural heritage, and gain access to the technology necessary to preserve an oral heritage (Buck, 1993; Kanahele, 2001).

This analysis indicates that conflict theory faces the same basic dilemma as functionalism in its explanation of cultural change. It is supportive of indigenous people's efforts at cultural preservation but at the same time recognizes that this very preservation serves to isolate and marginalize them, especially if they are denied access to technology and education. The Raute of Nepal have been foragers for centuries, but dwindling forests and wildlife are threatening their nomadic life. They have resisted assimilation into the underclasses of neighboring Hindu farmers

In America and many places in Europe, cultural beliefs about attractiveness propel people to sit in the direct sunlight for hours to obtain a bronze body. This cultural practice persists in spite of widespread knowledge that premature aging and skin cancer are common results.

by changing methods of hunting, bartering for food, and even by begging (Fortier, 2001). A degree of ethnic autonomy is maintained, but they remain poor, children are unlikely to attend school, and they do not benefit from even the minimal services offered by Nepal's social development programs. Overall, the conflict approach favors the notion that cultural change is more beneficial than cultural continuity to oppressed people. The question is how much to emphasize cultural similarities, which functionalism does, and how much to emphasize cultural differences, which conflict theory does. Cultures continue to change because people are creative and inventive; they can adapt to natural and social forces, and they can adapt these same forces to their benefit.

Symbolic Interactionism

Not all sociologists and anthropologists agree that culture and its customs can be explained mainly in terms of adaptation (Sahlins, 1976; Murphy, 1994). There is broad consensus that cultural values and attitudes can help or hinder progress and development (Harrison & Huntington, 2000). A large number of inefficient, disadvantageous, and even dangerous customs persist in most cultures. In cultures where malnutrition is common, taboos against eating certain foods put children at risk for illness and death. Eggs are regarded as a cause of late speech development in Korea and of mental retardation in East Africa. In some tropical areas the belief persists that the plentiful papaya causes worms in children. In some rural areas in Nigeria women believe that eating arsenic and castor oil seeds or drinking water used to wash dead bodies will prevent pregnancy (Keller, 1996; Latham, 1997). Similarly, Western conceptions of beauty propel Caucasians to spend hours in the sun or in salons in search of a perfect tan, a practice that has drastic health consequences. Rates of skin cancer continue to increase in the United States, Western Europe, and Australia even with more media attention about the devastating effects of overexposure to the sun as well as increasing risk with even lower sun exposure because of ozone layer depletion (Chapter 22) (de Bendern, 2000). And multimillion dollar media campaigns on the health risks of smoking and excessive alcohol consumption often do not dissuade young people from the belief that these are needed to be cool and have fun.

Those in the same culture often disagree about why they choose certain types of cultural behavior. Symbolic interactionists suggest that people often present views that are flexible and pragmatic, and that vary according to their personal situations. Their reasons for how and why they do things change as their cultural circumstances change. The Tsimihety people of Madagascar represent this view:

> Some villages irrigated their rice fields while others relied upon rain. Some organized cooperatives that exchanged labor; others worked on their own. Some men performed a certain ritual using a prayer; others omitted the prayer or used a different one. (Cited in Vayda, 1994:321)

Symbolic interactionists also point out that a people may consciously and deliberately reject an innovation that they recognize as adaptive. The Rwala Bedouins of Saudi Arabia retain ancient camel herding practices that require long training in difficult environmental conditions. Lifestyle pressures make camel herding an arduous occupation, both physically and economically. Since sheepherding now offers these people a less strenuous existence and future economic advantages that they clearly recognize, why do so many Rwalas still herd camels? The answer seems to be that they like camels and don't much like sheep. Their reason is an emotional one and not an economic one. Camel herding also helps them retain a greater sense of independence and cultural integrity (Lancaster, 1997).

Functionalists might view the Tsimihety culture as disintegrated and Rwala camel herding as maladaptive. Symbolic interactionists would disagree. In their view, what matters is that people attach particular meanings to what they do and why they do it.

CULTURAL DIVERSITY

Cultural elements such as technology, media-based popular culture, tourism, immigration, the uprooting of people due to war and politics or disaster and famine, and most important, the requirements of a global economy, affirm that cultural diversity is rapidly becoming a fact of life in even the most remote areas of the world. Cultures that were traditionally patterned primarily according to kinship, gender, and age are now incorporating new elements into their cultural mix. As a result, groups may form around these newer patterns. However, the principle of adaptation suggests that new patterns form but traditional patterns are not erased. Groups within a society may maintain as well as develop distinctive cultural identities.

Subcultures: The Significance of Being Different

A **subculture** is a segment of a culture sharing characteristics that distinguish it from the broader culture. Subcultures often have distinct values and norms that set them apart from mainstream culture. Ethnic subcultures are a clear example; immigrants often settle in the same areas and neighborhoods, and maintain many elements of their native culture in their new setting, at least among themselves. These characteristics can include dress, food, style of language (or even a different language), economic activity, dating patterns, and child-rearing practices. Many immigrant groups adapt to the broader culture in their work lives but effectively return to their original culture in their homes and neighborhoods.

Subcultures are typically based on race, social class, ethnicity, age, religion, gender, or occupation. But the key principle of how subcultures evolve is that attitudes and patterns of behavior are distinctive enough, or important enough, to unite people. As will be discussed in Chapter 5, in highly diverse societies such as the United States and Canada, race and social class may trigger subcultural formation to the degree that children are explicitly socialized into race and class norms. There are also subcultures based on sexual orientation, art and music, sports, and physical

disability. Your college functions as a strong subculture—a lifestyle shared with college students across the country, even around the globe. You dress, speak, and act a bit differently in the college subculture than in any other subcultures to which you belong. Like culture, subcultures provide guidelines for effective interaction in diverse societies.

Subcultures are also found in smaller, homogeneous societies that are uniform in terms of race and religion and whose members may not differ significantly in terms of social class and economic functions. In such societies, age and gender usually form the most important criteria in which subcultures evolve. The Masai of the opening vignette are a pastoral people of cattle herders living in Kenya and Tanzania who remain culturally distinctive despite years of colonial rule, political upheaval, and tourist invasions (Coast, 2002). Masai legends trace their culture back 300 years, although anthropologists believe they migrated to the region about 1,000 years ago. They exist as a traditional subculture in the rapidly developing political states in which they are legally contained (Marks, 1999; Shaw, 2002). But within Masai subculture, another powerful age- and gender-based subculture also thrives, with such practices as the circumcision rites of Masai males mentioned earlier. The life of Masai males, especially, follows a prescribed progression based on culturally determined age grades (Peatrik, 1995). A male's life is distinguished by elaborate ceremonies, or *rites of passage*, that mark the transition from one life stage to another—from childhood to boyhood, to warriorhood, to elderhood. The tribe is structured around these rituals, because from birth boys grow up with their peers in an age-set to which they belong throughout their lives. Although not as formally restricted to interaction with their age-mates as boys, Masai females are socialized into their primary roles as lover, wife, and childbearer (Hodgson, 1999). For both males and females, the subculture they inhabit is mysterious to members of the other gender.

Countercultures: Different but Opposed

Sometimes the distinctiveness of a subculture puts it in such sharp contrast with the broader culture that it becomes a **counterculture**, with values and norms in opposition to the dominant culture. The term was popularized by Theodore Roszak (1969) during the student protest movement against the war in Vietnam. This movement was also associated with rock music, sexual experimentation, and illegal drug use, particularly marijuana—all of which parents and society as a whole viewed as subversive, dangerous, and wrong. Most important, the protest movement generally gained its recruits from white, middle-class families

Although multicultural diversity is common in many colleges, the students who study in them are drawn together in a common subculture. Unlike the countercultural college students in the 1960s and 1970s who rejected materialism and traditional values associated with the American Dream, today's college students embrace these values.

that were the supposed standard-bearers for the American Dream. Resistance to fighting a war many considered unjust coincided with the emergence of a radically different vision of "the good life." Members of the counterculture questioned traditional values such as nationalism and patriotism. They questioned the belief that science and technology represented progress. And they rejected materialism as a guideline for living, and valued individualism—"Do your own thing"—over conformity and traditional measures of success. Some pursued alternative lifestyles based on interdependence and affection in rural communes or in large cities such as San Francisco. The critical factor, however, was that large numbers of young people rejected conventional lifestyles and the "work ethic" that held that the primary goal of life was to work hard in the present to secure material benefits for oneself and one's children in the future. When many literally "dropped out" in rejection of the American cultural standard for achievement and in favor of instant gratification, the counterculture was born (Braunstein & Doyle, 2001). The power of sheer numbers in mass protest played a key role in the eventual pullout of the United States from Vietnam (Appy & Bloom, 2001; Morrison & Morrison, 2001; Streitmatter, 2001).

The youth countercultures that have since evolved are still made up mostly of teenagers and young adults who strive for immediate gratification of goals, with a number of them organized around the music and drugs themes similar to the earlier groups (Sirius, 1998; Temple, 1999; Markert, 2001). But the similarity stops there. Contemporary youth countercultures are smaller, more homogeneous, and more

organized. They are not interested in broad-scale social reform and are likely to be racist, anti-Semitic, or overtly intolerant and suspicious of any ethnic or racial group different from their own. They do embrace important American cultural goals, such as material comfort and power through competition, at least for their specific group, but they achieve these goals through illegal and often violent means. Tattoos, graffiti, group identity, secret signs, specialized language, and dangerous rites of passage are associated with countercultures across the globe.

Gangs and gang violence are not new. What is new, however, is that the violence is less contained and more lethal with easy access to guns and recruitment of increasingly younger members. Some countercultures may not be engaged in illegal activities but operate on the fringes of the law. Skinheads, the Ku Klux Klan, and antigovernment militia groups have been implicated in many violent activities, including the 1995 bombing of a federal building in Oklahoma City (Zellner, 1995; Southern Poverty Law Center, 2002). On a global level, countercultures may come together to become larger, more organized terrorist organizations such as the Peru's Shining Path, the Irish Republican Army, and Al-Qaeda (*Frontline*, 2001; U.S. Department of State, 2001). Despite recent crackdowns, many countercultures manage to survive as distinct groups. Although hate crimes appear to be decreasing, evidence suggests that hate group activity is increasing (Blazak, 2001). Like other subcultures and the broader culture in which they exist, countercultures provide values and guidelines for behavior. However, contemporary countercultures ultimately socialize members into a set of values

Like the Masai of East Africa, many cultures have strong norms about gender and age segregation. Traditional Masai culture is being eroded by the forces of modernization.

that is dysfunctional for counterculture members as well as for society as a whole.

LIFE CONNECTIONS

Who Is an American?

Culturally diverse since its founding, the United States has always struggled with the question, Who is an American? For most of the 20th century, the dominant image was of the United States as a melting pot—a giant cauldron where people of diverse backgrounds would be submerged and then reemerge as a unified group known as "Americans." In this hypothetical melting pot, immigrants would shed previous cultural identities and embrace the culture and values of their new homeland. This ideal held sway, although it was never fully achieved in practice. Some ethnic groups were not considered 100 percent American—whether they were deliberately and forcibly excluded from mainstream society (especially African Americans and Native Americans), chose to maintain their distinctive ethnic identity (Latinos, to some degree Italian Americans, as well as groups such as the Mormons and Amish), or both. Chinese Americans, for example, encountered strong prejudice and discrimination and also chose to "keep to themselves." Immigrant and second-generation Chinese children are often caught between broader American norms and values and those of their cultural heritage (Sung, 1994; Glenn et al., 2000). How much are they culturally "American," culturally "Chinese," or culturally "Chinese American?"

In recent decades, the question of who is American—and of maintaining some degree of cultural integrity in an increasingly heterogeneous society—has taken on new meaning. Over the last two decades, not only has the United States experienced one of the highest rates of immigration in its history, but these immigrants are from countries that are culturally less similar to the United States than are immigrants of the past (see Chapter 12). At the same time, established groups such as African Americans, Native Americans, and other formerly excluded peoples are reclaiming their heritages and reasserting their distinctive cultural identities. Always "a nation of nations," today the United States is more multicultural than ever before.

Multiculturalism

The term *multiculturalism* has two levels of meaning. First, it is the existence of different cultural groups side by side in the same culture. These different groups are basically subcultures. Second, multiculturalism refers to the emerging value of *cultural identity*, a belief that the ethnic heritage of all groups should be understood and respected—whether in the folkways of food and dress or the mores of religion and morality. However, the equal respect owed to other subcultures does not mean that critical judgment of these subcultures should be suspended. If different cultures are to be equally respected, then they must also be "worthy" of critiques by outsiders. All practices of all subcultures do not have to be accepted as right and proper by everyone for multiculturalism to flourish in the United States. Multiculturalism does not imply relativism. While the value of cultural identity is an emergent

GLOBAL CONNECTIONS

The Exotic Nacirema

In studying cultures throughout the globe, social scientists encounter an extraordinary array of exotic customs, superstitious beliefs, and magical behaviors. A half century ago, anthropologist Horace Miner encountered a culture so remarkable that his description of it remains one of the most significant contributions to cultural understanding. As described by rituals involving the body, we provide Miner's portrait of the Nacirema, a people still inhabiting the territory between the Canadian Cree and the Yaqui Indians of Mexico in North America.

The Nacirema believe that the human body is ugly and that its natural tendency is to debility and disease. The only way to avert these characteristics is to use powerful rituals and ceremonies in special shrine rooms all households have devoted solely to this purpose. The rituals carried out in the shrine room are not family ceremonies but are private and secret. The focal point of the shrine is a box that is built into the wall. The box contains many charms and magical potions that the natives believe they cannot live without. These preparations are obtained from powerful healers who must be rewarded with expensive gifts. The healers do not provide the potions directly to their clients but decide on what the ingredients should be. They write them down in an ancient and secret language and then send their clients to herbalists, the only ones who can interpret the language and, for another gift, provide the required potion. After the potion serves its purposes, it is placed in the charm box in the wall. These magical materials are specific for certain ills. Since the real or imagined maladies of the Nacirema are many, the charm box is usually full to overflowing. The magical packets are so numerous that people forget what their purposes are and fear to use them again. The natives are very vague on why they retain all the old magical materials in the charm box, before which the body rituals

are conducted. In some way, they must protect the worshiper.

Beneath the charm box is a small font. Every day, family members separately enter the shrine room, bow their heads before the charm box, and mingle different sorts of holy waters secured from the Water Temple of the community, where priests conduct elaborate ceremonies that make the liquid ritually pure. Another daily ritual performed in the shrine room font is the mouth-rite. The rite involves a practice that strikes the uninitiated stranger as revolting. The ritual consists of inserting a small bundle of hog hairs into the mouth, along with certain magical powders, and then moving the bundle in a highly formalized series of gestures. In addition to the daily mouth-rite, the natives seek out special holy-mouth-practitioners once or twice a year for the exorcism of the evils of the mouth.

Holy-mouth practitioners use an impressive set of paraphernalia that involve almost unbelievable ritual torture of the client, especially when magical material is put in the holes of clients' teeth. Clients endure the torture because they believe it will arrest decay and draw friends. It is suspected that the mouth practitioners have a certain amount of sadism as they watch the tortured faces of their clients. In turn, most of the Nacirema population show definite masochistic tendencies. The theoretically interesting point is that what seems to be a preponderantly masochistic people have developed sadistic specialists.

The exotic behavior of the Nacirema described by Miner 50 years ago has intrigued sociologists so much that there has been continuous research on this culture. For example, a Portuguese anthropologist studied their complex and contradictory cultural traits, including language use. The Nacirema delight in using the word *nice,* as in: "Nice to meet you"; "Have a nice day"; "How do you like Nacirema? Oh that's nice!" Their abuse of the word "nice" shocks the hearing of a visitor. Either their language

doesn't have the richness to avoid repetitions, or the Nacirema have a mental laziness that keeps conversation very simplistic. Perhaps the Nacirema are so anxious to please newcomers and be friendly that words such as "nice" are overly used. A Polish sociologist living among these people notes that they do exhibit much friendship and kindness. "Everyone wants to help me, to thank me for calling or for stopping by. They become my friends very quickly." The Nacirema call one another by their first names and commonly avoid distinctions and titles based on rank and age. Teachers are often addressed by their first names, and nicknames are given to foreign visitors to show informality and cement friendship.

But closer examination of the Nacirema reveals many contradictions. The use of first names does not necessarily indicate a close relationship. In Nacirema, quality friendships that are lasting, intimate, and emotionally involving are difficult to develop. Nacirema say they have many friends. But for both the Polish sociologist and a sociolinguist from central Africa who lived in Nacirema for many years, the word "acquaintance" would probably be a better term to describe these relationships.

As Miner suggested, "The ritual life of the Nacirema has certainly showed them to be a magic-ridden people." Later research on the contradictions in Nacirema culture may agree with his conclusion that it is difficult to understand how they have managed to last so long under the burdens they impose on themselves. As you have probably already figured out, Nacirema is American spelled backwards.

1. Does this portrait arouse any emotions about your own culture, whether it is American or not?

2. How can sociologists studying other cultures remain objective in their reporting when they encounter cultural traits vastly different from their own?

Sources: Adapted from Miner, 1956; Mucha, 1998; Mufwene, 1998; Ramos, 1998.

one, the challenge of incorporating it into the core value set of the United States is as old as the nation itself. How can unity be maintained in the face of increasing cultural diversity?

LANGUAGE The unity–diversity issue is highlighted in regard to language (Crawford, 2000). Which groups of Americans speak which language? Many believe that if Americans all spoke the same language, then cultural unity would be easier to accomplish, regardless of a person's cultural heritage. This belief fueled the "Official English" movement in the 1980s, seeking to make English the official language of the United States through a constitutional amendment (Lewelling, 1997; Crawford, 2000). Twenty-seven states have passed laws making English their official language, although two have since overturned the laws and court challenges in others are pending (CMMR, 2002). California recently made English the standard language in schools despite the growing Asian and Latino populations who retain and speak their native tongues. The issue is especially important for the estimated 25 million Spanish speakers in the United States, half of whom regularly speak Spanish at home.

English fluency is associated with educational achievement and higher paying jobs, and bilingualism increases opportunities for higher paying jobs. Research also shows that bilingual children have enhanced self-esteem, positive social and psychological adjustment in school, and earn higher grades overall than children who speak only one language, a pattern found both in the United States and Canada. (Savoie, 1999; Krashen, 2001; Montero-Sieburth & Batt, 2001; Suarez-Orozco & Suarez-Orozco, 2001). Although for Latinos the Spanish language is the distinguishing marker for cultural identity, Latinos are clearly aware that fluency in English is vital for success in the United States (Barker et al., 2001). Also, Spanish language groups do not represent a significant challenge to English dominance in the United States. Contrary to what many people believe, all available evidence suggests that while the number of minority-language speakers is increasing, so is the rate of linguistic assimilation into English. Immigrants are losing their native tongues more rapidly than ever before in U.S. history (Crawford, 1997, 2002). Latinos are similar to other groups who wish to preserve some cultural distinctiveness within a society as diverse as the United States. Research also shows that a combination of ethnic and national identities, which language offers, promotes the best adaptation to the host culture (Phinney & Liebkind, 2001; Bhatia, 2002). Although the language issue is far from

INTERNET CONNECTIONS

In the text there is a discussion of the concepts cultural relativism and ethnocentrism. To explore the concepts in more depth go to the Nacirema Web site: **http://www.beadsland.com/FCT/nacirema/html/shome/** click on launch of institute for Nacirema studies it will take you to another page. On the right side of the new page under related articles click on Miner, Horace [1956], "Body Ritual Among the Nacirema." After reading the article answer the following question. What examples of ethnocentrism can you identify in the study of the body ritual of the Nacerima?

resolved, multicultural appreciation is now a significant part of all levels of education, a topic we will discuss further in Chapter 16.

POPULAR CULTURE Multiculturalism fuels an appreciation of ethnic diversity and is taking hold in places beyond classrooms. Chinese immigrants to the United States, and their patterns of adjustment, are good examples of how a subculture has maintained a visible presence but, until recently, an obscure one. Tourists flock to the Chinatowns of New York, Chicago, Honolulu, and San Francisco for food and souvenirs but usually have little knowledge about how and why such communities developed. However, knowledge about various subcultures, such as Chinese Americans, is also gradually being introduced to broader American culture, with popular culture as a major vehicle. The movie adapted from Amy Tan's novel, *The Joy Luck Club*, offers complex and touching portrayals of three generations of Chinese families in their struggle to adjust and succeed in the United States. Coupled with popular and critically acclaimed movies such as *The Last Emperor*, *Xiu Xiu*, and *Crouching Tiger, Hidden Dragon*, these elements of popular culture lay the groundwork for understanding the traditions and lifestyles of contemporary Chinese Americans.

Movies spotlighting multiculturalism are increasing in number, and many of the newer images of cultural diversity are undoubtedly offering challenges to once prevalent but demeaning stereotypes. The acclaimed 1970s television movie *Roots*, based on the novel by Alex Hailey, portrayed the slavery-to-freedom existence of one African American family. Alice

Walker's *The Color Purple* in the 1980s showed the misery and triumph of an African American girl growing up in the rural South during the Depression. *Amistad*, filmed in the 1990s, traced the legal battle of shipwrecked slaves in their attempt to be defined first as human beings and only secondly as slaves. Newer movies such as *Do the Right Thing* and *Waiting to Exhale* spotlight African American culture through family and community in mainstream cinema. Kevin Costner's film *Dances with Wolves* provided a glimpse of 19th-century Native America—both brutal and humane—that was largely unknown to most Americans. The 2002 film *Windtalkers* demonstrates how Native Americans used their languages to devise codes in World War II that were never broken by the enemy, offering a glimpse into the Native American cultures surrounding the languages. *El Norte* and *Lone Star* offer realistic and complex character portrayals of Latinos (Mexicans) who share community life and personal history in their challenges on the U.S.–Mexican border.

Although stereotypes of America's subcultural groups still abound in movies and other aspects of popular culture, the new value of multiculturalism has fueled portrayals that are more accurate and positive. More important, these portrayals highlight the fact that cultural differences can be appreciated rather than scorned, and that there are many kinds of Americans. Although it is always evolving, a distinctive "American" identity does exist, and it is a growing identity. The number of people who wrote "American" as their ancestry increased to 20 million in 2000 from 13 million in 1990 on the last census (American Identity, 2002). This identity can only be understood in the context of the extraordinary multicultural heritage of the United States (Wucker, 200; Teicher, 2002; Triandis & Suh, 2002).

SOCIETY CONNECTIONS

Cultural Change and Cultural Survival

Through the lens of sociology, a picture of culture emerges that focuses on two central images: cultural diversity and cultural change. These features represent contemporary cultures at all levels and at all stages of development. Although the degree of cultural contact varies from society to society, it is virtually impossible for even the smallest culture in the most remote area of the world to remain immune to outside influences. The globe is already economically and environmentally interdependent, a trend that can only increase in the future. Some cultures may be on the verge of extinction because their way of life and cultural identity cannot be preserved. Sociologists emphasize that because of the profound interconnectedness of all things, cultures will always be challenged in how they deal with change.

Maintaining Cultural Identity

Sometimes cultures resist change, and sometimes they do not. Outsiders to the cultures may speak of cultural "subversion" when they see technology eroding traditional cultures of indigenous people, even when the people themselves are using technology in the way they see fit. Eskimo cultures of North America use modern fishing and hunting technology, including citizen-band radios, aircraft, all-terrain vehicles, and rifles to catch, process, and store fish and game in ways allowing them to engage more effectively in the global economy. They take whatever technology works for them and shape it to their purposes, to the dismay of outsiders who want them to remain "pristine" (Cited in Sahlins, 1999). Another example involved a Save the Rainforest campaign in Brazil spearheaded by the rock star Sting. The Kayapo Indians of the rainforest were granted rights to a large protected area of rainforest that Sting and western environmen-

---

TABLE 3.1

Language Spoken at Home

English only	209,860,377
Language other than English	44,885,797
Speak English less than "very well"	19,492,832
Spanish	26,745,067
Speak English less than "very well"	12,463,516
Other Indo-European languages	9,479,670
Speak English less than "very well"	3,103,665
Asian and Pacific Islander languages	6,864,461
Speak English less than "very well"	3,395,653
Other languages	1,796,599
Speak English less than "very well"	529,998

Source: U.S. Census Bureau, "Profile of Selected Social Characteristics, Census 2000." Adapted from Supplementary Survey Summary Tables. http://factfinder.census.gov/servlet.

talists believed would end the massive logging and mining of the area. However, Kayapo chiefs had already been logging the area and complained that the "protection" would deprive them of their livelihood. Again to the dismay of the outsiders, "Kayapo, Inc." ensured that the logs continued to fall (Whelan, 1999).

A major cultural transition is also occurring among the !Kung (the exclamation point is pronounced as a click in their language), hunter-gatherers of the Kalahari Desert region of southern Africa, one of the few known remaining hunter-gatherer societies on earth. In recent years the !Kung have begun settling down, adopting the horticultural way of life of neighboring Bantu tribes and now intermarrying with them. With no written language, the !Kung transmit their culture orally. With !Kung assimilation into neighboring societies on the horizon, an entire way of life—the way our ancestors lived for millions of years—is disappearing (Shostak, 1994; Robbins, 2001; Lee, 2003). Around the globe, traditional indigenous cultures are disappearing. The Penan of Borneo, the Masai of East Africa, the Yaqui of Guadalupe, Arizona, the New Guinea Kalam, and other New Guinea tribes may also be losing the battle (Gray, 1996; Trujillo, 1998; O'Hanlon, 2000; Phillips & Bhavnagri, 2002). It is not coercion through war, forced migration, or starvation that is responsible for this transformation. It is part of a peaceful, largely voluntary process of gradual but accelerating cultural change that appears to be inevitable.

For the Eskimos, Kayapo Indians, !Kung, and all traditional societies undergoing rapid cultural change, the thorny issue that must be resolved is how to safeguard traditional cultures in the global economy and keep those safeguards in line with the choices of the people in those cultures (Seitel, 2001).

Human Rights

The extinction of a culture through conquest and often deliberate genocide is called *ethnocide* by anthropologists. The first culture conquered by the Europeans was probably the Guanache, the native people of the Canary Islands of Africa's northwest coast. After resisting numerous waves from invaders, the Guanache succumbed to full Spanish control by 1496, and 50 years later virtually disappeared (Crosby, 1986). Although deliberate ethnocide is frequently attempted today, it rarely succeeds for two main reasons. First, because of advances in communication, isolation can no longer be ensured by geography. Global culture, by definition, is a con-

nected one. Second, there is global consensus on **human rights,** those rights inherent to human beings in any culture, including but not limited to the right to dignity, personal integrity, inviolability of body and mind, and those civil and political rights associated with basic democratic freedoms. Torture, state-supported terrorism, forced labor, and rape of refugees are human rights violations. The global media commonly spotlight human rights violations, as we have recently witnessed in Afghanistan, Bosnia, Sudan, Somalia, and Indonesia. Safeguarding minority subcultures is a human rights concern (Easterly, 2001).

The global culture, like any other culture, has a core value set. In addition to the value of human rights, the global culture has economic values related to free trade based on capitalistic models. Another value affirms each culture's right to make its own decisions regarding how to participate in the global economy, an endorsement of cultural relativism. Respect for all cultures leads, in turn, to the principle that one society should not interfere with the rights of another.

Today's world has many borders but fewer boundaries—it is impossible to separate what goes on inside a culture from what goes on outside it (Lopez et al., 1997). As we have already seen, core values in any culture, including the global one, are not necessarily consistent and can be contradictory.

Cultural relativism is often used to the disadvantage of minorities within a culture. People throughout the world are denied education, food, and opportunities for livelihood because they are affiliated with certain subcultures. These subcultures are usually minority ones. Yet the state tells the rest of the world that there should be no "interference" in their internal affairs (Lerner, 2000). A good example is the use of religion to deny women access to education or employment—in countries such as Afghanistan, Sudan, Pakistan, Iran, and Saudi Arabia. Religion enables such cultures to maintain a distinct cultural identity in the face of frightening globalization, while still participating fully in the lucrative global economy.

The tide is against those who defend obvious human rights violations by raising the charge of cultural interference (Turner & Nagengast, 1997; Korey, 1998). For example, the weight of global public opinion is against religion when it is used to restrict human rights, usually women's rights (Mayer, 1999; Peters, 1999). The theme that human rights are also women's rights has struck a resonant chord worldwide, ensuring it a place in the core value set of the dawning global culture.

SUMMARY

1. Culture is a shared way of life that includes everything from material objects to intangibles such as values, customs, and symbols. Culture is learned and, because of its symbolic basis, is possessed only by humans.

2. Most people consider their own culture superior to other cultures, a view known as ethnocentrism. Sociology is based on cultural relativism, the principle that all cultures must be understood and respected on their own terms.

3. Values are the ideals that underlie a culture's moral standards. Values are expressed through rules of conduct, called norms, and penalties for violating those rules, called sanctions. Norms include both the folkways that regulate daily life and stronger mores on which a society's laws are based.

4. Shared symbols, such as a flag or a language, distinguish one culture from another. Language is a key marker that provides distinctive cultural identity and can bias one's perceptions and behavior. Language use varies with gender, based on cultural norms and roles prescribed for men and women.

5. Humor is based on a shared knowledge of cultural stereotypes. While functionalists see humor as a kind of social glue, conflict theorists see jokes based on ethnic and racial slurs as masked aggression.

6. Culture is always changing due to contact with other cultures, environmental change and innovation. Cultural integration is the process by which cultural elements become interdependent when culture changes.

7. Technology and popular culture are cultural elements spread through the media that fuel both cultural integration and cultural change. Both elements are integrated more quickly than the values associated with them, creating cultural lag.

8. The spread of culture from one society to another, called diffusion, occurs directly through contact between people or indirectly, where goods and ideas are exchanged without firsthand contact. Culture changes through invention—the novel use of existing cultural elements—or through discovery—the creation of new cultural elements.

9. Functionalism suggests that cultural universals shared by all cultures, such as the incest taboo and religious rituals, aid in cultural survival. Conflict theorists suggest that the ideology of the dominant group in a culture controls its value system. Symbolic interactionists point out that cultures often retain dangerous or disadvantageous customs because of socially constructed emotional attachments.

10. A subculture is a group whose values, norms, and mores set it apart from mainstream culture. A counterculture is a subculture in which the values and norms are opposed to those of the dominant culture.

11. The United States is becoming more diverse, both culturally and linguistically, creating a highly multicultural society. An emergent value of respect for cultural identity is entering the set of core U.S. values.

12. Globalization and human rights violations are threatening the survival of indigenous and minority cultures. However, there is global consensus that human rights violations should not be tolerated and that minority cultures must be protected.

KEY TERMS

adaptation 78
beliefs 66
counterculture 81
cultural integration 76
cultural lag 76
cultural relativism 64
cultural universals 77
culture 63
culture shock 64

diffusion 77
ethnocentrism 64
folkways 68
human rights 87
language 70
laws 69
material culture 63
mores 68
nonmaterial culture 63

norms 68
popular culture 76
sanctions 68
Sapir-Whorf hypothesis 70
subculture 81
symbol 69
technology 76
values 66

CRITICAL THINKING QUESTIONS

1. Based on your understanding of the role of culture in attitudes, language, and behavior, argue for or against the idea that "we are all prisoners of our own culture."

2. How do sociologists explain cultural change from the perspectives of functionalism, symbolic interactionism, and conflict theory?

3. How does cultural diversity both fuel and slow down cultural change? In the United States, how can cultural unity be strengthened when multicultural diversity is also valued?

4. How do sociologists deal with violations of human rights that continue in the name of "noninterference" in another culture? How does the general public view the same issue?

INVESTIGATE WITH CONTENT SELECT

Journal Research Collections from
ContentSelect

Begin your research using Content Select for this chapter by following the directions found on page 27 of this text to visit Prentice Hall's Research Navigator website. Enter these search terms into the search field:

Ethnography
Qualitative Analysis
Wage gap

4
SOCIAL STRUCTURE

Joining the Crips

I never saw the blow to my head come from Huck. Bam! And I was on all fours, struggling for my equilibrium. Kicked in the stomach, I was on my back counting stars in the darkness. Grabbed by the collar, I was made to stand again. A solid blow to my chest exploded pain in bold red letters on the blank screen that had now become my mind. Bam! . . .

In the heat of desperation I struck out, hitting Fly full in the chest, knocking him back. Then I just started swinging, with no style or finesse, just anger and the instinct to survive. Of course, this did little to help my physical situation, but it showed the others that I had a will to live. And this in turn reflected my ability to represent the set in hand-to-hand combat. (Shakur, 1993:8–9)

These are the words of Kody Scott, a former member of a street gang in South Central Los Angeles. Kody is describing part of the initiation ritual he endured at the tender age of 11 in order to join a local branch (or "set") of the Crips. First, he stole an automobile in order to demonstrate his "street smarts" and willingness to break the law. Then he allowed himself to be beaten, showing both that he was tough and that he was ready to do whatever the gang required of him. He completed the process by participating in a "military action"—killing a member of a rival gang. Initiations like this are by no means uncommon in gangs today. (Curry & Decker, 1998)

A New Nation

The past decades have seen the birth of over a dozen new countries. Each represents the successful efforts of a smaller society to shake off the political domination of a larger and more powerful one. Among the best-known examples are states such as Georgia, Uzbekistan, Croatia, and Montenegro, which came into existence as a result of the disintegration of the Soviet Union and Yugoslavia.

The newest nation in the world is East Timor, which officially gained its independence on May 20, 2002, after over four centuries as a Portuguese colony and 24 years of domination by neighboring Indonesia. In ceremonies in the capital city of Dili, attended by former U.S. President Bill Clinton and U.N. Secretary General Kofi Annan, poet and former guerilla leader Xanana Gasmao was sworn in as East Timor's first head of state.

Despite its small size and population—24,000 square miles and just 800,000 inhabitants—the new nation is a separate society with its own distinct culture, as are the other countries that have recently gained independence around the world. Few, however, face as daunting a future as East Timor, the poorest country in Asia. About 40 percent of its population is illiterate, and much of its infrastructure was destroyed in 2 years of conflict with Indonesian-backed militias that temporarily displaced a third of the population. ("East Timor Gains . . ." 2002)

Although societies like East Timor are vastly larger and more complex than street gangs such as the Crips, they are both examples of social structures. Sociologists use the term **social structure** to refer to the relatively stable patterns of social interaction that characterize human social life (Smelser, 1988; Mark, 1998). Culture and social structure are intimately interconnected. Culture provides the blueprint or programming for the ways people behave. Social structure provides the setting in which culture is acted out.

We begin our analysis at the microsociological level by discussing how people participate in social structure as individuals. Then we gradually expand our scope to examine social groups and larger types of social structures, including institutions and entire societies. The chapter concludes with a consideration of how social life changes as societies evolve from relatively simple systems to the complex patterns typical of the developed world and a brief discussion of some new forms of social structure that may develop in the coming decades.

STATUS AND ROLE

The smallest components of social structure are statuses and roles, two closely related concepts that constitute the basic building blocks of all social life.

Status

Obviously, a group (or any other type of social structure) is made up of interacting people. However, sociologists prefer to initially analyze social structures as composed of a number of interrelated *positions* and only later to factor in the personal characteristics of the individuals who happen to be occupying those positions at any given time. Thus, a street gang might be made up of Cody, Jamal, Clarence, and many other specific individuals, but sociologists would analyze it as composed of positions such as president, warlord, or initiate. We adopt this approach because we are more interested in studying groups in general than in learning about the specifics of any particular group.

Sociologists use the term **status** to refer to a social position that an individual occupies (Linton, 1936). Your statuses largely define who you are in relation to other people, especially when you do not know the others intimately. At home, an individual is usually treated as a unique person, but at work that same person interacts with others mostly in terms of his or her occupational status—clerk, police officer, nurse, or CEO. Note that from this perspective, a group, or any larger type of social structure, is simply a set of interrelated statuses.

This usage of the term status is somewhat different from the meaning it has in everyday speech, where it usually refers to an individual's level of prestige. Thus, people may say that a physician is high in status and a fast-food worker is low. Sociologists recognize that many social statuses are ranked—generals over privates, seniors over freshmen—but this comparative aspect of status is secondary to its core meaning: a social position that people occupy. After all, some important social statuses are not ranked—basketball players are not generally seen as superior to football players, or Methodists as inferior to Presbyterians.

All of the statuses that an individual occupies make up that person's **status set.** Thus, every member of a juvenile gang also has a gender status (male or female), an ethnic or racial status (African American, white, Latino), an age status (teenager, young adult), a religious status (Baptist, Catholic), a class status (lower or working class), a sexual orientation status (straight or gay), various family statuses (father, cousin, brother), perhaps an occupational status (burger flipper, auto mechanic), and many others. Note also that not all of the statuses an individual occupies are necessarily relevant to any given interaction; for example, the fact that someone is a Baptist is relatively unlikely to influence his or her behavior in a street gang.

Sometimes the different statuses that make up an individual's status set do not fit together smoothly because they are ranked at different levels, a condi-

The military may be viewed as a complex system of ranked statuses. Individuals occupying the status of drill sergeant command more power and prestige than those occupying the position of boot camp trainee.

tion called **status inconsistency.** Examples include a 12-year-old attending college and a Ph.D. working behind the counter of Burger King. Such situations can be quite uncomfortable for the individuals involved.

We often interact with others on the basis of the statuses they occupy rather than who they are, especially in the modern, impersonal world. When you renew your driver's license, the clerk does not know you personally and you do not know him or her, yet the interaction usually goes smoothly because it is based on the statuses of clerk and applicant. Because so much interaction is status specific, people frequently display *status symbols* that identify the statuses they occupy and thus suggest how others are expected to interact with them. Note that contrary to the everyday usage of the term, a status symbol may denote either a prestigious position (a wealthy person's

People experience status inconsistency if they simultaneously occupy two distinct statuses that are differently evaluated. Female attorneys such as Supreme Court justice Ruth Bader Ginsburg frequently have to cope with the incongruity between their highly prestigious occupational status and their lower-ranking gender status.

sports car) or one that many people look down on (a street person's tattered clothes).

ACHIEVED AND ASCRIBED STATUS Some of our social statuses are **ascribed statuses,** those into which we are born and that we cannot change, or that we acquire involuntarily over the life course. Gender, race, or ethnicity, certain family statuses (eldest sister, son), and life cycle statuses such as adolescent or senior citizen are all ascribed statuses. Although we cannot change these statuses, we can work with others to try to increase the esteem with which they are viewed. This has been a primary objective of the feminist and minority liberation movements of recent decades.

We also occupy **achieved statuses,** positions acquired over time as a result of our own actions. Examples of achieved statuses include social class position, occupation, educational status (college graduate or high school dropout), some family statuses (wife or father), and political affiliation (Democrat or Independent). Achieved statuses may be high (physician) or low (convict) in prestige. The important point is that we are not locked into them at birth, although in some cases we may inherit an initial status placement (such as Methodist or lower class) that may or may not change later in life.

MASTER STATUS Not all statuses are equally important. A **master status** is a social position that is exceptionally powerful in determining an individual's identity, often to the point where other statuses are virtually ignored (Hughes, 1945). For example, someone who occupies the status of Catholic priest or president of the United States is likely to be treated as a priest or president in almost all interactions. Master statuses may also be negative, in which case they are called **stigmas** (Goffman, 1963b). Thus, blemishes of character, such as a conviction for a serious crime, often function as master statuses.

The ascribed statuses of race and gender have commonly functioned as master statuses, especially when most members of the group an individual is joining are of a different race or the other gender (Webster & Hysom, 1998). Thus, the first female executive in a firm is often dealt with more on the basis of her gender status than as an executive; such an individual is sometimes described as a *token* (Kanter, 1977). Male nurses or the first few African Americans who join a previously all-white fraternity may experience similar treatment. However, as more women and minorities enter positions from which they were previously excluded, these identities are gradually becoming less likely to function as master statuses.

Other master statuses are somewhat less pervasive but still important. Occupation is frequently a master

THEN AND NOW

Status Symbols

Most sociologists tend to favor a relatively broad definition of the concept of status symbol. In this view, anything that identifies any position or status that an individual occupies to those with whom that person is interacting, thereby facilitating interaction, is a status symbol. It doesn't matter how that status is evaluated. Thus, diamond jewelry is a status symbol, but so is a prisoner's uniform. Status symbols may be physical objects, people (servants, "trophy wives"), or even accents (a key symbol of class position in Britain).

In everyday usage, however, most people use the term primarily to refer to symbols that are *high* in prestige. It is this meaning that captured the attention of Thorsten Veblen (1857–1929), a noted economist and sociologist who developed an incisive analysis of social behavior in the United States during the early decades of the 20th century.

Veblen was especially interested in the status symbols employed by the wealthy of his era. Of course, then as now, large homes, expensive clothing, and fine furniture were obvious marks of the social elite. Veblen coined the phrase *conspicuous consumption* to refer to the ostentatious and public display of luxury goods as a claim to high status. He also noted that the wealthy of his day demonstrated their status by *conspicuous waste*. Although the father of the family generally had to work, his status and that of his dependents would be raised if his wife did not work, even in the home (that was what servants were for!); if he could afford to allow his children to study obscure subjects like medieval poetry that were unlikely to be of much value to them in the marketplace; and if he could throw lavish parties and employ workers to do frivolous things such as trim shrubbery into elaborate topiary sculptures. It is no surprise that Veblen used the con-

temptuous term "the leisure class" to refer to the elite.

How have status symbols changed since Veblen wrote? Some recent trends may provide insight into how society has changed over the past few generations.

Status symbols seem to have become far less subtle. For example, in Veblen's day, you often had to know just what to look for to evaluate the social meaning of clothes. Today, after almost a century of the growth of the mobility-oriented *Gesellschaft* model of society, class lines are less clearly drawn and higher status people seem to need to assert and defend their rank more aggressively and unambiguously by such means as displaying highly visible brand-name labels on their clothes, shoes, and automobiles. Two generations ago, this overt a display of status symbols would certainly have been regarded as vulgar or uncouth.

This trend toward the overt display of brand names may also suggest that, perhaps as a result of a gradual increase in the prestige of business in society since the 1970s, more people seem comfortable displaying a level of commercialization that might well have struck previous generations as crass. Few in Veblen's day would have been willing to become unpaid "walking billboards" advertising high-status brand names.

Conspicuous waste is still with us, but in a somewhat different form. Reflecting the greater egalitarianism, individualism, and competitiveness of the modern era, spouses and children of upper-crust families are no longer expected to publicly display their idleness. But early retirement after a productive career has become an increasingly potent status symbol. Hundreds of thousands of people, some as young as their 30s, have made their fortunes (especially in sports, entertainment, or high-tech industries) and then simply quit working. What more powerful and visible statement could you make to oth-

ers of having "made it" than to say that not only do my spouse and children not have to work (unless they want to), but neither do I?

In Veblen's day, status symbols seemed to "trickle down" over time. For example, the clothing styles worn last season by the elite were often adopted the following year by the middle classes—forcing the upper strata to find some new way of dressing to display their rank. Today, however, we occasionally see exactly the opposite pattern: clothing styles (like blue jeans) or music that was previously identified with the lower classes (folk, jazz, blues) suddenly become "cool"—it "trickles up" and becomes accepted by and even symbolic of the elite. This may reflect our current emphasis on egalitarianism and the more negative connotations of snobbery that have resulted from the successes of the women's and minority liberation movements.

The more frequent use of "ethnic identifiers" as positive status symbols has been another consequence of the continuing empowerment of minorities and other groups. Examples include the spread of braided or natural "Afro" hairstyles among African Americans and the resurgent popularity of distinctively ethnic names among a number of ethnic minorities.

1. What are some of the symbols used by your friends and family to announce their social status? Speculate on the underlying social meanings of these particular symbols.

2. Some elite symbols are easily imitated. Examples include knock-off designer clothing and fragrances, and Chevrolets that look a lot like last year's Cadillacs. What problems are created for the elite by such imitations? Can you think of some elite status symbols that cannot be so easily copied?

Sources: Lerner, 1948; Ridgeway, 1991; Davis, 1992; Lipovetsky, 1994.

status; it tends to be the first thing we ask about when we meet someone, and its significance often lingers after we have left our jobs: People are commonly introduced as former teachers or ex-military officers.

Role

The concept of role is closely related to that of status. A **role** consists of the norms associated with a particular status—norms that specify the behavior required of an individual occupying that position. Thus, the role of a gang member consists of all the expectations that people have about how such an individual should act. Role is the dynamic dimension of status. Like all norms, roles are learned through socialization. They represent the intersection of culture and social structure. The concepts of status and role are easy to confuse, but you can keep them straight by always remembering that we *occupy* a status but we *play* or enact a role (Linton, 1936).

Most important statuses are accompanied by a cluster of related but somewhat distinct roles that may be referred to as a **role set** (Merton, 1968). For example, someone who occupies the status of college professor may be simply said to play the role of professor, or we may dig deeper and identify the various elements of this person's role set, which include distinct norms guiding such activities as preparing lectures, teaching classes, advising students, conducting research, and doing committee work. Similarly, the role set of parent includes being a teacher, nurse, cook, disciplinarian, and chauffeur.

The notion of role is obviously based on an analogy between social life and the theater. This is the basic insight behind Erving Goffman's dramaturgical perspective discussed in Chapter 6. As on the stage, there is often a difference between what is formally expected of a social actor (*role expectations*) and how the role is actually played (*role performance*). However, social actors have considerably more freedom than actors on a stage because the "scripts" for social roles nearly always allow a good deal of room for improvisation. In fact, as the symbolic interactionist perspective would emphasize, people are constantly engaged in the process of *role making*, negotiating with other role players how they will perform their parts (Turner, 1962; Strauss, 1977; Wasserman & Faust, 1994).

As mentioned in Chapter 1, one of the advantages of acquiring the sociological imagination is learning to debunk. Role expectations do not always have to be rigidly obeyed. Role making and negotiation are especially common when role definitions are in flux (as is the case with contemporary gender roles, a central topic of Chapter 13), or when a new role is emerging, such as holistic health counselor or "partner" in a committed gay relationship.

ROLE STRAIN Sometimes people experience **role strain,** difficulty adequately performing all the elements of the role set connected to a single status (Goode, 1960; Gigliotti & Huff, 1995). For example, a police internal affairs agent is expected to be a loyal member of the police and also to root out corruption on the force (Mulcahy, 1995). Foremen and military chaplains may experience similar problems. Role strain is especially likely to arise when role sets are complex (Coser, 1991).

ROLE CONFLICT In contrast to role strain, **role conflict** arises when the expectations for the roles connected to one status clash with those associated with one or several entirely separate statuses coincidentally occupied by the same person (Lang, 1992; Gigliotti & Huff, 1995). This is sometimes a problem of a lack of time, as anyone knows well who has ever tried to work, go to school, and raise children.

Role conflict may also result from status inconsistency, as previously discussed. In addition, it may arise because of direct clashes between the requirements of two role sets, as may occur if a basketball coach is also the mother of one of the players. A coach is required to treat her players evenhandedly, whereas a mother is generally expected to favor her own children.

There are a number of ways to resolve role strain and role conflict (Goode, 1960). Determining which roles (or elements of the role set) are most important and which are secondary allows a person to concentrate on only the most important role demands; parents who decide to reduce their involvement at work in order to spend more time with their children are adopting this strategy. *Compartmentalization* or *role segregation*, playing your different and conflicting roles at different places and in front of different audiences, also can help. An individual who is a street gang member and an A student is unlikely to play both roles in front of the same audience.

People who are having role problems sometimes experience *role embracement*, the feeling that they are nothing more than the roles they are expected to play (Goffman, 1961b). A good antidote is provided by *role distance*, a process by which an individual deliberately communicates, either in words or in body language, that he or she is indeed much more than a simple role player: "I may be waiting on tables, but I'm really an actor."

The topics of roles and role playing will be explored more fully in Chapter 6.

Physicians and other professionals must modify their role performance when interacting with people from different social backgrounds in order to best meet the needs of their clients.

SOCIAL GROUPS

Groups are essential to human life. They shape our goals, our values, our behavior, and our self-concepts. In a very real sense, we are different people in different groups: Compare what you are like at home with how you behave as a member of a team or among your close friends. The differences result from the fact that we occupy different statuses and play different roles in different groups.

As sociologists use the term, a **social group** consists of two or more people who interact regularly and feel some sense of solidarity or common identity. Group members normally share some values and norms and often work to achieve common goals.

INTERNET CONNECTIONS

After reading about social groups in the text go to the following Websites:

http://www.spc. uchicago.edu/ssr1/PRELIMS/Theory/thmisc1 .html

and

http://www2.pfeiffer.edu/~lridener/DSS/Cooley/PRIMGRP .HTML

Read what Charles Horton Cooley and others had to say about social groups and then write a short report on the topic.

Families, sports teams, religious congregations, and street gangs are all examples of social groups.

We should differentiate between social groups and two other closely related concepts, aggregates and categories. **Aggregates** are collections of people who are physically at the same place at the same time, but do not interact in any meaningful way; examples include people in an elevator or those standing on a street corner waiting for a bus. Aggregates lack not only interaction but also appreciable feelings of solidarity. However, if they are given a common focus of attention—if the elevator jams or the bus fails to arrive on time—the members of an aggregate may start to interact and become a group.

Categories are collections of individuals who share a social status, such as people with red hair, Asian Americans, Bruce Springsteen fans, college freshmen, or sociologists. Members of a category may share some vague sense of solidarity, but because they are not physically in each other's presence, they do not interact and accordingly are not a group.

Types of Groups

People join social groups for two principal reasons: (a) to relate to others in order to enjoy a measure of intimacy and combat loneliness, and (b) to accomplish goals they would have difficulty achieving on their own—editing a newspaper, raising a barn, or robbing a bank. Groups tend to specialize to some extent in one or the other of these functions, as explained in the next section.

PRIMARY AND SECONDARY GROUPS Charles Horton Cooley (1909) used the term **primary group** to refer to small groups characterized by warm, informal, and long-lasting interaction. People in primary groups know each other well, interact on the basis of their entire identities and personalities rather than just as role players, and are not easily replaced. Primary groups generate high levels of solidarity and loyalty. They are ends in themselves, not means to an end. The most common examples are families and groups of friends, but many work groups, sports teams, small classes, and military units also have most of the characteristics of primary groups. Figure 4.1 illustrates how gender affects participation in various types of primary groups.

Cooley called such groups "primary" for two reasons: They are the *first* kind of group we experience, and they are *central* to our lives. The people who make up our primary groups are, by definition, important to us. For this reason they are often called *significant others*. Our membership in these groups is a cornerstone of our identity and absolutely vital to our mental health (Messeri et al., 1993; Egolf et al., 1993).

Obviously, not all primary groups are equally warm and caring and supportive. Instead, groups and the relationships that comprise them fall along a scale or continuum (see Figure 4.2). Relationships that closely fit the definition of primary groups, like those

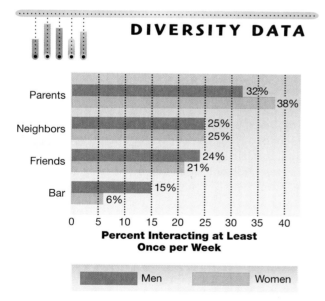

DIVERSITY DATA

FIGURE 4.1 How Does Gender Influence Where and With Whom People Interact? Women are more likely than men to spend leisure time with their parents. Men tend to interact more frequently than women in bars or with friends. Both genders are equally likely to spend time with neighbors. What do these data suggest about the relative strength of the ties of women and men to their parents?

Source: NORC. General Social Surveys, 1972–2000. Chicago: National Opinion Research Center, 2000. Reprinted by permission of NORC, Chicago, IL.

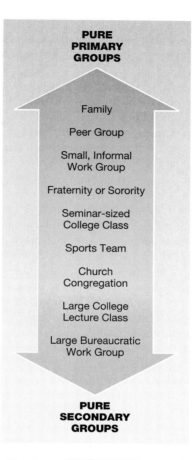

FIGURE 4.2 The Continuum from Primary to Secondary Groups.

among close friends, would fall toward the top of the scale. Those that lack some but not all primary characteristics would be located toward the center. Street gangs probably belong here. Groups and relationships at the bottom end of the continuum are secondary in character.

Secondary groups tend to be formal, emotionally cool, and often temporary. Interaction in secondary groups is typically role-specific, and individual members are easily replaced. In contrast to what is typical of primary groups, people's involvement in secondary groups is rational and calculative; they value these groups chiefly as a means to accomplish a particular task or end. Examples include most classrooms, offices, and voluntary associations such as PTAs or church congregations. Bureaucratic formal organizations, one of the principal topics of Chapter 21, are also secondary groups.

While the emotional tone of secondary groups is cool, members may be strongly committed to the group, not so much because of their personal interest in their fellow members, but rather because they strongly desire the goals toward which the group is working.

Secondary groups may be either large or small, although they are most characteristically large. Some small secondary groups may become increasingly primary over time as the members get to know each other better (S. Marks, 1994). Furthermore, primary groups are often embedded in or emerge from secondary groups. Thus, large classes are secondary groups, but smaller, more primary groups of friends, study partners, and students working together on a class project are normally present within them.

One of the most important patterns of change in today's world is a gradual but substantial decline in the time most people spend in primary groups and a corresponding rise in their secondary involvements. This change accompanies the shift from farming to industry and the growth of the modern city. Closely connected with the shift towards more secondary group memberships is a move away from ascribed and toward achieved statuses. The result is that people today are much freer to be individuals, but they are often left feeling more lonely and isolated.

Voluntary associations such as social clubs, service organizations, and youth groups, although essentially secondary, can provide some primary interaction for their members, helping to counter contemporary trends toward isolation. Figure 4.3 documents how gender affects membership in such associations.

Sociologists have identified several other types of social groups. The most important are in-groups, out-groups, and reference groups.

IN-GROUPS AND OUT-GROUPS   As you might expect, **in-groups** are the groups to which individuals belong and toward which they feel pride and loyalty, while **out-groups** are groups to which they do not belong and toward which they feel disdain and perhaps hostility (Sumner, 1960). Of course, the distinction between in-groups and out-groups is entirely relative. A Texan may normally view a New Yorker as a member of an out-group, but when that same person is traveling abroad, everyone from the United States is likely to be seen as part of his or her in-group.

Group membership tends to bias our judgments and perceptions: In-group virtues are often seen as out-group vices (Merton, 1968; Tajfel, 1982). *We* are intelligent, dedicated, and consistent; *they* are cunning, fanatical, and rigid.

Commitment to in-groups tends to be strengthened by conflict with out-groups (Lamont & Fournier, 1992) and by the presence of visible "markers" that identify members of the two groups to each other and to outsiders. Almost anything can serve as a marker: skin color, gang "colors," a distinctive T-shirt, or even sitting at a particular table in the school dining hall.

In-groups, whether primary or secondary, provide positive feelings of solidarity and self-worth (Coser,

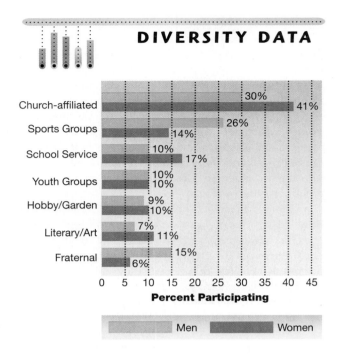

FIGURE 4.3   Membership in Voluntary Associations, by Gender. Women are more likely than men to participate in literary and artistic, school-related, and religious organizations. Men tend to be more active in fraternal and sports groups. These patterns are clearly in line with traditional gender roles. Do you think they may change as gender roles continue to become less rigid and more egalitarian?
Source: NORC. General Social Surveys, 1972–2000. Chicago: National Opinion Research Center, 2000. Reprinted by permission of NORC, Chicago, IL.

1956). Membership in them is frequently an important element of our social identity. But they have a dark side as well. Especially if in-groups are competing for scarce resources, conflict between them can be bitter and violent, promoting extreme forms of ethnocentrism (see Chapter 3), as is evident in the contemporary Palestinian–Israeli struggle over the occupation of the West Bank or in conflicts between street gangs (Noel, 1991; Bobo & Hutchings, 1996).

REFERENCE GROUPS   **Reference groups** serve two closely related but distinct functions: They provide us with guidance concerning how to behave (the *normative function*), and they allow us to evaluate how well we are living up to our role expectations in comparison with other people around us (the *comparative function*) (Hyman, 1942; Merton & Kitt, 1950). When these two functions are provided by a single person, we sometimes call that individual a *role model*.

At any given point in time, most people are guided by several different reference groups. Because of this, they may sometimes receive contradictory messages. For example, law students who have a big

A church choir is a good example of a small group. Choir members interact regularly, feel a sense of solidarity, share common values and norms, and cooperate to achieve mutual goals.

exam the next day may be torn between following the lead of friends who are settling in for a long night of studying and the model of another group of friends who are heading out to the bars.

Sometimes we are actually members of our reference groups, as in the case of a newly hired nurse who looks to his or her fellow nurses for reference group functions. Or we may choose reference groups to which we do not belong, as when a young basketball player copies the behavior of NBA stars. Some reference groups are even fictional—"What would Captain Picard do in this situation?"

Group Dynamics

Social psychologists have devoted a great deal of attention to the study of *group dynamics*—the reciprocal influence between the individual and the small group (Homans, 1950; Hare et al., 1994). *Small groups* are those in which each member can interact regularly and directly with all of the other members—a situation that becomes difficult once the group is larger than about twelve. Among the major topics studied by students of group dynamics, four are especially important: the impact of group size, leadership, conformity, and decision making (Levine & Moreland, 1998).

GROUP SIZE Any sociological consideration of the effects of group size must begin with the work of the German sociologist Georg Simmel (1858–1918). Simmel (pronounced *Zim-mel*) identified several crucial differences between *dyads* (two-person groups) and *triads* (three-member groups) (Simmel, 1950).

The dyad is simultaneously the most intimate group experience possible and the most fragile one.

Think of a husband and wife or two very close friends. Members of a committed dyad may give themselves to the other more completely and fully than ever occurs in a larger group. It is in the dyad that individuals can experience the most intense primary relationship possible. But if the relationship sours and one member leaves, the group disintegrates. This fragility is why virtually all societies back up the dyadic marriage bond with legal and religious injunctions against leaving the marriage except under extreme circumstances.

If we add a third member to a dyad, the group becomes less intimate but also less fragile; no longer does the loss of one person end it. There are now three relationships in the group where before there was only one (see Figure 4.4 on page 101). The third member may play several different roles. He or she may further unify the group, as sometimes occurs within a family after the first child is born. Or the new member may form a coalition with one of the others, usually the weaker of the two, against the third. Or the third member may try to "divide and rule," forming and breaking alliances in a way that works to his or her advantage (Simmel, 1950).

When groups grow beyond three, the basic principle that intimacy and intensity decline and stability increases continues to hold true. Also, as group size increases, the number of relationships in the group increases geometrically. There is only one relationship in a dyad and there are only three in a triad, but there are six in a four-person group and ten in a group with five members (see Figure 4.4) (Palazzolo, 1981).

When groups exceed five or six members, they become more formal. People *address* larger groups rather than talk to them conversationally (Bales,

Originally a dyad, a couple becomes a triad after the birth of their first child. The addition of a third member to a group may either strengthen or weaken its cohesiveness.

1951). Furthermore, as group size increases, more formal rules develop and the group's leaders may become more powerful because it becomes easier for them to simply ignore dissenting members.

LEADERSHIP Are leaders born or made? Many people, perhaps most, would probably choose the former option, especially if they are thinking about great historical leaders such as Abraham Lincoln, Nelson Mandela, or Mahatma Ghandi. However, research strongly suggests that group leadership is less a quality of a particular individual than a two-way relationship between leaders and followers that rests heavily on the leader's effectiveness in interacting with the members and the extent to which he or she is seen as committed to the group's goals and values (Stogdill, 1974). Someone who is an excellent leader in one context may be utterly ineffective in another. In other words, leadership is best understood as a characteristic of social structure rather than as an attribute of particular individuals.

Nevertheless, leaders do often share certain characteristics. Leaders tend to be original problem solvers who are comfortable acting on their own initiative, and they tend to be self-confident and good at living with a certain amount of frustration (Stogdill, 1974). They are typically taller and more talkative than their followers. They also tend to be perceived as attractive (Crosbie, 1975; Kalick, 1988).

Every small group tends to develop not one but two distinct leaders. One, the **instrumental** (or *task*) **leader,** is primarily concerned with making the decisions that will help the group achieve its goals; the other, the **expressive** (or *socioemotional*) **leader,** concentrates on keeping the group's morale high (Bales, 1950, 1953; Fiedler, 1981). Both types are crucial if the group is to function effectively. Occasionally, one person may fill both roles, but this is rare because an instrumental leader must sometimes ruffle people's feathers in order to keep the group moving in the right direction—a responsibility that makes it difficult to be well-liked enough to be an effective expressive leader (Olmstead & Hare, 1978). Good instrumental leaders earn the respect of their followers; good expressive leaders receive their affection.

Group dynamics researchers have identified three types of instrumental leaders based on how directive they are (White & Lippitt, 1960). An **authoritarian leader** assigns tasks, makes the major decisions for the group, pays relatively little attention to the concerns of the followers, and praises or criticizes group members without adequately explaining the criteria on which they are being judged. In contrast, a **democratic leader** encourages group discussion and input, works to build group consensus, and tries to explain why members are being rewarded or punished. A **laissez-faire leader** (from the French term for "let it be") is highly nondirective, letting group members make their own decisions without much help or input.

As you might expect, laissez-faire leaders are the least effective and sometimes the least popular (Fiedler, 1967), but the relative advantages of authoritarian and democratic leadership are more difficult to determine (Fiedler, 1981). Authoritarian leaders are generally not well liked, and members of groups under their direction usually report lower morale. At the same time, authoritarian leaders are good in a crisis, when decisions must be made quickly and obeyed without question. Democratic leaders often do not fare well in emergencies. On the other hand, when there is time for discussion and when a certain amount of dissent can be tolerated, democratic lead-

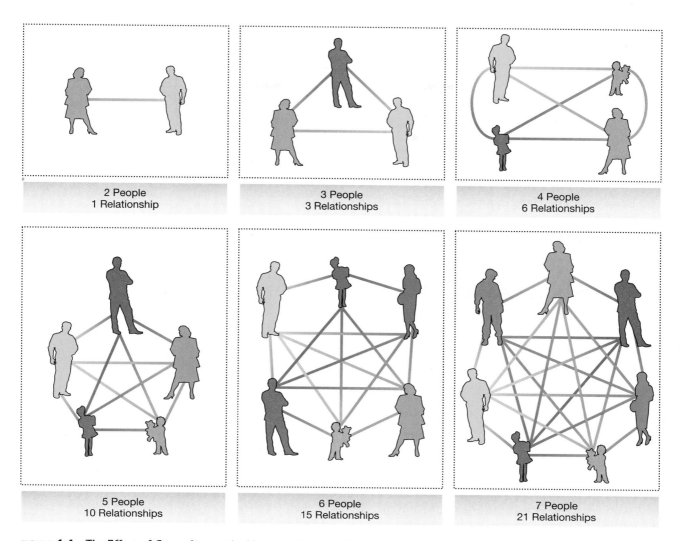

| 2 People
1 Relationship | 3 People
3 Relationships | 4 People
6 Relationships |

| 5 People
10 Relationships | 6 People
15 Relationships | 7 People
21 Relationships |

FIGURE 4.4 **The Effect of Group Size on the Number of Possible Relationships.**

Source: "Three Models of Minority-Dominant Group Relations" from *American Pluralism: A Study of Minority Groups and Social Theory* by William M. Newman. Copyright © 1973 by William M. Newman. Reprinted by permission of Addison-Wesley Educational Publishers, Inc.

ership creates groups that are more satisfied, work better without direct supervision, and in many cases are more productive (Tjosvold et al., 1992).

It should be noted that these findings are primarily based on research conducted in societies like the United States in which there is a strong cultural bias toward democratic leadership (Olmstead & Hare, 1978). It may be that in nations with weaker democratic traditions, authoritarian leadership is more popular and effective. The key point is that leaders must be seen to accept the group's values, whatever they are.

Gender and Leadership In the traditional family, as in many other types of groups, instrumental leaders have historically tended to be male, and expressive leaders, female. This pattern persists to some extent today because of enduring expectations and socialization patterns, but it is gradually weakening as

the importance of the ascribed status of gender declines.

Most research into small-group leadership has been androcentric in that it has focused primarily on males. Traditionally, people in this society have displayed a cultural bias toward male leadership, a reality that works very much to the advantage of men. In fact, men and women have been repeatedly shown to be roughly equally effective as leaders (Eagly & Johnson, 1990).

Early research suggested that women and men tended to display somewhat different communication patterns and leadership styles. In line with the instrumental/expressive distinction, male leaders were found to be relatively directive or authoritarian, whereas women were more democratic, collaborative, and participatory (Eagly & Karau, 1991). Women were described as seeking leadership roles out of a desire to be helpful, whereas men were more commonly driven by the need to achieve and dominate (Bridges, 1989). However, newer research suggests that such distinctions are fading as more women enter leadership positions (Klenke, 1996).

Interestingly, women who adopt a directive approach are commonly judged by their subordinates as too harsh, perhaps because this leadership style clashes with their stereotypical gender role. But the same principle does not seem to hold for men: Supportive male leaders, whose leadership style violates traditional male role expectations, are more likely to be appreciated than are more authoritarian male leaders (Butler & Geis, 1990).

CONFORMITY The way in which individuals interact in a group is determined not only by the size of the group and its leadership, but also by group pressures toward conformity. A classic study by social psychologist Solomon Asch (1952) illustrates this fact.

Imagine that you are a participant in Asch's experiment. You arrive at a social science laboratory and are told to sit at the end of a row of six other people whom you assume to be fellow research subjects. In fact, however, they are working with Asch: You are the only person being tested.

You are told—falsely—that you are participating in a study of perception. You are then shown a sample card (see Figure 4.5) and told that your task will be to decide which of the three lines on the bottom (X, Y, or Z) is the same length as the one on the top (A). As it happens, the correct answer is obvious. During the first "trial run," everyone announces the correct answer, one at a time. You give your answer next to last because of where you are sitting in the row.

Then the real experiment starts. You are shown a total of eighteen cards. In every case the correct answer is obvious. But on the third card, and eleven times thereafter, everyone in the group gives the wrong answer and then they all look at you to see what you will say.

What do you think you would do in this situation? Asch found that about one-third of his subjects went along with the group—giving an answer they knew was wrong—at least half the time. Another 40 percent conformed less frequently, and just 25 percent gave the correct answer throughout the experiment. Through interviews, he found that almost all the conformers knew they were answering incorrectly but were not willing to openly defy the expressed opinion of the rest of the group.

The real significance of this research is evident if we reflect on the fact that this was a very artificial situation. The experimental subject did not even know the other people in the group. Consider what happens

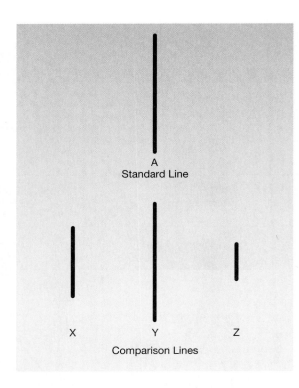

FIGURE 4.5 *An Example of the Cards Used in the Asch Experiment.*

when we are in real groups that are important to us, like our families and peer groups, and you will get a sense of how easily groups can affect behavior.

DECISION MAKING Do groups make better decisions than individuals? With several people working on a problem, you have a larger pool of knowledge to draw on, and the chances increase that someone will detect errors in the group's collective thought process. However, these advantages may be short-circuited by groupthink (Phillips & Wood, 1984; Watson et al., 1991).

Groupthink, a phenomenon first identified by Irving Janis (1972), refers to the tendency of highly cohesive groups to make poor decisions because the members are unwilling to threaten the group's solidarity. As a consensus emerges, dissent is stifled because of conformity pressures similar to those studied by Asch (Hart, 1991; Kameda & Sugimori, 1999). Self-appointed "mindguards" arise who pounce on anyone who disagrees with the collective mindset of the group and label dissenters disloyal.

Janis and other researchers have identified groupthink as a key factor in a number of disastrous governmental decisions, including the failure to prepare Pearl Harbor for a Japanese sneak attack, the Kennedy administration's decision to invade Cuba that led to the Bay of Pigs fiasco (McCauley, 1989),

Groupthink may occur when conformity pressures in highly cohesive groups prevent members from questioning an emerging group consensus.

Watergate (Hart, 1991), and the explosion of the space shuttle *Challenger*.

Now that sociologists have identified the symptoms of groupthink, steps can be taken to prevent it. Future leaders in business, politics, and the military are being formally taught to solicit and reward well-considered opposition to an emerging consensus (Aldag & Fuller, 1993). This is another example of how applying the sociological imagination can improve people's lives.

LARGER SOCIAL STRUCTURES

Many of our most important social interactions take place within small groups, but these groups are located within the context of various larger social structures, including networks, formal organizations, communities, strata, institutions, and, finally, entire societies.

Networks

A **network** is a broad web of social ties that radiates out from a given individual, linking that person with a large number of others (Doreien & Stokman, 1997). Networks are person-specific; that is, they are different for each individual. They include our primary and secondary group memberships, but they also connect us with many people whom we know more or less well but with whom we only occasionally interact. Networks are looser and less coherent than groups, lacking clear boundaries or any appreciable sense of collective identity. They tend to be quite large, typically varying from 500 to perhaps 2,500 people (Milgram, 1967).

The study of networks is a relatively new but rapidly expanding topic in sociology. Stanley Milgram's "small world" study was one of the first major research projects concerning networks (Travers & Milgram, 1969; Kochen, 1989). Milgram randomly selected individuals from all across the United States and designated them as either "starters" or "targets." The starters were given a letter that was addressed to one of the targets. However, the starters could not simply mail the letter to the target, but instead were required to send it on to someone they knew on a first-name basis and who might personally know the designated target. Successive members of the chain followed the same instructions. Most of the letters did eventually reach their final destinations, and it typically took only between five and seven links for them to do so.

Networks include both *strong links*, connecting people who know each other well (Fischer, 1982) and *weak links*, between individuals who know each other less intimately (Granovetter, 1973; Montgomery, 1992). People with smaller and weaker networks tend to be more vulnerable to physical and mental health problems (Seeman et al., 1985). Highly educated people usually have more strong ties and a larger number of ties to non-kin—both factors that increase their ability to accomplish their goals. Older people and individuals living outside of urban areas have fewer strong ties (Fernandez & Weinberg, 1997; Podolny & Baron, 1997). The *Diversity in Focus* box in this chapter explores the impact of gender, race, and class on occupational networking.

When people use the term "networking" in everyday speech, they are usually talking about business and professional networks (Granovetter, 1995). People with extensive work-related networks are at a distinct advantage in advancing their careers (Marsden, 1992). Studies show that most job seekers find their positions through networking rather than by responding to advertisements (Granovetter, 1995; Biari, 1997). Thus, the cynical saying "It's who you know,

DIVERSITY IN FOCUS

Beyond the Old Boys' Network

As anyone who has searched for a job in today's economy knows, personal contacts are often crucial. This is a reality that has traditionally worked against women and people of color. However, as in so many other areas of life, the times are changing.

Feminist researchers first called attention to the existence of "old boys' networks" in many businesses and other employing organizations. Pioneering work by Rosabeth Kanter showed that informal networks among male executives routinely provided their members with valuable information concerning job openings as well as helpful hints about how to achieve occupational success. Because much of the content of the informal interaction that occurred within these networks concerned stereotypically masculine topics like sports, few women felt comfortable participating in them even if the men were willing to allow them to do so—which was generally not the case in any event. Although these old boys' networks were not necessarily set

up to deliberately exclude women, in practice that became one of their key functions.

As women began to compete for high-level positions, they developed their own parallel "new girls' networks," which were explicitly designed to help their members get ahead. Recent research demonstrates that women's networks, previously more likely to contain relatives and lower status people than those of men, are becoming much more like those of men. While women's networks are today typically the same size as those of men, they may remain less effective: A 1997 survey of executives found that 63 percent of the men but only 41 percent of the women had found their current jobs through networking.

African Americans and other people of color are following suit by establishing their own networks; in fact, one study suggested that three-fourths of the U.S. black leadership either knew each other personally or were linked through a common friend. However, to the extent that racial and ethnic minorities are dispropor-

tionately found in the lower and working classes, their efforts to network may be limited by the fact that people who are toward the bottom of the class ladder tend to have more local (face-to-face) ties, whereas those in the middle and upper classes enjoy more cosmopolitan (long-distance) networks. Local networks provide strong personal support but are much less effective than cosmopolitan ones in the workplace.

1. Why do the networks of women and racial minorities still tend to be less effective than those of white men? Do you expect that they will achieve parity in the near future? Explain your answer.

2. Is your personal network composed mostly of people very much like yourself? If so, can you think of any advantages of trying to recruit a more diverse network?

Sources: Kanter, 1977; Moore, 1991; Taylor, 1992; Montgomery, 1992; Reskin & Padavic, 1994; Wright, 1995; Ibarra, 1995; Jackson et al., 1995; Gabor, 1995; Carey & McLean, 1997.

---

not what you know" is frequently quite true (Luo, 1997; Hagan, 1998).

However, it's not just professionals who network. Research shows that networking is important among such diverse groups of people as organized criminals (Block, 1983; Chambliss, 1988), top civic and political leaders (Domhoff, 1974; Useem, 1984), maids (Hondagneu-Sotelo, 1994), and Asian businessmen (Gerlach, 1992; Kotkin, 1993).

Since the next four larger types of social structure are discussed at length later in the text, we will only briefly introduce them here.

Formal Organizations

A **formal** (or *complex*) **organization** is a large secondary group that is explicitly designed to accomplish specific tasks by means of an elaborate internal divi-

sion of labor (Etzioni, 1964). Examples include General Motors, the University of Kentucky, the World Health Organization, and the government of the state of Missouri. Most modern formal organizations are structured as bureaucracies. Chapter 21 examines bureaucratic formal organizations in depth, with special attention to the workplace.

Communities

Traditionally, the term *community* has been used to refer to a relatively large number of people who live in one geographic area and are connected to each other by a variety of social bonds (Poplin, 1979; Lowery, 1993). More recently some sociologists have dropped the requirement that members of a community must share a territorial base, as reflected in the fact that we often use expressions like "the business community" to describe people who do not necessarily live anywhere near one another but who regularly communicate and share various concerns. More conventional examples of communities includes cities, towns, villages, and neighborhoods. Chapter 22 includes a sociological analysis of this topic.

Strata

Strata (singular: stratum) or "layers" are segments within a large population that receive different amounts of scarce and valued resources (property, prestige, and power) by virtue of their position in a ranked system of structural inequality. Examples include social classes, castes, genders, racial and ethnic groups, and different age categories. Chapters 10 through 14 examine these different types of strata.

Institutions

Social institutions were defined in Chapter 1 as predictable, established ways to provide for one or more of a society's basic needs. They are composed of interrelated statuses, roles, norms, values, and groups. Most sociologists identify five core social institutions: the family, religion, the economy, the political institution (or polity), and education.

These institutions must fulfill five critical needs, present in all societies, that are sometimes referred to as the *functional requisites* (Aberle et al., 1950; Mack & Bradford, 1979):

1. Replacement of members. This is a primary responsibility of the family.
2. Socialization of new members. The family, education, and religion accomplish this function.
3. Production and distribution of goods and services. This is the principal task of the economy.
4. Preservation of social order. This is accomplished by the political institution, in particular by the specialized institutions of law, the criminal justice system, and the military.
5. Provision of a sense of meaning and purpose. Religion has traditionally fulfilled this function.

A number of other institutions, including medicine, science, law and the criminal justice system, sport, the media, and the military, have emerged as distinct systems separate from the five core institutions in the modern era. Eight major social institutions are explored in detail in Chapters 9 and 15 through 21.

Societies

Societies are the largest elements of social structure. A **society** is defined as a sizable number of people who interact, share a culture, and usually live in a sin-

gle geographic territory. A society is, at least in principle, self-perpetuating and independent of all other societies, although in the modern world virtually all but the most isolated societies are in reality highly interdependent. Many societies are equivalent to nation-states—France and Japan are examples—but in some instances one nation-state incorporates two or more distinct societies. For example, the former Yugoslavia encompassed Croatians, Bosnian Muslims, Serbs, and Montenegrans; both Tutsis and Hutus live in the nation-state of Rwanda. The account at the beginning of this chapter recounted the successful struggle of the people of East Timor to gain political independence from Indonesia. In other instances, members of a single society may be spread out among several nation-states, as is the case with the Kurds, who live as a minority group in Iraq, Pakistan, and several other countries.

THE EVOLUTION OF SOCIETIES

The study of how societies change is one of sociology's most important objectives. Chapter 24 is devoted exclusively to this topic. In this section we introduce three classic theories of societal change that will prove useful at several points later in the text.

Early sociologists Émile Durkheim and Ferdinand Tönnies developed theories of change that continue to be useful today. After introducing their work, we turn to Gerhard and Jean Lenski's more recent theory of sociocultural evolution.

Durkheim: Mechanical and Organic Solidarity

Émile Durkheim (1933), one of the founders of the functionalist perspective, observed that most societies throughout history have been characterized by high levels of **mechanical solidarity,** a form of internal cohesion that results from people being very much like each other. In societies with a limited economic division of labor, almost everyone of the same gender and approximately the same age does pretty much the same sort of work. For example, in most agrarian cultures, nearly all adult men work in the fields and most adult women stay at home, cook, tend to other household tasks, and look after the children. Durkheim maintains that people who play the same economic role tend to share very similar values and general understandings of the world, and these similarities directly bond them. We experience a degree of mechanical solidarity when we are part of a crowd cheering for the home team. Think about how much stronger our feelings of solidarity would be if

In traditional cultures, people of the same gender and age generally share the same values, norms, and world-view. These similarities strengthen the social bond between them, a phenomenon that Durkheim calls mechanical solidarity.

these other people were similar to us in almost every way.

As societies grow, economic competition combined with larger population size leads to an increase in the division of labor and the emergence of different occupational specialties. Shoe salespeople and nurses and farmers and college professors live in different social worlds and have relatively little in common with one another. Consequently, mechanical solidarity weakens, although it does not disappear.

Instead, a new type of social bond called **organic solidarity** arises in order to keep the society functioning. Organic solidarity is based not on similarity but rather on difference and interdependence. Unlike the era of mechanical solidarity when each family was substantially economically independent, in modern times we must directly or indirectly rely on thousands of other people to provide the goods and services we need. The organic solidarity that results from economic interdependence may not leave us feeling warm and emotionally bonded to our fellows, but it does oblige us to maintain close connections with them simply because we need them.

Tönnies: *Gemeinschaft* and *Gesellschaft*

The German sociologist Ferdinand Tönnies (1855–1937) studied the same broad processes of societal change as Durkheim, but he took a slightly different approach (Tönnies, 1963). Tönnies started at the microlevel by comparing social interaction in traditional and modern societies. He argued that most relationships in premodern societies displayed a high level of *natural will*, by which he meant that they were generally considered to be ends in themselves rather

than means to an end. Cooley would have thought of them as primary relationships.

Tönnies called a society constructed primarily on the basis of natural will relationships a *Gemeinschaft*. A *Gemeinschaft* is typically small, rural, strongly committed to custom and tradition, and centered on kinship and other ascribed statuses. Most relationships are personal and long-term. Because everyone knows everyone else, there is little privacy, and conformity is promoted largely by gossip. The community is more important than the individual. Everyone sees the world the same way, and each individual's principal responsibility is to be like everyone else.

There are still some true *Gemeinschafts* left in the United States—the Amish, for example (Hostetler, 1980; Kraybill, 1989; Zellner, 2001)—but most of us no longer live that way. Today most social interactions reflect *rational will*, meaning that relationships are chiefly means of obtaining what we want. Business transactions are rational will relationships, and of course this style of interaction is especially characteristic of secondary groups.

Tönnies used the word *Gesellschaft* to designate a society based largely on rational will. A *Gesellschaft* such as the contemporary United States is normally large, urban, strongly oriented toward change, and centered on achieved statuses. Many relationships are impersonal and short-term. Since people are always trying to maximize their personal advantage and there are few widely accepted moral values, conformity is generally enforced by formal agencies such as the police and the courts. The individual is more important than the community, and people's primary responsibility is to look out for themselves.

The contrast between this traditional Amish buggy and the modern world that surrounds it suggests how difficult it has been for members of this Gemeinschaft *community to preserve its distinctive way of life into the twenty-first century.*

Gerhard and Jean Lenski: Sociocultural Evolution

Contemporary theorists Gerhard and Jean Lenski provide a third, more detailed perspective on the historical transition from mechanical to organic solidarity or from *Gemeinschaft* to *Gesellschaft* (Nolan & Lenski, 1999). They divide the process of sociocultural evolution into five stages. Each reflects a fundamentally different subsistence strategy, or method of obtaining food.

HUNTING AND GATHERING SOCIETIES From the beginning of human life on earth until about 12,000 years ago, every society employed a subsistence strategy called *hunting and gathering*; in other words, their sole sources of food were wild animals and plants (Service, 1966; Nolan & Lenski, 1999). This economic base limited the size of these cultures to small bands of 25 to 50 people. Also, because food resources became depleted over time in any particular area, almost all hunter-gatherers were nomadic.

Hunting and gathering societies have a very simple division of labor, with men normally responsible for hunting and women for most domestic tasks and gathering wild plants. Anthropologists believe that many early hunter-gatherers lived in very fertile environments and thus probably devoted less time and energy to food production and the other necessities of daily life than members of any other type of society (Sahlins, 1972). Still, everyone except very small children had to spend a certain amount of time every day finding food. This meant that these societies could not develop any full-time specialists such as toolmakers, and in consequence their level of technological development was very low.

At this stage of societal evolution, all of the needs met in modern societies by specialized institutions are provided by the family. For example, children do not go to school; they learn everything they need to know from their relatives. Although the dominant males within each family hold a certain amount of political power, their ability to compel obedience is very limited. For the most part, they can do little more than encourage people to follow long-established traditions. As in any *Gemeinschaft*, deviance is controlled informally. Food and craft goods are produced and distributed within the family; there is no concept of money or of profit. There are no full-time religious specialists, although some individuals, called *shamans*, do claim special knowledge of the supernatural, which they use to heal the sick.

Because hunter-gatherers are nomadic, they do not accumulate much property. Consequently, these societies are highly egalitarian, with no social classes and hence no wealthy or poor people. Gender relations also tend to be quite equal, in part because women make substantial contributions to economic subsistence—usually more than the men (Lorber, 1994; Volti, 1995). Finally, collective violence is limited to occasional feuds and raids; there is no war as we know it (Sahlins, 1960).

If this description makes hunting and gathering life sound idyllic, bear in mind that these cultures had little medical knowledge and virtually no ability to control nature. As a result, over half the people in hunting and gathering societies of the past died before reaching the age of 20 (Nolan & Lenski, 1999).

Today only a handful of hunting and gathering societies survive. The best known include the !Kung and the Mbuti in southern Africa, the Australian Aborigines, and the Semai of Malaysia. It is very doubtful

GLOBAL CONNECTIONS

Worlds Apart: Gopalpur and Walnut Grove

As members of a postindustrial, future-oriented, urban society, or *Gesellschaft*, people in the United States take for granted numerous impersonal, short-term relationships and encounters with strangers, the existence of diverse lifestyles and occupations, and the pursuit of individual achievement. In much of the world, however, *Gemeinschaft* is (or was until recently) the norm. Most people live in small, traditional, rural villages where little changes from one generation to the next.

The village of Gopalpur in southern India is a good example of a *Gemeinschaft* (Beals, 1980). The same families have lived in Gopalpur for as long as anyone can remember. Few people travel as far as the nearest town, only 15 miles away. Men live and die in the village in which they were born; women, often betrothed in childhood, spend their adult lives in their husband's family's village.

Except for a few specialists (such as the village carpenter and the blacksmith, who inherited their trades), all the men in Gopalpur are farmers. Families grow their own sorghum, rice, and vegetables. Most also plant fruit trees and keep at least one water buffalo for milk plus a few sheep, goats, and chickens for feasts and sacrifices. The pace of life is slow and the work hard.

While the men are working, the women go about their chores: hauling water from the river, carrying rubbish and cow manure to a compost heap outside the village, tending the cooking fire, grinding grain and mixing dough for flatbread, and preparing pots of beans, chili, and vegetables for the family's main meals. This routine is broken only during harvest time when, in addition to these chores, women work in the fields alongside men, and on special occasions such as weddings.

Each extended family has its own house—typically a windowless 30-by-40-foot stone and mud structure with holes in the roof for light and air and a raised veranda across the front. The entrance is a set of carved, heavy wooden double doors that open onto a courtyard. Beyond, in the darkness, is a raised platform with millstones and mortars for processing grain. A door on the left leads to a washing and cooking area. Not homes in the Western sense, Gopalpur houses are more like storehouses or small forts. There are no living rooms or bedrooms. The family eats on the front veranda and, at night, sets up cots outside.

Privacy is nonexistent in Gopalpur. Social life takes place on the streets under the watchful eyes of men gathered under shade trees and women working and chatting on verandas as their babies doze in hammocks and small children play nearby. During the hottest months, villagers sleep by day and socialize at night. This is the season for visits by elders from another village to discuss marriage arrangements with the father of a village girl, for wrestling matches and drama competitions, for feasts and festivals, and for predawn expeditions to collect firewood.

The rules of life in Gopalpur are so well known that they are rarely discussed. A man must find a bride, father children (especially sons), accumulate enough wealth to arrange proper marriages for

that this style of life can endure anywhere for more than another generation because of the constant incursion on their territories by the rapidly growing, technologically advanced societies that have come to dominate the planet (Haviland, 1999).

HORTICULTURAL SOCIETIES Between 10,000 and 12,000 years ago, hunter-gatherers in the Near East and later in several other parts of the world learned to domesticate various species of animals and plants. This development led to the emergence of *horticultural society*.

Horticulturalists supplement hunting and gathering by raising crops in small garden plots using simple hand tools such as digging sticks and hoes. These people generally stay put for several years until the fertility of the ground is exhausted, at which time they move to another site. They often return to areas where they lived previously when the soil there has become productive again. Many horticulturists use a "slash and burn" technology, cutting down ground cover and burning it to increase the soil's fertility.

This technology may sound primitive, but it leads to some truly dramatic changes in social life. Most significantly, horticultural societies produce substantially larger amounts of food than is possible by hunting and gathering. This surplus allows small bands to grow into tribes of up to several thousand people. Furthermore, horticulture is productive enough so that a few individuals in every community are freed from daily subsistence work and can focus all their attention on crafts and making more sophisticated tools.

The process of institutional differentiation begins at the horticultural stage (Parsons, 1966). A few full-

them, and make more friends than enemies so that his funeral will be well attended. A woman's duty is to obey her father, then her husband and mother-in-law, and to bear and raise children. To be sure, individuals stray—but not for long.

Men keep daggers in their house for protection against roving bandits, but violence toward neighbors is rare. Crops sometimes fail, but no one is homeless or hungry. "[P]eople do not regard Gopalpur's pattern as something to be changed, improved, or fought. Things, both good and bad, are as they always have been and as they always will be" (Beals, 1980:11).

Walnut Grove, an [hypothetical] apartment complex in the San Francisco Bay area, has about the same number of residents as Gopalpur—but the similarity ends there. Residents of Walnut Grove have little in common beyond their address. None grew up in the complex, though some are native Californians. Most will move again as their job opportunities and family lives change. Tenants include families with young children; singles of various ages living alone, with

roommates, or with a partner; middle-aged couples in first or second marriages; and retirees. Unlike the extended families of Gopalpur, each household is independent. Some residents phone family members every week and visit on holidays; others rarely do. Also unlike the villagers of Gopalpur, they practice different religions; work at different jobs; and have different tastes in clothes, music, and books.

Privacy and anonymity are as highly valued in Walnut Grove as sociability and familiarity are in Gopalpur. Residents do not view one another as part of a community. Indeed, most prefer to remain strangers. Neighbors observe a polite distance, not inquiring into the personal details of one another's lives. Mothers with children the same age or singles who enjoy hiking may become friends, but they are the exception. For the most part, residents lead separate lives; many do not know their next-door neighbor's name. Printed rules posted in the mail room and hired security guards relieve tenants of the need to resolve conflicts face to face.

Furthermore, at Walnut Grove different elements of each person's life are compartmentalized. On weekdays individual family members go their separate ways: children to day care or school, each parent to his or her job. The roles individuals play at work are distinct from the roles they play at home. Weekends are set apart as a time to relax, pursue hobbies, entertain friends, do chores, and go shopping. Individuals are expected to have unique needs, interests, and goals.

Gopalpur and Walnut Grove are worlds apart—socially and culturally as well as geographically.

1. Would it be easier for an Indian villager to adapt to life in Walnut Grove or for a modern American to learn to live in Gopalpur? Explain your answer.

2. Do you think the residents of Gopalpur feel confined and constrained by their lack of privacy?

3. What is gained and what is lost as societies evolve from the traditional agrarian pattern to modern postindustrial structures?

Source: Beals, 1980.

time religious specialists emerge, and while the power of political leaders remains limited, some men become chiefs. However, the extended family continues to be the primary setting for social life.

The semisedentary lifestyle typical of horticulturalists permits the accumulation of personal property, as does the existence of a predictable food surplus. These developments in turn lead to greater social inequality. Wealthier and poorer families start to appear. However, women continue to enjoy substantial equality in most societies at this level, again because they usually assume the primary responsibility for raising crops once the men have done the heavy work of clearing the land.

The existence of a surplus also allows horticulturists to trade with other societies, which in turn stimulates the more rapid diffusion of new ideas and technologies. It is also at this stage that warfare and

slavery appear (Harris, 1977). In societies that are particularly warlike, women's status starts to erode (O'Kelly & Carney, 1986).

Like hunting and gathering cultures, horticulturalists are becoming increasingly rare in the modern world. Among the most extensively studied are the Yanomamo of Brazil and Venezuela and the Truk of the Caroline Islands in the western Pacific.

PASTORAL SOCIETIES At about the same time that horticultural societies were appearing in the more fertile parts of the world, people living in arid regions of North Africa, the Middle East, and parts of Central Asia were domesticating herd animals such as cattle, sheep, goats, and camels, and developing a style of life known as *pastoralism*. Pastoral societies are thus an environmentally mandated alternative to horticulture rather than an advancement over it.

Shamans play an important role in traditional societies, using their special connections to the spirit world to perform a variety of healing rituals.

Pastoralists are mostly nomads, following their herds as they migrate with the seasons, although they may be sedentary at certain times of the year. They frequently establish ongoing trade relations with more settled peoples. Pastoral societies have roughly the same level of institutional differentiation as horticultural ones. They, too, generate a regular surplus and can support some full-time specialists (Evans-Pritchard, 1940). Social inequality increases as wealthy families accumulate larger herds than their poorer fellows. Gender inequality is usually moderate.

One of the most interesting historical developments at this stage concerns religion. Three of the great world religions—Judaism, Christianity, and Islam—developed in pastoral societies. This helps explain many passages in the Bible, such as "The Lord is my shepherd," and why the word *pastor* is used to refer to certain religious leaders.

Pastoral societies endure, often in the places where they first developed, in large part because the land they occupy has not until recently been seen as worth very much. But this is changing. As the world population has soared in recent decades, pastoralists have found their lifestyles increasingly constrained by the outside world (Bacon, 1980). Contemporary examples of pastoral societies include the Basseri of Southern Iran and the Karimojong, who live in Uganda.

AGRARIAN SOCIETIES   In the valleys of the Tigris and Euphrates Rivers, in what is now Iraq, the invention of the plow and the refinement of metallurgical technology about 6,000 years ago led to the agrarian revolution (Childe, 1951). Similar developments took place in Egypt, in India, along the Yangtze River in China, and, much later, in Peru. *Agrarian societies* use animal power to produce levels of surplus food, especially grains, far beyond anything previously possible. In a relatively short period of time, society changed beyond recognition.

Perhaps most obviously, the agrarian revolution led to unprecedented increases in the size of the population, with the largest societies swelling to several million members. The first cities arose at this time. In them, substantial numbers of people, freed from the requirement that they contribute to the production of food, became full-time specialists in fields such as metallurgy, woodworking, and pottery. Human knowledge expanded rapidly, leading to the invention of writing and mathematics and ultimately to "high culture" in the form of philosophy, theology, literature, art, architecture, and science (Jacobs, 1970). Trade grew, further quickening the pace of social change, and money was developed as a universal medium of exchange.

In agrarian societies, religious and political institutions became substantially differentiated, although they were often intermingled in the form of a *divine kingship* in which the leader of the society was not only a monarch but was also viewed by his subjects as a god. The state grew in power, sometimes basing its legitimacy on control of the elaborate irrigation systems that were often needed for large-scale agrarian production (Wittfogel, 1957). The first universal legal codes were written. The scale of war expanded as great empires such as Rome rose and fell. The family continued to be important, but more aspects of daily life were becoming increasingly independent of kinship.

The immense productivity of agrarian society accelerated the trend toward social inequality; most societies became divided into a small, extremely wealthy elite and a great majority of poor peasants (Pirenne, 1937). Removed from the core productive process by male-dominated agriculture, women saw their status decline sharply (Boulding, 1976; Fisher, 1979).

Many nations of the world today remain heavily agrarian, but none have escaped the impact of the next great societal revolution, which began in England in the middle of the 18th century.

INDUSTRIAL AND POSTINDUSTRIAL SOCIETIES
Industrial society is based on the use of non-animate sources of energy for economic production. Its origin a little less than 200 years ago transformed human society even more radically than the agrarian revolution 6,000 years earlier.

In pastoral societies, life is organized around the daily and seasonal needs of the animals. Pastoralists around the world keep a number of different species of herd animals, including oxen, goats, sheep, llamas, and camels.

Once again, the scale of society changed. Science led the way to a dramatic expansion of life expectancy and an unprecedented population explosion. Cities mushroomed. Mechanical solidarity and *Gemeinschaft* waned. The five major institutions became fully differentiated from each other. The importance of the economy, the government, and education greatly increased, while the family and, to a lesser extent, religion declined. New institutions such as medicine and criminal justice emerged.

As populations grew and physical mobility increased, many societies became far more culturally and racially diverse. Modern class systems emerged during the industrial era. Levels of social inequality initially expanded, but this trend seems to have reversed itself and the extremes of early industrial-era poverty have been substantially reduced (Critchlow & Hawley, 1989). The importance of ascribed status is gradually declining in industrial societies as women, ethnic and racial minorities, and other previously devalued groups have demanded and often received more equal treatment.

Today we are on the threshold of yet another dramatic transformation. Advanced industrial societies are moving rapidly toward a *postindustrial* model (Kumar, 1995; Bell, 1999). Whereas in industrial societies most people worked with relatively simple machines to produce physical goods like automobiles and toasters, in the postindustrial economy workers use computers and other advanced electronic technologies to provide information and services.

Table 4.1 on page 112 summarizes the main points of the Lenskis' theory of sociocultural evolution.

The transition to a fully postindustrial society will likely be as wrenching—and at least as radical—as the Industrial Revolution. It will be a primary task of sociology in the 21st century to analyze the character of the new computer-mediated society that has begun to take shape in the last few decades. The final sections of this chapter briefly examine the impact of the Internet on both social structure and culture in the early postindustrial era.

LIFE CONNECTIONS

Social Structure and Technology

Through most of history, nearly all social interaction took place on a face-to-face basis. This began to change only with the invention of the movable type printing press in the 15th century. Communication by means of the written word allowed a sort of slow-motion, long-distance interaction, but it lacked the instantaneous give and take that is possible in more personal contexts.

Subsequent technological developments—first the telegraph, then the telephone, and now the Internet—have made long-distance interaction much faster and easier and have greatly altered the character of social life. Because over half of all U.S. households now own personal computers, *virtual interaction* (as opposed to face-to-face interaction) has become increasingly common.

These developments have led some sociologists to rethink the concepts of groups and more generally of social structure (Meyrowitz, 1984; Hafner, 1994; Castells, 1996). Some maintain that online multiuser domains like chat rooms meet all the traditional defining criteria of social groups: They sustain continuous two-way interaction, they foster a sense of solidarity,

TABLE 4.1

Gerhard and Jean Lenski's Stages of Sociocultural Evolution

	When Stage First Appeared	Economic Basis of Society	Settlement Size
Hunting and Gathering	250,000 years ago or more	Hunting wild game, gathering wild plants, fishing	25–100
Horticultural	12,000–10,000 years ago	Gardens tended with hand tools	100–2,000
Pastoral	12,000–10,000 years ago	Domesticated herd animals	100–2,000
Agrarian	6,000 years ago	Fields plowed by draft animals	Up to 1 million
Industrial	200 years ago	Factories powered by non-animate energy sources	Millions
Postindustrial	Now emerging	Services and information, computers	Millions

Source: From *Human Societies: An Introduction to Macrosociology,* 8th ed. by Patrick Nolan and Gerhard E. Lenski. Copyright © 1999 by McGraw-Hill Book Company. Reprinted by permission of The McGraw-Hill Companies.

their members share norms and values, and they work toward shared goals (Turkle, 1995; Casalego, 1996).

Computer-mediated, diffuse interaction is emerging as a critically important sociological research topic in the postindustrial era. Here are some of the issues that will need to be explored:

- How does interaction change when people cannot physically observe each other? The fact that women, minorities, the physically disabled, and occupants of other traditionally stigmatized statuses can conceal most aspects of their identities online is often experienced as liberating (Turkle, 1995; Donath, 1997). In addition, diffuse interaction allows us to experiment by trying on new identities (Waskul, 1997). A 45-year-old white male can present himself online as a 12-year-old Latino girl if he wishes to do so. However, the very anonymity of cyberspace makes it difficult to evaluate the authenticity of an individual's presentation of self, a process that is much easier when the social cues provided by people's social statuses, expressions, gestures, and other forms of nonverbal behavior can be observed directly (Rhinegold, 1994; Schellenberg, 1996; Kollock & Smith, 1997).
- People communicating online can be amazingly open about revealing personal details of their lives (Marriot, 1998). One source describes virtual interaction as "a moderately strong, intimate secondary relationship" (Wellman et al., 1996). Sociologists wonder whether online groups can ever be truly primary in character. Is the sense of closeness that many participants experience genuine or illu-

sory? (Cerulo et al., 1992; Gabriel, 1996; Parks, 1996) Can a truly intimate relationship develop when each party can end the interaction with the click of a mouse? (Kraut et al., 1998)

- Today, entire "virtual communities" are coming into existence (Nie, 1999; Wellman, 1999). At most colleges, students can now access library materials, chat with fellow students, ask professors questions, download music, and order pizza, all without ever leaving their dorm rooms. Is it possible that a new form of social solidarity, neither mechanical nor organic, may emerge from this sort of online interaction? (Hornsby, 1998) If so, what would it be like?

SOCIETY CONNECTIONS

Inequality, Globalization, and the Internet

The dramatic growth of the Internet has created a number of important social issues, including equality of access to the "information superhighway" and the possible development of a single world society at some point in the future.

Access to the Internet

Conflict theorists are concerned that the computer revolution may be intensifying the division between the haves and the have-nots in a world in which eco-

Geographical Mobility	Extent of Institutional Differentiation	Extent of Structured Inequality	Status of Women
Nomadic	All institutions contained within the family	Egalitarian except for gender and age distinctions	Substantial gender equality
Semisedentary	Government and religion begin to emerge as specilized institutions	Substantial inequalities emerge	Women beginning to lose status
Mostly nomadic	Similar to horticultural	Similar to horticultural	Similar to horticultural
Sedentary	Family losing some importance; most institutions distinct	Great extremes of wealth and poverty; estates and castes; little mobility	Women occupy clearly subordinate role
Sedentary	Family loses many roles; full institutional differentiation	Reduced inequality; social classes; substantial mobility	Movement toward increasing equality of the sexes
Sedentary	Full institutional differentiation	Too early to determine	Probably highly egalitarian

nomic success is increasingly linked to the ability to use computers effectively. U.S. Internet users are 95 percent white and 60 percent male (Edmondson, 1997). Just one-quarter of those lacking high-school degrees use computers regularly compared with 82 percent of people with graduate degrees. Computer games, which often get youth hooked on cyberspace, are generally designed to appeal to boys, and males dominate most college computer science departments.

Globally, many of the nations of the developing world are lagging behind in computer technology (Wresch, 1996). Currently, well over 30 percent of the people in the United States use the Internet compared with 0.1 percent of those in sub-Saharan Africa and just 0.04 percent in South Asia. Ninety-three percent of the world's Internet users live in the developed countries, which account for only one-fifth of the world's population (United Nations, 1999). In addition, only 7 percent of computer users in China and 4 percent in the Arab world are women (United Nations Development Programme, 1999:63). If something is not done soon to change these patterns, billions of people may be left behind.

Toward a Global Society?

There can be no doubt that the Internet has promoted the emergence of a global culture, a trend that has been labeled *cultural leveling*. Much of this global culture originates in the United States. English is well on its way to becoming a universal second language: Worldwide, about 90 percent of the messages posted on the Internet are in English. Some concerned observers describe this trend as a sort of worldwide *cultural imperialism* in which diverse lifestyles are being lost beneath a numbing tide of CNN, Disney, and Hollywood (Kuisel, 1993; Pollack, 1996).

While there is some truth to these charges, the cultural influence does not flow in only one direction. Virtual groups, like La Francophonie in France, have been formed to resist the dominance of English

INTERNET CONNECTIONS

The "Society Connections" feature in this chapter deals with the relationship between globalization, the Internet, and social inequality. The gap between people who have access to the Internet and those who do not has been referred to as the *digital divide*. The Clinton Administration established a Digital Divide Website:

http://www.ntia.doc.gov/ntiahome/index.html

and it has been continued by President George W. Bush. From the opening page, click on "U.S. Households with a Computer and with Internet Access." For past reports and studies click on *Previous Statistical Reports on Computer and Internet Use in the U.S.* Describe the pattern of inequality as it relates to computer use and Internet access. What are your personal thoughts about this "new" form of social inequality?

New electronic technologies such as teleconferencing allow face-to-face interaction between people located thousands of miles apart. Sociologists are exploring how these new media-mediated patterns of interaction differ from traditional patterns.

online. More generally, increasing numbers of people in the United States are eating sushi and Thai food, listening to "world music," and watching Hong Kong action movies (Lyotard, 1993).

Globalization and the Internet are reshaping social structure as well as culture. A world economy is emerging, dominated by a handful of immense multinational corporations. Regional trade agreements such as the European Union and the North American Free Trade Agreement (NAFTA) are reducing the economic significance of the nation-state. Military interventions are increasingly conducted under the banner of the United Nations or other multinational consortiums. Hundreds of international nongovernmental organizations (NGOs) have been established to work for change in areas such as women's rights, the environment, and the refugee crisis. Regular global conferences link key government and NGO decision makers all around the world, connections easily maintained through the Internet.

Will a world society ever emerge? Some observers believe that such a development is quite possible at some point in the future as the full potential of the computer revolution manifests itself. Others, however, point to the resurgence of ethnic nationalism and regionalism in the former Soviet Union, Yugoslavia, and elsewhere as evidence that globalization has clear limits.

The most likely outcome is that global culture will continue to evolve but that regional cultures will also survive. Both local and transnational levels of social structure will gain in importance, while the traditional nation-state may weaken (Kennedy, 1993).

SUMMARY

1. Social structure consists of the relatively stable patterns of social interaction that characterize human social life; it is within the context of social structure that people enact culture.

2. Statuses, the key components from which larger units of social structure are constructed, may be either ascribed or achieved. When a status is es-

   pecially important in determining an individual's identity, it is called a master status.

3. Roles are the dynamic aspect of statuses. We occupy a status, but we play a role.

4. Role strain and role conflict can result when people play several roles at the same time.

5. Social groups consist of several people who regularly interact and feel some sense of solidarity or common identity.

6. Primary groups provide warmth and intimacy, whereas secondary groups are important for accomplishing specific objectives.

7. In-groups, out-groups, and reference groups are other important types of social groups.

8. The size of a group is crucial in determining how it functions.

9. All groups have two types of leaders: instrumental leaders, who concentrate on achieving group goals, and expressive leaders, who maintain group morale.

10. People in small groups feel strong pressure to conform to the expectations of others and to obey group leaders.

11. Groupthink can interfere with the ability of a cohesive group to make wise decisions.

12. Networks are an increasingly important type of relatively diffuse social structure.

13. Larger elements of social structure include formal organizations, communities, strata, institutions, and societies.

14. Durkheim identified a historical transition from mechanical to organic solidarity; Tönnies analyzed the same shift using the terms *Gemeinschaft* and *Gesellschaft*.

15. Gerhard and Jean Lenski argue that sociohistorical evolution proceeds through several stages: hunting and gathering, horticultural or pastoral, agrarian, industrial, and postindustrial.

16. New forms of computer-mediated social structure are emerging that are raising issues such as differential access to cyberspace and the possible emergence of a single world society.

KEY TERMS

achieved status 92
aggregate 96
ascribed status 92
authoritarian leader 100
category 96
democratic leader 100
expressive leader 100
formal organization 104
Gemeinschaft 107
Gesellschaft 107
groupthink 102
in-group 98

instrumental leader 100
laissez-faire leader 100
master status 93
mechanical solidarity 105
network 103
organic solidarity 106
out-group 98
primary group 96
reference group 98
role 95
role conflict 95
role set 95

role strain 95
secondary group 97
social group 96
social structure 91
society 105
status 92
status inconsistency 92
status set 92
stigma 93
strata 105

CRITICAL THINKING QUESTIONS

1. The general trend in modern societies is toward an increase in the importance of achieved statuses and a decrease in the importance of ascribed ones. Why do you think this change is taking place? Who stands to lose and who stands to gain as a result of this transformation?

2. The Asch experiment shows that people are strongly inclined to conform to the expectations of others. Does this tendency contribute to social problems as well as to social order? Should we try to make people less willing to conform? How might we go about such a task?

3. Is the balance between primary and secondary interaction about right in most people's lives, or have we swung too far toward the latter type? Explain your view.

4. How do diffuse, computer-mediated groups differ from conventional face-to-face groups? What is gained and what is lost as we move toward a society in which more and more interaction is diffuse?

INVESTIGATE WITH CONTENT SELECT

Journal Research Collections from ContentSelect

Begin your research using Content-Select for this chapter by following the directions found on page 27 of this text to visit Prentice Hall's Research Navigator Website. Enter these search terms into the search field:

Stigma
Postindustrial
Status

5
SOCIALIZATION

Extreme Human Isolation

Anna lived with her mother and her grandfather in rural Pennsylvania. She was born out of wedlock and kept in an attic room, deprived of normal human contact and barely kept physically alive. When Anna was discovered just before her sixth birthday, she was emaciated and could not talk, walk, or do anything that showed intelligence. When she died at age 10, she had progressed to about the mental level of a 2½-year-old. Anna was born in the 1930s, but numerous cases since document virtually the same results of extreme isolation early in life: the prevention of a child's human capacity for mental development. Even minimal isolation and interaction in infancy leads to increased biological risk and social withdrawal later in life. Like humans, monkeys also cannot develop normally if separated from other monkeys. Female monkeys raised in isolation abuse or neglect their offspring. They never learn from other monkeys how monkeys are "supposed" to behave. The very rare documented cases of "feral" children kept alive by animals also confirm these patterns. In India in the 1920s, two girls, about age 8 and 1½ were captured among wolves and brought to an orphanage. "Wolfish in appearance and behavior, they walked on all fours, their tongues permanently hung out, and they prowled and howled at night." These girls survived with the wolves because the older girl had some "human" inclinations and apparently cared for the younger one before they were abandoned. But their "wolf" upbringing doomed them to a short life of physical deformity, mental retardation, and abnormal social behavior that could not be overcome. (Davis, 1947; Harlow & Harlow, 1970; Candland, 1995; Newton, 2002; Texdorf et al., 2002)

Generation X: Coming of Age in America

Sometime between 1960 and 1980 a unique generation was born. Generation X—a label inspired from a novel with adult characters portrayed as overeducated, underemployed, intensely private, and unpredictable—was brought up on television, personal computers, and visions of unlimited economic success. Media creations of Generation X painted its members as materialistic overconsumers. In the scornful humor of the media, "Gen Xers" are often referred to as "slackers" and the "Me" generation, disconnected from one another and society. Gen Xers may have experienced a sense of disconnectedness until very recently. But contrary to the stereotype, data show that they value family commitment more than career goals and will do what they can to ensure a healthy work–family balance, even if it means sacrificing material comfort. Bombarded by the Internet and feeling the pain of "information overload," they also appear to be retreating from the view that technology is the quick fix for personal turmoil and social problems. Like the Baby Boomers a generation or two before them, Gen Xers are concerned about social injustice, environmental degradation, and national security—concerns that have increased since September 11. Gen Xers are buffeted by the same set of social, political, and economic forces as everyone else, but they will experience and respond to the forces differently because of their unique place in time. (Coupland, 1991; Greenberg, 2002; Silbiger & Brooks, 2002; Yin & Gardyn, 2002)

Both in humans and in social animals, such as monkeys, social interaction is needed to learn about ourselves and about others. How do we learn to become human? Since we are born as human beings, the question at first seems contradictory. But sociology approaches it from a different view. The tragic cases of Anna, the feral children, and other children raised in isolation clearly demonstrate that social contact is necessary for learning and the development of the self. **Socialization** is the lifelong process whereby we learn our culture, develop our sense of self, and become functioning members of society. Until we are socialized, we have not "learned" humanness. Socialization shows why children reared with little human contact cannot seem to grasp the meaning of acceptable human behavior. The biological being who emerges from the womb possesses the physiological readiness to learn, but only through sustained, structured interaction with a culture and a social environment will an individual be able to demonstrate his or her humanness. As this chapter shows, the self is also developed by many other forms of social contact, such as interaction with parents and media, and the peers of our generation.

The theme of gender socialization is applied throughout this chapter to illustrate these issues. **Gender socialization** is the process by which individuals learn the cultural behavior of femininity or masculinity that is associated with the biological sex of female or male. Socialization becomes the key factor that determines the directions we take as we individually progress through life. Sociology provides a critical lens for viewing this remarkable process.

THEORETICAL PERSPECTIVES ON SOCIALIZATION

All theories of socialization begin with the notion that social interaction is necessary for the development of our human potential and sense of self. In addition to social interaction, socialization is mediated through other important elements, such as biology, personality, and various social structures—including family, school, and media. Different theories give different weight to each element. These theories also demonstrate the importance of interdisciplinary work. In the area of socialization, significant bridges have been built between the social and behavioral sciences.

Nature Versus Nurture

How much of our behavior is determined by nature (heredity), and how much is determined by nurture, the environment or culture in which we live and learn? The discipline of sociology is rooted in the nurture side of this question. Social interaction is the essential element for triggering the development of human potential that is rooted in "nature." As explained in Chapter 3, animals are unlike humans because they cannot symbolize and therefore do not possess culture. Sociologists do recognize that nature plays an important part in ex-

plaining key aspects of human social behavior, such as intelligence and sports ability. Other scientists, however, believe that humans and animals are much more alike than sociologists claim (Boesch & Tomasello, 1998; Eriksen, 2001; Brumann, 2002).

Sociobiology. The field of **sociobiology** addresses the question of how human behavior is determined, but it is rooted in the nature side of the question in its examination of the biological roots of social behavior. Sociobiology originally developed out of research based on insects (Wilson, 1975). Sociobiologists argue that the theory of evolution can be used to draw conclusions about humans from studies of social animals. According to sociobiological reasoning, human behavior is largely determined by genes because humans, like other animals, are structured by nature (biology) with an innate drive to ensure that their individual genes are passed on to the next generation. It is as adaptive for a mother to care for her children as it is for men to be promiscuous, in order to pass on their genes successfully. Each sex evolved these attributes to increase its reproductive success (Low, 2000). As a natural result, the separate worlds of male and female emerged (Udry, 2000).

CRITIQUE Sociobiologists have been successful in applying evolutionary theory to animal behavior, but empirical support for their arguments about human behavior is weak and have not had much following in the social sciences. Social scientists suggest that ex-

During their first school experiences, children are socialized into new roles and learn to interact and cooperate with peers who may be different than themselves.

INTERNET CONNECTIONS

The text discusses the nature versus nurture issue. One very interesting example of the nature–nurture debate involves the cause(s) of *alcoholism*. Do people "learn" to be alcoholics, or are they biologically predisposed to become alcoholic? Christa Gerrish's Web site, "Alcoholism: Nature or Nurture," offers evidence on both sides of this debate:

http://www.umm.maine.edu/BEX/students/ ChristaGerrish/cg320.html

After you have read the contents of her discussion, write a brief position paper explaining the role of heredity and environment on alcoholism.

tending the theory of sociobiology to humans makes faulty assumptions about human behavior and disregards well-documented research about animals. For example, it ignores the fact that the female chimp is notoriously promiscuous. Sexual selection in sociobiology emphasizes competition and aggression in male chimps, but neglects the other part of the process, in which female chimps make choices among males. Female chimps can be sexually aggressive and competitive, just as male chimps can be nurturing and passive (Hrdy, 1999). Also, the latest evidence now suggests that aggressiveness in primates is rare (probably less than 1 percent of all activitites), with affiliated, friendly behavior, such as grooming and playing, probably 100 times more frequent. These researchers state that the the dominant belief that animals compete with one another to gain resources and repro-

INTERNET CONNECTIONS

Another interesting topic in the nature versus nurture debate centers on intelligence, heredity, and environment. To find information on the topic, go to the personality project Web site:

http://pmc.psych.nwu.edu/personality.html

Under recommended readings, click on intelligence. After browsing the site, write a report on the role of environment and heredity on IQ.

duce more is a narrow and unsophisticated view of evolutionary theory (McGinn, 2002).

As you will learn in Chapter 13, the nature versus nurture debate is perhaps a false one. Scientists in all disciplines recognize that both ingredients are needed to explain human social behavior, but they differ by discipline in their emphasis on one or the other. Sociologists emphasize that social interaction makes us human, or, stated another way, it humanizes us. Biology (nature) makes us ready for socialization. But the process of social interaction (nurture) activates it. The theoretical perspective of symbolic interactionism clearly illustrates this activation process.

Sociology: Symbolic Interactionism and the Development of the Self

Sociologists and psychologists agree that the **self** is the unique sense of identity that distinguishes each individual from all other individuals. The self is a key element of **personality**, the distinctive complex of attitudes, beliefs, behaviors, and values that makes up an individual. Personality and self come together to form *personal identity*, which gives each individual a sense of separateness and uniqueness. No one else is quite like you.

Whereas psychology highlights the role of personal identity in explaining attitudes and behavior, sociology emphasizes *social identity*, the part of the self that is built up over time through participation in social life (Capozza & Brown, 2000). We derive pleasure from a sense of community, the feeling of belonging and having things in common with others. Your social identity as a college student is celebrated when your school wins a football game. Social identity as a fraternity member is celebrated when your chapter is recognized for its efforts at raising money for charity. When you are a member of a number of groups that overlap and are important to you, social identity is strengthened (Roccas & Brewer, 2001). Since your college life provides many opportunities for such overlapping group memberships—through academics, sports, fraternity, volunteer, and social activities—college has a major influence on the development of the self.

Social identity is linked to what biologists and psychologists say is a human need for affiliation, the desire to seek relationships with others. We suffer great psychological anguish if this need is denied for an extended period. For this reason, solitary confinement is considered the harshest possible punishment for prisoners.

WHAT WE THINK OTHERS THINK OF US The emergence of the self over time in interaction with others is an active process. As children we quickly learn that what others think of us has major consequences on our lives. As a pioneer of the symbolic interactionist perspective, Charles Horton Cooley (1864–1929) provided a major tool for sociology with his concept of the **looking-glass self.** Cooley explained this as the idea that we use other people as a mirror to ourselves. We imagine how others see us and we imagine their judgment of that appearance. Our image of ourselves then develops based on that imagination (Cooley, 1902/1983).

If in class you imagine that your professor sees you as bright, attentive, and interested, and gives you positive signs that reflect that perception, you begin to develop a positive self-view in regard to the academic side of your college life. From the professor's viewpoint, when students stifle yawns or appear bored and disinterested, the professor may question his or her ability to teach effectively and may develop a negative self-view in regard to the academic side of the professor's life. This reality highlights symbolic interactionists' idea that only through interaction can we learn about ourselves and make social comparisons necessary to acquire a sense of self-esteem.

THE IMPORTANCE OF ROLE-TAKING   Perhaps the most influential player in forging the symbolic interactionist perspective and its connection to socialization is George Herbert Mead (1863–1961), who was responsible for a rather simple but important assertion. He maintained that the self is made up of two components. The first, he called the **I,** that aspect of self that is spontaneous, creative, and impulsive, and sometimes unpredictable. It shows itself when feelings of emotion arise—excitement, anger, joy—and you want to express yourself openly. Imagine that you have just received an A in a difficult course and want to share your triumph with others. Yet, in line with

the looking-glass self, symbolic interactionists argue that your behavior is influenced by how you imagine others view you, so you reconsider how to share the accomplishment. Mead called this second aspect of self the **me,** the socialized self that makes you concerned about how others view and judge you. To not appear too boastful, you decide to express your elation over the good grade by bringing it up over coffee in the student center with a close friend. Even in Arab and South American cultures in which bragging about accomplishments is more acceptable, there are limits to how much bragging is tolerated. The *me* helps us control our impulses and allows us to choose our behavior rationally (Mead, 1934). The socialized self helps us think before we act.

Both the *I* and the *me* continually interact to help guide behavior. There are links among all the concepts discussed so far. Mead's *I* is similar to personal identity, and the *me* is similar to social identity. Cooley's idea of the looking-glass self is more closely linked with social identity because it focuses on the development of self based on imagining how others view us—part of being connected rather than being separate. Misinterpretation of such views does not diminish the power of this process. As discussed in Chapter 6, we continually reevaluate and alter our behavior based on social interaction.

This process is a complex one. First, all of these "others" are not the same. We pay more attention to how some people judge us than we do to how others judge us. Those people whose approval and affection we most desire and who are therefore most important to the development of our self-concept are called **significant others.** Parents, for example, are a child's first significant others. Second, not only do we imagine what others think of us, but we imagine what it is like to be in their shoes as well. When we engage in such **role-taking,** we begin to develop empathy for others as well as to increase our social connectedness; role-taking inevitably draws us closer to other people. Another practical benefit of role-taking is that mental rehearsals allow us to anticipate others' behavior. Suppose you want to ask a classmate out on a date. You imagine several possible responses and are therefore prepared to modify your own response according to the one that occurs.

Third, as we mature we recognize that all the separate impressions we have of others and the world we live in eventually form a pattern. By age 12, most children have developed an awareness of the **generalized other**—the ability to understand broader cultural norms and judge what a typical person might think or do. After asking a number of people out on dates, gaining information from friends on their dating successes, and learning about dating norms, you will probably be more successful in

 INTERNET CONNECTIONS

There is a discussion in the text of the contributions of George Herbert Mead and Charles Horton Cooley in the area of social development. To obtain some in-depth articles on what they had to say about social development, go to the Mead project Website:

http://paradigm.soci.brocku.ca/~lward/

and click on Mead and Cooley. After perusing the contents of the Website, write a short description of the contributions of Mead and Cooley.

predicting who will go out with you and whether it is likely to be a satisfying experience. The next potential dating partner becomes a generalized other.

Mead believed that children learn these abilities in stages as they mature and expand their social world. As described below, these stages can also be viewed in relation to other components of socialization.

1. *Preparatory Stage (to about age 3)*. Children interact through imitation but do not understand the meaning of the interaction. They identify significant others, usually their parents, and seek their approval. Rewards and punishment nurture the development of the *I*, but the *me* is forming in the background and with it the grains of a sense of self. All these ingredients are necessary to prepare a child for later role-taking.

2. *Play Stage (about ages 3 to 5)*. Children model others in their play ("I'll be the mommy and you be the daddy"), so they are now moving beyond simple imitation of others to acting out imagined roles, but only one at a time. Significant others become the most important models to imitate. The *me* grows stronger because children are concerned about the judgment of significant others. Language is used more accurately at this stage; it must be mastered in order for a stable sense of self to emerge.

3. *Game Stage (early school years)*. The ability to take on the roles of several people at once emerges along with the generalized other. Complex games such as team sports require this ability. The game stage is developed in school, but its abilities are readily transferred to other real-life situations. Thus children develop the *me* and a relatively stable sense of self (Mead, 1934).

The game stage does not end the process of socialization or the continued development of the self. **Primary socialization,** in which language is learned and the first sense of self is gained, occurs mostly during the early years of life. Later experiences can modify this sense of self. *Continuing socialization* is thus a lifelong process and provides a basis for the later, varied roles individuals are expected to fulfill. Nonetheless, primary socialization puts an indelible mark on a person. Symbolic interactionism emphasizes the social construction of reality and how individuals continually create and re-create it. An illustration is **anticipatory socialization,** in which we practice what we want to achieve, such as excelling in college, being invited to pledge the best fraternity, or landing a good job.

Because socialization is an ongoing process that occurs in an ever-changing social world, other forces are at work that make the process uneven both for individuals and for the categories to which they belong. For example, some evidence suggests that boys advance to the game stage more quickly than do girls. At an earlier age boys play games, such as kickball, that have more participants and are more complex, competitive, and rule-governed than games played by girls (Lever, 1978; Benenson et al., 2001). Girls play ordered games like hopscotch and jump-rope, taking up less space than boy's games, in groups of two or three, which tend to minimize competitiveness (Lansford & Parker, 1999; Kelle, 2000). Through the games they play, boys may learn role-taking associated with a generalized other sooner than do girls. Yet this learning process may have negative effects for *both* girls and boys. Compared with the games of young girls, the games of young boys provide earlier guidelines that are helpful for success later in life, such as the importance of striving for individual excellence through competition, as emphasized in American culture. However, boys may be at a disadvantage because it takes them longer to learn values such as cooperation and intimacy, which are essential to interpersonal and economic success.

Psychology: Socialization as Crisis

Psychology contributes a great deal to our understanding of socialization, and certain psychological theories help clarify sociological thought on the topic. Symbolic interactionism views socialization as a normal process that is not particularly stressful. People may move through its various stages at different rates and still end up as fully functioning members of society. But most psychological theories acknowledge that while people eventually learn what they need to learn, the process itself creates inner conflict. Socialization is marked by a series of predictable crises that must be resolved in order for people to have a productive and successful life.

PSYCHOSEXUAL DEVELOPMENT The work of Sigmund Freud (1856–1939) has had a profound impact on the social sciences. According to Freud, humans have basic biological needs or drives that conflict with one another. Biology is an important part of human behavior, but unlike animals, who exist solely on inborn traits, humans have only a few general (but powerful) instinctive forces. Freud's model of personality is built around this clash of forces (Freud, 1961, 1963).

The model has three parts. The **id** is Freud's term for an individual's biological drives and impulses; the id is selfish, irrational, ever-striving for pleasure and gratification, and it is unconscious. The id is not necessarily antisocial as much as it is nonsocial; it has no regard for anyone or anything but pleasure and gratification. Newborns are totally id-driven, as are some adults who were isolated or abused as children or who are developmentally disabled. Others may have the capacity for learning but may not have

Freud believed that biological drives related to sexual attraction are kept in check by social norms. Dancing is an activity that allows some sexual expression but in a socially acceptable way.

developed a capacity for language. Helen Keller, for example, blind and deaf from infancy, could be said to be id-driven until she was able to grasp the idea of language. Until then she lived in a world of wordless sensation, made up only of attempts to remove any feelings of discomfort.

Since parents must inevitably begin to say "no" to young children, the unsocialized drives propelled by the id come into conflict with another part of the personality, the **superego.** This is Freud's term for all the norms, values, and morals that are learned through socialization. Essentially, these form the demands of society and are internalized as a person's conscience. For successful socialization, the id must be controlled, and it is the task of the superego to do so. Since pleasure and gratification are always lurking in the unconscious, the road to the socialized personality is not an easy one. The third part of the personality, the **ego,** acts as a mediator between the biological drives and the society that would deny them. The ego is largely conscious and reality-based, which means it provides rational plans to get what the individual wants, but in a socially acceptable way (Freud, 1961).

Freud was particularly concerned about the impact of the sex drive on the mediation process. His five stages of psychosexual development (see Table 5.1) revolve around attempts to satisfy id-driven sexual needs. He believed that even very young children experience sex-related pleasure, an idea that was quite scandalous in the Victorian era when he lived.

Of Freud's five stages of psychosexual development, the one that has received the most attention is the *phallic stage*, especially as it relates to gender socialization. At age 3 to 5, children focus gratification on the genitals (the clitoris for the girl and the penis for the boy), and masturbation and sexual curiosity increase for both sexes. According to Freud, girls come to believe that the penis, unlike the barely noticeable clitoris, is a symbol of power denied to them. Freud argued that the result is *penis envy*, which culminates in a girl's wish that she could be a boy (Freud, 1962). She views her mother as inferior because she, too, does not have a penis. The girl's *libido*, or sexual energy, is transferred to the father, who becomes the love-object. Later writers called this experience the *Electra complex*. The resolution occurs when the girl's wish for a penis is replaced by the wish for a child. A male child is even more desirable than a female because he brings the longed-for penis with him.

A boy also experiences conflict during the phallic stage, when his libido is focused on his mother, and his father is the rival for his mother's affections. Freud called this experience the *Oedipus complex*. When a boy discovers that a girl does not have a penis, he develops castration anxiety, according to Freud. The psychic turmoil a boy experiences during this stage leads to the development of a strong superego. Freud believed that girls have weaker superegos, since the resolution of the Electra complex occurs with envy rather than fear.

TABLE 5.1

Sigmund Freud's Stages of Psychosexual Development

Stage	Age	Description	Crisis to Resolve
Oral	0–1	Infants gain pleasure through the mouth. Feeding and sucking are key activities. Dependency and trust begin.	Weaning must not occur too early or too late or child may become a hostile, mistrustful, or gullible dependent adult.
Anal	2–3	Toilet training occurs. Child tests independence and is developing a sense of self.	Child must learn to control a biological urge. Either too much anxiety or not enough parental control can create a compulsively clean or overly messy adult.
Phallic	3–5	Feeling of sexual attraction toward same-sex parent occurs. Pleasure is transferred to genitals. Masturbation is common. Superego develops.	Boys must resolve castration anxiety and girls must resolve penis envy.
Latency	6–11	Gender identity develops. Boys and girls seem to ignore one another and sexual needs. Biological urges are lurking in the background.	Child focuses on learning skills and confronting issues to become a productive member of society.
Genital	Adolescence	Puberty occurs, focus is again on genitals. Normal interest in other sex develops.	Need to control sexual stirrings. Search for love and a marriage partner.

CRITIQUE The sexism in Freudian theory is obvious, even though its unfortunate effects concerning the idea of female inferiority far exceeded the intentions of Freud himself (Millett, 1995:61). He wrote during a period that embraced strict gender differentiation based on traditional roles for men and women in a patriarchal world. Freud was severely criticized for his ideas about infantile sexuality and the psychosexual stages of development but gained quiet acceptance for his comments on the biologically inferior design of females. However, feminist scholars do recognize that Freud's ideas give some insight into the way in which gender role socialization is also a power process. Freud offers a way of viewing domination not so much as a problem of human nature, but as one of human relationships (Benjamin, 1988:5).

Many of Freud's concepts are so well known that even though most remain as untestable assumptions, people typically use Freudian terms in describing others. How many times have you heard someone described as having a big ego, being anal-retentive, or being stuck in the oral stage? These expressions are examples of "pop-Freud." Even with Freud's insistence that social interaction is necessary for socialization, the "nature" side of the nature–nurture debate is given more weight in the media than scientific evidence suggests.

SOCIAL LEARNING THEORY Unlike Freud's psychoanalytic approach, which focuses on powerful biological drives and internal conflict, social learning theory focuses on observable behavior. The key idea is that behavior is shaped by early experiences. Once behavior is learned, it becomes habitual. Socialization is considered in terms of reinforcing appropriate behavior or extinguishing inappropriate behavior through the use of rewards and punishments. Specifically, social learning theory is concerned with the ways children model the behaviors they view in others, such as cooperation and sharing or selfishness and aggression. At first, imitation and modeling are spontaneous in children, but patterns of behavior develop through reinforcement.

As with other behaviors, gender roles are learned directly, through reprimands and rewards, and indirectly, through observation and imitation (Bandura & Walters, 1963; Mischel, 1966). The logic is simple. In gender role socialization, there is differential reinforcement for doing either "boy" or "girl" things. For example, a boy is praised by his peers for changing a flat tire but laughed at for playing with dolls. A girl is praised by her peers for knitting a sweater but laughed at for playing with toy soldiers in the mud.

Children associate the label of boy or girl with the rewards that come with the appropriate behavior. This association is the basis for gender identity. Children develop **gender identity** when they become aware that the two sexes (male and female) behave differently and that two different gender roles (masculine and feminine) are proper. Once we develop our gender identity, we perceive ourselves as either male or female. We then act out gender roles according to that perception. As parents and teachers model gender roles during the critical primary socialization years, children imitate accordingly. Continued reinforcement of the valued gender identity results.

According to social learning theory, gender-appropriate behavior is strongly associated with social approval for both genders. For males, masculine gender roles are more inflexible than those offered to females. Social learning theorists suggest that gender role inflexibility is a critical factor that makes male socialization difficult. For females, the socialization path is also difficult, but for a different reason. Even young children are bombarded by messages indicating that higher worth, prestige, and rewards are accorded to males than to females. Gender expectations lead to a preference for characteristic male behavior. Girls are offered subordinate roles that encourage deference and dependence (Geis, 1993). If modeling and reinforcement are as compelling enticements to behavior as social learning theory suggests, a girl could understandably become quite anxious when she must perform roles held in lower esteem. For socialization overall, girls have the advantage in gender role flexibility, but boys have the advantage in higher prestige associated with their gender role.

CRITIQUE Social learning theory provides a foundation for explaining much research on socialization, especially when it is combined with a symbolic interactionist perspective emphasizing the importance of role-taking. Role-taking allows opportunities for behavior to be rewarded or punished; it also allows behavior to be imitated. But reinforcement and modeling are more complex than social learning theory proposes for two important reasons. First, children may not model same-gender parents or may choose other-gender models outside the family (Lott & Maluso, 1993). Second, children model their parents, but parents also model their children. Parents often use their children as barometers of changing gender roles. Social learning theory minimizes the importance of social change as well as a child's ability to choose behavior. And regardless of the differences, both girls and boys learn to prefer their own sex and the gender roles associated with it. Other theoretical views help explain why.

COGNITIVE DEVELOPMENT Jean Piaget (1896–1980) was interested in how children gradually develop intelligence, thinking, and reasoning. His work is consistent with symbolic interactionism in two important ways. First, he starts with the idea that cognitive abilities are developed in stages through ongoing social interaction. Second, behavior depends on how a person perceives a social situation. Social learning theory suggests that children are passive learners who behave according to the stimuli presented to them. Cognitive theory stresses a child's active role in structuring and interpreting the world.

The child's level of understanding of the world varies with the stage of cognitive development (see Table 5.2). In the first, *sensorimotor stage*, infants learn their world through sight, sound, and touch. They begin to form attachments to parents or other caretakers. **Schema,** cognitive structures used to understand the world and process new information, begin to be formed. By the time children reach age 2, Piaget's *preoperational stage*, they begin to use pretending and imaginary play. Since the preoperational stage occurs during early childhood, most children are not yet capable of creating many new schema, so they tend to rely on those they have already developed.

Sociologists are particularly interested in the latter two stages of cognitive development, when new schema are developed more rapidly. From age 7 to 11, a time Piaget refers to as the *concrete operational stage*, children have developed a range of schema to classify material. They begin to use logic and reasoning to solve problems, and their mental images of the world become more complex. According to Piaget, the capacity for abstract reasoning develops at around age 12, a time he calls the *formal operational stage*. Adolescents at this stage can consider several alternative solutions to problems and can imagine a number of abstract possibilities. Since the mind matures through interaction with the environment, each stage of cognitive development provides necessary tools for proceeding to the next stage (Piaget, 1950; Piaget & Inhelder, 1969).

Social learning theory suggests that children model the behavior of others. The way parents act out aggression according to gender roles will be acted out similarly by their children.

TABLE 5.2

Stages of Cognitive and Moral Development

Jean Piaget: Cognitive Development

Sensorimotor (0–2 years)
Infants explore their world through their senses and motor activities: They touch, hear, smell, grasp, suck, and shake objects. Object permanence and emotional attachment to a few important people form.

Preoperational (2–7 years)
Children learn language to represent objects and begin to use pretending and thinking about things they cannot see. They are egocentric (self-centered) at this stage, seeing things only from their own perspective.

Concrete operational (7–11 years)
Logical reasoning develops, but is very concrete and linked to objects they can see. They learn to add and subtract and figure out the principle of conservation—physical properties of objects (weight, volume) are the same (conserved) even if appearance (form, shape) changes.

Formal operational (12 years to adult)
Abstract thinking develops. Concepts are manipulated and problem solving is thought out in advance. Historical time can be fully understood. Adolescents are cognitively *capable* of such thinking, but some adults do not become fully formally operational.

Lawrence Kohlberg: Moral Development

Preconventional (beginning at about age 7)
Moral reasoning develops based on meeting personal motives to obtain rewards or avoid punishment.

Conventional (about age 10 to adolescence)
Moral dilemmas are resolved by established social convention, the law, or other sources of authority. Social approval for moral behavior is sought.

Postconventional (adulthood)
Morality is linked to universal ethical principles—equality, justice, reciprocal rights and responsibilities—that may transcend authority. Conscience may override law. Some adults do not advance to the postconventional level.

Building on the work of Piaget, Lawrence Kohlberg (1969, 1981) surveyed the responses of people who were confronted with moral dilemmas they were asked to resolve. Kohlberg suggests that like cognitive ability, moral development also occurs in stages (see Table 5.2). To determine which stage of moral development a person is in, a scenario is presented to subjects involving a dying woman whose husband cannot afford a life-saving drug and a pharmacist who refuses to sell it at lower cost or let the husband pay for it later. The husband breaks into the pharmacy and steals the drug. According to Kohlberg, adolescents are at the *conventional stage* of moral development. They are likely to take a "law and order" view of the world, condemn the husband's actions, and believe that moral behavior is what is approved and necessary for the broader social good. Kohlberg's conventional stage of moral development corresponds to the start of Piaget's formal operational stage of cognitive development. Individuals need to achieve a certain level of cognitive development before they reach an advanced level of moral development.

According to Kohlberg (1966), children also learn their gender roles according to their level of cognitive development. One of the first ways a child organizes reality is through the self, a highly valued part of the child's existence. Anything associated with the self becomes highly valued as well. By age 3, children begin to self-identify by gender and accurately apply gender-related labels to themselves and often to others. By age 6, a girl knows she is a girl and will remain one. Only then, Kohlberg asserts, is gender identity said to be developed. Gender identity becomes a central part of self, invested with strong emotional attachment (Martin, 2000).

Once gender identity is developed, much behavior is organized around it. Children seek models that are labeled as girl or boy and female or male. While children base much of their behavior on reinforcement, cognitive theorists see a different sequence in gender socialization than do social learning theorists. This sequence is "I am a boy, therefore I want to do boy things, therefore the opportunity to do boy things (and to gain approval for doing them) is rewarding" (Kohlberg, 1966:89). Reinforcements are important, but the child chooses behavior and roles according to the sense of self (Serbin et al., 1993).

Gender schema theory, an important offshoot of cognitive development theory, suggests that once the child learns cultural definitions of gender, these schema become the core around which all other information is organized (Bem, 1981, 1983). The schema tell children what they can and cannot do according to their gender. They affect their behavior and influence their self-esteem. An individual's adequacy as a person is linked to how closely his or her behavior matches accepted gender schema. The influence of gender schema may help explain why it is so difficult to dislodge gender stereotypical thinking.

There is fairly wide support for the cognitive development approach to gender role socialization. Research consistently finds that children's choices, interests, and activities—such as play, toys, and friendships—are made according to beliefs about gender compatibility (Caygill et al., 2002; Martin & Dinella, 2002; Monsour, 2002). Children, especially boys, begin to value their own sex (gender) more than the other and believe theirs is superior to the other. As age increases, there is an increasing agreement with adult gender role stereotypes (Liben et al., 2001; Egan & Perry, 2001; Tenenbaum & Leaper, 2002). This research suggests that early in life children develop the ability to classify characteristics by gender and choose behavior according to that classification.

CRITIQUE The cognitive development model overall has been criticized on several grounds. First, it cannot account for all of gender role socialization. Second, it is difficult to test what comes first, gender identity or the child's understanding of gender constancy (that he or she will remain either a boy or girl) (Intons-Peterson, 1988:44). For the model to fit neatly with the stages outlined in cognitive development, gender identity must come first. To date, research has been unable to confirm this sequence.

More damaging to the legitimacy of Kohlberg's work is the fact that he used exclusively male subjects; generalizing the results to females is not warranted. Carol Gilligan (1982) presented the moral dilemma scenario in a modified form to girls and boys of the same age and social class. Gilligan found that when informed choices must be made and no clear-cut answers are suggested, moral reasoning differs by gender: Boys are more likely to choose on the basis of the norm of justice (people meet the needs of others because they deserve it), and girls are more likely to choose according to the norm of social responsibility, also called the *care ethic* (people should help those who are dependent on them, regardless of how the needs came about). Both norms are activated at the final stage of moral development, where morality is linked to ethical principles that may supersede the law.

The claim that men predominantly follow the justice norms and women the care norm is not as strongly supported today (Jaffee & Hyde, 2000). When controlling for social class, for example, a study of moral dilemma in dating situations shows that both male and female seventh graders respond generally according to the justice norm. The same study shows, however, that girls but not boys combine justice and care in their responses, regardless of social class (Weisz & Black, 2002). Women may be using both norms more because they seek economic self-sufficiency at the same time are largely responsible of caring for others independent of their paid work roles (Gerson, 2002).

Although the differences between the genders may be lessening in some situations, the key claims of Gilligan are still supported from both the psychological and sociological viewpoints: Men do not have "higher" levels of moral reasoning compared to women, and women have fewer personal boundaries in their understanding of morality, whereas men remain abstract and detached. Both men and women

Gender schema theory suggests that children match their behavior to their gender identity, such as boys choosing trucks and girls choosing dolls for toys.

THEN AND NOW

Childhood as Innocence or as a World of Little Adults

A legislator in Texas recently proposed that the death penalty be extended to 11-year-olds. According to this view, young children have advanced from being schoolyard bullies to being murderers. If they act like adults, they should be treated like adults. Childhood, after all, is a modern invention.

For centuries, children around the world were treated as little adults by the time they reached age 7 or 8. A close look at medieval paintings shows children depicted as little adults in costume and expression. The art, language, and literature of the times gave little thought to children. Toys and games were not designed for children, but to be used by people of all ages. Age as an indicator of personal identity did not exist. Age was not even recorded in family and civil records. Through the 19th century, children were expected to participate in the economic life of their families, whether it was working in the field, the home, or the factory.

The idea that children have a unique nature separate and different from that of adults was ushered in with the Enlightenment in the 17th century. A century later, the belief that childhood should be a period of innocence, and that children should be spared as long as possible from the turmoil faced by adults, became entrenched in the Western world. In the United States the belief in childhood innocence probably reached its peak at the beginning of the 20th century. It was

during this period that child labor laws, universal education, and juvenile justice systems were put into place. With new theories of childhood development to draw on, families and schools would guide the innocent child into adolescence and productive adulthood.

At the beginning of the new century, the clock may be turning backwards. Children today are under tremendous pressure to show off their accomplishments as soon as possible. Childhood is associated with day care, preschool, and latchkey homes where peers rather than adults exert powerful influences. The media have also reshaped childhood identity. The medieval portraits of children as little adults are showing up again as sexualized images of younger and younger children in ads for cologne and underwear. We are haunted by the image of murdered 6-year-old Jon Benét Ramsey in her showgirl costume and resplendent makeup. Virtually every state now has laws allowing 14-year-olds to be tried and sentenced as adults. For the death penalty to be carried out, some states do suggest waiting until the felon reaches age 18 or 21.

Throughout history, children were included in the world of adults in both knowledge and practice. Fueled by media, today they are excluded from adult practices but not from adult knowledge. Children know about violence, sex, drugs, and AIDS. The television shows most popular with children, such as

South Park and *The Simpsons,* are replete with wisecracking and foul-mouthed elementary and high-school students. Third graders worry about attractiveness and dating. Seventh graders worry about getting into medical school. Because of the sheer number of activities parents feel their children need to participate in to be successful as adults, children's lives have become stressed and overscheduled. Youthful innocence, if it occurred at all, is a hallmark only of the 20th century. Experts in child development suggest that a rich sense of adulthood depends on the play of childhood. The question is how socialization can be balanced to account for the blurring of childhood and adulthood, sometimes referred to as "kidult culture." By viewing the history of childhood, symbolic interactionists point out that childhood is as much a social construction as it is a biological one. Childhood is not destined to end, but a different kind of childhood is on the horizon.

1. How can parents help their children prepare for adult roles that are now demanded at an earlier age, but still allow them to experience the freedom associated with childhood?

2. At what age(s) did you realize that adulthood was looming? Do you believe your own childhood socialization adequately set the stage for your current roles?

Sources: Aries, 1962; Graff, 1995; Applebome, 1998; Steinberg & Kincheloe, 1998; Katrowitz et al., 2001; Seaford, 2001.

have the potential of understanding each other's views, but gender role socialization restricts that potential becoming actualized in behavior (Gump et al., 2000; Mitchell, 2002; Tagney & Dearing, 2002; Weisz & Black, 2002). Claims of moral superiority become ingrained in scientific theories of human development because the theories were constructed without diversity in mind and failed to account for the lived experiences of the people they were supposed to represent (Jaffee & Hyde, 2000). Different moral

choices need to be traced to the key influence of gender socialization and then to other influences, such as race and social class.

Gender schema theory may provide the best way to explain how people develop gender identities. It also bridges the gap between psychological and sociological approaches, because it assumes that as people interact with their environments, they actively construct mental structures (schema) to represent their awareness of the events around them

(Intons-Peterson, 1988:48). Other schema can also be identified, such as those based on age, ethnicity, or religion. These ideas are at the core of symbolic interactionism and provide a good intersection for sociological and psychological research on socialization.

SOCIALIZATION AND THE LIFE COURSE: CONNECTING SOCIOLOGY AND PSYCHOLOGY

The **life course** perspective of socialization is another strong link between psychology and sociology for several reasons. First, this view considers the roles people play over a lifetime and the ages associated with those roles. It stresses the importance of continuing socialization and the varied paths individuals take due to individual experiences as well as to broader social change. Whereas both Freud and Mead focused on primary socialization, the life course view argues that all stages of life are important for personality development, self, and identity (Owens, 2000; Pulkkinen & Caspi, 2002). Second, because the life course is broken down into a number of separate stages, a range of research can be incorporated into the various stages, using age as the key variable.

Third, along with age, the life course view accounts for attitudes and behavior influenced by one's **birth cohort,** all the people born at a given period of time who age together and experience events in history as a group. When people live through events or time periods that become historically significant, their perception of the world is affected. Some research shows that personality is also influenced by cohort effects (Twenge, 2002). A birth cohort is made up of individuals in an age group. But they are linked together in a *generation* when they develop a shared consciousness about powerful historical events. The birth cohort born during the 1920s focuses on their experiences during the Great Depression and World War II. For Americans, the Baby Boomers born during the 1950s vividly recall President John F. Kennedy's assassination as well as Woodstock, hippies, and the Vietnam War protests. Until September 11, the Generation X birth cohort born mentioned in the vignette as well as "Generations Next," current high-school and college-aged students, would have had difficulty identifying life-changing historical events that linked them together as a "true" generation. Evidence suggests, however, that Generation X is transforming itself from the Me generation to the "We" generation (Schanberg, 2002). Interest in careers related to social justice in nonprofit agencies and government-related services, such as Americorps and Peace Corps, homeland security, and diplomacy, has

skyrocketed for college students and recent graduates. Many Gen Xers in the first decade of their careers say they are seriously considering changing career paths in light of September 11 (Brooks, 2001; Hawn, 2001; Kantrowitz & Naughton, 2001).

Finally, while psychology provides the springboard into life course explanations, sociology provides the link between micro and macro perspectives. The intersection between a birth cohort and a generation is a good example of such a link. In this way, then, a new *sociological psychology* emerges. It is through such interdisciplinary links that the best theories of human social behavior are built.

Psychosocial Development

Freud's work is the foundation of Erik Erikson's (1902–1994) view of development. Like Freud, Erikson believed that early childhood experiences are important for personality development and that socialization is marked by crises in which conflict between the individual and society must be resolved. Unlike Freud, Erikson argued that culture rather than biology plays the biggest part in socialization. Also unlike Freud, Erikson argued that later life experiences that come with continuing socialization can significantly alter personality (Erikson, 1963).

Erikson proposed eight life stages that all people must go through from infancy to old age. The stages are called "psychosocial" by Erikson because they reflect both the psychological and social challenges everyone faces during the life course. Each stage is marked by a crisis (see Table 5.3). For example, during the first year of life, the crisis of *trust versus mistrust* occurs. This is the stage in which infants depend on others for basic physical and emotional needs. When parents are warm, nurturing, and responsive, infants develop confidence or trust that their needs will be met—a trust that is extended throughout their lives. While these crises imply that stresspoints are normal throughout life, they are not necessarily filled with turmoil. They represent turning points where different roads may be taken. And since they do not occur suddenly, people can use anticipatory socialization to help them in their choices. Erikson's theory of socialization is similar to symbolic interactionism in that behavior is consciously chosen and influenced by significant others.

If children learn to trust others during infancy, and that sense of trust is nurtured throughout the next life stages, by puberty they should be better prepared to deal with one of the most stressful times in their lives—the adolescent identity crisis. Between about ages 13 and 19, Erikson believed, adolescents must confront the challenge of creating a sense of personal identity. Referred to as *identity versus role*

TABLE 5.3

Erik Erikson's Stages of Psychosocial Development

Stage	Age	Crisis to Resolve
Infancy	0–1	*Trust vs. Mistrust* Infants depend on others and learn to trust that their needs will be met; otherwise they become fearful, mistrusting their environment.
Toddler	2–3	*Autonomy vs. Shame or Doubt* Children learn to do things on their own and control their behavior. Encouragement and consistent discipline builds self-esteem and protects them from shame and humiliation.
Early childhood	3–5	*Initiative vs. Guilt* Exploration, role-playing, and inquisitiveness are invited by parents; if not, children feel guilty when they initiate new behaviors.
Elementary school	6–12	*Industry vs. Inferiority* Children need recognition in school and at home for achievements and support for failures; otherwise feelings of inadequacy result.
Adolescence	13–19	*Identity vs. Role Confusion* Young people deal with sexual maturity and impending adult roles. They must integrate previous experiences to develop a sense of personal identity. Without an identity compatible with who they believe they are, role confusion occurs. They act in ways to please others but not themselves.
Young adulthood	20–40	*Intimacy vs. Isolation* A strong personal identity helps develop the intimacy needed for commitment to others, such as a spouse; otherwise a person can become lonely and isolated.
Middle adulthood	40–65	*Generativity vs. Stagnation* Career, marriage, and children are central. Contributions to the next generation occur. Value is placed on what he/she is doing for others; otherwise, a person is resigned, unproductive, and may feel worthless.
Late adulthood/ old age	65 and over	*Integrity vs. Despair* A life review finds meaning or lack of it in accomplishments. Was life worthwhile or full of disappointments and failure?

---

confusion, much of the focus of Erikson's work has been on this stage.

Puberty transforms the child into an adult in the sexual sense, but social roles during this stage are not so transformed. As explained in Chapter 4, all roles include both privileges and obligations. Regardless of biological maturity, these "new adults" find that childhood obligations far outweigh adult privileges. This realization results in role confusion until a stable ego-identity can be formed. The following account of a 16-year-old's memories of this time of life illustrates the turmoil:

I was losing myself. The ground, once so firm beneath my feet, quivered. . . . And then I met the abyss, where my own name and possessions became strangers, unfamiliar baggage in this formless place. But this very abyss, where all was lost, somehow, somewhere gave rise to what I now dare call "me." (Kroger, 1996:174)

There is no roadmap to matters of maturing (Kroger, 1996). Yet social resistance is high when teens experiment with new roles, especially if the roles are associated with rebellion against established norms and a focus on peers rather than on parents or teachers as confidants and role models. If parents and teens can maintain close emotional ties during this time, adolescent self-esteem is bolstered. Research shows that enhanced self-esteem during adolescence carries through to adulthood (Roberts & Bengston, 1996). This finding supports Erikson's idea that a successful resolution of the identity crisis has long-term positive effects.

Today sociologists have turned attention to applying Erikson's model to later life. Adulthood ushers in *maturity*, not simply in terms of age but in terms of emotional readiness to deal with the next stages of life. Maturity is an honest appraisal of one's own experience and the ability to use that knowledge caringly in relationship to one's self and others (Hoare, 2002). For sociology, although maturity is a necessary factor, social roles and social institutions take center stage in explaining transitions throughout the life course. As people move through the life course, continuing socialization occurs. Erikson's work serves as a vital sociological link in understanding this process.

The Sociology of Adult Development and Aging

Life is an ongoing process of development, socialization, and adaptation. Personality is important in determining how we adapt to the different stages of life. Our personality gives us an overall direction when choices for behavior arise. People do not undergo sudden personality shifts in confronting new or stressful situations. They do not lose their capacity to learn or change; this capacity is at the core of adult development (Atchley, 2000:121). The sociology of adult development looks at how people adapt to ongoing role changes, especially those associated with age roles and age norms.

EARLY ADULTHOOD   Young adults, those between the ages of about 18 and 22 and who are also in college, confront a later version of role confusion than that occurring in adolescence. Sometimes referred to as boys and girls, at other times as men and women, even among themselves, the confusion associated with the status of college student underscores that in the United States there is no single identified marker between being a minor and being an adult. Being able to vote at age 18 and consume alcohol legally at age 21 suggest adulthood. But for full-time students living away from home, college is also described as "never-never" land—a semiprotected, artificial world shielding its inhabitants from the responsibilities as well as the privileges of full adulthood. First-year students

are honored for being on their own, and professors confirm adult status. But these same messages can be experienced as abandonment and a refusal to care.

Clearly, these young adults are not children, but they do not yet fit various criteria for defining adulthood, such as financial independence or emotional readiness for marriage and family. New experiences bring about both stability and change in personality traits for young adults (Robins & Roberts, 2001). In college, personality is in a state of flux—the newer one based on the college experience has yet to form, but the messages from the older one of high school are still in place. Colleges report major increases in demands for therapeutic services for students over the last decade. The typical concerns about leaving home, getting good grades, and career preparation are complicated by economic uncertainty, information overload, too many rather than too few choices, family breakup, and the events of September 11 (Glover, 2000; Berger, 2002). The increased suicide rate of college students, concerns over campus drinking and drug use, and fears of lawsuits are bringing together parents, college administrators, and even students—all who desire more supervision over college life (Bronner, 1999; Furr et al., 2001; Sontag, 2002). The in-between world of adolescence and adulthood ends at graduation. College graduation terminates the student role, not just for the previous four years, but for the previous 16 years, and brings with it the yawning "abyss of freedom" (Gutmann, 2002:32). Seniors often express gladness, sadness, and anxiety in what they see as extraordinary changes in post-college life.

Beginning at about age 20, the phases of adulthood can be marked according to age-related norms. This assumes that there is an accepted sequence of events and life activities appropriate for each age. The pattern in the United States is for early adulthood to include the completion of formal schooling, marriage,

People in a birth cohort frequently come together in social movements to express concerns over social issues. Like the Baby Boomers before them who protested the Vietnam War and fueled the feminist and civil rights movements, these young adults protesting at the World Economic Forum are the core birth cohorts who are leading the environmental, economic, and social justice movements.

raising children, and becoming established in a career. Because the career commitment of women is severely compromised by their roles as wife and mother, they are often caught in an age and gender norm dilemma: Early adulthood is a time when raising a family and establishing a career occur simultaneously, and both are desired (Kirkpatrick, 2001). A typical resolution of the work–family dilemma—or crisis, in Erikson's words—is that women, regardless of race or ethnicity, end careers, put them on hold, or change directions (Brown, 2002; Mennino & Brayfield, 2002; Veiga et al., 2002). Whether the resolution is successful depends on the woman's long-term self-esteem and the couple's marital satisfaction level.

MIDDLE ADULTHOOD Middle adulthood, ages 40 to 60, is marked by the last children leaving home and the birth of the first grandchildren, increased career commitment, and planning for retirement. This phase also heightens concern for maintaining health as the first signs of physical aging, such as gray hair and the need for reading glasses, become noticeable.

Gender role–related crises that occur during middle adulthood may affect men and women differently. For women, the moderate to severe depression that supposedly occurs when the last child is launched, or moves away from home, is referred to as the *empty nest syndrome*. Research shows, however, that the empty nest syndrome is largely a myth. Contrary to the stereotype, most women experience an upturn in life satisfaction and psychological well-being when children are launched (West, 2000; Dennerstein et al., 2002). Most women look to the "empty nest" stage of life as offering opportunities to engage in activities that might have been put on hold during child raising. They generally seek expanded roles in a society increasingly receptive to women like themselves, who are venturing outside the traditional confines of the home. Reduced work and parental responsibilities help explain increased marital satisfaction in later life for white, African American, and Mexican American couples (Mackey & O'Brien, 1999; Zuker, 2001). The empty nest is something that parents look forward to.

Professionals have debated the idea that men experience a midlife crisis with physical and emotional symptoms, such as night fears, drenching sweat and chills, and depression. The psychological and social turmoil associated with these symptoms are often linked to hormonal changes, such as a drop in testosterone level (Fischman, 2001). Gender scripts linking masculinity to sexual performance create a fear of impotence, which may come true not because of hormones but because of the fear itself (the massive sales of Viagra, the drug that enhances the sexual performance of men, may be linked to this fear). Thus, biological changes must be seen in the light of social and psychological factors (White, 1998).

The debate continues over whether midlife is an unsettling transition or a normal, even healthy stage of life that allows people the opportunity to make choices and life changes. According to Daniel Levinson (1978, 1986), a wide variety of issues confront adults at this stage, with career and family taking precedence. For both men and women, the relationships that emerge inside and outside the family and the changes that occur shape every aspect of a person's life. Socialization continues, along with the reestablishment or renewal of self-concept (Sheehy, 1976; Edeslstein, 1999; Hermans & Oles, 1999). Midlife is a time for re-evaluation. Decisions made at this stage strongly influence the rest of life .

LATER ADULTHOOD AND OLD AGE Later adulthood marks the beginning of the last stage of life, that of old age. In the developed world, 60 to 65 is usually the age marker of this stage. Of course, old age is as much personal and cultural as it is biological. Unlike other phases of adulthood, transition to old age is often noted by formal **rites of passage**—a retirement dinner, a gold watch, or a special birthday celebration.

As with other stages of life, adaptations to old age are based on earlier patterns, but there are some important differences. First, old age for most people is now the longest stage of life, lasting an average of thirty years. These years can be subdivided into phases with certain features in common. Research on the "young" elderly (age 65–75), for example, shows high levels of life satisfaction and activity. The "middle" elderly (age 75–85) experience more physical slowdown and loss of some activities. But the majority of both these groups live independently. Only about 5 percent of those over age 65 live permanently in long-term care facilities. As would be expected, the oldest old, 85+, are the most likely to require such care (Chapter 14).

These phases highlight another important difference compared with earlier life: The path of old age needs much more exploration. We know a lot about children and teenagers, less about adults at middle age, and the least about the elderly. It is clear that many elderly are reshaping their personal identities in their old age but are themselves confused about issues related to age. This confusion is expressed by "Daphne," in her mid-70s, who received her Ph.D. at 70:

> I'm in the later years. But I'm still young in many ways . . . women my age are withdrawing, but I'm not. I don't consider myself old, although I know I am old. (Cited in Sadler, 2000:189–90)

The exploding field of *gerontology*, the scientific study of aging with a focus on the elderly population, is remedying this situation, offering new data and insights on people entering later years of life (see Chapter 14). Already, data suggest that the last stage

Adulthood is marked differently in different cultures. In the United States, voting is one marker.

of life is associated for most people with productivity and activity rather than depression and dependency (Morrow-Howell et al., 2001).

However, a key feature does distinguish this stage from previous ones: role loss rather than role entry. Although mental decline is not the rule, loss of physical strength, especially among the oldest old, means that fundamental lifestyle changes are on the horizon. Life is stretching out behind rather than in front.

Although there is some slowdown, most elderly people have active lifestyles and high levels of life satisfaction.

SOCIALIZATION INTO DEATH AND DYING The stage of dying is mostly associated with the final stage of old age. In societies with high life expectancy, there is less of an ongoing connection between life and death. People usually do not experience the death of a loved one until they are young adults. Coupled with physicians trained to consider any death as failure, death denial is the norm (Seymour, 2001). With medical technology keeping people physically alive for extended periods of time, societies such as the United States, Britain, and Japan are both death-denying and death-defying (MacLeod & Potter, 2001; Clark, 2002; Sasaki et al., 2002).

At middle age, people experience the first real physical declines associated with aging. It is also the time when most confront the loss of parents. These become the personally significant ways in which people are socialized into death. Among the elderly, the reality of death becomes a fact of life.

The dying process itself has been extensively studied through the pioneering research of Elisabeth Kübler-Ross (1969). Through interviews with many terminally ill people, she determined a pattern, or series of stages, that people go through when they are dying. Like a life course, there is a death course. The sequence of stages is as follows:

1. *Denial.* People who are told they have a terminal illness experience shock and disbelief. Aside from the personal horror of the news, in a death-denying society this is clearly a logical response.
2. *Anger.* Individuals express hostility and resentment, often toward others who will live on. "Why me?" they ask, with a strong sense of injustice.
3. *Bargaining.* Bargains are made, usually with God. "I will be a better person if only I can live, so please spare me."

GLOBAL CONNECTIONS

Planning for Death in the Netherlands

It appears from the results of the study that intravenous administration of thiopental followed by a muscle relaxant is the most reliable route for producing euthanasia.

The quote above is from a study conducted by the Royal Dutch Society for the Advancement of Pharmacy that determined the best drugs to administer to a dying patient so that death is painless and quick. The Netherlands (Holland) is the only country in the world where euthanasia, assisted suicide by a doctor, is legal. Dutch law protects doctors practicing euthanasia who follow official guidelines. Doctors will not be prosecuted if they meet the following requirements for euthanasia set by the Royal Dutch Medical Association:

1. The patient makes a repeated, voluntary request to die.
2. The request must be explicit, well informed, strong, and enduring.
3. The patient is in unacceptable suffering with no prospect for relief.
4. All other options for care have been exhausted or refused by the patient.
5. Euthanasia is administered by a physician.
6. The physician has consulted a colleague who agrees with the proposed euthanasia.

How many people choose euthanasia in the Netherlands? The answer depends on how euthanasia is defined and how the death is reported. Assisted suicide is called active euthanasia. When life support or extraordinary forms of treatment are withdrawn, passive euthanasia occurs. Between 5 and 10 percent of Holland's population are thought to end their lives by this practice, commonly reported as cardiac arrest.

Since death by euthanasia is culturally permissible and guided by standard medical procedures, planning for the end stage of life is common. Although some Dutch religious groups and other organizations are appalled by the practice, they appear to be fighting a losing battle. Public opinion is that euthanasia can be the last dignified act in the health-care process. Socialization for death in the Netherlands includes euthanasia as a legitimate alternative.

The first Dutch physicians violated the ban on euthanasia over 40 years ago to draw attention to the plight of dying patients, and now physicians in other countries are following suit. In the United States, the infamous Dr. Jack Kevorkian, inventor of the "suicide machine," has been convicted of murder after innumerable arrests for assisted suicide. His sentence of 10 to 25 years in prison has been called harsh and unjust by assisted suicide advocates. Several states have issued challenges to the constitutionality of laws against assisted suicide. Australia passed a law allowing euthanasia, but the law lasted only 6 months before angry opponents had it rescinded. Scotland is doing major research on euthanasia and testing public opinion on the subject.

Although death socialization via euthanasia may be common in the Netherlands, other factors may make the Netherlands a less compatible role model for other countries. For example, Holland has one of the highest standards of medical care in the world. Over 95 percent of the population is covered by private medical insurance. In addition, the level of trust between doctor and patient is very high. During the Nazi occupation, Dutch doctors went to concentration camps rather than divulge the names of their patients. Patients often keep the same doctor over a lifetime. Most important, Holland has one of the world's highest life expectancies. These specific characteristics of Dutch culture show that countries need to find their own solutions to the euthanasia issue rather than try to import the Dutch system wholesale.

1. Given that euthanasia is widely accepted in the Netherlands, do you think that the choice for euthanasia could become a prescription for it? What will prevent abuses in the system?

2. How does your own culture socialize its people into death? Could euthanasia become an acceptable alternative for dying patients?

Sources: Royal Dutch Society, 1994; Cohen-Almagor, 2002; Dutch Legalize Euthanasia, 2002; de Haan, 2002; Hendin, 2002; Welie, 2002.

4. *Depression.* When the realization comes that they cannot negotiate their way out of the situation, depression occurs. Sorrow, guilt, and shame are linked with this stage.
5. *Acceptance.* By discussing their feelings openly, dying persons move into a final stage in which death is accepted. Kübler-Ross believes that only with acceptance can inner peace be reached.

Kübler-Ross established the idea of *dying trajectories,* the courses dying takes in the social or psycho-logical sense. Her model has been used not only to describe the sequence of dying, but also to suggest a set of therapeutic recommendations for how dying "should" take place. Hospital staff are often taught to interpret terminally ill patients' behavior according to the stage theory and to work with them as well as their families so that they will eventually move into stage 5 and accept their inevitable death (Kammerman, 1988; Paci et al., 2001). Symbolic interactionists suggest that such therapeutic recommendations socially construct the process of death; a description *of* the reality of dying according to stage theory becomes a prescription *for* reality—how dying a "good death" is supposed to occur (Hart et al., 1998). As with other roles, a cultural standard for dying gradually emerges.

But research also shows that while there are categories of behavior and adaptations that dying people exhibit, they do not usually occur in predictable stages (Corr & Corr, 2000; Corr & Doka, 2001). Denial and depression, for example, occur at all points in the dying process (O'Leary & Nieuwstraten 2001; Olson et al., 2001). Socialization into death is similar to other socialization experiences during the life course. The right to choose the way we want to die is compromised by the social roles we take on and the way others define these roles during the dying process. An "appropriate" death becomes a negotiation between these roles.

Coming to terms with death could be a ninth category in Erikson's model. At the end of life, there is the struggle (crisis) to affirm both individual choice (dying the way we want to) and social constraints (dying the way society tells us we ought to). Our funeral, another rite of passage, provides a socialization experience for those left behind.

The Life Course: A Critical Review

A sociological view of an age-based life course adds to an understanding of the process of socialization. All cultures have some type of an age-based sequence. However, cautions must be noted. Sociology recognizes that any society constructs stages according to what is important to that society. The identity crisis, for example, has attracted a great deal of research and popular attention. Parents and teachers routinely lament to sympathetic listeners about the unrest of the teenagers in their lives and the toll exacted on everyone concerned. Teenagers in turmoil become the accepted norm.

While all people in all places must be socialized, contrary to Erikson's assertion, the stages are not culturally universal. The identity crisis for American adolescents is particularly stressful. College continues the struggle to define adult status. In some African cultures, however, there is no time for an identity crisis. One afternoon a 13-year-old boy is defined as a child. That evening he undergoes a circumcision rite of passage and is an adult. On the same day a 13-year-old girl is betrothed in another rite of passage. Two hours later she is an adult. Period.

Moreover, massive social change has altered the notion that people should accomplish certain developmental tasks at certain life stages, radically altering age-related norms. Examples of emerging norms are divorce and remarriage, grandparents taking on full-time parenting roles, adult children moving back with parents after divorce or job loss, women of all ages entering the paid labor force, and people changing careers several times in their lives (Amato & Booth, 2000; Bryant & Conger, 2002; Smith & Drew, 2002). Compared to the last generation, the social circumstances under which many children live have changed dramatically (Myers, 1999; Hochschild, 2000; Chase & Rogers, 2001). More and more of the elderly are exhibiting characteristics that were previously hallmarks of middle adulthood and even young adulthood. Does this mean they must go through the crises associated with these stages over again? Probably not. Age is only one way to monitor time-related changes

The identity crisis may be a Western invention. Among the Masai of East Africa, a young girl's bethrothal marks her as an adult. She has no time for an identity crisis.

and the developmental tasks involved. It is likely that along with age, new criteria will emerge that will also define the life course.

This section demonstrated that individuals must complete certain tasks in order to become functioning members of society. Principles consistent with symbolic interactionism provide the foundation for this discussion. But these tasks are embedded in broader social structures that also serve as socialization agents. Like the theories of socialization, most life course research is based on samples made up of white, middle-class males. However, research on primary socialization linking race, gender, and class is rapidly emerging.

AGENTS OF SOCIALIZATION: RACE, CLASS, AND GENDER DIVERSITY

Agents of socialization are the people, groups, and social institutions that provide the critical information needed for children to become fully functioning members of society. If these agents do not carry out their socialization tasks properly, individual and social integration may be compromised. These agents do not exist independently of one another. What happens at school affects the child and family in the home. Loss of a job and a paycheck has repercussions for both the individual and society. Functionalist theorists are particularly concerned about these agents. They emphasize how the various agents should work together so that society operates smoothly and social equilibrium is not jeopardized. From the viewpoint of conflict theory, the various agents may work to the benefit of one group but against another.

The Family

The family plays the pivotal role in primary socialization. In a child's first years of life, the family is largely responsible for the emerging identity, self-esteem, and personality of the child. The first values and attitudes you embrace as a child are from your family. Language learning and cognitive development reinforce these elements. In addition, the family is the source of a child's race, ethnicity, religion, and socioeconomic status. These forms of *cultural capital* provide for the child's first social placement and greatly influence how a child is raised (Bradley & Corwyn, 2002; Tardiff et al., 2002).

Both cultural capital and racial differences in socialization have been accounted for in examining opportunities that affect the races differently. For example, while the majority of both African American and white adolescents live in relatively advantaged homes, whites are much more advantaged. For African Amer-

icans, family advantages in social class may not make up for disadvantages in the larger society (Cornwell et al., 1996; Brody et al., 2001; Rankin & Quane, 2002). However, African Americans possess cultural capital related to their racial and ethnic heritage. When racial socialization messages are relayed with pride in African American culture by parents, the self-esteem of their children increases (Constantine & Blackmon, 2002; MacKinnon-Lewis et al., 2002). Chinese American children are also strongly influenced by ethnic heritage, especially about traditional beliefs related to respect for parents and older people, as well as about their family and kinship obligations. These beliefs and obligations are important for socialization of Chinese American children into their ethnic identity (Zhou, 2000). However, children may react negatively when they perceive too much parental pressure to maintain this identity if it restricts the time and energy they can devote to nonfamily activities (Cheng & Kuo, 2000; Fuligni et al., 2002). Socialization is a rocky path for all children but probably more so for children from racial minorities and immigrant families.

The first socialization into attitudes related to gender also occurs in families. Gender roles are more flexible in middle-class families than in working- and lower-class families in both the United States and Britain (Brigham, 2001; Sharpe, 2001). In terms of race, African Americans are less stereotyped than whites in role expectations regarding gender. African American married couples are more egalitarian than families in other racial groups. African American working- and middle-class females are regarded as more independent and assertive than white females of similar class status (Dill, 1999; Hill, 1999, 2001). The degree of socialization for role flexibility in childhood carries through to adulthood for both men and women or all races.

Data from Puerto Rican and Mexican American samples of lower- and working-class people show stronger support for deferential, subordinate female roles than is the case with African Americans or whites. Female roles are bolstered by powerful religious socialization within some Latino subcultures that promotes women's subservience to men (Anzaldua, 1995; Kane, 2000; Hunt, 2001). This pattern among Latinos specifically indicates how race, class, religion, and gender intersect in socialization.

Although the media have popularized the belief that the family is on the verge of collapse, it is still *the* critical socialization agent in the United States and throughout the world. While other institutions may be extending the work originally done in the family, sociological studies clearly show that the family still oversees the socialization process. Family socialization enhances a child's life prospects—both psychologically and socially. Children draw on cultural capital in the years ahead. Socialization experienced in the family is never erased.

Education

The family paves the way for the next major agent of socialization, the school. In contrast to the intimacy of the family, the school evaluates children on the basis of what they do rather than who they are. Children acquire necessary knowledge and skills, but also learn new social roles by interacting with teachers and peers (Brint et al., 2001; Foster, 2001). In the United States the socialization function of education emphasizes that children learn academic content, social skills, and important cultural values. Core cultural values help prepare children for life in a democratic society that stresses free enterprise and capitalism. These core values include the three "I's"—initiative, independence, and individualism. Schools in the United States are also expected to play a major role in *assimilation*, bringing together children from diverse cultures and subcultures and transforming them into committed Americans. For 12 to 20 years, school plays a dominant role in socialization.

Besides the formal academic curriculum, schools also have a powerful *hidden curriculum*, which includes all the informal, unwritten norms that exist both inside and outside the classroom. This hidden curriculum plays an important part in gender role socialization. Teachers who care deeply about their students, and who believe that they are treating girls and boys the same, are often unaware that they transmit gender-based stereotypes. The hidden curriculum may also be responsible for teachers inadvertently transmitting beliefs to poor children and racial minorities that they cannot succeed in school (Gadsden, 2001; Dumais, 2002) (see Chapter 16).

Although research shows that schools can unintentionally socialize children into ways that may perpetuate stereotypes, schools genuinely strive to use their socialization function to the benefit of children and society. Sociology recognizes that schools today are shouldering a bigger share of the socialization function in the United States than at any point in history.

Peers

As children are gradually introduced to the world outside the family, peers take on a major role in socialization. **Peer groups** are made up of people who are the same age and generally share the same interests and positions. Schools provide the setting for hierarchies of peer groups to form quickly. By fourth grade, children firmly identify with particular groups (Fletcher et al., 2001; Farkas et al., 2002). While parents and teachers mold identity and self-esteem, peer groups are also leading players in the process.

Parents initiate the first peer relationships; school allows children to select friends from a wider range of peers. Parents both encourage and fear this prospect, especially during the middle-school and high-school years. As life course research suggests, the pull of the peer group during adolescence can be stressful for everyone. Patterns of early peer relations continue into the later school years. The self-esteem of students suffers for those with unstable friendships or who have had many negative interactions with friends, and in turn they report poorer adjustment to school (Fuligni et al., 2001; Hussong, 2000a, 2000b). Adolescents with friends who are disruptive in school increase their own disruptiveness (Masini, 1998; Henry, 2000). Less attachment to parents and greater attachment to friends may predict antisocial behavior in middle-school students (Marcus & Betzer, 1996; Ary et al., 1999). These findings support the wealth of research suggesting that peer involvement is the key ingredient in adolescent drug use and other forms of delinquent behavior. However, as we will see, parents' fear of peers is probably more stereotyped than real.

Since the first peer groups are largely formed through school and neighborhood contacts, they are usually made up of people from similar races and social classes. Whereas race and social class segregation is thus the peer group norm, it is a norm that is usually not purposely chosen by members (Boyle & Lipman, 2002; Wade & Okesola; 2002). Peer groups segregated by gender, however, is purposely chosen behavior. Regardless of race or social class, boys interact in larger

"How is it gendered?"

Source: © The New Yorker Collection 1999 Edward Koren from cartoonbank.com. All rights reserved.

groups and have more extensive peer relationships. Girls have more intensive ones. Female peer groups have higher levels of self-disclosure, intimacy, and trust (Fagot & Leve, 1998; Maccoby 1998, 2000). Once same-gender relationships are formed, gender boundaries are monitored and enforced by peers. One consequence of this process is that having learned different styles of interaction, girls and boys may meet in adolescence virtually as strangers (Fagot, 1994:62).

Media

Like the schools, the media have gradually taken on a stronger role in socialization. But in the media, the socialization function is more subtle, much of it occurring without conscious awareness.

Television is by far the most influential of the media. Television establishes standards of behavior, provides role models, and communicates expectations about all of social life. Note how these are the very terms used in describing all theories of socialization. We rely more and more on the mass media, especially television, to filter the enormous amount of information we receive. When television images are reinforced by other mass media, the impact on socialization is substantial.

In the United States, over 98 percent of households have at least one television, almost 70 percent have cable, and the average number of sets per home is 2.4, one of which is turned on an average of 7 hours per day. These figures translate to about 3,500 hours of viewing time per person per year in the United States (U.S. Bureau of the Census, 2001: Tables 1125 & 1126). Although people over age 55 watch the most television, preschoolers and young children may spend up to one-third of the day in front of the set. Children from poor homes watch television more than those from affluent homes, working- and lower-class children more than those whose parents have higher education and income, and African Americans and Latinos more than European Americans, even when controlling for SES (Kotler et al., 2001; Certain & Kahn, 2002). Television does provide models of prosocial behavior, in which people help others out of unselfish motives. It also offers programming designed to help children learn to read and to fuel their interest in current events, nature, or the arts (Nathanson, 2001; Salamon, 2002). However, such programming is extremely limited when considering all the options television offers.

As expected, young children are the most vulnerable to television images, since they may not be able to distinguish fantasy from reality, are still in the formative stages of their identity, and use television more for role-modeling patterns found for both genders and for children of all races in the United States

(Cantor et al., 2001; Murray & Mandara, 2002; Shrum, 2002; Smith & Wilson, 2002). Critics of the media use these facts when considering the relationship between television and aggression. More than 2,000 studies conducted over three decades have documented a clear and consistent correlation between the two. Extensive research evidence indicates that exposure to violent media can contribute to aggressive behavior, desensitization to violence, nightmares and fear of being harmed, and engaging in high-risk behavior related to alcohol, drugs, gun use, and driving (Singer et al., 1999; American Academy of Pediatrics, 2001; Villani, 2001; Wilson et al., 2002). Even those who continue searching for irrefutable causal links cannot dismiss the following facts:

- Two out of three television programs contain violence that threatens or actualizes hurting and killing.
- By sixth grade, the average child has witnessed at least 8,000 television murders and 100,000 other violent acts.
- Nearly 70 percent of children's programs contain physical aggression—an aveage of 14 violent acts per hour of typical programming (Wilson et al., 2002).

Other forms of media violence repeat and even exaggerate many of the patterns found on television. As is exposure to television, exposure to movie and video game violence is linked to increases in aggressive behavior (Anderson & Bushman, 2001; Unsworth & Ward, 2001). Because of the ability to manipulate characters, violent video games may have even a stronger connection to aggression in children (Griffiths, 1998; Bensley & Van Eenwyk, 2001).

Socialization into gender roles is also influenced by the media. While portrayals of racial minorities have gradually become less stereotyped, such portrayals related to gender have increased (Berry, 1998; Graves, 1999; Brand et al., 2002; Palmer, 2002). One result of this increase is that as unrealistic as these stereotyped gender role images are, they are depicted as normal and typical of the real world and provide strong gendered messages for both boys and girls (Pearson, 2000). Boys identify with characters possessing physical strength and girls with those who are physically attractive (O'Reilly, 2001; Scharrer, 2001). Much media violence is directed toward women. White adult males and attractive white boys are more likely to be involved in violence and to get away with it, with girls and women of color, older women, and foreign women the most likely victims (Media Awareness, 2000; Smith et al., 2002). Even young children learn the gendered media messages that men are aggressive and women are vulnerable (see Chapter 13).

Viewing violence increases violence, and the more violent the content, the more aggressive the child or adolescent (Bushman & Huesmann, 2001; Smailes et al., 2002). From what we have learned about socialization, it is easy to understand how we can become desensitized to violent images, especially when the media glamorizes dehumanization. Contrary to news reporting about the link between media violence and aggression, "the scientific confidence and statistical magnitude" of the link has been clearly positive and shown consistent increases over time (Bushman & Anderson, 2001). While television is not *the* cause of violence, it is certainly *a* cause.

Other Agents

Socialization continues throughout life and on multiple fronts. While the family and the school are held most accountable for socialization, other agents contribute to the process. Religious institutions reinforce earlier moral development and messages from families. Family socialization related to religion have a dominant influence on future religious commitment (Sherkat, 1998; Mahoney et al., 2001). Throughout the life course people also join a variety of organizations through schools and workplaces. In elementary and high school they learn the rules of cooperation and competition through participation in sports. College students join fraternities and sororities that emphasize family-like relationships. Professional associations provide networking and mentoring opportunities to enhance job achievement. These agents provide opportunities for continuing to mold identity and self-esteem well into adulthood. However, all socialization experiences at any point in the life course will be directly influenced by peers.

LIFE CONNECTIONS

The Fear of Peers in American Socialization

Age segregation is a fact of life in the United States. Most people spend most of their time outside their families with those who belong to the same age groups. Since schools organize childhood and adolescence according to age, peer influences in socialization are very powerful (Zaff & Hair, 2002). When parents realize they no longer have control over whom their children interact with or become friends with, the dreaded "fear of peers" phase of parenthood begins. Parents worry that their children will get involved with the "wrong" crowd, who can be defined as unsavory, untalented, unimaginative, or simply poor. Parents may see peer groups propelling children to engage in all kinds of antisocial acts, from

talking back to teachers and cheating on exams to shoplifting or gang violence. Fueled by media images, the distinction between a peer group and a gang is a blurry one in the minds of many parents.

Peer groups are the first ways children learn to exert some control over their lives. Adolescents say they can be themselves only when with their friends; they do not have to show deference to adults and can use the peer group to mock adult authority, particularly as represented by school. By joining forces, children learn they can often get what they want from otherwise reluctant adults (Strouse, 1999). Adolescents realize their potential power when they congregate in front of a movie theater, at a fast-food restaurant, or in a mall, which often prompts a call to security to disperse them. But the fear of peers cuts both ways. Parents worry when their children spend more time with their peers than with their families. Young people worry that they will become social outcasts if they do not spend enough time with their friends. Codes of conduct in peer groups are rigid, and the threat of exclusion is usually enough to enforce peer-approved behavior (Horne, 2001; Finkenauer et al., 2002). To be "themselves" in the peer group, young people must dress and speak a certain way and possess what the group defines as important—whether in appearance, material possessions, sexual prowess, or sports talent.

For children in the United States, peers set standards of physical attractiveness that are strongly related to popularity. If you look good, people like you and want to be around you. If you do not look good in the eyes of your peers, you can be shunned. Peers assign many negative traits to unattractive children. Often a self-fulfilling prophecy occurs: Children as young as age 3 actually display some of the negative behaviors peers attribute to them. Discipline from parents—having allowance withheld or being grounded—is exchanged for discipline from peers—name-calling, ridicule, or at worst, social isolation (Lease & Axelrod, 2001; Baker et al., 2002; Axelrod et al., 2002). Even young children have an accurate notion about peer acceptance and will passionately work to protect it. Peer acceptance is a major factor in a child's self-esteem and can predict both adjustment in school and well-being later in life (Buhs & Ladd, 2001; Ryan, 2001).

However, data also show the positive impact of peers on adolescent self-esteem and prosocial behavior, particularly when adolescents are close to parents and other family members, a pattern that holds true across all races in the United States as well as in other Western cultures (Franco & Levitt, 1998; Eisenberg, 2002; Keltikangas-Jaervinen et al., 2002; Meeus et al., 2002). African American and Latino adolescents from low-income neighborhoods who demonstrate high levels of commitment to others describe themselves in terms of

Peer groups in school strongly influence identity. Children usually form gender-segregated peer groups even if they differ in age.

moral personality traits and goals and think of themselves as melding their own ideals with positive images provided by their parents (Hughes, 2001; Newman, 2001). Peer groups come together for support of one another and others outside their group in times of crisis and are often called upon by their schools for help in peer counseling programs related to suicide, drug abuse, family problems, and violence (Stevenson, 2002). Peer influence is also a major positive motivator in encouraging friends to continue to develop their talents in sports and the arts (Patrick et al., 1999). These adolescents are applauded for their prosocial behavior by schools, communities, and their peers.

We have seen that children the world over are socialized by a number of agents, but peer groups in the United States are becoming more and more important. Teenage recreation in the United States is now focused outside the home—in malls, video arcades, and movie theaters. Within the home, middle-class teens and their friends can retreat to rooms that are replete with color televisions, VCRs, phones, stereos, and personal computers with Internet access. As in the United States as a whole, the media and electronic gadgetry children and adolescents use for recreation are also age-based. The childhood and teenage niche in media and electronics is a multimillion-dollar industry (Kinder, 1999).

Since socialization in the United States hinges more on peer groups than ever before, the fear of peers may be justified. Peers come later in a child's life, and they offer a way for young adolescents to achieve a sense of positive belonging and social connection (Giannetti & Sagarese, 2001; Newman & Newman, 2001). However, the family is not only the first socialization agent, it is also by far the most im-

portant. Both parents and their children may worry about peer influences; in the long run, however, sociological research shows that it is highly unlikely that peer group values replace parental values.

SOCIETY CONNECTIONS

When Socialization Fails

Some people cannot make their way through the socialization process or are thwarted at some stage. Biological limitations, such as severe birth defects that compromise a child both physically and mentally, and social factors, such as the extreme isolation experienced by Anna and the feral children in the chapter-opening vignette, can interrupt the process. People may have accidents or experience medical problems such as strokes; in such cases mental and physical capacities may be so compromised that simple patterns of behavior must be relearned. In all these cases, socialization failed because of circumstances beyond the individuals' control. In other cases, however, socialization can fail because people choose behavior that is destructive to themselves or to society. Since the key role of socialization is to make a person a fully functioning member of society, behavior that goes against this process cannot be ignored.

Resocialization: Voluntary or Involuntary

When socialization fails, most people must go through the process of **resocialization** in order to remedy patterns of behavior that society finds destructive, or on the positive side, to alter behavior to make it fit with other personal or social goals. In the case of destructive behavior, this process may mean entering a drug rehabilitation program for heroin addiction or going to jail for theft. For altering behavior to fit with other goals, the military resocializes recruits so that they act according to rigid group-oriented rules necessary for war and other emergency situations.

Gender role resocialization may occur when a woman enters a culture that offers severely restricted roles for women. When Betty Mahmoody (1991) moved with her husband to Iran, she had to learn totally new patterns of behavior expected of Iranian women. Completely veiled when outside the home and restricted by extended family inside as well, she was effectively shut off from her old friends and prevented from establishing new ones other than through family links. Social disapproval and legal sanctions literally made her a prisoner in her new culture. Only after a dangerous journey was she able to escape from what she experienced as an intolerable life. Resocialization into her new culture was unsuccessful.

In most cases of resocialization, people are stripped of their old identity so that it can be rebuilt according to other standards. Much resocialization takes place in what Erving Goffman (1961a) termed **total institutions.** These are places of residence and work that are "total" because they exert complete control over the people they contain. Life is enclosed and supervised, and residents, or inmates, learn that it is easier to adjust than to rebel against the restrictive round of life. People may enter total institutions for voluntary resocialization, as in a religious community or in the military in countries without a draft. They may also voluntarily enter a mental hospital when they judge themselves as needing psychiatric therapy because they cannot cope with daily life.

However, although people may enter total institutions voluntarily, numerous barriers exist to keep them confined in these places until administrators grant approval to leave. A request for discharge from a mental hospital, the army, or even a convent is not automatically granted. A mental hospital may house people who are seen as a threat to themselves or others but who have not committed any crime. Regardless of whether they chose to enter the mental hospital, until they display "acceptable" behavior, they may not be released. In some instances, people become stripped of their freedom because others judge them to be mentally ill. Their freedom rests on being "cured" of mental illness (Szasz, 2000). Even a college campus has some qualities of a total institution, such as restricting activities on campus that could occur off campus or by putting up hurdles making it difficult to transfer credits or change schools altogether. Total institutions are by definition restrictive, and people simply do not enter or leave them arbitrarily.

Although there are many unresolved questions related to voluntary resocialization, there is not a great deal of public concern about them. As you would expect, this is certainly not true for issues related to involuntary resocialization due to criminal behavior. Prisons are total institutions where retribution rather than rehabilitation is the norm. As discussed in Chapter 9, not only are criminals punished, but incarceration keeps them from committing more crimes, at least outside of the prison. High rates of recidivism—returning to prison—imply that total institutions may not radically change behavior and that resocialization has failed. The public generally supports

Total institutions show similar patterns globally, such as in this mental ward for female patients in Afghanistan. However, grinding poverty, war, and a collapsed infrastructure have made such mental institutions more prison-like than hospital-like, with supervision and confinement more important than efforts at resocialization and rehabilitation.

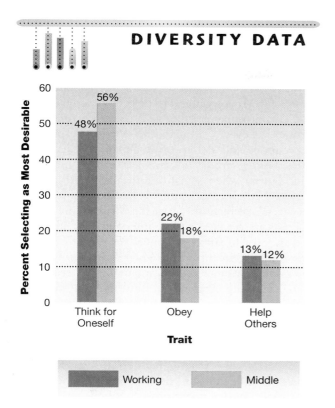

DIVERSITY DATA

FIGURE 5.1 **Percent Selecting the Three Most Desirable Qualities for a Child to Have, by Social Class.** Both working- and middle-class people select thinking for oneself as a child's *most* desirable quality, followed by obeying and helping others. However, thinking for oneself is selected significantly more often by the middle class, and obeying and helping others are selected slightly more often by the working class. What do these differences suggest about a child's socialization for independence and autonomy in these two social classes?

Source: NORC. General Social Surveys, 1972–2000. Chicago National Opinion Research Center, 2000. Reprinted by permission of NORC, Chicago, IL.

the punishment orientation, so longer sentences and increased security become hallmarks of criminal justice in the United States (Bureau of Justice Statistics, 2000).

The Insanity Defense

Controversy over the *insanity defense* is a good example of issues surrounding failed socialization—such as criminal behavior (voluntary choices) and mental illness (involuntary choices). In the United States, insanity can be used as a defense against criminal prosecution if the person is judged not to have been in his or her right mind at the time the crime was committed. If successfully employed, the verdict is that the person is "not guilty by reason of insanity." Although

insanity is a legal term and not a psychiatric one, psychiatrists are routinely called as expert witnesses to determine the state of mind of the accused. The insanity defense skyrocketed in public awareness in 1982 after John Hinckley attempted to assassinate Ronald Reagan. Hinckley was found not guilty by reason of insanity—he was diagnosed with schizophrenia—and sent to a mental hospital rather than a prison. The verdict and sentencing caused such public outrage that many states either modified or abolished the insanity defense altogether. Today the typical insanity defense is referred to as *guilty but mentally ill* (GBMI), and in death penalty states conviction for murder can result in execution (Palmer & Hazelrigg, 2000). More recently the insanity defense was used for Andrea Yates, who was convicted of drowning her five children in the bathtub. A Texas jury took 35 minutes to spare her from the death penalty but sen-

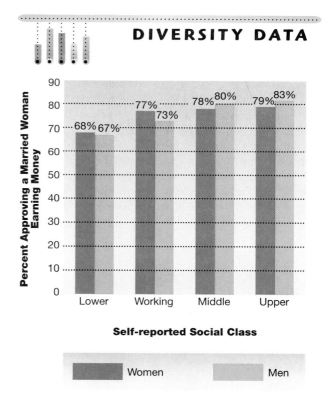

DIVERSITY DATA

FIGURE 5.2 **Should a Married Woman Earn Money If Her Husband Can Support Her?** As self-reported social class increases, both men's and women's approval of a married woman earning money increases. Although a large majority of people approve married women earning money, the lowest approval is from lower- and working-class men. Do you think children in these households will be socialized into these expectations more by their mothers or their fathers?

Source: NORC. General Social Surveys, 1972–2000. Chicago National Opinion Research Center, 2000. Reprinted by permission of NORC, Chicago, IL.

tenced her instead to life imprisonment (Charatan, 2002).

The public may believe that John Hinckley "got away with attempted murder" and that Andrea Yates did not receive the death penalty because of GBMI, but contrary to public belief, the insanity defense is rarely used (in less than 1 percent of all cases), and when it is used, it is rarely successful. When it is "successful," a person can be confined to a mental institution for the criminally insane or in a psychiatric ward of a prison indefinitely—for as long as it takes until the person is considered "cured." The insanity defense can backfire. Not only is it more likely to be used by nonviolent offenders, but people are often locked up in hospitals longer than in prisons (Kirschner & Galperin, 2002; *Mental Health Weekly*, 2002). As one law expert noted, the insanity defense is not used most of the time because juries don't accept it—they are afraid of insane people (Axtman, 2002).

Sociologists offer two important messages about the insanity defense. First, in the Hinckley and Yates cases, they may or may not have realized that they were doing something wrong when they committed the acts. If Hinckley and Yates represented failed socialization, they were either not capable of understanding their actions or capable of understanding but still willing to carry out the act, regardless of consequences. Whether they are regarded as criminal, mentally ill, or both, socialization was a still a failure. Second, what are the appropriate interventions for failed socialization? Should rehabilitation occur in a mental hospital or a prison? Should the person be released if "cured" of the illness, released because a sen-

tence was served, or not released at all? How does the state know if resocialization (rehabilitation?) is indeed successful? Should punishment and retribution rather than rehabilitation be the goal for all criminals, regardless of their level of mental competency? Although GBMI is supposed to help solve some of these problems, it remains laden with confusion and ambiguity in the eyes of all involved—victim, perpetrator, prosecution, and defense (Gesalman & Clemetson, 2002; *Mental Health Weekly*, 2002). The important point is that when socialization fails for reasons of criminal behavior, the state has a responsibility to intervene. Total institutions such as prisons and mental hospitals are set up for these interventions. The public is in favor of stiffer sentences for repeat offenders who commit violent crimes and of separating those who commit violent crimes, including the criminally insane, from other offenders. But there is a great deal of disagreement over what constitutes punishment and what constitutes rehabilitation, especially when mental illness and mental retardation are involved and especially when conviction could mean the death penalty (*American Demographics*, 2001; Perske, 2001; *Lancet*, 2002). Punishment and rehabilitation exist side by side in total institutions. Symbolic interactionists argue that total institutions such as prisons and mental hospitals must resocialize patients and inmates into a radically altered view of themselves that extends after release. Whether such resocialization can be successful in reducing crime is addressed in Chapter 9.

SUMMARY

1. Socialization is the lifelong process through which individuals acquire culture, develop their sense of self, and become functioning members of society.

2. Sociobiologists believe that human behavior is determined genetically, according to evolutionary principles. There is little evidence supporting this view.

3. Symbolic interactionists stress the importance of role-playing and the looking-glass self—imagining what others think of us—in developing social identity.

4. According to Freud, socialization is a multistage process in which the child struggles to reconcile basic biological drives with conflicting social norms and values.

5. Social learning theorists hold that children are socialized both directly, through rewards and punishments for specific behaviors, and indirectly, through observation and imitation of others.

6. Jean Piaget proposed a multistage theory of cognitive development that became the foundation for several studies of moral development. Best

known are Lawrence Kohlberg's research suggesting that boys reach a higher stage of moral development than do girls, and Carol Gilligan's critique, suggesting that girls use different but equally valid norms in their moral reasoning.

7. The life course perspective on socialization is an interdisciplinary approach that stresses adult as well as child development. Life course theorists are particularly interested in the attitudes and behaviors of birth cohorts, those who age together and experience events in history as a generation.

8. Erik Erikson proposed that human development occurs through eight life stages, each marked by special challenges and a central developmental crisis that must be resolved.

9. Compared with early and middle adulthood, later adulthood and old age are a time of role loss, although new roles may be substituted.

10. Elisabeth Kübler-Ross identified five stages people go through in coming to terms with death. Research suggests, however, that the dying do not necessarily progress through those stages in a set sequence.

11. The family is the primary agent of socialization, especially in the first years of life, providing cognitive development, self esteem, language, and cultural capital. Schools are important socialization agents, teaching social skills and communicating core cultural values and gender role expectations to students.

12. The mass media, especially television, may socialize young viewers negatively through their portrayal of violence and gender stereotyped role models.

13. American parents often fear that their children will be unduly harmed by peer groups. However, peer values rarely replace parental values.

14. Resocialization, a process designed to eliminate destructive behaviors or alter behavior to fit new goals, is often pursued in total institutions such as mental hospitals and prisons that exert control over people's lives.

KEY TERMS

agents of socialization 135
anticipatory socialization 121
birth cohort 128
ego 122
gender identity 123
gender schema theory 125
gender socialization 118
generalized other 120
I 120

id 121
life course 128
looking-glass self 120
me 120
peer groups 136
personality 119
primary socialization 121
resocialization 139
rites of passage 131

role-taking 120
schema 124
self 119
significant others 120
socialization 118
sociobiology 118
superego 122
total institutions 140

CRITICAL THINKING QUESTIONS

1. Explain the following statement: Socialization requires group experience, and social isolates fail to develop a normal personality.

2. Demonstrate how the life course is a continuous process of development, socialization, and adaptation.

3. Identify the similarities and differences in the sociological and psychological approaches to socialization.

4. Considering the different agents of socialization and how they are interdependent, which one agent do you believe is the most important for both the individual and society?

INVESTIGATE WITH CONTENT SELECT

 Begin your research using Content-Select for this chapter by following the directions found on page 27 of this text to visit Prentice Hall's Research Navigator Website. Enter these search terms into the search field:

Birth cohort
Learning theory
Sigmund Freud

6
SOCIAL INTERACTION
Constructing the Meaning of Everyday Life

Pygmalion: Transforming Eliza Doolittle

You see, really and truly, . . . the difference between a lady and a flower girl is not how she behaves but how she's treated. I shall always be a flower girl to Professor Higgins, because he treats me as a flower girl . . . but I know I can be a lady to you because you treat me as a lady.

Eliza Doolittle speaks these words in the play *Pygmalion* by George Bernard Shaw. Eliza tells us that the expectations about how she is perceived make a difference in how she is treated. She also tells us that she changes her own expectations about herself when she is treated differently. A "Pygmalion effect" occurs—she is transformed from a flower girl into a lady.

"Honkey"

I grew up in an inner-city housing project, were most everyone was black or Hispanic, and started first grade at P.S. 4 across the street. Teachers usually did a good job of ignoring the fact that one kid was shorter or fatter than another, but it was they, not the other students, who made my skin color an issue. The kids had only picked up on the adult cues and reinterpreted them. Height and weight were relative but race was a matter of kind, not degree. Some of the kids were *blancitos*—light skinned Puerto Ricans—but that didn't mean they got rapped on the knuckles any softer than the darker skinned kids. Every kid, boys and girls alike, received some form of corporal punishment. I was the only one who escaped the yardstick, and not because I was particularly well-behaved. The kids never resented me for this. Either you were black or you weren't. By the time I left the first grade, I knew what the concept of race meant. I now knew that, based on the color of my skin, I would be treated a certain way. I enjoyed a range of privileges that were denied my friends and neighbors but that most Americans take for granted. I am white. After first grade at my new school, the name of the game was class. That brought a whole new set of rules. Race and class are nothing more than a set of stories we tell ourselves to get through the world, to organize our reality. (Adapted from Dalton Conley, *Honkey*, 2000:x–xii, 46–54.)

When people interact, they bring to the interaction their own definitions about what is considered appropriate behavior. These vignettes suggest that not only can definitions change during the course of the interaction but that the definitions themselves influence the outcome of the interaction. Eliza Doolittle was gradually transformed from a flower girl into a lady when people treated her like a lady. Dalton Conley's recount of his childhood on New York's Lower East Side reflects a journey of discovery that unveiled the hidden rules surrounding race and class. He learned the taken-for-granted perils and privileges associated with race and class as a white middle-class male growing up in a "bad neighborhood" in the midst of a community of color. Eliza Doolittle, Dalton Conley, and all the participants in their social interactions constructed their own reality. This chapter explains how people construct social reality whenever interaction occurs, including sites of social institutions such as school and workplace, and through media sites such as television. It also shows that these constructions are based not just on what we say when we interact but also on *how* we say it, that is, through nonverbal communication. Finally, we show that social reality can also be *reconstructed*, as in the case of sexual harassment. Our discussion is guided by symbolic interactionism, the most widely used theoretical perspective in sociology for explaining social interaction. Because symbolic interactionists focus on the details of the interaction between two people or in other small groups, the *microsociological* level of analysis (Chapter 1) is used to examine it. However, since social interaction cannot be separated from the larger cultural context in which it occurs, we also show that the *macrosociological* level of analysis, particularly conflict theory, offers insight into understanding interaction. Sociologists are keenly interested in social interaction because of its enormous influence in how we conduct our everyday lives as individuals and in how the groups that makes social life possible are formed.

THEORETICAL PERSPECTIVES ON SOCIAL INTERACTION

As we saw in Chapter 5, the process of socialization explains the intersection of individual and group life. We now explore this intersection further by describing how sociologists view social interaction in everyday life. **Social interaction** refers to the way in which people behave toward and respond to one another in a reciprocal manner. When people meet, therefore, their behavior is influenced by the behavior of those they meet as well as by others around them. Social interaction occurs directly, such as in face-to-face encounters, and indirectly, such as by telephone or email. Another example of indirect social interaction is the observation of the interactions of others, such as when viewing television or simply watching people interact in a mall or park. Observing these and other types of social interaction helps us gain a better understanding of what is considered appropriate social behavior.

Understanding social interaction is a key goal of *social psychology*, a field of scientific study that intersects the disciplines of sociology and psychology. However, social psychologists from each discipline define the field differently according to how this goal is approached. Social psychologists who adopt a *psychological* view of social interaction focus on the individual and define the field according to how social interaction shapes his or her feelings, thoughts, and behaviors. Social psychologists who adopt a *sociological* view of social interaction are more interested in the ongoing social interaction in social situations and define the field according to how individuals change because of the interaction. The psychological view of social interaction dominates social psychology (Schwartz, 1998). Some social scientists therefore prefer the term *sociological psychology* to reflect a distinctly sociological understanding of social interaction, in which participants are active and dynamic rather than actors who merely respond to others in the environment (Cahill, 1995a; Charon, 1995). The sociological view becomes clear when we examine how reality can be socially constructed.

The Social Construction of Reality

Social interaction is a process governed by norms that are largely determined by our culture. But because people are not robots, they may act out the norms in various ways. Although cultural norms guide our behavior, we have many choices from a range of behaviors, some of which may be appropriate at one point in time and inappropriate at another. Cultural norms are modified whenever social interaction occurs because, as the vignettes suggest, we also bring our own definitions about appropriate behavior to the interaction. These definitions shape the way we see and experience the world. Symbolic interactionists refer to this shaping process as the **social construction of reality**—the shaping of our perception of reality by the subjective meanings we bring to any experience or social interaction.

A simple illustration of the social construction of reality is the response of two students in the same class to the actions of a professor, depending on the grade received on the last exam. The student who received an A on the test sees the professor's smile to him or her as an affirmation of a good grade. The student who received a D may interpret the smile as a sign of pity or disgrace. The professor's "real" intentions remain unknown, but the A student smiles back and the D student turns away in apparent embarrassment. In turn, the professor's interpretation of the behavior of the A student as positive and the D student as negative may influence how the professor will later interact with both of them. Every time social interaction occurs, people creatively construct their own understanding of it—whether "real" or not—and behave accordingly.

Since the social construction of reality is considered a part of all social interaction, it is a key feature of the symbolic interactionist perspective and cannot be separated from the perspective as a whole. The principle that society is socially constructed will be applied throughout the chapter.

Symbolic Interactionism

Symbolic interactionism is at the heart of the sociological view of social interaction. With its focus on people's behavior in face-to-face social settings, symbolic interactionists explain social interaction as a dynamic process. People continually modify their behavior as a result of the interaction itself. Herbert Blumer (1900–1987), who originated the term symbolic interactionism, emphasized that people do not respond directly to the world around them, but to the meaning they bring to it—such as the encounters between the students and professor. For Blumer and symbolic interactionists, society, its institutions, and its social structure exist—that is, social reality is bestowed—only through human interaction (Blumer, 1969).

Since people interact according to how they interpret situations, if the interpretation changes, so does the social reality. This principle accounts for a wide range of social interaction, including *dyads*—two person groups—as well as in groups with larger numbers of people. It also accounts for social cohesion. Regardless of the number of people in a group, when they interpret an event the same way, the common interpretation will tend to unite the group. Symbolic interactionists are concerned with explaining not only how human interpretation makes social life possible, but how social life is organized and constructed, and how it changes over time.

To illustrate these important principles of symbolic interactionism, let's take the notion of the social construction of reality a step further. We have seen that people interact according to how they perceive a situation. Their perception is based on how they understand the social encounter and the meanings they bring to it. But there is an additional step in the process: how they *think* other people who are part of the interaction also understand the encounter. Each person's *definition of the situation* (Chapter 1) influences others' definitions, so the negotiation of social reality is ongoing. The advice a columnist gave to a 17-year-old gay male who asked if he should "come out" (admit his homosexuality) reflects how the definition of the situation can be used to negotiate and change social reality:

> If you decide to come out, I'd suggest going first to the family member who you believe loves you the most—usually Mom. Tell her the news with warmth and good spirit. That is, present yourself in a light in which you want others to see you. Ask her to allow you to tell her the news in the best way—then go to the person you believe loves you the second most, and so on. (Savant, 1999:8)

The columnist's advice is for him to be positive so that in turn his mother will be positive. Although we do not know what her reaction will be, it is expected that engaging in the negotiation process, especially with a positive attitude about its outcome, will result in a more favorable perception of his coming out.

Although the social construction of reality is a dynamic, negotiated process, symbolic interactionists assert that it is a rational one. People choose their behavior very carefully. We saw in Chapter 5 that socialization is necessary for a person to develop a sense of *self*, the identity that distinguishes each individual from all other individuals. Social interaction allows us to learn about ourselves and make the social comparisons that are necessary to acquire a self-concept. A person will invest a great deal of effort to protect his or her self-concept and maximize self-esteem.

Constructing Social Difference: Race, Gender, and Class

Starting with the everyday interactions between people in small groups, symbolic interactionists tell us that society as a whole is constructed through the subjective meanings brought to all social interactions. They assert that we are not born with the social statuses of gender, race, social class, or sexual orientation; they are given meaning only through social interaction. Dalton Conley learned to define himself as "white" because people treated him differently than they treated the people of color surrounding him. He also realized that "whiteness" provided a certain degree of power and privilege that, unlike his African American and Latino friends, he did not have to earn. The power that his "lack of color" offered was an inevitable part of all his social interaction even before he figured out he was white. As we will see, the ability to define reality a certain way and then convince everyone else that your definition is the best or proper one reflects your power or the power of a group to which you belong.

Like race, gender is another inevitable part of social interaction, and also like race, symbolic interactionists assert that gender emerges through a socially constructed process. Research on men and women in various social networks—such as groups formed at school, work, and in volunteer activities—illustrates this process. From early childhood these groups are usually gender segregated. Gendered subcultures emerge, which strengthens the perceptions of gender differences and erodes the common ground upon which intimate, status-equal friendships between the genders are formed (Ridgeway & Smith-Lovin, 1999). Differences rather than similarities are much more likely to be noticed, defined, and acted upon. When cross-gender social interaction occurs, such as in the workplace, it is unlikely that men and women hold similar degrees of power and prestige. Once the genders are socially constructed as different, it is easier for those with more power (men) to justify inequality toward those with less power (women). Social difference is constructed into social privilege.

Symbolic interactionists emphasize that choices of behavior in social interaction are optional, but since race and gender cannot be disguised, people invariably use these categories to help structure their interaction. Class is less obvious and can be disguised or eliminated a variety of ways, such as learning appropriate class-based behavior. Eliza Doolittle was elevated to a much higher social class by changing her language, clothing, and "lower class" behavior.

Professor Higgins may agree she is no longer the pitiful flower girl he found on the street, but she will *always* be a women and relegated to the less privileged category designated by the social construction of her gender. The last line of the movie *My Fair Lady* illustrates the class-gender distinction in terms of privilege when Professor Higgins calls out imperiously, "Eliza, bring me my slippers."

Conflict Theory and the Social Construction of Privilege: The Case of the Homeless

Conflict theory views society principally from a macrosociological perspective, but it offers great deal to the study of social interaction. Focusing on inequality and the manner in which resources are distributed in society, conflict theory suggests that those who wield power in broader society—such as the major institutions—can also influence the way people think about those who do not have such power, such as homeless people.

The social construction of reality assumes that inequality between whites and people of color, men and women, and the middle class and lower class reflects the ability of those with power to control and shape the definitions of reality. This power to define yourself and have others accept your definition is well illustrated by considering the plight of homeless people. Accurate data are difficult to collect, but estimates of the numbers of homeless range between 1 million and 3 million, with another 5 million to 10 million so poor that the loss of a minimum wage job would force them on the streets (HUD, 1999). Although they are common sights on urban street corners and people are clearly aware of their presence, for the most part the homeless are invisible. When they do become visible, it is usually because of politicized accounts in the media. Media accounts are powerful in shaping the public opinion that will determine the destiny of the people portrayed. (Anastasio et al., 1999). More important for symbolic interactionists is that media also shape a person's perception about what *other* people who watch, read, or listen to the same media accounts are thinking. (Gunther, 1998). Although public opinion polls do show that most people in the United States support measures to end homelessness, anti-homeless laws which either criminalize the homeless or force them to leave an area are increasing (NLCHP, 2000a; 2000b). Media constructions of the homeless range from sympathy and pity to fear, disdain and anger. Often they are defined as "undeserving," and lumped together with drug abusers, panhandlers, and slackers who refuse to work (Blasi, 1994; Borchard, 2000).

RACE AND GENDER Once the homeless are constructed as undeserving, they have neither the power nor the resources to challenge the definition. Patterns of gender and ethnicity among the homeless further reinforce this lack of power. Estimates suggest that 70 percent to 80 percent of the homeless are men, but in many cities, over half of the men are African American and Latino, most of whom have some form of disability. But the ranks of homeless women and children are growing. Homeless women are likely to be younger than homeless men and even more likely to be members of a racial or ethnic minority. Single mothers with children, now represent over 30 percent of the homeless, are most likely to be African American (HUD, 1999; Nunez & Fox, 1999). The concentration of African Americans among homeless women parallels their concentration in the ranks of the extremely poor. The intersection of key social statuses—young, female, African American, single mother, and most important, extreme poverty and homelessness—is clearly linked to those who have the least amount of power in broader society.

The meaning attached to important social statuses invades all social interaction. People's social statuses make a difference in how we, as individuals, choose to interact with them. We may take into account their gender, race, age, social class, religion, or ethnicity before we act. We may consider how our culture offers us various ways to rank the statuses. Although females hold less power than males in almost every culture, in some cultures a woman's wealth may be more important than her gender in her degree of power. In those cultures the choice may be to interact with her as a wealthy person rather than as a female who happens to be wealthy. Symbolic interactionists recognize that it is necessary to account for such elements of social structure (macrosociological view) to understand social interaction between a few people (microsociological view). Both conflict theorists and symbolic interactionists agree, for example, that without the necessary power behind them, homeless people as a group cannot seriously challenge how they are defined by individuals or by broader society. The key point is that the reality of everyday life is continually shaped, modified, constructed, and reconstructed.

Everyday life may always be changing, but the changes are not haphazard—there is a structure to them. A fundamental task of symbolic interactionism is to determine the rules that people use when they select their behavior and under what conditions the rules are accepted, modified, or broken. The field of ethnomethodology offers a research strategy favored by symbolic interactionists that helps to uncover the rules of social interaction.

Ethnomethodology

Ethnomethodology is the study of how people socially construct their everyday world and give meaning to their experiences and interactions. There is a great deal of flexibility in the choices we make as we interact in our daily lives, but these choices are guided in patterned ways. In uncovering such patterns, ethnomethodologists are also interested in understanding social interaction from the person's own frame of reference. An outsider's view is not as valid, since, as we have already seen, people bring their own personal and social identities into the interaction. Thus, ethnomethodologists want to discover the hidden rules in social interaction—what is taken for granted when we interact. Over time, many of our actions become routine. Only when these habitual behaviors are challenged or when expectations are shattered do they resurface in our consciousness. When this happens, we need to regain a sense of control, a rule-governed process that ethnomethodology can uncover.

Understanding the informal rules of language is one of those powerful but habitual processes studied by ethnomethodologists. People attach their own meanings to any social interaction. Then they transmit these meanings through language to others as the process of interaction continues (Howard, 2000). The interaction is smoother when people share expectations that the words they utter will be "understood" by all participants in the interaction. Harold Garfinkel (1967), a pioneer in ethnomethodology, asked his students to break some taken-for-granted rules of communication in social interaction. The following was reported by one student (Ray):

FRIEND: Hi Ray. How is your girlfriend feeling?"

ME (RAY): What do you mean, how is she feeling? Do you mean physical or mental?

FRIEND: I mean how is she feeling? What's the matter with you? (He looked peeved.)

ME: Nothing. Just explain a little clearer, what do you mean?

FRIEND: Skip it. How are your med school applications coming?

ME: What do you mean, "How are they?"

FRIEND: You know what I mean.

ME: I really don't.

FRIEND: What's the matter with you? Are you sick? (Adapted from Garfinkel, 2001:382)

In asking the friend what he meant by *What do you mean, how is she feeling?* and then asking, "What do you mean, How are they?" Garfinkel's student challenged the usual definition of the situation, causing uneasiness and bewilderment. In seeking to regain control and figure out what was going on between them, the friend answers, "You know what I mean." Ethnomethodology shows that we are often unaware of the rules, or their power, until the rules are violated. If rules break down, new rules need to be negotiated and agreed upon and a new social reality built before communication can be successful.

Life-as-Theater

Another way to understand social interaction is to look at it as a play being acted out on a stage. This **dramaturgical approach** describes Erving Goffman's (1922–1982) view of social interaction. Like other symbolic interactionists, Goffman was searching for the rules that govern social interaction. Goffman believed that the underlying structure and process of social interaction could be found by considering social life as a staged drama or performance in which people act out certain roles (Goffman, 1959, 1974). Perhaps Goffman took his lead from Shakespeare: "All the world's a stage and all the men and women merely players."

Symbolic interactionists maintain that there are a number of competing "realities" in our lives, and we are constantly moving from one to the other. Using the life-as-theater metaphor, these transitions are marked by the rising and falling of symbolic curtains. In a "real" theater we are spectators transported to another world with its own meaning and order (Berger & Luckmann, 1966:25). When we return to our "real everyday" world, another meaning and order takes over. Just as in the theater, we construct our social realities through role playing. To test these ideas, think about your social status as a college student and the roles you play that confirm that status. The curtain rises when you enter the classroom, and you adjust your behavior to the audience of professor and classmates. The curtain falls as you leave that class, and it rises again when you enter another "social reality," such as sports practice, part-time job, or coffee with friends. Roles are added or discarded in a never-ending process as you move on and off various social stages.

The dramaturgical approach to social interaction in everyday life is expanded by Goffman through his model of *interaction ritual*—all the "small behaviors" that make up encounters, such as glances, gestures, positionings, and verbal statements. As social actors, we perform such rituals in deference to others and in light of cultural expectations and social norms. Interaction ritual determines what is needed to help make social order possible. As a result, social interaction is cooperative. A good demonstration of interaction ritual is the two taken-for-granted rules of elevator riding:

1. When you get on a small elevator with one other person, you each retreat to different sides of the car. A third person goes to the middle. Additional riders fill up middle space.
2. All elevator occupants must gaze at the floor numbers flashing by.

Nonverbal interaction is a powerful element of all social interaction. How would you react if someone stared at you throughout your ride? Modern society increasingly puts us in the company of strangers, and interaction rituals are performed to deal with any resulting discomfort. People find themselves in crowded elevators and subways with strangers, or in locker rooms waiting for others to vacate showers. Parents deal with unmanageable children in the candy aisles of grocery stores. To stare at each other in these situations is considered rude, embarrassing, or even threatening. We practice what Goffman calls civil inattention, a quick glance to acknowledge another's presence and a glance away just as quickly. In this instance, interaction ritual keeps discomfort at a minimum, even when acknowledging the presence of strangers. But, what if a homeless person carrying all his or her possessions in plastic bags stares fixedly at

passersby who will not return the eye contact? In this case, the homeless person breaks the ritual, perhaps intentionally, and creates discomfort.

Everyday life is made up of interaction rituals, all of which have subtle meanings and patterns. These everyday rituals provide us with the tools to engage meaningfully in a vast array of social interaction. The potential chaos of interacting with strangers and others who are different from us is transformed into a comfortable routine and is a testimony to the "genius of human sociability" (O'Brien & Kollock, 2001:199).

IMPRESSION MANAGEMENT Interaction rituals and the life-as-theater view of social interaction describe what we do. Symbolic interactionists offer explanations of why we do it. They believe that how we behave in social interaction is determined a great deal by efforts to protect our self-esteem. In social encounters we use strategies of **impression management** to provide information and cues to others that present us in a favorable light. The "self" that we present to others is designed to give them what we consider to be the most desirable impression.

Impression management is practiced routinely in the classroom. Students who usually come to class in tattered jeans and t-shirts will put on "nicer" clothes for a class presentation. In Goffman's theatrical terms this "frontstage" behavior is performed in a manner others expect (Goffman, 1959). By altering clothing and grooming, students send messages that the presentation is an important event. In contrast, "backstage" behavior refers to actions that are hidden from others, where people can just "be themselves" and where the audience is restricted, such as having pizza with a close friend in the dorm or chatting on the phone while your roommate is watching television. But even during these backstage performances, people are still playing roles. The concern for impression management follows people to whatever stage they are on.

Another side to impression management involves presenting ourselves in ways others *want* us to be—not just in ways they expect us to be. And not only do we perform for others, we are the audiences for their performances as well (Cahill, 1995b:188). When you introduce your girlfriend to your parents for the first time, you, your date, and your parents all practice impression management. Each person evaluates the performance of the others. Your date's performance takes center stage—she wants to present herself according to the way both you and your parents want her to be. All the roles we play come together to form a *negotiated* self. Through processes like impression management, "selves" are crafted and we gain a sense of control in social interaction. The ideal result is that we get what we want, and in doing so, our self-esteem is elevated.

Social interaction, including nonverbal interaction is in part based on how we perceive social statuses, such as age, gender, race, and social class, as well as nonverbal cues of others. The nonverbal interaction between these two people suggests positive regard for one another. They are linked by gender, age, and possibly sports affiliation which helps minimize racial differences.

Symbolic interactionism's principle of the *definition of the situation* (Chapter 1) can also be applied to impression management. If you believe the person sitting next to you in your sociology class is attracted to you, and you believe yourself to be attractive, you may decide to ask him or her out for coffee. Your definition of the situation suggests that this perception will result in a successful date. In contrast, shyness, averting eye contact, or displaying behaviors that suggest you are ill at ease can be interpreted as disinterest at best or hostility at worst. If you believe you lack self-confidence, it in turn increases the risk that the person you are asking out will decline the offer. A **self-fulfilling prophecy** occurs: Your expectations about others lead them to behave in ways that confirm the expectations. In other words, predictions shape actions. In the dating example, you have verified your own sense of inadequacy by your original definition of the situation. The result is that the other person doesn't go out with you. First impressions of others toward you, as well as how you think you are coming across to them, shape all later social interaction. This process is also a likely reason, for example, for the strong correlation between low self-esteem and loneliness in adults (Olmstead et al., 1991).

The concept of a self-fulfilling prophecy can also be applied to specific expectations you have of yourself, such as your expectation that you will fail a difficult exam. Acting on the expectation of failure, you do not study and hence fail the exam. However, symbolic interactionists generally use the concept to explain social interaction rather than individual behavior.

Critiquing the Social Construction of Reality

Symbolic interactionism's explanation of social interaction is widely accepted by sociologists, but there are some criticisms of the approach. First, since reality is socially constructed, it assumes that undesirable behavior may be changed by altering the construction, our perceptions about others as well as about ourselves, in social interaction. By this reasoning, mental patients would only need to be recast from mentally ill to mentally healthy, and then treated as mentally healthy, for their destructive behaviors that created the diagnosis of mental illness to disappear. Research suggests, however, women in certain diagnostic categories, such as eating disorders, require much more therapeutic intervention than simply treating them as if they were not ill. Eating disorders, like many forms of mental illness, must be considered in many ways—personal, social, and perhaps biological in origin—to effectively help a patent (Cosgrove, 2000). While it is clear that mental illness is *stigmatized*—negative labels are applied to the mentally ill—removing the label, a

stigmatized label or not, does not remove the mental illness.

Second, even with the benefit of a macrosociological injection of conflict theory, symbolic interactionists tend to minimize the impact of broader social structure on behavior choices. Herbert Blumer himself must have recognized this very criticism, since he called social structure a "straitjacket" that intrudes on behavior (Blumer, 1969). Social statuses such as race, class, and gender are central features of this structure. The very fact that we take into account the social statuses of others in social interactions show that they are key determinants of our behavior. In terms of race, for example, the social construction of reality emphasizes the influence of prejudice in social interaction, focusing on individual perception and outcomes of such perceptions. But there is minimal attention paid to the influence of discrimination, focusing on social structure (Link & Phelan, 2001).

Social institutions are also part of social structure and regulate behavior choices. As pointed out in Chapter 4, society is organized according to long-established social institutions that macrolevel sociologists say are difficult to change. For example, there are newer perceptions about women entering high-powered careers such as law or medicine. Even though women define themselves as talented, confident, and assertive, and others accept that definition, women must contend with law firms and hospitals that still perceive them primarily according to roles of wife, or potential wife, and mother. Recent research shows, for example, that female attorneys are not given the same assumption of competence as men, and they also face resistance to requests of flexible work schedules (Rhode, 2001). And as we will see, the perception of women as sex objects still haunts many work settings, where sexual harassment remains widespread. Workplaces developed around these definitions and have not changed significantly to account for the newer perception that women can be talented physicians and attorneys as well as talented mothers. Western European nations have offered paid maternity leave for several decades, and in Scandinavia it is especially generous for both men and women (Sidel, 1999). But in the United States it took over three decades to enact the *Family Leave Act* under President Bill Clinton, which allows limited *unpaid* leave for child care or family responsibilities. Workplaces that offer more flexibility to mothers are also associated with lower pay and insecure employment conditions (McCall, 2000). In universities, flexibility and "family-friendly" polices are not associated with tenure for female faculty. The economic institutions in the United States are built around the definition of an ideal employee who works full time, overtime, and in an uninterrupted career path—an idealized pattern few

SOCIOLOGY OF EVERYDAY LIFE

Pygmalion in the Classroom

Sociologists are keenly aware that since things are not always as they seem to be, it is often difficult for us to paint an accurate portrait of even the small portion of the social world we occupy. The portraits that we do paint, however, are largely based on expectations we have about other people's behavior. Like Eliza Doolittle's transformation from flower girl to lady, these expectations can alter the way we treat one another. A self-fulfilling prophecy can result—a positive one in Eliza's case. Although Eliza Doolittle is a fictional character, by understanding how her transformation occurred, the positive results accrued to Eliza might be reproduced in real-world settings. As documented in the following experiment, a typical elementary school classroom offers one such setting to study self-fulfilling prophecies.

During the spring semester, all the children in grades one through six at Oak School in San Francisco were administered a test that was supposed to predict those students who were on the verge of an intellectual growth spurt. In each of the 18 classrooms, 20 percent of the children were designated academic "spurters," and their names were given to their new teachers the following fall. At least this is what the teachers were told. The test was really a standardized IQ test, and the stu-

dents were selected randomly—no test scores or student grades were used to designate the "spurters." Four months after the teachers had the names of the "special" children, students took the same form of the test again; a third test was administered after another 4 months.

The results were amazing. Almost half the children in the experimental group, the spurters, gained 20 or more IQ points; only about 20 percent in the control group (all the other children at the school) made such gains. The greatest gains occurred among first-grade and second-grade spurters. Compared to the other children, teachers described the spurters as having a better chance for success in the future and as being significantly more curious and happy. Spurters were described as better adjusted, more affectionate, and with lower needs for social approval. The results were clear. In both IQ test scores and social behavior, children from whom intellectual growth was expected became more intellectually alive. Teachers who defined children as bright acted toward them on the basis of that definition. Their expectations clearly had a powerful influence on student performance in this experiment, and more important, the experiment has been replicated many times in many different schools. Positive outcomes from such guided self-fulfilling prophecies are both

common *and* expected. Sociologists who study social interaction are often called upon to provide guidelines for encouraging positive classroom outcomes. Their task is to provide teachers with tools for discovering the hidden dimensions of social interaction that profoundly impact their students. As this chapter suggests, symbolic interactionism in particular provides many such tools, including an understanding of the dynamics of impression management and nonverbal communication. Teachers can also use ethnomethodology to discover what they and their students take for granted in classroom interaction. Some teachers may have lower expectations for disadvantaged or minority students, so they demand less and do not push them to take challenging classes. Students in turn may demand less of themselves.

The Pygmalion effect—a self-fulfilling prophecy—occurs all the time in classrooms, sometimes to the detriment rather than the benefit of students. When sociological insight is applied to social interaction in schools, teachers may paint a more accurate portrait of the classroom world they and their students inhabit.

1. As a sociological consultant, you have been hired by a suburban school district to help determine why fifth graders are performing lower than the state average in math and reading. As a specialist in symbolic interactionism, what suggestions would you offer to these fifth-grade teachers to increase math and reading proficiency?

2. Provide an example of a guided self-fulfilling prophecy that can be used to enhance the self-esteem of people who must move from welfare to meaningful work roles. Justify your approach by applying principles based on the social construction of reality.

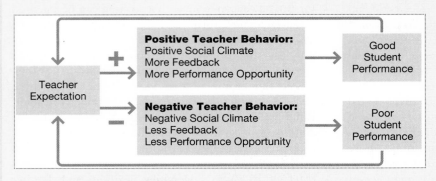

Teacher Expectations Can Affect Student Performance Holding a positive or negative expectation about a student can actually bring about student behavior consistent with the expectation.

Sources: Rosenthal & Jacobson, 1968; Rosenthal, 1995; Hacker, 2000.

mothers actually fit. The pattern is virtually nonexistent for women of color and women from lower SES groups (Williams, 2001). Most mothers do work outside the home, and some workplaces may be more supportive of the needs of these mothers. But although there are plenty of good intentions, the research clearly indicates they have not been translated into practice in a significant way. The family and the economy are established social institutions that are resistant to change. It may take decades before competing perceptions of women's talents outside the home change the practices of social institutions.

Third, behavior is supposed to be selected from a continuous stream of choices. We think before we act in ways that are supposed to protect our sense of self-esteem. However, our actions often reinforce inaccurate perceptions. Impression management inevitably masks who we "truly" are, and role performances ultimately seek to deceive others. Even Goffman (1959) pointed out that people can be so caught up in their own performances that in seeking to deceive others they deceive themselves. People may end up with "negotiated" selves that alienate them from their "true" selves. Rather than promoting self-esteem, these very behaviors can lead to anxiety, uncertainty, and depression.

Overall, interaction as socially constructed can be viewed in two competing ways: (1) the cynical views that social interaction is inaccurate, deceptive, and self-defeating, and (2) a more liberating view that suggests social interaction celebrates human creativity, choice, and freedom. The choice of one view over another is a philosophical one that sociologists cannot address. However, sociologists can address the useful-ness of the social construction of reality in assessing research on other types of social interaction, including nonverbal communication.

NONVERBAL COMMUNICATION

In Chapter 3 we learned that language is a system of symbols that enables even diverse subcultures to be bound together as a single culture. Language also creates barriers between cultures. Learning a language means learning a culture. In foreign language classes you probably first concentrated on vocabulary, grammar, and phonology (sound or dialect). These are the key elements of spoken language and provide the necessary tools for formal language learning. However, to truly understand how a culture is reflected in its language, it is also necessary to understand the complexity of the unvoiced element of the symbol system—its nonverbal aspect. What we say is often interpreted according to how we say it. Socialization into your culture and those subcultures of which you are a member assumes you learn how to communicate both verbally and nonverbally.

Nonverbal communication is the variety of ways in which people communicate without words—using body movements such as gestures, facial expressions, eye contact, use of personal space, and touching. It also includes use of paralanguage, length and rate of speaking, tone of voice, loudness, hesitation, and amount of interruption. If you can communicate appropriately using both verbal and nonverbal elements, you have made a giant leap in learning any culture.

Impression management during a job interview is a key factor in its success. The interviewer will notice not only what is said, but how the candidate acts nonverbally.

GLOBAL CONNECTIONS

Impression Management in the Global Workplace

When Fred Bailey was offered the position of managing director of his firm's Japan office, he saw it as an unbelievable opportunity. It meant moving from Boston to Tokyo, but it was a career opportunity too good to pass up. The benefits package for overseas employees—"expatriates"—was generous. Fred and his family had about 3 weeks to prepare for the move.

The first week on the job, Fred and his management team met with a team from a Japanese firm, an important prospective client. Not wanting to waste time, and being anxious to show how well prepared they were, Fred's team immediately laid out the proposal and asked for a reaction from the Japanese. When the Japanese did not respond, Fred summarized the proposal again, thinking that the translation was insufficient. Again, there were only vague responses.

Fred decided that the problem was lack of knowledge about the prospective client. The proposal would have to be repackaged. They chose a promising

young research associate, Tashiro, to prepare the report, which was needed in a week. "Can you do it?" Fred asked Tashiro. Tashiro hesitated, and then responded, "I am not sure what to say." Fred smiled, walked over to Tashiro, extended his hand, and said "Hey, there. Nothing to it. We're just giving you the opportunity you deserve." A week passed with no word from Tashiro on his progress. Tashiro did not complete the report on time. He was chewed out because at the outset he knew he couldn't do it but did not tell his supervisors.

Fred could not understand why Tashiro didn't speak up. No one, including the other Japanese employees, offered any answers, and the incident left everyone suspicious and uncomfortable with one another. Other incidents, big and small, occurred. Fred felt that working with the Japanese was like working with people on another planet. Fred had intended to stay 3 years in Japan but left within a few months.

Fred Bailey's problem of adjustment is typical of expatriates who enter settings

in which new behaviors are expected but the expatriate does not understand the culture enough to interact appropriately with host nationals. Fred applied American business rules to the Japanese firm—getting to the point, making decisions quickly, asking direct questions while expecting immediate answers, and showing confidence in employees, all sound practices for businesses managed by Americans. For the Japanese, however, such an approach is counterproductive. Not only are the Japanese much more indirect in questions and answers, they take time to discuss proposals and come up with consensus before a decision is made. A Japanese manager would have found out how much time Tashiro needed for the report, but in a manner that would allow Tashiro to "save face" if it would take longer than expected. Japanese do not single out employees for either special opportunities (Tashiro deserved it) or punishment (Tashiro was chewed out), especially in front of other employees.

When people from different cultures come together in the workplace, new

INTERNET CONNECTIONS

Sociologist Erving Goffman wrote extensively about the process of *social interaction,* including his distinction between "front-stage" and "back-stage" behavior. Drawn from his book, *The Presentation of Self in Everyday Life* (1959), a description of the process of Goffman's theory of dramaturgy may be found at:

http://www.westmyth.freeserve.co.uk/ISA/goffman.html

After you have browsed through the information contained in the links at the Website write a short description of Goffman's approach to interaction.

Evaluation of nonverbal communication is a good illustration of the process of impression management. Too much discrepancy between verbal and nonverbal language can generate mistrust and suspicion. For American couples, nonverbal signals are the first to show a decline in romantic attachment, especially by the person who would like to pull back or out of the relationship. There is less touch and more physical distance between the couple, eye contact is averted, posture is more rigid, and speaking is slower, with less fluency (Arliss, 1991; Wood, 1994). Such nonverbal cues eventually become so obvious that the inevitable question (What's wrong?), occurs most often initiated by the person who wants the relationship to continue. This question allows the initiation of verbal communication. It also serves as a face-saving device for the person who wants out of the relationship. You can probably predict the next sentence in this interaction:

rules of impression management need to be learned. Fred Bailey may have wanted to create a favorable impression, but his lack of understanding about Japan and its management style did just the opposite.

Multinational firms are aware of cultural barriers within their organizations. But research shows that these firms are not very successful in coming up with procedures that are satisfactory to employees from all the cultures represented in the firm. For example, Japanese typically want more participative management techniques than American managers. Too much participation makes Americans dissatisfied because decisions are too slow. Too little participation makes the Japanese dissatisfied because decisions are too fast. Hungarians who work in Japanese firms find the emphasis on teamwork problematic; they are even more individualistic than Americans, preferring to make decisions without consulting anyone.

Language barriers, both verbal and nonverbal, are ranked the number one problem among employees in multinational firms. Other issues routinely reported are differences in work method, differences in how employees are ranked, and differences in perspectives on time. Employees also frequently report that they cannot convince upper-level management that cultural differences are important.

The workplace is rapidly becoming more diverse. Over half of the labor force in the United States is made up of women, racial minorities, and immigrants. A similar trend is occurring in countries throughout the world. Training employees in impression management benefits both employees and the firms they represent in the following ways:

1. Employees from all parts of the globe can learn to respect, understand, and appreciate the values and traditions of one another's cultures.
2. The negative effects of culture shock for expatriates can be overcome or reduced.
3. Feelings of confusion, surprise, or indignation when people like Fred Bailey are trying to adapt to new environments may also be reduced.
4. Communication is helped by creating a healthy work setting for collaboration between expatriates and host nationals.

For firms to be economically successful, employees must be interculturally successful. Culturally appropriate impression management is now recognized as a key to this success.

1. From your knowledge of impression management, what advice would you give to an American employee who has been hired by a Japanese firm, with headquarters in London, to market its products in Germany, Brazil, and Indonesia?

2. What can businesses do to transfer positive social interaction among employees of different cultures in the workplace to outside the workplace? What would be an incentive for business to do this?

Sources: Child & Markoczy, 1993; Lichtenberger & Naulleau, 1993; Giacalone & Beard, 1994; Mendenhall & Wiley, 1994; Lindsey, 1997.

"Well, since you brought it up, we need to talk about our relationship."

Nonverbal Communication as a Polygraph

As mentioned earlier, there is some controversy as to whether role performances are meant to deceive others. Since nonverbal communication may be unintentional, it provides a good test for how well we can manage our impressions and detects the emotions of others. In this way it can be used as a polygraph, or lie detector. For example, enlargement or dilation of the pupil of the eye is a sign of attraction to someone or something. Once we learn our culture's beliefs of what is considered attractive (Chapter 3), this physiological response is almost impossible to disguise. People who are romantically attracted to each other have dilated pupils. When women see pictures of babies and infants, their pupils dilate, a sign of interest. Men's pupils get smaller, a sign of disinterest. Even the best poker players cannot conceal a good hand, because their pupils tend to dilate (Kleinke, 1986; Stiff et al., 1989). When an emotion cannot be masked completely, *leakage* occurs and the hidden emotion "drips" out (Goffman, 1961b; 1967).

Expressions of genuine happiness or devastating grief are betrayed by leakage through facial characteristics. The facial patterns of a true smile and one intentionally designed to conceal negative emotion differ (Ekman et al., 1988). Unlike smiling, laughter is more spontaneous; because it reflects emotion more than a rational act, it is difficult to fake. A great deal of evidence shows that lying is also revealed nonverbally through leakage. Interestingly, it is detected more easily in people who are the most motivated to get away with their lies (Forrest & Feldman, 2000)!

Cultural Variations in Nonverbal Communication

Research suggests that the facial patterns of some emotional expressions, such as fear and joy, are similar crossculturally. But because nonverbal communication is learned largely through socialization, only an observer who knows the culture very well can detect leakage of other hidden emotions. If deception *can* be uncovered, then impression management may fail. Among many Asian cultures, including Korea, Japan, and Thailand, displays of emotion such as broad grins or angry outbursts are considered impolite. It is also rude to show disagreement with another person's behavior in these cultures. Middle Eastern and Latin cultures expect such displays as signs of interpersonal closeness.

In the United States smiling is associated with friendliness and happiness, but not necessarily so in

In Korea, smiling in public is not all that common. This man would be viewed as unfriendly in the United States and other countries where smiling is more the norm.

Korea. Korean retailers in the United States are viewed as hostile by non-Korean customers because they do not smile (Dresser, 1994). Smiling is a taken-for-granted cultural norm in most parts of the United States, especially by a shopkeeper hoping to make a sale. Some consequences of breaking norms of nonverbal behavior are even more unsettling. People who do not show emotions—referred to as *flat affect* by psychologists—in situations that call for emotional expression may be considered mentally ill because they violate taken-for-granted cultural rules of nonverbal communication. Since some cultures may view flat affect as the appropriate response, cultural background must be taken into consideration in the diagnosis of mental illness.

There are other practical purposes for becoming knowledgeable about nonverbal behavior, especially in the context of a culture different from your own. In the United States a thumbs-up sign indicates victory and the circular A-OK sign formed by the thumb and forefinger means affirmation or giving the go-ahead. In much of the Middle East and South Asia these two signs are the nonverbal equivalent of "giving the finger." You can see how these innocent gestures might provoke a physical fight. The way to hail a taxi in the United States is to wave your hand above your head, usually with your index finger pointing up. In Greece this same gesture is extremely offensive. So if you hail a taxi in Greece the way you hail a taxi in the United States, don't be surprised if you don't get a ride!

Understanding the sexual implications of nonverbal behavior is crucial to success as our world becomes increasingly globalized. A man's steady gaze at a woman is interpreted as threatening in many cultures. Even a man's glance at a completely veiled Muslim woman in North Africa can be seen as a sexually provocative act and could make him the target of a physical attack by the woman's male companions. Modestly dressed Western women traveling in South Asia and the Middle East report that men routinely pinch, touch, and fondle them as they walk through crowded streets. Media stereotypes in those regions reinforce the belief that any adult female who is unveiled and not in the company of a male relative is either a prostitute or "loose" woman and therefore fair game for curious men. Unless they are corrected, misinterpreted nonverbal patterns can become part of the overall communication system. All these cases indicate the potential dire consequences of nonverbal misunderstanding.

Gendered Nonverbal Communication

Understanding nonverbal communication is important to sociological analysis because it serves as an excellent mirror of *social stratification*—that is, how people are ranked according to the various social statuses they hold (Chapter 10). Nonverbal behavior can show which groups wield power and which groups are subject to it. In all cultures, differences in power between females and males are clearly reflected in nonverbal communication. The following list summarizes some of the important differences in nonverbal communication between men and women in the United States. Although some nonverbal patterns are typical to the culture as a whole, a narrower pattern reveals the existence of a gender subculture. Distinct patterns of behavior in the interactions between females and males, including communication, differ from those present in the broader culture. Some of the items on this list may surprise you because of prevalent but inaccurate gender role stereotypes.

1. Men interrupt women more than women interrupt men, especially to change topics. When women interrupt conversations, they do so to indicate interest in the topic, to respond, or to show support (West & Zimmerman, 1983; Stewart et al., 1990).

2. Men verbally dominate women in conversation, especially in arguments. Structured conversations with an explicit agenda, such as at a meeting or in a work-related brainstorming session, are dominated by men. Women have more control over free discussion, where there is no agenda, such as colleagues having lunch together (Kimble & Musgrove, 1988; Woods, 1988).

3. Women engage in more eye contact than men. In both same-gender and other-gender conversational pairs, women will look at the other person more and retain longer eye contact. Men have more visual dominance than women—a pattern of looking at others when speaking but looking away from them when listening (Ellyson et al., 1992; Tannen, 1994).

4. Research on paralanguage indicates that men are more talkative than women in mixed-gender groups. Men also talk at a faster rate than women. In classroom interaction at all educational levels, male students talk more and for longer periods than female students. Interestingly, higher levels of male talkativeness as well as remaining silent are associated with power and dominance. Men can control conversations by either dominating conversations or not talking at all (Kimble & Musgrove, 1988; Crawford, 1995; Cameron, 1998).

   Even when men speak two to three times longer than women, the men believe they do not have their fair share of conversation. As the research notes, "If a woman is expected to be quiet, then any woman who opens her mouth can be accused of being talkative" (Spender, 1989:9).

Within same-gender groups, women talk for longer periods, enjoy it more, and converse on a wider variety of topics. For women, talk is a preferred social activity (Coates, 1988; Johnson, 1996).

5. Women more openly express emotions than men. For example, women smile more than men. Just look at your high school yearbook. The notable exception to male lack of emotional expression is anger. It is more acceptable for males than for females to display anger. Anger may be masked in females by another emotion, such as crying, which is generally more acceptable for women than for men (Ekman & O'Sullivan, 1991; Kinney et al., 2001).

6. Females are better than males at successfully decoding the nonverbal cues of others, because they rely more on facial expressions learned early in life. There is one major exception to this pattern: Women are superior to men in detecting truth-telling, but men are better at detecting lying. Why? Some social psychologists speculate that since women are more polite than men, a woman's generally superior ability to decode is suspended for some speakers. A norm of politeness keeps them from confronting the lying, so instead they simply avoid eavesdropping on nonverbal cues (DePaulo et al., 1993; McClure, 2000).

7. Men touch women more than women touch men. Since touch can suggest a range of motives, such as affection, dominance, aggression, or sexual interest, the context of the touching is important. Superiors touch subordinates with a hand on the shoulder or a pat on the back. But when passengers poke and pinch flight attendants or when a man fondles a status equal in the office, sexual overtones cannot be dismissed easily. Women tend to view touch as harassing when men use it to establish power (Poire et al., 1992; Snodgrass, 1992).

   Men rarely touch each other. Even intimate displays of physical contact during sports events have limits. Soccer players from various nations who compete under the guidelines of the International Soccer Federation were told that their outbursts of jumping on top of one another, kissing, and embracing were excessive and inappropriate. They were reminded to "behave like adults" (cited in Parlee, 1989:14) when they were actually being told to behave like males.

8. Men are more protective of their personal space and guard against territorial invasions. Men invade intimate and personal space of women more than the reverse, perhaps reflecting the fact that such invasions are tolerated more by women. The

space privilege by males is taken for granted. The next time you are on an airplane or in a theater, note the gender differences in access to the armrests. In walking or standing, women yield their space more readily than men, especially if the approacher is a man. Men retreat when women come as close to them as they do to women and feel provoked if other men come as close to them as they do to women (Payne, 2001). Space invasions by men are a rarely challenged and taken-for-granted form of social interaction.

Theoretical Perspectives on Nonverbal Communication

The various sociological theories can explain the patterns of nonverbal communication outlined above as well as others. Knowledge about culture and social stratification, especially related to gender, race, and class, is important in these explanations.

FUNCTIONALISM Functionalists maintain that nonverbal communication serves to bind people to their culture. Social equilibrium is helped when one language, including its nonverbal elements, is used and accepted by everyone. Functionalists would suggest, therefore, that any gender differences in nonverbal communication are useful for maintenance of this equilibrium. When couples communicate nonverbally in ways that reinforce traditional gender roles, there is less possibility for disrupting social patterns.

CONFLICT THEORY Conflict theorists look at gendered nonverbal communication patterns quite differently. According to the conflict perspective, men's interruption of women indicates the right of a superior to interrupt a subordinate, in the same way that children (subordinates) are interrupted by parents (their superiors). Space invasion offers another example. Subordinates are expected to give up space to superiors—in the workplace, on an airplane, or in a classroom. An employee must be anxiously watchful of the employer to determine what comes next in the interaction, such as a secretary waiting for directives from the boss. The boss, on the other hand, does not need to look at the secretary while issuing these directives. Direct eye contact by employer and employee can serve to diminish the employer's superior status. Type of posture also conveys messages about who's in charge. With the expectation that the subordinate will be prepared to respond to any immediate demands, the subordinate posture is more rigid and tense. The superior's, in contrast, is more relaxed. Overall, because women are more likely than men to be employee subordinates, they are also more adept in ad-

justing their nonverbal behavior, whether in posture, eye contact, or conversational strategy. A woman's advantage in decoding nonverbal cues is beneficial, because some research shows that gender differences in nonverbal behavior persist even when men and women occupy the same status (Hall & Friedman, 1999). However, other studies show that there are fewer gender differences in nonverbal behavior when men and women hold more equal social statuses (positions). Conflict theorists need to account for the specific context of the interaction as well as the degree of power other social statuses give men and women (Burgoon & Dunbar, 2000; Algoe et al., 2000).

LINKING GENDER AND RACE: SYMBOLIC INTERACTIONISM Symbolic interactionism interprets nonverbal communication patterns by focusing on the setting of the conversation and on impression management. For all races, nonverbal behavior enhances interpersonal intimacy and friendship; this is especially true for women. For both genders, interpersonal intimacy is enhanced in contexts in which power and domination are less important. Nonverbal behaviors between people who are equal in status tend to affirm and cement relationships.

The situation is different in exchanges between persons of unequal status. For example, a greater amount of direct eye contact may be interpreted as assertive, with strength rather than meekness being communicated. Status equals look directly at one another. Status unequals do not. Women who want career advancement can adjust their eye contact so that they appear not quite as watchful, but still deferential, to their superior. Thus, a female executive in the boardroom adjusts her nonverbals, such as amount of eye contact, to the situation according to the image she wants to project. She is practicing impression management to highlight her (superior) executive status and de-emphasize her (subordinate) gender status.

When the nonverbal situation involves people of different races, the gender pattern varies. A common testimonial from African American men is that white women plant broad grins on their faces when passing them, supposedly as a sign of trust. But the recipients of these smiles see it as fear and deference (Anderson, 1995). Another pattern is for white women to walk past African American men with eyes straight ahead, appearing to ignore them. Both patterns are illustrated by the following encounter in New York City reported by Mitchell Duneier, a sociologist doing a participant-observation (Chapter 2) study on sidewalk life.

Out on Sixth Avenue one day I ask Mudrick (an African American man) about his relationships to women on the street. Since most women ignore him, he says he talks to all of them. Three white women in their twenties approach, and I am given a demonstration. "Hi ladies. How you-all feeling, ladies. You-all look very nice, you know. Have a nice day." (Then) a white woman . . . approaches with her friend. "Hey, you, with the shades on. You look very nice." "Thank you," she says. "Your friend look nice, too." "Thank you." "Hey pretty," says Mudrick to a white woman in her thirties with blond hair. "Look at her smiling! Anybody look back at me and smile. I say, I'll get you when I catch you by yourself. I'm taking you to bed." I ask him what's the worst thing women will do when he says that. "They can't do anything. Because the words I say, they don't have any choice." He claims that the women he addresses never feel harassed because he gives them respect, and he can tell from their smiles that they like the attention. "I get a kick out of it. . . . It makes me feel good and I try to make them happy. The things I say, they can't accept. They gotta deal with it." (Adapted from Duneier, 1999:193–96)

While Duneier reports that rarely women verbally respond to Mudrick, it is very clear that they are not ignoring his remarks either. They are playing the game of civil inattention. They will do what they can to get through an encounter that is likely perceived as both unpleasant and threatening, maintain some degree of control, and do it in a manner that supposedly hides their true emotions.

Another example is from an African American male who came across a white woman late one evening on a deserted street in Chicago.

As I swung onto the avenue behind her, there seemed to be a discreet, uninflammatory distance between us. Not so. She cast back a worried

glance. To her, the youngish black man . . . seemed menacingly close. After a few more quick glimpses, she picked up her pace and was soon running in earnest. (Staples, 1997:228)

These nonveverbal exchanges reflect several points about how race, gender, and class are socially constructed as well as ranked by subtle but powerful definitions of the situation. First, all people react to African Americans in the context of the street. While whites are more afraid of blacks than the reverse, it has been shown that "blacks are more wary of blacks in some public places than they are of whites, including in black neighborhoods (Duneier, 1999:304). Regardless of where the interaction occurs, it is the definition of race that first conditions how the interaction will proceed. Second, race is a more important variable than gender, since the supposedly "higher" social category of white defers to the "lower" social category of black. The exchanges also reinforce the stereotypes associated with the danger of African American men to white women. Finally, but contrary to symbolic interactionism, such nonverbal exchanges correlate with research suggesting that the harmful effects of stereotypes cannot be completely overcome with individual attempts at impression management (Riordan et al., 1994). In these instances the women reinforced stereotypes by their failure to convince the African American men—or themselves—that they were unafraid. To effectively attack such stereotypes, all social institutions at all levels must be part of the effort. The mass media is one institution where definitions about race and race stereotypes appear to be changing, as you will see in the following section.

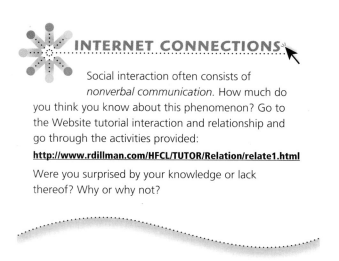

INTERNET CONNECTIONS

Social interaction often consists of *nonverbal communication.* How much do you think you know about this phenomenon? Go to the Website tutorial interaction and relationship and go through the activities provided:

http://www.rdillman.com/HFCL/TUTOR/Relation/relate1.html

Were you surprised by your knowledge or lack thereof? Why or why not?

LIFE CONNECTIONS

Constructing Social Class on Television

What are your earliest childhood memories? Chances are, in addition to family, neighbors, and friends, your favorite television character or show is among them. The mass media have an extraordinary influence on our social constructions of everyday life. Symbolic interactionists point out that like the larger society in which they are created, media classify people according to various cultural categories, especially those based on race, gender, and social class. Mr. Rogers is a white, middle-class male and his class, race, and gender are the media norms around which a great deal of television programming is based. As ethnomethodologists would suggest, since these norms dominate television programming, viewers are not apt to even notice the norms unless they are violated. It is

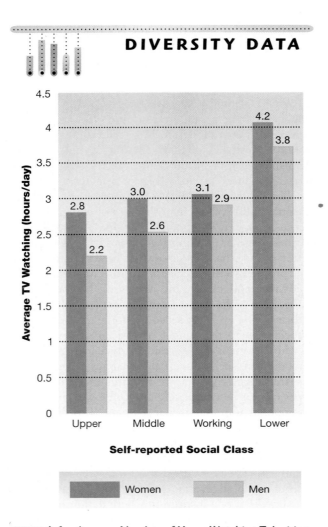

DIVERSITY DATA

FIGURE 6.1 **Average Number of Hours Watching Television, by Social Class and Gender.** Both women and men in the lower- and working-class watch television more than those in the middle and upper class. However, the working- and lower-classes are portrayed less and stereotyped more in social interaction. Do you think that a high level of television watching by the working class strengthens or weakens their agreement with these portrayals?

Source: NORC. General Social Surveys, 1972–2000. Chicago: National Opinion Research Center, 2000. Reprinted by permission of NORC, Chicago, IL.

section of the cultural categories of social class and race in prime time television provides an excellent demonstration of the social construction of everyday life.

The Intersection of Race and Class on Television

Like *Mr. Rogers' Neighborhood*, until the mid-1960s, prime time television was mainly inhabited by white, middle-class, professional and managerial men of generic northern European background. They were married to women of similar backgrounds who were depicted as full-time homemakers. When people of color were seen, they usually fell into three categories: African American chauffeurs and maids, Asian cooks and gardeners, and Latino desperados and drug lords. However, the next two decades saw a marked shift for people of color in both numbers as well as type of roles, a pattern that continues today. Not only have the number of nonwhite characters jumped to well over 10 percent, a wider range of roles—including more positive portrayals—accompanied the increases. African Americans are the biggest beneficiaries, with a 14-fold increase. Asians come in second in both numbers and positive portrayals. Latinos, however, remain a distant third. Some increase in numbers is noted, but Latinos are largely supporting players and background figures and are much more likely to be portrayed as poor, deviant, or criminal compared to all other racial and ethnic groups. (For more on the television image of Latinos, see Chapter 20.)

A gradual but steady blurring of racial differences is occurring on prime time television. However, as racial differences steadily decrease, a corresponding increase in class differences is occurring. Gone are the struggling working-class African American families of 1970s television. The laborers, servants, and junk collectors of the Evans family (*Good Times*) and *Sanford and Son* were replaced in the 1980s with business owners, attorneys, and other professionals (*The Jeffersons* and *The Cosby Show*). The 1990s gave us leading roles for African American secret agents, doctors, lawyers, and police officers in shows such as *ER*, *The Practice*, and *NYPD Blue*. For the white working class, a similar pattern occurred, especially for women. The struggling waitresses of *Alice* and assembly-line workers of *Laverne and Shirley* have been supplanted by the professionals of *Ally McBeal*, *Friends*, and *Sex in the City*.

As people from all races moved up in social class, they left their working-class counterparts behind. By the end of the 20th century, television became a virtual haven for the middle class (*Judging Amy*, *Spin City*, *West Wing*, and *Third Watch*). Many of the middle-class people shown on prime time television are

the norm violation that becomes the basis for the entertainment. Television slots people into convenient, taken-for-granted categories. These categories are constructed so that differences rather than similarities among people are highlighted. By emphasizing differences between various cultural categories, the media send messages about their value or importance. The media therefore construct and reinforce beliefs about differences as well as inequality in society. The intercollege-educated men and women who lead interesting and productive lives and have disposable income to travel and buy expensive artifacts for their tastefully decorated homes. Some even have servants and household helpers. They attend art shows and concerts and sit in box seats at sporting events. The desire of advertisers to show a full range of products used by glamorous people is often catered to. The result is television shows built around rather affluent middle-class characters (Butsch, 2000). The psychiatrist brothers of Frasier represent the middle-class standard of prime time television. Racial stereotypes are still very apparent, but class stereotypes appear to be on the fast track in overtaking them.

Television's Working Class

Middle-class roles offer a great deal of diversity and less negative portrayals overall than television's portrayal of the working class. In the real world, people in the working class are those who lift, bend, drive, keyboard, clean, load, unload, provide physical care for others, cook, and serve (Ehrenreich, 1998). They are likely to be high school graduates working for a wage rather than a salary and employed in blue-collar positions, retail sales, and lower level white-collar clerical occupations. Although they represent over two-thirds of employed Americans (Chapter 11), the working class of prime time television is mostly invisible. A study of 262 situation comedies from 1946 to 1990 found working-class household heads at only 11 percent of the total. Blue-collar families were the most underrepresented at 4 percent. Even more recent data on situation comedies featuring working-class families show slightly fewer upper-class than working-class families. The majority of sitcom families remain middle class and above, with the working class relegated to the category of "other" (Butsch, 2000; Scharrer, 2001).

Prime time television's construction of this small group of working-class families is a vastly different reality than that of the television's middle class. For example, compare *King of Queens* to *Will and Grace*. Blue-collar workers especially are depicted as needing supervision, and it is up to middle-class professionals to provide it. Working-class characters have few starring roles and are usually depicted as friends or relatives of the main characters in situation comedies (*Becker, Everybody Loves Raymond*) or as unsavory characters lurking in the background of police precincts, courtrooms, schools, and hospital waiting rooms in prime time dramas (*CSI, Gideon's Crossing, Boston Public*). News media representation of the working class as "irrelevant, outmoded, and a dying breed" reinforce these images (Mantsios, 2001: 565).

Unlike racial portraits, working-class portraits have remained virtually the same throughout television's relatively young history. Ralph Cramden, Fred Flintstone, and Archie Bunker have been replaced by Homer Simpson and Drew Carey's semiliterate friends. The few shows that portray working-class people in lead roles have prototype characters: They are white males depicted as lovable but incompetent, as clowns but losers. They are parochial, inarticulate, and have poor or questionable taste in all things. These middle-aged men are "addicted to cigarettes, Budweiser, polyester, and network television" (Ehrenreich, 1998: 148). The men are basically insecure but hide it beneath a thin veil of exaggerated masculinity that is easily unwoven by their ever-suffering wives. Wives hold the family together as their husbands bumble their way through get-rich schemes. Working-class families are seen to be less functional than middle-class families (Lichter et al., 1994; Douglas & Olson, 1995). What is perhaps most revealing, however, is that the male household heads of television families in situation comedies over 50 years are not only portrayed more foolishly than in shows featuring middle-class to upper-class families, but the pattern has actually increased over time (Scharrer, 2001). The most recent shows have the most foolish fathers, and they are likely to be members of the working class. The debut of *The Man Show* on cable television in 1999 is not a situation comedy but a talk-variety show that is geared to the 18- to 34-year-old male audience and to date has a wide and growing audience. Entertainment spots focus on working-class settings. It is billed as a show where "men are men, women are bouncy, and beer is beer" (McAdams, 1999). While middle-class men may enjoy watching the show, they are less likely to see themselves portrayed as laughably as their middle-class counterparts. The significant holdout to this pattern was *Roseanne*, which for a decade was one of most popular shows on television and is currently one of the most popular series in syndication. Roseanne's family deviated from the working-class norm by demonstrating diverse roles and dealing sensitively with a range of difficult issues all families face. Comedy was not sacrificed for such diverse portrayals.

As you would expect, producers defend portrayals of social class in the name of profit. Advertisers desire to spotlight a wide range of products, so series that revolve around working-class families who have less disposable income are not encouraged. In capitalist societies, commercial television and other media can exist only because of advertising, so the media will create products—news and entertainment programs—to suit advertisers. Prospects for television's less stereotypical images of the working classes remain dim (Blumler & Spicer, 1990; Butsch, 1992).

SOCIOLOGY **OF EVERYDAY LIFE**

The Good, the Bad, and the Ugly

"Beauty is only skin deep." "You can't judge a book by its cover." "The worth of people is not in their faces and figures but in their hearts and minds." Parents and teachers use such messages to guide children in humane ways of social interaction, but children also receive messages that counter good intentions. Throughout life, media bombard us with messages that beauty does count and we are judged by our looks and the looks of our friends—and woe to those of us who are not at least "minimally" attractive. Fortunately, there are ways to remedy our physical misfortunes. We can buy cosmetics, wrinkle-removing cream, hair-regrowth salve, diet pills, and exercise equipment. If these are not enough, there is always plastic surgery.

Television portrays attractive and unattractive people quite differently. Unattractive people are used as contrasts to other, more attractive characters. The unattractive are often cast as friends of the beautiful. They are likable, but bumbling and socially inept. They have intellectual flaws and often fail to see that others make fun of them. Examples include George

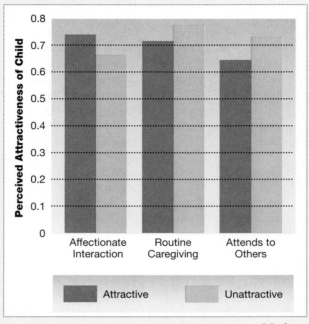

Attractive Children Can Even Affect Their Parents. Mothers of more attractive infants show them more affection and are more playful with them, whereas mothers of less attractive children are more likely to pay greater attention to people other than their infants.

Source: Graph from, "Infant Attractiveness Predicts Maternal Behaviors and Attitudes" by J. H. Langlois, J. M. Ritter, R. J. Casey and D. B. Sawin in *Developmental Psychology*, *31*, 1995, pp. 464–472. Copyright © by the American Psychological Association. Adapted with permission.

Costanza and Kramer in the long-running *Seinfeld* series, Bulldog in *Frasier,* and Bob, the short and out-of-style friend of *Becker.* The unattractive are also cast in bad guy (mostly male) roles. The murderers, drug addicts, and robbers who inhabit the wards of *ER* and the precincts

of *Law and Order* and *Judging Amy* can be described as "unattractive." "Ugly" may be a better word.

Research suggests that standards of attractiveness are strongly media based. After years of watching television and movies and viewing thousands of ads in magazines and on billboards, people gradually learn which types of faces and figures are considered to be the most attractive. These features may change over time, but people within a culture generally agree on beauty standards. Standards of beauty have powerful influences on how we perceive ourselves and others and on our social interactions. Research on the influence of attractiveness in social behavior centers on the "beautiful-is-good" (BIG) stereotype. BIG means that people associate beauty with an amazing variety of positive characteristics. As reinforced in the media, what is beautiful is also good. The "good" characteristics of the physically attractive compared to the less attractive include the following:

1. Throughout their lives, people who are physically attractive are liked bet-

Social Construction of Class on Television

Television perpetuates the myth that America is a classless society—everyone is middle class. As we have seen, the few portrayals that are not so middle class are exceptions. A media subculture made up of Hollywood executives and creative personnel determine television programming. This small, closed community is responsible for what we see or do not see on

television. Most television messages are openly and explicitly delivered—audiences have little trouble deciding, for instance, whether the portrayal of most television characters is positive or negative. But some messages are delivered much more subtly—audiences may not have enough information about some characters to make a reasonable judgment about who they are and whether they are to be liked or disliked. Invisibility sends just such a subtle message that those who

ter. They are often held to a different standard of judgment. When attractive people do negative things, their behavior is often described with excuses such as "they had a bad day." When unattractive people do the same things, their behavior is viewed in terms of "who they are," symptoms of larger personality problems. Mimi of the *Drew Carey Show* is obese and has outrageous hair, clothing, and makeup. She is bizarre, even psychotic, in her behavior. What she does is who she is—ugly.

2. Attractive people are rated higher on kindness, strength, sexual responsiveness, social skills, and intelligence. The strongest ratings come from teens. The popularity of shows such as *Friends* among college students and *Dawson's Creek* among high schoolers—with casts of exceptionally beautiful people—reflect such ratings. Vanity is the major variation to these beliefs. Beautiful people are rated as more conceited, such as Nina, the ex-model in *Just Shoot Me.*

3. Higher ratings sometimes translate to advantages for the physically attractive. They are more popular, get more dates, and are more favorably treated in school and work. *Happy Days,* also in reruns, had virile and handsome Fonzi, with women falling all over him, in contrast to physically plain Ralph Malph, who strived, but was usually unsuccessful, in finding women to date. The new millennium's record holder for "lack of success in love for unattractive people" must surely be awarded to Kevin, the nerdy and ill-kempt mailroom guy in *Just Shoot Me.* Kevin's record may be unchallenged now, but the century is still young.

BIG may be unfair and unkind, but is it accurate? Remember that stereotypes are largely inaccurate but persist because they also contain some grains of truth. BIG is no exception. Emotional stability and dominance are unrelated to attractiveness, as are intelligence and academic ability. Attractiveness has no influence on ratings of concern for others or level of integrity. The physically attractive have better social skills and experience less loneliness than the less attractive, but these differences are small. The grains of truth in BIG include higher popularity and higher work evaluations for the attractive compared to the unattractive. The most important finding about BIG, however, is that the more we get to know others through social interaction, concern for physical attractiveness, both theirs and others', fades. BIG oversimplifies ratings of others when information about them is limited.

Symbolic interactionism can explain why BIG is inaccurate but persistent. When first meeting an attractive person, we have a positive definition of the situation that may have been media inspired. People who are as handsome as Tom Cruise or as beautiful as Gwyneth Paltrow are also seen to possess heroic (good) behaviors. This definition creates favorable circumstances for the beautiful to "become" good. The good traits we first associate with beauty are reinforced in our social interaction and may create a self-fulfilling prophecy. Media may be the most powerful socialization factor for the BIG stereotype. Positive portrayals of people with less-than-perfect faces and figures will help break down BIG.

1. Do you think that two equally qualified people, one who is attractive and the other who is not, who apply for the same job, will be on an equal playing field for hiring? Would an unattractive interviewer—male or female—be more or less influenced by the attractiveness of the interviewee?

2. Media portrayals of women and racial minorities are becoming more positive. Do the media have any social responsibility in altering how people are portrayed based on their level of attractiveness—such as making unattractive people more positive?

Sources: Eagly et al., 1991; Feingold, 1992; LaRose et al., 1993; Jackson et al., 1995; Langlois & Musselman, 1995; Smith et al., 1999; Ruscher, 2001.

are not seen are less important than those who are seen. Children overwhelmingly say that they need to see their own race on television, and children of color are most likely to state this. Children of all races associate having money, education, being a leader, and being intelligent with the white people they see on television and breaking the law, being lazy, having little money, and acting goofy with the minority characters they see (Chen et al., 1999). Seldom seen groups, such as Latinos and working-class people, are much more likely to be portrayed stereotypically and unfavorably. Messages about minority status may be lost on adults, but children are keenly aware of these portrayals. Their perceptions can be summarized as follows: I love watching TV, I love what I see, I'm still looking for ME! (Chen et al., 1999).

Symbolic interactionists would argue that the elite media subculture is made up of middle-class

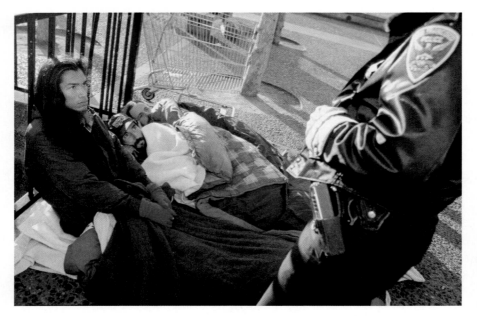

When the homeless are socially constructed as undeserving, they may be treated as social threats to society and may be forced to leave an area or be arrested.

people who reproduce class stereotypes in the shows they create, write, and produce. News and talk shows also bolster a middle-class programming bias. The counterparts to the Hollywood media subculture in other mass media are the owners, publishers, and editors of major channels of information and opinion, such as *The New York Times* and *The Wall Street Journal* (Blasi, 1994). If they hear only the opinions of their own members and look to the very media created by their middle-class predecessors to reinforce these opinions, media subcultures are effectively shielded from other views. As mentioned earlier, the media construction of homelessness has shifted over time. The homeless are the nameless and faceless murder victims on television, whether in "true" news stories or in fictionalized accounts. Rarely are they called upon by the media to comment on decisions made by others that will profoundly impact their lives. The working class and everyone below them in the stratification system are judged through the experiences of those middle-class people who socially construct them for the viewing public.

And since the media are owned by corporations and dependent on the advertising dollars of other corporations, conflict theorists assert that media content is shaped more by corporate interests than by the interests of the viewing public. The goal is to sell products to people who can afford to buy them—the middle class. Therefore, constructions of the working class are not likely to change unless social reality becomes profitable and society overcomes its disdain of those who are different from "us" (Nardi, 2000).

SOCIETY CONNECTIONS
Reconstructing Social Reality

According to the symbolic interactionist perspective, social issues arise through a process of collective definition. Only when enough people become aware that a social condition is harmful and should be remedied can we identify it as a social problem. Thus, social problems are socially constructed. Poverty, for example, is a long-standing social condition. When poverty is elevated from a social condition to a social problem, there is a consensus that poverty is harmful not only to some members of society, but to the society as a whole. Poverty is discovered and rediscovered as a social problem over time as the public shifts its attention from one issue to another.

Often, the definition of the situation from one important individual can help shape the collective definition. Activists in the areas of animal rights, food and nutrition, and health and environmental concerns have succeeded in getting their causes into the public consciousness because celebrities, politicians, or other notables have embraced the causes. For example, people in the United States expect the First Lady to take on a "cause" during her White House stay. Her high public profile allows for a swift transformation of an individual definition of the situation to a collective one, and the elevation of a social condition to a social problem. Lady Bird Johnson raised the nation's collective consciousness regarding littering and the environment, Jacqueline Kennedy did the same for mental retardation, Barbara Bush promoted child welfare,

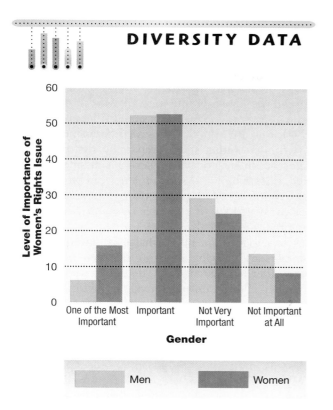

DIVERSITY DATA

FIGURE 6.2 **Percent of Respondents Stating Level of Importance for Women's Rights, by Gender.** Women are more likely to say that women's rights is one of their most important or important issues. Men are more likely to say the issue is not very important or not important at all to them. The specific women's rights issue of sexual harassment has an even wider difference in attitudes between men and women. On which women's rights issues do you think men and women have the least amount of difference?

Source: NORC. General Social Surveys, 1972–2000. Chicago: National Opinion Research Center, 2000. Reprinted by permission of NORC, Chicago, IL.

and Hillary Clinton focused the nation's attention on women in poverty. Laura Bush, a former teacher and librarian, has an education and literacy agenda for her tenure as First Lady. Symbolic interactionists point out that all of these social conditions may have caused suffering and deprivation before they gained public attention, but they did not emerge as social problems until they became defined as social threats and were thrust into the spotlight. There is no objective reality; social problems are matters of collective definitions.

Sexual Harassment

We conclude with a topic that illustrates well sociology's approach to social interaction and draws together many of the concepts discussed in this chapter.

By examining the issue of sexual harassment, we can better understand the process of redefining behavior from acceptable to unacceptable. Compared to other social problems such as the health consequences of smoking, there is less agreement about what constitutes sexual harassment. This was made abundantly clear in 1991 during the confirmation hearings for Supreme Court Justice Clarence Thomas, when Professor Anita Hill testified that he had sexually harassed her when he was her superior. The public furor over the hearings showed that a virtual chasm existed between women's experiences of sexual harassment and how it was understood by the wider society. Indeed, although women had experienced sexual harassment for decades, until collective definitions identified it as a social problem, it was all but ignored. Since the Hill-Thomas controversy, sexual harassment has become a major issue. Media continue to fuel the issue by spotlighting a number of alleged sexual harassment cases during the last decade: the "Tail Hook" scandal where women were sexually assaulted at a convention of Navy pilots, the extreme sexual bullying of the first female cadets admitted to the Citadel and Virginia Military Institute (VMI), Air Force pilot Kelly Flinn's discharge for adultery following her charges against the Army's highest ranked enlisted man (for which he was acquitted), and Paula Jones' case against Bill Clinton when he was governor of Arkansas, leading to later impeachment hearings. The media frenzy surrounding sexual harassment continued in the new millennium with independent counsel Kenneth Starr's investigation of President Clinton's affair with Monica Lewinsky. Regardless of the outcome, all of these cases illustrate one critical fact: Most people now denounce sexual harassment, but they still are unsure exactly what is being denounced.

Sexual harassment is a form of sex discrimination that is prohibited under Title VII of the 1964 Civil Rights Act. According to the Equal Opportunity Employment Commission's (EEOC) definition, **sexual harassment** consists of "unwelcome sexual advances, requests for sexual favors, and other verbal or physical conduct of a sexual nature" that are used as a condition of employment or a basis for employment decisions. Such conditions can also create an intimidating, hostile, or offensive work environment. The Thomas confirmation hearings allowed firsthand view of the extent of sexual harassment. A poll conducted immediately after the hearings found that well over half of women in the military and those who worked in federal agencies had experienced it (*Parade Magazine,* 1991). Research conducted over the past decade confirms that sexual harassment remains widespread in schools and workplaces. It is safe to conclude that well over half of all women have experienced it in some form in their lifetimes, a pattern found in the United States, Britain, and Canada (Se'ver, 1999; Wilson, 2000).

The EEOC regulations were approved in 1980, but until the Thomas hearings they were routinely ignored, both by those being harassed and by their employers. Sexual harassment has been linked to emotional problems, compromised work productivity, absenteeism from work and school, a deterioration in morale, and long-term depression, all of which can have a serious impact on a person's work and private lives. Retaliation by employers and coworkers can amount to career suicide; fear of such a backlash is a commonly cited reason for the failure to report it (Martin, 1995; Dansky & Kilpatrick, 1997; Schneider et al., 1997; Welsh, 1999). As pointed out by both conflict theory and symbolic interactionism, the reason sexual harassment is so hard to identify and resolve is because of accepted definitions of sexuality that disguise and dismiss sexual domination and exploitation in the workplace and elsewhere.

Gender, Race, and Sexual Harassment in Schools

Sexual harassment in schools is so widespread that one researcher has dubbed it a "pervasive folkway" (Steinberg, 1999). This is especially true in elementary schools where sexual harassment takes the form of bullying behavior by boys toward girls—accepted by the boys, tolerated by the girls, and ignored by the teachers. When adults hear comments and do not intervene, both boys and girls believe that the behavior is appropriate (Bailey, 1998; Stein, 1999). Whereas racial comments are swiftly censured, sexually harassing ones are usually dismissed. Surveys of female high school students report that over one-third had observed or experienced it (Sauerwein, 1996). Examples from these students included "taking about people with large chests," "pinching butts on the bus," and "half of everything said on the Commons." Research reviews of colleges indicate that between 30 percent and 75 percent of female faculty and female students report some form of sexual harassment ranging from everyday jokes about body or physical contact, demeaning images, negative remarks, and sexist comments to unwanted advances, demands for sexual favors, and sexual aggression or victimization (Welsh, 1999; Riger, 2000; Wilson, 2000).

Some studies report higher rates of sexual harassment of women of color with African American women experiencing the highest rates, followed by Latino, white, and Asian/East Indian women (Mecca

& Rubin, 1999; Paludi, 1996). Compared to white women, African American women may identify their experiences with sexual harassment differently as well. For example, African American women mention comments about racially based physical features and stereotypes about promiscuity of African Americans as demonstrating sexual harassment (Mecca & Rubin, 1999). Research on race in sexual harassment is still very limited. Other studies report no significant race difference in level or type of sexual harassment. However, since white and African American women perceive it differently, the race-gender intersection in social constructions of sexual harassment needs to be explored (Kalof, et al., 2001).

Sexual harassment of males is infrequent, but numbers are growing. Bullying behavior by boys toward other boys is common, decreases with age, and is usually ignored unless it involves physical fighting. It can be brutal and humiliating, but it is not considered sexual harassment (Stein, 1999), even when boys bully other boys by verbally using sexually derogatory comments that compare them to girls or gay men or boys. At military schools such as the Citadel and VMI, male cadets can be expelled for sexually harassing female cadets only if bullying becomes sexualized. Boys do not report bullying from other boys for the same reason girls do not report sexual harassment—fear of reprisal, especially from peers. Males are even less likely to report sexual harassment by females. Norms about masculinity make it difficult for males to admit that they may be intimidated by females (Dziech & Hawkins, 2000; Lee, 2000). A few years ago the media gave a great deal of attention to an incident in which a young boy in elementary school who kissed a girl was expelled for sexual harassment. The loud media message was that sexual harassment will not be tolerated in school. The media ridicule of the incident also sent a second, more subtle message: Sexual harassment was exaggerated and unfounded. Symbolic interactionists suggest that the second, more subtle message was the more powerful one. If this is sexual harassment, are there other claims that are also false?

The Hill-Thomas confrontation resulted in a large increase in sexual harassment lawsuits, prompting companies to adopt more rigorous policies to protect employees. It challenged the taken-for-granted belief that women in school or workplace roles could expect to be sexually harassed. In a straightforward and unanimous Supreme Court ruling, Justice Sandra Day O'Connor stated that targets of sexual harassment do not need to show they suffered psychological damage to win their suits. The court upheld the notion that sexual harassment violates workplace equality. Despite the court rulings, confusion still exists about acceptable and unacceptable behavior that has sexual overtones. Like rape, it is the issue of sexual consent that underlies whether sexual harassment has occurred or not. From a feminist perspective, women should be able to enjoy sexual freedom, but sexual harassment is sexism—not sex (Chaucer, 1998). Sexual harassment allegations in the media about Bill Clinton's affair with Monica Lewinsky were quickly dropped, since there was mutual consent. Sexual harassment is offensive "not because it is sexual per se" but because it does damage to a woman's life (Williams, et al., 1999).

Many men polled about sexual harassment report sympathy but also bewilderment about the sexual harassment claims made by women. Men and women talk about and construct sexual harassment differently. Women are angry and fearful when they are sexually harassed. Both men and women, however, are socialized into powerful beliefs that define women largely in terms of their sexuality (Clason, 2000; MacKinnon, 2000a; 2000b). Such social definitions are reinforced by *institutional sexism*, the subordination of women embedded in social institutions. We have seen how this kind of sexism plays out at school and work regardless of some legal protection. To combat institutional sexism, definitions of social reality need to be reconstructed at both the individual and societal levels. Symbolic interactionists tell us that sexual harassment will be dislodged through its social reconstruction from an acceptable social condition to an unacceptable social problem. Conflict theorists tell us that institutional sexism will stall the process of reconstruction until women gain more power in their schools, workplaces, and families. Both perspectives agree that women can then gain a sense of *empowerment* when they first redefine and then realize their own power. They become agents in control of their destiny. These new definitions help women gain ground in their challenge to institutional sexism. In Chapter 13 we will consider the success of such challenges.

There is a final note on the Hill-Thomas case. In 1991 the public and Congress was split on whether they believed Anita Hill lied and perjured herself during the hearings. The fact that Clarence Thomas was confirmed by the narrowest margin ever for a Supreme Court Justice (52–48) clearly indicated this split (Anderson, 2001). In 1997 over 80 percent of the public believed Anita Hill told the truth, and in 2001 new information emerged that allegedly confirms her testimony (Brock, 2001). The validity of this new information remains to be determined. Whether the government, media, or a public are willing to investigate it may depend on social constructions of race, gender, and class—and how they are ranked—as they relate to Anita Hill and Clarence Thomas.

SUMMARY

1. Social interaction is an active, dynamic process in which participants may choose from a range of appropriate behaviors. In doing so, people construct social reality and modify existing cultural norms.

2. According to symbolic interactionism, people interact on the basis of their own definitions of a situation and their assumptions about others' definitions; the broader statuses of race, class, and gender also intrude on social interaction, and behavior is selected based on subjective meanings given to people in those statuses.

3. Ethnomethodology is the study of how people socially construct their everyday world and give meaning to their experiences and interactions. By uncovering the hidden rules of social interaction, we better understand how communication occurs and how social reality is constructed.

4. According to Erving Goffman's dramaturgical approach, social interactions are similar to theatrical performances and are culturally and socially prescribed. People play roles conferred on them by their social status and try to manage the impressions they give others in order to protect their self-esteem and to please others.

5. Self-fulfilling prophecies can result when people are led to behave in ways that confirm your expectations about them. Symbolic interactionists

believe that predictions about behavior shape behavior.

6. The social construction of reality approach has been criticized for minimizing the importance of social structure, such as institutions, in interaction.

7. Nonverbal communication—gestures, facial expressions, eye contact, touching, tone of voice, and speed and volume of speech—is socially constructed and varies between cultures. Nonverbal messages are often more important than verbal ones in social interaction. Functionalists suggest that gender differences in nonverbal communication help to maintain social equilibrium by reinforcing differences in gender roles, but conflict theorists see such differences as evidence of differences in power between men and women.

8. Television in the United States portrays people according to race, class, and gender stereotypes. Although racial stereotypes are declining, class stereotypes are not, especially for the working class. Shows about the middle class dominate television.

9. According to symbolic interactionists, social problems such as poverty and homelessness are socially constructed. Only when they are defined as social threats by large numbers of people do these social conditions become social problems.

10. Sexual harassment has been redefined from a social condition to a social problem, but there is disagreement about its definition. Institutional sexism can be combated when people agree on the definitions of sexual harassment and women gain power in the various social institutions.

KEY TERMS

dramaturgical approach 149
ethnomethodology 149
impression management 150

nonverbal communication 153
self-fulfilling prophecy 151
sexual harassment 165

social construction of reality 146
social interaction 146

CRITICAL THINKING QUESTIONS

1. From a symbolic interactionist view, explain how social interaction is characterized by cooperation. Include the definition of the situation and impression management in your explanation.

2. Demonstrate how social interaction forms our identities as individuals and also creates society.

3. Children voluntarily segregate themselves by gender, a pattern that increases as children get older. How is this fact explained by a social psychologist who adopts a psychological perspective and by a social psychologist who adopts a sociological perspective?

4. Describe a college classroom according to the dramaturgical approach. Provide examples of role playing, frontstage and backstage behavior, and impression management other than those given in the chapter.

5. From a symbolic interactionist perspective, what suggestions would you offer to make television less stereotyped in terms of race, class, and gender, but still entertaining and provocative?

INVESTIGATE WITH CONTENT SELECT

Begin your research using Content-Select for this chapter by following the directions found on page 27 of this text to visit Prentice Hall's Research Navigator Website. Enter these search terms into the search field:

Social construction
Sexual harassment
Social interaction

7
SEXUALITY

What Sexual Revolution?

Baby boomers supposedly started the sexual revolution to give in to their appetites for sex, drugs, and rock and roll—especially sex. Compared to world of the pre-1960s, men and women, married and single, younger and older, have more sex, more sex partners, more sexual variety, and more sexual satisfaction. But does this mean there has been a sexual revolution? Humorist Garrison Keillor puts it this way:

> There is an incredible amount of normality going on in America these days. America is not so obsessed with sex. To the contrary, we wear ourselves out with work; we are surrounded with all manner of entertainment. Considering what the American couple is up against, it's astounding to think that maybe once a week or month or on holidays or whenever the coast is clear they actually have sex. It's worth becoming middle-aged to be able to enjoy it utterly.

Sex makes people happy but it is doubtful if they have been revolutionized by it. (Adapted from Keillor, 1994; Grant, 1993; McClaren, 1999)

On Virginity

> I asked him to give me a reason why I should have sex . . . and he said it would feel good. I said, "But you can't guarantee me, give me something concrete." I knew I didn't want my first experience with a guy that would view me as a notch on a bedpost. (Female, African American, straight)

> I thought it would make me feel better love for him . . . (but) there was nothing added to the relationship. No more caring, no more nurturing, no more nothing. (Female, white, straight)

> I was nervous, it was my first time . . . I didn't want to look foolish . . . . She was totally dissatisfied and I had no control. (Male, white, straight)

> The first time I heard the word virgin was in elementary school . . . used as a cut-down. Virgin equals bad, laughed at. (Male, African American, gay)

These quotes are from four young adults reflecting on their experiences with virginity when they were in their teens. Their perceptions on the experience differ, but a common message comes through: Ideas about sex impacted their youthful lives and ideas about *first* sex will be vividly recalled. (Adapted from Carpenter, 2002:354–57)

When people talk about sexuality and the sex act itself, they often accept the idea that sex and the pleasure it brings come "naturally"—that it is completely driven by biological makeup and physiological urges. As the vignettes demonstrate, however, sexuality is not as "natural" as people believe. **Sexuality** is a type of social interaction through which we perceive, experience, and express ourselves as sexual beings. Through culture we learn what kinds of experiences are important, such as loss of virginity. Our culture teaches us how to experience sexual pleasure, who is sexually attractive, and how sexual intercourse should be conducted. Time and cultural constraints may keep us from it. Therefore, although sexual intimacy is intensely private, our sexual lives are encroached upon by society in part because sexual expression is organized and governed by social rules and cultural stereotypes.

In this chapter we expose common beliefs about human sexuality to the lens of sociology. Sociological data and explanations for the data will allow us to accept or thoughtfully reject preconceived notions about sexuality. Such data are most often based on the sexual interaction and intimate activities of couples, so a microlevel perspective is very useful in explaining sexuality. Symbolic interactionism is by far the most important microlevel theoretical perspective in this explanation and will guide much of this chapter's discussion of the topic.

GLOBAL CONNECTIONS

Female Genital Mutilation

It looked as though thieves broke into my room and kidnapped me from my bed. My thighs were pulled wide apart, gripped by steel fingers. A knife dropped between my thighs and a piece of flesh was cut off from my body. I screamed with pain despite the tight hand held over my mouth and saw a pool of blood around my hips. I wept and called to my mother for help. But the worst shock was when I saw her at my side surrounded by strangers, talking to them and smiling to them, as though she had not participated in slaughtering her daughter just a few moments ago. They carried me to my bed. They caught hold of my sister sleeping next to me, who was two years younger.

A 6-year-old Egyptian girl had just been "circumcised." It was about to happen to her 4-year-old sister as well.

Do people have a right to sexual pleasure? Westerners believe that not only is sexual pleasure a right, but that both men and women are entitled to it with a consenting partner they freely choose. In many parts of the world, however, sexual pleasure—if seen as a right at all—is reserved for men. For millions of the world's women, sexual pleasure is effectively eliminated by the procedure now commonly referred to as *female genital mutilation* (FGM). FGM is justified in many cultures by the belief that women are more promiscuous and sexual than men. A girl's virginity must be protected. The "protection" takes two forms. One is by *purdah*—secluding women in their homes or veiling them when they venture outside. The second is by FGM—a variety of genital operations designed to reduce or eliminate a woman's sexual pleasure and ensure her virginity. If virginity is safeguarded, then she is marriageable.

Otherwise, she can be condemned and live the life of an outcast. Sometimes she is murdered.

FGM is routinely performed without anesthetic and in unsanitary conditions. Referred to incorrectly as female circumcision, FGM is not at all equivalent to the far less radical procedure of male circumcision. FGM may range from a partial clitoridectomy to full removal of the clitoris, a woman's most erotically sensitive organ. In its more extreme form, FGM removes the clitoris and then the vagina is sewn almost completely shut, leaving an opening just large enough to release urine and menstrual blood. The vagina is cut open again on the woman's wedding night. FGM is believed to make childbirth easier and enhance male sexual pleasure. Whether men actually experience greater sexual pleasure is debatable, but many women die in childbirth as a direct result of botched FGM when they were younger. FGM is practiced in parts of the Middle East, throughout North Africa, and in some sub-Saharan regions. The total number of living females who have undergone FGM range from 80 to 100 million, including 4 or 5 million children as young as age 4. It is practiced by Muslims and Christians, by the wealthy and the poor, and in rural and urban areas. FGM's past is untraceable. It predates Islam, although some Islamic cultures justify it today on religious grounds. As brutal as the practice is, FGM continues because it forms the core cultural identity of many traditional people. Like the mother of the Egyptian girl, women who themselves were forced to undergo the painful procedure are often its strongest advocates.

Three United Nations Conferences on Women took up the FGM issue. In 1980 African delegates argued that FGM was essential to guarantee a girl's marriage-

ability. Delegates from Western culture, appalled by FGM, thought it should be eliminated and were accused of interfering with hallowed cultural traditions. Dialogue remained open, and five years later the issue was discussed with much less confrontation. A decade later the conference reached consensus that FGM was a human rights violation. Egypt, Nigeria, and Ghana have banned the practice. The United States may grant asylum to keep a girl from returning to a country where FGM is practiced.

The controversy over FGM illustrates symbolic interactionism's "definition of the situation" in two ways. First, what used to be named female *circumcision* has been renamed female *genital mutilation*. The former name suggests something mild or benign. The latter name clearly does not. Second, the movement against FGM has been redefined as a defense of human rights rather than as cultural interference. The new definition of the situation is fast becoming the reality, so that in the last decade all major international bodies and governments have committed to its suppression. However, cultural beliefs regarding women remain strong, and despite laws to the contrary, the practice continues in many areas.

1. How does the FGM case apply to the movement to eliminate male circumcision in the United States, one of the few countries that still practices it? Why does it continue when it is no longer justified on medical grounds?

2. Is sexual pleasure a human right? If so, what culturally acceptable changes must occur to ensure this right in the United States and in North Africa?

Sources: El Saadawi, 1980; Caldwell et al., 2000; Rahman & Toubia, 2000; Shweder, 2000; Eyada, 2001; UNICEF, 2002.

SEXUALITY IN A DIVERSE WORLD

Research reveals remarkable variability in human sexuality. As emphasized by symbolic interactionists, what one culture views as erotic or sexually stimulating might be disdained or even forbidden in another culture. In addition, our cultures provide powerful messages about physical attractiveness. A person we believe is physically attractive is also sexually attractive.

Sexual Stimulation

Human females are born with the capacity to experience the sexual pleasure that comes with orgasm. However, research reviewing sexuality in many cultures, including the United States, reveals that female sexual pleasure is associated more with the culture's beliefs about the purposes of sexual intercourse and the appropriateness of sexual pleasure (Laumann & Mahay, 2002; Middleton, 2002). The So people of Uganda believe that only males experience orgasm (the climax of sexual arousal). Genital touching is forbidden. These So women do not enjoy sex, but they tolerate it in order to conceive. On the other hand, among the Mangaian people of Polynesia, children are socialized to give and receive the pleasures of sexual intimacy. Girls in particular are sexually active early in life and encouraged to have intercourse with a number of boys. Through these experiences they select the best match for a spouse who gives the most sexual enjoyment. Unlike So women, who believe female orgasm is impossible, Mangaian women are thought to have triple the number of orgasms as Mangaian men (cited in Allgeier & Allgeier, 2000:38).

If there are strong cultural beliefs about what is sexually stimulating, it follows that there are also strong beliefs about what is sexually repulsive or dangerous. The fear of menstrual blood is fairly common around the world and is associated with many beliefs about the dangers of sex when a woman is menstruating. The *Mae Enga* people of New Guinea, for example, believe that if a man has sex with a menstruating woman, he will become so sickened that he will

vomit, his flesh will waste, and his wits will be permanently dulled, all leading to his decline and death (Pasternak et al., 1997:36). Another repulsive act for some cultures is kissing. Kissing is the norm in almost all cultures today, due mainly to Western influence. Traditionally associated with savagery, it has only been practiced in Japan in the last several decades, and in remote parts of China today it is virtually unknown. Kissing is widely practiced in Japan today, but as a sexual act it is still associated with uncertainty and strangeness (Ishii, 2001). The earlier traditional beliefs have not been eradicated. As a form of sexual foreplay, kissing occurs less often than genital manipulation in many cultures. Conducting cross-cultural research in sexuality is difficult at best, but knowledge of what other cultures believe to be sexually stimulating provide insight into our own beliefs (Frayser, 2002).

Sexual Attractiveness

Cultural differences abound when considering what is sexually attractive and erotic. A 12th-century Chinese emperor was said to have been erotically aroused by tiny feet in women, and so the practice of footbinding ensued. Thus, for centuries Chinese men have been socialized to believe that tiny feet are sexually attractive, and Chinese women have undergone this painful and crippling procedure. Although footbinding has been banned only relatively recently, tiny feet are still seen as erotic by Chinese men. For the Abkhasians of Russia, the female armpit is just as arousing, and viewing it by anyone except the women's husband is forbidden (Frayser & Whitby, 1995; Wang, 2002).

Throughout the developing world, particularly in North and Sub-Saharan Africa and the Middle East, heavier people are considered the most attractive. In the Tonga Islands of the South Pacific, the most attractive men are built like football linebackers, and the women are expected to be round and chunky (Cobb, 1997:8T). Weight is associated with wealth in many of these societies. Stouter people are those who can afford to eat more. In the West, the reverse is true. Both men

For Better or For Worse®   **by Lynn Johnston**

Due mainly to media images showing ultra thin models and actresses, teenage girls usually want to be thinner than they are—even when they are of normal weight. Weight obsessed adolescents and young women are at risk for eating disorders such as anorexia.

Source: "For Better or For Worse" copyright 1992 Lynn Johnston Productions, Inc. Reprinted with permission of Universal Press Syndicate. All rights reserved.

and women subscribe to the adage "you can never be too rich or too thin." The result has been a dramatic increase in eating disorders such as anorexia nervosa, a disease of self-induced severe weight loss, primarily in young women. A thin woman with large, but not too large, breasts is sexually idealized in the West. Obsession with thinness and breast size is definitely media based. Evidence for Western media influence on other cultures is suggested by a global increase in eating disorders and cosmetic breast surgery in societies where they were previously unknown (Kelly, 1997; Pacey, 1999; Bilukha, 2002).

Attitudes and behavior regarding sexuality change gradually. It took nine centuries before footbinding was banned in China. Since change is gradual, the idea of a sexual revolution is misleading—an idea confirmed by the opening vignette that asked, "What sexual revolution?" A revolution assumes an abrupt and usually reversed change of behavior. In the United States, changes in patterns of sexuality became evident in the 1920s, when women from all social classes began entering the labor force in greater numbers. Higher rates of premarital sex and out-of-wedlock births were reported. The divorce rates began to increase. Small but noticeable increases in tolerance related to attitudes toward unmarried couples living together, sex education, and homosexuality occurred. Baby boomers accelerated the patterns, but the earlier patterns were not completely abandoned. Change as well as continuity characterized the sexuality of this period. Sociologists accept the notion that sexual *evolution* is perhaps a better way than sexual *revolution* to describe patterns of human sexuality over the last century.

Chapter 3 showed us that there are important cultural universals related to sexuality, especially regarding its regulation. However, as we will continue to document, both within and between cultures, sexual attitudes and behaviors vary widely, but our humanness unfolds only by culture and socialization.

SEXUALITY AS SOCIALLY CONSTRUCTED

According to the symbolic interactionist perspective, we interact on the basis of how we perceive the interaction, including the expectations we perceive others have of us. Sexual interaction is no exception to this rule; sexual beliefs and behaviors are built up (constructed) over time. Culture is the major influence in providing the meanings people use to distinguish their sexual feelings, identities, and practices (Levine, 1998). For symbolic interactionists, the sexual excitement that appears to be naturally driven by biology is a learned process (Eagly & Wood, 1999; White et al., 2000).

Defining Sex, Gender, and Sexual Orientation

Sex and gender are now regarded by scientists in all disciplines as two different realities. **Sex** is described as those biological characteristics distinguishing male and female. Males and females are biologically distinguished, for example, by differences in chromosomes and hormone levels. **Gender** is described as those social, cultural, and psychological characteristics linked to male and female that define people as masculine and feminine.

Two other areas of human sexuality are particularly important to symbolic interactionists. The first is *gender identity*, discussed in Chapter 5 as a person's awareness that the two sexes behave differently and that two *gender roles*—one emphasizing masculinity and the other emphasizing femininity—are proper. The second is **sexual orientation,** a person's preference for sexual partners, usually of one gender. We will see, however, that these categories overlap much more than most people realize. Many of the vast differences in human sexuality can be traced to how gender identity and sexual orientation are socially constructed.

Gender Identity

The overlap of sex and gender identity is one good way to show how symbolic interactionists discuss human sexuality. By age 6, children have developed gender identity, a general pattern found throughout the globe. Gender identity is a central part of self and is invested with strong emotional attachment. Biological sex does not automatically grant gender identity. It is something that must be learned through socialization. You become aware that you are a girl or boy (gender identity), then you construct your behavior, including sexual behavior, around that awareness (gender role). Males and females have many ready opportunities for the social construction of gender roles, such as through their own families, peer interaction, schools, and the media (see Chapter 13). Information from these and other social sources is also selected for how the sexual part of their gender roles will be played out.

Data on **hermaphrodites,** infants born with both male and female sexual organs or ambiguous genitals (such as a clitoris that looks like a penis), tend to support the social construction of gender identity. Sometimes referred to as *intersexed*, they are assigned one sex at birth; the child's genetic sex is often discovered later. Studies point out that hermaphrodites are likely to take on the gender identity of whichever sex is assigned, regardless of the genetic sex. The age of the child is the crucial factor in adjustment *if sex reassignment surgery* (SRS) is an option. In SRS, genitals are surgically altered so that a person changes from one biological sex

Gender identity for males is constructed around sexual scripts often associated with violence, such as learning to use firearms. Military training allows other opportunities for reinforcing masculine sexual scripts since in most nations women are exempt from a draft.

to the other. By age 4, a child acquires both language and a sense of self. Gender identity is developing. Powerful social definitions related to appropriate gender role behavior have already occurred. In a case of sex reassignment, not only must the child change his or her gender identity, but others who know the child as one sex must now start treating him or her as the other sex (Money & Ehrhardt, 1972; Dreger, 1998).

The decision by parents to alter the sexual organs or genitalia of their intersexed child to fit either the appearance of one sex or the other or to correspond to the child's male or female genetic code is controversial. The child has no choice in the decision, and the surgery may not be reversible. Current advice is to assign a sex at birth, provide appropriate information and counseling about the intersex condition as the child is growing up, and then have the mature person decide on what action to take, if any, for surgery. Timing of the surgery in conjunction with hormonal therapy are important ingredients for the development of gender role behavior and gender identity of hermaphrodites (Dittman, 1998).

SEXUAL SCRIPTS **Sexual scripts** are shared beliefs concerning what society defines as acceptable sexual thoughts, feelings, and behaviors for each gender (Gagnon, 1990). For example, gender roles are connected with different sexual scripts—one considered more appropriate for males and the other considered more appropriate for females. Although the world has supposedly witnessed a sexual revolution, sexual scripts continue to be based on beliefs that for men sex is for orgasm and physical pleasure, and for women sex is for love and the pleasure that comes from intimacy. While people may desire more lati-

tude—such as more emotional intimacy for men and more sexual pleasure for women—they often feel constrained by the traditional scripting of their sexuality. When both men and women accept such scripts and carry their expectations into the bedroom, such as described in the vignette, gendered sexuality is being socially constructed. Beliefs about gendered sexuality contribute to sexual dysfunction and increased sexual violence toward women. Such beliefs also hold disadvantages for *both* men and women by constraining their sexual pleasure (Wiederman, 2001). Gendered scripting illustrates that biology alone cannot explain human sexuality (Frayser, 1999). Indeed, the evidence is overwhelming that biology is a player in the sexuality game, "but it is not the only player or even captain of the team" (Schwartz & Rutter, 1998:28). Sexuality is much less spontaneous than we think.

Sexual scripts may provide the routes to sexuality, but symbolic interactionists also assert that over time new paths offering new directions for sexuality can be built. It is unlikely that gendered sexuality will be eliminated entirely. However, it is likely that as gender roles become more egalitarian, the sexual lives of both men and women will be enhanced.

SEXUAL ORIENTATION

Like gender identity, sexual orientation is not automatically granted by biological sex. Humans share the same anatomy and have the same capacity for sexual pleasure, but there is a great deal of variation in how and with whom people experience sexual pleasure. According to symbolic interactionists, sexual orientation, like gender identity, is a social construction built

THEN AND NOW

Does Nature Rule? A Case of Sex Reassignment

On August 22, 1965, Janet and Ron Reimer of Winnipeg, Canada, became the parents of identical twin sons named Bruce and Brian. Eight months later, to correct a minor urination problem, the babies were to be circumcised. Circumcision is not routinely performed in Canada. Baby Bruce was picked up first by the nurse. A few minutes later, Ron and Janet were informed that an accident occurred—an electric current was set too high and Bruce's penis was burned off. When Janet looked at what was left of his penis, she described it as "blackened, a little string." It could never come back to life. Baby Brian was whisked away without the circumcision. The teams of Canadian and U.S. physicians who examined Bruce came to the same discouraging conclusion: Constructing an artificial penis was possible but not promising.

Ten months after the accident, Janet Reimer happened to watch a talk show where Dr. John Money, one of the world's foremost experts on gender iden-

tity, spoke of encouraging results with sex reassignment surgery (SRS) for children born with ambiguous genitalia. According to Money, gender identity was solely shaped by parents and environment. The topic of sexuality is now standard fare for the talk show circuit, but imagine Janet Reimer's discovery 30 years ago about a technique that might change the life of her son. Dr. Money agreed to take on Bruce's case. Just before his second birthday, Bruce underwent surgery to remove the remaining penile tissue. Bruce became Brenda.

The transformation from Bruce to Brenda was not an easy one. She rebelled almost from the start, tearing off dresses, preferring boy toys, and fighting with her brother and others. There was nothing feminine about Brenda. She had a masculine gait and was teased in school. At age 8 she had a nervous breakdown. But with strong support from Money, the Reimers were convinced that Brenda could be "taught to want to be a girl." Vaginal surgery was the next step. But any time the topic was broached, she

would adamantly refuse to accept the possibility. Mere mention of the word "penis" or "vagina" induced explosive panic. In most therapy sessions she was sullen, angry, and unresponsive. At times she would "play the game" and give them the answers they wanted to hear: "I want to be pretty; I'm a girl, not a boy." At age 12 she began estrogen therapy and breasts formed. She binge ate and gained weight to cover them up. In the meantime, Brenda's case became famous in scientific circles as proof that a child could be taught the gender identity corresponding to a new sex. All reports said she was adjusting nicely and acting out typical female roles—that she accepted her gender identity as a female.

When did Brenda learn that she was born Bruce? At age 10, in an embarrassed and fumbled attempt, her father told her that she needed surgery because a doctor "made a mistake down there." Brenda's sole response: "Did you beat him up?" Although Brenda did not understand what her father was saying, some believe that at this point Brenda

---

during social interaction. Like heterosexuals, both men and women who see themselves as homosexual maintain a gender identity consistent with their biological sex. They are socialized into prevailing gender roles except for their sexual orientation (Lippa & Tan, 2001; Philaretou & Allen, 2001). This socialization helps explain why homosexuals prefer for sexual partners those men or women who fit the standards of masculinity or femininity defined by the culture (Roof, 1997; Mutchler, 2000). However, since it is accompanied by gender roles that are defined as masculine or feminine, gender identity is much more susceptible to change over time than is sexual orientation. In the middle of the 19th century a masculine gender role was associated with employment that included elementary school teaching and clerical work. Today these same jobs are associated with a feminine gender role.

INTERNET CONNECTIONS

In the text there is a discussion of issues surrounding *sexual orientation*. You may wish to explore these issues further by accessing:

http://psychology.ucdavis.edu/rainbow/index.html

click on get the facts and then the two links on sexual orientation. After you have examined this Website, answer the following questions. What is the relationship between socialization, biology, and sexual orientation? How does sexual orientation and sexual identity overlap?

subconsciously knew she was a boy. At age 14 she was finally told the truth. Her response this time was anger, doubt, and amazement—but mostly relief. She vowed to change back to a boy. His new name would be David, since he felt the name Bruce was too "geeky." At age 18 at a relative's wedding, he made his public debut as a boy. He married in 1990.

In 1952 when George Jorgenson was surgically transformed in Denmark to become Christine Jorgenson, the world's most well-known transsexual was "born." The first complete transsexual surgery performed in the United States was not until 1965. David Reimer had a rudimentary penis and testicles constructed in 1981, requiring eighteen hospital visits. Just before his 22nd birthday, new techniques for microvascular reconstruction were used with much better results.

Most children who have SRS are born with ambiguous genitals, so David's case is very rare. The current advice for such children is to assign a firm sex at birth—the child must be raised as either a boy or girl. Any irreversible surgery must wait until children are old enough to know and say which gender they feel closer to. "Rear the child in a consistent gender—but keep away the knife." While not a perfect solution, it does consider biological, psychological, and social forces at work on the child.

In the media frenzy that followed David's "coming out" as a boy, the public heard only that gender identity is a natural, inborn process. The role of nurture is given little credit in the process. For many, the case seemed to "prove" that if nurture plays a role in shaping masculinity and femininity, nature is by far stronger.

Sociologists never discount biology as a key factor in explaining human behavior, especially related to sexuality. Although David's case questions the belief that gender identity is learned, it cannot be totally rejected. Symbolic interactionists focus on the critical role of socialization in learning gender identity. Consider, for example, that Bruce became a girl nearly two years after everyone, including twin brother Brian, treated her like a boy. Interviews with Brian showed him confused as well. He was also embarrassed by Brenda's tomboy behavior, which no one accepted. Two years of gender socialization cannot be easily erased—if at all. At one point the Reimers moved to get away from "ghosts and doubters." The media also never questioned the ability of a host of players to carry out a giant pretense. There are good arguments for the contributions of both biological and cultural factors to gender identity. Both need to be considered. Everybody may have been playing a game of science fiction—but the game of social reality was largely ignored.

1. Do you think the Reimers made the correct decision when they agreed to have Bruce undergo SRS? If not, what advice would you have offered to them?

2. What does "real gender" mean to you? Even if people can change biological sex, can they ever change gender identity?

Sources: Money & Ehrhardt, 1972; Money & Tucker, 1975; Diamond & Sigmundson, 1997; Colapinto, 2000.

Problems with Definitions

Public interest on the topic of sexual orientation is reflected in its coverage in the mass media. Terminology to describe the topic, once familiar mainly to scientists, has made its way into public usage. However, even scientific nomenclature about "sexual orientation," including this very term, is offensive to many therapists as well as to those in the homosexual community. Challenges to these offensive labels can help shape discourse about homosexuality by scientists, teachers, physicians and therapists, and the media (Pierce, 2001; Taubman, 2001).

Sexual orientation is divided into the categories of heterosexual and homosexual in most Western cultures. **Heterosexual** is the category for people who have sexual preference for, and erotic attraction to, those of the other gender. Heterosexuals are also referred to as *straight*. **Homosexual** is the category for people who have sexual preference for, and erotic attraction to, those of their own gender. Homosexual males are referred to as *gay men* and homosexual females as *lesbians*. The term *gay* is often used to include both gay men and lesbians. **Bisexual** is the category for people whose sexual orientations may shift and who are sexually responsive to either gender. Experts disagree as to whether bisexuality represents a distinct sexual orientation or is simply "homosexuality in disguise" (Drescher, 2002; Friedman et al., 2002). The last point about bisexuality highlights an important problem when identifying categories of sexual orientation. Science requires such categories for accurate reporting of research, but there is a major pitfall: They overlap a great deal. Is it accurate to say that heterosexuals only have sexual relations (behavior) with and sexual fantasies (attitudes) about the other

Although many churches offer marriage ceremonies to celebrate and publicly acknowledge unions between gay men and lesbians, to date marriage between homosexuals is not legally recognized in the United States.

sex (Katz, 1995; Neighbors, 2001)? Whether experts agree, the public tends to put bisexuals in the homosexual category (Omoto, 1999; Angelides, 2001).

So Who Is Gay? A Continuum of Sexual Orientation

For the first time, the 2000 U.S. Census allowed people to identify themselves as members of same-sex couples, revealing about 600,000 gay or lesbian couple-led homes nationwide. The three most populous states—New York, California, and Texas—also had the highest percentages of same-sex couple households (Amras, 2001). But the total homosexual population is much larger because the census does not allow for a person to identify sexual orientation and does not count homosexual partners who do not occupy the same household (see Technical Note, 2000). Like many other organizations and agencies that collect such figures, the U.S. Census Bureau assumes that people can be easily divided into two categories of sexual orientation—heterosexual or homosexual.

This dividing line masks accurate numbers on sexual orientation.

The pioneering work of Alfred Kinsey and his associates (1948, 1953) led to a scientific assault on the view that sexual orientation is *either* heterosexual *or* homosexual. According to Kinsey's research, sexual orientation can be measured by degrees on a continuum of sexual behavior involving one's own or the other gender (Figure 7.1). Later research added a psychological dimension to the continuum. People could be rated according to level of erotic attraction to, and fantasies about, their own or the other gender, disclosures to others about same-gender feelings, and timing of self-identified sexual orientation (Ellis & Mitchell, 2000; Floyd & Stein, 2002). As you would expect, this modification of Kinsey's continuum further decreases the numbers of people who may be exclusively heterosexual.

The original Kinsey data on sexual behavior showed that 37 percent of men and 13 percent of women said they achieved orgasm with a person from their own gender after puberty. Correcting for sampling bias (he overrecruited gay men, for instance), later research in 1970 showed this figure to be about 20 percent for men (Fay et al., 1989). When erotic attraction to own gender is added to sexual behavior, some data show about one-fifth of both men and women reporting homosexual activities (Sell et al., 1995). Data consistently report that gay men are likely to be exclusively homosexual in behavior, but less than half say they are exclusively homosexual in feelings. Lesbians report significantly more heterosexual feelings and behavior. However, for both men and women who experiment with homosexuality, very few decide to repeat the experience and even fewer identify themselves as exclusively homosexual. People who experiment with homosexuality often themselves believe that such sexual relationships are inappropriate or even pathological (Yip, 2002).

Instead of asking about sexual behavior and attitudes, some surveys simply ask people to state their sexual preference. One such poll showed 5 percent of respondents self-identifying as gay, lesbian, or bisexual, more than triple the number who self-identified when a similar poll was conducted only two years before (Riggle & Tadlock, 1999). Results also change when surveys ask about the timing of first same-gender sexual experience(s), the continuity of the relationship(s), and the type and frequency of erotic attraction without sexual experiences (Horowitz et al., 2001; Klentrou et al., 2002).

Since Kinsey's study, surveys on sexuality have become much more sophisticated in both sampling and types of questions asked. Overall, from reviews of studies over a half century using various definitions and data collection, it is safe to conclude that in Western cultures, more or less exclusive homosexuality ranges from

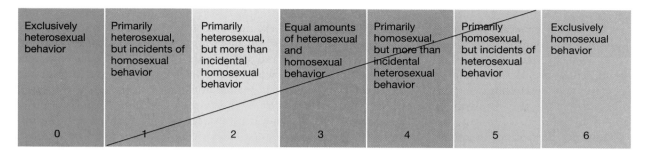

FIGURE 7.1 The Kinsey Continuum of Sexual Orientation.

Source: "Kinsey's Sexual Behavior Continuum" from *Sexual Behavior in the Human Male,* The Kinsey Institute (William B. Saunders), Copyright © 1948. Reprinted by permission of The Kinsey Institute.

5 percent to 10 percent for men and 3 percent to 5 percent for women (Laumann et al., 1994; Bagley & Tremblay, 1998; Kinsey Institute, 1999).

So, do these numbers tell us who is gay? Symbolic interactionists think not for one major reason. According to their perspective, what you are is what you think you are—both in identity and way of life. Even when carefully constructed polls ask people to "self-identify" their sexual orientation, the relationship between identity and way of life is usually absent. The term homosexual refers to people who both define themselves as gay men or lesbians and adopt behavior corresponding to this identity. Asking whether a person is gay, straight, or "bi" obscures the personal, cultural, and social roots of sexual orientation (Meyers, 2000).

Global Patterns

Historical and cross-cultural research support Kinsey's contention that sexual orientation, like other forms of human sexuality, is extremely varied. Research shows that the conceptual distinction between gender identity and sexual orientation is a blurry one. For example, **transgender** describes people who do not conform to culturally defined traditional gender roles associated with their sex. Transgendered people may or may not identify themselves as homosexual and may or may not choose to "pass" for the other sex in appearance (Roen, 2002). The ancient Greeks, for instance, accepted both homosexuality and heterosexuality as "natural" relationships, with no moral overtones. A man's preference for males or females was seen as a matter of taste and desire; the enjoyment of one over the other did not categorize men according to a gender preference for sexual interaction. A man who pursued males did not see himself as any different from one who pursued females. It was common for a man to change his sexual preference to women after spending his youth loving boys (Foucault, 1990; Murray, 2000). For the Greeks, gender identity existed but sexual orientation did not. Many of these Greek males may be described as transgendered people who moved between gender roles in ways that suited their sexual preferences and lifestyles at the time.

Transgendered people who perform specific social functions are found throughout the world today. In India, men known as *hijras* dress up in women's clothing and are called upon to bless newborn infants. In order to become a hijra and perform this important cultural role, most of these men by choice have been emasculated—their testicles have been removed. Hijra are not homosexual. They think of themselves more as females and thus prefer heterosexual men as sexual partners. They generally live and dress as females, often in a separate subculture. In the rural areas of India where hijras practice their trade, sexual orientation and gender identity do not appear to be concerns (Nanda, 1997). Hijras are ambivalent figures in India. They are teased and mocked but also valued and esteemed (Ward, 1999). The hijras have a gender role that legitimizes their function as ritual performers. This role forms the core of their self-definition and the basis of their positive, collective self-image.

Unlike hijras, who live openly as females, some people go through life with "mixed" gender identities. A number of Native American tribes believe sex and gender are not always the same. Until they were colonized by whites, some tribes accepted the cross-gender role of biological female who performed male duties. The role of *berdache*, a title conferred on males who do not exhibit masculine traits, still exists in some tribes. In tribal mythology, berdache may act as mediators between men and women and between the physical and spiritual worlds (Jacobs et al., 1997; Roscoe, 1998). Native Americans refer to those who act out cross-gender roles as having "two spirits." The *xanith* of the Arab state of Oman are also biological males. They work as homosexual prostitutes and skilled domestic servants. Described as a "third" gender, they have male names but distinctive dress and hair styles, unlike that of either men or women. Xanith are not men because they can interact with women and are not women because they are not restricted by purdah, the system of veiling and secluding women (cited in Lips, 2001:161). The term transgender may also describe the *mahus* of Tahiti. Mahus are usually young boys who adopt female gender roles early in life and eventually find jobs usually performed by women. However, female mahu are emerging shaped by gay and lesbian influences that are coming into Tahiti. In both male and female mahu, the status is viewed as naturally evolving from childhood roles. They have sexual relations with those of their own sex, but not with other mahus. Their preferred sexual partners are those from the other gender. Mahu sexuality, therefore, is "same-sex but opposite(sic)-gender" (Elliston, 1999:238). Though Tahitians may poke fun at mahus, they are accepted members of society (Stanley, 2000).

The hijra, berdache, xanith, and mahus are roles associated with approval, and sometimes honor, rather than disdain and immorality. These transgendered people violate the principle of **sexual dimorphism,** the separation of the sexes into two distinct groups, and show that what is socially defined as sexually unacceptable in one culture can be defined as sexually acceptable in another. Symbolic interactionists emphasize that these roles attest to the powerful impact of culture on both gender identity and sexual orientation.

Transsexuals

Unlike hermaphrodites, *transsexuals* are genetic males or females who psychologically believe they are members of the other gender. They feel "trapped" in the wrong bodies and may undergo SRS to "correct" the problem. Only then can their gender identity and their

biological sex be consistent. By this reasoning, transsexuals are not homosexuals. They are newly minted males or females who desire sexual intimacy with the other gender. Their ideal lover would be a heterosexual man or woman. The reality, however, is that most heterosexuals would not choose transsexuals as lovers. *Transvestites*, mostly males who are sexually aroused when they dress in women's clothing, are not transsexuals. Transsexuals are rare in society. The numbers worldwide are thought to be 1 in 100,000 males and 1 in 130,000 females (cited in Miracle et al., 2003:316).

Psychotherapy aimed at acceptance of a transsexual's biological sex instead of sex reassignment surgery is generally unsuccessful (Smith et al., 2001). The outcomes of SRS are mixed. Research from the United States in the 1970s showed overall negative results. Some transsexuals believed the surgery was a mistake and others reported no better adjustment after than before surgery. With better surgical techniques, more knowledge of transsexualism by therapists and social workers, and increased tolerance in society, later research report much more positive outcomes. International data indicate that the majority of transsexuals report satisfaction with their choice of sex reassignment (Landen et al., 1998; Rachlin, 2002; Smith & Cohen, 2002).

Discrimination and Diversity

Western societies, including the United States, are primarily *heterosexist*—people tend to view the world only in heterosexual terms. In doing so, other sexual orientations are devalued. At various times in history homosexuality was a sin, a disease, a crime, a mental illness, an immoral choice, an alternative lifestyle, and a health threat (Mondimore, 1996; Rupp, 1999). **Homophobia,** negative attitudes and overall intolerance toward homosexuals and homosexuality, is expressed by a wide spectrum of the U.S. public. However, people in some demographic categories are more homophobic than others. People with higher levels of homophobia share a number of characteristics: They are likely to be male, heterosexual, elderly, not college educated, living in the South, and religiously, sexually, and politically conservative. They also tend to be more authoritarian and believe in rigid gender roles (Lienemann, 1998; Kaminer, 2000; Basow & Kelly, 2000; Cohler & Galatzer-Levy, 2000). Negative attitudes are also associated with having few or any gay friends or acquaintances. Knowing gay people personally increases positive attitudes toward homosexuals as a group (Yang, 1997; Kantor, 1998). Those who believe that homosexuality is due to biology or uncontrollable factors express more tolerant attitudes (Hegarty, 2002; Sakalli, 2002). Homophobia translates to stigma, depression, and fear in the lives of gay men and lesbians. Most disheartening

INTERNET CONNECTIONS

As discussed in your text ("Problems with Definitions"), there is a great deal of misinformation surrounding human sexuality. After reading this chapter, are you clear on the distinction between a homosexual and a transsexual? Even if you think you are well informed, go to the site:

http://www.transsexual.org/

Click on "What Exactly Is Transsexuality." After you have read the contents, write a brief essay on the distinction transsexual and the other sexual orientations discussed in the text. What are some of the conceptual problems associated with sexual orientation?

Widespread homophobia in the United States is associated with violence toward homosexuals with almost all the violence perpetrated by heterosexual males on gay males. Matthew Shepard, a 21-year-old student was tortured and beaten to death by two men because he was gay.

is that in groups with high levels of homophobia, violence against homosexuals is an all too common outcome (Pinar, 2001; Mason, 2002).

RACE AND ETHNICITY Racial and ethnic minorities in the United States are subject to prejudice and discrimination (Chapter 12). When the minority status of "homosexual" is added, their already disadvantaged position gets worse. Those disadvantages may be higher *within* their own ethnic subcultures as well. African American gay and bisexual men, for example, may be at higher risk for violence and HIV infection because of their wish to maintain a facade of heterosexuality and to present masculinity norms in their homophobic communities. Although secrecy may protect them against violence, it does not protect them against HIV risk because unprotected sex is another example of a masculinity norm that works against all men, but especially gay men (Lichtenstein, 2000; Constantine-Simms, 2001). Among Latinos, a similar scenario is played out, but the HIV risk extends to both young men and women, heterosexual as well as homosexual. Throughout Latino cultures in the United States and Central and South America, Latino males are expected

to be dominant, tough, and fiercely competitive with other males. This exaggerated masculinity, referred to as *machismo*, is displayed more frequently in poor and working-class neighborhoods. Unprotected sex with multiple partners is proof of virility and masculinity, and therefore *not* homosexuality. Young Latinos are aware of the dangers, but cultural norms about manhood and homosexuality continue, especially those reinforced by religion (Schifter & Madrigal, 2000; Rodriguez & Ouellette, 2000). Latinas are expected to be submissive to men and remain virgins until marriage. Although homophobia in Latino communities is very strong, and male-to-male sexual liaisons are kept secret, they may be accepted as transitory until marriage because they say a sexual outlet is needed. A gay identity, however, is not acceptable. In addition, while some people believe that the machismo tradition makes it more disgraceful for men than for women to be gay, others disagree. Latinas who take on a lesbian identity not only are stigmatized as lesbians, but their status also challenges the machismo of male dominance (Trujillo, 1991; Sue & Sue, 1999; Diaz et al., 2001).

We saw earlier that many Native American tribes accepted those with mixed-gender identities. During the colonial period, Catholicism prevailed and eventually eliminated many of these traditions. It remains to be seen if acceptance levels will be higher for gay men and lesbians living on reservations where ancient traditions are being revitalized. Among Asian Americans, especially in Chinese communities, gender roles are extremely rigid. Since a woman's fundamental role is to ensure the family line through conceiving sons, gay men and lesbians pose major threats. They are likely to be isolated from their families unless they give up their "gayness" and return to traditional roles. Gay Chinese Americans express high levels of anguish because they were socialized for strong family ties, but are now rejected by their families. The gay subcultures cannot offer the sense of family and community they desire (Chan, 1992; Sue & Sue, 1999). Evidence is mixed for African Americans. Some studies find whites having more homophobic attitudes than African Americans and others find no significant differences (Simon, 1998; Lewis & Rogers, 1999). Though it is difficult to generalize about levels of homophobia within different racial and ethnic groups, it is clear that gay men and lesbians must contend with another layer of minority status that will undoubtedly impact their lives.

GENDER Over time homophobia has declined significantly for most demographic categories, especially in the areas of support for rights related to employment and military service (Haeberle, 1999). Some states now allow gay couples to have "official" civil unions similar to marriages and adopt children under the same rules as unmarried couples (see Chapter 15). Over the last 25 years there has been a steady decline in willingness to restrict the civil liberties of homosexuals. However, although more Americans say that sexual relations between adult gays should be legalized, this attitude has not declined as quickly. Some sociologists suggest that legalizing sexual relations may be more of a moral issue on which Americans are more conservative than a civil liberty issue on which they are more liberal (Loftus, 2001). Overall, the population of young adults can be described as somewhere between "tolerant" and "accepting" of homosexuals (NORC, 2000).

Gender differences in level of acceptance of homosexuality is the single most important contradiction to the trend. Males may be less homophobic than in the past, but they have been slower to change than other groups. In fact, the "homophobic gap" between men and women is actually widening, specifically in attitudes toward gay men (Kite & Whitley, 1996; Lewis & Rogers, 1999). Both genders appear to hold similar views about lesbians—with men generally as accepting of them as women. Sociologists explain this trend by highlighting contemporary notions about masculinity.

MEN AND MASCULINITY Sociological research linking homophobia to a masculine gender role supports the following conclusion: Homophobia is such an integral part of heterosexual masculinity that being a man means *not* being a homosexual (Badinter, 1995:115). One example is the "antifeminine standard"—the male rejection of any behavior that has a feminine quality. Data from the United States, Britain, and Australia suggest that homophobia is learned early through the media and at school (Clum, 2002; Keller, 2002). Homophobia endorses antifemininity with devastating labels such as sissy, queer, pervert, or simply girl. Homophobia is learned early. Most teenage males express high levels of intolerance concerning images of homosexual men (Plummer, 2001;Thurlow, 2001). As adults, men still fear being labeled a homosexual. Homophobia among men is related to heightened levels of masculinity used to dispel any notion that they may be viewed as feminine, hence homosexual (Zeichner et al., 2002).

The traditional male gender role encourages homophobia for several reasons. First, women and anything perceived as feminine are less valued than men and anything perceived as masculine. Second, men generally accept stereotypes about gays and homosexuality. These stereotypes are negative but also very powerful. Men see little need to seek out facts, because just by doing so, they may be threatened with a homosexual label. Finally, early socialization offers few alternative models for boys (Chapter 5). An often

rigid standard of masculinity is upheld. Boys learn quickly from their peers that gestures of intimacy with other males are discouraged and that expressions of femininity, verbally or nonverbally, are not tolerated. Male role models—fathers, teachers, and brothers—provide the cues and the sanctions to ensure compliance on the part of the young boy (Strikwerda & May, 1992; Plummer, 1999).

GAY RIGHTS The emergence of a gay rights movement has helped gays to affirm positive identities and the right to sexual self-determination (Kinsman, 1992:49). Patterned somewhat after the women's movement, one faction of the gay rights movement is working to escape the bonds of a sexist culture. This faction recognize the common oppression and levels of discrimination they share with women. On the other hand, some gay men recognize that since women and gay men are both subordinate in society, it may be better to capitalize on their advantage of being male—regardless of how it undermines women. From this "male advantage" view, a gay male executive moving up the corporate ladder can wield power over any competing female. As conflict theory suggests, males are higher in the stratification system than females. Males are socialized into accepting masculinity norms—whether they are gay or not (Clendinen & Nagourney, 1999; Andryszewski, 2000). As we will see in the next section, these standards show up in all forms of sexuality.

SEXUALITY: ATTITUDES AND BEHAVIOR

Until fairly recently, beliefs about human sexuality were shrouded in myth and superstition. Just as Sigmund Freud stunned the scientific world and then the general public with his pronouncements on sexuality, the original Kinsey study revealing sexual behavior in the United States in the mid-1900s sent similar shockwaves throughout the country. Not only were Americans much more sexually active than most people realized, but those activities strayed far from what people thought were sexually appropriate norms. A half century later, another major sex survey showed a rather startling twist. In the century of sexuality, Americans were less sexual then previously thought (Laumann et al., 1994). This section explores changes and continuities in sexual behaviors and attitudes.

Gendered Sexuality

The original Kinsey data revealed that 92 percent of males and 58 percent of females used masturbation (sexual self-stimulation) to achieve orgasm. Males

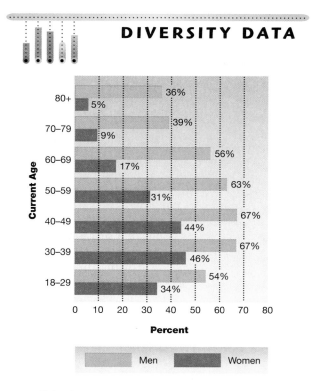

DIVERSITY DATA

FIGURE 7.2 **Percent Reporting Four or More Other-Sex Partners Since Age 18, by Age and Gender.** At all age levels, men are significantly more likely than women to report having four or more other-sex partners. However, other data show that in the last two decades women are gradually increasing their number of sex partners. Do you think that the gender double standard in number of sex partners will eventually be eliminated?

Source: NORC. General Social Surveys, 1972–2000. Chicago: National Opinion Research Center, 2000. Reprinted by permission of NORC, Chicago, IL.

begin to masturbate during early adolescence. Females begin to masturbate later than men, often in their 20s and 30s. These patterns have not changed significantly since Kinsey's original research (Hunt, 1974; Laumann et al., 1994; Hyde, 1996).

During intercourse men are more likely to have an orgasm than women. Kinsey found that over one-third of married women never had an orgasm prior to marriage and that one-third of married women never had an orgasm. Later data show that almost 90 percent of all women experience orgasm, whether married or not, and virtually all married women (98 percent) do reach orgasm, although not with every sexual intercourse. Husbands generally would like more frequent intercourse than their wives, especially early in the marriage. Later in their married life this trend may reverse; married women report more positive

perception of their sexual behavior and men report a more positive perception of their marital life. However, for both men and women, marital satisfaction and sexual satisfaction are highly correlated, and the more frequent the sex, the higher the level of marital satisfaction (Young et al., 2000; Trudel, 2002). If sex keeps people happy in their marriages, sexual satisfaction is also a good predictor of divorce.

PREMARITAL SEX Kinsey's (1953) data reported that one-fourth of unmarried women born before 1900 had experienced coitus (sexual intercourse). He found that one-third of young women reported premarital sex by age 25. Premarital sex for men was 77 percent. Today the differences between men and women in premarital sex have all but disappeared. Men may have sex earlier than women, but by the time they graduate from college, virtually all men and women are sexually experienced (Kamen, 2000; Rouse, 2002). Females do have fewer sex partners than men, but they will plan for their first intercourse. About half of all teenagers age 15 to 19 have had sexual intercourse at least once. However, people are surprised to learn that during the last decade, sexual activity among teens has significantly declined. As you would expect, this decrease resulted in fewer teenage pregnancies and a decrease of sexually transmitted disease (Abma, 2002). What is perhaps more surprising is that the number of teenage boys reporting sexual intercourse has dramatically decreased—white, African American, and Latino alike. For girls, the rate of sexual activity has remained relatively stable. The only change to this pattern is for African American girls, who reduced their sexual activity at levels comparable to white and Latino girls (Risman & Schwartz, 2002:18).

The overall rate of sexual risk-taking among teens has appeared to decline. Why? Sociologists suggest that norms about gendered sexuality explain the new pattern. While girls have increased their sexual behavior, it is still within the bonds of a romantic relationship. A decade ago, a boy was likely to have his first sexual intercourse with a pickup or casual date. Girls whose first intercourse occurred before age 16 are more likely to report that it was not voluntary. Today, boys are likely to have their first intercourse with a girlfriend (Risman & Schwartz, 2002).

Since most people have several sexual experiences with people whom they will not likely marry, the term "premarital" sex is inaccurate. A more accurate term to refer to these experiences is *nonmarital* sex.

EXTRAMARITAL RELATIONSHIPS Once called adultery but now commonly called affairs, this form of nonmarital sex is exceedingly varied. Extramarital relationships involve different degrees of openness and

SOCIOLOGY OF EVERYDAY LIFE

The Sexualization of America

America has a message about sex. The message says that almost everyone but you is having endless, fascinating, varied sex. This message opens one of the most important studies on sex in the United States since Kinsey—the mid-1990s version, rather than the 1950s version. This and more recent studies provide data that test what we call the "sexualization thesis"—that Americans are preoccupied with sex; they eagerly engage in frequent sex with a variety of interesting partners. The media are seen as fueling this belief. Does the sexualization thesis have merit? Review some of the latest data on sexuality in the United States to determine if the thesis is indeed correct.

Sex is for pleasure: Virtually all surveys report that Americans have sex mainly for erotic pleasure. Sex for reproduction takes a distant second place. U.S. Catholic couples, for example, typically use contraceptives even though the rhythm method is the only form of birth control sanctioned by the Catholic church. The sex that Americans have is also more frequent and more varied than in the past. They ex-

periment with different sexual techniques more than their parents did and certainly more than their grandparents did. Masturbation and oral sex are common and accepted. **BUT:** Over three-quarters of adults say that media concentrate too much on sex. Advertising, movies, videos, and television overdo the showing of breasts and buttocks, nudity and near-nudity. Americans are used to these images but would prefer fewer of them. And even if people are personally more open to sexual experimentation, traditional vaginal intercourse tops the list of the most appealing sexual practice for the vast majority of adults—regardless of gender, race, class, or age.

First sex: Age for first intercourse has steadily declined. The average age of lost virginity for people born in the 1930s and 1940s was 19. Today it is 16. Women who were either virgins when they turned 20 or had sexual intercourse with only one person declined from 84 percent for those born before 1953 to 50 percent for those born after that date. About four-fifths of U.S. teens have their first intercourse before they turn 20. **BUT:** More teens in the 1990s reported that

they intended to abstain from sex before marriage than those in the 1980s. Data are still incomplete to determine if they "do not practice" what they preach. However, the good news is that high-school students who report they had any sexual intercourse dropped by 5 percent in the last decade.

Sex partners: Americans have more sex partners than just two decades ago. About a third of people over age 50 say they had at least five partners in their lifetimes, but about half of people between age 30 and 50 report this. The highly educated have more partners over their lifetimes than the least educated. About one-third of those who did not finish high school report having had more than five partners, compared to about half of those finishing college. Does this pattern mean that "smarter" people are more sexually active? Probably not. A better explanation is that people with more education postpone marriage to finish school, so they have more time and chances to meet and date a variety of people, many of whom become sex partners. **BUT:** For data on number of sex partners in the past year, 70 per-

include married as well as single people. They may or may not include sexual involvement. The emotional involvement with a partner other than one's spouse can be more threatening to the marriage than sexual involvement. Despite the fact that most people claim to disapprove of affairs in any form, Kinsey's data indicated that 50 percent of males and 26 percent of females engaged in extramarital sex by age 40. Currently, estimates are that about 25 percent to 35 percent of men and 15 percent to 25 percent of women have had an extramarital affair (Norman, 1998; Treas & Giesen, 2000; Atkins & Jacobson, 2001). It is clear that while most people disapprove of affairs, a significant number engage in them (see Figure 7.3 on page 186).

There are a number of problems with these data. First, although extramarital relationships are likely to

be discreet, they vary in degree of openness. Sometimes the spouse and other friends are aware of the relationship. Sometimes the awareness translates to either tolerance or acceptance, especially if physical abuse, mental illness, or alcoholism are evident in the marriage. In this sense, the label of "affair" is a false one, since it implies secrecy. Second, single women and men are involved with married women and men, but figures usually give only the married estimates. Third, as we have already discussed, sex may or may not be a part of an extramarital relationship. Fourth, reporting on these kinds of relationships is often threatening to respondents who are engaging in them. Although later research validated Kinsey's data, the high percentage of affairs he reported was suspect. It is also clear that when respondents report their

cent say they had one and 12 percent say none.

Sex frequency and cheating: About two-thirds of all people have sex from a few times per month to several times per week. Sex is probably with the same partner and with a spouse if they are married. **BUT:** About 20 percent of married Americans report that they have had an affair, showing a steady increase over the last two decades. While the large majority of married couples do not cheat on their spouses, it is clear that affairs are becoming more acceptable.

Sex knowledge: Compared to past generations, U.S. teenagers know more about sex and understand what they know. Beginning at about age 12 through age 17, their levels of sexual understanding increase dramatically. At every age, girls know more than boys and know more on every topic. For both genders, their bodies are physically changing and they talk about these changes with their friends and families. Adolescents report good communication with their parents on sexual matters. Sex education is moving to lower grades, so knowledge and communication are reinforced. In the 1950s, 15-year-olds may have had basic sex education. Today it is taught in more depth to 11-year-olds. **BUT:** The majority of all teens believe that boys can't control their sex urges and girls can. They also believe that a girl cannot get pregnant unless a boy has an orgasm and ejaculates directly into her vagina.

Sex and disease: Not only do teens have more formal sex education, the sex and health link is clearer for them. For example, most high-school students understand how HIV is transmitted and what they need to do to protect themselves and their partners from the disease. **BUT:** Regardless of age, risky sexual behavior is common. Some studies show only 20 percent of nonmarried couples use condoms. Those under age 19 are less likely to use them, even during anal intercourse. Women often report that their boyfriends do not like condoms, so they go along with these preferences. They do, however, take oral contraceptives. Safe sex to them means not getting pregnant.

Clearly, there is a great deal of evidence supporting the sexualization thesis.

But the data also show that Americans are much less "sexualized" than people believe. The sexual lives of ordinary men and women revolve around sex with a spouse or in a committed relationship, which provides them with erotic pleasure and excitement. The sexualization of the United States is associated with erotic pleasure but also moral panic. It is associated with fascination with sexual things but also disdain when these very things surround them too much, especially through the media. As this chapter shows, cultural beliefs explain much of the inconsistency.

1. From the patterns of sexuality described here, do you think the United States will become more or less sexualized? What factors prevent or promote sexualization?

2. From the conflict and functionalist perspectives, explain why many do not act on their sex knowledge, even when health is at risk.

Sources: Janus & Janus, 1993; Laumann et al., 1994; McClaren, 1999; Pearson, 1999; Kamen, 2000; Atkins et al., 2001; Amba, 2002.

knowledge of affairs others are having, the numbers increase. Finally, the fact that divorce is less stigmatized is also associated with openness to extramarital relationships. Thus, it is probable that reported figures for extramarital relationships are lower than the actual numbers.

THE DOUBLE STANDARD. A *double standard* that men are allowed to express themselves sexually and women are not has traditionally existed in the United States. Since the level of nonmarital sexual behavior for males and females is now similar, does a double standard still exist? The answer is yes when considering biological sex—but no when considering gender. Data on sexual behavior has changed dramatically. It was assumed that compared to men, women had weaker sex drives, were more difficult to arouse sexually, and became aroused less frequently. These assumptions have all been proven false (Foley & Sugrue, 2002; Leiblum, 2002). It is the clitoris, not the vagina, as Freud insisted, that is responsible for the multiple orgasms experienced by women. Prompted by feminist social scientists, new models about female sexuality from women's own voices are evolving. In stark contrast to Freudian views, they offer an understanding that sexuality for women is pleasurable, fulfilling, and desired (Kleinplatz, 2001).

Major gender differences in sexual attitudes do persist. For more women than men, emotional closeness is a prerequisite for sexual intercourse. Men give sexual pleasure and conquest as the main motives.

DIVERSITY DATA

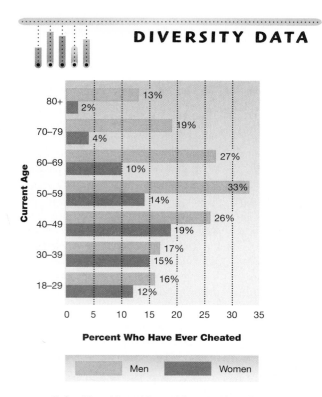

FIGURE 7.3 **How Many Married People Have Ever Had Sex with Someone Other than Their Spouses?** At all age levels men report significantly higher levels of extramarital sex than women, but especially during middle age. What explains the large difference for this age group? Do you think that the numbers are higher or lower for both genders because it is difficult to collect accurate data?

Source: NORC. General Social Surveys, 1972–2000. Chicago: National Opinion Research Center, 2000. Reprinted by permission of NORC, Chicago, IL.

They prefer more partners over a shorter period of time than women (Buss et al., 2001; Abma, 2002). Women adopt a more "person-centered" approach to sex; men adopt a more "body-centered" approach. Most important, males are less likely than females to be criticized or to feel guilty about their sexual activities (Allyn, 2000; Scott & Sprecher, 2000).

Such gendered attitudes are especially clear for extramarital relationships. Both genders act on their desire to have affairs, but men express a greater willingness. The idea that women are sexual beings who can and should experience sexual pleasure is relatively recent. Symbolic interactionists highlight the fact that pleasurable sexual activities are gendered—conditioned by sexual scripts defined as acceptable for men or women. The double standard, which reinforces a woman's passivity during the heterosexual sex act, is one such script. The data on female sexuality are still viewed in light of male dominance in sexuality.

Women and men both believe that her orgasm is a sign of his success as a lover.

Ironically, the disappearance of a sexual double standard may not be desirable. The absence of significant gender differences in frequency of nonmarital sexual activities, number of partners, or degree of emotional involvement with partners could trigger a lifetime of more sex with not only more people, but more people who are less known to their partners. Given the risks to both genders related to health and sexually transmitted diseases, sexual violence, and unplanned pregnancy, the disappearance of a sexual double standard may be hazardous to your health and to society.

Sexuality in Later Life

The cultural barriers, gender norms, and behavior–attitude discrepancy also apply to sexuality in later life. For the elderly, an already difficult situation is made worse by a combination of age and gender-related stereotypes. As with gender, there is a sexual double standard regarding age and sexuality (McCarthy, 2001). Because it is associated with youth and virility, sexuality among the elderly has been ignored

Despite the popular belief that elderly people are "sexless," the vast majority of older couples remain sexually active and sexually responsive to their partners throughout their lifetimes.

or demeaned. The elderly are perceived to be sexless. If elderly males show sexual interest, they are labeled as "dirty old men." Once childbearing and mothering are completed for women, they are expected to retreat to a sexless existence. Women and men also age differently in their sexuality. Women experience more comfort and less anxiety about sex as they age, thereby increasing their desire for intercourse and sexual intimacy (Rice, 2001). On the other hand, widows significantly outnumber widowers, so options for sexual activity decline for women, despite the fact that sexual desire remains strong.

Research by two other pioneers of sexuality, William Masters and Virginia Johnson (1966, 1970), shows that when advancing age and physiological changes influence sexual ability for men, performance anxiety increases. A man's wife may believe his "failure" is a rejection of her. Men are socialized early in life to believe that they will be judged by their sexual potency and talents. As suggested earlier, when a couple accepts such beliefs, a cycle of less sex, less interest in sex, and increased emotional distance is perpetuated. The irony is that it is easier to cope with these incorrect beliefs if society assumes the elderly are not supposed to be sexually active anyway.

Research clearly illustrates that men and women of all age groups are far less sexually different from one another than once thought (Hillman, 2000). Consistent with symbolic interactionism, they differ more in how they negotiate sexual activities and in the kinds of sexual relationships they seek. The social construction of women as passive sexual beings and men as sexual conquerors can be reconstructed to make them partners in a mutually pleasurable experience.

MACROLEVEL PERSPECTIVES: FUNCTIONALISM AND CONFLICT THEORY

Although the microlevel perspective of symbolic interactionism provides an excellent framework for understanding human sexuality, macrolevel perspectives also have much to offer on the subject. The macrolevel perspectives of functionalism and conflict theory emphasize how sexuality is located and arranged in large-scale social structures, such as social institutions. Both perspectives also emphasize that sexuality is a legitimate area of public debate, since it is associated with a host of social issues, including nonmarital pregnancy, sex education, prostitution, sexual victimization, the rights of homosexuals, and the spread of AIDS. Because social structures are interdependent, the sexual attitudes and practices occurring at one level in society will eventually influence other levels. For example, the increased pregnancy rate for unmarried teens has major economic consequences for the fami-

lies of the young couple if the child is not put up for adoption. Welfare and health benefits may be necessary, especially if the couple remains unmarried. High schools may offer babysitting for mothers so a diploma can be earned. All social institutions are impacted. Functionalism and conflict theory focus on different elements of this impact.

Functionalism

Functionalists maintain that society experiences the least disruption when sexuality is regulated by custom and law. Social equilibrium is maintained when people know the normative rules of sexuality and follow these rules. Many problems can arise with the violation of sexual norms, such as those mentioned above, but functionalists emphasize disruptions related to marriage and the family as critical to social stability. Functionalists suggest that sexual relationships occurring between adult, heterosexual married couples offer the best opportunities for social equilibrium. Other types of sexual relationships, from heterosexual cohabitation to homosexual liaisons, are potentially disruptive of this equilibrium, since they counter traditional beliefs about how marriage and family are defined (Chapter 15).

An illustration of the functionalist approach to explain the social disruption that occurs when sexual norms are violated is child sexual victimization, especially incest. Cases of sexual victimization of children in families are not only increasing, but are much higher than would be predicted by a culturally universal incest taboo (Chapter 3). Since child victimization also includes neglect, psychological abuse, and other kinds of physical abuse, figures on sexual victimization are often included with these cases. However, reasonable estimates of incestuous relationships of children in the United States range between 10 percent and 17 percent (Browning & Laumann, 1997; Gorey & Leslie, 1997). Given the profound personal and social results, it follows from functionalist theory that perpetrators of childhood sexual victimization need to be dealt with harshly. When perpetrators are publicly condemned, models for positive adult–child intimate standards are reinforced. Public consensus denouncing childhood sexual victimization is built voluntarily. Sexual order—therefore social order—is maintained.

Conflict Theory

Conflict theory also explains sexuality in terms of social location, arrangement, and the impact of sexuality on all the social institutions. But conflict theory focuses on how this arrangement is based on a hierarchy—how sexuality is stratified by degree of power. According to conflict theory, sexuality is embedded in larger social structures in which some groups wield more power than others. Inequality between groups is the inevitable result of these arrangements. The inequality existing in other social structures intrudes into the sexual lives of all members of society. Thus, sexuality is defined more by degree of power than degree of cooperation.

To return to the child victimization example, conflict theorists focus on the adult as wielding power over the child. Age is one form of accepted inequality that obviously puts children under the authority of parents and other adults. The most common form of child victimization involves younger females as victims and older males (including father, stepfather, and brother) as perpetrators. The more patriarchal—male-dominated—the society, the higher the level of female subordination. Father–daughter/stepdaughter is the most common form of incest in both the United States and globally (Herman, 2000; Sheinberg & Fraenel, 2000; Itzin, 2001). In larger society, females are subordinate to males. Thus, conflict theorists suggest that when a father engages in incest with his daughter, he expresses the right of access to any female. All types of sexual terrorism, whether incest, rape, the threat of violence, or even the nonviolent sexual intimidation of women, are reinforced by patriarchal attitudes (Sheffield, 1995).

Conflict theorists also suggest that power is a shifting resource. When powerless people join forces, they begin to amass resources to challenge existing power relationships, sexual or otherwise. Incest survivors speak out, rape victims bring rapists to trial, and sexual harassment in school or the workplace is reported. Both conflict theorists and feminists point out that when men and women share sexual power more equally, sexual conflict is reduced and the joy of sexual intimacy is enhanced (Schuiteman, 2001).

LIFE CONNECTIONS

Sex and the College Student

The pattern of nonmarital sex is alive and well on college campuses throughout the United States. Patterns of nonmarital sex among college students are based on decades of data suggesting that college functions as the key marriage market for middle-class Americans. A number of important factors—such as romantic love, commitment, emotional attachment, physical attractiveness, and demographic similarity of partners—connect with sexuality when the marriage market is navigated. These factors are explored in detail in Chapter 15. For now, however, the focus is on the "sex" in sexuality. As reflected in a major study of college students by Michael Moffatt, sexual chastity for the unmarried is "almost as dead as the dodo" (Moffatt, 1989).

Because of ads like this one, college students have a great deal of knowledge about sexually transmitted diseases, especially AIDS. However, college students are less likely to use condoms and rely more on birth control pills for "safe sex"—which may prevent pregnancy but not AIDS.

Exploring Sexuality

The major influence on the sexuality of the students Moffatt studied was American popular culture. Their sexual ideas came almost entirely from the mass consumer culture of movies, popular music, advertising, and television—from sex manuals and sex surveys in popular magazines to *Playboy* and *Penthouse* for men and *Harlequin* romance pulp fiction for women. Even sex education and popular psychology are filtered through these mass media sources. More recent research supports these ideas. The sexual images of television and other media are major factors in the increased sexual permissiveness among college students (Weinberg et al., 1997).

Sex is important for college students, even if they are not very sexually active—the shy worry about not having it, and those who opt for limited sex often give up the battle. These ideas are reflected in the following comments:

From a male junior: I have never had sexual contact of any kind . . . and I am not proud of this fact. I just haven't been fortunate enough to have any. I consider sex a basic need in life, comparable to food and shelter.

From a female sophomore: I personally prefer sex not too often. My boyfriend is just the opposite . . . I think (it might be) . . . that I am not ready to handle being sexually active. Don't get me wrong. I do enjoy sex and I do need it.

Both women and men celebrate sexual pleasure, but in Moffatt's study women promoted the value of sexual pleasure more than men. He suggests that these women may be making a deliberate effort to deny what they view as the outmoded "nice girls don't" stereotype. On the other hand, some women were afraid to talk about sexual pleasure or sexual experiences because, as one woman stated, "I am basically afraid of what people might think of me if they knew about my sexual experiences." Even for those who celebrated the value of sexual pleasure, it was not easy to achieve it. Orgasm through intercourse was especially troublesome. Half of women reported they were still "failing" in achieving orgasm. For males, sexual pleasure was discussed less often either as an actuality or a problem. Moffatt believes that the male unspoken view on sexual pleasure is "Of course I enjoy sex. I'm a normal guy. It goes without saying!"

The celebration of sexual pleasure is backed by other data showing that college students are increasing the number of their sex partners and having sex both with and without emotional involvement. Casual sex just for the pleasure of it is also increasing. However, women still report fewer partners, more emotional involvement, and engage in less risky sexual behaviors with their sexual partners than men. Male college students engage in riskier sexual behavior more often than females and have less knowledge about their sex partners (Poppen, 1995; Weaver & Herold, 2000; Moore et al., 2000). One caution needs to be addressed here. These data reflect the sexual attitudes and behaviors of a large and growing segment of college students in the United States. They may not be representative of students attending colleges that are more conservative or religiously oriented. However, the broader generalization that college life typically includes an exploration of sexuality cannot be dismissed. Overall, these findings reflect that the celebration of sex as well as the sexual double standard are alive and well on college campuses.

Nonconsensual Sex

The exploration and celebration of sexuality just described are in stark contrast to the dark side of sexuality existing on contemporary college campuses. Both in the United States and Canada, between 25 and 35 percent of college women report a rape or attempted rape. The typical pattern reported by college women is that nonconsensual or pressured intercourse occurs through the use of physical force, drugs, alcohol, and psychological intimidation (Elliott & Brantley, 1997; DeKeseredy & Schwartz, 1998; Ottens, 2001).

Date or acquaintance rape is a fact of life on college campuses. About half of college men have engaged in some form of sexual aggression on a date; between one-fourth and one-half of college women report being sexually victimized (Finley & Corty, 1995; Johnson & Sigler, 2000). Despite these high numbers, when victim and offender know one another and alcohol is involved, the incident is less likely to be reported to school officials or the police and even less likely to gain a criminal conviction. (Cowan 2000a; Shook et al., 2000). Date rape is also associated with alcohol for both victim and perpetrator, the belief that men are entitled to sex after initiating and paying for the date, fraternity parties, and length of time the couple has been dating (Abbey et al., 1998; Lonsway, 1998; Binder, 2001). The new "date rape drugs" used to plan a rape are becoming more widespread on college campuses (Zorza, 200). And despite substantial empirical evidence to the contrary, the rape myths outlined in Table 7.1 are widely accepted,

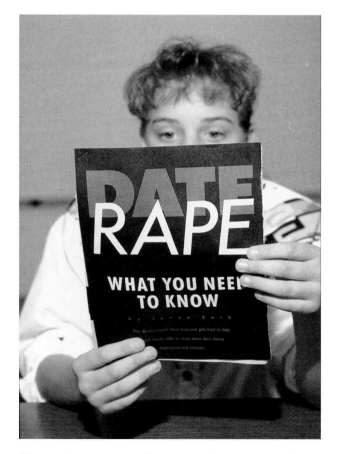

Date rape is common on college campuses but most women do not report the offense to either the police or to campus authorities. College personnel now routinely offer information to all students about the causes and consequences of date rape.

TABLE 7.1

Myths of Rape

Myth	Reality
1. Rape is a sexual act.	Rape is an act of violence to show dominance of the rapist and achieve submission by the victim.
2. Rapes are committed by strangers.	Rape is more likely to occur between acquaintances. Date rape is an example.
3. Most rapes are spontaneous, with the rapist taking advantage of the opportunity to rape.	Rape is likely to be pre-planned. If spontaneity occurs, it may be part of another crime, such as robbery.
4. Women wear provocative clothing or flirt with men.	This is the classic blaming the victim myth. Since most rapes are preplanned, the rapist will strike regardless of appearance.
5. Women enjoy being raped.	The pain, violence, degradation, and psychological devastation experienced by the victim are overwhelming.
6. Most rapists are psychopathic or sexually abnormal.	It is difficult to distinguish the rapist from other men in terms of personality or ideas about sexuality.
7. When she says no to sex she really means yes.	When she says no she really means no.

Source: Table on p. 237 from *Gender Roles: A Sociological Perspective,* 3e by Linda L. Lindsey. Copyright © 1997 by Prentice Hall, Inc. Reprinted by permission of Prentice Hall, Inc. Upper Saddle River, NJ.

but more so by male college students than females (Cowan, 2000b; Van Wie & Gross, 2001).

According to the feminist perspective, increasing sexual violence and rape are spurred by a number of elements in society. Media representations often legitimize male aggression and reinforce gender stereotypes, especially in college life. Movies such as the classic *Animal House* seem to legitimize men's engaging in sexual "antics" that are hurtful to women and may even be criminal offenses. Feminists suggest that culturally condoned relationships put men in dominant and aggressive roles and women in passive and submissive ones, and regard women as the sexual property of men (Anderson & Swainson, 2001). To support their view, they mention that some states do not have laws against marital rape. Sex is seen as part of the marriage agreement, whether the wife wants it or not. Both genders are socialized with these standards in mind. This view allows the victim to be blamed and justifies the crime (Morry & Winkler, 2001).

College men and women bring their socialization experiences with them to campus life. Their sexual behavior is shaped by these prior experiences as well as ongoing cultural influences. By studying sexual interactions on campus, sociologists help debunk long-held beliefs and hope to give students a sharper awareness of their social environment.

SOCIETY CONNECTIONS

Sex for Profit

Catering to the sexual tastes and desires of people around the world has turned into a multibillion dollar industry. The two most profitable enterprises related to sexuality are *pornography*, the sale of sexually explicit material designed to enhance sexual arousal, and *prostitution*, the exchange of sex acts for money. *Sex workers* are those who engage in sexual activities for commercial purposes and include people who work in bars, strip clubs, massage parlors, and as models for pornography. Prostitution is the largest category of sex work. Because sexual expression is always regulated, broader society may find unacceptable and illegal those activities the sex industry finds profitable and acceptable for its customers.

Pornography

Since ideas about sexual attractiveness are so diverse, a large variety of products and sexually stimulating material are produced for entertainment of people across the globe. These include magazines, films, books, and sexual toys that are developed for customers who form distinct niches based on what they find sexually appealing or arousing. Pornography is big business and becoming bigger with the ease of Internet access for producers, distributors, sex workers, and customers. In the United States alone it is a $20 billion industry (Lane, 2001). Pornography has come under a great deal of scientific and legal scrutiny because of its link to sexual aggression.

Pornography can be categorized according to two major factors—degree of depiction of sexual acts and depictions of aggression in these acts. "Hard-core" pornography often depicts genitalia openly and shows sex acts that are aggressive and violent. Women are uniformly the objects of the violence. Rarely are men portrayed in this manner. In experimental research, sexually suggestive but nonviolent "soft-core" pornography appears to have no direct effect on sex crimes or attitudes toward rape. However, aggressive sexual stimuli or hard-core pornography showing rape scenes heightens sexual arousal, desensitizes viewers to violent sexual acts, and leads them to see rape victims as less injured and less worthy (Milburn et al., 2000; Sharp & Joslyn, 2001). Although it is still un-

These teens have been arrested for prostitution. Did they engage in prostitution out of absolute economic deprivation—they had no choice—or did they freely choose to sell their services to willing clients?

clear if the arousal actually leads to later aggression, one study showed that almost one-third of women who were sexually abused and/or raped reported that their abuser used pornography, and 12 percent said it was imitated during the abusive incident (Bergen & Bogle, 2000).

The issue of what actually constitutes pornography and whether it should be illegal is hotly debated (MacKay, 2001). One side of the debate focuses on pornography as implicitly condoning the victimization of women, arguing that sexual violence against women is increasing and pornography fuels the desensitization to sexual violence and rape. Video pornographic images are certainly more powerful than photos. But consider the implications of a cartoon in *Hustler* (a pornographic magazine), which shows two "plain looking" women jogging through a park together; one says to the other, "The trouble with rapists is that they're never around when you need them" (cited in Russell, 1998).

The other side contends that pornography may actually reduce sex crimes by providing a nonharmful release of sexual tension. Proponents of this view do not deny the association of pornography with women's degradation, but assert that campaigns against it obscure more urgent needs of women. For instance, making pornography illegal denies income for women who are pornographic models and actresses. There is concern in both camps that banning pornography amounts to censorship in a free society. All factions do agree, however, that child pornography should be censored. There is also some consensus on distinguishing pornography according to its degree of violent imagery.

People may not agree on the definition of pornography, and the empirical evidence of the causal link between pornography and sexual violence remains undetermined, but this lack of agreement does not justify ignoring social issues related to pornography (Russell, 1998).

Prostitution

Since sexual behavior is so diverse, prostitutes cater to that diversity. Some work occasionally as prostitutes as an aside to their roles as hostesses and adult entertainers. Others derive their total income from prostitution. Male prostitutes representing all sexual orientations cater to specific clienteles. Heterosexual men usually offer services as escorts and sex partners for wealthy women. Some of these men are referred to as *gigolos* and are the male counterparts to mistresses who are "kept" by wealthy men. More common among male prostitutes are those homosexual or bisexual men who frequent gay bars to ply their trade. They engage in prostitution for money as well as for sexual pleasure.

Children, especially young girls, are also recruited, or forced, into prostitution. Conservative estimates globally are that more than 2 million children, with an average age of 13 or 14, work as prostitutes (Barnitz, 2001). Between 200,000 and 300,000 children under the age of 18 are estimated to be working as prostitutes in the United States (Youth Advocate Program International, 2001). In some parts of the developing world, girls are often abducted from their villages by owners of brothels dotting the sprawling urban slums. A common pattern is that these girls are sold into sexual slavery by impoverished parents (UNICEF, 2002). Sex tourism flourishes across the globe and many young prostitutes are paid for specific sex acts requested by men from Western Europe, the United States, and Japan. A key reason behind the increased demand for child prostitutes is the AIDS scare—there is a false sense of security that minors are less likely to be infected. Girls as well as boys are being marketed as "virgins, free of AIDS," so an even higher price is paid for their virginity (Flowers, 1998, 2001).

Historically, poverty-stricken women turned to prostitution as a means of survival, a pattern that continues today. Attitudes toward these women have shifted among acceptance, toleration, and outright condemnation. Prostitution flourished throughout the Roman Empire and declined when Christianity enveloped Europe and stamped the practice as irrevocably immoral for both prostitute and customer. But morality had a practical side as well. In 19th century Europe, an alarming rise in sexually transmitted diseases was traced to prostitutes whose clients were sailors returning from the New World (Bullough & Bullough, 1987). Today the global AIDS epidemic has fueled public urgency to deal with all categories of sex workers, but particularly prostitutes (Murray, 2001).

Prostitution is fundamentally a female occupation. Two-thirds of the white males in Kinsey's sample said they had seen a (female) prostitute at least once, and almost one-fifth said they did so regularly. Greater sexual freedom combined with the fear of AIDS have dramatically decreased these percentages. Although you might expect that feminist sociologists would condemn prostitution, since women are sold as sexual objects, there is ample disagreement about the reason women become prostitutes: Do they offer their services because of financial desperation or as a freely chosen occupation?

One faction argues that prostitution exists due to male demand, a need to subordinate women to male sexuality. She is vulnerable to rape, sexual violence, and exposure to HIV infection, especially in war-torn areas with a history of human and civil rights abuses (Beyrer, 2001). If a woman chooses prostitution because of economic needs, then it is not a free choice. Therefore, sex traffickers and buyers should be criminalized and prostitution eliminated (MacKinnon, 1989; Barry, 1979,

INTERNET CONNECTIONS

What are your attitudes toward sex for profit? Do you think prostitution should be legalized? With the disclaimer that some may find the contents offensive, you may wish to access the Website Coyote:

http://www.bayswan.org/COYOTE.html

"call off your old tired ethics" an organization devoted to the legalization of prostitution and the rights of prostitutes. Click on the statements The North American Task Force on Prostitution, and The International Committee for Prostitutes' Rights. What are your views on the legalization of prostitution?

1995). The other faction argues that sex workers are free agents who choose the best job they can of the gendered work available. The sexism in prostitution is no different than sexism in the rest of society. Although the feminization of poverty may be a factor in a woman's choice to become a prostitute, women should not be further impoverished by denying them income from prostitution. Like other service industries, prostitution and its traffickers and buyers can be regulated, but laws against prostitution oppress sex workers the most. Prostitution therefore should be decriminalized (Jenness, 1993; Doezema, 1998; Simmons, 1999). As with pornography, there are no easy answers to how the various factions will resolve the issues to everyone's satisfaction.

SUMMARY

1. Sexuality is social interaction in which we perceive, experience, and express ourselves as sexual beings. Most data on sexuality come from intimate activities of couples, so the microlevel perspective of symbolic interactionism is most useful in its explanation.

2. Sexuality is very diverse around the world—what one culture views as erotic, attractive, or sexually stimulating, another culture may disdain or even forbid.

3. Symbolic interactionists state that sexuality is socially constructed; sexual excitement that appears to be naturally driven by biology is a learned process.

4. Sex describes the biological characteristics distinguishing males and females, while gender is the social, cultural, and psychological characteristics defining masculinity and femininity. Sexual orientation is the preference for sexual partners, usually of one gender. All these categories overlap more than most people realize.

5. People construct their gender roles around their gender identity. Hermaphrodites, those born with both male and female or ambiguous genitals, often construct their gender identity based on the sex assigned to them at birth.

6. Sexual scripts are beliefs about acceptable sexual behavior for both genders. These beliefs contribute to "gendered" sexuality and may serve to undermine options for different kinds of sexual expression for men and women.

7. Heterosexuals have sexual preferences for the other gender; homosexuals have sexual preferences for their own gender. Bisexuals are sexually responsive to either gender. There are problems with these definitions, especially since the categories overlap a great deal.

8. Sexual dimorphism, the separation of the sexes into two distinct groups, is violated by groups such as the berdache, hijra, mahu, and xanith. Transsexuals and transvestites may also violate the principle.

9. Homophobia—negative attitudes toward homosexuals—is widespread. Males are more homophobic than females because of masculinity norms. However, tolerance and acceptance of homosexuals is increasing, especially among young adults.

10. Kinsey's original data found relatively high rates of masturbation, orgasm, and premarital sex for both genders, patterns that persist and have increased since. Extramarital sex is disapproved of, but a high percentage of people engage in it.

11. Both men and women have similar rates of non-marital sex, but the double standard, which discourages sexuality for women and encourages it for men, persists. The elderly are particularly vulnerable to gendered stereotypes about sexuality.

12. Functionalists and conflict theorists view sexuality in terms of how it is located in large-scale institutions. Functionalists believe custom and law must regulate sexuality to keep society from the least disruption. Conflict theorists look at people's location in the social structure, which puts some more at risk for sexual violence than others.

13. College students explore and even celebrate sexuality. But the double standard in sexuality persists for men and women. College life may also be sexually violent, with many women reporting a rape or attempted rape.

14. According to feminist sociologists, the media and U.S. culture condone relationships in which men are aggressive and women are submissive, contributing to sexual violence.

15. Pornography and prostitution profit through sex. Defining pornography and deciding what types should be illegal is hotly debated. The legalization of prostitution hinges on beliefs about whether prostitutes freely choose their occupation.

KEY TERMS

bisexual 177
gender 174
hermaphrodites 174
heterosexual 177

homophobia 180
homosexual 177
sex 174
sexual dimorphism 180

sexual orientation 174
sexual scripts 175
sexuality 171
transgender 179

CRITICAL THINKING QUESTIONS

1. Explain how research on sexuality can be used to claim that there *has* been a sexual revolution as well as that there *has not* been one. What research would you focus on to justify one or the other claim? How do the media influence the beliefs about sexuality?

2. Speaking as a sociologist who is also a symbolic interactionist, what would you say to a person who states that sexuality is solely a biological fact?

3. From the research on hermaphrodites, gender identity, and sexual orientation, demonstrate how the principle of sexual dimorphism may be violated.

4. Show how sexuality is "gendered" with reference to sexuality inside and outside of marriage and issues surrounding "sex for profit."

INVESTIGATE WITH CONTENT SELECT

Journal Research Collections from *ContentSelect* Begin your research using Content-Select for this chapter by following the directions found on page 27 of this text to visit Prentice Hall's Research Navigator Website. Enter these search terms into the search field:

Sexual orientation
Pornography
Masculinity

8
DEVIANT BEHAVIOR

Peyote on the Reservation

Joseph, an 18-year-old Navajo boy, recently joined a 125-year-old Christian sect called the Native American Church that uses the bud of the peyote cactus in its sacred rituals. Although considered a dangerous drug by many people because of the vivid hallucinations it produces, peyote has long been familiar to Native Americans as a traditional means of promoting healing and self-knowledge (Aberle, 1982). Before the reservation era, it was expected that young members of a number of different tribes would engage in "vision quests," periods of prolonged fasting and self-denial that led to hallucinations much like those Joseph is now seeking through peyote. Indeed, in some traditional Native American cultures, youths who were not successful in evoking visions of ancestor spirits were considered deviant, or at least less than full adults. (Lame Deer & Erdoes, 1972)

Coca Cola in Utah

As a Mormon living in a small town in Utah, Susan knows that her spiritual well-being depends on, among other things, following her church's teachings requiring abstinence from drugs—including not only alcohol and tobacco (to say nothing of peyote!), but also caffeine-laden drinks such as tea, coffee, and some soft drinks (Whalen, 1964). But sometimes it's hard to live up to these ideals. Earlier today Susan drank a Coca Cola, and now she can't stop worrying about her lapse into "drug abuse."

Both of these young people have used a mood-altering drug. In each case, some people would consider the behavior wrong while others would see it as perfectly normal. This chapter examines how behaviors such as drug-taking come to be socially de-fined as unacceptable. We also present a number of different explanations for why people engage in such activity.

WHAT IS DEVIANCE?

Deviance consists of behavior, beliefs, or conditions that are viewed by relatively powerful segments of society as serious violations of important norms. Let's look at each element of this definition more closely.

When most Americans think of deviants, they probably visualize drug addicts, rapists, or child molesters. This view emphasizes behaviors that involve *major* violations of *important* norms. People are not generally defined as deviant for such minor violations as not applauding at the end of a play or wearing mismatched clothes.

But note that under the sociological definition, deviance may consist not only of *behaviors*, but also of *beliefs*—atheism and communism come to mind—and *conditions*, such as being physically handicapped, mentally ill, HIV-positive, or morbidly obese (Degher & Hughes, 1991).

Students are frequently uncomfortable with the fact that sociologists classify people who are physically disabled or mentally ill as deviants. Such an interpretation seems unjust: These people did not choose to be different. Yet it is clear that because of their conditions, they are denied full acceptance in society in much the same way as bank robbers and bigamists—people who are generally believed to have chosen to violate norms—are looked down upon. The extent to which an individual's behavior is voluntary may affect how negatively he or she is viewed, but it is not necessary that nonconformity or difference be freely chosen for it to be classified as deviance (Link et al., 1987; Gortmaker et al., 1993; Crandall, 1995).

Along the same lines, note that an individual need not cause appreciable harm to anyone in order to be regarded as deviant. Most mental patients, many drug users, and the vast majority of the members of unconventional religious groups harm no one except,

195

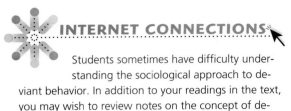

INTERNET CONNECTIONS

Students sometimes have difficulty understanding the sociological approach to deviant behavior. In addition to your readings in the text, you may wish to review notes on the concept of deviance that will serve as another useful "Introduction to Deviance." Go to:

http://www.umsl.edu/~rkeel/200/200lec.html#disclaim

After you have completed a review of the information, write a brief report on the sociological meaning of deviance.

arguably, themselves, yet they are clearly deviants in many people's eyes.

Deviance should be differentiated from the related concept of crime, which we discuss in the next chapter. A **crime** is a violation of a formal statute enacted by a legitimate government. Acts such as homicide, arson, or rape are clearly both criminal and deviant. However, some criminals are not treated as deviants, including most traffic offenders and people who cheat on their income taxes. Furthermore, many types of deviance, such as mental illness or not bathing regularly, are not covered by the criminal statutes (see Figure 8.1).

The Relative Nature of Deviance

The vignettes that opened this chapter illustrate an important point: *Deviance is relative.* What is regarded as deviant in one society may be accepted or even honored in another (Goode, 1997). Using peyote is seen as seriously deviant by most citizens of the United States but not by many traditional Native Americans; drinking Coca Cola is mildly deviant for a Mormon, but not for a Catholic or Jew.

Some of the most striking examples of the relative nature of deviance concern sexuality, the topic of Chapter 7. Some cultures are extremely repressed by the standards of most residents of the United States, regarding as seriously deviant many behaviors that we consider quite normal. Among the traditional Cheyenne, for example, a girl who lost her virginity was permanently dishonored and considered unmarriageable (Hoebel, 1978). Residents of Inis Beag, an island off the west coast of Ireland, were even more conservative, traditionally disapproving of nudity even in the marital bed (Messenger, 1971).

On the other hand, about 25 percent of all societies fully accept premarital sex by both genders (Rathaus et al., 1997). In the developed world, the Scandinavians are widely known for their sexual openness. The least sexually repressed people in the world may well be the Polynesians of Mangaia in the Cook Islands; early field work among these people reported intense sexual activity among both women and men, largely devoid of romantic attachment and beginning well before puberty (Marshall, 1971; see Harris, 1995, for a more skeptical account).

What is regarded as deviant also changes over time within any particular society. A hundred years ago, child-rearing practices that would be seen as abusive today ("Spare the rod and spoil the child") were not only accepted but frequently encouraged. Racial discrimination was legal and widely endorsed. And millions of respectable Americans routinely used drugs that are illegal today: Opium was a common ingredient in over-the-counter medications, and Coca Cola originally contained a small dose of cocaine.

People with serious physical disabilities are often treated as deviants. However, a record of outstanding personal achievement can help to overcome the stigma. Former Senator Max Cleland of Georgia is an excellent example.

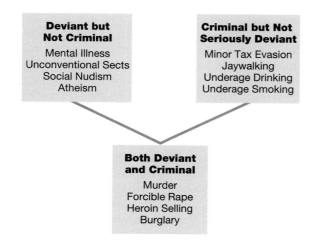

FIGURE 8.1 The Relationship Between Deviance and Criminality.

and groups with high levels of power and prestige. In the United States today, this means that the definition of what is deviant is more heavily shaped by the rich than by the poor, by men than by women, and by whites than by people of color. The definition of deviance is thus a political process: Behaviors that are accepted by the powerful are likely to be regarded as normative, while those that are common among the powerless may well be stigmatized (Schur, 1971).

There is widespread agreement in modern societies that certain types of behaviors, especially predatory crimes like robbery and forcible rape, are seriously deviant. But in other areas where value-

On the other hand, many practices that most people in the United States now take for granted were once regarded as deviant, including participating in lotteries, women smoking and wearing pants in public, and unmarried couples cohabiting.

Deviance is relative in other ways as well. Behavior that is generally acceptable for one gender—such as asking a friend to accompany you to a public restroom—is unacceptable for the other. Similarly, behavior that is strongly encouraged in one subculture may be just as strongly rejected by another. For example, members of street gangs are expected to fight—but the Amish embrace strict norms opposing physical combat.

Deviance also varies by place—language heard in a football locker room would be most unseemly at a church social. Class also matters. Although standards are currently changing, bearing children out of wedlock continues to be more acceptable in the lower class than in the middle and upper strata of U.S. society. Figure 8.2 illustrates how class affects drinking, smoking, and attitudes toward the decriminalization of marijuana.

The extent of these variations in what is considered deviant strongly suggests that *no behavior is inherently deviant*. While some actions, such as incest within the nuclear family, are condemned by nearly all cultures, researchers have not been able to identify any universally deviant behaviors.

Since deviance is a relative concept, the question of who decides what will and will not be considered deviant is a crucial one. In small, traditional societies displaying a very high level of consensus regarding norms and values, it may be reasonable to say that the society as a whole makes this decision. However, in modern societies where disagreement about norms is widespread, deviance is often defined by individuals

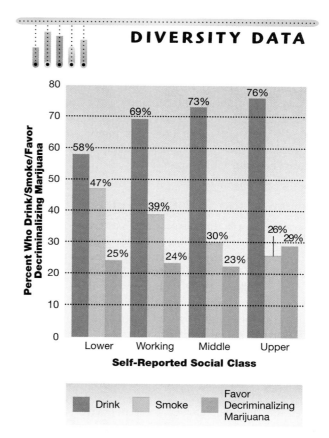

FIGURE 8.2 Percentage of the U.S. Population Who Drink, Smoke, and Support Decriminalizing Marijuana, by Social Class. As self-reported social class position rises, people tend to be more likely to drink and less likely to smoke. Attitudes toward decriminalizing marijuana do not vary sharply by class, although the elite is slightly more supportive of decriminalization than any other class. Given the fact that the upper class tends to have a disproportionate ability to affect the way laws are written, what do these findings suggest about which substances are likely to remain legal?

Source: NORC. General Social Surveys, 1972–2000. Chicago: National Opinion Research Center, 2000. Reprinted by permission of NORC, Chicago, IL.

consensus is lacking, such as attitudes toward recreational drug use, soft-core pornography, and homosexuality, the preferences of the powerful usually dominate. Thus, for example, the primary reason why one drug—say, marijuana—is generally considered deviant, whereas another drug—say, whiskey—is widely accepted, is not because of the relative dangerousness of these substances but rather because the most powerful members of society—typically older, middle- and upper-class white males—are much more likely to relax after work with a few drinks than with a joint. (The *Global Connections* box on page 216 in this chapter discusses how some European nations respond to drugs in very different ways than does the United States).

Finally, *deviance is a cultural universal.* In other words, deviance can be found in every society (Durkheim, 1897/1964). Even in a culture with a high degree of normative consensus and virtually no serious crime, there is occasional misbehavior. However, as the story of Susan (the Mormon girl who indulged in a forbidden soft drink) suggests, in a strongly moralistic society, what outsiders might consider to be a minor type of deviance will likely be viewed as a relatively major violation.

Deviance and Social Control

Sociologists use the term **social control** to refer to measures taken by members of society intended to encourage conformity to norms. In other words, the purpose of social control is to reduce, if not eliminate, deviance (Gibbs, 1989). This can be done in three general ways: through formal social control, informal social control, or internalized normative standards.

Formal social control consists of efforts to discourage deviance made by people such as police officers and college deans whose jobs involve, in whole or in part, punishing nonconformity and rewarding obedience.

Punishments, referred to as **negative sanctions,** are especially important at the formal level. Negative sanctions range from a parking fine or academic probation to the total ostracism of a deviant by an entire community (Hostetler & Huntington, 1971). The ultimate negative formal sanction is, of course, execution.

Formal social control may also involve **positive sanctions** or rewards, such as a good conduct medal or an A on an examination. In either case, the purpose of the sanction is the same: to promote conformity and to discourage deviance.

While formal social control is necessary to restrain the most serious deviants, no society could survive if people conformed only to avoid formal sanctioning. A far more effective way to reduce deviance is through **informal social control**—positive and negative sanctions applied by friends and family. The desire for approval from significant others can be a far stronger motive for conformity than the fear of negative formal sanctions. After all, while the authorities may have a great deal of power over us, it is usually the opinions of those who are closest to us that really matter. The *Then and Now* box on the facing page entitled "Informal Social Control: Shunned at Berkeley" discusses a modern example of informal social control.

However, neither formal nor informal social control is society's main line of defense against deviance. Most conformity results from the *internalization of norms* during the process of moral socialization. Fear of externally imposed sanctions is often far less powerful than the desire to avoid feelings of guilt. Similarly, the pleasure obtained from positive sanctions can rarely compare with the sense of self-esteem that comes from living up to the demands of one's conscience (Berger, 1963:93).

FOUR QUESTIONS ABOUT DEVIANCE

Sociologists who study deviance are generally interested in answering one or more of four important theoretical questions:

1. *Who decides what behaviors, beliefs, and conditions will be defined as deviant?*
2. *What are the social functions of deviance?*
3. *Why do people deviate?*
4. *How do people react to deviants, and how do these reactions in turn affect the behavior of the deviants?*

Later in this chapter, we will explore these issues in some depth. However, before we proceed further, we need to introduce one of the most widely read research studies in the sociology of deviance, William Chambliss's (1973) analysis of two groups of juveniles he called the Saints and the Roughnecks. Despite the fact that this study was carried out more than a generation ago, its central findings remain as valid and relevant as they were when it was first published. We will use this research to illustrate a number of important theoretical points throughout the remainder of the chapter.

The Saints and the Roughnecks were two groups of boys who attended the same high school. The Saints grew up in middle-class families. The other clique, the Roughnecks, came from lower-class backgrounds.

Both groups of boys were fairly seriously delinquent. The Saints cut school regularly, drank excessively, drove recklessly, and committed various acts of petty and not-so-petty vandalism. The Roughnecks, too, were often truant and stole from local stores, got

THEN AND NOW

Informal Social Control: Shunned at Berkeley

Informal means of controlling deviance have been far more common throughout history and often much more effective than the formal controls applied by the police, courts, and prisons. Small, traditional societies, or *Gemeinschafts* (see Chapter 4), relied especially heavily on informal social control.

The Amish are arguably the most traditional subculture that still exists in the United States. They may be viewed as a kind of living fossil, allowing us to experience firsthand something of what it was like to live in a true Gemeinschaft. The Amish custom of *meidung,* or shunning, is a classic example of the sorts of informal social control mechanisms that were widely employed by societies before the industrial era (Wasilchick, 1992). When an Amish individual violates important religious rules, the faithful—including the person's immediate family—are forbidden to speak to that person, eat at the same table with him or her, or even, in the case of a spouse, engage in marital relations. Shunning is the ultimate penalty: Imagine living in a community where everyone behaved as if you no longer existed.

Even in modern *Gesellschaft* societies in which elaborate formal social control mechanisms are present, informal social control remains important. On Memorial Day weekend, 1997, University of California student David Cash and his best friend Jeremy Strohmeyer visited a casino outside Las Vegas. Around 3:30 AM, Strohmeyer lured a 7-year-old girl into a

ladies room. Cash followed, watched as his friend forced the child into a stall, then walked outside. Not long afterward, Strohmeyer rejoined Cash and confessed that he had raped and murdered the girl. Cash had made no effort to stop the assault; nor did he report the crime—out of loyalty to his friend, he later claimed. Strohmeyer was arrested a few days later. To avoid the death penalty, he pleaded guilty and was sentenced to life without parole. But prosecutors could not bring charges against Cash because he had not broken any law (Hammer, 1998).

During his freshman year at Berkeley, Cash went unnoticed. That August, however, he appeared on a popular radio talk show, defended his behavior, and proclaimed, "the university officials are behind me, baby." And they were. Because he had not committed a crime or violated campus codes, university officials (agents of formal social control) had no grounds for expelling him or even reviewing his case. In the chancellor's words, "We cannot set aside due process based upon our outrage over a particular instance." But Berkeley students who learned about the case disagreed. Soon after the talk show, a large demonstration alerted other students to Cash's presence on campus. He was thrown out of a fraternity party and chased to his dormitory room by an angry mob. Overnight, spray-painted graffiti reading EXPEL DAVID CASH appeared all over the campus. The Berkeley student senate passed a bill asking Cash to withdraw voluntarily. Invoking due process, the president of the senate vetoed the

bill. In his words, "David Cash is morally repugnant. But if you don't like him, don't talk to him. That's all you can do."

Cash continued to attend classes at Berkeley, but as an outcast, shunned (in Amish tradition) by fellow students. No one spoke to him, though some students muttered obscenities when he passed by. Everywhere he went, he confronted graffiti calling for his expulsion. He avoided major gatherings. When he walked into a nearby 7-Eleven store, a stranger spat in his face. Thus, when formal social controls failed to satisfy public outrage, Berkeley students applied informal controls.

The shunning of David Cash shows that even in a modern, heterogeneous society, there is a high level of consensus on certain issues, such as child molestation. Berkeley has a reputation as an exceptionally tolerant campus where widely different points of view are respected. But even there, Cash found few defenders. Just as prisons isolate child molesters from other inmates for their own protection, so Cash was accompanied everywhere by a plain-clothes police officer.

1. Do you think Cash would have been more likely to have come to understand the seriousness of his failure to act had he simply been expelled from Berkeley rather than being shunned?

2. Can you think of examples from your own experience of informal social control? Were they effective?

Sources: Wasilchick, 1992; Hammer, 1998.

drunk, and fought with other youths. But despite these similarities, the two groups were regarded very differently by social control agents, particularly by the police and school authorities.

The middle-class Saints were perceived as basically good boys. This image was partly a direct reflection of the respectability of their parents, but it was also influenced by other class-based factors. The Saints had learned during primary socialization to treat authority figures with the appearance of respect. When they cut school, they arranged for fake excuses; when stopped by the police, they were always polite and deferential. Further, since they could afford cars, their deviance was generally carried out in other towns or at least well away from the eyes of their neighbors. When the Saints were caught misbehaving, social control agents consistently made excuses for them.

In contrast, the Roughnecks were viewed as no-good punks heading for trouble. Again, this label was both a direct and an indirect consequence of their class status. Their socialization had not prepared them to sweet-talk the authorities; instead, they tended to be insolent and aggressive when confronted. Lacking the means to own cars, they hung out on a centrally located street corner where everyone in the community could see them. When they were caught in some criminal or deviant act, nobody was inclined to go easy on them.

Which group was more deviant? In the eyes of the community, clearly the Roughnecks. Yet, according to Chambliss, the Saints caused at least as much harm as the Roughnecks, and they probably committed more criminal acts. But the fact that the Roughnecks were labeled as deviant had devastating consequences. Seven of the eight Saints finished college, and most established themselves in careers as doctors, politicians, and businessmen. Two of the seven Roughnecks never graduated from high school, three became heavily involved in criminal activities, and only two achieved stable, respectable community roles.

Now we will return to the four questions that opened this section and explore how sociologists respond to them, making reference to the Saints and Roughnecks as appropriate. This discussion will also illustrate how many sociological explanations of deviance are linked to the major theoretical perspectives that were introduced in Chapter 1.

WHO DEFINES WHAT IS DEVIANT?

The first question sociologists must consider in explaining deviance is how—and by whom—certain behaviors, beliefs, and characteristics come to be understood in a given society as deviant. This question has principally been addressed by conflict theorists (Lynch, 1994). Their answer, in short, is that societal elites control the definition process (Turk, 1977; Chasin, 1997).

You will recall that conflict theory is based on principles first developed by Karl Marx, who maintained that the ruling class in a capitalist society controls all the major institutions and uses them to protect its interests (Lynch & Groves, 1989). Their control of the political institution is especially significant. The legal statutes that define what will be considered criminal deviance clearly reflect the values and interests of the ruling class (Quinney, 1970;

Many behaviors are regarded as more deviant in some cultures than in others. This tourist from San Francisco is taking advantage of the relatively tolerant attitudes toward marijuana use currently prevalent in Holland; back in the United States such a public display of drug use would very likely result in his arrest.

Greenberg, 1981). Crimes committed mostly by the poor—robbery, burglary, larceny, aggravated assault—carry heavy penalties, while offenses most commonly committed by elites, such as price-fixing, dumping hazardous wastes, or maintaining unsafe working conditions, carry lesser penalties (Reiman, 1995). Conflict theorists also charge that the police and courts routinely discriminate in the application of the law, a problem we will take up in Chapter 9 (Arvanites, 1992; Lynch, 1994).

The elite also control the schools and the mass media, two additional important social institutions, and use them to shape people's understandings of what sorts of behaviors and ideas ought to be considered deviant. These definitions are biased in favor of the capitalists' interests and emphasize the seriousness of types of deviance that are especially common among the poor and minorities (Quinney, 1970). Note that these insights concerning how deviance is defined reflect a synthesis of the conflict and symbolic interactionist perspectives.

Richard Quinney is an important modern conflict theorist who has addressed these issues. He notes that the fact that the ruling class defines deviance and enforces laws in a self-serving manner actively promotes norm violation among both the wealthy and the poor (Quinney, 1977). The elite commit what Quinney calls "crimes of domination and repression," which are designed to increase their wealth and power and to control the middle and lower classes, with relative impunity. After all, writes Quinney (1972), ". . . those in power, those who control the legal system, are not likely to prosecute themselves and define their official policies as crime."

At the same time, the poor have little choice but to engage in predatory deviance in order to survive. Most of their acts are property crimes such as larceny and burglary. The lower classes also engage in a great deal of violent personal crime, which Quinney sees as an expression of their anger and frustration. Crime thus makes sense for both the upper class, because they can get away with it, and for the poor, because they have few other options (Gordon, 1973).

According to conflict theorists, mainstream sociologists are too willing to accept the elite's definitions of deviance. As a result, many do not devote sufficient attention to the great harm that results from the misbehavior of elites and from the inequities of the criminal law (Liazos, 1972).

For example, America's current drug laws mandate much more severe penalties for the possession or sale of crack cocaine than for the powdered form of the drug (Smolowe, 1995). Crack is used primarily by lower-class African Americans, while the majority of powdered cocaine offenders are white. The average prison sentence for crack is three to eight times longer, yet the two forms of the drug are, in essence, chemically identical (Kappler et al., 1996). Similarly, the police are much more likely to arrest streetwalkers, who are heavily minority, than to go after call girls, who are mostly white. They also rarely arrest female prostitutes' male customers (Riccio, 1992).

Conflict theory can be applied easily to the Saints and the Roughnecks. The middle-class Saints misbehaved extensively, yet they suffered no lasting consequences because the authorities identified them as "our kind" and treated them with a presumption of innocence. Conversely, the lower-class Roughnecks were defined as members of the "dangerous classes" and treated accordingly. No conflict theorist would be at all surprised by the different paths these two groups traveled after high school.

CRITIQUE Conflict theory's great strength is that it directs our attention to the importance of power in shaping social definitions of deviance. It has also highlighted the biases present in our criminal justice system. Yet the conflict approach enjoys only limited acceptance among sociologists and has had little effect on the general public.

This lack of acceptance is congruent with the central point made by conflict analysis. Most Americans, including many sociologists, have internalized elite definitions of deviance and are thus likely to believe that the conflict perspective is "radical." But this belief may lead sociologists to concentrate their attention on "real" crimes like robbery or assault, crimes committed principally by the poor, while largely overlooking white-collar crimes like the recent Enron scandal which, as conflict theorists are quick to point out, are actually far more costly than any street crime.

There are, however, some real problems with conflict theory (Toby, 1979; Inciardi, 1980; Sparks, 1980; Gibbs, 1987; Gibbons, 1994). First, its observation that the elite often control the definition of deviance makes the most sense with regard to acts such as insider trading or drug use. It is hard to support when applied to predatory crimes such as murder, forcible rape, or robbery, which almost everyone, regardless of class, regards as seriously deviant.

In addition, the primary policy implication of conflict theory is that economic inequality must be substantially reduced in order to prevent the dominant class from distorting the definition of deviance to its own advantage. Most conflict theorists believe that this can only be achieved by a fundamental shift of the U.S. political economy away from capitalism and toward some form of democratic socialism (Pepinsky & Quinney, 1993; Milovanovic, 1996). However, such an economic transformation is not only unlikely to be achieved in the United States (Owomero, 1988), but it also did not appear to be effective in reducing deviance and crime in the old Soviet bloc nations.

WHAT ARE THE FUNCTIONS OF DEVIANCE?

The conflict perspective, as we have just seen, is useful for answering the first of our key questions: Who decides what is deviant? The second question, however, is best addressed by functionalism.

Following the lead of Emile Durkheim, functionalists maintain that any aspect of a society that fails to contribute to its stability tends eventually to fade away. Since deviance is a cultural universal, it follows that although it is socially devalued, it must serve some functions (Durkheim, 1897/1964; Erickson, 1966). There are four especially important positive functions of deviance:

1. *The Boundary Setting Function.* In complex modern societies, the *real* rules are frequently unclear. How often and how much can students cheat before they are expelled? How fast can you really

THEN AND NOW

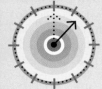

From Getting High to Getting Drunk: Changing Styles of Campus Deviance

The marijuana "epidemic," as some called it, peaked in the mid-1970s (Akers, 1992). Study after study in this era found that two out of three college students had used pot, up from a mere 5 percent in the mid-1960s. Prior to this era, marijuana use had been largely confined to "outsiders," especially Mexican American laborers and jazz musicians, whom respectable people did not consider "one of us." Use of the drug by these groups merely confirmed their otherness; it was not a cause for public alarm.

When middle-class college students—presumably the best and the brightest American youth and the nation's future leaders—began using marijuana, it was a different story. As part of the hippie rebellion, college students were also experimenting with cocaine, LSD, amphetamines, and other illicit substances. Clearly, the nation's youth were at risk. And so campaigns like DARE and Just Say No were born.

Over time, the use of marijuana and other illicit drugs by college students declined. But a new epidemic was on the horizon. In 1994 the Harvard School of Public Health issued a report on the use of alcohol on college campuses. A survey of 140 campuses found that almost half of all students engaged in "binge drinking" (consuming five or more drinks at one sitting for men, four or more for women). Even more alarming, half of students who binge do so regularly. Binge drinkers are far more likely than other students to engage in unprotected sex, drive while intoxicated, miss classes, and experience memory lapses. They are also more likely to commit acts of vandalism, get into fights, and injure themselves.

Indeed, drinking too much too fast can be deadly. Each year an estimated 50 students die from bingeing, either be-

cause they pass out and choke to death on their own vomit or because their blood becomes so thick that oxygen can't reach their brain (alcohol poisoning). The effects of binge drinking are not limited to participants. At schools with high binge rates, a majority of students who don't drink report such second-hand effects as not being able to sleep or study, enduring insults or unwanted sexual advances, and having to care for drunken friends. Recent studies have found that despite campaigns publicizing the dangers of alcohol abuse, the percentage of binge drinkers on college campuses has been increasing as has the proportion of students who admit they drink specifically to get drunk (not because they enjoy the taste of beer, wine, or whiskey).

The shift from getting high to getting drunk lends support to the functional view that although patterns of deviance change over time, the overall level of deviance remains more or less constant. When frequent use of marijuana on college campuses declined, heavy drinking replaced it. This pattern also suggests that public perception of deviance remains steady. During the marijuana years, alcohol did not disappear on campuses, but most people did not consider college drinking a problem. After all, alcohol wasn't a "drug" in the social sense of being an illicit substance. Likewise, marijuana hasn't disappeared from college campuses, but the public is now somewhat less likely to view cannabis as dangerously addictive and morally subversive. To the contrary, possession of small quantities of marijuana has been decriminalized in a number of states and reduced from a felony to a misdemeanor in others. At the same time, attitudes toward alcohol, and particularly toward drunken drivers, have changed. Once viewed as a matter of personal choice,

heavy drinking has been redefined as a public health issue.

Why do college students engage in high levels of deviance? From the functionalist perspective, societies need a certain level of nonconforming behavior in order to test and reaffirm the boundaries of acceptable behavior. College students are well situated to perform this function. As young adults, they are no longer expected to accept their parents' authority without question; nor do they have as many responsibilities as they will when they embark on careers, marry, and become parents. In effect, the college years are a "time out" when the penalties for nonconformity are reduced. Students are expected to question ideas and engage in critical thinking; that some question society's norms and values should not be a surprise. Most people who frequently smoked pot in college do not become life-long drug users; nor do most college binge drinkers continue to abuse alcohol. Having tested the boundaries of acceptable behavior, most choose respectability. But the next generation of college students, and the next, reenact the cycle.

1. Is binge drinking widespread on your campus? How do participants explain and excuse their behavior? What additional interpretations might be suggested by a sociologist?

2. Do you believe that programs like DARE and groups like MADD and SADD are effective in combating alcohol abuse? Discuss.

3. What should be the goals of a sociologically informed campus-based campaign to oppose binge drinking? How would you structure such an effort?

Source: Akers, 1992; Goldberg, 1998; McCormick & Kalb, 1998.

drive on the interstate without getting a ticket? How much can you drink before people will start thinking of you as an alcoholic? In some cases, there are no official rules; in others, there are formal rules but they are enforced with a degree of tolerance, which means that there is a difference between the *formal* and the *actual* boundaries of acceptable behavior.

We learn the real boundaries by observing what happens to people who deviate: We know that we cannot go as far as they do unless we are willing to risk punishment ourselves. In other words, publicly labeled deviants define the range of acceptable behaviors by exceeding that range, and they encourage conformity by showing what happens to people who fail to conform.

It can be argued that one reason why there are so many portrayals of deviance in the mass media is to spread public awareness of the true limits of tolerance. Thus, ironically, one of the principal functions of deviance is to encourage conformity!

2. *The Solidarity Function.* Nothing unites a group of people more strongly than their shared opposition to an enemy; this phenomenon is especially evident in societies engaged in warfare. For example, most Americans experienced a surge of patriotism following the September 11, 2001, terrorist attacks. Deviants provide a domestic equivalent of Osama bin Laden.

3. *The Warning Function.* When any type of deviance becomes substantially more common, it sends a signal that something is wrong in society. Examples include escalations in the frequency of inner-city riots or a sharp increase in the use of illegal drugs by teens. The authorities may respond to the warning in one of two ways: They may modify the rules or laws to fit changing circumstances, or they may simply step up their social control efforts.

4. *The Innovation Function.* Sometimes deviance can be highly functional in promoting social change. For example, the nonviolent tactics employed by the Southern civil rights movement of the 1960s, including sit-ins and freedom rides, were widely viewed at the time as being beyond the conventional limits of political activity, but were nevertheless very effective in bringing about racial integration. Similarly, people in formal organizations sometimes find that they must break some of the formal rules (or "cut through the red tape") in order to achieve important ends.

Chambliss's study of the Saints and the Roughnecks nicely illustrates the boundary setting and solidarity functions of deviance. The official response to

On February 4, 1999, New York City police fired 41 shots into the home of unarmed African immigrant Amadou Diallo, killing him instantly. Shared opposition to this act of apparent police brutality unites the members of this protest crowd.

the misdeeds of the Roughnecks clarified the actual limits of toleration for other youths, and the community clearly was united in condemning the gang's deviance.

The fact that deviance serves positive functions implies that societies may take covert steps to ensure that they do not "run out" of deviants (Erickson, 1962). For example, we claim that prisons are designed to reduce crime. Yet, since there is little emphasis on rehabilitation in modern prisons, what inmates actually learn while incarcerated often consists largely of tips picked up from fellow inmates about how to become better—more effective—offenders. Because of the severe stigma associated with having been incarcerated, ex-prisoners often find it extremely difficult to find honest employment after they are released, strongly pushing them toward illicit sources of income. In light of these facts, it seems possible that prison is really less about reducing crime than about perpetuating it (Reiman, 1995).

Of course, deviance also is dysfunctional for society. In addition to the numerous direct physical and economic injuries that result from acts such as robbery, arson, manufacturing hazardous products, or domestic violence, deviance has at least three important general dysfunctions. First, it makes social life problematic because it reduces our certainty that others will obey the norms. Much like someone driving in the wrong lane of a highway, the presence of criminals and deviants makes our lives less predictable.

Second, if deviance is seen to be rewarded, it reduces people's willingness to play by the rules. If your neighbor gets away with cheating on her income tax, why should you report every penny? If your friends get A's by cheating, why study?

Finally, deviance is dysfunctional because it is very costly. The United States loses more than $450 billion annually due to crime, including both direct costs and social control expenditures (Mandel & Magnusson, 1993). These resources could be used for other, more constructive purposes.

The most important policy implication of the functional approach is to remind the authorities that it is not possible, or even desirable, to attempt to eradicate all deviation. Certainly, we should try to reduce serious predatory crime as much as possible, but at the same time we need to recognize that a certain amount of relatively harmless nonconformity has positive social value. In fact, there is some evidence that if one sort of deviance is sharply reduced, whether by effective social control or by redefinition, some other type of deviance is likely to become more common (Erickson, 1966). This strongly suggests that "zero-tolerance" efforts to completely end drug abuse, juvenile gangs, or other forms of deviance are most unlikely to succeed.

WHY DO PEOPLE DEVIATE?

Through most of history, the usual answer to the question of why people violate important norms was a religious or moralistic one. Thus, deviance might be explained by demonic possession or by a simple declaration that deviants and criminals were "evil" or "sinful" or "bad" people.

But in the late 18th century, Enlightenment thinkers such as Caesare Beccaria and Jeremy Bentham challenged these early explanations by asserting that deviance could best be understood as a consequence of the exercise of free will (Bentham, 1967; Devine, 1982). Deviants, they maintained, consciously assessed the costs and benefits of conformity and nonconformity and chose the latter only when it seemed advantageous to do so. This perspective, known as *classical theory*, has enjoyed renewed popularity in the past two decades under the name **rational choice theory** (Cornish & Clarke, 1986). Early classical theory led to more humane social control efforts than moralistic theories, but it fell into disfavor late in the 19th century with the rise of positivistic thinking in the social sciences.

Positivism is an approach to understanding human behavior grounded in the scientific method.

Positivistic theories are research-based, concentrate on measurable aspects of empirical reality, and aim to identify the causes of behavior. They are strongly oriented toward reducing deviance: If we can identify what causes a behavior pattern, we can use that knowledge to change the behavior. Classical theory simply states that people choose crime because they think such a choice will benefit them. Positivistic theories, in contrast, explore the underlying *reasons* for the choices that people make, thereby allowing us to develop more effective techniques of social control.

It is important to recognize that in contrast to classical theory, positivism does *marginally* reduce the degree to which deviants are considered responsible for their behavior. If deviance is *purely* a result of free will, then deviants are entirely responsible for their actions. If, on the other hand, the decision to deviate is influenced by biological, psychological, or social factors—which are to some extent beyond the deviant's ability to control—then individual responsibility is somewhat lessened. But this does not mean that, in practice, positivists regard criminals as personally blameless.

Positivists therefore see punishment as part of an appropriate response to misbehavior, but they insist that society needs to go beyond negative sanctioning and consider causal factors in order to reduce deviance more effectively. Failing to consider factors that shape the decision to deviate places too much weight on the shoulders of the individual; it is a form of victim-blaming (Ryan, 1971).

Biological Explanations

The first positivistic theories of deviance arose when Darwin's theory of evolution was having a profound influence on European and American intellectual thought and were thus strongly grounded in biology. The most popular of these approaches was a theory developed by Italian criminologist Caesare Lombroso, who maintained that many criminals were born rather than made (Lombroso-Ferreo, 1972). Without altogether denying the importance of other factors, Lombroso argued that some lawbreakers were genetically inferior throwbacks to an earlier, more brutal type of humanity. Defective in reasoning power and physically distinctive, sometimes deformed, these individuals could not be reformed or even reasoned with.

Some early 20th century theorists continued to search for a general genetic cause of deviation that would allow them to put deviants and nondeviants into two distinct categories. However, most of this early work was marred by serious methodological weaknesses, and biological positivism lost popularity early in this century, only to be revived in a more sophisticated form during the last 40 years (Wilson, 1975; Fishbein, 2000).

Instead of arguing that misbehavior is directly caused by biology, modern biological theories generally maintain that certain physical traits, acting in concert with psychological and social factors, increase the chances that an individual will engage in deviance (Ellis & Hoffman, 1990). The key factor is often aggressiveness. The physical factors that may contribute to a violent temperament include dietary deficiencies, hypoglycemia (low blood sugar), allergies, hormonal abnormalities, environmental pollution, abnormal brain wave patterns, and tumors (Siegel, 1995: 138–150).

Other biological research posits a connection between deviance and physiologically based difficulties in learning. Some evidence suggests that offenders are likely to exhibit various forms of learning disorders, often linked to minimal brain dysfunction or to attention deficit disorder (Monroe, 1978; Farone et al., 1993; Hart et al., 1994). Researchers maintain that children who have difficulty learning will become frustrated and consequently hostile in the classroom. This in turn may promote deviance by alienating the child from the conformist world and closing the doors to the educational achievement necessary for economic success.

CRITIQUE While research strongly suggests some link between genetics and deviance, this does not mean that any significant amount of violent crime is caused exclusively by physiological factors. Sociological critics say that biologically oriented theorists overstate the importance of genetics. They also argue convincingly that there are serious methodological problems in many biological studies, including excessively small samples and a tendency to study only in-carcerated male offenders, a nonrandom subset of the larger category of all offenders (Curran & Renzetti, 2001).

In addition, the policy implications of biological theories are potentially disturbing. While some biological problems can be remedied with improved diet and medical treatment, others cannot. Moreover, we are not even close to being able to accurately predict people's future behavior on the basis of inborn physiological variables. If we treat someone like a potential deviant, aren't we running a risk of creating a *self-fulfilling prophecy*? And even if we could accurately identify at-risk individuals, what should we do with them? Psychological therapy or social reform will be, by definition, inadequate. Should we sterilize them? And who decides?

Psychological Explanations

Unlike biological positivism, psychological positivism does not consider deviance inborn. Rather, the tendency toward deviance is seen as developing in infancy or early childhood as a result of abnormal or inadequate socialization by parents and other caregivers (Andrews & Bonta, 1994). Each of the several branches of psychology takes this fundamental insight in a different direction.

The *psychoanalytic approach*, based on the work of Sigmund Freud, holds that criminals typically suffer from weak or damaged egos or from inadequate superegos that are unable to restrain the aggressive and often antisocial drives of the id (Byrne & Kelly, 1981). The *cognitive school* assumes that deviants have failed to reach more advanced stages of moral reasoning (Kohlberg, 1969; Veneziano & Veneziano, 1992)

Children who suffer from biologically-caused learning disorders may become frustrated and even hostile at school. Further deviance becomes more likely if a poor academic record makes it difficult for such children to achieve economic success later in life.

or that they have difficulty properly processing the information they receive. *Social learning* theorists maintain that children learn how to act by observing the kinds of behaviors that are rewarded. If deviance is positively reinforced, whether in real life or in the media, it is likely to be imitated (Bandura, 1973). Finally, *personality theorists* search for personality traits that are disproportionately present among deviants, such as aggressiveness or the inability to defer gratification (Andrews & Warmith, 1989; Curran & Renzetti, 2001).

CRITIQUE Sociologists generally acknowledge the value of psychological positivism, especially in analyzing the origins of some of the more extreme types of deviance. Serial killers, for example, are often diagnosed as *sociopaths*, individuals with highly antisocial personalities lacking any appreciable conscience (McCord & Tremblay, 1992; Hickey, 2002).

However, critics note some serious problems with the psychological approach. The worst may be that there is no one-to-one correspondence between any particular personality pattern and a given type of deviance. Thus some people who are impulsive, immature, defiant, and destructive as youths may grow

All children act out their aggressive impulses from time to time, but social psychologists have found that those with sociopathic tendencies are unusually prone to violent behavior.

up to be career deviants, but others with the same characteristics as youths become conforming citizens. Conversely, some thieves or drug addicts may display certain distinctive personality patterns, but others do not. As a result, psychologically oriented researchers are rarely able to accurately predict which youths will become seriously deviant, missing some and mislabeling others (Tennenbaum, 1977).

The policy implications of psychological positivism appear humane. Instead of punishing deviants in order to deter them, as classical theory mandates, or subjecting them to medical intervention, as the biological school may suggest, psychologists recommend various forms of therapies, often combined with tranquilizers and antidepressants. Their goal is to reform or rehabilitate deviants. (This approach may not be as progressive as it seems, however; this is a controversial issue that we address toward the end of this chapter). Yet the idea of rehabilitating deviants, widely endorsed by social control agencies through most of this century, is perceived by the general public as not just humane but indeed "soft." Most people appear to believe that the therapeutic approach to criminality has been ineffective, which partially explains the renewed popularity in recent decades of harsher crime-control policies based on biological and free-will understandings.

There are other problems with psychological positivism. Like biological theory, traditional psychological theory tends to ignore the social context in which deviance occurs. Both approaches also accept the definition of crime and deviance as given, meaning that—as conflict theorists are quick to point out—they devote little attention to elite deviance. In sum, both biological and psychological positivism provide useful but incomplete paths to understanding why some people deviate.

Sociological Explanations

Whereas biological and psychological positivism locate the cause of deviation *inside* the individual, sociological approaches focus on the influence of the *external* social environment in the causation of deviance.

There are two major types of sociological theories of deviant behavior. *Social structure theories* explore the reasons why different rates of deviance and criminality are found in different sectors of society. *Social process theories* examine how particular people learn to think about and evaluate deviance within a given social setting (Akers, 1997).

SOCIAL STRUCTURE THEORIES Observers have long noted the heavier involvement in deviance among persons occupying certain social statuses. (see

Figure 8.3). In our society, the highest rates of officially recorded crime occur among young, lower income, minority males. Conflict theorists argue that this pattern is primarily a result of the inability of the relatively powerless segments of society to influence the official definition of deviance or the actions of the criminal justice system. Without necessarily denying the value of this insight, social structural theorists think it is still well worth investigating why so many young, poor, minority males break the law.

The connection between social structure and individual behavior was first explored by the early functionalist Émile Durkheim. As discussed in Chapter 1, Durkheim's study of suicide rates emphasized that people who are strongly integrated into social groupings that disapprove of suicide are unlikely to take their own lives (Durkheim, 1897/1964). But when people become less involved in such groups or when the group's commitment to a particular normative position weakens, the suicide rate rises. In Durkheim's terms, a weakened collective conscience leads to the dysfunctional state of *anomie*, a situation of normative ambiguity in which people are unsure of how they should behave. Society no longer offers adequate guidelines for behavior and, naturally, deviance increases (Durkheim, 1897/1964).

Anomie is generally low in traditional cultures, but industrialization and urbanization break down normative consensus and promote nonconformity. Deviance is particularly likely to occur today among young people, the poor, and minorities precisely because these groups tend to experience significant levels of anomie (Menard, 1995).

Strain Theory In the late 1930s, Robert Merton extended Durkheim's functionalist observations into a widely known sociological theory of deviance (Merton, 1938). He started with the observation that virtually everyone in the United States accepts the desirability of attaining certain "success goals," especially wealth. While some may have stronger needs to succeed than others, almost everyone is socialized in the family, at school, and through the mass media to desire material success. We also learn that only some means are appropriate or legitimate ways to seek this goal. One can properly obtain wealth by inheriting it, working hard, going to school, or perhaps by winning the lottery, but not by selling drugs, holding up banks, or printing hundred dollar bills in the basement.

However, according to Merton, social structural factors limit the ability of many people—especially the poor and minorities—to seek wealth effectively through the approved means. Merton refers to such a situation as a *blocked opportunity structure*. This lack of equal opportunity is dysfunctional and throws society out of balance or equilibrium. People who are blocked experience anomie because they are not sure how to behave; Merton refers to this feeling as strain.

Such people may try to reduce their strain in five different ways (see Table 8.1 on page 208). First, they may continue to slog away in pursuit of success using only the legitimate means despite the fact that their opportunities to succeed are severely limited. Merton terms this response *conformity* and notes that it is fortunately the most common pattern among members of at-risk groups.

Second, individuals experiencing strain sometimes become *innovators:* They continue to desire to attain the success goals but they reject the established ways of doing so and substitute illegitimate means— they embezzle, they kidnap the children of the rich and hold them for ransom, they join an organized crime family. This response is clearly deviant.

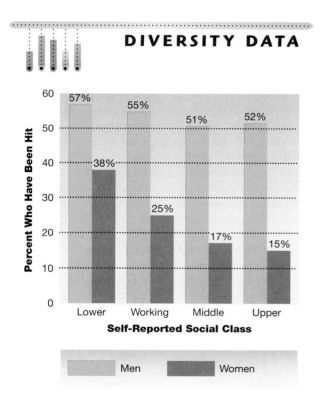

DIVERSITY DATA

FIGURE 8.3 *Chances That Someone Has Ever Been Hit, by Gender and Class.* As the self-reported social class position of women rises, the likelihood that they have been hit declines sharply. A similar pattern is apparent among men, but the differences between the classes are much less substantial. At all class levels, men are considerably more likely than women to have experienced interpersonal violence. What social factors explain why violence seems to be more common among men and the lower classes?

Source: NORC. General Social Surveys, 1972–2000. Chicago: National Opinion Research Center, 2000. Reprinted by permission of NORC, Chicago, IL.

TABLE 8.1

Robert Merton's Strain Theory of Deviance

Form of Adaptation	Attitude Toward Conventional Success Goals	Attitude Toward Legitimate Means to Achieve Success Goals	Deviant?	Examples
Conformity	desire	accept	no	work hard; earn a college degree
Innovation	desire	replace	yes	drug dealer; counterfeiter
Retreatism	reject	reject	yes	crack addict; dropout
Ritualism	reject	accept	maybe	Ph.D. in unmarketable discipline; bureaucrat mired in red tape
Rebellion	replace	replace	yes	political revolutionary; full-time environmental activist

Third, people trapped in a blocked opportunity situation may become what Merton calls *retreatists*—they drop out and stop seeking any goals beyond immediate self-indulgence. Retreatists often are heavily involved in drugs and alcohol. They are generally regarded as deviants.

Ritualism is a fourth way of responding to a blocked opportunity structure. Ritualists abandon the idea of achieving economic success, but they still go through the motions of striving for it. They are not seriously deviant, though we may consider them a little eccentric. A graduate student toiling away for a Ph.D. in an obscure discipline with very limited employment possibilities would be a ritualist.

Finally, people may respond to strain by becoming what Merton terms *rebels*. Like retreatists, rebels turn their backs on established goals and the legitimate means to reach them. But, unlike retreatists, they substitute new goals and new ways of attaining these new goals, often in the company of like-minded others. Individuals who channel virtually all of their time into the environmental movement are a good example of what Merton means by rebellion, as are political revolutionaries. Rebels may or may not be considered seriously deviant.

Merton's theory can be applied to the Roughnecks, but strictly speaking, not to the Saints, since the latter group did not have to deal with the strain of blocked opportunities. The Roughnecks, raised in the lower classes, responded to structural strain through innovation, in the form of theft, and retreatism, in their continual truancy from school and frequent indulgence in alcohol.

Critique Merton's theory highlights the importance of social factors and is supported by a good deal of empirical research (Cohen, 1965; Passas & Agnew, 1997). In particular, the finding that deviance thrives where there is a great disparity between rich and poor is in line with his work. This relationship holds both within the United States (D. Jacobs, 1989; Simons & Gray, 1989) and globally (Archer & Gartner, 1984).

However, it is not clear that everyone is equally committed to striving for material success. Some maintain that the working and lower classes aspire to a somewhat different and more realistic set of goals—not to become fabulously wealthy, but simply to own a home and make enough money to live fairly comfortably (Matza, 1969; Messner & Rosenfeld, 1994). Others question whether Merton's theory can be applied to women without substantial modification, since at least traditionally, marriage has been the primary legitimate route by which females have achieved economic success (Pollock, 1999). This is a good example of the androcentric orientation of most traditional theories of crime and deviance (Naffine, 1996).

In addition, Merton does not adequately specify the conditions under which people who are experiencing strain come to choose one or another of the five resolutions. Neither does he explain why most people abandon deviance as they become older. Finally, Merton does not address the deviance that occurs among societal elites like the Saints; he seems to uncritically accept the view that only lower-class deviation needs explanation.

The primary policy implication of Merton's theory is that the structural factors that contribute to deviance by blocking opportunity must be opened up. At a minimum, this means expanding educational opportunities for the lower classes and attacking racist and sexist discrimination.

Lower-Class Focal Value Theory In another influential variation of social structure theory, Walter Miller (1958) agrees with Merton that deviance is concentrated in the lower classes, but he denies that it results from a socially imposed inability to live up to internalized cultural values. Rather, Miller thinks deviance reflects the acceptance by poor young males of a lower-class subculture. The norms and values of this subculture are not entirely distinct from those of the mainstream culture, but the lower class tends to more wholeheartedly accept certain orientations that are less important to members of the higher classes. Accepting these subcultural patterns does not necessarily lead directly to deviance, but it can promote such an outcome. Miller identifies several "focal concerns" as particularly relevant to the lower-class subculture. They include

- *Trouble*—Both getting into trouble and dealing with it effectively are highly valued.
- *Excitement*—Lower class youth put a lot of importance on "kicks" and excitement.
- *Smartness*—Book learning is not necessarily disparaged, but "street smarts," the ability to manipulate others and not be taken advantage of, is strongly emphasized.
- *Fate*—Members of this subculture believe that much of what happens in life is due to factors beyond their control.
- *Autonomy*—Independence from external control is highly valued.
- *Toughness*—Frequently raised in female-dominated families, lower-class boys struggle to affirm their masculinity; this effort often leads to an exaggerated "macho" emphasis on fighting and physical strength.

Both the Saints and the Roughnecks valued excitement, street smarts, trouble, and autonomy. However, the middle-class Saints placed less emphasis on physical toughness and fate than the Roughnecks. As a result, the Saints generally avoided physical confrontations, which reduced their chances of coming into contact with formal agents of social control. Furthermore, believing they were in control of their own destiny, they did a much better job of planning their misbehavior to avoid apprehension.

Critique The key issue in assessing Miller's theory is whether the subculture of the poor is guided by its own relatively distinct set of norms and values. Research on this issue is inconclusive. Some scholars find solid evidence of different norms and values in the lower class (Banfield, 1974; Gaines, 1991), while others reach the opposite conclusion (Cernovich, 1978; Einstadter & Henry, 1995). Critics have also pointed out that Miller's work is focused exclusively on the values of lower-class males; women are again left out of the picture (Pollock, 1999).

The most obvious policy implication of Miller's focal value theory is that if the value system of the lower class could be changed, deviance would decline. However, in order to do this, it would probably be necessary to institute the sorts of reforms implied by Merton's theory. Thus all varieties of social structure theory ultimately lead to the same conclusion: We must reduce inequality and lower the barriers to social mobility in order to combat deviance.

SOCIAL PROCESS THEORIES Social structure theories help explain the higher rates of deviance in some sectors of society, but they do not address the micro-level question of why some individuals growing up in high-crime areas resist temptation and, conversely, why some of the privileged go astray. To answer such questions, we must consider how individuals learn attitudes regarding deviance and conformity from the people around them. Social process theories focus on socialization and incorporate aspects of psychological learning theory, but they also include elements of the symbolic interactionist perspective. They are sometimes called *cultural transmission theories*. We will discuss two representative social process theories: differential association theory and control theory.

Differential Association Theory Writing around the same time as Merton, criminologist Edwin Sutherland addressed the question of how particular individuals, regardless of their place in the social structure, acquire positive attitudes toward crime and learn the skills they need in order to be successful criminals (Sutherland, 1940).

The result was the theory of differential association, which is ultimately based on the everyday observation that deviants and conformists tend to hang around mostly with other people like themselves. Sutherland argued that

- Deviance is learned, not inherited.
- It is learned primarily through interaction in small, intimate groups. Media influence is indirect or filtered through the attitudes of the members of the group.
- A person becomes deviant because he or she encounters more definitions favorable to violation of norms than definitions unfavorable to violation of norms.
- The relationships in which these definitions are transmitted may vary in *frequency* (how regularly a person interacts with a particular individual), *duration* (how long each interaction lasts), *priority* (how early in life the relationship begins), and *intensity* (how important the relationship is to the individual).

Differential association theory clearly applies to the Saints and the Roughnecks. Both groups absorbed definitions favorable to deviance from their peers, but the Saints also learned effective techniques for avoiding social control agents, which the Roughnecks did not acquire.

These children are getting help with their homework from an adult volunteer. Differential association theory suggests that at-risk youths who are exposed to positive role models are less likely to become delinquent.

Critique Differential association theory makes strong intuitive sense. Moreover, unlike social structure theory, it explains both conformity and deviance and applies equally well to both men and women and to members of all social classes. In fact, one of the reasons Sutherland developed it was to explain white-collar crime, which he believed was more likely when cohesive peer groups that endorsed unethical business practices arose in corporations (Sutherland, 1940).

The idea that deviants generally associate with and learn from other deviants has been widely supported by research both in the United States (Short, 1960; Smith et al., 1991; Kandel & Davies, 1991; Heimer, 1997) and abroad (Cheung & Ng, 1988). The major criticism of this theory is that the terms frequency, duration, priority, and intensity are imprecise. For example, it would be difficult to empirically measure the intensity of a relationship. Differential association theory also fails to account for solitary deviants, such as check forgers and embezzlers.

The primary policy implication of Sutherland's theory is that potentially wayward youth need to be encouraged to spend more time with conformist peers. For example, offering recreational programs like basketball leagues potentially weakens the hold of the deviant peer group.

Control Theory Instead of assuming that obeying the rules is normal and that deviance is what must be explained, control theorists think it is *conformity* that must be explained. This perspective is congruent with many nonsociological views of human nature, especially that of Sigmund Freud, but is relatively uncommon within sociology. According to control theory, we all experience strong pushes toward nonconformity. Deviants are people who lack adequate internal or external controls (or containments) against norm violation (Reckless, 1969).

The most widely cited social control theory was developed in the late 1960s by Travis Hirschi (1969) and revised by Hirschi and Michael Gottfredson (Gottfredson & Hirschi, 1990). The original theory suggested that people were more or less successfully insulated from deviance by four types of social bonds:

- *Attachment*, a feeling of emotional connection with parents, teachers, and peers. The desire not to disappoint people one cares about provides a good reason to avoid deviance.
- *Commitment*, a strong interest in achieving goals—for example, attending a good college or becoming a police officer—that might be blocked by a criminal record or a reputation as a deviant.
- *Involvement* in the busy routines of everyday life may not leave youths with enough free time to become deviants.
- *Belief*, the acceptance of conventional values.

Hirschi and Gottfredson's revised theory retains the emphasis on social bonds but adds the idea that these social bonds will be less effective in restraining people whose parents failed to develop in them an adequate level of *self-control.*

The key insight that control theory provides regarding the Saints and the Roughnecks concerns the variable of commitment. While neither group accepted very many conformist beliefs or was tightly bonded to parents or teachers, and both seemed to find time to misbehave, the Saints' middle-class background gave them a reasonable expectation of attending college, a career path that might have been closed off if they had been tagged as serious deviants. In fact, all but one of the Saints completed college, while only two of the Roughnecks were able to do so, both of them on football scholarships.

Critique Researchers have found substantial support for control theory (Grasmick et al., 1993; Nagin & Paternoster, 1993; Free, 1994). Unlike some of the other theories, it has the virtue of explaining why criminality tends to decline as people move past their teenage years: Unlike adolescents, most adults acquire high levels of attachment, commitment, and involvement as they marry, take full-time jobs, and start raising families. Furthermore, like differential association theory, control theory explains both conformity and deviance and applies to everyone regardless of class or gender.

Hirschi and Gottfredson's work suggests that in order to reduce crime, we need to strengthen social bonds with conformist others and improve the quality of child socialization in order to increase people's self-control. Required parenting classes in high school might be a step in this direction.

WHAT IS THE SOCIAL REACTION TO DEVIANCE?

An innovative approach to deviance, called **labeling theory,** emerged in the 1960s. This perspective explores how the label "deviant" is applied to particular people and the ways in which this devalued identity influences their subsequent behavior—a way of thinking that is deeply grounded in the symbolic interactionist perspective that was discussed at length in Chapter 6.

Labeling theorists emphasize the difference between *deviant acts* and a *deviant role* or *deviant identity* (Becker, 1963; Schur, 1971). All of us commit acts that could be defined as deviant from time to time,

but most people do not become publicly known as deviant role players. Thus most students cheat on occasion but only a few acquire the identity of cheaters; many youths experiment with illegal drugs but only some come to be labeled "stoners."

The purpose of labeling is to apply a *stigma*, a powerfully negative public identity, to an individual who is believed to have violated important norms (Goffman, 1963b). The stigma dramatically influences the way others view the labeled individual. Instead of being seen as someone who occasionally has a few drinks or uses drugs now and then, the stigmatized individual becomes a "drunk" or an "addict."

A label may be acquired in three ways. First, some people voluntarily engage in *self-labeling*. Often, they take this step because concealing their true identity requires a great deal of time, energy, and hypocrisy. People may self-label because they may find that it is easier to bear others' negative comments than to continue to hide their deviance.

Others self-label because they have fully rejected the conventional point of view and actively embrace their deviance; examples include some atheists and motorcycle outlaws like the Hell's Angels (Thompson, 1966; Watson, 1988).

Second, people acquire labels *informally*, from family and friends. For example, many prostitutes are labeled as such by their peers long before they come into contact with the criminal justice system. This form of labeling can have a tremendous influence on an individual, since almost everyone cares about the opinions of the people they are close to and with whom they regularly interact (Matsueda, 1992).

Labeling theory has traditionally put the strongest emphasis on the third way that people acquire labels—*formally* (Lerman, 1996). Formal labeling involves a type of public ritual called a **degradation ceremony**

An informal label like "class clown" or "troublemaker," which is acquired in small peer groups like this one, can be an important factor pushing a youth toward criminal or deviant activity.

INTERNET CONNECTIONS

Labeling theory is one of a number of theories on deviance. After reading about the theory, go to the Website CrimeTheory.com:

http://www.crimetheory.com/Archive/Response/SR2.htm

Browse through the information but make sure that you click on the parts that are underlined. What sociological question is labeling theory trying to answer? What are some of the weaknesses of the labeling approach to understanding deviance?

(Garfinkel, 1956). Degradation ceremonies, such as criminal trials, sanity hearings, and court martials, officially devalue a deviant's identity, imposing a stigma that may be difficult or impossible to escape. Consider, for example, these words from the prosecution's closing argument in the trial of Oklahoma City terrorist bomber Timothy McVeigh:

> Take a moment and look at Timothy McVeigh. Look into the eyes of a coward and tell him you will have the courage. Tell him you will speak with one unified voice, as the moral conscience of the community, and tell him he is no patriot. He is a traitor, and he deserves to die. (Annin & Morganthau, 1997:41)

What influences the chances that someone will acquire a deviant label? Because we all prefer to believe that we live in a just world, we like to think that people who acquire a stigma must have repeatedly committed serious and harmful deviant acts. Though there is certainly a good deal of truth to this claim, other factors also enter in, principally social power.

Blending themes from the conflict, feminist, and symbolic interactionist perspectives, labeling theorists note that in U.S. society, wealthy, white, male, middle-aged, heterosexual individuals are better able to resist stigmatizing labels than are the less socially empowered (Schur, 1984; Adams et al., 1998). Edwin Schur (1984) was one of the first sociologists to observe the ways in which patriarchal society uses the threat of labeling as an effective means of keeping women from challenging oppressive gender roles.

Other important factors influencing whether a stigmatizing label is applied include (a) how closely a person matches the popular (often media-generated) stereotype of a particular kind of deviant (Surette, 1998; Bailey & Hale, 1998); (b) how concerned formal social control agents currently are about any given type of norm violation (Margolin, 1992); and (c)

how experienced the deviant is—beginners are more likely to be caught, all other factors being equal.

Edwin Lemert (1951) introduced the terms primary and secondary deviance to convey the importance of labeling. **Primary deviance** refers to any deviant act that is not followed by some form of labeling, or to the period of time during which such acts occur. Lemert's point is that primary deviance, even if engaged in for a very long time, rarely affects a person's life very much. You may shoplift, vacuum your apartment naked, smoke crack, or worship the devil for years, but so long as nobody knows about it—or at least nobody who is inclined to publicize this knowledge—it won't have much effect on your life.

On the other hand, once your norm violation is known, you enter into **secondary deviance,** that period of time in which you are compelled to reorganize your life around your devalued identity. Now everything changes. First of all, you may discover that many of your old friends are uncomfortable around you. They may engage in *retrospective reinterpretation* (Scheff, 1984) of their past interactions with you: "Last week she fell asleep in class; I thought she was just tired but now that I know she uses drugs, I realize that she must have been high."

Such reinterpretations may or may not be factually accurate, but once labeled, you have little ability to correct them. You will probably find yourself in the market for new friends, and you are particularly likely to recruit them from fellow deviants who tend not to judge you negatively. Note, however, that in line with Sutherland's differential association theory, deviant friends are likely to propel you toward increased involvement in deviance.

Secondary deviance also requires changes in your major life roles. Labeled deviants frequently lose their jobs, are forced to move, drop out of school, and may become estranged from their families. Such changes combined with the direct effects of stigmatization lower the chances of obtaining legitimate success (Schwartz & Skolnick, 1962). In Merton's terms, your opportunity structure becomes blocked and, again, you are pushed toward deviance.

Finally, secondary deviance also tends to change your self-image, even if you initially resist thinking of yourself as a deviant. A damaged self-image yet again increases the chances that you will move farther into deviance. As a symbolic interactionist would say, the deviant label becomes a self-fulfilling prophecy. The ultimate consequence of secondary deviance is *role engulfment*—deviance becomes your master status (Schur, 1980).

Chambliss's study of the Saints and the Roughnecks is a classic example of the power of labeling. The lower-class Roughnecks were probably no more delinquent than their middle-class counterparts. But, in part because they lacked the social power that would allow them to own cars and hence escape the relentless observation of the police and townspeople, they became known as no-good delinquent punks. This label then affected virtually everything that happened to them. The Saints were also labeled—as basically good kids who occasionally sowed a wild oat or two—a label that also had a great impact on their lives, but in quite the opposite direction.

CRITIQUE   One of the most serious criticism of labeling theory is that research has not clearly demonstrated that formal labeling necessarily promotes greater commitment to deviance (Wellford, 1975; Sherman & Smith, 1992; Cavender, 1995). While some studies strongly support this role engulfment thesis (Ageton & Elliott, 1973; Ray & Downs, 1986), others refute it (Tittle, 1975). As Hirschi would argue, it may be that people who have a strong attachment to conformist others and to conformist goals respond to the threat of labeling by reaffirming their commitment to conventional norms, whereas people lacking such controls are pushed toward deviance by labeling.

The primary policy implication of labeling theory is that in order to avoid role engulfment, we should minimize the number of people who are publicly labeled, a policy termed *radical nonintervention* (Schur, 1973). In particular, while we must label and punish serious predatory criminals, we must not create a self-fulfilling prophecy by tagging young people who are not yet committed to crime as juvenile delinquents. In fact, not publically revealing the names of juvenile offenders, a practice now under attack, was originally intended to minimize destructive labeling (Kratcoski & Kratcoski, 1996).

Critics charge that labeling theory's heavy emphasis on the relative nature of deviance and on radical nonintervention seem out of step with the law and order, "lock 'em up" mentality of the United States today. Certainly the notion that a rapist or murderer whose crime goes undetected (that is, who avoids being labeled) is not really a deviant seems to violate the core understandings that most people hold concerning deviance.

Table 8.2 summarizes the principal theories of deviance that have been discussed in this chapter.

TABLE 8.2

Theories of Deviance

Type of Theory	Questions Addressed	Major Observations	Policy Implications	Representative Theorists
Classical Theory/ Rational Choice Theory	Why do individuals deviate?	People calculate the costs and benefits and rationally decide whether or not to deviate. Deviance is freely chosen.	Increase negative sanctions for deviance.	Caesare Beccaria, Jeremy Bentham, Marcus Felson, James Q. Wilson
Conflict Theory	In whose interests is deviance defined?	The rich and powerful define deviance to benefit themselves.	Reduce the power of elites.	Willem Bonger, Richard Quinney, Steven Spitzer
Biological Positivism	Why do individuals deviate?	Deviants are physically different than conformists.	Medical treatment, drugs, perhaps sterilization.	Caesare Lombroso, William Sheldon, Hans Eysenck
Psychological Positivism	Why do individuals deviate?	Deviants are psychologically different than conformists.	Better child rearing; psychological therapy.	Sigmund Freud, Lawrence Kohlberg, Stanton Samenow
Sociological Positivism (*Social Structure Theory*)	Why are some categories of people more deviant than others?	Certain social environments encourage deviance.	Change the social environment; offer more opportunity.	Robert Merton, William Miller, Albert Cohen
Sociological Positivism (*Social Process Theory*)	Why do individuals deviate?	People learn from others around them whether or not to deviate.	Provide more chances to learn from and bond with conformist others.	Edwin Sutherland, Travis Hirschi, Walter Reckless
Labeling Theory	What are the consequences of the ways in which members of society react to deviance?	Labeling people as deviants can reinforce their deviant identity and become a self-fulfilling prophecy.	Minimize labeling; radical nonintervention.	Edwin Lemert, Howard Becker, Harold Garfinkel

LIFE CONNECTIONS

Mental Illness as Deviant Behavior

What is the difference between a mentally healthy person and one who is mentally ill? This is not an easy question to answer, in large part because our understanding of what is and is not normal is heavily influenced by the social and cultural context in which a particular act takes place. For example, members of some religious groups are expected to enter trancelike states in which speaking in tongues is encouraged. So long as such behavior is defined in religious terms, most people in the United States would probably regard it as a little strange but basically normal. If, however, the same behavior were observed in a poorly dressed person standing on a street corner, many of us would have little difficulty labeling that individual "crazy."

The media have a strong influence on our understanding of mental disorders, sometimes in unfortunate ways. Media imagery of the mentally ill tends to stereotype them as violent and dangerous. In fact, the vast majority are neither.

Mental illness is widespread in modern societies. If it is defined as exhibiting severe enough symptoms to require ongoing treatment, then about 15 percent of all people in the United States suffer from mental illness. If it consists of having some difficulty coping with everyday life due to stress, anxiety, or depression, then as much as 80 percent of the population may be affected (Dohrenwend & Dohrenwend, 1974; Gallagher, 1987; Regier, 1991; Coleman & Cressey, 1999). However mental illness is defined, most of the people who suffer from it go untreated (Mechanic, 1989; Barker et al., 1992).

Most people understand mental illness in terms of the *medical model*, which interprets it as a disease with biological or genetic causes that is best treated by a psychiatrist or psychologist. While there is clear evidence that some forms of mental illness, especially the more serious ones such as schizophrenia, are indeed caused partly by biological factors, it is equally clear that many other types do not result from organic defect (Gatchel et al., 1989; Berrios, 1995).

Many sociologists find labeling theory to be more useful than the medical model as a means of understanding psychological disorders (Rosenfeld, 1997). This perspective interprets mental illness as a status with attached role requirements that are first internalized and then acted out. Although most norm violations evoke labels such as strange, eccentric, or criminal if people violate certain basic and taken-for-granted expectations, they are likely to be labeled as mentally ill, an identity that is typically very difficult to change. Examples include people who fail to observe basic principles of personal hygiene or who carry on animated conversations in public with individuals who are not present. Thomas Scheff (1963) refers to such violations of basic social conventions as *residual deviance*.

Some labeling theorists go even further, claiming that the very idea of mental illness is a myth. Thomas Szasz (1961, 1994b) embraces this view, maintaining that the people we call mentally ill are in fact simply experiencing what he calls "unresolved problems in living." He strongly criticizes psychiatrists, who he claims "know little about medicine and less about science," for labeling people as mentally ill and then taking away their freedom in the name of curing them (Szasz, 1994b:36).

D. L. Rosenhan (1973) conducted a classic study that supports the conclusions of labeling theory. Rosenhan and seven of his colleagues presented themselves at a number of different mental hospitals claiming to hear voices. In fact, none of the "pseudopatients" had any history of mental disorder. All were admitted with a diagnosis of schizophrenia; all stopped claiming to hear voices or displaying any other psychiatric symptom immediately upon entering the hospital.

Rosenhan suggested that if psychiatric diagnoses were objective, the pseudopatients would soon be detected by the staff. This did not occur. The researchers' stays in the hospitals varied from 7 to 52 days; all were released with the diagnosis "schizophrenia in remission." The doctors and nurses never detected the deception, although some of the "real" patients did, an outcome Rosenhan attributed to the power of the label of "mental illness" to frame virtually all perceptions of the patients by the medical staff.

In a second stage of the study, Rosenhan told staff members at a prestigious mental hospital who were skeptical of the results of the initial research that he would be sending them more pseudopatients and asked them to identify any they detected. Over the next 3 months, 41 of 193 new patients were identified as fakes with a high degree of confidence by at least one staff member; in fact, Rosenhan sent no pseudopatients!

Sociologists have consistently found an inverse relationship between mental illness and social class. This is true for both treated and untreated populations and has been found in many societies, including Britain and Canada (Turner & Marino, 1994; Armstrong, 1995; Cook & Wright, 1995). Although the connection between class and diagnosed mental disorder is firmly established, there is some disagreement as to whether mental illness is a cause or a consequence of being relatively low in class. The *drift hypothesis* suggests that people move (or "drift") downward on the class ladder because they are mentally ill.

They are unable to function normally, and in particular to hold a job, because of their psychological problems. A number of research studies support this view (Turner & Wagonfeld, 1967; Harkey et al., 1976; Miech et al., 1999). On the other hand, it is intuitively obvious that the strain of living in or near poverty can directly contribute to poor mental health.

Many forms of mental disorder appear to be more common among African Americans, Native Americans, and some other minority groups than among whites, but most research suggests that this is principally a consequence of the generally lower social class ranking of the members of these racial and ethnic groups (Williams et al., 1992; Gaw, 1993; Miech et al., 1999).

There appear to be no significant gender differences in overall *rates* of mental disorder, but there are consistent differences in *type*. Women are more likely to suffer from affective and anxiety disorders, while men are more likely to be diagnosed with personality disorders (Rothblum, 1982; Chino & Funabiki, 1984; Darnton, 1985; Carson et al., 1988). Most sociologists suspect that these differences result more from the ways that therapists perceive men and women than from innate differences between the genders.

It is better for your mental health to be married, especially if you are male. Never-married, divorced, and single men have higher rates of mental illness than those who are married (American Psychological Association, 1985; Steil, 1995). But married women suffer more mental health problems than married men (Gove & Tudor, 1973; Steil & Turetsky, 1987; Rosenfield, 1989; Simon, 1995). For both married men and women, working outside the home contributes to better mental health (Campbell, 1981; Sloan, 1985; Thoits, 1986). Female single parents, especially those who are living in poverty, are particularly likely to suffer from mental illness.

Two generations ago the stigma associated with homosexuality was so strong that the vast majority of gays and lesbians chose to keep their sexual orientation carefully hidden. Today, same-sex couples are an increasingly familiar sight, especially in larger cities, as homosexuality gradually moves through the repression-medicalization-acceptance cycle.

SOCIETY CONNECTIONS

The Repression-Medicalization-Acceptance Cycle

There is a high level of agreement in modern societies concerning most forms of serious, harmful deviance. We may debate exactly how we should respond to acts such as murder, forcible rape, treason, and child abuse, but almost everyone agrees that these behaviors are thoroughly despicable. However, there is much less consensus regarding many other acts that were once more widely condemned, such as alcoholism and homosexuality.

How is it that some behaviors once considered deviant become acceptable? This process is an excel-

lent example of a changing *definition of the situation*, a symbolic interactionist concept that was introduced in Chapter 6 in reference to the issue of sexual harassment. Initially, people *condemn and repress* deviant behaviors, frequently with religious justification. Deviants are seen as evil, sinful people unfit to enjoy normal status in society.

As the values of society become more diverse, however, commitment to traditional forms of religion weakens and a few voices are heard calling for change. Gradually, as moral consensus declines, repression is

GLOBAL CONNECTIONS

The Social Control of Drugs: European Alternatives

For over 80 years, the United States has been guided by these three basic principles in its efforts to control drugs:

- The drug problem is primarily a criminal justice issue.
- The ultimate goal is to end all illicit drug use.
- There are just two kinds of drugs: legal (alcohol, nicotine, caffeine) and illegal. No significant distinctions need to be drawn between different types of illegal drugs.

Policies based on these principles have led to an extremely costly and, in the eyes of many critics, largely futile war against drugs.

On the other hand, many European nations proceed from a very different set of assumptions:

- The drug problem is primarily a public health issue. As Germany's drug czar put it, "Consumers of drugs are not criminals and should be exempt from criminal prosecution. Addiction is a disease and not a crime." (Power, 1999:54)
- Drug use can be minimized but not eliminated; the primary goal is to *reduce the harm* that is done by drug abuse.
- There are profound differences between "soft drugs" (marijuana, hashish) and "hard drugs" (heroin, cocaine, amphetamines) that must be reflected in national drug policies.

These principles have led to a variety of innovative approaches to the drug problem. The policies of the Netherlands have been especially widely publicized. While hard drug sales are severely punished—persons who deal heroin or cocaine may receive 12-year terms in prison—the sale and use of small quantities of soft drugs, while technically illegal, are in fact tolerated. Beginning in 1976, marijuana and hashish could be openly purchased and used in coffee shops in Amsterdam and other Dutch cities.

Dutch policies regarding hard drug users (as opposed to sellers) strongly reflect the harm reduction philosophy. Methadone (a legal heroin substitute) is widely and legally available and there are numerous free needle exchanges designed to reduce the risk of AIDS. There are even ATM-style needle-dispensing machines for use late at night. In addition, the government funds extensive drug education programs and even helps finance the *Junkiebund,* a sort of union of hard drug users.

The results of the Dutch experiment have been generally encouraging. The addict population is small, and few youth seem motivated to try hard drugs; marijuana use is increasing, but still considerably less common, especially among teenagers, than in the United States.

Both Switzerland and the United Kingdom have experimented with supplying not only methadone but also heroin to some hard-core addicts. The Swiss have established 16 clinics where registered long-term addicts who have tried to quit but failed may legally inject heroin as often as three times a day. Both crime rates and unemployment have fallen among patrons of these clinics.

The British also occasionally supply users with heroin, but put much more emphasis on methadone maintenance programs. Addicts obtain methadone prescriptions from their physicians and buy the drug at their corner pharmacy.

Similar policies are in force in some German states, where the government has shifted its drug control efforts from its criminal justice system to its health ministry, and in France, where judges lock up people who sell drugs, but not those who use them. As Nicole Maestracci, director of the French Interministerial Mission Against Drugs and Addiction, puts it, "Sure, a society without drugs would be wonderful. But nobody believes such a society can exist anymore." (Power, 1999:53)

1. What do you think would happen if the United States adopted the European approach to drug control?

2. Do you think it is possible to stop all drug abuse? Explain your answer.

Sources: Trebach, 1989; Beers, 1991; Huber, 1994; Perrine, 1994; Nadelman, 1995; Barnard, 1998; MacCoun & Reuter, 1999; Power, 1999.

replaced by medicalization (Conrad & Schneider, 1980). The **medicalization of deviance** involves a redefinition of the character of the deviant from "evil" to "sick." Note that the behavior has not changed—only the label has. Instead of punishing alcoholics and gays, we try to help them "get well." Alcoholics Anonymous has been especially effective in promoting the "disease theory" of alcoholism.

This shift in labels has several consequences. It relocates social control efforts from the criminal justice system to the medical establishment, replacing punishment with therapeutic intervention. Medicalization promotes more humane treatment of deviants, but it also redefines the deviant as less morally responsible for her or his behavior and less personally competent to make decisions about the future. Some critics charge that the medicalization of deviance has simply replaced cops in blue coats with cops in white coats. Furthermore, these critics claim, our society protects the civil rights of "evil" criminals better than the rights of "sick" deviants (Szasz, 1961). In this sense, the medicalization of deviance may be less of a humane advance than it seems at first.

In response to such concerns, some organized groups of deviants have campaigned for yet another redefinition, this time from medicalization to acceptance. John Kitsuse (1980) calls such group efforts to achieve acceptance **tertiary deviance.** This shift has not occurred with alcoholism, but it has regarding homosexuality. In 1974 the American Psychiatric Association formally voted to redefine homosexuality as a variant type of sexual behavior, not a form of mental illness. The general public's attitude toward homosexuality is clearly moving toward toleration if not full acceptance. Figure 8.4 summarizes the repression-medicalization-acceptance cycle.

It is important to note that not all forms of deviance shift smoothly from repression to medicalization and then on to acceptance. Some, like pedophilia, remain in the repression stage despite the best efforts of groups like the North American Man-Boy Love Association. Others, like alcoholism, move only to medicalization. Substantial percentages of the population continue to endorse repression of abortion despite its legalization in the 1973 *Roe v. Wade* decision.

FIGURE 8.4 The Repression-Medicalization-Acceptance Cycle.

And the popular reaction to a few types of behavior—as we will document shortly—is moving in the opposite direction, toward repression.

The point is not that movement toward acceptance is in any way inevitable, but rather that in modern societies shifting norms make it difficult to define deviance. We conclude this chapter with a brief discussion of some contemporary efforts to reverse the direction of the repression-medicalization-acceptance cycle.

Reversing the Cycle

While the dominant trend in modern society is away from defining various forms of deviance as evil and toward seeing them as signs of sickness or as acceptable alternatives, some behaviors that were accepted in the past are being redefined as more seriously deviant.

For example, campaigns by groups like MADD (Mothers Against Drunk Driving) have had a considerable effect on public attitudes toward driving under the influence of alcohol. While there has been no dramatic reduction in the incidence of drinking and driving (J. B. Jacobs, 1989; Mastrofski & Ritti, 1996), some jurisdictions have made taverns legally liable if they continue to serve obviously intoxicated customers who later have auto accidents. Similarly, naming a "designated driver" who abstains from alcohol in order to drive others home safely is now a widely accepted practice.

Perhaps the most interesting example of the increasing stigmatization of behavior in American society concerns smoking. For centuries, using tobacco has been regarded as acceptable, at least for adult men; since the 1920s it has been generally allowed for women as well. In fact, during much of the 20th century, smoking was widely viewed as a sign of maturity and sophistication. However, this is now changing.

The public's increased willingness to view cigarette smoking as deviant has a number of causes. Chief among them is the great emphasis that an aging population puts on good health combined with an ever-increasing body of research substantiating the damaging effects of smoking. A National Institute of Drug Abuse study found that for every death caused by cocaine, there were 300 tobacco-related deaths (Reinarman & Levine, 1989). People have historically resisted seeing tobacco as an addictive drug, but many are coming to realize that it is in fact just that. Thus, the current "war on drugs" campaign may well be having an anti-tobacco spillover effect.

The signs of this shift in attitude are everywhere. Laws now ban the practice in offices, airplanes, restaurants, and many other public places. A decade or two ago, asking someone to extinguish her or his cigarette in a public place would have been considered pushy and ill-mannered; now it is the smoker who is considered rude. The Clinton administration placed a high priority on trying to keep cigarettes out of the hands of children and adolescents and attempted to give the FDA the power to regulate tobacco as a drug. Spokespersons for the tobacco industry express fears that we may be moving toward some form of legal prohibition of their product.

The bottom line is that smoking is being redefined as mildly deviant behavior. The small clusters of people huddled together just outside the doors of smoke-free buildings are visible proof of this change. It is not clear at present how far this trend will go. The fact that many respectable middle-class people still smoke and the substantial political clout of the tobacco lobby suggest that tobacco users probably do not face full criminalization of their habit. However, they may well have to accept the medicalization of their behavior—they will need to convince the rest of us that they ought to be regarded as nicotine addicts—sick—rather than as immoral devotees of the demon weed.

SUMMARY

1. Sociologists consider deviance a relative concept; therefore, no behavior is seen as inherently deviant. Deviance is found in all societies.

2. Deviance may be interpreted as a negative label established and applied by the socially powerful to a variety of disapproved actions, beliefs, and conditions.

3. Social control consists of actions intended to encourage conformity and to discourage deviance. It may consist of either punishments or rewards. Social control may be exercised by formal or informal agents and is also a consequence of moral socialization.

4. Conflict theory emphasizes the ability of social elites to define what is regarded as deviant in line with their own interests.

5. Although deviance makes social life problematic, erodes trust, and is very costly to control, it also serves several positive functions. It sets the boundaries of what is regarded as acceptable behavior, encourages solidarity, and warns that change is needed.

6. Biological and psychological positivism explain the origins of deviance in terms of internal factors; sociological positivism emphasizes the importance of factors located in the external social environment.

7. Social structure theories, such as Merton's strain theory and Miller's lower-class focal value theory, explain the high rates of deviance among the poor and minorities by reference to broad structural factors such as blocked opportunity and distinctive subcultural values.

8. Social process theories, such as Sutherland's differential association theory and Hirschi's control theory, explain individual decisions to deviate by reference to factors such as social learning and bonds to conventional society.

9. Labeling theory explores the consequences of applying deviant labels to individuals. It assumes that a stigma is likely to become a self-fulfilling prophecy.

10. In modern societies, which are characterized by considerable normative ambiguity, many forms of behavior once considered severely deviant and repressed come to be redefined as illness rather than sin. In some cases, these behaviors are later further reinterpreted as nondeviant and hence worthy of acceptance.

11. However, sometimes the repression-medicalization-acceptance cycle reverses, and previously accepted behaviors such as drunk driving or tobacco smoking come to be seen as deviant.

KEY TERMS

crime 196
degradation ceremony 212
deviance 195
formal social control 198
informal social control 198

labeling theory 211
medicalization of deviance 216
negative sanction 198
positive sanction 198
positivism 204

primary deviance 212
rational choice theory 204
secondary deviance 212
social control 198
tertiary deviance 217

CRITICAL THINKING QUESTIONS

1. Why do many people have trouble accepting the idea that all deviance is relative? Can a person be a good sociologist and at the same time be personally committed to an absolute moral standard? Explain your answer.

2. What sort of social control is usually most effective: formal, informal, or internalized? Similarly, do you think positive or negative sanctions normally work better to reduce deviance?

3. Rational choice and biological theories of deviance seem to be more widely accepted than psychological and especially sociological theories. Why do you think this is the case? How do these preferences affect our social control efforts?

4. Which of the theoretical approaches to deviance strikes you as most useful in interpreting the case of the Saints and the Roughnecks? Explain your choice.

5. What types of behavior, other than those discussed in this chapter, are either becoming more or less accepted in contemporary society? How do you account for these trends?

INVESTIGATE WITH CONTENT SELECT

 Begin your research using Content-Select for this chapter by following the directions found on page 27 of this text to visit Prentice Hall's Research Navigator Website. Enter these search terms into the search field:

Positivism
Medicalization
Strain theory

9

CRIME AND CRIMINAL JUSTICE

America's Toughest Sheriff

Opinion polls showed Maricopa County, Arizona, Sheriff Joseph Arpaio to be the most popular elected official in the state after he housed jail inmates in tents without air-conditioning during the searing Phoenix summer. Arapio also banned cigarettes, coffee, videos, and most television programs, and cut the cost of meals to 30¢ each by supplying prisoners with food such as moldy bologna. In addition, he issued pink underwear to male inmates. In a patriarchal culture like that of the United States, forcing men to wear a color traditionally identified with women is a tactic designed to further humiliate them. ("Arizona Sheriff . . . ," 1996)

Getting Soft on Crime

The Mutter-Kind-Heim (Home for Mothers and Children) in Frankfurt, Germany, is a halfway house built to accommodate a maximum of 23 nonviolent female offenders together with their children under the age of 3. The facility is pleasant and homelike, with its own play yard, kitchen, and flower garden.

This arrangement prevents the traumatic separation of mothers and children that so often occurs in prisons in the United States. Allowing the inmates to continue to nurture their babies appears to increase their self-respect and confidence. The mothers also receive educational, medical, and psychological assistance, learn work skills, and accumulate earnings that will help them adjust after they leave the institution. Upon release, they receive a welfare grant and free rent. Recidivism rates for this program are extremely low (Douglas, 1993).

Virtually every poll shows crime at or near the top of the public's list of concerns. As Figure 9.1 on page 222 illustrates, in recent years between 40 and 45 percent of Americans have reported that there is at least one neighborhood within a mile of their homes where they are afraid to walk at night for fear of being victimized (Ferraro, 1995; Blakely & Snyder, 1998).

Is this level of concern justified? Official data suggest that violent street crime has declined sharply since 1991. However, this downturn follows a long period during which the crime rate rose sharply. Between 1960 and 1994, while the American population grew 39 percent, reported crime increased roughly fivefold even though law-enforcement spending quadrupled (Lindgren, 1995).

Despite recent reductions, the magnitude of the crime problem remains staggering. In 2000, for example, about 15,520 people were murdered and almost 11.6 million major crimes were reported to the police (Federal Bureau of Investigation, 2001). The total annual cost of street crime is estimated at roughly $18 billion, an enormous figure that is dwarfed in turn by the cost of white-collar crime, which may be as high as $472 billion per year (Donziger, 1996).

Many people believe that such figures demonstrate the need for a larger and more punitive criminal justice system. Support for hard-line policies such as those of Sheriff Arpaio has boomed. These sentiments have fueled unprecedented increases in the prison population, measures such as mandatory sentencing provisions for habitual criminals, and the 1994 federal Omnibus Crime Bill, which established 52 new capital crimes (crimes punishable by the death penalty) and increased spending by $30 billion, mostly to hire more policemen and build more prisons.

However, as the account of the Mutter-Kind-Heim suggests, some European societies have been moving in the opposite direction. They base their policies on the assumption that crime can best be reduced by treating offenders with dignity, which will in turn increase their chances of being rehabilitated.

Maricopa County, Arizona, Sheriff Joseph Arpaio exemplifies the popular "get tough" approach to crime control, having instituted such harsh measures as chain gangs for female prisoners.

Which approach makes the most sense? This chapter explores a number of issues that may help us to answer this critical question. After a brief discussion of two ways crime may be defined, we overview the extent of crime in the United States and other societies. Next, the chapter introduces some of the major types of crime and discusses selected aspects of the criminal justice system. After presenting an analysis of how the sociological factors of race, gender, class, and age affect involvement in crime for both offenders and victims, we will conclude by outlining the contemporary policy debates concerning capital punishment and the control of drug abuse.

DEFINING CRIME

In Chapter 8, *crime* was defined as a special type of deviance involving the violation of formal statutes enacted by a legitimate government. This definition reflects a *legalistic approach* because it takes the common-sense view that a crime is whatever the law defines as a crime at a given time and in a particular place. Just as what is defined as deviant is relative (see Chap-

ter 8), a wide variety of different behaviors have been considered to be criminal at some place or at some time.

In contrast, some people prefer a *natural law approach*. In the past, natural law definitions generally interpreted crime as a violation of divinely inspired guidelines. Today, advocates of this approach are more likely to see crimes as acts in opposition to universal secular principles of human rights. The Nuremburg trials following the end of World War II, during which many leading Nazis were found guilty of war crimes for their involvement in the Holocaust in which millions of Jewish people and other minorities were exterminated, reflected secular natural law. Had the judges used a legalistic definition instead of the natural law approach, they could not have found

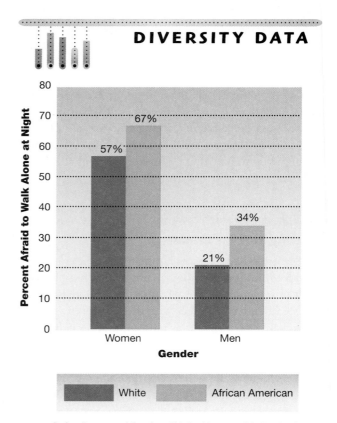

FIGURE 9.1 **Percent Afraid to Walk Alone at Night, by Race and Gender.** Women are consistently more likely than men to say that there are some places within a mile of their homes where they would be afraid to walk alone at night. Levels of fear appear to have declined slightly among women over the past 30 years while they have increased marginally among men. Will the sharp decreases in the crime rate that began in the early 1990s result in declines in public fear of crime?

Source: NORC. General Social Surveys, 1972–2000. Chicago: National Opinion Research Center, 2000. Reprinted by permission of NORC, Chicago, IL.

these men guilty as their acts did not violate the laws of Nazi Germany.

RATES OF CRIME

After briefly introducing some of the problems sociologists encounter in determining how much crime occurs, this section examines the current rate of crime in the United States and then compares the U.S. crime rate with those of other similar societies.

Sources of Data

Sociologists who wish to study crime in the United States rely heavily on two sources of official statistical information. Unfortunately, both have serious limitations. The most widely used source is the *Uniform Crime Reports* (UCR), which have been compiled and published annually by the FBI since 1930. These reports are based on information provided by roughly 17,000 local police agencies covering better than 95 percent of the U.S. population (Federal Bureau of Investigation, 2001). Eight street crimes, called **index crimes,** are given special attention in the UCR. They include four personal or violent crimes: homicide, robbery, aggravated assault, and forcible rape (as opposed to statutory rape—intercourse between an adult and a minor); and four property crimes: burglary, larceny-theft, auto theft, and arson. Data recorded for these crimes include the number of offenses reported, the number of people arrested, the number of cases sent to trial, and selected demographic information concerning individuals who have been arrested and convicted.

There are serious problems with the UCR (Biderman & Lynch, 1991). Most crimes are never reported to the police, principally because many people don't think their victimization is important enough or because they doubt the police can help them. Additionally, changes in police recording procedures, such as those resulting from the introduction of computers, can significantly influence crime rates, making it difficult to compare UCR data across time. And, finally, only about one-fifth of all crimes reported to the police are actually solved by arrest. In sum, the UCR figures are not very reliable (Kempf, 1990).

The FBI is in the process of developing a National Incident-Based Reporting System that should correct some of the UCR's failings. However, no police-derived database will ever provide information about crimes that are not reported—the so-called "dark figure of crime." To investigate unreported crime, researchers use the *National Crime Victimization Survey* (NCVS), which is based on regular interviews conducted with a random sample of Americans aged 12 and over.

The NCVS began in 1972. The adult members of 86,800 households—about 159,470 individuals—are asked about their experiences with crime victimization over the past six months. Six of the eight index crimes are covered; arson and homicide are not. The NCVS is probably a more useful source of information than the UCR, but it is not without its own problems. For example, people often have difficulty applying official definitions to their experiences and may be hesitant to report particularly embarrassing victimizations.

Crime Rates in the United States

Table 9.1 summarizes trends in arrests for UCR index crimes between 1990 and 2000. Two points stand out:

TABLE 9.1

Changes in Official Arrest Rates for Selected Index Offenses, 1986–2000 (per 100,000 People)

Offense	1986	1990	1996	2000
Homicide	8.1	9.5	7.6	4.8
Forcible Rape	15.7	16.0	12.8	9.8
Robbery	62.6	70.4	64.1	39.7
Aggravated Assault	148.1	194.8	204.1	173.9
Violent Crime	**234.5**	**290.7**	**288.6**	**228.2**
Burglary	189.2	176.3	139.1	104.0
Larceny/Theft	596.6	641.4	577.3	429.5
Auto Theft	64.7	87.0	69.5	54.2
Property Crime	**857.3**	**912.5**	**793.2**	**593.6**

Sources: Maguire, Kathleen, and Ann L. Pastore, eds. (2001) *Sourcebook of Criminal Justice Statistics* [Online]. Available: http://www.albany.edn/sourcebook/ Table 4.2; Federal Bureau of Investigation (2001). *Crime in the United States, 2000.* Washington, DC: U.S. Department of Justice.

- About 88 percent of all arrests for index crimes are for property offenses; statistically speaking, violent crime is relatively uncommon.
- Arrests for virtually all crime categories have declined dramatically since 1990. A comparison between UCR data for 1996 and 2000 shows that arrests for violent index crimes dropped 15.6 percent. Homicide and robbery arrests declined 25.6 percent and 28.2 percent respectively. Arrests for index property crimes went down 18.9 percent during this same period.

How can we explain these decreases, which are unprecedented in modern times? Criminologists argue that the reduced crime rate is partly a result of changing demographics. Since most street crimes are committed by people in their teens and early 20s, in an era such as 1960 to 1975, when the baby boom generation was young, the crime rate naturally rose (Steffensmeier & Streifel, 1991). Today the youth population is relatively small, leading to lower crime rates (Steffensmeier & Harer, 1991; Klofas & Stojkovic, 1995).

Demography is only part of the story. The recent drop in crime may also be attributed to increasing rates of imprisonment. With roughly 2 million people behind bars, the criminal justice system may have finally managed—although at enormous cost—to incarcerate a large enough number of career criminals to affect the national crime rate. The economic boom of the 1990s also may have played a role in reducing the crime rate.

However, projected demographic trends for the next two decades as well as recent scattered increases in certain types of crime suggest that there may be trouble ahead. Homicide rates in Boston and Phoenix increased roughly 60 percent in 2001, and they grew between 10 and 20 percent in several other cities (Tyre, 2002). Preliminary figures for the 2001 UCR, released as this text was going to press, showed major crimes rising by 2 percent—the first increase since 1991. Except for aggravated assault, which dropped 1.4 percent, every category of crime grew, led by a 5.9 percent increase in car theft, a 3.9 percent increase in robbery, and a 3.1 percent increase in murder. If the deaths from the 9/11 terrorist attacks had been counted as homicides, the murder rate would have jumped 26 percent (Holland, 2002). There are presently about 40 million children in the United States under the age of 10—an unusually high number. As these children start moving into their teens, the nation's adolescent (and hence crime-prone) population will grow substantially (Morganthau, 1995). As a result, many sociologists expect crime to increase over the next few years.

Crime Rates in Cross-Cultural Perspective

Cross-cultural comparisons of crime rates are always difficult, in part because different nations define particular crimes quite differently and also because the accuracy of data collection varies sharply around the world. Comparisons are probably easiest concerning homicide because most nations take special pains to investigate murders and to record their findings accurately, although certain murders—such as the "honor killings" of women and female infanticide (see Chapter 15)—may not be reflected in the official statistics.

As Figure 9.2 shows, a few nations report higher homicide rates than the United States, but the U.S. rate substantially exceeds those of most other industrialized societies (Ellis & Walsh, 2000). For example, despite a 50 percent increase over the past decade, the violent crime rate in Japan is still six times lower than the rate in the United States. Tokyo, a city of 12 million, experienced 133 murders in 1987; New York, with 7 million people, recorded 1,672 homicides in the same year (Yanagishita & MacKellar, 1995; "Once-Safe Japan," 2000).

More generally, in recent decades U.S. violent crime rates have been three to four times higher than those of other modern societies. However, cross-cultural differences in the rates of major property crimes are much less substantial, and a number of European nations have seen marked increases in both violent and property crime during the same years that crime declined in the United States.

Many sociologists are convinced that the single most important factor underlying the high rate of violent crime in the United States is this nation's fascination with guns (Wright et al., 1983; Davidson, 1993). Between 60 and 70 million handguns and automatic weapons are currently in circulation in this country, and about 15,000 people die each year as a result of gun homicides—well over 400,000 since John Kennedy was assassinated in 1963 (Fingerhut, 1993). Homicide is now the number one cause of death among African American youths, and close to 90 percent of these murders involve guns.

But the proliferation of guns is not the whole story. Several nations, including Switzerland, have high rates of gun ownership and low levels of personal crime. Could the pervasive violence in our media be a contributing factor? Possibly, but low-crime Japan is also known for its violent popular culture. High levels of drug use in the United States, frustration resulting from extensive economic inequality (see Chapter 11), and the high level of cultural heterogeneity in the United States also play a part (Currie, 1998).

Many researchers have studied Japan in order to understand how a modern society can keep its crime

GLOBAL CONNECTIONS

Religious Law in Iran

The September 11, 2001, terrorist attacks on the World Trade Center and on the Pentagon led to a marked increase in the level of interest in the Islamic world among many citizens of the United States. One of the least well understood aspects of Muslim culture may be its criminal law. The legal system of the Islamic republic of Iran provides an excellent example of the religious law tradition.

At the heart of the Iranian criminal justice system is a blurring of the distinction between government and religion (Entessar, 1988). The leaders of the Iranian Revolution of 1978–1979 believed that secular governments, which rely on humanly made laws, inevitably fall victim to corruption and degeneration. Only by rejecting foreign influences and adhering to the God-given laws, or *Shari'a,* spelled out in the Koran, could their nation become whole again.

Islamic law has remained virtually unchanged for centuries. Muslim "fundamentalists" hold that when conflicts arise between Islamic law and the needs of a changing society, society must change to conform with the law, not the reverse. A key principle of the Islamic government of Iran is that legislative and judicial bodies exist not to create laws, but solely to enforce them. In most cases the punishment for a category of crimes is specified in the Koran and is nonnegotiable. Iran's Revolutionary Court, led by the supreme *faaih* or "just jurist," has the authority to issue *fatwahs* (or edicts) and to decide cases deemed a threat to the Islamic state; its decisions are final, with no right of appeal. More routine cases are heard and decided by *ulema,* religious scholars, or in some cases, by self-appointed neighborhood tribunals.

The Islamic penal code followed in the Republic of Iran recognizes three general categories of crimes. The first, *hudud* offenses, are acts including theft, adultery, heresy, and drinking alcoholic beverages prohibited by God; these offenses carry mandatory penalties. If the accused is found guilty, the judge has no discretion regarding punishment. Theft is punishable by amputation of the hands; adultery, by stoning to death. Other *hudud* offenses, such as *mofsed-e fil arz* (earthly corruption) and *mohareuh ba Khoda* (hostility to God)—both of which carry a mandatory death penalty—are largely undefined, allowing judges to exercise vast and arbitrary power with no semblance of impartiality.

The second category of crimes, *qisas,* includes murder, manslaughter, battery, and mutilation. Under Islamic law, such acts are considered crimes against the victim *and his or her family,* not solely against the individual or society. The family has the right to personally enact vengeance, inflicting injury or death on the culprit equal to that experienced by the victim. Although the Koran urges forgiveness, the victim is entitled to retribution in kind, or "an eye for an eye."

The third category, *ta'zir* offenses, are roughly equivalent to misdemeanors: They include immoral behavior, wearing immodest clothing, and the like. Here, judges do have options. Depending on how disruptive they consider a transgression, they may issue a rebuke or a warning, impose a fine, seize property, or order a public flogging (the most common form of punishment in Iran today).

Divat refers not to a type of crime but to a form of punishment. If the victim of a *qisas* offense (or the victim's family) chooses not to exact retribution, he or she is entitled to compensation or "blood money." The Iranian government has established clear rules for the amount of *divat* due for various crimes as well as schedules for its payment.

The first *fatwah,* issued by the late revolutionary leader Ayatollah Khomeni in 1979, declared all prerevolutionary laws null and void. Since then, Iranian authorities have consistently asserted that divine law overrides international law and widely shared Western standards of human rights and just procedure. To outsiders, the Islamic penal code may seem barbaric. To Iranians, strict penalties are just, not only to the victim but also to the criminal, who, having paid for his or her sins, is more likely to ultimately receive mercy from God.

1. What are the advantages and disadvantages of explicitly grounding a legal system in a particular religious tradition? Should the United States attempt to integrate Christianity into its criminal justice system, as some conservatives recommend? Explain your reasoning.

2. The Iranian legal system is more focused on protecting the rights of crime victims (and their relatives) than is the law in the United States. Should our courts move in this direction?

Source: Entessar, 1988.

rate low. The most important factors retarding crime in Japan appear to be (1) a high level of ethnic and cultural homogeneity; (2) a strong cultural emphasis on conformity, which is reinforced in the family, in the schools, at work, and through religion; (3) a relatively strong economy and a moderately generous welfare state that together have greatly reduced poverty; (4) strict gun control laws; and (5) an innovative criminal justice system that is strongly supported by the populace and that solves a very high percentage

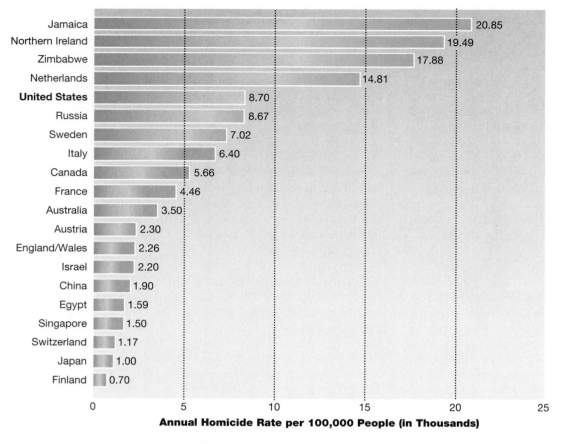

FIGURE 9.2 Homicide Rates per 100,000 People for the United States and Selected Additional Countries, 1996

Source: Lee Ellis and Anthony Walsh. 2000. *Criminology: A Global Perspective.* Boston: Allyn and Bacon: p. 59.

of its cases (Westerman & Burfeind, 1991; Miyazawa, 1992; "The Secret of Japan's Safe Streets," 1994; Terrill, 1999).

MAJOR TYPES OF CRIME

This section examines some of the important characteristics of violent street crime, elite crime, and victimless crime.

Violent Street Crime

Only about 12.3 percent of all index offenses are violent crimes, but this is the type of offense that arouses the deepest fear and is most frequently reported in the mass media (Warr, 1995). Violent crime also creates the most serious and lasting trauma for its victims (Parker, 1995).

HOMICIDE In 2000, 15,517 Americans were murdered, an average of 300 per week. Although the per-

centage of murders committed by strangers is on the rise, most homicides still take place between people who know each other—family members, friends, neighbors, and drinking buddies (Wilson, 1993). What some criminologists call the "common homicide" occurs as a result of everyday interpersonal conflict between two or more young lower-class men that gets out of hand, typically late on Friday or Saturday night and after heavy use of alcohol by both participants.

Almost all homicides committed by women are defensive attacks against abusive husbands or boyfriends rather than drunken barroom brawls. Many stranger murders are committed accidentally in the course of other crimes such as robbery or burglary. Others, such as "drive-by" shootings, are related to turf conflicts between rival drug-distribution syndicates. Very few, despite what Hollywood tells us, are carried out by professional hit men, serial killers, or mass murderers.

RAPE Forcible rape, perhaps the most feared of all crimes, was discussed in Chapters 7 and 8. It is un-

Japan's police force is widely regarded as one of the most effective criminal justice agencies in the postindustrial world; it is one of the primary reasons why the Japanese crime rate, although currently on the rise, remains among the world's lowest.

doubtedly the index offense for which the official data are least reliable. Several decades ago, it was estimated that up to 90 percent of all rapes were not brought to the attention of the authorities. Today, a comparison between UCR and victimization figures suggests that about 30 percent of rapes are reported (Bureau of Justice Statistics, 2001). This increase is primarily a consequence of changes in the way the criminal justice system processes rape complaints. All-female police rape squads, reductions in requirements for corroborating evidence, and *shield laws*, which prohibit attorneys from probing into victims' private lives, have all increased rape survivors' willingness to report (Allison & Wrightman, 1993).

In searching for the causes of rape, many sociologists have been struck by research that shows many offenders are not severely psychologically disturbed. There also appear to be no significant personality traits that clearly distinguish rapists from other men.

These findings strongly imply that some aspects of mainstream culture promote rape. In particular, the feminist perspective suggests that both men and women may be, in a sense, socialized for rape: Women traditionally have learned to be passive and agreeable while men have been taught to be aggressive and to look at women as sex objects to be conquered. Rape is not, in this view, about passion but rather about power. This interpretation is further supported by the observation that the primary function of homosexual rape in prison is clearly the establishment of a hierarchy of dominance, not the provision of sexual gratification.

The legal penalties for rape are severe: It is one of the small number of crimes for which offenders have historically been sentenced to death in the United States. This seems surprising at first glance. Why would a man, an occupant of the more highly ranked gender status, be severely punished for a crime against a woman, an occupant of a less valued gender status? The feminist perspective provides a chilling explanation for this apparent contradiction. In this interpretation, the law treats rape not as a *personal crime* but rather as a *property offense* in which one man, the rapist, despoils a valuable possession of another man, the victim's father or husband. This may be the ultimate expression of how sexist culture treats women as objects rather than as people.

Elite Crime

Most of the people arrested for violent street crimes are lower-status individuals. However, criminal acts perpetrated by the well-to-do, which some have called "crime in the suites" (Nader & Green, 1972), cause far more financial harm and take far more lives than do the crimes that show up in the UCR. We will

INTERNET CONNECTIONS

The FBI has an interesting Website at
www.fbi.gov/ucr.htm

From the most recent "Uniform Crime Reports," find how much crime there was in your city and compare the rate of crime in your area with national trends. What accounts for the difference? (If you need to download Acrobat Reader, simply follow the instructions on your screen.)

Women who have been raped sometimes hesitate to report their victimization to the police because they dread talking about their traumatic experience; some even blame themselves for what was done to them. Rape crisis centers like this one in Cambridge, Massachusetts, have played an important role in encouraging rape victims to press complaints against their attackers.

briefly consider two types of elite crime: organized crime and corporate crime.

ORGANIZED CRIME **Organized crime** is criminal activity conducted by relatively large-scale and highly structured gangs or syndicates that routinely use corruption and violence to maximize their profits. Most, but not all, organized crime groups are involved in providing illegal goods and services to the public (Abadinsky, 1990; Block, 1991; McCaghy & Capron, 1997). Popular understandings of organized crime tend to reflect the "Godfather" image, or more formally the *alien conspiracy model*, which suggests that most local criminal gangs are controlled by a single national organization of Sicilians called the Mafia or *La Cosa Nostra*. Whether organized crime in the United States was ever this highly centralized is debatable, but there is no doubt that the alien conspiracy model is no longer accurate.

INTERNET CONNECTIONS

Go to the Web of Justice site:

http://www.co.pinellas.fl.us/bcc/juscoord/eorganized.htm

on organized crime. Click on some of the links to obtain information not presented in the text on organized crime. Write a short report on some of the primary sociological features of organized crime.

Organized crime arose in the United States long before the immigration of large numbers of Italians. Early in the 19th century, Irish and later Jewish gangs functioned as criminal syndicates in many large cities. They were displaced early in this century by Sicilian groups, but the era of Italian control over organized crime has now ended (Block & Chambliss, 1981; Albanese, 1989). Today's gangs are increasingly run by members of ethnic groups such as African Americans, Chinese (Chin, 1990), Cubans, Colombians, Jamaicans, and many others (Elliott, 1993). Some of these groups are strictly local, while others have national and international connections (Delattre, 1990; Ryan & Rush, 1997).

The general process whereby groups of different national origins assume control of criminal syndicates is termed *ethnic succession* (Bell, 1953). Members of ethnic groups migrate to this country only to find their opportunities for upward mobility limited. Refusing to abandon the American dream, many respond by innovating; in Robert Merton's terms, they find illegitimate ways of achieving success goals (see Chapter 8) (O'Kane, 1992). Over time, as legitimate opportunities gradually open up, newer immigrants take their place in the syndicates.

Syndicated crime is by no means found only in the United States. It thrives throughout Europe (Fijnaut, 1990), in Russia (Bartos, 1995), and in Japan, where about one-third of all prison inmates are believed to be members of a syndicate called the *Yakuza* (Bryjak & Soroka, 1994: 274). Latin American and Southeast Asian syndicates are heavily involved in exporting drugs to the United States.

Efforts to control syndicated crime are hampered by these groups' very deep leadership hierarchy, which makes it extremely hard to convict the top bosses. Systematic and widespread corruption of local, state, and federal officials is another barrier to effective prosecution (Newfield & Dubrul, 1979). However, in the past two decades, federal prosecutors have successfully gone on the offensive against the leaders of the old-line Sicilian groups. Armed with the witness-immunity program and the Racketeer-Influenced and Corrupt Organizations Act (RICO), officials have substantially weakened the *Cosa Nostra* in the United States, but they have not prevented new ethnic gangs from taking its place.

CORPORATE CRIME Over 50 years ago, Edwin Sutherland directed sociologists' attention to a problem he called **white-collar crime,** criminal acts committed by high-status people in the course of their occupations (Sutherland, 1949). Sutherland's concept lumps together several very different types of crime. The most fundamental distinction is between **occupational crimes,** acts such as embezzlement committed by individuals against their employers, and **corporate crimes,** criminal acts committed by businesses against their employees, customers, or the general public (Clinard & Quinney, 1973).

There are four principal types of corporate crime. *Financial offenses* involve acts such as insider trading, price fixing (Baker & Faulkner, 1993), bribery, kickbacks, and corporate tax evasion. The savings and loan scandal of the 1980s is a good example (Waldman & Thomas, 1990; Weisburd et al., 1991). During the Reagan era, the government relaxed regulations on the savings and loan industry, and some 500 executives began an orgy of what has been termed "collective embezzlement" (Calavita & Pontell, 1991). They paid themselves exorbitant salaries, made bad loans to

friends and relatives that were covered by federal insurance programs, falsified records, and in some cases simply absconded with depositors' funds. It is impossible to know how much the S&L scandal will ultimately cost the taxpayers; estimates vary between $300 billion and $1 trillion (Newdorf, 1991; Kettl, 1991). Using a relatively conservative figure of $500 billion, each man, woman, and child in the United States will eventually pay $2,000 in taxes to make good the stolen funds.

The recent Enron scandal may also be classified as a financial offense. However, the behavior of top Enron executives, who secured windfall profits while millions of smaller investors went broke as the company collapsed, may be more precisely characterized as extremely unethical rather than openly criminal given the very broad range of actions considered legal under current regulations, which are supposedly intended to control corporate misbehavior (Fineman & Isikoff, 2002).

A second type of corporate crime involves *hazardous working conditions* (Frank & Lynch, 1992). Although aware of the health dangers of asbestos since the 1930s, the Johns Manville corporation refused to make the modifications in its plants that would have protected workers. The consequence was many thousands of painful and premature deaths from preventable lung diseases (Brodeur, 1985; Mokhiber, 1988). Not one Johns Manville executive went to jail for these crimes, and the corporation avoided full financial responsibility by declaring strategic bankruptcy and reorganizing itself (Calhoun & Hiller, 1988; Delaney, 1992).

Third, many corporations have been found guilty of *manufacturing unsafe products.* In a classic case, Ford

The 2002 Enron scandal directed a great deal of public attention to the issue of corporate crime. Here former Enron employees picket the firm's Houston headquarters.

executives rushed the Pinto into production in 1970, even though they knew that when the car was struck from behind, the doors jammed and the fuel tank exploded. Ford calculated that it would cost $137 million to repair the problem, but only $49.5 million to settle claims resulting from the design flaw. In the end, 500 people died, but Ford's profits were not affected (Downie, 1977). The seriously defective tires marketed by the Firestone corporation provide a more recent example of the manufacture of unsafe products.

Finally, corporations have been heavily implicated in air and water pollution, toxic waste dumping, and other *environmental crimes*. The poisoning of the Love Canal district in upstate New York by the Hooker Chemical Company is one well-known example (Simon & Eitzen, 1986). Another is the release of poisonous gas from a Union Carbide plant in Bhopal, India, that killed over 2,000 people in 1984.

The overall cost of corporate crime is enormous (Moore & Mills, 1990). The annual losses resulting from white-collar crime, most of which is corporate, have been estimated at 50 times the cost of conventional property crime. Avoidable workplace hazards are responsible for one-third of all work-related deaths (Hills, 1987; Rosoff, et al., 1998).

Corporate crime is extremely widespread. In a study of 600 of the largest manufacturing companies in the United States, researchers found that over a 2-year period, 60 percent were charged with some sort of violation and 43 percent with more than one offense. Just 13 percent of the companies—concentrated in the oil, automobile, and pharmacy industries—were responsible for over half of the violations, suggesting that, like some street criminals, some corporations are, in effect, hardened and habitual offenders (Clinard & Yeager, 1980; Friedrichs, 1996).

Can corporate crime be controlled? There has been some movement in the direction of stiffer penalties in recent years, but overall, the powerful are still punished less severely than the poor (Braithwaite, 1985; Pearce & Tombs, 1997). Many harmful business practices are controlled by regulatory agencies whose sanctioning power is largely limited to fines (Hawkins & Thomas, 1984; Gray & Scholz, 1993). Furthermore, these fines, while sometimes substantial, are minimal compared to the profits that result from corporate crime. Executives often regard them as part of the cost of doing business; some fines are even tax deductible!

When corporate offenders *do* end up in criminal court, the penalties tend to be mild. In part this is because corporations can easily afford top-flight legal representation; in addition, the law is more easily applied to individuals than to corporate entities (Reiman, 1995). Most cases are settled out of court, and fines (often paid by the firm), probation, or at the

worst short prison sentences served in minimum-security facilities are the usual punishments.

Why such easy treatment? For one thing, corporate offenders simply don't fit our stereotypes of criminals: They are mostly otherwise respectable, church-going, middle-aged, white suburban homeowners. Judges seem to find it difficult to send people much like themselves to jail for long terms—almost no matter how serious their offenses (Wheeler et al., 1988; Coleman, 1998). Moreover, the victims of corporate crimes are usually, though not always, difficult to identify. Industrial pollution kills far more people than muggers, but no one can point to a single polluter as specifically responsible for a given death, a fact that reduces public outrage against corporate criminals.

Victimless Crime

A third major type of crime consists of acts such as drug sales and possession, prostitution, pornography, and illicit gambling. **Victimless crimes** are created when the criminal law is used to attempt to prohibit the exchange of strongly desired goods and services between willing adults (Schur, 1979).

Some say victimless crimes are efforts to "legislate morality" (Jenness, 1990). Of course, most laws have a moral dimension, but those prohibiting other types of crimes are generally based on substantial social consensus. In contrast, there is considerable disagreement in modern societies concerning whether drug use, prostitution, and gambling are acceptable behaviors.

Because neither party in the exchange of outlawed goods and services feels victimized, there is generally no one to complain to the police. This makes victimless crime laws extremely difficult and costly to enforce. Not only must the authorities apprehend the offenders, they must also investigate in order to find that an offense has taken place. Although between 25 and 30 percent of all arrests are for victimless crimes, the overwhelming majority of all instances of drug use, prostitution, and illegal gambling do not come to the attention of the authorities. In practice, the police and courts generally realize that they can never substantially reduce these outlawed practices. Their periodic crackdowns are primarily intended to demonstrate to conservative moralists that the law is still on their side.

The sexually oriented victimless crimes of prostitution and pornography are discussed in Chapter 7.

THE CRIMINAL JUSTICE SYSTEM

All modern societies have developed elaborate institutional structures to identify suspected offenders, determine their guilt or innocence, and punish the guilty. A structure of this sort, consisting of the police, the courts, and correctional institutions, is called a *criminal justice system*. This section examines selected aspects of the criminal justice systems of the United States and of other nations around the world.

The Police

Because the public sees the police as front-line troops in the "war against crime," hiring more police officers is one of the most politically popular anticrime measures. The number of police in the United States has roughly doubled over the past 20 years (Carter & Radelet, 1999). There are presently over 660,000 full-time sworn officers in this country, or about 24 police per 10,000 people (Federal Bureau of Investigation, 2001).

Is increasing the number of police the most effective way to spend our crime-prevention dollars? Research shows that police rarely spend more than 20 percent of their time in crime control; most of their day is devoted to routine public order activity—directing traffic, dealing with public nuisances, controlling crowds—and completing routine departmental paperwork (Siegel, 2000). Police officers rarely witness crimes, and unless they do, they must depend on the testimony of victims and witnesses in identifying suspects.

The fact that the public expects so much of them, coupled with their having surprisingly little ability to actually reduce crime, contributes to the heavy stress many officers experience. Rates of marital violence, divorce, suicide, and alcoholism are all high among the police. Although the public by and large supports the police, officers spend much of their time in contact with young, poor, minority males who, as a category, are especially prone to antipolice attitudes; such constantly negative interactions add to the strain police feel (Wilson, 1983; Skolnick, 1994). This strain promotes the development of a strong, isolated police subculture that is extremely suspicious of outsiders (Crank, 1997).

In the past two decades, many U.S. police departments have moved towards *community policing*. In this approach, officers institute neighborhood watch programs and walk beats rather than stay in their patrol cars as they drive through the streets of urban neighborhoods (Kelling & Coles, 1996).

Community policing is an international movement found, among other places, in Canada (Normandeau, 1993) and Germany (Brown, 1983). It is especially popular in low-crime Japan (Westerman & Burfeind, 1991; Terrill, 1999). Most urban Japanese police are assigned to mini-stations called *kobans*, which are scattered throughout the nation's cities. Officers in these neighborhood police stations become intimately familiar with the people in their districts. They work 56 hours per week and may stay in the same *koban* for several years. Their duties include not just crime control but also helping people with everyday problems, such as finding addresses and locating misplaced property. If a police officer in the United States is like a firefighter, who appears only when there is a problem, a Japanese officer is more like a letter carrier, part of the daily life of the community. As a result, most Japanese readily cooperate with the police rather than seeing them as outsiders.

Neighborhood watch programs have been established all across the country in the past few decades. They reflect the simple fact that the people who live in a neighborhood are far more likely to detect criminal activity than are the police.

We cannot solve our crime problems by simply copying the Japanese. Our culture is not prepared to allow police to enter unlocked homes at will, stop and question citizens on the street without cause, or conduct highly personal crime surveys of neighborhood residents, as the Japanese police do. Few people in this country would feel comfortable allowing the police to hold suspects for up to 23 days and to deny them food, sleep, and toilet privileges during interrogation, even though such practices help the Japanese criminal justice system achieve a better than 99 percent conviction rate. We are simply too individualistic and too culturally heterogeneous to trust the police as much as the Japanese do. But certain aspects of Japanese community policing have been accepted in the United States and seem to have improved the quality of law enforcement in this country (Kelling & Coles, 1996).

The Courts

The legal system of the United States is grounded in the English **common law** tradition. In this arrangement, the law develops gradually over time through the accumulation of many cases. Legal principles are based on precedent. Thus, in applying common law, a judge is guided by rulings made by other judges concerning similar cases in the past.

Such a system seems natural to us, but it is by no means universal. There are, in fact, three distinct families of criminal law in the modern world (Fairchild, 1993; Reichel, 1994). Most of the world's societies follow the **civil law** tradition, which is *code-based* rather than *case-based*. Instead of developing gradually from the bottom up, case by case, in the civil law tradition the law (or code) is written by the ruler, a legislature, or a judicial panel and imposed on society from the top down. For example, most European nations derive their law from the Code Napoleon, which was drawn up in France in 1804.

The world's third major legal family is **religious law.** Like the civil law tradition, it is constructed mostly from the top down. However, the source of the law is believed to be divine will rather than custom or human reason. Iran, where criminal law is based on the *Shari'a* ("the way") as revealed by Allah to the prophet Mohammed in the *Qur'an* (Koran) and other sacred writings, is a good example. The Iranian legal system is discussed in the *Global Connections* box on page 225 of this chapter.

Common law societies, including the United States, structure their courts according to the **adversarial principle.** That is, defendants are, in theory, considered innocent until proven guilty, and their guilt or innocence is determined through a contest between the defense and the prosecution with a neutral judge making the final decision (Eitzen & Zinn, 1992).

Unlike common law societies, civil law nations such as France and Germany are based on the **inquisitorial principle** rather than the adversarial one. In this tradition, the judge's role is greatly expanded. Both before and during the trial, a civil law judge determines the truth of the matter at hand rather than simply mediating between two contesting sides. It is therefore the judge who calls and questions witnesses. Trials in the inquisitorial system avoid the long delays and courtroom dramatics that often occur in the adversarial system, but they do reduce the defendant's presumption of innocence.

The media present a very idealized image of how the courts function in the United States. Criminologists Lawrence Friedman and Robert Percival use the concept of the *criminal justice wedding cake* to describe how our system really works (Friedman & Percival, 1981; Gottfredson & Gottfredson, 1988; Walker, 1994). As depicted in Figure 9.3, this model suggests that there are four fundamentally different types of crimes, each of which is treated somewhat differently in the courts. At the top are the highly publicized "celebrated cases" such as the O.J. Simpson or Rodney King trials, which are processed in a fully adversarial fashion. Next come the serious felonies, like

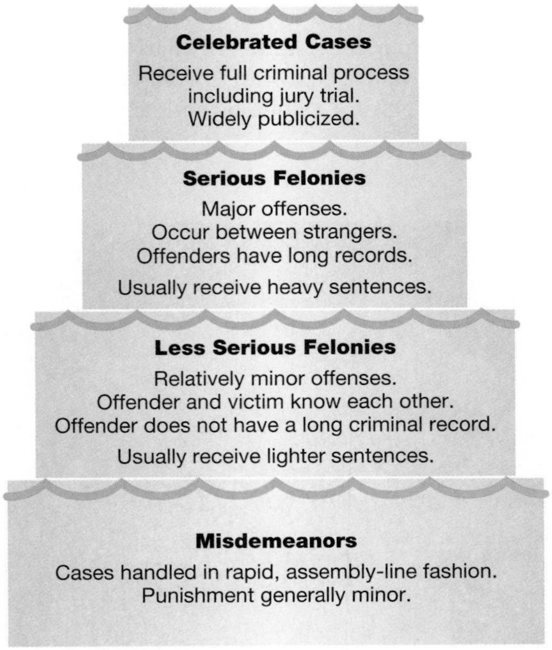

Celebrated Cases
Receive full criminal process including jury trial.
Widely publicized.

Serious Felonies
Major offenses.
Occur between strangers.
Offenders have long records.
Usually receive heavy sentences.

Less Serious Felonies
Relatively minor offenses.
Offender and victim know each other.
Offender does not have a long criminal record.
Usually receive lighter sentences.

Misdemeanors
Cases handled in rapid, assembly-line fashion.
Punishment generally minor.

FIGURE 9.3 *The Criminal Justice Wedding Cake.*

Source: Figure 2.2, p. 32 from *Sense and Nonsense About Crime and Drugs.*, 5th edition by S. Walker. Copyright © 2001 by S. Walker. Reprinted by permission of Wadsworth, a division of Thomson Learning. www.thomsonrights .com. Fax (800) 730-2215.

murder, forcible rape, and burglary, especially those committed by strangers; they also are handled adversarially, though somewhat less so.

The vast majority of criminal cases are minor felonies or misdemeanors—crimes like simple assault, theft, or vandalism—often occurring between people who know each other. They are resolved in an assembly-line fashion with the judge, prosecutor, and defense attorney working together rather than as opponents. Their goal is to ensure that defendants, who are in practice assumed to be guilty, receive a "going rate" sentence, neither harsher nor less severe than sentences given to similar defendants.

The primary means by which this assembly-line justice is accomplished is **plea bargaining,** a process by which defendants plead guilty to a lesser charge rather than go to full trial. There is little doubt that if it weren't for plea bargaining, the overloaded American court system would simply grind to a halt. But it is equally clear that innocent defendants are sometimes pressured to accept a plea bargain, which amounts to a denial of due-process rights guaranteed by the Constitution (Schulhofer, 1992).

The Purposes of Punishment

Why do we have prisons? There are at least four distinct answers to this surprisingly difficult question: retribution, deterrence, rehabilitation, and incapacitation (Conrad, 1983; Siegel, 2000).

RETRIBUTION The purpose of retribution is to restore the moral balance of society. Because a criminal has caused innocent victims to suffer, proponents of retribution believe it is morally necessary that the offender suffer in turn. Thus, retribution is based on the ancient principle of *lex talionis*, "an eye for an eye."

Note that punishment as retribution is not a means of reducing crime. If our motive in executing a murderer is purely retributive, then it does not matter whether the murder rate decreases after the execution. What is important is that the murderer has been punished.

This is the oldest of the four rationales for punishment. As modern societies strove to develop effective means of reducing crime over the past century, simple retribution came to be seen by many as bloody-minded and barbaric. But the sharp pre-1991 increases in the crime rate eroded many people's faith in the efficacy of contemporary crime-control measures and led to a resurgence of retributive thinking.

DETERRENCE The logic of deterrence rests squarely on the classical theory of criminality introduced in Chapter 8. If potential offenders think care-

fully and rationally about the risks and benefits of their actions and decide to violate the law only if the positives outweigh the negatives, then strengthening the penalties will change this "mental calculus" and reduce the crime rate (Gibbs, 1975).

There are two kinds of deterrence: **Specific deterrence** is punishment of a particular individual intended to keep him or her from violating the law in the future. **General deterrence** shows people who have yet to commit crimes what is done to offenders in the hope that they will decide not to break the law.

Does deterrence work? Will Sheriff Arpaio's moldy bologna eventually reduce the crime rate? This question has aroused passionate debate. Supporters point to research that shows that criminals generally avoid victimizing individuals whom they know to be armed. This implies that they are rational enough to avoid crime if the price tag is high enough (Greenberg & Kessler, 1982; Pontell, 1984; Hook, 1989). Opponents note that the United States already has extremely severe criminal penalties, yet it also has a very high crime rate (Savelsberg, 1994). They argue that deterrence theorists overestimate the rationality of criminals (Aday, 1989; Pepinsky & Quinney, 1993; Chambliss, 1994).

It is difficult to research how well general deterrence works because there is no accurate way to count the number of people who have not committed crimes for fear of punishment. Specific deterrence can, however, be studied by interviewing offenders. Unfortunately, most of this research is not very encouraging. For example, Kenneth Tunnell (1992) interviewed 60 men imprisoned for repeated property offenses. These career criminals had collectively committed almost 50,000 criminal acts. Tunnell investi-

INTERNET CONNECTIONS

The death penalty is a very controversial issue in American society. After reading about the topic in the text go to the Human Rights site: **http://www.derechos.org/dp/and** one of the most exhaustive sites on the internet on the topic of the death penalty. Click on some of the links and after reading the information presented answer the following questions. What are your views on the death penalty? What reasons can you site for or against the death penalty (according to the principles of punishment presented in the text)?

gated the process by which they decided to commit the crime for which they were currently incarcerated. He reached the following conclusions:

- Because most of these men had limited education, few conventional job skills, and lengthy criminal records, there was no legitimate way they could have earned even a minimally adequate living in today's economy. Only four even briefly considered working rather than committing crimes.
- Many of them were addicted to expensive drugs, making legitimate low-wage employment an even less viable alternative to crime.
- Most underestimated their chances of getting caught, did not know how long their sentences were likely to be if apprehended and convicted, and had not found their previous prison experiences intolerable.
- Finally, virtually all of them deliberately avoided thinking about the possible risks of crime by numbing themselves with drugs and alcohol or building up their confidence by talking with more experienced criminals. Just as a tightrope walker doesn't obsess over the pain of a possible fall, these men, having no real alternative to crime, did everything they could to put the possibility of failure out of their minds.

It seems clear that some crimes—and criminals—are more deterrable than others (Smith & Gartin, 1989). Much of the popular support for deterrence theory is based on the fact that most of us can remember times when the threat of punishment kept us from shoplifting, trying drugs, or committing some other minor criminal act. As Travis Hirschi's social control theory (see Chapter 8) would suggest, basically law-abiding people who would lose a lot if they were labeled criminals are generally quite effectively deterred by the threat of punishment. But skeptics ask how much most career criminals have to lose if punished; for them, prison is simply an occupational hazard. Furthermore, many of the violent street crimes we fear the most are committed in the heat of passion, when rational calculation is largely or entirely blocked by emotion (Bouffard et al., 2000).

Five conditions must be met for a sanction to effectively promote deterrence. First, punishment must be *certain*. It should also be *swift*, *public* (so that general deterrence can operate), and perceived as *just*. Finally, deterrence theory holds that punishment should be *severe enough* to outweigh the rewards of crime (Sherman & Berk, 1984; Decker & Kohlfeld, 1990; Nagin & Paternoster, 1991).

Unfortunately, none of the first four conditions can be easily met in today's criminal justice system. Since most crimes are never even reported to the police, certainty of punishment is obviously impossible.

The sheer volume of crimes that are reported slows down the system, making swiftness unlikely and reducing the chances that the punishment given for any particular crime will be publicized. And, finally, class-based and race-based differences in how the law is applied—an issue to be discussed shortly—reduce the chances that a given sentence will be seen as just.

REHABILITATION The growth of positivism in the social sciences (see Chapter 8) led directly to the concept of rehabilitation: If the decision to commit crime is caused by some combination of biological, psychological, and sociological variables, then therapeutic intervention should be able to "cure" the criminal. This optimistic philosophy has played an important role in criminal justice for most of the past two centuries, as is suggested by the use of words like *reformatory* and *correctional institution*. It underlay the development of the juvenile justice system in the late 19th century. It is clearly the guiding philosophy of Frankfurt's Mutter-Kind-Heim. Only in the past 30 years, because of the very high levels of public concern over crime, has the rehabilitative ideal become less popular (McCorkle, 1993).

Critics point to the fact that between 60 and 75 percent of all offenders commit new crimes within 3 years after they are released from correctional institutions in asserting that efforts at rehabilitation are usually futile (Gottfredson, 1995). Some go farther, claiming that the very idea of rehabilitation excuses criminals from full responsibility for their acts (Methvin, 1997).

As they are now run, do prisons rehabilitate? Almost certainly not. As Sutherland's theory of differential association suggests (see Chapter 8), if prisoners associate primarily with other unreformed offenders, then the only thing they are likely to learn is how to become better criminals. *Could* prisons rehabilitate? Perhaps. We do know that inmates who participate in well-constructed vocational and educational programs are substantially less likely to return to prison (Keller & Sbarbaro, 1994).

INCAPACITATION In the 1970s, many observers began to doubt whether prisons could either deter or rehabilitate; some skeptics began to argue that "nothing works" (Martinson, 1974). But even if we cannot reform offenders or frighten them into conforming, prisons can at least perform the function of incapacitation. We can keep the most dangerous criminals locked away where they cannot hurt anyone except each other.

It is this bottom-line rationale that dominates current correctional thinking in the United States. As noted criminologist James Q. Wilson wrote, "Wicked people exist. Nothing avails except to set them apart

Group therapy sessions such as this substance abuse class offered at a women's prison in Alabama represent a popular method that many correctional institutions use to attempt to rehabilitate their inmates.

from innocent people" (Wilson, 1983). And that is exactly what the United States has been doing, in unprecedented numbers and at unprecedented cost.

Corrections

In 2000, nearly 6.5 million people in the United States were living under some sort of correctional supervision—prison, jail, probation, or parole. This amounted to one in every 150 citizens. Of these 6.5 million people, 3.83 million were on probation, 726,000 on parole, 1.31 million in federal and state prisons, and 621,000 in local jails (Maguire & Pastore, 2001). This figure was over three and one half times the 1980 total, reflecting an average annual growth rate of 7.4 percent over the 20-year period (see Figure 9.4). Only in the past few years has this growth begun to slow, with a 4.8 percent increase between 1997 and 1998 and just a 3 percent expansion between 1999 and 2000.

One major consequence of this rapid growth in corrections has been serious overcrowding, since prison construction has failed to keep pace with the increasing number of inmates. State prison systems have been operating about 25 percent over capacity in recent years; in some states, cells constructed for a single occupant were housing two or even three inmates. Such conditions not only violate basic constitutional guarantees of humane treatment, they also encourage inmate violence. In some cases, the courts have taken control of the prisons and reduced overcrowding, usually by giving relatively minor criminals early releases.

The expansion of the prison population has also caused financial havoc. The total cost of building and maintaining our correctional system is about $30 bil-

lion annually—$4 billion in California alone. At an average cost of $17,000 per inmate per year, a 25-year-old given a life sentence without parole will ultimately cost taxpayers over $1 million (Mandel & Magnusson, 1993).

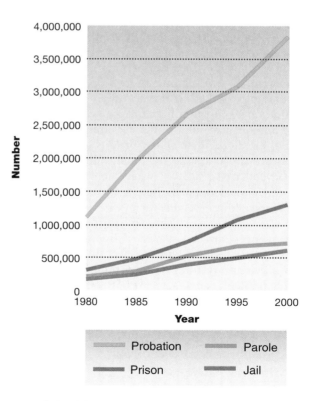

FIGURE 9.4 Adults Under Correctional Supervision, 1980–2000.

Source: From *Sourcebook of Criminal Justice Statistics,* 2001 ed. by Kathleen Maguire and Ann L. Pastore. Copyright © 2001. Reprinted by permission of Ann L. Pastore.

Why has this unprecedented expansion occurred? Not, as we have already seen, because crime is increasing rapidly. Nor is it because sentences are longer or because convicts are serving a higher proportion of their terms. The key is that several changes in the criminal justice system have sharply increased the chances that an individual who is convicted of a crime will actually be sent to prison (Langan, 1991). In particular, mandatory sentencing for drug offenses and, secondarily, for violent index crimes has swollen the population behind bars. In 1980, 19 of every 1,000 persons arrested on drug charges were eventually imprisoned; by 1993, the comparable figure was 104 per 1,000. Laws that mandate long prison terms for persons convicted of three felonies over their lifetimes (popularly called "three strikes" rules) have also contributed to the enormous growth of the prison population (Irwin & Austin, 1994).

Who actually ends up in prison? Inmates are 95 percent male, most have not completed high school, and 80 percent have previously been incarcerated. Over half are serving time for offenses the public considers minor, such as petty theft or the possession of marijuana (Austin & Irwin, 1989). Although African Americans make up only 12.8 percent of the U.S. population, 46 percent of all prison inmates are black (Beck & Harrison, 2001). The *Diversity in Focus* box on page 238 of this chapter entitled "A Generation Behind Bars" further examines the disproportionate imprisonment of lower-income African American males.

If we look to European prisons for alternatives, we find vastly less punitive correctional institutions. For example, in the Netherlands there is an absolute prohibition against putting more than one inmate in a cell; consequently, minor offenders frequently wait to serve their time. Most Dutch prisons are small, sentences are short, and correctional officers are highly trained and well paid. Extensive therapeutic services and educational opportunities are available, and inmates are allowed regular conjugal visits. Prisoners even wear their own clothes and earn decent pay for their labor (Downes, 1992). Most people in the United States would probably reject the Dutch model as insufficiently retributive, even though it costs less, is less violent, and achieves a somewhat lower *recidivism* rate (the rate at which released prisoners are incarcerated for new crimes) than does our system.

The Fundamental Dilemma of Criminal Justice

The most important underlying policy issue in the sociology of crime is balancing short-term and long-term solutions. Short-term approaches tend to be "hard-line" strategies, emphasizing incapacitation and (perhaps) deterrence: more cops, more prisons, longer sentences. These steps are popular with the public, and no one can deny that some career offenders simply must be locked away. For example, Inciardi (1992) studied 254 cocaine users in Miami and found that each had committed an average of 880 crimes, including 37 major felonies, in the past year. Obviously, some people must be confined to protect the public.

But if we devote nearly all our energies to hardline responses, most sociologists believe that we will continue to be plagued by high levels of crime as far into the future as we can see. Perhaps we should direct more attention to remedying the underlying causes of crime. For example, a study conducted by the RAND Institute found that, dollar for dollar, programs that encourage at-risk youth to stay in school and avoid trouble prevent five times as many crimes as mandatory sentencing laws. Similarly, teaching parents of aggressive youth how to control their children is three times more cost effective (Montgomery, 1996).

Everything we know about deviance suggests that informal social control is more effective than formal control. In particular, we need to help integrate at-risk individuals into small groups that oppose criminality (Heckathorn, 1990). Informal control through small groups is the cornerstone of the Chinese criminal justice system. Workplace and neighborhood-based "study groups" teach their members about the law and routinely intervene to censure even rather minor attitudinal or behavioral deviance. Formal authorities are used only as a last recourse. Can we learn anything from this?

More generally, many sociologists feel that reducing economic inequality is the best long-term solution to the crime problem (Messner & Rosenfeld, 1994). Conflict theorist Elliott Currie (1998) recommends fighting crime through large-scale government programs that reduce poverty, improve the wages and stability of low-skill jobs, strengthen community ties, and restore the vitality of the family.

LIFE CONNECTIONS

Diversity and Crime

Crime is not a random phenomenon. Some people are far more likely than others to commit offenses and, similarly, some people are more likely than others to be victims. In this section we investigate the demographic characteristics of criminals and of crime victims, with particular emphasis on race, gender, social class, and age.

TABLE 9.2

Percentage of Persons Arrested for Index Crimes By Age, Race, and Gender, 2000

By Age	under 18	18–24	25–44	45–54	55–64	65+
Murder	10.8	42.0	39.4	6.3	1.8	1.1
Forcible Rape	16.4	29.0	44.5	7.0	2.0	0.9
Robbery	25.2	37.6	33.5	3.0	0.4	0.1
Aggravated Assault	13.8	26.0	43.1	8.0	2.0	0.8
Burglary	33.0	30.7	31.7	3.6	0.5	0.2
Larceny-Theft	31.1	25.7	37.7	6.2	1.4	0.7
Auto Theft	34.2	32.2	30.2	2.7	0.4	0.1
Percent of total population	25.7	10.4	30.2	13.4	8.6	12.4

By Gender	male	female
Murder	89.4	10.6
Forcible Rape	98.9	1.1
Robbery	89.9	10.1
Aggravated Assault	79.9	20.1
Burglary	86.7	13.3
Larceny-Theft	64.1	35.9
Auto Theft	84.9	15.1
Percent of total population	48.9	51.1

By Race	white	black	other
Murder	48.7	48.8	2.5
Forcible Rape	63.7	34.1	2.2
Robbery	44.2	53.9	1.9
Aggravated Assault	63.5	34.0	2.5
Burglary	69.4	28.4	2.2
Larceny-Theft	66.7	30.4	2.0
Auto Theft	55.4	41.6	3.0
Percent of total population	82.2	12.8	5.0

Source: Federal Bureau of Investigation (2001). *Crime in the United States, 2000;* and U.S. Census Bureau (2001). Statistical Abstract.

Who Are the Offenders?

Table 9.2 presents UCR data on the age, gender, and race of persons arrested for index crimes. It is apparent that offenders are predominantly young males and that minorities are heavily overrepresented. The UCR does not collect information on social class, but a walk through any prison will confirm that most inmates are drawn from the bottom of the economic ladder.

RACE Probably the single most prominent element in the popular stereotype of street criminals concerns race: Many Americans, regardless of their own race, tend to visualize criminals as minorities, particularly African Americans. Both UCR and victimization data lend some support to this stereotype. As Table 9.2 suggests, although only 12.8 percent of the U.S. population is African American, 28 percent of all persons arrested for index crimes in 2000 were blacks. In the

same year, 48.8 percent of those arrested for murder and 53.9 percent of those arrested for robbery were African Americans. Latinos, who make up about 13 percent of the population, are apprehended for 10 to 15 percent of all serious violent crimes.

To a considerable extent, the high African American crime rate reflects the great number of blacks in the poorer classes, whose members are, as we have just indicated, particularly likely to be apprehended by the criminal justice system (Sampson, 1987; Hagan, 1994). But poverty among African Americans is especially strongly associated with crime, principally because black poverty tends to be more severe than it is among other segments of the population. There are several reasons for this:

• The declining availability of low-skill, decent-paying jobs, a problem throughout the United States but a particularly severe one for minorities

DIVERSITY IN FOCUS

A Generation Behind Bars

The expanding racial and ethnic diversity of the United States is apparent throughout society, but perhaps nowhere more than in the nation's jails and prisons. Minorities, especially African Americans, are greatly—and increasingly—overrepresented in the criminal justice system.

Some specifics: Blacks, who make up just under 13 percent of the total population of the United States, constitute 46 percent of all prison inmates. Eighteen percent of all prisoners and about 13 percent of the general population are Latino. In contrast, whites account for 71 percent of the population but only one-third of all prisoners. For males in the age range 20 to 29, 1 out of every 16 whites, 1 out of every 8 Latinos, and 1 out of every 3 African Americans is in jail, in prison, on probation, or on parole.

In the juvenile system, African American youths without prior records are six times more likely to be incarcerated than white youths who also lack a previous criminal history and have committed similar crimes. A young African American male currently faces a 28 percent likelihood of being imprisoned at some time in his life. The estimated cost of confining African American inmates in jails and prisons is currently $11 billion per year. Furthermore, the number of blacks who have been in trouble with the law has been growing rapidly: If the current rate of increase were

to continue, by 2020 two-thirds of all young black men would be under some form of correctional supervision.

If we ask why poor black men are being imprisoned at such a high rate, we will find a number of contributing factors. While there is no doubt that this population does commit an unusually large percentage of the more serious and violent crimes for reasons discussed elsewhere in this chapter, this is not enough to adequately explain the huge numbers of African American prisoners.

For one thing, the war on drugs has clearly targeted minority populations. Twenty-eight percent of African American inmates have been sentenced for violent crimes and 38 percent for drug offenses, mostly nonviolent. While research shows that far more drug users are white than African American, and also that on the average whites are more likely to use illegal drugs than blacks, African Americans make up 79 percent of all drug offenders in state prisons. Nationally, black men are 13 times more likely then whites to be sent to state prisons for drug offenses; in Maryland the ratio is 28 to one.

Second, because of their generally higher rate of offending, African Americans have been differentially impacted by mandatory sentencing laws. In California, for example, where they make up only 7 percent of the population, blacks constitute 43 percent of those sentenced under "three strikes and you're out" statutes.

Significantly, 83 percent of all three-strikes felons are nonviolent offenders.

Finally, a certain amount of the difference must be explained by simple bias. A study by Alfred Blumenstein found that 24 percent of the sentencing disparity between African Americans and whites could not be explained by severity of offense or prior record. Race appears to be a particularly important biasing factor for drug offenses.

Many sociologists fear that our imprisonment binge has doomed an entire generation of poor young African American men to a marginal existence. The effects of poverty, low levels of education, and racial discrimination combined with the lingering stigma of prison will make it extremely difficult for millions of African American men to ever find a secure place for themselves in the world. Already, there are eight states in which at least one-quarter of all adult black males have lost the right to vote as a result of felony convictions; nationally, 13 percent are barred from voting.

1. How could the criminal justice system be altered in order to eliminate or at least reduce current racial disparities?

2. Should convicted felons be punished by permanently losing the right to vote, or would allowing them to regain this privilege help to reintegrate them into society?

Sources: Blumstein, 1993; National Criminal Justice Association, 1996; Mauer, 1999; Finley & Schinder, 1999; Baum, 2000; Human Rights Watch, 2000; Gullo, 2001.

who still sometimes experience racist discrimination.

- The large numbers of single-parent, female-headed families in poor African American communities—largely due in turn to the lack of decent jobs that would allow young men to support their families (Wilson, 1987). These single-parent families are less able to supervise their chil-

dren or to provide positive male role models for them. Furthermore, single-parent families are very likely to fall below the poverty line, especially if headed by a female.

- The out-migration of nearly all working- and middle-class African Americans from the highly segregated inner-city neighborhoods where crime is at its worst (see Chapter 12). This exodus of individuals who have achieved success legitimately means that youth growing up in these neighborhoods may see crime, especially drug dealing, as the only viable route out of poverty. As Sutherland's differential association theory would predict (see Chapter 8), when there is nobody to hang out with except criminals, crime becomes normative.

These factors work in concert to intensify poverty and promote crime. Furthermore, although some sociologists deny that the criminal justice system is biased against minorities (Wilbanks, 1987), substantial evidence suggests that, above and beyond issues of class, the system stacks the deck against persons of color (Tonry, 1995). Research shows, for example, that African American youth are more likely to be arrested than whites for the same crime (Krisberg et al., 1987). Young African Americans are also between 5 and 13 times more likely than whites to be killed by the police on the street (Brown, 1993). African American youth are also more likely than whites to be tried as adults (Mauer, 1994; Free, 1996).

While some studies have found that race has no effect on sentencing (Dannefer & Schutt, 1982; Miethe & Moore, 1986), others show clear evidence of bias, especially in the case of juveniles (Tonry, 1995). Furthermore, research confirms that even if sentences do not differ substantially by race, African Americans actually end up serving more time for the same crimes (Huizinga & Elliott, 1987; Klein et al., 1988; Bridges & Crutchfield, 1988). African Americans are also disproportionately likely to be sentenced to—and to receive—the death penalty.

Most studies conclude that racial bias in the criminal justice system has probably diminished in recent decades and that most of the reason for the large number of minorities in the courts and prisons is due to their greater criminality (Balkwell, 1990). At the same time, some bias persists, at least at some times and in some places. Worse, perhaps, many minorities perceive the system to be unfair, a view that can easily become a self-fulfilling prophecy.

AGE   With the exception of white-collar offenders, most criminals are young people, often only a few years past childhood. In 2000, 33 percent of all arrests for burglary, 25 percent of those for robbery, and 31 percent of those for larceny-theft were of persons under 18. These figures are congruent with a point made earlier in this chapter, that the surge in crime between 1960 and 1975 occurred largely because the enormous baby boom generation was passing through

its teenage and young adult years. In fact, the generalization that most criminals are young appears to be broadly true in all historical eras and societies (Hirschi & Gottfredson, 1983; Land et al., 1990). Why should this be so?

The vigor and physical strength associated with youth is doubtless one factor, especially with regard to index street crime. However, two sociological theories introduced in Chapter 8 also help to explain this pattern. One is Travis Hirschi's control theory of deviance. Hirschi believed criminal impulses are restrained by an individual's social bonds. These bonds are typically weaker for teenagers than for adults. Adolescents often seek to establish their independence from their parents; normally lack the obligations associated with having spouses or children; often do not realistically consider that they may be caught and stigmatized as criminals; and tend to have plenty of spare time. In short, they are much less restrained than adults and are correspondingly more likely to gravitate toward crime.

Edwin Sutherland's differential association theory provides further insight into why most criminals are young. Sutherland emphasizes the importance of significant others' attitudes toward crime in shaping our own feelings and behaviors. In line with their desire to break away from their parents, teenagers often spend a great deal of time in the company of their peers; they also care deeply about what their friends think of them. But peers frequently propel youths toward deviance (Agnew & Petersen, 1989).

The significance of age is underscored by the fact that crime declines sharply after the mid-30s, a phenomenon known as **aging-out** (Hirschi & Gottfredson, 1983; Wilson & Herrnstein, 1985). Only 3.5 percent of all robbers, 4.3 percent of burglars, and 3.2 percent of auto thieves arrested in 2000 were over 44. As people acquire adult responsibilities, spend more time with their families and less with peers, and obtain the means to get what they want legitimately, they are less likely to turn to crime.

GENDER   Most crime is committed by male perpetrators. This generalization applies to all major crimes except prostitution. Males constituted 99 percent of all rapists, 89 percent of all murderers, and 90 percent of all robbers arrested in 2000. As with the tendency for criminals to be young, this overrepresentation of males is apparent worldwide (Heidensohn, 1991).

Most females who *are* criminals are guilty of relatively minor crimes. For example, women who commit larceny-theft, the only index crime with substantial female involvement, are mostly small-time

While women continue to be substantially less likely than men to commit virtually every crime other than prostitution and shoplifting, the rate at which women offend has been rising much faster than the equivalent rate for men. The women shown here are inmates at a prison in Russia.

shoplifters. Female crime rates are gradually rising, but they remain much lower than male rates, and women's crimes continue to be primarily nonviolent (Pollock, 1999).

How do we account for women's lesser involvement in crime? Early explanations emphasized what were believed to be innate psychological and biological differences between the sexes. These theories have generally been abandoned for lack of empirical support (Klein, 1995), although men's larger physical size and higher levels of testosterone may well contribute to their overrepresentation in violent crime.

Sociological explanations for women's lower crime rates are more compelling. Traditional female gender role socialization, as discussed in Chapter 5, emphasizes conformity and passivity while discouraging aggressiveness. Drawing again on the work of Hirschi and Sutherland, women tend to be more tightly bonded to parents and less involved in potentially delinquent peer groups (Hagan et al., 1985). They also may have more to lose if they acquire a criminal identity: Our culture considers criminality more compatible with the male role, so female criminals are particularly likely to be viewed as seriously deviant.

Feminist theorists have emphasized the importance of studying how gender influences criminality, because women very rarely become involved in serious crime (Naffine, 1996). Can we learn something from this that can be applied to both men and women? Feminists also maintain that the success of rehabilitation-oriented women's facilities such as the

Mutter-Kind-Heim may indicate some ways in which the U.S. system might be improved.

It has also been suggested that women, particularly white, working- and middle-class minor offenders, historically were treated gently by the courts because of their gender, a view known as the **chivalry hypothesis** (Feinman, 1994). However, recent sharp increases in the number of incarcerated females suggest that this hypothesis is no longer valid (if indeed it ever was). These increases may in part reflect the criminal justice system's acceptance of the feminist movement's demand for equal treatment. But they are also the result of new mandatory sentencing laws for repeat offenses and drug-related crimes.

SOCIAL CLASS Research strongly supports the popular image of criminals as not only young and male but also disproportionately poor (Braithwaite, 1981; Wolfgang et al., 1987; Hsieh & Pugh, 1993). Such findings fit well with Robert Merton's anomie theory of deviance (see Chapter 8). Like everyone else, members of the lower classes desire material success. But, opportunities to achieve success goals are often blocked, and some people respond to a blocked opportunity structure by innovation—adopting alternative, illegitimate, and often criminal ways of obtaining desired goals.

In support of this notion, a good deal of research suggests that when employment declines, crime usually—but not always—rises (Carlson & Michaloski, 1997). While most poor people remain basically honest, a substantial percentage are drawn to crime, and

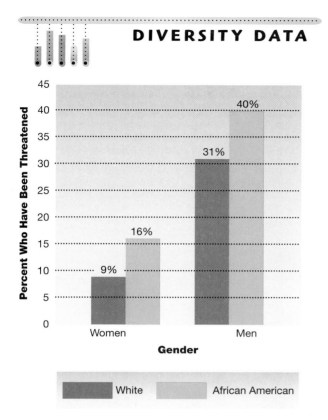

DIVERSITY DATA

FIGURE 9.5 **Percent Who Have Been Threatened by a Gun, by Gender and Race.** In general, men are much more likely than women to have been threatened with firearm violence, but African Americans of either gender are at greater risk than their white counterparts. Why do women generally report greater fear of violent crime despite the fact that they are at less risk of experiencing it?

Source: NORC. General Social Surveys, 1972–2000. Chicago: National Opinion Research Center, 2000. Reprinted by permission of NORC, Chicago, Il.

many of these people show up in the UCR. The class–crime connection is particularly obvious among adults: While youth of all classes commit some acts of minor delinquency, class differences in official criminality are pronounced among people over 18.

If we broaden our inquiry into the relationship between class and crime, the situation becomes more complex. Self-report studies show that serious street crimes are indeed concentrated among the poor, but as we have already discussed, lawbreaking occurs much more frequently among the privileged classes than UCR data suggest. In fact, there may be very little overall correlation between class and criminality

(Hirschi, 1969; Tittle et al., 1978; Tittle & Meier, 1990). Some researchers have even suggested that crime may be more common among the elite (Reiman, 1995).

In part, the disagreement over the extent of criminality in different classes reflects the use of different definitions of crime by different observers. Scholars who ignore the UCR's bias toward street crimes come up with strikingly different conclusions than do those who also take into account violations of trust, such as embezzlement, price fixing, environmental crime, and the manufacture of substandard or hazardous products (Williams & Drake, 1990). Thus, if we broaden our working definition of crime, we find criminals at all class levels, although members of different classes commit quite different crimes. But even if we focus primarily on traditional predatory crimes, there is good reason to believe that the criminal justice system is more likely to apprehend and process the poor (Chambliss, 1969; Forer, 1984; C. E. Smith, 1991).

Who Are the Victims?

Historically, criminologists have focused their attention almost exclusively on offenders. But the last 25 years have seen the birth of **victimology,** a subfield of criminology devoted to the study of the victims of crime (Karmen, 1995). NCVS data, as summarized in Table 9.3 on page 242, allow us to compare the demographic characteristics of crime victims with those of offenders for selected crimes, as reported in Table 9.2. (Note that homicide is not included in Table 9.3, as it cannot be studied using the methodology of the NCVS).

The similarity between these two populations is striking: Both victims and offenders are predominantly young, lower-income males, with minorities strongly overrepresented. The similarities are greatest for violent personal crimes, which is not surprising, since most homicides and many rapes and assaults grow out of ongoing relationships, and since most people associate primarily with people much like themselves. It is less obvious, and certainly ironic, that victims of property crime frequently turn out to be as disadvantaged as the people who prey upon them. Robbers, thieves, and burglars tend to find it easier to victimize people who live near them, which generally means in poor neighborhoods. Wealthy people may have more property, but they also have a much greater ability to safeguard their possessions.

Crime victimization figures strongly illustrate the combined effects of minority status, poverty, and gender. For example, African American men experience an exceptionally high risk of homicide—six to eight times that of young white men. Young African Ameri-

TABLE 9.3

Victimization Rates per 1,000 People by Age, Race, Gender, and Household Income for Selected Crimes, 2000

By Age	12–15	16–19	20–24	25–34	35–49	50–64	65+
Rape	2.1	4.3	2.1	1.3	0.8	0.4	0.1
Robbery	4.2	7.3	6.2	3.9	2.7	2.1	.7
Aggravated Assault	9.9	14.3	10.9	6.8	4.7	2.8	0.9

By Gender	male	female
Rape	0.1	2.1
Robbery	4.5	2.0
Aggravated Assault	8.3	3.2

By Race	white	black	other
Rape	1.1	1.2	1.1
Robbery	2.7	7.2	2.8
Aggravated Assault	5.4	7.7	5.2
Burglary*	29.4	47.6	32.4
Theft*	136.0	151.4	128.6
Auto Theft	7.9	13.2	10.4

By Household Income	less than $7500	$7500–14,999	$15k–24,999	$25k–34,999	$35k–49,999	$50k–74,999	over $75,000
Rape	5.2	1.7	1.4	1.9	0.8	1.0	0.2
Robbery	7.1	4.7	3.2	4.2	2.3	3.6	2.0
Aggravated Assault	14.7	9.5	6.1	6.2	6.2	3.8	4.4
Burglary*	61.7	41.1	39.3	33.3	32.0	24.0	27.7
Theft*	151.2	116.8	143.8	149.4	151.4	147.9	167.5
Auto Theft*	7.9	9.1	9.9	9.5	9.6	10.0	7.0

*per 1000 households.
Source: U.S. Bureau of Justice Statistics (2001). *Criminal Victimization, 2000*. Tables 2, 3, and 6.

Victims' assistance programs have expanded dramatically over the past 20 years. Here a counselor helps prepare a crime victim to testify in court.

can women are between three and four times as likely to be murdered as are their white counterparts (Karmen, 1996). And while female victimization rates remain well below those of males for all index crimes except rape and some types of larceny-theft, their fear of crime is much greater (Kennedy & Sacco, 1998). In part, this is due to their greater physical vulnerability, but it may also reflect the fact that the patriarchal logic of the criminal justice system has tended to deemphasize the seriousness of domestic violence, a crime that disproportionately impacts women.

SOCIETY CONNECTIONS

Capital Punishment and the Decriminalization of Drugs

Of all the subfields of sociology, criminology is probably the most strongly oriented toward finding practical solutions to social problems. Two of the most intensely debated crime-control issues concern capital punishment and the decriminalization of drugs.

Capital Punishment

The continued popularity of the death penalty among the majority of the citizens of the United States stands in stark contrast to the views of the people of virtually every other modern Western nation in which capital punishment has either been abolished outright or is, in practice, never used (Wood, 1996). The only nations that currently execute more offenders than the United States are China, Iran, Saudi Arabia, and the Congo. International criticism of the United States has been particularly intense regarding this nation's willingness to execute people who are mentally retarded or who committed their crimes as juveniles.

Most of this concern is expressed in moral terms, but from a social science perspective, the most important issue is whether the death penalty is an effective deterrent. The evidence is mixed. Some research does support a deterrent effect, especially immediately after widely publicized executions (Phillips, 1980; Stack, 1990). But the clear majority of the evidence leads to the opposite conclusion (Schonenbaum, 1998). States with the death penalty tend to have higher murder rates. Furthermore, internationally, the abolition of capital punishment has generally been followed by a drop in homicide rates (Archer & Gartner, 1984).

Why does capital punishment apparently fail to deter? In part, it may be because most murders are crimes of passion and the offender is not thinking ra-

tionally. Furthermore, the death penalty is neither swift—it commonly takes at least 10 years to exhaust a prisoner's appeals—nor certain—if we execute 100 murderers annually, then the odds of any particular offender actually being killed are about 250 to one.

There are several arguments in favor of the death penalty. It certainly provides both incapacitation and retribution. Relatives of homicide victims frequently, but not always, report a sense of relief after an execution. Capital punishment is also supported by public opinion, never irrelevant in a democratic society.

On the other hand, in addition to the weak evidence for deterrence, there are other problems with the death penalty. It is irreversible, and as discussed in the *Then and Now* box on page 244, in the 20th century alone, about 400 Americans were sentenced to death and at least 18 executed who were later found to be innocent (Radelet & Bedau, 1992). Furthermore, it is actually more expensive to provide full rights to appeal a capital conviction than it is to keep an offender locked up for a lifetime.

Finally, evidence of class and racial bias continues to be a concern. Between 1977 and 1997, 37.5 percent of all executed offenders were African Americans. Of those convicts on death row in 2000, 42.7 percent were African American and 55.4 percent were white (Sness, 2000). However, research suggests that the key variable is not so much the race of the offender as the race of victim: People who kill whites are 4.3 times more likely to be executed than those who kill African Americans (Jackson, 1996; Cole, 1999). However, on numerous instances the current Supreme Court has refused to consider such statistical evidence as proof of injustice (Joseph, 1996)

Drug Decriminalization

The war on drugs has had a major impact on the criminal justice system. Court dockets and prisons are overflowing with drug cases. About 57 percent of all federal prisoners and 22 percent of the inmates in state prisons—a total of over 251,000 people—are classified as drug offenders, most of them nonviolent. Arrests of adults for the sale and possession of illegal drugs doubled in the late 1980s and early 1990s, even though drug use was declining (U.S. Bureau of Justice Statistics, 2000).

People who question the wisdom of using the criminal justice system to attempt to reduce drug use offer Prohibition as an example of the ineffectiveness of this strategy. Outlawing alcohol apparently did somewhat reduce consumption, since cirrhosis of the liver declined during the 1920s (Goode, 1989). But Prohibition did not end alcohol use in this country, and it ate up a tremendous amount of the time and resources of the criminal justice system (Musto, 1987).

THEN AND NOW

Changing Views on Capital Punishment

The death penalty has been used in this country since colonial days. A total of 3,859 prisoners were executed between 1930 and 1966 alone. However, increasing concern over both the morality of capital punishment and its effectiveness as a deterrent led to a marked decline in its popularity in the years after World War II. Opinion polls showed that just 42 percent of the public backed the death penalty in 1966.

In 1972, the Supreme Court voted 5–4 in the case of *Furman v. Georgia* that capital punishment as it was being applied was both cruel and unusual. The Court's rationale was heavily based on sociological research that showed African Americans were disproportionately likely to be given the death penalty. For example, between 1945 and 1965, 13 percent of blacks but only 2 percent of whites convicted of rape were sentenced to die. This ruling voided capital punishment in 39 states and permanently blocked the execution of over 600 convicts, including Sirhan Sirhan and Charles Manson.

After *Furman,* most states rewrote their capital punishment statutes to increase the court's ability to take aggravating or mitigating circumstances into account. In 1976, the Supreme Court determined in *Gregg v. Georgia* that these rewritten laws passed constitutional muster. Over the next two decades, fueled by a rising crime rate, public opinion swung sharply in favor of the death penalty. As of the beginning of 2000, 38 states had reinstated capital punishment, 632 people had been exe-

cuted (214 in Texas alone), and 3,652 inmates were housed on death rows around the country.

However, between 1976 and early 2000, 87 condemned inmates were released from prison because it was determined that they did not commit the crimes of which they had been convicted. How many other convicts awaiting execution are innocent? No one knows, but research making use of advances in forensic science (especially DNA tests) suggests that there may be quite a few more.

For example, in 1988, Dennis Fritz and Ronald Williamson were convicted of the brutal rape and murder of a 21-year-old barmaid in a small town in Oklahoma. Fritz was sentenced to life imprisonment and Williamson received the death penalty. Scientific evidence helped to convict them: Experts testified that body hair and semen found on the victim could only have come from these men. However, in April 1999, both were exonerated on the basis of DNA tests that were not available at the time of their trial.

Why have so many people been wrongfully condemned to death? The main reason appears to lie within the legal system itself. Most people accused of capital crimes cannot afford to hire their own lawyer, much less a "defense team." The states that rarely hand down death sentences, such as New Jersey and New Hampshire, have strong public defenders' offices with sufficient financial resources to attract experienced lawyers and to allow them to follow a case from the initial trial through appeals and even up to the Supreme Court. And two-thirds

of the 4,578 capital cases that were appealed between 1973 and 1995 were overturned.

In states such as Texas and Alabama, public defense is not coordinated or funded at the state level; instead, a county judge appoints a lawyer who is paid according to a fixed scale that does not cover federal appeals. As a result, accused murderers often are represented by inexperienced lawyers who lack the resources and incentive to mount a vigorous defense. Whether verdicts are rechecked and new evidence is uncovered is largely a matter of luck.

Public opinion is beginning to shift once again in response to such concerns. Once backed by as much as 80 percent of the public, capital punishment today is favored by a two to one margin. Significantly, in January 2000, Illinois Governor George Ryan suspended all executions in his state pending a careful reappraisal of the procedures by which the death penalty is applied.

1. Why do you think the United States is the only remaining postmodern nation that retains the death penalty?

2. If you support capital punishment, would you be willing to abandon it if convicted murderers could be sentenced to life imprisonment with absolutely no chance of parole? Similarly, if you oppose the death penalty, would you change your opinion if evidence emerged that proved that it really was an effective deterrent?

Sources: Wolfgang & Reidel, 1973; Johnson, 1990; Bell, 1992; Snell, 1996; McCormick, 1998, 1999; Dedman, 1999; Alter, 2000; Alter & Miller, 2000.

People on both sides of the capital punishment debate often express their feelings with great passion. Currently, a sizable majority of Americans support the death penalty, and the number of executions is rising each year.

The current antidrug crusade faces similar criticisms. For example, between 1985 and 1988, despite the fact that federal antidrug expenditures tripled, cocaine use is believed to have increased by over 30 percent (Vacon, 1990). More recently, despite 25 years of Just Say No programs, adolescent drug use increased in the late 1990s (Johnson, et al., 1997).

No one disputes the desirability of reducing drug abuse. The question is whether the criminal law is the best means of achieving this end. One alternative is **decriminalization,** a policy whereby currently illegal drugs would be treated much as alcohol and tobacco are now: prohibited to children but available to adults under certain conditions. Decriminalization is based on reducing *demand*, not cutting off *supplies*. Under this policy, much of the money currently used by the criminal justice system for the "war against drugs" would go to expanding educational and therapeutic programs, an approach which has been found to be seven times more cost-effective in reducing drug use than law enforcement strategies (Rydell & Everingham, 1994).

Does decriminalization make sense? In discussing this issue, it is important to focus on the positive and negative consequences of the law rather than on the negatives of the drug. The issue is not whether drugs are harmful—they are. It is whether decriminalization is a rational way of trying to reduce drug use.

Opponents of decriminalization argue that existing laws reduce drug use even if they do not come close to ending it (Goode, 1997). Decriminalization, they claim, would open the floodgates to an unprecedented increase in addiction because drugs would be cheaper and easier to obtain and because drug use would be less stigmatizing. It would send precisely the wrong moral message, especially to impressionable youth.

Supporters of decriminalization doubt that drug use would sharply increase if the laws were changed

(Baum, 1996; Rosenberger, 1996). They point to the example of Denmark, which decriminalized pornography and saw usage decline (Little, 1995: 49). Certainly, most people who currently wish to purchase drugs are able to obtain them easily enough. And the simple fact that drugs are illegal makes them "forbidden fruit" and thus even more attractive to some youth.

Decriminalization would greatly reduce the amount of police time devoted to trying to track down drug sellers and users, leaving the criminal justice system far more able to deal with predatory crime. It would come close to eliminating police corruption, which almost always occurs in the context of victimless crime laws. It would have the potential of dealing a death blow to organized crime, since the current laws create what amounts to an operating subsidy for the syndicates. The end of Prohibition led to dramatically reduced profits for the Mafia. Decriminalization would also cut down on theft to obtain money to buy drugs. If sales of drugs were taxed, those revenues could be used to fight abuse. Decriminalization would also save the lives of users who buy impure drugs or share needles, thereby risking AIDS and other serious diseases.

The key question is how much use would increase if drugs were decriminalized. If the upswing were moderate, then the advantages would seem to outweigh the costs; on the other hand, this country certainly cannot afford to triple or quadruple its drug-dependent population. We won't know which side of this debate is right and which is wrong any time in the near future, since only about 15 percent of the public currently approves of across-the-board decriminalization.

SUMMARY

1. The legalistic approach defines crime as any violation of a law enacted by a legitimate government. In contrast, the natural law approach sees crime as a violation of an absolute principle.

2. Most sociologists rely on information from the Uniform Crime Reports (UCR) or from the National Crime Victimization Survey (NCVS), although both sources have serious weaknesses.

3. Street crime has been declining in the United States since the early 1990s although this trend apparently ended in 2000. Demographic changes and sharp increases in imprisonment help explain this trend.

4. Rates of violent crime are much higher in the United States than in other developed countries, especially Japan.

5. Homicides typically occur between people who know each other, often arising out of ongoing conflicts.

6. Organized crime consists of large-scale and highly structured gangs or syndicates that routinely use corruption and violence to maximize their profits. It is often a means by which immigrants and minorities can succeed when legal opportunities are blocked.

7. The four major types of corporate crime are financial offenses, maintaining hazardous working conditions, manufacturing unsafe products, and environmental crimes.

8. Victimless crimes, created when the law attempts to prohibit the exchange between willing adults of strongly desired goods and services, are extremely difficult to control.

9. Many nations, including the United States, are currently experimenting with community policing.

10. The United States follows the common law tradition in which numerous cases accumulate to form a coherent set of legal principles based on precedent. Most other societies embrace civil law or religious law traditions.

11. Courts in the United States operate according to the adversarial principle, but in practice most cases are plea bargained. In contrast, many European societies use the inquisitorial model.

12. Punishment is based on one or more of four rationales: retribution, deterrence, rehabilitation, or incapacitation.

13. The U.S. prison system has become enormously overcrowded over the past decade.

14. Societies must choose an appropriate balance between short-run solutions to crime and long-run solutions that address crime's underlying causes.

15. Persons who commit major street crimes tend to be young, lower-class males; a disproportionate number are members of minority groups. Most victims of street crimes come from the same demographic categories as the offenders.

16. The United States is virtually alone among the highly developed nations in using capital punishment.

17. Many sociologists believe that the decriminalization of drug use would allow the criminal justice system to concentrate its energies and resources on more serious crimes.

KEY TERMS

adversarial principle 232
aging-out 239
chivalry hypothesis 240
civil law 232
common law 232
corporate crime 229

decriminalization 245
general deterrence 233
index crimes 223
inquisitorial principle 232
occupational crime 229
organized crime 228

plea bargaining 233
religious law 232
specific deterrence 233
victimless crime 220
victimology 241
white-collar crime 229

CRITICAL THINKING QUESTIONS

1. How do you think the United States should balance the public's pressure for short-term solutions to the crime problem with the need to address the underlying causes of crime?

2. How much emphasis do you think the criminal justice system ought to put on each of the four possible rationales for punishment: retribution, deterrence, rehabilitation, and incapacitation?

3. Can you think of factors other than those mentioned in this chapter that help explain why the U.S. crime rate is so high?

4. Are the policy debates about the death penalty and the decriminalization of drugs primarily moral or practical?

INVESTIGATE WITH CONTENT SELECT

 Begin your research using Content-Select for this chapter by following the directions found on page 27 of this text to visit Prentice Hall's Research Navigator Website. Enter these search terms into the search field:

Capital punishment
Rehabilitation
Organized crime

iNTERSECTIONS

EXERCISE 2. SATISFACTION WITH FRIENDS

Outside family, our most important relationships are with friends. They are among the strongest influences on our thinking and behavior, far more than professors or television. For most of us at any given time, the quality of our friendships is one of the primary reasons we are happy or depressed.

Respondents in the General Social Surveys were asked how much satisfaction they got from their friendships. Here answers are collapsed into two categories, either "a very great deal," or less than a very great deal. Thirty percent of respondents reported a very great deal of satisfaction from their friends, leaving 70 percent reporting less satisfaction.

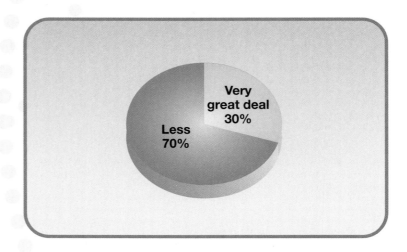

To further analyze satisfaction with friends, go to the Companion Website for this text at http://www.prenhall.com/lindsey, and select this exercise from the drop-down menu at the top.

Do you think men are more or less satisfied with their friends than women are? See if you are correct by comparing the satisfaction level among men and women. Recall from Exercise 1 that the computer program CHIP will do this for you if you select Gender as its Column Variable. (Make sure CHIP is set for % Down, and its Row Variable is Satfrnd.)

In interpreting the difference in views between men and women, remember these percentages are based on random samples. Any randomly drawn sample will differ somewhat from any other randomly drawn sample (this is called "sampling error"). In the GSS sample, 32.7 percent of women reported a very great deal of satisfaction with their friendships, but if we had another random sample of American women, the corresponding number might be, say, 29.9 percent, and in a third sample it might be, say, 33.8 percent. Therefore we shouldn't regard any percentage from a sample as *exactly* representing the population from which the sample is drawn. These percentages are only approximations.

If the percentage of men and the percentage of women who are very satisfied with their friendships are approximations for the U.S. population, then we shouldn't take seriously a small difference between them. (Make sure you understand this.) Only if the difference were sizable would we regard women and men as having different views about their friendships. But how big is "sizable"? Recall from Exercise 1 the "10 percent rule": *A difference less than 10 percent is too small to be important, while a difference of 10 percent or larger should be taken seriously.* Here the difference between women and men is 32.7 percent − 26.8 percent = 5.9 percent. Since this is less than 10 percent, experienced analysts would say gender makes little if any difference in satisfaction with friendships.

Do you expect any racial difference in satisfaction with friends? If so, whom do you think reports higher satisfaction, white or black respondents? Check the difference, using Race as the Column Variable. Is it more or less than you expected?

Do younger people report higher or lower satisfaction with friends than older people do? Here the GSS respondents are divided into three age categories: young, middle age, and older.

Finally, see if there is any social class difference in satisfaction with friends. Respondents were asked to place themselves in one of four social classes: lower class, working class, middle class, or upper class. Do people who give themselves different class labels also differ in their evaluation of satisfying friendships?

Write a brief summary of your findings. Try to explain the differences you found. Did you expect these differences, or are they surprising?

10
ECONOMIC STRATIFICATION

Clothing and Class

People who think that social class is unimportant should study the history of fashion. Many cultures have used clothing style as a highly visible symbol of class position because we need to be able to identify someone's class on sight in order to know how to interact with that individual.

For example, in many traditional cultures, low-ranking commoners typically wore little more than loincloths, while aristocrats and members of the royal family favored much more extensive and elaborate garb. Laws commonly restricted certain clothing styles to the higher classes and prescribed substantial punishments for people who dressed inappropriately for their station.

Similarly, for centuries wealthy Europeans publicly identified themselves as such by wearing clothes made of damasked satins, patterned brocades, and handwoven velvets—expensive fabrics that the middle or lower classes could never afford to purchase. Today, inexpensive copies of designer clothes are readily available in any Wal-Mart. In response, many manufacturers prominently display their "elite" brand name labels on the outside of their clothing rather than hiding them inside. You may enjoy knowing that you're wearing Nike athletic shoes and a Tommy Hilfiger sweater—but it's *essential* that everyone else knows that you're wearing them! (Lurie, 1981)

The Time Machine

One of H. G. Wells's best known novels is entitled *The Time Machine.* On one level it is a simple science fiction story, but on another, it is a cautionary tale about the widening of class inequality in late 19th century England (Wells, 1969). In the novel, a time traveler finds himself in a future populated by two cultures: the beautiful, delicate Eloi, who live on the surface of the Earth, and the brutish Morlocks, who

dwell in subterranean caverns. At first the traveler cannot imagine how this arrangement could have come about, but when he observes that the Morlocks do all the work to support both communities, he realizes that the explanation lies in

> . . . the gradual widening of the present . . . difference of the capitalist from the laborer. . . . The exclusive tendency of richer people . . . is already leading to the closing of considerable portions of the surface of the country against these latter. . . . So, in the end, you would have above ground the Haves, pursuing health, comfort and beauty, and below ground the Have-nots, the workers. . . . (Wells, 1969:55–56)

The Morlocks, denied the opportunity to live in the sunlight, regularly kidnap and consume the Eloi—a uniquely vivid expression of class hostility!

These two brief accounts demonstrate the significance of **social stratification,** the division of a large group or society into ranked categories of people, each of which enjoys different levels of access to scarce and valued resources, chiefly property, prestige, and power.

Social stratification may be based on any number of different social statuses. The most important of these are economic status (income, wealth, and property), gender, race or ethnicity, and age. The study of stratification is an investigation into the social factors determining who gets what, when, and why (Lenski, 1966). Sociologists who are interested in this topic attempt to explain questions such as why elites enjoy so many privileges—including luxurious clothes—that are not available to the rest of us. Why are some people Morlocks and others Eloi?

Social stratification is sometimes called *structured social inequality* in order to emphasize the important point that the rewards allocated to occupants of different statuses are *built into* society. That is, they are supported by widely accepted norms and values, and

251

they endure from generation to generation. By and large, stratification has surprisingly little to do with individual differences in ability. High-ranking persons, even those lacking outstanding intelligence or ability, generally find it far easier to obtain property, prestige, and power than do even the most capable individuals who hold lower ranking statuses.

Let's look a little more closely at the main types of stratification. *Gender* and *age stratification* are cultural universals (Rossides, 1990; Nolan & Lenski, 1999). In every known society, men and women and people in different age categories—at a minimum, children, adults, and the elderly—have different levels of access to scarce and valued resources. We will discuss gender and age inequalities in Chapters 13 and 14, respectively.

We may be particularly aware of *racial and ethnic stratification* in the United States because of the unusual diversity of our society. This form of social stratification—widespread in the modern world but uncommon in earlier eras when people were less geographically mobile—is the subject of Chapter 12.

This chapter and the next are devoted to the topic of *economic stratification*, which involves the division of society into two or more social classes. A **social class** may be defined as a category of people who share a common position in a vertical hierarchy of differential economic reward. This chapter concentrates on theories of economic stratification. Chapter 11 discusses the class structure of postindustrial societies such as the United States.

This chapter also overviews **global stratification,** the division of the nations of the world into richer and poorer categories. Just as the people in any particular society belong to wealthier and less-advantaged social classes, countries may be ranked by their differential access to valued resources.

LEGITIMATING STRATIFICATION

One of the first questions that arises in the study of social stratification is, Why does structured inequality persist? Many—usually most—people in society do not seem to benefit very much from it. There are tens of millions of children, elderly people, and racial and ethnic minorities in the United States; most people are female and middle, working, or lower class. Yet society continues to be structured in a way that confers substantial advantages on males, whites, adults, and members of the upper class.

The elite in most societies do not maintain their position through force. While the upper classes do occasionally resort to the military to protect their privilege, it is generally as a last resort and extremely costly. A far more efficient method is to convince lower ranking people that their lack of rewards is just and proper. This is the role of ideology.

Ideology

An *ideology*, in this context, is a belief that legitimates existing patterns of structured social inequality (Lipset, 1963; Marger, 2002). It is easy to see why elites would accept ideology, but why would other members of society do so?

The answer is that the groups at the top of stratification systems generally enjoy a tremendous ability to shape how people think, an ability called *ideological hegemony* (Gramsci, 1959; Robertson, 1988; Abercrombie et al., 1990). People are socialized—in school, in church, by the media, and by their parents—to accept a worldview that leads them to see their relative lack of success as natural and proper.

Historically, most ideologies have been religious. The traditional Indian caste system (Milner, 1994; Beteille, 1996; Sekhon, 2000) and the very rigid class structure of ancient China were considered expressions of divine will. Modern ideologies are more often supported by science, or pseudoscience, like the "scientific" proofs of racial inferiority that were widely believed earlier in the last century.

In recent decades, many people have become more aware of the bias inherent in the ideologies that have traditionally supported racial, gender, and age inequality. Later chapters introduce the terms racism, sexism, and ageism for these belief systems. Interestingly, though, there is no generally accepted equivalent term to identify the ideology that legitimates economic inequality. We will call it **classism.**

Classism

Classism has been called "the ideology of competitive individualism" (Lewis, 1978). Others refer to it as the "Horatio Alger myth," after a 19th-century author whose heroes invariably rose from poverty to wealth by virtue of unrelentingly hard work. Some simply define classism as excessive faith in the American Dream.

Classism begins with acceptance of the idea that the capitalist system of the United States offers, if not completely equal opportunity to achieve success, at least sufficiently equal opportunity so that everyone who works hard has an excellent chance of acquiring wealth (Ritzman & Tomaskovic-Devey, 1992). Most sociologists think this claim is greatly exaggerated. However, right or wrong, if it is accepted, classism leads to two important conclusions: first, that the wealthy deserve their privileges, and second, that the poor are largely responsible for their plight.

Classism thus promotes a narrow and stereotyped way of thinking. It suggests the poor are lazy, stupid, immoral, and without ambition (Huber & Form, 1973; Ladd & Bowman, 1998). It largely ignores structural barriers to upward mobility and implies that success or failure depends almost entirely on what individuals do—or fail to do. For this reason many sociologists see

Clothing is often a useful symbol of an individual's class position. Uniforms, like those worn by these domestic workers, usually—but not always— indicate relatively low status.

classism as a form of victim blaming (Ryan, 1971). Figures 10.1 and 10.2 on page 255 demonstrate how the variable of race influences the way people think about the factors that affect how well individuals do in life.

Like other ideologies, classism is first learned in childhood (MacLeod, 1987; Ridgeway et al., 1998). In addition, it is continually reinforced in media imagery, especially that concerning the poor (Herman & Chomsky, 1988; Mantsios, 1995; Domhoff, 1998).

In addition to socialization, there is another reason why many people accept classism: There is a kernel of truth buried within its distortions. Some poor people who work hard *do* get ahead, and some poor people *are* held back by their own personal limitations. However, such instances are more likely to be publicized in the capitalist media than are the counterexamples—the many capable individuals who work hard yet still fail. People use the media's selective presentation to validate their classist worldview and lose track of how rare dramatic upward mobility really is.

Furthermore, the idea that hard work is sure to be rewarded appeals to people who want to believe they live in a just world, that if they simply apply themselves with enough diligence, they need not worry about falling behind (Kluegel & Smith, 1986; Ritzman & Tomaskovic-Devey, 1992; Jasso 1999).

Not surprisingly, after a lifetime of exposure to classist thinking, most people are not especially interested in changing the rules of the game. Instead of seeking structural changes that would modify capitalism to make competition fairer, they simply want their share of the economic pie. Not only the advantaged, but also many poor people accept this view. Those who question it tend to be viewed as left-wing radicals (Bobo, 1991).

What are the consequences of accepting classism? First, most people in the United States underestimate the importance of class in shaping people's lives. They also resist identifying themselves by their class position (Langston, 1992; Wright, 1997). In addition, classism often leads people to reject policies that could help the disadvantaged to overcome the structural factors that limit their opportunities for upward mobility. Examples of such policies include proposals for universal health care, extensive job-training programs, or marked increases in the progressivity of the income tax.

Some trends suggest that classism is being challenged more frequently today. Awareness of class, while muted, is by no means absent in the United States (Jackman & Jackman, 1983; Beeghley, 2000). Educational levels are rising, and the information revolution makes it easier for disenfranchised groups of poor people and minorities to spread counter-ideologies that challenge popular misconceptions about class. Finally, the poor are more likely than members of other classes to view the class system as unfair. They commonly understand that hard work often is not enough to ensure success (Kluegel & Smith, 1986; Polakow, 1993).

SYSTEMS OF ECONOMIC STRATIFICATION

Historically, systems of structured economic inequality have varied greatly. Sociologists do, however, distinguish between two major types. *Closed systems* are based on ascribed statuses and permit very little if any social mobility. Relatively *open systems*, on the other hand, focus more on achievement and permit substantial upward and downward mobility (Tumin, 1985). The United States is generally classed among the more open societies in the world today (Grusky &

Learning About Structured Social Inequality: Resistance, Paralysis, and Rage

How has reading this chapter made you feel? Angry? Uncomfortable? Frustrated? It's not easy to learn that some of your most cherished beliefs—such as the notion that we live in a land of unlimited opportunity—not only may be factually inaccurate but may actually contribute to the oppression of your fellow citizens.

Sociologists often find that teaching about class, gender, and race—that is, the various forms of social stratification—is one of the most difficult tasks they confront. Yet helping students to debunk popular miusunderstandings about structured social inequality is one of the most important functions of the discipline, especially for sociologists who feel that they have an obligation to try and correct what they see as social injustice.

Nancy Davis has identified three general ways in which her students respond when they are first exposed to the realities of social stratification: resistance, denial, and rage. The most common is *resistance*. Many students simply deny the existence or at least the importance of structured social inequality in today's society. They tend to see racism and sexism as history: problems that existed in the past but are no longer of much importance. They view classism as foreign. After all, the United States, they have been taught, is a land where the streets are paved with gold. If opportunities were limited in this country, why would millions of immigrants come here each year?

Other students may recognize the enduring inequalities in our society, but attribute them exclusively to individuals' personal weaknesses (in the case of poverty) or personal strengths (in the case of wealth). Very few have thought about the possibility that our emphasis on individualism—and the belief that anyone who works hard can get ahead—are components of an ideology that actually helps keeps the poor down.

Davis points out that the cultural and political climate in which today's students grow up glorifies self-sufficiency and the pursuit of personal wealth. Most of our heroes and heroines are self-made multimillionaires, especially in sports, entertainment, and computer technology. The poor have been stereotyped as perpetrators of welfare fraud. Sympathy for the homeless has declined; people in line at soup kitchens are criticized as misfits and freeloaders.

Students may resist the concept of structured inequality because the picture sociology paints is gloomier than the images they see every day in the mass media. TV sitcoms that focus primarily on middle- and upper-middle-class individuals whose problems are largely interpersonal, self-inflicted, and resolved within a half-hour reinforce classist attitudes. By implication, this is what the United States is about: being middle-class and taking care of your own problems. Programs like *Survivor* extol the virtues of rugged individualism and denigrate compassion and sharing. Popular magazines headline articles about how, with the right "packaging," anyone can be a success. Self-help books dominate best-seller lists, implying widespread discontent on the one hand, and on the other, the belief that the solutions to most problems lie with the individual.

Students from advantaged backgrounds may feel that members of the group from which they come, or perhaps even they themselves, are being cast unfairly in the role of exploiters. But less advantaged students are often equally resistant to discussions of structural barriers to success, as if acknowledging their problems would be admitting their own failure.

Not all of Davis's students are resistant. She describes some as *paralyzed*. Although they are aware that the deck is stacked against certain categories of people, they tend to see the current system of stratification as inevitable and themselves as powerless. Although outraged by poverty, sexism, and other forms of injustice, they may feel utterly helpless to do anything about them. Some may have personally experienced poverty, racism, or sexism. Others may have seen a parent or friend who was laid off slip into depression and alcohol abuse. Having kept these "guilty secrets" to themselves, they may withdraw when what they have thought of as personal problems become the subjects of analysis in a sociology class.

The opposite of paralysis is *rage*. Some students enter stratification courses already nursing powerful feelings of injustice and indignation. They tend to blame everything that is wrong in the world on sexism, racism, or a capitalist conspiracy, and to see the world (and even members of their sociology class) as divided into exploiters and the exploited, victimizers and victims. Their anger is easily understood, but it can lead to self-righteousness rather than to becoming actively engaged in trying to improve the situation.

Rage, paralysis, and resistance are not unique to students, but reflect attitudes held by the public at large. By uncovering the truth regarding power and privilege, advantage and disadvantage, and the ideologies that support structured social inequality, sociology gives its students the opportunity to examine their own biases and assumptions and, in the end, to learn how to work more effectively for a fairer society.

1. Did your high school classes fully explore the realities of structured social inequality, or did they gloss over them? Would a teacher at your school have been allowed to critically discuss these issues?

2. If resistance, paralysis, and rage are all ultimately inappropriate responses to learning about the inequalities of class, gender, race, and age, then how should students be encouraged to respond when they learn about these issues?

Source: Davis, 1992.

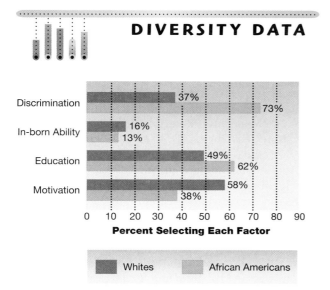

FIGURE 10.1 How Does Race Influence Opinions About Why African Americans Generally Have Lower Incomes and Poorer Jobs and Housing Than Whites? Whites tend to emphasize the individual attributes of motivation and innate ability as factors that contribute to African Americans' lower income and poorer jobs and housing. In contrast, African Americans are more likely to stress the impact of discrimination and quality of education. Given these findings, how likely is it that most whites will enthusiastically support social programs designed to reduce discrimination?

Source: NORC. General Social Surveys, 1972–2000. Chicago: National Opinion Research Center, 2000. Reprinted by permission of NORC, Chicago, IL.

Hauser, 1984). While some societies have been almost completely closed, none has ever been anywhere near completely open. In part, this is because elite parents can use their wealth and power to send their children to expensive, prestigious universities and secure advantageous marriages for them, thereby greatly increasing their chances of future success.

In addition to being more or less open, societies also vary over time in the extent of inequality they display—that is, in the size of the gap between the rich and the poor. Economist Simon Kuznets (1955) developed an influential theory concerning how inequality changes as societies evolve. Referred to as the **Kuznets curve** (see Figure 10.3 on page 256), the theory suggests that inequality mounts steadily as societies develop until they pass through the early phases of the industrial revolution, after which it tends to decline.

Gerhard and Jean Lenski's evolutionary theory of social development, which was discussed in Chapter 4, can help illustrate the dynamics of the Kuznets curve (Nolan & Lenski, 1999). *Hunting and gathering societies*

were very open and nearly classless, although structured differences based on age and gender did exist in them (van den Berge, 1973; Harris, 1979). Some people may have had somewhat more power, property, and prestige than others, but these differences were relatively minor, were based chiefly on talent, and could not be easily passed on to the next generation.

It was in *horticultural societies* that significant social stratification first emerged. At this stage of social development, enough food could be produced in intensively cultivated garden plots to yield a fairly predictable surplus. Particular kinship groups came to control the surplus and used it to elevate themselves over their fellows and to ensure a head start for their children (Nolan & Lenski, 1999). Horticultural societies were thus much less open and more sharply stratified than the hunting and gathering cultures

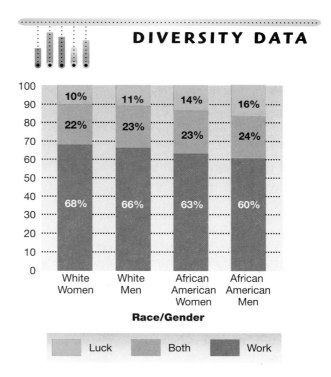

FIGURE 10.2 How Do Race and Gender Influence Opinions About Whether People Mostly Get Ahead Due to Hard Work or Good Luck? While whites and women put slightly more emphasis than African Americans and men on hard work and African Americans and men consider luck slightly more important than whites and women do, all the differences are small. Most people of both races consider hard work to be the most important factor explaining success. Would conflict theorists consider this an example of false consciousness among African Americans? Do you agree?

Source: NORC. General Social Surveys, 1972–2000. Chicago: National Opinion Research Center, 2000. Reprinted by permission of NORC, Chicago, IL.

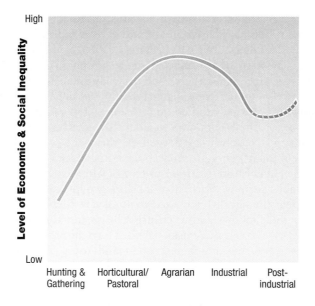

FIGURE 10.3 The Kuznets Curve. The Kuznets curve allows us to visualize the relationship between societal complexity and overall level of economic inequality. Hunting and gathering societies are highly egalitarian, but as horticulture and then agriculture emerge, a chasm opens up between the wealthy elite and the impoverished masses. This gap substantially narrows with the emergence of industrial society due to a dramatic expansion of education and the greatly increased productivity of the economy. However, some evidence suggests that inequality may be increasing once again as we move into the postindustrial era.

Source: Atkinson et al., 1995: 40.

they replaced. The first distinct political systems—hereditary chiefdoms—arose in part to help the new horticultural elites safeguard their advantages.

Horticultural societies also saw the rise of *slavery*, a distinctive system of stratification based on the ownership of one group of individuals by another (Patterson, 1982). Slavery was common throughout the ancient world—including Greece, Rome, and Israel—and continued to be legal in some nations until the late 19th century. As the *Diversity in Focus* box on the facing page suggests, slavery persists even in the 21st century (Jacobs & Athie, 1994). Some estimate that as many as 3 million people may be slaves around the world today.

Agrarian societies are characterized by very high levels of structured social inequality (Dalton, 1967; Nolan & Lenski, 1999). At this stage, new technologies greatly expanded food production, which allowed elites to accumulate a massive surplus. At the same time, new agricultural technologies freed many people from working in food production. These people flocked to the newly founded cities to become specialized workers such as tool makers, weavers, and potters. Greatly expanded governments and new religion-based ideologies emerged to protect the privileges of the dominant

strata. The elites, who often made up less than 2 percent of the population, typically held as much as half of the society's wealth.

Slavery reached its greatest extent in agrarian societies. In addition, several new types of stratification developed. Most notable were **caste systems,** made up of a number of sharply distinct groups or castes whose membership is determined entirely by birth or ascription (Berreman, 1987; Fuller, 1996).

By definition, caste systems allow virtually no social mobility. They are justified by a very strongly held legitimating ideology, nearly always religious in character. An individual's caste is absolutely central to her or his identity; it determines much of everyday behavior, from clothes to marriage patterns.

The best known example of caste in the world today is found in India. As early as 350 B.C.E., Indian society was divided into four great castes or *varnas:* Brahman, Kshiatriya, Vaishya, and Shudra. Each caste is loosely associated with a general type of work—priests and scholars, nobles and warriors, merchants and artisans, and cultivators and laborers, respectively. A fifth group, the Harijan or "untouchables," technically not even part of the caste system, occupy the lowest rung on the ladder. The Harijan were traditionally responsible for sweeping streets, removing the corpses of dead animals, and other types of labor considered degrading. Each varna is subdivided into many hundreds of subcastes or *jati,* whose members are expected to specialize in a specific occupation.

Caste membership is hereditary, and although individuals within a given group may become richer or poorer, they can never change their varna or jati identity except through rebirth at a higher or lower level in the next life. Furthermore, each caste possesses a certain level of prestige or ritual purity, and an extremely elaborate set of rules dictates how the different caste groups must act toward each other. These rules cover virtually every aspect of life, but are especially detailed concerning food preparation and service (Wolpert, 1991). For example, a high-caste Brahman may receive an unhusked coconut from a Harijan, but not one whose meat has been exposed (Tyler, 1986). Violation of these rules creates "ritual pollution" and requires a sacred cleansing ceremony (Lannoy, 1975).

Although the Indian caste system was formally abolished half a century ago, it continues to thrive in the villages and also influences the modern sectors of the society. Legislation cannot easily erase thousands of years of tradition, especially when customs are legitimated by the Hindu religion. However, urbanization and industrialization have greatly increased geographic mobility, making it increasingly difficult to maintain traditional caste relations. Expanding educational opportunities encourage members of low-ranking castes to challenge age-old restrictions in the polit-

DIVERSITY IN FOCUS

Modern Slavery

The phrase "modern slavery" sounds like an oxymoron: Surely this ancient and despicable practice could not continue to exist in the same world as microwave ovens, space shuttles, and MTV . . . right?

Christi Elangwe, a 23-year-old native of the West African nation of Cameroon, knows better. Six years ago she emigrated to the United States to work as a domestic in the $280,000 home of a Cameroonian family that had moved to Germantown, Maryland, years earlier. Her employer led her to believe that she could attend school and eventually fulfill her lifetime ambition of becoming a nurse, but soon after she arrived she realized that he had lied to her. For the next 5 years, she was held as a virtual captive, forbidden for the most part to use the telephone, to leave the house unescorted, or even to talk with outsiders. Christi worked 16 hours a day, 7 days a week, was not allowed to see a doctor or a dentist, and was never paid a penny.

This is the face of slavery in the 21st century, an ancient custom that endures both in the United States and in other parts of the world, especially North Africa, Southeast Asia, Latin America, and Western Europe. Most contemporary examples of the practice are not traditional *chattel slavery,* in which one person owns another outright, but rather some form of *bonded labor,* such as that endured by Christi Elangwe, in which the slaves are obliged to labor long hours for minimal (if any) wages in order to pay off an accumulated debt of as much as $30,000. Because bonded laborers commonly must reimburse their employers inflated sums for room, board, and other expenses, in practice many have little or no hope of ever obtaining their freedom.

What sort of people are victimized by the slave trade? Overwhelmingly, they are the poor, often youngsters growing up in remote villages in the developing world who are lured into slavery as Christi was with deceitful promises of opportunities in the city or abroad. Many are members of minority groups: In Mauritania and the Sudan, two African nations where widespread slavery persists, slaves are usually dark-skinned members of indigenous ethnic groups and their masters are generally lighter-skinned Muslims.

No one knows how many people are living in slavery around the world; if the term is defined broadly to include marriages in which wives have virtually no freedom, there may be as many as 400 million, although most sources put the number at somewhere between 25 and 100 million. Theresa Loar, director of the U.S. Inter-Agency Council on Women, estimates the value of the global slave trade at $9 billion.

Many modern slaves work as agricultural laborers or in sweatshops; others, like Elangwe, are domestic servants. Millions of girls as young as 10 or 11 are held as sex slaves. Some are kidnapped and others are sold into slavery by their desperately poor parents. In Thailand, some 10 percent of the female population—2 million women—work in brothels servicing both local men and tourists who come from all over the world. Not only is the work exhausting and demeaning, but over 40 percent of Thailand's prostitutes are estimated to be HIV positive.

There are probably between 50,000 and 70,000 slaves in the United States, although some estimate that the number may be as high as 1 million. Some are undocumented Latin American field workers. Some are employed as maids. Others,

especially young women from Southeast Asia, toil as much as 84 hours per week sewing clothes for hourly wages as low as $1.65. Many thousands of Asian and East European women work in the sex trades: The Immigration and Naturalization Service (INS) has identified 250 brothels in 26 states that are suspected of using immigrant women as prostitutes.

All of this continues despite the 1948 U.N. Declaration of Human Rights, which states that "no one shall be held in slavery or servitude. Slavery and the slave trade shall be prohibited in all their forms." The practice is illegal in every nation in the world, yet it continues, in part because its victims are impoverished and ethnically or racially distinct and thus largely powerless to protest against their treatment.

In 1998, a federal task force was organized in the United States to fight slavery; 2 years later the U.N. Crime Commission drafted an international treaty to aid in the struggle against the practice. President Clinton signed a bill that same year that gives temporary asylum to victims of slavery and allows for the possibility of a life sentence for persons caught trafficking in human beings. Adopting a more aggressive approach, the Zurich-based group Christian Solidarity has freed 10,000. Dinka slaves in the Sudan by paying Arab "retrievers" $50 for each person they buy or abduct from their masters.

1. How does modern slavery differ from the African American slavery characteristic of the antebellum Deep South?

2. What can college students do to help end the practice of slavery in this country and around the world?

Sources: Patterson, 1982; Janus, 1996; Burkett, 1997; Crossette, 1997; Bales, 1999; Mabry, 1999; France, 2000; Richard, 2000.

In traditional India, the caste into which people were born shaped virtually every aspect of their lives. Although the system was formally abolished half a century ago, it continues to have a powerful effect on the lives of hundreds of millions of Indians, whether they are very wealthy or completely destitute.

ical arena. The Indian government has even sponsored affirmative-action plans on behalf of the untouchables, now referred to as the scheduled castes. Still, caste endures in Indian culture, most visibly in the context of marriage, which still largely occurs only within castes.

Other examples of caste in the modern world tend to be linked with race. Until recently, South Africa was characterized by a racial caste system called *apartheid* that divided the population into four distinct groups: whites, (Asian) Indians, Coloureds (people of mixed European and African ancestry), and blacks. Apartheid required that the four groups remain almost completely separate from each other (Frederickson, 1981; Wilson & Ramphele, 1989). The system strongly favored the whites. After decades of protest, it was formally abandoned in the early 1990s.

Many sociologists believe race in the United States has a distinctly castelike quality. This was certainly true in the post-Reconstruction South. People were legally prohibited from marrying outside their race, ascribed identity shaped virtually all aspects of life, and an elaborate etiquette defined relations between blacks and whites (Stampp, 1956). For example, African Americans were expected to step aside to allow whites to pass them on the street, and they were required to address all whites formally ("Yes, Mrs. Jones"), while whites were free to call all African Americans, regardless of age or occupation, by their first names. As in India, these rules both reflected and reinforced the caste system.

Industrial and *postindustrial societies* typically grow increasingly open to social mobility, and the gap between elites and the rest of society narrows. However, the increased economic inequalities in many postindustrial nations since the early 1970s suggest that Kuznets's hypothesis may need revision.

The primary reason economic inequality declines in industrial societies is that a modern economy requires highly educated workers to operate its increasingly sophisticated machinery. With expanded education comes a better understanding of the inequities of class. In addition, education helps poor people learn how to use an increasingly democratic political system in order to seek fairer treatment (Lipset & Bendix, 1959; Drucker, 1969).

In addition, industrialization is linked to a dramatic rise in urbanization. As workers become geographically concentrated in cities, they can more easily organize to demand reforms. The legalization of unions, unemployment compensation, welfare programs, and other political changes, taken together, tend to reduce economic inequality (Nielsen, 1994).

Finally, the greatly increased productivity of the industrial system yields so much wealth that elites can permit an improved standard of living in the classes below them without making appreciable sacrifices

themselves. As a result, even the poor in modern societies are generally much better off than much of the population in earlier eras.

With slavery largely eliminated and caste systems fading, industrial societies are characterized by class systems, which are based principally on achievement rather than ascription and hence are relatively open, especially in the middle ranges (Berger, 1986; Marger, 2002). However, downward mobility from the extreme upper class and upward mobility from the very bottom remain uncommon. In addition, the lines between the classes in the middle become blurred, and awareness of class distinctions tends to decline.

Table 10.1 summarizes the characteristic changes in stratification systems that occur as societies develop.

EXPLAINING STRATIFICATION

Sociologists who study social stratification are principally interested in two questions: First, *is structured social inequality inevitable?* And second, *are its effects on society basically positive or negative?* If stratification is inevitable, then efforts to eliminate or greatly reduce inequality are pointless. If it is not inevitable, but its consequences are primarily beneficial, then movements toward equality may succeed but are misguided. Finally, if structured inequality is not inevitable and also harmful, then efforts to reduce it are not only possible but badly needed.

Keep these questions in mind as we examine four theories of social stratification. We begin with deficiency theory, a widely accepted but seriously flawed non-sociological approach. Then we look at sociological explanations based on the functionalist, conflict, and symbolic interactionist perspectives.

Deficiency Theory

Deficiency theories of stratification explain differences in property, power, and prestige as the direct consequence of individual variations in ability. As such, they are not really sociological, since they focus on the biology or psychology of particular people rather than on the social origins of structured inequality. Elites obtain and retain their advantages

TABLE 10.1

Societal Development and Structured Economic Inequality

Stage	Patterns of Inequality
Hunting and Gathering	Very little economic inequality. That which exists is based on personal talent with little if any inherited advantage or disadvantage.
Horticultural/Pastoral	Some kinship groups secure control over surplus production, producing substantial structured inequality. Slavery emerges in some societies.
Agrarian	Very high levels of structured inequality with an enormous gap between a small, highly privileged elite and the masses. Strong religious ideologies justify unequal arrangements. Slavery endures; caste systems dominate.
Industrial	Expansion of education spurs discontent among the masses; tremendous increases in economic productivity allow genuine improvement in the living standard of all groups. Gap between rich and poor narrows. Class systems replace castes.
Postindustrial	Some indication that economic inequality may increase; emerging patterns remain unclear.

Source: Table adapted from *Human Societies: An Introduction to Macrosociology,* 8th edition by Patrick Nolan and Gerhard E. Lenski. Copyright © 1999 by McGraw-Hill Book Company. Reprinted by permission of the McGraw-Hill Companies.

This classic 1888 photograph was taken by Joseph Riis in one of the worst slums in London. Many Victorians made use of Herbert Spencer's concept of Social Darwinism to justify their refusal to help people living in desperate poverty.

because they are better—smarter, harder working, more moral—than everyone else. Clearly this point of view is highly compatible with the interests of the upper classes. It also fits well with the ideology of classism. It suggests that social inequality is not only inevitable, but also desirable, since inherently inferior people obviously do not deserve equal rewards.

Deficiency theory was immensely popular in the later 19th century. Its principal spokesman was the British theorist Herbert Spencer, who was for a time the world's best-known sociologist. Spencer's philosophy came to be known as **Social Darwinism;** in fact, it was he, not Darwin, who coined the phrase "the survival of the fittest" (Turner et al., 2002).

The policy implication of Social Darwinism is clear. Just as weaker animals must die in order to keep a species' genetic stock strong, the poor must be allowed to suffer and expire. Keeping them alive may seem humane, but in the end, it will only weaken civilization and decrease the human race's chances for survival. In Spencer's own words, poverty is nature's way ". . . of excreting . . . unhealthy, imbecile, slow, vacillating, faithless . . ." people. Governments and other institutions must maintain a *laissez-faire* (hands-off) attitude to the lower classes. And the same goes for individuals: People should resist the impulse to

help the poor, with the possible exception of "blameless" widows and orphans (Sumner, 1883).

Social Darwinism fell into disfavor early in the 20th century as sociological interpretations grew in popularity. However, during the past two decades deficiency theory has become more widely accepted in a slightly different guise. In 1969, educational psychologist Arthur Jensen published an intensely controversial article that claimed about 80 percent of the variation in IQ scores is explained by genetic differences. A generation later, Richard Herrnstein and Charles Murray (1994) presented a broadly similar argument in their book *The Bell Curve*.

CRITIQUE Opponents of deficiency theories are particularly concerned because minorities are disproportionately represented in the "inherently inferior" lower class. They point out that the IQ tests that Jensen and his followers take as accurate measures of ability are in fact biased against persons not raised in a white, middle-class environment (Fischer et al., 1996).

If deficiency theorists are right, then helping the disadvantaged is a waste of money. If they are wrong, then their primary policy recommendation—to abandon programs like Head Start and affirmative action—amounts to kicking people who have already fallen due to factors that are largely beyond their control.

Most sociologists believe that deficiency theory is fundamentally off track. If society does not aid the poor and they fail, does this prove that deficiency theory is right, or does it simply amount to a self-fulfilling prophecy? Deficiency theories are a classic example of blaming the victim. They ignore the critical role of structural factors that very strongly influence an individual's chances of success or failure (Kerbo, 2000).

Unlike deficiency theory, sociological interpretations of social inequality emphasize its structural

INTERNET CONNECTIONS

After reading about the different theoretical models of global stratification in the text go to Sweatshops:

http://www.sweatshops.org/

and click on the different links. Gather some facts and then answer the following questions. 1. How would you explain what you saw on the sweatshop Website? 2. How do we in the West (Developed Nations) contribute to global inequality? Support your comments with facts and/or theories from the text and Website.

character. That is, they view stratification as a characteristic of society rather than of individuals. People in different classes receive different levels of reward primarily as a result of the way society is organized, not because of differences in individual ability or effort. This way of thinking does not deny that individuals may have different talents, but it suggests that conditions of the social structure determine which abilities are considered important and how much opportunity different groups of people have to develop their skills.

Functionalism

The most influential functionalist theory of stratification was developed by Kingsley Davis and Wilbert Moore (1945). The **Davis-Moore thesis** maintains that inequality serves two vital functions: It motivates people to work hard, and it ensures that key statuses in society will be occupied by highly capable people. Davis and Moore assume that certain occupational positions in society are critically important. Some of these positions, such as garbage collector, must be filled (lest we end up hip deep in orange peels and coffee grounds), but they need not be filled by highly qualified people. Other positions, such as surgeons, corporate executives, or generals, absolutely must be staffed with highly capable individuals. The key is replaceability—garbage collectors are much easier to replace than brain surgeons (Weslowski, 1966).

These critical positions typically require not only considerable talent but also years of preparation and hard work. How can we ensure that highly capable people are recruited into these demanding statuses? Davis and Moore reply that we accomplish this by giving the people who occupy these important positions more rewards—more possessions, more prestige, and more power. The rewards compensate for the difficulty of preparing for and working in these jobs.

CRITIQUE The Davis-Moore argument is compelling, but it has also been widely criticized. (The following discussion is based on Tumin, 1953, 1963; Simpson, 1956; Wrong, 1959). First, according to Davis-Moore, inequality is beneficial only when it ensures that the most capable people occupy the most important positions. However, one of the rewards elites receive is the ability to help their offspring attain the good life. The problem is that the children of highly capable people are not necessarily highly capable themselves. The result is a situation in which many people enjoy upper-class status, not because of their merit, but because of that of their ancestors. Heavy inheritance or estate taxes might correct this problem, but the wealthy generally have enough political clout to keep their taxes low.

Second, the fact that modern societies continue to allow ascriptive factors such as gender and race to substantially limit access to elite positions, even for highly talented people, also challenges the logic of Davis-Moore. The relatively low salaries of such socially critical but traditionally female-dominated occupations as social workers, teachers, and child-care providers clearly demonstrate the extent to which gender bias rather than functional importance often determines salary levels.

Third, there are serious questions about which positions ought to be highly rewarded. In a capitalist economy, a given occupation's pay is chiefly determined by the market, not by a rational assessment of its value to society. The result has been extremely high salaries for rock stars, athletes, and movie actors whose social contribution is debatable.

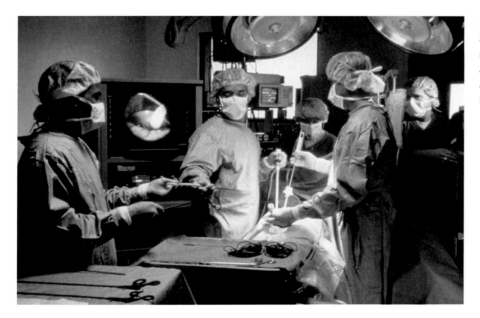

The Davis-Moore functional theory suggests that the medical professions are well paid and carry high prestige so that highly capable people will be attracted to these important and demanding occupations.

Critics argue that the relatively low salaries of teachers, especially in comparison to the astronomical earnings of film stars like Jennifer Lopez, keep many talented people from entering critically important fields like education.

Fourth, Davis and Moore ignore the role that power plays in determining how well various occupations will be rewarded. Professional associations, such as the American Medical Association and labor unions, have artificially driven up the wages of their members by restricting the supply of workers.

A final criticism concerns the *extent* of social inequality. Even granting the basic Davis-Moore argument, are the extremes of wealth and poverty that characterize the United States really functional? Major film stars can earn over $20 million per movie. Physicians' annual salaries commonly exceed $200,000. The CEOs of major corporations routinely make several hundred times more than their entry-level employees. At the same time, 32 million people are living below the poverty line, and hundreds of thousands are homeless. Perhaps society needs inequality—*but this much?*

The Davis-Moore thesis does make some good points. The relatively low wages paid to scientists and

engineers in the former Soviet Union did seem to make them less willing to work hard (Aganbegyan, 1989). And survey research has found that 75 percent of the people of the United States agree that "no one could be expected to study for years to become a doctor or lawyer unless they expected to earn a lot more than ordinary workers" (Stark, 1996a). However, the theory ignores the negative impact of structured inequality on the working and lower classes (Grimes, 1991). To balance the picture, we need to consider the conflict approach.

Conflict Theory

The conflict perspective is based on the assumption that all social life is a struggle for scarce resources. Applied to social stratification, this interpretation suggests that the social classes actively compete against each other in a battle that will inevitably produce winners and losers. Conflict theorists generally believe class inequality is harmful, but they disagree as to whether it is inevitable.

KARL MARX Karl Marx (1818–1883) is the most important figure in the conflict analysis of social stratification. He believed that class inequality was neither desirable nor inevitable. Writing in an era of extreme inequality and widespread class conflict, Marx argued that sociologists must not only study society as it is, but must also work actively to end any injustices they uncover. This commitment to activism led him to become closely involved with the political revolutionaries of his day (Berlin, 1963).

For Marx, all of social life was shaped, and in some cases determined, by the relationships people establish between each other in the process of economic production (McLellan, 1977). Class was no exception to this general principle. Marx suggested that stratification originated in the struggle to control the surplus that accumulated when society moved beyond a subsistence economy. The groups involved in this struggle are social classes, which Marx defines as people who share a common relationship to a society's *means of production*—that is, to whatever is used in that society to create wealth. The nature of a society's means of production changes as its technology advances. In the Middle Ages, land was the most important form of productive property; in Marx's day, it was factories; today it is computers and communications systems. But the basic definition of social class remains the same.

Because individuals may be related to the means of production in a number of ways, there are a number of different social classes, but the most crucial distinction is always that between those who *own* the means of production, the dominant or ruling class, and all of the classes that *do not own* productive resources and are therefore subordinate to the owners.

In Marx's day, the ruling class, the **bourgeoisie** or capitalists, were the owners of large factories. The other major class, the **proletariat,** were industrial workers who had to sell their labor power to the bourgeoisie, generally on very disadvantageous terms, in order to survive. Other minor classes existed, including a remnant of the old feudal nobility, the *petit bourgeoisie*, who owned shops but did not employ workers (Robinson & Kelley, 1979), and the *lumpenproletariat* or urban underclass. But Marx considered their roles in history to be secondary to those of the bourgeoisie and the proletariat.

It is important to note that, for Marx, the interests of the social classes are, by definition, incompatible. The dominant class benefits from maintaining its position of control and extracting as much profit as possible from the workers. The subordinate classes can improve their lot only by overthrowing the ruling class and taking its place at the top of the stratification ladder. Without real power, they will never get more than the crumbs from the tables of the rich (McLellan, 1977).

Marx saw all of history as a series of revolutions in which ruling classes were overthrown and absorbed into newly ascendent elite groups. These conflicts were generally violent because no elite would willingly give up its position of advantage. In order for a revolution to take place, the subordinate class must gain **class consciousness.** For Marx, this meant not only knowing what class you are in but also becoming aware of the true implications of your class position. In the case of a subordinate class, class consciousness meant realizing that you will never prosper so long as you are under the heel of the ruling class, that revolution is essential (Ossowski, 1983). For the ruling class, it meant understanding that you must never lift your heel.

Obviously, it is not in the interests of the ruling class for members of other classes to gain class consciousness. The bourgeoisie work against this possibility in many ways. For one thing, they try to lock up the agitators. They are aided greatly in this effort by their control of the state and of the "state machinery"—police, prisons, the military—which they use to protect their class interests.

But it is always easier to head off dissent before it arises. The bourgeoisie do this by promoting **false consciousness,** narrowly defined as anything that retards the growth of class consciousness. More generally, false consciousness refers to any ideology that convinces subordinate groups that their lack of property, prestige, and power is proper. Marx particularly stressed how religion strengthens false consciousness by encouraging poor people to focus on the supposed rewards of the next life instead of trying to change things in the here-and-now (McLellan, 1977).

Some modern conflict theorists argue that unions and democratic politics play a similar role, giving subordinate classes the illusion of real power in their relations with the elite. Above all, the fact that the ruling class controls the means of socialization—the schools, churches, and mass media—allows it to convince others to accept ways of thinking, classist ideologies, that defend its class advantages (Marger, 1993).

In opposition to false consciousness, Marxist revolutionaries like Lenin developed and popularized their own ideas or counter-ideologies that were designed to challenge classism. One of Marx's most important contributions is his insight that ideas are rarely neutral; they are weapons used to promote the interests of particular classes.

Critique Marx's work led directly to the development of the conflict perspective in sociology. His emphasis on the economic basis of society and on the importance of social class in history has been immensely influential (Gilbert & Kahl, 1993). His interpretation of the state as the agent of the ruling class is widely accepted by conflict theorists. The notion of false consciousness has been applied in many different contexts, perhaps most usefully in regard to gender and racial or ethnic oppression (Parenti, 1995). When women accept sexist ways of thinking or minorities learn racist ideologies and attitudes, the effects are similar to those that follow from the internalization of classism by the poor: Their willingness to fight oppression is weakened. These issues are discussed further in Chapters 12 and 13.

On the other hand, Marx was a poor political prophet: The United States and other postindustrial societies have not, at least until recently, experienced a widening gap between the rich and the poor—or a communist revolution—as he predicted would occur. What happened in the United States to confound Marx's expectations? (The following discussion is based on Gurley, 1984; Edwards, 1985; Rubin, 1986; Wright & Martin, 1987; Wright, 1989; Kelley & Evans, 1995; Parenti, 1995).

For one thing, since Marx's day governments have learned to actively intervene in the economy in order to smooth out the cycles of boom and bust that contributed heavily to the miseries of the 19th-century working class. Even more important, capitalist economies have become vastly more productive than Marx thought possible. This has been partly the result of globalization, which has opened up vast new markets for exploitation, and partly due to the rapid development of new technologies.

These stable and highly productive economies have, until recently, allowed the real incomes of the workers to rise rather than fall and even, during some parts of the past century, somewhat narrowed the economic gap between the classes. Individual upward mobility has been a real possibility for many workers, especially union members, a factor that has greatly weakened the development of class consciousness. Furthermore, the growth of the welfare state, made possible by escalating economic productivity, has smoothed out the rough edges of capitalism by providing such benefits as unemployment insurance, worker's compensation, and expanded aid to the poor.

Finally, Marx did not foresee the emergence of an enormous middle class of managers, professionals, and technical workers—often called the "new class"—who are structurally proletariat in that they do not own the means of production, but who identify more with the interests of the bourgeoisie than with those of the industrial workers. This new class has been a particular focus of attention among modern conflict theorists who have attempted to adapt Marx's analysis to the present era.

MAX WEBER Weber believed that Marx's exclusive emphasis on people's relationship to the means of economic production resulted in a limited and simplistic theory. He also argued that Marx's passion for abolishing class inequality led him to confuse his own value preferences with objective social analysis. For Weber, Marx's dream of achieving a classless utopia was far from inevitable. In fact, Weber thought that social stratification was, at least implicitly, unavoidable.

The central point in Weber's (1947) analysis is that social stratification is *multidimensional*. Societies, he maintained, are indeed divided into economic classes, much as Marx believed, but they also have separate and distinct stratification systems based on two factors other than property: prestige and power. In addition, Weber saw the lines separating the different strata as less sharply drawn than Marx believed to be the case. Most sociologists have found Weber's analysis to be more useful than that of Marx in understanding contemporary society, although Marx's influence remains substantial. Let's briefly examine each of the three systems of structured inequality Weber identified.

Property Weber's understanding of economic class was loosely similar to Marx's. However, he placed less emphasis on people's structural relationship to the means of production and more on the characteristics that allow different groups to participate in different ways in the market. For example, Weber distinguished between *entrepreneurs*, such as merchants and factory owners, who actually produce something of value, and *rentiers*, who live off the return from their investments. Marx would have classified both groups as bourgeoisie.

Weber thought economic class was relatively unimportant because most people do not consciously think of themselves in terms of their class identity. That is, they lack class consciousness, which Weber saw as simply the way things were rather than as Marx saw it—as a problem in need of correction.

Prestige People may rarely think of themselves in class terms, but most are very much aware of their membership in what Weber called **status groups.** Status groups are ranked strata based on different lifestyles or patterns of consumption that are accorded different levels of honor, esteem, or prestige.

Examples of status groups abound. Some are based on ethnicity: African Americans, WASPs, Hispanics. Some are religious: Jews, Southern Baptists, Catholics. Some reflect recreational lifestyle choices: skydivers, fitness buffs, Star Trek fans. Some are based on subcultural occupational groupings: manual laborers, academics, professionals. Note that members of a single economic class are typically drawn from many different status groups and, similarly, that several classes are typically represented in any given status group.

People frequently act collectively on the basis of their status group membership, something that rarely occurs with economic classes. Furthermore, members of status groups regularly interact with each other and, in the process, build up a shared culture (Marger, 2002). Some subcultural patterns are accorded more prestige than others. For example, the lifestyles of motorcycle gang members are generally considered less honorable than the lifestyles of, say, stockbrokers or school teachers. According to the contemporary French sociologist Pierre Bourdieu (1984, 1987), the shared subcultures of high-ranking status groups constitute valuable **cultural capital,** defined as those aspects of people's lifestyles—including values, attitudes, language patterns, and consumption preferences—that help to define their class location.

The *Global Connections* box on page 266 summarizes some of the results of a study concerning the different sorts of cultural capital valued by upper-middle-class men in France and in the United States.

Power Finally, Weber noted that different groups of people could be ranked not only on the basis of economics and honor, but also in terms of how much power they had over others. For Weber, **power** was the ability of one social actor to compel a second social actor to behave in a way in which the latter would not otherwise have acted. Weber used the term "party" to refer to the various strata within

Many urban residents in low-income nations make their homes in shacks and makeshift shelters like this one, which people in the developed world would find entirely unlivable.

society that were determined by different levels of power. But a party may also be called simply a "power group." Just as status group membership often cross-cuts economic class, membership in Weber's power groups does not necessarily correspond to membership in either social classes or status groups.

The importance of power groups in modern society is most clearly seen in the context of bureaucratic organizations (see Chapter 21). Upper managers in government and some other large bureaucracies may not earn enormous salaries and may occasionally be members of devalued status groups. But the power they derive from their bureaucratic status requires that we acknowledge their high ranking on at least this dimension of stratification. Similarly, the elites who ruled the Soviet Union did not occupy a class position that was, in Marx's terms, different from anyone else's, yet they derived enormous power from their authority within the state bureaucracy. Although relatively classless, the Soviet Union was in no sense unstratified, a fact that Weber's theory can explain easily but one that Marx did not foresee (Hurst, 1992).

The fact that Weber identifies three distinct systems of stratification opens up the possibility of *status inconsistency*, a situation in which an individual occupies several ranked statuses, some of which are evaluated more positively than others (Kerbo, 2000). For example, most ministers are high in prestige but fairly low in economic class. Many high-status professionals are women or members of devalued minority groups. A mortician may be wealthy, but the job is not highly esteemed because it requires close contact with the dead. Or, as we have just noted, government bureaucrats may have great power but enjoy only limited economic rewards.

Most people display a reasonably high level of status consistency, especially at the top and bottom of society (Gilbert & Kahl, 1993). However, many others experience serious inconsistency. Generally, people who are caught in this sort of situation wish to be seen overall in terms of their most highly valued status. Thus, college professors expect to be treated as highly educated professionals, not as people who earn only middling salaries. But many of those who come into contact with such individuals emphasize their lower status identity, probably in order to feel as good as possible about themselves (Lenski, 1954, 1956).

TOWARD A SYNTHESIS Can the functionalist and conflict perspectives be combined? Macrosociologist Gerhard Lenski thinks so (Nolan & Lenski, 1999). He suggests that in simple societies with little or no surplus, where most valued resources are necessities, the distribution of rewards will be reasonably egalitarian. This is necessary to keep everyone adequately fed, clothed, and sheltered. However, just as Davis and Moore argued, individuals who contribute more to the common good will be given extra shares as a reward. Thus, functionalism provides a good explanation for the *origins* of structured inequality.

At later stages in sociocultural evolution, a surplus becomes available. There is no particular societal need for an egalitarian distribution of this surplus, so under these circumstances power determines who will enjoy society's luxuries. Thus, according to Lenski, conflict theory provides the most convincing explanation for the *persistence* and *intensification* of social stratification.

GLOBAL CONNECTIONS

Upper-Middle-Class Culture in the United States and France

Possessing the right kind of what the contemporary French sociologist Pierre Bourdieu calls *cultural capital* is a critical resource for anyone hoping to achieve upward social mobility. This is because people commonly look at an individual's cultural capital to determine if he or she is "one of us." If you display the right lifestyle, it will be far easier to be accepted into the "right" social circles.

However, the specific content of what is seen as the appropriate cultural capital to validate membership in a given social class varies greatly from society to society. Michael Lamont interviewed members of the upper-middle class in the United States and in France and discovered sharp differences in the sort of cultural capital that validated an individual's membership in that class in the two societies. He focused on three general categories of cultural capital: moral character, images of success, and cultural sophistication.

Moral character. Americans place a high value on honesty—or more precisely, they look down on people whom they consider dishonest. They particularly dislike phonies (who pretend to be something they are not), social climbers (who are blatantly ambitious and forget or drop people who helped them in their scramble to the top), and "low types" (who lie, cheat, and steal in their personal lives as well as in their business dealings).

The French share their American counterparts' dislike of insincerity and social climbing. But they view other American moral standards, especially those regarding sex, as puritanical and outdated. In the words of one interviewee, a literature professor,

> . . . I am completely indifferent to whether or not the president of the United States

has one, two, three, or ten mistresses, whether he likes little boys, or is homosexual or bisexual. I would simply ask that he not spend too much time at it. . . .

He went on to explain that the French value honor, a complex concept involving being true to oneself, sincere in relations with others, and trustworthy in financial dealings.

Success. Both the Americans and French tend to judge other people's worth in terms of such external status symbols as what they do for a living, where they live, where they vacation, and the like. But Americans place more emphasis on financial success. To upper-middle-class American men, wealth—measured in terms of the items an individual can afford, including cars, homes, trips, electronic equipment, and, not least of all, advantages for one's children—is both the symbol of and the reward for achievement.

In contrast, many French respondents considered questions about whether they themselves or their friends are "successful" to be uncouth. They view the pursuit of money for its own sake as debasing. Success, said one French entrepreneur, "is the full realization of oneself." Others value money not so much as a symbol of success, but as a means of maintaining their social identity and supporting a comfortable lifestyle, by which they mean being able to eat out regularly, go to the theater and other cultural events, and offer hospitality to friends and kin. They value inherited wealth and homes, art, and furniture that have been in the family for generations above "earned" money and recent purchases. Upwardly mobile, *nouveau riche* individuals who indulge in conspicuous consumption do not quite belong; they are "too American."

Cultural Sophistication. Both the Americans and the French see educational level and intelligence as important.

But here again, their criteria differ. Upper-middle-class U.S. men respect people who have a wealth of information—not only about their particular area of expertise, but also about the world at large—and the competence to translate this knowledge into action. They tend to see people with only "book learning" as lacking in common sense; their heroes are individuals like real estate magnate Donald Trump or Microsoft founder Bill Gates.

Upper-middle-class French are more likely to cite intellectuals like Raymond Aron and Jean-Paul Sartre as their heroes. They value *un sens critique* (a critical approach), combining intellectual playfulness, a capacity for abstraction and eloquence, and a distinct personal style above factual or practical knowledge. While Americans often say they feel inferior in the company of individuals who are more financially successful or more politically powerful than they, the French are awed by "people who strictly at the intellectual level make me feel very small . . . because I think they have succeeded at what I am trying to achieve."

In short, Lamont found that the heroes and models of upper-middle-class life in the United States would be considered vulgar and even mildly offensive in the equivalent French social circles.

1. What are some of the sociohistorical differences between the United States and France that might help to explain Lamont's findings?

2. What kinds of cultural capital are important in achieving entry into your campus's elite social circles?

Source: Lamont, 1997.

Symbolic Interactionism

Symbolic interactionists approach the issue of social stratification quite differently. Instead of speculating about its inevitability or its value to society, they are principally interested in how class affects patterns of everyday social life. Symbolic interactionism pays special attention to *status symbols* (Berger et al., 1992). Not all status symbols indicate an individual's class position, but many of the most important ones do.

Status symbols are especially important in the modern urban world. In rural areas and small towns, most people's class position is well known within the community. This is not true in large, anonymous cities. Urban life also allows people greater freedom to present a false front by concealing symbols of their low status and appropriating those denoting a higher class position than they actually hold. All of us are familiar with people who drive cars they can't afford or wear imitation designer clothes. Consequently, people are somewhat skeptical concerning displays of the more readily obtained symbols of elite class status.

Nevertheless, some physical objects remain quite effective as cues to people's class position, especially at the extremes of the stratification ladder. A person's home is a good example. People who live in mansions located in gated communities with private security forces are making an unambiguous statement about their class position, as are people who live in shacks or public housing projects. As noted at the beginning of this chapter, clothing is another good example (Mazur, 1993), especially clothes worn on the job. There is a good deal of truth to the old line that in the working class, your name goes on your shirt; in the middle class, on the door of your office; and in the upper class, on your company.

Some important symbols of class position are nonmaterial. In England, where the class lines are more sharply drawn than in the United States, accent is a reliable cue to class position. The popular 1950s musical *My Fair Lady* is about a gentleman named Henry Higgins who sets out to teach Eliza Doolittle, a woman from the lower classes, to speak with a "proper" accent in order to "pass" in genteel society.

Generally, lower status people coming into contact with their "betters" are expected to respond with deference, another nonmaterial symbolic representation of status differences. We have already mentioned examples of deference in relations between castes in traditional India and between the races in the old South. A good contemporary example concerns waiting: The lower your status compared to that of the person you are waiting to see, the longer you usually have to wait (Schwartz, 1975; Henley, 1977; Levine, 1987). In fact, the long waits in welfare and unem-

ployment offices and Medicaid clinics are among the most stigmatizing aspects of poverty status.

Here's another good example of class-linked deference: In many languages, speakers use different terms to address persons higher in status than they use with class equals and inferiors. In German, for example, the equivalent of the English "you" when addressing someone who is higher in rank is *Sie*. *Du* is a less formal term that is used only with intimates. The equivalents in Spanish are *usted* and *tu*.

Table 10.2 on page 268 summarizes the various theoretical perspectives on social stratification.

GLOBAL STRATIFICATION

The study of social stratification is not limited to consideration of the divisions between categories of people within a single society. It also encompasses *global stratification*, the separation of nations into ranked categories of wealth and power.

For many years, sociologists used the terms first, second, and third worlds to identify three broad "classes" of nations. In this scheme, the *First World* referred to the industrial and postindustrial "advanced" societies, including the United States, most of Western Europe, Canada, Australia, New Zealand, and Japan. All of these nations industrialized early and are characterized by technologically sophisticated, capitalist economies. All have high standards of living and democratic governments, and all but Japan reflect European cultural patterns. In a global context, these nations made up the world's upper class.

The *Second World* consisted of the Soviet Union and its satellites in Eastern Europe. These nations featured state socialist economies, intermediate levels of industrialization, moderate standards of living, and authoritarian governments. The Second World was equivalent to a global lower-middle class.

The world's poorer societies were lumped together as the *Third World*. Located principally in South America, Africa, and Asia, the Third World includes most of the world's people. These nations have low levels of industrialization and concentrate on subsistence production, their governments tend to be nondemocratic, and most of their citizens live in extreme poverty, although there usually is a small, highly privileged indigenous elite. The Third World nations were the global poverty class.

In recent decades, this typology has become outdated (Harris, 1987). This is partly a result of the Soviet system's collapse. But it is also because scholars realized that the Third World was an excessively broad and rather ethnocentric category. It lumped together all the following: rapidly developing nations

TABLE 10.2

Theories of Stratification Compared

Type of Theory	Origins of Inequality	Policy Implications	Representative Theorists
Deficiency Theory	Differences in individual ability	Social Darwinism; efforts to lessen the distress of the poor are misguided and socially harmful	Herbert Spencer Richard Herrnstein and Charles Murray
Functionalism	Necessary in order to promote efficient functioning of society	Reducing extreme poverty is desirable but society needs substantial inequality	Émile Durkheim Talcott Parsons Kingsley Davis and Wilbert Moore
Conflict Theory	Imposed by the powerful to promote their own interests	Dramatically reducing or even eliminating economic inequality is essential	Karl Marx Max Weber Ralf Dahrendorf
Symbolic Interactionism	Symbolic representations of inequality influence everyday interaction	None	Thorsten Veblen

such as South Korea and Singapore, which appear well on their way to First World status; oil-rich states such as Saudi Arabia and Kuwait whose citizens enjoy high incomes but that are structurally far from modern; relatively poor but economically developing nations such as Brazil and India; and the poorest of the poor, nations such as Somalia and Rwanda that cannot even feed their own people. The old scheme was also clearly value driven, implying that the First World was superior and the Third World backward.

No equally widely accepted typology has yet emerged. One alternative scheme, generally used in this text, divides nations into *developed* (or postindustrial), *developing*, and *underdeveloped* categories. The middle group includes most of the old Second World, the rapidly expanding economies of the Pacific Rim nations, and intermediate states such as Argentina and Turkey.

This model reflects contemporary geopolitical realities, but it does implicitly suggest that all societies are following the same general path, a path that will eventually lead every nation to resemble the industrial West. This implication has led some observers to charge that it is ethnocentric. Moreover, there are solid reasons to doubt that full industrialization is possible for many of the world's poorer societies.

Another option simply divides nations into high, medium, and low income categories on the basis of their citizens' wealth (World Bank, 1995). Figure 10.4 shows how the world's societies may be classified according to this scheme. Like all such typologies, this model is ultimately arbitrary. It is, however, relatively value-neutral (Sklar, 1995).

Sociologists have developed three different theoretical explanations of global stratification: modernization theory, dependency theory, and world systems theory.

Modernization Theory

Modernization theory originated in the United States during the 1950s (Weiner, 1966). Its central argument is that the less-developed nations may be placed somewhere along an evolutionary path moving toward full modernization and that all will eventually come to closely resemble the United States and other "advanced" nations.

In this model, modernization is seen as not only inevitable, but also desirable and irreversible. Low-income nations are believed to be slow in developing because of internal problems: inadequate infrastructure, lack of investment capital, inefficient governments, and, above all, a traditional culture that is fatalistic and highly skeptical of new technologies and institutional arrangements (Eisenstadt, 1973; Inkeles, 1983; Rostow, 1978, 1990; Bradshaw & Wallace, 1996). High-income nations can, it is believed, help developing countries by supplying capital and knowledge needed to expand their manufacturing sectors. Equally important, contact with developed nations will help overcome cultural inertia.

CRITIQUE. Modernization theory is accepted by many scholars in the developed world (Moore, 1979; Berger, 1986; Firebaugh & Beck, 1994; Inglehart & Baker, 2000). It is often used to justify the foreign policies and cross-national investment practices of the rich nations. This perspective assumes that contact between developed and developing societies normally benefits both. Modernization theory is often used to explain the success of the "Asian Tigers"—especially South Korea, Hong Kong, and Singapore. Their rapidly developing economies have strong links to the fully developed U.S. and Japanese economies.

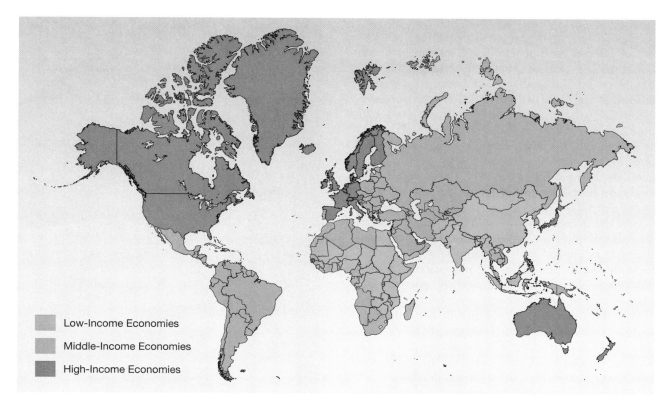

FIGURE 10.4 *Global Stratification: Low-, Middle-, and High-Income Countries, 1995.*
Source: World Bank (1995).

Low-Income Economies

Middle-Income Economies

High-Income Economies

But some scholars point out that many of the world's poorest nations, especially those in Latin America, do not seem to be moving toward prosperity despite their close ties to the industrial West (Isbister, 1998). The theory ignores the crucial fact that when the high-income nations modernized, they were not competing with powerful and wealthy nations, as is the case with today's developing world (Walton, 1987). In addition, the modernization process in countries such as France and England was greatly aided by **colonialism,** a system whereby certain high-income nations seized political, economic, and cultural control over most of the world's less developed societies (Bell, 1981; Worsley, 1984; Harrison, 1993). The easy availability of inexpensive labor and raw materials in their overseas colonies gave these nations a critical advantage that is not available to the once-colonial nations currently attempting to develop.

The critics are also uncomfortable with the implicit assertion that all nations ought to emulate countries like the United States, pointing to the numerous serious problems in our society. They also reject the notion that the problems keeping low- and middle-income nations undeveloped are all internal, which can be seen as a form of cross-national victim-blaming (Jaffee, 1998). In fact, there is considerable evidence that some traditional values, including a religiously motivated work ethic and a tradition of obeying paternalistic authority, may actually promote modernization (So, 1990).

Dependency Theory

Dependency theory emerged in the 1960s, especially in the work of Andre Gundar Frank (1966, 1967, 1980, 1998). It amounts to a fairly direct translation of conflict theory into the global arena. High-income nations play the role of the ruling class and the middle-income and especially the low-income nations serve as the equivalent of the proletariat.

According to dependency theorists, the relationship between these two groups of societies is far from mutually beneficial; in fact, it is very one-sided, with the wealthy countries reaping almost all of the advantages. The continued prosperity of the industrialized world comes from the exploitation of lower income nations. According to this perspective, these countries were often better off before they were drawn into ongoing economic interaction with the world's wealthy societies (Brown, 1994).

This pattern of dependency originated under colonialism. Indigenous peoples were denied the right to govern themselves. The economies of the colonies were also restructured to benefit the "mother nation," usually by serving as a source of minerals, agricultural raw materials, and cheap labor (Gill & Law, 1988).

Sometimes colonial economies became focused almost exclusively on the production of cash crops for export. Coffee in Brazil, bananas in Nicaragua, and rubber in the Congo are examples. Because so much land was devoted to the production of these crops, everyday foodstuffs that could otherwise have been grown in the colony had to be imported and tended to be more costly then they would have been if grown locally.

The colonial powers also encouraged the growth of a small, indigenous elite with strong cultural connections to the mother country. These people handled most of the day-to-day job of running the colony in the interests of the colonizers.

In the decades following World War II, almost all colonial societies gained political independence. But they continued to be economically and technologically dependent upon the old colonial powers. Today the colonial powers have been partially supplanted by vast multinational corporations (Webster, 1990). This pattern of continued dependency is known as **neocolonialism** (Harrington, 1977). Local governments, often controlled by the indigenous elite created by the colonizers, continue to allow their countries' economies to serve foreign interests.

According to dependency theory, the high-income nations benefit greatly from their relationship with low-income countries. They obtain raw materials and cheap labor (Clinard, 1990). They can unload products they cannot sell at home, including flammable sleepwear, hazardous pesticides, and tobacco. They can relocate manufacturing plants that create pollution because low-income nations lack both the political will and the ability to enforce even minimal environmental regulations. In some cases, hazardous wastes are shipped to these countries and simply dumped (La Dou, 1991). The primary negative effect on the high-income societies is unemployment, as manufacturing jobs move to developing countries.

From the perspective of the poor nations, the relationship looks even less positive (Brecher & Costello, 1994; Shen & Williamson, 1997). In addition to distorting local economies by concentrating on a single cash crop, paying low wages, and polluting the environment, other problems commonly arise:

- It is difficult for a large, stable middle class to develop. In part, this is because the multinational corporations pay low wages and oppose organizing by unions. Poor countries therefore tend to remain divided between a very large lower and working class and a small, highly privileged elite. Further, the ruling elite tend to become corrupt in defense of their advantages (Bradshaw, 1988).
- When high-income nations, often acting through international organizations such as the International Monetary Fund or the World Bank, extend

One of the most obvious signs of the global reach of modern corporation is the appearance in recent decades of fast food franchises all around the world. Kentucky Fried Chicken is becoming as popular in Beijing as it is in Louisville.

development loans to poorer nations, they often do more harm than good. The problem is that the recipients frequently are unable to repay the loans. The debt crisis worsens as interest charges spiral upward (Tordoff, 1992; Akinsanya, 1994).
- The continuing influence of high-income countries keeps the cultures of their former colonies from developing, a situation termed **cultural imperialism.** The language, religion, and customs of the high-income countries are considered, at least by local elites, to be superior to their own (Harrison, 1993; Barnet & Cavanagh, 1994; Sklar, 1995).

CRITIQUE Dependency theory corrects some of the excessive optimism of modernization theorists. However, the theory has limitations. In particular, it assumes that all low-income countries face similar problems as a result of their unequal relationships with the developed world. It cannot therefore explain the rapid progress of former colonies such as the previously mentioned Asian Tigers (Hill, 1994).

Many scholars maintain that if poorer nations proceed wisely, neocolonialism is not necessarily a fatal obstacle to modernization (Fallows, 1994). Studies strongly suggest that foreign investment can promote growth, not dependency (Vogel, 1991; Firebaugh, 1992; Bollen & Appold, 1993; Firebaugh & Beck, 1994). Thus, it is possible for both wealthy and poorer nations to benefit from economic interactions in some cases.

World Systems Theory

International economist Immanuel Wallerstein (1974, 1979, 1990, 1991) has developed a third theory of global stratification. His world systems theory combines the functionalist theme of the interdependence of the components of a social system with several elements of the conflict perspective. Its purpose is to explain the *origins* of the present international economic order.

World systems theory proposes that, over the past 450 years, all the world's nations have become integrated into a single system of capitalistic economic interdependency, with different nations and multinational corporations playing different roles in a global division of labor. In effect, world systems theory visualizes the global economy as a kind of gigantic assembly line where workers in many different nations contribute in different ways to the productive process (Bornschier, 1995).

Wallerstein identifies three distinct groups of nations in the world system—the core, semiperiphery, and periphery—each playing a different role in the global division of labor. Over time, some nations have moved from one group to another, but the basic distinctions remain (Arrighi, 1994). Within each of these three categories, there is a tendency for nations to gradually become more similar.

The *core* is world systems theory's term for the high-income nations located mainly in Europe and North America. They control the global economy (Chase-Dunn, 1990), were the first to industrialize, and retain technological and managerial superiority. Most of the profits generated by the world system flow back to the core, and especially to the huge multinational corporations headquartered there. Less than 25 percent of the world's population lives in the core, but they consume up to three-fourths of the planet's resources (Mingione & Pugliese, 1994).

At the other extreme, the *periphery* consists mostly of former colonial nations whose primary role in the world economic system is to supply raw materials and labor for the global assembly line (Shannon, 1989). The periphery participates in the world economic system only on terms set by and favorable to the core. The problems faced by the nations of the periphery are essentially the same as those that dependency theorists have identified as plaguing the world's poorer societies: unbalanced economies, low wages, pollution, rule by a small and unrepresentative elite, the lack of a stable middle class, high levels of foreign debt, and rampant cultural imperialism.

The nations of the *semiperiphery* stand in an intermediate position. This category includes, among others, Mexico, Argentina, Brazil, Russia, most of Eastern Europe, Ireland, Portugal, Greece, Spain, South Africa, the industrializing Pacific Rim nations, and the oil-producing states of the Middle East. Some, such as South Korea, are moving toward core status; others, such as Portugal, have been downwardly mobile. The semiperiphery is actively involved in the global economy but does not significantly shape it.

CRITIQUE World systems theory is a good middle ground between modernization and dependency theories. One of its strengths is its emphasis on the structure of global economic relations. Another is its extended time frame, which takes into account the centuries-long changes in the international economy that other theories tend to miss. Its weaknesses are that it ignores the positive aspects of contacts with the core for the economies of the periphery and the semiperiphery and that it downplays the importance of factors internal to the low-income nations that retard development (Brenner, 1977; Cockerham, 1995b).

Table 10.3 on page 272 summarizes key features of the three major perspectives on global stratification.

LIFE CONNECTIONS
The Homeless

While theory is important, we need to always bear in mind that sociologists study economic inequality because it has such enormous consequences for the lives of real people. In this section we illustrate the impact of social class by exploring the life circumstances of the poorest of the poor, the homeless.

No one really knows how many homeless people there are; the fact that they have no fixed place of residence makes it very difficult to count them accurately, although a number of attempts have been made to do so, both by sociological researchers and by the Census Bureau (Jencks, 1994). Conservative estimates suggest that perhaps 250,000 people are homeless on any given day, whereas poverty advocates have proposed numbers as high as 3 million. In the late 1980s, a group of researchers carefully enumerated Chicago's homeless and then extrapolated their findings to the national level, yielding an estimate of about 350,000 homeless people in the entire country, a figure that still seems roughly accurate (Rossi et al., 1987). But the number of people who are homeless at some point during any

TABLE 10.3

Theories of Global Stratification Compared

Type of Theory	Theoretical Orientation	Explanation for Poverty of Some Nations	Solution for Poverty	Representative Theorists
Modernization	Functionalist	Failure to modernize, mostly due to internal cultural and structural inadequacies	Emulate fully industrialized nations	Walt Rostow
Dependency	Conflict	Colonial and neocolonial domination by the developed nations	Resist neocolonial domination	Andre Gunder Frank
World Systems	Blends functionalist and conflict themes	Disadvantageous location in the periphery of the world system	Attempt to relocate to semiperiphery or core	Immanuel Wallerstein

given year is much higher, almost certainly exceeding 1 million, and the total number of people who have ever been homeless is estimated at 13.5 million, 1.75 million of whom have lived on the streets for longer than one year (Link et al., 1994).

There have always been homeless people in the United States, but prior to the mid-1970s they were principally unmarried elderly men, often with serious alcohol problems. Most spent their time working sporadically as laborers and living in the skid row districts of the nation's larger cities.

These men remain as a component of the homeless, but they have been joined by several other groups. A recent survey found that 46 percent of the urban homeless were single men; 14 percent were single women; 36.5 percent were families, almost all female-headed; and 3.5 percent were runaway and throwaway children (Worsnop, 1996). Families are the fastest growing part of the homeless population: Roughly one-third of the homeless are women and 25 percent are children.

Women and children suffer disproportionately from homelessness. One study found 89 percent of homeless mothers come from backgrounds of family violence and sexual abuse (Browne & Bassuk, 1997). Many leave home to escape these problems. Once on the street, they are highly vulnerable to rape and other forms of criminal victimization (Liebow, 1995). Their children often suffer serious health problems and have great difficulty concentrating on schoolwork.

A recent study found that 56 percent of the homeless are African American, 30 percent are white, and 10 percent are Hispanic (U.S. Conference of Mayors, 1996). The average age of homeless adults is in the mid-30s. About one-quarter are seriously mentally ill and another 25 percent show some mental impairment (Tessler & Dennis, 1992; Shinn & Weitz-

man, 1996). Most estimates suggest that over one-third of the homeless have major substance abuse problems. These are often the same people who are suffering from mental problems. Most of the homeless are high school graduates and some have attended college. A quarter are veterans (Edmonds, 1993). As many as 25 percent work, mostly part-time at minimum wage jobs (Shinn & Weitzman, 1996).

When the problem of homelessness first began to be publicized in the 1980s, the public was generally sympathetic, but in more recent years we have seen a great deal of what some have termed *compassion fatigue* (Smolowe, 1993). Cities around the nation have strengthened anti-loitering laws, closed shelters, and passed new ordinances against panhandling (National Law Center on Homelessness & Poverty, 1996).

These harsh measures doubtless reflect the fact that most people explain homelessness by reference to the personal failings of the homeless (Lee, 1992; Phelan et al., 1997), who are widely believed to be lazy, mentally ill, addicts, or drunks. In contrast, sociologists put much more emphasis on structural factors (Burt, 1992). While a minority of the homeless are indeed mentally ill or substance abusers, most are not, and the vast majority of Americans who suffer from serious personal problems do not end up on the streets. Some of the mental problems of the homeless are better viewed as consequences rather than causes of their extreme poverty (Golden, 1992). The following social factors seem central in explaining the growth of the homeless population over the past three decades (Elliott & Krivo, 1991):

- *Persistent and severe unemployment.* The homeless are the poorest of the poor. The kinds of low-skill, decent-paying jobs that they might have been able to find in the past have largely disappeared due to globalization and the rise of a postindustrial economy (Katz, 1995). Many live with family or friends, typically for 4 years after they lose work, but eventually their safety net collapses and they find themselves on the street (Snow & Anderson, 1993).

- *Loss of affordable housing.* America's stock of low-cost rental housing has been declining for decades due to abandonment, arson, demolition, and *gentrification* (the upgrading of units so that they can be rented or sold to middle-class people). At the same time, the number of very poor families and individuals has been increasing. As of 1995, there were 4.4 million more needy families than available low-rent housing units (Janofsky, 1998). People living below the poverty line usually pay between 50 and 75 percent of their after-tax income for housing—when they can find a home at all (Dolbeare, 1995; Koegel et al., 1996).
- *Cutbacks in government aid.* Direct federal aid for low-income housing dropped from $30 billion in 1980 to $8 billion in 1988 under the Reagan administration (Morganthau, 1988). Few of these cuts have been restored. Fifteen million families currently qualify for federal housing aid; fewer than one-third of them actually receive any (De-Parle, 1998).
- *Deinstitutionalization of the mentally ill.* A movement to reduce the number of people in mental hospitals began in the late 1950s, but it was not until the mid-1970s that substantial numbers of patients who could not care for themselves were released. Many ended up homeless (Patterson, 1994; Jencks, 1994).

The theoretical approaches to economic stratification introduced in this chapter may help explain homelessness. The widespread belief that the homeless are responsible for their own plight is a classic example of a victim-blaming ideology and very much in line with deficiency theories. Functionalists might point out that believing the homeless to be exclusively responsible for their plight allows those opposed to aiding the poor to successfully oppose welfare initiatives that would raise their taxes (White, 1992). Conflict theorists see the homeless as the ultimate losers in the struggle to get ahead; Marx would define them as *lumpenproletariat*, and Weber would note that they were on the bottom of the class, status, and power rankings. Symbolic interactionists would emphasize the consequences of the heavy stigma they bear (Phelan et al., 1997).

Extreme poverty is not a problem that is limited to the United States, of course. The concluding section of this chapter briefly examines poverty in Brazil.

SOCIETY CONNECTIONS

Wealth, Poverty, and Class Conflict in Brazil

Brazil, a country of 176 million people, is an excellent example of a developing nation located in what world systems theory calls the semiperiphery. Earlier in the 20th century, its economy was slow-growing and largely agricultural but in recent decades it has been industrializing rapidly and is now the world's 10th largest. The Brazilian government has attracted foreign investment by improving transportation and communication systems, outlawing labor unions, and offering tax credits and low export fees to investors (Evans, 1979).

Development has not come without problems, however. The annual inflation rate was 66 percent in 1995 (although it was only 7 percent in 2000), and the Brazilian foreign debt currently exceeds $244 billion, the highest figure outside of the core nations. In the early 1990s, the government privatized many public services and laid off some 250,000 civil service workers (Brooke, 1990). Nevertheless, the overall economic picture is quite encouraging for some Brazilians, although not for everyone.

Brazil displays one of the widest gaps between the rich and the poor in the contemporary world (Soares, 1996; Sernau, 2001). According to the most recent census, the top 10 percent of Brazilian society controls 49 percent of the nation's wealth and the bottom 10 percent owns less than 1 percent of it. Collectively, the upper 20 percent of the population owns 32 times as much as the bottom fifth. Half of the cultivable land is owned by less than 1 percent of the nation's landowners. Brazil's average annual income is $5,370, but people in the bottom 10 percent earn an average of only $564 (Passell, 1996).

The Brazilian upper class, about 1 percent of the total population, enjoys tremendous power and privilege. The middle classes—the next 26 percent of the population—are well educated, travel widely, and lead comfortable lives by North American standards. But for the remaining 73 percent of the population—and especially for the 47 percent who are classified as poor—living conditions are dreadful (Wood & de-Carvalho, 1988; Harrison, 1992).

Some of the worst conditions are found in the *favelas*, shantytowns housing hundreds of thousands of recent arrivals from the countryside who are seeking a better life. Large families and limited job skills doom most of the poor to a marginal existence. One-fourth of Brazil's people go to sleep hungry every night.

Instead of clamoring for policies to reduce this misery, the middle and upper classes seem utterly unmoved by it. In fact, many appear far less concerned about the suffering of the poor than about the possi-

Children like these who grow up in the slums of Brazil's large cities face a perilous, hand-to-mouth existence.

bility that they might be inconvenienced by efforts to help the lower classes. This is especially evident in the way many elite Brazilians respond to the millions of street children living in the nation's large cities (Sanders, 1987). Armed guards patrol municipal dumps lest children make off with scraps of edible garbage. And despite ongoing protests by interna-

tional human rights organizations, thousands of poor Brazilian children have been murdered since 1985 by police and vigilante death squads hired by shopkeepers who don't want the sight of a begging child to scare off tourists and other middle-class customers (Larmer, 1992; Michaels, 1993).

SUMMARY

1. All but the simplest societies are characterized by social stratification based on variables such as gender, age, race or ethnicity, and economic status.

2. Systems of social stratification are legitimated by widely accepted belief systems termed ideologies.

3. The ideology that legitimates economic inequality in modern societies may be called classism. It suggests that because there is widespread equal opportunity, both the wealthy and the poor deserve their fates.

4. Structured economic inequality generally increases as societies develop until they reach the industrial stage, when this trend reverses.

5. Historic patterns of social stratification include slave and caste systems; contemporary developed societies emphasize class rather than more ascriptive patterns of structured economic inequality.

6. Deficiency theories, generally regarded by sociologists as inaccurate and misleading, explain social stratification in terms of differences in individual ability.

7. Functionalist theory as developed in the Davis-Moore thesis argues that economic stratification is inevitable and that it serves the positive function of ensuring that the most important statuses in society are filled by the most capable people.

8. Conflict theorists disagree with the functional view that the effects of stratification are generally positive.

9. Karl Marx believed social classes, composed of people who share a common relationship to the means of production, are locked in irreconcilable conflict with each other. In order to win this struggle, subordinate classes must attain class consciousness; the dominant class attempts to retard class consciousness by encouraging various forms of false consciousness.

10. Max Weber identified three overlapping systems of stratification in modern societies: economic classes, status groups, and parties or power groups.

11. Symbolic interactionists emphasize the importance of status symbols and other ways that class differences influence everyday patterns of social life.

12. The modern world displays a pattern of global stratification into several distinct groups of na-tions: fully developed, developing, and underdeveloped, or high-, medium-, and low-income.

13. Modernization theory suggests that all of the world's societies will eventually become fully developed and argues that the failure of poor societies to develop is largely due to their own inadequacies.

14. Dependency theory explains the poverty of many nations as a consequence of their economic domination by the developed world.

15. World systems theory divides the world's nations into three categories—core, semiperiphery, and periphery—with each group playing a different role in a global assembly line.

16. While the homeless make up a relatively small percentage of the U.S. population, they illustrate the human consequences of living at the bottom of the stratification hierarchy. Sociologists generally see homelessness as more the result of structural than individual causes.

17. Extreme poverty is a very serious social problem worldwide, as illustrated by the condition of Brazil's underclass.

KEY TERMS

bourgeoisie 263	**Davis-Moore thesis** 261	**proletariat** 263
caste system 256	**deficiency theory** 259	**social class** 252
class consciousness 263	**false consciousness** 263	**Social Darwinism** 260
classism 252	**global stratification** 252	**social stratification** 251
colonialism 269	**Kuznets curve** 255	**status groups** 264
cultural capital 264	**neocolonialism** 270	
cultural imperialism 270	**power** 264	

CRITICAL THINKING QUESTIONS

1. How deep is the average American's support for classist ideology? Do you think support for classism is currently increasing or weakening in this country? Why?

2. Functionalists and conflict theorists disagree regarding whether economic stratification is inevitable and also regarding whether its consequences are primarily positive or harmful. What is your view? Do you think you would have given the same answer if you had been born into a different social class?

3. What are the implications of the three global stratification theories for U.S. policy toward the world's poorer societies? Which view do you find most convincing? Defend your choice.

INVESTIGATE WITH CONTENT SELECT

Journal Research Collections from *ContentSelect* Begin your research using Content-Select for this chapter by following the directions found on page 27 of this text to visit Prentice Hall's Research Navigator Website. Enter these search terms into the search field:

Caste system
Homelessness
Karl Marx

11
SOCIAL CLASS IN MODERN SOCIETIES

Three Social Classes—Three Different Worlds

William Wharton was born into an upper-class family living in Lake Forest, an exclusive North Shore suburb of Chicago. After attending an excellent (and very expensive) preschool, he was enrolled in a private elementary academy and later on in an exclusive Connecticut prep school. The distinctive language patterns and lifestyle preferences that William had learned at home were continually reinforced at his schools. Although he maintained only a B average, he was accepted at Cornell, the same university his parents had attended and to which they had made substantial donations. After completing college, William entered Yale Law School; when he graduated he secured a position in a major law firm whose controlling partner was a good friend of the family.

Susan Gonzales was born in Chicago on the same day as William but to a middle-class family. She attended public schools and graduated in the upper 15 percent of her high-school class. In order to save money, she attended a local community college for two years before transferring to the University of Illinois, where she majored in secondary education. After graduation, she married and taught high school in a Chicago suburb.

Jamal Smith was born to an impoverished Chicago family on the same day as William and Susan. Unable to adequately support his family, his father left home six months later. When Jamal turned 4, a social worker helped enroll him in a Head Start program. He showed high intelligence and did well initially when he entered elementary school, but after the fourth grade he began falling behind. He successfully completed middle school and two years of high school, but his grades were low, in part because he worked long hours at a local grocery store in order to help his mother pay the bills. He dropped out early in his junior year to go to work as a full-time stock clerk at the supermarket.

William, Susan, and Jamal are not real people; they are fictional composites reflecting common—but by no means universal—life experiences of young people born into the upper, middle, and lower classes. The reason we have begun this chapter with their stories is to emphasize a crucial point: *Class matters.* Your class location affects almost every aspect of your daily life—not just your school experience and career opportunities, but also such factors as your political preferences, the way you socialize your children, which church you attend, and the likelihood that you will be victimized by crime.

Gender and racial/ethnic stratification also profoundly affect our lives, especially as they interact with the effects of social class. These types of structured social inequality will be the topics of Chapters 12 and 13; in this chapter we concentrate on economic stratification in modern societies. The chapter begins by considering how sociologists determine an individual's class position. Next, we examine the U.S. class system, discuss social mobility, and explore how class affects life chances and lifestyles. The chapter concludes with a critical look at recent changes in the welfare system.

MEASURING CLASS

Many important sociological variables, including race, age, gender, and religion, are relatively easy to study because most people have a good idea of the categories in which they belong. Fewer people in the United States are sure of their class position. Researchers may use one or more of three distinct means of *operationalizing* the variable of class—that is, of defining class in such a way that it can be used in empirical research. These means may be termed the subjective, reputational, and objective approaches (Runciman, 1990).

The Subjective Approach

The **subjective approach** to identifying class—also called the self-placement approach—is the simplest of the three. It consists of nothing more than asking

The lifestyles of people belonging to different social classes are so distinct that it is sometimes possible to get a fairly accurate idea of what class people are in by looking at their clothing and physical appearance alone.

people to which class they think they belong. The data in Figure 11.1 reflect the use of the subjective approach.

In some cases, this methodology can be quite effective. If researchers provide respondents with a set of possible answers, then most people can manage to sort themselves out into classes. For example, in a recent national survey, 5 percent of males and 4 percent of females identified themselves as upper class, 45 percent of both genders called themselves middle class, 46 percent of men and 44 percent of women described themselves as working class, and 4 percent of men and 7 percent of women chose the label lower class (NORC, 1996). These findings suggest that people in the United States *are* aware that there are different classes and also that they have at least some idea of how they should be classified.

The problem with this approach is that many people do not have a *clear* understanding of particular class labels. Researchers cannot be sure that what one respondent means by, say, working class, is identical to what other respondents or sociologists might mean by that label. Another problem is that some people may identify with a class to which they aspire rather than with the one in which they are actually located.

Furthermore, when no structured responses are provided, a sizable majority of the respondents typically identify themselves as middle class. (Vanneman & Cannon, 1987; Simpson, et al., 1988; Marger, 2002). Some wealthy people may call themselves middle class to avoid appearing arrogant. Working- and lower-class individuals may choose this label because, given the widespread acceptance of classism (see Chapter 10) in U.S. society, to admit being less than middle class is to acknowledge a personal failing. Similar results have been found in contemporary Western European societies (Kelley & Evans, 1993).

Clearly, for many people "middle class" is a catch-all category that applies to everyone except those at the extreme top and bottom of society. This suggests that there is a relatively low level of class awareness in the United States, making the subjective approach of only limited value to researchers studying this society.

The Reputational Approach

Some 20th-century sociologists studied class in smaller communities by asking well-informed local "judges" to place their fellow citizens into such classes

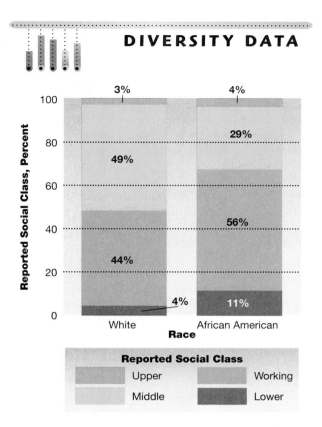

DIVERSITY DATA

FIGURE 11.1 *Self Perceived Social Class, by Race.* White people are substantially more likely than African Americans to describe themselves as middle class, while African Americans are more likely than whites to report that they are either working or lower class. Why might respondents of either race resist seeing themselves as lower class?

Source: NORC. General Social Surveys, 1972–2000. Chicago: National Opinion Research Center, 2000. Reprinted by permission of NORC, Chicago, IL.

as "people who are doing very well" or "hard-working regular folks" or "trailer-park residents." The best-known research using this **reputational approach** was carried out in the 1930s by W. Lloyd Warner and his associates in a New England town he called "Yankee City." Warner identified six "prestige classes" ranging from the upper upper to the lower lower (Warner et al., 1941, 1949).

The reputational approach remains useful in small communities with little population turnover where most residents know each other. However, the number of such communities has decreased sharply in the modern world. Most contemporary sociologists reject both the subjective and the reputational approaches in favor of the objective method.

The Objective Approach

In the **objective approach,** sociologists ask their respondents for several facts about themselves and then use this information to place them into social classes. The most commonly used objective definition of class is called **socioeconomic status (or SES)** (Gilbert & Kahl, 1993). It is made up of three loosely related *indicators* (or measures): income, occupational prestige, and education.

All three indicators are necessary because any one may be misleading. For example, most people without a high-school diploma are low in class, but there are some individuals who become millionaires even though they never graduated from high school. Money is not the whole story either: Drug lords may earn vastly more each year than ministers, but they enjoy much lower occupational prestige rankings.

Dual Earner Households

As married women have flooded into the job market in recent decades, the task of measuring social class position has become more complicated (Beeghley, 2000). Researchers who use the objective approach have developed new methodologies that not only take into account the income contributed by both earners but also factor in both the husband's and the wife's occupational prestige and educational attainment. Wives interviewed using the subjective approach traditionally tended to classify themselves solely in terms of their husband's job and education, but now they are more likely to consider both their own attributes and those of their spouses (Davis & Robinson, 1998).

PROPERTY AND PRESTIGE: DIMENSIONS OF CLASS

The popularity of the objective approach has led many sociologists to focus principally on three dimensions of class in modern societies: property, occupational prestige, and, to a lesser extent, power. Chapter 18 addresses the distribution of power in the United States; here we will discuss property and prestige.

Property

Property is a critical indicator of class position. Sociologists divide it into two general categories: **income,** consisting of salaries, rents, and interest and dividends received from stocks and bonds; and **wealth,** net accumulated assets, including homes, land, automobiles, jewelry, factories, and stocks and bonds (Keister, 2000). The distribution of both income and wealth is markedly unequal in modern U.S. society.

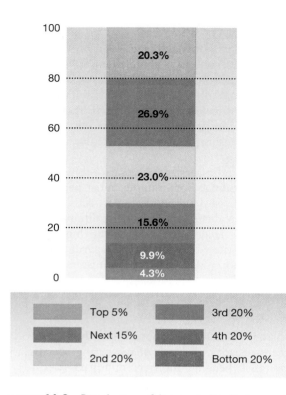

FIGURE 11.2 Distribution of Aggregate Family Income in the United States, 1999.

Source: U.S. Census Bureau (2001), Statistical Abstract, Table 670.

INCOME Figure 11.2 helps us to visualize the extent of income inequality in the United States. The top 20 percent of families received 47.2 percent of all income in 1999, while the bottom 20 percent earned just 4.3 percent. Collectively the top 20 percent was paid substantially more than the bottom 60 percent. The top 5 percent of U.S. families received 20.3 percent of all income; minimum earnings for this group were $155,040 compared with an average for all families of $48,950. The minimum income of families in the top one half of one percent was $1.375 million!

Looking even higher up, in 2001 the median annual compensation package for the top executives of the 350 largest public corporations was $2.9 million, 90 times the average worker's pay ("The Boss's Pay," 2001). Citigroup CEO Sanford Weill led the pack, receiving $224 million. In the words of noted economist Paul Samuelson, "If we make an income pyramid out of a child's blocks, with each layer portraying $500 of income, the peak would be far higher than Mount Everest, but most people would be within a few feet of the ground" (Samuelson & Nordhaus, 1989:644). In fact, the stack of blocks representing the average American family would be just 12 feet high in this model.

Both race and gender strongly influence earnings. In 1999, the median income of white families was $51,224 compared with $56,316 for Asian and Pacific Islander families, $31,778 for African Americans, and $31,663 for Latinos. In that same year, two-parent families earned a median of $56,676, single-parent male-headed families received $37,396, but single-parent female-headed families earned just $23,732.

The United States displays the most extreme income inequality in the developed world: People in the top 20 percent earn an average of 11 times more than the typical individual in the bottom 20 percent (Freeman, 1999). In contrast, Sweden's ratio is less than 4 to 1 (Beeghley, 2000). On the other hand, inequality is much more extreme in many developing nations than in the United States—the ratio in Brazil is 32 to 1 (Passell, 1996).

How have patterns of U.S. income inequality changed over recent decades? Figure 11.3 shows that between 1950 and 1970, the share of all income earned by the top 20 percent of U.S. families dropped from 42.7 percent to 40.9 percent, while the share of the bottom 40 percent grew from 16.5 percent to 17.6 percent. Since then, however, the pattern has reversed (Danziger & Gottschalk, 1995; Auerbach & Belous, 1998), with the top group earning 47.2 percent and the bottom just 14.2 percent by 1999.

In the 1990s alone, the number of millionaires in the United States quadrupled to 5 million (D'Souza, 1999); 86 percent of the growth of the economy during the stock market boom of this era went into the pockets of the top 10 percent of earners (Mischel et al., 1999).

On the other hand, the real earnings of the poorest fifth of the population rose less than 1 percent between 1988 and 1998. Between 1980 and 2000, the average worker's pay increased 66 percent (not adjusted for inflation), while the average salary of CEOs of the nation's 365 largest corporations rose 1,996 percent (Overholser, 2001).

Source: DILBERT reprinted by permission of United Features Syndicate, Inc.

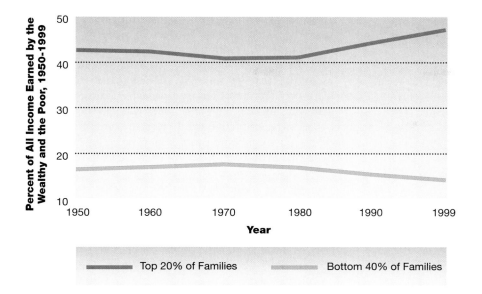

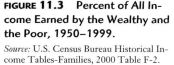

FIGURE 11.3 Percent of All Income Earned by the Wealthy and the Poor, 1950–1999.

Source: U.S. Census Bureau Historical Income Tables-Families, 2000 Table F-2.

The reasons for these trends are complex, including changes in the structure and health of the economy, in tax laws, and in welfare spending. We discuss these factors later in the chapter when we analyze the shrinking of the U.S. middle class.

WEALTH The distribution of wealth in the United States is much less equal than that of income. The top 20 percent controls about 80 percent of all wealth. Another 15 percent is in the hands of the second 20 percent; the rest own virtually nothing. In fact, if we consider debts as well as assets, the lowest two-fifths of the population owe more than their total wealth (Beeghley, 2000).

The concentration at the extreme top is staggering. The top 1 percent of the population holds almost 40 percent of all wealth in the United States, more than is held by the entire lower 90 percent. The top 12 families control over $300 billion; in contrast, the average household is worth about $72,000 ("The Forbes 400," 1999). In 2000 Microsoft CEO Bill Gates headed the *Forbes* list of the wealthiest people in the United States with estimated holdings of $63 billion.

As with income, the distribution of wealth in the United States is more unequal than in any other comparable country (Wolff, 1995). For example, in the United Kingdom, historically one of Europe's less egalitarian nations, the top 1 percent held about 18 percent of private wealth in the early 1990s; the U.S. figure was 34 percent.

Also as with income, the distribution of wealth has become even less equal in the United States over the past two decades (Wolff, 1995). Between 1992 and 1998, the share of wealth held by the top 1 percent increased from 37.4 percent to 39.1 percent.

How should we interpret these income and wealth trends? In line with the Davis-Moore theory

discussed in Chapter 10, some functionalists see increases in economic inequality as a spur to ambition: The rewards of getting to the top are greater than ever. Others, especially conflict theorists, are uneasy about the concentration of power that accompanies increasing inequality in income and wealth. They fear that tens of millions of people at the bottom have become so poor that, whatever their talents and motivation, they will have great difficulty getting ahead.

Occupational Prestige

In everyday life, we usually ask what someone does for a living in order to identify his or her class position. We do this, in part, because it is considered impolite to ask people about their income and wealth, while it is socially acceptable to show interest in a person's work. But this is also a reflection of the fact that people generally agree about how much prestige accompanies various occupations. Table 11.1 on page 282 summarizes the findings of recent research into occupational prestige rankings.

Take a few minutes to study this table. What seems to influence how people evaluate different jobs? Certainly money is part of the equation—most of the occupations toward the top of the list pay more than those near the bottom—but there are a number of exceptions to this rule: For example, truck drivers and carpenters may earn more than social workers or grade school teachers, two occupations whose wages are affected by the fact that they are predominantly female (Nakao & Treas, 1994). Jobs that are primarily held by minorities also tend to be less well paid and prestigious (Oliver & Shapiro, 1995).

High-status occupations normally involve substantial autonomy and authority; being closely super-

TABLE 11.1

Prestige Rankings of Selected Occupations

Physician	86
Lawyer	75
University professor	74
Architect	73
Dentist	72
Pharmacist	68
Registered nurse	66
High school teacher	66
Accountant	65
Elementary school teacher	64
Computer programmer	61
Police officer	60
Librarian	54
Firefighter	53
Social worker	52
Realtor	49
Mail carrier	47
Secretary	46
Welder	42
Farmer	40
Carpenter	39
Child-care worker	36
Truck driver	30
Cashier	29
Garbage collector	28
Bartender	25
Farm laborer	23
Janitor	22
Shoe shiner	9

Source: NORC. General Social Surveys, 1972–1998. Cumulative Codebook. Chicago: NORC, 1999. Reprinted by permission of NORC, Chicago, IL. pp. 1223–1241.

own means of creating significant wealth and (b) whether they exercise substantial *authority* over others. Figure 11.4 summarizes Wright's model.

At the top, like Marx (see Chapter 10), Wright identifies a powerful *capitalist class* that owns productive property and exercises extensive authority. At the bottom, there is a class of *proletarian workers* who neither own productive property nor exercise authority. The most interesting elements of Wright's model are the two groups that occupy what he calls "contradictory class locations" because they have some characteristics in common with the capitalists and in other ways resemble the workers. The *petite bourgeoisie* are the small shopowners and other entrepreneurs who own capital but employ few if any workers and so exercise little authority. This group makes up about 5 percent of the population. The fourth class, *managers,* work in firms owned by the capitalists but have authority over a large number of workers. Most members of this managerial group identify with the capitalists, and yet ultimately they are as expendable as any other employees. This fact has become a bitter reality to large numbers of middle managers during the current era of corporate downsizing (Uchitelle & Kleinfeld, 1996; see Chapter 21).

Concerning the three individuals introduced at the beginning of this chapter, Wright would classify William Wharton, the lawyer, as a manager. Susan Gonzales, who teaches high school, and Jamal Smith, who works in a supermarket, are both workers.

Though Wright's model has much to recommend it, other sociologists prefer to analyze the U.S.

vised and taking orders lowers occupational prestige. Most highly ranked jobs also require extensive education and are usually "clean" in that they involve working with people or ideas rather than with things (MacKinnon & Langford, 1994). Research shows that occupational prestige rankings have changed very little during the past century (Nakao & Treas, 1994). These rankings are also surprisingly similar around the globe (Lin & Xie, 1988).

THE CLASS SYSTEM IN THE UNITED STATES

Sociologists take several different approaches in describing the U.S. class system (Lucal, 1994). Some follow the lead of Erik Olin Wright (1979, 1985; 1997; Wright et al., 1982), who identifies four principal classes based on the four possible combinations of two key factors: (a) whether the members of a class

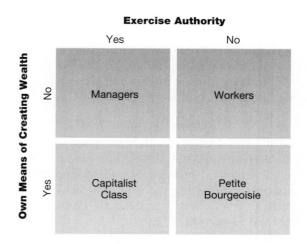

FIGURE 11.4   Erik Olin Wright's Model of the U.S. Class Structure. Wright identifies four classes based on the intersection of two factors: ownership of the means of creating wealth and exercising authority over others.

Source: Wright (1979, 1985); Wright et al. (1982).

THEN AND NOW

Lifestyles of the Robber Barons

The late 19th century resembled the present era in that the top leaders of the business community were becoming fabulously wealthy. These individuals, known popularly as "robber barons," accumulated vast fortunes through such tactics as the establishment of monopolies, intimidation, brutal exploitation of their workers, and in some cases overt violence. Their abuses went largely unchallenged except by a few crusading reformers and newspapermen; the industrialists' control over government was sufficient to guarantee that there would be no significant interference with their affairs.

This was an era in which labor unions were widely outlawed, when there were no large-scale governmental welfare programs, and when there were no progressive taxes. While millions of the poor lived in misery and squalor, the robber barons enjoyed a lifestyle of almost unimaginable luxury. Sociologist Thorsten Veblen referred to this group as the "leisure class" and characterized their lifestyle as "conspicuous consumption."

Here is a description of a fancy-dress ball given by the Vanderbilt family in March 1883 at their New York mansion:

Mrs. William K. Vanderbilt was costumed as a Venetian princess, Mr. Cornelius Vanderbilt as Louis XVI, and his spouse as "The Electric Light," in white satin trimmed with diamonds, and with a superb diamond headdress. In the drawing rooms of the Vanderbilt palace, with its cluttered interiors in Japanese or in French style, hung with flowing masses of pale red velvet drapery which was embroidered with foliage and jeweled butterflies, the noble throng ate, drank, and danced through the night. For the six quadrilles which represented the high moments of the ball, the dancers formed in the gymnasium on the third floor, moved down the grand staircase of Caen stone (fifty feet high), and swept through the great hall (sixty-five by twenty feet) into a drawing-room (forty by twenty feet whose wainscoting of carved French walnut had been torn from a French chateau and hauled across the ocean). (pp. 331–332)

The meals served to New York's elite were even more opulent:

At one, each lady present, opening her napkin, found a gold bracelet with the monogram of the host. At another, cigarettes rolled in hundred dollar bills were passed around after the coffee and consumed with an authentic thrill. One man gave a dinner to his dog, and presented him with a diamond collar worth $15,000. At another dinner, costing $20,000, each guest discovered in one of his oysters a magnificent black pearl. (p. 338)

Were the robber barons entirely unaware of the suffering of the poor?

Not quite.

. . . In later years the "Poverty Social" came strongly into vogue. At one such reunion held in the home of a Western millionaire, the thirty guests came attired in rags and tatters. At a cost of $14,000 . . . scraps of food were served on wooden plates. The diners sat about on broken soup boxes, buckets, and coalhods. Newspapers, dust cloths and old skirts were used as napkins, and beer [was] served in a rusty tin can. (pp. 339–340)

1. Is there anything wrong with wealthy people spending their money any way they wish?

2. How do the lifestyles of today's rich and famous differ from those of the 19th century robber barons?

Source: Josephson, 1934.

---

class system in terms of a somewhat simpler scheme represented by the work of Dennis Gilbert and Joseph Kahl (1993) among others. The following discussion of the U.S. class system is based on this interpretation.

The Upper Class

Although only about 1 percent of the U.S. population is in the upper class, their influence is hard to overestimate, as is implied by the income and wealth data presented previously (Hacker, 1997; Domhoff, 1998). Though members of this class earn large salaries, their chief economic resource is accumulated wealth rather than income. More than half of all upper-class

INTERNET CONNECTIONS

After reading the section on the upper class, go to *Forbes* Website,

http://www.forbes.com/2002/02/28/billionaires.html

and read the articles on the richest people in the world. Also, click on some of the interactive graphics. After browsing the Website, write a short description about the characteristics of the richest people in the world. In what way are they different from other social classes?

Corporate entrepreneur Bill Gates, the wealthiest individual in the United States, achieved an elite class position by virtue of the extraordinary success of the Microsoft corporation, which he founded.

families were born into the bulk of their wealth; about 40 percent inherited all of it (Keister, 2000; McNamee & Miller, 1998). William Wharton, the successful lawyer discussed at the opening of this chapter, clearly is a member of the upper class. In recent decades, the elite has used its political power to reshape the tax code so that most pay at lower rates than the rest of the population; a few take advantage of so many loopholes that they pay no federal taxes at all (Barlett & Steele, 1994).

Members of the upper class distinguish between two groups within it (Allen, 1987; Dye, 1995). At the extreme top are the "old rich," families like the Rockefellers, Fords, and duPonts, who have been wealthy for generations (Aldrich, 1988). Below them are people like Bill Gates or Steven Spielberg, who earned their wealth more recently. This group also includes a few highly paid athletes and actors as well as top professionals.

Members of the old rich may work, but many simply manage their investments, while many "new rich" occupy top executive positions in the largest corporations. For this reason, the latter group is sometimes called the "corporate class." In many cases, the new rich actually are wealthier than the old, but members of both groups generally acknowledge the higher status of the old rich.

Members of the upper class generally feel a strong sense of class consciousness (Baltzell, 1990). Traditionally, they were almost entirely white Protestants of British descent. Today, their lower ranks are opening to Catholics and some European ethnics, but there are still very few African Americans or Hispanics among them. They tend to live in a small number of elite communities, marry other members of the upper class, send their children to the same prep schools and top private colleges, join the same clubs, and vacation in the same exclusive spots (Baltzell, 1990; Domhoff, 1998). More than any other class, members of the elite form distinct social networks.

Historically, many members of the old rich felt a strong sense of *noblesse oblige*, a belief that in return for being born to privilege, they ought to support charitable organizations and the arts (Lapham, 1988). However, according to some critics, this orientation seems to be diminishing among many members of the modern corporate class (Dye, 1995).

The Upper-Middle Class

Most people have little contact with the upper class; the very rich tend to use their wealth to protect their privacy (Fussell, 1992). Not so the upper-middle class, whose members are usually highly visible. Lack-

Men and women in the upper-middle class can afford to enjoy sports like tennis and golf, which require expensive equipment and are popular at country clubs.

Members of the upper class are able to afford to live in luxurious mansions that the rest of us can only dream about.

ing significant power at the national level, these are the movers and shakers of the local community (Marger, 2000).

Making up about 14 percent of the population, this class consists of high-level professionals and managers typically earning between $100,000 and $300,000 per year. Upper-middle class women typically work, although more from choice than necessity. These families do not hold enormous wealth, but they are financially secure, drive new cars, and live in substantial homes. Their class position depends heavily on their education: Virtually all hold degrees and many have completed graduate work at high-quality colleges and universities. Most live in the suburbs, where they play a central role in groups such as the Chamber of Commerce and the local country club and often in local government as well. Although mostly white, they are more ethnically diverse than the upper class.

The Lower-Middle Class

About 30 percent of the U.S. population falls in the lower-middle class. These are the lower managers, small-business operators, nonretail sales workers, upper clerical workers, and minor professionals such as teachers. Most people at this level have at least some postsecondary education, but many have not completed their degrees. Their family incomes range from about $30,000 annually to perhaps $80,000 (Marger, 2000). Susan Gonzales, the Chicago high-school teacher, belongs in this class.

Normally, both husband and wife must work in order to maintain a moderately comfortable lifestyle, although one that is relatively insecure, since people at this level do not have substantial investments or savings. Most can take occasional vacations, eat out fairly regularly, drive inexpensive late-model cars, and send their children to public universities or at least to community colleges. Historically, most have owned (or been buying) their own homes, although this goal is becoming increasingly difficult in the contemporary economy (Cassidy, 1995).

Members of the lower-middle class typically encourage their children to complete their education in hopes of moving up; they are also deeply concerned about the possibility of sliding back into the working class. The vast majority of the members of this class are essentially powerless at the local and national levels, as well as in their jobs, where they follow rules established by their upper-middle class superiors.

The Working Class

Roughly 30 percent of people in the United States are in the working class. However, the line between the lower-middle and working classes is very indistinct. Most of the members of this class earn between $25,000 and $45,000 annually, but some, especially unionized production workers and skilled craft workers such as carpenters and electricians, earn substantially more. Those with higher incomes are characterized as working class mainly because their lifestyle is similar to that of others in this group (Beeghley, 2000)

Most members of the working class are skilled and semiskilled manual workers. The working class also includes low-level clericals, sales workers, and many female *pink-collar workers* such as waitresses and cooks. Most working-class jobs are highly routine

Members of the petite bourgeoisie resemble the bourgeoisie in that they are not compelled to sell their labor to others in order to survive, but they differ from them because they employ few workers and accumulate little capital.

and closely supervised. The large majority of wives in this class must work outside the home in order to help pay household bills (Rubin, 1994).

Working-class people usually complete high school, but relatively few go on to college. Perhaps half of them own their own homes, but they have no other significant assets and are vulnerable to a financial crisis resulting from illness or unexpected unemployment (Rubin, 1994). The real (inflation-adjusted) income from most blue-collar jobs has been declining in recent years. Most working-class people drive used cars, live in modest neighborhoods, and must sacrifice in order to eat out or take a vacation.

While upward mobility is encouraged in the working class, many people in this stratum emphasize the importance of conventional respectability in order to underscore their superiority over the lower classes.

The Working Poor

Perhaps 22 percent of the population may be classified as the working poor. As the term implies, members of this class work, sometimes full time and sometimes part time, but receive such low wages that they live in or near poverty. An individual who worked full time at the 2002 minimum wage of $5.15 per hour for 50 weeks would earn just $10,300, well below the poverty line. In fact, 2.9 percent of all full-time workers were classified as poor in 1998. So much for the bumper sticker that reads "I fight poverty—I work!"

But doesn't the American Dream promise a decent life to anyone who is willing to work hard? Part of the problem is that the minimum wage has failed to keep pace with inflation. If it had been automatically adjusted to reflect increases in the cost of living, as Social Security is, then in order to have given workers the same purchasing power in 1994 that they had in 1968, the minimum wage would have had to have been $6.29 per hour. In fact, it was $4.25, where it stayed until 1996, when Congress approved an increase in two stages to $5.15; it remains at that level today, although a number of states have independently raised their minimum standards to a higher "living wage." In 2000, 866,000 workers were receiving the minimum wage, and 1,844,000 more earned less than the federal minimum. Compared with 2.6 percent of men, 4.8 percent of women paid hourly rates fell at or below the minimum wage level.

Lacking any accumulated wealth whatsoever, these people exist from paycheck to paycheck. Jamal Smith, the supermarket stock clerk, is in the working poor. Members of this class have sometimes completed high school, but they commonly lack advanced job skills. Most of the working poor hold low-pay, dead-end service jobs, often on a temporary basis, that rarely offer health insurance, pension plans, or other benefits. In fact, about 80 percent of the 44.3 million people who lacked health insurance in 1998 were full-time workers or their dependents (Westphal, 1999).

When families are intact, both parents work, but female-headed single-parent families are disproportionately common among the working poor, a fact that worsens their economic dilemma, since wages received by women are typically lower than those earned by men. Though the majority of the working poor are white, minorities are disproportionately represented, and of course minorities, like women, are typically paid less. Members of the working poor

often live in rental units in undesirable neighborhoods; drive old, unreliable cars if any; and cannot afford any appreciable luxuries (Marger, 1998).

The "Underclass"

About 3 percent of the population is locked into long-term, chronic poverty. Sociologists disagree about what to call this group (Bagguley & Mann, 1992). Some use the term *underclass* (Myrdal, 1962; Glasgow, 1981; Auletta, 1982), but others argue that this word is stigmatizing, a real concern given the classist attitudes of most Americans (Gans, 1996). Similar criticisms apply to the terms *welfare class* and *lower lower class*. William Julius Wilson favors the term *ghetto underclass*, but this phrase falsely implies that everyone in this group is African American (Wilson, 1987, 1991).

Whatever we call them, the members of this class lack employable skills and have little or no experience in the job market. Unless given extensive training, many are nearly unemployable. Their household income is typically below $10,000 per year; the only legitimate source of support for most of them is public assistance. Many survive only through an elaborate network of sharing based largely on kinship ties (Stack, 1975).

The underclass is primarily, but not entirely, minority (Jencks & Peterson, 1991). Most of its members are women and children living in single-parent households. The combined effects of gender, race,

and family status have a devastating effect on the incomes of underclass families. Many experience a wide range of social problems, including crime, drug abuse, malnutrition, violence, gangs, and disease.

The dilemma of the underclass may be the most serious social problem facing the United States. For this reason, we turn next to a more detailed consideration of their plight.

POVERTY

How needy must people be before they are considered poor? This is by no means a trivial question, because the way we define poverty determines who is eligible for government assistance (Walker & Walker, 1995). There are two ways to define poverty: absolute and relative.

Absolute poverty refers to a life-threatening lack of food, shelter, and clothing. This definition has

Some members of the underclass are so poor that they cannot even afford a place to live. In recent years, homeless individuals have become a common sight in large American cities.

been used by the government since 1955. The official *poverty line* was originally computed by estimating the bare minimum cost of food necessary to keep people alive—a "short-term emergency diet"—and then tripling this figure, based on the assumption that poor people spend about one-third of their income on food (Orshansky, 1969). This figure is adjusted annually for inflation and has been modified in line with recent research that suggests food expenses make up only one-fourth of poor people's total budget. In 2000, the poverty line for a nonfarm family of four was $17,608. Remember that almost all officially poor people make less than this; about 40 percent of the poor earn under $8,000, less than half of the poverty threshold.

The absolute approach to poverty has generated considerable controversy (Walker & Walker, 1995). Conservatives argue that the official definition is faulty because it does not consider food stamps, rent subsidies, or the cash value of Medicaid and Medicare benefits as income (Whiteman, 1994). If it did, the number of poor might drop by some 5 million people.

On the other hand, advocates for the poor maintain that the official figure is, in fact, set too low (Michael, 1995; Schwartz & Volgy, 1993). They cite research that suggests poor families typically spend only about one-sixth of their income on food because the rapidly escalating cost of housing consumes between 50 and 70 percent of their total budget (Dolbeare, 1995). Furthermore, the current scheme does not allow for child-care expenses, which is especially unreasonable given the large number of women with young children among the poor.

These critics believe **relative poverty** is a more realistic approach. By this definition, individuals who make substantially less than most of the people around them and who cannot afford purchases that most people take for granted are poor, even if they can afford the necessities of life (Ropers, 1991). Supporters of this method of defining poverty sometimes suggest that people who earn less than half the national median family income are poor.

The official poverty line in the 1960s was indeed roughly 50 percent of the national median income. However, since then it has dropped to about 42 percent. By the relative standard, close to 20 percent of the population would be considered as poor today, an unacceptably high figure for national policymakers.

How Many Poor?

The highest rate of poverty in the 20th century occurred during the Great Depression of the 1930s when almost half of the U.S. population was in need.

By 1960, the year John Kennedy became president, the rate was slightly over 22 percent. In 1978, the figure had dropped to just 11.4 percent of the population, or 24.5 million people. This improvement was partly due to a very strong economy, which created the sorts of jobs that help poor people become self-sufficient. It was also due in part to substantial increases in government spending for social welfare (Gilbert & Kahl, 1993).

But in the 1980s the numbers turned upward until, by 1993, the United States was experiencing a poverty rate of 15.1 percent and had the largest absolute poverty population (39.3 million) since the 1950s. These figures reflected a worsening economy combined with dramatic cuts in social services under presidents Reagan and Bush. Since 1993, the economy has performed relatively well and the poverty rate declined to a 26 year low of 11.2 percent—roughly 28 million people—in 2000.

However, the U.S. rate remained high compared to that of other Western postindustrial societies: Using a relative definition of poverty, a U.N. study found that the U.S. poverty rate was 17 percent com-

TABLE 11.2

Selected Characteristics of the Poverty Population 2000

Category	Percent below the Official Poverty Line
Race	
All Races	11.3%
Whites	9.4
African-Americans	22.1
Hispanics	21.2
Asian and Pacific Islanders	10.8
Age	
Under 18	16.2%
18 to 24	14.4
25 to 34	10.4
35 to 44	8.2
45 to 54	6.4
55 to 59	8.8
60 to 64	10.2
65 up	10.2
Household Composition	
All Families	8.6%
Married Couple	4.7
Single-parent, Female-headed household	34.1

Source: U.S. Census Bureau (2001), Poverty in the United States: 2000.

pared with between 11 and 13 percent in the United Kingdom, Canada, Australia, and Italy (UN Development Programme, 2000).

Who Are the Poor?

Sociologically, the most important characteristics of the poor are their gender, family status, race, and age. Table 11.2 provides current data concerning the impact of these variables on poverty.

GENDER AND FAMILY STATUS   Sociologists use the phrase the **feminization of poverty** to refer to the growing percentage of the poverty population that is made up of women. Other societies as well as the United States are experiencing this trend, but it is especially serious here. In the United States today, almost two-thirds of all poor adults are women.

In 2000, 34.1 percent of single-parent, female-headed families were poor compared with just 8.6 percent of all families. Young, unmarried, lower-income women who become mothers are in a particularly difficult situation. Most lack the job skills to earn enough money to pay for day care as well as maintain a minimally adequate standard of living. The problem is intensified by the low wages typically paid to women. Marriage is often not a viable option; even if the father is willing, he is usually unable to earn enough to keep the family out of poverty. Many of these women end up on welfare, not because of some character flaw—unless wanting a family is a character flaw—but because welfare is the only way they can avoid destitution.

RACE   About two-thirds of all poor people are white, but minorities are disproportionately likely to be poor. Specifically, in 2000, 9.4 percent of whites, 22.1 percent of African Americans, and 21.2 percent of Latinos were below the poverty line. None of these figures has changed substantially over the past three decades. If we factor in the effects of gender and family status, we find that 44 percent of African American female-headed single-parent families and 43.3 percent of Latino female-headed single-parent families lived below the poverty line in 2000. The comparable figure for whites was 29.2 percent. Chapters 12 and 13 further examine the impact of the combined variables of gender and race on class position.

AGE   As late as 1967, almost 30 percent of the elderly were poor, but the indexing of Social Security to the inflation rate and the expansion of Medicare have reduced this figure to 10.2 percent. In fact, although many older people live just above the poverty line, today the elderly are actually less likely to be poor than the average member of the general population.

On the other hand, the United States has long had the worst child poverty problem in the developed world (Duncan et al. 1998). Poverty among children grew tremendously in the 1980s (Lichter & Eggebeen, 1993) but has been slowly declining in recent years. In 1999, 12.9 percent of all white children, 29.6 percent of all Latino children, and 32.7 percent of all African American children lived below the poverty line. Roughly 4 out of every 10 poor people are children. Even worse, about half of all poor children live in families with incomes below 50 percent of the poverty line.

Explaining Poverty

There are two general approaches to explaining the causes of poverty (Harris, 1993). The first, more widely accepted by the general public, looks to factors within poor individuals themselves. These theories are sometimes called *kinds-of-people* explanations; in Chapter 10 we introduced them under the heading of deficiency theories. The second approach, more in line with sociological understandings and research findings, directs attention to conditions of the larger social structure. These are *system-blaming* perspectives.

The crudest version of the kinds-of-people approach simply claims that poor people are poor because they are lazy and immoral (Mead, 1992). Since the United States is the land of opportunity, anyone who doesn't get ahead must have some serious character flaw. Exceptions are made for certain traditional categories of people—widows, orphans, the severely disabled—who are defined as "the deserving poor"; but most poor people are considered "undeserving" (Gans, 1996). This point of view is a consequence of classist ideology, and people who accept it tend to perceive programs designed to aid the poor as "handouts" to the unworthy.

Sociologists have found little or no evidence to support this interpretation (Fischer et al., 1996; Fraser, 1995) and commonly see it as a classic example of **victim blaming** (Ryan, 1971). If it were generally valid, then how could the size of the poverty population change as rapidly as it has in recent decades? Did half of all poor Americans move out of poverty in the 1960s because they suddenly became more virtuous? Or did structural factors change—with more good jobs created and more government aid available—allowing millions to work their way up out of poverty? Certainly, some poor people are lazy; there are lazy people at all economic levels. But personality flaws are not the primary cause of poverty.

A substantially more sophisticated version of the kinds-of-people approach focuses on certain subcultural values that are said to be common among the poor. The **culture of poverty** perspective suggests that the poor are socialized in childhood by their parents and peers to accept a distinctive way of looking at the world. In particular, they do not learn deferred gratification, the ability to forego immediate pleasure in order to work toward long-range goals (Lewis, 1966; Banfield, 1974). Middle-class people, the argument goes, learn to save money, study, and work hard in order to attain future success. None of these activities is much fun, but in the end, they pay off. On the other hand, the culture of poverty is radically present oriented. Thus, short-run hedonism locks the poor into poverty.

This thesis seems less biased against the poor than the view that they are simply lazy, but it still interprets poverty as a personal rather than structural problem. Considerable evidence suggests that many of the long-term poor—a small minority within the poverty population—do indeed have difficulty deferring gratification (Mayer, 1997). But is this a cause or a consequence of poverty? Life has taught the persistently poor that the future is unpredictable. Even if they try to save for the future, something beyond their control—sudden unemployment, illness, car problems—nearly always ruins their plans. Their experiences teach them over and over that gratification deferred is gratification lost (Liebow, 1967).

INTERNET CONNECTIONS

After reading about the poor and poverty in the text, go to the Institute for Research on Poverty:

http://www.ssc.wisc.edu/irp/

and click on the links under frequently asked questions. You should find information beyond what is in the text. After reading the information, write a short report on attributes of the poor. What, if anything, could be done to improve poverty-based programs? Base your answer on information from the Website or text.

There *is* a culture of poverty and it *can* trap people, but this culture is best understood as a consequence of and a reaction to life at the bottom of the class ladder; values are not the primary cause of poverty (Harvey, 1993). Change the structural realities, and in time the culture will change. But it is unrealistic to try to change the culture first. In fact, to take such an approach is a subtle form of victim blaming.

The second general explanation for poverty focuses on economic and social conditions. People who support this position acknowledge that personal and subcultural factors may be relevant at times, but overall, poverty is primarily the result of structural factors (Wilson, 1989).

One key structural variable promoting poverty is the loss in recent decades of millions of well-paying factory jobs as a result of *deindustrialization*, an issue that is discussed in some detail in the next section (Rifkin, 1995). The poor lack the skills to compete for the new high-skill technical jobs, leaving them only dead-end service jobs, often at minimum wage. But, as we have seen, these jobs cannot lift families out of poverty, especially since so many of the poor are women and people of color who tend to receive lower wages than whites and males. Furthermore, even low-wage jobs can be hard to find in poverty neighborhoods, and many poor people do not have reliable transportation that would allow them to work miles away from their homes.

A comprehensive antipoverty program could help compensate for structural factors that cause poverty, but the majority of the people in the United States clearly oppose such programs (Shapiro & Greenstein, 1991; Phillips, 1991). Recall that poverty declined during the 1960s, the decade of the Great Society programs, and soared when social welfare spending was sharply reduced in the 1980s. Many people believe that welfare spending encourages dependency and poverty, but research suggests otherwise. One major study found that the poor would have almost doubled to some 27 percent of the population if the relatively meager safety net provided in the 1980s had not been in place (Coder et al., 1989).

SOCIAL MOBILITY

Social mobility is a change in an individual or group's position in a stratification hierarchy, most commonly a class system (Sorokin, 1959). **Intergenerational social mobility** refers to an individual's class position compared to that achieved by his or her parents or grandparents. In contrast, **intragenerational social mobility** refers to changes in people's social standing over their lifetimes.

GLOBAL CONNECTIONS

How Do Other Nations Fight Poverty?

What would an effective antipoverty program look like? Successful programs in European social democracies such as Sweden, Norway, and the Netherlands generally incorporate most of the following features:

1. A universal children's allowance paid by the government to all families regardless of income.
2. National health care.
3. Government-subsidized child care.
4. Extensive low-income housing subsidies.
5. High-quality public education for all.
6. Ongoing efforts to reduce discrimination against women and minorities.
7. Job creation programs in both the public and the private sectors.
8. Minimum wage adequate to allow a decent existence.
9. Progressive taxation at all levels, with the wealthy paying at a much higher rate than the poor.
10. A centralized, federal welfare system that eliminates inequities between states.
11. Welfare benefits that at least bring recipients up to the poverty line.
12. Training programs to prepare people for jobs that pay better than poverty-level wages.

1. Do you think a real antipoverty program would make people dependent on the state? Or would it provide enough stability so that they could work to improve their future? Explain your position.

2. Why do you think most of these reforms have been accepted in nations like Denmark, Germany, and Sweden, while they remain politically unpopular in the United States?

Source: Sidel, 1996.

Sociologists who analyze social mobility usually study people who have moved up or down, such as an individual whose father was a bricklayer but who has become a corporate executive, or the daughter of a doctor who is clerking in a convenience store. These are intergenerational examples of **vertical mobility.** Sociologists also sometimes study **horizontal mobility,** which occurs when someone moves from one status to another that is roughly equal in rank—for example, if a carpenter's son or daughter becomes a plumber.

Most people in the United States assume that those who get ahead do so mainly on the basis of their ability, dedication, and hard work. Sociologists, however, see most mobility as structural (Levy, 1988). **Structural mobility** is most often a consequence of a change in the range of occupations that are available in a given society (Lipset, 1982; Gilbert & Kahl, 1993:145–156).

To better understand the concept of structural mobility, look at Figure 11.5 on page 292. Note that

The military continues to be an important means by which men (and, increasingly, women) from humble backgrounds can achieve significant upward social mobility.

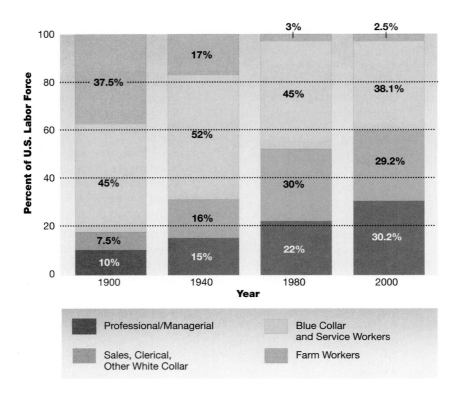

FIGURE 11.5 **The Changing U.S. Occupational Structure, 1900–2000.** Between 1900 and 2000 there was a major shift in the kinds of jobs available in the American economy.

Source: U.S. Bureau of the Census, *Historical Studies of the United States*, Vol. 1, 1975; U.S. Bureau of Labor Statistics, *Employment & Earnings*, 1993, Statistical Abstract, 2000.

over the course of the 20th century there was a major shift in the *kinds of jobs* provided by the U.S. economy. In 1900, only 17.5 percent of all jobs were classified as white collar, whereas by 2000 that figure had risen to 59.4 percent. A shift like this means that many people will experience upward social mobility simply because there are *more good jobs* and *fewer bad jobs* than there were previously.

Does this mean that hard work and ability are irrelevant? Not at all. At the individual level, which people are able to take advantage of structural changes in society and move up is determined in large part by talent and drive. But if the structure of society had not changed, then all the individual hard work and ability in the world would not have produced the massive upward mobility that has characterized most of U.S. history (Archer & Blau, 1994).

Overall, then, upward social mobility in the United States was substantial, at least until the early 1970s. Before that decade, about half of all Americans experienced some degree of upward intergenerational social mobility, about one-third stayed at about the same level as their parents, and perhaps 1 in 6 moved downward (Blau & Duncan, 1967). Almost half of all men in the middle class today had working-class fathers (Gilbert & Kahl, 1993:147).

Most social mobility is incremental; dramatic leaps in one lifetime from rags to riches—or from riches to rags—occur, but they are rare (Solon, 1992;

Gottschalk, 1997). In addition, most social mobility does not involve the extreme top or the extreme bottom. A very high percentage of people born into the upper class stay there, or at worst move down into the top levels of the upper-middle class (Oliver & Shapiro, 1995). Similarly, while a majority of the people born in the underclass do escape it, few rise farther than the lower rungs of the working class (Marger, 1998).

Rates of upward social mobility among African Americans remain generally lower than those among whites (Davis, 1995; Fosu, 1997). Patterns of intergenerational mobility among women are broadly similar to those of men, although women continue to experience substantial levels of occupational discrimination, as discussed in Chapter 13 (Biblarz et al., 1996).

Americans like to believe their nation offers unparalleled opportunity, but research shows that U.S. mobility patterns are broadly similar to those of the other Western democracies (Gottschalk, 1997; Smeeding, 1998). However, there is one important exception to this generalization: People born in blue-collar families have historically had a much better chance of climbing into the upper managerial or professional classes in the United States than in comparable countries.

Structural factors in the United States allowed a good deal of upward mobility, at least prior to the early 1970s (Archer & Blau, 1994). Since then, however, the trend has been generally downward (Kacapyr, 1996; Thurow, 1999). In particular, the middle class has been shrinking, a pattern some have called the "middle-class slide" (Duncan et al., 1992).

A critical factor in this slowdown of mobility has been a decline in real wages. Between 1958 and 1973, the real (inflation-adjusted) income of a typical 50-year-old man increased 50 percent; over the next 21 years, it did not grow at all (Russell, 1995). The problem has been most severe for those lacking college degrees: In 1980, male college graduates earned 36 percent more than male high-school graduates; the gap grew to 68 percent by 1998 (Danzinger & Reed, 1999).

These trends have hit the young especially hard. Moreover, they have occurred even though an increasing number of families have more than one earner, and the average number of hours worked per week has steadily increased (Burtless, 1990). In fact, wives in dual earner families worked an average of 223 hours more in 1997 than they did in 1983; men worked 158 more hours (Sklar, 1999).

There are many individual exceptions to this pattern of downward mobility, of course. But many observers foresee an end to the easy assumption that un-

ending upward mobility is the natural order of things in the United States. Today's youth could be the first generation in U.S. history that does not do as well on the average as its parents. Remember too that these patterns of substantial downward mobility are taking place at the same time that the elite are becoming more wealthy. If this trend continues, the class structure of the United States could end up much like that of Brazil (see Chapter 10), with a small but very wealthy elite group and a large majority of the population living in poverty or, at best, barely making ends meet.

Why has social mobility stalled out over the past three decades? This is a complex question, but three factors seem especially relevant. Most importantly, the globalization of the economy has led to **deindustrialization** (Barnet, 1993), a process in which the manufacturing sector of the economies of the developed nations declines while the service sector expands (Myles & Turgeon, 1994). This transformation has substantially reversed the patterns of upward structural mobility characteristic of the United States prior to about 1973. Millions of good-paying, mostly unionized, jobs have been lost, in large part because corporations have been shipping them to less-devel-

As in many developing societies, the distinction between the small elite class and the very large lower class is extremely sharp in Brazil.

oped nations in order to take advantage of inexpensive foreign labor (Reich, 1991). These are the jobs that traditionally allowed working-class people to move up the ladder.

In their place, two very different kinds of jobs are now being created in large numbers (Farley, 1996; Mischel et al., 1999). First, the number of well-paid, highly technical service jobs is increasing. Most of these positions are taken by children of the middle and upper-middle classes, who can obtain the necessary skills and education. Unfortunately, not enough of these jobs are being created to replace the desirable manufacturing jobs that have been exported. The people who have lost these jobs, along with their children, often end up in the second type of position now being created in the U.S. economy—low-skill service jobs. These "McJobs" pay barely enough—or not enough—to keep workers out of poverty. Moreover, they offer few if any benefits or opportunities for upward mobility. Of course, some individuals still manage to move into the middle class because of luck or outstanding ability, but they are swimming against the structural tide.

A second factor explaining the decline of the middle class is also linked, although less directly, to the globalization and deindustrialization of the economy: corporate downsizing (Uchitelle & Kleinfeld, 1996). Since 1980, about 25 percent of all executive positions have been eliminated. Not only do these reductions further restrict upward mobility from the working class, they also force large numbers of formerly middle-class managers downward. Middle-class workers who lose their jobs tend to stay unemployed even longer than their working-class counterparts, and when they do find work, it is usually at lower pay. Many downsized workers are rehired by the same firms that fired them, but as part-timers or consultants, at lower salaries than they earned previously, and with few benefits, if any (Newman, 1999). (See Chapter 21 for additional discussion of downsizing).

A final factor contributing to the decline of the middle class is the revised federal tax code. Under the Reagan administration (1981–1989), the top tax rate was cut from 70 percent to 28 percent while federal taxes overall rose for the bottom 90 percent of the population (Phillips, 1991). These changes were supposed to spur the American economy by giving the rich more money to invest so that new jobs could be created. The economy indeed thrived, but as we have seen, the mix of jobs that resulted has contributed to the middle-class slide. The tax policies were intended to create a rising tide that would lift all boats, but in reality, the people in yachts are doing well while a lot of those in rowboats are scraping the bottom.

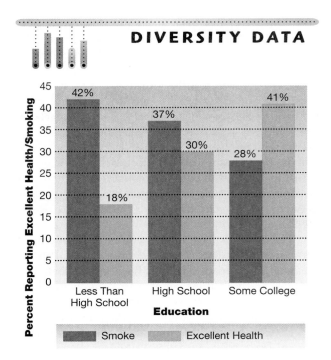

DIVERSITY DATA

FIGURE 11.6 How Does Education Affect Smoking and Assessment of Health? As education—a rough measure of social class—increases, the percentage of people who smoke goes down and the percentage who say that they are in excellent health increases. Why are better educated people less likely to be tobacco users?

Source: NORC. General Social Surveys, 1972–2000. Chicago: National Opinion Research Center, 2000. Reprinted by permission of NORC, Chicago, IL.

LIFE CONNECTIONS

The Difference Class Makes

Class matters because it affects so many aspects of our lives. Along with gender, race, and age, it strongly influences *life chances*, the likelihood that you will lead a successful and rewarding life (Gerth & Mills, 1958:181), and also *lifestyles*, the subcultural patterns that characterize the different classes.

Life Chances

William, Susan, and Jamal—the subjects of the vignettes that opened this chapter—experienced different life chances because they were born into different social classes. Not only was their schooling different, so were many other aspects of their lives. In this section, we'll briefly overview research on the effects of class on life chances.

PHYSICAL HEALTH AND MORTALITY Poverty is easily the number one social factor associated with ill health (World Health Organization, 1995; Syme & Berkman, 1997). At any given time, about 12 percent of the general population is sick; among the poor, that figure rises to 32 percent; among the homeless, it is 44 percent. Figure 11.6 illustrates how education, a key indicator of social class position, influences smoking and subjective assessment of health.

Not only does class affect physical health, it also influences how long people live. On the average, the poor die 7 years earlier than the rest of the population as a result of inadequate medical care, poor nutrition, unhealthy lifestyles, and other factors common among this group. The infant mortality rate among African Americans, who tend to be disproportionately poor, was 14.3 per 1,000 compared with a white rate of 6.0 in 2000.

The relationship between social class and health is discussed in greater detail in Chapter 19.

MENTAL HEALTH Extensive research shows that the poor are substantially more likely to suffer from mental problems (Faris & Dunham, 1939; Srole et al., 1962; Lynch et al., 1997). The best explanation seems to be that the stress associated with living in poverty contributes directly to mental illness. In addition, poor people who develop psychological problems are more likely to be treated with drugs or surgery than with less intrusive approaches such as counseling and psychotherapy (Goldman et al., 1994).

SELF-ESTEEM In a classic study, Richard Sennett and Jonathan Cobb (1973) conducted in-depth interviews with 150 working-class men and women in Boston and found a strong sense of inferiority among them. They were beaten down by the daily difficulties of making ends meet, but the main source of their low self-esteem came from internalizing classist ideology. They were convinced, on at least some levels, that their failure to succeed was their own fault. These attitudes, which are even more common among the poor than among the working class, can create a fatalistic hopelessness that can lead to a self-fulfilling prophecy.

EDUCATION Life chances in education vary sharply by class. Because public education is supported primarily by local property taxes, the schools attended by middle-class children generally provide better prepared teachers and more extensive and up-to-date educational technologies than schools in lower-class neighborhoods (Kozol, 1991). Furthermore, tracking, or ability-grouping in schools, tends to be strongly influenced by class, with lower and working-class

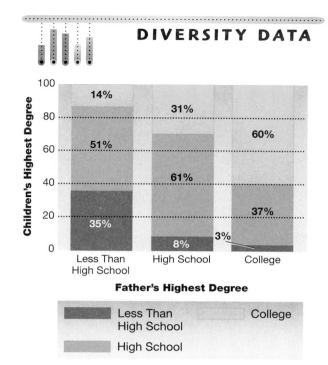

DIVERSITY DATA

FIGURE 11.7 How Does a Father's Level of Education Affect His Children's Education? Well over half of all children with college-educated fathers finish college compared with just 14 percent of those whose fathers did not graduate from high school. On the other hand, only 3 percent of the children of college graduates lack high-school diplomas compared to over a third of the children of high-school dropouts. Do these figures challenge the widespread belief that every child has a good chance to get ahead in life?

Source: NORC. General Social Surveys, 1972–2000. Chicago: National Opinion Research Center, 2000. Reprinted by permission of NORC, Chicago, IL.

students disproportionately channeled into noncollege tracks. As a result of such factors, educational attainment is markedly lower among poor children (Marger, 2002). Figure 11.7 shows that the children of well-educated fathers tend to go much farther in school. All in all, the facts show that contrary to popular opinion, schools are more important as a means of reproducing the existing class structure than as a way of allowing individuals to achieve upward mobility (Bowles, 1977; Kozol, 1991).

CRIME VICTIMIZATION Poor people are substantially more likely to become victims of crime. This is particularly true for violent offenses, but it is also the case for property crime, despite the fact that the poor have far less to steal than the middle and upper classes (Karmen, 2000). (See Chapter 9.)

At Fairfield Country Day School, an elite all-male prep school in Connecti-cut, every student is provided with a wireless laptop computer. Few if any public schools can match the quality of the education available in the private schools to which the wealthy send their children.

Lifestyles

Different behavioral patterns are associated with each class. In this section, we look at research concerning several important aspects of social life, starting with socialization and the family.

The contrast between the typical leisure-time activities of members of different classes is often quite dramatic.

CHILD SOCIALIZATION A classic study by Melvin Kohn (1977) demonstrates the existence of marked differences in childrearing patterns among classes. Compared to those in the middle class, working-class parents tend to stress obedience over self-direction and intellectual curiosity in their children. Working-class gender roles are relatively inflexible, and parents in this class are less likely to consider children's motivations when determining how to punish them. Working-class parents are also somewhat more likely to spank their children than are middle-class parents.

Kohn notes that these socialization patterns make sense in light of the jobs children will probably enter. Whereas middle-class jobs typically demand originality and creativity, working-class employment more often requires reliability and obedience to authority. The implication is that working-class children may be virtually locked out of more prestigious and rewarding occupations.

FAMILY In general, the farther down the class ladder, the earlier couples marry and the larger their families. Middle- and upper-class women are typically more knowledgeable about birth control and more consistent in using it, factors that reduce family size.

Style of marital interaction also varies by class. Men and women in working-class families live rather separate lives compared to couples in the middle and upper classes, who interact more with each other and typically have both male and female friends (Rubin, 1976). Working-class men are also more likely to assume patriarchal authority in the family. This fact, along with the stress of trying to survive on a limited income, may help explain the substantially higher divorce rate in the lower classes (Martin & Bumpass, 1989).

POLITICS The Republican party has long been more closely associated with the interests of the wealthy and the Democrats with those of the less affluent. These orientations are reflected in class-based voting preferences. More specifically, wealthier people tend to be conservative on economic issues, opposing such measures as government regulation of business and increases in the minimum wage. On the other hand, the higher classes are usually more liberal on social issues such as free speech, abortion, and separation between church and state (Lipset, 1959; Hout et al., 1995; Wright, 1997). As for political participation, the lower classes are less likely to vote or become involved in community political life, which only intensifies their powerlessness (Conway, 1991; Rosenstone & Hansen, 1993).

VOLUNTARY ASSOCIATIONS The lower classes are not just less likely to be politically involved, they are less likely to join any organizations other than unions and churches. This reluctance to join groups is significant, because only by working together with others can people safeguard their rights and achieve social change.

RELIGION Different denominations appeal more to some classes than to others (Roof, 1979; Johnstone, 1997). Episcopalians and Presbyterians gener-

ally come from higher-class backgrounds than Methodists, Lutherans, and Catholics, who are, in turn, typically better off than Baptists and members of religious sects. The church services of the poor tend to be more emotional and more focused on the rewards of the next world than are the services of middle-class congregations.

COMMUNICATION STYLES People in different classes learn to express themselves differently as they grow up. Some research suggests that working-class people are less direct and self-assured than people in the middle class (Schatzman & Strauss, 1972). But even if the communication styles of all classes were equally effective, to middle-class audiences the speech patterns typical of the lower classes would still carry a stigma.

SOCIETY CONNECTIONS

Welfare

In discussing the welfare system, it is important to keep two points in mind. First, the vast majority of government spending for social needs is relatively noncontroversial because it is not **means-tested.** This means that people do not have to fall below a particular specified income level in order to be eligible for the program. Roughly 80 percent of all government benefits are paid to the non-poor (Barlett & Steele, 1994). The amount of money the government spends on Social Security,

Well-constructed welfare programs can help children to overcome the disadvantage of being born in poverty, but the stigma attached to public assistance sometimes keeps poor families from accepting assistance from the government.

DIVERSITY IN FOCUS

Getting Off Welfare

Shari Pharr, a 28-year-old African American mother of two, was angry and scared. Two weeks earlier, the state of Wisconsin had begun requiring welfare recipients to earn their monthly checks by attending job-training classes or performing community service while they looked for work.

Shari came from a "welfare family." Her mother, who had six children with five different men, had been on disability since her last husband shoved her out of a moving car. Shari only met her father once, when she was 5 years old. Following her mother's pattern, she became pregnant before her junior year of high school. Her boyfriend denied he was the father of their son, yet berated her for being on welfare. When she criticized him for losing one job after another because of his drinking, he abandoned her. For a short time, Shari worked for a company that made decorative candles for K-Mart, walking 40 minutes to and from work to save the cost of bus fare. When the company moved and Shari, who was pregnant again, lost her job, she went back on welfare. The father of her second child became addicted to crack and increasingly abusive. Shari later recalled, "I kept asking, what's wrong with me? Why is my life not working out?" She and her mother often cried about the bad men they had known. She hated the stereotype of the "welfare queen," collecting checks and spending all day in a bathrobe watching TV. Shari got up at 7:00 each morning, got dressed, and went out with her children, even if she had nowhere particular to go.

When the state of Wisconsin initiated welfare reform, Shari began attending job-training classes at the Milwaukee Job Center North, which emphasized speaking conventional English and dressing properly. Like many others in the class, she found the experience patronizing. "They called us lazy," she said. Told that until she got a real job, she would have to sort and fold old clothes donated to Goodwill, Shari demanded to see her caseworker.

Preston White had grown up in the same neighborhood in which Shari now lived. He had been a case manager for five years, an easy but boring job that entailed little more than adding up benefits for poor women on the dole, or the "grant" as welfare was known in Wisconsin. At first, White was opposed to welfare reform: He was afraid that he couldn't make himself cut benefits for poor women and "throw their kids into the street" and afraid that he would lose his job if he didn't. But his attitude slowly changed. Many of his clients saw themselves as victimized by racism, the men in their lives, and the system, and therefore as entitled to welfare. They viewed getting an entry-level, "McWork" job as giving into "the Man." And this attitude was a main obstacle to finding employment. White began to see welfare as an addiction and himself as an enabler.

When Shari entered his office in March 1997, White recognized the resentment in her folded arms and hunched shoulders. He also noted that she was neatly dressed and had a small scar above her eye (inflicted by a former boyfriend). When she declared that she would not fold laundry, he challenged her to organize his office. In two weeks, she put his files in order, cleared the clutter on his desk, and began doing the same for other caseworkers. Soon after, Shari applied for a job at a warehouse, sorting and packing chemicals for shipment. The interviewer found her bright and eager. A supervisor passing through his office asked, in jest, "Hey, I need another truck driver. Can you do that?" Without hesitation Shari responded, "No, but I can learn if that's what it takes." She was hired on the spot.

Shari now earns almost $10 an hour—enough to save for the house she hopes to buy one day. She is seeing a man she met at work who respects her as a working mom. Shari knows that if she loses this job or if her 10-year-old son, Charlie, gets into trouble, she could fall back "into that bad life." But her eyes sparkle when she describes a planned trip to a lake over Memorial Day weekend—her first real vacation in many years.

Her caseworker, White, has also changed. Welfare reform forced him to get involved and made him feel that he could change lives. Instead of just pushing papers, he was actually using his training as a social worker. About three-quarters of White's clients have found at least part-time work, but he worries about those who have serious drug or alcohol problems, do not show up for appointments or job training, and will soon lose all their benefits.

1. Were there any factors that made it easier for Shari Pharr to get off welfare than it might have been for some of Preston White's other clients? What were they?

2. What widely believed myths about welfare are challenged by Shari's story?

Source: McKormick & Thomas, 1997.

Medicare, unemployment compensation, public education, mortgage subsidies through tax deductions, and other similar social programs dwarfs what most people think of as "welfare" (Goodgame, 1993). Public debate becomes intense primarily when programs are proposed to assist the poor.

Second, we must distinguish between two kinds of means-tested welfare efforts: *antidestitution programs*, which simply supply poor people with enough money to make ends meet, and *antipoverty programs*, which, in addition to meeting people's immediate needs, also help them obtain job skills and attempt to address the structural factors that promote poverty.

Large-scale means-tested welfare programs began only after tens of millions of hard-working Americans became impoverished in the early 1930s. Only then did most people begin to acknowledge that poverty does indeed have structural causes. Some of the earliest welfare programs consisted of simple cash grants to the poor, in particular the Aid to Dependent Children (ADC) program, which began in 1935. But others, such as the Civilian Conservation Corps and the Works Project Administration, provided both jobs and training and were therefore true antipoverty programs.

When the Depression ended, most of the work-training programs were phased out. ADC, however, was retained, and in 1950 it was renamed Aid to Families with Dependent Children (AFDC) to reflect the fact that caregivers, usually mothers, could now also receive government assistance. In time, AFDC became the cornerstone of the nation's welfare system.

In the 1960s, a number of innovative antipoverty programs were developed. However, they weren't fully funded, at least in the eyes of their supporters, and most, with the exception of Head Start, were dismantled as the country swung to the right in the later 1970s. The 1960s also saw the startup of food stamps, another major antidestitution program.

By the early 1990s, hard economic times had substantially increased the welfare rolls (DeParle, 1992). AFDC was supporting over 13 million individuals in 5 million families, two-thirds of them children. In 1994, 27.5 million people received food stamps. Although the benefits of both programs had already been sharply reduced by the Reagan and Bush administrations—the real cash value of the average AFDC award had declined by 40 percent since 1972—the public enthusiastically supported even broader changes in the welfare system.

How may we explain the political popularity of President Clinton's promise to "end welfare as we know it"? Widespread misunderstandings concerning public assistance contributed heavily to this political mood. Here are some of these misunderstandings—and the facts.

1. *Most poor people get welfare.* Just 25 percent of all families below the poverty line were receiving means-tested cash benefits in 1999. Thirty-one percent used food stamps, 44 percent were enrolled in Medicaid, and only 21 percent lived in public housing (2001 Statistical Abstract).

2. *Most welfare recipients are black.* In fact, only 46 percent of the people on welfare in 1999 were African Americans; 18 percent were Latino and 33 percent were white. Thirty-six percent of food stamp recipients and 35 percent of the children in Head Start were black.

3. *Welfare is a very expensive program.* In 1999 the total federal and state expenditure for TANF (Temporary Assistance to Needy Families), the program that replaced AFDC in 1996, was $22.6 billion. Food stamps cost $15.7 billion. In contrast, social security expenditures were nearly $403 billion, Medicare cost $208 billion, and the defense budget was $275 billion.

It is worth noting that the nations that provide the most generous welfare benefits—Sweden, Norway, and Germany—are the best both at moving the poor into jobs and at keeping overall poverty rates low, often below 6 percent.

4. *Life on welfare is easy.* Welfare benefits vary by state, but in no state does welfare plus food stamps bring recipients up to the poverty line (Sidel, 1996). The average AFDC payment in 1996 was slightly over $400 per month. Furthermore, the real value of public assistance has been declining for decades. Measured in constant dollars, the typical family enrolled in both AFDC and the food stamp program received $10,133 in 1970 and $7,657 in 1992.

5. *Welfare promotes poverty because most recipients become dependent on it.* The truth is, the sizable majority of recipients do not stay on the welfare rolls very long. Individuals on TANF are allowed only 5 years of assistance in their lifetimes. Most become eligible for aid because of some sort of life crisis—unemployment, illness, divorce—and get off it as soon as they are back on their feet again (Bane & Ellwood, 1994). Seventy percent of all AFDC recipients left the program within 2 years, and 85 percent did so within 4 years (Bane & Ellwood, 1994). Some of these people may need help again when another crisis comes along, but the vast majority of recipients do not become deeply dependent upon government aid. The benefits are too low, staying eligible is a bureaucratic hassle, and the stigma of being on welfare is too great.

It is true that some people are long-term welfare dependent. Roughly 2 million people, less than 1 per-

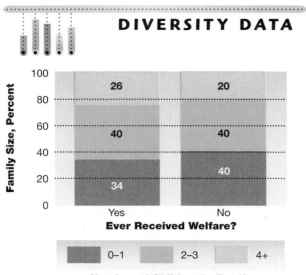

DIVERSITY DATA

Number of Children in Family
0–1   2–3   4+

Ever Received Welfare?

FIGURE **11.8** **How Long Are Families on Welfare?** Families that have received welfare are only slightly more likely to have four or more children and only slightly less likely to have no more than one child than are families that have never received public aid. Why do so many people still believe that many women on welfare deliberately have large families in order to increase their benefits?

Source: NORC. General Social Surveys, 1972–2000. Chicago: National Opinion Research Center, 2000. Reprinted by permission of NORC, Chicago, IL.

cent of the population, are locked into persistent poverty. Seven percent of the welfare population in the mid-1990s had received aid for at least 8 straight years (Dalaker, 1999). Studies of these "hard-core" poor show that most are unmarried African American women with children, many of whom were raised in welfare families and became eligible for aid when they became pregnant as teenagers. They typically have low levels of education and minimal job skills.

However, 80 percent of daughters whose mothers received AFDC for at least 8 consecutive years became self-supporting as adults (Ruggles, 1989). So, it is true there are people for whom welfare becomes a way of life, and they are a genuine challenge to public policy. But they are a relatively small and quite atypical group compared to most welfare recipients. To remake public policy on the assumption that most welfare families are like them is irrational.

6. *Welfare promotes poverty because it encourages single-parent families.* Until the 1990s, state laws generally denied welfare to families in which an adult

male was present. These policies were based on the assumption—far more valid in the past than today, given the nation's changing occupational structure—that virtually any man could find work that would keep his family out of poverty. Under these circumstances, welfare did encourage family breakup. But this situation was the result of an ill-conceived policy; it was not an inevitable consequence of giving aid to the poor.

More generally, the trend toward single parenting is by no means limited to the poor. Female-headed single-parent families are becoming increasingly common at all class levels. The fact that they are especially prevalent among poor people is primarily due to the lack of decent jobs in the U.S. economy. Men who are unable to adequately support their families do not make attractive potential husbands. Thus, single-parent families are not a major cause of poverty; they are mostly the result of larger structural factors (Sidel, 1996).

7. *Welfare promotes poverty because it encourages out-of-wedlock births.* A final popular myth is that unmarried poor women deliberately have large families in order to bring in larger benefit checks. In fact, the average size of welfare families has been shrinking since the early 1970s (see Figure 11.8).

Research shows no connection between the amount of welfare grants and the size of families among the poor. States whose payment levels are low tend to have higher rates of illegitimacy. Furthermore, women have been shown to be less likely to have another child while on welfare than are other low-income mothers (Rank, 1989). This should not be surprising: Welfare payments are far from generous and recipients know well that the cost of raising another child exceeds any increase in benefits.

Despite the facts, many people believe some or all of these myths. Only about 30 percent of the public realizes that most recipients truly need the welfare benefits they are receiving ("Welfare Mistrust," 1996). Quite simply, the popular definition of the problem has shifted: Until recently, the problem was poverty; now it is welfare.

The mid-1990s saw enormous changes in welfare. The 1995 federal budget cut spending for means-tested welfare programs by $54 billion over the following 6 years, while leaving other entitlement programs, such as Social Security, Medicare, and unemployment compensation, largely untouched. The food-stamp program was especially deeply cut. And, in 1996, President Clinton signed into law a bill ending the federal government's 60-year formal commitment to aiding all poor people.

This legislation terminated the AFDC program and restructured remaining federal welfare funds as bloc grants to the states for TANF. It lifted most previous restrictions and encouraged the states to develop new approaches to fighting poverty. All recipients (except for a few hardship cases) are required to take jobs no later than 2 years after their public aid begins. TANF also mandated that the states must move 25 percent of welfare recipients into jobs or work-related activities (including job training) by the end of 1997 and 50 percent by 2002.

The 1996 bill also denied welfare aid to legal immigrants and established a lifetime limit of 5 years of federal funding for any particular individual. States can exempt up to 20 percent of their clients from this requirement if they wish, but they also may reduce the lifetime assistance limit to less than 5 years. TANF allows states to reduce benefits by 25 percent to the children of single mothers who refused to name the fathers. States may also deny assistance to unmarried teenaged mothers unless they agree to live at home and enroll in school (Alter, 1996). TANF did not explicitly allocate federal money for job training, job creation, health insurance, or child care, although individual states may fund such programs if they wish (Church, 1996).

What are we to make of these changes? They seem unlikely to result in a stronger antidestitution program, since the overall level of funding for means-tested benefits has decreased slightly since 1995. Nor is TANF at the federal level in and of itself an antipoverty program; it does nothing to directly address the structural causes of poverty. It can easily be argued that TANF is less an antidestitution or an antipoverty program than an *antiwelfare program.*

A number of states have chosen to go beyond what the federal government requires and adopted true antipoverty strategies, but history suggests that only the more progressive ones are likely to fund such programs adequately. For example, Wisconsin and Illinois, among the national leaders in the antipoverty effort, have spent many millions of dollars on job training, child care, and expanded health benefits. Research clearly shows that these provisions work. But how many states will make such an effort?

The 1996 welfare bill clearly assumes that the primary cause of poverty is individual, not structural. This interpretation suggests that what is mostly needed is a "big stick"—a threat of utter destitution—to motivate welfare recipients to get a job, any job. And it is succeeding in achieving this limited goal: Whereas in 1992, just 7 percent of welfare recipients were working, by 2000 that figure had jumped to 33 percent (U.S. Department of Health & Human Ser-

vices, 2000). Furthermore, the number of people receiving AFDC/TANF dropped from 14.1 million to 5.9 million between 1994 and 2000, an unprecedented decline of 59 percent (Hopper, 2000). As this text went to press, the government was debating the reauthorization of TANF, with many voices (including that of President Bush) calling for reduced funding and even stronger work requirements.

The long-term prospects for the success of the new system remain unclear, especially now that the high rate of economic growth which characterized the 1990s has begun to falter (Dervarics, 1998; Zedlewski & Alderson, 2001; Sawhill, 2001). Ominously, welfare rolls in some states started to climb again in 2000 (Meckler, 2001). Each state will respond somewhat differently if this trend continues. Fortunately, there are enough loopholes built into the law so that many of the harshest provisions are likely to be moderated in practice (Kaus, 1997).

The old AFDC program certainly had its weaknesses, and as we have seen, TANF has moved many poor mothers into the labor force. However, most of these women take low-paying jobs, often with few benefits and limited career opportunities. More specifically, between 50 and 60 percent of the adult women who have exhausted their welfare benefits are in the work force, earning an average of between $5.50 and $7.50 per hour ("Life After Welfare," 1999). On the other hand, many are unable to make the transition: One study found that over half of a group of women who had left welfare to work in 1996 were unemployed 5 years later (Children's Defense Fund, 2001).

Without adequate job training and having to pay for child care, health insurance, work clothes, and transportation from their meager paychecks, many of these women—and their children—will probably remain poor. The annual report of the Children's Defense Fund (2001) noted that most former welfare recipients who were now in the work force were experiencing difficulty paying for rent, food, medical care, and utilities.

In addition, because they will be working full time and also raising children, these women are unlikely to be able to attend school—their best hope of improving their future job prospects (Harris, 1993). And what of those who simply are not employable? The people who are still receiving TANF are, in general, poorly prepared to enter the job market. Most have no work experience and little education; many have criminal records and drug habits (Hargrove, 2001).

Today, poverty is not a major item on the national agenda. If we ask why not, the answer is evident: Political priorities are determined by the upper and upper-middle classes, the classes that have power to shape the political process. The situation is not hopeless; the lower classes have successfully affected political decision making at times in the past. The *Global Connections* box, "How Do Other Nations Fight Poverty?" discusses some experiences of other

societies from which Americans might learn. But, in the end, we come back to where we began this chapter, with the observation that in the battle against poverty—or welfare—as in every other aspect of social life, *class matters!*

SUMMARY

1. Most sociologists use the objective approach to operationalize the variable of class; others prefer the subjective or reputational approaches.

2. Property—both income and wealth—is an important objective dimension of class. The gap between the rich and the poor, especially with regard to wealth, is greater in the United States than in other modern societies, and it is currently increasing.

3. Occupational prestige is a second important objective factor separating social classes.

4. Erik Olin Wright identifies four classes in U.S. society: capitalists, managers, the petite bourgeoisie, and workers.

5. Theorists such as Gilbert and Kahl divide U.S. society into ranked groups: the upper, upper-middle, lower-middle, and working classes, the working poor, and the "underclass."

6. Poverty may be defined in either absolute or relative terms.

7. The percentage of people living in poverty declined in the 1960s and early 1970s, but since then it has fluctuated at a somewhat higher level than previously. Currently, it is at a relatively low level.

8. Poverty is concentrated among children, minorities, and women. It is an especially serious problem in single-parent female-headed families.

9. Sociologists find more evidence supporting system-blaming explanations of poverty than kinds-of-people approaches such as the culture of poverty theory.

10. Most social mobility in modern societies is structural mobility.

11. The United States has historically offered substantial opportunities for upward social mobility, but recent trends suggest that downward mobility, especially out of the middle class, may be increasingly common in the immediate future.

12. Social class strongly influences people's life chances regarding such matters as physical health and mortality, mental health, self-esteem, education, and crime victimization.

13. Class also affects lifestyle patterns of child socialization, family life, politics, voluntary association membership, religion, and communication styles.

14. Public policies concerning poverty can be categorized as antidestitution, antipoverty, or antiwelfare approaches.

15. Many widely held but inaccurate beliefs strongly influence public responses to the problem of poverty.

16. TANF has substantially reduced the number of people on welfare, but it is unclear whether it will be effective in actually fighting poverty.

KEY TERMS

absolute poverty 287
culture of poverty 290
deindustrialization 293
feminization of poverty 289

horizontal mobility 291
income 279
intergenerational social
    mobility 290

intragenerational social
    mobility 290
means-tested 297
objective approach 279

relative poverty 288
reputational approach 279
social mobility 290

socioeconomic status (SES) 279
structural mobility 291
subjective approach 277

vertical mobility 291
victim blaming 289
wealth 279

CRITICAL THINKING QUESTIONS

1. If current predictions about increasing rates of downward social mobility in the United States are borne out, how do you think most people will react?

2. Can you think of any important aspects of social life that are not affected by social class?

3. What are some reasons many people believe some or all of the welfare myths discussed in this chapter?

4. Why do you think the United States is characterized by more inequality and fewer public efforts to reduce inequality than any other developed nation?

INVESTIGATE WITH CONTENT SELECT

Begin your research using Content-Select for this chapter by following the directions found on page 27 of this text to visit Prentice Hall's Research Navigator Website. Enter these search terms into the search field:

Socioeconomic status (SES)
Social mobility
Welfare

12
RACIAL AND ETHNIC MINORITIES

Racial Profiling

In the late 1990s a new name—racial profiling—emerged to describe a familiar practice. Police were being accused of indiscriminately stopping minority drivers and searching their cars for illegal drugs. Many victims felt that they had been "pulled over for a DWB" (driving while black—or brown). The language was ironic, but the problem was real.

For example, Dr. Elmo Randolph, a 42-year-old African American dentist from New Jersey, complained that his gold BMW had been stopped at least 50 times over the past 8 years, yet the police had never issued him a ticket. Research by Temple University psychologist John Lamberth revealed that while 85 percent of the motorists on one section of I-95 were white, 35 percent of those pulled over and 75 percent of those arrested were African Americans.

From the perspective of blameless minority drivers who found themselves hassled by the police, racial profiling was just the latest indignity in a long history of oppression. On the other hand, although few law enforcement officers openly defended the practice, the fact that African Americans and Hispanics are arrested and convicted for drug offenses at much higher rates than whites seemed to justify giving special attention to minority drivers. Critics responded by noting that racial profiling sets up a self-fulfilling prophecy: If the police disproportionately investigate African American or Hispanic suspects, then they will primarily apprehend minority offenders, thus distorting the racial composition of the official crime data, which they in turn use to justify their biased practices. (Cannon, 1999; Hosenball, 1999)

Diversity in the Heartland

Latinos have just recently become the largest minority group in the United States. They no longer live almost exclusively in southern Florida, along the Mexican border, or in metropolitan *barrios;* more and more, they are finding their way to smaller towns in the South and the Midwest. For example, the Hispanic community in the states of Arkansas, North Carolina, and Georgia has increased by between 300 and 400 percent over the past 10 years.

In some cases, the growth has been even more rapid. The Latino population of Rogers, Arkansas, expanded 15-fold during the 1990s; today the town of 39,000 is nearly 20 percent Hispanic. Drawn principally by the opportunity to work in local poultry plants, these new immigrants have met with a mixed reception from the community's Anglo majority.

Critics charge that the influx has raised the crime rate, and the town's long-time mayor was defeated in 1998 by a challenger who took a strong position against illegal immigration. In March 2001, the Mexican American Legal Defense and Educational Fund filed a class action suit against the local police force, alleging a continuing pattern of racial profiling. But there are also signs of progress. Over half of Rogers' Latino residents own their own homes, many Anglos join in celebrating Cinco de Mayo, and a girl named Jessica Diaz, who was raised in Mexico and is of black and Puerto Rican ancestry, was chosen as Miss Rogers High School in 2001. Adjusting to change is often difficult, but it is essential as the United States becomes ever more diverse. (Campo-Flores, 2001)

Much more than most of the world's societies, the United States is a complex mosaic of racial and ethnic minority groups. Some, like Native Americans, African Americans, and many Latinos, have lived here for centuries or even millennia; others, like the new residents of Rogers, Arkansas, are much more recent arrivals. All have endured discrimination such as the racial profiling experienced by African Americans and Latinos, and also by many Arab Americans after the terrorist attacks on the

Latinos are now the single largest minority group in the United States. Their numbers are growing, not only in states like California and Texas where they have traditionally settled, but also in small towns in the Midwest and the South.

World Trade Center and the Pentagon. All have had to strike a balance between trying to fit into the dominant culture and maintaining their own distinctive lifestyles and identities.

We begin this chapter by discussing the key concepts of race, ethnicity, minority groups, prejudice, discrimination, and racism. Next, we consider the various ways that dominant and minority groups interact and take a brief look at the history and present circumstances of selected minorities. The chapter concludes with a discussion of the emergence of multiracialism in the United States and a critical assessment of the policy of affirmative action.

RACE, ETHNICITY, AND MINORITY GROUPS

Any discussion of minority relations must begin with the traditional distinction between races and ethnic groups.

Race: A Social Construction

Contrary to what most people believe, race is a sociological rather than a biological concept. Races are *social constructions*. They are ways of conceptually grouping together large numbers of people, often in reality displaying highly divergent physical characteristics, so that they can be treated as a single category

and, commonly, so that they may be kept in subordinate positions. This process of defining a group of people as a race has been called *racial formation* (Omi & Winant, 1994). Following this logic, we define a **race** as a category of people who have come to be identified as sharing physical characteristics such as skin color that are believed to be socially meaningful.

There are several fatal problems inherent in attempting to argue for the biological significance of race. In the first place, there is no agreed-upon number of races (Montagu, 1964; Cavalli-Sforza et al., 1994). Furthermore, the physical variations among the people who are regarded as being of a single race are frequently greater than those that are believed to exist between the members of different races (Malcomson, 2000). For example, the physical characteristics of the people popularly classified as Caucasians range from the blond hair and very light skin of Scandinavians to the dark skin and black hair of Asian Indians. Even more significantly, the biological differences between groups identified as races are trivial. There is no credible evidence that people of different races are innately different from each other in any significant way, either in temperament or in mental or physical abilities (Shanklin, 1993).

To the extent that they do exist, "racial" characteristics are nothing more than the incidental consequences of the historic geographic isolation of human populations in different physical environments. Over the millennia, adaptations to environmental factors produced localized groupings of people with distinctive skin colors, facial features, and so forth—group-

INTERNET CONNECTIONS

Chapter 12 begins with a discussion of *racial profiling* and the predicament faced by some African-Americans known as "DWB" (Driving While Black). The American Civil Liberties Union (ACLU) hosts a Website that deals exclusively with the phenomenon of racial profiling, instructively entitled, Arrest the Racism: Racial Profiling in America:

http://www.aclu.org/profiling/

When you access the opening page, click on one or more news articles within the "What's New" section. These installments illustrate racial profiling in action and highlight some of the legal and constitutional issues involved. Do you agree or disagree with the practice of racial profiling and why? What do you think the long-term implications of this practice will be?

ings that are now gradually fading away as a result of increased rates of geographical mobility and inter-marriage (Smedley, 1999).

However, the fact that race is biologically meaning-less does not mean that it is sociologically insignificant. As we discussed in Chapter 1, the Thomas Theorem holds that what people believe to be real is real in its consequences. The view that races were biologically real and that they were important determinants of human behavior emerged only in the late 1700s as part of the Europeans' justification of their colonial domina-tion of nonwhite people around the world (Reynolds, 1992). In the United States, this way of thinking became a cornerstone of the intellectual defense of slavery (J. Marks, 1994). Even after slavery ended, whites treated people of color differently, refusing them op-portunities that members of the dominant group took for granted.

Ethnic Groups

Ethnicity is a matter of culture. An **ethnic group** is a category of people who are seen by themselves and others as sharing a distinctive subculture, somewhat different from the way of life of the dominant group (Alba, 1992; Feagin & Feagin, 1999).

Of course, most racial groups are also culturally distinct, which is why the line between races and eth-nic groups is unclear—but because race is so visible, racial identity usually overshadows ethnicity in the popular mind (Castells, 1997). Most people who are popularly classified as ethnics in the United States are whites identified by their country of origin: Irish Americans, Italian Americans, Mexican Americans, and so forth. As these terms suggest, ethnicity is

closely linked to migration (Handlin, 1992). When culturally distinct immigrants arrive in a new society, they commonly share a strong sense of ethnic identity or peoplehood. This is especially true if they come in large numbers, are quite different culturally from the dominant group, and experience substantial prejudice and discrimination (Doane, 1993).

If, however, succeeding generations adapt the dominant culture and start climbing the social class ladder, ethnic identity may start to fade (Gordon, 1964; Gans, 1979). This has already occurred among many European ethnic groups. In fact, children of the third and fourth generations often consciously seek to recapture the identity their grandparents and great-grandparents abandoned, an activity sociologists refer to as *ethnic work*, the ongoing effort to maintain or rediscover one's ethnic heritage.

Minority Groups

A **minority group,** whether racial or ethnic, is de-fined above all by its lack of power—economic power, political power, or simply the ability to define what it means to be a member of the group. For this reason, sociologists often refer to minority groups as *subordinate groups* (Feagin & Feagin, 1999).

Most minority groups are smaller in number than the people who hold the majority of the power, known as dominant groups. In the United States, the dominant group—whites, especially those of North-ern European heritage—has historically outnumbered African Americans, Latinos, and other minorities. However, there are some exceptions to this rule. Blacks in apartheid-era South Africa provide a good example.

The members of many ethnic groups, even those who have lived in this country for several generations, keep the traditions of their homeland alive through street festivals such as this fi-esta in Los Angeles, which features Mexican clothing, dances, and foods.

Because of their powerlessness, minorities experience both prejudice and discrimination—concepts we will explore more fully shortly. Members of a minority group are, by definition, stigmatized in the eyes of the dominant group. They are often treated not as individuals, but as members of a category. Further, most minority groups are based on ascribed (inherited) statuses and tend to be *endogamous;* that is, members usually marry within their own group. Most minorities also develop a strong sense of in-group solidarity (Wirth, 1945; Wagley & Harris, 1958).

Around the world, minority groups are defined by various physical and cultural characteristics. Differences in skin color are particularly familiar to Americans, while Canadians usually think first of language (French versus English) and the North Irish of religion (Catholic versus Protestant). For the most part, the more visible the defining characteristic, the more sharply minority and dominant groups are separated from each other and the more harsh the *stigma*—or negative social label—borne by the minority.

Note that women, the elderly, and members of the lower social classes share some, but not all, of the attributes of racial and ethnic groups. However, although these categories of people are clearly subordinate in terms of power, sociologists generally do not use the term minority groups in referring to such strata, preferring normally to limit the application of that concept to racial and ethnic groups.

DOUBLE JEOPARDY: THE ADDITIVE EFFECTS OF MULTIPLE SUBORDINATE GROUP MEMBERSHIP

The important concept of **gendered racism** (Collins, 1990; Essed, 1991) calls our attention to the fact that women who are members of racial or ethnic minority groups tend to encounter high levels of prejudice and discrimination based on the sum of both of their devalued identities. For example, note that while the median individual income in 1999 was $28,564 for white males and $20,579 for African American males, African American females earned an average of only $14,771 in that year (2001 *Statistical Abstract*, Table 676).

PREJUDICE, DISCRIMINATION, AND RACISM

Both race and ethnicity are frequently *master statuses*—the primary determinants of how people are thought of and treated. Minority group members commonly find that as a result of their master status they are viewed with prejudice and experience discrimination.

Prejudice

A prejudice is, literally, a prejudgment. Sociologists define **prejudice** as a negative attitude toward an entire category of people (Allport, 1958; Jones, 1997). Prejudice involves two components: a negative emotional reaction toward a group and a cognitive or intellectual element, usually called a stereotype.

Stereotypes are overgeneralizations about a category of people that are applied to all members of that category. Stereotypes may be accurate descriptions of some members within a group, but assuming that everyone in a certain category displays a particular trait limits our ability to understand social reality. Stereotypes may become self-fulfilling prophecies if they are accepted by those who are their subjects (Begley, 2000). Even positive stereotypes, such as the common belief that Asian Americans are highly intelligent, force people into pigeonholes and distort our perceptions of them (MacRae et al., 1996; Cashmore, 1996).

People who think in stereotypes tend to ignore evidence that contradicts their assumptions. When presented with an individual whose behavior does not fit the stereotype—for example, a Rhodes scholar who is a member of a minority group thought to lack intelligence—prejudiced people generally respond in one of two ways. They may say that the person is "the exception that proves the rule" (an absurd notion when you think about it), or they may redefine the behavior so that it fits their prejudgment: "It's amazing how cunning some of them are" (Jenkins, 1994a).

Is prejudice declining in the United States? There is no doubt that the *public* expression of stereotypes and prejudiced attitudes is less acceptable in many circles today than it was a generation or two ago. Research suggests that younger and better-educated people are especially likely to reject prejudice (Sniderman & Piazza, 1993; Glover, 1994). But do these findings accurately reflect people's real feelings (Bakanic, 1995)? Quite a bit of evidence suggests that they do not: Hate crimes have apparently been increasing—about 10,000 are reported annually—and researchers continue to find high levels of prejudice on college campuses (Allen et al., 1997; Southern Poverty Law Center, 1998).

Prejudices are, by definition, attitudes, not actions. But insofar as they confirm dominant group members' assumptions of superiority, they can lead to unequal treatment of minorities, a type of behavior sociologists call discrimination.

Discrimination

Discrimination is the unequal and unjust treatment of individuals on the basis of their group memberships (Feagin & Feagin, 1996). In modern societies, widespread norms mandate equal treatment of all people. Teachers and employers, for example, must not let ascribed factors such as race, ethnicity, and gender influence how they treat their students and employees. Anyone who violates these norms is guilty of discrimination.

Historically, however, most Americans openly accepted and indeed encouraged certain types of discrimination (Rose, 1990). For example, the Constitution denied African Americans the right to vote until 1865. Well into the 1960s, courts allowed restrictive covenants in real estate, which stipulated that house buyers would not resell to African Americans, Jews, or other "undesirables." Sociologists refer to discrimination that is required by law, or that results from the lingering consequences of such laws, as *de jure* discrimination; all other types of unequal treatment are *de facto* or customary discrimination.

A given act of discrimination may be further classified as individual, direct institutional, or indirect institutional. **Individual discrimination** is familiar to everyone (Carmichael & Hamilton, 1967). If your uncle refuses to hire an accountant to do his taxes because she is Latina or female, his behavior is clearly discriminatory. Today, few Americans publicly condone individual discrimination, although many still practice it (see Figures 12.1 and 12.2 on page 310).

Direct institutional discrimination (Davis, 1978; Feagin & Feagin, 1999) refers to the openly biased practices of an institution. A bank that refuses to hire someone because he or she is African American is guilty of direct institutional discrimination. Collectively, these two types of deliberate discrimination may be termed *dominative racism* (Jones, 1997).

However, contrary to what many people believe, even if we could abolish all dominative racism, discriminatory behavior would persist. This is because of **indirect institutional discrimination**—policies that appear to be neutral or colorblind, but in practice result in the unfair treatment of minority groups (Carmichael & Hamilton, 1967).

Here's how indirect institutional discrimination works: Suppose, for example, that a bank has recently hired a number of minority accountants, perhaps in response to pressure from civil rights groups. But now it must downsize its staff. If the bank directors simply fire the minorities overtly, they are guilty of direct institutional discrimination and might well be in trouble with the law. But if, instead, they announce that the layoffs are based on the "last hired, first fired" principle, then they do not appear to be discriminating, but the result is exactly the same: The minorities lose their jobs. Note that it is perfectly possible that the bank directors do not intend to be unfair—but, again, the result is the same.

Consider another example. Suppose that a law school announces that it will admit any student whose grades and law board scores meet a given standard. This sounds nondiscriminatory, but it fails to take into account the consequences of prior deliberate discrimination against groups such as African Americans. Compelled for generations to attend underfunded, segregated schools, until very recently few African Americans had a realistic opportunity to prepare for college or do well on standardized tests. Real progress has been made in correcting these injustices, but to assume that the legacy of 400 years of discrimination can be entirely undone in two generations is wildly

The legally required racial segregation that was universal in the American Deep South prior to the late 1960s is an excellent example of direct institutional discrimination. While discrimination against minorities endures in the United States, it is no longer this blatant.

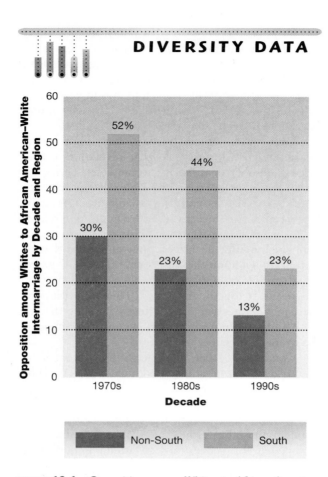

FIGURE 12.1 **Opposition among Whites to African American-White Intermarriage, by Decade and Region.** Over the past thirty years, racially mixed marriages have become more acceptable to all white Americans. However, Southerners remain less tolerant of such marriages than people from other parts of the country. What changes might lead to greater levels of acceptance of racially mixed marriages?

Source: NORC. General Social Surveys, 1972–2000. Chicago: National Opinion Research Center, 2000. Reprinted by permission of NORC, Chicago, IL.

optimistic. Given these realities, colorblind treatment is in fact often discriminatory against minorities.

THE RELATIONSHIP BETWEEN PREJUDICE AND DISCRIMINATION Is someone who discriminates necessarily prejudiced? Most of us assume that people's actions accurately reflect their inner feelings, but this is not necessarily true. Suppose, for example, that you were a totally unprejudiced white person living in the Deep South early in this century. If you owned a restaurant, would you serve African Americans? Not if you wanted to stay in business! If the Klan didn't shut you down, the local government would, since *de jure* (legally required) segregation was in effect at the

time. Similarly, suppose that you are a restaurant owner today in Madison, Wisconsin, and you just hate members of some ethnic group—say, the French. Are you going to post a big sign on your door saying "No French people admitted"? Again, not if you want to stay in business, because such a sign would offend many people's sensibilities and might also get you in trouble with the law.

The point is that you cannot always infer behavior from attitudes or vice versa. Sociologists have long known that what people think, say, and do often do not coincide (LaPierre, 1934; Kutner et al., 1952; Eagly, 1992). As Robert Merton (1948) pointed out, people can be not only prejudiced discriminators and

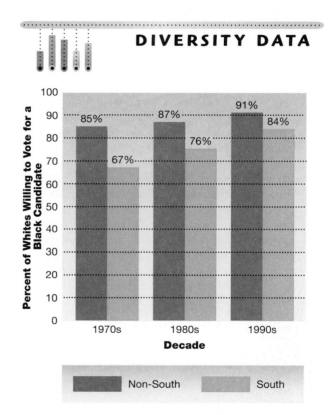

FIGURE 12.2 **Willingness among Whites to Vote for an African American Candidate for President, by Decade and Region.** Over the past thirty years, white people throughout the country have indicated greater willingness to vote for a qualified African American candidate for president. Opposition to an African American candidate remains strongest in the South. Southerners in the 1990s were about as willing to support a black for president as non-Southerners were in the 1970s. Do you think that the people answering this question were being honest, or might some of them have just been trying to appear unprejudiced?

Source: NORC. General Social Surveys, 1972–1996. Chicago: National Opinion Research Center, 1996. Reprinted by permission of NORC, Chicago, IL.

Does the Person Discriminate?

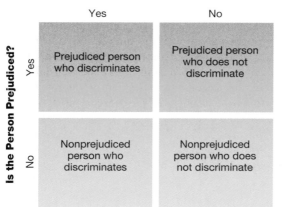

	Yes	No
Yes	Prejudiced person who discriminates	Prejudiced person who does not discriminate
No	Nonprejudiced person who discriminates	Nonprejudiced person who does not discriminate

Is the Person Prejudiced?

FIGURE 12.3 **The Relationship Between Prejudice and Discrimination.** *Source:* Merton, 1948.

unprejudiced nondiscriminators, but they may also be, as suggested above, prejudiced nondiscriminators or nonprejudiced discriminators (see Figure 12.3). In fact, there is substantial evidence that prejudice is not the main cause of discrimination.

Racism

In recent decades, the term *racism* has been tossed around so freely that some sociologists now hesitate to use the word at all. However, it does have a core meaning that continues to be of value. In sociology, racism is understood to be an *ideology*, a way of thinking that justifies unequal treatment. More formally,

racism is the ideology that maintains that one race is inherently superior to another (Miles, 1989).

Racist thought assumes that the concept of race is biologically meaningful and that race is directly related to ability (Ezekiel, 1995). It has been used to defend virtually every form of discrimination from genocide to casual social exclusion (Feagin & Vera, 1995; Doob, 1999).

THEORETICAL PERSPECTIVES ON PREJUDICE AND DISCRIMINATION

Sociologists and social psychologists have proposed a number of theories to explain prejudice and discrimination.

Social Psychological Approaches

One of the earliest attempts to understand the origins of prejudice suggests that people who are frustrated, whether by a difficult home life, poverty, or some other factor, and who are unable to strike back at the real cause of their frustration, often seek out **scapegoats,** individuals who are unfairly blamed for other people's problems (Dollard et al., 1939).

Minorities are convenient targets for scapegoating. They are relatively powerless, and there are often widely held beliefs among dominant group members that can be used to justify blaming them (Blackwell, 1982). A classic example is Hitler's scapegoating of the Jews for the ills that Germany experienced after

The Ku Klux Klan has long been America's best-known openly racist group. Today, the Klan is widely regarded as extremist and most people reject its views. However, more subtle forms of racism are widespread throughout American culture.

its defeat in World War I. A far less extreme example is provided by the numerous attacks against Arabs and other Muslims after the destruction of the World Trade Center.

A second social–psychological perspective is based on the concept of the *authoritarian personality* (Adorno et al., 1950; Ray, 1991; Jones, 1997). According to this view, relatively harsh child-rearing practices tend to produce people who are attracted to prejudiced patterns of thought. Uncomfortable with moral and ethical ambiguity, authoritarians tend to perceive people as either good or bad and to evaluate others as either their superiors or their inferiors. Minorities, of course, tend to fall in the latter category.

The reason we know that authoritarianism is a personality trait, not just a matter of learned bias, is that authoritarians tend to be willing to declare themselves opposed to *all* out-groups: African Americans, Latinos, gays, Jews, and even, in one classic study, nonexistent groups such as Danireans and Wallonians (Hartley, 1946; Sniderman & Piazza, 1993).

What are the policy implications of using social–psychological perspectives to understand prejudice? They are twofold: We need to help people find less harmful ways of coping with daily frustrations, and many parents need to modify their child-rearing practices.

Symbolic Interactionism

Symbolic interactionists, like all sociologists, take the social environment into account in constructing theories of prejudice and discrimination. In particular, they point out that attitudes toward minorities are *learned*. Research shows that by age 4 or 5, children have acquired attitudes concerning different racial and ethnic groups from the people around them (Fishbein, 1996).

If prejudiced attitudes and discriminatory behaviors are consistently reinforced, people learn to limit their perceptions of minorities in such a way that they never have to confront realities that might challenge their preexisting assumptions (Ehrlich, 1973). Learning theories take on particular significance when people grow up in cultures that embrace racist worldviews, such as the historic Deep South and South Africa.

Some symbolic interactionists go further and point out that the English language itself covertly supports racism. Suppose you were growing up as a person of color and learned that white was generally considered to be a symbol of virtue (the white dress worn by a virginal bride) whereas darkness often carried negative connotations ("a black mark on his character" or "to blackball a candidate"). Could you ignore the implications of such symbolic expressions?

The primary policy implication of learning theory rests on the observation that if prejudice is learned, it can be unlearned. According to the **contact hypothesis,** intergroup interaction can reduce prejudice. However, members of each group must have equal status, be working together toward a common goal, and receive positive reinforcement for appropriate attitudes and behaviors (Sigelman & Welch, 1993; Sigelman et al., 1996).

Functionalism

Functionalists believe racist ideologies and the prejudice and discrimination that they encourage persist because they promote social stability. Minorities who have been socialized into accepting racist belief systems are unlikely to challenge the existing arrangements. Furthermore, discrimination is clearly functional for dominant groups in that it tends to perpetuate the status quo.

However, functionalists also note that discrimination has several dysfunctions (Rose, 1951). It keeps society from making full use of the abilities of all of its citizens, and it aggravates social problems such as poverty, crime, and family instability. Discrimination also requires substantial social control expenditures to keep down those discontented minorities who do not accept the dominant ideology.

The main policy implication of the functionalist approach is that we must recognize the dysfunctions of prejudice and discrimination and find less destructive ways of fulfilling the stabilizing functions they now serve.

Conflict Theory

Conflict interpretations assume that conditions of unequal power and competition generate discrimination and emphasize the structural arrangements that create such conditions. There are several schools of thought within conflict theory.

According to the *split labor market perspective*, modern societies are characterized by two distinct types of jobs. *Primary labor market* jobs generally pay well and offer fringe benefits and a chance for advancement. *Secondary labor market* jobs offer none of these advantages. Minorities and other subordinate groups, including women, are disproportionately channeled toward the secondary labor market, a pattern that benefits the entire dominant group, but particularly white male workers (Bonacich, 1972; Lind, 1995). White men historically defended their advantage by keeping people of color and women out of their unions, a phenomenon which still occasionally occurs (Mladenka, 1991).

In contrast, *Marxist exploitation theory* sees an economic elite rather than the entire dominant group benefiting from discrimination (Cox, 1948; Hunter, 2000). Exploitation theory maintains that the ruling class deliberately promotes prejudice and discrimination in order to divide the workers. Whites and people of color are taught to see each other rather than the dominant class as the enemy. As a result, workers are less likely to join unions and similar organizations to demand fair treatment (Olzak & Nagel, 1986), and wages remain low. If white workers do unionize, factory owners can hire African Americans and members of other minority groups as strikebreakers because they are desperate for any kind of work (Bonacich, 1976). The big winners are the wealthy owners of the means of production. Workers—all workers—lose.

The policy implications of the conflict perspective are clear: The power differential between the elite and the masses must be sharply reduced. In such a restructured society, prejudice and discrimination would diminish greatly.

Table 12.1 summarizes and compares the views of the major theoretical perspectives concerning prejudice and discrimination.

PATTERNS OF MINORITY–DOMINANT GROUP RELATIONS

Dominant groups and minority groups can interact in many different ways. According to Simpson and Yinger (1985), most historical cases can be classified into one of six general categories: genocide, expulsion or population transfer, open subjugation, legal protection, assimilation, and pluralism.

Genocide

Genocide is the extermination of large numbers of the members of a minority group (or of any large group of people). It is most likely to occur when the dominant group is much larger than the minority, when the minority is of little or no economic value to the dominant group, and when the dominant group needs a scapegoat to blame for economic or military setbacks (duPreez, 1994).

The most widely known example in the last century is the Holocaust, Hitler's "final solution" to the "Jewish problem." Six million Jewish men, women, and children (as well as hundreds of thousands of Roms (Gypsies), homosexuals, and other groups) died in Nazi Germany's concentration camps (Baumann, 1991). Unfortunately, this was by no means the only instance of genocide in the 20th century.

For example, the "ethnic cleansing" of Muslims and Croats by Serbian forces in Bosnia in the early 1990s cost several hundred thousand lives (Rieff, 1995). In 1994, the dominant ethnic group in the African nation of Rwanda, the Hutu, massacred almost a million Tutsi (Block, 1994; Gourevitch, 1995, 1998).

The principal victims of genocide in the United States were the Native Americans. By 1890, the Indian population had been reduced by more than 90 percent (Garbarino & Sasso, 1994; Oswalt & Neely, 1999). Most of these deaths were accidentally caused by diseases such as smallpox against which Native

TABLE 12.1

Theoretical Explanations of Prejudice and Discrimination

	Specific Theories	Basic Logic	Policy Implications
Social Psychological Approaches	Scapegoat theory Authoritarian personality theory	Prejudice satisfies distinctive personality-level needs	Improve child-rearing practices and help people find more appropriate ways of dealing with everyday frustrations
Symbolic Interactionism	Learning theory	People learn prejudice and discrimination from those around them	Increase contacts with members of different groups; work to reduce biases inherent in culture
Functionalism	Functionalism	Prejudice and discrimination provide positive functions for some people and groups	Find less harmful functional alternatives to prejudice and discrimination
Conflict Theory	Split labor market theory, Marxist exploitation theory	Prejudice and discrimination help powerful groups maintain their advantages	Reduce power inequalities in society

Americans had no resistance. However, the view that "the only good Indian is a dead Indian" was widely endorsed among whites in the 19th century (Dudley, 1998).

Expulsion and Population Transfer

Sometimes, under much the same circumstances that can lead to genocide, the dominant group forces a minority to emigrate (expulsion) or confines it to a limited territory (population transfer). The decision to favor one of these strategies instead of genocide may be due to some mix of morality and practicality, but the goal is essentially the same: to remove the minority group from society.

Expulsion is responsible for the millions of refugees who wander the globe today, from the former Yugoslavia to Central Asia, the Middle East, and sub-Saharan Africa. In the 19th century the United States government practiced population transfer when it forced hundreds of thousands of Native Americans onto isolated and barren reservations, while whites grabbed the valuable land the Indians had "abandoned."

During World War II, over 110,000 men, women, and children whose ancestry was at least one-eighth Japanese, most of whom were U.S. citizens, were forced to sell their homes and most of their possessions and move to detention camps in remote areas of the West (Kitano, 1980). None of these people had been found guilty of disloyal activities, and white-skinned Germans and Italians, some of whom were known to be Axis sympathizers, were never subjected to similar treatment. This forced relocation was declared unconstitutional by the Supreme Court in 1944, but it was not until 1989 that Congress voted reparations to the victims (Takezawa, 1995). The *Diversity in Focus* box on page 323 discusses the related issue of reparations for slavery.

A more recent example of large-scale forced migration occurred in 1999. Slobodan Milosevic's Serbian government used military force to put down an independence movement among Islamic ethnic Albanians in the province of Kosovo—despite the fact that they constituted roughly 90 percent of the population of the region—ultimately forcing roughly 1 million people to abandon their homes and become refugees.

Open Subjugation

When the dominant group views the minority as economically valuable, it is unlikely to kill or expel them. Instead, it commonly forces them into a situation called *open subjugation* in which no pretense is made that the minority is in any way equal to the dominant group.

Slavery in the Old South and *apartheid* in South Africa prior to 1993 are historic examples of open subjugation. Labor was needed to work the plantations of Virginia and Georgia and the mines and factories of the African Transvaal. Prior to 1865, African Americans were subjected to the ultimate degradation of being owned; under apartheid, South African blacks were technically free, but their rights to live, work, and travel where they wished were greatly limited (Fredrickson, 1981; Sparks, 1990). In both cases

Since the end of the Cold War, ethnic conflicts have broken out in many parts of the former Soviet bloc. Some of the most intense struggles took place in 1999 in the province of Kosovo, when Serbian forces compelled hundreds of thousands of ethnic Albanians to flee their homes.

The Confederate flag is an intensely controversial symbol. Many blacks and liberal whites see it as a holdover from the days of slavery, but some Southern whites insist that it represents only regional pride, not racism.

the workers were regarded as less than fully human, denied most or all civil rights, and frequently treated with great brutality.

Legal Protection—Continued Discrimination

In this pattern of dominant–minority relations, the government claims to protect the basic civil rights of all of its citizens, but in reality substantial discrimination continues. African Americans entered this phase at the end of the Civil War and it continued until at least the passage of the 1964 Civil Rights bill.

It is under these circumstances that segregation is most visible. **Segregation** is the physical and social separation of dominant and minority groups. In the segregated South prior to the civil rights revolution, African Americans were compelled to attend inferior all-black schools, to live only in their own neighborhoods, and to sit only in the back rows on buses.

Under open subjugation, it is convenient for minorities to live with or near dominant group members so that they can serve them day and night, as during slavery. But once the state endorses the legal equality of all citizens, dominant groups tend to force—or at least encourage—minorities to keep to themselves in order to symbolically protect their higher status.

Assimilation

As dominant–minority relations improve, a real possibility arises of **assimilation,** the process by which minorities shed their differences and blend in with the dominant group. Assimilation is generally easier and more rapid under certain conditions: (1) if minority group members migrated voluntarily (Blauner, 1972), (2) if they are not sharply distinct physically from the dominant group, (3) if they are relatively small in number, (4) if they arrive when the economy is doing well, and (5) if they are culturally similar to the dominant group (Yinger, 1985).

There are two competing images of assimilation (Gordon, 1978). Most people in the United States are more comfortable with the *melting pot model,* which suggests that various racial and ethnic groups come to this country and then lose their distinctiveness and "melt" into a single group of "Americans." This view is represented in Figure 12.4 on page 316 by the equation A + B + C = D, in which A represents the British-descended or Anglo settlers, B and C represent other immigrant groups, and D represents generalized Americans (Newman, 1973).

In contrast, the *Anglo-conformity model*—A + B + C = A'—suggests that immigrants lose most of their ethnic identity and learn to act and think like the British-descended Anglos who traditionally dominated U.S. society. Thus, Italian immigrants, for example, became fluent in English and abandoned nearly all of their own culture, while the Anglos learned to like pizza—hardly an even trade!

The melting pot model is in line with egalitarian U.S. values and is widely endorsed in the media (Parrillo, 2000). Most sociologists, however, think that melting pot assimilation is more myth than reality.

We may further distinguish between three levels of assimilation: cultural, structural, and biological (Gordon, 1964). *Cultural assimilation,* also called *acculturation,* comes first: The minority accepts the dominant group's language, clothing styles, food preferences, many of its values and norms, and sometimes even its religion. This process initially creates people who are marginal—not fully accepted by either the dominants or by their original subordinate group (Weisberger, 1992)—but over time marginality declines as the dominant culture is more fully assimilated.

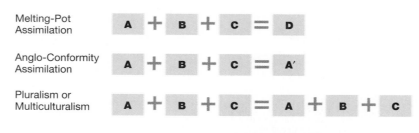

FIGURE 12.4 **Three Models of Minority-Dominant Group Relations.**

Source: Figure, "Three Models of Minority-Dominant Group Relations" from *American Pluralism: A Study of Minority Groups and Social Theory* by William M. Newman. Copyright © 1973 by William M. Newman. Reprinted by permission of Addison-Wesley Educational Publishers, Inc.

Cultural assimilation often leads to *structural assimilation*, whereby minorities live in the same neighborhoods, worship at the same churches, and work for the same firms as members of the dominant group.

The final step is intermarriage, referred to as *biological assimilation* or *amalgamation* (Spickard, 1991). As discussed later in this chapter, sociologists expect amalgamation to increase in future decades.

Pluralism

The final pattern of minority–dominant relations is **pluralism,** sometimes also called *multiculturalism*. In this model, minority groups maintain much of their cultural identity, yet do not experience significant discrimination and participate in common economic and political institutions (Taylor, 1995). Pluralism is summed up in Figure 12.4 by the formula A + B + C = A + B + C (Newman, 1973). Rather than a melting pot, the multicultural ideal visualizes America as a salad bowl where various elements mix together without losing their distinctiveness.

Pluralism is widely endorsed in U.S. society today (Glazer, 1997). It is easiest to achieve when there are no sharp economic differences between the groups. Switzerland is a substantially pluralistic society. Each of Switzerland's three major ethnic groups—German, French, and Italian—maintains its own language and traditions. None of the three constitutes a numerical majority, and none is much better off than the others. Each lives mostly in its own part of the nation, but all Swiss interact regularly with each other on a roughly equal basis.

Minority Responses to Subordination

When the dominant group insists on population transfer, open subjugation, or legal protection, minorities have few options. Some individuals, unfortunately, accept the ideology that defines them as inferior and do not actively resist oppression. A few are able to hide their minority-group membership and "pass," although often at great psychological cost, because it means turning their backs on most or all of

Pluralism is an arrangement in which members of ethnic and racial minorities are encouraged to retain their distinctive patterns regarding matters such as food and dress while participating as full equals in the larger economic and political system.

their friends and family. Some choose to emigrate. Others accept their devalued status publicly but not in private; for example, some slaves appeared resigned to their condition yet nurtured hope for eventual freedom while occasionally resisting through sabotage and work slowdowns. And still others actively work to change their status through social movements.

Once dominant–minority relations improve, however, minorities may choose between three principal alternatives: assimilation, pluralism, and separatism.

ASSIMILATION Assimilation holds forth the promise of complete acceptance by the dominant group, and for this reason, it has probably been the most widely embraced option among minorities in the United States (Hirschman, 1983; Pedraza & Rumbaut, 1996). However, there are serious doubts about whether racial minorities will be allowed to—or even want to—assimilate. Will most whites ever believe that people of color are just as good as they are (Zweigenhaft & Domhoff, 1991; Lawrence & Matsuda, 1997)? In addition, many minorities wonder whether they should assimilate if it means abandoning a culture that their ancestors treasured (Nagel, 1994).

PLURALISM Pluralism responds to some of the problems posed by assimilation. But the question arises regarding this strategy, as it does with assimilation, as to whether whites can transcend racism and permit minorities true equality (Shorris, 1992). Skeptics point out that white commitment to multiculturalism is relatively weak, as suggested by California's efforts to dismantle its bilingual education programs and by continuing efforts to dismantle affirmative action initiatives. Even if pluralism can be achieved, some people question the ultimate wisdom of the policy. In a multicultural society, will dominant groups maintain their power by "playing off" other groups against each other, as predicted by Marxist exploitation theory (Marden et al., 1992)? Furthermore, in a truly pluralistic culture, will there be enough common values to hold the society together, or will it fall apart, as has happened in the former Yugoslavia or as threatens to occur in Canada?

SEPARATISM Today many minorities, especially people of color, do not believe the dominant group will ever allow them to assimilate or to construct a truly pluralistic society (Brooks, 1996). This view has led some to embrace **separatism,** also sometimes called *ethnic nationalism,* a policy of voluntary structural and cultural isolation from the dominant group. Superficially similar to segregation imposed by the majority, separatism is initiated by the minority group in defense of its own cultural integrity (Delgado, 1995).

Separatism has been a fairly popular option among African Americans ever since Marcus Garvey's "back to Africa" movement of the 1920s (Cronin, 1969; White, 1990). Today, Louis Farrakhan's Nation of Islam advocates this model. Separatists generally recognize that they must remain enough in the mainstream culture so that they don't disadvantage themselves economically, but otherwise they try to distance themselves as much as possible from the dominant group. The widespread self-segregation of minority groups in dorms and cafeterias on many U.S. college campuses is a good example of separatism (Jordon, 1996).

IMMIGRATION

Most minority groups in the United States and throughout the world occupy that status as a result of immigration. Many migrated to new countries in search of freedom and economic opportunity. Others, like Native Americans or Catholics in Northern Ireland, became minorities when outsiders came to their land and settled.

Not even the Native Americans originated here; their ancestors came to the Western Hemisphere from Siberia at least 14,000 years ago (Oswalt & Neely, 1999). European settlers from Spain, France, Holland, and England arrived in the 16th and 17th centuries, subdued the indigenous peoples, and established themselves on these shores. Africans were brought to the Americas by slave traders beginning in the early 1600s. Over the past two centuries, numerous additional waves of immigrants have arrived (Jacobson, 1998). Figure 12.5 on page 318 shows the historic changes in immigration patterns since 1820.

In 1965 a new act was passed that allowed far greater numbers of non-Europeans to enter the United States than had previously been admitted. Between 1981 and 1990 roughly 10 million people immigrated to the U.S., 7.3 million of them legally (Frey & Tilove, 1995). The pace increased even more rapidly between 1991 and 1998, with 7.6 million people officially admitted during these 8 years.

The Census Bureau predicts that non-Hispanic whites, who made up 71.4 percent of the population in 2000, will barely be a majority in 2050. While the African American population will grow slightly, from 12.8 percent to 14.7 percent of the total, Latinos will increase from 11.5 percent to 24.3 percent; they will become the United States' largest minority group early in this century. This growth is due both to immigration and to the young age and high fertility rate of the Latino population. The Asian American population will also grow rapidly, roughly tripling to nearly 10 percent of the total by 2050.

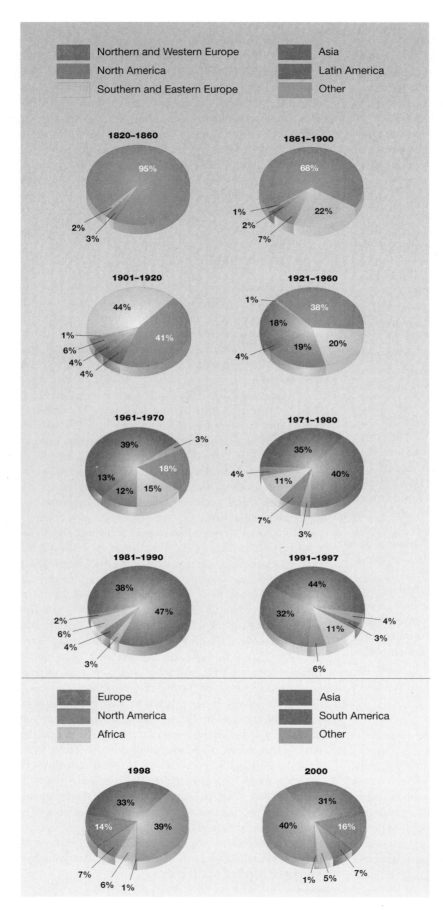

FIGURE 12.5 National Origins of Legal Immigrants Admitted to the United States, 1820–1997.

Source: Bouvier, Leon F., and Robert W. Gardner. 1986. "Immigration to the U.S.: An Unfinished Story." *Population Bulletin* 41 (November). 1999 *U.S. Statistical Abstract*, Table 8.

Quite simply, the United States is very close to the end of the era in which most citizens could trace their roots to Europe (O'Hare, 1992). Shortly after the midpoint of this century, a small majority of Americans will be ethnic or racial minorities.

Immigration has become a very controversial issue in the United States in recent years. Some critics charge that immigrants take jobs away from citizens and that they use more than their share of public services such as education and welfare. Research on these issues is inconclusive. It is clear, however, that many immigrants hold jobs that few others would accept, and many thousands of additional jobs are created by immigrant entrepreneurs each year (Cole, 1994).

Some anti-immigrant feeling doubtless reflects little more than *xenophobia*, an irrational fear of foreigners (Portes & Rumbaut, 1990). Whatever its origin, anti-immigrant sentiment has been very evident in recent years. Polls show that a sizable majority of Americans support restrictions on immigration (Suro, 1999). A nationwide English Only movement has led over 20 states to declare English their "official language," endangering bilingual education and other immigrant-friendly programs in these states.

One of the clearest signs of this anti-immigrant backlash occurred in California: In 1994, 59 percent of the voters in that state approved Proposition 187, which denied public education, nonemergency medical services, and welfare assistance to illegal immigrants. Although the courts blocked implementation of Proposition 187, similar legislation has been passed at the federal level. In 1996, all illegal immigrants and most legal immigrants who were not yet citizens were barred from receiving Social Security and most forms of public assistance.

A CLOSER LOOK AT SELECTED MINORITY GROUPS

In the following discussion, we will limit ourselves to a few key points regarding selected minority groups in the United States and Europe. In addition, the *Global Connections* box on page 123 discusses the status of minority groups in Japan. Tables 12.2 and 12.3 present important data concerning the size and social circumstances of the major U.S. minority groups and will be referred to regularly in the following sections.

African Americans

The first Africans to arrive in America in significant numbers landed at Jamestown, Virginia, in 1619, centuries before the ancestors of most white Americans came to these shores. These earliest immigrants were temporarily indentured servants, but by 1661 lifelong

TABLE 12.2

Size of Selected Ethnic and Racial Groups in the U.S., 2000

Total Population	**281,422**
European Ancestry	
German	32,529
Irish	20,575
English	19,153
Italian	12,771
Polish:	6,287
French	5,755
Norweigan	3,056
Dutch	2,922
African American	34,648
Native American	2,475
Latino	
Mexican	20,640
Puerto Rican	3,406
Cuban	1,241
Asian	
Chinese	2,432
Filipino	1,850
Asian Indian	1,678

Source: U.S. Census Bureau (2001). Detailed Data Table DP-1 and Table PCT02.

slavery was legally established in the colonies (Sowell, 1981). Of all American minorities, Africans were the only group to be enslaved in large numbers, the only group forced to entirely abandon its traditional culture, and the only group whose families were deliberately broken up (Franklin, 1967).

African American slavery was an important factor in the U.S. Civil War, certainly the most pivotal event in the history of this nation. Following the war, black–white relations continued to define the culture and identity of the South, and in some ways of the nation itself, as the United States moved through the post-Civil War Reconstruction era (1865–1876), the subsequent Jim Crow years (when segregation was supported by state laws), and the civil rights revolution of the 1960s.

Beginning in the 1920s, after laws were passed to curtail European immigration, African Americans started migrating north in search of economic opportunity and in order to escape the pervasive segregation of the Deep South. In the 50 years between 1920 and 1970, the black population was transformed: Once overwhelmingly Southern and rural, it became urban and widely distributed throughout the nation (Lemann, 1991).

During the civil rights era, Dr. Martin Luther King, Jr., worked to establish a society in which race

---

TABLE 12.3

Social Characteristics of Selected Racial and Ethnic Groups

	Median Family Income	Percent of Individuals Below the Poverty Line	Percent of Two-Parent Family Groups	Percent of Persons 25 and Over Completing High School	Percent of Persons 25 and Over Completing College
Non-Hispanic whites	$51,244 (2000)	9.8 (2000)	74.7 (2000)	84.9 (2000)	26.1 (2000)
African Americans	31,778 (2000)	23.6 (2000)	38.6 (2000)	78.5 (2000)	16.5 (2000)
Latinos	31,663 (2000)	22.8 (2000)	63.5 (2000)	57.0 (2000)	10.6 (2000)
Native Americans	21,619 (1989)	31.2 (1989)	n. a.	65.6 (1990)	9.4 (1990)

Source: U.S. Census Bureau (2001). Statistical Abstract, Tables 215, 57, 41, and 38.

---

was no longer a stigma. In sociological terms, he envisioned the United States as a multicultural society with a good measure of assimilation. But as early as 1968, it was apparent that his dream was imperiled. In that year, the Kerner Commission, established to investigate the urban riots that were sweeping the nation, concluded that the United States was rapidly becoming ". . . two societies, one black, one white—separate and unequal" (National Advisory Commission on Civil Disorders, 1968). Twenty-five years later, another national commission, once again organized in response to urban rioting, concluded that the Kerner Commission's analysis remained highly accurate (Milton S. Eisenhower Foundation, 1993). While real progress has been made, discrimination endures and in some case is even becoming worse: The racial profiling discussed at the beginning of this chapter is one example as is the fact that racial discrimination in

mortgage lending was found to be increasing in the late 1990s (Turner & Skidmore, 1999).

A glance at Table 12.3 provides a starting point for understanding the current situation of African Americans. In 2000, the median family income for blacks ($31,778) was just 62 percent of the figure for non-Hispanic whites. Only about 30 percent of all African American men and 60 percent of black women are currently employed in professional, technical, managerial, and administrative jobs, compared with roughly 50 percent of white males and 75 percent of white females. Over 23 percent of African Americans—and about two-thirds of those in single-parent families—live below the poverty line. Black unemployment figures are consistently more than twice the white figures, and the teenage unemployment rate tops 40 percent in some cities.

These problems have endured despite rapid improvements in median levels of education. In 1980,

Despite the growth of a sizable African American middle class, roughly half of all black children are still born into families living below the poverty line.

THEN AND NOW

African Americans Move Back South

Seventy-one-year-old Bennie Rayford, whose parents were sharecroppers, grew up in a county in rural Mississippi where black children didn't go to school until all the cotton was picked. Beating the odds, he finished high school, earned a college degree in education, and became the principal of a run-down, segregated school in his home state. In 1957, when Rayford organized his students' parents to petition for a new school bus, the county superintendent fired him. "You're too smart a nigger," his termination letter read. "We no longer need your services" (Smith & Pedersen, 1997, p. 36). He and his wife Hilda, also a teacher, decided then and there to head north and settled in Toledo, Ohio. When they retired, however, they moved back to Tchula, the small town in rural Mississippi where they both grew up; three of their adult children have now joined them there.

When the Rayfords moved to Ohio, they were participating in the largest internal migration in U.S. history. Between 1940 and 1970, more than 5 million African Americans left the rural South for cities in the North in the hope of finding better jobs and less discrimination. In the mid-1970s, however, this pattern began to reverse. During the decade of the 1990s alone, the African American population of the South grew by 3.6 million people.

For hundreds of years the South humiliated African Americans—first through slavery, then through sharecropping and segregation. For most of this century Southern blacks were not allowed to vote, were forced to attend segregated schools, and were systematically denied good jobs and housing. Why would anyone return to the scene of so much misery?

Young, middle-class African Americans are moving to the South for the same reasons other people are: better jobs, affordable housing, cleaner air, and a more laid-back lifestyle. Atlanta, a magnet for both whites and blacks, is today one of the fastest-growing metropolitan regions in the country. Beth Griffen visited Atlanta out of curiosity and decided to stay; so did her fiancé, Rick. They stayed because they felt there were better career opportunities for black men and women in Atlanta than in the North. Today Beth is a senior financial analyst for Coca-Cola and Rick works as a computer-software consultant. The Griffens believe they enjoy a better life here than they could elsewhere. Equally important, they want to raise their child in a city where there are a significant number of African American professionals, business owners, and other successful role models.

The Rayfords returned to Mississippi for much the same reason they left: Life in Toledo had become intolerable. Both taught in inner-city schools, where students brought guns into the classroom; the schools had become almost as dangerous as the streets at night. In some ways, Tchula hasn't changed much since they left more than 45 years ago. People still sit on their porches, go for strolls, or visit neighbors at night without fear of being mugged. As before, the town is 80 percent black; also as before, most of the residents are poor and undereducated. In other ways, however, Tchula has changed: Both the local police force and the county board, once all white, are now largely African American. Equally important, the Rayfords have changed: Both have the experience and contacts needed to get things done. Hilda has started a learning center for adults as well as for young people. Bennie, who chaired Jesse Jackson's presidential campaign in Ohio in 1984, is the head of a local health center and vice chair of the Holmes County Republican Party.

Not all participants in the reverse migration South are as financially secure or sophisticated as the Griffens and the Rayfords. In her book *Call to Home* (1996) anthropologist Carol Stack tells the stories of African Americans who left crowded inner-city apartments for trailers, cabins, and small brick houses on dusty roads in rural North and South Carolina. Many had spent their childhood or their summers with relatives in the South, sent their children to be raised in the South, and on some level had never left the region. Second-generation migrants to the North, they found that the "promised land, the land of freedom and opportunity, had become the Rustbelt" (Stack, 1996:48). The only jobs available to them didn't pay living wages; their marriages weren't holding together; their children were out of control; their lives weren't working out.

The migrants Stack got to know did not romanticize the rural South as a "paradise lost"; they knew that life there was as hard as ever. Certainly, they did not want to turn back the clock to the days of segregation and humiliation. But they missed the network of kin and neighbors who come to one another's aid in hard times. In Stack's view, "What people are seeking is not so much the home they left behind as a place they feel they can change, a place in which their lives and strivings will make a difference—a place in which to create a home" (1996, p. 199).

1. What, if anything, do these reverse migrants lose by returning to the South?

2. How much change do you believe has taken place in the racial attitudes of white Southerners in recent decades? What are the primary factors that have produced this change?

Sources: Stack, 1996; Smith & Pedersen, 1997; Cohn, 2001.

about 50 percent of all African Americans over 25 had completed high school; by 2000, 78.5 percent had graduated. College enrollments have also substantially increased, although a dropout rate of almost 70 percent (compared with 40 percent for whites) lowers the percentage of African Americans who earn their degrees (Allen & Jewell, 1995; Leslie, 1995). Unfortunately, education often has less payoff for blacks: White male high-school dropouts earn almost as much as black high-school graduates, and white high-school graduates earn only slightly less than African Americans who have attended (but not completed) college (Schaefer, 2000).

Saddest of all, African Americans continue to lag behind whites in vital statistics. In 1998, 14.3 out of every 1,000 African American children died in their first year of life; the figure for whites was 6.0. In 1999, black men could expect to live, on the average, 68.7 years compared with 74.7 years for white men. The figures for females were 75.4 and 80.2, respectively.

Remember also that the negative effects of race and ethnicity are amplified in complex ways when we consider the combined impact of the variables of race, gender, class, age, and sexual orientation on the ways in which individuals are treated in society, a reality that has shaped a great deal of contemporary sociological research and theory construction (Anderson & Collins, 1998; Rothenberg, 1998).

A closer look at the African American population reveals a critical point that is not apparent from aggregate statistical data: Major changes have occurred in the African American class structure over the past 40 years. Before the 1960s, the black middle class was small and composed largely of marginally well-paid government employees and free professionals. Today, about 40 percent of African Americans are middle class (Landry, 1988; Takaki, 1993), and although they hold only about 15 percent of the wealth that the average white middle-class family controls (Oliver & Shapiro, 1995) and continue to experience a measure of discrimination (Feagin, 1999), they are beginning to approach a degree of parity with the dominant group.

On the other hand, the African American lower class has also expanded, and by almost any measure, its life circumstances have worsened. The black poverty rate has increased by almost 50 percent since 1988, and roughly half of all African American children are now born into poverty (Pinkney, 2000).

William Julius Wilson (1978), a prominent African American sociologist, has long supported the controversial position that the most critical factor affecting blacks today is class rather than race (Steffensmeier & Demuth, 2000). He maintains that the key to understanding the plight of the contemporary inner-city poor lies in two factors: deindustrialization and the exodus of the black middle class (Wilson, 1987, 1996).

By deindustrialization, Wilson means the steep decline in recent decades in the availability of decent jobs to inner-city black men. Two or three generations ago, capable and ambitious young African American men could find work near where they lived on assembly lines or operating machines. These jobs were far from ideal, but they provided a decent level of support, adequate to allow them to marry and father families and to seek further education for themselves and their children. But over the years, most of these jobs vanished, moving abroad or to the suburbs, out of the reach of people lacking access to reliable transportation (Kasarda, 1989; Massey & Denton, 1993).

An increasing number of African Americans have turned to drug sales and property crime or taken marginal service jobs that simply do not pay enough to support a family. At the same time, the percentage of two-parent families in some sections of the inner city has declined precipitously (Pinkney, 2000). Today, most lower-class African Americans simply do not make enough money to support a family. Welfare policies, which traditionally denied benefits to intact families, only intensified the problem by encouraging the further fragmentation of the black family. The high numbers of single-parent families are not unrelated to the problems of the inner city, but Wilson insists that family structure is more a *consequence* than the primary cause of African American poverty.

According to Wilson, a second factor complicating the problems of the inner-city poor is the out-migration of the African American middle class. Since desegregation opened up much of the housing market in American cities, black families with adequate incomes have streamed out of the inner city. In the process, poor neighborhoods have lost the mainstays of local institutions, from PTAs to political organizations to churches. These moderately affluent African Americans were also the people who helped finance local businesses and community projects. Once, there were hard-working, conventional role models living on almost every block; now drug dealers and professional athletes are often the only economically successful black people visible in the inner city (Crane, 1991).

The implications of Wilson's analysis are clear. Programs preaching against drugs, crime, and pregnancy outside of marriage are not the answer, because they focus on symptoms, not causes. The recent dramatic cuts in welfare (see Chapter 11) are also unlikely to reduce poverty. Providing decent jobs for the inner-city poor, jobs that pay enough to allow for the

DIVERSITY IN FOCUS

The Debate Over Reparations

Should African Americans be paid monetary compensation—reparations—for the harm done to them by 200 years of slavery? This question has sparked one of the most heated debates in minority–dominant relations in recent years.

The issue is not a new one. At the end of the Civil War, Union General William T. Sherman ordered that all newly-freed slaves be given 40 acres of farmland and a mule, but President Andrew Johnson vetoed his plan. A century later, during the civil rights movement, activist James Foreman asked that the white churches pay $500 million in reparations for slavery. Michigan Representative John Conyers, Jr., sponsored an act in 1989 calling for the establishment of a federal commission to study the effects of slavery and to recommend ways of repaying the debt, legislation that has been endorsed by the NAACP, by the National Bar Association, and by nearly a dozen city councils.

Supporters of reparations stress that they are not asking for charity, but rather for a balancing of accounts based on the fact that a great deal of white wealth—some estimate as much as 20 percent—was accumulated as a direct result of unpaid slave labor. Whites were able to invest this wealth and thereby to augment their fortunes. Much white wealth is thus, in the eyes of the supporters of reparations, unjust enrichment. The capital that African Americans could have accumulated and used to advance themselves and their descendants was appropriated and used to their own benefit by whites. As a result, while the gap between white and black *incomes* is gradually narrowing, the difference in accumulated *wealth* between the two communities remains enormous. Victoria Barnett puts it this way: "The legacy of their

crimes continues to benefit those who inherited the power and privileges that emerged from that injustice."

Most activists are not asking for payments to individual African Americans, but rather for a massive government commitment to strengthening the black community, above all by helping African Americans secure access to large blocks of investment capital that would allow them to expand their collective wealth until it reaches the level it would have attained had slavery never existed. Other proposals endorse using reparations to enhance education and job training programs in poor African American neighborhoods.

Advocates such as attorney Adjoa A. Aiyetoro, co-founder of the National Coalition of Blacks for Reparations in America, cite a number of historical precedents for their position. The German government has paid reparations to individual Jews and to the state of Israel for the Nazi Holocaust; Australia and New Zealand have paid compensation for the historical harm done to their indigenous populations; and in 1987 the U.S. Congress awarded $1.2 billion in reparations to Japanese Americans who were interned during World War II—$20,000 to each individual. The state of Florida paid $2.1 million in 1994 to the descendants of African Americans killed in a brutal 1923 race riot in the town of Rosewood.

Opponents of reparations raise several objections. In particular, they argue that no whites living today benefit directly from slavery, which ended in 1865; indeed, the ancestors of most contemporary whites had not even emigrated to the United States when the slaves were emancipated. Practical questions also arise concerning such issues as exactly how much money should be paid, over what period of time, and to whom.

Critics also ask whether we should be focusing on the wrongs of the past at this late date; some charge that the demand for reparations promotes a counterproductive "victimization" mentality among African Americans. Reparations supporters reply that ignoring historical injustices such as slavery will not make their modern-day consequences vanish, and that the moral inhumanity of the crime of slavery absolutely demands compensation.

A final issue concerns the probable reaction among whites and other minority groups were reparations to be granted. Such a policy might well increase racist sentiments among whites. Given the high level of opposition to affirmative action programs, is it likely that most whites would accept the moral need to balance the scales through reparations, or would they see this proposal as nothing more than another demand for special treatment? There could also be dissent from other minority groups, including Latinos and Native Americans, who might feel that the historical injustices perpetrated against them are being ignored or trivialized. Should backlash be allowed to carry the day? What is ultimately more important to African Americans—justice or maintaining the goodwill of the dominant community?

1. Are there other groups besides African Americans and Japanese Americans that deserve reparations for the way in which they have historically been treated by the dominant group in the United States?

2. Is there any way by which most whites can be convinced that reparations for slavery are fundamentally just?

Sources: America, 1995; Barnett, 2000; Brain, 2000; Smith, 2001.

formation of stable families, would be the most promising solution to the problems of the African American lower class.

Latinos

The Latino (or Hispanic) population of the United States is both large and diverse (Shorris, 1992). The 2000 census classified 11.8 percent of the U.S. population as Hispanic, but this count missed large numbers of undocumented immigrants. The true total is probably higher by about 8 million. The Latino population is young and, as was noted in the vignette about Rogers, Arkansas, that opened this chapter, it has recently overtaken the African American community as the largest single minority group in the United States.

Figure 12.6 shows the national origins of the Latino population of the United States. While roughly two-thirds of all Hispanics trace their roots to Mexico, substantial numbers come from Puerto Rico, Cuba, and other Central and South American nations. There are many social and cultural differences between the members of these groups; in fact, most refer to themselves by their country of origin, not as Latinos (Heyck, 1994; Romero et al., 1997). However, some common patterns can be identified.

Most obviously, the fact that Latinos are Spanish-speaking people has affected their experiences in the United States. Many Hispanic students enter school poorly prepared in English, contributing to high-school dropout rates of about 30 percent and relatively low levels of educational attainment. As shown in Table 12.3, only 10.6 percent of Latinos over 25 hold college degrees.

Because Latin America is so close to the United States, Hispanics, especially Mexican Americans and Puerto Ricans, often return home, sometimes temporarily, sometimes permanently. This, along with the language factor, often makes it more difficult for Latinos to assimilate well enough to allow upward economic mobility. Thus, overall, Latinos earn just 61.8 percent of the median non-Hispanic white family income, although the figure for Cuban-Americans is much higher and that for Puerto Ricans is much lower. Roughly 22.8 percent of all Latinos live below the poverty line, and median Latino household wealth actually declined 24 percent between 1995 and 1998 ("Latinos Failing . . .", 2000).

Religion is another common factor among Hispanics. Protestant denominations are making inroads, but about 85 percent of Latinos remain Catholic. The church has helped immigrants settle in their new land, but Catholic doctrine opposes all forms of artificial birth control, materially contributing to the larger family size and indirectly to the relatively low economic standing of most Latino groups. On the other hand, religious beliefs have doubtless helped strengthen the family; according to Table 12.3, 63.5 percent of all Latino families are intact.

Native Americans

Although they were not subjected to large-scale slavery, the trauma inflicted on the Native American population is not dissimilar to that experienced by African Americans. In at least one regard, their experience was worse. Slaves were economically valuable and their population increased in America, whereas the vast majority of the Native American population died as a result of contact with whites: Between 1500 and 1900 their numbers declined from between 2 and 3 million to about 240,000 (Brown, 1991).

White–Indian relations can be divided into three broad historic periods (Nichols, 1992; Hoxie & Iverson, 1998). Until 1871, the government made treaties with tribes as if they were conventional foreign nations, though it never fully honored those treaties and relentlessly pushed the Native Americans westward across the Mississippi. Between 1871 and 1934, official policy shifted to forced assimilation. Individual families were given plots of reservation land in the hope of turning Native Americans into small farmers, and many thousands of children were sent away to boarding schools where they were taught white cul-

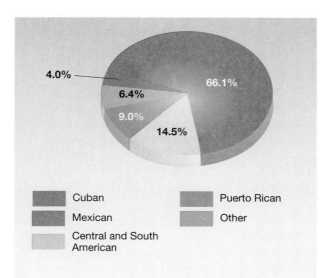

FIGURE 12.6 National Origins of the Latino Population, 2000.

Source: U.S. Census Bureau (2001). The Hispanic Population in the United States. Figure 1.

Inadequate housing is only one of the major social problems commonly experienced by Native Americans who live on reservations.

ture and punished if they did not abandon their traditional ways (Noley, 1990). Since 1934, government policy has gradually shifted toward pluralism, with the aim of incorporating Native Americans into national life, but as Native Americans. Tribal governments have been established, and today most Native American groups enjoy considerable autonomy (Bordewich, 1996; Nagel, 1996).

Native Americans are generally considered the most disadvantaged of all minority groups. Overall, 31.2 percent of all Indians lived below the poverty line in 1989, the last year for which census data are available (see Table 12.3). But on the reservations, where about one-third of all Native Americans live, the poverty rate often exceeds 50 percent. School achievement, although increasing, remains low (Cage, 1993). Unemployment and infant mortality are exceptionally high, and the life expectancy of men on the reservation is just 45 years; for women, the average is 48 years (Churchill, 1994). Mental illness, suicide, and alcoholism are all too common (Bachman, 1992; Lester, 1997).

One of the most serious issues confronting Native Americans today is the choice between the reservation and the city (Dudley, 1998). On the one hand, city life promises much greater economic opportunity, but it is difficult for small, isolated groups of urban Indians to maintain their cultural heritage. On the other hand, the reservation offers a more sheltered and nurturing environment but few decent jobs other than those provided in the casinos that have been established by some tribes. Many young Native Americans shuttle back and forth between city and reservation, never fully committed to either (Iverson, 1998).

Asian Americans

Like Latinos, Asian Americans are entering the United States in great numbers, and they are a tremendously diverse group. Figure 12.7 identifies the principal countries from which Asians have immigrated. The number of Asians living in the United States increased from 7.5 million to 11.2 million in the 1990s alone; it is expected to more than triple by 2050 (Lee, 1998). Each group has had unique experi-

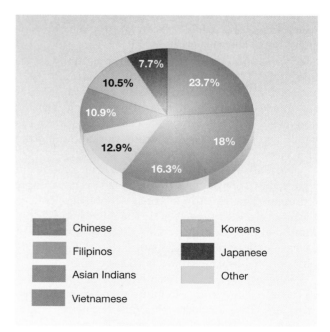

FIGURE 12.7 National Origins of the Asian American Population, 2000.

Source: U.S. Census Bureau (2001). Statistical Abstract, Table 24.

ences; yet, as with Latinos, there are certain common themes.

Most Asian Americans, especially those who arrived on the West Coast in the 19th century, met substantial hostility (Parrillo, 2000). For example, the first major wave of Chinese immigrants came to build the railroads and to participate in the 1849 California gold rush, but they were so hard-working that many whites came to consider them dangerous economic competitors. These fears, intensified by the marked physical and cultural differences between whites and Chinese, led to the 1882 Chinese Exclusion Act that ended Chinese immigration until the early 1940s (Chan, 1991).

Japanese Americans, who arrived somewhat later than the Chinese, fared marginally better until they were forced into internment camps during World War II. More recent arrivals, especially refugees from the Vietnam War era, have continued to face opposition from time to time.

From a sociological perspective, what is remarkable about Asian Americans is how many of them have become economically successful and how quickly this success has come. Remember, this is a highly visible racial minority whose culture of origin is very different from mainstream culture in the United States. Yet the median family income of Asian Americans is 110 percent of that of white families; they have the lowest unemployment rate of any group; and just over half of them own their own homes—a higher percentage than any group other than non-Hispanic whites and Cubans.

How can we explain these statistics? For one thing, the level of discrimination experienced by Asian Americans, while substantial, has been considerably less than that suffered by African Americans and Native Americans. In addition, the family structure of most Asian American groups is typically very strong. Nearly 80 percent of Asian American families are intact—a very high rate. Divorce and teenage pregnancy are uncommon. Socialization within the family tends to stress a very strong work ethic and the importance of education (Caplan et al., 1992).

Not all Asian Americans excel in school, of course, but so many do that they are very strongly represented at the top of high school and college classes (Gibson & Ogbu, 1991; Rong & Grant, 1992). Almost 44 percent of Asian Americans over the age of 25 have college degrees, far more than the 26.1 percent of non-Hispanic whites in this age range.

Furthermore, most Asian American groups initially settled in strong, supportive communities that provided a base for developing new businesses (Light & Bonacich, 1988). Today, many Asian Americans have become highly assimilated—culturally, structurally, and, given their high intermarriage rate, biologically, as well (Nee et al., 1994).

Because of their successes, Asian Americans are sometimes called "model minorities" (Winnick, 1990; Lee, 1996). Although there is considerable truth to this label, it is an oversimplification (Woo, 1985; Tyson, 1994). For one thing, many of the more recent arrivals from Asia are still living in Chinatowns or Little Saigons, experiencing considerable discrimination, and earning modest incomes or barely surviving on welfare. The Asian American poverty rate (10.7 percent in 2000) is still above the non-white figure of 9.8 percent. In addition, the high median family income of Asian Americans reflects a larger number of wage earners per family than is typical of whites (Barringer et al., 1993; Takaki, 1993).

Catholics in Northern Ireland

For hundreds of years, Northern Ireland has been—and to a considerable extent remains—a segregated society, even more so than the U.S. South before the civil rights era (Harris, 1972). Working-class Catholics and Protestants normally grow up in separate neighborhoods, attend different elementary and secondary schools, play different sports, support different political parties, work for different employers (although this is gradually changing), and even use different names for the province: Protestants call it Ulster, while Catholics prefer Northern Ireland.

The Catholic population of Ireland has lived there for over 1,000 years. Most of the ancestors of the present-day Protestant community emigrated to the northern coast of the island from Scotland in the early 17th century, displacing thousands of Catholic families from their land. Relations between the two groups have generally been hostile ever since, with the Protestants occupying the dominant role and the Catholics the subordinate one (Ruane & Todd, 1996).

The conflict in Northern Ireland is not really about religion. Rather, it is a struggle for political and economic power between two ethnic groups that happen to be identified by their faiths (Beach, 1977). Structurally, the North Irish situation resembles white–Indian relations in the United States in that, in both cases, the minority group has been subjugated in its own land by foreign invaders. The critical difference is that Native Americans constitute less than 1 percent of the population of the United States, whereas Catholics make up about 46 percent of the population of the province (Darby, 1995).

The present configuration of interethnic relations was established in 1922 when the overwhelmingly Catholic southern 26 counties of Ireland won political independence from Britain. Because the Protestants of the North feared discrimination in an independent, all-Ireland Catholic state, they estab-

GLOBAL CONNECTIONS

Minorities in Japan

While virtually every modern society is characterized by minority groups, some include far more than others. The United States, Canada, and Australia, nations that have historically encouraged immigration, lie toward one end of this continuum. On the other hand, Japan is the most homogeneous of all developed societies. No more than 4 million Japanese—4 percent of the population—are considered to be racial or ethnic minorities. However, their small numbers do not seem to have lessened the extent to which these people have experienced discrimination at the hands of Japan's collectivistic and strongly conformist dominant culture.

The *Burukumin* are Japan's largest and most severely stigmatized minority, despite being physically indistinguishable from other Japanese. Members of this group, who make up about 2 percent of the population, are believed to be the descendants of ancient outcastes who were looked down upon because they did "unclean" jobs like butchering or leatherworking.

The Burukumin were granted legal equality in 1871, but this did not end their minority status. To this day they are widely regarded as unsuitable marriage partners and continue to experience discrimination in employment. Burukumin are relatively less educated, more than twice as likely to be on welfare, and three times as likely to be arrested as other Japanese. They even score substantially lower on IQ tests.

The fact that the Burukumin are physically identical to everyone else creates problems for prospective employers and in-laws, who sometimes violate the law by hiring private detectives to check out the backgrounds of job applicants and the would-be spouses of their children. In the modern era, Burukumin liberation movements have successfully campaigned for government-sponsored scholarship programs and affirmative action initiatives, and today both college attendance and intermarriage rates are increasing rapidly.

Additional Japanese minority groups include:

- The *Ainu,* a racially distinct group of some 20,000 individuals descended from the aboriginal inhabitants of Japan, most of whom live in the remote northern islands.
- Koreans, numbering a little less than 1 million. Most came to Japan in the decades before World War II. Although most Koreans have adopted Japanese names and some conceal their ancestry, members of this ethnic group experience substantial discrimination. Only about half of all Korean boys in Japan finish high school (compared with 97 percent of other Japanese), Koreans are rarely welcomed as prospective spouses, and they tend to work in marginal blue-collar occupations.
- The 265,000 *Nikkeijin* are persons of Japanese heritage whose ancestors emigrated to Brazil, Peru, and other parts of South America but who have returned to Japan since 1989 in search of employment. Like the Burukumin, they are physically indistinguishable from the general population, but they are ethnically distinct, speaking loudly in public, openly embracing each other, and holding street festivals featuring Latin music.

In addition, about 1.5 million foreigners reside legally in Japan and there are another half million undocumented resident aliens.

Japanese women may also be analyzed as a minority. As noted in this chapter, women in Japan and elsewhere meet many defining criteria of a minority group: They occupy an ascribed status, are relatively powerless, experience prejudice and discrimination, and have some degree of solidarity.

Japanese women have enjoyed formal equality under the law since 1947, but they continue to be limited by a strong cultural separation of spheres that allows them control over the household while defining the outside world as the man's arena. Half of all Japanese women work, but employment discrimination is rampant. Women earn only about one-third of all wages and are very rarely found in prestigious jobs, especially in business. They are socialized to see themselves as mothers and wives, not as workers, and to subordinate themselves to the needs and desires of their families. The Japanese feminist movement is probably the weakest of any in the developed world, and the prospects for significant improvement in the treatment of women in Japan in the near future are quite dim.

1. Reflect on the case studies presented in this box and elsewhere in this chapter and see if you can develop some general principles about how the relative size of a minority group seems to affect how it is treated.

2. Should women be analyzed as a minority group, or does this improperly blur the lines between gender, race, and ethnicity? Explain your position.

Sources: Lindsey, 1997; Weiner, 1997; Kerbo & McKinstry, 1998; Schneider & Silverman, 2000; Wehrfritz & Takayama, 2000.

Conflict between the Protestant and Catholic communities in Northern Ireland has continued for over 350 years. Outdoor murals cover the walls of many working-class homes throughout the province, proudly and aggressively identifying the ethnicity—in this case, Protestant—of the area's inhabitants.

lished a six-county province that remained part of the United Kingdom and in which they enjoy a 54 percent majority (O'Malley, 1990).

In the 50 years between 1922 and the dissolution of the North Irish parliament in 1972, Protestants held complete control over Northern Ireland. They gerrymandered electoral boundaries and manipulated the franchise in order to maintain political control even over heavily Catholic areas. Catholics were openly discriminated against in employment and housing. The police were overwhelmingly Protestant, recruited in some cases directly from the ranks of the aggressively anti-Catholic Orange Order (Ruane & Todd, 1996).

The tenacity and longevity of this conflict has few parallels worldwide. For over 80 years, a Catholic-based group called the Irish Republican Army employed force to attempt to oust the British from the island and end Protestant domination. A majority of the voters in the North approved a historic restructuring of the government in May 1998, but extremists on both sides have continued to resist any changes that might strengthen the opposition.

LIFE CONNECTIONS

Toward Multiracial Society

In the United States, traditional thinking long suggested that there were only a small (and fixed) number of races, that everyone could be unambiguously defined as a member of one of these races, and that anyone who had virtually any nonwhite ancestry was nonwhite—the "one drop" principle (Wright, 1994;

Malcomson, 2000). As recently as 1983 a Louisiana court ruled that a woman who was the great-great-great-great-granddaughter of a slave, but all of whose other ancestors were white, was officially an African American (Marger, 2000:434).

However, since race is a social construction rather than a biological concept, racial labels are not fixed but are rather constantly changing. There appears to be increasing public support in the United States today for a new "multiracial" category (Cose, 2000).

The key factor promoting this change is doubtless the increasing number of marriages across racial lines. In 1980, 1.3 percent of all married couples were interracial; by 2000, the percentage had risen to 2.5. In 1970, only 1 out of every 100 children was biracial or multiracial; today 1 in 19 is—1 in 10 in California and Washington. The total multiracial population of the nation has been estimated at 16.5 million people (Clemetson, 2000).

Another factor contributing to this change may be the popularity of multiracial golfer Tiger Woods, whose ancestry is one-eighth white, one-eighth Native American, one-fourth African American, one-fourth Thai, and one-fourth Chinese. Although the press often still follows the "one drop" rule and refers to him as black, Woods prefers to define himself as "Cablinasian"—Caucasian, black, Indian, and Asian (White, 1997).

As the numbers and visibility of mixed race individuals increase, they are beginning to form a distinct subculture with their own magazines, Web sites, and chat rooms. Over 30 universities now sponsor mixed-race student organizations (Clemetson, 2000).

While most people still resist changing their understanding of race, a substantial and increasing minority is unhappy with the traditional categories. About 10 million people refused to check a racial/ethnic category on the 1990 census (Feagin & Feagin, 1999), leading to the demand that the option "multiracial" be included in 2000 (Della Piana, 1995; Kalish, 1995).

Instead, the government compromised by allowing respondents to check as many races as they felt applied, and about 6.8 million people chose multiple categories. Although this change may make it more difficult for researchers to compare the results of different censuses—63 combinations of racial identifications are now possible—it does seem to reflect the beginnings of a shift in the way race is perceived in the United States. In fact, the American Anthropological Association recently recommended that the term race be eliminated from the 2010 census. Table 12.4 illustrates the changing racial categories used by the census between 1890 and 2000.

Symbolic interactionists in particular would argue that this shift is not a trivial matter. As we have emphasized throughout this text, according to this theoretical perspective, the linguistic categories that people use shape the way they think. If race is concep-

---

TABLE 12.4

U.S. Census Classifications, 1890–2000

Census Date	White	African American	Native American	Asian American	Other Categories
1890	white	black mulatto Quadroon Octoroon	Indian	Chinese Japanese	
1910	white	black mulatto	Indian	Chinese Japanese	other
1930	white	Negro	Indian	Chinese Japanese Filipino Hindu Korean	Mexican other
1950	white	Negro	American Indian	Chinese Japanese Filipino	Hawaiian other
1970	white	Negro black	American Indian	Chinese Japanese Filipino Korean	Hawaiian other
1990	white	black Negro	Indian Eskimo Aleut	Chinese Japanese Filipino Korean Asian Indian Vietnamese	Hawaiian Guamanian Samoan Asian or Pacific Islander other

2000	white	black
		African
		  American
			American Indian
			Alaska Native
				Chinese
				Japanese
				Filipino
				Korean
				Asian Indian
				Vietnamese
					Native Hawaiian
					Guamanian
					Samoan
					Asian or Pacific
					  Islander
					other

Sources: Lee, Sharon. 1993. "Racial Classification in the U.S. Census, 1890–1990," *Ethnic & Racial Studies* 16(1): 75–94. *2001 Statistical Abstract,* Table 22.

tualized as a matter of degree and choice, not as an absolute biological category—if we start thinking as Tiger Woods does rather than in terms of black-OR-white dichotomies—then the social meaning of race will be gradually transformed.

Perhaps the United States will eventually come to resemble truly multiracial societies like Brazil, in which innumerable intermediate statuses are recognized between white (*branco*) and black (*preto*) (Page, 1995; Marx, 1998). This does not mean that Brazil is a society without racial discrimination—it is well understood there that it is better to be light skinned—but it does mean that the boundaries between the races are less rigid, that the impact of race on people's lives is less dramatic, and even that race becomes to a certain extent an achieved status: Brazilians often say that "money whitens" and that "a rich Negro is a white man (sic)." (Marger, 2000:434). Of course, skin color does not actually change with wealth, but people's perceptions do, and that makes all the difference.

The goal of affirmative action is to help minorities ovecome the lingering consequences of prior discrimination. These demonstrators are concerned because recent rulings have suggested that an increasingly conservative Supreme Court may soon declare some or all affirmative action measures unconstitutional.

SOCIETY CONNECTIONS

Affirmative Action

For several decades, the United States has been engaged in efforts to increase the opportunities available to minorities. The most controversial of these programs is **affirmative action,** public and private efforts to recruit people of color and women into educational programs and jobs in which they have traditionally been underrepresented. At a minimum, affirmative action involves no more than being sure that members of these groups are made aware of the opportunities available to them. But many programs go further and give preferences to certain people and groups.

Through the later 1960s and 1970s, every president and both major political parties supported the principles of preferential hiring and admissions. By the early 1970s, the use of quotas had become fairly common in affirmative action programs. However, in the 1978 *Bakke* case, in which an unsuccessful white applicant to medical school sued the University of California-Davis because it had rejected him and accepted several less qualified applicants of color, the Supreme Court ruled by a 5–4 vote that quotas were generally—but not always—inappropriate. At the same time, the court reaffirmed that race could properly be taken into account in admissions and hiring.

The picture changed in 1980 with the election of Ronald Reagan, a dedicated opponent of preferential hiring and admissions. As the courts became more conservative during the 1980s, successive rulings began to erode affirmative action. In the 1970s, a lack

INTERNET CONNECTIONS

A number of controversies were discussed in the chapter on the impact that immigrants have had on American society. Go to the Website Population Reference Bureau:

http://www.prb.org/Content/NavigationMenu/PRB/AboutPRB/ Population_Bulletin2/Immigration_to_the_United_States.htm

and click on the different links. After reading the information, write a short response to each of the following questions. Describe the pattern of change where do immigrants come from today in comparison to past decades? What impact will this change have, if any, on society? What is the economic impact of immigrants?

of minority employees or students was generally enough to justify affirmative action (Commission on Civil Rights, 1981). More recently, the courts have generally required evidence of intent to discriminate, evidence which is often extremely difficult to obtain.

In 1995, the Supreme Court further limited affirmative action by ruling that federal programs may include racial preferences only if they are "narrowly tailored" to accomplish ends that are of "compelling government interest" (Greenhouse, 1995). Also in 1995, California's governor acceded to conservatives' demands that all affirmative action in admissions to the state's public colleges and universities be ended.

One year later, in 1996, a federal appeals court ruled that racial preference in admissions at the University of Texas Law School was unconstitutional. This ruling applied only to Texas, Louisiana, and Mississippi, but it has set an important precedent (Morganthau & Carroll, 1996; Schrag, 1996). Also in 1996, 54 percent of the voters in California approved Proposition 209, which prohibits all affirmative action programs (Ayres, 1996).

Affirmative action is, by definition, a temporary policy, to be used until the playing field is truly level. But have we reached that point? Can we abandon affirmative action programs without unduly harming women and people of color? (Curry, 1996) Opponents of affirmative action raise the following points (Sowell, 1972; Glaser, 1976; Puddington, 1995; Crosby & VanDeVeer, 2001):

- Affirmative action is reverse discrimination. The white males who lose opportunities have done nothing personally to merit not being hired, promoted, or admitted.
- It is demeaning to minorities and women. Saying that they need extra consideration is tantamount to saying that they are incapable. People who are hired under affirmative action programs never escape a cloud of suspicion about their abilities (Steele, 1990).
- Affirmative action can result in hiring marginally less qualified people (Belz, 1991).
- Finally, affirmative action helps only people who are qualified for hiring or admission, mostly educated upper-working- and middle-class women and people of color. But these groups have made significant progress in recent decades and may not need additional help. Meanwhile, affirmative action does little or nothing to help the poor and uneducated.

Advocates of continuing affirmative action respond as follows (Ezorsky, 1991; Wilkins, 1995; Crosby & VanDeVeer, 2001):

- Reverse discrimination, if it occurs at all, is very rare (Burstein, 1991). Of some 3,000 affirmative action cases heard in the courts between 1990 and 1994, only 100 involved claims of reverse discrimination, and only six of these charges were upheld ("Reverse Discrimination . . .", 1995).
- Claiming that affirmative action is no longer necessary assumes that individual and direct institutional discrimination no longer exist in areas such as employment and housing. This is a widespread view among whites (Blauner, 1989; Kluegel, 1990; Hoschschild, 1995). But numerous studies demonstrate that both individual and direct institutional discrimination most definitely endure (Feagin & Vera, 1994).
- Given the existence of indirect institutional discrimination, colorblind and gender-neutral policies are actually discriminatory in favor of white males. As Lyndon Johnson said, "You do not take a person who for years has been hobbled by chains, and liberate him [sic], bring him up to the starting line, and then say 'You are free to compete with all the others'" (Hacker, 1992). In other words, to get past race, we must first take race into account. Affirmative action makes up for the lingering consequences of earlier deliberate discrimination.
- Finally, much evidence shows that affirmative action works, especially for college graduates (Beggs, 1995; Reskin, 1998). Institutions that have followed affirmative action guidelines have hired or admitted women and people of color in larger numbers and more rapidly than similar institutions without such policies. When the law schools at the University of California and the University of Texas stopped following affirmative action guidelines, the percentage of minorities enrolling dropped sharply (Torry, 1997; Bowen & Bok, 1999).

The debate continues, but the future of affirmative action looks dim, given current trends. If it is, in the end, abolished, supporters say the most promising alternative approach would be either some form of class-based affirmative action program or a substantial strengthening of educational opportunities for the poor. Both schemes are colorblind, which is probably necessary to gain public acceptance (W. J. Wilson, 1990). Still, some observers doubt if either would help minorities as much as traditional affirmative action programs have (Lively et al., 1995).

SUMMARY

1. Although most people think of race as a biological concept, it is a social construct. Ethnic groups share a common subculture, somewhat distinct from the culture of the dominant group.

2. Minority groups lack power compared to dominant groups. They also experience prejudice and discrimination, feel a sense of solidarity or peoplehood, are defined by ascription, and usually marry endogamously.

3. Prejudice is a negative attitude toward an entire category of people. There are two components of prejudice: an emotional reaction and a cognitive stereotype.

4. Discrimination consists of differential treatment on the basis of category membership. It may be *de facto* or *de jure*; it may also be individual, direct institutional, or indirect institutional.

5. Prejudice and discrimination often occur independently of each other.

6. Racism is a widespread ideology that maintains one group is inherently superior to another.

7. Prejudice and discrimination may result from personality-level processes, social learning, or economic conflict; they serve a number of functions as well as dysfunctions.

8. Negative patterns of dominant–minority group relations include genocide, expulsion, population transfer, open subjugation, and legal protection combined with de facto discrimination.

9. Assimilation is a process whereby minorities shed their differences and adopt the characteristics of the dominant group. There are three levels of assimilation: cultural, structural, and biological.

10. Under pluralism or multiculturalism, minorities retain their cultural identity yet peacefully coexist with other minorities and the dominant group.

11. Some minority group members seek assimilation, some prefer pluralism, and others advocate separatism.

12. Most people living in the United States—or their ancestors—entered the country as immigrants. Since 1965, immigration from Latin America and Asia has been very substantial. By the middle of the new century, only a numerical minority will be able to trace their ancestry back to Europe.

13. As a result of rising intermarriage rates and changing social definitions, multiracial identity has become more widely accepted in the United States in recent years.

14. Affirmative action is a controversial policy designed to remedy the consequences of prior discrimination, generally through giving preference to women and people of color.

KEY TERMS

affirmative action 330
assimilation 315
contact hypothesis 312
direct institutional discrimination 309
discrimination 308
ethnic group 307
gendered racism 308

genocide 313
indirect institutional discrimination 309
individual discrimination 309
minority group 307
pluralism 316
prejudice 308

race 306
racism 311
scapegoat 311
segregation 315
separatism 317
stereotype 308

CRITICAL THINKING QUESTIONS

1. Can the unequal treatment of minority groups be adequately addressed without responding to indirect institutional discrimination? Why do so many people, especially members of the dominant group, resist accepting the fact that this type of discrimination exists?

2. Which of the various theories of prejudice and discrimination offers the most promise for reducing the inequities experienced by minorities?

3. Do you believe that assimilation, pluralism, or separatism is the most appropriate policy for the various minority groups discussed in this chapter? Explain your choice.

4. Should the United States continue to offer affirmative action programs for minority groups? Why, or why not?

INVESTIGATE WITH CONTENT SELECT

Begin your research using Content-Select for this chapter by following the directions found on page 27 of this text to visit Prentice Hall's Research Navigator Website. Enter these search terms into the search field:

Affirmative action
Segregation
Native Americans

13
GENDER

Nature Versus Nurture Revisited

Famed anthropologist Margaret Mead journeyed to New Guinea in the 1930s to learn about the different tribal groups comprising the nation. She lived with three different tribes. Among the gentle, peace-loving Arapesh, both men and women were nurturant and compliant, spending time gardening, hunting, and child rearing. Arapesh children grew up to mirror these patterns and became cooperative and responsive parents themselves. By contrast, the fierce Mundugumor barely tolerated children; they left them to their own devices as early in life as possible and taught them to be as hostile to, competitive with, and as suspicious of others as their elders were. Both mothers and fathers showed little tenderness to their children, commonly using harsh physical punishment. The Tchumbuli exhibited still a different pattern. Their women were practical and unadorned. Their men were passive, vain, and vindictive. Women's weaving, fishing, and trading activities provided the economic mainstay for the community; men remained close to the village and practiced dancing and art. Women enjoyed the company of other women. Men strived to gain the women's attention and affection, a situation women took with tolerance and humor, viewing men more as boys than peers. Contrary to her original belief that there were "natural" sex differences, Mead concluded after visiting these tribes that masculine and feminine are culturally, rather than biologically, determined. (Adapted from Mead, 1935)

Girls and Boys Together . . . But Mostly Apart

In elementary school, eating and walking are not sex-typed activities, but in forming groups in lunchrooms and hallways, children often separate by gender. On the playground similar patterns show up. Boys control the large fixed areas for team sports such as soccer and football. Girls play closer to the building, using cement areas for jumprope and hopscotch. A boy watching girls playing jumprope offers to swing the rope. The girls respond, "No way, you don't know how to do it. You gotta be a girl." Boys who move into female-marked space, such as the cafeteria line or female lunch table, are teased by other boys: "Look, Mike's in the girl's line" or, pointing to a boy at an all-female table, "That's a girl over there." Relaxed interactions between girls and boys often depend on adults, such as teachers, to set up and legitimize contact. But children are strongly oriented to segregation by gender and often resist adult interference into their segregated activities. (Adapted from Thorne, 1997:179)

These vignettes highlight several key themes of this chapter. First, attitudes and behavior regarding gender are taken-for-granted assumptions about human social life. Second, when such assumptions are challenged, people have a variety of responses, ranging from puzzlement and disbelief to scorn and ridicule. Third, a change in gender roles is often resisted not only by those who hold power (mostly men), but also by those who have the lesser amount of power (mostly women). Finally, other patterns of behavior develop when gender intersects with race, class, ethnicity, and other categories of social life. Sociologists provide a number of explanations for all these patterns.

SEX AND GENDER

The study of gender emerged as one of the most important trends in sociology in the 20th century. Once a marginal concept, it is now a central feature of the discipline. Although all social relationships are ordered in some manner, gender is a key component of that ordering. Social institutions, as the key agents of socialization, are structured significantly according to attitudes and behaviors regarding gender.

In sociology, the terms sex and gender refer to two different content areas. As defined in Chapter 7, *sex* refers to the biological characteristics distinguishing male and female. This definition emphasizes male and female differences in chromosomes, anatomy, hormones, reproductive systems, and other physiological components. *Gender* refers to those social, cultural, and psychological traits linked to males and females through particular social contexts. Sex makes us male or female; gender makes us masculine or feminine. Sex is an ascribed status—a person is born with it. Gender is an achieved status—it has to be learned.

This relatively simple distinction is nonetheless loaded with problems because it implies unambiguous "either-or" categories. Recall from Chapter 7 that sexuality itself is culturally conditioned. *Sexual orientation,* how people experience sexual pleasure, varies considerably. People such as *hermaphrodites,* who are born with ambiguous sex characteristics, may be assigned one sex at birth but develop a different gender identity. And many cultures allow some people to move freely between genders. Sociology emphasizes how gender is learned, how it changes over time as cultural definitions change, and its variations from culture to culture. Margaret Mead's work in New Guinea undeniably supports such an emphasis. **Gender roles,** then, are the expected attitudes and behaviors a society associates with each sex. This definition puts gender squarely in the sociocultural context.

Some biological differences must be accepted as given. But equally problematic is a model with too strong a focus on biological differences and insufficient attention to the institutionalized sexism that transforms male–female differences into male advantage and female disadvantage (Bem, 1996:11). As detailed in Chapter 5, although sociology certainly does not dismiss biology, the strength of its perspective on gender rests with the social side. Sociologists favor theories that account for a range of variables rooted in sociocultural factors, explanations that suggest that female or male physiology does not limit achievement. Biology may tilt people in certain directions related to gender, but social influences direct them to the countless ways gender is expressed across the globe (Baldwin & Baldwin, 1997; Kennelly et al., 2001).

Scientists in all disciplines now agree that both biology and culture are necessary variables in explaining human social behavior. However, the biological differences between the sexes continue to be used to justify gender inequality. One major result of such a justification is **sexism,** the belief that one sex, female, is inferior to the other sex, male. Sexism is most prevalent in societies that are **patriarchal,** in which male-dominated social structures lead to the oppression of women. Patriarchy goes hand in hand with **androcentrism,** in which male-centered norms operate throughout the social institutions and become the standard. Sexism is reinforced by both patriarchy and androcentrism, and by the belief that gender roles are determined by biology and therefore cannot be significantly altered. The sociological perspective shows how sexism is maintained even when the majority of both men and women wish to eliminate it.

THEORETICAL PERSPECTIVES ON GENDER ROLES

Early sociological explanations related to gender roles evolved from work on the sociology of the family. These explanations centered on why men and women hold different roles in the family that in turn impact the roles they perform outside the family. This early work on the family has continued to inform current sociological thinking on gender roles.

Functionalism

The functionalist theoretical perspective suggests that separate gender roles for women and men are beneficial. In preindustrial societies, the most useful way to maintain order is to assign different tasks to men and women. In hunting and gathering societies, men were hunters, were away from home more, and were expected to hunt and bring food to their families and to protect them from harm. It was functional for women, more limited in mobility by pregnancy and nursing, to be assigned tasks related to child rearing and household maintenance. Women also obtained food by gathering or through subsistence agricultural activities (Wiesner-Hanks, 2001). Children, especially girls, were needed

In many cultures women are likely to work outside the home, but they still have responsibility for household tasks associated with traditional gender roles.

Functionalists suggest that families can be disrupted when men and women do not adhere to traditional gender roles, such as when a husband is the homemaker and a wife is the breadwinner.

to help with agricultural and domestic activities. Similar principles apply to families in contemporary societies. Disruption is minimized and harmony is maximized when spouses assume complementary and specialized roles, such as breadwinner and homemaker (Parsons & Bales, 1955). If there is too much overlap in these roles, competition between spouses increases and the family system can be disrupted.

CRITIQUE Functionalism offers a reasonably sound explanation for the origin of gender roles and demonstrates the functional utility of assigning tasks on the basis of gender, particularly in societies where children are needed for agricultural work. Overall, however, functionalist views of gender and the family have not kept pace with rapid social change and the move toward more egalitarian attitudes. Functionalism is based on a traditional white middle-class family structure in which women are in the home or, if outside the home, only as part of a paid reserve labor force or in unpaid voluntary roles, and where men are separated from their families because of career commitment. Contemporary families, especially in the developed world, simply do not fit this pattern.

Conflict Theory

Conflict theory reflects Marxian ideas about class conflict and the relationship between the exploiter and the exploited. Marx's collaborator, Frederick Engels (1884–1942), extended this idea to the family. According to Engels, after the introduction of private property and capitalism, a woman's domestic labor

was less valued compared to the household need provided by men. Women, therefore, are subordinate to men in the autocracy of the household and can never be emancipated until they can take part in paid production, with domestic work taking an insignificant amount of their time. Contemporary conflict theory concurs that men's economic advantage provides the basis for gender inequality both inside and outside the home. The conflict perspective is evident in research suggesting that household responsibilities have an effect on occupational location, work experience, and number of hours worked per week, all of which are linked to the gender gap in earnings (Shelton & Firestone, 1989). Undesirable work will be performed disproportionately by those lacking resources to demand sharing the burden or purchasing substitutes (Spitze, 1986). Since household labor is unpaid, and thus associated with lack of power, the homemaker (wife) takes on virtually all domestic chores (Lindsey, 1996a; Riley & Kiger, 1999).

CRITIQUE Conflict theory has been criticized for its overemphasis on the economic basis of inequality and its assumption that there is inevitable competition between family members. It tends to dismiss the consensus among wives and husbands regarding task allocation. In addition, paid employment is clearly not the panacea envisioned by Engels in overcoming male dominance. In the old Soviet Union women had the highest levels of paid employment in the world, retained more household responsibilities than comparable women in other countries, and earned two-thirds of the average male income. In post-Communist Russia, there is no change in women's domestic work, but women now earn less than half of men's average earnings (Hockstader, 1995; Stanley, 1997; Vannoy et al., 1999). Research unanimously concludes that even in those cultures where gender equity in the workplace is increasing, employed women globally take on a "second shift" (Hochschild, 1989) of domestic work after returning home (see Chapter 17).

Symbolic Interactionism

Symbolic interactionism asserts that gender is a social construction and that people called "females" or "males" are endowed with certain traits defined as feminine or masculine. Concepts like gender must be found in the meanings people bring to them (Denzin, 1993). Gender emerges "not merely as an individual attribute but something that is accomplished in interaction with others." People "do" gender (West & Fenstermaker, 1995:21). In doing gender, symbolic interactionism takes its lead from Erving Goffman (1959a, 1963a), who maintains that when we want to create certain impressions, we act out various roles, similar to what would occur in a theatrical performance (see Chapter 6). Research on singles bars typifies this approach. Both men and women "stalk" for partners, but they do it according to agreed-upon rules. A man, who usually comes to the bar alone, operates from a script in which he makes the first move. A woman, who is more likely to be with a female friend, must disengage herself from that friend if she is "selected" by the man. In places where men and women who do not know one another meet, a process of unspoken negotiation and choice based primarily on gender roles is operating (Laws & Schwartz, 1981; Rouse, 2002).

Gender roles are structured by one set of scripts designed for males and another designed for females. Although each script permits a range of behavior options, the usual result is that gender labels promote a pattern of between-sex competition, rejection, and emotional segregation. This pattern is reinforced when we routinely refer to those of the other sex (gender) as the "opposite" sex. Men and women label each other as opposite to who they are, then behave according to that label. The behavior serves to separate rather than connect the genders.

CRITIQUE Symbolic interactionism's approach to understanding gender role behavior is criticized for its lack of attention to macrolevel processes that often severely limit choice of action and prompts people to engage in gendered behavior that counters what they would prefer to do. In some cultures, for example, women and men are dictated to by both law and custom to engage in certain occupations, marry others they do not like, or be restricted from going to school, regardless of a family's ability to pay.

Feminist Sociological Theory: Linking Race, Class, and Gender

The most useful sociological theories take into account the ways people are alike and the ways they are different. Feminist sociologists were among the first in the discipline to account for similarities and differences, specifically as related to race, social class, and gender. The feminist perspective is based on **feminism,** an inclusive worldwide movement to end sexism and sexist oppression by *empowerment*, allowing women to have a measure of control over their own destinies.

The race–class–gender link originated with African American feminists in the 1960s. These women recognized that using this link to analyze social behavior is necessary not only for scientific understanding, but also to determine how women are alike and how they are different. If the real differences among women in terms of race and class are ignored, feminism will falter. For example, when the issue of poverty becomes "feminized," the issue is defined primarily by gender—women are at a higher risk of being poor than men. A focus on the feminization of poverty ignores the links among race, social class, and marital status that put at higher risk certain categories of women, such as single parents, women of color, and elderly women living alone. To explain

INTERNET CONNECTIONS

In the text there is a discussion of different views of feminism. Go to the following Websites:

http://www.feminist.com/ and **http://www.now.org/**

the sites will provide you with information and articles of interest on feminist issues. Do you think feminism reflect the interest of women and men today? Why or Why not?

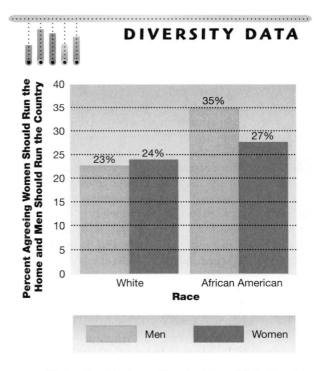

DIVERSITY DATA

FIGURE **13.1** *Should Women Run the Home While Men Run the Country?* About one-fourth of white men, white women, and African American women believe women should run the home and men should run the country. However, over one-third of African American men believe this. How do gender and race intersect to account for this important difference between groups?

Source: NORC. General Social Surveys, 1972–2000. Chicago National Opinion Research Center, 2000. Reprinted by permission of NORC, Chicago, IL.

Feminism has prompted sociological theory to account for the ways race, class and gender are linked and challenges the white, middle-class male norm for explaining social behavior.

poverty, racial and class oppression must be considered along with gender. When white, middle-class feminists focus on oppression of women, they sometimes have difficulty recognizing the privileges that come with their own race and class (Collins, 1996).

Thirty years ago the women's movement did not recognize that these intersecting categories can divide women. An African American woman living in poverty might be more concerned about the disadvantages associated with her social class and race than the disadvantages associated with gender (Jackson, 1998). Although the movement today specifically addresses the concerns of women interconnected to various subcultures, a feminist agenda that speaks to the needs of *all* women is still being built (Acker, 1999; Cole et al., 2001). Feminist sociological theory that accounts for both the similarities and differences among women offers a good start in helping create that agenda (Foster, 1999; Marshall, 2000).

BRANCHES OF FEMINISM The large majority of feminists accept the goal of ending sexism by empowering women. However, the feminist movement is not completely unified, in part because it is inclusive, and that very inclusiveness makes it difficult for agreement on some issues. As a result, the movement has several different branches divided according to general philosophical differences. Different formal and informal groups of feminists are regarded as falling under one of the following general branches.

Liberal Feminism Also called egalitarian or mainstream feminism, the philosophy of this branch is based on the simple idea that all people are created equal and should not be denied equality of opportunity because of gender. Since both genders benefit from eliminating sexism, numerous men also identify with this branch. The work of this branch is largely based on eliminating sexism in the overall social

structure. The National Organization of Women is the formal group that represents this branch.

Socialist Feminism Also called Marxist feminism, this branch believes that the inferior position of women is linked to class-based capitalism and the structure of the family in capitalistic societies. Capitalism is supported by women's unpaid household work and underpaid work in the labor force. Male supporters agree that the privileges they receive in the home are unjust to women. This branch works to adapt socialist principles to both workplace and home to increase gender equity.

Radical Feminism This branch believes that sexism is at the core of patriarchal society and all social institutions reflect that sexism. Women's oppression is from male domination, so neither capitalism nor socialism will solve it. Radical feminists desire to create separate institutions that are women-centered—those that rely on other women rather than on men.

Multicultural and Global Feminism This branch of feminism explicitly acknowledges that gender intersects with race, class, issues of colonization, and the exploitation of women worldwide. Gender, however, is the overarching concern that unites the men and women in this branch. They seek to work together across national boundaries to change patriarchy. They contend that no woman is free until the conditions that oppress women worldwide are eliminated. The people who came together for the United Nations Conferences on Women (see Global Connections box) support this view.

Despite the philosophical differences, clearly these branches overlap a great deal. Feminists can agree to disagree. As psychologist Judith Worrell (1996:361) points out, "Although we have joined a common parade, we do not all march to the same music."

GLOBAL CONNECTIONS

The United Nations Conferences on Women: Beijing and Beyond—A Personal Perspective

"Development, if not en-gendered, is endangered."

United Nations Development Program, 2000

In its Charter of 1945, the United Nations announced its commitment to the equality of women and men. The year 1975 was declared as International Women's Year, and the years 1976 to 1985 were recognized by the United Nations (UN) General Assembly as the United Nations Decade for Women. Official conferences to mark the decade and work on a global agenda of women's issues were held in Mexico City in 1975; Copenhagen, Denmark, in 1980; and Nairobi, Kenya, in 1985. Under the banner of "equality, development, and peace," each conference assessed the progress of commitments made on behalf of women by various nations.

Alongside each official UN conference ran a forum consisting of hundreds of nongovernmental organizations (NGOs) that brought together women from all over the world and all walks of life, representing a wide diversity of opinions and agendas. Inclusiveness brings dissent, and the conferences were marked by political, religious, and economic factionalism, which, unfortunately, became media

In 1995, the UN Conference on Women in Beijing brought together 50,000 of all races, classes, and nations and adopted a platform of action calling for gender equality, development, and peace.

highlights. Efforts by conservative groups to discredit and interrupt the proceedings also occurred. Many women who attended the NGO Forum in Copenhagen were discouraged by the amount of friction that appeared to separate rather than unify women. Some women felt that the Copenhagen conference did not focus enough on the intersection of class and race with gender. They wanted to

address issues relevant to all groups of women, especially women in the developing world. By Nairobi, friction was reduced and dialogue was opened. A fundamental change was the recognition that the women's movement is fundamentally a political movement.

In 1995, the international women's movement took center stage when Beijing, China, hosted the largest UN confer-

GLOBAL PERSPECTIVES: WOMEN AND DEVELOPMENT

The United Nations has spearheaded major efforts to reduce the gender gap in areas such as literacy, access to health care, job training, and family planning. Women in the developing world are the most restricted in almost all these areas. The good news is that since 1985 the gap in education and health has been cut in half. The bad news is that patterns of gender inequality continue to have dire consequences on the lives of women and girls (SIGI, 2001; United

Nations Development Program, 2001; World Bank, 2002). These include the following:

1. Seventy percent of the 1.3 billion people worldwide who live in abject poverty (living on less than one dollar a day) are women and girls.
2. Almost two-thirds of the 854 million illiterate adults worldwide are women.
3. If the unpaid work women perform—such as subsistence farming and domestic labor—was counted in economic terms, the world's gross domestic product would increase by almost one-third.

ence in history. With an attendance estimated at 50,000, Beijing was historic not only in terms of numbers, but because the women's agenda moved to the center of global debate. Beijing served as a watershed for the women's movement worldwide.

International media attention again focused on controversy and conflict—rather than on the more pervasive atmosphere of unity and support. Yet the truly remarkable events in Beijing finally managed to alter this trend. Even while attending the conference, many of us were acutely aware that the international media were dwelling on issues that generated the most controversy. Demonstrations by those representing conservative groups were frequently staged. The Iranian delegation of fully veiled women and their male "escorts" provided the media with much camera time. Their efforts were met by what many women there described as "bemused toleration." But television crews willingly followed them and reported on the nightly news that religious fundamentalism was tearing the conference apart.

This could not have been further from the truth. While religious fundamentalism was certainly one of many controversial topics, the NGO Forum was remarkable

in its ability to bring together women of all faiths to engage in dialogue about matters that affected their daily lives, such as reproduction, parenting, family violence, and health, all of which have religious overtones. When politics, religion, and cultural tradition were met head on, as between Palestinian and Israeli women or between African and western women who supported or opposed female genital mutilation, toleration and understanding emerged. What did become clear, however, is that the die is cast against religious fundamentalism when religion is used to deny women's human rights.

The norm of the NGO Forum sessions was to ensure that everyone had the opportunity to voice opinions; thus, complete unity was rare. However, when people "agree to disagree," the stage is set for a better understanding of the issues and more toleration of dissenting opinion.

What is the legacy of Beijing? I speak from the perspective of attending the gatherings in Copenhagen, Nairobi, as well as Beijing. While the Beijing conference was marked by negative international media attention, Chinese obstructionism, logistical nightmares, and inadequate facilities, the ability and perseverance of the women who attended

and worked to get the Platform of Action adopted was nothing short of spectacular. As Hillary Clinton stated in her address to the Forum, "NGOs are where the action is."

With thousands of NGOs as watchdogs, governments are now held accountable for the pledges made to women and their families throughout the world. Bolstered by NGO advocacy, more girls are in school, more women receive development funds, and more families are intact as direct effects of the conferences; human rights violations of women and girls garner worldwide attention. The gathering of women in all four U.N. conferences attests to the recognition that women's empowerment is beneficial to everyone.

1. What international events might alter the positive directions women's rights took after the Beijing conference?

2. Demonstrate how sociological knowledge of level of power between men and women and between the developed and the developing world can be helpful in predicting the future course of the women's movement.

Sources: Crossette, 1998; Thom, 2000; U.N. Development Program, 2000; Walt, 2000; Walter, 2001.

4. Women grow three-fourths of the world's food but receive less than 10 percent of agricultural assistance. Eighty percent of Africa's food is grown and processed by women.
5. Eighty percent of the world's 50 million uprooted people or "official" refugees are women and children.
6. Ninety percent of all countries have organizations that promote the advancement of women, but women make up about 10 percent of the world's legislative seats.

Overall, the underlying cause of the inequality of women is that their roles are primarily domestic

(mother, wife, homemaker), and although these are vital to the well-being of society, they are undervalued and unpaid (Lindsey, 1997). Other social institutions, especially the economy, reinforce the existing inequality.

Women's Economic Activities

In the developing world, the role and status of women in the process of economic development has emerged as a major issue that now advises many development assistance programs. Beginning with Ester Boserup's (1970) pioneering study on women in development,

Females are less likely than males to attend school in developing societies when they are needed for domestic tasks, such as gathering cow dung patties for fuel in India.

resources available to women. Subsistence farming is vital to the livelihood of a family. But because subsistence agriculture is defined as domestic work and there is no cash exchanged and no surplus for profit in the marketplace, it is not considered "productive" in traditional economic definitions of labor (Waring, 1988; SIGI, 2001). Development programs typically rely on standard international economic definitions, which exclude the majority of work women perform, such as child care, domestic labor, and subsistence farming.

In addition to farming, development policies have also ignored the gender implications of other labor-force activities. At the family level, the "trickle-down model" is supposed to operate. Policies are designed to upgrade the economic standards of families by concentrating on the assumed male head of household, who is the breadwinner, with his dependent wife in the homemaker role. Development programs often assume that by improving employment of men, the whole family will benefit. The problem with this assumption is that it is based on an urban, middle-class model that fails to acknowledge the varied productive roles of women, especially rural women. As a result, women's work remains undercounted, undervalued, and underpaid (Staudt, 1998).

In addition, men often migrate to cities in search of paid work, leaving women with loss of help in

the argument that development has an adverse effect on women has been well documented (Lindsey, 1996b; Kurian, 2000; Rai, 2002). The path leading to negative development outcomes for women is a deceptively simple one. "As development proceeds, women are denied access to productive sources and new technologies," which then "serves to lower their relative, if not absolute, productivity" (Norris, 1992:183). In societies characterized by powerful patriarchal institutions, men and women rarely share equally the limited resources available to families, a situation that deteriorates with development.

The hardest hit are rural women whose nondomestic work consists of subsistence farming. Even though they were not landowners, before cash crop-farming, Latin American and African women for several centuries managed farms and retained control over their produce. Colonialism and subsequent agricultural development projects introduced technology and cash-crop farming, which undermined farming practices and virtually eliminated the traditional economic

Women in the developing world have similar roles worldwide. Among subsistence farmers in Nepal, women are responsible for both agricultural production and household work.

remaining subsistence activities. Paid employment available to rural women usually consists of low-paid domestic work or work on commercial farms. Others are recruited for work in the assembling and light-manufacturing plants that multinational corporations are building on the fringes of urban areas in less-developed countries. Multinational corporations favor young women, most between ages 13 and 25, for their willingness to work for low wages in substandard conditions and their presumed docility that keeps them from challenging the conditions. Others migrate overseas to join the massive ranks of domestic workers employed in the households of the world's wealthy. Overall, development planners have failed to account for the various ways that women and their families are impacted by the global economy and the supposed economic benefits that come with it (Moghadam, 1999; Çağatay, 2001; Chang, 2000).

On the positive side, the correlation between women's impoverishment and development is no longer ignored. Propelled by the international women's movement, strong women-oriented non-governmental organizations (NGOs), and the Platform of Action adopted at the United Nations Conference on Women in Beijing, gender analysis in development planning has moved from the fringes to the center (Staudt, 1998; Institutionalizing Gender Equality, 2000). All development projects funded through the United Nations and World Bank must now do a gender analysis at the planning stages to determine how the project may differentially impact the lives of women and men.

GENDERED SOCIAL INSTITUTIONS

Like all socialization, gender socialization must be transmitted so that people learn what is expected of them. Social institutions are important vehicles for demonstrating gendered social behavior. In Chapters 5 and 6 we learned how primary socialization and social interaction are significantly influenced by gender, especially in language and early sibling and peer relationships. Learned first in the family and then reinforced by other social institutions, gender is fundamental to the shaping of all social life.

Family Life

The infant's first artifacts are clothes and toys. If the sex of a baby is not known in advance, friends and relatives choose gender-neutral gifts to avoid giving clothes or toys suggesting the "wrong" gender. Teddy bears and clothing in colors other than pink and blue are safe bets. But within weeks after the baby's arrival, the infant's room is easily recognizable as belonging to a girl or a boy. Color-coded and gender-typed clothing for infants and children is widespread and taken for granted. If her gender is not readily identifiable by her clothing, an infant girl of 3 months will often have a velcro bow attached to her bald head in case onlookers mistakenly think she is a boy.

Toys for girls encourage domesticity, interpersonal closeness, and a social orientation. Boys receive more categories of toys, their toys are more complex and expensive, and they foster self-reliance and problem solving. Both parents and children express clear preferences for gender-typed toys. These preferences reinforce the persistent gender-related messages that are sent to children through the toys. On your next outing to a toy store, note how shelves are categorized according to gender and how pictures on the boxes suggest how boys and girls should use the toys. Little Jane uses her tea set to give parties for her dolls in her room, while same-age Dick is experimenting with sports or racing trucks outside in the mud. Siblings and peers ensure that the children will play with toys or stage games in gender-specific ways. The gender-related messages, in turn, show up in differences between girls and boys in cognitive and social development in childhood as well as differences in gender roles as adults. And research continues to show that even with massive social change impacting the genders, gender-typed preferences persist and may be growing (Witt, 2000; Lueptow et al, 2001; Serbin et al., 2001).

Dolls for girls, especially Barbies™, and "action figures for boys" (advertisers will never call them dolls) are standard gifts to children from parents. One study reports that virtually every girl in the United States between ages three and ten, from all social classes and races, has at least one Barbie; the average girl has eight (Rogers, 1999). Not only are messages about beauty, clothing, and weight sent to girls via

Owned by Taiwan, managed by Americans, and located in the People's Republic of China, the largest Nike factory in the world employs 70,000 people. The vast majority of these employees are young women in their teens and early twenties, most who are recruited from rural areas in south China.

Barbie, but girls also learn about options in life. A glance at Barbie's shortened resume shows unsteady employment in a variety of fields, indicating her lack of direction and career commitment (Urla & Swedelund, 2000:403–404). She would not do well in jobs requiring analytic skills, since she says math is hard for her.

1959 to present: fashion model
1961–present: ballerina
1965: teacher and fashion editor
1966: stewardess (Pan Am)
1973–75: flight attendant (American Airlines)
1984: aerobics instructor
1985: fashion designer, television news reporter, and corporate executive
1989–present: animal rights volunteer

A generation ago, the male counterpart of Barbie was G.I. Joe™. Although today G.I. Joe is sold mainly to nostalgic adult men, it was the prototype for subsequent action figures. The action figures currently sold to boys have larger body frames and show more muscles than the figures of a generation ago (Klugman,

1999; Powers, 2001). Girls equate beauty with Barbie. Boys equate handsomeness and ruggedness with heroic action figures. Messages about masculinity and femininity ideals are sent to both boys and girls through these toys. Combined with an entertainment-based youth culture, gendered toys are another link to lower self-esteem and the origins of eating disorders in children (Vallone, 1999; Grogan & Richards, 2002; Kenway & Bullen, 2001). The play activities of children also predict the kind of recreational roles they choose later in life (Giuliano et al., 2000). The development of gender-role identity is linked to the child's perception of his or her parents' behavior; the toys, clothes, and other objects given to children serve as important gender reminders.

Parenting practices vary according to not only the gender of the child but also the gender of the parent. Gender is one of the strongest predictors of how parents will behave toward their children. Children of all ages are seen more frequently with mothers than with fathers. Mothers talk to their children more and stay closer to them than do fathers. Both parents are responsive to their infants, but as expected, as children get older, fathers are more involved with their

Children the world over are socialized for future roles according to their gender. This girl from Mali is playing "house" with a baby on her back and her tunic pulled over her breasts like the adult woman.

sons. Mothers show more expressive and emotional support regardless of the child's gender. Household chores are usually divided according to gender, but mothers are more likely than fathers to encourage both their sons and daughters to take on chores that would usually be assigned to the other gender. This pattern of gender intensification increases as children get older (Cunningham, 2001; Turnbull & Carpendale, 2001; Leaper, 2002). Research also suggests that parents' commitment to gender equity varies according to whether they have sons only or daughters only. Parents, especially fathers, have less support for gender equity when they have sons only, but more support when they have daughters only (Warner & Steel, 1999). Thus, patterns of child rearing that are influenced by both gender of parent and gender of child can greatly impact social change in attitudes and behavior regarding gender.

Family life offers children powerful gender-role socialization messages. The gendered socialization messages that children receive in their families are also occurring along with messages related to social class, race, religion, and notions about sexual orientation (Chapter 5). However, research clearly demonstrates that in family life, gender messages dominate and are among the best predictors of a range of later attitudes and behavior (Rosier, 2000; Hill, 2001).

Education

When children enter the classroom, earlier gender-role patterns follow them. Americans wholeheartedly embrace the belief that education is the key to success and the vehicle for social mobility. Gender equality in education is assumed. Yet when the female kindergarten teacher first removes Dick's mittens and helps Jane off with her coat, by virtue of gender alone, their long educational journey will contain essential differences.

KINDERGARTEN In kindergarten Jane gains approval from peers, parents, and teachers for her quiet demeanor and studiousness. Toys in kindergarten are likely to be a familiar extension of those at home. They encourage quiet play, especially the doll corner and minikitchen. Jane can pretend to cook, set the table, and clean with miniature household artifacts constructed for small hands. Girls may envy the boys as they display more power and freedom in their play behavior, but that envy is tempered by the teacher's obvious disapproval of the boys' boisterous classroom behavior. Jane rarely plays with the boys and prefers playing house or jumprope with a few friends. Kindergarten continues a process of self-selected gender segregation that increases during the school years. Gender is a better predictor of choice of playmates

than is race (Haynes, 2001; Hoffman & Powlishta, 2001). Gender-segregated play groups during preschool have powerful socialization outcomes. Children are acquiring distinctive interaction skills that can hamper cross-gender relationships later in life (Wood, 2000).

Meanwhile, Dick enters the classroom more unprepared for the experience than Jane. His higher level of physical activity is incompatible with the sedate nature of school. Dick soon becomes aware that the teacher approves of the quieter children—and the quieter children are usually the girls. But the teacher pays attention to the children who are more disruptive—and the more disruptive children are usually the boys. Dick may believe it is better to be reprimanded than ignored. When boys wander into the doll corner, they use the area for nondomestic games, mainly based on fighting and destruction. They invent "warrior narratives" to structure their play—games involving good and bad, such as pirates and police—and they alter the domestic artifacts to fit their needs (Jordan & Cowan, 1995). Although teachers maintain that they do not treat girls and boys differently, aggressive boys and dependent girls gain teachers' attention. Begun in kindergarten, this pattern continues in elementary school (Sadker & Sadker, 1994; Strauss, 2000).

ELEMENTARY SCHOOL For girls, elementary school is a vehicle for achievement. They receive higher grades than boys, and they exceed boys in most areas of verbal ability, reading, and mathematics. With a premium on being good and being tidy, high achievement coupled with low criticism should be an ideal learning environment. Yet the message that is communicated to girls very early in their education is that they are less important than boys. In curricular materials, for instance, over 30 years of research demonstrates that girls are virtually invisible, or at best, play insignificant roles. Boys do interesting and exciting things; girls do not. Although curricular material is more egalitarian today, stereotyped gender portrayals are prevalent. For example, children's books show girls as brave, but still needing rescue. They show boys babysitting, but unable to express a full range of emotions. Boys see active and resourceful males who build, create, and discover, and who protect and rescue girls. Despite publisher's guidelines and political pressures, textbooks are still highly stereotyped in gender portrayal (Orenstein, 1997; Evans & Davies, 2000; Levstik, 2001).

Teacher behavior reinforces such messages. Girls are called on less frequently than boys; they receive less criticism but also less instruction. When teachers criticize boys for inadequate academic work, they suggest it is because of lack of effort rather than an intellectual flaw, a point girls are less likely to hear. Girls who do poorly in math, for instance, are less likely than boys to believe more effort will produce success (Helwig et al., 2001; Burnett, 2002; Fredricks, 2002). Research demonstrates that elementary school teaches boys that problems are challenges to overcome; it often teaches girls that failure is beyond their control.

HIGH SCHOOL Intellectual achievement and superior grades in elementary school do not predict academic success in high school. As might be expected, girls' standardized test scores decrease, especially in mathematics (Osborne, 2000). Whereas in elementary school girls are confident and assertive, they leave adolescence with a poorer self-image, with the sharpest drop in self-esteem occurring between elementary and middle school (Prettyman, 1998). It is even more pronounced for Latino girls who start out with the highest levels of self-esteem for all races. African American girls retain higher levels of self-esteem compared to white girls, but positive feelings about their teachers and their academic work drop significantly (Daniel, 1999; Guinn & Vincent, 2002; Benjet & Hernandez-Guzman, 2001). On the other hand, boys experience consistent gains in self-confidence and believe they are good at a lot of things. They are able to demonstrate their talents in courses (shop and automobile mechanics) and sports (wrestling and football) specifically designed for them (Eder & Kinney, 1995; Newberger, 1999). By high school, scholastic achievement for girls tends to decline in reading and writing, but especially in mathematics, where boys are beginning to excel.

The finding that girls do not do as well in math as boys has led some to conclude that there are biologically based sex differences in analytic ability. The bi-

ology argument in explaining gender differences in math and science has used everything from chromosomes, hormones, and brain organization, to genetic codes to explain the slight male edge (Halpern, 2000). In terms of spatial ability, no gene has been identified that traces the ability from mother to son, and researchers are skeptical that such a "complex ability as spatial reasoning could possibly rest in a single gene" (McLoughlin, 1988:55). Biology cannot be completely discounted, since mathematics and spatial tests are related, and there are gender differences in rate of development. However, since even the small gender differences in mathematics have been steadily decreasing, researchers lean toward the counterargument that sociocultural factors propel boys but deter girls in mathematics (Orenstein, 2001). When verbal processes are used in math questions, girls outperform boys. When spatial-visual processes are used, boys outperform girls. When the number of math courses taken is controlled for and female teachers and other role models are available for girls, gender differences in math performance are not significant (Henderson, 2001; Quaiser-Pohl & Lehmann, 2002). Any existing male–female difference in math and science is best explained by *gender* factors, due to culture, rather than *sex* factors, due to biology.

HIGHER EDUCATION If high school has done its job well, the best and the brightest students will pursue a college education. Since World War II there has been a steady increase of both men and women attending college. Women are now enrolled in greater numbers than men, in part because of women over age 35 who attend part time (Chapter 16). Ideally, college should be the one educational institution that

When girls take more math and science courses in high school, they are better prepared for entering certain high-paying research, engineering, and medical careers.

evaluates students solely on criteria related to academic achievement and the potential for success. But the gender lessons of elementary school and high school are not easily forgotten.

In college, as in high school, girls' popularity is associated with how popular they are with boys. In tracing the experiences of even high-achieving college women, research suggests it is difficult to resist the "culture of romance" that serves to lower their ambition and academic achievement. Romantic ideals often propel young women into marriage and child-bearing earlier than they intended and changes their career direction, which impacts them throughout their lives (Holland & Eisenhart, 1990; Fishel, 2000). College men are also not immune to gender-role changes regarding love and romance, which put some men in a double bind. Men value intelligence, competence, and originality in their female classmates much more than they did in the past, yet many are unable to relinquish the internalized norm of male superiority. This norm makes it difficult for true egalitarian relationships to be established.

Compared to men, women perceive that the campus climate is a "chillier" one. Over one-third of women report gender discrimination in and outside of the classroom by instructors and classmates. The impact of this perception is greater in the second and third years of college compared to the first year. This chilly climate can negatively affect a woman's personal and intellectual development (Association of American Colleges & Universities, 1999).

College women may find it easier to choose the well-traveled gender road of majoring in the arts and humanities. Almost half of women who enter college with science-related interests switch to other majors. The math-gender link described above comes into play. Insufficient precollege preparation in math and science and lack of peers in the field are key factors in explaining this switch. When girls believe they cannot succeed in math and science, they do not take the courses necessary to prepare them for many high-paying careers such as in engineering and computer science (Correll, 2001). However, they earn slightly more than half of all doctorates in fields other than science and engineering. Gains in professional degrees have been steady; about one-half of law degrees and over forty percent of medical degrees are awarded to women (U.S. Bureau of the Census, 2001:Table No. 289). Considering that opportunities for women to pursue higher education are relatively recent, these numbers are impressive. But compared to women, men are distributed in a wider variety of majors, and these majors lead to jobs in expanding, more lucrative technical fields such as engineering and computer science. Men dominate the most influential fields where graduate work is required and are at the top of the prestige hierarchy within them (Chapter 16). In medicine, men are surgeons and women are pediatricians. Men practice international law and women practice family law. Female nurses are in clinical roles; male nurses are in administrative roles. The culmination of college or graduate school, whether as holder of B.A., M.D., or Ph.D., is also the culmination of a lifetime of attitudes and behaviors regarding gender.

THE LESSONS OF TITLE IX Title IX of the Educational Amendment Act of 1973 addresses many of the educational patterns described here. It prohibits sex (gender) discrimination in schools receiving federal funds. Title IX has helped alter blatant gender discrimination related to areas such as school admissions, financial aid, promotion and tenure of faculty, dress codes, counseling, and housing. Title IX is a major effort in dealing with gender equity in education. Despite political compromises, it has had a large impact on college athletic programs. Instead of equal redistribution of financial resources—which critics argue would hurt "big ticket" men's sports such as football and basketball—Title IX calls for "reasonable opportunities" for financial assistance for each sex in proportion to the numbers participating in intercollegiate sports (Sigelman & Wahlbeck, 1999). Before Title IX, few colleges offered female athletes adequate facilities, and college athletic scholarships for women were virtually nonexistent. Although women still receive only one-fourth of college sports operating budgets, there has been an impressive increase in sports' participation. About half of women students, for example, participate in college sports (Women's Sports Foundation, 2002). Title IX has come under attack by those who say it may help females but at the expense of males (Koszczuk, 1999). Research shows, however, big-ticket sports programs are largely immune when female athletic programs get more of a school's budget. Many of the men's programs ran into deficit spending years *before* Title IX (Rishe, 1999; Title IX at 30). Title IX is unquestionably responsible for the dramatic success of U.S. women in worldwide competitions such as the Olympics and World Cup soccer.

Gender and the Workplace

Throughout history women have made major economic contributions to society, doing unpaid domestic work, producing goods or services at home for sale or exchange (cottage industry), and providing food for their families and villages (subsistence farming) (Christie & Lindsey, 1997). The Industrial Revolution opened up the world of paid work outside the home or farm for both men and women. Globally, the ratio of women to men in paid labor has jumped over 25 percent since

1970. In the United States, 60 percent of all women 16 years of age and over are in the labor force (Table 13.1). The participation rate of married women with very young children has doubled since 1975. This has had profound consequences for all social institutions, especially family and school. Sociologists are interested in examining the type of paid work men and women do and why the work is differentially valued. For this reason, the workplace has become the strategic location for determining advances toward gender equality.

THE WAGE GAP Research consistently shows that even when controlling for education and work experience, and as measured by median annual earnings of full-time employees, women earn less than men, a global pattern that holds across all racial and ethnic groups and throughout occupations. In the developed world, the United States and Canada have the highest wage gap (about 75 percent) and the Scandinavian countries the lowest (between 80 and 90 percent, with Iceland at a remarkable 94 percent) (United Nations Development Program, 2001; U.S. Bureau of the Census, 2001). A sociological perspective on gender roles helps explain why men are paid more.

As expected, the genders are not evenly distributed across occupations (see Table 13.2). When the majority of a particular occupation is made up of one gender, it becomes a normative expectation. This **gender-typing** of the occupation reinforces the segregation of the occupation by gender. If women are the majority of an occupation, the job is associated

with fewer rewards. In the professions, accountants, architects, and engineers are predominantly male; teachers, nurses, and social workers are predominantly female. Males in female-dominated occupations have more advantages than women doing the same jobs. Referred to as the "glass escalator effect," this pattern means men take their gender privileges with them and experience upward mobility as a result (Williams, 1992). Women are clustered in overcrowded, less-prestigious specialties. The result for women: less pay, less prestige, and less authority.

Race and ethnicity add double or triple jeopardy. Occupational distribution of minority women reflects changes in the labor force as well as gender inequality. After World War II, large numbers of African American women moved into government white-collar and clerical jobs and the lowest level private sector jobs, such as data entry or filing clerks (Glenn & Feldberg, 1995). Wage levels of minority women are less than those of men of the same group. African American, Asian American, and white women earn two-thirds to four-fifths of what men earn, with the greatest disparity occurring between white men and women. Rooted in a tradition valuing economic opportunities for women, African American middle-class women moved into the professions earlier than white women. Like white women, they are steered into traditionally female occupations, but they have an added race liability. Concentrated in the public sector, such as teaching and social work, there is less discrimination but also less pay (Higginbotham, 2002). Although

TABLE 13.1

Characteristics of Women in the Labor Force, Selected Years

Status	1970	1975	1980	1985	1990	1995	2000
Total employed women 16+	43.3	46.3	51.5	54.5	57.5	58.9	60.2
Total unemployed women 16+	5.9	9.3	7.4	7.4	6.4	5.6	4.1
Total employed men 16+	79.7	77.9	77.4	76.3	76.1	76.7	74.7
Total unemployed men 16+	4.4	7.9	6.9	7.0	5.6	5.6	3.9
Female employment by age							
16 to 19	44.0	49.1	52.9	52.1	51.8	52.2	51.3
20 to 24	57.5	64.1	68.9	71.8	71.6	70.3	73.3
25 to 34	45.0	54.9	65.5	70.9	73.6	74.9	76.3
35 to 44	51.1	55.8	65.5	71.8	76.5	77.2	77.3
45 to 54	54.4	54.6	59.9	64.4	71.2	74.4	76.8
55 to 64	43.0	40.9	41.3	42.0	45.3	49.2	51.8
65+	9.7	8.2	8.1	7.3	8.7	8.8	9.4
Female employment by marital status							
Single	56.8	59.8	64.4	66.6	66.9	66.7[a]	69.0
Married with spouse	40.5	44.3	49.8	52.8	58.4	60.7[a]	61.3
Other	40.3	40.1	43.6	45.1	47.2	47.5[a]	49.4

[a]1994 data

Source: U.S. Bureau of the Census, *Statistical Abstract of the United States,* 1991, 1995, 1998, *Employment and Earnings,* U.S. Bureau of Labor Statistics, Vol. 43(1), January 1998. U.S.Census Bureau, 2001: Tables 568, 575, 576. U.S.Census Bureau, 2001: Tables 568, 575, 576.

TABLE 13.2

Occupational Distribution of Labor Force by Percent Female in Selected Occupations for 1983, 1997, and 2000

Occupational Category	1983	1997	2000
Executive, administrative, and managerial	32.4	48.9	45.3
Officials and public administrators	38.5	49.5	52.7
Personnel and Labor relations managers	43.9	63.4	61.8
Professional specialty	48.1	53.3	53.9
Engineers	5.8	9.6	9.9
Dentists	6.7	17.3	18.7
Nurses (RNs)	95.8	98.5	92.8
Physicians	15.8	26.2	27.9
University teachers	36.3	45.7	43.7
Elementary school teachers	83.3	83.9	83.3
Secondary school teachers	51.8	58.4	57.9
Clergy	5.6	13.6	13.8
Lawyers	15.3	26.6	29.6
Technicians, sales, and administrative support	64.6	64.1	63.8
Health technicians	84.3	80.2	80.5
Science technicians	29.1	39.5	41.4
Sales occupations	47.5	50.2	49.6
Real estate sales	48.9	50.0	54.3
Cashiers	84.4	78.4	77.5
Administrative support, including clerical	79.9	78.8	79.0
Secretaries	99.0	97.9	98.9
Computer operators	63.7	58.4	48.7
Service occupations	60.1	59.4	60.4
Child-care workers	96.9	96.8	97.5
Cleaners and servants	95.8	94.0	94.8
Police and detectives	9.4	16.4	16.5
Firefighting, fire prevention	1.0	3.4	3.0
Precision production, craft, and repair	8.1	8.9	9.1
Construction trades	1.8	2.4	2.6
Carpenters	1.4	1.6	1.7
Operators, fabricators, and laborers	26.6	24.7	23.6
Textile furnishing machine operators	82.1	72.1	69.2
Truck drivers	3.1	5.7	4.7
Farming, forestry, and fishing	16.0	19.8	20.6
Farm operators and managers	12.1	23.0	25.4
Farm workers	24.8	19.0	18.7

Source: U.S. Bureau of the Census, *Statistical Abstract of the United States,* 1995, 1998, 2001. Adapted from Table No. 649 (1995), No. 672 (1998), and No. 593 (2001).

white women are also segregated in female-dominated professions, they are represented throughout the private sector where pay is higher.

The wage gap is also associated with the *human capital model.* According to this view, the gender gap in wages is due to individual choices in matters of education, family, and occupation. If women choose to interrupt schooling or careers for marriage and family reasons, experience and productivity are compromised and wages are lower (Mennino, 2002; Metz et al., 2001). In addition, the human capital model is consistent with the law of supply and demand. Women can be paid less because they choose occupations and work schedules that make fewer demands on their family responsibilities

(Aronson, 1999; Gutner, 2002). These are the very jobs that have an abundance of workers. The result is lower pay. If there is artificial intervention to make jobs equitable in terms of wages, such as setting quotas for certain jobs for men and women, the law of supply and demand will be compromised. To intervene will do more harm than good (Becker, 1994).

On the other hand, the wage gap can be explained according to the power relationships between men and women. This view of the wage gap suggests that men exercise power in a way that maintains their wage advantage. A good example is a protégé system in which an already powerful member serves as a sponsor for entry and upward movement of a novice. An effective

Although gender segregation dominates the workplace, especially in schools, policies such as Title IX and affirmative action are encouraging more and more people to enter fields that are dominated by the other gender, such as this early childhood education teacher at a school in rural Wyoming.

"old boy system" keeps power in the hands of a few men. This system also operates on norms that support cultural notions of masculinity and femininity that often bar women from meaningful participation in informal work groups. Women will not be accepted if they are "too masculine" but are taken less seriously if they are "too feminine." Mentors and role models are essential for upward corporate mobility (Reeves, 2000; Bannerjee, 2001; Mattis, 2001). Until women's networks include people of high rank, the corporate advancement of women will be stalled.

Regardless of how the wage gap is explained, its persistence is clearly linked to three factors:

1. The work women do, regardless of content, skill, or functional necessity, is less valued overall than the work men do.
2. The higher the number of women in the occupation, the lower the wages; the converse is true for male-dominated occupations. One-third of the wage gap is correlated with gender segregation.
3. Regardless of the law, gender discrimination in the workplace endures.

Overall, research suggests that men are paid more than women for what they do largely because they are men (Burt, 1998; Portes, 1998; Hesse-Biber, 2000). Women's patterns of employment are different from men's, but for equal work there is not equal pay.

Women in Business

There have been steady increases of women into management positions in businesses throughout the United States. However, although women have made strides in middle management, they are deserting the ranks of larger organizations because they continue to be denied access to upper management (Rosener, 1995). The **glass ceiling** is a term that describes women's failure to rise to senior-level positions because of invisible and artificial barriers constructed by male management. Recruits into upper management are imaged, although unintentionally, according to a "white-male model," which excludes all women as well as men of color. Studies conclude that for women at all ranks, but particularly women managers, many barriers to upward mobility exist, including career stagnation, role conflict, isolation, gender stereotypes, and lack of feedback and training. Women continue to report gender discrimination as the most frequent barrier to their advancement, patterns found in the United States, Britain, and Australia (Stewart, 1998; Liff & Ward, 2001; Metz & Tharenou, 2001). In cooperation with private enterprise, the federal government initiated a number of programs to counter the glass ceiling and provide incentives for businesses to be more flexible for women who are juggling career and family responsibilities. These family-friendly policies have also benefited men, who may apply for leave or flexible work schedules on the same basis as women (Kelly, 1999; Mennino & Brayfield, 2002). For women, the government's message is that companies will ultimately lose if they continue to limit the talent and ambition of their female employees. If women leave a company to start their own businesses, or if they jump to another company, former employees will be competitors. As one female executive of a top global-assets management firm suggests to women who feel thwarted in job advancement:

> If you're at a firm that's not interested in creating a culture where you can grow, cut out of

there fast . . . find a place that wants you. (Ligos, 2001)

Since companies are clearly aware of the research confirming that the loss of female talent is bad for business, they are now much more enthusiastic about seeking ways to shatter the glass ceiling (Abelson, 1999; Kelly, 1999; Meyerson & Fletcher, 2000).

GENDERED MANAGEMENT STYLES: THE PARTNERSHIP ALTERNATIVE Despite past barriers to success, some research now suggests that a woman's socialization pattern may offer an advantage to modern corporations. In sharp contrast to the traditional corporate hierarchy, women tend to develop "web-like" leadership structures, relying on skills and attitudes valuable to a workplace in which innovation and creativity are demanded but where an authoritarian chain of command is obsolete (Helgesen, 1990:37). The woman's web extends to roles outside the corporation. Women bring interpersonal skills gained outside the organization back into the organization. They tend to form friendships in their workplace that extend outside the workplace and endure even after leaving a job. In contrast, men give up significant parts of their private lives for corporate success in traditional business hierarchies, a situation detrimental to themselves, their families, and their employers (Gerstel & McGonagle, 1999; Faludi, 2000). For companies more receptive to alternative visions of corporate life, the distinctive management styles of women are encouraged. Women managers tend to adopt styles compatible with overall gender socialization patterns of females, such as encouraging participation, mentoring, sharing power and information, and interacting with all levels of employees.

These are the very patterns that are the hallmark of Japanese Style Management (JSM). JSM encourages a sense of community in the firms in which employees work, an interest in employees' lives outside of the office, consensus building, socioemotional bonding between employees and between management and labor, and a flattened management structure that is more egalitarian than hierarchical (Sasaki, 1990; Miwa, 1996). Principles of JSM are compatible with American gender-role socialization patterns for females (Lindsey, 1992, 1998). JSM also fits with partnership models emerging in innovative corporations that emphasize linking rather than ranking, interactive and participative leadership styles, teamwork, and sharing (Eisler & Loye, 1990). A problem may arise when the "celebration" of the female advantage in the workplace leads to increased stereotyping and a reaffirmation of the differences between women and men. The image of women as nurturers who smooth over problems is as stereotypical as the image of men who create the problems. On the positive side, with workplaces becoming increasingly multicultural, businesses today recognize that difference does not imply better or worse or stronger or weaker.

REDUCING GENDER STRATIFICATION: POLITICS AND THE LAW

In 1776 Abigail Adams wrote the following letter to her husband John who was attending the Second Continental Congress:

> In the new Code of Laws . . . I desire you to remember the ladies and be more generous and favorable to them than your ancestors. . . . That your sex is naturally tyrannical is a truth so thoroughly established as to admit of no dispute . . . so whilst you are proclaiming peace and good will to men, emancipation for all nations, you insist on retaining an absolute power over wives. But you must remember that arbitrary power is like most other things which are hard, very liable to be broken.

John Adams, who became the nation's second president, dismissed these warnings in his reply:

> As to your new Code of Laws, I cannot but laugh. . . . We know better than to repeal our masculine system. (Adapted from Norton & Alexander, 1996)

Unlike John Adams' response to his wife when she asked him to "remember the ladies," the political institution in the United States is firmly committed to policies promoting gender equality. Americans have no desire to eliminate social stratification, but they believe that any inequality that exists should be due to talent, ability, and motivation, and not to ascribed statuses such as gender, race, or ethnicity (Chapters 11 and 12). The principle of gender equality is a strong one in America's legal structure.

Employment

Title VII of the 1964 Civil Rights Act makes it unlawful for an employer to refuse to hire, discharge, or discriminate against a person because of race, color, religion, sex, or national origin. The Equal Employment Opportunity Commission (EEOC) is the federal agency overseeing the enforcement of Title VII. EEOC was created primarily to protect minority men. Through efforts of groups like the National Organization of Women (NOW), EEOC now protects women as well. Besides NOW's strategies, the mushrooming of sexual harassment cases has increased EEOC's responsibility considerably. Beginning with the testimony given by Anita Hill during the hearings for Clarence Thomas's confirmation to the United States Supreme Court and culminating with allegations against President Clinton, the 1990s was the decade in which sexual harassment was defined as a social problem (Chapter 6).

In employment, the only way that Title VII can be legally circumvented is through the *Bonafide Occupational Qualification* (BFOQ), which, for gender, means that one or the other sex is necessary for carrying out a job. A movie role calling for a male actor and a female clothing model are BFOQ examples. The courts have ruled that "customer preference" is not a BFOQ exemption; men cannot be denied jobs as flight attendants, for example. BFOQ is very narrowly interpreted and is seldom used as a defense against charges of sex discrimination in hiring.

The Equal Pay Act (EPA) of 1963 requires that females and males receive the same pay for the same work. Despite the passage of this legislation, the wage gap has only improved slightly in the last four decades. Interpreted through Title VII provisions, **comparable worth** is the idea that male and female jobs should be assessed according to skill level, effort, and responsibility. Equal pay should be given for equal worth. In an early comparable worth suit, a federal court in Washington ruled in 1983 that the state had to raise the wages of 15,500 employees in predominantly female occupations. Two years later a higher court overturned the decision, stating that market forces created the inequity and that the government had no responsibility to correct it. The later decision is based on the presumed gender neutrality of the human capital model; if women get paid less, they either prefer less demanding jobs or are less productive in the jobs they have (Rhoads, 1993). Research in the United States and Canada measuring the impact of gender on jobs refutes the market-driven, human capital model. These studies show that wage discrimination exists because employers use gender to assign people to jobs, a technique limiting a woman's financial and career success (Sorensen, 1994; Ranson & Reeves, 1996). In addition, when jobs are assigned on the basis of gender, occupational gender segregation increases and it is even more difficult to determine comparable worth. Overall, comparable worth has had some positive effects on reducing the gender wage gap but has done little to alter gender segregation in jobs (Wolbrecht, 2000).

Another cornerstone of federal law concerning gender and employment is *affirmative action* (see Chapter 12). With media attention focusing on quotas (not a provision of affirmative action), preferential hiring, and government control of private businesses, the policy has come under attack. People generally support government objectives, but not quotas, to increase employment opportunities for women and minorities

(Stryker, 2001). Nonwhite women and women in management have benefited directly from affirmative action, but all women may benefit indirectly in its call for a fairer distribution of social benefits, a principle that has been constitutionally accepted and applied throughout U.S. history (Bergmann, 2002). The self-esteem of women hired through affirmative action should also be a consideration. There may be psychological pain at being a "twofer," or a token employee on two counts: for example, a woman of color accepted into a male-dominated field. Despite outstanding credentials, her status is still defined by race and gender. Stigma is a double-edged sword: When former Assistant Attorney General Barbara Babcock was asked how she felt about gaining a position because she was a woman, she answered, "It feels better than being denied the position because you're a woman" (Rhode, 1993:263).

Domestic Relations

Domestic law, more than any other area, demonstrates glaring gender inequity. Legal statutes regarding wife–husband roles are based on three general models (Stetson, 1997):

1. Unity: The husband is dominant, and the wife has few rights and responsibilities.
2. Separate but equal: The husband is the breadwinner and the wife is companion and nurturer of children, but they share similar legal rights. This is also referred to as the reciprocity model.
3. Shared partnership: The husband and wife have equal rights and overlapping responsibility.

The third notion (shared partnership) is the most equitable, but contemporary law is a mixture of all three, with separate but equal dominating.

DIVORCE Property division in divorce is a good example. In a *community property* state, all property acquired during the marriage is jointly owned by the spouses. In a divorce, each partner is entitled to half the property. Community property implicitly recognizes the unpaid homemaker role. In a divorce, however, a woman is often forced to sell her share of the home, the only real property she has, while still maintaining responsibility for children. Other states are *common law*, with property belonging to the spouse in whose name it is held. Common law severely penalizes women economically, since men are more likely to have property in their name both before and during a marriage. To remedy the problem, "equitable distribution laws" are required. According to these laws, courts consider other factors, such as length of marriage, contributions of both partners to child care, earning capability, and health. Unpaid homemaking roles are also considered. The problem, nonetheless, is that since the

In uncontested divorces a mother usually gains custody, regardless of whether a child appears to dislike one parent over another.

separate but equal doctrine still underlies much domestic law, the way couples determined how they distributed household assets during the marriage makes a difference in how assets will be divided in a divorce. For example, if the husband is the wage earner, he may give "his" paycheck to his wife for household expenses, or he may give her an allowance for household or personal needs. In most situations, therefore, the result is that women rarely receive half of the assets.

Confusion reigns in divorce law because of legislation that is both punitive and sexually biased. When a divorce involves children, the mother usually gains custody, the preferred pattern for both mothers and fathers. There is immense gender disparity in terms of child custody and support, and the economic consequences of a divorce for a woman and her children are often disastrous. For example, while half of all custodial mothers are awarded child support, half of the mothers usually receive it from nonresidential fathers. When child support enforcement occurs and the court reorders it, only one-fourth of men actually pay. Over 11 million families are owed support, forcing 10 million children into welfare (Turestsky, 1999; Sorenson & Zibman, 2000). Although the courts have been more vigilant in tracking down these nonpaying fathers, welfare reform focuses more on putting women with children into the labor force to get them off welfare.

Considering the reciprocity (separate but equal) model, it is understandable that the courts have also been inconsistent in efforts to prosecute cases of wife abuse. Much of U.S. law is based on English common law and still reflects certain of these patterns. Until the middle of the 19th century, in the United States men had the right to beat their wives. This was a legally sanctioned practice dating back to feudal times under the infamous "rule of thumb" allowing a man to beat his wife as long as the stick was no bigger than his thumb. Today all but a few states have adopted laws that allow a charge of rape to be brought by spouses. The notion of marital rape is so recent because historically sexual intercourse has been viewed as "his right and her duty," again traced to English common law. For other cases of domestic abuse, which may or may not involve rape, judges have been reluctant to temporarily bar a husband from his home because his due process rights may be violated. Judges may accept the stereotype that her behavior was responsible for his abuse (Dalton & Schneider, 2000).

GENDERED MESSAGES IN MEDIA

All institutions socialize people into attitudes and behavior regarding gender. Although families provide the earliest gender messages, the mass media, especially television, quickly follow. Heavy television viewing is strongly associated with traditional and stereotyped gender views, a pattern that is demonstrated for all races and age groups (Chapter 5). Children are especially vulnerable in believing that television images represent truth and reality. Television is supported by magazines, newspapers, books, and music that present the genders in stereotyped ways. For all mass media forms, these stereotypes are reinforced by advertising.

Print Media

Of all types of print media, magazines and newspapers are extremely powerful in presenting views about gender roles. Gender stereotypes persist and thrive in print media across the globe, even when media

SOCIOLOGY OF EVERYDAY LIFE

Men's Images in the Media

Compared to men, women have not fared well in the media. Men star in more television series, sell more records, make more movies, and are paid more than female media counterparts. But men, too, must pay a price for that popularity. From the media's standpoint, a man is a breadwinner who cheats on his wife, is manipulated by his children, has no idea how to use a washing machine or vacuum cleaner, and uses violence and force to solve his problems and demonstrate his masculinity. On the other hand, a man is the voice of authority to be admired and respected. How do the various media contribute to these images?

Advertising

Advertisers classify products as masculine or feminine. Cars, life insurance, and beer are masculine, so men do the selling to other men. Men do most of the selling on television, as evidenced by voiceovers. More than all other types of advertising, beer commercials portray men as "good old boys" who are adventurous, play hard at sports, and have a country spirit. Men are portrayed as mature, successful, and strong. Advertisers do not often show men in family roles and prefer instead to associate them with entertainment and sports. One result is that portrayals of men as sex objects are increasing.

Movies

Films routinely portray men in two thematic ways. The first is the hero theme. They are hard-living and adventurous tough guys who quickly move in and out of relationships with women—but all the time righting wrongs and saving the day. John Wayne and Gary Cooper of the past have been replaced by Mel Gibson, Tom Cruise, Will Clark, and Jean-Claude Van Damme. Often, men are linked in "buddy" movies. The plot calls for them to be competitive on the surface and then gradually move toward genuine—if begrudging—respect and camaraderie. They learn to admire one another for traits they see lacking in their own personalities. *Blues Brothers, Batman and Robin,* and *Men in Black* suggest this theme.

Second is the violence theme. Both heroes and villains are violent, and violence is needed to end violence as in *Star Wars* and the Jackie Chan movies. The kill-and-maim plots of films like *I Know What You Did Last Summer, Halloween,* and *Friday the Thirteenth* show that revenge and violence in the name of a "good" cause are acceptable to men.

Television

Men on prime-time dramas are portrayed as in control of most situations. These men recognize that power may bring adversity, but they are willing to accept the consequences. Television men are active, independent, and can solve their own problems. The major exception to this image is the situation comedy where men may take on a childlike dependence on their wives in household functioning, as in *Everybody Loves Raymond.* Some shows are now depicting men in loving and nurturing relationships with their children, but historically men are rarely shown as competent dads who can raise children without the help of women. Even single dad Andy Griffith had Aunt Bea.

Growing support for nontraditional media images of masculinity is evidenced by the popularity of films such as *A Beautiful Mind* and *Shine* and TV shows exploring the many sides of fatherhood such as *Malcolm in the Middle.* However, stereotypes still account for the vast majority of male images. "Bad dads" (Homer Simpson, Jack Gallo, *Just Shoot Me,* the dads in *King of the Hill,* and *Titus*) overwhelmingly outnumber "good dads" (*Seventh Heaven*). Evidence suggests that men want to be portrayed differently and are angered when seen as both success objects and sex objects. These hopes, however, are apparently not in the intent of the media. The sensitive man image popularized a decade ago is retreating fast, and as one researcher notes, "Cradling a newborn is out, and guy stuff is back." Until men are portrayed as loving fathers, compassionate husbands, and household experts, stereotypes about masculinity will resist change.

1. How do these themes about male roles appear in the television and movies you watch? What messages do these themes provide for men and women about masculinity and femininity?

2. How would a symbolic interactionist respond to television and music producers who say that they are only giving the public what the public wants?

Sources: Kanne, 1995; Eschholz & Bufkin, 2001; Mathewson, 2001; Williams, 2001.

---

content is adapted to a culture's values and norms (Walker, 1998; Al-Olayan & Karande, 2000; Munshi, 2001). For example, compared to male politicians, female politicians in the United States and Europe are much more often represented in newspapers according to characteristics associated with their gender. Women are discussed according to their hairstyles, clothing, how they juggle motherhood and politics, and their overall femininity. In many media accounts, women are not treated as "persons" in politics but as part of the larger category of "women" (Fabjancic, 1999; Sreberny & van Zoonen, 2000). This lack of personhood also shows up in print media related to sports. Coverage of female athletes often focus on their attractiveness to the exclusion of their athleticism (Knight & Giuliana, 2001).

ADVERTISING Advertisers exert much control over article content in magazines (Steinem, 1995). In women's magazines, an article about beauty will appear next to an ad selling makeup, and it is highly unlikely that any psychological or medical downside to makeup would appear anywhere in the magazine. Consistent with symbolic interactionism's view of the self-fulfilling prophecy, the advertising–article connection promotes almost narcissistic self-absorption, particularly in teenage girls who read magazines such as *Seventeen, Elle, Sassy,* and *Vogue.* Print ads emphasize women as sex objects. Females represent "body-isms" or "partialisms," in that parts of their body are shown, often without a face. These "partialisms" are in contrast to "face-isms." When males are shown in ads, they are much more likely to reflect "face-isms," in that their faces are photographed more than their bodies are. A body part without a face is the classic example of a sex object. A face identifies a person as a subject, a real person (Hall & Crum, 1994; Andersen, 2002).

Print ads tell girls and women how to become more beautiful so that they can attract and keep a man (Wolf, 1991; Saltzberg & Chrisler, 1995; Kang, 1997). Women of color must also deal with stereotypes that link race, ethnicity, and gender in how a product is suggested to them, even in race affirmative magazines such as *Ebony* and *Essence* for African American women and in *Moderna* and *Estylo* for Latino women. Of all racial and ethnic groups, Latinas are the most sexualized in the print media (Bettivia, 2000; Valdivia, 2000; Thomas & Treiber, 2000; Beer, 2002). But for all females, the message is that money, men, romance, and success come with beauty.

NEW DIRECTIONS Some changes are on the horizon related to these stereotyped portrayals. For example, to encourage women to buy athletic wear, advertisers have discovered that they need to feature strong women in the center of meaningful activities (Cunnen & Claussen, 1999). Type of magazine also makes a difference in how products are sold. Magazines such as *Working Women* offer advertising images of women in both workplace and home that contrast sharply the demeaning ads found in fashion and beauty magazines. Other independent magazines with a feminist claim directed to women in their 20s and 30s have sprung up with titles like *Bust* ("For Women with Something to Get Off their Chests"), *Bitch* ("Feminist Response to Popular Culture"), and *Moxie* ("For the Woman Who Dares"). These magazines are viewed as a backlash against magazines like *Cosmopolitan* and *Glamour,* although, like them, they sell mascara and sexuality. At the same time, they send feminist messages about the downside to these very items and also discuss issues related to pay equity, sexual harassment, victimization, and all levels of health—sexual, physical, and emo-

tional. Whether these magazines can attract a mainstream audience and more advertisers remains to be seen. Once they get too big, they may become indebted to advertisers and will be unable to write about what they want. As author Erica Jong points out, "Women's magazines tend to be indebted to the corporations that advertise in them" (Kuczynski, 2001:8).

Television

As discussed in Chapter 5, in most American homes the television is turned on an average of 7 hours a day, and preschoolers and young children may spend one-third of their day in front of television. Viewers of all ages find some characters personally meaningful. Women are more likely to identify with less-than-perfect rather than glamorous characters; the women of *Friends* are less likely to be role models than the women of *The Practice.* While some television shows, such as *Oprah Winfrey,* are recognized for confronting gender-related issues openly, television overall influences *misogyny,* defined as the dislike, disdain, or at the extreme, the hatred of women.

PRIME TIME AND SOAPS Television prime time revolves around men, with male characters outnumbering female over two to one. Males dominate dramatic shows, often playing tough and emotionally reserved characters who remain unmarried but have beautiful female companions. In crime shows women are usually the victims (Clory, 2001).

In many shows, female characters are simply bystanders who add sex appeal. When race is added as a variable, some research suggests that African American women are shown more favorably but in less varied roles than their white counterparts (Goodwin, 1996). In soap operas women appear slightly more frequently than men. Soap opera women are likely to be portrayed as schemers, victims, bedhoppers, and starry-eyed romantics. But they are also shown as intelligent, self-reliant, and articulate. Soaps appear to both engage and distance their primarily female viewers while keeping them entertained. The strong soap opera women who question the gender status quo and challenge patriarchy show some progressive change regarding gender roles on television. However, with new television niches geared to women who work outside the home, the traditional daytime soap opera may be on the verge of extinction.

CHILDREN'S TELEVISION Young children are entranced by *Barney* and *Sesame Street.* Both these shows have earned high marks for their prosocial and educational messages as well as for portraying inclusiveness in terms of race, ethnicity, and disability. However, both shows still provide gender stereotypical images.

The make-believe characters are more likely to be male and to have girls in helping roles and boys in leadership roles. *Sesame Street* has been criticized because even today there are few female muppets. Cartoon shows for children have male characters significantly outnumbering female characters. In some cartoons for young adolescents, males outnumber females 10 to 1. Females are portrayed more in family roles and are more physically attractive than male characters (Klein et al., 2000).

ADVERTISING Like in the print media, gender stereotypes dominate television advertising. Beauty and anti-aging products dominate the commercials targeted to young girls and women (Clory, 2001). Male voiceovers have decreased in the last decade from 90 percent to 70 percent, but they still have an overwhelming presence on television, even when the central figure is a woman. In commercials, males are underrepresented for domestic products (toilet tissue and detergent) and females underrepresented for nondomestic products (automobiles and computers) (Artz et al., 1999; Bartsch et al., 2000). Men are rarely shown taking care of children, and it is even rarer to see them taking care of girls. Men are shown in family life commercials teaching, reading, and talking and playing with children. However, they still are portrayed in activities that are stereotypically male (Kaufman, 1999). In television commercials for children, research concludes that boys are depicted as more knowledgeable, active, and instrumental than girls. Dominance and control are associated with boys, and dependence and passivity are associated with girls (Browne, 1998).

When race is factored in, television commercials tend to depict powerful white men, aggressive African American men, white women as sex objects, and African American women as inconsequential. These commercials perpetuate not only gender stereotypes but also race stereotypes, since cultural differences are exaggerated and positive emotions are denied for people of color (Coltrane & Messineo, 2000).

MOVIES White men are overrepresented in movies. With white men in control of most movie studios as both directors and producers, movie images of the genders reflect their images of society in general and gender roles in particular. Although over two-thirds of the public in the United States believe that many movies are demeaning to women, gender stereotypes are a staple of American cinema (O'Toole, 2001; Riordan, 2002).

Mainstream films are often more violent than pornographic films. "Slasher" movies, which appeal to adolescent males, regularly send the message that sexual violence is normal and acceptable. Well-known movies routinely portray scenes of graphic violence against passive female victims (Mediascope, 2000). Movie plots often revolve around a hero who links up with a beautiful woman to support him in his exploits (see *Sociology in Everyday Life* box on page 356). Perhaps more than television, movies provide strong gender-role images to both males and females about unattainable ideals of attractiveness, especially in terms of body size (Hall, 1999; Spitzer et al., 1999). Movie heroism is associated with a lean, muscular body image for a male at least 6 feet tall and a thin female with a larger-than-average breast size who is at least 5 feet 7 inches tall. Propelled by movies and gender-stereotyped mass media, eating disorders are increasing among boys and show no signs of slowing down among girls. A new term to describe these disorders is "media-induced body image disturbance" (Harrison, 2001; Posavac et al., 2001).

Music

Overall, popular music is the most stereotyped of all media in its gender portrayals. In the last half century, popular music of all types and targeted toward all age categories has played to the sex appeal of women who use it to control men or who are victimized by men. Strong women prevailing in the face of adversity or those who "stand by their men" regardless of how they are used by the men are country music traditions. Such music portrayals influence the way people view acceptable roles of men and women in the United States (Andsager & Roe, 1999).

Rock music has emerged as music's major artistic force and has promoted the restructuring of all types of music (Regev, 1995). Since the 1950s, views of women in rock music have become increasingly associated with sexuality and sexual violence. The misogyny in many lyrics is unconcealed. Music videos provide a visual extension and support a gender ideology of male power and dominance, reinforcing misogyny. Videos routinely depict women as emotional, illogical, deceitful, fearful, dependent, and passive, and men as adventuresome, domineering, aggressive, and violent. Although over half show no women or place women only in background shots, those videos that do show women usually combine sexual images with acts of violence (Alexander, 1999; Kalof, 1999). Heavy metal and rap display the most violent lyrics and images; women are routinely depicted as sex objects on whom violence is perpetrated, with increasing numbers of rape scenes being enacted (McLeod et al., 1997; McLeod et al., 2001). The song title "Stripped, Raped and Strangled" by Cannibal Corpse and "Smack My Bitch Up" by Prodigy, and the following lyrics from "I Want Action" by Poison, are typical of the rape themes of best-selling albums (Mediascope, 2000): "I want action tonight, If I can't have her, I'll take her and make her."

Research shows that men and women receive these messages differently. Women read the female images in music videos as powerful and suggestive of control or as vulnerable and weak. Men read the same images as teasing and hard-to-get or as submissive and indecisive (Milburn et al., 2000). There are no significant gender differences in interpretations of male images (Kalof, 1993). Consistent with symbolic interactionism, this research suggests that gender is a social construction shaped by social myths articulated in popular culture (Denzin, 1992). The gender role effects are negative for both men and women.

A number of bands either led by women or with female and male lead singers and musicians have emerged. Madonna, Tori Amos, Alanis Morrissette, Paula Abdul, k.d. lang, and Britney Spears are recognizable as leading women of popular music. However, many of their songs still portray women in stereotyped ways. They too sing of love and pain, and about vulnerable women being abandoned by men. Until recently, women artists have had little power in altering the sexist material of their bands and still being commercially successful. With the rise of female superstars, this situation is changing. Women artists are creating new identities that challenge male domination in mainstream rock culture and are gaining control over their own images (Katovich & Makowski, 1999; Schippers, 2002; Grajeda, 2002). A major result of attaining economic independence is that they are seriously challenging rock's misogyny.

LIFE CONNECTIONS

The Men's Movement in the United States

The first men's movement began on college campuses in the 1970s as men began to come together in response to the feminist movement. These men reacted to feminism in a positive way by forming "anti-sexist" men's groups and supporting their female friends and partners in feminist efforts. Support for feminist causes encouraged their reflection on how ideals about masculinity influenced their own self-image and their behavior toward other men. They were aware, for example, that men who reject sexual bravado and oppressive behavior toward women are targets for ridicule and exclusion by other men and that definitions of masculinity that deny men expressions of vulnerability, nurturing, and caring serve to undermine psychological and physical well-being (Chapters 7 and 19). These men formed the National Organization of Changing Men and have organized yearly conferences on themes related to parenting, sexism, violence against women, sexuality, sexual orientation, and friendship. Although profeminist and gay affirmative in stance, these conferences focus more on personal or social rather than political change. This branch of the men's movement works on male liberation by consciousness-raising related to the negative effects of striving for power and the disabling effects of rigid masculinity. In 1990 they changed their name to the National Organization of Men Against Sexism (see NOMAS) and remain a viable presence on college campuses throughout the United States. Overall, only a minority of men have been attracted to the goals of NOMAS.

The lack of public awareness of the first men's movement is revealed in how the media have publicized later men's "movements." In 1990 media attention focused on poet Robert Bly's (1990) belief that men are caught in a toxic masculinity that demands efficiency, competition, and an emotional distance that separates them from one another. In Bly's view, rooted in a competitive work environment that keeps fathers absent from their families, boys turn to women to meet emotional needs. Using myths, art, and poetry as vehicles to access inner emotions, men must unearth and celebrate their lost natural birthright of righteous anger and primordial masculinity, which can be regained only in communion with men (Barton, 2000). Communication between men is encouraged, but the "soft male" who is out of touch with his masculinity and turns to women as authority figures as substitutes for their absent or distant fathers is denounced. Through rituals of wounding and healing at weekend retreats, men become aware of their animal instincts and come to embrace their full masculinity (Wilson & Mankowski, 2000). Today it is referred to as the *mythopoetic* branch of the men's movement, and its healing techniques have been embraced by some psychotherapists who believe that many men can be helped when they rediscover and repair the damage

INTERNET CONNECTIONS

The life connections section of the text discusses the men's movement in American society. To find out more about the men's movement go to:

http://www.vix.com/men/index.html

Browse the links and articles and then write a short report on issues related to men in society. Are the issues presented on the site related to the interest of men and women? Why or why not?

caused by father deprivation. Unlike the first movement, which is profeminist and argues against men's privilege, the mythopoetic movement is promasculinist and seeks to heal men's pain by distancing them from women. The men attracted to the mythopoetic ranks tend to be powerful, straight, middle-class, and white (Morton, 2000). Working-class men and men of color are virtually nonexistent in this movement.

Another branch of the men's movement focuses on the African American male experience. Research shows that African American males tend to construct definitions of masculinity in direct opposition to Euro-American male models (Franklin, 1994; Harris et al., 1994). Feeling blocked in achieving masculine goals offered by mainstream society, these men may initially adopt views of masculinity similar to Euro-American males. Their values change, however, as they get older (Hunter & Davis, 1994; Roberts, 1994). The 1997 "Million Man March" in Washington, D.C., organized by controversial Black Muslim leader Louis Farakhan, was an effort to bring together African American men in support of one another and to offer role models to young people and their communities. The effort was largely successful (Gabbidon, 2001). However, the luster was tarnished by its antiwoman thrust. While all the national and international women's conferences welcomed men, the Million Man March did not invite women to join. And Farakhan later applauded Iran for setting a shining example to the world on behalf of democratic principles. Iran's unquestionably brutal record regarding both women and democracy intensified any existing schism between men and women.

The newest branch, the Promise Keepers (PK), is by far the largest, drawing over 2 million men to large stadium events and small group meetings in the 1990s. Founded by Bill McCartney, former head football coach of the University of Colorado, Promise Keepers is an evangelical Christian organization dedicated to reestablishing male responsibility in the family and overcoming racial divisions (Claussen, 1999). Media coverage of PK has been so positive that some research suggests it is less like news and more like advertising (Claussen, 2000). Similar to both the mythopoetic and African American branches, PK sees the fatherless home as the source of America's problems. It is different, however, in that its foundation appears to resonate with many more men. To become Promise Keepers, men must pledge their commitment to seven "promises," including honoring Jesus Christ, practicing spiritual and sexual purity, and building strong marriages and families. PK is also founded on the goal to reconnect men to their families and to take back family leadership that "sissified men" abdicated, leaving women to fill the vacuum of leadership. As one PK leader suggests, men should

not *ask* for their role back but are urged to *take* it back (Healey, 2000:221, orig. ital.). Although PK has carefully avoided political affiliation or involvement, and its members are not completely in agreement with its gender ideology, its goals for asserting Christianity into home and society strongly parallel the agenda of the political right (Quicke & Robinson, 2000). This political avoidance has allowed many middle- and upper-class Protestant men who would not have likely joined to become involved with the movement (Bartkowski, 2000; Lockhart, 2000; Lundskow, 2002).

All branches of the men's movement believe women will be the ultimate beneficiaries of their agendas. All the branches except NOMAS share a promasculinist stance that supports traditional and non-overlapping gender roles and largely excludes women from their ranks except as volunteers. In general, the media have given a high approval rating to PK but have tended to dismiss criticisms that the ultimate effect will be to subjugate women. Promise Keepers leaders say that women need not be threatened, because in the kingdom "there is no male or female." Feminists point out, however, that patriarchy and not partnership is the logical outcome. PK would agree.

Feminism is supportive of the idea of men coming together in exclusive male groups for healing and sharing, but the promasculinist themes in all but NOMAS suggest that women are responsible for the problems of men. Blaming serves to undermine dialogue, reinforce sexism, and distance men and women from one another.

Do these gatherings of men suggest that a mass-based men's movement, whether profeminist or promasculinist, has occurred? Three decades of evidence suggest that it has not. Although these are referred to as "branches" of a larger movement, there is virtually no overlap in membership, ideology, or goals. The first three do share prosmaculinist ideology but not in a way that would unite them under a common banner. Because of the small groups that come together outside of the large stadium events, PK is probably the most viable of the organizations. However, it is difficult to predict its long-term success, since members and finances have fallen considerably since its 1996 peak, and unity is being eroded by differing beliefs about masculinity, evangelism, and religious inclusiveness (ecumenism) (Cole, 2000; Reynolds & Reynolds, 2000; Lundskow, 2002). Its goal of racial unification is suffering, since it has failed to attract a significant number of men of color to its ranks (Hawkins, 2000).

NOMAS has not received the publicity or attracted the numbers of the other three groups, but after 30 years it is still convening conferences and drawing together men who are supportive of partnering roles with women. On college campuses across the country, young men are dialoging with one another and with men about issues related to sexual violence, sowing the seeds for a new generation of potential supporters. Latino men are gathering in small groups and discussing how the concept of "machismo" has harmed them and relationships with the women in their lives (Mena, 2000; Stasio, 2001). It remains to be seen if the other three groups will be as successful over the long run. The women's movement has touched the lives of millions of women; the same cannot be said for the men's movement.

SOCIETY CONNECTIONS

The Gender Politics of Biology and Religion

A newspaper columnist advocating the belief that women should not be in the military supported her claim with the statement, "Men are physically stronger than women, and if women object to that reality, their complaint is with God" (Charon, 1997). God and biology are consistently used to support sexism, just as they were used to support racism in the past. The biology–God link is a recurrent theme used in political agendas. The controversy surrounding reproductive rights clearly demonstrates this link.

Until the 19th century a woman's right to an abortion in the United States was legal as long as the procedure was prior to "quickening" of the fetus, when the mother felt the first movements. By 1900 abortion was banned in every state, except to save the mother's life. This changed on January 22, 1973, with two landmark Supreme Court decisions. In *Roe v. Wade* and *Doe v. Bolton*, a seven-to-two vote supported a woman's right to privacy, which allowed for a (now) legal abortion. Women did not have the absolute constitutional right to abortion on demand, but a broadening of the legal right to abortion was established. This right has been challenged ever since.

Bolstered by the reaffirmation of divinely ordained sex and gender differences, the New Christian Right, headed by conservative political leaders and aligned with fundamentalist churches, has been effective in challenging abortion rights. The association of their moral stance with religion is clear by the term "pro-life," adopted as a label for their group. Stronger religiosity for the pro-life group is a key element separating these people from the general public. In the United States, Canada, and Europe, a higher degree of religious fundamentalism is clearly associated with lower support for reproductive rights (Marshall, 2000; Wolbrecht, 2000; Kuttner, 2001).

With religion as the factor that distinguishes pro-life activists from others, it is understandable that their antiabortion work is viewed as "God's work." As

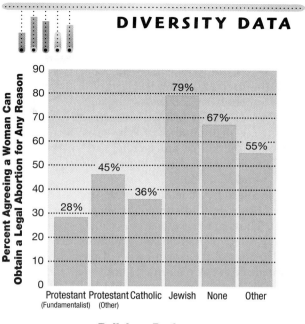

DIVERSITY DATA

FIGURE 13.2   Percent Agreeing That a Woman Should be Able to Obtain a Legal Abortion if She Wants It for Any Reason, by Religion. About half of people believe that a woman should be able to get a legal abortion for any reason. However, Catholics and Fundamentalist Protestants have the lowest approval rates for abortion for any reason and Jewish people and those with no religious preference have the highest approval. Other Protestants fall in between. What accounts for both the similarity between Catholics and Fundamentalist Protestants and the differences between them and other religious groups on this issue?

one pro-life activist said after her arrest for illegally blocking entrance to a clinic that performed abortions, "I know murder is against God's commandments. . . . These children we 'rescue' are the children of God. It's God's will" (cited in Ruth, 1998: 253). Pro-life activists have succeeded in lobbying for legislation restricting government-funded abortion services to poor women. However, they were less successful in the 1992 Supreme Court decision of *Planned Parenthood v. Casey*, which said that a state cannot place substantial obstacles in the path of a woman's right to choose an abortion prior to fetal viability—the ability of the fetus to survive outside the womb. However, states can still restrict pre-viability abortions as long as the health of the mother and fetus are promoted (Thomson, 1998).

Antiabortion activists lobby tirelessly against funding for any national or international agencies offering abortion counseling, even if such counseling is only a small part of a broader program of family planning. Tactics to limit or eliminate abortion rights have ranged from gruesome antiabortion films and television commercials and the boycotting of facilities where abortions are performed, to death threats and bombing of abortion clinics (Press & Cole, 1999). After the murder of physicians in Florida and New York, antiabortion activists were quick to point out that these tactics are neither advocated nor supported, although a small number of extremists in their ranks condoned the killing and publicly stated that it was justifiable homicide (Russo & Horn, 1995; Poppema, 1999; Samuels, 1999).

On the other side, and just as tireless, are "pro-choice" activists who cite public support for abortion rights. Those in this camp argue that abortion rights is actually a referendum on how much women have the right to control their own bodies (Luker, 1978, 1984; Cannold, 2000). A majority of both men and women voters believe that abortion should be legal and safe, but the percentage for men is higher. Adolescent males have the highest percentage of pro-choice supporters of all age groups of males. Yet such numbers mask the complexity of the issue. For example, whites are more supportive of abortion rights than are African Americans, but there are no significant differences between the races for females of childbearing age. For all races, three-fourths approve of abortion when the mother's life is endangered or when pregnancy resulted from rape. Severe fetal deformity is also a major reason for women to elect abortion. A significant minority of Catholics also take a pro-choice stance (Welch et al., 1995; Dombrowski & Deltete, 2000; Greenberg, 2001; Roberts et al., 2002). It is clear that Americans are deeply ambivalent about abortion. A majority believe that some restrictions should be placed on abortion, but few want it outlawed.

Although the abortion issue has been presented to the public as representing two intractable sides, there is agreement that preventing unwanted pregnancy is a desirable option to abortion. People on both sides of the issue are beginning to discuss positive alternatives to abortion, such as sex education, easier access to birth control, and better financial support for parents. Theological debates are also starting to yield common ground (Kelly, 1999; Cannold, 2000; Chesler, 2001). There is indication that the so-called "abortion pill"—RU-486—that can terminate a pregnancy within a week of unprotected intercourse is gaining acceptance (Talbot, 1999; Mann, 2000).

But how these goals are to be achieved again relates to the intersection of gender, religion, and politics. Since antiabortion activists argue that life begins at conception, they promote abstinence for the unmarried and only certain types of contraception for the married. The feminist view is that sex education and availability of contraception should be expanded for young people, married or not. However, at least by beginning with the idea that abortion is not in anyone's best interests, there is a glimmer of hope for consensus.

SUMMARY

1. Sex is a biological category. Gender is a social and cultural category that is learned, varies between cultures, and changes over time as cultural definitions change. Gender roles are expected attitudes and behaviors associated with each sex.

2. According to functionalism, gender roles developed as a practical way of dividing labor in preindustrial societies. Conflict theorists assert that in capitalist societies, gender inequality is largely explained by women's unpaid work in the home and men's economic advantage both inside and outside the home. Symbolic interactionists view gender roles as social constructions based on agreed upon definitions of masculinity and femininity.

3. The new feminist theoretical perspective accounts for the links between race, class, and gender and how women are both alike and different. The branches of feminism—liberal, socialist, radical, and multicultural/global—demonstrate these similarities and differences.

4. Women in the developing world have been adversely affected by development strategies that were supposed to help them, but nongovernmental organizations (NGO's) are helping women and families worldwide.

5. The family is an early and powerful source of gender socialization. Children as young as 2 years display gender roles learned through differences in ways parents interact with boys and girls, and in toy and clothing selection.

6. Gender stereotypes are reinforced at all educational levels, through interaction with teachers, curricular material, and choice of majors. Title IX has helped reduce gender discrimination in education, especially in sports.

7. Men earn significantly more than women; this inequity persists despite women's education and work experience. Gender-typing of occupations, the lower value placed on women's occupations, and gender discrimination help explain the gap.

8. Gender inequality has been addressed with a number of laws and programs, including the Equal Employment Opportunity Commission, the Equal Pay Act, and affirmative action.

9. Domestic law is based on three models: the dominant husband, reciprocal rights for spouses, and a shared partnership between spouses. Divorce law especially is punitive and sexually biased.

10. Mass media, from magazines to television to popular music, send gendered messages that suggest women are defined mainly by their appearance and that violence toward women by men is pervasive. Rock music is the most gender-stereotyped of the mass media. Many women rock artists are emerging but to date have not been able to challenge gender stereotypes.

11. The first men's movement in the United States was accepting of feminism and worked for male liberation against rigid masculinity. Later and much larger men's movements organized around Robert Bly, the Million Man March, and Promise Keepers tend to exclude women or blame women for men's problems.

12. The abortion rights debate involves two major groups—pro-life, supported by fundamentalist religious groups that advocate traditional gender roles, and pro-choice, supported by feminists and those who want to keep the right to abortion legal. There is some agreement between both sides that preventing unwanted pregnancy is a desirable option to abortion.

KEY TERMS

androcentrism 336
comparable worth 352
feminism 338

gender roles 336
gender-typing 348
glass ceiling 350

patriarchal (patriarchy) 336
sexism 336

CRITICAL THINKING QUESTIONS

1. Demonstrate how the development process has an adverse affect on women. What suggestions would you offer to make this process beneficial rather than detrimental to women, but at the same time not make it detrimental to men?

2. How do functionalism, symbolic interactionism, and conflict theory explain the persistence of the wage gap in light of laws that require equal pay for equal work? Compare these explanations with the feminist theoretical perspective.

3. Of the various social institutions discussed in this chapter, which one institution do you believe has the most impact on gender-role socialization? Which one institution do you believe is the most amenable to change for gender equity?

4. Describe how the law is gender biased and how this gender bias is disadvantageous to both men and women.

INVESTIGATE WITH CONTENT SELECT

Journal Research Collections from ContentSelect Begin your research using Content-Select for this chapter by following the directions found on page 27 of this text to visit Prentice Hall's Research Navigator Website. Enter these search terms into the search field:

Patriarchy
Glass Ceiling
Title IX

14
THE AGED AND SOCIETY

Live Long and Prosper?

Leah is a 71-year-old widow living with her two dogs in a large trailer home in Florida. She moved to Florida when arthritis forced her to quit her job as a dietician. Her disability benefits ended when she turned 65 and became eligible for Social Security. She supplements her $440 Social Security check with her job as a hostess at Burger King. She needs knee and hip replacement surgery but fears she cannot pay the medical bills and will lose her job if she takes time off for surgery.

Also living in Florida, in a pleasant condominium community, are Nate and Selma Fiske. They spend summers in their hometown of Springfield, Massachusetts. The Fiskes live comfortably on two pensions, investment income, and Social Security. They play golf and bridge with their many friends and enjoy visits from their children and grandchildren. (Adapted from Quadagno, 1999:62–63)

Aging in Native America

"People come to him and ask him things—how to do things in the old way."

Among two rural, nonreservation Oklahoma Indian tribes, the Oto-Missouri and Ioway, attitudes toward elders reflect respect, power, and prestige. These tribes define being old by roles and functions, not by chronological age. Knowledge about tribal ways and customs, the role of grandparent, or the head of a family line bring honor and prestige. The elderly are the religious and ritual specialists of their culture. They preserve a vital oral history, passing down songs and legends to the younger generation. As one grandmother said, "Old people are useful in many ways. Grandparents . . . patch clothes, sew on buttons, [and] look after the children when the

mother and father have to go somewhere." To be seen as old means you cannot take care of yourself, whether you are 40 or 85. The elderly accept dependence on family members if necessary, but even then, they retain the right to make their own decisions. (Adapted from Schweitzer, 1983)

The Fear of Growing Old: The !Kung of South Central Africa

"I have gone far and killed lots of meat. My bones are hurting me and I am almost old."

"Now I am too old. Who will give me food to eat?"

The middle-aged !Kung men quoted above are already worried about old age. In their culture physical strength is essential for survival. The !Kung live in small, kin-based villages, subsisting on the food and using the tools they produce themselves. In the struggle for survival, they continually face obstacles having to do with physical strength. They have nothing good to say about old age. The !Kung value independence and see children and old people as not fully "whole" persons because they must rely on others. As one older woman says, "Life is with me. I can get up and do the things I need to do. I can take care of myself. I can cook and sew and still have strength." She is still a "whole" person.

Although the !Kung fear old age, they do not resent helping elderly kin. The old should benefit from the work of those who are younger. Your hard work is returned at old age. As expressed by a !Kung man, "If they have a mother, they love her. They love to be with and take care of relatives." Older people live with their kin and participate fully in village activities. !Kung fear the loss of physical independence, but do not see reliance on others as a problem. (Adapted from Keith et al., 1994)

here are many faces to the aged and the aging process. In Oklahoma Native America, the aged are valued. Among the !Kung of Botswana, aging itself is feared. Leah and the Fiskes represent the potential for either the liability or the leisure that are associated with being old in the United States. Although aging is neither uniformly positive nor uniformly negative, there are patterns to the process of aging that sociological research has uncovered and sociological theories can explain. In describing these patterns, this chapter focuses on the key factors of family, money, and health that help explain why there are so many faces to aging and the aged worldwide. As discussed in the first chapter, sociology is a "debunking" science. Our analysis of the aged and society also debunks the widely held stereotype that the elderly are "all alike."

THE PROCESS OF AGING

There is a shared cultural universal in regard to the process of aging—every society marks the stages of the aging process in some manner. For example, some cultures mark the transition to old age simply in terms of whether the person has the physical capability to work on a subsistence farm. If a person does not have the physical stamina to continue such work, he or she is considered "old" and must be cared for by the family or community. But since the process of aging also involves biological, psychological, and social factors, different societies put more or less emphasis on different factors. We now explore these factors through the sociological perspective as well as through explanations from other disciplines. We also show how these factors relate to the process of aging throughout the world.

Defining Old Age

We all age—but our society tells us when we reach old age. Western opinions of old age are chronologically based. This kind of classification is important in bureaucratic societies that must determine eligibility for a variety of services. In the United States, 65 is the standard for old age simply because the Social Security Act of 1935 originally set it to establish mandatory retirement and the age when benefits could begin. But the norm of 65 had already been established in parts of Europe in the 19th century, so most of the developed world is now accustomed to using it. However, as life expectancy continues to increase throughout the world, and as people begin to retire earlier, the "age 65" standard is likely to change. In the United States, for example, some people may now draw Social Security as early as age 62.

In addition to chronological age, old age may be defined by certain life passages or events. Recall from Chapter 5, that from the life course perspective, as we age we progress through a sequence of statuses that require certain kinds of role behavior. These include *rites of passage* to formally mark the transition from one status to another. These generational events, such as high-school graduation or a retirement dinner, help us understand how our own individual histories are linked to the larger groups to which we belong.

The scientific study of aging is called **gerontology**; it focuses on that population referred to as "aged" or "elderly." These terms are used interchangeably throughout this chapter. Researchers generally use age 65 to put a person in those categories. The label "oldest old" describes people who are over age 80. If life expectancy rates continue to increase, this group may become the "young old" or the "middle old." Sociologists are also interested in how others in the population define and label old age. Terms range from very negative to more positive—"coot,"

Depending on a person's culture and his or her place in it, aging may be associated with uncertainty, fear, power, or contentment.

"geezer," "old-timer," "elder," "golden ager," and "senior citizen." Even the terms selected for use in this book, "elderly," and "the aged," may be seen negatively or imply infirmity. The terms used to describe "old people" have not kept up with their incredible diversity. Their active lifestyles, lifelong learning, and improved health are challenging traditional views and call for different sociological descriptions (Rosenthal, 2000). The key point is that there is confusion between being old chronologically and being old in terms of obsolete or abandoned.

Throughout the world, old age is associated with role transitions that may occur at different chronological ages. Many of the indigenous peoples in Mexico use age 52 as the beginning of old age. This age is marked as the "binding of years," followed by the period before death called "fulfillment of old age" (De Lehr, 1992). In some Native American tribes, a person cannot participate in certain rituals until designated an elder. In the age-graded systems of East Africa and the Amazon Basin, young people cannot become adults and adults cannot become elders until an elaborate series of rituals occurs. Elder status brings power, prestige, and material wealth in the form of cattle (Sokolovsky, 2000). Seniority has its advantages.

Views from Other Disciplines

Aging is a multidimensional process. The best way to understand the process is to integrate material from a variety of disciplines. **Primary aging** involves the physical changes that accompany our body's biological processes. Changes such as decreased bone density, thinning hair, and hearing loss are included here. **Secondary aging** involves the lifetime of stresses our bodies are subjected to. These include everything from childhood diseases and emotional trauma to lack of exercise and cigarette smoking. From a sociological point of view, secondary aging includes how our bodies and minds react to the social consequences, such as age prejudice, of growing old.

BIOLOGICAL VIEW OF AGING Biologists and physiologists have developed a number of theories that attempt to explain the aging process, but some offer better explanations than others. Genetic theories focus on inherited characteristics that program an individual to a specific aging pathway. Like a biological clock that is ticking, this genetic pathway will determine how long you can expect to live and what you are likely to die of. A pattern of heart disease in your family may have a genetic basis, increasing your risk of developing heart problems.

Other biological theories focus on aging as an outcome of all the external stresses on our bodies.

Gerontologists demonstrate that the aged exhibit a wide range of behavior patterns and lifestyles often associated more with race and social class than with age per se.

The "wear and tear theory" points out that any living organism is like a machine, and after extended usage its parts inevitably wear out. "Free radical theory" assumes the culprit in aging can be traced to the damaging effects of unstable atoms in the cells. "Cross-linkage theory" concentrates on connective tissues such as collagen and elastin. As we age, changes occur in these tissues that result in wrinkled skin, sagging

Some elderly people in all ethnic groups in the United States, such as these Cuban Americans in Miami, prefer to give up the stressful roles they filled earlier in life. They are unlikely to be fully disengaged from younger people but prefer to interact in satisfying activities with like-minded age peers.

muscles, loss of elasticity in blood vessels, and slower healing of wounds. The "autoimmune theory" emphasizes breakdowns in the body's immune system so it can no longer produce the antibodies needed to protect against invading microorganisms and the body's own mutant cells (Cristofalo et al., 1999; Masoro, 1999). Each of these theories offers some help in explaining the mysteries surrounding the physical process of aging. Probably no single biological theory will be able to explain the entire process.

Although biologists still cannot agree on *why* we age, the physical patterns of *how* we age are very clear. We are all aware of the external signs of moving into middle and old age—gray hair, stiffening joints, wrinkled and blotchy skin, increase in weight, and decrease in height. More subtle changes such as decreased need for sleep, higher frequency of urination, and lessening visual and hearing acuity are also likely. And depending on the habits developed over a lifetime, changes in physical energy, mobility, and coordination may be noticeable.

The important point to remember, however, is that while these changes are associated with aging, they are not necessarily associated with either illness or disability. Most elderly people are not in poor health. The onset of physical problems is probably due more to secondary aging, which is dependent on the habits we have developed over a lifetime. We *can* predict that age-related physiological changes will occur, although there is considerable variation in rates of aging. However, many age-related pathological changes are not directly tied to the aging process itself (Masoro, 1999; Miller, 1999). Thus, we *cannot* reliably predict which of us will experience poor health or disability in old age.

PSYCHOLOGICAL VIEW OF AGING The psychology of aging emphasizes age-related changes in cognitive functioning, creativity, and personality. One of the most important elements of cognitive functioning is intelligence. Research on changes in intelligence over the life course concludes that intelligence is generally stable and predictable throughout adult life, peaking in late middle age. Declines after age 60 occur on timed tests, word fluency tests, and tests of spatial abilities. But tests related to primary mental abilities, such as verbal reasoning and learning performance, show no decline in most people until advanced old age. Unless they are connected to physical problems, the declines that do occur are not major disrupters of daily activities (Schaie, 1990; Baltes, 1997; Li, 2002). Overall, age-related changes in intelligence occur gradually, the degree varies from person to person, and changes are associated with both long plateaus and declines.

Like intelligence, changes in creativity are also difficult to measure. While psychologists debate the meaning of creativity, most agree that its expression varies with age, increasing gradually and then declining. The age at which this happens appears to vary by individual, but also by gender and by type of creative discipline. Artists and laboratory scientists tend to peak in their 30s and early 40s but women artists peak later than men artists. Scholars, architects, and writers tend to peak later, many into their 70s (Adams-Price, 1998; Edelstein, 1999; Simonton, 2002).

Whether a peak time also produces the most significant work of one's career is also debatable. Grandma Moses, Benjamin Franklin, Claude Monet, and Irving Berlin continued high-quality work well into old age, making some of the most valuable contributions in their fields at this stage of life. Young creative people become old creative people. Even with some decline, the creative urges remain strong and can even resurge at old age (Simonton, 1990; Ravin & Kenyon, 1998). If poor health and age prejudice do not interfere, the creativity of the elderly may not be significantly hampered.

THE CONVERGENCE OF BIOLOGY AND PSYCHOLOGY: ALZHEIMER'S DISEASE The fields of biology and psychology converge in discussing the impact of age on personality. Old age is not associated with personality discontinuity. Once personality traits are developed, they remain remarkably consistent (Caspi & Roberts, 1999). The emergence of psychiatric symptoms such as severe depression and noticeable personality change that may occur in old age can be a form of psychopathology (Adams, 2001). Alzheimer's disease is one such form. Since all studies show that Alzheimer's disease increases with age, people with the disease are likely to be in the "oldest old" category, age 80 and above. With increased longevity, the projection is that by 2050, unless a cure is found, 14 million Americans will have Alzheimer's disease. Currently, only 1 in 10 people over age 65 have Alzheimer's disease, but half of those over 85 have the disease (ADRDA, 2002). Keep in mind, however, that while this disease is almost unique to older people, it is not part of normal aging.

Alzheimer's disease is a type of organic brain syndrome: It is a progressive and irreversible decay of brain tissue that significantly impairs mental functioning. It is characterized by short-term memory loss, confusion, impaired judgment, inability to concentrate, and personality change. As the disease progresses, memory loss can be complete and the patient becomes totally dependent, both physically and psychologically. The effects are devastating for both patient and caregivers (Quinn, 2002). The patient may forget how to urinate or open a door. The deterioration of the brain eventually leads to death. But since the disease is usually one of gradual onset, people can live for up to 20 years after symptoms appear (ADRDA, 2002). Thus, in most cases, the patient is keenly aware that the mind as well as the body will succumb to the disease (Wilkinson, 2002). As described by a retired sociologist a year after his diagnosis:

> Now how do I live? I have lost the normal feeling of moving forward with life, which I used to take for granted . . . I want, as long as possible, to maintain a quality of life [of] dignity, integrity, and responsibility . . . I want deep communication and closure with those I love, and to make well the decisions leading to a "good death." (Friedell, 2000:381, 382)

Given the dependency that accompanies the disease, Alzheimer's patients are the people already likely to be institutionalized. Half of all people in long-term care (nursing homes) have Alzheimer's disease or a related disorder. With Alzheimer's disease costing $100 billion a year in the United States, both the financial and psychological costs associated with the disease are formidable (Alzheimer's Disease, 2002).

Global Graying

The world is experiencing enormous growth in the population over age 65 (Figure 14.1 on page 368). This growth is one of the greatest success stories of all

Caregiving for Alzheimer's patients is made more demanding because of impairment in both the mind and the body. Caregivers are usually the spouse or the female children of the patient.

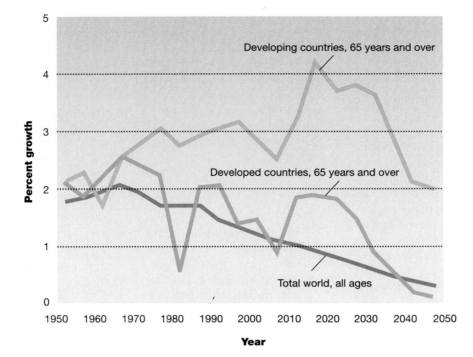

Percent Elderly by Age: 2000 to 2030

Region	Year	65 years and over	75 years and over	80 years and over
Europe	2000	15.5	6.6	3.3
	2015	18.7	8.8	5.2
	2030	24.3	11.8	7.1
North America	2000	12.6	6.0	3.3
	2015	14.9	6.4	3.9
	2030	20.3	9.4	5.4
Oceania	2000	10.2	4.4	2.3
	2015	12.4	5.2	3.1
	2030	16.3	7.5	4.4
Asia	2000	6.0	1.9	0.8
	2015	7.8	2.8	1.4
	2030	12.0	4.6	2.2
Latin America/Caribbean	2000	5.5	1.9	0.9
	2015	7.5	2.8	1.5
	2030	11.6	4.6	2.4
Near East/North Africa	2000	4.3	1.4	0.6
	2015	5.3	1.9	0.9
	2030	8.1	2.8	1.3
Sub-Saharan Africa	2000	2.9	0.8	0.3
	2015	3.2	1.0	0.4
	2030	3.7	1.3	0.6

FIGURE 14.1 **A Global View of the Growth of the Elderly Population.**

Source: Kinsella & Velkoff, 2001: 9. U.S. Census Bureau.

times. It attests to tremendous global gains in providing healthier and more secure living conditions. The technological change and advances in health and medicine that are associated with modernization have set the stage for this increase. As detailed in Chapter 22, countries with the highest proportion of the elderly are in the last phase of the *demographic transition*, with lowered birthrates and death rates.

In addition to the global increase in the over-65 population, the percent of the oldest old is dramatically increasing (see Figure 14.3 on page 372). Almost 40 percent of the world's oldest old live in the three most populous countries in the world: China, India, and the United States. By the year 2030, as a percentage of elderly in their nations, Japan will have the highest share of the oldest old in the world (11 percent), followed by Italy (9 percent), Greece (7.8 percent), and then other Northern European countries in the 7 percent range. The United States is projected to have about 5.3 percent in the oldest old category by 2030. Although the industrialized nations of the developed world have higher percentages of people over 65, almost two-thirds of the world's elderly now live in the developing world. Thus, even in the poorest regions of Asia, Africa, Latin America, and the Caribbean, where life expectancy is much lower, the elderly population is growing at an astounding rate, often at a faster rate than in the developed world. Within the next two decades, the percent of the elderly population over 65 is projected to double from about 4 to 6 percent to 8 to 12 percent in many of these regions (Kinsella & Velkoff, 2001). The percent of those in the oldest old category are projected to increase between 1 and 2 percent in these regions as well. While the growth may appear small, even a 1 percent jump over a 20-year period profoundly affects a country's infrastructure (Kinsella, 2000). As we shall see, the impact on the family and health care systems is significant.

GENDER When gender is added to the profile, the graying world becomes a female world. The current elderly population throughout the world is predominantly female, and it is projected to become even more so (see Figures 14.2 and 14.3 on pages 370 and 372). In less than a decade, many countries will have only 5 men to every 10 women over the age of 80. In the developed world the gender gap in mortality is declining slightly. Compared to women, men are making some gains in living longer. But the gap widens again at the oldest age. As the demographic transition proceeds, the developing world should also experience the same pattern. However, the gap may remain wider in those places of the world where the sex ratio is artificially altered through such methods as sex-selective abortion and abandonment of both infant and elderly females.

THE DEVELOPED WORLD A rapidly growing elderly population represents opportunities as well as challenges for the developed world. The overall picture of the aged is one of health, adequate economic resources, and connectedness with family but independence in lifestyle (Wenger, 1992; Grundy, 2001; Greengross, 2002). Families still provide a great deal of care and support to the elderly when needed, but these are in addition to an array of substantial health care benefits, particularly for those who live alone (OECD, 2000). The elderly receive help, but also return it. Mutual help is a historical pattern and continues today. In the United States and in most Northern European countries where independence is a strongly held cultural value, intergenerational helping assures that neither group becomes totally dependent on the other.

Led by Germany, the welfare systems of Western Europe were first to help the poor. Today they have broadened their mission to deal with other issues of social and economic inequality, including the aged (Stanovnik et al., 2000; Barnighausen & Sauerborn, 2002). Sweden, for example, provides the elderly with a network of publicly funded home and community services that are coordinated with the health and welfare system. Informal care by families and friends is bolstered by government help (Tornstam, 1992).

These opportunities for the elderly in the developed world—to enjoy an enhanced quality of life—are not without liability. The good news is that people are living longer and healthier lives. The bad news is that as they near the end of those lives, they are likely to require an enormous output of resources—financial, social, and psychological. As discussed in Chapter 19, expensive health care options, whether home-based or not, are consuming vast amounts of public funds and contribute to the fiscal crisis facing all the nations in the developed world.

THE DEVELOPING WORLD Most countries in the developing world have no real infrastructure that formally supports services to their growing elderly population. In Asia, for example, the population age 65 and older is projected to more than quadruple by the year 2050 (Mason et al., 2002). Families are the indispensable caregivers, yet those families are changing (Tan, 1999; Johnson & Climo, 2000). Evidence from India and China suggests that traditional respect for the elderly is also declining and caregiving is eroding, since children, especially females, are seeking jobs and education away from home with many not returning. The result is that old people are experiencing increasing loneliness and alienation (Kumar, 1998; Sung, 2000). A similar pattern is occurring throughout Africa, where massive migration of young people to urban areas in search of jobs has left the elderly behind in rural areas with little remaining family support. If the elderly join

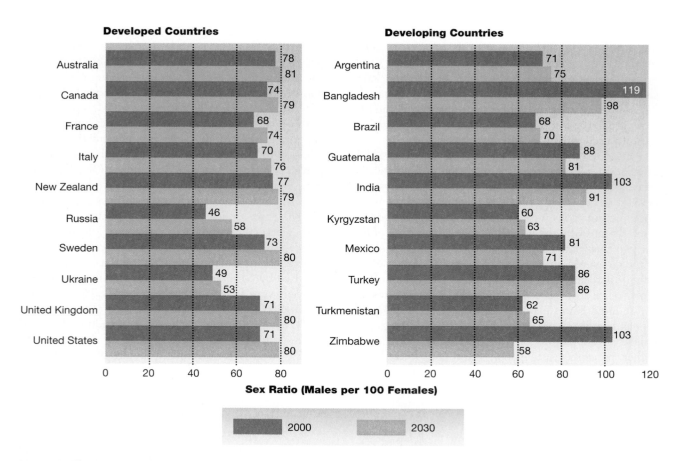

FIGURE 14.2 Sex Ratio for Population Age 65 and Over: 2000 and 2030 in Selected Developed and Developing Countries.

Source: Kinsella & Velkoff, 2001: 58. U.S. Census Bureau.

their families in the cities, they relinquish community ties and are displaced at perhaps the most vulnerable times in their lives (Brown, 2000; Apt, 2001).

Among the very poor in rural areas and subsistence cultures, the elderly are at risk for abandonment, suicide, or even killing when they and others believe they are burdens on their families and communities. In China and South Asia, increasing poverty among the rural elderly is clearly associated with suicide and lack of economic resources when they can no longer contribute to farming and household tasks (Lester, 2000; Yip, 2001; Zhao & Lester, 2001). In some cultures, the elderly person decides that death is necessary and a close relative is chosen to do the killing. It is also interesting that respect for the elderly can coexist with killing or abandonment, as it does among the subsistence !Kung in the vignette. Aging is feared, but there is no resentment involved in the care of elderly kin (Keith, 1992).

Overall, however, elderly people in the developing world who live in extended families in rural areas have high prestige and respect. This prestige is preserved through ownership of land, continued productivity,

and norms that reinforce reciprocity (Lloyd-Sherlock, 2000). A proverb from Ghana captures this norm: "If your elders take care of you while cutting your teeth, you must in turn take care of them while they are losing theirs" (Apt, 1992:206). As we will see later, attitudes toward the aged in the United States show some important similarities to those in the developing world.

SOCIOLOGICAL THEORIES OF AGING

With global graying on the horizon, there has been an explosion of sociological interest in the field of gerontology. While the major sociological theories had implications for the study of the life course and aging, it was not until the early 1960s that the first formal theories related to a sociology of aging emerged.

Disengagement Theory

With the functionalist perspective as its foundation, disengagement theory is an influential view of the aging process. **Disengagement theory** views aging as

TABLE 14.1

Living Arrangements of the Elderly by Gender and Age Category, 2000.

Characteristic	Number in thousands		Percent	
	Men	**Women**	**Men**	**Women**
65 years old and over				
Total	13,886	18,735	100.0	100.0
Living alone	2,355	7,427	17.0	39.6
Married, spouse present	10,084	7,743	72.6	41.3
None of the above	1,447	3,565	10.4	19.0
65 to 74 years old				
Total	8,049	9,747	100.0	100.0
Living alone	1,108	2,983	13.8	30.6
Married, spouse present	6,170	5,156	76.7	52.9
None of the above	771	1,608	9.6	16.5
75 years old and over				
Total	5,837	8,988	100.0	100.0
Living alone	1,247	4,444	21.4	49.4
Married, spouse present	3,914	2,587	67.1	28.8
None of the above	676	1,957	11.6	21.8

Source: Fields & Casper, 2001: 12 U.S. Bureau of the Census.

the gradual, beneficial, and mutual withdrawal of the aged and society from one another (Cumming & Henry, 1961; Neugarten & Weinstein, 1964). As older people inevitably give up some of the roles they have filled—as paid workers, for example—society replaces them with younger, more energetic people. Both groups benefit: The aged shed the pressures of stressful roles, and the young find their own places in society. Society is less disrupted, since the elderly relinquish these roles for the next generation. Ideally, the process is adaptive and benefits the elderly, the young, and society as a whole.

Disengagement theory also assumes that the life course follows a normative sequence of age synchronization that determines the appropriate age for life activities (Cox, 2000:131–132). In the United States people expect to marry in their 20s, have their last children in their 30s, be in their top jobs in their 40s, and retire in their 60s. If the timing of major life events is modified too quickly by too many people who make other choices, the stability, integration, and order that functionalism emphasizes are compromised.

Disengagement theorists emphasize role loss, but they do suggest that temporary role substitutions may serve as buffers until complete disengagement from previous roles occur. For example, a teacher who formally retires may decide to tutor on a self-determined schedule that is more flexible and less demanding. However, even when some role substitutions are suggested by disengagement theorists, the major thrust of

the theory is that disengagement from previous roles must occur. Role loss is inevitable and even positive.

CRITIQUE Often called the "rocking chair" approach to aging because withdrawal is the key to "successful" aging, disengagement theory is also seen as a blueprint for the elderly to follow to their deaths. This blueprint may not be beneficial to the aged. What happens to the people who do not want to give up—voluntarily disengage from—their roles or find that role substitutions are not satisfying? Are they aging "unsuccessfully"? Should they be forced out of paid work or community roles they wish to keep? Should the needs and desires of the elderly be abandoned to satisfy the needs and desires of younger people? To satisfy the assumed needs of society? Would the social order be compromised even when the aged work to keep themselves or their families out of poverty?

These questions point to another issue: They demonstrate how a theory, which is supposed to be a neutral, objective explanation of a social phenomenon, can become a philosophical justification for behavior. For example, older people who want to retain their jobs may be under pressure from their companies to retire early. Disengagement theory offers a justification for a retirement policy that does not serve the interests of some older workers. In Chapter 5 we saw how an influential theory of "dying in stages" became an accepted standard for "successful" dying. Disengagement theory has been criticized for

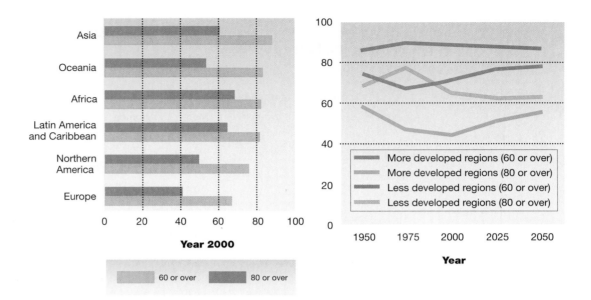

Year 2000

FIGURE 14.3 Current and Projected Sex Ratios for Elderly and Oldest Old by Region of the World.

Source: World Population Aging 1950–2050, p. 26, United Nations Population Division. Copyright © 2002 by United Nations. Reprinted by permission of United Nations, Population Division, New York.

doing the same thing: offering an accepted standard for "successful" aging. The problem is that theories can become cultural prescriptions about what people are supposed to do when they turn the magic age of 65 or when they are faced with dying.

Another criticism of disengagement theory is that the theory assumes there is an age-based orderly progression through the life course. Research does not support this assumption. There is such a great deal of individual variation presently that age patterns are tentative at best. People grow old in many different ways (Quadagno, 2002:33). Given the massive changes occurring in economic and family institutions, it is even less likely in the future. Although disengagement theory offers a reasonably sound rationale for why people select certain roles at old age, sociologists are looking to other theories for more convincing interpretations of the aging process.

Activity Theory

In direct contrast to disengagement theory, **activity theory** suggests that successful aging means not only that role performance and involvements continue, but that new ones—not simply substitutions for old ones—are developed (Havighurst, 1963; Havighurst

Theories of aging have focused on whether the aged disengage or reengage in productive and satisfying roles.

GLOBAL CONNECTIONS

The Elderly of China

Respect, honor, reverence. These words describe the view of the elderly in traditional Chinese culture. Yet Zhao Chunlan, a 73-year-old widow, had her son and daughter-in-law sign a formal support agreement assuring that they would provide for her needs—from cooking special meals and giving her a color television and the largest room in the house to never making her angry. If respect for the elderly is so much a part of Chinese culture, why is a formal agreement needed that requires family members to take care of their elders?

Respect for the elderly is based on two principles: *filial piety,* which is the duty and subordination of the son to the father, and *xiao,* showing one's parents respect and obeying them without question. Dating from 800 B.C.E., these principles give the oldest men the most respect. In practice, all elderly—both men and women—gained. In traditional Chinese families, a woman's life is severely restricted. However, an elderly woman obeys her husband, but commands respect from her children. Although under communism new marriage laws to upgrade the position of women in their extended families were enacted, old age is the best way for a woman to gain some limited authority in traditional families.

The family is the key institution around which support for the elderly is organized. Each generation rears the one behind it, which then becomes responsible for support of the preceding generation. The elderly remain in the family until death and provide valuable feedback in how the next two generations are reared. Violations of filial piety, such as failure to support the elderly, are illegal, but in rural areas public opinion, which denounces the violator to the community, carries more weight.

Traditions of filial piety and *xiao* are being eroded by a massive increase in China's elderly population. By the year 2025 this age group in China will double. When China's baby boomers reach old age, the social and economic burden will be enormous, quadrupling for urban families and doubling for rural families. China's economic resources are limited; it is the family that is still expected to be the major source of support for the elderly.

But the Chinese family is changing. It varies from smaller, nuclear families in urban areas to larger extended families in rural areas where the elderly are expected to live with their adult sons. In many rural areas and those regions with high percentages of indigenous minorities, people are often allowed to have more than one child. Since these areas produce their own food, they can also support larger extended families. In urban areas, China's one-child policy is more strictly enforced, so there will be fewer children available to care for the next generation of elderly.

On the other hand, elderly Chinese contribute to their children and their community. Extended family life in rural areas allows opportunities for elderly men and women to engage in farming as long as they are physically capable. In urban areas, a retired man may work on neighborhood committees and in cultural organizations. Women withdraw earlier from the workforce after the birth of the first grandchild to focus their time and energy on household tasks and child care. In fact, elderly women perform most housework. Women continue economic activities longer than men and seem to willingly accept a life of "ceaseless toil." A lifestyle of leisure is neither available nor desired.

China has gained economically from the unpaid productive work of the elderly. When their "ceaseless toil" must finally cease, government help is limited. Any public assistance to the elderly will also mean bolstering the family in their caregiving roles. Zhao Chunlan knows that her son loves her and is bound by traditions of filial piety and *xiao.* But she is well aware that the formal support agreement will make him "conscious of his commitment" to her as well as legally responsible. Support for the elderly will be shaped by ancient traditions for their respect in the family and the economics of caring for the globe's largest percentage of elderly population.

1. Do you think that the tradition of honor and respect for the elderly in China will be eroded? What works for and against changes in this tradition?

2. Given the increase of the elderly population and the decrease in the birthrate, what policies related to support for the elderly could China adopt that would serve the needs of families and communities?

Sources: Sun, 1990; Davis-Friedmann, 1991; Fang et al., 1992; Hare-Mustin, 1992; Jiang, 1995; Lindsey, 1999.

et al., 1968). According to this theory, successful aging is linked to substantial levels of interpersonal, physical, and mental activity that help resist a potentially shrinking social world. The choices made at this stage of life will depend in part on opportunities for continued involvement in work or leisure activities that are not regulated by law or limited by cultural beliefs about the aged.

Activity theory assumes that the elderly have the same social and psychological needs as middle-aged persons, so these norms become the guideposts for behavior. In the United States, for example, consistent with a value system that supports keeping busy and staying young, activity theory is widely advocated among both gerontologists and the elderly themselves. The late science fiction writer Isaac Asimov would be an excellent representative of the thrust of activity theory. In reflecting on more than a half century of writing with over 365 published books and additional volumes on the horizon, he stated that "naturally there's got to be some limit, for I don't expect to live forever, but I do intend to hang on as long as possible" (Asimov, 1988:x). Isaac Asimov died at age 72 in 1992.

There is a strong correlation between activity level, happiness, morale, and life satisfaction in late middle age and old age (Sheehy, 1995). Both the men and women who emerge in old age as psychologically healthiest use activities to shape a "new" self, as their expectations and goals change. When disengagement occurs, it is most often due to poor health or a major life change rather than any desire to limit activities or withdraw from social interaction. While involuntary role loss may occur, such as compulsory retirement, activity theory offers a variety of mechanisms to offset role loss. For example, roles may be consolidated. Rather than searching for new roles, time and energy may be redistributed to remaining roles (Ferraro, 2001). Retirement may be an opportunity to expand time on enjoyable activities, such as cooking, reading, or volunteering, that before were minimized due to paid work and family obligations. Role consolidation can result in an activity level equal to that of preretirement. Thus, a new sense of self based on such activities can be crafted (Diehl, 1999; Whitbourne, 1999).

CRITIQUE While activity theory is certainly appealing, it has its critics. Some elderly prefer to give up the pressures and high levels of activity associated with middle age, especially if they felt overinvolved during this time. Self-esteem may be compromised if problems related to health, income, or family limit desired activities. A feeling of controlling one's life and destiny may be considered a measure of self-esteem. Compared to their younger counterparts, older Americans who have increasing physical impairment and low levels of education report a substantial reduction in sense of control (Mirowsky, 1995). Activity theory cannot easily explain the intentional isolation that becomes the preferred lifestyle of some elderly. Finally, with its emphasis on "staying young," disdain for aging itself is reinforced and may deprive the elderly of one of their most hard-earned resources: their age (Andrews, 1999).

Continuity Theory

Continuity theory, offering more of a social psychological perspective in explaining the aging process, suggests that individual personality is important in adjusting to aging, with previously developed personality patterns guiding the individual's thinking and acting (Neugarten et al., 1968; Bengston et al., 1985). More recent versions of the theory emphasize the evolution of adult development and our capacity to always learn from ourselves and our environments (Atchley, 1999). We adapt to change based on these patterns as well as on social structural factors, such as race, gender, and class. In other words, while we do not become different people simply because we are growing old, we have an overall developmental direction that we call upon when the opportunities for role choices arise. For instance, how do you spend your leisure time? Proponents of continuity theory would argue that if bicycling or hiking is your preference now, you are beginning to establish patterns of selection that will become stabilized by middle age. How do you deal with interpersonal problems? If talking things over with close friends is your solution, it is likely that this pattern will continue.

At the core of adult development is the ability to preserve our adaptive capacity (Atchley, 2000:158). By middle age we know our strengths and weaknesses and make our choices accordingly. The loving behavior of a grandparent toward a grandchild suggests to continuity theorists that the loving older person was also a loving younger person. When the grandchildren are grown, the loving grandparent may turn to volunteer work with children. Like activity theory, continuity theory suggests that when roles are lost, similar roles are substituted.

CRITIQUE The strength of continuity theory as an explanation for adult aging lies in its interdisciplinary scope. It allows for the linking of individual personality and social structure in determining the attitudes and behaviors of the elderly. By adding the notion of ongoing adaptation to new situations, it overcomes the criticism that it is too deterministic and that we are caught in particular patterns of behavior that may be more detrimental than beneficial. The problem is that it is difficult to test empirically. We need longitudinal data to fully understand how people adapt psychologically, physically, and socially. This means studying those entering middle age now and following them through the rest of their life course. The premise of continuity theory is evident in these lines from Maya Angelou's (1978) poem, "On Aging":

> I'm the same person I was back then,
> A little less hair, a little less chin,
> A lot less lungs and much less wind.
> But ain't I lucky I can still breathe in.[1]

Age Stratification Theory

Using the wealth of sociological work on class stratification as a foundation, gerontologists have developed models of stratification based on age (Riley, 1987;

---

[1]From Maya Angelou, *And Still I Rise*. New York: Random House, 1978.

Riley et al., 1988). With sociological conflict theory as its foundation, we have seen how stratification systems are cultural universals that emerge when societies use certain social characteristics such as social class, race, age, and gender to rank members and determine their roles and statuses. Chronological and biological age are associated with a set of behavioral expectations or **age grades** that change as we get older. When a child is told to "act her age," it is in relation to what is expected for the age grade in her culture. She is part of a *birth cohort* of people born at a given period who age together and experience events in history as an age group.

The explosion of interest in gerontology, for example, is a direct result of the large cohort of baby boomers—those born between 1946 and 1964—who will be reaching retirement age within the next two decades. A cohort's "societal significance" is judged by the influence one cohort exerts over others (Uhlenberg, 1988). As illustrated by the protest movements of the 1960s and 1970s, baby boomers have had a major impact on social institutions and public policy, not only in the United States but with their age partners throughout the world.

Using both cohort analysis and conflict theory as bases, **age stratification theory** seeks an understanding of how society makes distinctions based on age. Gerontologists are interested in that period of life referred to as "old age." As social change continues to alter patterns of aging, age cohorts exhibit both similarities and differences (Riley, 2000). People are not only living longer and healthier, they are more affluent, with age norms modified accordingly. Marketing strategies target the affluent aged, offering them a tantalizing array of consumer goods and services, from luxurious condominium living to adventure-oriented vacations. What is age-typical for you at age 75 will be different from the pattern of your parents, just as it differed from the pattern of their parents.

The cohort analysis approach of age stratification theory offers a valuable tool for understanding the aging process. When tied to the broader conflict perspective in sociology, age stratification theory provides a more complete picture. All forms of social stratification produce social inequality. In much of the world the period of old age is associated with an unequal portion of societal resources, such as less money, power, and prestige compared to other periods of life.

AGE AS BENEFIT OR LIABILITY   However, age itself can bestow power. When age and gender are combined so that the most powerful positions are assigned to the oldest men, the result is a **gerontocracy**. As mentioned earlier, this is the case in some East African cultures where reaching a certain age means automatically becoming part of the ruling elite. When age and social class are combined so that property remains in the hands of the oldest males, they can use it both to control other family members, especially their sons, and as leverage against being abandoned or mistreated if they become infirm.

Although the elderly may benefit from age stratification and the inequality that elevates their position in some cultures, conflict theory suggests several reasons why this situation rarely exists. First, modernization has transformed much of the world and weakened those economic and kinship structures where the

In some Pacific Islands, the role of village chief and the power associated with it resides with the oldest male.

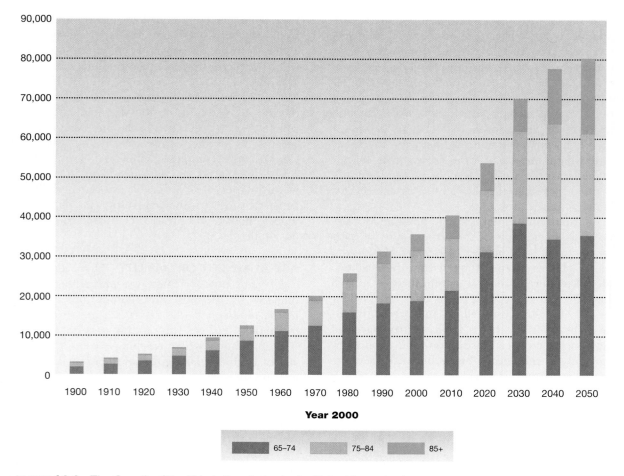

FIGURE 14.4 **The Growth of the Elderly Population in the United States by Age Category, Selected Years.**

Source: Administration on Aging, 2002. U.S. Department of Health and Human Services.

elderly have been accorded power and prestige. With modernization come industrialization, urbanization, mass education, scientific technology, highly individual roles, migration to urban areas, and increased mobility. Such processes literally can leave the elderly behind with fewer resources to compete effectively with younger age cohorts.

Second, age stratification leads to age segregation and greater social distance between age cohorts. Whether it is a retirement community for the more affluent or a transient hotel in an inner-city slum for the poor, isolation and separation from younger people can occur. Third, compulsory retirement and the lack of skills to maintain a current job or successfully compete for another one put the elderly at financial risk. This problem is particularly acute considering that the current generation of elderly relies on Social Security as the most important source of income (see Figure 14.5 on page 377). Social Security accounts for over 90 percent of the income for about 30 percent of the elderly, most of whom are very poor (Social Secu-

rity Administration, 2001). Finally, some argue that age-based social inequality increases the potential for tension between the aged, who have lost valued roles and resources, and the younger persons who have gained them (Hall, 2001).

Thus, conflict theory focuses on the elderly's loss of resources and the inability to either retain or retrieve them. Power is transferred to another group, in this case a younger age cohort. A modified stratification system based in part on age discrimination is institutionalized. Once in place, this discrimination is difficult to eradicate. This cycle leads to **ageism,** the devaluation and negative stereotyping of the elderly.

CRITIQUE One problem with age stratification theory is that it is based on the assumption that age stratification is the dominant force in the distribution of resources in a society. The variation within cohorts may be as important as the variation between them (Riley, 2000). Age is one of many social divisions, but gender, race, class, and even health are other variables

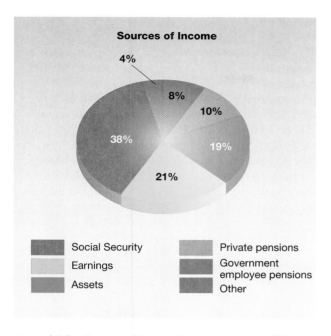

Sources of Income

4%

8%

10%

38%

19%

21%

Social Security

Earnings

Assets

Private pensions

Government
employee pensions

Other

FIGURE 14.5 Sources of Income for Americans Age 65 and Over.

Source: Social Security Administration, 2001.

that reap social rewards and liabilities. Another problem is that there is contradictory evidence that modernization ushers in devaluation of the elderly. As societies continue to modernize, the quality of life improves for the aged. Higher prestige for the elderly is now associated with societies that are the most modernized. Social policies have been developed to the benefit of the aged (Kingston & Williamson, 2001; Lockhart, 2001). In the United States, for example, there is widespread support for public funds used for those who are no longer able to work because of age. There is a tradition of respect for the elderly, so programs such as Medicare have been put in place to allow them some freedom from the stigma that may come from dependency. By bolstering income and health support, retirement becomes a time for self-fulfillment and self-sufficiency.

Symbolic Interactionism

Like continuity theory, symbolic interactionism takes a social psychological perspective on aging. It resonates with that part of continuity theory that emphasizes adaptation and the ability to choose behavior. If we are constrained by our environment, then we modify it. If we are constrained by our individual needs, then we adjust them. A retired elementary school teacher, for example, may start a preschool, which sustains her or his individual need to help children. These choices are not made in a vacuum. As dis-

cussed throughout the text, symbolic interactionism argues that behavior is for the most part rationally chosen, based on our interpretations of others' attitudes and behaviors and the symbolic meanings we share.

Symbolic interactionism also capitalizes on the work of conflict and age stratification theory by focusing on the impact of ageism and how it can force the elderly into devalued age strata. Old age is socially constructed, and this construction results in less economic power and social prestige for the elderly (Irwin, 1999; Quadagno & Reid, 1999). As a subset of symbolic interactionism, labeling theory asserts that the elderly are stereotyped through ageism. Media views of the elderly, for example, fuel ageism. A wealth of research demonstrates that even with some notable exceptions, the message of aging on film, television, and in print celebrates youth and laughs at stereotypes, marginalizes, or simply ignores the elderly. Older women are virtually invisible (Markson & Taylor, 2000; Krueger, 2001; Signorielli, 2001; Healey & Ross, 2002). While there is no strong, cultural disdain of the elderly in the United States, there is an acceptance of negative beliefs about them reinforced by the ageism of the media (Carrigan & Szmigin, 2000; Levy & Banaji, 2002).

The elderly may internalize the negative labels and learn to act in the manner the stereotypes suggest. By being labeled as incompetent, for example, the elderly can begin to question their ability to learn new skills or hone old ones. If the cycle continues, complete disengagement may occur, compromising the elderly person's capacity to take care of himself or herself. Labeling can usher in a self-fulfilling prophecy and lead to *social breakdown syndrome* (Kuypers & Bengston, 1973). This means that when we tell the elderly they are incompetent to do anything but "relax" in the rocking chair, they may never again be able to leave it. In this way, labeling, ageism, and disengagement theory go hand in hand.

CRITIQUE Overall, symbolic interactionism adequately deals with how we perceive the elderly and how labeling can be detrimental or beneficial to them. And like continuity theory, it helps explain individual variations in behavior, from the aged person's point of view as well as that of other age cohorts. But because of its microlevel focus, symbolic interactionism minimizes the impact of the broader social structure on behavior. Once ageism becomes institutionalized, it is difficult to dislodge it without a concerted attack on all social institutions. As we will see, ageism can be reversed, and positive labeling can occur when the elderly build their resources and form a power base to challenge age-discriminatory practices.

A PROFILE OF THE AGED IN THE UNITED STATES

When profiling the aged in the United States, the portrait that emerges is a positive one. Most elderly people are married, are relatively secure financially, and live in their own homes or apartments. They have frequent contact with other family members and see their children regularly. They describe their health as generally good, and they view any problems related to health as not severe enough to significantly compromise their lifestyle, a pattern found in both the United States and Canada (Rosenthal, 1997; Nemeth, 1998; Gutman et al., 2001). This section focuses on the diversity in those social institutions that have important consequences for the lifestyles of the elderly in the United States.

Links to Diversity: Social Class, Gender, and Race

The United States is a very diverse society, and age is only one of many categories of social structure in which people may be placed. There are a number of possible outcomes for the aged related to that diversity. For example, many elderly face "multiple jeopardy" because they fall into other categories that are associated with financial risk. The *theory of cumulative disadvantage* takes into account the social categories that increase inequality throughout the life course (Quadagno, 2002:221). Advantages or disadvantages based on social class, gender, and race early in life carry through to old age (Calasanti, 2000).

SOCIAL CLASS Financial security is a key factor in maintaining a healthy and independent lifestyle during old age. As a group, the elderly have experienced a major decline in poverty since the 1960s. Coupled with economic growth and better pension plans, this decline is primarily due to the expansion of

INTERNET CONNECTIONS

To obtain more information on the profile of the aged in the United States go to the Administration on Aging Website:

http://www.aoa.dhhs.gov/default.htm

and click on statistics about older people. Browse through the site and write a descriptive report on the elderly population in the United States.

federal programs such as Medicare. Medicare is available to virtually all American citizens age 65 and over as a health insurance program that covers significant health care costs (Chapter 19). Before Medicare, health care costs propelled many of the elderly into poverty. Since 1960, poverty among the elderly has declined from 30 percent to under 10 percent (see Figure 14.6 on page 379). Children under age 18 are more likely to be poor than people over the age of 65. There is substantial evidence that economic hardship actually declines with age (Mirowsky & Ross, 1999). Despite this success story, however, the figures mask a number of factors that not only keep many elderly in poverty but put certain groups at risk for poverty when they reach old age.

GENDER Income declines with age among the elderly. The younger elderly, age 65 to 80, have more resources than the oldest old, age 80 and above; recall that the latter is the fastest growing age population in the United States. This decline is associated with changes in sources of income and, more important, with marital status. The oldest old are also likely to be widows who experience severe economic consequences at the loss of their spouse. Spouse benefits provide some help for older widows, but they are at best uncertain. In addition, marriage has a health benefit for both elderly men and women, but this is especially true for women. Elderly widows and divorced women of all races are at high risk for chronic illness, functional limitations, and disabilities (Morgan, 2000; Pienta et al., 2000). Minority women in the oldest old category who live alone and are psychologically or physically impaired have the fewest financial resources of any age group. And we will see that a lifetime of employment does not protect women from poverty at old age.

THE MINORITY AGED The minority elderly face multiple jeopardy for poverty. As with the elderly population as a whole, older African Americans have improved economically since the 1960s. Although about 10 percent of the elderly are below the poverty level, these numbers double for African American and Latino elderly (U.S. Bureau of the Census, 2001). Poverty is most pervasive for elderly African American and Latino women who head multigenerational households, who have limited education, or who live alone (Rudkin & Markides, 2001). Poor health often forces African Americans from paid employment earlier in their careers than whites, since they are likely to work in more physically demanding jobs. Unemployment reduces pension and Social Security benefits and puts them in a precarious economic position because they lose health insurance, lack access to quality health care,

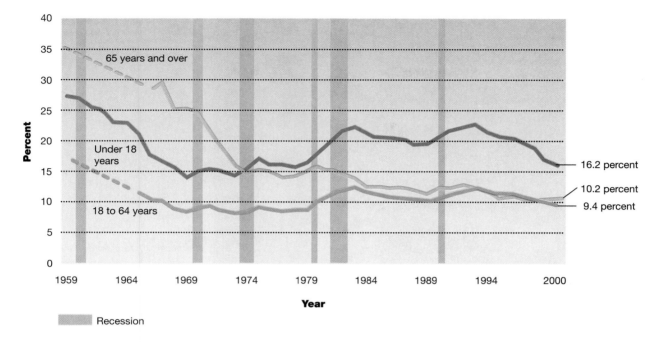

FIGURE 14.6 Poverty Rates by Three Age Groups (Children, Adults to Age 64, and Elderly, 65 and Over), Selected Years.

Source: Dalaker, 2001: 4. U.S. Census Bureau.

and are likely to have more dependents than whites (Williams & Wilson, 2001). Compounding this situation is the fact that they were often employed in low-paying jobs that provided little in the way of economic security or retirement benefits (see Chapter 12). Retirement in the conventional sense is less applicable.

Interestingly, these economic disadvantages do not necessarily mean that African Americans face old age with misery. Although the oldest old African Americans are in poorer health and have lower incomes than comparably aged whites, they have significantly better morale. Objectively, they are in ill health and poverty. Subjectively, they believe their situation is better than what they expected; they survived a lifetime of racial discrimination and economic hardship (Johnson, 2000). As suggested by symbolic interactionism, it is the perception that their present lives are better than their past—the difference between expectation and reality—that determines their attitudes.

Elderly Latino Americans fall between African Americans and whites in poverty. Like the elderly of all races, these Latinos have experienced a steady decline in poverty, but their poverty rate is still twice as high as that of elderly whites. Gender again increases risk for poverty. When compared to African American and white women, census figures show that elderly Latino women have the lowest median incomes.

The high poverty rate of elderly Latinos is affected by unique cultural influences. Latino cultures are described as extremely family oriented, with an expectation that kin will be available for support. Despite a strong belief that these families must care for the needs of their elderly, the intent to help depends on the income and availability of family members to do so. Even when formal sources of help are available, elderly Latinos prefer to rely on family and fear the prospect of living in a nursing home. The elderly themselves perceive that formal services are insensitive to their individual needs and ignore the cultural and language issues they face. However, the traditional extended Latino family is eroding, and family members may no longer be able to give the care required of elderly relatives (Mutchler & Angel, 2001; Wilmoth, 2001; Beyene et al., 2002).

Native American elderly also see kinship as central to their economic and social lives, and they enjoy a highly revered status within their communities, perhaps higher than any other category of minority elderly (Baldridge, 2001). However, since the Native American population remains the poorest of all ethnic and racial minorities, this poverty carries over into old age and is associated with a series of chronic health problems. Unlike the Latino elderly, they readily seek and use formal support services and any financial help provided through such services (Bell et al., 2000; John, 2000). Most elderly can still be found on reser-

Although African American elderly are likely to have low incomes, they express relatively high levels of life satisfaction and well-being.

vations. Those who migrated to urban areas often return to spend their old age closer to kin. Reservation living is also associated with higher poverty. An interesting pattern of financial support has occurred among those elderly who qualify for some pension and welfare benefits. Many have voluntarily shared even these meager incomes with younger family members and grandchildren who come to rely on this steady support. In doing so, they uphold ancient traditions of sharing and interdependence, and the prestige of the elderly is further enhanced (Jackson & Chapleski, 2000; Weibel-Orlando, 2001; Gardiner et al., 2002).

Retirement

The prospect of retirement presents a dilemma. Americans subscribe to a strong work ethic from which they gain a sense of identity and self-esteem. The transition to retirement requires major adjustments in all segments of life. It restructures daily living and alters family relationships and spending patterns. Retirement produces psychological stress and contributes to economic and social inequality. With senior citizens leading the way, the 1978 Amendments to Age Discrimination in Employment Act (ADEA) increased the mandatory retirement age to 70. Amendments to ADEA in 1986 ended mandatory retirement entirely. Comparative research in the United States, Germany, Australia, Japan, and Great Britain show that Americans are the most strongly opposed and the British the most accepting of mandatory retirement (Hayes & Vandenheuvel, 1994; Traphagan, 2000). Americans seem to be captivated with the prospect of work.

Other evidence suggests that captivation with work has changed to work as captivity. Retirement has become part of life's expectations, and norms for early retirement are rapidly being established. The stressful transition between work and retirement is eased by retirement seminars and financial counseling. Companies are offering benefit packages to encourage early retirement, and workers are receptive to them. If financial security is ensured, they prefer early retirement. For postindustrial nations, retirement has emerged as a basic right that is embraced by most workers (Ekerdt, 1998; OECD, 2000).

Although retirement is something most workers now look forward to, several factors are important in adjustment to and satisfaction with this life stage. Despite the role loss involved, a large majority of retirees do not experience a great deal of difficulty when they exit their jobs. Retirement correlates positively with self-esteem and negatively with depression (Reitzes et al., 1996). As predicted by activity theory, many find substitute roles that offer alternative sources of productivity, such as becoming entrepreneurs in home-based businesses. When social contacts are maintained or expanded, satisfaction with retirement and leisure activities also increases. Higher levels of education and occupation offer more flexibility and variety in pursuing retirement opportunities and contribute to better adjustment (Reeves & Darville, 1994; Pillemer et al., 2000). Such retirees have adopted a "busy ethic" rather than a work ethic and begin to experiment with new roles. As one researcher reports on American retirees who are active and satisfied in their retirement, they have "defined retirement rather than letting retirement define them" (Savishinsky, 2000:29).

GENDER AND RETIREMENT   Gender is another variable that affects the retirement picture. Gender role differences predict that men would have a more difficult time with retirement than women, since men are expected to be the primary breadwinners in a household. Paid work, therefore, provides not only the practical benefit of income but also a sense of purpose and intrinsic satisfaction. However, available data suggest that retirement satisfaction is based on the same factors for women and men. Like men, career women anticipate retiring at an earlier age, but they use the resulting free time differently. Men take on more extra-domestic roles and activities. Women restructure domestic lives that were constrained because of work and spend more time with family and on home-related activities (Choi, 2001; Barer, 2002; Kim & Moen, 2002). Working-class women who would like to retire early have little choice but to stay in the labor force for as long as possible. Low earnings in gender-segregated jobs throughout their careers take their toll on retirement. Poverty at retirement is a common result (Olson, 1999; *Research Dialogues*, 1999). Like other aspects of aging, retirement needs to be more widely viewed from a model that incorporates the experiences of both men and women.

Yet research consistently shows that difficulty or satisfaction with retirement have less to do with gender and more to do with the health and income of the retiree. Both male and female workers are less satisfied if poor health forced them to retire or if deficient economic resources forced them to remain on the job. While it is a myth that retirement harms health, poor health obviously will impact what they do in retirement, just as it impacts the lifestyle of younger people. A question women confront more frequently than men is whether they must return to the world of paid employment for economic survival. But a question both men and women confront is whether they are physically fit enough to return. Acceptable options in health and wealth profoundly impact retirement adjustment and the lifestyle that results (Schulz, 2001; Vierck, 2002).

Living Arrangements

Our living environments at any age have a major impact on our lives. How we use and share our physical space make a difference in our behavior, quality of life, and sense of well-being. For the elderly in the United States, such issues are perhaps more important because at the last stages of life their choices for living arrangements may be severely curtailed. Two questions need to be addressed in this regard: Is it better for the elderly to live independently but alone? Is it better to live with people their own age? Sociological research provides some answers to these questions.

The vast majority of the elderly—both couples and widows or widowers—not only live in their own homes and apartments, they are also likely to own them free of any mortgage (U.S. Department of Housing and Urban Development, 1999; Casper & Bianchi, 2002). They are fully capable of functioning independently, even when living alone, and they strongly prefer to remain in their own homes, especially when they are modified to accommodate physical needs (Tabbarah et al., 2000). This preference is tied to a "loss continuum" that reduces social participation and increases social isolation (Pastalan, 1982). Elderly persons experience losses through widowhood, retirement, and the death of friends and siblings. The number and quality of

Residential options for the elderly include apartment complexes and "leisure villages" where activities are offered with age peers that are associated with enhanced life satisfaction.

relationships shrink (Pillemer et al., 2000). A move from a home and community where they spent major portions of their lives represents another loss. On the death of a spouse, the attachment to familiar surroundings becomes even more important.

Residential segregation of the elderly has received a great deal of research attention. Age-segregated housing offers both psychosocial benefits and costs. It can be attractive to those of the same birth cohort who share similar interests and lifestyles. Residences designed specifically for the elderly are usually safer, accessible to public transportation, and offer a range of services and recreational activities. After the move, residents often report higher levels of social participation, an improved sense of well-being, and satisfaction with housing (Castle, 2001). On the down side, the elderly may be more subject to isolation because they are separated from the larger society, caught in a narrow corridor where they interact only with other age peers (Hickey, 1999; Folts & Muir, 2002; Streib, 2002). When younger people are deprived of contact with elders, ageism and negative stereotypes may be heightened for both groups. Consistent with age stratification and conflict theory, residential segregation can produce social inequality.

A RANGE OF HOUSING ALTERNATIVES The last two decades have witnessed a boom in housing alternatives for senior citizens. A range of housing options is shown in Figure 14.7. This classification indicates that the elderly represent a diverse population. The options are based on the degree of physical and psychological impairment—the critical factor in determining which services need to be provided within each alternative (Lindsey, 2000).

Many of the facilities are multipurpose; they offer a variety of assistance, such as food and cleaning services, health and security checks, recreational activi-

ties, and volunteer opportunities. An example is *congregate housing* that serves the elderly who are impaired but not ill (Long, 2001; Carder, 2002). For the elderly who are less capable and live with their working children, day-care centers can provide for their maintenance and supervisory needs for portions of the day (Lindsey, 2000). In all cases, maximizing independence is critical.

Too often, those who plan living arrangements for the aged, despite the best of intentions, do not recognize the diversity of their elderly clientele, especially in terms of income and health. At a minimum, housing must be affordable and must accommodate any medical challenges that residents may face (Moore, 2001). As these needs are being met, factors related to gender, ethnic, and sexual diversity must be recognized. The pervasive myth that the elderly are all alike still persists, even among those who work in gerontology. For those who do require support, individual wants and needs should be carefully considered when determining living arrangements.

INSTITUTIONALIZATION Most people overestimate the percent of the elderly population who reside in long-term care facilities (LTCFs) or nursing homes. Less than 5 percent of people over age 65 are in continuous long-term care. But the percentage increases dramatically for many in the oldest old category. Half of those over 85 reside in nursing homes. Nearly three-fourths of all LTCF residents are women. And Alzheimer's disease residents are fast becoming the majority (Pandya, 2001). If more noninstitutional options and social support networks were available for non-Alzheimer's elderly, this number could be significantly reduced. But for those elderly who are fully dependent, with extensive physical and psychological impairment, and who require round-the-clock care, admission to an LTCF may be the only realistic alternative.

An LTCF is another example of a *total institution* (Chapter 5). It is "total" because, like a prison, it exerts complete control over the individual. Can an LTCF institution both carry out administrative functions efficiently and take into consideration individual wants and needs? Research suggests the answer is yes. For example, most nursing homes now have resident councils with some decision-making authority. Residents of LTCFs are also protected by federal legislation, such as the Older American Act passed in 1965, which established the Administration on Aging and allowed grants for planning, training, and coordination of services to the elderly. Most important, the 1975 amendments to this legislation established an *ombudsman* program designed to serve as a liaison between LTCF administration and residents. Ombudsmen are both paid and volunteer staff from outside

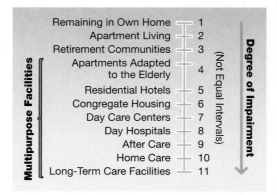

FIGURE 14.7 Housing Options for the Elderly.
Source: Adapted from Lindsey, 2001:91.

the LTCF who serve as advocates and investigate complaints, bringing in legal counsel if necessary.

Although most elderly desperately wish to maintain at least a semi-independent existence in their own homes, some do prefer an LTCF where social isolation is reduced and they can live among peers. It is also difficult to rely completely on outside caretakers for all basic needs. Patient-centered approaches can make life better for those who reside in LTCFs. The key factor in the well-being of nursing home residents is their perception of how much control and choice they have over their lives. It is clear that LTCFs can offer residents a great deal of this control (Mitchell & Kemp, 2000; Frank, 2002; King & Johnson, 2002). Staff can assure that residents make the most of the gift of time as they move from independence to dependence.

LIFE CONNECTIONS

Later Life in American Families

Marriage is highly correlated with happiness at all life stages. As mentioned above, most elderly are married. This translates to about two-thirds of elderly men and two-fifths of elderly women (U.S. Bureau of the Census, 2001). Indeed, of today's elderly, less than 5 percent have never married. With increased longevity, couples can expect to spend about one-fourth of their married life together after the departure of the last child from the home.

The Marriage Relationship

For the married elderly, marital quality is high. Research consistently demonstrates the same overall conclusion: that marital satisfaction is as high or higher in later life as it was at the beginning of the marriage (Barrett, 1999; cited in Quadagno, 2002:231–33) (see Figure 14.8 on page 385). When combined with good health and financial security, retirement and the last child leaving home allow the older couple more opportunities for shared activities and a re-exploration of the marriage. Leaving a high-stress job actually improves marital quality (Myers & Booth, 1996).

At that point, the marriage relationship itself again becomes the focus of life, another "honeymoon stage" when the couple can finally do the things they always wanted to do. When asked what contributes to marital stability and satisfaction, both older men and women suggest similar things, including seeing your spouse as your best friend, sharing the same goals, involvement in a social network that reinforces the marriage, having a sense of humor, viewing marriage as a

Most elderly are married and exhibit high levels of marital satisfaction, which may actually increase at this stage of life.

long-term commitment, and wanting the relationship to succeed (Lauer et al., 1990, 1995; Bryant & Conger, 1999). There is consensus among all age groups on what is important for a good marriage (Chapter 15).

REMARRIAGE While most elderly couples express a reasonably high degree of marital satisfaction, there is a small but growing percentage of divorces within this age group. In 1980, 3.5 percent of people over age 65 were divorced; by 2000 the rate almost doubled (U.S. Bureau of the Census, 2001). Age itself is probably less of a factor than the fact that people of all age groups are now more likely to see divorce as an acceptable option. This suggests that the elderly of today may not be subscribing to traditional values that would make divorce out of the question. Another factor is that the next generation of elderly will consist of a majority of women who have not only worked outside the home but may have retired from successful careers that offered retirement benefits. Their financial security may allow them the choice to end a marriage, particularly when "staying together for the sake of the children" may have kept the marriage intact.

Given the satisfying marital relationships that typify older couples, it is not surprising that many choose to remarry. Not only do later life remarriages have a better chance of success after a divorce, but couples also report that their marriages are happier. Remarriage rates are higher for those who have divorced compared to those who are widowed, with age, income, and gender explaining most of the differences. Women are at a disadvantage both as widows and if divorced because men marry younger women, and women outlive men on the average by about 7.5 years. On the other hand, a woman may be reluctant to remarry if she must again take on a significant caretaking role, whether it means attending to the domestic daily needs of a husband or caring for him if he becomes debilitated. For men the opposite is true. Men who are inexperienced in looking after themselves or are physically impaired in some way want to remarry in part because their wives can provide domestic and caretaking services (Stroup & Pollock, 1999; Davidson, 2001).

Whereas the intense emotion associated with romantic love impels younger couples to marry, older couples express a simple desire for companionship and affection (Bengston et al., 1990). Sexuality, however, is still expressed as an important desire and is not necessarily compromised by old age (Chapter 7). Successful remarriages are associated with similarity of background, long-term prior friendship, often including the former spouse, and approval of family and friends. Marriage is associated with companionship, affection, and interdependency for all age groups. These characteristics appear to be even more important to those who remarry in later life.

Cohabitation

Just as higher divorce rates in the overall population are showing up among the elderly, so are rates of cohabitation, or living together without marriage. This may be surprising to those who believe that such a lifestyle is attractive only to younger people and college students. Although younger cohabitants eventually get married (though not necessarily to those with whom they are living), this is generally not true for the elderly. Other incentives propel elderly people to choose cohabitation rather than marriage. Many originally chose this lifestyle to avoid a reduction of Social Security benefits that, until the law changed in 1984, penalized those who remarried after age 60. Widows and widowers may still lose rights to their former spouses' pensions and health benefits, and inheritance of assets within a family may be jeopardized (Kaplan, 1999). Other older couples may simply want companionship and a sense of security without the legal entanglements of marriage (Cooney & Dunne, 2001; Quartaroli, 2001).

The children of these couples face a dilemma. Do they sanction the arrangement or encourage their parents to marry? It is difficult for adult children to envision a parent in such a relationship. And older couples who grew up at a time when such liaisons were frowned upon may feel compelled to hide the arrangement from their peers. Yet as norms are relaxed and cohabitation becomes more of an acceptable lifestyle among younger people, acceptance will probably increase among the elderly as well.

Grandparenting

Families in later life are also shaped by both the delights and burdens associated with grandparenting in America. With so many baby boomers becoming grandparents and so many grandparents becoming caretakers of grandchildren, there is an explosion of research on the grandparenting role. Three common grandparenting styles have been identified (Bengston & Robertson, 1985; Cherlin & Furstenberg, 1992). First, the *companionate* or *formal* grandparenting style stresses independence for grandparents but lots of love and companionship between grandparents and grandchildren. Grandparents do not interfere with the parents' authority. They clearly keep parenting separate from grandparenting. Second, in sharp contrast to the companionate style, is the *involved* or *surrogate-parent* role, in which grandparents, usually grandmothers, care for grandchildren who often live with their grandparents. They therefore have a great deal of control over them. Third, the *remote* style of grandparenting occurs when grandparents have limited contact and are distant figures with their grandchildren, usually seeing them only on holidays or special occasions. Giftgiving and kindness are common, but the grandparent vanishes until the next family event. Overall, grandparenting for most older people allows them to engage in productive roles when other social roles may be shrinking and clearly contributes to life satisfaction.

These styles are not mutually exclusive and are altered as family circumstances change. With its emphasis on companionship, the companionate style is the ideal in the United States—loving grandparents who may indulge their grandchildren and help out their children when necessary but who leave parenting to the parents. However, much research is now focusing on the rapidly increasing involved/surrogate-parent style. Divorce, death, drug use and AIDS, out-of-wedlock births, safety concerns, and escalating day-care costs often result in grandparenting becoming a full-time job. When parents are not financially or emotionally capable of caring for their children, grandparents are frequently gaining custody. About 6.3 percent of all children under the age of 18 are living in grandparent-headed homes, a 30 percent in-

Grandparents are likely to be central to the lives of their grandchildren, although they leave the parenting up to their children.

crease from 1990 to 2000 (AARP, 2002a). There is still too little research on what happens to families when grandparents "are pressed into service as parents" (Ehrle, 2001). However, while love and support characterize their roles, when grandparents become the parents of their grandchildren, role strain, depression, lack of privacy, and emotional problems are frequent byproducts.

Widowhood

As age increases, so does the number of elderly living alone (see Table 14.1 on page 371). Widowers are much more likely to remarry; thus, among the elderly, the large majority of widows reside alone. Although most older adults return to earlier levels of physical and emotional health within 18 months after the loss of their spouse, social isolation and loneliness are frequent outcomes of widowhood. The surviving spouse is at higher risk for physical illness and even death (Smith, 1996; Carr, 2001). If a caregiver-spouse dies, the already debilitated surviving spouse is left in an even more dependent and vulnerable position. Suicide rates among the elderly have increased since the 1980s, and they remain the highest for all age groups. Men account for 84 percent of all suicides. White males in their 80s have the highest suicide rates of all races and both genders (National Strategy for Suicide Prevention, 2001). Suicide attempts by younger people (those under age 35) are likely to fail; suicide attempts rarely fail for the elderly (Hendin, 1995).

WIDOWS Although the death of a spouse has a profound and devastating effect on the surviving partner, becoming a widow is a qualitatively different experience than becoming a widower. Older women are more likely to form their identity around marriage, so

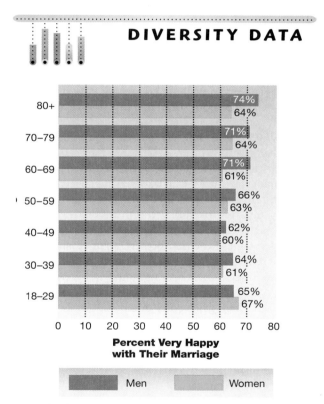

FIGURE 14.8 **Percentage of People Describing Their Marriage as Very Happy, by Age and Gender.** Although the majority of both men and women at all age levels describe their marriages as very happy, people over 60 have the highest ratings for very happy marriages. Since the factors for a happy marriage are the same for the young and the old, why do people believe that elderly married couples are "different" from their younger married counterparts?

Source: NORC. General Social Surveys, 1972–2000. Chicago: National Opinion Research Center, 2000. Reprinted by permission of NORC, Chicago, IL.

losing a spouse literally means loss of a central life role. Widows are likely to experience a sudden decrease in standard of living, and for working-class women, widowhood can quickly result in poverty. Isolation increases and support networks decrease (Meyer, 1996; Hungerford, 2001). These are worsened if the couple has moved away from her family for his career advancement. Finally, if a widow feels emotionally secure enough to venture into dating, prospects for male companionship and remarriage are limited.

On the other hand, the widow may be guided by the many others with whom she can share her experiences, memories, and activities (DeSpelder & Strickland, 1996). Due to their numbers alone, a variety of productive roles have been carved out for widows. These role choices may not be completely clear, and may depend upon previous interaction with husbands, family members, and friends, as well as the ability to cope with crisis. But some expectations can help map out the road ahead. One role may allow for a widow's desire to keep the memory of her husband alive, particularly if the family supports the effort. Another is volunteer or even paid work. Since married women know that widowhood is probable, they may begin to actually mentally rehearse it, another example of *anticipatory socialization*. Consistent with continuity theory, adjustment is related to both social and psychological factors.

WIDOWERS   The role of widower is much more vague than that of widow. At first glance, it would seem that adjustment is more difficult because men lose their most important source of emotional support and probably their major, if not their only, confidant. Wives typically take responsibility for maintaining the couple's social calendar and network of friendships. Lacking the strategies for either preserving or reestablishing intimate relationships, widowers have reduced social contacts. Elderly men are also guided by traditional norms of masculinity, which may prevent them from talking out their grief with others (Doka & Martin, 2001). Retirement increases social isolation. Widowhood intensifies it. The net result is a loss of significant personal relationships. Older men are also less likely to be prepared for the everyday domestic responsibilities necessary for taking care of themselves. When ongoing relationships and customary responsibilities are shattered, anomie (normlessness) can follow. This pattern helps explain the high suicide rate of elderly males.

On the other hand, marriage prospects remain bright for widowers, with many embarrassed by all the attention they receive from widows who want to "do" things for them. In addition to the numbers of women of their own age or younger who are available to widowers as potential dating and mating partners, men are better off financially to actually support another spouse. Finally, men may have a stronger need

to be remarried, so they quickly move through the dating stage to make remarriage a reality (Moore & Stratton, 2002). Overall, adjustment to widowhood may be different for men and women, but it remains unclear as to which gender fares better.

SOCIETY CONNECTIONS

Later Life as Risk or Opportunity

We have seen that throughout the world people are living longer and healthier lives. But opportunities for reaping the benefits of longevity are weakened with the increased assistance required as the elderly age. Whether they live independently or in a group setting such as a nursing home, they must rely on caregivers to provide for their basic needs. Caregiving has emerged as a major issue in the demographic revolution that is producing global graying.

Caregiving

The spouse is the first to provide care for the elderly (Greenberg, 2001). The next level of responsibility falls to adult children. For the poorer elderly, the next level is the network of extended family and kin.

While type of care and patterns of caregiving in families vary greatly, women are the primary caregivers to elderly parents, whether they are daughters or daughters-in-law (Abel, 2001; Moen et al., 2000). They have been called the **sandwich generation** because they are caught between caring for the older and younger generations at the same time. Many of these women are middle-aged, in the workforce, and still have children at home. Caregiving may provide opportunities to grow together to explore reciprocal relationship needs of elderly parents and their adult children in their final years together (Greenberg, 1994).

Love, commitment, and responsibility can describe caregivers. Other words to describe caregiving are guilt, burden, depression, and strain. Assistance to the elderly produces higher levels of caregiver strain and work interference than when providing assistance to younger adults (Scharlach & Fredriksen, 1994). The stress of the elder-care role for women is associated with compromises in both emotional health and psychological well-being. Time away from spouse and children can negatively affect their marriages, and guilt is produced when caregiving results in less affection to the parent (Moen et al., 1995; Rossi, 2001).

ELDER ABUSE AND NEGLECT   Even with the vast literature on quality-of-care issues in nursing homes (LTCFs), the data on elder abuse in these facilities is difficult to document. While the majority offer competent and loving care to residents, a recent federal study finds about one-third of all LTCFs in the United States cited for abuse over a two-year period. Typical problems include untreated bed sores, dehydration, and poor hygiene. Other research suggests that 10 percent of staff commit at least one incident of physical abuse, such as slapping or punching residents. Psychological abuse, including scolding, use of degrading language, and neglect, is more common, 80 percent of staff have witnessed other staff committing such abuse (Wolf, 2000, 2001; Ruppe, 2001). Investigations of LTCFs and stricter standards for those receiving federal funds have resulted in a decline of the most glaring offenses (Rosenbaum et al., 2001). For elder care occurring in domestic settings, usually in their own or their children's homes, between 4 and 6 percent of older adults report abuse. This abuse most commonly takes place as passive neglect, verbal and psychological abuse, and financial exploitation (Wolf, 2000; 2001). Unfortunately, today's elderly are also likely to be abused by their own spouses and other caregivers in the home.

Physical abuse of the elderly by adult children and spouses who serve as caregivers is common and is correlated with caring for mentally confused elderly, especially Alzheimer's patients. Alzheimer's disease is associated with uncontrolled outbursts of anger and unpredictable behavior that creates the most stress for the caregiver. Caregivers may counter with violence (Carp, 2000; Conner, 2000; Schiamberg & Gans, 2000). Another pattern of elder abuse fits with data on "traditional" domestic violence where the abuse is rooted in power and control over the elderly victim rather than caregiver stress (Brandl, 2000).

Caregivers may be puzzled when charged with abuse. In the first systematic studies of elderly abuse in the home from the eyes of the caregivers, some reasons for this puzzlement surfaced (Steinmetz & Amsden, 1983). In-depth interviews of caregivers and their definition of the situation revealed the difficulties in separating victims from perpetrators. A daughter who had been caring for her 72-year-old mother for eight years exclaimed:

> I ripped her dress off when she refused to get ready to go out. I was sorry right after to think that I let her get to me. . . . (Steinmetz, 1988:180)

The daughter is sorry for her behavior not because of what she did to her mother, but because she let her mother provoke the aggression. The daughter sees herself as the victim. While it may seem contradictory, the vast majority of interviewees were caring and loving children who were doing everything to ensure the best care for their parents. This interpretation

INTERNET CONNECTIONS

The text discusses some of the issues surrounding *elder abuse and neglect.* Public service organizations in many American communities specialize in disseminating information related to this topic. One of these organizations is located in the East Bay region in California (Richmond). Go to their Web-site, "Elder Abuse Prevention," at

http://www.oaktrees.org/elder/

Click on "What is elder abuse?"; "How is it recognized?"; and "What should I do?" After you have reviewed the contents of this Website, respond to these questions:

1. Describe what elder abuse is and is not.
2. Try to imagine that you are an elderly citizen who is dependent on others for your care. What standards should apply to caregivers?

of the data supports the symbolic interactionist view that the definition of the situation is critical in understanding elder abuse.

It is clear that as life expectancy increases, caregiving responsibilities for family members will also increase, raising the question, How will we care for the caregivers? More than at any other time in history, adult children are providing not only more care, but more humane care, but we cannot assume this will continue without adequate resources. The caregiving role needs to be assessed in this light.

Advocacy and the Elderly: Senior Power

This chapter has demonstrated that throughout the world many contradictory attitudes are associated with being old. Respect for the wisdom of the aged is countered by disdain for the burdens they may create for others. Positive labels to describe the elderly (independent, capable, strong, senior citizen) appear alongside negative ones (disabled, decrepit, frail, burdensome). The sociological perspective helps explain these apparent contradictions. Research demonstrates that many of the beliefs about old age are false, especially the myth that old people are abandoned by their families. Applied sociology shows how such findings can be used to benefit the aged.

Combating ageism in our social institutions requires scientific data and a way to use it to the advan-

SOCIOLOGY OF EVERYDAY LIFE

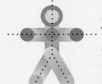

Seniorcitizen.Com

When grandmother Betty Fox began exploring the Web in search of sites dedicated to senior citizens, she discovered thousands of sites on an amazing array of topics—everything from supplemental medical insurance, Alzheimer's disease, and retirement relocation to investments, Elderhostel adventure travel, and Scrabble clubs. However, she also realized that the sites were in such a chaotic state that frustration rather than enlightenment often resulted from her Web surfing. She decided to set up her own Website to help older people navigate the Internet—www.grandmabetty.com. Today she not only offers links to other sites of interest to seniors, she peppers her senior-friendly Website with lifestyle tips, jokes, and news of senior activities throughout the globe. Her work has certainly paid off—she gets over 30,000 hits a day.

Betty Fox's successful foray into the Internet on behalf of senior citizens underscores an important point highlighted in this chapter: The elderly are an extremely diverse group of people who continue to learn and are enhanced by that learning. For example, most colleges now offer programs for lifelong education designed to enhance knowledge and update existing knowledge. In college classrooms, particularly in sociology classes, older adults offer insights about career experiences and raising children that are valued by their younger classmates. Outside the classroom, the elderly can log on to SeniorNet, a national nonprofit organization offering courses to help older adults learn computer and Internet skills. Keeping in touch with family and friends who do not live close by is the most cited reason for seniors' going online. Courses fill quickly, and keeping up with the demand for new courses attests to SeniorNet's popularity. Nearly 80 percent of its students are over 65; SeniorNet has a membership of over 39,000 and boasts over 220 learning centers throughout the United States.

The homebound, disabled, and elderly in long-term care facilities also benefit from the wired world, especially if nonprofit organizations provide the necessary technology. Research indicates that the elderly can be successfully introduced to what computers can do, particularly when conducted in a safe, supportive setting, allowing any problems with memory or new learning to be handled in a nonintimidating manner. People who may feel outmoded are brought to the present and eagerly anticipate the future. The image of the elderly as disinterested, fearful, and disengaged from the computerized world is simply not supported.

Consider the following facts related to computers and the elderly:

- Age is one of the best predictors of computer and online technology use. Baby boomers and young adults dominate use. However, over one-fourth of adults over age 50 use the Internet regularly and spend more time online than any other group. These are the baby boomers on the cusp of changing careers and early retirement. As early as 1996, another survey reported that one-third of seniors already use a computer, 9 percent use a modem, 4 percent use the Internet, and 11 percent say they intend to buy or

Although age alone does not uniformly separate people into voting blocs, it is clear that the elderly represent an important constituency that politicians are paying close attention to, especially in relation to income and health related issues such as Medicare, prescription drugs costs and Social Security. Many advocacy organizations led by the elderly have mobilized to fight efforts to privatize Social Security.

upgrade a computer. There is every reason to predict even higher computer usage as these groups age.

- The Internet has been used by senior citizens long enough to show distinct patterns about the sites they visit. As Betty Fox discovered, these marketers are developing senior-friendly messages and sites making it easier for seniors to smoothly navigate their sites.

- Senior citizens are overrepresented in visiting sites related to health care, pharmaceuticals, comparison shopping for older adult-based goods and services, and products designed to help with disabilities associated with aging, such as arthritis-friendly thermostats and home appliances, smoke alarms with lower frequency sounds for the hearing impaired, and voice-activated electronic memory devices to help older patients take medications on time and in proper dosage. Funeral-related sites are also extremely popular. Online wakes and, for the more traditional, live video feeds from the chapel, are being marketed to well-heeled and savvy older consumers.

Although many elderly benefit from computer technology, there still exists a "digital divide" between the "well-off and savvy" group and a significant number of their age-mates who are left out of the wired world. First, those over age 65 are the most underrepresented of all age groups in significant computer use. Of the one-third of senior citizens mentioned above who regularly use computers, most of them are financially secure and learned computer basics during middle age. Second, for the financially strapped elderly, a home computer with Internet access is considered an unaffordable luxury. Nonprofit groups providing computer hardware to the homebound can only service a small percentage of those who could benefit from the technology. When coupled with other disabilities such as visual impairment, arthritis, or paralysis of the upper body, even free services offered at senior centers and libraries are out of reach. The computer world remains a graphically intense world and, even with visual improvements on the horizon, reasonable eyesight, for example, is vital to computer usage.

Internet access is increasingly necessary to fully participate in today's society—and it will be even more important in the future. Elderly who have been bypassed due to disadvantages related to education, money, health, and age discrimination may not have enough time left to glimpse, much less access, the Internet phenomenon. The good news is that the digital divide is narrowing as the most well-educated population in American history—the current baby boomers—makes its way to senior citizen status.

1. Based on your current computer and Internet knowledge, predict your own use and capability when you reach the golden age of 65. What do sociologists suggest that will enhance or deter your computer literacy at that stage of life?

2. What suggestions would you offer to bridge the digital divide that separates some seniors from others in computer usage? Consider enterprises that are both profit and nonprofit in your suggestions.

Sources: Henderson, 1998; Russell, 1998; Whelan, 1998; Cleaver, 1999; *People,* 1999; Goldsborough, 2000; Perry, 2000; "Senior Net," http:www.seniornet.org.

---

tage of senior citizens. In general, older people are more interested in politics, are better informed, and have higher voting rates than younger people (Binstock, 2000). However, this profile has not translated into a voting bloc that is exercised on behalf of their age peers (Kleyman, 2000).

This lack of a voting bloc does not mean that the elderly cannot or will not come together as an age-specific political group or that age is not significant in how political issues are debated. Their numbers are growing. They are becoming better educated. They are an informed citizenry. Politicians recognize the potential for senior power. Recent debates over changes in Medicare and health policy, and especially over the cost of prescription drugs, have been geared toward senior citizens. If an age-based consciousness is lacking, politics will help create one.

But the real nurturers of a shared consciousness based on old age are the strong advocacy groups that have brought to the public's attention issues that impact senior citizens. Voluntary associations allow people to come together to work for morally worthwhile goals. On an international level, these associations are referred to as nongovernmental organizations (NGOs). There are a number of such associations working to advance the cause of older people, including the National Council of Senior Citizens, National Council of Retired Federal Employees, National Caucus and Center on the Black Aged, and National Senior Citizen's Law Center. An advocacy group more focused on fighting ageism is the Gray Panthers, with its motto of "age and youth in action." Founded by the late charismatic Maggie Kuhn, and with the assistance of thousands of volunteers, the Gray Panthers have been responsible for exposing scandalous conditions in nursing homes, monitoring the media on stereotypical portrayals of the elderly, fighting for housing suitable for older people and those who are physically challenged, and ensuring the political and economic rights of the aged. The Older Women's League (OWL) targets issues that perpetuate the double discrimination of gender and age, such as differential Social Security and pension plans, health insurance, and caregiving.

By far the largest and most influential advocacy organization for senior citizens is in the United States is the American Association of Retired Persons (AARP), which boasts a membership of over 35 million, one-third of whom are under age 60, but almost half between age 70 and 74 (AARP, 2002b). AARP has served to keep issues related to the aged in the public eye, especially in terms of health care. AARP has been successful in mobilizing support for a bill to add prescription drug coverage to Medicare (Barry, 2002). While age-based voting on issues is not the historical pattern in the United States, the drug coverage issue, still uncertain in outcome, is poised to become a major political issue in the next election. Some polls indicate that the party winning the prescription drug argument will control Congress (Machacek, 2002). AARP will assure that the issue remains in the public's eye.

The productive-aging theme is one that is likely shared by all of the advocacy groups mentioned above (Freedman, 2001). These groups demonstrate that the possibility for a stronger social movement based on senior power exists. Many associations in the United States have joined with their international counterparts to raise a global consciousness about old age. As activists in their own countries and with their allies abroad, they have the potential to become formidable NGOs. This chapter has shown that the elderly are not all alike. However, by capitalizing on their increasing numbers, they can gain improvements that will be beneficial for their age-mates in all social categories.

SUMMARY

1. Old age is defined differently in various cultures. In Western cultures old age is usually defined chronologically, but all cultures mark the aging process with role transitions.

2. Aging is a natural process that is influenced by stresses such as emotions and health habits. Primary aging refers to the physical changes that accompany aging; secondary aging refers to the life stresses that involve how our bodies and minds react to the social effects of growing old, such as age prejudice.

3. In general, old age is not associated with a significant decline in intelligence or with changes in personality. Psychological impairment is associated more with poor health and age prejudice.

4. Alzheimer's disease is an organic brain syndrome characterized by progressively deteriorating mental functions. It is not a normal part of aging. Most people who suffer from Alzheimer's disease are in the oldest old category, age 80 to 85 and above.

5. The elderly population is growing worldwide. Women outlive men all over the world. People are living longer and healthier lives, but care for the elderly toward the end of life strains resources of the developed world, which often relies on public funds for support.

6. Disengagement theory sees successful aging as the voluntary, mutual withdrawal of the aged and society from one another. In contrast, activity theory sees successful aging as a continuation of the usual roles and substitution of new ones if role loss occurs.

7. Continuity theory, a social psychological perspective, suggests that adjustment to old age is an extension of earlier personality development. Race, gender, and SES affect the aging process more than personality.

8. Age stratification theory emphasizes generational differences such as birth cohort in the aging process and the effects of separating the young and the old. Symbolic interactionism emphasizes adaptation and choices of behavior in old age. It also focuses on ageism and the effects of labels on these choices.

9. Most elderly people in the United States are married, live in their own homes, report good health, and are not isolated from their families.

10. The poverty of the aged was cut in half by the advent of Medicare. However, widows, racial minorities, and the oldest old are most likely to be poor. Many elderly are in multiple jeopardy because of several minority statuses.

11. Most Americans look forward to retirement. The most important determinants of satisfaction with retirement are health and financial status.

12. The majority of the elderly live in their own homes; only 5 percent are in long-term care facilities. The loss of a spouse produces such emotional distress that the surviving spouse is more susceptible to illness and death, especially suicide among widowers.

13. Later life in U.S. families shows high marital satisfaction for elderly couples. However, divorce and cohabitation are becoming more common.

The remarriage rate is higher for elderly men; for both genders, remarriage is higher for the divorced compared to the widowed. Grandparenting roles for the elderly are expanding so that many are now primary caregivers for their grandchildren.

14. Women tend to be the primary caregivers for elderly parents and relatives. Because many are juggling responsibilities of parenthood and elder care, they have been dubbed the "sandwich generation." About 4 percent of the elderly are abused or neglected by spouses or caregivers in all settings.

15. Many advocacy groups such as the Gray Panthers have been formed to combat ageism and promote positive thinking about the aged and the roles they can play in society.

KEY TERMS

activity theory 372
age grades 375
ageism 376
age stratification theory 375

continuity theory 374
disengagement theory 370
gerontocracy 375
gerontology 364

primary aging 365
sandwich generation 386
secondary aging 365

CRITICAL THINKING QUESTIONS

1. Demonstrate how biology, psychology, and sociology can work together to provide the best explanations for the process of aging. What theory from each discipline offers the best approach for interdisciplinary work?

2. Which social categories put people at most risk for social and individual problems when they become elderly? What social policies can be developed to reduce these risks to the benefit of all age groups?

3. What information can sociologists offer to the sandwich generation that can be helpful in deal-

ing with caregiving? What information can be offered to those elderly who face dependence on caregivers, whether these caregivers are family members or not?

4. Given your knowledge of family patterns in later life, how would you respond to an elderly relative, perhaps your own widowed parent, who reports to you that he or she wants to cohabit or remarry?

INVESTIGATE WITH CONTENT SELECT

Begin your research using Content-Select for this chapter by following the directions found on page 27 of this text to visit Prentice Hall's Research Navigator Website. Enter these search terms into the search field:

Ageism
Elder abuse
Retirement

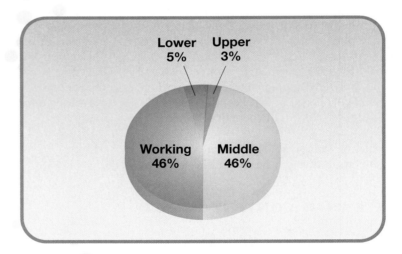

iNTERSECTIONS

EXERCISE 3. SELF-PERCEIVED SOCIAL CLASS

The United States is sometimes regarded a classless society, and indeed it is compared to many traditional societies that distinguished between a small aristocracy and the much larger peasantry. Even among Western industrialized nations, Americans are less divided by class lines than, say, citizens of Great Britain or France. Nonetheless, if you ask them, nearly all Americans have some notion of where they stand in the social hierarchy.

Interviewers for the General Social Surveys asked respondents, "If you were asked to use one of four names for your social class, which would you say you belong in: the lower class, the working class, the middle class, or the upper class?" By far the most popular choices are middle class (chosen by 46 percent of respondents) and working class (also chosen by 46 percent). Relatively few respondents rank themselves at the very bottom of society (only 5 percent chose lower class) or the very top (3 percent chose upper class). Why do you think GSS respondents so rarely place themselves in the highest or lowest social class? Where would you place yourself and your family?

For the remainder of this exercise, the four class categories are collapsed into two: "middle" (middle plus upper classes) and "working" (working plus lower classes).

We can examine determinants of social class perception at the Companion Website™, http://www.prenhall.com/lindsey. Click on the cover of this book, and select the appropriate INTERSECTIONS exercise from the drop-down menu at the top. (Make sure CHIP is set for % Down, and its Row Variable is Class.)

How does race affect perception of social class? It's an easy guess that white respondents tend to see themselves in a higher class than black respondents do, but how big do you think the race difference is? CHIP will tell you if you select Race as its Column Variable. Is the difference more or less than you expected?

In an idealized picture of American society, children from the poorest families have a chance when they grow up to move into the middle class, even into the upper class. But to what extent does that actually happen? How much does the social class of one's parents affect one's own social class? Answering this requires that we have a measure of parental social class. Family income is often used for this purpose. GSS respondents were asked to estimate their family's income as low, average, or high (relative to other families) when they were 16 years old. This variable name is abbreviated as Incom16. Using CHIP, see how a respondent's perceived class is affected by his or her family income when a teenager.

Another measure often used to represent a family's social class is the amount of education of the parents. All respondents in the GSS were asked the highest degree in school attained by each parent. The variable name for father's highest degree is Padeg. Using CHIP, see how respondent's social class depends on the father's highest school degree. Then see how respondent's social class depends on the mother's highest school degree (abbreviated Madeg). Whose educational level most affects the respondent's social class, the mother or the father?

Do you think this effect might work differently for men than for women? Perhaps the gender of respondents affects the relationship between father's education and the respondent's own social class. (Perhaps a father's educational level has more influence on his sons than on his daughters.) To check this requires a slightly more sophisticated analysis than we've been doing so far. The basic idea is to look for a relationship between Padeg and social class, as you did before, *but for each gender separately*. Then you can see if the relationship between Padeg and social class is stronger for one gender than the other.

To do this with CHIP, you start as before, choosing Padeg as your Column variable, then clicking "Crosstab." Now, in the box to the right of "Control by," highlight "Gender," then click "Control by," then click "Crosstab." The screen will display results labeled separately for men and for women. (You may have to use up or down arrows to see the entire display.)

What do you conclude about the effect of family background on one's own social class? Does the effect depend on the gender of the respondent?

15
THE FAMILY

9/11

"If I survived, I knew I would be a better brother."

Gedeon Naudet spoke these words as he waited for his brother Jules to return from the World Trade Center on September 11, 2001. He and his brother were filming a documentary about New York City firefighters. Jules was on a routine call 10 blocks from the World Trade Center on the morning of 9/11. He shot the pictures of the plane hitting and followed the firefighters as they rushed into Tower 1. Gedeon was at Engine Company 7; he raced to the scene and filmed the plane hitting Tower 2. Both Jules and Gedeon stayed to film the horrors that followed. Each brother thought the other was dead. Family members of the victims who saw the video expressed sincere appreciation to the Naudet brothers for risking their lives during the filming. Did 9/11 impact ideas and ideals about families? While the answer is a resounding yes, the value of a "family orientation" began quietly during the economic turmoil of the late 1990s as more and more people began to refocus their lives on what they say is important. Family and parenting is overtaking wealth and work for first place. Perhaps 9/11 was the culmination of this trend. On 9/11 Gedeon Naudet vowed to be a better brother. Whether other people's actions about families will match their words about families remains to be seen. (Jacoby, 2000; CBS News, *9-11*, March 10, 2002; Shellenbarger, 2002)

A Daughter's Story

I am a Chinese-Korean-American young woman. I was born two days before International Woman's Day, always a hectic time because my mother was busy going to meetings and organizing IWD pro-

grams. We weren't always close. As a young child I was resentful that she didn't spend more time with me. I felt closer to my father; he did things with me. My parents were probably gone the same amount of time but I blamed my mother more. She was supposed to be around. Looking back, I realize my mother made sure we had quality time together, while my father and I were content to bum around the house. I am a feminist by my own interpretation. Activism is definitely part of me. I would like to have the kind of relationship my parents have. They love, respect, and support each other but are not joined at the hip. They have learned, changed, and grown both as individuals and "together as one." (Adapted from Miriam Ching Yoon Louie and Nguyen Louie, 1998)

The family is not only a cultural universal (Chapter 3), it is the oldest and most conservative of the social institutions, the basic unit around which all social organization is built, and fundamental to the process of meeting social needs. In cultures that have relatively undifferentiated social organization, the family *is* society. As the vignettes suggest, family bonds are strengthened in adversity. If families are strong, then society as a whole will benefit from their strength. Also, expectations about how married couples should treat each other and how parents should treat children are learned in the family. This chapter examines the remarkable diversity of the family and how social change accelerates this diversity. It also sheds light on why such diversity can be viewed either as a threat to social stability or an opportunity for family enhancement and individual growth.

WHAT IS A FAMILY?

Sociologists who study families find it easier to describe what families do than what they are. Identifying the functions of the family first gives us a better idea of what they are; it is also a springboard for assessing how well they are accomplishing their tasks and how they are responding to the impact of social change.

Family Functions

Almost a century of data suggests near consensus in both sociology and anthropology that the family carries out vital social functions (Ogburn, 1938; Parsons & Bales, 1955; Dreman, 1997). A review of these functions includes some key terms sociology applies to the social organization of the family.

1. *Reproduction.* In a fundamental sense, the future of the society is in the hands of the family. Families ensure that dying members of society will be replaced in an orderly fashion so there is a new generation to carry on. In most societies, the **family of procreation** is established at marriage and is the culturally approved sexual union that legitimizes childbearing.

2. *Regulation of sexual behavior.* All societies restrict sexual relations and reproduction among certain family members. The incest taboo is a powerful cultural universal (Chapter 3). **Exogamy** is a cultural norm in which people marry outside a particular group. For the family, exogamy is a mandate forbidding marriage between close kin. In the United States, for example, 30 states do not allow first cousins to marry (Willing, 2002).

3. *Socialization.* The **family of orientation** is the family in which children grow up; it is the vehicle for primary socialization of children, providing both social and individual benefits. In the family of orientation, children learn basic competencies, such as language, sexual rules, gender roles, and other behavioral norms that allow them to become fully functioning members of society. In the process, they also develop a sense of self. As we saw in Chapter 5, the self-esteem that is fostered in the family becomes a defining characteristic of people as they move into adulthood.

4. *Protection, affection, and companionship.* The family provides the essential economic and emotional support to its members during all the events and inevitable crises in a typical family life cycle. To augment support for family members, roles are assigned. In traditional families, the husband–father usually takes the *instrumental role*, in which he is expected to maintain the physical integrity of the family by providing food and shelter and linking the family to the world outside the home. In the *expressive role*, the wife–mother is expected to cement relationships and provide emotional support.

The "traditional" family has taken several forms, such as the 1930s extended family of The Waltons *and the two-parent–two-child model today. However, neither form was or is the American norm.*

5. *Social placement.* Families provide ascribed status, which places children in various social hierarchies from birth. Children are born into the same place in the stratification system occupied by their parents. This social location is related to **endogamy**, a cultural norm in which people marry within certain groups, with social class, race, and religion among the most important elements. Social placement is also tied to patterns of descent and inheritance. In societies that use **patrilineal descent**, common throughout Asia, Africa, and the

Middle East, the family name is traced through the father's line, and sons and male kin usually inherit family property. In **matrilineal descent**, the least common pattern today and throughout recorded history, the family name is traced through the mother's line, and daughters of female kin usually inherit family property. **Bilateral (or bilineal) descent** uses both parents to trace family lines and is most common in Western societies. In the bilateral pattern women typically assume their husband's surname at marriage, but family connections are recognized between children and the kin of both parents. Bilateral systems do not ensure that females can inherit property, but they are the least restrictive in this regard. The critical point is that family name is significant in social placement and can enhance a child's prospects for upward mobility. This is clear, for example, when a Smith or a Jones marries a Rockefeller or a Roosevelt.

Family Structure

Families carry out these social functions within a variety of family structures. In many regions of the developing world, large families are functional for subsistence agriculture, to produce goods for family use or for sale or exchange when surpluses are available. As long as it can feed itself, a larger family unit of production provides an economic advantage. In the developed world, the family has been transformed from a unit of *production* to one of *consumption*. **Extended families**, consisting of parents, dependent children, and other relatives, usually of at least three generations living in the same household, are typical in rural areas throughout the world. In urban areas, larger families are at an economic disadvantage, since families consume but do not produce goods. Thus, **nuclear families**, consisting of wife, husband, and their dependent children who live apart from other relatives in their own residence, are more typical globally in urban areas.

Family structure has been profoundly altered by industrialization and urbanization, the two key elements of the process of modernization (Chapter 22). Modernization in the developed world followed a typical pattern: As industrialization accelerated, more and more families moved from farms into cities, families became smaller, and men and women became wage earners. Evidence shows that the nuclear family structure was typical in urban areas in Western Europe as early as the 17th century (Lasch, 1979; Berger & Berger, 1991). We can draw several implications from this pattern:

1. Modernization processes continue to modify a nuclear family model that is at least 300 years old.

2. Modifications show up as changes in the roles of husband and wife in nuclear families. Today, nuclear families with dual-earner couples in more egalitarian gender roles are normative.

3. Modifications also show up as changes in the structure of nuclear families. Examples of such changes include increased numbers of single-parent families, cohabiting couples with children, blended families, and gay and lesbian families.

The contemporary reality is that the "traditional" nuclear family is but one of many variations on a theme. Since the conventional definition is too limited to encompass the structural diversity of U.S. households (Figure 15.1), especially those without marriage partners, a more inclusive definition is needed. For example, the U.S. Bureau of the Census (2001) uses the term *family* to describe a group of two or more persons related by blood, marriage, or adoption who reside together. A *subfamily* consists of a married couple and their children *or* one parent with one or more never-married children under 18 living in a household. The term subfamily, then, combines the traditional nuclear family with other family forms. Finally, notice that all varieties of "families" are not the same as households. A **household** is a person or group of people who occupy a housing unit. There are family households, nonfamily households, and households made up of both family and nonfamily members. These definitions may appear overly picky, but as we will see, how a family is defined makes a profound difference in the lives of many people.

THEORETICAL PERSPECTIVES ON THE FAMILY

All theoretical perspectives in sociology recognize that the family is pivotal in carrying out the functions described above. There is also general agreement that the functions can be carried out within a variety of family structures found across the globe. However, sociologists disagree about the benefits and liabilities to the family associated with social change.

Functionalism

The functionalist perspective highlights family tasks as vital for social stability. If the institution of the family is ineffective in carrying out requisite social "duties," and other institutions have not picked up the slack, social equilibrium will be compromised. From the functionalist perspective, the socialization of children into non-overlapping and accepted social roles—instrumental for boys and expressive for girls—is central to social stability. Role change and ambiguity of

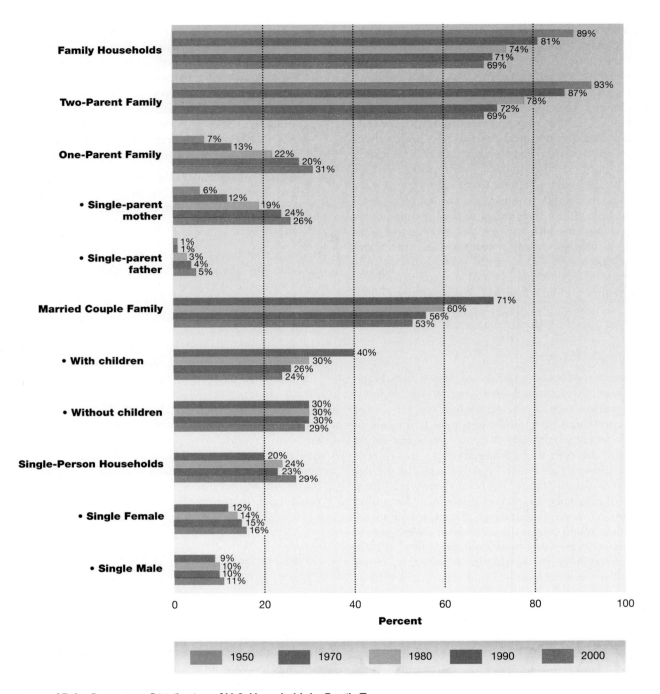

FIGURE 15.1 Percentage Distribution of U.S. Households by Family Type by Selected Years

Source: Adapted from Tables 54 and 57, U.S. Bureau of the Census, 2001.

roles are disruptive to family harmony and also to broader social harmony. Functionalists feel strongly that families must somehow be made immune to social change. Functionalists favor a traditional family model with a wage-earning husband who has final power over decisions, and a dependent wife and children. This model becomes the ideal to which all families should adhere.

CRITIQUE The problem with the functionalist view is that change is inevitable, so what is "traditional" changes over time. Although the traditional model is believed to be both the historical and contemporary norm in the United States, it emerged only a century ago, was associated with white, middle- and upper-class families, was never the norm, and is far from the norm today (Coontz, 1992, 1997). Nostalgia is expressed for a family unit typifying only a minority of Americans. Functionalist snapshots of families taken at different times in history show that the model for the traditional family varies over time. The three-generation family living in the same household was believed to be normative in the early 20th century. This belief was perpetuated by television shows such as *The Waltons*, which depicted a three-generation farm family surviving the Depression by hard work, faith, and devotion to family. A "new" traditional family emerged in the 1950s and has served as the ideal ever since, when television gave us *Leave It to Beaver* and *Father Knows Best*. These shows portrayed a patriarchal family model with a bread-earning husband, a homemaker mother, and their at-home children.

Conflict Theory

Conflict theory focuses on the social placement function of the family in preserving existing inequality and power relations in the broader society. According to this perspective, social class endogamy and inheritance patterns ensure that property and wealth are kept in the hands of a few powerful families. Inequality becomes institutionalized through socialization, so the notion that family wealth is deserved is perpetuated—that those born into poor families remain poor because they lack talent and a work ethic. The structural conditions that sustain poverty are ignored. When social placement operates through patriarchal and patrilineal systems, wealth is further concentrated in the hands of males, which promotes female subservience, neglect, and poverty. Conflict theorists suggest that when women gain economic strength by also being wage earners, their power inside the home is also strengthened and can lead to more egalitarian arrangements.

CRITIQUE With its focus on control of economic resources in the family and the jealous guarding of family property both between and within families, conflict theory has been criticized for disregarding the cooperation that is also part of family life. Family members are highly altruistic and kin and nonkin networks offer major sources of support to families in a variety of ways—even when their own well-being is compromised. Also, research shows that a paycheck for women may not bring with it egalitarian roles in their homes.

Feminist Perspective

Feminist scholars in the 1960s and 1970s viewed the traditional patriarchal family as a major site for the oppression of women. Feminists expressed concern that when the patriarchal family is viewed as beneficial to social stability, it hampers the movement into egalitarian roles desired by both men and women. Since the 1980s, the feminist perspective broadened considerably to include not just gender, but race, class, and sexuality as other avenues of oppression to women in the family.

Feminists recognize that gendered family relations do not occur in a vacuum and that lives are helped or hurt by the resources outside the family that shape what is happening inside the family (Baca Zinn, 2000). Along with gender, for example, single-parent African American, Latino, and Native American women are disadvantaged by race when they seek employment necessary to support their families. Lesbians must deal with a system that represses same-sex relationships when they fight for custody of their children. However, feminists suggest that women may be doubly or triply disadvantaged by their race, class, or sexuality, but they are not helpless victims: they possess *agency*—the power to adapt and even thrive in difficult situations.

CRITIQUE With a view of marriage and the family focusing on oppression of women, feminists tend to minimize the practical benefits of marriage, including economic resources and social support (Waite & Gallagher, 2000). Feminist scholars also find it difficult to reconcile research suggesting that women in traditional marriages are as satisfied with their choices as women in egalitarian marriages. Finally, the acceptance of all forms of family diversity that highlight informal power and human agency may disregard situations such as domestic abuse, where both law and custom maintain women's victimization (Umberson et al., 1998).

Symbolic Interactionism

Symbolic interactionists suggest that there are many subjective meanings attached to what a family is "supposed" to be and what its members are "supposed" to do. But in our daily lives we adapt these beliefs to fit our own definitions and accommodate our own needs. As we saw from the census classifications, the definition of a family is not written in stone. It shifts with the broader social changes. These shifts show up in how people are labeled. The offspring of unmarried women are less likely to be referred as "illegitimate," for example. Symbolic interactionists also focus on how couples take on family roles that become traditionally gendered, even when they desire egalitarian marriages. The definitions of what a man and woman are "supposed" to do in the home are powerful and are reinforced every time we carry out our family roles. However, since family members can negotiate these definitions, over time the roles may change to what a couple desires rather than what they currently have.

CRITIQUE As a microlevel perspective, symbolic interactionism tends to downplay larger social structures in explaining family dynamics. Men and women interact not only as individual family members but according to other roles they play in society and the prestige associated with those roles. For example, a wealthy white man who holds a powerful position in a corporation does not dissolve those roles when he walks into his home. They shape his life at home, in the workplace, and the other social institutions in which he takes part. Race, class, and gender offer a range of privileges bestowed by the broader society that also allow for a power base to be established in his home. Power and privilege can result in a patriarchal family regardless of the couples' desire for a more egalitarian arrangement.

GLOBAL PERSPECTIVES ON THE FAMILY

What you have learned about the diversity of family forms common to Western cultures will make it easier to grasp the extraordinary global variations in families. This section provides examples of marriage and family forms typical of other societies across the globe.

Marriage Forms and Residence Patterns

Cultural norms (exogamy and endogamy) and legal requirements determine who is allowed to marry whom. Most Western societies enforce **monogamy**, marriage to one spouse at a time. **Polygamy** means marriage to more than one spouse at a time. Although most non-Western societies allow for polygamy, plural marriages are infrequent. Polygamy is usually associated with extended families and with either **patrilocal residence**—the couple moves into the husband's home at marriage—or **matrilocal residence**—the couple moves into the wife's home at marriage. The cost of providing for the large extended families that accompany polygamy explains why this form is so infrequent even in societies that allow it.

The most common form of plural marriage is **polygyny**, in which a man can marry more than one woman at a time. In sub-Saharan Africa, South Asia, and the Middle East, polygyny correlates with high levels of gender inequality. For polygynous marriages in Ghana, for example, women have less communication with their spouses, less control over family planning, and are viewed by their husbands as easily replaceable (Agadjanian & Ezeh, 2000). In the United States an estimated 100,000 Mormon dissidents residing primarily in Utah, Arizona, and Idaho live in polygynous families. Polygamy is a felony, but in areas with large numbers of polygynists the police do little to enforce the law. It is only when cases of forced marriage, domestic abuse, or incest surface that the law takes a serious look at polygyny (Egan, 1999).

A rare form of plural marriage found in less than 1 percent of the world's societies is **polyandry**, in which a woman can marry more than one man at a time, usually brothers. It exists today among the remaining few hundred people of the Toda tribe in south India, among some isolated Tibetan peoples, among the Marquesan Islanders of the south Pacific, and among the Surui of the Amazon region of Brazil. Plural marriage, especially polyandry, is linked to high degrees of female subordination that produces an almost insurmountable chasm separating the gen-

Polygamy still exists in the United States even though it is illegal. Here, Alex Joseph sits surrounded by his nine wives.

GLOBAL CONNECTIONS

The Second Wives of Hong Kong

Every Friday evening the trains between Hong Kong and Mainland China are filled to capacity. People crammed into second-class coaches bring huge bags of clothing, food, and household utensils to kin on the Mainland. These people are noticeable because their clothing is threadbare, their backs are humped, and their skin is weathered from a life of physical labor. In the first-class cars are another group of people—mostly men—also bringing items to the Mainland. Their well-appointed suitcases are filled with exotic food, luxury household products, and designer clothing. They wear expensive leisure clothes, sport Rolex watches, and if their skin is weathered, it is because of too much time on a sunny golf course. These Hong Kong men will spend the weekend with their "second wives" across the border in Shenzhen. Sometimes referred to as "China's Tijuana," Shenzhen was decreed in 1980 a Special Economic Zone where capitalism is allowed to thrive unfettered. The result, according to one journalist, is that Shenzhen is a city of "laissez-faire business and institutionalized lust." Thousands of women from impoverished areas migrate to Shenzhen in search of love and money. Hong Kong men flock to Shenzhen for the same two reasons. Shenzhen offers extraordinary business opportunities for men enthusiastically pursuing China's mandate that "to get rich is glorious." They find young, attractive, and eager Mainland women willing to exchange love for the chance to become the second wife of a rich man. For the most part, the second wives are in stable relationships and are provided apartments, gifts, and generous monthly allowances to support themselves and the children that they often have with their "husbands" from Hong Kong.

Why does a man want a second wife? From his perspective, she is affordable and available. She gives him what he regards as "needed" psychological and sexual release when he is away from home. And because a new family is established and provided for by the liaison, he justifies the union as legitimate. Peer pressure also plays a role. The "good boys" *(houdzai)* are teased by other men and told that the first wife *(silai)* is getting old, dull, and dumb, and losing her feminine qualities. Why does a woman agree to be a second wife? From her perspective, being a second wife is far superior to being a sex worker or having a passionate but brief extramarital affair. Even if she is "less than" a wife, she is "more than" a mistress. More important, compared to her impoverished existence before she migrated to Shenzhen, this new life offers her higher status, stable income, and upward mobility. Her children could become Hong Kong citizens. When he dies, she may inherit half his wealth, with the other half going to his legal wife across the border. China's effort to outlaw second wives is reflected in a sweeping new marriage law, the first since 1980, to shore up unstable marriages and deal with a divorce rate that has quadrupled in two decades. The law stresses "mutual responsibility and faithfulness in marriage." However, it has not had much success in cracking down on Hong Kong's philandering husbands. While the law gives first wives some legal recourse, it is costly and embarrassing to track down the "second" families, prove bigamy, sue their husbands, and deal with a court system in Mainland China where officials are routinely paid off for rulings that benefit husbands. In addition, media accounts seldom blame the men for their cross-border lives. It is the first wife who is at fault—she needs to be retrained to serve her husband better. The law has been unable to deal with strong cultural beliefs that implicitly condone the behavior of these men.

1. Do you think that a law requiring "faithfulness in marriage" will be successful? How would functionalists and feminists view such a law?

2. What suggestions would you offer to Hong Kong first wives when they suspect their husbands have second wives? How do you think the second wives view the first wives?

Sources: Fan & Huang, 1998; Daswani, 1999; Gittings, 2000; Perry, 2001; So, 2001; Pomfret, 2002.

---

ders in virtually all aspects of their lives (Cassidy & Lee, 1989; Calafell et al., 1999).

Dowry Marriage Customs

In many cultures a woman's value is determined by what she can bring to the family in the form of a *dowry*, a payment from the bride's family to her husband's family to compensate them for her support. Dowry customs contrast with the less common custom of *bridewealth*, where the groom's family transfers goods or money to the brides' family to compensate them for the loss of her services (Scupin, 1998). Dowry systems dominate in cultures where arranged marriages are normative, women's status is low, and the bride takes up residence in the groom's household. They existed in colonial America and are found throughout contemporary Asia and the South Pacific, the Middle East, and Eastern Europe. In almost all cultures, marriage unites families as well as couples. Dowries are critical in determining how well the bride will fare in her new extended family and the degree to which the families will cooperate with one another (Watson & Ebrey, 1991; Dubey, 2001).

India is a case in point. Dowry deaths have increased 15-fold since the mid-1980s in all castes. When dowries are considered too paltry, the torture or death of the bride can occur. In many cases the bride is doused with kerosene and set on fire so that the death looks like a cooking accident. Official figures from cities like Bombay show that one in four deaths of young women is due to so-called "accidental" incineration. Unreported dowry deaths, plus cases of abuse, neglect, and female infanticide, are most likely involved in cases of the 22 million Indian females who are simply "missing" (Breakaway, 1995; Hitchcock, 2001). Dowry systems remain strong in the developing world, especially in rural areas. Abuses are clearly tied to women's subservience and persist in those societies that severely restrict women's roles.

Communal Families

Both globally and in the United States, communes have existed throughout history; like families overall, they vary considerably in structure and function. **Communes** are collective households in which people who may or may not be related share roles typically associated with families. During the turbulent era of the 1960s, many young people in the United States deserted conventional marriage and family practices and opted for different styles of cooperative living. Communal arrangements in the United States are usually short-lived, however, since utopian visions and beliefs about family relationships are at odds with the rest of society (Smith, 1999; Sosis, 2000). In Denmark and Sweden, on the other hand, communes are institutionalized as alternatives to nuclear families. For many young people, communes represent a normative stage in marriage and family formation that allows them to live cooperatively and intimately with others who may become marriage partners.

Dating from almost a century ago, the largest secular communal type is the *kibbutz*, an Israeli agricultural collective in which children are raised together in an arrangement that allows their parents to become full participants in the economic life of the community. Until about 1970, kibbutzim (plural form) were characterized by collectivization in family and work life that minimized gender role differences. Today, however, agriculture is no longer profitable enough to sustain the strong egalitarian ideology of the traditional kibbutz, and gender stratification has increased (Gavron, 2000). Second and third generations of kibbutzim children are abandoning the kibbutz in favor of urban living and nuclear families. Currently, the communal kibbutz family is neither extended nor completely nuclear. In most kibbutzim,

the child-centered approach is being gradually replaced by the family-centered approach—"nuclear-like" in structure—with children raised by their parents and living at home (Fidler, 1999). Although it is uncertain what the kibbutz family will look like in the future, kibbutzim members are equipping themselves with the social and economic tools to bolster community survival (Mort & Brenner, 2000).

LOVE, MARRIAGE, AND DIVORCE— AMERICAN STYLE

Americans are so accustomed to viewing love and marriage as inseparable that it is rather startling to realize that they have been paired only recently in the United States. Romantic love as an ideal existed in Europe centuries ago, but it was not seen as a basis for marriage. Marriage was an economic obligation that affected power, property, and privilege and could not be based on something as transitory or volatile as romantic love. Marriage was the mundane but necessary alternative to the enchantment of feudal romance and courtly love games reserved for the aristocracy. For the vast majority of people, personal fulfillment and compatibility of the couple were irrelevant. The decision to marry was rational rather than romantic.

The Puritan era in the United States ushered in the revolutionary idea that love and marriage should be tied together. This was a radical departure from early church teachings, which warned men that even looking on their wives with lust made them sinners. In the new ideal, if love was not the reason for marriage, it was expected to flourish later. Parental control over approval of marriage partners remained the norm, but the belief that love should play a part in the process became etched into the fledgling American consciousness. Today the idea of love as a factor in assessing a marriage partner is gaining worldwide popularity, but initially it was a phenomenon uniquely associated with the United States.

Mate Selection

Love can make you want to die, but it can also make you want to live. (Anonymous)

Since love is one of the most complicated emotions, beliefs about love have produced many myths (Table 15.1). Our attitudes and behaviors about gender roles, marriage, and the family are impacted by romantic ideals that are not enough to sustain couples for the adaptability and long-term commitment necessary for marriage. Although romantic love is idealistic, it is also very structured. Social structural characteristics such as age, race, and social class of potential

TABLE 15.1

How Do I Love Thee? Myths of Romantic Love

Sociological research shows that what we often believe to be true about love is in reality romantic myth.

Myth	Reality
1. Love conquers all.	1. A person's partner cannot fulfill all needs and make all problems disappear.
2. Women are the romantic gender.	2. Men fall in love sooner and express love earlier in the relationship than do women.
3. Women are more emotional when they fall in love.	3. Related to #2, men are more idealistic; women are more pragmatic about love.
4. Love is blind.	4. The process of falling in love is highly patterned.
5. Opposites attract.	5. We fall in love with people similar to ourselves.
6. Love and marriage are prerequisites for sex.	6. Sex is likely in a relationship regardless of love, and premarital or nonmarital sex is now normative.
7. Absence makes the heart grow fonder.	7. Out of sight, out of mind. This is the problem with high school romances and leaving for different colleges. It is also the problem with commuter marriages.
8. The opposite of love is hate.	8. The "opposite" of love is more likely to be indifference—emotions are neutralized.

partners are of enormous importance in mate selection. Sociology documents the impact of **homogamy**, becoming attracted to and marrying someone similar to yourself. If romantic love were the sole basis for mate selection, coupling would occur by chance; instead, homogamy results in **assortive mating**, coupling based on similarity. Assortive mating assumes that people who are culturally similar to one another have more opportunities to meet people similar to themselves than more dissimilar to themselves (Kalmijn & Flap, 2001). College, for example, is a powerful marriage market where people meet, date, fall in love, and marry. Parents send children to certain colleges with the expectation that they will not only receive an excellent education but will meet potential partners from similar backgrounds.

AGE, RACE, AND SOCIAL CLASS   The critical variable influencing mate selection is age. Most people marry others within a few years of their own ages. If there is an age difference, the man is usually older than the woman. Traditional gender expectations

In the United States, the large majority of people select marriage partners from others in their own race, but interracial marriages are rapidly increasing. A common interracial pattern is a Caucasian woman marrying a man of color, such as an African American man, or as shown here, a Jamaican-American man.

dictated that men must gain the requisite education and job skills necessary to support a family, thus keeping them out of marriage longer than women. Today women represent half of all college students and half of the labor force (see Chapter 13), so traditional gender roles are being altered significantly; as a result, women's age at first marriage is approaching that of men (Bonds & Nicks, 1999).

Of all demographic variables, homogamy is strongest for race. Between 1970 and 2000, interracial marriages tripled. In Hawaii, almost half of all marriages are interracial (Fu & Heaton, 2000; U.S. Bureau of the Census, 2001: Table 50). Since the U.S. Census now allows an option of multiple racial responses, it is certain that the numbers of interracial marriages will surge. However, interracial marriages are still relatively rare, accounting for about 3 percent of all marriages (Table 15.2). Of these, less than 1 percent are African American–white marriages, with about 70 percent of these consisting of a white wife and an African American husband. The remainder are between whites and nonblacks, the two most typical patterns being Asian and Native American women marrying white men.

When comparing race and class in these marriages, the data generally support homogamy in socioeconomic status (Kalmijn, 1998; Root, 2001). When differences in socioeconomic status do occur, the woman's socioeconomic status is usually lower than the man's, a pattern that cuts across all races. When African Americans and whites are attracted to one another, the reasons are generally the same as in racially homogeneous couples—they share similar

interests, values, and background (Chrohn, 1995; Brown, 2000) As one couple reported,

> . . . everyone else was looking at us as a Black and white couple, which I think is really stupid because we are just a married couple. We're just a couple who decided we want to be with one another. (Rosenblatt et al., 1995:25)

THE MARRIAGE SQUEEZE   For both genders, age at marriage is also affected by the proportion of women and men who are available. When there is an unbalanced ratio of marriage-age women to marriage-age men, a marriage squeeze exists, in which one gender has a more limited pool of potential marriage partners. Figure 15.2 shows that most people marry in their mid-20s and men marry women who are a few years younger than themselves. After World War II the birthrate increased considerably (the "baby boom" era). There were more women born in 1950 than men born in 1940. By the 1980s there was a shortage of marriageable men. Because of the sharp decline in birthrates in the 1960s and 1970s, men now in their mid-20s face a shortage of women (Eshleman, 2000).

GENDER   Whereas homogamy is the mate selection norm, it is filtered by the *marriage gradient*, in which women tend to marry men of higher socioeconomic status, the conventional practice used by women for upward mobility. Although this practice is weaker today, data still clearly support that "marrying up" is the path many women choose to bolster economic security. The marriage gradient is functional for women—even for college-educated women—who prefer men with the earnings capacity necessary to support a family (Melton & Lindsey, 1987; Albrecht et al., 1997; Coltrane, 1998).

Both men and women pay close attention to physical attractiveness in assessing potential mates, but men place a higher value on it than women (Regan & Berscheid, 1997; Subramanian, 1997). For a quick confirmation of this fact, pick up any newspaper devoted to ads for dating partners. Men's ads are more likely to mention "beautiful and slender" or "weight in proportion to height" as desired traits. Women are more likely to mention affluence, success, and interpersonal understanding as desired traits (Smith et al., 1990; Cicerello & Sheehan, 1995; Fetto, 2000). Male preoccupation with physical attractiveness cuts across race and social class. In addition, since men value it more than women and it is the first trait they notice when checking out possible dating partners, physical attractiveness is an important factor in explaining why men fall in love sooner than women.

Theoretical perspectives in sociology explain the marriage gradient. According to functionalists, tradi-

TABLE 15.2

Interracial Marriages for Selected Years (in thousands)

	1980	1990	2000
Same race couples	48,264	50,889	55,033
Interracial couples	651	964	1462
Black/white	167	211	363
Black husband/white wife	122	150	268
White husband/black wife	45	61	95
White/other race*	450	720	1051
Black/other race*	34	33	50
Hispanic/non-Hispanic origin	891	1,193	1,742

* Excludes white and black.
Source: Adapted from Table MS-3, U.S. Bureau of the Census, 2001.

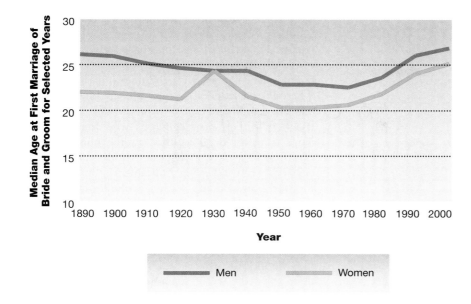

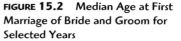

FIGURE 15.2 **Median Age at First Marriage of Bride and Groom for Selected Years**

Source: Adapted from Table 159, U.S. Bureau of the Census, 1998 and Table MS-2, U.S. Bureau of the Census, 2001.

tional gender socialization—expressive roles for women and instrumental roles for men—contribute to social stability. An attractive woman may have more of an advantage in "marrying up," but she, her family, and society as a whole will benefit. According to conflict theorists, men do not need to be as attractive, because they possess greater economic power than women. Once economic power is in place outside the home, men will use it to maintain dominance within the home. The feminist perspective suggests that when excluded from power, women become objects of exchange. The marriage gradient in mate selection serves to reduce women to objects based on appearance and disregards their other statuses, such as personal accomplishments and occupational success. Symbolic interactionists assert that the marriage gradient may produce a self-fulfilling prophecy: Women may come to view themselves the way they are viewed by men—merely as objects of exchange based on varying degrees of beauty.

Successful Marriages and Families

Marriage is satisfying for most couples; both wives and husbands express happiness with their spouses (Michael et al., 1994) (see Figure 15.3). Married people, particularly men, are more physically and emotionally healthy than the unmarried (Gove et al., 1990; Wickrama et al., 1997; Waldron et al., 1998). For marriages based on romantic love, the happiest families are those with high levels of respect, sharing, physical intimacy, communication, trust, loyalty, sacrifice, and emotional support (Klagsbrun, 1995; Barich & Bielby, 1996). Higher education, income, and approval of the marriage by the couples' parents also have beneficial effects on marital quality and stability, especially in societies where marriages are arranged by parents or matchmakers (Smith & Moreau, 1998; Bloch & Ryder, 2000; Pimentel, 2000).

Children bring joy to a couple but also increased marital tension. The easygoing B.C. (Before Children) couple in the first years of marriage can decide on an hour's notice to go to the mountains for the weekend. Children change everything. Work, commitment, time, and energy are needed to keep the marital relationship healthy and strong. Focusing on couplehood in turn allows for better parenting. The B.C. life is gone forever, even after children leave home (Baldwin, 1988). Some couples express fear that raising children hurts their expectations for romantic marriage that must be put on hold until after the children leave home (Weiss, 2000:128). While more energy is expended on children-related issues than on marriage-related ones, tension is balanced by the gratification that comes from being parents (Belsky & Kelly, 1995; Cushman et al., 1996; Rogers & White, 1998). There is life after parenthood. Successful couples do not take their relationship for granted even when their stress as parents is high. Sociologists consistently document that marriage and family are what most people want and that they are happy with their choices (Michael et al., 1994; Boyer-Penninton et al., 2001).

Egalitarian Marriages

The alternative to the traditional family desired above is one where the marriage, hence the family, is egalitarian in both structure and function. In an **egalitarian marriage**, partners share decision making and assign family roles based on talent and choice rather than on traditional beliefs about gender. The Scandinavian countries, specifically Norway and Sweden, consistently rank the highest in all measures of human development, including gender role egalitari-

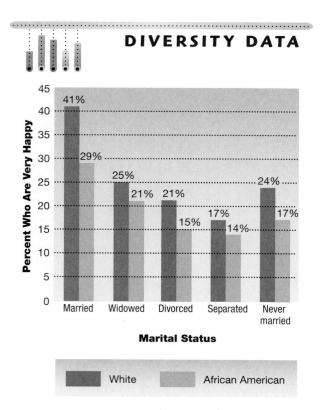

DIVERSITY DATA

FIGURE 15.3 **How Do Marital Status and Race Relate to Happiness?** For all categories of marital status, both African American and white married people report the highest happiness level. Surprisingly, widowed people are happier than those who are divorced, separated or never married, regardless of race. What are the happiness "benefits" of marriage? Do the benefits carry over even when the spouse dies? Do you think that divorced and separated people would have reported lower levels of "very happy" *during* their marriage?

Source: NORC. General Social Surveys, 1972–2000. Chicago: National Opinion Research Center, 2000.

anism and public policies designed to bolster it in the family (Eisler et al., 1995; United Nations Development Program, 2001; Wennemo, 2001)

Instead of ranking husband over wife, egalitarian marriage means that a partnership pattern emerges, one that is strongly associated with paid employment for wives. This pattern suggests that when wives contribute financially to the family, their decision-making powers are enhanced. Perceived imbalance in decision making lowers marital satisfaction for both husband and wife (Knudson-Martin & Mahoney, 1998; Rogers & Amato, 2000). Egalitarian marriage fosters better communication and sharing. It may be described as a "peer marriage," which builds on a strong, empathic friendship between spouses (Schwartz, 1994). Conflict may occur, but it allows for

open communication (Burleson & Denton, 1997; Guilbert et al., 2000). Children also benefit from egalitarianism, since parents share the joy and burden of childrearing more equitably, and the needs of the couple are balanced with the needs of their children. The two sets of needs cannot be separated. This balance is very important to women who are happy in their egalitarian marriages but who must deal with what is referred to as the "motherhood mandate" (Hoffnung 1995). As suggested by Susan Maushart's (1999:3) research, egalitarianism "unmasks" the motherhood mandate because women can openly talk about both the joys and turmoil of motherhood. The mask of motherhood is revealed in cultural values glorifying its ideal, but takes for granted its work. The mask shows up in debates about child care that pass judgments on "what's best for the child," as if the child's needs were separable from those of the mother, father, and siblings.

The benefits of egalitarian marriages are bolstered by longitudinal research on children of all races that compares them according to whether their mothers worked outside the home or not. The results show that on measurements of self-esteem, academic achievement, and behavior problems in both family types, children are not harmed in their development. This study is important because the results applied to mothers who worked outside the home when their children were babies and preschoolers (Harvey, 1999). To the relief of egalitarian couples, results such as these continue to be confirmed. Motherhood and working for pay does not harm children—to the contrary, it often improves their social and intellectual development (Chira, 1998).

For both men and women, attitudes about gender roles in marriage are shifting toward an egalitarian model (Cherlin, 1998; Botkin et al., 2000). However, the goal of behavior change remains elusive. Over 30 years of research shows that egalitarian marriages remain compromised when wives work full time outside the home and husbands do not share domestic roles with them on anywhere near an equal basis (Geerkin & Gove, 1983; Press & Townsley, 1998; Coltrane, 2001; Walzer, 2001). Most employed wives of all social classes walk into their homes to what sociologists now refer to as a "second shift" of unpaid household work after a day of paid employment (Hochschild, 1989). According to women, "helping out" at home is not the same as true task sharing, especially if their husbands' share of the domestic division of labor is taken up by child care and traditional male chores. According to men, wives have such high standards for housework that whatever they do is not good enough. "Chore wars" remain the thorn in the side of making egalitarianism work for both men and women (Kluwer et al., 1997; Lasswell, 1997).

Despite the household task overload women face, the trend toward egalitarian marriages is unlikely to slow down (Fan & Marini, 2000). We have seen that marital satisfaction, gender equity, and communication are enhanced when men and women are partners, when women engage in satisfying employment, and when men get involved in housework (Hoffman & Kloska, 1995; Peters, 1998; Risman & Johnson-Summerfield, 2001). As society becomes more gender equitable, marriages will become more egalitarian.

Divorce

An enduring marriage is not necessarily a successful one. People often stay together in conflict-ridden or devitalized marriages for the sake of children or because of other obligations (Amato, 2001; Furstenberg & Kiernan, 2001). Children display greater behavior problems after separation and divorce, but may have even greater behavior problems and psychological symptoms when couples with high levels of marital conflict do not break up (Morrison & Coiro, 1999; Kelly, 2000; Sun, 2001). Longitudinal research following divorced people over a 30-year period concludes that divorce may be tragic at the time, but families are resilient, people rebound, and divorce can have positive effects in the long run (Amato, 2000; Hetherington & Kelly, 2002). On the other hand, clinical researchers claim that divorce causes pervasive harm to children and their later marriages (Wallerstein et al., 2000). While a complete picture of the impact of divorce on children and their parents is still lacking, we do know that emotional divorce precedes a legal one. Since Americans say romantic love is the primary reason for marriage, "falling out of love" becomes a reason for divorce. Though subject to anomalies like the Depression and World War II, the divorce rate has steadily increased throughout the last century; it rose rapidly during the 1970s, peaked in the early 1980s, and has modestly decreased since 1990.

Depending on which standard for calculating divorce rates is used, the future of marriage for U.S. society as well as for individual couples appears rather bleak. When you compare the number of divorces to the number of new marriages (Table 15.3), it is fair to say that half will end in divorce. The problem with this comparison is that it does not account for how long a couple was married, so it may inflate the failure rate of new marriages. It is more informative to look at annual divorces per 1,000 married women (half of a married couple), which is presently at about 20 (Hughs, 2002). This indicates a less discouraging 4-in-10 marriage failure rate. By all measures, the divorce rate is rising throughout the world, but the United States remains near the top with one of the world's highest rates (Divorce, 2002).

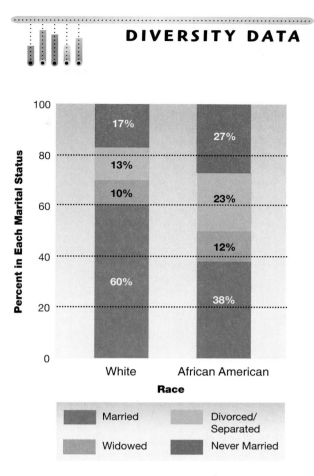

DIVERSITY DATA

FIGURE 15.4 Marital Status by Race. Whites are significantly more likely to be married than African Americans. Half of African Americans are single or divorced/separated compared to about one-third of whites. Demographic variables are powerful indicators of social trends such as marriage and divorce. What other variables could be added to this figure to make understanding of race and marital status more meaningful?

Source: NORC. General Social Surveys, 1972–2000. Chicago: National Opinion Research Center, 2000.

PREDICTING DIVORCE Research has identified several key variables in a couple's vulnerability to divorce. The two that in combination most consistently predict divorce are age and social class. Teenage marriages of couples from lower socioeconomic groups are the most likely to dissolve, probably within the first 5 years (Sassler & Schoen, 1999; Rank, 2000). For teenage couples who start out with less education, fewer economic resources, and less emotional maturity, love quickly fades when confronted with the stark reality of married life.

Sociologists suggest other important predictors of divorce. First, we have seen that homogamy predicts

In a divorce, mothers usually have custody of children, and children often visit their fathers on weekends. If men remarry, their contact with and financial support of their children decline.

Finally, when parents divorce, their offspring face increased risk of divorce. Children of divorced parents learn behaviors that may actually prevent mutually rewarding intimate relationships, which in turn contribute to an even higher divorce rate for remarried couples (Jacobson, 1995; Amato & Sobolewski, 2001). The effects of divorce on young people may already be in place before they begin dating (Amato & Booth, 2001; Jacquet & Surra, 2001). These findings suggest a self-fulfilling prophecy at work: The very visibility of divorce contributes to its intergenerational transmission, reduces its stigma, and sets the stage for the next divorce wave.

GENDER, DIVORCE, AND THE FEMINIZATION OF POVERTY Divorce has profound effects on the divorcing couple and their families. Research also shows that it has different consequences for women compared to men. Certain categories of women appear to adjust better than men: those who are younger, those married for shorter lengths of time, those with higher self-esteem, those who adopted nontraditional gender roles in marriage, and those who initiate the divorce (Hackstaff, 1999; Simon & Marcussen, 1999; Zimmer, 2001). African American women also appear to fare better—have higher levels of personal mastery over their situation—compared to white women (McKelvey & McKenry, 2000).

with whom we will likely fall in love. When couples are demographically parallel in age, race, and religion, and are culturally comparable in attitudes and values, their chances for marital satisfaction and marital permanence are enhanced. Second, since women today are likely to be employed, they may have the financial latitude to end unhappy marriages. Although an employed wife contributes to her happiness and well-being, when her income begins to match her husband's income and his share of household work is low compared to hers, his sense of well-being is lowered (Hiedemann et al., 1998; Rogers & DeBoer, 2001). The most dissatisfied couples are those in which wives want joint decision making and household task-sharing by husbands, while husbands prefer a more traditional, patriarchal style of family functioning—a pattern that holds for couples of all races (Lawson & Thompson, 1999; Kroska, 2000; Stohs, 2000). Third, legal barriers to ending a marriage have eased considerably with *no-fault divorce*, which allows one spouse to divorce the other without placing blame on either. Divorce is readily available to those who want it, such as women in abusive marriages and young couples who married quickly and confronted marital conflict just as quickly (Glenn, 1997; Rodgers et al., 1999).

TABLE 15.3

Marriages and Divorces, Selected Years (Rates per Thousand Population)

	Marriage	Divorce
1960	8.6	2.2
1970	10.6	3.5
1975	10.0	4.8
1980	10.6	5.2
1984	10.5	4.9
1990	9.8	4.7
1992	9.3	4.6
1994	9.1	4.4
1996	8.8	4.3
1998	9.0	4.3
2000*	8.7	4.1

*Estimated.
Sources: Monthly Vital Statistics Reports, Vol. 42–44, 1993–1995, U.S. Public Health Service: Adapted from Table 156, U.S. Bureau of the Census, 1998; *National Vital Statistics Report,* 50(1), U.S. Bureau of the Census, 2001.

However, while women may adjust better psychologically than men after divorce, the financial consequences are devastating for women as a group. Divorce is a principal reason for the high poverty rate of single-parent women and their dependent children, a factor contributing to what we identified in Chapter 13 as the "feminization of poverty." When a divorce involves children, mothers gain custody about 90 percent of the time, usually without further legal action by fathers (Gordon, 1998). Regardless of race, divorce increases a woman's financial burdens in two important ways. First, child support payments do not match expenses of maintaining the family, and second, women are expected to work outside the home, but their salaries are low, a situation compounded by both race and gender discrimination (Kurtz, 1995; Smock et al., 1999; Molina, 2000a). Older women, homemakers, and those reentering the labor force are at a disadvantage in the job market at the exact time they need an adequate income to support their family.

No-fault divorce makes a bad economic situation worse for women when courts mandate an equal division of assets, such as the family home and savings. No-fault divorce is increasingly linked to the rise of *joint custody* arrangements, where parents share decisions related to their children, including how much time children will spend in the home of each parent. While the psychological benefits for parents and children are still being debated (Kurdek & Kennedy, 2001), it is already clear that joint custody puts women at great financial risk. Most women do not have the economic resources to co-parent on an equal basis with their ex-husbands.

The severe economic consequences of divorce are played out among women of all races. Although young minority men are not well off economically, their postdivorce financial situation tends to be better than that of their ex-wives. Gender more than race is probably the important variable, however. Some data now show that a man's standard of living increases about 10 percent to 15 percent following a divorce; other data show that it decreases by about the same percent (Gordon, 1998; McManus & DiPrete, 2001). While declines in women's postdivorce income are less than in years past, the data still show decreases and losses much greater than men's postdivorce income. A loss of half the family income is typical (Amato, 2001; Josephson, 1997; McKeever & Wollinger, 2001). The risk of poverty for children living with single-parent mothers dramatically increased between the 1970s and 1990s because of many of these trends. The feminization and *juvenilization* of poverty go hand in hand (Bianchi, 1999).

To help get divorced women off public assistance, some states are more vigilant in enforcing child custody orders. But the benefits of getting men to live up to their financial obligations may be greater when men are nurtured in their identities as fathers by meaningful welfare reform programs. Welfare programs that reconnect poor, absent fathers to their children may be more successful than programs criminalizing fathers when they do not or cannot pay (Samuel, 1999; Curran & Abrams, 2000).

Single-Parent Families

In single-parent families, economic vulnerability is often a way of life. *Single-parent families* are those in which one adult, usually the mother, is responsible for caring for one or more children. Since 1950, the number of single-parent households has doubled. In 1950, 7 percent of families were headed by single parents. This figure skyrocketed to 27 percent a half century later, with single-parent mothers outnumbering single-parent fathers 4 to 1 (Bianchi & Casper, 2001; Simmons & O'Neill, 2001). The staggering statistic today is that half of U.S. children live in a single-parent household before age 18. When accounting for race, about 40 percent of African American children live in families headed by women, compared to 20 percent Latino, 15 percent Asian, and 12 percent white children. For all races, African American children are most likely to live with a female grandparent (Office of Child Support Enforcement, 2000; Population Reference Bureau, 2002). Because media tend to focus on "illegitimacy rates" of single-parent mothers, people often forget that single parents include divorced parents. About half of all single parents are divorced; the other half have never been married. The divorced half of single-parent mothers appear to fare better economically than their never married counterparts (O'Connell, 1997). If children from divorced homes are living with their fathers, the median family income is $30,753; if they live with their mothers, it is $19,917 (U.S. Bureau of the Census, 2001: Table 663).

Not only are single-mother families the fastest growing type of family, but the odds that these families are in poverty approach one in two. Almost half of all poor children in the United States live in families headed by women, whose median income is a whopping four times lower than in husband–wife families (Costello et al., 2002). When race is factored in, the poverty rate of single-mother families for whites, African American, and Latino families is 22.5 percent, 39.2 percent, and 38.8 percent respectively (National Center for Children in Poverty, 2000). Financial uncertainty heightens the physical and emotional demands on single-parent women. Compared with married couples, they rely more on children for housework, have fewer social supports, and raise children who are also more likely to become single parents. Single mothers report higher rates of depression and lower levels of self-esteem than married mothers, especially if they were teenage mothers—a pattern

Single-parent families headed by divorced and never married women are increasing. Among African Americans, a female grandparent is often a child's guardian.

found in both the United States and Canada (Davies et al., 1997; Solomon & Liefeld, 1998; Sarlo, 2000). Money is the key factor in this pattern. Not only do women who are more financially secure adjust better to single parenting, their children tend to have better educational outcomes and fewer behavioral problems overall than in intact families marked by high levels of conflict (Chollar, 1995; Winkler, 1995).

As single parents, men face a situation far different from that of women. About 4 percent of children live with their fathers only. This number is expected to increase in the next decade as more fathers gain sole or joint custody of their children (Center on Budget and Policy Priorities, 2001; Coltrane, 1996, 2001). Fathers are usually better educated, have higher level occupations, and continue their careers after becoming single parents. Financial strength is one reason why fathers are increasingly awarded sole custody when they request it. Like single mothers, single fathers report problems balancing work and family. For child-care and household tasks, single fathers appear to adapt well, perceive themselves as competent, share tasks with their children, and do not rely extensively on outside help (Greif, 1995; Pasley & Minton, 2001). When fathers take on the role of "primary" parent, they report close ties to their children and high levels of family satisfaction. But they still must deal with gender role stereotyping that assumes they cannot be as competent as women in the parenting area (Gardner, 1995).

Regardless of race and gender, the data suggest that the prospects parents and their children face in single-parent families appear bleak. There is some good news on the horizon, however. For the first time since 1940, the number of children born to unmarried parents is leveling off. The teenage birth rate also dropped substantially by the mid-1990s. Compared to unmar-

ried white women, the birth rate for unmarried African American women has also narrowed considerably. These trends are predicted to increase over the next two decades (Ventura & Bachrach, 2000; Bramlett & Mosher, 2001). For children from current single-parent homes, research is countering the notion that single parenting puts these children at high risk in their social development. Despite economic hardship, recent data show that children in single-parent and two-parent homes have no significant differences in social skills or overall well-being (Hilton et al., 2001; Kesner & McKenry, 2001). But perhaps the most heartening statistic is that median income for single-parent women—particularly African American women—is steadily rising (Holmes, 1998). Although the booming U.S. economy of the last decade explains part of this income rise, programs that help with child care so young mothers can finish school are starting to pay off.

Blended Families

While the United States has the world's highest divorce rate in the developed world, it also has the world's highest remarriage rate. Almost 75 percent of divorced people remarry, and now almost half of all marriages are remarriages (Kim & Cole, 2000; Bramlett & Mosher, 2001). The marriage–divorce–remarriage pattern is called **serial monogamy**. Remarriages are the primary reasons for the formation of **blended families** in which children from parents' prior relationships are brought together in a new family. This new form of kinship affects half of children in the United States today, and it is predicted that by 2005 almost half of families with children will be blended families (Bold, 2001). This rapidly growing family form has a major impact on childrearing, family organization, and marital satisfaction (Ganong & Coleman, 1999; Arnaut et al., 2000). Children must adjust to a new parent and siblings in a newly created family. They often report feelings of rejection from siblings and intense competition for parental attention and affection (Wallerstein et al., 2000). Some counselors go so far as to suggest that as loving as stepparents can be, they are not the same as biological parents: "Merging families is like living in a foreign country: It takes time to learn the customs and language, and it is essential not to expect too much too soon" (Robinson, 2000:147).

However, remarriages at midlife when children are older or have left the nest may be more stable, especially in couples with higher levels of education and income. Both children and their biological and stepparents in blended families do adjust, and a "successful" family can be established (Herbert, 1999; Coleman et al., 2000). Compared with children in first-marriage homes, children in blended families have only a slightly higher risk of emotional problems (Hetherington, 2001).

GENDER, AGE, AND RACE About 75 percent of divorced men remarry and about 66 percent of divorced women remarry. The majority of men usually remarry within 5 years of their divorce. Most divorced men with children are free from sole custody and economically better off than their ex-wives, allowing for greater latitude in the remarriage market. Men have an age advantage as well. There is more acceptance of the older man–younger woman pattern than the reverse. A 10-year age difference favoring men is common in remarriages. About 75 percent of divorced women remarry within 10 years of their divorce. Women who are poorly educated are most likely to remarry. Their remarriage chances decrease if they have dependent children, since they represent a financial liability for men. Financially independent women are attractive to men for remarriage, but these women have less to gain in a remarriage, especially if they do not want to raise children (Sweeney, 1998; Coleman et al., 2000). When adding race to the remarriage picture, African American women are the least likely to remarry and white women the most likely. Latino women fall in between (Bramlett & Mosher, 2001).

Sociologists find that these remarriage rates are best explained by the influence of race, class, and gender in combination. Among women of all races, marriage and remarriage offer opportunities for economic stability. But low-income African American single mothers report that autonomy in their lives is more important. Low-income white single mothers mention trust and freedom from domestic violence as more important. The meaning of marriage differs for these women. Many believe that marriage will make their lives more difficult, hence choose to remain single (Edin, 2000a; 2000b).

Finally, remarriages are more fragile than first marriages—regardless of gender, age, race, or class. Whereas about half of all first marriages fail, the rate climbs to over 60 percent for remarriages (Maudlin, 2001). Since homogamy predicts mate selection, the likelihood is that a marriage will be successful. Since remarriages create blended families, they start out as less homogeneous, which in turn increases the likelihood of divorce. Although the statistics may be grim for remarriage, the lure of marriage remains strong, and generally people believe it is better to remarry than remain single.

EMERGING LIFESTYLES

We have seen that both globally and in the United States, the family is an immensely varied social institution. It is inevitable that changes in family structure will produce changes in households. Rapid social change provides new paths for those seeking alternatives to conventional *family*—rather than *household*— arrangements.

Singlehood

Nonfamily households have grown rapidly since 1960, and that increase is largely due to the growth of one-person households. Today about one-fourth of all nonfamily households are one person (see Figure 15.1). Women living alone represent over half (58%) of nonfamily households and include those who are widowed, divorced, and single. In 1900, only 1 in 10 adults were unmarried; today it is almost 1 in 4 (Caplow et al., 2001; U.S. Bureau of the Census, 2001: Table 48). The large majority of both genders marry, but the percent of never-married people, especially women, continues to increase.

Historically, "failure" to marry was seen as caused by personal or social deficiencies. For women the stigma was "She was never asked," and for men, "He's probably gay." Bolstered by the women's movement and gay rights activism, today these stigmas have all but disappeared. College students in particular say that while they plan to marry, it is not in their near future. Finishing college and getting a good job are more important, so for now they favor a lifestyle free of long-term commitments (Levine & Cureton, 1998).

Highly educated, financially independent women are likely candidates for choosing singlehood. For every age category, the higher a woman's income, the lower the rate of marriage. These women express a sense of control in their lives that remaining single offers (Lloyd & South, 1996; Clements, 1998; Edwards, 2000). Men are also choosing singlehood at increasing rates. For men, singlehood frees them from financial burdens associated with their instrumental role

(Nakosteen & Zimmer, 1997). There are no significant gender or race differences in terms of what is liked or disliked about being single. Both men and women of all races enjoy its mobility, freedom, and social options. But they must deal with times of loneliness and being single in a "couples" world. Many singles, particularly men, report higher levels of emotional distress than married people (Davies, 1995; Phillips, 1999).

As the current generations of never-married people age, it is likely that many will remain unmarried. Contemporary singlehood represents opportunities for happiness for a significant subset of the population who may reject marriage and any permanent and/or exclusive sexual relationship. It is clear that the increase of singles in the United States is also associated with the increase in cohabitation.

Cohabitation

Until relatively recently, *cohabitation*—an unmarried couple living together—was cause for condemnation. As increasing numbers of people choose cohabitation as their preferred lifestyle, this is no longer the case. Social support does vary, however, and as expected, younger people are more accepting of cohabitation than older generations. Such support may account for the dramatic increase of cohabitants and the slight decrease in the marriage rate (Lipke, 2000). The number of cohabiting couples has soared from about half a million in 1970 to almost 4 million couples today, representing close to 4 percent of all households in the United States. The U.S. Census Bureau admits that these are conservative numbers, since people may be reluctant to report themselves as "cohabiting" and may call themselves roommates. In addition, these figures do not include gay and lesbian couples, since, to date, homosexual couples cannot be legally married. The U.S. Census Bureau considers cohabiters as POSSLQ's—People of the Opposite Sex Sharing Living Quarters (Casper & Cohen, 2000). Today, half of all couples married since 1985 have lived together at some point before marriage (Fields & Casper, 2001).

There are striking gender differences in cohabiting couples. Unlike married couples, in cohabiting couples women tend to be younger, have higher levels of education, and earn more money than their partners (Fields & Casper, 2001). Males also express less commitment to the relationship than females (Brown & Booth, 1997). Women tend to view the relationship as temporary and leading to marriage. Men tend to view it as temporary but not leading to marriage. If children are involved, marriage is the more likely outcome (Wu, 1995; Smock, 2000; Elizabeth, 2000).

Contrary to popular belief, cohabitation is not a good screening device for a later successful marriage. Research concludes that cohabitants who marry have lower marital satisfaction, adjustment, and commitment to marriage than noncohabitants, and perhaps more significant, have divorce rates that are equal to or higher than noncohabitants (Bauman, 1999; Jabusch, 2000). Both male and female cohabitants who break up are likely to cohabit again, setting up a cycle in which one failed relationship may predispose them to another one. Living together lessens total commitment—the door to leave is always open. Playing house and keeping house are fundamentally different.

U.S. FAMILIES IN MULTICULTURAL PERSPECTIVE

The multicultural heritage of the United States is reflected in its families (see Table 15.4). Because this heritage is linked to race and ethnicity, minority families are impacted by the same disadvantages that affect them in their other roles in society (see Chapter 12). This section highlights data that show minority families to be at risk for a number of family-related social problems. However, as you will see in this section, even with risks, families are very resilient.

African American Families

Contrary to stereotypes, there are two parents present in over half of African American families and over half of the fathers in these families work full time (Center on Budget and Policy Priorities, 2001; U.S. Bureau of the Census, 2001: Table 60). African American families do exhibit a wider variety of family and household structures and a greater degree of role sharing by wives and husbands than other racial groups. The key factors in the development of these patterns are the impact of slavery and economic oppression rooted in discrimination. The half of African American households that do not have two parents present are those headed by single parents, about 90 percent of whom are single-parent women (U.S. Bureau of the Census, 2001: Adapted from Table 58). The households are likely to consist of both kin and nonkin.

Economic need is the harsh reality in many single-female parent households, so there is an advantage to accommodating household structure to meet various stressors. African American families demonstrate a strong willingness to absorb others into kin structures by creating a network of **fictive kin** in which friends who are not related by blood or marriage "become" family. African Americans tend to define the boundaries of their families more flexibly than do white families, so distant kin become primary kin and close friends and neighbors become fictive kin (Johnson, 1999). Fictive kin bring an array of exchange and support, such as child care, that benefits all household members. In

TABLE 15.4

Selected Family Characteristics (percent) by Race, 2000

Race	Married Couples	Female-Headed Single-Parent Families	Families Below Poverty Level
White	80.9*	14.7*	7.3**
Black	47.8*	48*	21.9**
Hispanic origin	67.8*	25.6*	20.2**
American Indian†	65.8	26.2	27.2
Asian and Pacific Islanders	79.6*	12.0	10.3**

** 1999 data from Table 37. U.S. Bureau of the Census, 2001.
* Data from Tables 53, 54, 57. U.S. Bureau of the Census, 2001.
† 1990 data.

turn, children are offered a diversity of parenting models, which are seen as enriching children (Dill, 1994; Hasell & Scanzoni, 2000).

Overall, role flexibility has strengthened African American families in three fundamental ways. First, African American women have traditionally taken on provider roles essential to family stability and survival. The legacy of institutionalized racism and the deterioration of the economic position of African American men created many fatherless families (Wilson, 1996). Second, working-class and middle-class married couples are likely to have an egalitarian family structure where husband and wife are dual earners in stable employment (Staples, 1997). Egalitarian arrangements are bolstered by middle-class African American women who work outside the home by choice and who do not view their wife–mother and wage earner roles as mutually exclusive (Higginbotham, 2000). Recent research by sociologist Burt Landy (2000) argues that these women were practicing an egalitarian lifestyle decades before it was even envisioned by white couples. Third, African American middle-class husbands appear to be more willing than white husbands to adapt themselves and the household to the needs of their employed wives (Staples, 1997). This last pattern is interesting, since African American working-class and lower-class men tend to hold traditional ideas about gender roles (John & Shelton, 1997). More data are needed to determine if it is race, social class, or a combination of both that accounts for the pattern.

Latino Families

Latinos, also referred to as Hispanics, represent diverse social, cultural, and historical legacies that are readily distinguished from one another (see Chapter 12). There are now slightly more people who identify themselves as Latino or Hispanic (12.5%) than who

identify themselves as black or African American (12.3%), making them the largest minority in the nation (Grieco & Cassidy, 2001). The terms we use to refer to them as a group often gloss over differences, particularly those related to immigrant status, nationality, number of generations in the United States, and

Multi-generational Latino families are common in the United States and demonstrate strong kinship bonds emphasizing the needs of the family over the needs of the individual. This three generation Mexican-American family shares the same household and all its members share in household tasks.

DIVERSITY IN FOCUS

African American Women and the Marriage Squeeze

Eligibility in the U.S. marriage market is determined by strong cultural norms regarding who is "appropriate" to marry—norms that direct us toward some people and away from others. Some people can be "squeezed" out of the marriage market because they find fewer eligible partners of their own race and near their own age. When considering African American women as a subgroup, the marriage squeeze is acute. Several factors explain this:

1. For both race and sex, life expectancy rates are lowest for African American males (Chapter 19). African American women outnumber men at age 18; for whites it is age 32. It is estimated that there are now 8 black men for every 10 African American women.

2. Education and income are also important. For every 10 college-educated African American women, there are fewer than 2 comparably educated men. African American women outnumber employed African American men in every age category by 2 to 1. Remember that education is an indicator of social class, and in turn social class is used for determining marriage

eligibility. Since women tend to marry "up," the field of eligible men is further narrowed.

3. Interracial marriages, although infrequent, are increasing, but the pattern of African American men marrying white women has not changed significantly (see Table 15.2 on page 409). African American men who marry women of other races are also likely to be highly educated. Highly educated African American women are less likely to intermarry (as are highly educated white men).

These patterns significantly restrict the field of eligible partners for African American women. As a result, in comparison with white women, African American women are more likely to marry men who are older, are of a lower educational level, and have been previously married. If African American women select mates of their own race who are otherwise significantly different than themselves, there may be a negative impact on marital stability and happiness.

It is easy to explain the marriage squeeze for African American women simply according to unbalanced age, sex, and education ratios. However, sociology

offers additional insights. The marriage squeeze is a byproduct of cultural beliefs determining who is "acceptable" as a marriage partner in the first place. It is not as much an objectively determined process as it is a socially constructed one. As beliefs about acceptability are altered, the norms surrounding eligibility will also be altered. The marriage squeeze may be responsible for the hard choices African American women must make in today's marriage market. But shifting cultural definitions of what is "valued" in a prospective partner can loosen the current marriage squeeze or even make it obsolete.

1. What would you predict to be the basis for a future marriage squeeze, and which groups will most likely be affected?

2. Do you think that any marriage squeeze could narrow the field of eligible partners so much that people would choose to remain single rather than marry someone so "different" from themselves? Why or why not?

Sources: Cready & Fossett, 1997; Crowder & Tolnay, 2000; Collins & Coltrane, 2001; U.S. Bureau of the Census, 2001

---

economic well-being. Economic status is a key variable in viewing Latino families. As discussed in Chapter 12, the largest subgroups are Mexican Americans (Chicanos), Puerto Ricans, and Cuban Americans, all of whom suffer the economic consequences of minority status. Poverty is most acute for Puerto Ricans and least acute for Cuban Americans. Mexican Americans hover near the poverty line but have the widest variation in economic well-being. Latinos share a heritage of Spanish colonialism, and through this, a solid connection to the Roman Catholic Church. Several fundamental values related to family life link these diverse groups. First, family relations are characterized by respect and honor. Second is the notion of *familism*, a strong cultural value emphasizing the family and its collective needs over personal

and individual needs. Familism creates strong bonds between nuclear and extended family members in terms of support, loyalty, and solidarity (Magana, 1999). Third, there is a strong adherence to patriarchal gender roles in a well-defined system of mutually exclusive beliefs that separate men and women; these roles are found throughout all social classes in Latino cultures. The man's role is associated with *machismo*, seen to include virility, sexual prowess, and the physical and ideological control of women. The woman's role is associated with *marianismo*, seen to include the beliefs of spiritual and moral superiority of women over men, the glorification of motherhood, and the acceptance of a difficult marriage (Stevens, 2000). The beliefs that support marianismo remain strong, but changes in what were entrenched patriarchal gender roles in the family are appearing (Mirande, 1997; McLloyd et al., 2000). Factors such as socioeconomic status and degree of acculturation affect how these values are translated into the home.

PUERTO RICAN FAMILIES   Most research on family relations in Latino subcultures centers on the relationship between employment and home, especially for employed women and their families. The low income of Puerto Ricans is explained by critical gender–family linkages. Almost half of Puerto Rican households are headed by women, only half of Puerto Rican women are high school graduates, and there has been declining demand in those industries in which women have traditionally been employed (Zambrana, 1994; Lichter & Landale, 1995). Families are often divided, with children raised by grandparents in Puerto Rico, mothers residing in New York City, and husbands migrating back and forth between there and Puerto Rico depending on employment options. Marriages are fragile. Often, couples remain legally married but separated. Half of all heterosexual couples form *consensual unions.* These are different from cohabitation in that they are more recognized as an informal marriage and often produce children (Manning & Landale, 1996). Women who have recently migrated to the United States strive to maintain a continuity of family life. Better-educated women are more likely to value both career and family roles. Traditional gender roles are common, but in families with dual-earner couples, some erosion of the double standard is evident (Toro-Morn, 1995).

MEXICAN AMERICAN FAMILIES   Mexican American families are also tied to familism and the machismo–marianismo ideology, factors that keep divorce rates low. The nuclear family is embedded in kin networks, which maintain intergenerational ties by passing on cultural traditions and serving as social and economic support (Dietz, 1995). Men control the household, and subordination of women to men in families is evident, but newer studies question the concept of the all-dominant and controlling male. These data suggest a trend toward more gender equity in Mexican American households. Couples report that fathers and mothers are increasingly sharing household tasks and that joint decision making is increasing, especially for dual earners (Herrara & Del-Campo, 1995).

Familism with traditional ties to older generations are also weakening (Baca Zinn & Wells, 2000). Unique among Mexican American families is a *horizontally extended family*, which consists of members of the same generation—typically brothers and sisters and their spouses—who live in the same household and share household responsibilities. Such ties are extremely helpful to new arrivals from Mexico who are likely to enter the labor force with minimum wage jobs and in a very precarious economic position (Glick et al., 1997).

Children born in the U.S. are moving up economically and in educational attainment. Compared to their parents, there is less poverty and higher levels of education. Young adults are entering college at increasing rates and are being trained for well-paying jobs. On the negative side, more Mexican American women are becoming single parents, and they have overtaken African Americans in teen birth rates (Mathews et al., 1998). Issues related to class, race, ethnicity, and gender will determine if the economic prosperity of second-generation Mexican Americans can be sustained.

CUBAN AMERICAN FAMILIES   Cuban Americans enjoy the highest standard of living of all Latino groups. Immigrants in the 1960s were highly educated, many drawn from Cuba's professional ranks. Even though women were not likely to be in the labor force, education for middle and upper class women was encouraged and helped bolster the prestige of the family (Chilman, 1995). Later immigrants were poorer, marriages more prone to breakup and women in the workplace more common, a trend that continues today. However, compared with other Latino subgroups overall, Cuban American families have fewer children, are economically stronger, and are more likely to be headed by a married couple. Married couples with higher levels of education are less traditional in their gender roles and there is a move toward more egalitarian relationships (Jimenez-Vasquez, 1995). Unlike European Americans, Cuban American families are more likely to be extended and children are expected to live with their parents until they get married. The elderly in these families offer child care services and in turn expect to be taken care of as they become more feeble (DeGenova, 1997).

Asian American Families

Due to high rates of immigration, Asian Americans are the fastest growing of America's racial minorities. Even more so than Latino families, Asian American families exhibit striking cultural diversity—by language, religion, and culture—all of which have powerful influences on family life (Chapters 3 and 19). However, evidence does suggest several interrelated patterns shared by Asian American families (Fuligni et al., 1999; Rastogi & Wampler, 1999; Chen et al., 2001; Lee & Liu, 2001).

1. Collectivistic kinship traditions—sacrificing personal needs to family needs—from the originating Asian cultures live on in America.

2. Marriages are routinely arranged by kin rather than left solely to the devices of the couple.
3. Extended families are normative.
4. Children are socialized to be obedient in the family and loyal to parents and elders.
5. Gender roles emphasize female subordination to all males and older females in a patriarchal family structure.
6. Asian Americans, especially Chinese, Japanese, and Filipino Americans, have the highest number of married couples and the lowest divorce rate of all other racial minorities at numbers similar to European Americans.

The extent to which each of these patterns occurs is linked to length of residence in the United States. Recent arrivals are strongly connected to their ethnic community, which provides social support and jobs in family businesses. Chinese and Koreans in particular appear to benefit from community ties—they have low divorce rates, high levels of education, and enjoy relatively fast upward mobility (Ishii-Kuntz, 1997). However, traditional expectations for marriage are eroding, and emerging norms are now emphasizing choice of partners based on romantic love. While still quite low, the divorce rate and number of female-headed households are steadily increasing among all Asian American groups. When children become more "Americanized," intergenerational conflict increases (Kitano & Daniels, 1995; Jain & Belsky, 1997). Among Chinese Americans, for example, children will gladly provide economic help for their parents but resist their parent's advice on personal matters, such as who they choose as friends, dates, or marriage partners. The Chinese-Korean-American daughter in the opening vignette is the exception to many of the traditional characteristics described here—egalitarian parents, a father very involved in his parenting role, and a desire for a relationship based on love.

Native American Families

Native Americans comprise less than 1 percent of the U.S. population and include those reporting American Indian and Alaskan (Eskimo and Aleut) origin. About a third of Native Americans are Navaho or Cherokee (U.S. Bureau of the Census, 2001). Although there is a great deal of tribal diversity, Native Americans share some key patterns related to family life.

About one-third of Native American households are female headed; most of these are in poverty. The remaining two-thirds are made up mostly of married couples (Table 15.4). These households are at risk for social problems related to their poverty status, such as unemployment, dropping out of high school, illiteracy, and alcoholism. Current government policy, em-

Many Native American women hold positions of power and prestige, both inside their families as well as in community and spiritual roles.

bedded with historic roots, is fundamentally responsible for the economic plight of Native American populations (U.S. Commission on Human Rights, 2001).

Colonialism, which was accompanied by Christianity, altered ancient tribal patterns drastically, especially those related to gender roles in the family. Women's power and prestige varied by tribe, but historical evidence indicates that women lost status with colonialization. Many tribal units were matrilineal and matrilocal. Although gender segregation was the norm, complementarity, balance, and gynocratic (female-centered) egalitarianism also existed (Kuhlmann, 1996). To assimilate native people, the U.S. government first sought to obliterate ancient traditions—a policy that became known as *cultural genocide*. Altered family patterns was its first manifestation, and a generally egalitarian family structure changed to a patriarchal one (Harjo, 1993).

Cultural genocide did not succeed. Ancient tribal customs were altered, but not eradicated. Women retain roles offering prestige and power in their families and communities (Joe & Miller, 1994; Cheshire,

2001). Families are often extended and exist in strong kinship networks that serve as sources of intergenerational support and repositories of tribal knowledge (Yellowbird & Snipp, 1994).

Native Americans are being assimilated rapidly into majority culture, and high rates of intermarriage are eroding tribal integrity. In 1970, one-third of all Indians were married to non-Indians. It is estimated that 19 out of 20 Native Americans are related to someone of a different racial group (Goldstein, 1999). At the same time, resurgent cultural pride has contributed to a rise in the number of people claiming Native American origin. It remains to be seen whether Native Americans will "intermarry themselves out of existence" (Yellowbird & Snipp, 1994:239). The strength of family kinship will play a large part in that outcome.

LIFE CONNECTIONS

Family Violence in the United States

The view of the family as a safe and loving haven is in stark contrast to the dramatic increase in domestic violence that makes the family home one of the most lethal environments in the United States. Privacy of the family and the reluctance of the police to get involved in family disputes make it difficult to get accurate statistics on all forms of family violence and abuse. However, for the typical forms of domestic violence, research shows the following:

1. Both men and women assault one another in marriage, and mutual abuse is more common than either alone. However, the consequences to women are much more lethal. Domestic abuse is the leading cause of injury to women in the United States, and wife battering is the most common and most underreported of all crimes, including rape (Gelles & Straus, 1995; Dobash et al., 2000).

2. One-third of all women who are murdered die at the hands of husbands or boyfriends. A woman's risk increases if she threatens to leave, files for divorce, or calls the police, although physical attacks will most likely continue if she stays. Half of all homeless women and children are fleeing domestic violence (Thomas-Lester, 1995; Hague & Malos, 1999).

3. Reported cases of violence against children are over 2 million per year. An estimated half million cases of child neglect occur. Between 1,300 and 2,000 children per year are killed by parents, relatives, or boyfriends of single mothers. Domestic violence against wives heightens the risk that children will also be abused (Gelles, 1997; Rumm et al., 2000; McGuigan & Pratt, 2001).

4. Some studies estimate that approximately one-fourth of girls and one-fifth of boys have experienced incest, sexual abuse, and/or sexual victimization in their families. Father–daughter/stepdaughter and brother–sister sexual abuse are the most common (Finkelhor et al., 1990; Morrison & Clavenna-Valleroy, 1998).

Family violence cuts across all demographic categories, although it is more prevalent in families with low income and unemployment and is associated with alcohol use, drug abuse, and family isolation (Gelles &

Domestic violence in the United States has increased over the last several decades. Mutual abuse by spouses is common, but the effects of wife-battering are much more lethal. One-third of all murdered women die at the hands of husbands and boyfriends, usually in their own homes.

Straus 1995; Currie, 1998; Molina, 2000b). In addition, coming from a violent family of orientation increases the risk that one will become violent in the family of procreation. In other words, a violent past can lead to a violent future (Gelles & Straus, 1995:377).

Functionalists would suggest that the social organization of family life, with its intimacy and intensity of relationships, lays the groundwork for family violence. However, cross-cultural research shows that in a number of societies, family violence as well as rape are rare (Levinson, 1989; Sanday, 2000). The Semai of West Malaysia, for example, are nonviolent, and physical punishment is virtually nonexistent (Robarchek & Dentan, 1979). Sweden has legally banned the use of physical punishment to discipline children. Rather than being fined or jailed for breaking the law, offenders are sent to classes to learn more effective parenting skills.

Public education about family violence has been most effective in dealing with child abuse. Feminist and conflict theorists argue that wife battering has not gained as much attention because it remains subtly condoned and there is inconsistency in enforcing the law (Dalton & Schnieder, 2000; Nabi & Horner, 2001). From these perspectives, the element of power offers the best explanation for family violence and wife battering (Frug, 1998). Violence is most common in patriarchal systems in which men hold power over the women and children in their families (MacKinnon, 2001). In contrast, egalitarian families have the lowest rates of violence. The greater the inequality (the more power held by one person), the greater the risk of violence. The power inequity is expressed sexually in violence against women.

Families are changing as society is changing, and new family structures will develop as a result of this social change.

SOCIETY CONNECTIONS

Gay and Lesbian Families and the Family Values Debate

As society's most conservative institution, the family is the most resistant to change. When social change finally filters down to the family, it indicates that profound change is going on in society as a whole. Because changes in family structure and function are embraced by some but feared by others, they are often the focus of contentious debate.

Gay and Lesbian Families

In 1995 Utah became the first state to expressly prohibit same-sex marriages. In 1996 Hawaii became the first state to legalize same-sex marriage but reversed the ruling 2 years later. In 2000 Vermont allowed same-sex couples to enter *civil unions.* Although Vermont's statute still refers to "marriage" as a union between a man and women, civil union is a new legal classification entitling same-sex couples to the rights and responsibilities available to married partners, such as inheriting a partner's estate and filing joint tax returns (CNN, 2000). If any one state upholds same-sex marriages, reciprocity with other states will be a major issue.

The European Union is already confronting this issue. By the 1990s, same-sex marriages were legal in Denmark, Norway, and Sweden, but in all three countries same-sex couples do not enjoy the complete range of marriage benefits heterosexual married couples receive. In 2001 the Netherlands approved a bill to legally recognize same-sex marriages and same-sex adoptions. It is the first country in the world with full marriage rights for gay and lesbian couples (Eskridge & Hunter, 2001). Reciprocity is expected between member countries (Schwartz & Rutter, 1998). In the United States the fallout from any legal recognition of same-sex unions is far from over. A "federal marriage amendment" to the Constitution is making some headway in Congress; the amendment would define marriage strictly between a man and woman

INTERNET CONNECTIONS

Family violence continues to be a very hot topic today. The text's discussion presents a broad range of statistical data demonstrating the extent of violence among intimates in American society. *U.S. Department of Justice* (http://www.ndvh.org/) Web site offers the opportunity to examine facts and policies on family and relational violence. From the opening page, try clicking on "Dom. Viol Information." You will find some information here that is not presented in the text. Then, try clicking on "Teens and Dating Violence." Click on "DV in the Workplace" to take a look at the problem of family violence at work. After you have thoroughly perused the contents of this Website, answer the following questions:

1. Exercise your sociological insight: What patterns did you find? What are the underlying forces behind family violence?

2. The text observes that *egalitarian* families are less likely to experience family violence. What explanations can you offer for this fact?

and would invalidate legal protections for unmarried couples, regardless of whether or not the couple is homosexual (NOW, 1998).

Whether it is referred to as a civil union or a marriage, legal acceptance does not mean social acceptance. A small but growing number of gay men and lesbians have gained custody, have adopted children, and live in permanent households with their homosexual partners and their children. These families face hostility and suspicion with society's stereotypes about homosexuality as well as idealized notions about families (Ryan, 2000; Clarke, 2001). And even with legal recognition, rights may be denied. In custody cases, for example, interpretations of family law work against gays and lesbians by defining them as unfit to raise children.

The families and stepfamilies formed by gay men and lesbians tend to incorporate a network of kin and non-kin relationships, including friends, lovers, former lovers, co-parents, children, and adopted children. These families are organized by ideologies of love, social support, and rational choice (Erera & Fredriksen, 1999). Notice how this structure is similar to the fictive kin and familism evident in African American and Latino families. The first comprehensive study that compared homosexual and heterosexual couples concluded that homosexual couples were more egalitarian

(Blumstein & Schwartz, 1983). The egalitarian pattern tends to occur for both lesbians and gay men, although lesbians are more successful in maintaining it over the long term (Huston & Schwartz, 1996; Kurdek, 1998). However, research does challenge some aspects of this egalitarianism. As heterosexual couples, in "lesbigay" couples one partner takes on more domestic responsibilities. Also as in heterosexual couples, domestic work is hidden and devalued. The partner doing the most housework is also likely to be the one with less decision-making power. Egalitarianism may be more evident in lesbigay families, but as in heterosexual families, the disadvantages associated with the partner who carries out the expressive role have not been eradicated (Carrington, 1999).

The debate about levels of egalitarianism in lesbigay couples has implications for the same-sex marriage issue. If same-sex couples are more egalitarian, would legally recognized marriage make them less so? From a feminist perspective, marriage is more likely to be patriarchal than egalitarian, so legally married same-sex couples may succumb to patriarchy (Stiers, 2000). The debate can be resolved only when same-sex marriages become normative. This is unlikely to happen any time soon.

The Family Values Debate

The issue of legal recognition of gay and lesbian families is also a feature of the "family values" movement that has gained political momentum in the last decade. The theme of the movement is that family breakdown and the support for "alternative lifestyles" are creating social havoc and neglect of children. It advocates a return to the traditional family as a solution. Led by the New Right linkage of conservative politicians and fundamentalist Christian churches (Chapter 17), "family restorationists" are united around the idealization of the traditional, patriarchal, nuclear family (Cohen & Katzenstein, 1991). They suggest that males are disempowered in *companionate marriages*, those based on romantic love, equality, and an emphasis on balancing individual needs with family needs. Such marriages and families, they believe, undermine traditional Victorian values of self-sacrifice and family commitment. As a result, the welfare state has taken over roles the family once had. Sweden typifies this process (Popenoe, 1993, 1996, 2000).

The shortcomings of the family restorationist model center on five key points. First, how a family is defined has changed and will continue to change over time. The demand of the restorationists is for a family ideal that has never been normative (Stacey, 1996). Second, the family values movement calls for a form that is rarer today than ever, due as much to economic necessity as to feminist progress (Schwartz & Rutter,

1998:43). Data show that divorce was increasing even before women's widespread entrance into the labor force. And as we saw in the link between patriarchal families and domestic violence, this family form can have lethal consequences. Third, data from four industrialized societies, including Sweden, show that the connection between family decline and child well-being is far more complex than the sweeping negative effects family restorationists emphasize (Coltrane, 1997; Cherlin, 1999). Fourth, American couples increasingly desire gender-role egalitarianism in their marriages, in direct opposition to the patriarchal family model advocated by restorationists.

Finally, and most important, the model ignores the reality of social change. Restorationists consider traditional families in modern societies to be "in decline," regardless of the extent of change over time (Houseknecht & Sastry, 1996:727). As this chapter documents, there are all kinds of "new" traditional families depending on the timeframe used.

With media influence and ongoing legal and political challenges to extending the rights of the married to the nonmarried, the issue of "what a family is" will be kept before the public. The focus in this chapter has been on macrosociological perspectives that suggest that families will continue to evolve new structures as they face the challenges of an increasingly diverse society. The nuclear family has undergone change but remains vital and functional. Most sociologists specializing in family studies would agree that the family entering the 21st century is neither doomed nor the fundamental cause of current social problems (Johnson, 1997; Mason et al., 1998). They would agree with the columnist and humorist Erma Bombeck:

> The years have challenged families in ways no one would have thought it possible to survive. They've weathered combinations of step, foster, single, adoptive, surrogate, frozen embryo, and sperm bank. They've multiplied, divided, extended, and banded into communes. They've been assaulted by technology, battered by sexual revolutions, and confused by role reversals. But they're still here—playing to a full house. (Adapted from Erma Bombeck, 1987:11–12)

SUMMARY

1. Sociologists agree that the family is responsible for accomplishing important social functions, including reproduction, regulation of sexual behavior, socialization, protection, and social placement.

2. Family structure has been altered by the processes of industrialization, urbanization, and overall modernization.

3. Functionalists argue that social stability is disrupted if families do not adequately carry out their functions. Many people are seeking alternatives to conventional household arrangements. Conflict theory focuses on the family's role in preserving inequality in the broader society. Feminists argue that viewing the patriarchal family as beneficial for social stability hampers the movement into egalitarian families. Symbolic interactionists focus on the subjective meanings attached to definitions of the family and family roles.

4. Marriage patterns vary considerably across the globe. Polygamy (multiple-spouse marriages), extended families, dowry customs, and communal families, such as the Israeli kibbutz, are examples.

5. Rather than a purely emotional process, romantic love is structured. People fall in love with those who are similar to themselves (homogamy), especially in terms of race and age.

6. Women tend to marry men who are higher in socioeconomic status. Women put a higher value on interpersonal understanding, and men put a higher value on physical attractiveness in mate selection.

7. Most couples express satisfaction in their marriages. Successful marriages and families have high levels of caring, communication, trust, loyalty, and emotional support.

8. Many people are seeking alternatives to conventional household arrangements. Singlehood, cohabitation, and single-parent families are all

increasing. Egalitarian marriages based on shared decision making and nontraditional beliefs about gender are also increasing.

9. The United States has the highest divorce rate in the world. Although the divorce rate steadily increased throughout the last century, it is leveling off.

10. Teenage marriages among couples of lower socioeconomic status are the most likely to end in divorce. Marital permanence is helped when the couple is similar in age, race, religion, attitudes, and values.

11. Divorce is a principal reason for the high poverty rate of single-parent women and their dependent children. No-fault divorce and joint custody contribute to the "feminization of poverty."

12. The remarriage rate is lower for women than for men. Men are more likely to be free from sole custody and to have an age and economic advantage in remarrying.

13. America's multicultural heritage is reflected in its families. The four largest groupings are African American, Latino, Asian American, and Native American families. Their marriages and families are greatly influenced by their minority status.

14. Intimacy and intensity of relationships lay the groundwork for family violence. Family violence is associated with low income, unemployment, alcohol use, drug abuse, and family isolation.

15. Gay men and lesbians are challenging traditional views of marriage and family to receive benefits previously available only to married couples.

16. The family values movement calls for a "family restorationist" model centered around the ideal of the patriarchal nuclear family. Sociological critiques of the model focus on its failure to account for social change.

KEY TERMS

assortive mating 403	family of orientation 396	nuclear family 397
bilateral (bilineal) descent 397	family of procreation 396	patrilineal descent 396
blended families 410	fictive kin 412	patrilocal residence 400
commune 402	homogamy 403	polyandry 400
egalitarian marriage 405	household 397	polygamy 400
endogamy 396	matrilineal descent 397	polygyny 400
exogamy 396	matrilocal residence 400	serial monogamy 410
extended family 397	monogamy 400	

CRITICAL THINKING QUESTIONS

1. Discuss the evidence (both pro and con) related to the following statement: "We are socialized to fall in love with only certain people; therefore, the notion of romantic love is a myth."

2. Review the positive effects of egalitarian marriage for the couple, their children, and society as a whole. Given these effects, what prevents or encourages the formation of more egalitarian marriages?

3. How do family restorationists view the emerging lifestyles that compete with the traditional family? What sociological perspective best supports their view?

INVESTIGATE WITH CONTENT SELECT

Journal Research Collections from **ContentSelect** Begin your research using Content-Select for this chapter by following the directions found on page 27 of this text to visit Prentice Hall's Research Navigator Website. Enter these search terms into the search field:

Nuclear family
Cohabitation
Divorce

16
EDUCATION

The Challenges of Classroom Diversity

Diversity is valued at Prior Lake High School in suburban Minneapolis. Students at Prior Lake—less than 1 percent of whom claim non-European or non-Christian heritage—are required to take a 12-week social studies course devoted to India, Africa, Russia, and Latin America. The choir sings in French, Spanish, and Ibo, and will go to Harlem in New York to sing with a gospel choir. But students are keenly aware that there is a disconnect between practices and attitudes about diversity. When Hmong and Latino residents began fishing along Prior Lake, the parking area was eliminated. A new low-income apartment complex housing many Somalis alarmed the school board, since the district would need an English as a Second Language program and added classrooms. The season's first football game was scheduled on Rosh Hashanah and the community fest on Yom Kippur. All required books for the 3-year literature program were written by white males. The dozen or so Asian students created a separate, remote society in school. The school's few African Americans functioned in a kind of "high-school social limbo," except for one, whose wealth made up for his race.

In a sixth grade classroom in California, Arlene and Juan are classmates. Arlene is bright, eager, and attentive, with parents who carefully oversee her schooling. Juan lives with his grandmother and three younger siblings, each of whom has a different father. His grandmother cannot speak English. Juan's attendance is poor, but he is often drawn to class because of a free breakfast. All teachers have their Arlenes and Juans. They also have Japanese to whom a pat on the back is an insult; Jehovah's Witnesses who will not salute the flag; and Muslims who fall asleep in class due to fasting during the holy month of Ramadan. They have Native American children who are suspicious of white teachers, African American children suspicious of their Korean classmates, and children in wheelchairs who cry when it is time for recess. A teacher' mission is to educate everyone—and to do so without ignoring individual student differences, whether the differences are cultural, racial, religious, economic, or even physical. Teachers are passionate about their students and their profession. They embrace the growing diversity they see in their classrooms and believe that the school can forge the path for tolerance that will follow their students throughout life. (Rasch, 1999; Smith, 1999; American Council on Education, 2001a; Burkett, 2001:116–17)

Violence at School

It was Adolph Hitler's birthday. Armed with a semi-automatic rifle, two sawed-off shotguns, and dozens of homemade bombs, two 17-year-old boys opened fire on classmates at Columbine High School, located in suburban Denver, Colorado. The massacre ended with 14 students (including the gunmen) and one teacher dead. Three years and one week later, a 19-year-old student expelled from his high school in Erfurt, Germany, killed 13 teachers, a police officer, 2 students, and then himself. The boys in both the United States and Germany were later described as lonely, frustrated, and withdrawn—with revenge on their minds.

When Mara took her daughter to enroll in a small Catholic school in Chicago, she was given a form called a Zero Tolerance Agreement. The principal told her that the school has a "first-strike and you're out" policy. "First strikes" may include fighting, offensive language, weapons possession, drug use, and gang activity. "You're out" ranges from expulsion to arrest. All Mara could think of was that her daughter was only 5 years old. (Mitchie, 2001; Andrews, 2002)

Education has changed enormously. Teachers at all levels face far different classrooms than their predecessors did only a generation ago—classrooms that defy all stereotypes. Diversity is happening in classrooms throughout the United States and across the globe. And while the mass violence described here is rare, its high visibility has altered perceptions about the school as a place of safety and security. The challenges educators face related to classroom diversity, school violence, and helping their students face life in the global economy are daunting.

The sociology of education focuses on how schools meet these challenges to serve the needs of society and the needs of individual learners. Teachers are the critical link between students and society. We will see in this chapter that while education is a sorting process designed to benefit society and learners, with benefits also come liabilities. A sociological perspective helps assess the benefits and liabilities associated with the process of education. Such an assessment is vital in ensuring that schools prepare students for the increasingly diverse world they will face outside the classroom.

SOCIOLOGICAL PERSPECTIVES ON EDUCATION

Sociology has made major contributions to understanding the process of education and how it affects various groups. The functionalist perspective has dominated this understanding because the first question functionalists ask is, What are schools expected to accomplish for society? All sociological perspectives accept certain functions of the school, but they disagree about how much to emphasize each function and how the functions should be carried out. Thus, functionalism can serve as a springboard for evaluating other theoretical approaches.

Functionalism and the Functions of Education

The functionalist perspective provides a clear and powerful explanation of the importance of education for both society and the individual. Its focus is on how education serves as a force in social integration. At the turn of the century Émile Durkheim (1898/1956) suggested that schools are necessary to build a community and a society. When children begin formal education outside their families, they enter a society where what they do is more important than who they are. It is their first experience in a society of equals. The classroom reflects the values and norms of wider society, including ways in which its members are ranked. In the United States, as in most of the world, pupils are evaluated on the basis of their achievement. These grades are the first formal indicators of what is believed to be the child's potential. In the United States, people firmly believe that education is the key to success and will translate to economic rewards, social prestige, and an enhanced self-concept.

The numerous functions of education can be grouped under a number of broad, interrelated themes. Consider how each of the following themes emphasizes the functionalist view of how society is integrated, interdependent, and maintained in a state of equilibrium: socialization, transmission of culture, innovation, and social placement.

EDUCATION AS SOCIALIZATION Schools continue the socialization process that begins in the family; they introduce children to a distinct set of values, attitudes, and norms. Not only do children acquire knowledge and skills, they take on new roles and learn proper behavior in interacting with peers and teach-

A key function of schools is to ensure that children are prepared for the rapidly changing world they will face outside of the classroom. Since that world is now a technology-driven one, students are taught computer literacy at earlier ages. Students in this fifth-grade computer class are sharpening the skills they learned in earlier grades.

ers. Schools transmit knowledge in a social context: Dick and Jane are taught computer literacy and also how to share the computer with others.

EDUCATION AS TRANSMISSION OF CULTURE

Schools are the formal channels for passing the fundamental values of the culture to the next generation. In the United States, the core cultural values emphasized in schools help prepare children for life in a democratic society where free enterprise and capitalism are dominant. These values include competition, individualism, respect, self-discipline, and achievement. Globalization has added a new dimension to these values. Schools in the United States are now stressing cooperation, teamwork, and group decision making, values that have played a critical role in Japan's ascendance as one of the world's richest nations. Schools have the difficult task of simultaneously teaching children the benefits of traditional ways of thinking and acting (core values) and challenging those very traditions with new, emergent values such as those inspired by Japan. Core values are not abandoned but supplemented, and a uniquely American value system continues to evolve.

By transmitting core values, education plays a key role in assimilation, the shaping of children from many diverse cultures and subcultures into committed Americans. Because the United States is a nation of immigrants, mass education has been driven by the need to Americanize its arrivals with the heart and will to become good citizens (Graham, 1995). Schools require students to pledge allegiance to the flag each morning and to understand the basic elements of the U.S. Constitution and the political system flowing from it. If the transmission of culture is successful, another educational function is served—that of social control. Dick and Jane meet Ricardo and Noriko in school; together they learn to be proud of the American heritage they all share.

EDUCATION AS INNOVATION

Schools provide students with the attitudes and skills needed to adapt to a rapidly changing world. Today's curriculum reflects the needs of a changing family and population structure. Boys take home economics, girls take shop classes, and both learn sex education. Throughout U.S. history, the face of the population has constantly altered, but today at an even faster rate. Estimates indicate that by 2025 half of the U.S. population and a majority of elementary and secondary school students will be people of color—most of whom will face some form of inequity in their schooling (Lewis, 1996; Education Reforms and Students at Risk, 1996; Green, 2001). Multiculturalism and global interdependence are facts of modern life. Cooperative learning, group problem solving, and student-directed school projects are innovative ways children can learn about others and themselves. With a set of core values as a foundation, children are provided with creative and beneficial tools for confronting social change and for life in a diverse society and a shrinking world.

Innovation means more than adapting to change. Children also learn to become agents of change. They mold their world according to their individual desires and talents. In schools that emphasize multicultural education, Ricardo, Noriko, Dick, and Jane can learn to appreciate both their diversity and their common identity. If schools carry out this function properly, social change can be empowering rather than overwhelming or fearful for children.

EDUCATION AS SOCIAL PLACEMENT

Education is the key institution that functions to nurture talent and achievement in children, preparing them for their future roles in society. All functions of education reinforce this mandate. Americans firmly believe that their children's success in life is fundamentally linked to their success in school. The social placement process serves the needs of both the individual and society. In school, Ricardo's ability in art and Jane's athletic prowess are discovered and developed. When education guides children to fulfill their goals and hone their talents, society will also benefit.

According to the concept of **meritocracy,** society rewards people on the basis of ability and achievement—on what they can do. Schools are a microcosm of society—talent is not wasted, competence is rewarded, and students are motivated to achieve at their highest levels. Schools reward students with grades for academic work and with praise for athletic ability. As discussed in Chapter 10, *social stratification* ranks people according to a number of criteria, the most important of which is income. Just as employed people are ranked by income, students are ranked by grades.

This social placement function of education—and the meritocracy that is supposed to develop from it—lends itself to an emphasis on credentials. Referred to as **credentialism,** an individual's qualification for a job or social status is based on the completion of some aspect of formal education. A credential may be college credit for a sociology course, a certificate for continuing education in word processing, or board certification for an MD in cardiology. The most important credential in the United States is the college degree. Functionalists argue that credentials based on merit are essential for filtering people and assigning them to appropriate roles and statuses, justifying the resulting social stratification.

MANIFEST AND LATENT FUNCTIONS OF EDUCATION

As discussed in Chapter 1, *manifest functions* are those consequences of social life that are explicit, intended, and recognized. As such, they contribute to social integration. *Latent functions* are those that are unintended and often unrecognized. Sociologists generally agree on the functions of education, but disagree on which are manifest and which are latent. Part of the reason for this is that as society changes, so does its needs. A function that was latent at one time can become manifest at another time, or vice versa. For example, schools have always provided a latent babysitting function, but this has become a manifest function in many schools. Latchkey programs and after-school activities occupy children at school until their parents come home from work. In violent neighborhoods, school athletic programs for teenagers are manifestly responsible for the safety and well-being of many teens, merely by keeping them off the streets and under supervision. Such programs are vital for working parents. Schools provide social networks in which lifetime friendships are likely to form. Along with the manifest function of higher education, colleges also have latent functions, such as marriage markets and a vehicle of social placement. When parents pick schools precisely because of the social and business networks they offer their children, these latent functions become manifest functions. For example, in Japan, college friendships are expected to evolve into long-term business relationships.

DYSFUNCTIONS Modern functionalism recognizes that when schools perform their functions, dysfunctions—which may be damaging—may occur. For example,

1. Education transmits culture, but what is transmitted and how it is transmitted has created tension among various groups who are scrambling for visibility in the curriculum. How much U.S. history can be devoted to any one group without slighting another? As we will see, a curriculum that is designed in part to enhance tolerance may latently contribute to intolerance.
2. Bringing masses of youngsters together as peers has contributed to a weakening of parental authority. By the middle-school years, parents find themselves competing for time and authority with their children's friends.
3. Schools led by concerned administrators and caring teachers provide an organized and predictable day for those children who come from disruptive or even violent homes. But some parents believe that inflexible school bureaucracy and teacher demands interfere too much in their family's life.

It is impossible to do society's work without creating some negative results. As long as the functional advantages of education outweigh the dysfunctional disadvantages and the dysfunctions are dealt with effectively, society still benefits. A fundamental principle

of functionalism—that the social system will return to a state of equilibrium—is not violated. Core values instilled in schoolchildren and reinforced in the other institutions provide the foundation for this equilibrium.

Although schools have their problems, functionalists suggest that the U.S. educational system as a whole is doing its job. Literacy and high-school graduation rates are going up, the racial gap in dropout rates is narrowing, and college attendance and degree completion are increasing for both genders and all races (see Table 16.1). Even with the economic downturn, unemployment is at a low level. Schools must be given credit for successfully transferring classroom learning to paid employment. On tests of verbal ability, social class differences have continued to narrow, making a plausible argument that meritocracy is alive and well (Weakliem et al., 1995). Despite the dysfunctional aspects, the functions of education are being carried out effectively.

CRITIQUE Many sociologists of education question the core functionalist view that social stability rests with transmitting culture from older to newer generations. These sociologists believe that the process of education is neither linear nor uniform and that some of the functions of education, such as skill-based schooling, are becoming obsolete in a rapidly changing society. Functionalist explanations for education do not adequately account for the dynamics of race, class, and gender that profoundly influence any student's educational outcome. For example, the socialization function of schools does not benefit many low-income children of color, especially if they are taught to follow orders when jobs now call for workers who can think critically and act independently (Torres & Mitchell, 1998). Emerging perspectives in the sociology of education emphasize that schools should promote social justice and diversity that challenge the status quo functionalists see as vital to social order.

Conflict Theory and Educational Inequality by Class, Race, and Gender

The rather glowing portrait of education in the United States painted by functionalists can be viewed quite differently from a conflict perspective. Conflict theory focuses on the social placement function of education. According to this perspective, a principal function of schooling in the United States is to reproduce and reinforce inequality. Rather than assigning future roles to students based on talent and motivation, the critical factors for achievement are social class, race, and gender. Of these three, social class appears to be the best overall indicator. In the landmark study published over three decades ago, based on family background and achievement test data from over half a

TABLE 16.1

Educational Attainment by Race and Gender, Selected Years

	White		African American		Hispanic*	
Year	Male	Female	Male	Female	Male	Female
Completed 4 Years of High School or More						
1965	50.2	52.2	25.8	28.4	(NA)	(NA)
1975	65.0	64.1	41.6	43.3	39.5	36.7
1985	76.0	75.1	58.4	60.8	48.5	47.4
1995	83.0	83.0	73.4	74.1	52.9	53.8
2000	84.8	85.0	78.3	78.3	56.6	57.5
Completed 4 Years of College or More						
1965	12.7	7.3	4.9	4.5	(NA)	(NA)
1975	18.4	11.0	6.7	6.2	8.3	4.6
1985	24.0	16.3	11.2	11.0	9.7	7.3
1995	27.2	21.0	13.6	12.9	10.1	8.4
2000	28.5	23.9	16.3	16.7	10.7	10.6

NA-Not Available

*Persons of Hispanic origin may be of any race.

Source: Adapted from Table 261, U.S. Bureau of the Census, 1998; Table 216, U.S. Bureau of the Census, 2001.

million students at 4,000 schools nationwide, sociologist James Coleman (1966) and his colleagues came to an inescapable conclusion: The single most important criterion for school achievement was socioeconomic status (SES), especially related to a child's home environment. Children with lower levels of achievement came from homes that lacked such things as an automobile, vacuum cleaner, or record player. Reading materials—books, magazines, newspapers, and encyclopedias—were also largely absent from these homes. Since children from poor families are likely to live in neighborhoods with other poor families, they attend schools with students who also lack material resources. Coleman's report found that the social class background of fellow students was highly related to a student's achievement. The poverty surrounding a student's life translates to lower levels of achievement. Low-achieving children attributed success and failure to luck rather than motivation or ability.

Coleman's findings from almost 40 years ago continue to be confirmed. As elements of SES, parental education, family income, and peer family income are the most powerful predictors of a child's success in school. Such is the power of SES that even when variables such as race, immigration status, and measured intelligence are accounted for, upper- and middle-class children still achieve at higher overall levels than do working- and lower-class children (Chaplin & Hannaway, 1998; Rusk, 1999; Kahlenberg, 2001a). But a poor child's failure in school cannot be attributed entirely to the home environment. Conflict theory argues that the schools these children attend also discourage learning. They are poorly funded, inadequately maintained, located in high-

crime areas and staffed by overworked and underpaid educators. They function primarily as institutions for social control and conformity rather than achievement and innovation.

Some classical conflict theorists take this scenario a step farther. From a Marxist perspective, educational content is intentionally designed by the upper class to perpetuate their dominance as a capitalist economic elite (Bowles & Gintis, 1976). Marxian conflict theorists argue that inequality in SES and education serves to obstruct the aspirations of lower-class children, thus reproducing the existing class structure.

Conflict theorists also emphasize the role of the hidden curriculum in persuading poor and working-class children to accept their place in life on the lowest rungs of the stratification ladder. The **hidden curriculum** includes all the informal, unwritten norms that schools use to keep students in line. Working-class students go to schools that stress rote learning, obedience, and little freedom of choice. Middle-class schools ensure that students follow directions but permit more student decision making. Schools catering to the elite—generally, expensive private schools—encourage creativity, divergent thinking, and independence. Although almost half of students in privileged, private schools are of average academic ability, they achieve at much higher levels than comparable students in public schools (Powell, 1996). Conflict theorists maintain that aspects of the hidden curriculum ensure that class position is maintained from one generation to the next.

Schooling is supposed to enhance opportunities for all to succeed, but conflict theory suggests that it actually does the opposite. The elite and a very few others are destined for success; many others encounter mediocrity and failure. This system remains unchallenged in part because the "nonelite" who do succeed become role models for the others. The schools are not responsible for the failure of the other students; something must be inherently "wrong" with the students themselves.

In his bestselling work *Savage Inequalities* (1991), author and social critic Jonathan Kozol examined the massive inequality in U.S. education. Kozol contrasts several New York City public schools—those in neighborhoods of poor and heavily nonwhite residents—with others where well-educated families and few low-income students live. One school in a poor Bronx neighborhood with a capacity of 900 students serves 1,300. Students share textbooks, the library has only 700 books, 26 computers and no encyclopedias. There is no recess because there is no playground. Four kindergartens and a sixth-grade class of Spanish-speaking children are packed into a single room. In another part of the Bronx, by no means its richest area, a public school serves 825 kindergarten through sixth grade students. The school is surrounded by large, expensive, and beautiful homes, and the excellence of the school adds to the property values. Classrooms are clean and well maintained. Dedicated parents and volunteers donate time, money, and school materials. The library has 8,000 volumes and every class has at least one computer. The district cannot afford a librarian, but educated parents volunteer as library staff. Fundraisers by the parents' organization enhance resources. What does Kozol's analysis tell us about inequality?

TRACKING: SOCIAL CLASS AND RACE Even in wealthier schools, children of all races and social classes may occupy the same building but experience the learning process quite differently. Latino and African American children, who are disproportionately poor, are far more likely to be assigned to "special" classes, including lower level nonacademic or vocationally oriented ones. This practice of grouping children according to an assessment of their ability is called **tracking**. These special classes for the lower "tracks" are often overcrowded, have inadequate facilities, and are staffed by rotating teachers. The opposite is true of the higher or "gifted" tracks. The children in higher tracks are far more likely to learn critical thinking and logic; the children in lower tracks are far more likely to learn by rote memory and practice obedience to authority (Finn, 1999). A result, according to conflict theorists, is that high-tracked students are prepared to be managers in the global economy and lower tracked students are prepared for a life of wage labor.

With an elementary school legacy already in place, conflict theorists maintain that tracking in high

When schools cannot offer an adequate learning environment, conflict theorists argue that schools are warehouses of social control rather than sites for student achievement.

school operates to separate the college and noncollege bound. Some educators justify tracking by arguing that the college bound are more ready to learn, learn more rapidly, and should not be restrained by the slower progress of other students. Critics argue that students in lower level tracks are actually discouraged from living up to their potential. Research shows that class and race have a great impact on tracking, regardless of past achievement, ability, and IQ. Nonwhite and poor children more often find themselves in non-college-bound tracks where they encounter a less rigorous and less rewarding curriculum (Oakes & Lipton, 1996; Lucas, 1999). Although the number of high-school dropouts has decreased and the number of high-school and college graduates has increased, there remains a continuing education gap based on both race and social class.

Conflict theorists argue that tracking is a barrier to equal opportunity for lower- and working-class children and children of color. However, most research today finds that bias in tracking is now likely to be more class-based than race-based (Kahlenberg, 2001b). For example, affluent parents will work to assure their child gets into higher level tracks even when the child's test scores do not warrant the placement. To the dismay of teachers seeking to modify tracking so that all students benefit, these parents work to keep the system in place. Since their children benefit at the expense of others, a class-based tracking system is maintained (Wells & Oakes, 1998; Yonezawa & Oakes, 1999). Although segregation of students by ability is supposed to be an advantage of tracking, its cumulative effects can be destructive (Ansalone, 2000; Page, 2001). Since tracking encourages learning for some children but discourages it for others, the standard of equal opportunity in education is compromised.

GENDER Along with social class and race, gender is another important factor that influences the educational process. According to conflict theory, schools put girls at a major disadvantage in the opportunity to compete economically. High-school girls are tracked into academic courses such as English and vocational courses such as word processing and home economics more often than are boys. While more girls graduate from high school, a greater number are also enrolled in vocational education courses. Overall, high-school vocational education for girls is geared to the noncollege bound who either marry or wind up in low-paying, dead-end jobs. Girls take courses that prepare them to be employed right out of high school. The overwhelming majority of students in courses geared to retail sales, health assistance, and secretarial and other office occupations are female. This pattern is especially true for working-class and minority girls (Weiler, 2000). Historically, vocational education has been reserved for the less powerful in society, whether they are women, the working poor, or other skilled laborers (Conroy, 1998; Kincheloe, 1999). Conflict theorists also suggest that those women who do go on to college receive less faculty encouragement for their work, have fewer female role models, and will be listened to less by faculty and interrupted more by their male classmates (Condravy et al., 1998; Gumbiner, 1998; Canada & Pringle, 2000). Both high-school and college classrooms serve to perpetuate gender stratification.

Men and women who graduate from college enter a gender-segregated workforce. When an occupation is dominated by one gender, its pay and prestige reflects that pattern. Gender contributes more to a wage gap than race, ethnicity, or years of schooling (Chapter 13). Conflict theorists argue that "gendered" education ensures that men, especially white men, maintain dominant economic positions that perpetuate both racial and gender inequality in all parts of society.

CRITIQUE The strength of the conflict approach to education lies in the abundant evidence showing that

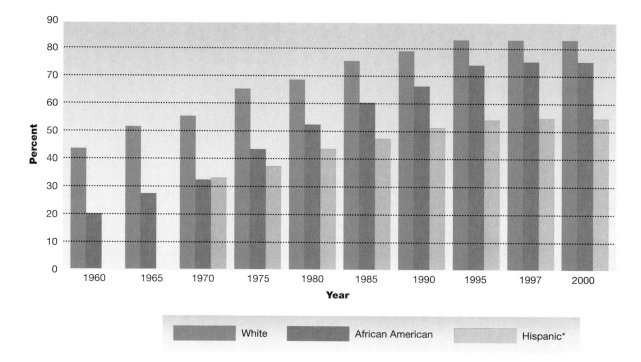

FIGURE 16.1 Percentage of Students in the United States Who Completed Four Years of High School or More, 1960–2000 (for persons 25 years and older), by Race.

*Persons of Hispanic origin may be of any race.

Source: Adapted from Figure 4.1, p. 158, U.S. Bureau of the Census, 1998; and Table 215, U.S. Bureau of the Census, 2001.

SES is a powerful variable to explain school achievement in the United States as well as throughout the world. In both developed and developing countries a "wealth gap" and gender gap stratify children by access to quality education and school achievement (Filmer & Pritchett, 1999). In his pioneering work, Brazilian educator Paolo Freire (1970) bluntly stated that schools provide a "pedagogy of the oppressed." He indicated that the oppressed are a social class unspecified by race, gender, ethnicity, language, and culture (Freire & Macedo, 1995).

However, the view that schools intentionally serve the interests of the ruling elite is not verified.

Although Freire's work has stimulated over three decades of international dialogue on educational philosophy, teachers do not see themselves or their schools as passive tools to maintain the class status quo. They want all students to achieve at the highest level possible. In addition, the notion that tracking by ability groups disproportionately harms poor and minority children is countered by other evidence showing that achievement is enhanced when teachers tailor instruction to the level understood by most children in a class (Loveless, 1999a). As we will see later in the chapter, tracking is also an issue related to diversity and school reform that is far from resolved.

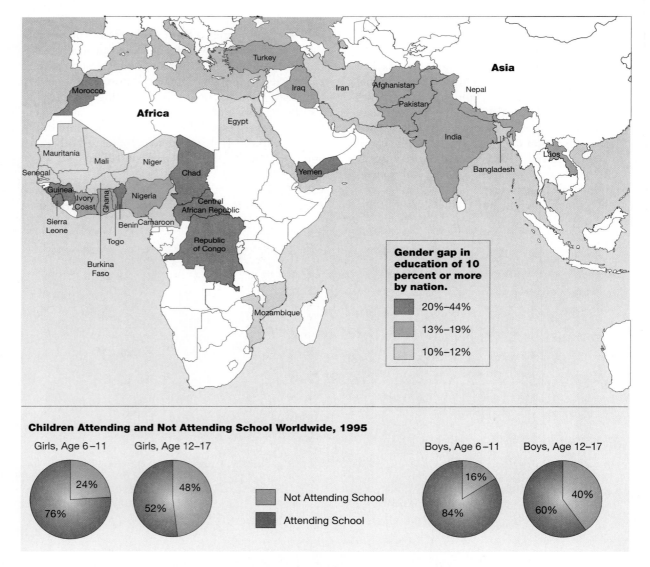

FIGURE 16.2 The Global Gender Gap in Education. The gender gap averages the difference between enrollment rates for boys and girls in primary and secondary schools. The larger the gap in percentage points, the more disadvantaged girls are relative to boys. In developing nations in Africa and Asia the wealth gap also increases the gender gap in education.

Source: Adapted from "Education: Gains and Gaps" in *The Washington Post*, October 24, 1998. Copyright © 1998 by *The Washington Post*. Reprinted with permission.

Symbolic Interactionism: Education as Socially Constructed

Symbolic interactionism focuses on the socialization function of schools and how a child is transformed into a student. Like other roles, the student role is socially constructed. Children, teachers, and student peers actively engage in a process of mutual interaction; the roles they carry out in the school are subject to continual negotiation and definition. Recall from Chapter 5 that for symbolic interactionists, socialization is a dynamic, reciprocal process. Children actively participate in defining their student role.

THE POWER OF LABELS Labeling in the classroom plays a key role in the way children define themselves at school. Different expectations based on labels assigned by teachers and other students lead to different outcomes. Research demonstrates the idea that students develop their own culture and actively participate in constructing their own set of labels at various points in their schooling. For example, when entering middle-school, a new identity as a seventh grader is forming, as a middle-school student suggests: "Teachers don't always talk to you as a little kid. . . . You have to act more mature 'cause we are growing up and becoming young adults." On entering high school, the freshman identity is being built: "Little kids will look up to me . . . You feel older and more sophisticated" (Staton, 1990:81, 106).

Another consequence of labeling is that both students and teachers may eventually give in to negative labels. For students, assigning a negative label may produce such a stigma that their self-esteem suffers. For teachers in working class schools who use curriculum guides referring to their students as "educationally deficient," teaching is compromised. If teachers believe children are not interested in learning and there is less resistance to easy work, then they demand less from their students. As one researcher notes (Finn, 1999:59),

> Schools have little to offer so they offer little in return. They stop asking for real effort on the part of students. In return, the students offer enough cooperation to maintain the appearance of conducting school.

Students and teachers alter their behavior to fit the negative label in a self-fulfilling prophecy. Why should students even try to achieve when they and their teachers believe they are not only incapable of learning—"educationally deficient"—but not interested in learning in the first place? Opponents of tracking believe that children assigned to low tracks are negatively labeled and that tracking leads to lower self-esteem, lower aspirations, and lower academic achievement (Nicholson, 1998).

But even a self-fulfilling prophecy is not a completely passive process. A student who is labeled an underachiever will resist the increased workload that a concerned teacher assigns, but may also resist being labeled a failure. Ongoing negotiation creates a working relationship. Students may continue to behave as "underachievers" in the teacher's estimation, but the student modifies his or her behavior through mutual interaction and ever-changing definitions of the situation. The modification of behavior by the student illustrates the concept of the **end point fallacy**—new labels produce new behavior in an ongoing process. Behavior continues to be modified in a never-ending process—there is no end point.

An understanding of the end point fallacy is important because it alerts us to potential results of labeling. Labeling can be used in positive as well as negative ways. **Mainstreaming,** the integration of special-needs students into the overall classroom or

Symbolic interactionists suggest that students learn to adapt to a classroom according to how they define and act on the expectations of their teachers and their classmates.

school, recognizes the power of labeling. Mainstreaming was not meant for children identified as mentally retarded or having severe behavioral or emotional disorders. It is designed to reduce the stigma and negative outcomes of isolating children who may have learning disabilities, mild academic handicaps, or physical handicaps. Prior to mainstreaming, students with such disabilities were served primarily through special-education programs. These included "pull-out" programs in which students were pulled from regular classrooms for up to one hour a day to receive remedial instruction in small groups (Slavin & Fashola, 1998; Ruder, 2000).

In this sense, mainstreaming is the opposite of tracking. The idea is to provide as much "normal" school life and peer interaction as a special-needs student can handle. Ideally, a three-step process occurs: Mainstreaming reduces stigma, enhances self-confidence, and generates higher expectations for achievement by both teacher and student. The process is associated with positive student outcomes both educationally and socially, and therefore, the risk of failure is reduced (National Research Council, 2000; Westling & Fox, 2000). Mainstreaming got a big boost with the passage of the federal Individuals with Disabilities Education Act (IDEA) in 1997. Among its provisions, IDEA is explicitly designed to promote practices providing access to services *without labels*, focusing on child and family assets rather than deficits. High achievement through quality education will be fostered with high expectations by the teacher that will transfer to the learner (Telzrow, 1999; U.S. Department of Education, 2000a).

Tracking, special education, and pull-out programs are designed to serve the needs of underachieving students or those with varying levels of disabilities by separating them. But evidence suggests that these programs often limit rather than enhance learning opportunities, children are further marginalized, and the stigma of "being different" is increased (Fisher et al., 1999; Sizer & Sizer, 1999; Nordmann, 2001). The words from Emily Kingsley's poem "Like Me" reflects this idea of marginalization. "He" is a new kid at school with a disability:

> He studies all day in a separate class,
> And they say that it's called "Special Ed."
> And sometimes I don't understand what he's said,
> And he's nothing at all like me, like me,
> No, he's nothing at all like me.
>
> *From "Like Me" by Emily Perl Kingsley.*
>
> Copyright © 1987 by Emily Perl Kingsley. Reprinted by permission of the author.

Bolstered by IDEA, mainstreaming is now being enlarged to incorporate an *inclusiveness* model—ensuring that all students benefit from their education by becoming important and productive members of their school communities (Ferguson et al., 2000). Inclusive schools embrace mainstreaming—schooling special needs and other students together—as well as individualized learning—all students receive a learning experience that fits their special needs (Schuster et al., 2001).

Symbolic interactionism also emphasizes that since schools are part of the broader culture, programs to enhance school performance must be designed with cultural issues in mind. For example, Project Head Start, a federally funded preschool program to ensure that children are armed with the necessary skills for kindergarten, operates in hundreds of U.S. communities and assists a diverse population. Latinos, African Americans, and whites are about equally represented among the almost 1 million children enrolled in Head Start, but one-fifth enter the program speaking a language other than English (U.S. Department of Health and Human Services, 2002). For these children to be prepared for kindergarten, program development must account for how a child's cultural background impacts learning and how a teacher's cultural background impacts the way he or she teaches. Symbolic interactionism emphasizes that taken-for-granted cultural practices must be raised to the conscious level for children to be adequately prepared to participate in a democratic society (Lubeck et al., 2001:500).

CRITIQUE Symbolic interactionists point out that programs that integrate rather than separate students have an edge in reducing negative labeling and stigma for special needs students. However, the reduction of the stigma does not necessarily result in a positive self-concept for the special-needs child. Symbolic interactionists have difficulty accounting for data that teachers spend less individual instructional time with them, that they are less likely to be chosen by classmates for activities, and that students who were mainstreamed as children report a less than satisfactory quality life in adulthood (Maras & Brown, 2000; Pavri & Luftig, 2000; Hornby & Kidd, 2001). Most damaging is that special-needs children may have an eroded sense of self-esteem the more time they spend in inclusive classrooms (Loveless, 1999b; Wigle & DeMoulin, 1999). Also, symbolic interactionists tend to overlook the fact that mainstreaming-type programs work only if mainstreamed students are not too disruptive and teachers have the support and training to deal with the disruptions. If not, resources are drained and teachers focus too much attention on a few children to the detriment of the others (Everington et al., 1999; Holmes, 1999; Huber et al., 2001). While mainstreamed students do not rise to the level of the most talented, the most talented may suffer. As one advanced track gifted high-school student reported, "We're bored because we're pulled down to the level of the least intelligent and interested" (Burkett, 2001:88).

When special-needs children are mainstreamed whenever possible, such as this third grader in a music class, sociologists of education suggest that stigma toward these students is reduced and that their self-confidence is enhanced. They have more opportunities to interact with peers from all learning ability and physical ability levels.

Applying Sociological Theory to Education

Of all social institutions, education perhaps best illustrates the application of sociological theory to the real world. The most effective educational programs can incorporate the strengths of each major theoretical perspective, as well as account for the impact of the other social institutions on education. Each perspective helps answer the question, What can be done to prevent the risk of student failure? Research suggests that, at a minimum, programs that include the following elements will meet with the most success (Mehan & Rueda, 1997; Krovetz, 1999; Oakes & Lipton, 1999; Lynch, 2000). Notice how each element can be readily linked to one or more sociological theories.

1. Take a comprehensive approach. Recognize that educational disadvantages at home weaken attachment to school. Make parents partners in their child's learning. *(Functionalism)*
2. Keep the pedagogy of classroom learning relevant to the lives of all students so they do not feel isolated and marginal and so they see an end product, such as a good job, if they succeed. Cultivate school and business partnerships. *(Functionalism and symbolic interactionism)*
3. Raise expectations for at-risk students of lower SES backgrounds. *(Conflict theory and symbolic interactionism)*
4. Invest in schools with the highest dropout rates, not only with money, but through staff development, summer enhancement programs, and one-to-one mentoring. Show students that they are good investments. *(Conflict theory and symbolic interactionism)*

Sociological theory points to multiple levels of influence in dealing with student achievement. Education touches and is touched by every other social institution:

- families provide different levels of encouragement for their children to succeed in school;
- school funding rises and falls according to political interests and the health of the economy;
- religious leaders believe that moral education needs to be stronger in schools and encourage congregation members to advocate these wishes to school boards;
- schools are part of society, so the whole social system and not just pieces of it must be part of the process to improve student learning (Waddock, 1995:217).

A GLOBAL VIEW OF EDUCATION

Investing in education brings high returns globally. In the global economy quality education is the key to unlocking the door to economic prosperity. This key allows nations to compete in world markets and individuals to compete for the jobs demanded by the global economy. Whether the competitors are nations or individual citizens, education provides an asset, such as literacy, which can never be taken away. Education lasts a lifetime. Education is a social investment that adds to economic growth and enhances a person's quality of life. In the developing world, every year a child stays in school beyond grades 3 or 4 is correlated with higher wages, lower birth rates, and lower infant mortality (Academy for Educational Development, 2002). When nations fail to invest in education, not only is their competition in the global economy threatened, but within their borders inequality increases and more and more people are thrown into poverty (Birdsall, 2000).

Throughout the world, the role and content of education vary according to specific cultural, economic, and political demands. Education serves democratic and capitalistic interests in Costa Rica, Japan, and Singapore, and it serves socialist and authoritarian interests in Libya, Viet Nam, and North Korea. In Saudi Arabia and Israel education serves both religion and capitalism, but its content bolsters authoritarianism in Saudi Arabia and democracy in Israel. Education in Nicaragua, Nigeria, and Iran fostered swift and dramatic social and economic change (Najafizadeh & Mennerick, 1992; Spring, 1998). Education assures that there is no such thing as an "outside" world.

The Global Gender Gap in Education

One of the best ways to make economic development a success is to teach girls to read. Indeed, data suggest that with only a 10 percent increase in female literacy, family size shrinks 10 percent, child death rates drop 10 percent, and wages rise 20 percent. In the developing world it is estimated that gains in education for women and girls may account for almost a 40 percent drop in infant mortality (World Health Organization, 1999; World Bank, 2000). Education also influences rate of marriage (people marry later), patterns of work (people enter more white-collar than blue-collar jobs), health habits (people practice preventive health care), food consumption (people eat a healthier diet), and even leisure activities (people engage in recreation outside their homes and neighborhoods) (United Nations Development Program, 2001). A sociological perspective on education reveals many aspects of global interde-

pendence. An educated population can more easily accept new technology and can communicate with one another and the world more quickly and efficiently. Education creates more linkages to the "outside" world in an endless cycle of reciprocity.

One of the most important global demographic trends is that women's education level is the strongest predictor of fertility (birth) rate (Brown et al., 1999). This is true between countries and among women in the same country. This simple correlation masks its enormous impact, not only on the lives of individual women and their families, but on the world as a whole, confirming that education is inevitably an agent of social change.

Despite education's many benefits, and although it is no longer reserved for a culture's elite, there is a large and persistent global education gap. The largest gap is between the developed and developing world (see Table 16.2). Almost 97 percent of the world's 113 million children not enrolled in primary school are in the developing world. Of these children, 42 million live in sub-Saharan Africa and another 47 million live in South and West Asia (see Figure 16.2 on page 400). Most of these children are in poverty, most are in rural areas, and most of them are girls (Doyle, 1997; UNESCO, 2001). The adult illiteracy rate in China has been cut by two-thirds since 1949, but the gender gap in illiteracy remains large; only 9 percent of men are illiterate compared to 25 percent of women (World Bank, 2000). China reflects the larger global pattern; two-thirds of the illiterate adults in the world are women. The highest female illiteracy rates are in regions with the lowest indicators of human development, specifically in South Asia and sub-Saharan Africa. For example, Pakistan and Nepal have female illiteracy rates of 70 percent and 77 percent compared to about 40 percent for men in both countries. For Sub-

Education functions as both a powerful agent of socialization and a mirror to the society as a whole. This classroom in India reflects some gender segregation as well as less value put on a girl's education as compared to a boy's; fewer girls attend school— even at the primary levels.

TABLE 16.2

The Global Education Gap

A. Country Income Level and Education

Income Level (GNP)	Mean Years of Education by Age	
	15–19	45–49
Low Income	2.4	1.7
Lower-Middle Income	5.5	2.7
Upper-Middle Income	8.9	6.9
High Income	9.4	8.0

B. Adult Literacy Rate (ALR%) and Country Income Level (Selected Countries)

Country	ALR (%)	Income Level
Niger	16	Low
Togo	43	Low
India	45	Low
China	84	Lower-Middle
Singapore	88	Upper-Middle
South Korea	96	Upper-Middle
New Zealand	99	High

Examples of Low Income Countries:
Afghanistan, Bangladesh, Haiti, India, Malawi, Niger, Peru, Sudan, Togo, Uganda

Example of Lower-Middle Income Countries:
Bahamas, Chili, China, Ecuador, Jordan, Kenya, Philippines, Thailand

Example of Upper-Middle Income Countries:
Argentina, Czech Republic, Hong Kong, Hungary, Israel, South Korea, Poland, Singapore, Taiwan, United Arab Emirates, Venezuela

Examples of High Income Countries:
Australia, Britain, Japan, Kuwait, New Zealand, Northern Europe (all countries), United States

Sources: Lockheed & Verspoor, 1991; Kennedy, 1997; *United Nations Development Report,* 1998, 2001; World Bank, 2000.

Saharan Africa, the overall adult illiteracy rate is 50 percent for women compared to 34 percent for men. The African country of Niger ranks at the bottom on human development indicators and predictably has the worst adult illiteracy rates: 77 percent for men, but 93 percent for women (World Bank, 2000; United Nations Development Program, 2001; UNESCO, 2001). It is clear that in much of the developing world reducing the gender gap in education has not been a priority. Although the elimination of any education gap is in the best interests of a thriving global economy, sociology reminds us that even positive social change brings both benefits and liabilities, depending on how various social groups are affected.

Culture and Education

Culture has an enormous impact on education—how it is taught, what is taught, and who is taught. Although we are quick to applaud the achievements associated with education, there is another side to the coin. Consider what happens to those who are left behind when a culture shifts, first from an oral to a literate tradition, and then later when some languages are "selected" for literacy education and others are not. In an oral culture, knowledge is only what can be recalled and repeated to the next generation. There are many strengths in an oral tradition. When literacy replaces oral transmission, not only are sources of traditional knowledge lost, but languages can disappear when they are gradually absorbed into the standardized language of the literate culture (Jung & Ouane, 2001). Among indigenous peoples in Peru, Bolivia, and Chile, literacy offers both advantages and disadvantages. Literacy offers them the power to control their own destiny and to defend their right to remain different. Among the indigenous Guarani of Bolivia, for example, an ancestral language on the verge of extinction was reproduced in written form and introduced in schools as the primary language of literacy. For the first time, knowledge of their traditional culture that had been transmitted orally could now be transmitted to children in written form (Lopez, 2001). The asset of literacy also allows children the chance of a better life in the larger society. But the power literacy brings comes at a price. Guarani is taught along with Spanish, and it is inevitable that "literate culture" values will collide with the "oral culture" values and may serve to separate the literate from the illiterate, the old from the young, and the urban from the rural (Triebel, 2001). The Guarani, like many others who make the transition from an oral to a literate tradition, must deal with how their culture will be impacted.

Politics and Education

Educational programs in developing countries must also deal with broader social and political issues. Conflict theorists suggest that adult literacy, for example, may have low priority because it works against the interests of a ruling elite that depends on the low-paid services of the illiterate. Literacy would upset the balance of privilege and poverty on which some societies rest. For example, when women in the developing world are targeted for education, it is often nonformal and vocationally based (Stromquist, 1998). Education for women could challenge an entrenched gender stratification system that keeps women in low-paid jobs or out of the labor force entirely. This situation may explain the failure of literacy campaigns in parts of India (Ghose, 2001; Ramdas, 2001). Another consideration has to do with language choice and where a language fits in the hierarchy of languages. Only languages selected for school-based literacy have real survival potential. Very few of Africa's hundreds of indigenous languages will be incorporated in the schools, so if current trends in language policy continue, most African languages will be extinct by the next century (Prah, 2001).

The United States is not immune to the "language of choice" issue. Native American tribal governments are concerned that if children do not learn in their native tongue at the same time they are learning English, the culture will be lost (Demmert, 1996). The same is true for native speakers of Hawaiian, a language that has decreased in usage as a result of religious and political changes (Buck, 1993). In other states, bilingual education programs serving large Spanish-speaking populations have operated for decades. They are designed to prepare children for the transition to speaking and writing English. But critics of bilingual programs see them as nationally divisive. Supporters of bilingual education claim that students can adapt to a school's culture, even in language learning, without losing their own ethnic culture (Garvin, 2001; Smitherman, 2002). It is clear that increased cultural diversity in the United States will continue to fuel this debate. Also, it is clear that children who are bilingual will have an economic advantage when they leave school.

Even when the economic advantages of education are obvious, political issues remain. Can economic benefits be reaped but political power upheld? A case in point is how much an authoritarian regime can afford to censor its educational system when the regime needs an educated cadre to either maintain a prosperous economy or to develop an unprosperous one. Consider the enormous influence of the Internet. When some nations, such as China and Cuba, attempt to limit access to those sites that are "official," they may lose valuable sources of information that help with development. Bits of "unaccepted" knowledge will also inevitably slip through (Richard, 1998; Einhorn et al., 2001, 2001). With open access to the Internet, democratic societies must also confront the same issue. Should there be restrictions on Web sites related to information ranging from deviant (pornography or sexual misconduct) to deadly (how to build a bomb or engage in biological warfare)? The coordinated attack on the World Trade Center was planned and carried out largely through the Internet. With national and global security at stake, all nations—democratic or otherwise—must deal with issues of censorship in education.

EDUCATIONAL CHALLENGES FACING THE UNITED STATES

Diversity is a thread that runs through U.S. history and serves as a force for both unity and separation. Since it is clear that schools in the United States are being reshaped by diversity, schools are fertile grounds for debates on multiculturalism.

Multicultural Education: Schooling for Diversity

Over the next 30 years a gradual but dramatic change will occur in the racial and ethnic composition of children attending U.S. schools. The number of racial and ethnic minorities is expected to triple, with the largest increase among Latinos. Overall, Latinos will represent 25 percent of the U.S. population, with African Americans at 15 percent, and Asian Americans at 12 percent (Chapter 12). Because of the legal acceptance of declaring multiracial identity and the educational advantages of claiming Native American heritage, the Native American population is small but growing. Over the next half century immigration will account for about two-thirds of the population growth of the United States, with most of these immigrants coming from Asia, Africa, and Latin America. Because these groups are also younger than the national average, by 2025 a majority of the nation's schools will be made up of children of color. Although classrooms have always been heterogeneous, cultural sensitivity in the classroom is essential in serving children representing different racial and ethnic heritages. In addition to accommodating a range of ability groupings, the inclusiveness model described earlier also means inclusiveness in terms of race and ethnicity. Schools are fundamentally responsible for shaping positive or negative attitudes about an entire group, and understanding cultural diversity is now essential for effective participation in the global economy (Shaughnessy et al., 1998; Onyekwuluje, 1999). The need for multicultural education at all levels is obvious, essential, and urgent (American Council on Education, 2001a).

CURRICULUM ISSUES A multicultural curriculum highlights the ethnic heritage of all Americans—how an American identity is shaped based on this heritage and how this identity is represented globally (Jackson, 2001). Ideally, multicultural education seeks to offer children an appreciation of the heritage of other groups while at the same time fostering an appreciation of their own (Hyun, 2001). Parents and educators agree that multicultural studies should be infused into the school curriculum. But the curriculum of these studies is the subject of much debate among groups who differ on their moral visions of the United States. Each group would like to see its own vision implemented in the school curriculum, and these in turn can serve the political agendas of various groups (Sleeter & McLaren, 1995; Bernstein, 2001).

The changing demographic portrait of America is first reflected in elementary classrooms, where children from Latino backgrounds and other students of color will soon become the majority of students attending American schools.

The cultural content of a school's curriculum is perceived to elevate or diminish some groups at the expense of others. For example, until recently, history textbooks in secondary schools rarely acknowledged the actions of the federal government that served to conquer, subordinate, and kill Native Americans. Conflict theorists suggest that when a curriculum fails to account for the perspective of racial minorities in the historical record, the ideology of white supremacy becomes an accepted part of mainstream culture. Not only are racial differences talked about from a white norm, but the history of resistance to racism and oppression is virtually ignored (Parenti, 2002). In textbooks, the contributions of Native Americans, such as planting, cooking, food storage practices, herbal remedies, and hunting techniques adopted by settlers and infused into broader culture, were also ignored (Bordewich, 1996). Other formerly disempowered groups—African Americans, Asian Americans, women, the elderly, gay men and lesbians, to name a few—are advocating for space in the curriculum to highlight their history and achievements. As a result of this competition, schools are often sites for different groups to wage what has been termed "culture wars." At odds with the ideal of a multicultural curriculum, culture wars are fought under the banner that diversity is acceptable as long as my (cultural) group remains elevated and is portrayed in a manner to my liking. If not, multiculturalism represents reverse racism (Mio & Awakuni, 2000).

The majority of college students are now women, due mainly to a flood of "nontraditional" students—women who are returning to finish their degrees after raising a family.

DIVERSITY IN FOCUS

Desegregation and Resegregation: The Dilemma of Busing

"The judgment rendered this day, in time, will be . . . pernicious . . . In respect to civil rights, all citizens are equal before the law."

—Justice John Marshall Harlan, 1896.

In 1896 the United States Supreme Court ruled in *Plessy v. Ferguson* that states could legally separate the races (referred to at the time as "white or colored") in public facilities such as parks, schools, and buses, as long as those facilities were equal. Since existing racial **segregation** was now protected by federal law, this "separate but equal" doctrine served to reinforce it. Most states swiftly enforced the separation part of the doctrine but ignored the equal part. Although it took a half century, the prophecy suggested by Justice Harlan's lone dissenting opinion was finally fulfilled. In 1954 the Supreme Court reversed the 1896 ruling in the watershed case of *Brown v. Board of Education of Topeka,* which said that segregated schools are "inherently" unequal. Making school segregation illegal, however, did not make it nonexistent. In fact, since 1954 the percentage of children attending racially segregated schools has increased. Why? The racial segregation of

U.S. schools is probably the number one educational challenge facing all segments of society, from students and parents to educators and politicians. Life in a multicultural society requires better knowledge and understanding of differences in race, ethnicity, and social class. But because most people live in areas occupied by those of the same race and level of wealth, and children attend schools in these same areas, opportunities to interact with other races and social classes are limited. While there is widespread agreement that racial desegregation is desirable, there is often bitter disagreement on how to accomplish it.

Disagreement is obvious in the emotionally charged response to programs such as **busing,** in which children of different races are transported to schools according to a certain racial parity formula. Court-ordered desegregation efforts of the 1970s involved cross-town busing of African American and white children within the same school districts. By the 1980s, busing was expanded to include the transport of inner-city African American children to mostly white suburban districts and busing white children to newly created inner-city **magnet schools.** Because the magnet schools are selective, they recruit better students,

offer specialized programs, and provide higher quality instruction in superior facilities. For between-district busing, parents chose whether to allow their children to be bused or to remain in neighborhood schools.

Antibusing sentiment reached its height in Boston in the fall of 1974, when the nation witnessed appalling images of racial bigotry and violence perpetrated by both whites and African Americans. Opponents to forced busing saw it as a threat to their neighborhoods and lifestyles. Supporters saw it as a practical way to ensure civil rights, democratic principles, and understanding between races. If children of different races go to school together, their argument goes, they can adjust better when they meet up again in the workplace or other circumstances. Despite the high visibility of the earlier incidents such as those in Boston, only a few regions experienced any form of protest.

Busing was partly responsible for "white flight" to the suburbs and a resegregation of inner-city schools by both race and social class. Parents in more affluent areas were afraid that their children would be forced to attend poor quality schools. People with the most resources moved to the outer suburbs.

With its emphasis on social equilibrium, functionalists would be sympathetic to the view that multicultural education threatens the authority of the state, which in the United States is based on cultural ideals rooted in the philosophy, literature, and art of Western civilization (Bloom, 1987; Greene, 2001). Remember the controversy in 1992 marking the 500th anniversary of the "discovery" of America by Christopher Columbus? On one side were those who believed Columbus should be depicted as a hero who overcame massive obstacles to reach the New World. On the other side were those who believed Columbus should be depicted as a conqueror who should assume historical responsibility for the subjugation and murder of indigenous people. Depending on which view

of multicultural education is adopted, school children may be presented with a picture of Columbus that considers conquest and colonialism from the European perspective, from the perspective of the indigenous peoples of the Americas, or both.

THE IMPACT OF CULTURE Multicultural education at a minimum involves acknowledging the powerful role of culture on children—how it influences them and how their own subculture, race, ethnicity, and gender influence broader society. Multicultural education offers opportunities to examine diversity by providing a more level playing field on which no one group is better or worse than any other group (Jones & Clemson, 1996). Educators are moving away from

Thus, schools remain highly segregated because of residential segregation. Court-ordered busing was suspended in many cities by the late 1990s.

How successful was busing? It depends on how "success" is defined; both academic achievement and social equity must be considered. In schools where busing is voluntary, where schools offer supportive environments and meaningful activities to bring the races together, where parents are consulted and schools and communities work together, achievement levels of African American students are higher than those in segregated schools. On the social equity side, African Americans who attended "supportive" desegregated schools are more likely to have friends of other races, have better jobs, and be involved in activities and jobs that cross racial lines. Racial attitudes of both whites and African Americans who were schooled together also improved. On the other hand, busing is expensive and white suburban schools appear to benefit more than the inner-city schools reserved for the majority of children who were not bused. Also, African American parents are dismayed that their children cannot get into magnet schools due to spaces reserved for suburban whites. Others feel insulted when it is implied

that their children cannot adequately learn unless in the presence of white students. The nail in the coffin of busing had to do more with money and demographics than with achievement and equity. In the long run busing did little to change segregation by race and social class in schools or society. Not only has urban poverty increased with the end of busing, school resegregation is happening faster than at any time since the 1954 *Brown* decision.

Busing may be ending, but support for desegregation remains strong, especially when the focus is on high-quality schools for all children, no matter where they live or where their schools are located. Since race and social class are so connected, the new buzzword for desegregation is *economic integration,* a growing belief that money is a better predictor than race of academic achievement. San Francisco, one of the most racially diverse cities in the nation, has adopted a "diversity index," which accounts for race, economics, and family background in determining which schools children might attend. Since Latinos and African Americans are more likely than whites to be poor, when they attend more affluent schools, a measure of racial desegregation also occurs. But race and class are

not the same; some warn that such a diversity index is a weak alternative to true racial integration. It is much too early to say whether economic integration will serve as a meaningful option to racial integration. There is no consensus on a "best" method for desegregation, and there is no one way to measure success. However, we do have clear and consistent evidence that desegregated schooling has long-term benefits—enhancement of racial tolerance and understanding. In addition, a desegregated school is a meaningful path for a desegregated society.

1. What would the sociological response be to the argument that economic integration will not alter racial integration because race and class are not the same?

2. What programs involving schools, both public and private, would you suggest that could alter the path of a further resegregated society?

Sources: Olzak et al., 1994; Stave, 1995; Natale, 1998; Belsie, 1999; Pride & May, 1999; Eaton, 2001; Hamm & Coleman, 2001; Laosa, 2001; Orfield, 2001a, 2001b; *Plessy v. Ferguson,* 2001; Reid, 2001; Schofield, 2001; Walker, 2001; Fletcher, 2002.

the idea that a multicultural curriculum is merely about adding dark faces to the textbooks and new national holidays to the calendar (Boykin 1994:124). It seeks to work against prejudice and intolerance to prepare students to become critical agents of social change in the service of democracy.

Schools are expected to present "diversity within diversity," a monumental and conflicting task. They need to avoid substituting one set of stereotypes for another. All members of a particular group do not share the same view of their own culture. Schooling for diversity must also operate in harmony with democratic principles emphasizing equity and the right to learning (Gonzalez, 1995; Darling-Hammond, 1997). All this must be done in a limited amount of

time within an already packed curriculum. Schools must allow students from many subcultures to embrace their own history while at the same time arming them with necessary knowledge and skills to succeed once they leave school (Lloyd, 1999; Pacheco, 1999).

Culture does not merely mimic the past—it alters the present and transforms the future. Multicultural studies have impacted every level of education by putting "other" groups (such as women and people of color) on the same footing with dominant groups (whites, males, and those with European ancestry). In this way, the idea of "other" is eliminated, and diversity is presented within the framework of a commitment to social justice (Estrada & McClaren, 1993:31). Sociologists agree that even when schools simply add

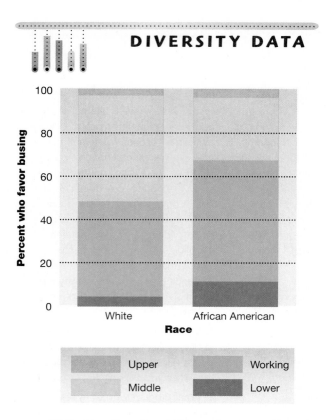

DIVERSITY DATA

Percent who favor busing (y-axis, 0–100)

White / African American (x-axis)

Race

Upper | Working
Middle | Lower

FIGURE 16.3 How Does Race Influence Support or Opposition to School Busing? Regardless of social class, African Americans are more supportive of busing than are whites. However, African American support for busing overall appears to be declining. What factors contribute to less support for busing than in the past for African Americans?

Source: NORC. General Social Surveys, 1972–2000. Chicago: National Opinion Research Center, 2000. Reprinted by permission of NORC, Chicago, IL.

multicultural studies with no real intent to transform the curriculum, the seeds for social change are planted. One educator's comment reflects the momentum multicultural education offers:

> America is not a private club defined by one group's historical hegemony. . . . multicultural education . . . defines demographic and pedagogical necessity . . . if we want youngsters from Los Angeles whose families collectively speak over 160 languages to be "Americans," we must first acknowledge their diversity and honor their distinctiveness. (Barber: 1997:29)

Violence in U.S. Schools

In 2000 violent crime rates in the U.S. reached their lowest level since 1973, and the risk of becoming a victim of violence was twice as likely outside of school (U.S. Department of Justice, 2001). The juvenile crime rate in the United States, including arrests for murder, has decreased in the last decade, and this decrease is reflected in juvenile crime in schools. However, this decrease may mask two other important trends. First, though the juvenile arrest rate for murder was lower in the mid-1990s than in 1989, it was still 50 percent higher than in the early 1980s. Thus, in the last two decades it showed both the greatest decline and the greatest increase (Snyder, 1999). Second, compared to all crime in schools, the proportion of serious violent crime (homicide, rape, sexual assault, aggressive assault) has remained constant over the past decade in most schools and has increased significantly in others (U.S. Department of Education, 2000b; Small & Tetrick, 2001). While theft and physical fights without weapons are the school crimes most commonly reported to police, about 10 percent of high-school students carry weapons—guns, knives and clubs—to school. In some inner-city schools, despite heightened security measures, 1 in 9 high-school students bring weapons to school and almost one-third carry guns to school. Although only 9 out of 1,000 students are victims of school-related serious violent crime, about 20 percent of middle- and high-school students report at least one violent crime while at school (Burke, 1998; Garrett, 2001; National Center for Education Statistics, 2001a; Small & Tetrick, 2001).

School violence tends to be concentrated in about 10 percent of schools, most of which fit the following profile: They are larger urban schools with older children; they serve children of color who are poor; they are located in high crime neighborhoods; they have high levels of school dropouts; most students have witnessed some form of violent crime both in and outside of school; and the most common reason for student expulsion is bringing guns or explosives to school. Victims and perpetrators are likely to be racial minorities. When homicide is involved, the most likely case is one teenage male killing another student or a teacher (U.S. Department of Education, 2000b; Garrett, 2001).

While this profile of school and killer fits the vast majority of school homicides in the past, and school homicide overall is rare, it does not fit a pattern of school violence that has emerged in the last decade, including the Colorado massacre mentioned in the chapter-opening vignette. Since 1991, multiple victim homicides occurred at schools in small cities in Kentucky, Arkansas, and Oregon, where boys opened fire on classmates and teachers. In the last 3 years throughout the United States, teenagers have been arrested for stockpiling weapons and explosives, building bombs, and allegedly planning to carry off multiple murders at school, some intending suicide in the aftermath (Bai et al., 1999; Associated Press, 2001; Sultan, 2001).

The tragedies and near-tragedies reported here suggest the emerging pattern. School homicides are likely to be multiple murders carried out by teenage

The use of guns and other weapons by American schoolchildren has prompted security measures such as daily weapons inspections of everyone entering a school building.

boys who are white, middle class to affluent; live in small cities or suburban areas; are bright, often high-achieving students; have no connection to violent gangs or drugs; and have few identified family background or personality characteristics that would link them to violent behavior. One researcher labels a student who fits the emerging profile as the "teenage suicidal terrorist" (Barr & Parrett, 2001:37). The search for reasons for school violence has produced much speculation but few definite answers. Sociologists point to four factors that offer reasonable indicators for violence in the schools.

1. **The Peer Connection.** The shootings and assaults were mostly done by boys identified as passive, alienated, and exhibiting little empathy for others. Later investigation marked them as ostracized or shamed by their peers—especially by the school's "popular" clique. Research suggests that isolation and humiliation by peers may have been the triggers for the violence. Regardless of race and social class, antisocial behavior is one result of low self-esteem and is the single best predictor of later aggression (Kerr & Nelson, 2002). Revenge followed by suicide is often how they settle "grudges" or deal with personal problems (Bai et al., 1999).

2. **The Drug and Gang Connection.** The world outside the school fuels school violence, with gangs and drugs as important sources. Although higher in inner-city areas, students in all locales say that gangs operate openly in their schools. While students report that the presence of street gangs in schools is down from about 30 percent in the early 1990s, gang presence is sill estimated at between 17

percent and 25 percent. Schools are also a convenient location to sell and distribute drugs. Marijuana use, for example, is increasing for 9th through 12th graders, and over 30 percent report that someone has offered or given them an illegal drug on school property (Kaufman et al., 2000; U.S. Department of Justice, 2000; National Center for Education Statistics, 2001a).

3. **The Media Connection.** Although the media is an easy scapegoat for violence, the link to the Colorado massacre is a particularly strong one. One of the killers was addicted to extremely violent video games, such as Doom and Quake. He regularly surfed hate Web sites, and his own Web site provided information about building bombs and lethal weapons. In addition, media attention to school shootings is clearly a factor in copycat crimes and teen suicide. Whether hours spent in a fantasy world of violent video games, movies, and the Internet increases adolescent isolation and encourages the vision they see on their computer screen remains unclear. Of course, millions of teens consume violent media and do not become killers. However, more and more evidence is accumulating that suggests the media connection as a key factor in school violence (Bai et al., 1999; Easterbrook, 1999; Johnson et al., 2002).

4. **The Gender Connection.** Gender role is also a critical factor in understanding school violence but one that is ignored by almost all media sources and most professional ones. Reporters, educators, parents, and scholars refer to the perpetrators as "violent youths," "isolated adolescents," "lonely teenagers" and "unhappy students" and rarely mention that virtually all the killers are male. Indeed, the gender connection is the only one that adequately links both the past and emerging patterns of violent perpetrators in school. Definitions of masculinity in the United States are associated with aggression—toward other boys as well as girls. Masculinity is celebrated through sexual harassment and bullying, often starting in elementary school (Chapter 6). The "boys will be boys" attitude, which condones male aggression, shows up in numerous incidents that have caused injury and death on high-school athletic fields, in all-male militant schools, and in college fraternities (Bronner, 1999; Jacobs, 2000; Martin & Hummer, 2001). And when tied to media, the gender connection is even stronger. Not only are violent video games marketed to adolescent boys, but gender role portrayals are highly stereotypical—depicting aggressive boys and helpless girls (Dietz, 1998).

Given these connections, sociologists suggest that dealing with school violence requires a coordinated effort at all levels. At the school district level, there are good arguments that zero-tolerance policies—no excuse will be accepted for violating certain school rules—actually fail to create safe environments. Although zero-tolerance policies usually start with the worthy intent of keeping weapons out of school, the vast majority of the 3.1 million suspensions or expulsions from school are for nonviolent acts (Schiraldi & Ziedenberg, 2001). "Get tough policies" such as facility lock-downs, metal detectors, armed guards in the hallways, and elimination of sports and after-school activities not only interrupt learning but produce mistrust, resistance, and fear, especially when they are applied along racial and class lines (Hyman & Snook, 2000; Fine & Smith, 2001; Skiba, 2001). From this perspective, militarized schools are less safe because the relationship between teacher and student is damaged—fear replaces trust for both (Ayers et al., 2001).

Humanizing schools by involving the community, teaching conflict resolution, improving school spaces, and using mentoring offer more successful strategies and have the additional advantage of public support. In the wake of the Colorado killings, polls showed that almost half the public believe the most effective way of preventing school shootings is to pay more attention to antisocial behavior, to identify those children who are ongoing targets of peer ridicule, and to intervene early when necessary (Browne, 2001; Noguera, 2001). This does not mean that "incorrigible," violence-prone students should be allowed to remain in the school. It does mean, however, that a self-fulfilling prophecy is a real possibility when coercion is the accepted method to combat violence.

At the teaching level, the threat of violence keeps many from entering the profession or pushes good teachers out. The following journal entry from a high-school teacher in Watts, a poverty-stricken community in South-Central Los Angeles that serves Latino and African American students, was written the second week of school:

> I've met a kid, Antonio, who claims to be involved with the "Mexican Mafia," says he is selling large amounts of coke and heroin, and tells me he wants to stop but cannot because of his Mafia connections. . . . I am not invincible. This kid could attack me simply to try to prove that his story is real. . . . My other kids are mostly gems, so lovely and energetic that I move at the speed of light to give them all I have. I so love to teach. I just think I'd feel a lot better about it if I weren't afraid of being killed. (Adapted from Diver-Stamnes, 1995:85)

Teachers must confront and openly respond to the daily reality of their students' lives, which often contain violence and death. Acknowledging and affirming the fears of both teachers and students should become part of teacher training and classroom pedagogy, and should be used as a basis for learning (Johnson, 1995; Palmer, 1998).

LIFE CONNECTIONS

Who Goes to College?

Higher education in the United States is also experiencing enormous change as multiculturalism and global interdependence combine with continuing challenges that influence higher education.

Diversity in Higher Education

The democratization of American higher education occurred after World War II, when the GI Bill enabled veterans to enter colleges. Before that time, institutions of higher learning were reserved for primarily white, Protestant men from affluent families (Brown, 1996:71). The college population today reflects a considerably different student composition, but the academic doors are still slammed shut for most children living in poverty. Cost restricts opportunities for working-class and lower-middle-class students, although they have a better chance to attend college than in the past.

The high-school seniors entering U.S. colleges in 2001 are the largest and most diverse group of students in history. Besides social class, college diversity has increased in terms of age, race, religion, gender, ethnicity, and number of international students. Racial minorities comprise almost 35 percent of college students, up from 28 percent just a decade ago. Almost one-fifth are bilingual or consider English to be their second language (College Board, 2001). Their share of degrees at every level increased between 2 percent and 4 percent per year over the last decade, accounting for about 25 percent of associate's degrees, 21 percent of bachelor's degrees, 15 percent of master's degrees, and 13 percent of doctoral degrees (Gehring, 2001; American Council on Education, 2002). For gender, due mainly to the influx of women in their 30s and 40s who resume college and attend part time, women now comprise 54 percent of all college students. This high level of female college enrollment is predicted to not only continue but significantly increase so that by 2011 women are expected to receive between 55 percent and 70 percent of all bachelor's degrees (College Board, 2001; National Center for Education Statistics, 2001b).

However, there are important patterns to this diversity. As we have seen throughout the text, demographic variables that now describe "diversity" are powerful determinants of behavior. For higher education, the variables of gender, race, and social class can predict the likelihood of entering college, where stu-

Students of color will make up the majority of the population in schools in the United States by 2025, but multicultural diversity in education is already rapidly occurring, as demonstrated by this recent college commencement at New York's Columbia University.

dents go to college, what they major in, the probability that they will graduate, and how much money their degree will be worth. Think about how these demographic variables apply to your own college experience. Sociology offers explanations for these patterns.

Community Colleges

Community or two-year colleges typically channel students into two major groups. One group attends for career education in semiprofessional and technical fields, where skills must be learned but a college degree is not necessary. These students earn an "associate's degree" as well as certification in a given pro-

INTERNET CONNECTIONS

The text discusses the issues surrounding school desegregation and the dilemma of busing. For a particularly critical and scathing point of view on *school busing*, go to:

http://www.adversity.net/special/busing.htm

("School Busing 25 Years Later: Good Riddance to a Bad Idea"). For a historical look at busing go to:

http://www.justicetalking.org/shows/show179.asp

After examining the content of both Websites, answer the following questions: Do you believe that busing was a "bad idea" from its inception? Do you think that busing is a "dead issue," or does this practice hold some value in certain areas? What is your opinion of "magnet schools"?

gram, such as health, computer technology, paralegal studies, or engineering technology. They are assured that a job is waiting for them at graduation. The other group of students at community colleges plans to transfer to four-year colleges. To the benefit of both groups, community colleges offer inexpensive courses, flexible schedules, and a variety of services to assess student interest and ability and to assist students in career choices. They serve the needs of a changing society that demands a pool of technically competent people and ongoing training and retraining programs. They also provide enrichment courses and continuing education for the community at large.

There is also a less optimistic view of community colleges. Community colleges may benefit students by their accessibility and career orientation but also may block students' advancement for the same reasons. College admissions tests and minimum grade-point averages are usually not required, so students enter with very different levels of preparation (Nettles & Millett, 2000). Bright and motivated community college students complain that when instruction is conducted at a high-school level, they will be inadequately prepared for the more academically challenging four-year college awaiting them. Another concern is that community college career-education programs prepare students for jobs offering less opportunity for advancement. Because career-education students take few liberal arts courses, they are less prepared to attend four-year college programs after they have been employed for a while. Many of their community college courses are not accepted for transfer at a four-year college, so they may have to start all over again. Even for those who intend to transfer and graduate from a four-year college, the reality is that a large majority do not. Many from this group eventually enroll in career-education programs. It is not surprising that

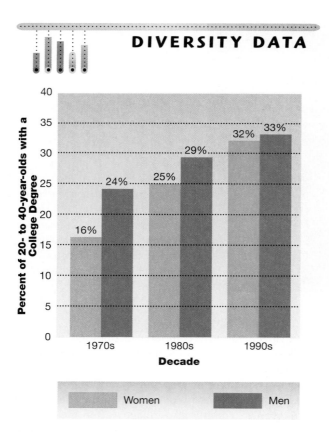

DIVERSITY DATA

y-axis: Percent of 20- to 40-year-olds with a College Degree

1970s — Women 16%, Men 24%
1980s — Women 25%, Men 29%
1990s — Women 32%, Men 33%

x-axis: Decade

Legend: Women, Men

FIGURE 16.4 **Percent of 20- to 40-year-olds with College Degrees, by Gender and Decade.** The college graduation rate for both genders has steadily increased since the 1970s so that today about one-third of men and women are college graduates. Since women are now enrolled in college in greater numbers than men, do you think women with college degrees will eventually outnumber men?

Source: NORC. General Social Surveys, 1972–2000. Chicago: National Opinion Research Center, 2000. Reprinted by permission of NORC, Chicago, IL.

women, racial minorities, and lower-SES students are disproportionately enrolled in community colleges and career-track programs (Hale, 2001; White, 2001). Although minority students have comparable or even higher educational aspirations as white students, they are least likely to transfer to four-year colleges. Community college enrollment may place limits on later career success (Rendon & Hope, 1996; Herideen, 1998).

A Bachelor's Degree and a Job

A college degree is key to economic success. The highest paying jobs all require a college degree, and throughout the economy, jobs requiring a degree are growing twice as fast as others (U.S. Department of Labor, 1999). For four-year colleges, both the job landscape and enrollment have changed radically in the past 20 years. The predicted decline of the tradi-

tional 18- to 21-year-old college population, including full-time students, occurred in the 1980s, forcing some smaller colleges out of business. By the 1990s, however, this trend reversed, with the numbers of traditional age students entering college at record levels and at numbers predicted to increase significantly into the next decade (Jamieson et al., 2001). But the decline of the traditional age students in the 1980s altered the way many colleges delivered undergraduate education. Colleges responded with renewed efforts to bring in "nontraditional" students, especially "re-entry" women and adults whose degrees are being paid for by their current employers. Recruitment of minority and international students was also accelerated with a wide array of programs and services designed to meet their learning needs. Most of these programs remain in place even as full-time traditional age students return to college in record numbers. In this sense, multiculturalism and diversity allowed many institutions not only to survive, but to grow.

This change has been a mixed blessing. There is concern that some colleges have lowered standards to become "diverse" for reasons of economic survival, especially in terms of federal support (Hardaway, 1995; Zwerling, 1996). Social justice issues take a back seat. Another concern is that in catering to the workplace, colleges are abandoning liberal arts missions. Employers who pay for educational expenses desire skill-based programs that are readily transferred to the workplace. They often will pay for courses in accounting and marketing but not for courses in history and literature—but both are needed for the degree. Thus, colleges have been forced into a version of the career-education dilemma faced by community colleges. The paradox is this: Career success requires a liberal arts-based education from a four-year college, but students are reluctant to major in areas that do not offer "practical" skills. The dilemma is reflected in often-heard comments during registration, such as "Why do I have to take philoso-

INTERNET CONNECTIONS

There is a gender gap in education throughout the world. To explore this issue a bit more beyond the text go to:

http://www.oxfam.org.uk/policy/papers/gendgap/gendgap.htm

You can read a short description about the gender gap in education and also obtain a more comprehensive report by downloading some of the rtf. files. Write a short descriptive summary of the global gender gap.

phy? I'm going to be an accountant." This orientation has led to an explosion of some majors, such as business and preprofessional studies, and a decline of others, such as literature and the humanities.

Another element of the paradox is that businesses are reluctant to hire graduates who come from programs that are too skill-based. Many of the flood of business majors vying to enter the corporate world have found themselves less competitive precisely because they did not have a strong liberal arts background. The demand for broadly educated rather than narrowly trained graduates has increased. Beyond necessary technical competence in some areas, such as computer programming, businesses provide the job-specific training that students cannot get in college anyway. If students are trained for what is relevant today, they may be shut out of the workplace tomorrow, when "relevance" changes and there is no core knowledge base to fall back on. The trend in majors has shifted, with an increase in liberal arts fields and a decline in business areas (Table 16.3).

Sociologists are interested in yet another important factor that links race and class to this shift in majors. African Americans and Latinos more likely to major in business than are Asians, Asian Americans, and whites (Leppel, 2001). Race is also a strong correlate of who goes to public universities compared to private colleges, and choice of major. Asian Americans and whites are not only more likely to attend private colleges, especially elite ones, but are more likely to major in liberal arts and sciences (Trusty et al., 2000; U.S. Department of Education, 2000c; College Board, 2001). Both major and type of college one attends translate to different economic payoffs. There is strong evidence that, regardless of race, graduating from an elite private college with a degree in liberal arts or science has significant economic returns—and that this premium has increased over time (Brewer et al., 1999).

Popularity of majors is also due to marketplace realities and to the repackaging of college courses to appeal to students faced with an uncertain economic future. Recognizing this paradox, many colleges are now designing unique programs that combine ingredients of professional and liberal learning. On the applied side, curriculum requirements for a variety of majors now include an internship or volunteer work that can be highlighted as "practical experience" on a new graduate's résumé. On the liberal arts side, courses in multicultural, gender, and global studies are now required. Interdisciplinary programs, particularly between professional schools and colleges of arts and science, are gaining in popularity.

Overall, while there are clear race, class, and gender linkages that serve as advantages or disadvantages regarding who goes to college, there has been a steady rise in the expectation of attending college among all groups (Bennett & Xie, 2000; Reynolds & Pemberton, 2001). This rise in aspirations is realistic for one key reason: A college degree is now essential for career success in the global economy.

SOCIETY CONNECTIONS

Student Achievement

Any complacency Americans may have had about the quality of their schools was severely jolted by a 1983 report, *A Nation at Risk*. Although this study is now 20 years old, it continues to serve as the benchmark for assessing school quality (Spring, 1998; Sizer, 1999). According to the authors, educational achievement in the United States experienced a steep, 20-year decline. Several measures were used to support their assertion. Scores on standardized tests, such as the Scholastic Aptitude Test (SAT) taken by college bound seniors, which are now the norms for assessing education quality, decreased sharply. **Functional illiteracy,** the inability to do the reading, writing, or basic math necessary to carry out daily activities, increased dramatically. Achievement of children in the United States lagged far behind those in other nations, especially in mathematics and verbal skills.

TABLE 16.3

Bachelor's Degrees Earned, Selected Fields

	1990	1995	2000
Business and Management	246,698	234,323	233,119
English Language and Literature	47,519	51,901	49,708
Liberal and General Studies	27,985	33,356	33,203
Philosophy, Religion, and Theology	12,068	12,854	14,110
Social Sciences and History	118,083	128,154	125,040

Source: Adapted from Table 325. U.S. Bureau of the Census, 1998; Table 287, U.S. Bureau of the Census, 2001.

Mediocrity ruled. The report indicated that the United States was "at risk"; if schools produce people who cannot be competitive, the very future of the nation is at stake (National Commission on Excellence in Education, 1983).

The good news is that for the first time since 1967, SAT scores have risen. Since 1991, verbal scores have increased by 7 points and math scores by 14 points. However, this rise in scores masks another important reality: There is a persistent race and gender gap in scores. Although the gap has decreased somewhat, men continue to outperform women, and racial minorities lag behind whites. In the math section, Asian Americans students outperform all other groups (College Board, 2001). Data from the National Assessment of Educational Progress (NAEP) show that in overall achievement, children do better in the earlier grades, but by high school, performance in most subjects drops considerably (Ravitch, 2001). NAEP as well as the U.S. Bureau of the Census (2001) data indicate that declines in mathematics and science appear to have reached a plateau, but verbal scores still show decline (SSBR, 2000). Even the plateau in math scores may be an artificial marker of achievement. Between 1999 and 2000, more students were barred from taking the NAEP than in the past because of limited English skills or significant physical and mental disabilities, so data are from a larger pool of better students. And as for SAT scores, NAEP data show a significant racial gap in achievement generally favoring whites over children of color (Grissner & Flanagan, 2002). Finally, although the number of years of schooling has increased, reading levels have stagnated and functional illiteracy continues to increase. Almost 90 million Americans lack basic literacy skills. Functional illiteracy translates to poverty (42 percent are below the poverty line), unemployment (they work an average of 19 weeks per year), and crime (7 in 10 prisoners are illiterate) (First Book, 2001). At the global level, the United States ranks 10th out of 17 industrialized nations in adult literacy (Bernstein, 2002).

Global Comparisons

Given its legacy of economic superiority and educational excellence, it is quite a shock to see how public schools in the United States stack up in a global comparison. In almost all measures, achievement levels of children in the United States are far lower than those in many other nations, including some in the developing world. Among thousands of students throughout the world at different ages and school levels, U.S. high-school seniors are typically at the lower end of the measurement scale (United Nations Development Program, 1998).

The greatest gaps are in mathematics and science, with the United States continuing to lag behind (see Table 16.4 on page 448). Overall, Japanese and Chinese students outperform U.S. students in these areas. Math scores for Asian American students are higher than for European Americans, but *lower* than for students from East Asia (Chen & Stevenson, 1995). This pattern suggests the importance of cultural influences on academic performance. A major study of attitudes and achievement finds that Asian American and East Asian parents believe that effort is the road to success. Americans in general believe that hard work pays off, but they also believe more strongly in limits due to natural ability (Stevenson & Sigler, 1992). According to symbolic interactionists, the results are explained by parents' messages to their children: East Asian and Asian American students get the message that hard work and diligence are the keys to learning. Other American students get the message that talent is limited by ability, so they may be discouraged from pursuing subjects their parents perceive are too difficult for them.

This rather dismal picture of student achievement in the United States brightens when we examine the data through sociological eyes. First, a wider range of students are now in school and are staying in school longer. While only 50 percent of high-school aged children were in school in the 1930s, 95 percent of that age group attends school now (Kaestle, 1995:343). Rates of school attainment, high-school graduation, and college attendance have increased steadily (National Center for Education Statistics, 2000; Baron, 2002). A more diverse student population is taking achievement tests today. As an example, nearly one in four students in U.S. elementary and high schools are from homes where English is either not the dominant language or not spoken at all, and these numbers are expected to increase (LaCelle-Peterson, 2000). The United States is educating more students and more difficult students to levels that a generation ago would have been available only to a favored elite (Kennedy, 1999; College Board, 2001).

Second, educational standards have not decreased but increased. For example, the definition of literacy has been continually modified to account for social changes that call for new skills not only for reading but for the ability to digest massive amounts of information (Kleiman, 1998; Kirsch et al., 2001; Goad, 2002). A person defined as literate in 1990 may be redefined as illiterate today. Also, data show no decline in reading among fourth graders for almost a decade (Christie, 2001). While "no decline" is not necessarily cause for celebration, the data must also be viewed in terms of how student achievement is assessed. When the method of instruction takes more of a "student-centered" than "teacher-centered" approach, when

GLOBAL CONNECTIONS

Examination Hell in Japan

The expression *shito goraku* guides Japanese students as they prepare for university entrance exams: "Those who sleep four hours a day will pass; those who sleep five hours will fail." Often referred to as "examination hell," the competition for entrance into the most prestigious universities in Japan is cutthroat. In Japan, the important thing is the university one graduates from; the subjects one studies are secondary. Success or failure on an entrance examination affects a student's entire future, since the prospect of finding a good job depends on the school attended. Indeed, major corporations restrict recruitment to a few select universities. Therefore, the Japanese believe that this cutthroat competition for university slots is necessary.

Japan's public schools are staunchly egalitarian and have a high commitment to mixed ability students. Students are not tracked by ability, either high or low, and individualized learning is rare. Students are expected to work together and cooperate not for individual praise but for the good of their classroom and the school. Homogeneity and sameness, not diversity and difference, are valued in education. Students are expected to work together and to cooperate in all school activities. Disabled students, for example, are often rejected for high school in Japan, regardless of their scores on entrance exams. In fact, many Japanese believe diversity and catering to individual differences has hurt U.S. education. Less than half of Japanese people see the United States' educational system as admirable. Although this view of our education system may be offensive, the Japanese point out that 95 percent of Japan's students graduate from high school.

The egalitarian system of Japanese education is highly effective for the majority of students. There is a tendency to pass students to the next grade so that they can stay with their grade cohorts. But when university entrance exams determine a person's future economic life, parents are willing to spend a great deal of money for special advantages for their children. Without supplemental lessons, some students would fall behind in the competition for entrance into the best universities. To meet the need for supplemental learning, *juku* ("cram schools") have become a thriving business throughout Japan; 90 percent of urban students in Japan are in some form of *juku*.

By the eighth grade, ambitious students are beginning to prepare seriously for high-school entrance exams. *Juku* likely begins here. For the most motivated students, tutoring programs lasting 4 to 5 hours a day after school and 8 to 10 hours on weekends are common. High schools are ranked according to their academic standing in the community, and as for the university, examinations are the main basis for admission. The best high schools better prepare students for the university exams. All Japanese high-school students are affected by the competition for college admission, but only 10 percent can be said to experience the intense competition for entrance into the most prestigious universities.

A version of the cram school is called *yobiku* and exists solely for the purpose of preparing students for university entrance exams. *Yobiku* primarily cater to *ronin,* who in Japan's feudal times were masterless samurai, wandering warriors. Today this term refers to students who wander between schools, having graduated from one without being admitted to another. Often they have failed the entrance exam to the university of their choice once or twice. Families pay as much as $5,000 a year for a first-rate *yobiku* where students may stay for a year or two to try for the necessary grade. Cram schools have created an enormous financial burden for Japanese parents and a psychological burden for children. Suicide rates for Japanese adolescents, for example, are highest in April when grades are posted and the educational fate of the young test-takers is publicly acknowledged.

Japan now recognizes the national obsession with university admissions tests as a social problem. Attempts to defuse the examination war have centered on dialogues between corporations, schools, and parents. Corporations are encouraged to move away from limiting the universities from which they will hire graduates. Smaller corporations that want to attract students from the best universities are joining the dialogue. These smaller companies argue that the current university–corporation link limits overall competition. Also, the downturn in the Japanese economy and a decline in the Japanese birth rate have had fewer students chasing university acceptance. The doors are opened for students who may have been denied entrance in the past. While cram schools are still common, universities are becoming more flexible. It may be that Japan's economic downturn will prompt more dialogue to resolve this social problem. To date, however, examination hell is a fact of student life in Japan.

1. What fundamental social values in Japan are reflected in the rise of cram schools and an acceptance of examination hell?

2. How would functionalists and conflict theorists explain the successes and failures of Japan's egalitarian public school system and its *juku* counterpart?

Sources: Kenmochi, 1992; McAdams, 1993; Halloran, 1994; Kristof, 1997; Keizai Koho Center, 1999 *Taipei Times,* 2001.

TABLE 16.4

Average Mathematics and Science Achievement* of Eight-Grade Students, by Nation: 1995 and 1999

1995				1999			
Maths		**Science**		**Maths**		**Science**	
Nation	Average	Nation	Average	Nation	Average	Nation	Average
1 Singapore	643	Singapore	607	1 Singapore	604	Chinese Taipei	569
2 South Korea	607	Czech Republic	574	2 South Korea	587	Singapore	568
3 Japan	603	Japan	571	3 Chinese Taipei	585	Hungary	552
4 Hong Kong	588	South Korea	565	4 Hong Kong SAR	582	Japan	550
5 Belgium (F+)	565	Bulgaria	565	5 Japan	579	South Korea	549
6 Czech Republic	564	Netherlands	560	6 Belgium-Flemish	558	Netherlands	545
7 Slovakia	547	Slovenia	560	7 Netherlands	540	Australia	540
8 Switzerland	545	Austria	558	8 Slovak Republic	534	Czech Republic	539
9 Netherlands	541	Hungary	554	9 Hungary	532	England	538
10 Slovenia	541	England	552	10 Canada	531	Finland	535
11 Bulgaria	540	Belgium (F+)	550	11 Slovenia	530	Slovak Republic	535
12 Austria	539	Australia	545	12 Russian Federation	526	Belgium-Flemish	535
13 France	538	Slovakia	544	13 Australia	525	Slovenia	533
14 Hungary	537	Russia	538	14 Finland	520	Canada	533
15 Russia	535	Ireland	538	15 Czech Republic	520	Hong Kong SAR	530
16 Australia	530	Sweden	535	16 Malaysia	519	Russian Federation	529
17 Ireland	527	**United States**	**534**	17 Bulgaria	511	Bulgaria	518
18 Canada	527	Canada	531	18 Latvia	505	**United States**	**515**
19 Belgium (W+)	526	Germany	531	19 **United States**	**502**	New Zealand	510
20 Thailand	522	Norway	527	20 England	496	Latvia	503
21 Israel	522	Thailand	525	21 New Zealand	491	Italy	493
22 Sweden	519	New Zealand	525	22 Lithuania	482	Malaysia	492
23 Germany	509	Israel	524	23 Italy	479	Lithuania	488
24 New Zealand	508	Hong Kong	522	24 Cyprus	476	Thailand	482
25 England	506	Switzerland	522	25 Romania	472	Romania	472
26 Norway	503	Scotland	517	26 Moldova	469	(Israel)	468
27 Denmark	502	Spain	517	27 Thailand	467	Cyprus	460
28 **United States**	**500**	France	498	28 (Israel)	466	Moldova	459
29 Scotland	498	Greece	497	29 Tunisia	448	Macedonia, Republic of	458
30 Latvia	493	Iceland	494	30 Macedonia, Republic of	447	Jordan	450
31 Spain	487	Romania	486	31 Turkey	429	Iran, Islamic Republic of	448
32 Iceland	487	Latvia	485	32. Jordan	428	Indonesia	435
33 Greece	484	Portugal	480	33 Iran, Islamic Republic of	422	Turkey	433
34 Romania	482	Denmark	478	34 Indonesia	403	Tunisia	430
35 Lithuania	477	Lithuania	476	35 Chile	392	Chile	420
36 Cyprus	474	Belgium (W+)	471	36 Philippines	345	Philippines	345
37 Portugal	454	Iran	470	37 Morocco	337	Morocco	323
38 Iran	428	Cyprus	463	38 South Africa	275	South Africa	243
39 Kuwait	392	Kuwait	430				
40 Columbia	385	Columbia	411				
41 South Africa	354	South Africa	326				

*Third International Maths and Science Study International Average = 1995 average = 500 (41 nations); 1999 average = 487–488 (38 nations).

NOTE: It should be noted that the set of 38 nations who participated in 1999 was different in important ways than the 41 nations who participated in the 1995 TIMSS. Several European countries (such as Switzerland, France, Austria, Ireland, Germany, Spain, and Portugal) did not participate, while many developing countries joined the study. At the same time, however, the highest scoring countries in 1995 also participated in 1999.

Sources: World Education League, 1997: 21; National Center for Education Statistics, 2000. http://nces.ed.gov/ssbr/pages/Math8_r.asp.

cultural background of students is accounted for in the tests, and when forms of assessment other than standardized test are used, such as simulations and observations of students in individual and group problem-solving situations, student achievement tends to increase (Chall, 2000; Hanson, 2000; National Center for Education Statistics, 2001). Correlated with statis-tics that fewer than 20 percent of seniors say they do *not* plan to go on to college, the proportion of high-school students enrolled in core areas of science, math, and foreign language have also increased (Angus & Mirel, 1995; Waldman, 1999). However, educational needs are rising so fast that the schools can barely keep up. The illusion is one of decline because more demands are placed on the schools. For example, the foundation for 21st century work is computer literacy, but there are massive costs to keep teachers current with the needs of an information-driven society and to provide the latest technology for students (Goad, 2002). If the gap widens between what is demanded and what is produced in education, real decline may occur. U.S. school policy needs to address such gaps to keep competitive with other industrialized nations in the global economy.

Third, global comparisons must account for the proportion of students who continue school beyond a certain age. It is methodologically unsound to simply compare countries without considering the average number of years most students remain in school. As noted above, illiteracy rates in many parts of the developing world exceed 70 percent. In rural areas, very few children advance beyond primary grades, especially the girls. As in an earlier United States, schools in developing nations are reserved for the elite. Level of economic development in each country is probably a better indicator of achievement levels (Buchmann & Hannum, 2001).

Fourth, both globally and nationally, tests need to be constructed so that they are as culturally unbiased as possible. The same questions are read by students of very different backgrounds, making it difficult to know whether test scores are due to a student's achievement or to a student's culture or subculture. Since race, class, ethnicity, religion, and gender are also culturally relevant, this becomes a monumental task, especially in the multicultural classrooms of the United States. Some believe that it is impossible to construct a completely unbiased test, so additional measures of achievement are needed. *Triangulation*, the use of multiple indicators and methods for data collection, adds to validity or accuracy of the results (Chapter 2).

The state of student achievement in the United States is complex, and it is difficult to determine whether the reported decline is empirically justified. What is clear, however, is that the nation cannot afford to be complacent about its schools. Perhaps the storm of controversy erupting from the reports of educational decline has provided a valuable lesson. Educational reform is now near the top of government and community agendas.

Toward Educational Reform

Both the George H. W. Bush Administration (*No Child Left Behind*) and the Bill Clinton Administration (*Goals 2000*) set ambitious educational priorities for the United States that include the following:

1. Ensure that all children start school ready to learn.
2. Eliminate the racial achievement gap.
3. Eliminate illiteracy.
4. Maintain drug-free and violence-free schools.
5. Assess student achievement with competence testing throughout their schooling.
6. Develop centers to bring families, schools, and communities together to increase student achievement.
7. Build a world-class education system available to everyone.

These goals involve determining what children should know and how to provide that knowledge. Reform efforts by schools to achieve these goals are extremely varied. They center on stronger links to family, businesses, and communities; stricter discipline; better teacher training; upgrading buildings; increased homework; a longer school year; higher levels of student responsibility; and less school bureaucracy. High-school graduation requirements have been expanded to include more knowledge in core areas. This is the "back to basics" curriculum embraced by many school districts with the blessing of parents. What the "basics" include, in terms of both subject area and content, remains unresolved (Abelson, 2001; Osborne, 2001).

While such reforms look great on paper, critics charge that they are merely technical and bureaucratic adjustments that do not address the "real" reasons for lack of student achievement. These critics suggest that the real reasons are due more to individual student characteristics than to broader social circumstance; government intervention, including more public funding, will not solve the problem (Grubb, 1995; Ravitch, 2000; Frammolino, 2001). However, as sociology continually reminds us, to regard social institutions such as education, family, and government as separate from one another is not only unrealistic, it is impractical. For example, when student achievement is based solely on improving the school environment, the home environment may be ignored. School facilities may be improved, but when a child comes to school with no breakfast, even the best teachers will find that what the child can achieve is limited. Private schools are often held up as models for student discipline. But when private school students have discipline problems, they are often shunted off to public schools where admission cannot be refused. Schools can be restructured to make them less bureaucratic, but higher achievement and more equity is associated with smaller schools, highly paid teachers, excellent facilities, and an active and involved community of teachers and learners (Lee, 2001; Bracey, 2002). These are matters of money and politics, not bureaucracy.

At the individual level, there are differences in a child's *readiness* to learn and her or his *opportunity* to learn. The former deals with an individual approach to learning; the latter deals with the impact of social structure on that approach. Only one of the goals on the educational priorities' list deals squarely with this issue.

The Carnegie Foundation has expanded the "readiness to learn" goal to provide an educational mandate for the nation (Boyer, 1994). Note how the Carnegie list accounts for differences in opportunity as well as linkages with other institutions. As such, it offers a sound sociological model for educational reform:

1. A healthy start. To be ready to learn, every child must have a healthy birth, be well nourished, and be well protected in the early years of life.
2. Empowered parents. Since parents are the first teachers, children should live in secure homes that encourage language development.
3. Quality preschool. All school districts should establish preschool programs.
4. A responsive workplace. Employers need family-friendly policies, such as access to quality day care and flexible scheduling.
5. Television as teacher. Children should be exposed to educational and enriching television.
6. Neighborhoods for learning. Children must have safe, friendly, and improved places to grow and explore. Facilities such as museums and libraries should be accessible.
7. Connections across the generations. Children need a sense of security and continuity. Schools, day-care centers, and retirement villages should be linked to bring together young and old.

The Carnegie Foundation also suggests programs that can help implement these goals. Examples include federal initiatives such as WIC (Women, Infants, and Children), a nutrition program for eligible mothers and infants, and Head Start. Undoubtedly, the goals are overly ambitious, but they carry forth the recurring sociological theme that schools cannot be held completely responsible for the rise or fall of student achievement.

The problems facing academic achievement cannot easily be put aside. Any reforms designed to deal with the problems must be viewed in light of an increasingly diverse society in which the value of quality schooling for all is passionately embraced. Schools must ensure that uniform standards are maintained so that all students from all backgrounds receive the same quality of education. Schools must also nurture individual talent and interest but in a socially responsible yet academically sound manner (Oakes, 2000; Lee, 2001). This list also demonstrates that schools *should* bring students together but also separate them so they can realize their potential in life.

There is a movement to create a uniform set of national standards to which all public schools must adhere, but local control of schools is fiercely upheld. Even with state standards, compared to other nations, the United States virtually stands alone in allowing the public schools to determine their own destinies. This freedom has also allowed parents and communities to consider an amazing variety of schooling options, including public funds for home schooling and for vouchers that parents can apply toward tuition at private schools, which operate fairly independently of the school district in which they are located (McGrath, 1999; Meeks et al., 2000; Moe, 2001). Options such as these are consistent with capitalism—they are said to encourage competitive and creative alternatives for public policy (Friedman, 2001; Glassman, 2001). However, as pointed out in this chapter, the diversity of the school population in the United States makes it highly unlikely that more privatization of public education will serve the interests of the nation's schoolchildren any better (Wells & Oakes, 1998; Maran, 2000; Bracey, 2002). U.S. education serves a political agenda considered to be in the best interests of all the groups making up a democratic society. The school system—the one institution through which all children must pass—is expected to pursue this agenda.

SUMMARY

1. In the United States, education socializes children, helps the children of foreign-born parents to assimilate into mainstream society, and prepares the younger generation to adapt to a rapidly changing culture and economy.

2. While functionalists see the schools as nurturers of talent and ability, regardless of a child's social class, conflict theorists charge that the schools reinforce the social-class structure. Social class is, in fact, the best overall indicator of educational achievement.

3. U.S. schools mirror the communities in which they are located: Some are well staffed, well furnished, and well maintained, while others are rundown, ill equipped, and poorly staffed.

4. Research shows that within U.S. schools, students are tracked to different academic levels based more on their class, race, and gender than on their ability and past achievement.

5. According to symbolic interactionism, assigning students to lower levels, or tracks, reduces their self-esteem and their motivation to achieve. To avoid these effects, educators have adopted a policy of mainstreaming, inclusion of special-needs students in regular classrooms whenever possible.

6. A society's education system is a powerful agent of social change, affecting its level of economic development, its marriage and birth rates, and its income and nutritional levels.

7. Demographers predict that by 2025, slightly more than half the students in U.S. classrooms will be people of color. The realization that the racial and ethnic makeup of the nation's schools is changing has produced a shift in educational policy toward a multicultural curriculum.

8. Although the juvenile crime rate has decreased over the last several decades, the proportion of serious violent crime (homicide, rape, sexual assault, aggressive assault) has remained constant over the past decade in most schools and has increased significantly in others.

9. Though the student bodies at four-year colleges and universities have become more diverse, most are still drawn disproportionately from the middle and upper classes. Women, racial minorities, and working- and lower-class students are over-represented at community colleges.

10. Over the last three decades, standardized test scores declined and functional illiteracy increased among U.S. students compared to students in other countries. However, it is difficult to tell whether there has been a real decline in U.S. education, or whether the changes are a result of an increased student population.

11. Educational reformers are seeking to improve achievement through a "back to basics" approach and standards-based competency testing, but it must be recognized that the broader social structure impacts individual learning.

KEY TERMS

busing 438
credentialism 425
end point fallacy 431
functional illiteracy 445

hidden curriculum 427
magnet schools 438
mainstreaming 431
meritocracy 425

segregation 438
tracking 428

CRITICAL THINKING QUESTIONS

1. Given that diversity in education is now the norm, how can education serve individual students as well as broader social needs? How can educational equity be achieved for both the individual and society?

2. From a symbolic interactionist perspective, demonstrate how the labeling process involving teachers, peers, and parents can be used as an enhancement rather than as a liability for student achievement.

3. Efforts at desegregation of the public schools in the United States have revolved around busing. What other methods can schools use to increase interracial contact and understanding? How can the success of these methods be evaluated?

4. What proposals would functionalists, conflict theorists, and symbolic interactionists offer to decrease school violence? Consider the role of institutional interdependence in these proposals.

INVESTIGATE WITH CONTENT SELECT

Journal Research Collections from ContentSelect Begin your research using ContentSelect for this chapter by following the directions found on page 27 of this text to visit Prentice Hall's Research Navigator Website. Enter these search terms into the search field:

Illiteracy
School violence
Tracking

17
RELIGION

Faith in America

From a storefront church in a poor Los Angeles neighborhood, to a Buddhist temple in Honolulu, to a mosque in upscale suburban St. Louis, to St. Patrick's Cathedral in Manhattan, there are so many places of worship in the United States that they are almost too numerous to count. However, it is estimated that the United States is home to more churches, mosques, temples, synagogues, and churches than is any place on earth: about one for every 865 people. These sites of worship are home to adherents of every major world religion as well as thousands of smaller groups who come together to seek God in whatever manner they choose. The United States is not a melting pot when it comes to religion—it is one of amazing religious diversity, and perhaps more important, of amazing religious tolerance. In the aftermath of September 11 when cases of backlash against Muslims occurred, people of all faiths rallied in their support. People also retreated to places of worship to seek solace within their own community of believers. Others meditated, prayed, or sought spiritual guidance without ever stepping foot in a house of worship. Americans eagerly embrace science and technology to help with problem solving and to help ease the strain of fast-paced lives. Yet science is unable to relieve their deep desire for a spiritual anchor that they believe can only be provided by religion and spirituality. In the world's most modernized nation, religion and science exist side by side in apparently peaceful co-existence. (Eck, 2001; Sheler, 2002)

Among the Believers

An eager gathering of Christians in rural Alabama speaking in tongues . . . another group blocking access to a clinic that performs abortions . . . the rhythmic chanting of the crowd in Peshawar, Pakistan, celebrating the bombing of the World Trade Center . . . hundreds of "Moonie" couples at Madison Square Garden having their wedding vows blessed by Rev. Sun Myung Moon himself . . . the fervent worship of political leader Kim Il Sung by North Korean school children . . . women being beaten in Saudi Arabia and Iran because their veils left ankles uncovered . . . practitioners of Falon Gong, a banned religious cult, arrested in China with the support of Catholic priests . . . Buddhists in Tibet setting themselves on fire in protest of a crackdown on their religion. All these cases evoke a sense of unease. This is the world of the fundamentalist—no matter whether Allah, Christ, or a godlike political figure is being worshipped. Fundamentalists have no doubt about their beliefs and want to clear up any doubts you may have. (Swift, 1991: 99–100; Murphy, 2001; Wang, 2001)

All religions search for ways to reconcile faith with modern life, especially in societies experiencing rapid social change. As the vignettes indicate, there are disagreements regarding how best to harmonize religion and modernity. Some believe that religion must adapt to social change. For others, adaptation means surrendering the faith to the forces of **secularization,** the process in which religion, challenged by science and modernization, loses its influence on society, thereby threatening its very existence. The counterchallenge to secularization occurs with religious resurgence, mostly in the form of **fundamentalism,** a movement designed to revitalize faith by returning to the traditional ways the religion was practiced in the past. Traditional practices of fundamentalists are based on literal interpretation of religious doctrine. As we will see, although fundamentalists agree that "authentic" religious content has been lost and must be revitalized, they disagree on what this content should look like today. Can these two processes—secularization and fundamentalism—occur

GLOBAL CONNECTIONS

Violence in the Name of God

The images of peace and serenity religion evokes have been shattered throughout history, from the Spanish Inquisition and witch burning in Europe during the Middle Ages to Palestinian suicide bombers in Israel, murders of physicians who perform abortions, and the attacks of September 11. In the scramble for public support, money, and fresh recruits, the political and economic roots of religious violence are ignored. To save religion from the forces of secularization, violence is justified and people are rallied in the name of God. There are many examples of continuing feuds among the world religions and even among branches of the same religion.

One of the most horrifying examples occurred when Hindu India and Muslim Pakistan were separated into independent states in 1947, leaving many people trapped in regions under political control of the "other" faith. Over a million Hindus and Muslims slaughtered one another when they crossed lines in the flight to their new territory. Turkey, Algeria, and Malaysia are striving to remain secular states in the face of Muslim fundamentalists equally determined to transform them into Islamic states. In Malaysia, Sunni and Shiite Muslims are at odds about what the potential Islamic state should look like. Catholic and Protestant Christians in Northern Ireland engage in continuing, often violent, conflict over the issue of nationhood. A right-wing Jewish activist, who believed Israel had gone too far in compromising religious principles to meet political demands, was responsible for the assassination of Prime Minister Yitzhak Rabin in 1995. Jews in Israel and the United States are divided over how to stop the bloodshed and suicide bombings in the Middle East, and this in turn has spawned hatred and more violence among Jews.

The banner of religion often appeals to people who are marginal, poor, or who lack power in other parts of their lives. On the other hand, middle-class, educated people who have time and money are usually the planners of the violence. They are today likely to be the ones carrying out the violence as well. Osama bin Laden's brand of Islamic fundamentalism ignited religious passions in young, educated men who could be recruited for his al-Qaeda terrorist network. The less educated remained as Taliban fighters in Afghanistan.

Fundamentalists seek to contain the undesirable effects of globalization, such as secularization, modernization, and capitalism. The terrorism on 9-11 can be viewed as an attack on globalization itself. Airplanes, symbols of global mobility, were used to target the World Trade Center—the world's most powerful symbol of globalization. Other agents of globalization include multinational corporations like Nike and McDonald's, international organizations like the United Nations and World Trade Organization, economic institutions like the World Bank and International Monetary Fund, and entertainment industry corporations like CNN and Disney. Believing they may be targets of further violence, all these organizations are on heightened alert. Fundamentalists in both the developed and developing world argue that globalization is a major culprit in eroding traditional beliefs and moral systems. In order to stem the tide of globalization and restore core religious values, terrorism is justified. The irony is that religious terrorists use the tools of modernity and globalization to achieve their goals. Carrying out God's will requires more than religious passion—it also requires cell phones and computers.

1. How is violence in the name of religion used to both gain support and hurt support for its causes?

2. How would you respond to people who argue that religious violence is a way to stem the tides of globalization and secularization?

Sources: Stackhouse & Paris, 2000; Appleby & Marty, 2001; Armstrong, 2001; Dart, 2001; Jenkins, 2001; Khashan & Kreidie, 2001; Cox, 2002; PRNewswire, 2002.

at the same time in the same society? Can they both flourish in societies such as the United States where there are numerous religions from which to choose? These questions are addressed by examining secularization and fundamentalism, and the influence of both processes on the political setting, especially in the way a society accommodates different religions. Answers to these questions are vitally important in understanding the connection between religion and politics in the wake of the September 11 attacks on the World Trade Center and Pentagon. Besides seeking the hearts and minds of individuals, religions also seek the political blessings of the nation in which they exist.

Finally, this chapter shows that while the tides of secularization and fundamentalism may sweep through the United States, most people cannot be counted as either secular or fundamentalist.

THEORETICAL PERSPECTIVES ON RELIGION

Sociologists who study religion examine the social framework in which religion operates. In particular, sociologists are interested in how the processes of

Religion may be losing or winning in the battle against secularization. Christian revival meetings and gospel shows attract many people, but mainstream churches, especially in urban areas, are losing members.

fundamentalism and secularization are swayed by **religious pluralism,** the tolerance by society of many religions, which often compete with one another for members. Each sociological theory offers insights into why religious pluralism may or may not thrive in society.

Functionalism

Émile Durkheim's brilliant scientific study of religion, *The Elementary Forms of Religious Life* (1912/1954) is still regarded as the most important functionalist perspective on religion. His definition of **religion** as a "unified system of beliefs and practices relative to sacred things" is at the core of sociological thinking about religion.

This simple definition weaves together three important elements. First, religion must have beliefs and practices that are organized in some manner, usually in the form of a specific **theology,** a systematic formulation of religious doctrine. Individual expressions of spirituality do not become religion until they are organized around common denominators in some fashion. Second, the system of religious beliefs must be translated into behavior. Faith must be observable; the expression of religious behavior and practices is referred to as ritual. Third, Durkheim argues that all known religious beliefs, no matter how simple or complex, presuppose a classification of everything in the world into two distinct, nonoverlapping categories. One category represents elements that are considered religious or **sacred,** set apart from the everyday world, inspiring awe and reverence, and often imbued with transcendent qualities. The other, opposite category is the **profane,** the world of every-

day objects. In this context, profane does not mean "bad." It simply means anything that is not sacred.

Notice that Durkheim does not use the word "supernatural" in his definition; for him religious belief is not necessarily tied to belief in divinities such as gods. For example, supernatural beings may be absent or have minor importance to the religion, as in ancient Australian totemism, where animals or plants have a special relationship with a tribal group and act as its guardians. The key to religion, then, is not the existence of a god or gods, but that the sacred world is the world of religion and society agrees on the definition. In your classroom a desk is a profane object, but if the desk is used for a religious ritual, it becomes a sacred object. Like objects, certain places can be considered sacred. Jerusalem is a sacred place for Jews, Christians, and Muslims, who share common religious roots. There is a hierarchy of the sacred, in Durkheim's terms, "sacred things of every degree." Synagogues, churches, and mosques scattered throughout the world are considered less sacred than those in Jerusalem. Hindus make pilgrimages to the sacred waters of the Ganges in Varanasi, India, considered more sacred than in other places where the Ganges flows. Religion is a cultural universal, but its expression is extremely varied. Each society defines what belongs to the sacred world, and its religious rituals are conducted accordingly.

Functions of Religion

Durkheim's definition of religion is a good starting point for understanding the intersections among religion, society, and the individual. The interdependence of these elements is evident when we inspect the functions of religion.

In faiths around the world, such as in Eastern Europe or Southeast Asia, funerals are actually ways of celebrating a religion and serve to strengthen the social bonds of its believers.

1. **Social cohesion.** Religion allows believers to establish strong bonds that form a moral community. For Durkheim, this integrative function provides the "social glue" necessary to bring together even a diversity of people within a specific system of religious beliefs (Miller, 1996).

2. **Support system.** With the establishment of a moral community, people find strength, comfort, and support from one another in times of crisis. Their social bond is reinforced by celebrative rituals, like weddings, or those that are sorrowful, like funerals. Social support is also psychologically healthy.

3. **Emotional health.** By addressing "ultimate" questions that give life purpose and meaning, religion bolsters emotional well-being. Why am I alive? What is my purpose on earth? Why did my friend have to die? Religious faith can reduce the inevitable uncer-

tainty and anxiety that arise with such questions. In this regard, while science is religion's principal competitor, science has been unable to provide the definitive answers people seek to these questions.

4. **Social service.** Religion addresses social as well as "private" questions. Why do evil and injustice exist in the world? What does my religion tell me about helping others? Theology can be a moral pathway. In many societies, religion provides an enormous amount of voluntary service that is beneficial to the community (Maton & Wells, 1995; Ammerman, 1997; Greeley, 1997).

5. **Social control.** When government draws moral authority from religion, it legitimizes political authority. For centuries monarchs sought a religious seal of approval to "divinely sanction" their reigns. In contemporary religious states, political policies are dictated by religious interpretation; thus the government is imbued with the sacred. In these circumstances, a person who questions government authority is also questioning religious authority. The two social institutions—government and religion—come together as powerful mechanisms of social control (Turner, 1991).

6. **Social change.** The prophetic aspect of religion can influence social change. If a powerful religious leader emerges with a vision of an ideal reality as interpreted through a sacred text, a religiously based social movement may occur. Martin Luther King represents the prophetic function with the religious imagery in his "I Have A Dream" speech, which became a rallying cry for the civil rights movement, as did Mahatma Gandhi's message of nonviolence in India's struggle to be free of British colonial rule. Both leaders offered religously based nonviolent messages that became metaphors for an ideal society.

This funeral of a Palestinian killed in a clash with Israeli soldiers in the West Bank shows that religion can unite as well as divide people. The funeral unites Palestinians but also serves to widen the political chasm between Palestinians and Israelis.

CRITIQUE Although functionalists account for the fact that like other social institutions, religion can also have dysfunctional consequences, they have difficulty explaining the major social upheavals that occurred because of religion. Religion can also be dysfunctional when conflict among religious groups disrupts cohesion. The social glue that binds the people in one moral community also separates it from other such communities. A community may say "We are one in Christ," but there are also those who are "one" in Allah, Shiva, Buddha, or any of the contemporary religious leaders whose followers consider them divine in some manner. Consider the centuries of violence in the name of religion—from the Crusades and the witch hunts in medieval Europe to the Protestant–Catholic conflict in Northern Ireland and the ongoing Arab–Israeli conflict. In a religiously pluralistic state, people can move between religious groups fairly easily and even recruit followers to begin a new church or even a new religion. Growing spiritual diversity weakens social cohesion (Berger, 1967; Demerath & Williams, 1990; Wilson, 1996). Durkheim's cohesive moral community falters when it becomes a simple matter to walk across the street into another church or synagogue.

In addition, religion must compete with other institutional sources of identity, such as race, gender, social class, or nationality. For example, intermarriage rates between Protestants and Catholics, and Jews and non-Jews have steadily increased throughout the 20th century (Kalmijn, 1998). Married couples from different religions generally have less identification to a religion, lower levels of religiosity in their marriages, and put less emphasis on religion in raising children (Rebhun, 1999; Williams & Lawler, 2001). These couples may turn to sources other than religion for personal identity.

Conflict Theory and Social Change

Conflict theory recognizes that religion is integral to social functioning, but focuses on its role in maintaining a stratification system that is beneficial to some and detrimental to others, thus emphasizing the social control function of religion. In Karl Marx's (1848/1964) classic formulation, religion is the "opiate" of the people; he uses the symbol of the depressive drug to suggest apathy, lethargy, and a dulling of the senses. Religion lulls people into a *false consciousness,* Marx's term for the tendency of an oppressed class to accept the dominant ideology of the ruling class, thereby legitimizing oppression. A divinely sanctioned monarchy, for example, perpetuates the belief that God is on the side of the nobility and that God's will shuffles people into various social categories. As discussed later, Buddhist ideas about rein-

carnation and the Confucian concept of loyalty to rulers are other examples.

The potential for slave uprisings in the United States weakened when it was determined that slaves had souls just like white Christians and were subject to the same cycle of judgment and salvation. Christianity's notion that heavenly rewards come to those who lead humble, pious, and self-sacrificing lives bolstered in slaves an "other worldly" orientation that deterred efforts for change in this world. The religious opiate works for slaves and other people who are marginalized or poor; by consoling those who are deprived, religion denies the opportunities for social change necessary for greater equity. Pastors in churches made up of poor people may be so interested in uplifting their congregations' spirits that they inadvertently, and regrettably, bolster an unjust socioeconomic system.

CRITIQUE Conflict theory assumes that religion is used to serve prevailing economic or political interests. This view is accurate only if it can be determined

Religion benefits society in many ways, such as providing volunteers for services that help the community. Churches often become recruiting centers or headquarters for programs such as Habitat for Humanity and Meals on Wheels.

that religion is the effect rather than the cause of social change. As will be detailed in Chapter 22, Max Weber (1905/1954) challenged this thesis with his argument that religion served as the catalyst for the growth of capitalism early in U.S. history. According to Weber, the Protestant ethic stemmed from Calvinist beliefs in *predestination*—the belief that God already determined whether you were chosen for salvation. Hard work, discipline, and asceticism (austere practices involving self-denial, such as always favoring work over entertainment) allowed capital to be accumulated and then reinvested in business enterprises, whether farm or factory. While your actual place as one of the "elect" could never be known, earthly signs such as material success hinted at heavenly favor. For Weber, Calvinism and capitalism went hand in hand.

Finally, the role of religion as an agent of social change is demonstrated by religion's prophetic function. Rather than passively accepting the world as it is, religion is used in pursuit of social justice, as in the U.S. civil rights movement or religiously based movements in other parts of the world. For example, *liberation theology* is a religious fundamentalism movement grounded in literal interpretations of Christian scripture promoting social justice. Advanced mainly by Catholic clergy in Latin America who work directly with the poor, liberation theology challenges governments to redistribute wealth more equitably. But unlike Marx, it rejects the idea that religion, in this case Christianity, is an "opiate," using it instead to support economic equality through social change (Lynch, 1998; Dawsey, 2001; Martinez, 2001). In the Philippines Catholic clergy aligned with peasant groups played a powerful role in the downfall of the authoritarian regime of Ferdinand Marcos in 1986 (Andaya, 2002). Liberation theology may be strengthening in the United States with the increased numbers of Latino Catholic immigrants.

Religion as Socially Constructed

Sociologists who emphasize the social constructionist approach to religion suggest that religion is a human enterprise that is produced and then continually altered through social interaction. The symbolic interactionist concept of the *endpoint fallacy* fits this approach well; although religious truths and symbols are inherited from previous generations, these truths are always subject to change. People transform the truths and adapt the symbols to their own circumstances (Aldridge, 2000; Madsen et al., 2002). According to Peter Berger (1967), the most influential sociologist of the social constructionist approach to religion, this process of adaptation is very powerful because people are compelled to put a meaningful order—referred to as a *nomos*—on their experiences. Berger argues that

nomos is necessary because it protects people and the society of which they are part from the inevitable chaos presented in daily life. For example, when death, natural disaster, or terrorism threaten a sense of order, nomos is available to counter the threat. Of all the types of nomos that are socially constructed, religion is perhaps the most important one. Religion becomes a shield against terror and helps restore meaning and order to life (Hamilton, 2001).

Although religious truths and symbols are social constructions, they eventually take on a powerful reality, called *symbolic realism*, separate from the people who constructed them. The symbols of religion help people define their world, allow groups to be formed, and serve as bridges between the conscious and unconscious meanings people get from their religion. Symbolic realism assumes that symbols act back upon their creators (Bellah, 1970; Berger, 2001; Alexander & Sherwood, 2002).

A good example of symbolic realism is how veiling is perceived by men and women in Asian *purdah*-based Muslim societies, such as Afghanistan and Pakistan, and in Iran and Saudi Arabia where men and women are segregated by law and/or custom. When women venture into public spaces, gender segregation is symbolically maintained and traditional gender roles are not threatened (Chatty, 2000; Talbani & Hasanali, 2000). In Afghanistan today the harsh rules of the Taliban are gone. Although the new government has encouraged women to adopt clothing that is modest but does not fully envelop them, it is unusual to see a woman without a *burqa*, a veil that covers her entire body. Afghan men will still not allow their wives to show their faces in public, since they fear it will brand the women as "loose" and they (both wife and husband) will be taunted for it (Komarow, 2002). Even if not required to wear a burqa, many Muslim women say they do so willingly since the veil symbolizes their piety and obedience to God. For them, a burqa is a sign of their faith, not of their servitude (Bullock, 2000). Other Muslim women condemn the veil and see it as a symbol of their oppression, in their homes and in their broader society, that has little to do with their religion (Smith, 1999). Since the veil holds such powerful symbolic significance, a veiled woman or an unveiled woman is a symbol in the minds of every person who sees her, regardless of what the law says, what she believes, or how her religion is interpreted. The idea of symbolic realism is underscored because the veil is present—even in its absence (Lindsey, 2002).

CRITIQUE The social constructionist approach to religion has been criticized on two main points: First, the idea that people universally and inherently have a need for nomos can never be empirically verified.

Second, the emphasis on religion as producing order puts Berger more in the functionalist than the symbolic interactionist camp, and like functionalists, he discounts the chaos that may erupt from religion (Dorrien, 2001; Hamilton, 2001). This chaos serves to erode nomos, not strengthen it.

Rational Choice Theory

Emerging only since the 1980s, rational choice theory is now accepted as a new paradigm for sociologists of religion. Rational choice theory applies a marketplace approach to religion by assuming that people's choice of religion will be determined by its costs and benefits to them (Iannaccone, 1997; Bruce, 1999). Rational choice theory helps explain changes in membership patterns among competing religions in societies with high degrees of religious pluralism. Christianity, for example, must adapt itself to the needs of the religious consumer because if it does not, other new religions will emerge to "fill the gap" in the market (Stark & Bainbridge, 1987). Many churches offer a variety of religious services billed as traditional, modern, folk, gospel, spirit-filled, or meditative to cater to these consumers. Interviews with young adults in England suggest that they gravitate to congregations offering more lively, exciting, alternative, and youth-orientated religious experience, away from congregations that are dominated by older people and "old-fashioned" services (Richter & Francis, 1998). With the influx of recent immigrants to the United States, some congregations have transformed their structure and ritual, often returning to more traditional theological approaches (Yang & Ebaugh, 2001). Churches on the verge of collapse through loss of members have been revitalized. As in any free-market economy, the religious economy must adapt to the needs of its consumers. As a result, religions become more vitalized, and profits, in the form of new members, are increased.

Contrary to the predictions of secularization, rational choice theorists contend that religious pluralism actually increases religious adherence, because in many places of the world, especially the United States, there are no state-supported churches that interfere with a religious marketplace. Religion grows because of the rational choices people make to compensate for the trials and tribulations of life (Stark & Iannaccone, 1994; Young, 1997). Religion is the only institution that can serve intense, personal needs, so pluralism encourages a person's spiritual quests. A religious marketplace is readily available for them to purchase the services needed to fulfill this quest.

CRITIQUE While it is clear that religions compete with one another to attract and retain members, it remains doubtful that religion, especially in terms of membership, is energized by so much competition. When people shop around for spiritual options, religious switching may eventually lead to decreased rather than increased affiliation with a particular religious group (Olson, 1999; Chaves & Gorski, 2001).

RELIGIOUS BELIEFS AND ORGANIZATIONS

The enormous variety of religious beliefs makes any classification scheme tenuous at best. The most widely used schemes have been criticized for their basis in Western European conceptions of religion, which do not adequately account for spirituality in the non-Western world and among indigenous peoples (Cox, 1996; Bowie, 2000). Émile Durkheim's definition of religion, with its emphasis on beliefs about the sacred, is a good tool to help categorize systems of religious beliefs and the world religions that are grounded in them. The link between religious belief and institutionalized religion is an important one. As society becomes more complex and heterogeneous, social institutions become more specialized. Spirituality, which may be identified by certain beliefs about the sacred, becomes institutionalized as religion.

Expressions of Religious Belief

Early anthropologists attempted to solve the classification problem by proposing that religious beliefs could be categorized not only by type of belief but also along evolutionary lines. Edward Tylor (1871), a founder of the anthropology of religion, argued that religion evolves through stages. The first stage is **animism,** the belief that supernatural beings or spirits capable of helping or hurting people inhabit living things (plants and animals) and inanimate objects

Rational choice theory looks at religion as a marketplace. People can shop the yellow pages in the phone book for the kind of church that appeals to them. Churches that gain the most members might be the best advertisers.

(rocks and houses). Spirits have human emotions, so, like humans, they can be manipulated for one's own advantage or for the benefit of the community. Animist beliefs are among the earliest religious expressions, but continue today in many agriculturally based societies where various earth spirits are solicited in behalf of community needs for abundant crops, plentiful rain, or mild winters. In Durkheim's view, when spirits are beseeched for community rather than personal gains, animism plants the seeds for religion, uniting people into a moral community.

The next stage of religious evolution is characterized by **theism,** the belief in one or more independent supernatural beings (gods), who do not exist on earth and who are more powerful than people. **Polytheism** is the belief in many gods. In "diffuse" polytheism, all gods are equal; in "hierarchal" polytheism, the gods are ranked according to degree of importance or power. Hierarchal polytheism is associated with the emergence of a separate, political state, which uses the gods to the benefit of governing powers. The ancient Roman Caesars and Egyptian pharaohs embodied god, human, and government. Functionalists suggest that claiming godlike qualities allowed these rulers immense power, since they used religion as a social control function. Contemporary Hinduism, which has both diffuse and hierarchal qualities, is an example of a polytheistic religion that has thrived for centuries. When one all-powerful, all-knowing god replaces a hierarchy of gods, polytheism is replaced by **monotheism** in Tylor's evolutionary scheme.

Tylor's categories of religious beliefs remain useful, but his evolutionary scheme is no longer accepted. Neither societies nor religions evolve along a single line of development. Also, since the evolutionary scheme ranks monotheism "higher" than any earlier form, it implies that contemporary animistic and polytheistic religions are somehow less evolved or are substandard. Contemporary anthropology and sociology would never support such a position, but as we will see, adherents of many religious faiths do not share the cultural relativist view (Chapter 3) that "all religions are created equal."

Some sociologists use the concept of **civil religion,** also called **secular religion,** to describe a system of values associated with sacred symbols that is integrated into the broader society and shared by the society's members, regardless of their individual religious affiliations (Bellah, 1967, 1970; Coleman, 1970). In the United States, Judeo-Christian religious symbolism is tied to a belief in a divinely sanctioned political system. Like other religions, civil religion brings intense emotional feelings that come with patriotism, nationalism, and reverence for symbols such as a nation's flag. Within hours of the bombing of the World Trade Center and Pentagon, the American flag was unfurled in the largest, most spontaneous nationwide display of unity since the bombing of Pearl Harbor in 1941. With people of all faiths displaying the flag, it transcended religion yet functioned as a powerful symbol of civil religion. The Declaration of Independence, national shrines like the Washington Monument and Lincoln Memorial, and the "holy days" of the Fourth of July and Thanksgiving are other such symbols. Consider how each of the functions of religion mentioned above is met with these symbols of civil religion in the United States. In the former Soviet Union, communism as a civil religion was symbolized by Lenin's tomb; Mao's tomb has this same function in China today. If civil religion were factored into Tylor's evolutionary scheme, it would be the highest, most evolved level, because patriotism has a sacred quality but does not rely on the concept of a god or the supernatural.

Just as Tylor's scheme is unacceptable to contemporary social science, the very idea of civil religion with its "non-godlike" quality is offensive to many theologians and to those whose lives are centered explicitly around their faith. For them, civil religion is implicit religion and therefore not religion at all (Marty, 1959, 1974; Bruce, 1996; Noonan, 1998). While civil religion does meet Durkheim's definition of religion and can affirm common values, it is a weak competitor with any of the world's religions or most religious belief systems, because it lacks a transcendent quality and cannot deal as effectively with ultimate questions regarding life and death.

Types of Religious Organizations

Sociologists identify several types of religious organizations that help distinguish one belief system from another. The forms that religious organizations take provide clues for understanding how religions change and develop, and whether they grow or die.

CHURCH AND SECT A **church** is an inclusive religious body that brings together a moral community of believers in formalized worship and accommodates itself to the larger secular world. The church is an adaptive organization—an integral part of the social order that is organized similarly to other bureaucratic organizations in society. It employs educated, professionally trained clergy who are usually ordained in seminaries representing a specific theology. Membership grows as people are born into the church or if the church successfully competes with other churches to attract new members (Greeley, 1972; Swidler & Mojzes, 2000). Churches are most prevalent in societies with a high degree of religious pluralism. The extensive institutional fabric of a church and its acceptance

As a formal organization, a church trains its leaders not only in theology but also in administrative functions, such as connecting the local parish to the broader church. Women now represent over half of seminary students.

in wider society help minimize tension between it and the many other places and causes that also compete for a person's time, loyalty, money, or energy.

When a church is institutionalized as a formal part of a state or nation and claims citizens as members, it is an **ecclesia**, or state religion. By definition, an ecclesia does not exist in societies with high religious pluralism, but there is considerable variation according to degree of religious toleration and political influence in the society. The Church of Sweden is Lutheran and the Church of England is Anglican. Both are ecclesiae, both are secular states, and both allow other religious groups to worship and thrive in their societies. In contrast are the Islamic states of Iran, Saudi Arabia, and Pakistan, also ecclesia, but with low toleration of religious pluralism and with governments that are organized and interpreted according to Islamic principles. Violation of religious principles in some Islamic states can result in beating, imprisonment, or death.

Used in the context of religious pluralism, a **denomination** is a socially accepted and legally recognized body with bureaucratic characteristics similar to the larger church with which it has an official relationship. They are self-governing, multiple organizations of quasi-equal status that reflect an adjustment to religious pluralism (Greeley, 1972). The best examples of denominational societies in the Western world are the United States (see Table 17.1), Canada, the Netherlands, and Switzerland. Although the distinction between denomination and church is a blurry one, denominations are better devices than churches to classify the diversity encompassed in any world religion. Denominations of a particular religion share a common theology but interpret it differently. They are also divided according to how strongly they embrace traditionalism and how much accommodation they make to the demands of a continually modernizing society (Johnstone, 1992). A good example is reflected in the two major Lutheran denominations in the United States: the Lutheran Church Missouri Synod (LCMS) and the Evangelical Lutheran Church in America (ELCA). Both denominations share the theology of Martin Luther, but the LCMS denomination interprets it quite literally compared to the ELCA denomination. LCMS is also much more traditional than ELCA on issues related to social change. LCMS does not ordain women and does not share communion with nonmembers. ELCA ordains women and is actively engaged in *ecumenism*—promoting practices that bring Christian churches together, such as through joint worship and communion. According to Andrew Greeley (1972:1), "In the absence of understanding the denominations, one cannot understand American society either." The same can be said of any society with a high level of religious pluralism.

Unlike churches, ecclesiae, or denominations, a **sect** is smaller and is either aloof or hostile to the secular society surrounding it. Sects focus on salvation and otherworldly concerns, and renounce worldly gain. Since members are often drawn from the less privileged and marginalized, tension between sect and society is heightened (Sherkat & Ellison, 1999). Membership is exclusive and voluntary, determined usually by a conversion experience (Bainbridge, 1997a; Hunt, 2002). Whereas church is usually an ascribed status, sect is an achieved one. Often sects break away from a church, led by dissidents who believe that the parent church is not practicing the authentic or true religion as it was originally conceived (Stark & Bainbridge, 1985). Sects must exist in religiously pluralistic societies that tolerate them, but they are likely to maintain a judgmental attitude toward nonmembers who are not part of their exclusive community of believers.

TABLE 17.1

Largest Denominational Families in the United States, 2001[*]

Denomination	1990 Est. Adult Pop.	2001 Est. Adult Pop.	Est. % of U.S. Pop., 2001	% Change 1990–2001	% Weekly Church Attendance this Denom. 2001
Catholic	46,004,000	50,873,000	24.5	+11	48
Baptist	33,964,000	33,830,000	16.3	0	50
Methodist/Wesleyan	14,174,000	14,150,000	6.8	0	49
Lutheran	9,110,000	9,580,000	4.6	+5	43
Presbyterian	4,985,000	5,596,000	2.7	+12	49
Pentecostal/Charismatic	3,191,000	4,407,000	2.1	+38	66
Episcopalian/Anglican	3,042,000	3,451,000	1.7	+13	30
Judaism	3,137,000	2,831,000	1.3	−10	x[*]
Latter-Day Saints/Mormon	2,487,000	2,697,000	1.3	+8	71
Churches of Christ	1,769,000	2,593,000	1.2	+47	58
Congregational/ United Church of Christ	599,000	1,378,000	0.7	+130	30[**]
Jehovah's Witnesses	1,381,000	1,331,000	0.6	−4	[**]
Assemblies of God	660,000	1,106,000	0.5	+68	69

[*]No figures available
[**]Estimated based on sociologically similar Episcopalian/Anglican
Sources: Adapted from Barna, 2001; Kosmin & Mayer, 2001a.

Since spiritual perfection is a goal of sects, membership standards are high—a factor that functions to keep membership low. Leaders are often charismatic, and clergy may have no formal training. A high degree of spontaneity and participation of members is expected, both in worship services and to allow the organization to function. Sects often have one identifiable leader and emphasize a lack of hierarchy. Like churches, sects vary according to how many of these characteristics apply (Bruce, 1999; Aldridge, 2000). The Amish and Quakers are sects that are aloof but not necessarily hostile to the secular society, and their industriousness and piety have garnered a degree of respect from it. On the other hand, mutually hostile relations exist between the broader society and Mormons who split from the larger church, formed a sect, and still practice polygamy. However, as sects grow in size, they inevitably take on some of the bureaucratic functions they originally disdained. The result is that if sects are successful, they are likely to become more churchlike over time (Sherkat & Ellison, 1999; Finke, 2001).

CULTS AND NEW RELIGIOUS MOVEMENTS

Whereas sects often begin by splintering from an established religious body, a **cult** usually organizes around a charismatic leader who provides the basis for a new, unconventional religion. Max Weber (1925/1975) defined *charisma* as an aspect of personality that sets some people apart; these exceptional powers or qualities are often viewed as supernatural or superhuman. Charismatic leaders develop a special bond of trust and love with followers that reinforces loyalty and obedience. A cult is the only type of religious organization that relies solely on charismatic authority to maintain and legitimize its mission. All other social organizations, religious or not, receive their authority by tradition, such as a monarchy, or through a rational-legal system, such as constitutional authority given to a president (Chapter 18). Weber argued that unless charisma can be "routinized" so that stable social routines evolve along a road to institutionalization, a cult will not survive. Because it is so closely associated with a charismatic person who has virtually irreplaceable powers, a cult usually does not outlive its leader.

Most cults have no clearly defined structure and are associated with a great deal of tension, suspicion, and hostility toward the larger society. The definition assumes that cults have a specifically religious focus, although some do not—such as survivalists, militia-based groups, and astrology followers. Sometimes a cult that originates with a quest for spiritual truth transforms itself into a politically motivated group. In preparation for the mission of world domination, followers of Shoko Asahara's Aum Supreme Truth cult dispersed nerve gas in the Tokyo subway system in 1995, injuring thousands and causing the death of 12. The Aum cult murdered some of its members who appeared to be straying from the cult and who may

The Heaven's Gate cult Web site was designed to recruit new members, convince others outside the cult that their beliefs were rational, and reassure devoted cult members that their beliefs about the significance of the Hale-Bopp comet were about to come true.

have had doubts about its political goals (Trinh & Hall, 2000). Since most of these cults have all the characteristics of religion other than the transcendent, like a civil (secular) religion, they may be viewed as secular cults.

The media have characterized cults as brainwashing groups who prey on young people searching for alternative lifestyles and whose followers are led to their deaths through their fanatical devotion to the cult leader. Examples are numerous: In 1978, under the leadership of charismatic Jim Jones, who formed the People's Temple, over 900 Americans died of mass suicide–murder in a Guyana, South America, jungle settlement known as Jonestown—including over 200 children whose parents gave them poisoned fruit punch. In 1993, 80 members of David Koresh's Branch Davidians, including 19 children, burned to death in their Waco, Texas, compound when it was stormed by federal agents (Tabor & Gallagher, 1995; Hall et al., 2000). Others, such as the Heaven's Gate cult, under leader Marshall Applewhite, believed that angelic presences sending messages from space would offer an escape from earthly bonds. Thirty-nine people dressed themselves in black, ate drugged applesauce, and died in waves in an immaculately planned mass suicide. An entire space-related theology formed the foundation of Heaven's Gate (Schodolski &

Madigan, 1997). In Uganda, almost 1,000 adults and children died at the compound of the Restoration of the Ten Commandments of God. This cult believed that the world would end at the millennium. It is uncertain how many of the deaths were suicide and how many were murder, since many victims appeared to be strangled and mutilated (*Christian Century*, 2000). Media attention to these extreme examples reinforce stereotypes about cults.

Although it is true that cults successfully recruit from the disenchanted and those with fewer social ties, they vary considerably in terms of their religious emphasis as well as what must be surrendered to become a full-fledged member. Detrimental effects of cults are linked to the degree that members are cut off from wider society (Robbins, 1988; Stark, 1996a). Most cults do not demand such isolation, because they need the ongoing financial resources from members who work in the "outside" secular world. New Age cults, also referred to as the *New Age Movement*, are good examples. *New Age* is a catch-all term for loosely organized spirituality-seeking groups. Although there is no one set of consistent beliefs, New Age groups often focus on self-expression, a quest for inner peace, and a holistic framework that suggests unity between the individual, the planet Earth, and the universe (Heelas, 2000). They often gain members first as transient clients by selling a variety of services and products, such as alternative medicines and therapies, health foods, crystals, jewelry, and books. They tend to attract largely middle class people, especially women, who may be part of other New Age groups and may even belong to conventional religions. For example, eco-spirituality is a New Age religious movement seeking to encourage the protection of the Earth as God's creation and viewing all forms of this creation as interdependent, with humans not superior to any other forms (McFague, 1993; Rolmes, 1997). New Age groups in general are very pluralistic and are set up to meet a variety of individual needs (Hollis, 1998; Mears & Ellison, 2000; Woodhead & Heelas, 2000). Because the cults of the New Age Movement are so difficult to define and categorize, they have been described as a "cultural fog bank" (Bainbridge, 1997b:390). Cults exist in the hallways but not in the sanctuaries of more conventional religions.

Some cults can sustain themselves without a continuing charismatic leader if they begin to develop more sectlike qualities. Examples include the Church of Scientology and the International Order of Krishna Consciousness (Hare Krishna). It remains to be seen whether Reverend Sun Myung Moon's Unification church, founded in the 1950s and based in Korea, can survive beyond its leader's life. The Unification church is believed to be the world's largest Messianic religion with about 3 million members worldwide, and Moon proclaims himself as the messiah under which all religions and nations of the world will be united. A paid staff and highly effective administrative center, which distributes educational material worldwide, has kept the church economically stable. On the other hand, amid allegations of Moon's wife-beating and cocaine addition, membership and financial support are declining (Hong, 1998; Hoh, 1999). While it may have been on the road to becoming an established sect, Moon's financial woes coupled with the lack of an heir may herald the end of the cult (Shupe, 1998; Religious Movements, 2000).

Since there is disagreement among sociologists about the differences between a cult and a sect, the term *new religious movements* has gained acceptance as a substitute for cult (Dawson, 1998; Barrett, 2001; Hunt, 2002). Contrary to the examples above, most cults are peaceful and safe for their members. The millions of people attracted to various facets of the New Age Movement suggest this level of safety as well (Clark, 1993; Kloehn, 1997; Brown, 2000). The vast majority of cults do not end abruptly with the death of their members or the death of their leaders. They simply fade away.

The cult is a prime example of the difficulty of classifying religious groups because there is so much overlap between categories. We turn once again to Max Weber (1919/1946) for help. According to Weber, the distinction between church and sect can be conceived according to *ideal types*, the classification of information on a continuum between two poles. Idealized models of a church and a sect are at the two opposite poles of the continuum. Actual cases can be placed along the continuum according to how much or how little the religious organization represents either a church or sect. The same organization may be placed at different points on the continuum as its characteristics change. Ideal types are useful for showing how religious organizations evolve.

For example, a denomination can represent a midpoint on a continuum between church and sect. Like all contemporary world religions, Christianity began as a cult. Christianity then became a sect and then a church, and has since split into numerous denominations. Some of these denominations are now ecclesiae. On the other hand, denominations can split into sects or even cults if members feel there is too much accommodation to secular society. The way world religions are organized thus shifts according to the pressures of social change and secularization.

WORLD RELIGIONS AND SOCIAL CHANGE

The world's major religions are powerful institutionalized forces impacting social life. Religions function as agents of socialization, passing downs their beliefs from generation to generation. In addition to beliefs concerning the sacred, religions provide adherents with standards of social interaction in everyday life, especially those regarding the proper roles of men and women. As we will see in this section, both between and within religions, there are marked differences in these beliefs. When religious beliefs are linked to religious organizations, 19 major world religions have been identified; these are further divided into 270 large religious groups and thousands of smaller ones. About three-fourths of the world's more than 6 billion people identify with one of these world religions (see Table 17.2). Most of the remaining one-fourth are in spiritual traditions that have not been transformed by an "organized" formal religious organization. Less than 4 percent of all people are atheists (Adherents, 2001; Barrett, et al., 2001). Despite any secularization trends, almost 70 percent of the world's inhabitants identify themselves with one of five major world religions: Christianity, Islam, Judaism, Hinduism, and the ethicalist religions (Buddhism and Confucianism) (see Figure 17.1 on page 466).

TABLE 17.2

Worldwide Adherents of Selected Religions, in Millions by Six Continental Areas, Mid-2001

	Africa	Asia	Europe	Latin America	Northern America	Oceania	World	%
Christians	368,244	317,759	559,359	486,591	261,752	25,343	2,019,052	32.9
Roman Catholics	123,467	112,086	285,554	466,226	71,391	8,327	1,067,053	17.4
Protestants	90,989	50,718	77,497	49,008	70,164	7,478	345,855	5.6
Orthodox	36,038	14,219	158,375	564	6,400	718	216,314	3.5
Anglicans	43,524	735	26,628	1,098	3,231	5,428	80,644	1.3
Other Christians	87,978	160,126	29,456	47,316	91,779	2,004	414,479	6.8
Buddhists	139	356,533	1,570	660	2,777	307	361,985	5.9
Confucianists	250	6,277	10,800	450	0	24,000	6,313,000	0.1
Hindus	2,384,000	813,396,000	1,425,000	775,000	1,350,000	359,000	819,689,000	13.4
Jews	215,000	4,476,000	2,506,000	1,145,000	6,045,000	97,600	14,484,000	0.2
Muslims	323,556	845,341	31,724	1,702	4,518	307,000	1,207,148	19.7
New-Religionists[1]	28,900	101,065	160,000	633,000	847,000	66,900	102,801	1.7
Nonreligious[2]	5,170,000	611,876,000	105,742,000	16,214,000	28,994,000	3,349,000	771,345,000	12.6
Atheists	432,000	122,408,000	22,555,000	2,787,000	1,700,000	369,000	150,252,000	2.5

[1]New-Religionists. Followers of Asian 20th-century New Religions, New Religious movements, radical new crisis religions, and non-Christian syncretistic mass religions, all founded since 1800 and most since 1945.

[2]Nonreligious. Persons professing no religion, nonbelievers, agnostics, freethinkers, uninterested, or dereligionized secularists indifferent to all religion but not militantly so.

Source: Adapted from *Britannica Book of the Year,* 2002:302. Chicago: Encyclopedia Britannica.

Christianity ✝

From its origins 2,000 years ago as a Middle Eastern cult rooted in Judaism, Christianity developed as a result of the life events of its charismatic leader, Jesus of Nazareth, who was born a Jew. Christianity is the largest of the world's religions, representing about one-third of the world's population. Christianity's phenomenal growth rate is in part due to its early focus on class and ethnic inclusiveness (Stark, 1996b). This growth was triggered, first, by the 11th century split of Christianity into the Eastern Orthodox Church (based in Turkey) and the Roman Catholic Church, and second, by the Protestant Reformation led by Martin Luther in the 16th century.

Contemporary Christians separate themselves into an amazing variety of churches, denominations, and sects—34,000 separate Christian groups have been identified in the world with over half of them independent and not linked with denominations (Barrett et al., 2001). They are united, however, by the belief that Jesus is the son of God, the messiah who was crucified, resurrected from the dead, and will return as the salvation for the world. Jesus preached a gospel based on love, a belief in one almighty God, and the virtue of leading an ethically based life, and demonstrated miraculous healing powers that gradually attracted many followers. These stories are recorded in the New Testament of the Bible, the holy book of Christianity. Since adherents came mostly from the ranks of the numerous poor, discontented, and otherwise socially marginalized classes who abandoned conventional religious practices and the polytheism dictated by the Roman Empire, Jesus was perceived as a threat to the social order by both political and mainstream religious leaders. This resulted in mass arrests and persecution of his followers, driving the cult underground and activating what Christians believe to be preordained events, espcially Jesus' death and resurrection, on which Christianity is founded.

INTERNET CONNECTIONS

In the text there is a discussion of world religions. To find more information on global religions go to:

http://religion.rutgers.edu/vri/index.html

Scroll down and click on the links of different religions. After reading about two or more world religions answer the following questions. What are some common features that these different religions share? What are some differences? How do religions vary by type of society?

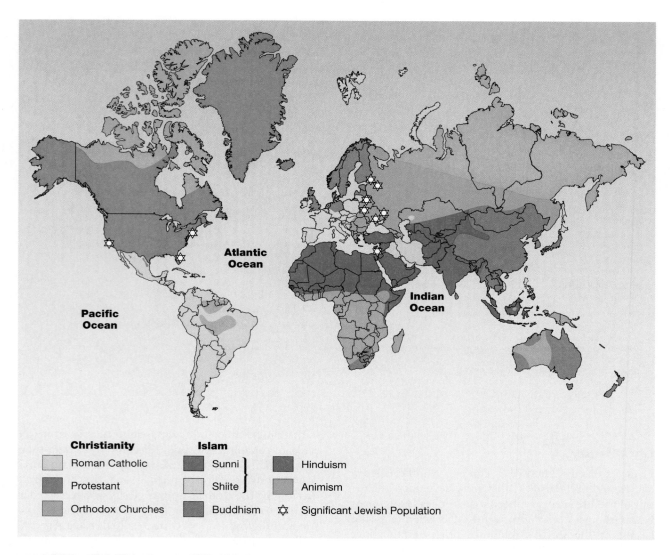

FIGURE 17.1 Global Distribution of World Religions.

Source: From *Human Geography: Cultures, Connections, and Landscapes* by Edward Bergman. Copyright © 1995 by Prentice Hall, Inc. Reprinted by permission of Prentice Hall, Inc., Upper Saddle River, NJ.

After Christianity became established as an institutionalized religion, missionary work and military conquest bolstered its expansion to the Western world. As functionalists maintain, the story of Christianity shows how politics and religion join forces to return the social system to a state of equilibrium. On the other hand, conflict theory points out that initially it did just the opposite: With its emphasis on inclusiveness of all people, regardless of class or ethnicity, the prevailing political and religious system was challenged.

Christians and Jews share the first five books of the Hebrew Bible and its images of women and men. One such image is that woman is made from the rib of a man, Adam, contrary to all subsequent natural law. Historically, the *androcentric*—male centered—passages have been emphasized: "the head of every woman is her husband" (I Corinthians 11:3); "wives be subject to your husbands" (Ephesians 5:22); "let a woman learn in silence with all submissiveness, permit no woman to teach or have authority over men" (I Timothy 2:11–12). Yet as women are being ordained in record numbers—with many seminaries now comprising well over 50 percent women—women have taken new leadership roles in their churches. As a result, the positive images of women found throughout the Bible are being highlighted (Zikmund et al., 1998; Brinton, 1999; Albee, 2000). Interpretation of scripture is more female friendly and gender equitable. For example, the "Adam's Rib" creation story ignores the earlier Genesis (1:27) account that God creates male and female in God's own image, a much more gender-equitable image. As told in the New Testament,

"There is neither Jew nor Greek, there is neither slave nor free, there is neither male nor female, for you are all one in Jesus Christ" (Galatians 3:28).

Islam ☪

The world's second largest and fastest growing religion is Islam, representing about one-fifth of the world's population (Barrett et al., 2001). Like Christianity, Islam has spread its message by both missionary and military means. Islam is an ecclesia in many nations of the developing world with higher birthrates than in those dominated by Christianity; thus most of the growth is due to those being born into the religion. The world *Islam* translates to *submission*, and Muslims, the adherents of Islam, are ones who have "submitted" to the will of God, or Allah (Johnstone, 2002:275). Founded in the seventh century, Islam is based on the teachings of Muhammad (570–632), the last and greatest among God's prophets whose revelations are recorded in the *Qur'an* (Koran), the holy book of Islam; other prophets include the divinely inspired (but not divine) Jesus, as well as Abraham and Moses. As governed by its pillars of faith, Islam is precise in what adherents must do to lead a godly life, such as praying five times a day, fasting during the month of Ramadan, and if able to do so, making a pilgrimage to Mecca (Muhammad's birthplace) at least once during their lifetime.

As Muhammad gained political and religious prominence, a death threat forced him to flee Mecca (now in Saudi Arabia) to Medina, where he founded a new community based on his revelations. Muhammad returned to Mecca in a bloodless conquest and established himself as a powerful leader of a religious state. Islam is divided into two major groups, Sunni and Shiite, who differ on beliefs about the leadership of the community after Muhammad (Feener, 2002). These two groups loosely fit the definition of denominations, with the Shia adherents generally more traditional, fundamentalist, and politically motivated than Sunni adherents (Armstrong, 2000a; Scupin, 2000; Johnstone, 2002). The large majority of Muslims, close to 90 percent, are Sunni. Muslims are not organized into churches, however, since formal religious structure is viewed as an obstacle between people and God. Note the continuities between the founding of Christianity and Islam, the effects of merging politics and religion, and how religion originally creates social disequilibrium and disorder. Once it becomes institutionalized, however, religion can be a force for social order.

Muslims vary considerably in how they interpret the Qur'an in regard to the roles of women. In the pre-Islamic Arab world, women had esteemed roles as soothsayers, priestesses, and queens. Islam arose in re-

The "Hajj," (pilgrimage) to religious sites in and near Mecca in Saudi Arabia is considered to be the culmination of Islamic religious duty. Although many Muslims can afford to make only one Hajj in their lifetimes, many others return to Mecca annually. The Saudi government estimates that annually over one-million Muslims visit Mecca for the Hajj.

sponse to unique cultural needs, including Muhammad's desire to aid the poor and protect widows, orphans, and unmarried women. The Qur'an shows a wide range of apparently contradictory practices concerning women. Women are seen as ideal, obedient, and gentle as well as jealous, conspiratorial, and having imperfect minds. By the third century (of the Muslim calendar) women were more secluded and restricted than in earlier Islamic decades (Mernissi, 1987; Minai, 1991). Although, contemporary Islam defines men and women as complementary rather than equal, passages from the Qur'an emphasizing inequality over complementarity are emphasized, such as "men are in charge of women, because God hath made the one of them to excel the other" (Qur'an IV:34). Since men are a step above women and the protectors of women, God gives preference and authority to men over women. Women have less freedom outside their homes and lower literacy rates in Islamic nations where the law is based on interpretations of the Qur'an. In Afghanistan under the Taliban, girls were denied schooling based on such interpretations even though Islamic tradition encourages female education so women can instruct their children in the words of the Prophet (Esposito, et al., 2001; Lakshmanan, 2002). Female ethnographers are documenting that numerous restrictions on women in the name of the Qur'an are much more likely the result of a nation's history and politics rather than of its religion.

In Malaysia and Indonesia women's Muslim groups are offering interpretations of Islamic law aimed at restoring gender justice (Anwar 2001; Feener, 2002). When women are educated in Islamic history and empowered to interpret the Qur'an, they not only offer more positive messages, but balance the distorted ones regarding the role and status of Islamic women.

Judaism ✡

Judaism is one of the oldest world religions; both Christianity and Islam sprang from Jewish roots. Despite its enormous global influence, it is by far the smallest, numbering about 18 million adherents (Robinson, 2001). Jewish history is recorded in the first five books of the Hebrew Bible, which Jews call the *Torah* (law). The Torah specifies that a Messiah will eventually bring Jews to a promised land—a state of paradise. The Torah also contains 613 commandments—including the Ten Commandments God gave to Moses on Mount Sinai—that are viewed as rabbinic law. These and other Jewish scriptures set down important beliefs and rituals, such as the promotion of community among all Jews, dedication to a synagogue or temple, doing *mitzvah* (good deeds), religious observances in families, and the belief that the human condition can be improved.

Judaism also shares with Christianity and Islam the teaching of the prophet Abraham. Judaism is traced to God's covenant with Abraham 4,000 years ago that allowed Abraham's descendants to be the chosen people and offered them permanent, exclusive rights over what would become the land of Israel in exchange for their allegiance. The original Jewish land in Palestine prospered until wars with neighboring kingdoms culminated in a final confrontation with Rome; their defeat resulted in the scattering of Jews throughout the world in the first century.

Almost 2,000 years passed before an independent Jewish state was regained—years marked by intense prejudice and anti-Semitism, including the Nazi Holocaust. A persistent Zionist movement to recreate the Jewish state in Palestine marked the last century of struggle. While Jews celebrated Israel's founding in 1948, displaced Palestinians and their Egyptian and Syrian allies, almost all of whom are Muslim, vowed revenge, leading to four wars that ended each time with less than satisfactory peace settlements and outbreaks of violence that continue today. Israel's strategic location and its profound importance as a religious site for Christians, Muslims, and Jews, make it a prime target for world conflict. The main Jewish denominations of Orthodox, Conservative, and Reform, as well as an emerging Reconstructionist branch, developed in response to this very confrontation—how much accommodation is necessary in one's religious life to suitably carry on other parts of one's life. As we will see later in this chapter, the latter three denominations are Jewish American adaptations to social change.

The ancient biblical world of Judaism was a patriarchal world. A strict gendered division of labor dictated family and religious life. Men's duties were to lead, teach, and legislate, and women to follow. Women's duties were confined to the household, including overseeing domestic religious rituals, such as preparing Sabbath meals. Ancient customs prescribed daily, rigorous religious duties for men from which women were exempt, since they could interfere with domestic roles. A woman required permission from her husband to engage in any outside activities, and she could divorce him only if he granted it. The "Texts of Terror," parts of four books of the Torah (Old Testament in the Christian Bible), that document abuse and sexual violence against women were often used as justifications for restricting women's lives (Trible, 1984; Fischer, 1994).

This situation changed dramatically when Jews entered modern, Western society in the late 19th century. The flexible, adaptive quality of Jewish beliefs and practices is again demonstrated in accommodating women's greater independence and higher levels of education (Glazier, 2000). The scriptural voices confirming God's high regard for women are being rediscovered (Shamir, 2002). In first-century documents, Eve is visioned as the mother of humanity who may have been naive, but certainly not wicked—an unselfish woman whose good character Satan abused. When Jews were scattered around the world, women had opportunities to climb to prestigious positions and assume leadership roles in their communities. Today not only are women allowed to take leading roles in public ritual life, but they are being ordained as rabbis in all branches of Judaism except Orthodoxy (Magonet, 2002).

Hinduism ॐ

Dating from about 4,500 years ago, Hinduism is the oldest and third largest of the world's major religions, with almost 800 million followers, most of whom live in India. Unlike Christianity and Islam, Hinduism does not *proselytize;* that is, it does not gain adherents through organized efforts to convert others to the religion. High birthrates in India and a negligible number of interfaith marriages among Hindu communities throughout the world function to steadily increase the number of Hindus. Hinduism is a polytheistic religion that has no one sacred text but uses a number of sources for guidance on morality in accordance with *dharma,* the moral responsibilities necessary for a godly life. Gods and goddesses are ranked, but there is no one supreme being who sits in judgment of every individual.

The goddess Dhurga serves as a powerful religious symbol for both Hindu men and women. Hinduism is the only contemporary world religion that has a long tradition and continuing practice of goddess worship.

It is impossible to separate Hinduism from the caste system in which it originated (Chapter 10) because of the link between the caste system and the Hindu belief in *reincarnation*, the cycle of birth, death, and rebirth into a higher or lower caste depending on how well an individual acts out the ideal life dictated by dharma. In each incarnation, the soul continues its journey toward *nirvana*, the point where spiritual perfection is achieved, the soul is absorbed into the universal spirit, and the reincarnation cycle ends.

Because Hinduism is based in India, one of the most ethnically diverse nations in the world, its practices have been adapted to suit a wide variety of cultural circumstances. Shrines erected to harvest and rain gods are numerous in rural villages. The image of Ganesh, the god of prosperity who is also the "great guide," with his elephant head and human body, is emblazoned on walls near ATM machines. His figure rests on computer terminals in businesses throughout Bombay and New Delhi. Just as St. Christopher medals are carried by Christian Catholics who travel, so are Ganesh images by traveling Hindus. Hinduism emphasizes virtues often associated with one of its great personages, Mahatma Gandhi, who epitomizes the dharma of service, courage, humility, and nonviolence. Mother Theresa of Calcutta, herself a Christian, demonstrated these same virtues in her work with the poorest of India's poor. Hinduism suggests that because both Ghandi and Mother Theresa led exceptional, even miraculous lives on behalf of humanity,

they may have reached nirvana, ending their cycle of earthly incarnations.

The oldest Hindu scriptures, the *Vedas* and *Upanishads* (1800–500 B.C.E.) provide images of women that have been interpreted in many ways. Some scriptures criticize women for being too ambitious, energetic, and masculine, which denies their "higher" level of womanhood in serving their families. Hindu religious rituals reinforce their roles as mothers, wives, and homemakers, and their connections to men for their well-being (Jacobson & Wadley, 1995; Weisgrau, 2000). When women became "unconnected" to men by widowhood, infamous practices such as *suttee*, widow burning, occurred. A widow could feel guilty all her life because her husband died before she did. Others, however, demonstrate an esteem for femininity and complementarity between spouses. Women are auspicious and vital to the well-being of the family and are celebrated by a number of prominent female deities who continue to be worshipped (Larson, 1994; Flood, 2002). Hinduism's continuing goddess heritage has always allowed women to serve in temples and lead religious rituals.

Ethicalist Religions: Buddhism and Confucianism

Most ethicalist world religions originated in Asia. These religions are identified not by their belief in divine beings or the manipulation of supernatural forces, but by their adherence to ethically based codes of behavior, culminating in the achievement of human happiness or a higher state of personal awareness or consciousness. The abstract ideals on which ethicalist religions are based provide prescriptions for moral living that not only aid individuals in their journey to higher consciousness, but also benefit those with whom they come into contact.

Buddhism, which grew out of Hinduism, claims almost 6 percent of the globe's population as members (Robinson, 2001). Buddhism was founded around 600 B.C.E. by Siddhartha Gautama, who became the "Buddha." He was a wealthy upper-caste Hindu who believed that ending human suffering rested on ending human desire. By following a rigidly prescribed path of righteous living focusing on meditation and proper conduct, an individual could achieve enlightenment, the highest level of human consciousness. Similar to Hinduism, the soul would be released from the reincarnation cycle into eternal bliss. This spiritual quest does not need gods as mediators, since godliness is considered the untapped potential in *all* humans.

The most secular of the ethicalist religions was founded by the Chinese philosopher Confucius (551–479 B.C.E.). Like Buddhism, Confucianism is

Tibetan Buddhism, which these monks represent, is the fastest-growing branch of Buddhism in the West. Buddhism is struggling to maintain its identity within Communist China.

based on a code of self-discipline and meditation designed to maintain proper relationships that enhance loyalty, respect, and morality. Reverence for ancestors is the closest Confucianism gets to the idea of worship. Proper conduct toward others is formed first in the family and then relayed to the broader community. Confucianism works toward earthly success rather than supernatural rewards. Confucianism for centuries was the philosophical foundation for both Chinese and Korean politics. Confucianism in Korea was adapted to virtually every aspect of social life, making Korea much more "Confucian" in ethical principles than China, a pattern that held until the arrival of Christianity in the 18th century (Breen, 1998; Grayson, 2002). Confucianism thrived in collectivistic societies like China and Korea, which emphasize hierarchy, harmony, and respect for authority and tradition.

In the strongly monotheistic Western world, there is often misunderstanding about ethically based religions, particularly since neither Buddha nor Confucius are elevated as gods in the religions they founded. To sociologists, it is not the supernatural elements that are important, but the consequences of religious behavior on the community of its believers.

Although they share similar roots in Asia, Confucianism and Buddhism have fairly different images of women. Confucius had a low opinion of women that cannot be easily dismissed from his writings, and the religion named for him is the most patriarchal of all world religions (Yao, 2002). A woman's life is carried out under the direct authority of her husband, sons, and in-laws. Confucianism has lost ground in contemporary China in part because it has not been able to accommodate changes to women's status and family life that are promoted by the Chinese government

(Zi, 1995). While women are certainly restricted in Buddhist areas throughout Asia, ancient Buddhist traditions supported women's quest for enlightenment. Buddha's disciples included both men and women, and spiritual paths were open to both. Women could be ordained as nuns just as men could become monks, practices that continue today (Calkowski, 2000; Corless, 2002; Ingram, 2002).

Global Fundamentalism

We saw in Chapter 3 that a culture must adapt to social change in order to improve its chances of survival. All religions provide guidelines for behavior, but the principle of adaptation asserts that as the world changes, religious guidelines must be modified accordingly. Compared to all other social institutions, religion is perhaps the most resistant to adaptation, as shown by the rise of fundamentalism worldwide. Religious resurgence rooted in fundamentalism is taking place among diverse cultures, in nations with very different levels of economic development and, most important for sociologists, in every major religion (Thomas, 1999; Armstrong, 2000b; Laqueur, 2001). The connection between globalization and fundamentalism is perhaps the most rapidly growing topic in the sociology of religion.

Fundamentalism grew out of a religious movement among American Protestants in the early 20th century who were concerned that modernization was eroding Christianity. Fundamentalism relies on the view that a golden age existed in the past and must be recovered. In this sense fundamentalism is more *reactionary*—a return to the past—than *conservative*—maintaining or conserving what already exists (Swift, 1991). According to fundamentalists, even conservatives have already gone too far in accommodating social change. With the worldwide resurgence in the 1970s of "militant" religiously based social movements designed to align government with religious scripture, the term fundamentalism is now applied much more extensively (Swatos, 1998). Fundamentalism is a broad movement comprising a number of different groups, and there is a great deal of disagreement about how religious scripture should be interpreted and what a religiously based government should look like.

All world religions exhibit some fundamentalist trends. Secularization is a threat to any religion, but how that threat is carried out varies considerably (Audi, 2000). Fundamentalists do not accept the functionalist view that adaptation is required to maintain religious integrity. They suggest the reverse: Adaptation is compromise in disguise and leads to the surrender of religious integrity. The benign, benevolent, and ethical focus on the universal "good" provided by religions contrasts sharply with the sectarian, fundamentalist side of religion, which fuels tension. In the name of religion, tension can escalate into violence.

But the large majority of adherents to the world's major religions are not fundamentalists, and those who *are* fundamentalist condemn the violence that is associated with their religions (Amaladoss, 2001; Es-

posito, 2002). Like the term *cult*, fundamentalism is linked to negative stereotypes in the media, which paint Muslims in particular as threats. Many fundamentalist groups, however, disdain political activism of any type, preferring instead to be left alone to pursue their religious vision in settings under their control (Shupe & Hadden, 1989; Friedland, 2001). Sects of ultra-orthodox Jews in Israel and the United States reflect this pattern, even as they struggle with needs for religious commitment and the economic realities of modernization (Heilman, 1999; Armstrong, 2001). As explained in Chapter 24, fundamentalism is one example of a countermodernization movement that promotes ways to minimize the effects of modernization. Even when violence may be propelled by religious fundamentalists, all major world religions promote faith for the purposes of peace and hope, not violence. Unfortunately, it is the violent arm of the fundamentalist movement combating modernization and globalization that has gained the world's attention (see Global Connections Box on page 454).

LIFE CONNECTIONS

Religious Diversity in the United States

The United States has the highest degree of religious pluralism in the world (Table 17.3). Religious toleration and the separation of church and state are hallmarks of American culture, so the various denominations often compete for members. Strong cultural values of individualism and personal autonomy may reduce religious commitment (Wuthnow, 1993; Madsen, 2002). Modernization contributes to this reduction by reinforcing faith in science rather than religion for problem solving. However, as we will see in this section, while there is a trend toward secularization that is fueled by pluralism, there are other processes at work that counter the trend.

Challenges to Secularization

American citizens are more religious than those in almost every other modern industrialized nation (Verweij et al., 1997). Two hundred years ago only 10 percent of people in the United States were affiliated with churches and only 20 percent attended (Hudson, 1973). Today, over 90 percent state a religious preference, 60 percent say they belong to a church, and regular church attendance is in the 40 percent to 60 percent range (Kosmin & Mayer, 2001a; U.S. Census Bureau, 2001: Table 66; Kohut & Rogers, 2002). While the 1950s witnessed the highest levels of attendance, there has been a pattern of steady increase with only slight fluctuations; when downturns occur, they tend to be short term (Roof, 1999). The vast majority

TABLE 17.3

U.S. Religious Affiliation, 2002

Self-Identification, American Religious Identity Survey (ARIS)

Religion	% of U.S. Pop., 2000	% Change 1990–2000
Christianity	76.5	+5
Judaism	1.3	−10
Islam	0.5	+109
Buddhism	0.5	+170
Agnosticism	0.5	−16
Atheism	0.4	
Hinduism	0.4	+237

Largest Branches of Christianity and Other Religions

	%, 1996	%, 2002
Protestant	53	52
Roman Catholic/ Orthodox	24	24
Mormon	2	2
Other Christian	2	2
Not practicing/ don't know	3	2
Other religions	16	18

Sources: Adapted from Adherents (ARIS), 2002; Kohut & Rogers, 2002; Sheler, 2002.

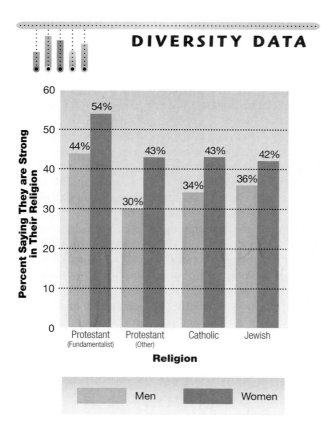

DIVERSITY DATA

FIGURE 17.2 Percent Who Identify Themselves as Strong in Their Religious Preference, by Religion and Gender. Among all religious preferences, women are significantly more likely to report they are strong in their religion compared to men, with Fundamentalist Protestant women at the highest levels. What explains the gender difference in strength of religion? How do gender and religious preference intersect to explain the difference?

Source: NORC. General Social Surveys, 1972–2000. Chicago: National Opinion Research Center, 2000. Reprinted by permission of NORC, Chicago, IL.

identify religion as important in their lives and believe in core religious doctrines, such as the existence of God and life after death (Niebuhr, 1999; NORC, 2000; Sheler, 2002). Atheism is at an all-time low. These patterns appear to refute the long-term trend toward secularization.

Religious roots stemming from a Judeo-Christian foundation are entangled in U.S. government. A number of state-sponsored churches existed in the United States until the adoption of the First Amendment at the end of the 18th century (Handy, 1991). Americans simultaneously support separation of church and state and the belief that good Christians (broadly construed) are also good citizens. God is at home in America, both in its churches and in its government (Wogaman, 2000; Hauerwas, 2002). Although belief in God is

firmly entrenched in the United States, there is little support for official government endorsement of a particular brand of religion (Audi, 2000). As we will see, even in the highly publicized political activities of various religious groups, the United States continues to embrace religious pluralism.

MEASURING RELIGIOSITY The question of whether the United States is undergoing secularization or religious resurgence can be answered in part by how religiosity is measured. Religions vary in organizational structure as well as in many other dimensions, such as amount and type of rituals, level that social justice is a part of the ministry, degree to which members openly express emotions, and expectations regarding religious knowledge (Glock & Stark, 1965; Steensland et al., 2000). There are also differences between ideal or official religion, which usually comes from the pulpit, and real or popular religion, which is expressed in the culture. Sociologists tend to focus on the ideal practices, such as church attendance and religious affiliation, and may overlook important popular indicators of religious experience, such as how religious artifacts (rosaries, bibles, gospel music CDs) are displayed, how non-churchgoers bring religion into their homes through prayer at meals or listening to religious music, and how religious beliefs propel people to volunteer for social, charitable, and civic causes (McDannell, 1995; Parris, 2000; Becker & Dhingra, 2001).

There has been a great deal of controversy about using Christian prayers at events in public schools. Although Christianity may be the dominant religion in these schools, such practices may violate the principle of the separation of church and state.

SOCIOLOGY OF EVERYDAY LIFE

Magic and Religion in America

Leo (July 23–August 22): Cycle is such that you land on your feet from no matter what height. Imprint style—don't follow others. You will come from behind to ultimately win the game. Aquarius, another Leo in picture.

Religiosity is strong in the United States, one of the top three countries in the world with the highest degrees of religious affiliation and belief. Yet Americans are also apparently quite comfortable with practicing rituals that might be defined as magical, superstitious, or occult. Beliefs in astrology, hexing, charms, witchcraft, water divining, and UFOs are quite strong. These beliefs contradict scientific or religious knowledge and are sometimes referred to as nonofficial religion. It is difficult to distinguish what falls within the categories of nonofficial and official religion. Consider the following statistics on the U.S. population:

1. One-quarter report seeing a ghost or spirit of the dead.
2. Thirteen percent have seen or been in the presence of angels.
3. Over one-third have had a mystical experience. Most believe it was religiously inspired.
4. Two-thirds have experienced déjà vu or ESP, a sense they are repeating an experience, being somewhere they have never been, or sensing things that are not immediately present.
5. Two-thirds believe that a prayer has been answered, such as using prayer for healing themselves or others.

Can these be interpreted and accepted (legitimized) according to official religion,

or do they fall in the unofficial realm? Are they magical or religious?

The above examples may be viewed positively by religion, but other practices are less likely viewed this way. Contrary to what their official religions expect them to practice or believe, Americans often, and routinely, engage in behavior that would be defined as religiously inappropriate. For example, most of us may quickly check out our horoscope as a form of entertainment as we peruse the daily newspaper. But 25 percent of the population in the United States say they believe in astrology and often make daily decisions based on it. Based on the horoscope above, astrology-believing Leos could be inspired to take a risk in love or finances and find another Leo or an Aquarius to help them out.

Other studies confirm belief in magic and superstition. New England commercial fishers admit that they would not break certain fishing taboos. The taboos include "don't turn a hatch cover upside down," "don't whistle on a boat," and "don't mention the word 'pig' on board." Why? Breaking a taboo risks personal safety and brings bad luck. When on shore these fishers express disbelief about the effectiveness of their taboos, but at sea and when in danger, anxiety levels rise and they will not risk breaking them. Anxiety increases the use of magic and superstition. A study of professional sports and Olympic athletes shows them to be under ongoing stress and often in physical danger. Auto racers, hockey players, and football players risk severe injury every time they engage in their profession. Magical

practices—whether skating three times around the ice before the game, having a teammate knock on a football helmet three times before a kickoff, or wearing blue underwear at every game—reduce their anxiety.

Superstitions are strong among Americans. While people may not say they believe in them, they routinely practice them. Ninety percent of people say they have personal items that they consider lucky, such as a four-leaf clover, rabbit's foot, or special amulet. Sports stars continue to wear the jewelry that they had on when they were on a winning streak. Studies of college students report that they wear certain jeans, shirts, or special clothing to exams to bring them luck. Most people would not walk under a ladder (probably a good idea regardless of superstition) and do not want a room on the 13th floor in a hotel. Indeed, hotels must also know something about superstitions and customer preferences, since many do not have a thirteenth floor!

Every time you take a sociology exam, make sure you reread this box. And knock on wood.

1. What magical and religious behaviors do you engage in routinely? Why do you engage in them, and how effective are they for your purposes?

2. How can magic and religion exist comfortably alongside one another in any society that defines itself as religious?

Sources: Poggie & Pollnac, 1988; Gallup & Castelli, 1989; Womack, 1992; Kantrowitz, 1994; Cunningham, 1999; Swidler & Mojzes, 2000.

Documenting religious pluralism would seem to be a simpler task than measuring religiosity overall. But religious structure in the United States is remarkably varied (Olson, 1999). The large number of religious subcategories together with the rapid emergence and decline of cults and other new religious movements compound the difficulty. We can say, however, that currently the religious salad bowl in the United States is largely comprised of three main ingredients—Protestant, Catholic, and Jewish—in proportions that until recently have remained relatively stable. However, immigration patterns are altering these proportions somewhat. Christians, especially Catholics, are arriving from Mexico and Latin America as well as from Christian regions of sub-Saharan Africa (Adherents, 2002). The portion of "other religions" is enlarging with Muslim, Hindu, and Buddhist immigrants arriving from Asia, North Africa, and the Middle East. While still quite small compared to other religions, Buddhism is also growing and includes those who may also be members of other religions (Wood, 1997). Muslims account for the largest portion of these new arrivals. Jews are slightly declining in numbers. Overall, while the Protestant and Catholic proportions are not expected to change significantly, the decrease in the number of Jews and increase in the number of Muslims will add Islam as the fourth major ingredient of the religious salad bowl in the United States (Barrett et al., 2001; Lindner, 2002).

Although these four groups testify to the religious pluralism in the United States, sociologists have identified other layers of diversity within each of them, especially related to race, social class, and gender. We have already seen how the roles of men and women vary in the major world religions. Since religions in the United States are also part of the world religions, similar gender patterns occur. However, this section will show that diversity has as much to do with adaptation to life in the United States and theology as with demographic variables.

Protestant Diversity

Protestants in the United States are so diverse they almost defy generalization. However, they do have two things in common: They are Christian and they are not Catholic. One-third are Baptists; one-third are in several "mainstream" denominations, including Methodist, Lutheran, Presbyterian, Episcopalian, and United Church of Christ; and the other one-third are a collection of small denominations, independent churches, and those not otherwise affiliated with any specific Protestant group. This last group includes many of the fundamentalist churches at the core of religious resurgence in the United States (Robinson, 2001; Adherents, 2002). Protestantism in the United

States is one of schism and divisions. This means that since Protestants are not a unified body sharing the same religious beliefs and practices, they are the group most likely to split into smaller independent churches and sects (Lindner, 2002). Clearly, schisms promote religious pluralism.

Mainstream denominations in the United States have disproportionately lost members to other groups since the 1960s. Similar to the larger churches they represent, these denominations are inclusive and liberal in their theology—they accommodate a variety of interpretations. Conservative churches are more likely to be absolutist in their beliefs—the Bible is the word of God and contains no errors. Liberal churches gain more members from conservative churches than the reverse, but not enough to offset overall losses. Conservative Protestants, including Baptists, are the winners in the membership race, but the biggest winners are in the one-third of churches that are likely to be conservative *and* fundamentalist. For example, the Pentecostal/Charismatic denomination is the largest and fastest growing one in this group and is positioned to outnumber Presbyterians in the near future (Hunt et al., 1998).

SOCIAL CLASS AND MEMBERSHIP Compared to other Protestants, mainstream Protestants tend to be older, have higher levels of education, earn higher incomes, come from the middle and upper classes, and hold more liberal theological and political views. They have a strong sense of personal autonomy and often come from upwardly mobile families in which religious switching occurred—from low-status to high-status denominations. Episcopalians, Presbyterians, and affiliates of the United Church of Christ are the best representatives of this profile. On the other hand, conservative churches are more likely to be made up of working-class and poorer people and, as we will see, they express a range of political views (Waters et al., 1995; Steensland, et al., 2000; Kosmin & Mayer, 2001a) (Figs. 17.3 and 17.4).

THEOLOGY Larger denominations of mainstream Protestants are theologically more tolerant than their fundamentalist siblings. Research shows that such broad-based theology, designed to be accepted by everyone, cannot capture the religious hearts of different groups, such as teenagers, college students, seminarians, and many African Americans. While they may have a strong identity as Christians, when asked what it means to be part of such denominations, most people simply say "nothing" (Carroll & Roof, 1993). These people more often identify with a specific congregation of close friends than with the denomination as a whole.

Because they are more absolutist and conformist, traditional sources of religious identity are easier to tap

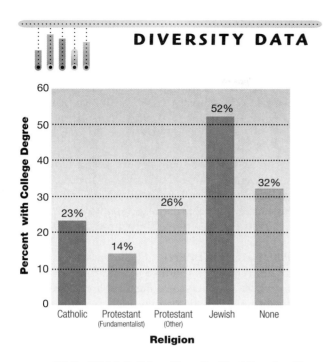

FIGURE 17.3   Which Religions Have the Most People with College Degrees? Over half of Jewish respondents have college degrees compared to just under one-fourth of those from other religions, including those who report no religion. What explains the high educational attainment of Jews compared to those in other religions? How can minority status be considered a factor in this explanation?

Source: NORC. General Social Surveys, 1972–2000. Chicago: National Opinion Research Center, 2000. Reprinted by permission of NORC, Chicago, IL.

for fundamentalists. Given the global resurgence of fundamentalism, however, sociologists are most interested in diversity *within* fundamentalist churches. This diversity is the key factor in understanding political views of fundamentalists, yet is usually overlooked in media accounts of Christian fundamentalism in the United States. Fundamentalism reflects two important sides of Christianity—salvation of souls (the evangelical side) and the improvement of society (the political side) (see Figure 17.5 on page 480). Both sides fear the effects of creeping modernization; they also believe that a personal experience with God is the key to salvation, that the Bible is absolutely truthful, and that they have an obligation to share their faith with others. Evangelical fundamentalists, however, are often content to retreat to their churches to praise God in the company of others like themselves in a manner of their own choosing. In contrast, politically oriented fundamentalists take their faith on the road, determined to convince others that government and society need an injection of Christian morality to save them from secular doom

(Aldridge, 2000; Hunt, 2002). Christian fundamentalism in the United States has a history of moving between "pious retreat and theocratic assault" (Bruce, 1999:155). When democracy and religious pluralism are linked, as in the United States, believers can leave their churches and begin a movement of their own, which accounts for the large variety of Protestant fundamentalist groups.

Another fundamentalist success story is research supporting the argument that the stricter the church, the stronger the church. Mainstream Protestant churches are more lenient—they encourage dialogue and theological debate. Strict churches are more absolutist and conformist. Fundamentalist churches are often sectarian and democratic in leadership. They require high levels of commitment, participation, and energy (Sherkat & Ellison, 1999; Sherkat, 2001). Theology and commitment work together to keep conservative churches strong.

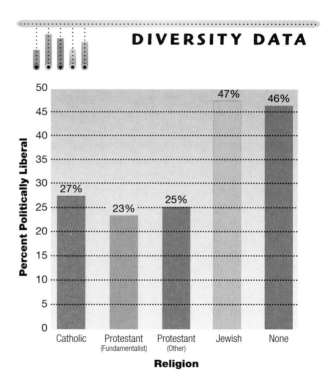

FIGURE 17.4   People Who Identify Themselves as Politically Liberal, by Religious Preference. Almost half of Jews and those reporting no religion identify themselves as politically liberal compared to about one-fourth of those in other religions. What political and social issues do you think separate Jews from other religious groups? How does religion intersect with other factors to explain these differences?

Source: NORC. General Social Surveys. 1972–2000. Chicago: National Opinion Research Center, 2000. Reprinted by permission of NORC, Chicago, IL.

INTERNET CONNECTIONS

In this chapter, various "challenges to secularization" are discussed. One of these challenges involves the issues surrounding *school prayer and religious symbolisms in school*. In order to acquaint yourself with the school prayer issue go to:

http://www.adherents.com/misc/fed_guidelines.html

The opening page has a list of federal guidelines on prayer in schools and links to a number of different sites on the topic. How do you feel about this particular issue involving secularization? Should there be a separation of church and state? Should individual schools be free to make their own policy regarding school prayer? How do you think the conflict might be rectified?

RACE AND ETHNICITY Religious identity is stronger in congregations that are ethnically homogeneous, especially as reflected in race, customs, and language. Ethnic diversity, like religious pluralism, has a substantial negative effect on church adherence, so stronger churches are likely to be racially segregated. African American congregations are overrepresented in fundamentalist churches. Compared to congregations from African American mainstream denominations, such as African-Methodist-Episcopal (A.M.E), African American fundamentalists engage in less denominational switching and have higher levels of religious participation. Religious involvement enhances feelings of psychological closeness and quality of life, social support, and shared interest with other African Americans and is a major factor in faith-based community service projects (Blake & Darling, 2000; Miller, 2000; Day, 2001; Hunt & Hunt, 2001). As a reflection of all these feelings, African American churches, for example, played a dominant political role as key sites for the civil rights movement (Calhoun-Brown, 2000).

Catholic Diversity

Religious homogeneity—both in theology and in the demographic composition of congregations—is more evident among Catholics than among Protestants. Nonetheless, a great deal of diversity exists. Several branches of Catholicism worldwide adhere to different interpretations of Jesus' teachings. The Roman Catholic Church is by far the largest, claiming about one-fourth of all Americans as members (Kohut & Rogers, 2002).

SOCIAL CLASS AND RACE In the 20th century, Catholics as a group generally moved from lower SES to middle SES categories. Today, however, this moderate class position is declining with the influx of poorer Catholic immigrants, mainly from Latin America. The vast majority of Catholics are non-Latino whites—less than 10 percent of Catholics in the United States are African American. African American Catholics have higher levels of education and income than their Protestant counterparts. However, perhaps reflecting a Protestant heritage, African American Catholics are more likely than white Catholics to engage their congregations in evangelical and social action ministries (D'Apolito, 2000; Franklin, 2000).

RELIGIOUS COMMITMENT Catholicism represents mainstream religion, but unlike in mainstream Protestantism where numbers of adherents are decreasing, membership in Catholic churches has remained fairly stable. In general, there is a decline in commitment to the church, as shown by less financial support, less expressed concern for the sacraments, and higher percentages who say that the church is out of date and not relevant in their lives. Like Protestants, Catholics are becoming more individual rather than collective in their attachments to the church. However, among Catholics in general, there is a shift to concern for social issues and social action (D'Antonio et al., 1989; Williams & Davidson, 1997; Christiano, 2000).

WOMEN AND SEXUALITY Probably the most important issues dividing contemporary U.S. Catholics from the authority of the broader Roman Catholic church are attitudes about women in general and sexuality in particular. This division shows up among both clergy and laypeople. For example, various orders of nuns have removed themselves from traditional patterns of Catholic hierarchy and worship; they take a distinctly female-centered view of religion, preferring to pray to "Her" rather than to "Him." Other parishes stretch church authority to allow altar girls, nuns as campus ministers, and women leading "priestess parishes" in rural areas where there are shortages of male priests (Wallace, 1992, 1993; Egan 1999). Among laypeople, a majority of Catholics practice birth control other than the rhythm method, support the use of condoms and sex education in schools, believe priests should be allowed to marry, do not believe political candidates should be judged solely on the abortion issue, believe that divorced Catholics need to be welcomed back into the church, and are receptive to women's ordination, all in direct contradiction to Vatican authority (Williams & Davidson, 1997; Lippy, 1999; Strange, 2002). Since so many Catholics have beliefs and practices that directly counter Vatican teaching, the church is reluctant to dismiss them from church rosters.

As the head of the Roman Catholic Church worldwide, when the Pope celebrates a mass, such as in Victory Square in Warsaw, Poland, thousands are in attendance, including many non-Catholics.

Regarding the issue of women in the priesthood, however, the church will not budge. For every proclamation that reasserts the Vatican's position that women can never be ordained, a worldwide outcry centered in the United States against the position occurs. Currently, the Vatican believes allegiance of Catholics can be maintained without women's ordination. Others take the view that this issue will eventually cause an irrevocable split in the church (Bohlen, 1995; Weaver, 1999).

Issues related to women and sexuality have been in the forefront of Catholic controversy for decades. However, a new twist on the sexuality issue recently exploded in the media when widespread sexual abuse by Catholic priests perpetrated on children was revealed. The shock that priests in both the United States and abroad engaged in "serial, predatory, and sexual abuse of minors" was magnified when it was learned that Roman Catholic officials who knew of abuse routinely shuffled "problem priests" to other parishes and ignored the problem. These cover-ups were as disturbing to many Catholics as the original abuse, and most people believed that the Church did a poor job in handling the scandal (Roane, 2002). In an unprecedented move, Pope John Paul II convened a meeting of U.S. cardinals at the Vatican to deal with the matter. Along with official apologies, counseling, and monetary compensation for victims, removal from the priesthood and criminal charges for perpetrators are offered as short-term solutions (CNN, 2002; Rice, 2002).

Regardless of the success of these solutions, the sex scandal will certainly magnify the existing split in the church. The church may have been so busy warding off hostile forces in society over their stand on women's ordination, birth control, and sexuality that "they neglected to root out the enemy within" (Stanley, 2002:3).

As we have seen from a sociological perspective on religious pluralism, for the Roman Catholic church to effectively deal with the issues that divide the church in the United States from Rome, it must adapt to social change and modernization but at the same time uphold religious traditions.

Jewish Diversity

In the United States, Jewish religion is strongly congregational—any group of Jews can organize a congregation in any way they see fit. The congregation is the core of Jewish communal life. Religion, ethnicity, cultural history, and anti-Semitism intertwine to make Judaism a stronger ascribed status than other religious groups (Elazar, 2000; Glazier, 2000) Jews represent about 1.5 percent of the U.S. population, and numbers are declining due mainly to lower birth rates, less immigration, and an increase of interfaith marriages (Waite, 2000; U.S. Census Bureau, 2001: Table 67; Mayer & Kosmin, 2001).

SOCIAL CLASS AND SOCIAL ISSUES Compared to Protestants and Catholics, there are far fewer demographic differences between Jews. Jews are highly urbanized: 90 percent live in metropolitan areas, and most reside in the New York City region. They top the social class hierarchy in income and educational level (NORC, 2000). Politically, most Jews are Democrats, identify themselves as liberal, and will work for causes that are central to Jewish identity, such as protecting religious freedom and support for Israel. However, the turmoil in the Middle East has weakened attachment to Israel and has divided American Jews on both religious and political grounds (Arian, 1999; Cohen, 2000; Freedman, 2000). Jews have also been strong advocates of minority rights initiatives and were among the earliest partners with African Americans in the civil rights movement. Despite their small numbers, Jews have been very influential in U.S. politics.

THEOLOGY It is not demographics but interpretation of theology that best describes Jewish diversity in the United States. As mentioned earlier, Judaism is divided into several branches. In the United States, of the approximate 2.8 million Jews, about 20 percent are Orthodox, 50 percent Conservative, and 25 percent Reform, with the Reconstructionists representing the other 5 percent (Wertheimer, 1997; Mayer & Kosmin, 2001; Adherents, 2002). Each branch varies according to the degree to which theology is literally interpreted and acted on in daily life. Orthodox Jews, for example, are sectlike and have the strictest interpretation, viewing the Torah as the absolutely binding word of God. This branch is attracting more members, especially among younger Jews who use Orthodoxy to rediscover their heritage. Nonetheless, diversity is also evident among Orthodox Jews. There is a split between those who want to engage more fully in activities outside the subculture and those who believe that to do so compromises Jewish law (Eisen, 1996; Klinghoffer, 1998). Those who identify as Conservative are less strict, allowing interpretation of the Torah in the context of modern life. Some religious traditions are maintained, and others are adapted to contemporary society.

Reform Jews, the most liberal and assimilated branch, are more churchlike. They accept the Torah's ethical guidelines but have lenient attitudes regarding obedience to rabbinic law. The Reconstructionist branch of Judaism is small but slowly growing. Embracing humanistic values and Judaism's historical and cultural heritage, Reconstructionists reject the traditional religious doctrines as set down in the Torah. Reconstructionism resembles a civil (secular) religion, since it cherishes the ethnic Jewish history and traditions, reveres science and intellectual curiosity, but does not believe in the divine, supernatural origin of the Torah (Yinger, 1994; Dershowitz, 1997). Given centuries of anti-Semitism, Jews agree that their safety is tied to the protection of religious pluralism, and they are politically active in ensuring that this continues. Jews in all branches are in congregations who are innovative in adapting their religious practices to modern life in the United States (Schwartz, 2000).

Islamic Diversity

The growing number of immigrants from Islamic countries is adding to religious diversity in the United States. Although there are only about 1 million Muslims in the United States, their numbers are rapidly increasing; they are expected to outnumber Jews within one or two decades (Barrett et al., 2001; Kos-min & Mayer, 2001b; Adherents, 2002). Like other religious groups in the United States, Muslims exhibit striking demographic and theological diversity. Reflecting the world pattern, the large majority of Muslims in the United States are Sunni and are less literal in their theological interpretation of Islam than are their Shiite counterparts.

RACE AND SOCIAL CLASS The 1870s witnessed the first significant waves of immigration of Muslims to the United States. These arrivals were mostly young, relatively unskilled single men from Turkey, Lebanon, and the Middle East. These men sought the jobs and economic opportunities offered by the rapid industrial expansion in the United States. However, there was no established religious community to which they could attach themselves, as there was for earlier Christian arrivals. Workplaces did not accommodate opportunities for prayer, fasting, or religious observances required by their religion. Some immigrants were able to start small businesses that gave them greater flexibility to practice Islam. Others, especially second-generation Muslims, tended to distance themselves from their Muslim and ethnic heritages by changing their names, abandoning distinctive clothing, and decreasing religious rituals. Muslims were also keenly aware of the strong race prejudice against people of color in the United States, especially African Americans (Haddad & Esposito, 1998; Smith, 1999). Muslims with darker skins were more likely to experience the double discrimination associated with religion and race.

Yet just when these Muslims were moving away from some practices of Islam, many African Americans were embracing it. In the mid-20th century, under the leadership of Elijah Mohammed, the son of a Baptist preacher, and Malcolm X, the Nation of Islam (NOI) was established. NOI is the first indigenous movement in the United States claiming to have an affiliation with Islam (Smith, 1999). However, unlike Islam, NOI is couched in openly racist terms. The world religion of Islam states that all people of all races are equal under God; NOI's stance that whites are evil contradicts this. During a trip to Mecca in 1964 Malcolm X realized that his understanding of Islam was severely limited. Disavowing NOI's racist ideology, Malcolm began to preach about Islam as an inclusive religion. Malcolm X was murdered a year later; his murder has never been solved. Today, Louis Farakhan leads a smaller NOI and one that is again associated with separatism and racism, although it has worked to improve the plight of poor, inner-city African Americans. The Sunni and Shiite communities have distanced themselves from NOI.

African Americans who convert to Islam are more likely to join the ranks of these much larger Muslim communities. Compared to NOI adherents, other

African American Muslims tend to be better educated and come from homes with less divorce and with stable employment, and to be engaged in a Muslim community of believers that includes people from other races. Early efforts by Muslim intellectuals in the United States provided centers for learning about Islam, helped increase inter-faith dialogue, and served as paths for some people converting to Islam (Esposito & Voll, 2001). As Jane Smith (1999:103) points out: "Immigrants, African Americans, and converts from other groups all combine to illustrate the many ways it is possible to be Muslim in America."

WOMEN'S ROLES The way in which women can contribute to the formation of American Islam is a major topic among Muslims. Muslim women are altering as well as affirming the traditional values of their religion. While women are denied the opportunity to be *imams*—religious leaders—there is strong support for the belief that Islam provides equal rights and responsibilities for women. Most Muslim women earn or expect to earn college degrees, and most work outside the home. But like women of other faiths, there is a debate about how women can reconcile employment and family roles, especially concerning child care. Another debate concerns the proper dress of Muslim women in certain settings (Anway, 1996). Unlike in South Asia and the Middle East, the debate in the United States is whether a woman's hair—not her whole body—should be covered (Smith, 1999; Scupin, 2000). Reflecting the unique, American stamp on Islam, Muslim women are actively engaged in these debates and may be empowered to resolve them.

SOCIETY CONNECTIONS

Challenges to Religious Pluralism

As this chapter has emphasized, the relationship of religion and political life is different in democratic, religiously pluralistic societies and in authoritarian religious states. Religion and politics have always intermixed in the United States, so the rise of Christian fundamentalism in the 1970s was not unusual (Marsden, 1991). What is different, however, is that a number of Christian sects may appear to be converging under one political banner. Fundamentalist resurgence is a global phenomenon, but Christian fundamentalism in the United States takes a unique path.

The New Christian Right

The **New Christian Right (NCR)** is a fundamentalist political movement composed of a number of mostly conservative Protestant groups with an agenda calling for the return of morality to U.S. society (Fig-

ure 17.5). Secular humanism, seen as rampant in politics, is a common foe that unites several Christian right-wing groups, including Jerry Falwell's Moral Majority, Pat Robertson's Christian Coalition, and although less political in tone, Bill McCartney's Promise Keepers (see Chapter 13). These groups do not demand that the United States become a religious state, but that the nation's Christian historical foundations be embraced in government policy. However, contrary to the principle of religious pluralism, NCR promotes a specific Christian brand of morality based on the Bible and God's will as the ultimate source for political life (Reed, 1996; Williams, 1999; Harding, 2001). While it is difficult to get statistics on NCR membership, estimates range from 10 to 15 million who explicitly identify as partisans of the religious right (Wacker, 2001).

Specific targets of NCR's political campaign include support for a Constitutional amendment allowing voluntary prayer in public schools; the teaching of creationism in biology courses; restrictions on sex education; and opposition to homosexual rights, abortion rights, and the Equal Rights Amendment (Chapter 13) (Moen, 1994; Jelen, 1999; Johnson, 2000; Williams 2000).

Women's role and status are at the core of the NCR political platform. Adherents of the NCR seek to reverse the tide of gender equity, which they believe has eroded the divinely inspired moral order, and to return the United States to its patriarchal roots (Bendroth, 1999). Similar to fundamentalists worldwide, NCR focuses on the traditional role of women because women's emancipation is seen as a hallmark of modernity and secularization (Armstrong, 2001).

TELEVANGELISM AND THE ELECTRONIC CHURCH

In Holyland, U.S.A., busloads of tourists walk through a sculpture garden depicting biblical scenes such as Noah's Ark, the Last Supper, and the Crucifixion. The gift shop sells postcards of all these scenes along with videos to help visitors relive their Holyland experience. Thousands of tourists visit the Crystal Cathedral in Garden Grove, California, home to Reverend Robert Schuller's television ministry; his books and tapes are sold at Christian bookstores across the country. An even larger variety of religious products are offered on the Internet. People of all religions can find their version of God or spirituality on television and radio and now throughout cyberspace (Castells, 1996; Connell, 1998). Most people who buy these products and are drawn to these sites are consumers of religious broadcasting.

As a newcomer to religious broadcasting, the Internet joins radio and television ("televangelism") as an important part of the "electronic church." Of all the parts of the electronic church, televangelism to date is by far the most commercially lucrative. The

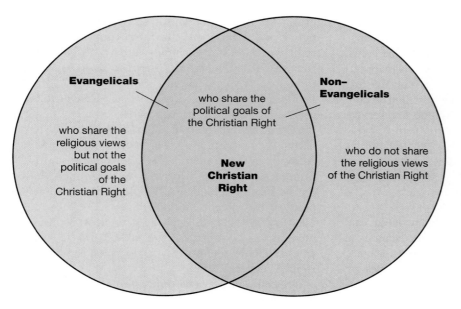

Evangelicals

who share the
religious views
but not the
political goals
of the
Christian Right

who share the
political goals of
the Christian Right

New
Christian
Right

Non-
Evangelicals

who do not share
the religious views
of the Christian Right

FIGURE 17.5 **Who Supports the New Christian Right?** *Evangelicals* generally describes people who believe the Bible is totally accurate (literal interpretation) and who state a need for a personal experience with God and an obligation to tell their faith to others. *Non-Evangelicals* includes politically conservative Catholics, Jews, Mormons, and some people who are secularist or who proclaim no religion.

Sources: Adapted from Wacker, 2000; Adherents, 2002.

sponsors and consumers of televangelism generally fit the two broad groups of fundamentalists mentioned above. The first group, the evangelicals, use religious media as the proclamation of the gospel and the drive to convert lost souls. Televangelism functions as the church for people who cannot get to a church on a regular basis; it targets people who are already religious and who share common symbols, values, and a belief in a moral culture (Hadden, 1993; Lyon, 2000).

Research on the success of televangelism suggests that while religious media may meet the goals of the evangelical group, the same cannot be said for the second group, the political activists. The composition of the electronic church's audience has not changed appreciably over the years, with the average audience size for the top televangelist programs not fluctuating much since its peak in the 1980s (Schultze, 1996; Lippy, 1999; Apostolidis, 2000). There is little evidence to suggest there has been a new surge in audience size when religious media are used for political purposes. It is estimated that no more than 200,000 adult Americans conform to NCR's political agenda in recent elections (Wacker, 2001). And it is doubtful that even this group received most of its political prompting via the electronic church. The evangelical and politically activist groups remain pretty much the same. If religious broadcasting is to be politically successful, it must do more than "preach to the converted." On the other hand, this broadcasting does pay off financially. Consumers of religious media buy religious products and support political causes, social service ministries, and the often lavish lifestyles of the preachers themselves, some of whom had to end their careers because of scandals and the abuse of funds en-

With his 700 Club *"televangelist" show as a major forum, Pat Robertson's Christian Coalition promotes the idea that Christian moral principles based on the Bible should be the foundation for government policy in the United States. Research shows that televangelism is more commercially than politically successful.*

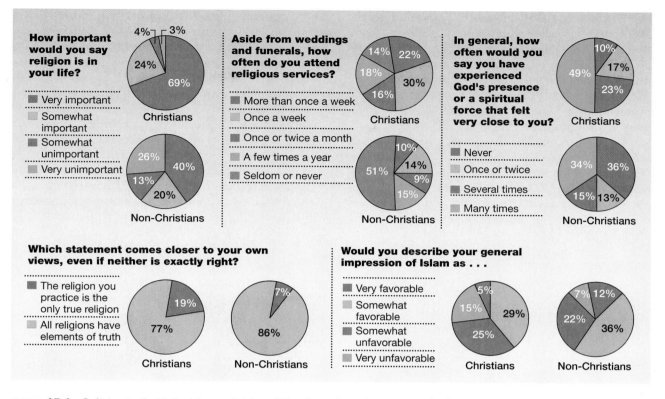

FIGURE 17.6 **Religion in the United States: Faith and Pluralism.** Americans express high importance of religion, engage in religious activities, are tolerant of other religions but express less favorable views of Islam.

Source: "Religion in America" from Faith in America (p. 42) by Jeffrey L. Schelor *U.S. News & World Report,* May 6, 2002. Copyright © 2002 by U.S. News & World Report, L. P. Reprinted with permission.

trusted to them (Buddenbaum & Stout, 1996; Coleman, 2002). Overall, it is profits and not politics that makes televangelism successful.

Secularization or Religious Resurgence?

This overview of the rise of Christian fundamentalism suggests why the secularization hypothesis is questionable, but also why religious pluralism is alive and well in the United States (Figure 17.6). Fundamentalist groups such as NCR represent religious resurgence, but its supporters are divided between the evangelical and political sides of the movement. In both ranks, there are people who are across-the-board conservatives and those who are conservative on some social issues but moderate on others (Regnerus et al., 1998; Woodberry & Smith, 1998). George W. Bush, an Episcopalian, supports a number of NCR fundamentalist goals. Former Presidents Jimmy Carter, born-again Christian and Baptist, and Bill Clinton, also a Baptist, were generally opposed to these same goals. Research on Protestant conservatives, for example, defies stereotypes by documenting relative liberalness on civil liberties and activism for the poor.

African American Protestants who are religious conservatives are more liberal than mainstream white Protestants and all varieties of Catholics. And Catholics who support fundamentalist calls for a return to morality disagree on such issues as the death penalty, social welfare net, and teaching of creationism (Miller, 1997; Bendyna, 2001). Being morally conservative does not make someone politically conservative (Kivisto, 1994; Goodstein, 1998). Religious pluralism ensures that the religious right cannot muster the strength it needs to sustain an ongoing, cohesive political movement of Christian fundamentalists. Research shows that mainstream denominations, especially among Protestants, are less vocal than fundamentalists but continue to exert a strong influence on public policy. They can be characterized as quietly "active" rather than as openly "activist" (Wurthnow, 2000).

Even if fundamentalists are not all that politically successful, does that mean that secularization is succeeding? For most sociologists, the answer is no. The secularization hypothesis has fallen on hard times (Stark, 1999). Peter Berger, the eminent sociologist who was influential in developing the secularization hypothesis in the 1950s, began to question it by the 1970s and has since disavowed it (Berger, 2001; Bruce, 2001). While it is clear that religion is expressed differently than in the past and that competition for members hurts religious participation, core religious beliefs continue to be embraced by people throughout the United States (Gallup & Jones, 2000; Chaves & Gorski, 2001; Sheler, 2002).

We have seen in this chapter that the sociology of religion has been a sociology of the churches. "Churchly" religiosity has declined, but religious participation has not. Televangelism reaches the homebound who may never step into a church. When measures are used to tap different dimensions, religiosity

emerges unharmed. Religion has been affected by a host of major happenings, such as modernization, politics, and gender role change. The effects of September 11 on religion will be felt for years to come—effects that brought Americans of all faiths back to their churches, synagogues, mosques, and temples, even if temporary. "Deep pluralism of America is compatible with equally deep religious conviction" (Stark, 2001). Sociology shows that religion has adapted and restructured, but has not necessarily been secularized; in the process it has enriched an already existing religious pluralism in the United States.

SUMMARY

1. According to Émile Durkheim, religion performs social functions: social cohesion, system of support, emotional health, social service, social control, and social change.

2. Karl Marx asserted that religion maintains the stratification system and serves its prevailing economic interests. He saw religion as an opiate—a depressive drug—because religion focuses people on the "other world" rather than on striving for change in this world. Max Weber argued that religion served as an incentive for the rise of capitalism and promoted social change.

3. Anthropologist Edward Tylor argued that religion evolved through stages, from lower to higher level forms: animism (supernatural beings and spirits that can help or hurt) to theism, belief in many gods (polytheism), to one god (monotheism). A final stage may be secular or civil religion—with sacred symbols shared by everyone in society regardless of their religion. The evolutionary view overall is no longer accepted by social scientists.

4. A church is an inclusive body integrated into larger society, with a specific theology and professionally trained clergy. Some societies have ecclesia, or state churches, with all citizens claimed as members. Churches may be organized into denominations, separate branches that emphasize different interpretations of the same theology.

Denominations are typical in societies with high religious pluralism.

5. Sects are small, exclusive, relatively informal groups, which have higher levels of tension with larger society. Sects often begin by splitting away from established churches. Cults are small groups who begin new or unconventional religions, usually founded by a charismatic leader. The term cult is being replaced by "new religious movement."

6. Christianity, Judaism, and Islam share common roots. Both Christianity and Islam began as monotheistic cults centered around charismatic leaders and survived to become world religions.

7. Hinduism is polytheistic and is the oldest of the world religions. India's caste system is consistent with many Hindu beliefs, such as reincarnation and dharma (service to others). Buddhism and Confucianism are based on ethical codes intended to promote human happiness, a higher state of consciousness, and self-discipline.

8. Fundamentalism is a religious trend found in all world religions; it seeks to curb modernization and return society to a previous religious golden age. Fundamentalists include evangelicals who believe in a personal experience with God; others are political activists who believe morality based on religion should be part of government.

9. Founded on the principles of religious tolerance and the separation of church and state, the

United States is the most religiously pluralistic society in the world. The vast majority of Americans are affiliated with religions, attend worship services, and believe in God. Secularization challenges occur, such as faith in science rather than religion for problem solving.

10. Measuring religiosity and religious pluralism is complex, but these indicate less secularization. The three main religious groups in the United States are Protestants, Catholics, and Jews, but Muslims will soon be the fourth.

11. American religious diversity shows up both between and within religions, especially in terms of class, race, and gender. Protestants are divided into many denominations. Mainstream Protestants tend to be more politically liberal than fundamentalist Protestants.

12. Like mainstream Protestants, Roman Catholics have declined in religious commitment and are more diverse than in the past. The number of Jews is declining, and Muslims are increasing in number. The Nation of Islam is made up of African Americans but it is not consistent with traditional interpretations of Islam.

13. The New Christian Right is a coalition of mainly Protestant fundamentalist groups seeking to incorporate their beliefs about Christian principles into broader life and government policy.

14. Religion in the United States has adapted to social change, and religious pluralism is increasing, but there is not a great deal of support for the secularization hypothesis.

KEY TERMS

animism 459
church 460
civil religion 460
cult 462
denomination 461
ecclesia 461
fundamentalism 453

monotheism 460
New Christian Right (NCR) 479
polytheism 460
profane 455
religion 455
religious pluralism 455
sacred 455

sect 461
secular religion 460
secularization 453
theism 460
theology 455

CRITICAL THINKING QUESTIONS

1. Based on your understanding of religious pluralism in the United States, argue for or against the secularization hypothesis.

2. How do functionalists, conflict theorists, and rational choice theorists explain trends toward fundamentalism as well as trends toward secularization? Which explanation is the strongest?

3. Demonstrate how world religions in the United States and abroad are similar and different in relation to the role and status of women. How can women who are in faiths that put more restrictions on women work for more gender role equity in their respective religions?

INVESTIGATE WITH CONTENT SELECT

 Begin your research using ContentSelect for this chapter by following the directions found on page 27 of this text to visit Prentice Hall's Research Navigator Website. Enter these search terms into the search field:

Fundamentalism
Denomination
Sect

18
THE POLITICAL ECONOMY

Emily's List

Fifteen years after the rebirth of the U.S. feminist movement, women had made substantial progress in many areas of public life, but elective politics remained an overwhelmingly male preserve, especially at the national level. Concerned over this poor showing in the political arena, 25 women activists met in 1985 to organize a support network that could identify promising pro-choice female Democratic candidates and help them to raise funds and conduct their campaigns.

The organization they founded was called EMILY's List (www.emilyslist.org). EMILY stands for Early Money Is Like Yeast—it makes the "dough" rise. The group has grown to become the nation's largest political action committee, with over 60,000 members, and it has played an important role in the recent increase in female representation to an all-time high of 13 senators and 61 representatives in the 107th Congress.

How Big Is Big?

You have doubtless used the phrase "big business," but how big have multinational corporations *really* become in the era of global capitalism? A little research suggests that many have become so enormous as to virtually surpass comprehension: General Motors, the world's largest company, took in revenues of $176,588,000,000 in 1999–2000, but what does that really mean?

One way to get a clearer understanding of the size of big business is to draw together a list of the world's 100 largest financial entities (Robbins, 2002). The first 24 are nation-states, led by the United States, Japan, and Germany. But 44 of the remaining 76 are corporations! General Motors, Wal-Mart, Exxon-Mobil, Ford, and Daimler-Chrysler all take in more revenue annually than the GNPs of Poland or Nor-

way. Toyota and General Electric are larger than Portugal. Honda and Nissan stand ahead of the Czech Republic and Hewlett-Packard tops Hungary.

This chapter examines the **political economy,** a term sociologists frequently use rather than speaking of the political and economic institutions as fully separate systems because of the distinctive ways that power and authority are structured at the macrolevel in the developed societies (Berberoglu, 1990; Kourvetaris, 1997). General Motors is, strictly speaking, an economic entity, but its enormous resources allow it to exercise a great deal of political power. EMILY's List is a political organization, but its primary activity is collecting and disbursing funds.

In traditional usage, politics concerns the struggle for control of the **state,** the institution that maintains a monopoly over the legitimate use of force within a given territory (Weber, 1947; Perdue, 1993). The **economy** is the institution that organizes the production, distribution, and consumption of goods and services (Boyes & Melvin, 1994). However, as suggested by the preceding accounts, the distinction between these two is becoming increasingly fuzzy.

The state is very involved in the economy in modern societies (Parenti, 1995). It guarantees property rights, regulates economic transactions, and imposes taxes. It provides social programs, trains people to use new technologies, owns productive assets, and even enters into partnerships with private businesses. It regulates international trade and may act militarily or diplomatically to protect its trade advantages.

On the other hand, the state is strongly affected by powerful economic actors such as corporations and, to a lesser extent, unions (Domhoff, 1998). Our use of the concept of the political economy thus underscores the interrelationship and interdependency of these two institutions.

This chapter begins with a theoretical consideration of the concepts of power and authority. Next, we examine three contrasting philosophical positions on which specific political economies may be based: liberalism, socialism, and conservatism. An investigation into the various types of economic and political systems and a review of several interpretations of the distribution of power in modern societies follows. We then consider three important current trends in the political arena: democratization, the participation of women and persons of color in politics, and the growing importance of the Internet in campaigning. The chapter concludes with a consideration of voter turnout trends and with discussions of two major threats to modern political economies: terrorism and nuclear proliferation.

POWER AND AUTHORITY

Max Weber (1947) defined **power** as the ability to achieve one's desired ends despite resistance from others. Power always involves interactions among at least two parties. It is also always hierarchical; one party or group is stronger than or controls another.

Most—perhaps all—power ultimately relies on force, either physical or psychological. But no society can be organized solely on the basis of force because, given the opportunity, coerced people tend to break the rules. Consequently, powerholders try to institutionalize their power; that is, they try to make it more stable by convincing subordinates that it is legitimate. This is usually accomplished by means of an *ideology* (Seliger, 1976) (see Chapter 10).

Authority is power that is perceived by subordinates as fair and just (Weber, 1947). Whether power is legitimate depends on the social context. In a college classroom, professors assign projects and, despite groans, students generally comply with these assignments. Professors can claim authority over their students because of the status that they occupy and the high level of expertise necessary to obtain that status, although the students retain the freedom to withdraw from the course. But there are limits to authority: Should instructors demand sexual favors or lack appropriate academic credentials, they lose their right to expect obedience.

Note that there are always at least two sides in an authority relationship—the *claimant* (here, the professor) and the *subordinate* (the students). In addition, third parties are often used to reinforce authority claims (Stinchcombe, 1968). In our classroom example, parents, college administrators, and the general public help indirectly to establish the legitimacy of professors' demands on their students.

Three Types of Power

There are three distinct types of power: decision-making power, agenda control, and systemic power (Lukes, 1974).

Most students accept social norms that justify the exercise of a substantial (but not unlimited) amount of power within the classroom by their professors. Max Weber refers to such legitimated power as authority.

Decision-making power is the ability to *directly* determine the behavior of others. For example, police officers or some claimants who hold important political offices are able to control subordinates, even against their will.

Agenda control is a less direct type of power, based on the ability to determine which issues will (or will not) be addressed. Agenda control has been called "nondecision-making power" because it allows powerholders to prevent issues from even being considered (Bachrach & Baratz, 1970). Thus, for example, the problem of increasing income inequality, central to much political discussion in this country in the 1960s, is rarely raised today.

The mass media are central in setting the political agenda in modern political economies (Denton & Woodward, 1992). But they in turn are heavily influenced by the government and the large corporations. Nearly 80 percent of all news stories in the United States are based on press releases and interviews with government officials, which gives these officials a major say over the content of the political agenda as it is presented in the media. In many other countries, the mass media are owned by the state, giving political officials nearly complete agenda control. Similarly, U.S. corporations maintain sizable public relations staffs that devote a great deal of time to promoting the ideology of free-enterprise capitalism and corporate preferences concerning public policy matters (Qualter, 1985).

Systemic power refers to advantages resulting from existing structural arrangements, such as the distribution of wealth. Systemic power typically results from the structural inability of subordinates to mobilize and press their claims. It also relies on claimants' ability to promote false or misleading beliefs. For example, under slavery, slaveowners promoted the idea that they were paternalistic father figures who cared for their slaves much as they did for their own children. Slaves who accepted this ideology saw no need to demand their rights. Similarly, large corporations today tell employees and consumers that they are acting on their behalf when in fact the bottom line is corporate profit, which often comes at the expense of both groups (Clawson et al., 1992).

Three Types of Authority

Max Weber (1947) described three types of authority: traditional, charismatic, and rational-legal. In the real world, individual leaders often combine two or even all three of these models, but we will discuss them separately, as ideal types.

Traditional authority is power legitimated by respect for long-established cultural patterns. The claimant's major argument is that power has always been distributed in a certain way and is therefore legitimate. In most cases, individuals who hold traditional political authority do so by virtue of their ascribed statuses; this type of authority is the basis on which kings and queens justify their rule.

However, industrialization and exposure to modern views tend to undermine traditional authority by encouraging subordinates to question long-standing customs. Thus, for example, patriarchy—the traditional dominance of men over women—persists in modern societies, but it is increasingly open to challenge. Most women no longer view themselves as inferior or properly subject to men, and most men agree, endorsing an egalitarian view of gender (Eisenstein, 1994). Social change thus may encourage subordinates and claimants alike to question traditional authority.

Rational-legal authority is power legitimated by legally enacted rules and regulations. It is generally associated with achieved statuses obtained by virtue of an individual's formal qualifications. It is especially characteristic of business and governmental bureaucracies. In order to be effective, the rules that underlie rational-legal authority must be universal (applying in every possible circumstance) and clear and comprehensible to all. In rational-legal authority, loyalty is owed to the impersonal state, corporation, church, or university rather than to a personal ruler.

Finally, **charismatic authority** is based on an individual's claim to possess extraordinary or unique leadership abilities. These claims are frequently justified by reference to the divine or transcendent. Charismatics lead independently of formal positions or offices. Political leaders such as Hitler, Gandhi, and Martin Luther King, Jr. are examples of charismatic authority, as are religious prophets and leaders like Joseph Smith (the founder of the Mormon church) or Reverend Moon. Such individuals frequently find themselves in conflict with traditional and rational-legal rulers.

Charismatic authority is inherently unstable because it depends on the claimant's ability to sustain belief in her or his special qualities. It cannot be passed on in its pure form to the next generation of leadership, but rather must be combined with other forms of authority in a process called the **routinization of charisma.** Christianity, for example, began as a sect based on the charismatic authority of Jesus. After his death, his disciples routinized the movement by developing rational-legal authority and bureaucracy,

Dr. Martin Luther King, Jr. was one of the most outstanding charismatic leaders of the twentieth century. Although he was president of the Southern Christian Leadership Conference, in reality Dr. King's authority was based more on the passionate commitment of his followers and on his magnetic speaking style than on his formal position.

TABLE 18.1

Three Types of Authority

Type of Authority	Definition	Strengths	Weaknesses	Examples
Traditional Authority	Authority based on respect for long-established cultural patterns.	Line of succession is unambiguous.	Authority holder may not be competent. Vulnerable to challenge in times of rapid social change.	Absolute monarchy. Patriarchy. Authority of parents over children.
Rational-legal Authority	Authority based on rules and regulations. Usually lodged in statuses achieved on the basis of competence.	Leaders are generally competent. Methods of replacing leaders are well established.	May become an oppressive "iron cage."	Superiors in any bureaucracy.
Charismatic Authority	Authority based on followers' perceptions of a leader's outstanding personal qualities.	Followers will do almost anything a charismatic leader asks. Leader can effectively promote sweeping social changes.	Difficulty replacing deceased or discredited leaders. Unstable charismatic leaders (e.g., Hitler) may create havoc.	Religious prophets. Gandhi. Martin Luther King, Jr.

eventually establishing the Catholic Church. Charismatic authority is present, although relatively uncommon, in both traditional and modern societies, and it has been a major force for social change throughout history. Table 18.1 summarizes and extends this discussion of Weber's three types of authority.

THEORETICAL MODELS OF THE POLITICAL ECONOMY

Since ancient times, political philosophers have argued about the structure of the ideal political economy. Three positions have dominated this debate: liberalism, socialism, and conservatism.

Liberalism

The core values of **classical liberalism** as developed in the 17th century focused on the rights of the individual, who was seen as ultimately autonomous from society and capable of reason (Gray, 1986). Philosopher Thomas Hobbes took the view that in a "state of nature," human appetites were unlimited, giving rise to endless competition and eventually a "war of all against all." In order to prevent this state of anarchy from making life "nasty, brutish, and short," Hobbes suggested that rational actors should and commonly do accept the external authority of the state. Thus, the state exists to create political order and to protect the rights of individuals against the dangers of anarchy.

Later classical liberal thinkers such as John Locke and Adam Smith were more skeptical about the power of the state. They argued that a limited government and a free-market economy were the best means of ensuring well-being. Locke believed that property ownership was the supreme natural right and that independent property holders would rationally choose to subordinate their interests to the rule of law. Adam Smith focused on the benefits of competition, maintaining that the "hidden hand" of the market provided the best assurance of peace and prosperity. The state, in his view, should limit itself to protecting individual rights, especially private property rights, and ensuring open and free market competition.

However, classical liberalism is not without its difficulties. First, it could not explain how a limited state could adequately fight certain collective problems. For example, how could a relatively weak state combat the environmental pollution that indirectly but inevitably results from market competition in industrialized societies? A competitive market rewards short-term individual efforts, but it may not adequately protect long-term collective goods such as clean air or national security.

In addition, classic liberalism did not seem capable of providing an adequate solution for the tendency of competitive markets to evolve toward **monopoly,** a situation in which a single provider dominates the market and reaps windfall profits. In the late 19th and early 20th centuries, industrialists in the United States—popularly known as "robber barons"—came to monopolize the railways; oil and gasoline, and electricity production; and telegraphy, exploiting consumers and small businesses alike.

Solutions to such failures of the market typically require a strong state. This reality prompted the emergence of **modern liberalism,** a philosophy that favors a powerful government existing alongside private property and market economics. Modern liberalism is characterized by a strong welfare state that lessens the harmful excesses of capitalism by providing basic citizenship rights such as a guaranteed minimum income, free public education, health care, and other benefits (Esping-Anderson, 1990).

Socialism

The central idea of **socialism** is that collective control of the economy by a very strong state reduces inequality and social injustice and contributes to peace and prosperity (Miller, 1991). The French philosopher Jean Jacques Rousseau argued that private property promotes greed, artificially separating the individual from the community and producing poverty and vice. His solution was an extreme form of socialism called *communism*, which mandates the collective ownership of all property. Instead of owning private property, under communism individuals transfer their wealth to collective control. They then receive back what they need from the community.

Twentieth-century efforts to establish socialism in the Soviet Union, Eastern Europe, and China revealed major flaws in the model. Most critically, it did not include adequate protection against the abuse of power by those controlling the state. Within a few years after the 1917 Russian Revolution, a totalitarian state had been established with virtually unlimited control over the mass media, civic organizations, and much of private life (Titma & Tuma, 2001).

A second major flaw of the socialist system concerns the failure of economic planning. The Soviet system centralized control over investment and production, abolishing market competition. Without the market to guide economic decisions, surpluses of some goods existed alongside major shortages of others. Soviet housing was notoriously inadequate, and long lines at grocery stores with empty shelves were common (Misztal, 1993). Furthermore, collectivized agriculture proved a colossal failure: Three-fourths of all production came from tiny private plots that represented less than 10 percent of all agricultural land (Titma & Tuma, 2001).

Conservatism

The third major model of the political economy is **conservatism,** a philosophy that emphasizes social order and sees the family, religion, and the local face-to-face community as the natural bases for that order (Gray, 1986). Early conservatives, led by the English thinker Edmund Burke, argued that gradual change was always preferable to the large-scale transformations associated with upheavals such as the French Revolution. They agreed with the classic liberals that the state was artificial and should be limited, and they agreed with the socialists that community and cooperation were critical values. However, conservatives believed that the competitive market favored by classic liberals could destroy the natural order of society by weakening the traditional bonds between people. Conservatives also opposed the socialist view that private property should be abolished, maintaining instead that property was a crucial means of reinforcing the social order.

Conservatism could not, however, respond adequately to one critical question: What if a particular political-economic system was grossly inadequate? Making many small changes over time would only reinforce a corrupt and inefficient system; yet conservatives strongly opposed revolutionary change no matter how desperately it might be needed.

The Monica Lewinsky scandal severely weakened the Clinton administration but it did not seriously threaten the stability of the U.S. system of government. Functionalists see this as evidence that the underlying legitimacy of the political system remains strong.

CONTEMPORARY ECONOMIC AND POLITICAL SYSTEMS

In this section we move away from pure theory and discuss the major types of economic and political institutions that exist in the world today. Economic and political systems are considered separately, but bear in mind that this is a somewhat artificial distinction. The two tend to be closely intermingled in real-life political economies, a theme to which we will return at the end of this discussion.

Economic Systems

There are two basic types of economic systems: capitalism and state socialism. Mixed economies attempt to blend elements of both.

CAPITALISM **Capitalism** is based on the private ownership of the means of production, hired workers, and commercial markets that are today increasingly international as well as domestic. It is compatible with either the liberal or the conservative theoretical model. The state plays a major role in regulating the market, but its importance is ultimately secondary. That is, major economic players take precedence over political powerholders (Lindblom, 1977). The United States, Western Europe, Japan, and much of the developing world are capitalist. In varying degrees, the countries of Eastern Europe and the former Soviet Union have also been reorganized along capitalist lines (Pohl, 1996; Buraway, 1997).

STATE SOCIALISM **State socialism** is a system whereby the state owns the means of production during a transitional stage between capitalism and communism. Workers are guaranteed basic food, housing, education, and health care. Markets play a secondary role at best because the state manages the economy through planning and political regulation (Lindblom, 1977; Lane, 1985). There may be small pockets of private enterprise, but they are subordinate to the public sector. Workers seek jobs much as in a capitalist economy, but employment is centrally planned so

The New York Stock Exchange is the nerve center of modern capitalism. As a result of globalization, the financial transactions that are conducted here influence the lives of virtually every person on the planet.

INTERNET CONNECTIONS

Socialism and capitalism represent contrasting economic systems. Many major economies found today share features of both. Visit the Website on capitalism:

http://capitalism.org/

and explore the site. It contains information on capitalism. What are some primary features of capitalism? How does capitalism compare with socialism from what you read in the text?

that the movement of workers from job to job is regulated, in part to prevent excessive migration from the countryside to the cities. Contemporary examples include China, Cuba, and North Korea.

MIXED ECONOMIES **Mixed economies,** also known as *social democracies*, combine significant state ownership and regulation of markets with some aspects of capitalism. In Sweden, Norway, the Netherlands, and much of the rest of northern Europe, strong welfare states provide education, health care, and social insurance, including generous family allowances for young children and the elderly. Taxes are quite high—as much as 60 percent or more of the incomes of top earners—but benefits are extensive. No one is truly poor. State industrial policies encourage private entrepreneurs to adopt new technologies and enter new fields. The government also attempts to plan investment by regulating interest rates and co-investing in new enterprises (Olsen, 1996).

How well do these various systems perform? State socialism creates more equal access to education, health care, and the like, but it also creates major inefficiencies and production bottlenecks. In the former Soviet Union, for example, the military and heavy industry were developed at the expense of consumer goods. Without market forces regulating investment and production, economic growth was overly concentrated in the sectors favored by political leaders, resulting in chronic shortages of many basic consumer items.

The capitalist countries show stronger overall economic growth and a greater emphasis on consumer industries. At the same time, they are characterized by greater class inequality and poverty.

Social democracy combines strong state regulation and a comprehensive welfare state with capitalism. It thus may be seen as blending the more desirable characteristics of the two basic economic systems. The northern European social democracies have greater equality than the United States and Britain but, especially in the past decade, their rates of economic growth have been lower.

Political Systems

As with economic systems, there are two basic kinds of political regimes: authoritarianism and democracy. (A *regime* is a system of government and the ideologies used to legitimate it).

AUTHORITARIAN REGIMES In **authoritarian regimes,** the people are excluded from any meaningful participation in decision making (Shils, 1962; Linz, 1964; Wesolowski, 1990). *Monarchies* are the oldest type of authoritarian regime, allocating formal power solely on the basis of heredity. Saudi Arabia is one of the world's few remaining traditional monarchies.

In *dictatorships*, a "strongman" rules on the basis of personal loyalties, favors, and threats of force. Dictatorships most often arise in the least developed countries, where literacy and political mobilization among citizens are low. They are relatively weakly institutionalized because they generally lack a strong appeal to tradition or charisma (Roth, 1968). Examples include Cuba, Libya, and Iraq.

In *bureaucratic-authoritarian regimes*, power is vested in a bureaucratic state dominated by the military and top government officials (O'Donnell, 1979). Because leaders use rational means of control—formal rules, a constitution—this form of government is frequently more stable than other types of authoritarian rule. A strong nationalistic ideology helps legitimate power. Elites from major institutions—the economy, education, religion—are brought into the system as consultants and advisors. A large professional military is also often important. A number of countries in the developing world, including Algeria, Myanmar, and Guatemala, fit this pattern.

The National Rifle Association is one of America's most vocal interest group organizations. Viewing almost any effort to regulate the sale of firearms as a threat to the Second Amendment, NRA members have successfully opposed numerous efforts to strengthen gun control laws over the years.

Totalitarianism is a type of authoritarianism in which, in contrast to monarchies and bureaucratic-authoritarian regimes, there are no formal limits on the extent to which the government can intervene in people's everyday lives (Friedrich & Brzezinski, 1965). In Nazi Germany, the government routinely entered private households and seized people and goods without warrants. The state controlled all the mass media and all associations, from the Boy Scouts to churches and sports teams. Similarly, at the height of the Chinese Cultural Revolution of the late 1960s, the Red Guards publicly humiliated critics of Mao Zedong, closed down major universities, and forced educated people into the countryside to work on communal farms. The former Taliban regime in Afghanistan is another example of totalitarianism.

Like some other totalitarian systems, the Soviet Union held formal elections in which citizens had the right to vote "yes" or "no" to a list of candidates, but there were no competing candidates and the Communist Party preselected everyone who appeared on the ballot. Thus, totalitarian systems may appear to generate popular participation, but it is false participation in that it does not actually allow the citizens to control the power of the state. Totalitarian regimes are ideologically diverse, from the ultra-right and racist Nazi government to the ultra-left Communist governments of the former Soviet bloc.

DEMOCRATIC REGIMES **Democracies** routinely include citizens in government, and their consent is the formal basis for the legitimacy of the state. Joseph Schumpeter (1942) distinguished between two ideal types of democracy. In a *participatory democracy*, citizens are personally involved in decision making (Barber, 1984), while in an indirect or *representative democracy*, citizens elect leaders who make decisions on their behalf.

Because of the size of modern political systems and the complexity of the decisions that they must make, participatory democracy is generally no longer a viable option. It worked well in small New England communities in the 18th century and in some utopian communes, but it is not feasible in modern states. Many of the liberation movements of the 1960s attempted to operate on the basis of participatory democracy, but they generally found the process unwieldy and inefficient (Anderson, 1995; Rosen, 2000).

Representative democracy is more practical. A healthy degree of democratic accountability is provided by competitive elections, universal adult suffrage, guaranteed rights of assembly and free speech, and the secret ballot. A representative democracy also requires an independent mass media accessible to all candidates and a voting system free of manipulation and bias (Dahl, 1958, 1982).

INTERNET CONNECTIONS

After reading the section in the text on voters go to the Federal Election Commission Website:

http://www.fec.gov/

and click on elections and voting. Click on recent election results and look at the geographical breakdown of the results. What patterns did you find? How would you explain the pattern based on what you read in the text?

Political Economies

Political sociologists have investigated the question of which types of economic and political systems are most likely to be combined. State socialism is typically associated with totalitarian regimes, although capitalist countries, such as Nazi Germany, may also be totalitarian. To date, no state socialist economy has coexisted with a fully representative democracy. In contemporary China, there are competing candidates and secret ballots in local elections, which help motivate officials to pay some attention to public opinion, but at the national level the Communist Party retains complete control.

Capitalism is compatible with a variety of political systems, but it is perhaps most often found in democracies. In fact, political scientist S. M. Lipset (1960) has argued that capitalism is a structural requisite for stable democracy. Not only is the populace in a capitalist society typically well educated and thus better able to mobilize politically, but affluence also makes economic conflicts easier to resolve because it creates a large middle class that may help find common ground between the extreme positions often favored by the rich and the poor.

THE DISTRIBUTION OF POLITICAL POWER

There are four basic schools of thought concerning how power is actually distributed in modern states such as the United States that embrace capitalism and democratic principles: pluralism, the power elite model, the ruling class model, and the state autonomy model.

Pluralism

Many political scientists and some sociologists accept **pluralism,** the view that competition among elites disperses power broadly among many different individuals and groups (Dahl, 1961, 1968; Rose, 1968; Pinderhughes, 1987; Rothman & Black, 1998). Pluralists claim that politics is a genuinely competitive arena. The large number of contending groups and the relative ease of mobilizing and influencing decision making ensure substantial access for all significant interests. Moreover, various types of resources—wealth, charisma, prestige—can be translated into power, and thus power may be dispersed even more widely.

Pluralists believe that the political system is structured around two key institutions: political parties and interest group organizations. *Political parties* compete for elective office, appealing to various constituencies in order to gain voter support. *Interest group organizations* are independent political associations that promote particular economic and social interests

George W. Bush meets with CEOs of some of the largest corporations in the United States. Pluralists see big business as just one among many interest groups while power elite theorists generally believe that the corporations are in a commanding position in the political economy.

(Walker, 1991). By lobbying, filing suits, contributing to political parties, and engaging in propaganda campaigns, interest groups such as trade associations, unions, and professional societies try to influence specific governmental decisions. Examples include the National Organization for Women (NOW), EMILY's List, the National Right to Life Committee, the Sierra Club, the National Association for the Advancement of Colored People (NAACP), and the National Rifle Association (NRA).

Pluralists suggest that interest group organizations focus on "single issues" such as the legality of abortion or highway construction in particular Congressional districts. Neither business nor labor ever mobilizes as a whole, but rather there is healthy competition among a number of relatively narrow interest groups. Businesses compete with other businesses, and labor unions are, at least theoretically, as likely to forge coalitions with businesses sharing similar interests as they are to align with other unions. In this way, multiple interest groups counter one another, keeping the more extreme factions in check and preventing polarization.

Pluralists also see the overall structure of the government itself as pluralistic, with the federal system being distinct from state and local governments and often competing with these other units for power. The result is a constant "checks and balances" process, whereby no one group consistently gets its way and all interests are kept from becoming too extreme.

Finally, the plurality of group interests means that there are strong *cross-cutting cleavages* in modern societies. Cross-cutting cleavages occur when individuals find themselves pulled in different directions at the same time. One might be a Catholic and thus attracted to a pro-life position but also be a feminist and on that basis be drawn toward pro-choice policies.

Cross-cutting cleavages encourage moderation and fluid political allegiances; they also help prevent polarization, which might lead to more intense and violent conflict (Lane & Ersson, 1991).

In sum, the pluralist model considers the U.S. political economy to be basically democratic and open, giving a measure of power to all competing groups. Although pluralists do not claim that power is fully equalized, they do maintain that the powerful do not consistently get their way and that the disadvantaged often are able to mobilize and have at least some of their interests addressed. Pluralists also contend that the U.S. system is relatively stable. This is an interpretation that is broadly compatible with the functionalist perspective.

Critics respond that pluralism paints a misleading picture of U.S. politics. First, they note that disadvantaged groups face major obstacles in mobilizing and therefore, in practice, are often entirely excluded from the decision-making process (Gamson, 1990; McAdam, 1982; Jenkins, 1985; Jordan, 1990). For example, although the civil rights movement of the 1960s was able to overturn Jim Crow laws mandating segregation, it had little success in challenging the more deeply entrenched economic and social disadvantages of African Americans (McAdam, 1982; Wilson, 1987).

Critics also point out that business and a significant portion of the upper-middle class can mobilize politically on a broader basis than can other interests. Big business funds a multitude of associations that represent the general business point of view (Useem, 1984; Parenti, 1995). Organized labor has the AFL-CIO, which lobbies on behalf of workers and consumers (Greenstone, 1968), but it is much weaker than the major business-oriented interest groups (Form, 1996). Similarly, the upper-middle class funds

Secretary of State Colin Powell, formerly a four-star general in the Army, shakes hands with Israeli Prime Minister Ariel Sharon. As predicted by elite theory, top leaders frequently shuttle back and forth between the political, military, and corporate sectors of the power structure in the United States.

a number of public interest groups promoting environmentalism, the rights of women and consumers, and related middle-class concerns. These middle-class lobbies are also more powerful than organized labor or any other groups representing the lower or working classes (Berry, 1997).

The Power Elite Model

The central idea of the **power elite model** is that power is concentrated in the hands of a single small, cohesive group holding numerous high-level positions. Common social backgrounds and socialization experiences make this elite cohesive and capable of unified action. Most conservatives who accept this view believe that this concentration of power is functional (Dye, 1995), but socialists and some modern liberals argue that it is exploitative (Mills, 1956).

C. Wright Mills was the major architect of this perspective, which presents a highly critical, conflict theory-oriented interpretation of the U.S. political economy. Mills (1956) argued that shortly after World War II, four major changes together created a U.S. power elite:

- *The growth of the modern megacorporation.* True market competition has largely been supplanted by corporate planning and the mass manipulation of consumers through advertising. The heads of the immense corporations are commonly involved in *interlocking directorates* or the practice of simultaneously holding seats on several different corporate boards of directors (Kono et al., 1998). This greatly increases elite coordination and cohesion.
- *The expansion of the mass media* after the second world war—especially television.
- *The growth of a huge and permanent peacetime military establishment.* At the end of World War II, the United States did not greatly reduce the size of its military as it had following every earlier war. A vast and seemingly permanent Pentagon bureaucracy arose and seized upon the nuclear threat of the Soviet Union as a rationale for unending military expansion. Defense spending became the primary basis for stabilizing the national economy, providing a boost during recessions and enormous profits for the large corporations.
- *The development of social institutions that forged an integrated national elite.* Attending Ivy League colleges and belonging to exclusive social clubs increased cohesion among the elite and helped develop an awareness of their mutual interests.

Together, these four changes created a single elite out of three formally distinct groups: (1) the leaders of the largest corporations; (2) key political figures who control the White House, Congress, and the federal bureaucracy; and (3) the top military leadership. The unification of this national elite was reflected in the phrase "the military-industrial complex," a term first introduced by President Eisenhower in 1958.

How well does the evidence support the power-elite thesis? The most systematic research on this question has been conducted by Thomas Dye (1995). Dye investigated the social origins, political and economic resources, career paths, and interconnections among 5,778 corporate, political, and military elites. He found that 5,700 persons occupied 7,314 key elite positions. He also found that these elites were significantly interlocked, with well over one-third of them belonging to exclusive private clubs and attending Ivy League colleges. Although almost 80 percent held only one command position at a time, almost half had held other elite positions during their careers. Among the "interlockers," an inner group held five or more elite positions simultaneously, integrating the corporate, governmental, and civic sectors.

Dye's work generally supports the power elite model, although it suggests that Mills may have been wrong about the military elite, who were overwhelmingly drawn from modest class origins, educated at the military academies, and rarely assumed elite positions in the government or large corporations. Mills also apparently overestimated the importance of being born into the upper class, as Dye found that less than a third of the elite had upper-class parents.

Some conservatives argue that elite cohesion is functionally necessary in modern complex societies (Dye, 1995). They suggest that Mills based his criticism on a romantic model of a decentralized society like the United States in the 19th century with its local markets, weak central government, and strong local communities, which does not adequately describe the modern world. Modern technology concentrates power, and the complexity of modern society mandates expertise. In this view, the existence of a sophisticated elite, with power based on knowledge and abilities and with sufficient cohesion to allow it to make complex decisions, is imperative in modern societies.

Some observers suggest that the power-elite model applies best to foreign policy, where public scrutiny is relatively weak and political secrecy is easier to justify. Citizens are more aware of their interests and better able to influence decisions regarding domestic policies. In addition, there is considerable evidence that the power elite thesis is more accurate at the national level than at the local one.

The Ruling Class Model

A number of sociologists support a **ruling class model** based in Marxist conflict theory, which argues that a cohesive upper class (as opposed to a power elite composed of people drawn from relatively diverse social backgrounds) dominates society (Domhoff, 1979, 1990, 1998).

The ruling class defends its power in four ways (Miliband, 1977):

- *The candidate-selection process.* The wealthy give money to candidates for high-level political office, effectively restricting competition to an acceptable field of contenders (Allen & Broyles, 1991).
- *The special interest process.* Businesses and other organizations controlled by the ruling class use their economic and political power to shape major governmental decisions. This mechanism resembles the interest-group politics of the pluralists, but in this view the interests of the wealthy generally (or always) dominate.
- *The ideological process.* Corporate elites and top government officials are responsive to ruling class pressure to encourage popular beliefs such as free-enterprise capitalism.

- *The policy planning process.* Corporate elites and the upper class develop long-term policy strategies to address the structural problems of the political economy.

Of the four, the policy planning process is probably the most important. It is carried out principally by a handful of business associations and research institutes that are funded and controlled by corporate elites and the upper class. Some, such as the Business Roundtable (made up of the top 100 *Fortune* manufacturing corporations) and the U.S. Chamber of Commerce, represent a wide range of business interests. They try to establish a consensus on policy options by sponsoring meetings, conferences, and private bargaining sessions. Others, such as the Brookings Institution, the Heritage Foundation, and the American Enterprise Institute, are large policy research organizations that accept funding from private foundations and wealthy individuals to develop solutions to what they see as pressing structural problems (Domhoff, 1998).

For example, policies promoted in the early 1980s by the Business Roundtable, the American Enterprise Institute, and the Heritage Foundation cut corporate taxes by over half and reduced the top personal tax rate from over 65 percent to 32 percent (Peschek, 1987; Akard, 1992). Earlier, the Social Security Act of 1935 was developed by upper-class policy experts who wanted to stave off the depression and co-opt popular support for more radical measures (Jenkins & Brents, 1989; Domhoff, 1990).

Critics raise three major arguments against the ruling class model. First, they say it underestimates the autonomy of high government officials and policy experts who are, in fact, usually the central architects of major policy changes. In this view, institutional precedents and political ideologies are often more important than upper-class interests. Second, critics argue, the upper class is rarely politically unified but is instead sharply divided by industrial and firm-specific interests (Berg & Zald, 1978; Wilson, 1989). Other players, including interest groups and public opinion, are more influential than the upper class in guiding policy decisions. Finally, although decisions regarding some types of public policy—for example, defense spending—are centralized and dominated by the upper class, critics suggest that others—for example, many of those concerning education—are made in a more pluralistic fashion (Laumann & Knoke, 1987).

The State Autonomy Model

According to the **state autonomy model,** top government officials and policy experts play the key role in the development of policy (Nordlinger, 1981; Skocpol, 1985; Rueschemeyer & Skocpol, 1996). Instead of being the tools of special-interest groups, as pluralists maintain, or of the upper class, as the ruling class approach would have it, government leaders develop policies largely on their own. They can do so because of the growing independence and increasing resources of the state. The state bureaucracy insulates government agencies from outside influences, making them increasingly independent.

The problem with this perspective is that it may overemphasize political power as distinct from economic and social power. This is a particularly serious weakness in analyzing the power structure of the United States, where "the business of politics is business." Hence, many critics suggest that this perspective is best combined with other theories of power (Hicks & Mishra, 1993) or that it is actually just a revised version of pluralism (Domhoff, 1996).

Toward a Synthesis

These four theories concerning the distribution of political power all have some merit. Scholars are currently trying to blend the insights of each into a broader theory of the political economy. For example, Alexander Hicks (Hicks & Mishra, 1993) has proposed a "political resource" theory. He contends that in a basically pluralistic state such as the United States, political leaders are relatively weak and most policy is initiated by interest groups and business-policy organizations. On the other hand, in France or Japan, where the state is more strongly institutionalized and political leaders can draw on substantial economic resources, they are more often the true architects of policy. This theory underscores two key points: We must look broadly at how different political economies are organized, and we must develop an inclusive framework that incorporates the insights of all of the theories of power.

CURRENT TRENDS IN THE POLITICAL ECONOMY

In this section, we consider three recent issues in the political economy: the worldwide movement toward democratization, the influence of gender and race/ethnicity on political participation in the U.S., and the growing importance of the Internet in campaigning.

Democratization

All around the world today, authoritarian regimes are undergoing a process of *democratization*—the transition from authoritarianism to democracy (Etzioni-Halevy, 1997; Freedom House, 1999). There are two main perspectives on how this occurs: the elite-pact thesis and the class-conflict thesis.

According to the *elite-pact thesis*, institutional elites more or less voluntarily decide that expanding popular participation is in their own best interest (Higley & Gunther, 1992). This usually occurs at a time of political or economic crisis. The leaders of the authoritarian regime make an implicit agreement or "pact" with their opponents that guarantees the leaders a substantial amount of continued power in exchange for a measure of democratization (Linz & Stepan, 1996; Sorensen, 1998). Most recent democratizations have been elite-guided and have occurred in semi-industrialized countries, especially in Latin America, with a substantial middle class, mass education, and market economies. This tends to support Lipset's claim that stable democracy requires capitalist economic development.

On the other hand, the *class-conflict thesis* explains democratization as a consequence of political pressure resulting from working-class mobilization (Rueschemeyer et al., 1992). Throughout Western Europe, working-class social movements have pushed to expand citizenship rights and promote the growth of the welfare state. Similarly, dissent by workers (as well as by intellectuals) has been critical in promoting democratization across Eastern Europe (Misztal & Jenkins, 1995).

What are the benefits of democratization (Etzioni-Halevy, 1997)? For one, democracies are historically less likely to engage in wars than are authoritarian regimes. However, the most important benefit is reduced internal state repression. Rudolph Rummel (1995) documents that this type of political violence is closely associated with totalitarian regimes, ranging from Stalin's Russia and Hitler's Germany to Cambodia under Pol Pot, the Rwandan genocide, and the revolutionary tribunals and purges in China. Authoritarian capitalist regimes in Argentina, Chile, and Brazil during the 1970s and Nigeria in the 1980s were also guilty of internal repression, although of a less extreme nature. Violence directed by states against their citizens claimed almost three times as many lives in the 20th century as did international war.

Gender, Race, and Ethnicity in the Political Economy

Throughout U.S. history, women and people of color have been more or less systematically blocked from assuming positions of real power in the political economy, a generalization that remains largely valid today despite the substantial progress that has occurred in recent decades.

WOMEN Feminist theoreticians emphasize that the political economy continues to be a highly gendered, distinctively masculine sphere of activity (MacKinnon, 1983; Haney, 1996). Modern governments routinely focus primarily on traditionally masculine issues of economic development and military preparedness while giving lower priority to issues such as education, welfare, and child care (Blankenship, 1993).

Women have made political progress, but it has been agonizingly slow (Zweigenhaft & Domhoff, 1998). They were first allowed to vote in the Wyoming Territory in 1869, but universal suffrage was only attained when the 19th Amendment was ratified in 1920. The first woman was elected to Congress in 1917. The first female governors were elected in 1924 (both were the wives of former governors). The first female senator was elected in 1931, and the first female cabinet officer was appointed in 1932. Sandra Day O'Connor became the first woman to sit on the Supreme Court in 1981, and Geraldine Ferarro was chosen as the first major-party vice presidential nominee in 1984.

No woman has ever been nominated to run for President on a major party ticket. Before 1955 a majority of Americans said that they could not support a qualified female candidate for the Presidency; as recently as 1987, 25 percent still said they would not do so (Farley, 1998). In contrast, 24 women served as heads of state internationally during the last century, representing nations as diverse as the United Kingdom, Israel, Norway, Turkey, Canada, Pakistan, India, and Nigeria.

Prior to the 1992 election, women held just two Senate seats and 29 in the House. By 2003, 13 of the 100 senators and 59 of the 435 representatives were female. This meant that women made up 13 percent of the 108th Congress. However, the United States ranks only 40th in percentage of female representation out of the 116 nations with democratic systems. Sweden leads the way with 43 percent (Norris, 1997; Inter-Parliamentary Union, 1999). At the other extreme, women are still denied the right to vote in Kuwait and the United Arab Emirates.

In general, women have been more successful running for state or local offices than at the national level. Between 1979 and 2001, the percentage of state legislators who were female rose from 10.3 to 22.8. Ninety-two women held statewide elective office in 2001, including five governors and 1,672 state legislators.

Women's voting rates, once lower than those of men, were slightly higher in the 2000 election—61 percent compared with 58 percent. Prior to the early 1980s, party preference did not vary appreciably by gender, but since then, college-educated women have tended to disproportionately favor the Democratic Party, a trend that has been called the *gender gap* (Ladd, 1993; Jackson et al., 1996; Wilcox et al., 1996). In the 2000 presidential election, Democrat Al Gore received 54 percent of women's votes but only 42 percent of those of men. Most analysts explain this pattern by the fact that national Democrats tend to emphasize health care, education, poverty, and gun control, all issues that are commonly of strong interest to women (Lake & Breglio, 1992). Interestingly, there is no gender gap between African American men and women; both strongly support liberal Democratic policies (Welch & Sigelman, 1989).

The glass ceiling is especially obvious in the corporate world where, although reasonably well represented at the lower executive levels, no more than 5 percent of top managers in America's 1,000 largest corporations are female (Rosenblatt, 1995).

AFRICAN AMERICANS While a number of former slaves were elected to Congress from the South during Reconstruction (1866–1877), once local whites regained control of the region, almost all African Americans were disenfranchised by means of poll taxes, literacy tests, and similar devices. It was not until the civil rights movement of the 1960s that African Americans regained the right to vote in the South (Morris, 1984; McKelvey, 1994).

The first important black electoral successes of the modern era took place in northern cities where white flight to the suburbs was changing the racial composition of the urban electorate. African American mayors were elected in Cleveland, Detroit, Chicago, New York, and Los Angeles, among other places. Today 47 cities with 50,000 or more people are led by black mayors.

In 1968, only 1,469 African Americans held elective office nationwide; by 2000, 9,040 did so. However, this figure still represented only about 4 percent of all elected officials. As of 2001, blacks, who constitute about 12 percent of the nation's population, held no Senate seats and 39 in the House. Two African Americans have been appointed to the Supreme Court and two sit in President Bush's cabinet. Only three African Americans are currently widely recognized as national political leaders: former Presidential candidate Jesse Jackson, leader of the Nation of Islam Lewis Farakahn, and Secretary of State Colin Powell. None has ever held major elective office.

Except during the late 1960s, African American voting rates have been lower than those of whites of similar age and class level, but the participation gap has been closing in recent years (Ellison & Gay, 1989). In the 2000 elections, 53.5 percent of all adult African American citizens voted compared with 56.4 percent of whites.

African Americans have been strongly identified with the Democratic Party since the New Deal era; in 2000, 90 percent of the black vote went to Vice President Gore. There is some concern that they have been so loyal to the Democrats that their support is sometimes taken for granted by party leaders (White, 1990).

While African Americans have made some progress in the political sphere, there are only three black CEOs heading Fortune 500 corporations, and they are dramatically underrepresented in corporate boardrooms.

LATINOS   Latino Americans are the fastest growing minority in the United States. They constitute nearly a quarter of all eligible voters in California, Texas, New Mexico, Arizona, and Florida, making them a potentially powerful voting bloc. Furthermore, recent controversies over bilingual education and "English only" laws have intensified many Latinos' interest in politics. Yet their turnout in recent presidential elections has been low—just 27.5 percent of all adult citizens in 2000. As of that year, there were 21 Latinos in the House and none in the Senate.

Like African Americans, most Latinos find the policies of the Democratic Party appealing and give it most of their support. Sixty-two percent backed Vice President Gore in 2000. However, the Cuban American population, economically better off than other Latinos and intensely anti-communist, has generally voted Republican (Welch & Sigelman, 1993).

OTHER RACIAL AND ETHNIC MINORITIES   Most other minority groups are too small in numbers to have much political impact except in local areas where they constitute a significant percentage of the population. Asian Americans are a partial exception: Despite making up only 3 percent of the population, there are six Asian Americans in the House and two in the Senate, most from Hawaii. One Native American has been elected to the House and another to the Senate, and Connecticut Senator Joseph Lieberman, an orthodox Jew, was Al Gore's running mate in the 2000 presidential election.

Figure 18.1 summarizes the representation of women and people of color in high positions in the U.S. political system.

Politics and the Internet

Democratic regimes like the United States have always been characterized by a substantial amount of grassroots political activism. This has traditionally involved such mundane activities as displaying yard signs or bumper stickers, manning phone banks, or going door-to-door in support of favored candidates. Recently, however, the computer has been enlisted in the service of political advocacy, promising to alter the character of campaigning in the future (Roberts, 1995; Wayne, 2000).

Six months before the 2000 presidential election, some 6,800 private citizens had already established Websites concerning one of the major party candidates. Some of the sites directly supported either Republican George W. Bush or Democrat Al Gore. Others were parody sites, mercilessly criticizing one of the candidates.

The established political parties are grateful for the support of activists on the Web, but they express some concern over the fact that people can post political information, no matter how inaccurate, on their personal Web pages without any control or regulation. The Democrats have asked the Commerce Department to

	Percent in Population	Percent in Office		
		Senate	House	Governors
Males	49.1	87	86.0	90
Females	50.9	13	14.0	10
Non-Latino Whites	70.4	97	84.7	96
African Americans	12.8	0	9.0	0
Latinos	11.8	0	4.8	0
Asian-Americans	4.1	2	1.4	4
Native Americans	0.9	1	0.1	0

FIGURE 18.1   Percentage of Persons Holding High Political Office, by Gender and Race/Ethnicity, 2000

Source: 2001 U.S. Statistical Abstract.

DIVERSITY IN FOCUS

Gambling on the Future, with Reservations

Are you looking for a different spot for your next vacation? Do you like to gamble? Perhaps you might enjoy visiting the Foxwoods Resort Casino in Ledyard, Connecticut. There you will find 3,900 slot machines, 15 restaurants, numerous shops, and an opulent spa. Entertainers who have appeared in its showroom include Frank Sinatra, Bill Cosby, and Ray Charles. Foxwoods employs about 10,000 workers. Unofficial estimates place its annual gross revenues as high as $1 billion. And the entire operation is under the control of the 350-member Mashantucket Pequot nation.

Native American casinos have proliferated since the late 1980s as a direct result of a special political relationship between the tribes and the federal government. Beginning with the Indian Reorganization Act of 1934, Native Americans have been granted a variety of political rights designed to help them to recover their economic and cultural vitality after several centuries of oppression. In particular, their sovereignty over the reservations allows Indian tribes to operate casinos that would be illegal if they were run by whites.

Modern era Indian gaming began with a high-stakes bingo parlor run by Florida's Seminole nation, which opened in 1979. In 1987, the Supreme Court case of *California v. Cabazon Band of Mission Indians* established that state laws limiting gambling could not be automatically enforced on the reservations. One year later, Congress passed the Indian Gaming Regulatory Act (IGRA), which provides the basic legal foundation on which Indian casinos currently rest. The IGRA requires that tribes and the states in which they are located enter into negotiations concerning how gambling operations will be run prior to opening casinos or bingo halls. As of 1999, over 150 Indian nations ran some 150 casinos and 220 bingo parlors in 24 states.

Gaming has dramatically transformed the previously dismal economic picture of some Native American tribes. Consider the Oneida nation of Wisconsin. Its tribal budget grew from under $50,000 in 1969, virtually all derived from the federal government, to $158 million in 1995, over 90 percent of which comes from its gambling operations, which attract some 6 million visitors each year. The tribe employed nine people in 1969; by 1995, that number had grown to 3,391, of whom 1,970 were Native Americans. Oneida unemployment dropped from 75 percent to under 5 percent over the same period.

Some tribes divide gaming revenues up evenly among enrolled members, occasionally resulting in annual individual stipends in the hundreds of thousands of dollars, but the wiser strategy appears to be to use the profits for the benefit of the entire group. Casino-generated profits have dramatically improved roads, health care, education, housing, and environmental conditions on a number of reservations. Some tribes have constructed new museums and cultural centers.

However, casinos are not a panacea for all Native Americans. Many such ventures have failed, often because they were located on reservations too far off the beaten path to attract sufficient numbers of paying customers. As of 1997, 40 percent of all revenues from Indian gambling came from just eight casinos.

Opposition from social conservatives and from the owners of off-reservation resorts and other tourist attractions has frequently been intense. In some cases outsiders contracted to run Indian casinos have raked off as much as 75 percent of the profits. State officials are endemically frustrated by their inability to tax the casinos. And there is always concern about the possibility of organized crime trying to muscle in.

In addition, by no means do all Native Americans themselves support the casinos. The more traditional tribal members are often opposed despite the fact that gambling was an integral part of most premodern Native American cultures. In 1994, the Navajo nation narrowly voted down a proposal to establish a tribal casino. There are also concerns among some opponents that it is risky to put so much emphasis on a single type of economic activity.

Still, for those tribes that have chosen to open gambling operations, the move has often paid off. Indian gaming provides an excellent example of how the political status and the economic activities of a community are often intimately interconnected.

1. Should Native Americans be granted privileges such as the right to run casinos based on their special political relationship with the U.S. government, or is this discriminatory?

2. Despite the success of Indian gaming, Native Americans remain the United States' poorest minority group. What additional strategies might help them to promote economic development on the reservations?

Sources: Rosecrance, 1988; Garbarino & Sasso, 1994; McCulloch, 1994; Johnson, 1995; Bordewich, 1996; Nagel, 1997; Iverson, 1998; Anders, 1999; Sutton, 2000; Larese, 2001.

consider assigning a special domain (*.elect* or *.pol*) to official Websites in order to differentiate them from the unofficial and uncontrolled Web pages.

The major parties are also hustling to catch up with the grassroots activists by improving the quality of their own Websites. The Republican National Committee has sponsored workshops to help both party organizers and local activists use cyberspace more effectively. Meanwhile, the Democrats sponsored parody sites such as www.MillionairesForBush.com, modeled after private anti-Bush Web pages.

Campaigning on the Web is in its infancy, and no one knows how it will evolve, but it seems clear that computer technology has the potential to be a powerful force fighting political alienation and apathy. As Robin Orlowsky, a junior at Texas Women's College and the sponsor of a liberal Website, puts it, "These sites will increase democracy in the long run. You don't have tightly scripted campaigns as the sole voice. You will have independent citizens voicing their opinions in a way they couldn't before. It's because the Internet is dirt cheap and it costs money to print campaign materials. The Internet is a great free opportunity" (Wayne, 2000).

LIFE CONNECTIONS

America's Low Voter Turnout

Did you vote in the last election? If you are typical of most college students, you probably did not (Leon, 1996). More generally, voting rates in the United States are much lower than they are in the other Western democracies. The 54.7 percent of the eligible electorate who made it to the polls in the 2000 presidential election represented a slight increase over the 54.2 percent who voted in 1996. Participation in local and state elections is typically much lower, ranging from 40 percent to below 10 percent. Figure 18.2 illustrates the effects of age and race on voting turnout. Why don't more Americans exercise their right to vote?

Some conservatives argue that political apathy is functional (Lipset, 1960). Nonvoters tend to be less educated, less politically informed, and more prone to extreme political views, so their failure to participate may actually stabilize the system or even reflect general satisfaction with it. Critics, however, suggest that nonvoting more often reflects the beliefs that one's vote doesn't matter and that public officials are unresponsive to the average citizen (Piven & Cloward, 1978).

Structural factors play a part in explaining low voter turnout. Laws that remove people from the voting rolls who have moved or who have not voted in recent elections contribute to low turnouts, as does

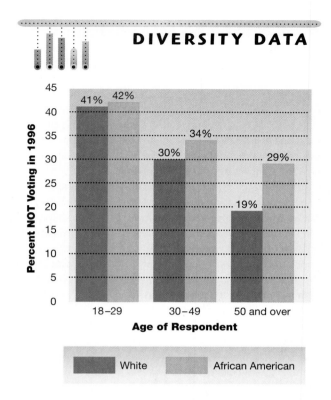

DIVERSITY DATA

FIGURE 18.2 How Do Age and Race Affect Voting Rates? In the 1996 Presidential election, older people were substantially more likely to vote than younger people. African American and white voting rates were similar among the young, but older African Americans were less likely to vote than older whites. Why do you think today's youths, especially African Americans, seem to be uninterested in voting?

Source: NORC. General Social Surveys, 1972–2000. Chicago: National Opinion Research Center, 2000. Reprinted by permission of NORC, Chicago, IL.

the U.S. custom of holding elections on workdays. In Europe, where three-fourths or more of the eligible voters typically go to the polls, elections are held on Sundays or on official holidays. In Italy, the state even levies fines against nonvoters.

Another structural reason why many Americans fail to vote is that the United States has a two-party system. This encourages Democrats and Republicans to compete for the middle ground and to blur their distinctiveness. By emphasizing high-consensus issues like crime control or the importance of education, parties downplay their differences and thus render elections largely meaningless (Lewis et al., 1994; Phillips, 1994). In Europe, strongly ideological parties engender intense loyalties that encourage high turnouts (Lind, 1995).

Why is the United States a two-party system? The U.S. government is structured around single-member districts and winner-take-all voting. Members of Congress represent specific geographic units. Majority rule (or, more correctly, plurality rule) means that a candidate needs only one more vote than the next closest opponent to win office. Voters rarely support third parties, because doing so splits the vote and may indirectly contribute to the success of their least favored candidate. For example, in the 2000 presidential election, Ralph Nader's candidacy clearly helped George W. Bush despite the fact that most Nader voters were ideologically closer to Al Gore. A successful third-party challenge for the presidency has occurred only once in U.S. history, in the 1860 contest won by Abraham Lincoln.

In contrast to the U.S. system, most representative democracies, especially in Western Europe, allow *proportional voting* in which the number of candidates a party elects is determined by the overall number of votes that it receives. This system encourages multiple parties, and it allows parties to take much clearer and stronger ideological stands on the issues and still be successful. Under these arrangements, voters typically are more interested in electoral outcomes and are more likely to vote.

Other equally persuasive explanations for the low turnout in U.S. elections focus less on structural factors and more on sharp declines in public confidence in major institutions, including not only government but also corporations, labor unions, education, and religion (Lipset & Schneider, 1983) (Figure 18.3). In the early 1960s, two-thirds of the general population expressed a high level of trust in most major institutions. By the late 1970s, barely a third did so, and the percentages continued to decline slowly through the 1980s and 1990s. There is some indication that this trend may have reversed in the period immediately following the September 11 terrorist attacks, but it seems likely that this was only a temporary interruption in a long-term decline. It seems that a very substantial and growing proportion of the U.S. electorate is alienated—they distrust the political system and consciously refuse to participate in it.

A number of factors have combined to create this crisis of confidence. They include major policy mistakes, such as the Vietnam War, Watergate, the savings and loan scandal, and the Monica Lewinsky affair. Most recently, allegations that the FBI, CIA, and NSA, arms of the federal government, failed to detect and process potential clues prior to the attacks of September 11 have added to this crisis of confidence. The fact that conservative Republicans have tended to portray government as the problem rather than part of the solution is certainly relevant here. Some argue that the mass media, by concentrating on negative stories in order to boost their audiences, have contributed to widespread cynicism about politics and society in general (Parenti, 1986). Others

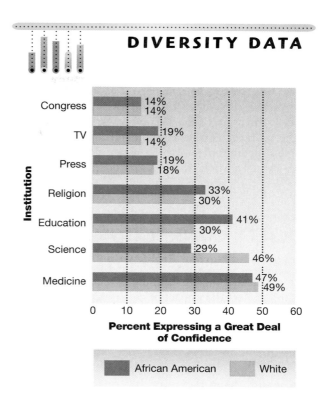

DIVERSITY DATA

FIGURE 18.3 **How Much Confidence People Express in Major U.S. Institutions, by Race.** Overall trust in medicine and science is relatively high whereas fewer than one in five respondents expresses a great deal of confidence in the press, television, or Congress. African Americans report greater trust of TV and education than do whites, while whites report more confidence than African Americans in science. There is no institution that inspires great confidence in more than half of the population. Why do you think so many people have become so skeptical?

Source: NORC. General Social Surveys, 1972–2000. Chicago: National Opinion Research Center, 2000. Reprinted by permission of NORC, Chicago, IL.

note that the U.S. public has become more highly educated and knowledgeable and therefore less trusting in recent decades. In the past, high levels of confidence may have reflected ignorance and blind trust in political leaders rather than an accurate assessment of reality.

This confidence gap raises questions about the legitimacy of the U.S. political system. It strongly suggests that certain groups, including many African Americans, other people of color, and the poor, view the U.S. political system as unresponsive (DeLuca, 1998; Fetto, 1999). The impact of class is especially powerful, with virtually all research documenting markedly lower rates of political participation among those toward the bottom of the class ladder (Verba & Nie, 1972; Orum, 2001). At the same time, many educated middle-class people also view politics skeptically and are increasingly unlikely to vote.

Some authorities contend that the confidence gap is not a true crisis of legitimacy (Lipset & Schneider, 1983). But the gap does suggest that should the U.S. political economy be challenged as it was, say, in the Great Depression of the 1930s—when over one-third of the workforce was unemployed and when most people's incomes dropped significantly—the possibility of a systemic breakdown might be quite real.

SOCIETY CONNECTIONS

Terrorism and Nuclear Proliferation

In this final section, we examine two critical social issues that reflect the impact of globalization on the political economy: terrorism and the threat of nuclear proliferation.

Terrorism

The world changed irrevocably on September 11, 2001. You remember where you were that morning; we all do. As these words are being written in January 2003, there is a nearly universal assumption that further large-scale attacks on the United States, perhaps suicide bombings (Taylor & Ryan, 1988), perhaps incidents involving biological, chemical, or nuclear weapons (Sanz, 1992; Taylor, 1998), are likely or even inevitable. Certainly the impact of the threat of terrorism on the political economy of the United States has fundamentally and perhaps permanently altered social life in this country.

Terrorism is not an easy concept to define (see Hoffman, 1999; Combs, 2000; White, 2002). Politicians frequently use the term to characterize any and all instances of violence perpetrated by individuals, groups, or nations with whom they strongly disagree, but they resist the label when referring to the actions of their supporters or allies (Cooper, 1978). It is a truism that one person's terrorist may be another's freedom fighter. For the purposes of this discussion, we will define **terrorism** as goal-oriented political action employing or threatening extreme violence against symbolic and often randomly selected victims. This definition makes three critical points.

First, terrorism is goal-oriented behavior, and the goal is a political one (Bryman, 1998). The al-Qaida attacks may appear senseless, but in fact they were intended to bring pressure on the U.S. government to withdraw its troops from Saudi Arabia and to reduce or end its support for the state of Israel.

Second, terrorism makes use of extraordinary forms of violence (Combs, 2000). This is necessary in order to agitate the citizens of the target nation so that they will put pressure on their government to give the terrorists whatever they are seeking (Jacquard, 2001). Unfortunately, this means that there is generally a pattern of escalation in the scale of the devastation, because attacks otherwise become routine and ineffective from the point of view of the terrorists (Jenkins & Alexander, 1987).

Finally, the targets of the extraordinary violence are generally chosen at random so that everyone has reason to fear that they are personally at risk (Combs, 2000). Anyone could have been visiting the World Trade Center that Tuesday morning. In this sense, the victims are symbolic.

The September 11, 2001, terrorist attacks on the World Trade Center and the Pentagon dramatically transformed the political landscape of the United States.

TYPES OF TERRORISM Researchers have identified a number of different types of terrorism, but three are particularly important:

- *Terrorism sponsored by political sects.* Small, radical political groups have long made use of terroristic tactics to call attention to their demands. Examples include European anarchist bombings in the 19th century, attacks by extreme 1960s student groups such as the Weathermen in the United States and by the German Bader-Meinhof gang (Becker, 1977), and the l995 destruction of the federal building in Oklahoma City by antigovernment extremist Timothy McVeigh (George & Wilcox, 1996; White, 2001). This form of terrorism may be extremely destructive, but it is somewhat limited by the fact that its perpetrators enjoy little support from the general public.
- *Revolutionary nationalist terrorism.* This is the type of terrorism that currently poses the greatest threat. It is practiced by organizations that claim to speak for the aspirations of national or ethnic minorities that see themselves as oppressed. The Palestinian terrorists (Nurse, 1999), the Irish Republican Army (Bell, 1975), the Basque ETA (Khatami, 1997), and Osama bin Laden's network (Reeve, 1999) are examples. While the relationship between the terrorist group and the people for whom it claims to be fighting may reflect a good deal of ambivalence, there is usually a substantial level of support for the group's goals if not for its methods, and this makes eradication of revolutionary nationalist terrorism particularly difficult (Seale, 1992; Alexander, 1994).

- *State terrorism.* Finally, there have been many instances in which governments have engaged in terroristic actions against their own citizens (Slann, 1993). Among the best examples are the death squads sponsored by a number of bureaucratic-authoritarian regimes in Latin America in recent decades and the genocide perpetrated by the Khmer Rouge government in which roughly one-seventh of the population of Cambodia perished.

Note that terrorism is generally a last-choice strategy of the weak against the strong. If political sects, revolutionary nationalist movements, or, to a lesser extent, repressive governments could accomplish their aims through more conventional (and generally more effective) means, they would surely do so. Terrorists are people who are unwilling to abandon their dreams despite the long odds against their success.

WHY NOW? Why has terrorism, and especially revolutionary nationalist terrorism, become more common in the current era?

First, and probably most important, are some unexpected consequences of the globalization process. Over the past 40 years, almost all of the formerly colonial nations in the developing world have achieved political independence. This has greatly raised expectations in these societies. However, most have remained poor and heavily economically dependent on the developed world, which has provoked widespread hostility among their inhabitants. Guided by widely accepted theories that attribute the failure to thrive of the developing nations to their unfavorable position in the world economic system (see

While most people in the United States paid little attention to the threat of revolutionary terrorism before the September 11 tragedy, the Israelis have lived with it for decades. This bus was recently blown to pieces in the streets of Jerusalem by a Palestinian suicide bomber. Nineteen passengers died and fifty-five people were injured in the attack.

Chapter 10), activists have channeled their frustration into attacks on the developed nations, and especially on the United States, which is the dominant power in the world system (Barber, 1995).

Other factors explaining the expansion of terrorism are mostly technological. The ever-increasing complexity and interdependence of the modern world's infrastructure has provided terrorists with numerous attractive targets. Strikes against power stations, airports, or buildings like the Pentagon or the World Trade Center have the potential of causing massive disruption yet are relatively easily and cheaply mounted. Modern technology also has provided terrorists with effective new weapons, such as plastic explosives and fuel-laden airliners (Laqueur, 1999). The Internet allows conspirators to coordinate their activities globally, and other advances in communications technology allow the media to provide immediate and graphic reports of terrorist activities.

WHO ARE THE TERRORISTS? Although their opponents often describe them as insane, in fact revolutionary nationalist terrorists are generally quite rational, although they are absolutely committed to a political goal that may be so unlikely to be attained that outsiders may regard it as hopeless (Hacker, 1978). Terrorism specialist Edgar O'Ballance (1979) suggests that in addition to passionate dedication to their cause, terrorists tend to display personal bravery, intelligence, sophistication, and a fairly high level of general knowledge. They also must possess the ability to totally suspend their capacity to empathize with their victims, which is usually accomplished by referring to them in very negative terms ("infidels"), and by either killing them at a distance or at least covering their faces before they are slain.

While the leaders of revolutionary nationalist terrorist groups are frequently drawn from middle-class backgrounds, their foot-soldiers are increasingly likely to be very young (sometimes barely more than children) and poorly educated (Laqueur, 1999). Modern terrorists also include a much higher percentage of women than has been the case in the past (Combs, 2000).

COMBATING TERRORISM Although there is considerable disagreement among experts about the best ways to respond to the threat of terrorism, there is little doubt that effective intelligence gathering is the most crucial means of deterring attacks. Well-trained military and paramilitary antiterrorist teams are also important, as are a variety of new law enforcement technologies (Buck, 1998).

Other strategies are more controversial. International agreements and blockades often fail because

INTERNET CONNECTIONS

Since September 11, an increased amount of attention is being focused on *terrorism*. Take the opportunity to have a look at U.S. State Department site on counterterrorism

http://www.state.gov/s/ct/c4291.htm

After browsing the site answer the following questions. What are the threats of today? Do you think appropriate steps are being taken by our government to avert future situations like the attacks on the World Trade Center and the Pentagon?

some governments overtly or covertly support groups that others regard as terrorists. Indiscriminately attacking citizens of states believed to support terrorism frequently builds popular support for the terrorists. Assassinations create martyrs. Granting some of the demands of terrorists, especially those that may be seen as just, or even negotiating with terrorist groups, may have the negative consequence of making these groups seem more legitimate, thus encouraging them to continue their campaigns.

The role of the media is particularly critical (Alexander & Patter, 1990; Schaffert, 1992; Perl, 1998). Terrorists and the media are in a *symbiotic* relationship: Terrorists must secure widespread publicity for their acts if they are to have the desired effect on the public, while the media can attract large audiences by airing graphic accounts of extreme violence.

After every major terrorist event, there are calls for restraint with regard to what is published or broadcast. There can be no doubt that the "media circus" that often accompanies coverage of major terrorist attacks works to the advantage of the terrorists (Kingston, 1995). Most critics encourage voluntary self-restraint on the part of the media aimed at reducing sensationalistic coverage. Some endorse government controls.

This is the dilemma: We cannot end terrorism, but we can dramatically reduce it if we are willing to allow censorship of the media, institute greatly expanded governmental surveillance policies, issue national ID cards, and so forth. But to do these things would amount to abandoning our democratic freedoms. There was little or no terrorism in totalitarian states like Hitler's Germany and the old Soviet Union—but are we willing to pay that high a price for a measure of security?

GLOBAL CONNECTIONS

The Structural Roots of Genocide in Rwanda

In 1994, the government of Rwanda, which was controlled at the time by members of an ethnic group called the Hutu, launched a ferocious campaign to exterminate the Tutsis, who had traditionally dominated the country politically. In just four months, over half a million Tutsis and moderate Hutus who opposed the genocide were slaughtered. Then, a rebel Tutsi army based in neighboring Uganda regained political control. In the ensuing upheaval, the Tutsis killed over a quarter of a million additional Hutu. The United Nations subsequently established a human rights court to try officials of the former, Hutu-dominated Rwandan government for crimes against humanity.

As much as a quarter of the population was directly affected by these events—some as victims, some as perpetrators, and some as refugees who fled the violence. The attacks on the Tutsis were deliberately planned by high-level Hutu government officials who used radio broadcasts to whip up ethnic antagonism and trained entire soccer teams to ritually kill Tutsi men, women, and children. The Rwandan genocide is unique in that it involved a larger portion of the population and was conducted much more openly than any previous act of mass extermination. How can we explain this intense outpouring of collective violence?

The history and political economy of Rwanda are critical factors. During the colonial era of the late 19th and early 20th centuries, the Belgian government legitimated the political power of the aristocratic Tutsis, who controlled the army and were the principal landlords. At this time, the Tutsis represented roughly 11 percent of the population. But then, when preparing to grant Rwanda its independence, the colonial government decided to democratize the country, allowing some real power to the majority Hutus. This decision sparked a civil war, which in turn produced a refugee army of Tutsis residing in nearby Uganda. Over the next two decades, these refugees, supported by the Tutsi-dominated government of neighboring Burundi, maintained a hostile relationship with the Hutu regime in Rwanda.

Despite significant levels of intermarriage between the Hutus and the Tutsi in Rwanda, the Hutu-controlled government overtly promoted the notion that the Tutsi were subhuman and constituted a dire threat to Rwandan society. Many Hutus opposed the genocide and tried to shelter neighbors and friends from the rampaging Hutu military, but long-standing ethnic hatreds ultimately prevailed.

Moreover, international isolation and indifference reinforced the crisis. Despite incontrovertible evidence that genocide was planned or underway, most Western governments maintained that they had no strategic interests in the region and that military intervention in the internal affairs of another country was unwarranted. The Western media ignored accounts of the slaughter for almost four months, thus eliminating the possibility of reliable reporting that might have led to effective international intervention. By the time the outside world began to take the situation seriously, the invading Tutsi army had already defeated the Hutu leaders and driven them from power.

What lessons can be learned from the Rwandan genocide? First, it proved once again that people can inflict unspeakable violence on each other. Most of the victims were killed face-to-face with pickaxes, shovels, and other hand weapons. Many of the murderers knew their victims personally.

Second, propaganda can legitimize unthinkable brutality. The Hutu government had practiced ritual killings and used hate radio and other dehumanization methods for several years in order to make the genocide appear reasonable and just.

Third, although the Hutu–Tutsi relationship was historically tense, particular decisions made by the extremist political leadership of the Hutus were critical in mobilizing the genocide. Simply referring to "ancient hatreds" and racial differences does not adequately explain the massacre.

Finally, the Rwandan genocide teaches us that foreign powers are unlikely to intervene to halt such outrages unless they feel that their own national interests are at stake. Despite the international conventions against genocide that grew out of the Holocaust, neither Western governments nor African powers stepped in before the carnage was largely ended. This is why many argue that the lack of political will is the chief obstacle to preventing genocide and lesser forms of political repression.

1. Why do you think the government of the United States refused to become involved in the Rwandan genocide, but did intervene a few years later in Kosovo?

2. Is an authoritarian or a democratic political system more likely to sponsor genocide? Explain your answer.

Sources: Hammer, 1994; Masland, 1994; Gourevitch, 1995; Purvis, 1996.

Nuclear Proliferation

While the threat of nuclear terrorism is very real, terrorists are by no means the only agents who have the potential of unleashing the unthinkable devastation of atomic warfare. At the end of the Cold War, the United States and the successor states to the USSR agreed to reduce their nuclear stockpiles and to attempt to deter the spread of nuclear weapons around the globe. Many people believed that the threat of species annihilation had finally ended and that nuclear weapons might soon become obsolete.

These hopes have proven premature at best. Although Russia and the United States have significantly reduced their arsenals, enough nuclear weapons still exist to destroy the world's population many times over. The international sale of plutonium and other nuclear components by financially strapped laboratories and military facilities in the former Soviet Union has created a major security worry. There is also an international market in nuclear engineers, and critical know-how is spreading throughout the globe.

As of 2002, there were seven openly declared nuclear powers (the United States, China, France, Russia, the United Kingdom, India, and Pakistan). Several additional states are suspected of possessing nuclear weapons (including Iran and Israel), and numerous others, including North Korea have the technological ability to develop a nuclear arsenal in a fairly short period of time (Jones & McDonough, 1998, p. 11; Smith, 1997, pp. 70–71).

What are the implications of the continued proliferation of nuclear weapons? What if a quarter of the nations of the world possessed nuclear capacity? Instead of just threatening South Korean and U.S. troops, North Korea could bomb them out of existence. Longstanding disputes between India and Pakistan or between Israel and much of the Islamic world could easily escalate to the nuclear stage. Because of international alliances, a regional nuclear war could spread quickly (Posen, 1991; Blair, 1993). Rogue states with unpredictable leaders might be joined by criminal syndicates involved in smuggling that would find it useful to use nuclear weapons as bargaining tools. As we move into the new century, the world remains an extremely dangerous place.

SUMMARY

1. The concept of the political economy emphasizes the fact that the economic and political institutions of modern societies are largely inseparable from one other, especially at the macrolevel.

2. Power is the ability to compel others to act as the powerholder wishes, even if they attempt to resist. There are three types of power: decision-making power, agenda control, and systemic power.

3. Authority is legitimate power. Max Weber identified three ideal types of authority: traditional, rational-legal, and charismatic.

4. There are three major philosophical models of the political economy: liberalism, socialism, and conservatism.

5. Most modern economic systems are capitalist, a few are state socialist, and some, termed mixed economies, are intermediate between the two polar types.

6. Political regimes may be authoritarian or democratic. Authoritarian regimes include monarchies, dictatorships, bureaucratic-authoritarian regimes, and totalitarian states. Democratic regimes may be either participatory or representative democracies.

7. There are four competing models of the actual distribution of political power in modern societies: pluralism, the power elite model, the ruling class model, and the state autonomy model.

8. In most cases, democratization, the transition from authoritarianism to democracy, is instigated by elites, although sometimes it is promoted by the lower classes.

9. Minorities and women have been systematically excluded from the top levels of the political economy, although both groups have made significant progress in recent decades.

10. The Internet is rapidly becoming an important means of disseminating political information.

11. Voter turnout in the United States is normally very low, especially among Latinos and the poor.

In part, this may be explained by the structure of the U.S. political institution, especially the two-party system. It also reflects the low levels of confidence many Americans express in major social institutions.

12. Terrorism is the political, goal-oriented threat or use of extraordinary violence against symbolic, often randomly chosen victims.

13. Nuclear proliferation is one of the most serious problems currently facing the world.

KEY TERMS

authoritarian regime 491
authority 486
capitalism 490
charismatic authority 487
classical liberalism 488
conservatism 489
democracy 492
economy 485
elite model 494

mixed economy 490
modern liberalism 489
monopoly 488
pluralism 492
political economy 485
power 486
rational-legal authority 487
routinization of charisma 487
ruling class model 495

socialism 489
state 485
state autonomy model 495
state socialism 490
terrorism 502
totalitarianism 491
traditional authority 487

CRITICAL THINKING QUESTIONS

1. Why do you think that rational-legal authority has largely replaced the traditional and charismatic types during the past two centuries?

2. Which of the four models of the distribution of political power do you believe most accurately describes your home community? The state in which you live? The United States as a whole? Explain how you arrived at your answers.

3. What do you believe is the best explanation for the low voter turnout in the United States? How do you think we could best attempt a long-term and substantial reversal of this pattern?

4. How will the ongoing threat of terrorism affect the political economy of the United States? Do you see most of these changes as positive or harmful?

INVESTIGATE WITH CONTENT SELECT

Journal Research
Collections from
ContentSelect

Begin your research using Content-Select for this chapter by following the directions found on page 27 of this text to visit Prentice Hall's Research Navigator Website. Enter these search terms into the search field:

Terrorism
Monopoly
Autonomy

19
HEALTH AND HEALTH CARE

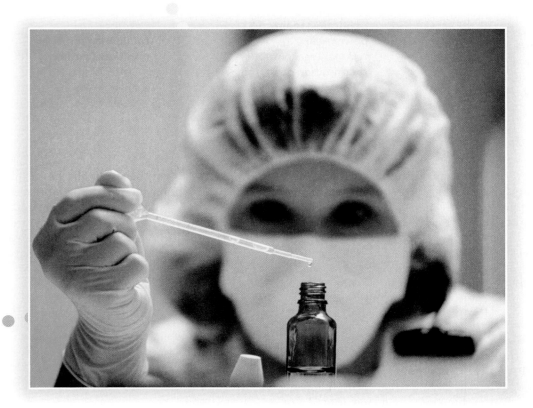

Organ Transplants: Rationing by Wallet

In Upper Marlboro, Maryland, William Dobbs, age 65 and retired, was bleeding internally and needed a liver transplant—a $200,000 operation. He no longer qualified for his former insurance, and his Medicare coverage denied the operation. Mr. Dobbs received his transplant because, in an abrupt change of policy, Medicare decided to pay for adult liver transplants. In Rockwood, Oregon, teenager Coby Howard died of leukemia, his death coming in the midst of a campaign to raise $100,000 for a bone marrow treatment. A year earlier there would have been no need for the effort. But Coby became the first victim of a policy set by the Oregon legislature to stop all organ transplants for welfare recipients and instead spend the money on prenatal care. Deciding who gets organ transplants has become a formal process based on medical judgments. But there is one nonmedical characteristic almost all who get transplants share: They have a way to pay for the operation. William Dobbs had health insurance and survived. Coby Howard had no insurance and died. (Adapted from Rich, 1993:228; Callahan, 1994:196)

Ancient Medicine in a Modern Hospital

For two weeks he was in a coma hovering on the brink of death in a San Francisco hospital. His fever hit 106. The 28-year-old Mohawk, Richard Oakes, was a leader in a Native American movement that was pressing claims for the return of California lands. These activities triggered an attack in which he was almost beaten to death. As skeptical doctors watched, Mad Bear the Medicine Man placed an ancient and mysterious medicine in his feeding tube. Within an hour a normal temperature and pulse returned. Mad Bear was allowed to treat Richard because it was a religious rite to be administered with Indian herbs. His condition was so bad that doctors reasoned, "What harm could it do?" and they were aware that medicine men are skilled in the use of curative herbs. Mad Bear refuses to say what medicine was placed in the IV tube. The tube in a modern hospital was used to convey the secret, potent drug. In this instance there was a blending of Native American and modern healing practices. (Adapted from Kane & Kane, 1994:172)

These vignettes illustrate that health and health care exist in a sociocultural context and cannot be separated from it. The values, beliefs, and norms of society—key elements of social structure—influence the organization and delivery of health care. When patients enter the health care system, they bring their social statuses with them. William Dobbs's life was saved by the advances of modern medicine. Because of his economic status, Coby Howard could not benefit from these same advances. The case of Richard Oakes indicates a newer trend in health care—practices that blend the traditional (indigenous) with the modern (scientific) in healing. All these people entered the health care system in the United States and had varying experiences with it. As this chapter shows, the care they and others like them receive is profoundly impacted by the structure of society in which the health care is delivered.

DEFINING AND MEASURING HEALTH AND DISEASE

The World Health Organization (WHO) defines **health** as a state of complete physical, mental, and social well-being, not merely the absence of disease or infirmity. This view of health is **holistic**—involving treatment of the "whole" person, with a focus on wellness and prevention rather than simply on disease and cure. The "holistic health" model is fast becoming an ideal for health care delivery in the United States and Britain, particularly with patients who have

The World Health Organization is responsible for monitoring the spread of disease worldwide. They also provide services to remote areas of the world where modern health care is unavailable.

chronic diseases that are both life threatening and socially stigmatizing, such as AIDS (Schilder et al., 2001). The delivery of health care is also based on the accumulation of accurate data.

Measurement Techniques

People who collect data on health usually work under what is referred to as a *negative health standard:* We are healthy because we are not sick; that is, we have no fever or pain and no interference in our daily activities. Although the "negative" health standard contradicts WHO's assumption that health is much more than the absence of disease, the standard is used because the "positive" standard of health based on wellness and prevention is too broad or vague. Disease indicators involving major physical illnesses with well-defined symptoms are easier to document. These are used in combination with other demographic characteristics, such as population growth or decline, age, gender, birth and death rate, marital status, and ethnicity (Chapter 22). Therefore, data on *health* are routinely collected based on measurements of *disease.*

Various measurement techniques have been developed to determine patterns of health and well-being in countries around the world, including the United States. The simplest measure, the **mortality rate,** is expressed as a percentage of the total number of deaths over the population size (x 1,000) in a given time period, usually a year. Calculating a **morbidity rate,** the amount of disease or illness in a population, is more difficult. Although illness may have well-defined symptoms, illness itself is in part subjective. Many people do not recognize their own sickness, may recognize it but refuse to alter their behavior, or

prefer to treat themselves. As a result, morbidity rates are often based on treatment, thus compromising the accuracy of the data.

The two most important status indicators of global health are the *infant mortality rate* (IMR) and the *life expectancy rate* (LER) at birth. IMR is the number of deaths in the first year of life for each 1,000 live births. It is a sensitive measure of overall inequality and reflects a country's success in fighting child deaths due to preventable diseases. LER at birth reflects both childhood and adult death rates. Once an individual survives childhood, the gap between the developed and developing world is narrower (Table 19.1).

Social Epidemiology

Epidemiology is the study of the causes and distribution of disease and disability in a given population. Since this study must include more than biological or physical factors, the discipline of epidemiology has expanded. *Social epidemiology* is its logical extension and includes the sociocultural and behavioral factors contributing to disease and disability.

The word "social" before the word "epidemiology" is actually redundant. Today epidemiologists draw upon the work of many disciplines, especially medical sociology, in constructing the complex web of the multiple causes of disease and disability (Syme & Yen, 2000). For all kinds of health planning, epidemiologists continually track diseases. The figures they use most are the **incidence** of disease, the number of new cases during a specified time period, and the **prevalence** of disease, the total number of cases during a specified time. Since prevalence rates are cumulative, it is essential to track them for highly

TABLE 19.1

Life Expectancy Rate at Birth (LER) and Infant Mortality Rate (IMR) of Selected Countries in Developing and Developed World

	LER		IMR	
Year	1998	2002[1]	1998	2002[1]
Developing World				
Africa				
Egypt	62.1	64	69.2	58.6
*Ethiopia	40.9	44.6	125.7	99.9
Kenya	47.6	47	59.4	67.2
*Rwanda	41.9	38.9	113.3	118.9
*Sudan	56.0	56.9	72.6	68.6
*Uganda	42.6	43.3	92.9	91.3
Asia				
Afghanistan	46.8	46.6	143.6	144.7
*Bangladesh	56.7	60.5	97.7	69.8
China	69.6	71.9	45.5	27.2
India	62.9	63.2	63.1	61.5
*Indonesia	62.5	68.2	59.2	40.9
Pakistan	59.1	61.8	93.5	78.5
South America				
*Argentina	74.5	75.2	19.0	17.7
*Bolivia	60.9	64	63.9	58.9
Brazil	64.4	65.5	37.0	35.9
Mexico	71.6	72.0	25.8	24.9
Peru	70.0	70.6	43.4	38.2
Developed World				
Canada	**79.2**	**79.7**	**5.6**	**5.0**
France	78.5	79	5.7	4.4
Germany	77.0	77.8	5.2	4.7
*Hong Kong	78.8	79.6	5.2	5.8
Italy	78.4	79.2	6.4	5.8
Japan	80.0	80.9	4.1	3.8
Spain	77.6	79.1	6.5	4.8
Sweden	79.2	79.8	3.9	3.4
Switzerland	78.9	79.4	4.9	4.4
United States	**76.1**	**77.4**	**6.4**	**6.7**

[1]Projected
*2001 data

Sources: U.S. Bureau of the Census, 1998 (adapted from Tables 128, 134, 135); *CIA World Factbook,* 2001; U.S. Bureau of the Census, International Data Base, 2002.

contagious diseases such as influenza, tuberculosis, and measles. This practice ensures that health care facilities are prepared for the influx of patients and that the public is made aware of any preventive measures they can take. Global cooperation is critical in reporting incidence and prevalence rates.

THEORETICAL PERSPECTIVES ON HEALTH IN THE UNITED STATES

Sociological theory has contributed significantly to our understanding of health and health care. As noted above, the social and cultural determinants of health are well documented and can be viewed sociologically at both the macro and micro levels. In addition, these theoretical perspectives can be readily applied to help understand the health care situation in the United States.

A Functionalist Perspective on Health

Why do people commit suicide? What happens when students call teachers to say they cannot take an exam because they are sick? Why are patients faced with a bewildering array of health care providers? As we have seen throughout the text, functionalists point out that when everyone acts in accordance with shared values and norms, the social system is in equilibrium. Patterns of behavior related to health also follow this rule. Various aspects of social structure guide people in their choices of health-related behavior. In this section, three of these aspects will be viewed: suicide, the sick role, and health care delivery.

SOCIAL STRUCTURE AND SUICIDE We saw in Chapters 1 and 2 that Émile Durkheim's (1897/1964) monumental work, *Suicide*, paved the way for the beginnings of sociology as a science. This work may also be viewed as the first systematic study of medical sociology, because it showed that even the most intensely personal act imaginable, suicide, is rooted in social causes. Although Durkheim's original data focused on Europe, his findings are still applicable over a century later to patterns of suicide in the United States. According to Durkheim, when the usual norms of society are severely disrupted or become ineffective, and *anomie* (normlessness) prevails, the resulting stress causes some people to take their own lives. For example, refugees and asylum seekers fleeing from violence, war, and famine that will forever alter or even wipe out their communities experience mental health problems so severe that they have high risk for anomic suicide (Lindsey, 1990; Hingorani, 2001). The social structure embedded in the community that these people knew literally disappeared.

Durkheim also explains *altruistic* suicide among those who belong to societies that strongly bind the individual to the group and hold values that emphasize group solidarity. This social structure helps explain the high rates of suicide in Japan, where individual shame reflects dishonor on the family or other important social groups, thus justifying suicide for the good of the group. Rather than creating social disruption, functionalism would explain altruistic suicide as reinforcing social cohesion. It contrasts with *egoistic* suicide, which is committed by those who are socially isolated and strongly adhere to the value of individualism. High rates of suicide among elderly widowers in the United States may point to social detachment (Mineau et al., 2002). Coupled with role loss due to retirement, the death of their wives creates a void that is difficult to overcome.

All three types of suicide—anomic, altruistic, and egoistic—are explained by the power of social bonds, according to the functionalist perspective. Over a hundred years later research continues to support Durkheim's original hypothesis that social isolation puts people at a much higher risk for suicide (Kawachi, 2000:59). This perspective is also evident in the growing research suggesting that social support is linked, both physically and mentally, to good health, as social isolation is linked to poor health (Berkman et al., 2000). People with devastating diseases such as cancer adapt better and live longer when they have high levels of social support. When social support is lacking, people also engage in more risky behavior that has negative health consequences, such as overeating, nicotine addiction, heavy alcohol consumption, and lack of physical activity (Berkman, 2000; Wills & Filer, 2001). Functionalists emphasize that health and well-being are enhanced when the individual receives support within a society that is performing smoothly, effectively, and with little disturbance to social equilibrium.

THE SICK ROLE The second area where the functionalist approach to health is evident is the concept of the sick role. As identified by the classic work of Talcott Parsons (1951, 1964), the **sick role** describes those behaviors that are socially expected of a sick person according to prevailing norms. Like other roles, it consists of privileges and obligations defined by the individual and society. Because the sick role exempts people from their normal roles and is not deliberate, it is considered to be a legitimate form of social deviance. In the United States this legitimacy is accepted as long as the person intends to get well by seeking help if necessary. Medicine exerts a strong mechanism of social control. Some teachers will exempt a student from an exam only with a written statement by a physician. Thus, how each individual performs the sick role will be strongly influenced by role partners, such as family members, nurses, and physicians. In addition, the longer a person is released from his or her typical role obligations, the greater the strain on the social system.

The sick role works well in explaining temporary sickness according to American conceptions of medicine and how illness as deviance can be brought under social control. However, it presents several problems. It does not consider how people can actively participate

Functionalists say that the sick role is associated with rights and responsibilities. Children are allowed to have longer sick roles, more rights, and fewer responsibilities than adults when they are sick.

THEN AND NOW

The Fall and Rise? of Midwifery in America

For a hundred years in the United States, childbirth was completely female-centered. New mothers delivered their infants with the support of midwives. The norm was that mothers and midwives worked together—before, during, and after the delivery—to make certain that mothers were both emotionally and physically prepared for birth and early motherhood. They served as role models and emotional supports, and helped socialize women into the status of motherhood. But by the early 20th century, midwifery was virtually eliminated in the United States.

Once childbirth became medicalized, women were seen as unsuited for independent medical roles, even with evidence showing that midwives attended deliveries that were safe for both mother and child. Obstetrics practiced by men replaced midwifery practiced by women.

However, "adequacy of nature" is making a comeback in the momentum toward holistic health. Midwives are growing in number. Certified Nurse Midwives (CNM's), most of whom have master's degrees, are trained through approved nursing programs and are growing in numbers. Another route to midwifery includes licensing or certification not through nursing programs. What a midwife can do depends on the type of license and the local restrictions. But an alliance is being forged by some obstetricians who deliver high-risk babies and do more costly cesarean sections and nurse-midwives who are attracting those who desire a more natural birthing experience.

Certainly there is no dispute that midwifery is an acceptable alternative to conventional obstetrics, but only if there are no foreseen complications. Advances in obstetrics have saved the lives of mothers and their newborns during higher risk delivery situations.

Conflict theory suggests that the medicalization of childbirth and the social control brought with it was accepted as legitimate over time. The comeback of midwifery, tentative as it is, also can be explained by conflict theory. Midwives offer an alternative ideology—translated as an alternative view of procreation—that is gaining its own power. It is fascinating that this alternative view is also an ancient one.

1. From the perspective of conflict theory, what do you think the success will be for the comeback of midwifery in the United States?

2. What role does the public play in determining the practice rights of midwives, and how does this role impact the AMA's position on the subject?

Sources: Mumford, 1983:273; Wertz & Wertz, 1990; Langton, 1994; Rothman & Caschetta, 1995:67–68; http://kidsdirect.net/BD/pregnancy/midwife-faq.

---

in their own healing, how their own actions, such as cigarette smoking, create their illness, or how they succumb to illness due to hazards over which they have no control, such as carcinogens in their workplaces.

Another problem with the sick role is that it fits only what today would be described as a rather narrow range of illness. **Acute disease** is characterized by sudden onset, rapid peak, and limited duration, resulting in either recovery or death. Influenza, appendicitis, and pneumonia are examples. In contrast, **chronic disease** is characterized by gradual onset, long duration, little chance for complete recovery, and often death. AIDS, Alzheimer's disease, heart disease, asthma, and some forms of cancer fall into this category. Chronic diseases have replaced acute diseases as the major killers in most of the world, including the United States. Caring for the chronically ill patient, especially if care is guided by a holistic model, impacts the entire health care delivery process. For patients with certain chronic diseases, the sick role is permanent and may exempt people from role obligations for as long as they live.

HEALTH CARE DELIVERY: HOW EFFECTIVE IS IT?

The third health area in which the functionalist model can be applied is in evaluating the performance of the health care delivery system in the United States. If sickness causes social disruption, it is imperative that an organized, effective health system provides the highest quality care to everyone. Functionalists would support this claim by viewing health care improvements in public health, technological advances in medicine and pharmacology leading to curing acute diseases, higher remission rates of chronic diseases, and increased life expectancy. While functionalists would not deny the fact that the health care system in the United States is in a state of crisis and some of the population is not served well, they would suggest that drastic changes in the current health care system could be dysfunctional, creating more problems than solutions. Instead, functionalists would recommend a gradual shift from a marketplace approach that views health care as a privilege to one that views it as a right.

The functionalist perspective can be applied in some instances even to those who may not be served well in the current health care system—for example, the uninsured chronic patient. Project Concern is a model of care services that fits well with the functionalist perspective. It provides direct assistance to low-income, pediatric asthmatic patients; it has been successful in alleviating both the physical and psychological problems experienced by chronic patients and their families who have no health insurance (Horst, 1995). The strength of the program is tied to cost effectiveness, expansion of traditional medical social-work practices, and a coordinated approach emphasizing a health care team concept. By focusing on chronic patients who take on a sick role periodically, and the strengths of an existing system that is interdependent, coordinated, and allows for gradual change, the Project Concern model conforms to the functionalist perspective.

A Conflict Perspective on Health

Like functionalism, conflict theory provides a macro view and centers on several important aspects of social structure to explain health-related behavior. But unlike functionalism, the element of social structure conflict theorists focus on is power.

PROFESSIONAL AUTONOMY AND ENCROACHMENT One way in which conflict theory links the notion of power to health care is through the issue of professional autonomy and the control it brings. With the American Medical Association (AMA) as the key lobbying agency, the medical profession has retained absolute control and jurisdiction over health care in the United States. The basic principles of the AMA, established in 1934, include the key ideas that health

INTERNET CONNECTIONS

The debate continues about whether the United States of America should have a national health care plan. There are a number of web sites that provide more information on the topic. Go to Physicians for a National Health Program:

http://www.pnhp.org/

and Americans for Free Choice,

http://www.afcm.org/

Scroll down and click on ideas. After you have had the opportunity to peruse the Web sites, write a brief report listing what you perceive to be the advantages and disadvantages of a national health care plan. Are you personally in favor of national health care? Why or why not?

care and medical practice should be controlled by a self-regulating medical profession, charge on a fee-for-service basis, and that there should be no interference in the physician–patient relationship (Starr, 1982; Baker & Emanuel, 2000).

Once in control of the health care system, professional autonomy allowed the medical profession to ward off *encroachment*, the invasion by others who would also deliver health care. Some were simply eliminated from practice, such as healers who used religion, faith, or magic in treating disease. Others who were not eliminated were severely restricted, such as midwives and chiropractors. Most were subordinated, including nurses, optometrists, pharmacists, medical technicians, psychologists, and physical therapists. By eliminating any threat in the provision of health services by potential competitors, the professional autonomy of medicine was secured (Freund & McGuire, 1999; McKinlay, 1999).

Conflict theory argues that physician control of health care can be sustained as long as physicians have the power and resources to successfully keep others from encroaching on their terrain. Fueled by massive increases in health care cost, challenges to their dominance are now coming from many fronts. A "buyer's revolt" from the patients, government, and insurers has led to more public scrutiny of what physicians do (Light, 2000). When the cost of adequate health care rises beyond the means of more and more citizens, the public demands more control of the terms, conditions, and content of medicine as a whole.

A better educated public is also supporting allied health practitioners who believe in a team approach to healing and illness prevention (Debehnke & Decker, 2002). Encroaching on the dominance hierarchy of medicine, nonphysician specialists are challenging the control of medicine's technical core. For example, nurse practitioners have gradually increased their diagnostic and treatment roles and are performing tasks such as physical exams once only the prerogative of MDs. Not only does this free physicians to do more of the specialized medicine appropriate for their training, it allows nurses to expand their own professional domains to help increase their status vis-à-vis that of physicians (Glazer, 2000).

MEDICALIZATION In the United States the social power exerted by the profession of medicine has also allowed it almost complete control over the organization and delivery of health care, the authority of other health care practitioners, and the definitions of health and illness. Taken together, this power has resulted in **medicalization,** a process that legitimizes medical control over parts of a person's life (Conrad & Schneider, 1980). Through medicalization, medicine in the United States becomes a major institution of social control.

There has been a massive increase in the medicalization of all kinds of mental disorders, maladies, and personal problems. Eating disorders, alcohol and drug addiction, attention deficit disorder, shyness, and shoplifting are routinely categorized as medical problems. Physicians use antidepressant drugs to treat people who report they are "unhappy." Medicalization of unhappiness may be responsible for the statistic that depression in the United States has doubled in the past thirty years (Dworkin, 2001). Even racism has been medicalized. If racists are labeled as "sick," the battle against racism and discrimination as a broader social problem is weakened (Wellman, 2000). The medicalization of the "disorder" of unattractiveness encourages cosmetic surgery among women who are aware that attractiveness is associated with better jobs and attracting desirable men (Dellinger & Williams, 1997; Ancheta, 2002). Health professionals who might otherwise be consulted in managing these types of problems, such as clinical psychologists, nurse practitioners, and social workers, are marginalized in the system. While medicine offers essential therapeutic techniques, the conflict perspective argues that its power in defining illness, especially mental illness, only in biological terms restricts other sociocultural avenues for exploration.

SOCIAL CLASS AND HEALTH Another way conflict theory links power and health is by viewing illness among the various social classes. As discussed later, there is a strong and consistent association between social class and health—lower SES people have less access to health care, less health insurance, and a higher risk of getting sick and not recovering completely. To understand how conflict theory uses social class to analyze health, consider how health is maintained. In Marxist terms, capitalism places the responsibility for health on the individual and downplays collective solutions to health problems (Navarro, 1986; Waitzkin, 1989). When you need health care, you must seek it in a monopolistic system designed to maximize profits in a seller's market. Health-related products and services are marketed the same way as other products that are sold for profit (Morton, 2001). The massive increase in direct-to-consumer advertising of prescription drugs in the media, to the tune of over one *billion* dollars a year, attests to this marketing approach (Pinto, 2000). Conflict theorists also suggest that the bombardment of influence by the drug companies puts physicians and consumers at risk because it blurs the lines between advertising, marketing, and medical education (Sluzki, 2001). Drug companies rather than professionals become the teachers of health care.

Conflict theory maintains that much of our lifestyle is not under our control. Capitalist society limits the control workers have over their lives, both at work and outside of it. Lower SES people work at jobs they can get and live in places they can afford. This may mean working and living in areas with high health risks. Daily ingestion of pollutants from work in a factory coupled with repetitive, physically demanding tasks that offer little in the way of either autonomy or pay contribute to poor physical and mental health among lower SES groups (Amick & Lavis, 2000). Poor people often live near toxic waste dumps or hazardous landfills where the rent is cheap but the health risks are costly. Conflict theorists assert that what is attributed to a voluntary lifestyle can better be credited to involuntary poverty.

Symbolic Interactionism: The Social Construction of Health

Like the other theories, symbolic interactionism begins with the idea of health as a social concept. In defining health and illness, we also define the roles we play as health professionals and patients. To some extent, the sick role concept from functionalism fits with this model. The difference is that for symbolic interactionists, the sick role is not a passive, prescribed role, but one involving continued negotiation and role definitions. How we perceive health and respond to sickness are the results of social interaction.

Studies of people with diseases like arthritis, multiple sclerosis, or epilepsy, for example, find that beyond the disabling effects, there are profound changes to their identity. People are literally ripped from their previous, taken-for-granted daily lives and must reconstruct identity to regain a sense of control (Bury, 2000).

LABELING HEALTH AND ILLNESS In explaining health, symbolic interactionism rests on three key notions. The first is labeling. People label health and illness as conditions according to their unique understanding of a situation and how social audiences react to them. These labels are social constructions that can be altered, such as the stigma associated with certain illnesses. For example, although breast cancer is associated with issues of women's attractiveness, the disease itself is much less stigmatized today. Women with breast cancer perceive that they have high levels of emotional support. Women have come together to create a breast cancer movement, which has heightened public awareness and sensitivity to the issues women and their families face when confronted with the disease (Brenner, 2000). Changes in norms regarding smoking provide another example. By making the health hazards of smoking and secondhand smoke a public issue, smoking has been transformed from an acceptable to an unacceptable behavior in specific contexts, such as in theaters, in hospitals, on airplanes, and especially around children. Smoking as a right has been relabeled smoking as a privilege.

DEFINITION OF THE SITUATION: BELIEVING IN THE LABELS

The second notion that symbolic interactionists rely on to explain health is the definition of the situation and its associated concept of self-fulfilling prophecy (Chapter 6). While medical science, for example, may be skeptical of the empirical basis for faith healing, it cannot be easily dismissed as simply a medical fluke. In such cases the self-fulfilling prophecy works to the benefit of the patient. On the other hand, patients who believe they are beyond healing and thus do not seek help are more likely to suffer the most negative effects of their illness.

Symbolic interactionism is rooted in the remarkable power of the human mind to create reality and alter it to conform to preconceived beliefs. It is interesting that science may doubt this power in healing, but in an important way symbolic interactionism is at the heart of *all* science. Medical investigations must conform to rigid guidelines based on experimental design. In a *double-blind* procedure, neither the subjects nor those conducting the research know to which experimental condition a subject is assigned. This procedure is essential to protect against the *placebo effect*, that a change will occur because of the mere suggestion that it will occur.

In medical research to test the effects of drugs, for example, both the experimental group and the control group used for comparison receive what they think is a "drug." But the control group receives a placebo. Without the safeguard of the placebo, any changes in health could be attributed to the subjects believing the drug or therapy is working. This is a clear example of the power of the definition of the situation.

HEALTH-RELATED INTERACTIONS

The third idea from symbolic interactionism centers on the roles involved in health-related (social) interactions. In the intimate encounters involving health and illness, such role playing is critical for both patients and physicians. Patients want to be treated as whole persons and maintain a sense of dignity and control; they feel marginalized when physicians do not respond to personal concerns. Physicians must respect these rights but do so in an objective manner that allows them to retain the degree of control they believe is ultimately beneficial to the patient. Health-related interactions between physicians and patients that enhance a feeling of partnership and where patients are involved in their decision-making about their care help decrease marginalization (Meldrum & Hardy, 2001; Leibovici & Lievre, 2002; Mead & Hahn, 2002).

In addition to feeling marginalized, patients often feel depersonalized in interactions with health providers. This depersonalization has serious consequences for health and overall patient satisfaction, particularly if it leads to poor patient–provider communication (Ganz, 2002; Kurtz, 2002; Kleinman, 1988; Haas & Shaffir, 1993). Reducing the social distance between patient and provider also reduces misunderstandings. Good health care outcomes for ethnic minorities, lower SES patients, and non-heterosexual patients require knowledge and understanding of their subculture as well as awareness of the stereotypes health care providers carry with them every time such patients come for medical treatment (Feinberg, 2001; Chevannes, 2002; Fuller, 2002). When health care providers base their interactions with patients on cultural misconceptions, patients are put at risk. Hospital staff in emergency rooms in public hospitals informally evaluate patients according to their belief about how

Health facilities in the developing world are often primitive and staffed by volunteers of NGOs. However, the services they provide are vital to the health and well-being of the people in the communities they serve.

worthy the patients are, how legitimate their health problems are, and how much of their behavior is socially acceptable. Children, middle-class people, people who are injured during work or in sports, and those who have health insurance tend to communicate well with staff and receive more staff support and sympathy during their emergency room encounters. Understandably, these people would report higher levels of patient satisfaction than those who staff view as "less worthy," even if all patients have their medical needs met. Along with medical diagnosis, patient background makes a difference in ER care (Lockey & Hardern, 2001; Darby, 2002; Hazelett et al., 2002).

Research concludes that there is an enormous gap in the way physicians and other health professionals think about disease and the way patients experience it. Symbolic interactionism supports the idea that health care providers need to listen carefully to their patients and to learn from other disciplines about the complexity of the illness experience that is usually not present within the mainstream medicine they are taught (Umberson et al., 2000).

THE CHALLENGE OF INTERNATIONAL HEALTH

International health is an idea whose time has come. In 1977 the United Nations (U.N.) called for "the attainment by all citizens of the world by the year 2000 of a level of health that will permit them to lead a socially and economically productive life." The "Health for All by the Year 2000" (HFA2000) campaign was waged for over twenty years and has had many successes, such as cutting the mortality rate in half in the developing world (Figure 19.1). Much of this reduction is due to better sanitation and nutrition programs and massive immunization for infants and children that largely ended deaths to some communicable diseases in certain regions. A campaign goal to eradicate polio is projected to succeed by 2005, making polio the second disease in history—following smallpox—to be virtually wiped off the planet (UNICEF, 2002a). In 1998 the World Health Organization reaffirmed its commitment to continue to work on "health for all" in the new century. Since the HFA2000 initiative, the U.N. convened the 2000 Millennium Summit and the 2002 World Summit on Sustainable Development in partnership with other international relief and development agencies. These conferences set ambitious goals to reduce poverty in order to sustain good health (United Nations Development Program, 2000a, 2000b; Goodburn & Campbell, 2001; Johannesburg Summit, 2002; UNESCO, 2002). Goals of both summits include reducing under-5 mortality and maternal mortality by two-thirds and three-fourths respectively by 2015, reversing the spread of HIV/AIDS, halving the number of people without access to safe drinking water, reducing the maternal mortality rate by 75 percent by 2015, and phasing out chemicals harmful to health and environment by 2020. The sociological perspective can help evaluate the success of these ambitious goals, both globally and in the United States.

Concern for international health began as a humanitarian issue, but with the rise of global interdependence it has become a survival issue. A college stu-

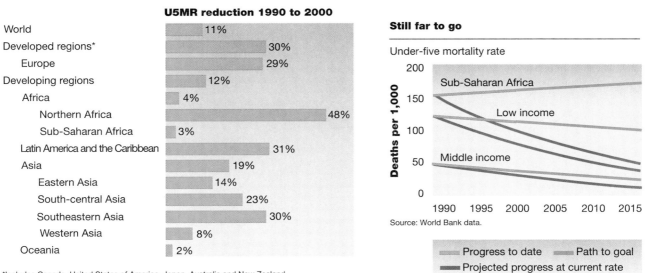

FIGURE 19.1 Progress for Under-Five Mortality Rate (U5MR) per 1,000 Live Births for 1990, 1995, 2000, and 2015 (Progress Needed to Reach Goal) by World Regions.

Sources: Adapted from United Nations Economic and Social Council, 2002; *World Bank Indicators,* 2002; http://www.developmentgoals.org/Child_Mortality.

GLOBAL CONNECTIONS

The AIDS Epidemic: Focus on Africa

Acquired Immunity Deficiency Syndrome (AIDS) is packed with cultural meaning. In the two decades since it erupted, it has become the worst of the global epidemics. There is no vaccine to prevent it, there is no cure for it, and care of its victims costs billions of dollars.

AIDS has emerged as a leading killer among young adults throughout the world and is spreading into what had been considered "safe" populations, such as married, heterosexual women with no history of drug use. In its path of destruction, infant mortality is rising and life expectancy is falling. In recent years life expectancy in some areas of sub-Saharan Africa has fallen by 10 years. Over 90 percent of people infected with HIV, the AIDS virus, are in the developing world. It is estimated that close to 40 million people are infected.

Sub-Saharan and Central Africa have the largest number of AIDS cases in the world. In Nigeria, more than 3 million people are estimated to be infected. In Uganda, rates are as high as 50 per 100,000 people in large cities and areas with high concentrations of migrant laborers. In South Africa 5 million people are living with AIDS, an astounding *1 in 9* of the population. Tests of pregnant women who come to clinics in Botswana, Zimbabwe, Congo, Cameroon, South Africa, and Uganda reveal rates for HIV in-

fection at 30 to 45 percent, up by as much as 5 percent in less than five years. Men pass it to their wives, who pass it to their babies. Other long-term health consequences involve the hunger and exploitation of remaining children and family members when parents die. Society also loses the strongest and most productive members of the labor force.

The condom is effective in the prevention of AIDS, but there are many cultural barriers to its use throughout the world. In Africa and Asia, the most common route of transmission is heterosexual, with half of all new HIV infections diagnosed in women. The year 2000 saw female AIDS victims exceeding males. Yet in these cultures, women have little power to alter sexual habits in their own families. Sexual intercourse is a husband's right, not to be vetoed by wives. Traditional African belief systems demand large families as ways to expand a lineage; childlessness and small families may be regarded as the work of evil spirits. Coupled with an AIDS epidemic in full force, the desire for large families leads to the worst possible outcome: family size larger than in most other areas of the world, increasing to millions the young Africans and their mothers who will be dying of AIDS.

The global AIDS crisis reflects what sociologists call a "functionalist challenge." In fighting AIDS, especially as a family disease, traditional values are compromised.

There is visible strain on social order. But more social disorder will occur if AIDS is left unchecked. To control the disease, culturally appropriate means must be developed that alter traditional values, especially regarding family size and the roles of women.

From the perspective of symbolic interactionism, the cultural meanings associated with AIDS need to be altered to fight the disease. AIDS has been labeled a "disease of the undeserving" because in the developed world, its first victims were gay men. Drug users were its later victims. The "undeserving" are now in the most impoverished regions of the world and include not only prostitutes but other heterosexual women whose only sex partner is their spouse. Isolating AIDS victims by labeling them undeserving denies the vulnerability and responsibility of the broader population. AIDS does not reflect national boundaries. It's increase in the world is a threat to everyone.

1. From the perspective of functionalism, what culturally acceptable guidelines can health workers use to prevent and treat AIDS in Africa?

2. From the perspective of symbolic interactionism, what can be done to alter the label of AIDS victims as undeserving?

Sources: Schiller et al., 1994; McGreal, 2002; UNAIDS, 2002.

dent in the U.S. Midwest or a subsistence farmer in Peru can be impacted by a cholera outbreak in North Africa, a nuclear accident in Russia, or the spread of AIDS in Thailand. Health policy is made by governments. By accepting WHO's definition of health, the governments of U.N. member nations also accept the idea that health is a fundamental human right and, as stated in the preamble to WHO's constitution, health is not restricted by race, religion, political belief, or economic or social condition.

Health and the Developing World

A half-hour airplane flight from Florida to Haiti represents a gap in life expectancy at birth of over nineteen years. Haiti is one of the globe's poorest countries, and like much of the developing world, it is characterized by high poverty rates that translate to malnourishment, lack of disease resistance, and about a 50 percent chance that children who survive to age 5 will live to see age 40. Preventable and treatable diseases, such as measles, are far more likely to be fatal in the developing world. Unclean water and poor sanitation are responsible for over 12 million global deaths per year, the vast majority of them from developing countries (United Nations Population Fund, 2002).

Countries with higher levels of economic development also have better overall health records (see Table 19.1). Countries of the developing world have shown major gains in increased LER and decreased IMR (see Figure 19.1). Between 1960 and 2000 the IMR gap between the developed and the developing world narrowed by half. But a chasm between the developed and developing world in IMR and LER still exists, and in many regions it actually widened. The AIDS epidemic is taking the lives of thousands of middle-aged parents throughout sub-Saharan Africa, which explains why 95

People whose lives depend on foraging for food and other resources from contaminated sources such as city dumps are susceptible to many health problems, such as diarrheal, parasitic, and respiratory diseases and skin infections. Children are the most vulnerable.

percent of the world's AIDS orphans live in this region (AVERT, 2002). Deaths due to malaria are increasing after having declined for several decades. In Africa every year, 2.5 million die of malaria, representing 90 percent of malaria deaths worldwide (Burka, 2002). In parts of the developed world only 6 out of 1,000 newborns die before age 5, but in the least developed countries, such as Afghanistan, Haiti, and Sudan, the rate is well over 150 per 1,000 children. Infant and child mortality are closely connected with the death of the mother due to childbirth (see Figure 19.2 on page 520). If a mother from a very poor family dies, her newborn may die because of starvation—her milk was the lifeblood of the infant. The lifetime chance of a women dying during childbirth in the developed world is 1 in 4,085; in the least developed countries worldwide it is 1 in 16 (UNICEF, 2002b). Overall, a person in a least developed country of the world can expect to live almost a third of a century less than one in a most developed country (World Bank, 2001; United Nations Population Fund, 2002).

In summarizing the state of the world's health, poverty is the world's biggest killer. Data from the World Health Report document the impact of poverty on health:

> Poverty is the main reason why babies are not vaccinated, why clean water and sanitation are not provided, why curative drugs and other treatments are unavailable and why mothers die in childbirth. It is the underlying cause of reduced life expectancy, handicap, disability and starvation. Millions of children under 5 years die from causes which could be prevented. . . . They die largely because of world indifference, but most of all they die because they are poor. (World Health Organization, 1995)

Although written a decade ago, the conclusions continue to hold true today. Given this stark reality, the Millennium Summit's goals rest on how the world will maximize health benefits with economic resources that are becoming more limited.

Health and the Developed World

The more developed countries of Western Europe, North America, and Japan enjoy health benefits unknown to most of the world's population. These countries share the health advantages that historically have accompanied the move from agricultural to industrial economies. This process is referred to as the *epidemiological transition*. In the process of this transition, the rates of population growth and IMR decrease considerably, with a corresponding rise in LER. Morbidity and mortality patterns are completely altered. Acute and infectious disease caused by famine and

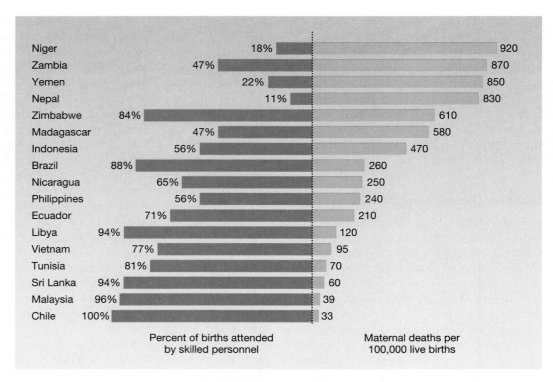

Country	Percent of births attended by skilled personnel	Maternal deaths per 100,000 live births
Niger	18%	920
Zambia	47%	870
Yemen	22%	850
Nepal	11%	830
Zimbabwe	84%	610
Madagascar	47%	580
Indonesia	56%	470
Brazil	88%	260
Nicaragua	65%	250
Philippines	56%	240
Ecuador	71%	210
Libya	94%	120
Vietnam	77%	95
Tunisia	81%	70
Sri Lanka	94%	60
Malaysia	96%	39
Chile	100%	33

FIGURE 19.2 Skilled Care at Delivery and Maternal Mortality Rate, Selected Countries in the Developing World, 1995–2000 Data.

Sources: Adapted from Sass & Ashford, 2002, and *World Development Indicators*, 2002.

malnourishment, pestilence, and poor sanitation are virtually eliminated as major threats to mortality, replaced by chronic and degenerative illnesses such as heart disease and cancer (Figure 19.3). Compared to the developing world, the United States is spectacularly healthy. But compared to many other developed countries, the United States lags far behind in critical health characteristics, such as IMR (see Table 19.1).

Most of the countries in the developed world have adopted policies that maximize advantages of the epidemiological transition, such as offering more housing options for the aged (Chapter 14). In every country of the developed world except for the United States, the major policy has been some form of **national health insurance** (NHI) financed through the government, which provides health care as a right of citizenship regardless of ability to pay.

National health insurance varies widely. Despite government funding, each government determines how much of the system is private and how much is public. At one extreme is Switzerland, which simply subsidizes private health insurance. At the other end are Britain, Spain, Italy, and Sweden, which have systems of nationalized hospitals with physicians paid directly by the government. Most other Western European countries, such as France, Germany, Belgium, and the Netherlands, fall in between. Despite govern-

ment involvement, most of these systems assure a great deal of autonomy in medical practice and allow physicians to take private patients on a fee-for-service basis (Schulte, 1998; Powell & Wessen, 1999). But even the richest countries are concerned about health care costs, which are increasing at rates that exceed gains in national resources.

Global Interdependence: Health and Technology

People in the developed world who can escape poverty cannot fully escape the health consequences of technology. Level of development is associated with degree of industrialization, urbanization, and technology. Because of this, the most developed nations of the world are especially vulnerable to the very processes that allow these economic advantages.

Initially, the population of the most developed nations is more vulnerable to radiation than the population of the developing world. Both worlds are exposed to radiation from natural sources such as the cosmos and radioactive materials in the earth's crust, but people in the developed world are also more likely to be exposed to artificial radiation from health care procedures, such as chest and dental x-rays.

Artificial sources of radiation are increasing mainly because of technology's impact on the ozone layer, industrial pollutants, problems related to nuclear energy, and contaminated soil and water. The earliest studies of the surviving victims of the atomic bomb blasts in Japan in 1945 showed an increased incidence of leukemia in the most heavily irradiated areas. Those who did not die of radiation poisoning within a few months of the explosions were likely to die of cancer or some cancer-related illness later in life (Wiesner, 1992; Akiyama et al., 1996). In 1979 at the Three Mile Island nuclear plant in Pennsylvania, a 52 percent meltdown of the reactor core occurred, making it the worst nuclear accident in the United States. Morbidity rates for those exposed to radiation up to twenty miles from the accident scene have been monitored ever since (Stencel, 1999). Nuclear fallout is associated with a weakened immune system. Nuclear testing in the United States and other Western industrialized countries between 1945 and 1965 is now held responsible for a rise in can-

cer and immune deficiency diseases in North America (National Cancer Institute, 1997; CNN, 2002).

Developing countries are suffering as well. In 1984 more than 2,500 people in Bhopal, India, died almost instantly and another 100,000 were injured when a deadly gas escaped from a faulty storage tank at a Union Carbide plant (Bryce, 1999). Air pollution—from both outdoor and indoor sources—kills more than 5 million people a year, the vast majority from the developing world (United Nations Population Fund, 2001). As nations in the developing world are used more as sites for dumping toxic waste and for building industrial plants where labor is cheap and safety standards are low, any "advantage" to a lesser level of development will be eliminated. The worst nuclear power accident in history occurred in 1986 at Chernobyl, in the former Soviet Union, when a reactor explosion caused the roof of the plant to cave in. Over 5 million people were affected by fallout, thirty-one officially recognized victims died in the accident,

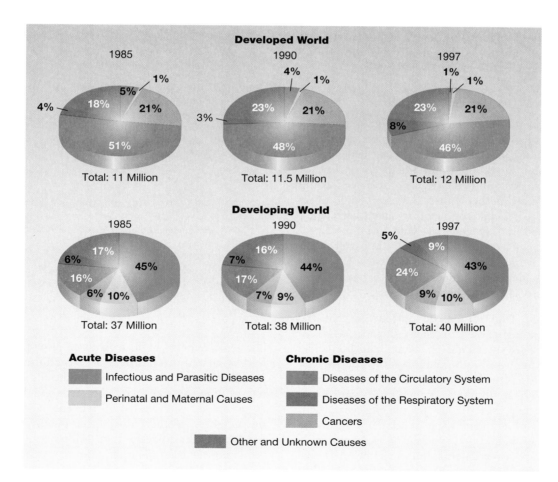

FIGURE 19.3 Main Causes of Death in the Developed and Developing World, Selected Years

Sources: Adapted from *World Health Report*, World Health Organization, 1998; http://www.who.int/1998/fig6e.jpg.

and two thousand cases of thyroid cancer have since resulted. With over 5 million people affected by the fallout, Chernobyl produced the biggest group of cancers ever from a single accident. Those who helped with the accident and those in the exposed surrounding areas still live in fear and uncertainty about their future. Farmland is also contaminated, with new areas of concentrated contamination "hot spots" still being discovered. The Russian media have labeled the mental health consequences of Chernobyl "radiophobia" because of the justifiable fear people have about radiation and its effects (BBC News, 2001; Environment News Service, 2001).

HEALTH IN THE UNITED STATES: LINKS TO DIVERSITY

Disease does not strike randomly. Key elements of social structure, such as social class, influence health. Another important factor that influences health is a person's unique set of social statuses within society. Demographers examine population characteristics that put some categories of people at higher risk for disease than others. Sociologists use demographic data to describe health in the United States.

The Demographics of Mortality

As we will see, mortality rates in the United States reflect what is happening globally. The most significant influence on the mortality rate has been the decline of infant deaths. A second trend has been decline of deaths due to acute diseases. Today, the three leading causes of death in the United States, chronic heart disease, cancer, and stroke, are correlated with aging and increased life expectancy (Table 19.2). This pattern reflects the benefits of medicine and better living conditions overall. But the downsides are the psychological and financial burdens for both patient and caregiver associated with chronic disease.

NONDISEASE DEATHS A third trend is that the fourteen leading causes of death include all three nondisease causes—suicide, accidents, and homicide. Many environmental and public health officials now view accidents as the most unrecognized public health problem. Vehicle accidents, including driving while intoxicated, kill over 40,000 people per year, with about the same number dying in accidents involving work, recreation, and fire. Nuclear disasters and toxic waste spills are also accidental but can show up as cancer deaths years later. Almost half the deaths of children are due to accidents, such as falls, drownings, and accidental shootings (Minino & Smith, 2001; McCaig & Ly, 2002).

Although deaths due to homicide have decreased to levels last seen in the 1960s, the mortality rate for

TABLE 19.2

Leading Causes of Death in the United States in the Twentieth Century

Rank	1990
1	Pneumonia and influenza
2	Tuberculosis
3	Gastroenteritis
4	Heart disease
5	Strokes
6	Kidney disease
7	Accidents
8	Cancers

Rank	Mid-Century
1	Heart disease
2	Cancers
3	Strokes
4	Accidents
5	Pneumonia and influenza
6	Disease of early infancy
7	Arteriosclerosis
8	Diabetes

Rank	2000
1	Diseases of heart
2	Malignant neoplasms (cancer)
3	Cerebrovascular diseases (stroke)
4	Chronic lower respiratory diseases
5	Accidents (unintentional injuries)
	Motor vehicle accidents
	All other accidents
6	Diabetes
7	Pneumonia and influenza
8	Alzheimer's disease
9	Kidney disease
10	Suicide
11	Chronic liver disease and cirrhosis
12	Hypertension and hypertensive renal disease
13	Pneumonitis (lung disease due to solids and liquids)
14	Homicide

Sources: Wright, 1997; *National Vital Statistics Reports,* 49(12): 5; Marks, 2002 (Center for Disease Control).

homicide remains high, with three clear trends. The first is that most murders are committed between people who know one another, especially in the context of domestic violence. The second is that murder is intraracial, with almost 90 percent of victims slain by members of their own race. Finally, murder is urban and firearm-related, most likely to be committed in poorer areas of larger cities (Canada, 1995; Fox & Zawitz, 2001).

Epidemiologists may add terrorism, including war, as another nondisease category in determining mortality rates. While they are intentional, deaths due to terrorist activities are probably counted as accidents or homicides. These include six deaths from the

1993 bombing of the World Trade Center in New York City, 168 people left dead and over 400 injured in the 1995 bombing of the federal building in Oklahoma City, and 2 dead (with 100 more injured) in the Olympic Park bombing in Atlanta in 1996. The addition of terrorism as a nondisease category has more urgency considering that the September 11 attacks on the World Trade Center and Pentagon and the four commercial flights involved in the attacks caused the deaths of 3,003 people (Spektor, 2002).

GENDER Females outlive males all over the world. In the United States, females live an average of about six years longer than males. When race is factored in, both African American and white females still have a clear advantage (Figure 19.4). Males have higher mortality rates at every stage of life (cited in Cockerham, 2001:42). Even at the prenatal stage, spontaneous abortions are more likely to occur with male fetuses. The first year of life is the most vulnerable for both genders, but infant mortality rates are higher for males. Males succumb earlier to virtually all causes of mortality, with the nondisease causes showing the greatest male–female differentials (Anderson, 2001).

Reasons for these differences are both biological and sociocultural. Females possess an additional X chromosome and protective sex hormones that are associated with a superior immune system. When men and women are diagnosed with the same disease, such as cancer, men are more likely to die from it than women. Added to this biological advantage is a gender-role benefit. Whereas the female gender role encourages women to seek help for health problems, the male gender role discourages men from seeking such help (see Chapter 13). For example, cancer therapies have benefited women in part because the disease is more likely to be diagnosed in earlier, more treatable stages. Gender roles also put more men than women in occupations that are potentially hazardous to their health, such as police and fire protection, the military, construction, and mining.

It is still unclear how much of the gender differential in mortality is biological and how much is sociocultural. For example, although adult men in all age groups continue to have significantly higher rates of cigarette smoking and excessive alcohol consumption, gender differences in rates for adolescent females and males are now almost equal (National Center for Health Statistics, 2001; SAMHSA, 2002). If these trends continue, mortality rates for men and women due to lung cancer, heart disease, and cirrhosis of the liver may also reach parity. However, even with the movement of women into such health-risky behaviors, gender differences in mortality rates have not changed significantly (Wasserman et al., 2000; Bolego et al., 2002; Maiese, 2002).

SES AND RACE There is a dramatic relationship between mortality and SES, both globally and in the United States. The higher the level of occupation, education, and income, the lower the death rate. Infant mortality rates are higher for poor children throughout the United States (Lynch et al., 1999; Berger, 2001). Since lower SES is associated with so many health-related factors, such as inadequate housing and nutrition, lack of health insurance, occupational risk, and exposure to violence, it is difficult to determine specific causes for this relationship (Ellen et al., 2001). As reflected in the IMR, we do know that SES is such a powerful indicator of mortality that the health of the poorest Americans is comparable to those in some developing countries.

Infant mortality is also associated with racial minority status. Infant, neonatal, and postnatal deaths for African Americans are double those for whites. Among African Americans, except for the very old, mortality rates are higher than for all racial groups. One of the most alarming statistics is that life expectancy for African Americans has shown less

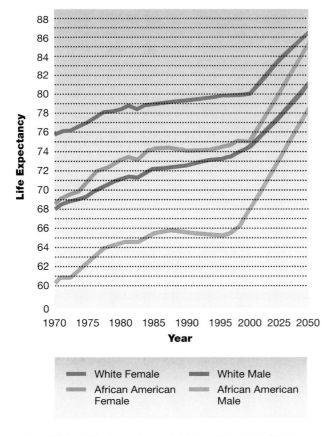

FIGURE 19.4 Life Expectancy at Birth in the United States by Gender and Race, (African American/White), 1970–2000 and Projections for 2025 and 2050.

Sources: National Projections Program, U.S. Bureau of the Census, 2000; *National Vital Statistics Reports* 59(12): 3, 2001 and 50(6): 4, 2002.

increase and may have decreased slightly in absolute terms (Smaje, 2000; Berger, 2001). Economic inequality and discrimination, which place a disproportionately higher number of African Americans and other people of color into lower SES groups, is a contributing factor (Shi & Starfield, 2001). However, persistent race differences are not simply a result of social class. Native Americans have lower neonatal death rates, indicating a possible genetic advantage, but higher postnatal rates, indicating a sociocultural (environmental) disadvantage. Both lower income Chinese Americans and higher income Japanese Americans have low infant mortality that is stable over a variety of conditions, suggesting a genetic benefit. However, even among those Americans who fall into "lower income" groups, Chinese and other Asians still have relatively higher incomes than African Americans, Latinos, and Native Americans (Hayward & Heron, 1999; U.S. Bureau of the Census, 2001: Table No. 37). While it may be difficult to determine the specific effects of SES and race on overall mortality rates, it appears that SES is nudging out race as the better explanation (Kaplan et al., 1999; Levine et al., 2001; Mathews et al., 2002).

The Demographics of Morbidity

If every disease could be calculated according to the proportion the mortality it causes, then mortality rates would be enough to determine the burden of illness on an individual, family, or community. But some chronic diseases, such as epilepsy, anemia, skin conditions, arthritis, and leprosy, cause substantial illness (morbidity) but little mortality. Also, since morbidity is largely subjective, measuring it is very difficult. Thus, in discussing morbidity it is important to use research that includes physical signs as well as those that are self-perceived.

GENDER A clear and consistent pattern emerges in gender differences in mortality and morbidity. Women have higher morbidity rates but live longer than men. Men have lower morbidity rates but do not live as long as women. One of the most striking features of these data is the trend of females to report more physical and mental disorders and use health services more than males. Females have more daily and transient illnesses such as colds and headaches and a higher prevalence of nonfatal chronic conditions such as arthritis, anemia, and sinusitis. Males have lower overall acute conditions but higher prevalence of chronic conditions that are life-threatening and associated with long-term disability, such as heart disease, emphysema, and atherosclerosis (Shinberg, 2001; Marks, 1996; U.S. Bureau of the Census, 1999).

Gender differences related to the use of alcohol and other drugs show up in morbidity as well as mor-

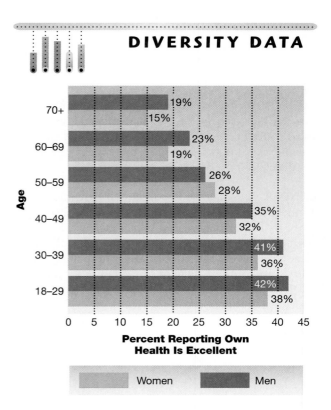

FIGURE 19.5 *People Reporting Their Own Health Is Excellent, by Age and Gender.* As expected, adults under 50 report significantly higher levels of excellent health than those over 50. At all age levels men report slightly higher levels of excellent health than women, but this difference has been declining in recent years. What do you think would be needed to further reduce the gender gap in excellent health? Could the age gap also be reduced?
Source: NORC. General Social Surveys, 1972–2000. Chicago: National Opinion Research Center, 2000. Reprinted by permission of NORC, Chicago, IL.

tality rates. Fetal Alcohol Syndrome is linked to mental retardation and low birthweight of infants. Men's higher rate of excessive alcohol use is a major factor in rape and spouse abuse. Women smoke less than men but have higher rates of nicotine addiction, with lung cancer rates doubling for women since the 1950s (MMWR, 2002a). When considering overall quality of life measures by gender, women appear to fare worse than men (Eckerman, 2000; Travis & Compton, 2001).

SES AND RACE People of low SES have higher morbidity rates for almost every disease or illness, especially in terms of higher rates of infectious and parasitic diseases and major mental disorders such as schizophrenia. Low income and low education are among the strongest predictors of poor health and the poor lifestyle outcomes it produces. This correlation

Health and the Workplace

In the United States, people are socialized into a strong work ethic. Work is healthy. It plays a valuable role in self-esteem, life satisfaction, and overall psychological well-being. The impact of work on personal identity is seen in Sigmund Freud's answer to the question of what a "normal" person should do well. His answer: "to love and to work." For Freud, normal psychological functioning emphasizes work and family. The ideal is to create an environment where work and family are not opposed to each other.

Achieving this ideal is becoming more difficult. Most couples voluntarily choose dual-earner roles, now the U.S. norm, but balancing work and family commitments may add to stress. In addition, occupational stress can be viewed as the overall illness people experience because of their work. The symptoms can be physical (headaches and fatigue), psychological (depression and anxiety), or behavioral (decreased job performance and low worker morale). Stress is associated with burnout, and is often accompanied by depression. People in the helping professions and those whose work involves life-threatening situations and fast decisions, such as in hospital emergency rooms, police and fire departments, and airlines, are particularly vulnerable to occupational stress. The "occupation" of college student is also susceptible. Illness plagues students near the end of the semester, when their physical and psychological resources are exhausted.

When violence enters the workplace, stress levels may rise so high that employees cannot continue on the job after the violent episode. In the last decade almost 2 million violent victimizations were committed against people at work. The increased incidence of shootings in schools and offices heightens fear of employees everywhere. In the wake of September 11 the insecurity and perceived vulnerability of those who work in public buildings, financial institutions, and any place where large groups of people gather skyrocketed. The 1980 and 1990s were called the stress decades in part because of work-related stress. Today it is the decade of work-related fear.

Sociologists emphasize the cultural value of work to explain its connection to health. Functionalism focuses on the problems that occur when the rapid changes in the workplace create too much anomie, which hurts smooth societal functioning. Conflict theory focuses on the struggle of workers at all levels to maintain their economic resources in an era of corporate downsizing and mergers. Symbolic interactionism focuses on how changing work roles are redefined and how we internalize these new labels. All three perspectives recognize that work and health and well-being are intimately connected.

1. What can employers do to create a workplace that enhances the physical and mental well-being of employees?

2. Which of the three theoretical perspectives best explains the fact that Americans find their work roles psychologically satisfying but also find them to be stressful?

Sources: Dunham, 2001; Siegrist, 2001; Theorell, 2001; Sygnatur & Toscano, 2000; McKenzie et al., 2002; OSHA, 2002.

---

has not decreased over time. SES is the vital link in understanding inequalities across diverse racial and ethnic groups in health and health care (Lantz et al., 2001; Thomas, 2001; Sturm et al., 2002).

With some notable exceptions, SES appears to be more important than race in explaining overall morbidity (see Figure 19.6 on page 526). African Americans have a higher rate of sickle cell anemia, which appears to be genetically based. They also experience higher rates of hypertension (high blood pressure) than whites, but those with low incomes have triple the rates of those who are more affluent. One earlier study suggested that this is due to the greater prevalence of obesity in the lower classes in general (Syme & Berkman, 1994). However, although African Americans have a higher rate of obesity than whites, the increase in obesity among all age and SES groups suggests that it is an "American" disease and not one of race or class. Obesity is increasing at such alarming rates that it is now considered an epidemic and a major health threat in the United States (Mokdad et al., 2000; Centers for Disease Control, 2002).

Finally, other research suggests that the culprit for the health disadvantage for African Americans and Latinos is psychological stress resulting from discrimination, cultural barriers, poor nutrition, and lack of medical care, many factors that can fall under the umbrella of racism (Pokras & Woo, 1999; Ruiz-Beltran & Kamau, 2001). As with mortality, while the reasons for these race and health differences are not completely clear, the better argument traces the differences to SES (Fiscella, 1999; Kawachi et al., 1999; Dearing et al., 2001; Ellen et al., 2001).

These race trends are in contrast to Asians and Pacific Islanders, who are the healthiest of all racial groups in the United States. And even with continu-

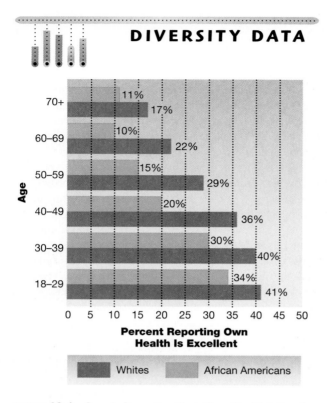

DIVERSITY DATA

Age

70+	11% / 17%
60–69	10% / 22%
50–59	15% / 29%
40–49	20% / 36%
30–39	30% / 40%
18–29	34% / 41%

0 5 10 15 20 25 30 35 40 45 50

Percent Reporting Own Health Is Excellent

■ Whites   ■ African Americans

FIGURE 19.6 People Reporting Their Own Health Is Excellent, by Age and Race. At all age levels whites are significantly more likely to report their own health as excellent compared to African Americans. What explains this major difference between the races? If income is taken into account, do you think that the race difference would disappear?

Source: NORC. General Social Surveys, 1972–2000. Chicago: National Opinion Research Center, 2000. Reprinted by permission of NORC, Chicago, IL.

ing health problems related to poverty, alcoholism, and accidents, there has been a significant improvement in the general health of Native Americans over the last half century (Indian Health Service, 1999; MMWR, 2002b). The evidence for a strong association between social conditions and morbidity remains, with SES as the most important indicator (Kawachi & Kennedy, 2002).

MENTAL ILLNESS Mental illness is one of the most serious health issues facing the United States, yet the public has little objective information about it. The scope of the problem is reflected in prevalence estimates. Excluding mental retardation, if mental illness is defined as those who exhibit symptoms severe enough to require ongoing treatment or hospitalization, about 15 percent of Americans have some type of mental illness. However, as many as 80 percent suf-

fer milder psychiatric symptoms where coping with everyday life becomes difficult due to stress, anxiety, or depression.

For those who do seek help, treatment ranges from large numbers in outpatient community facilities or private therapists' offices to smaller numbers who are institutionalized for severe disorders and to the vast majority who receive no treatment. Mental illness has physical, psychological, and sociocultural causes. Despite the complexities, over fifty years of research provides a good overview of the social epidemiology of mental illness (Chapter 8).

LIFE CONNECTIONS

Alternative Medicine in the United States

The number of Americans seeking out alternatives to conventional medicine is growing rapidly. They are referred to as "alternative medicine" because they are rarely encountered by medical students and seldom used in conventional medical treatment in hospitals (Cited in Weitz, 2001:379). Three important factors have fueled the trend toward alternative medicine. First, Americans are much more educated about health overall and take more responsibility for managing their health than in the past. In turn, physician dominance over patients is being challenged. Second, rapidly increasing multicultural diversity in the United States translates to a search for medical treatment consistent with various cultures and belief systems. Third, a holistic health model is rapidly making its way into public consciousness about what optimal health and health care should be.

Therapies such as herbal remedies, megavitamins, guided imagery, massage, acupuncture, yoga, chiropractic, and faith healing are included in alternative medicine. Medical doctors who integrate alternative and conventional medicine, who refer patients to alternative healers such as chiropractors or massage therapists, or who treat patients with pharmaceuticals as well as herbal and vitamin products do so outside of what they were taught in medical school. These physicians may choose alternative medicine for patients whose mainstream medical options have been exhausted because of their personal experiences with illness or because they embrace the holistic health model (Csordas & Kleinman, 1996; Gevitz, 1998).

Close to 100 million Americans use some form of alternative medicine, an increase of 20 million since 1990 (Grady, 1998; Fontanarosa et al., 2000). Today *most* Americans use vitamins and herbal supplements, experiment with diets outside of mainstream nutritional practices, engage in relaxation and exercise

The poorest of the poor are often homeless people. Poverty and homelessness are linked to high rates of infectious disease and mental disorders.

techniques they judge to be healthful, or seek out culturally supportive nonmedical people who offer a range of health-related assistance. Given these large numbers and the fact that people continue to see their physicians even when engaging in these practices, the term *complementary-alternative medicine* (CAM) is making its way into the research literature on the subject. Most people seek out CAM mainly to prevent illness or supplement physician prescribed therapies (Jones et al., 2001; O'Connor & Huford, 2001; Wellman et al., 2001). Although they continue to see their physicians, many patients do not tell their physicians they are using CAM (Adler, 2001; Mundell, 2002).

CAM is usually not covered by health insurance but is much less costly. The people who use such therapies are generally upper income and college educated—those who do have insurance and can afford conventional treatment. Users of these therapies are also more likely to be female, older, and have chronic health problems, a pattern found both in England and the United States. They choose CAM largely because they believe in its ease, effectiveness, and naturalness, and are treated as whole persons by those who provide it (Sharma, 1996; Eisenberg et al., 1998; Kessler et al., 2001; Vincent & Furnham, 2001).

Mainstream medicine can no longer ignore the statistics on CAM users and the potential for serious health consequences when patients are reluctant to discuss these practices with their physicians (McCarthy, 2002). The National Institutes of Health has established the National Center for Complementary and Alternative Medicine and in league with the American Medical Association is conducting research to determine the scientific basis of CAM. Through scientific research, some alternative therapies have

been reported not to work (for example, chiropractic manipulation for tension headaches and acupuncture for nerve damage caused by HIV), and some have been reported to work; such as yoga (for wrist pain associated with carpal tunnel syndrome), Chinese herbs (for hard-to-treat inflammatory bowel syndrome and rheumatoid arthritis), and acupuncture (for nausea associated with chemotherapy) (Grady, 1998; National Institutes of Health, 2002; Tao et al., 2002).

A key aspect of the scientific debate between CAM and conventional medicine has to do with the concern that alternative medicine is led by unlicensed practitioners who offer fraudulent, unsafe, and untested techniques for financial gain—referred to as "quackery" in healing. The AMA funds a special unit with the goal of investigating quackery, fraud, and malpractice among both alternative healers and MDs. It is probable that even with ongoing research supporting some CAM claims, tighter medical control on CAM is on the horizon (Marwick, 2002).

Holistic Health

It is apparent that beliefs about alternative medicine are altering patterns of health care practices among Americans. Close to one thousand licensed physicians belong to the American Holistic Medical Association—open only to licensed physicians—and the number is expected to increase (Weitz, 2001; AHMA, 2002). Sociologists and social epidemiologists have been in the forefront of providing data to the health community, focusing on the relationship between social life and health. One result is that there is understanding among physicians and the public that a "magic pill" will not be found for the chronic diseases

The health care crisis in the United States brings many diverse groups together to protest the high cost of health insurance that puts health care out of reach for many people. Groups representing women, racial minorities, and senior citizens are especially vocal—and powerful—in these protests.

that plague the United States and the world. The holistic health approach does not abandon the search for cures, but recognizes that health and health care need to be considered in terms of disease prevention and in light of the sociocultural circumstances of all patients.

SOCIETY CONNECTIONS

The Health Care Crisis

Health care in the United States is said to be in crisis. Of the many factors contributing to the crisis, the three most often cited are cost (the United States spends more on health care than any other country in the world, and health care costs continue to rise, outstripping inflation), access (a larger number of Americans have no health insurance and cannot get adequate health care in public or charitable facilities), and organization (health care occurs in a complex and confusing system of providers and facilities) (see Figures 19.7 and 19.8). Sociologists clearly demonstrate the interdependence of these three issues.

Health care has developed in response to emerging needs rather than to a rational planning process. In other words, the evolving health care system is crisis-oriented. Two factors help explain this evolution. First, the ways the crises (needs) are met are consistent with the values of the United States. For example, the organization of health care delivery reflects an American value system that emphasizes individualism and choice in a capitalistic economy. Second, health care has moved from a model where general practitioners

(physicians) provided almost all services to one in which most practitioners are now specialists, and physicians represent only a very small minority of all health care providers. This situation is tied to the fact that health care is information- and technology-driven. It is impossible for any one type of health care provider to have all of the knowledge now deemed necessary to treat many, if not most, patients. Both of these factors have created a uniquely American health system that has profound consequences for patient care.

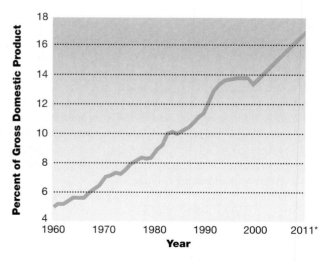

FIGURE 19.7 **National Health Expenditures as a Percentage of Gross Domestic Product (GDP), 1960–2002, and Projected 2011.**

Sources: Adapted from Centers for Medicare and Medicaid Services, 2002; Federal Reserve Bank of New York, 2002; Kaiser Family Foundation, 2002c: 6.

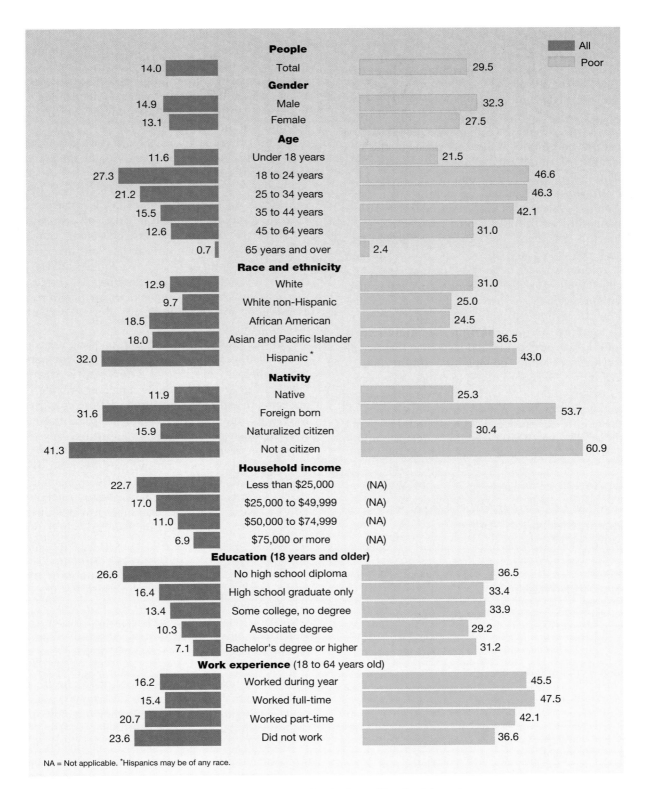

People

	All	Poor
Total	14.0	29.5

Gender

	All	Poor
Male	14.9	32.3
Female	13.1	27.5

Age

	All	Poor
Under 18 years	11.6	21.5
18 to 24 years	27.3	46.6
25 to 34 years	21.2	46.3
35 to 44 years	15.5	42.1
45 to 64 years	12.6	31.0
65 years and over	0.7	2.4

Race and ethnicity

	All	Poor
White	12.9	31.0
White non-Hispanic	9.7	25.0
African American	18.5	24.5
Asian and Pacific Islander	18.0	36.5
Hispanic*	32.0	43.0

Nativity

	All	Poor
Native	11.9	25.3
Foreign born	31.6	53.7
Naturalized citizen	15.9	30.4
Not a citizen	41.3	60.9

Household income

	All	Poor
Less than $25,000	22.7	(NA)
$25,000 to $49,999	17.0	(NA)
$50,000 to $74,999	11.0	(NA)
$75,000 or more	6.9	(NA)

Education (18 years and older)

	All	Poor
No high school diploma	26.6	36.5
High school graduate only	16.4	33.4
Some college, no degree	13.4	33.9
Associate degree	10.3	29.2
Bachelor's degree or higher	7.1	31.2

Work experience (18 to 64 years old)

	All	Poor
Worked during year	16.2	45.5
Worked full-time	15.4	47.5
Worked part-time	20.7	42.1
Did not work	23.6	36.6

NA = Not applicable. *Hispanics may be of any race.

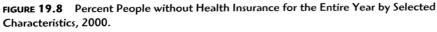

FIGURE 19.8 Percent People without Health Insurance for the Entire Year by Selected Characteristics, 2000.

Source: Mills, 2001: 5 (U.S. Bureau of the Census).

Cost and Access

The health care crisis is fundamentally a financial one. The technology, skill, and facilities to both treat and cure disease are available. When cure is impossible, the knowledge and compassion necessary for ongoing care are also available. Although the distribution of providers is uneven, there are enough to serve the current and future health care needs of the U.S. population. As noted in the opening vignettes, the problem is that these vast resources are reserved primarily for those who can pay for them.

About 10 percent of children under age 18 and about one-fifth of people 18 to 64 have no health insurance (Ni & Cohen, 2002). Over one-third of people under 65 who are in poverty and over 60 percent of all children who are defined as "poor or near poor" are uninsured (Table 19.3). About 60 percent of people without health insurance work full time, over one-third who are the "working poor" who receive no health insurance as a benefit from their employers or cannot afford even the minimal insurance they are offered (Kaiser Family Foundation, 2001a; 2001b). Lack of insurance is not limited to the poor, however, since many who do not have health insurance are well above the poverty line. However, these people could be "made poor" because coverage is climbing beyond their reach (Toner & Stolberg, 2002). People without

insurance also include the chronically ill and those with preexisting medical conditions. Without adequate health insurance, those who need health care try to receive help from public and charitable institutions, which are overburdened, understaffed, and under the constant threat that funding cuts will curtail or eliminate their programs.

Unequal access to health care is already a fact of life for many Americans. These people illustrate the problem of *allocative health care rationing* based on lack of insurance and high cost (Conrad, 1993). Health care rationing involves budget caps, insurance protocols, and limiting treatment by type and age. As indicated by the opening vignette, rationing translates into incredibly difficult ethical decisions determining who lives and who dies (Light & Hughes, 2001). Not only is the doctor–patient relationship harmed, but the most vulnerable segments of our population, such as the poor and the elderly, are prevented from receiving treatment.

Vulnerability of such groups is heightened because health care is rendered on a **fee-for-service** basis, where the patient pays for each service provided. Even when charitable agencies provide care, patients are expected to pay some of the cost. In this way, health care is a commodity, and patients are customers who pay for this commodity like any other product or service.

In reality, the cost of health care has risen so dramatically that fees cannot be paid for by patients directly. Most fees are billed to *third-party payers*, typically consisting of private insurance, provided through employers or purchased independently, and public agencies. Most patients pay some out-of-pocket expenses as copayments for third-party coverage.

The rising cost of health care can also be traced to the development of a system in which hospitals and providers have been allowed to set their own fees and third-party payers have been expected to pay them. When combined with the medicalization trend, the fee-for-service system encourages unnecessary services because of the profit motive. Hospital services continue to take the largest piece of the health care dollar (Figure 19.9). Physicians determine which patients get admitted and how long they stay. Any interference with this process by third-party groups is seen as an assault on the doctor–patient relationship, limiting patients in the choice of their physician, and an impediment to quality care. The system thus upholds the values of individualism, choice, and profit.

The American Medical Association originally resisted the passage of any legislation that was believed to endanger physician autonomy in a fee-for-service system, including workmen's compensation and Social Security at its early stages. As it became clear that a growing segment of the population was excluded from quality health care and some excluded from any

TABLE 19.3

Key Health Characteristics by Selected Race in the United States, 1990, 1995, 2000

	1990	1995	2000
Not Covered by Health Insurance			
White	12.9	14.2	12.9
African American	19.7	21.0	18.5
Hispanic*	32.5	33.3	32.0
Asian and Pacific Islanders	17.0	20.5	18.0
Infant Mortality Rate			
White	7.6	6.3	5.7
African American	18.0	14.7	13.6
Hispanic*	7.5	6.3	5.6
Asian and Pacific Islanders	6.6	5.3	4.9
Native American	13.1	9.0	8.3
Low Birth Weight			
White	5.7	6.2	6.2
African American	13.3	13.1	13.0
Maternal Mortality Rate			
White	5.4	4.2	5.8**
African American	22.4	22.1	20.8**

*Hispanics may be of any race.
**1997 data.
Sources: Mills, 2001 (U.S. Bureau of the Census); Mathews et al., 2002 (*National Vital Statistics Reports*); MMWR, 2002: 4.

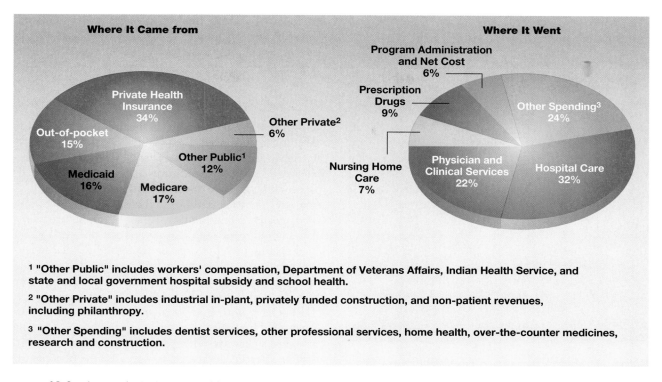

Where It Came from

Private Health Insurance 34%

Out-of-pocket 15%

Other Private[2] 6%

Other Public[1] 12%

Medicaid 16%

Medicare 17%

Where It Went

Program Administration and Net Cost 6%

Prescription Drugs 9%

Other Spending[3] 24%

Nursing Home Care 7%

Physician and Clinical Services 22%

Hospital Care 32%

[1] "Other Public" includes workers' compensation, Department of Veterans Affairs, Indian Health Service, and state and local government hospital subsidy and school health.

[2] "Other Private" includes industrial in-plant, privately funded construction, and non-patient revenues, including philanthropy.

[3] "Other Spending" includes dentist services, other professional services, home health, over-the-counter medicines, research and construction.

FIGURE 19.9 America's Health Dollar, 2000.

Source: Centers for Medicare and Medicaid Services, Office of the Actuary, National Health Statistics Group, 2002.

health care, and despite continued AMA resistance, two major pieces of federal legislation were enacted—Medicare and Medicaid. These programs have been a financial boon for health care providers.

MEDICARE Enacted in 1965 during the presidency of Lyndon B. Johnson, **Medicare** is a health insurance program funded through Social Security primarily for those age 65 and over, but with provisions for covering people of any age who have certain disabilities. Medicare is *not* welfare. It is the only program that has any resemblance to the much more comprehensive national health insurance programs in the rest of the developed world (Derickson, 2002). Part A of Medicare is premium free for most enrollees. Part B is an option paid largely by premiums of enrollees. In 2002 the monthly premium for Part B was $54, up from 45.50 in 2000 (Medicare, 2002). For those on limited incomes, even a $10 increase can become a burden when the choice is between paying rent or paying for health coverage, but almost all enrollees take Part B. Medicare to date does not pay for prescription drugs, but Congress will soon pass legislation offering some coverage. Medicare pays less than half of the total health care costs of the elderly, but it dramatically increased their health coverage and is responsible for cutting the poverty rate of the people over age 65 in half since the 1960s (DeLew, Nancy, 2000; Myers, 2000).

MEDICAID Unlike Medicare, **Medicaid** is a joint federal and state welfare program that provides medical assistance for certain people of any age with very low income. Medicaid is the third largest source of health insurance in the United States after employer coverage and Medicare. People move on and off Medicaid within any given year because their income and thus their eligibility changes. With higher employment rates and the downturn in the U.S. economy, Medicaid enrollees are expected to increase over the next several years beyond the original 1 percent forecast in 2000 (*American Medical News*, 2002). However, more stringent eligibility requirements may serve to offset the increase.

Of the approximately 44 million Medicaid recipients today, about half are children, and the other half are adults, including elderly, blind, and disabled individuals. For the elderly, Medicaid provides for long-term (nursing home) care, but only after a person "spends down" assets to get to an "acceptable" poverty level. Although the huge significance of Medicaid covering some health needs of the poor cannot be overstated, the majority of recipients today include the working poor and those made poor by health care costs due to disability, chronic illness, and custodial care needed in old age (HCFA, 2000; Kaiser Family Foundation, 2001b). Most poor and near poor people are not covered by Medicaid or any other private or public health insurance.

Medicare provides some services, such as rehabilitation and physical therapy, that allow the elderly to remain in their homes. These are less costly and more satisfying than long-term nursing home care.

Organization

Health care in the United States is delivered through a multibillion dollar industry consisting of hospitals, a complex array of outpatient facilities, and practitioners who are relatively autonomous in how they choose to deliver their services. These practitioners include those who deliver direct patient care, such as nurses and physicians, and those who organize the care that is delivered, such as hospital and home health administrators.

Fueled by a public with a great deal of faith in medical technology, the complexity of health care organization and the expansion of medical knowledge and technology has shaped how and where physicians practice and the health labor force as a whole (Mechanic, 2002). Total patient care at all stages—prevention, treatment, cure, and care—now requires the involvement of a number of specialized personnel. Optimal health care requires the coordination of such services to avoid unnecessary duplication.

The organization of health care delivery into autonomous, fragmented, self-regulated units often prevents this ideal. Patients are routinely shuffled from one provider to another and can literally get lost in the process. Duplicate medical and lab tests cause patient discomfort and drive up costs. Specialization also prompts an oversupply of physicians in some specialties, such as surgery, and an undersupply in others, such as general medicine. Research also shows that there is such an oversupply of physician specialists in

large urban areas that supply is driving demand. Health care spending is not only much higher in places with a glut of doctors but higher spending does not translate to better health overall (Kolata, 2002).

Toward Health Care Reform

Government involvement in health care, especially Medicare, has been financially lucrative for physicians, insurance companies, and hospitals. But skyrocketing health expenditures and the drive for a balanced budget have focused on cost containment. A major effort to curtail hospital costs was the initiation of *diagnosis-related groups* (DRGs). Hospitals are paid a fixed amount for each diagnosis, regardless of the actual cost incurred. Hospitals have the financial incentive to move patients in and out of the hospital quickly, since they can keep the difference if they spend less than the designated DRG allowance. DRGs have both functional and dysfunctional consequences. Home health services expand because people who are sicker are released earlier from hospitals and still need care. Medicare has increased the benefits for home health in order to meet these needs. Hospitals also take advantage of the system by avoiding patients with "less profitable" DRGs.

MANAGED CARE Cost-cutting is the major reason for the managed care trend in the United States. **Managed care** is a health care delivery plan designed to cut costs by requiring authorization prior to consulting a specialist, undergoing expensive tests, or hospitalization. Unlike traditional fee-for-service health care where a person with insurance could go to almost any doctor or hospital and then submit a claim for reimbursement, managed care plans have much more control over the health care choices of both patients and physicians. Physicians who contract with the plans agree to use the health care providers in the managed care network, and patients agree to use network providers for most of their health care. Most Americans who have health insurance from all sources, employer-sponsored or government, are enrolled in some type of managed care plan (NCQA, 2001).

Managed care plans differ according to how services are organized and how bills are paid. The most common plan is the **health maintenance organization (HMO).** HMOs are prepaid health plans offering comprehensive health care where physicians and other providers are either independently contracted or salaried employees of the HMO. Employers find HMOs appealing because they can buy services for even thousands of employees and decide on the range of care they can receive under the plan. Compared to traditional insurance, HMO health care costs to both employers and employees are cheaper. There are over 500 HMOs enrolling about 80 million members in the

United States (NCQA, 2001; *American Medical News*, 2002). HMOs provided the prototype for the emergence of other types of managed care plans. The *preferred provider organization* (PPO) is a plan in which employers buy discounted group health insurance packages that send employees to certain physicians and hospitals. There is also a *point of service* (POS) plan, which combines care in the network with some care outside the network. Most workers who are insured through their employers are in some type of managed care, with about half in PPOs, one-fifth in "standard" HMOs, and another one-fifth in POS plans (Kaiser Family Foundation, 2002). Nearly all managed care plans rely on general practitioners rather than more costly specialists, and they are expected to keep expenses low by keeping patients healthy.

How successful is managed care? It is clear that managed care plans are far less expensive than traditional insurance for enrollees and their employers. Physicians employed directly with HMOs or whose private practices are geared to managed care contracts have less demanding work schedules and less cost for maintaining their practices or starting new ones, and a steady source of paying patients is a major incentive with the current physician surplus.

But patients in managed care plans express dissatisfaction with limited health care choices as well as mistrust related to denial of coverage for catastrophic illnesses and putting company profits before patient needs (Goold & Klipp, 2002). Health insurance and out-of-pocket patient payments for services continue to rise at the same time that options shrink. Many patients who need specialized care often go unserved. Physicians complain that the doctor–patient relationship is intruded upon by too many regulations and that managed care plans limit autonomy (Scott et al., 2000). The rising dissatisfaction with managed care is likely responsible for the 1 percent to 2 percent decrease in number of people enrolled in HMOs over the last several years (*American Medical News*, 2002).

THE BUSH HEALTH INITIATIVES Although health care is a stated priority of President Bush, his health care initiatives are geared more to reforming specific sectors of health care than to overhauling it. The common themes of these initiatives are privatization and choice. For example, he believes consumers should be able to set aside money in tax-free medical savings accounts and that tax laws should change to help more people afford health insurance. He opposes national health insurance but believes that Medicare should be expanded to include coverage equal to what is available from private insurers. Prescription drug coverage would be provided as well. He has developed Medicare+Choice demonstration programs in about half the states modeled after PPOs; these programs offer access to a wider network of providers at lower cost than were previously available to Medicare beneficiaries (Issues, 2002; *HHS News*, 2002; White House, 2002). The success of initiatives related to privitization remains to be determined (Caro, 2001).

CANADA'S HEALTH CARE SYSTEM Because of similar political, cultural, and geographical features, the Canadian system of health care has been carefully scrutinized by policymakers in the United States as a potential model. The publicly administered Canadian National Health Insurance (CNHI) program covers all legal residents and all medically necessary services provided by a physician, including hospitalization and mental health services. Funding includes federal transfers favoring poor provinces, general provincial revenues, employer payroll taxes, and insurance premiums. No one is denied coverage, and special assistance is provided for those with low incomes. Similar to the United States, most hospitals are not government owned but profit-oriented, and physicians are reimbursed on a fee-for-service basis. A key difference is that hospital budgets and physician fees are negotiated in CNHI (Goering, 2000; Health Canada, 2001).

How successful is the Canadian model? Canada has been more successful than the United States in controlling costs, as reflected by percent of health cost per capita (Table 19.4). IMR and LER are also better in Canada (see Table 19.1). In addition, through federal-provincial effort and citizen participation in regional authorities, Canada's system has

TABLE 19.4

Total Expenditures on Health Per Capita, 2000. Selected Countries in the Developed World (In U.S. $)

Rank	Country	Per capita $
1	**United States**	4631
2	Switzerland	3222
3	Germany	2748
4	Iceland	2608
5	**Canada**	2535
6	Denmark	2420
7	Norway	2362
8	France	2349
9	Belgium	2269
10	Netherlands	2246
11	Australia	2211
12	Austria	2162
13	Italy	2032
14	Japan	2012
15	United Kingdom	1763
16	Finland	1664
17	Portugal	1441
18	Spain	155

Source: OECD Health Data, 2002: Table 9.

increased both equity and access to health care (Frankish et al., 2002). While quality is difficult to measure, the charge that American citizens would receive inferior medical care if universal coverage was in place is hard to justify given these comparisons.

HEALTH FOR ALL Regardless of which models are used and which elements are selected from them, it is clear that some type of health care reform is necessary and desired by the American public. The reform will account for a unique American value system in which both social and economic profit are demanded (Geyman, 2002). Underserved people will be served in a market-driven health care system. From a sociological perspective, conflict theory would support the notion that the health care system needs a major overhaul to make it more equitable. Bush's initiatives are more supportive of functionalism (the health care system is effective but some reform is needed to make it more equitable). Both perspectives agree that the health care dollar needs to be used more effectively (more money may not translate to better or more equitable health care). With issues such as drug coverage, a patient's bill of rights, inequality in health care access, and poverty due to the cost of health care, the drive

INTERNET CONNECTIONS

In the text there is a discussion about the health status of Americans. Go to The National Center for Health Statistics,

http://www.cdc.gov/nchs/

and click on the atlas of United States Mortality and some other links. Write a short report on the demographics of mortality. What are the regional patterns? Make sure to explain the patterns from the perspective of sociology.

toward a national health insurance program as a right for all Americans is gaining momentum (Gorin, 2001; Oberlander & Marmor, 2001; LeRoy, 2002). The "Health for All 2000" campaign is an initiative that applies as much to the United States as to the global community.

SUMMARY

1. The World Health Organization (WHO) defines health holistically, as a state of complete physical, mental, and social well-being. Health is a fundamental human right.

2. Health is often measured in terms of a population's mortality rate (the percentage of people who die every year). Globally, the two most important indicators of health are the infant mortality rate (IMR) and the life expectancy rate at birth (LER).

3. Epidemiology is the study of the causes and distribution of disease and disability in a given population. Epidemiologists are concerned with both the incidence of disease (the number of new cases reported over time) and the prevalence of disease (the total number of cases per period).

4. Functionalists view health as contributing to social equilibrium, and sickness contributing to disequilibrium. Émile Durkheim thought behaviors like suicide were caused by a lack of social sup-

port; Talcott Parsons identified the sick role as behaviors expected when a person is ill—a form of legitimate deviance.

5. Conflict theorists focus on power and social class to explain health care inequality. The professional autonomy of physicians gives them a great deal of power over definitions of disease and how health care is delivered. Lower SES people have less access to health care and insurance, and higher risk of sickness.

6. Symbolic interactionists see health as a social concept. The sick role is a negotiated one. Both physicians and patients label health and illness according to their own beliefs and act according to the labels. The interactions between patients and physicians are socially constructed.

7. A country's level of economic development has an enormous impact on health. Infant mortality rates are much higher, and life expectancy is much

lower, in developing countries than in developed nations, due mainly to poverty and a high rate of population growth. The developed world enjoys better health overall. Except for the United States, countries in the developed world provide national health insurance. But global interdependence and sources of risk such as radiation and pollution puts those in all countries at health risk.

8. In the United States, the leading causes of death are chronic disease and nondiseases, such as suicide, accidents, and homicide. Mortality rates are influenced by gender and race—women tend to live longer than men, and whites to live longer than African Americans. SES is the strongest influence on mortality rates—people of lower SES have higher mortality rates.

9. Women have higher morbidity (sickness) rates than men, though their mortality rate is lower. Race has some influence on morbidity, but SES is a stronger influence.

10. About 15 percent of Americans suffer from severe mental illness, which, like morbidity rates overall, is higher among people of lower SES.

11. Linked to holistic health, alternative medicine, such as chiropractic, acupuncture, and guided imagery, is growing in popularity. Those who use

alternative medicine tend to be middle class, educated, and using it for prevention of illness or for chronic illness; at the same time, they continue to see their physicians.

12. Though the United States spends more on health care than any other nation, millions of Americans do not have health insurance. Health care is rationed to those who are insured or who can pay for the care themselves on a fee-for-service basis.

13. Medicare is a health-insurance program funded through Social Security that primarily serves the elderly. Medicaid is a welfare program that provides medical assistance to low-income people of all ages.

14. Medical specialization, increased reliance on expensive technology, and a fragmented, uncoordinated system of competing providers are driving up health care costs in the United States. To lower costs, there is a move toward managed care using health maintenance organizations (HMOs).

15. The U.S. health care system is in a process of reform, as shown by Bush's health initiatives. The Canadian system is a potential model for national health insurance in the United States, but it is not likely, to develop in the near future.

KEY TERMS

acute disease 513
chronic disease 513
epidemiology 510
fee-for-service 530
health 509
health maintenance organization
(HMO) 532

holistic health 509
incidence 510
managed care 532
Medicaid 531
medicalization 514
Medicare 531
morbidity rate 510

mortality rate 510
national health insurance 520
prevalence 510
sick role 512

CRITICAL THINKING QUESTIONS

1. Demonstrate how global and U.S. patterns of health are both similar and different. What characteristics of social structure explain the patterns?

2. What explains the differences in mortality and morbidity between men and women and between the races? What interventions would reduce the disadvantages created by these differences?

3. How can both patient and health care provider needs be met in the movement toward holistic health and alternative medicine?

4. Which of the three theoretical perspectives could best be applied to resolve the crisis related to cost, access, and the organization of the health care system?

INVESTIGATE WITH CONTENT SELECT

Journal Research Collections from **Content**Select

Begin your research using ContentSelect for this chapter by following the directions found on page 27 of this text to visit Prentice Hall's Research Navigator Website. Enter these search terms into the search field:

Holistic
Health Maintenance Organization
Medicaid

20
EMERGING INSTITUTIONS:
SPORT AND THE MASS MEDIA

High School Football in Texas

A few years ago, the town of Odessa, located on the sparsely populated plains of west Texas, built a new football stadium for Permian High School. It cost $5.6 million and featured

> . . . a sunken artificial-surface field eighteen feet below ground level, a two-story press box with VIP seating for school board members and other dignitaries, poured concrete seating for 19,032, and a full-time caretaker who lived on the premises. (Bissinger, 1991:42)

The school flies the football team to away games on chartered airplanes, yet the English department can barely afford to supply students with textbooks. Players routinely pass their classes whether they have learned anything or not, and the primary route to popularity for girls at Permian is to become a "Pepette." Winning is so important that on the day after the team lost a big game, Permian's coach awoke to find a forest of "for sale" signs on his front lawn. (Bissinger, 1991)

Beam Me Up! The Star Trek Phenomenon

When NBC programmers decided to air a science fiction show called *Star Trek* in 1966, there was no way that they could have guessed that it would attract a fan base so large and so devoted that it would endure nearly 40 years and inspire four additional television programs and 10 major motion pictures. *Star Trek* fans wrote over half a million protest letters when the show was in danger of being cancelled. Since 1972—three years after the program left the air—thousands of commercial and amateur *Star Trek* conventions have been held across the country and abroad. Today there are several thousand Web sites devoted to the *Star Trek* universe, and a Google search of the Web reveals roughly 1.5 million references to the topic.

The commitment of *Star Trek* fans is truly legendary. A 1998 film called *Trekkies*, which documented some of the extraordinary lengths to which fans have gone in celebrating *Star Trek*, featured, among other displays of fan devotion, a woman who showed up for jury duty in 1996 in full uniform and carrying a phaser and a tricorder; the Interstellar Language School in Red Lake Falls, Minnesota, where you can learn how to speak Klingon; and a dentist's office in Orlando, Florida, where the staff dress like *Star Trek* characters (www.trekdoc.com/general).

Star Trek fandom and high-school football are just two examples of the many recreational and leisure-time activities enjoyed by members of modern societies. Traditionally, sociologists devoted relatively little attention to leisure, preferring to concentrate on more "serious" topics like the family, poverty, and crime (Ritzer, 2000). However, the intense passion with which enormous numbers of people participate today in recreational activities, such as attending *Star Trek* conventions and following high school football (at least in Texas!), strongly suggests that this topic is worthy of serious sociological attention.

Through most of history, recreational activities were largely uninstitutionalized, and most took place in the home. In the evening, family members might play games together or work on a group project. Mother would quilt while father whittled or carved. An older child might read aloud to the others. Neighbors would drop by and engage in unplanned and informal athletic contests (Fischer, 1989). But beginning early in the 20th century, large-scale recreational activities separate from the family arose in the developed world. Big-time sports and the mass media are prime examples.

Prior to the industrial era, most leisure-time activities took place within the family. This pattern continues today, but it is substantially diminished. More and more contemporary recreation is commercialized and set outside of the family.

Sociologists interpret sport and the media as *emerging institutions* because they have developed from small-scale and informal roots into their current increasingly formal and highly routinized patterns. They have also become much more important economically. Other institutions that have emerged within the past several centuries include criminal justice (see Chapter 9) and health care (see Chapter 19).

Sport and the media may also be understood as examples of modern **popular culture**: commercialized art and entertainment designed to attract a mass audience (Kammen, 1998). In this chapter we start by analyzing selected sociological aspects of sport and the media separately and then turn to a consideration of how these two emerging institutions are interrelated. The chapter concludes with discussions of deviance, racism, and sexism in sport, and of censorship of the electronic media.

SPORT

Sociologist Jay Coakley (2001:20) defines **sport** as an institutionalized, competitive activity involving rigorous physical exertion or the use of relatively complex physical skills by participants motivated by the desire for personal enjoyment and external rewards.

Sport may be thought of as a concept halfway between play and spectacle (Guttmann, 1978; Coakley, 2001). Pure *play*, as exemplified by a group of friends tossing a frisbee around the back yard, is spontaneous, voluntary, largely without rules, and enjoyed purely for its own sake. Progressing from play to sport, events are increasingly planned, formal rules emerge, and the activity becomes more relevant to the rest of

the players' lives. External rewards—money, prestige, college scholarships—become more important reasons for participating.

What happens when sport becomes so serious that playfulness and spontaneity fade away and participation becomes, for all practical purposes, work, as in the NFL or NBA? Sociologists use the terms **spectacle** or *corporate sport* for athletics at this level, implying that these activities have become corrupted or have lost some of the qualities we find most appealing about "true" sport (Hoch, 1982; Sage, 1998).

Sport has clearly grown increasingly significant in recent decades. As we have seen, it is often thought of as somehow less serious or important than longer established institutions like government or education, but its pervasiveness suggests that it merits close consideration.

About 70 percent of the U.S. public is involved in sports, either as participants, as spectators, or in both roles. In 1999, major league baseball attracted 71 million fans, NCAA men's basketball drew 29 million, 39 million people attended big-time college football games, and pro hockey drew 18 million spectators (U.S. Bureau of the Census, 2002: Table 1241). In the same year, roughly 58 million people swam, 27 million played golf, and 11 million played tennis (U.S. Bureau of the Census, 2002: Table 1245). Sports generate more than $212 billion in total revenue each year in the United States (Broughton et al., 2000). The sports section is by far the most widely read part of the daily newspaper, and about 15 percent of all major network television programming is devoted to athletics (Eitzen & Sage, 2003).

In addition, sport may be viewed as a microcosm of larger society, a lens through which we can gain perspective on other aspects of social life. For example, as we will see later in this chapter, the struggles that minorities and women fought in recent decades for full acceptance in the larger society were reflected by similar conflicts in sport. Jackie Robinson and Billie Jean King played roles roughly similar to those of Martin Luther King and Betty Friedan (Tygiel, 1983; Shropshire, 1996).

Sport is also intimately connected with other major social institutions. Governments use international competitions such as the Olympics to advance national prestige; religions use organizations like the Fellowship of Christian Athletes to build membership; events like the Super Bowl are big business in every meaning of the word; and universities rely on sports to bring them publicity and alumni donations.

If you still doubt the cultural significance of sport, consider how often you hear sports terms such as the following used in nonathletic contexts: ground rules, low blow, foul play, jump the gun, the bush leagues, game plan, cheap shot, touch bases, go to bat, and out of bounds.

The Functions of Sport

Sociologists who use the functionalist perspective maintain that sport fulfills a variety of needs at both the individual and the collective levels, thereby facilitating the smooth and predictable operation of society (Loy & Booth, 2000).

PROVIDING ENTERTAINMENT The most obvious or manifest function of sport is that it supplies pleasurable entertainment to many millions of people. This allows a temporary escape from real-life activities and problems.

PROMOTING SOCIALIZATION At a somewhat more latent level, sport is widely viewed as an effective means of socializing youth to accept key social values (Coakley & Donnelly, 1999). In this context, pioneering sport sociologist Harry Edwards (1973) identified what he called *the dominant American sports creed* as the widespread belief that sports promote discipline, competitiveness, physical and mental fitness, religiosity, and patriotism. In a classic study of Little League baseball as a means of socialization, Gary Fine (1987) identified four central themes that the participants are taught: personal effort, good sportsmanship, teamwork, and how to cope with both winning and losing.

Competition lies at the heart of this set of values. However, not all sport is organized exclusively around competition. Sometimes participation and cooperation are more strongly emphasized, as in the Special Olympics. Furthermore, athletes, especially in indi-

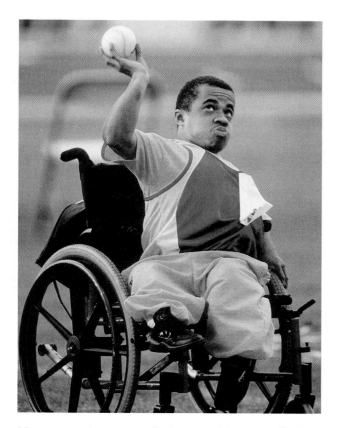

Not every sporting event emphasizes competition above all other values; the Special Olympics encourages winning but also stresses the importance of cooperation and of allowing everyone to have an opportunity to participate.

vidual sports, such as track, swimming, and golf, may choose to measure their performance against some abstract standard or against their own previous best mark rather than in simple terms of wins and losses (Kohn, 1994).

PROMOTING INDIVIDUAL AND COLLECTIVE IDENTITY At the individual level, sport can be a significant element in establishing one's personal identity. Commitment to a particular team can endure throughout one's life despite moves, career changes, and divorces, providing stability and continuity. Sport also allows people to validate their prestige claims, whether by virtue of personal athletic achievement, extensive knowledge of the history and current statistics of a favorite team, or just by wearing the "right" team jersey or basketball shoes.

Beyond this, whether as a participant or a spectator, commitment to a team connects us to other people who feel as we do, enhancing the social bond. High schools and colleges explicitly use sports to build solidarity among their students and alumni. Loyalty is encouraged by rituals like pep rallies, caravans to away games, and the wearing of team colors.

Brazilian soccer fans celebrate a key victory against Turkey in the 2002 World Cup semifinals played in Saitama, Japan. The Brazilian team won the championship match four days later.

Team logos take on a quasi-sacred quality, symbolizing the unity of the fans. Major college and professional teams frequently provide a similar function for whole communities, states, or regions (Eitzen & Sage, 2003).

In the emerging global society, sport promotes social integration and patriotism for cities, regions, and entire nations. This cultural identity function is well illustrated by soccer, which is by far the world's favorite sport. The sport is wildly popular in Brazil, winner of the 2002 World Cup, where it functions to simultaneously divide and unify the people of this large and very heterogeneous society (Lever, 1983).

Each major Brazilian city has numerous teams that compete fiercely with one another. The teams typically draw the core of their support from different social groups. For instance, in Rio de Janeiro different teams are identified with ". . . the old rich, the modern middle class, the poor, the blacks, the Portuguese, and a number of neighborhood communities" (Lever, 1983:146–147). At this level, team support mostly promotes social fragmentation.

But Brazilian soccer is also organized beyond the municipal level, with one team representing each city in a national championship series. During this tournament, everyone from a given city unites behind their team. This crisscrossing of loyalties helps unite the diverse populations of various cities and regions.

At an even higher level, people from all parts of Brazil passionately support their national team as it competes with other countries for the World Cup. The national team often makes allies out of bitter opponents. Thus, soccer in Brazil both reinforces internal social divisions and helps forge a sense of national identity and collective consciousness.

MILITARY PREPAREDNESS Sports directly affect people's physical health, which at the collective level may contribute to a nation's ability to defend itself militarily. During the 1950s, physical education programs in the schools were beefed up on the rationale that physically fit children would become fit adults and would help the United States respond to the Soviet challenge.

Conflict Interpretations

Conflict theorists generally maintain that sport benefits men more than women, whites more than people of color, the wealthy more than the middle and working classes, and owners and administrators more than athletes (Leonard, 1998). Consider, for example, the life of a major college football or basketball player. If you add up the total number of hours devoted to conditioning, practice, travel, and actual games, even student athletes who receive full scholarships are in effect being paid little more than a minimum wage salary. Meanwhile, a successful team may produce millions of dollars of revenue and publicity for the school that sponsors it (DeVenzio, 1986; Adler & Adler, 1991; *Top Players Produce . . ."* 1994; Sack & Staurowsky, 1998).

Moreover, many college athletes, especially those competing in the revenue-producing sports, have trouble keeping up with their studies. As a result, these athletes have lower graduation rates than other student-athletes or the student body in general (Suggs, 2000). It is easy to see why conflict theorists believe student athletes are being exploited.

Student athletes often accept such treatment as a necessary preparation for becoming highly paid professionals. But in most cases, this goal is unrealistic. There are, for example, some 40,000 college football players, but only about 2,300 slots in the NFL (Leonard, 1998).

At a more abstract level, big-time college and professional sports can be highly dehumanizing (Brohm, 1978). Athletes are often required to play despite painful injuries, to practice long after they have ceased to enjoy what they are doing, to use performance-enhancing drugs, and to regard their own bodies as little more than objects to be used in pursuit of an end (Sabo, 1995).

SOCIALIZATION REVISITED: WHAT VALUES DO SPORTS REALLY TEACH? As suggested above, most functionalists believe that the values promoted by sport are generally positive, but conflict theorists take a different position (Sage, 1998; Rigauer, 2000). For one thing, sports train athletes to submit without complaint to the arbitrary authority of their coaches, which may help prepare them to become docile, easily exploited workers and overly compliant citizens (Eitzen, 1999).

Furthermore, because success in sport (including team sports) is often based on individual effort, athletes may be led to adopt a radically individualistic global worldview in which the unequal levels of success enjoyed in the larger society by different classes, genders, and ethnic groups are explained solely by the efforts—or failings—of individuals.

As we have already noted, competition is the centerpiece of the American sports creed. When one individual or team wins, all the others lose. We give lip service to good sportsmanship, but most people agree with former Green Bay Packer coach Vince Lombardi, who said, "Winning is not everything; it is the only thing." Or, as another coach put it, "Show me a good loser and I'll show you a loser." This value, that winning is the only relevant goal in sport, is sometimes referred to as the **Lombardi ethic** (Eitzen, 1999).

What are the consequences of accepting this ethic? Does competition increase motivation? The answer is yes, under certain conditions: People who are raised in an environment that emphasizes competition, who have a competitive personality, who have some reasonable chance of success, and who participate in relatively familiar sports usually thrive on pressure to succeed. On the other hand, those who do not meet these criteria tend to find an emphasis on competition frustrating and counterproductive (Kohn, 1986; Eitzen, 1990). Thus, for example, Hopi Indians, who come from a strongly cooperative culture, may play high-school sports, but they often disappoint their coaches because they seem to lack a "killer instinct" (Garrity, 1989; Simpson, 2001).

Most Americans believe that successful athletes learn positive values through competition. Are the lessons the losers learn equally valuable, or does athletic failure primarily destroy young people's confidence in themselves?

Does the Lombardi ethic help people succeed in the real world? Success in some activities, especially sales work, requires competitiveness, but many businesses now put greater value on cooperation and teamwork. These qualities can be taught through athletics, but they are usually considered distant seconds to competitiveness.

Compare the U.S. emphasis on competition with the team orientation that is stressed in Japan, a society that generally values the group over the individual (Kerbo & McKinstry, 1998). Outstanding athletes are considered deviant if they brag or try to stand out as individuals by throwing temper tantrums or complaining to the media. Most Japanese baseball players are more willing than their U.S. counterparts to bunt to help their teams—and less likely to try for home runs (Coakley, 2001).

If, as conflict theorists maintain, big-time sports exploit and dehumanize athletes, teach them to obey authority without question, and mercilessly overemphasize competition, why do so many people persist in believing that sports are a good way to build character? One reason is because of the **halo effect.** When we see athletes perform well on the field and win, and when the media constantly associate winning with virtue, we generalize that people who are good in one area of life—in this case, sports—must be *generally* good people (Coakley, 2001).

Conflict theorists also emphasize that sport promotes commercialism. Everything seems to come down to money: Which star or player has the biggest contract? Who receives the most cash for endorsements? Corporate involvement in sport has reached unprecedented levels: Colleges routinely receive hundreds of thousands of dollars for outfitting their teams in particular brands of sports equipment. All of the major bowl games, like the *Sunkist* Orange Bowl, have accepted corporate sponsorship. In 1999, major league baseball seriously considered (but ultimately rejected) a proposal to allow teams to sell advertising space on their players' uniforms (Sage, 1998).

Finally, conflict theorists argue that sport encourages excessive nationalism, as exemplified by the violent attacks by British "soccer hooligans" on foreign nationals during international contests (King, 1995; Stott & Reicher, 1998). Consider also the euphoria aroused when the U.S. hockey team upset the Soviet Union in the 1980 Olympics and when the U.S. team advanced much farther than expected in the 2002 World Cup competition. Media coverage of such events triggers fervent nationalism that can promote ethnic and racial stereotyping at a time when global political challenges require understanding and cooperation (Wilson, 1994).

Symbolic Interactionist Views

Symbolic interactionists are interested in how both participants and spectators attribute meaning to athletes (Donnelly, 2000). In one study based in this perspective, Peter Donnelly and Kevin Young (1988) interviewed rugby players and mountain climbers to learn how they went about constructing the identity of "serious athlete." The researchers found that this was a rather long-term process and that it involved acquiring knowledge about the sport, becoming associated with athletes whose identity was firmly established, using these people as a reference group, and reconfirming the new identity by interacting regularly with more established athletes. Similar studies have explored topics such as how athletes learn to interpret the meaning of pain (Curry, 1993).

Symbolic interactionists have also explored how sports influence participants' gender identities (Brustad, 1996; Theberge, 1997; Dworkin & Messner, 1999). Michael Messner (1990) interviewed a sample of males heavily involved in athletics and found that success in sports confirmed these athletes' manliness in their own eyes as well as in the eyes of others (also see Lorber, 1994). Unfortunately, this process of identity construction may include the acquisition of sexist stereotypes: Some coaches habitually spur male

athletes on to better performances by calling them "girls" (Foley, 2001). Sexism in sport will be considered further later in this chapter.

Finally, symbolic interactionism also offers insights into issues such as Native American names for sports teams. Some maintain that team names like the Atlanta Braves, the Kansas City Chiefs, and the Washington Redskins demean Native Americans by depicting them in offensive and stereotypical terms (Sigelman, 1998; Spindel, 2000). Such concerns have led several universities to change their team names—for example, the Stanford Indians became the Stanford Cardinals and the St. John's Redmen are now the Red Storm—but professional teams have resisted changing their names. Some argue that these team names and mascots are well-intentioned or even meant to honor Native Americans, but other observers find these claims less than convincing:

> . . . Just for the moment of one game, put your feet into our moccasins. Watch the red-painted faces. Watch the fanatics in the stands wearing turkey and chicken feathers in their hair. Watch the fools doing the tomahawk chop and singing that horrible chant. Then picture that section of fans as people supporting a team called the African Americans. Imagine them doing the same things to black Americans as they are doing to Native Americans. (Giago, 1998)

In the following sections, we look at the role sport plays in two major aspects of social life: economic stratification and religion.

Sport and Economic Stratification

Sociologists have studied various issues concerning sport and social stratification, but two seem especially interesting. First, what is the connection between class and choice of sport? Second, does participating in sports promote upward social mobility?

Most studies show that wealthy men and women are more oriented toward sports participation and that the lower classes are more inclined to be spectators. As participants, the higher classes favor individual sports, whereas the lower classes prefer team games (Loy, 1972; Eitzen & Sage, 2003). More specifically, the wealthy are especially likely to enjoy golf, tennis, yachting, skiing, and polo. These sports require expensive equipment and extensive instruction, and they are often played at country clubs that the children of the elite frequent. Thorstein Veblen (1934) saw elite sports participation of this sort as a classic example of **conspicuous consumption,** activity undertaken to validate the social status of the upper class by demonstrating that they can afford to throw money away on nonessentials.

Modern commercial sports clearly reflect the reality of social stratification. Corporations and wealthy individuals relax in air-conditioned luxury suites, such as this one at the Toronto Skydome, while less affluent fans swelter in General Admission.

Less affluent people tend to go bowling or play basketball, baseball, and volleyball, none of which are expensive to learn or play. People toward the bottom of the class ladder often favor physically aggressive sports like wrestling, boxing, and demolition derbies. Perhaps this is because their life experiences leave them more frustrated and thus more in need of a safety valve to release their tensions (Zelman, 1976; Eitzen & Sage, 2003).

As for the major spectator sports, people from all classes enjoy football, basketball, baseball, and hockey. However, sports arenas are sharply segregated on the basis of class (Eitzen, 1996; Coakley, 2001). The corporate rich relax in "sky boxes," while the middle classes occupy the bulk of the seats. Most members of the working class can no longer afford to attend major league sports unless they come on bargain night or sit in general admission. And as for the poor, well, they can always watch the game on TV.

Does sports participation aid social mobility? Most studies show that both male and female high-school athletes have somewhat better grade averages than nonathletes. In part this is because they must keep their marks up in order to stay eligible. But they also tend to have higher educational aspirations and ultimately to do a little better in life (Sabo et al., 1993; Rees & Miracle, 2000). Perhaps sports really do build character. It may also be that the friendships that result from being on a team provide networking opportunities. The public visibility of star athletes may also help them in their search for good jobs.

Many college athletes, especially in the major sports, are first-generation college students. This factor alone explains why they often do better than their parents. However, these athletes are generally less likely to graduate than minor-sport competitors or nonathletes, partly because they tend as a group to be less well prepared academically and also because the rigors of big-time sports may leave them with little time or energy to apply themselves properly to their studies (Coakley, 2001).

A handful of the best college athletes make it into the professional ranks, but the vast majority do not. Even those who do become pros usually have short careers—averaging less than five years—and only a few superstars earn astronomical salaries. Some pro athletes, especially in football and boxing, suffer serious physical damage by the time they retire, and many lack the nonathletic skills that would allow them to make a good living after they leave sports. Finally, as we will discuss later in this chapter, opportunities for African Americans and other people of color, especially in coaching and administrative roles, remain relatively limited, and there are still very few lucrative positions in professional sport open to women.

Sport and Religion

The connection between sport and religion dates from prehistoric times. Many traditional cultures viewed athletic rituals as a way to honor the gods. The original Olympic games were dedicated to Zeus. In fact, when the Olympics were suppressed late in the fourth century, it was because they were seen by the Church as a pagan custom (Swaddling, 1999). Similarly, before the industrial era, Christians and especially Calvinist Protestants often considered sport a sinful celebration of the body and a waste of time that could better be spent working or in church (Brailsford, 1991; Overman, 1997).

This view began to change in the United States during the 19th century when a movement called *muscular Christianity* arose, in part as a result of concerns among the upper and middle classes about the enormous numbers of immigrants flooding into the larger cities (Ladd & Mathisen, 1999). This movement sponsored softball and bowling leagues and established the YMCA as a means of keeping the children of the new arrivals busy and distracting them from crime and radical politics. All of this was done in the name of vigorous physical activity combined with robust spirituality.

The tradition of using sports as a way to build religious commitment continues today in the activities of some evangelistic groups (Higgs, 1995). For example, the Fellowship of Christian Athletes, founded in 1954, is active in thousands of high schools and colleges. Athletes in Action, a similar organization, sends teams of young Christians out to play exhibition games and testify at halftime to their faith (Mathiesen, 1990). Religiously affiliated universities—most notably Notre Dame and Brigham Young—have also found that intercollegiate athletics programs can build loyalty to both their institutions and their faiths.

Just as religions sometimes use sport for their own purposes, athletes and teams often use religious rituals in hope of enhancing their performance. At church-affiliated institutions, formal prayers often precede games; in more secular settings, many athletes pray individually. Many basketball players make the sign of the cross before attempting a free throw (Gmelch, 1978).

At another level, sports often serve as a kind of secular religion for their followers, providing many of the functions of religion, even though they do not include a transcendent element (Prebish, 1993; Hubbard, 1998) (see Chapter 17). The ability of sport to perform this role stems from its collective identity function. In a religiously heterogeneous society, loyalty to a sports team may be one of the few factors that gives people a sense of commonality.

Along the same lines, sport provides numerous rituals—pep rallies, awards ceremonies, the games themselves—that bring people together in large numbers to celebrate their shared loyalties. Team logos and colors take on a kind of sacred quality, affirming each fan's loyalty to the team. The most dedicated supporters find that sport, like religion, makes their lives more meaningful.

Sport provides its "believers" with sacred days (Super Bowl Sunday), holy writings (statistics books), and shrines (halls of fame). Fans engage in sacred ritual cheers and sometimes make pilgrimages to watch their teams play away from home. Athletes are expected to purify themselves for the contest, if no longer by abstaining from sex, as once was common, at least by keeping regular hours and avoiding drugs and gambling. Players like former Cincinnati superstar Pete Rose, who violate important rules (in his case by betting on baseball games), risk being cast out of their sport just as heretics are likely to be excommunicated from their religions.

THE MASS MEDIA

As we have seen repeatedly in earlier chapters, the mass media have an enormous and ever-increasing impact on social life. This is true not only regarding the *content* of the media, but also in terms of the ways in which different types of media impact upon us. In the words of pioneering media scholar Marshall McLuhan (1964), the medium is the message.

Consider, for example, the transition from the oral tradition to the print media (newspapers and magazines) and then to the modern electronic media (especially television, and now the Internet). In what is sometimes called the *Postman thesis*, Neil Postman (1985) argues that these shifts have had a critical impact on our understanding of the nature of childhood, among other things. In preliterate times, all information was passed on by word of mouth, including that concerning topics such as sexuality and adult misbehavior. Even young children had easy access to the oral tradition, and as a result they tended to lose their illusions early in life, becoming in effect miniature adults.

But with the invention of the printing press, adult secrets could be hidden away in books, which allowed parents to keep their children much more sheltered. Only at this point, according to Postman, did we start to feel that children ought to be kept innocent of the dark secrets of the adult world and to see them as sharply distinct from older members of the community.

Cultural constructions of childhood began to change again with the rapid spread of television in the years following World War II. Early sitcoms like *Leave It To Beaver* and *The Adventures of Ozzie and Harriet* continued to depict children as innocents. This rapidly changed, however, because television was moving us back to the oral culture in the sense that once again adult secrets could no longer be easily hidden from children. In an era in which 4-year-olds could tune in to *The Jerry Springer Show* and *NYPD-Blue*, there was no way that they could remain sheltered. Today's children on television are nothing

TV's Forgotten Minority: Latinos

Who is your favorite Latino TV star? This is a surprisingly difficult question to answer for the simple reason that there are virtually no Hispanics in starring roles, and only a handful in featured ones, on prime-time television. Latinos are now the largest minority group in the country, yet they remain almost invisible on commercial television.

In the 1950s and 1960s, prime time television was virtually an all-white world. The most popular shows featured suburban, middle-class white families of no specific ethnic heritage: *Father Knows Best, Ozzie and Harriet,* and *Leave It to Beaver.* By implication, this was the "real" United States. Latino characters occasionally appeared as outlaws in the Old West or lounging under sombreros in the dusty squares of Latin American towns as background, not characters, waiting for the stars to appear. The principal exception was Cuban band leader Ricky Ricardo (played by Desi Arnaz) on the *I Love Lucy* show. Ricky's ethnicity added a comic touch: When totally exasperated by his wife Lucy's hairbrained schemes, he lapsed into Spanish and displays of stereotypical "Latin temper."

Television began to broadcast a new message about selected minorities in the early 1970s. The improbable pioneer in this trend was Archie Bunker—the narrow-minded working-class star of *All in the Family.* An equal opportunity bigot, Archie railed against virtually every minority group. Producer Norman Lear's goal was to "hold up a mirror to our prejudices," using humor to raise issues that had been taboo on television until then.

The huge success of this program led to any number of imitations and spinoffs, primarily African American family comedies. For the most part, Latinos did not participate in the 1970s ethnic revival. As in the 1960s, there was one major exception. *Chico and the Man* paired a young, high-spirited Mexican American man (played by Latino comedian Freddy Prinze) with an aging Anglo garage owner, Ed Brown. The irrepressible Chico taught the stubborn, ill-tempered Brown to relax, enjoy himself, and be more tolerant. Sadly, the show's success ended when its star, Prinze, committed suicide in 1977.

The popularity of shows with all or mostly black characters reached new highs in the 1980s with *The Cosby Show.* In some ways, the Huxtables resembled the happy prime-time families of the 1950s and 1960s. Despite high-powered careers (Cliff was a physician, Claire, a lawyer), their lives revolved around their family, whose lighthearted disagreements were always easily resolved. The show was widely criticized for presenting an idealized version of black families and ignoring serious racial issues.

In the late 1980s and early 1990s, the number of colorblind roles for African Americans crept upward. However, there was no Latino equivalent of *The Cosby Show.* To the contrary, during a decade when African Americans were being accepted (at least on television) into the mainstream, the stereotype of the Hispanic "bandito" was revived with markedly sinister overtones. On shows like *Miami Vice,* Latinos were frequently cast as drug lords rich and powerful enough to control entire cities and even small countries. Even on *Hill Street Blues, Cagney & Lacey,* and other shows that featured blacks and women in positions of authority, Hispanics lurked in the netherworld of small-time gangsters, junkies, and pimps. The best known Latino actor in this era was *LA Law* and *NYPD-Blue* star Jimmy Smits, whose mother was Puerto Rican but whose father was of Dutch ancestry.

A large-scale survey conducted during the 1994–1995 season found that about 2 percent of all characters on TV were Latino—far below the 12 percent of Americans who claim Hispanic ancestry in real life. Latino characters were more likely to be unskilled laborers than executives or professionals; they were twice as likely as white characters and three times as likely as black characters to be criminals. More recent research has reached similar conclusions.

More often than other characters, Latinos are shown as motivated by greed, pursuing their goals through violence or deceit, and generally failing to attain whatever goals they sought. Hispanic characters tend to be "ghettoized" into a small number of prime-time series. Finally, with rare exceptions, Latinos are portrayed as members of a single ethnic group, rather than as Cubans, Mexicans, Hondurans, and so forth—as members of a variety of Spanish-speaking ethnic groups with distinct cultures and experiences in the United States.

1. Why do you think that African Americans have been much more successful than Latinos, not only in obtaining parts on prime-time television programs, but also in being able to occasionally play relatively nonstereotyped roles?

2. What are the effects on viewers of the invisibility of Latino Americans on television?

3. How have other ethnic and racial minorities in the United States—including Jews, Asian Americans, and Native Americans—been depicted on television?

Sources: Castleman & Podrazik, 1982; Lichter & Amundson, 1997.

Numerous research studies suggest that violent television programming contributes to real-life violence, either through direct modeling or as a result of a gradual desensitization to aggressive content.

like the Beaver or Ricky Nelson: They are cynical, wise-cracking, and obsessed with sexuality. Once again, due to shifts in the media, they are little adults.

As the Postman thesis suggests, the social effects of television are exceptionally important (McDonald, 1994; Newcomb, 2000; Straubhaar & LaRose, 2002). Today, 98 percent of U.S. homes have at least one television set, and the average person watches 30 hours of television each week (see Chapter 5). Figures 20.1 and 20.2 illus-

trate the impact of age and gender on television viewing and, for contrast, on newspaper readership.

In the last 10 to 15 years, rapidly expanding access to computers has opened up the Internet, which promises to have even more radical social effects than the print media or television (Porter & Read, 1998). By the year 2000, over 40 percent of people in the United States had access to the World Wide Web at home, school, or work, a figure that is expected to

The gentle, non-controversial, family-based situation-comedies of the 1960s like Ozzie and Harriet *routinely portrayed children as innocents, unaware of the darker aspect of adult society.*

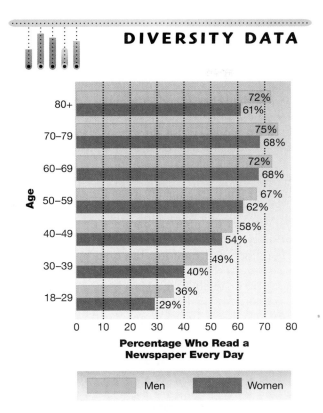

DIVERSITY DATA

Percentage Who Read a Newspaper Every Day

Age:
- 80+: 72% (Men), 61% (Women)
- 70–79: 75% (Men), 68% (Women)
- 60–69: 72% (Men), 68% (Women)
- 50–59: 67% (Men), 62% (Women)
- 40–49: 58% (Men), 54% (Women)
- 30–39: 49% (Men), 40% (Women)
- 18–29: 36% (Men), 29% (Women)

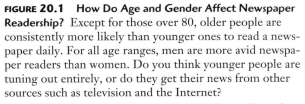
Men | Women

FIGURE 20.1 **How Do Age and Gender Affect Newspaper Readership?** Except for those over 80, older people are consistently more likely than younger ones to read a newspaper daily. For all age ranges, men are more avid newspaper readers than women. Do you think younger people are tuning out entirely, or do they get their news from other sources such as television and the Internet?

Source: NORC. General Social Surveys, 1972–2000. Chicago: National Opinion Research Center, 1996. Reprinted by permission of NORC, Chicago, Il.

continue to increase rapidly (Fidler, 1997; Straubhaar & LaRose, 2002).

In recent decades sociologists have devoted extensive attention to the effects of the media on society. Chapter 5 introduced research documenting the strong link between media presentations of violence and patterns of youthful aggression. It also discussed the effects of race, class, and gender stereotyping in the media, topics that were covered further in Chapters 6 and 13. In this chapter we extend these observations, focusing primarily on television and film, and organizing our comments around the three major theoretical perspectives. Before doing so, however, we must first turn to a brief discussion of how the media affect their audience.

Most early researchers accepted what was called the **hypodermic model,** which assumes that the media have a simple, direct, one-way effect rather than one that is mediated through primary group interaction (Croteau & Hoynes, 1997). The hypodermic model is grounded in psychological behaviorism (see Chapter 5), which sees human action as shaped by a simple stimulus-response process.

On the other hand, modern scholars generally believe that media messages are socially interpreted rather than absorbed directly (Lindlof, 1995). Media presentations are discussed and evaluated with peers and family. Length of exposure, type of content, and the social characteristics of the audience are all critical factors affecting how the media influence people's attitudes and behavior.

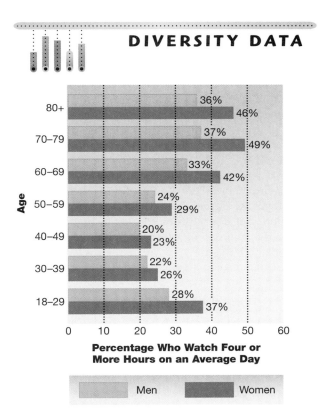

DIVERSITY DATA

Percentage Who Watch Four or More Hours on an Average Day

Age:
- 80+: 36% (Men), 46% (Women)
- 70–79: 37% (Men), 49% (Women)
- 60–69: 33% (Men), 42% (Women)
- 50–59: 24% (Men), 29% (Women)
- 40–49: 20% (Men), 23% (Women)
- 30–39: 22% (Men), 26% (Women)
- 18–29: 28% (Men), 37% (Women)

Men | Women

FIGURE 20.2 **How Do Age and Gender Affect Television Viewing?** Women are more likely than men to watch four or more hours of TV on an average day, with the largest gender gap among people who are under 30 and over 59. Viewership is heaviest among the elderly and lightest in the age range 30–59.

Source: NORC. General Social Surveys, 1972–2000. Chicago: National Opinion Research Center, 2000. Reprinted by permission of NORC, Chicago, IL.

Thus, for example, a steady diet of aggressive rap music, televised professional wrestling, and films that blur the distinction between the good guys and the bad guys is likely to cultivate violence among teenagers who already live in an aggressive environment (Huesmann, 1994; Gerbner et al., 1994). On the other hand, youth who grow up in a more prosocial setting, without being exposed to delinquent peers or abusive parents, will probably not be significantly impacted by media violence.

The Functions of the Media

The mass media serve a number of important social functions, most of which promote social stability.

ENTERTAINMENT   The media generally relax rather than excite; they put people at ease and even make them less alert. This is not necessarily negative. Tensions that mount up over the day can be eased by watching television; in a sense, it is a form of therapy for a stress-filled lifestyle.

ENCOURAGING SOCIAL INTERACTION AND SOLIDARITY   The media provide reasons for people to get together and furnish topics for conversation. They promote family activities, dating, and simply mingling with friends. College students watch MTV, pro wrestling, and even the news in their dorms. Groups of people read the latest book recommended on talk shows and then meet to discuss it. In times of crisis, like the September 11, 2001, terrorist attack, television coverage promoted a feeling of unity among the millions of people watching their sets in stunned amazement.

INTERNET CONNECTIONS

There has been a lot of criticism directed toward the effect of television on children's behavior. Go to parenting and babies Website:

http://babyparenting.about.com/cs/toddlersandtv/?once=true&

and read the articles on toddlers and television. What is the impact of television on the development of toddlers? Do you think television is a good thing or harmful to children? Provide support for your position.

SOCIALIZATION   As discussed in Chapter 5, although the family is the first agent of socialization that we encounter, the media, and especially television, quickly become critically important in a child's life. Children today spend far more hours watching television than they spend in school (Lemert, 1997). Television characters set standards of behavior for children to model, if not directly as the hypodermic model suggests, then certainly indirectly.

SOCIAL CONTROL   In authoritarian societies like China and Cuba, the media are under strict governmental control and are used to publicize the certainty of punishment for political deviance or lack of social conformity (Chen & Chaudhary, 1991). But the media present and reinforce the rules by which individuals are expected to live in all societies, whether democratic or totalitarian. Television programs such as *C.S.I.* and *Law and Order* that suggest that offenders are very likely to be apprehended and convicted are prime examples of this function. Thus, the media promote conformity and obedience to the law and other important societal standards.

This same function, interpreted differently, provides the starting point for a conflict analysis of the media.

Conflict Interpretations

For conflict theorists, the crucial issue is who the mass media benefit. We live in an era in which ownership of the major media is becoming increasingly concentrated in the hands of a small number of megacorporations (Aufderheide, 1997). Just 11 corporations collectively control over half of the newspaper market; comparable figures for other media are five for book publishing, four for film, three for television, and two for magazines (Croteau & Hoynes, 1997). These corporations are in turn run by and in the interests of a very small group of extremely wealthy individuals (Ryan & Wentworth, 1999).

These realities lead conflict theorists to the conclusion that the social control function of the media disproportionately works to the benefit of the rich and powerful (Gitlin, 1983; Ryan & Wentworth, 1999). The elites who control the media often use them to shape public opinion, deaden critical thinking, and legitimize existing power arrangements (Habermas, 1976; 1990). The media generally reproduce the status quo and discourage social change. They serve what Marx would call an "opiate" function because they distract people from paying attention to—and attempting to remedy—social injustice and political oppression.

In recent years computers have become an integral part of class-room instruction throughout the developed world.

For example, researchers have found that most people in the United States get their political information from television (Lee & Solomon, 1990). "Spin doctors" manage media campaigns so that sound bites become more important than serious political debate. Politics is reduced to "made-for-media" events (Croteau & Hoynes, 1997; Bucy & D'Angelo, 1999; Slayden & Whillock, 1999). Serious questions about issues such as the growing gap between the rich and the poor, which might lead to changes that could harm the powerful, are carefully avoided (Parenti, 1992).

In global perspective, conflict theorists study the impact of the U.S. and European media on the values and norms of developing societies. The enormous economic power of the Western media virtually assures that influences will originate there and flow outward to the rest of the world. This has been referred to as *cultural imperialism* (Kuisel, 1993). The potential impact of these media is so enormous that they have been banned as part of government anti-

modernization campaigns in some developing countries (Schiller, 1992).

Symbolic Interactionist and Postmodern Views

Symbolic interactionism is becoming an increasingly popular theoretical perspective from which to study the media. It focuses on how the meanings of cultural phenomena, especially those transmitted in the media, are constructed and interpreted by individuals whose consciousness has been in turn shaped by the distinctive symbolic and structural patterns of their society.

In one major line of inquiry, symbolic interactionist research by George Gerbner and his associates suggests that heavy television viewers tend to have markedly distorted views of the real world because they apparently believe that the world is very much like what they see on the tube (Signorelli & Morgan, 1990; Sparks, 1992; Gerbner et al., 1994; Burk & Shaw, 1995). Since television is overloaded with crime and violence, heavy viewers overestimate their risk of being victimized (Chirocos et al., 1997)— Gerbner calls this the "mean world" effect. Similarly, because there are large numbers of doctors, lawyers, and police on television, heavy viewers overestimate the number of people who actually work in these fields.

Symbolic interactionism raises a number of other important questions concerning the effects of the content of television programming. The negative and distorted images of minority and female characters on television and in films, which were discussed in earlier chapters, can affect how viewers see members of these groups. Research has clearly established, for example, that the more television people watch, the more conservative their gender role attitudes (Signorelli, 1989; Klein, 1996). Thus it is important to focus on how women and minorities (and other groups, such as the elderly or gays and lesbians) are portrayed in the media in order to understand how they are viewed and treated by the larger society.

MINORITIES Although some stereotyping persists in the movies, especially in comedies, significant gains have been made, especially among African Americans. In part, this is because blacks are now fairly well represented in most facets of the industry, from actors like 2002 Oscar winners Denzel Washington and Halle Berry to widely acclaimed directors like Spike Lee and the Hughes brothers (Johansen, 1997; Wells & Hakanen, 1997).

On television, on the other hand, while blacks are generally quite visible, most of the shows with predominantly African American casts are situation comedies (frequently on UPN and the WB) that attract very few white viewers, and many of these shows depict blacks in demeaning and stereotyped ways. Overall, 39 percent of all black actors on television appear in sitcoms, compared with 31 percent of whites (Elber, 2002).

Latinos continue to be almost invisible in both film and television, as is discussed in the *Diversity in Focus* box on page 545.

WOMEN Women have made less progress in film than have African Americans, and some of their earlier gains may be threatened. When the studio system was at its peak in the 1930s and 1940s, women were well represented among Hollywood's brightest stars, and they were frequently portrayed as strong and capable, especially during the 1940s. But today over 70 percent of all feature film roles go to men, male studio executives still outnumber females three to one, and top female stars are often paid as little as half what leading men make (Silvas et al., 1993; Lindsey, 1997).

Hollywood executives defend themselves against charges of sexism by saying that stereotyped female roles simply reflect male fantasies, and that films must appeal to a male audience in order to turn a profit. This claim may be reasonable considering that the average moviegoer is a male between the ages of 14 and 24 (Basow, 1992; Anderson, 1994). But if Hollywood expects to keep profits high, it will need to target the growing market of financially secure women who want more positive film portrayals of people like themselves.

The progress of women in television has also been slow. Although 59 percent of the prime-time audience is female, only 40 percent of the major characters on prime-time TV are currently female—about the same percentage as in 1990—and men continue to be more likely than women to be depicted as doctors, lawyers, or CEOs. In part, this is because only 21.5 percent of the studio brass in television are female. Female characters are more likely to be present and to be depicted in nonstereotyped ways when there is at least one woman among the top executives on a given show (Lauzen, 1999).

POSTMODERN THEMES Recently, extensive analyses of the media have been conducted by a number of postmodern sociologists who have been strongly influenced by the conflict and symbolic interactionist traditions. They have greatly broadened the symbolic interactionist critique, charging not only that media domination of people's consciousness influences how we think about women and people of color, but indeed that it has fundamentally altered and distorted our basic perceptions of social reality (Dandaneau, 2001).

The French sociologist Jean Baudrillard (1988, 1995) coined the term *hyperreality* to refer to the fact that, in his view, most people in postmodern societies and especially in the United States seem to experience simulated reality on television as somehow more authentic than real life. We relieve our loneliness by tuning in to *Friends,* and we accept television charac-

What are these children learning? Research by George Gerbner and his associates has consistently found that people who watch a great deal of television view certain aspects of society differently than do more moderate users of the medium.

Sports fans frequently engage in rituals such as cheering and painting their faces in team colors in hopes of spurring their team on to victory. Sociologists note that such actions have a religious quality to them.

ters as members of our reference groups as if they were real people. In short, we believe media portrayals of reality more than we trust our own experience.

For example, informal racial segregation is widespread in reality, but because most television shows idealistically portray a highly integrated world, we think there is more interracial interaction than there really is (Gates, 1992). Evidence that global warming is a real and very serious problem is all around us, in nature (melting glaciers, rising temperatures worldwide) and in scientific research reports, but because it is rarely depicted on television, most people are ignoring the problem, with potentially catastrophic consequences. The media create concepts like "Generation X," which do not really exist (unlike the Baby Boom, people born between 1964 and 1978 share relatively few common experiences)—but because we become familiar with these concepts through the media, they take on a kind of phantom reality, shaping the way we think about ourselves and the social world (Dandaneau, 2001).

In short, our minds have been colonized and are effectively controlled by the mass media, leading us to ignore critical realities. In Neil Postman's (1985) evocative phrase, we are "amusing ourselves to death."

SPORT AND THE MEDIA: A SYMBIOTIC RELATIONSHIP

Sport and the media enjoy a symbiotic relationship, each contributing directly to the growth of the other. Sports coverage attracts newspaper and magazine readers and television viewers, while media publicity promotes the popularity of sports (Lever & Wheeler, 1993; Wenner, 1998).

Newspapers began regular coverage of sports in the 1890s; today they take up about half of the space devoted to all hard news combined. Moreover, the sports section of the paper attracts about five times as many readers as any other feature (Lowes, 1999). The newsstands are filled with sports magazines; *Sports Illustrated*, with a weekly circulation of 3.5 million, is the most widely read.

Radio airs over half a million hours of sports coverage each year (Eitzen & Sage, 2003). But television is the real thousand-pound gorilla in the world of sports media. The major networks broadcast over 2,000 hours of sports programming annually. Even this figure is dwarfed by the 24-hour-per-day coverage of the several all-sports cable networks, most prominently ESPN, which was founded in 1980.

Although sport and the media are symbiotic, sports need the media more than the media need sports. The revenue that the media have made available to sport has radically transformed big-time athletics (Bellamy, 1998). The broadcast rights for the 2008 Summer Olympics will cost NBC $894 million. The right to televise the NFL between 1998 and 2006 sold for $17.6 billion, about 65 percent of all team revenues. Each team in major league baseball receives $13 million per year from the TV networks. A single 30-second commercial during the 2002 Super Bowl costs $1.9 million or more (Eitzen & Sage, 2003).

How have these economic realities changed sports? In almost every way imaginable (Wenner, 1998). Consider the following examples:

- The flow of media dollars has played a crucial role, along with the establishment of free agency, in increasing player salaries. In 1970, the average annual wage in the NFL was $23,000; in the NBA it was $40,000; and in major league baseball, $29,300. In 2001, the equivalent figures, not adjusted for inflation, were $1.269 million, $3.17 million, and $2.29 million (Eitzen & Sage, 2003).
- The number of franchises has expanded. Baseball, for example, has grown from 16 teams to 30. More teams mean more televised games and more money. For the same reason, the number of teams eligible for post-season play has increased in all major sports.
- Television has greatly reduced the popularity of minor league sports, especially baseball. Why watch second-rate players when you can turn on the television and see Alex Rodriguez and Randy Johnson? In turn, college sports have become de facto minor leagues, which has accelerated the commercialization of sport at this level.
- Numerous rule changes have been made, not because they necessarily enhance the game, but because they meet the needs of television. Many of these changes—such as the shot clock and the three-point shot in basketball—make games more exciting, especially to less-knowledgeable fans. Sudden-death tie breakers in football and tennis keep games predictable in length and thus allow them to fit better into broadcast schedules. In the NFL, official time-outs at the end of each quarter and the two-minute warning exist solely to allow more time for commercials (Coakley, 2001).
- Athletes have become far more flamboyant, diminishing, in some people's eyes, the dignity of sports. While the pros have always attracted characters—Ty Cobb, Babe Ruth, and Wilt Chamberlain certainly had their personality quirks—before television, their excesses were generally covered up by the print media. Today the unblinking eye of the television camera focuses on bizarre sports personalities like Allan Iverson, Mike Tyson, and Tonya Harding.

LIFE CONNECTIONS

The Dark Side of Sport

Unquestionably, sport pervades our lives. But despite the positive functions it provides, it also has a dark side, sometimes encouraging violence, racism, and sexism (Dunning, 1999).

Violence and Deviance in Sport

Decades ago, some social scientists thought that watching sports could serve as a *catharsis*, a release of emotional energy, especially violent and aggressive urges. The noted animal behaviorist Konrad Lorenz (1963) recommended expanding international athletic competition as an alternative to warfare. However, while some forms of vigorous exercise can reduce aggressiveness in some instances among participants, there is no evidence that watching violent sports has a comparable effect on spectators. In fact, androcentric but instructive research shows that men watching football games tend to become more aggressive, which is not true of male spectators of nonviolent sports like gymnastics (Berkowitz, 1993; Sipes, 1996).

Sociologists believe that violence is primarily learned, not innate, and that this learning usually occurs when an individual observes other people being rewarded for their aggressive behavior. This is true for both watching and playing sports. Sport is the only institution other than the military that routinely condones violence. Young athletes who have internalized the Lombardi ethic are often pressured to use violence in pursuit of victory, whether in the form of late hits in football, high-sticking in hockey, or deliberate fouls in basketball (Nixon, 1993; Sabo, 1995).

Not surprisingly, the result is frequently injury. Boxing is the most extreme case: Some 500 fighters died between 1950 and 1995 from ring-related problems. About one in five NFL players misses at least one game each year due to injury; two-thirds of retired pro football players believe the game has shortened their life expectancy (Huizenga, 1994). An average of eight high-school football players die annually. And most observers believe that the problem is getting worse, in part because of the constant emphasis on violence in the media.

In addition, players sometimes continue their aggressive behavior off the field. Recent studies document that male college athletes, especially those involved in contact sports like football, are considerably more likely than nonathletes to be involved in sexual assault (Welch, 1997; Benedict, 1998). One researcher found athletes were 5.5 times more likely than other students to admit having committed date rape (Crosset et al., 1995). This finding is congruent with the fact that sport is an important mechanism of male gender-role socialization. The roles that male athletes learn generally emphasize toughness, denial of empathy, and dominance. This construction of masculinity is clearly compatible with sexual assault (Nelson, 1994; Burstyn, 1999).

Deviance among athletes is by no means limited to violence. For example, one study showed that one-third of a group of NFL players received illegal money when they were in college (Sack, 1991). Even more seriously, the use of performance-enhancing drugs in sports has become increasingly common (Yesalis & Cowart, 1998). Such practices are not new; throughout history athletes have used everything from caffeine to nitroglycerine to strychnine to amphetamines to improve their performance (Eitzen & Sage, 2003). But the advent of anabolic steroids, extensive media coverage of their use, and the feverish intensity of the "war on drugs" have made the problem more visible.

There is no accurate way to estimate how many athletes abuse steroids. Research suggests that between 6 and 10 percent of male high-school students take them, as do roughly 30 percent of college football players, 15 percent of female track and field athletes, and 75 percent of NFL players (Lucas, 1994; Yesalis & Cowart, 1998). As usage rises—and is more widely publicized—pressure to take performance-enhancing drugs escalates, because if you don't use them and your opponent does, you are putting yourself at a disadvantage. The result, despite increased drug testing, may well be continued growth in the use of steroids and an increased incidence of their harmful side effects.

Racism in Sport

Before World War II, sports were almost completely segregated, with the exception of boxing with heavyweight champions Jack Johnson and Joe Louis. But when the Brooklyn Dodgers brought Jackie Robinson up to the majors in April 1947, the barriers to black participation began to crumble (Tygiel, 1983). By 1957, 12 percent of all major league baseball players were African Americans, the same percentage that blacks made up at that time in the society as a whole. The NBA reached that milestone one year later, and the NFL did so in 1960. Over the next 15 years, almost all formal resistance to black participation at both the amateur and the professional levels ended: In 2000, African Americans made up 77 percent of the NBA, 65 percent of the NFL, and 15 percent of major league baseball players. Latino participation remains minimal—less than 1 percent—in pro football and basketball, although major league baseball players are currently 26 percent Hispanic (Lapchick, 2002).

Sports were desegregated earlier than other sectors of U.S. life for several reasons (Edwards, 1973; Gnida, 1995). The competitive nature of sport meant that there would be strong support for nondiscrimination if minorities could help their teams win. Crucially, as was discussed in Chapter 1, performance in sports can be precisely and objectively mea-

sured, so bias is less of a factor than is the case in more subjective situations. Furthermore, success on the field does not require that athletes be friends. And, finally, the success of a minority athlete is not likely to lead to his or her promotion over whites, a significant way in which sport differs from most other careers.

Many people cite the success of minorities in sports as evidence that U.S. society is no longer discriminatory (Entine, 2000), but the truth is more complex. For one thing, a certain amount of **stacking** continues in college and professional football and baseball (Smith & Leonard, 1997). In this practice, minorities are disproportionately assigned to "non-central" positions low in outcome control and leadership responsibility (Loy & McElvogue, 1970). These positions are believed to require speed, aggressiveness, and good "instincts," whereas central roles call for intelligence and coolness under pressure (Williams & Youssef, 1975).

For example, in 2000, 21 percent of NFL quarterbacks were African Americans compared with 86 percent of running backs; in baseball, 4 percent of catchers and pitchers, but 40 percent of outfielders, were black (Lapchick, 2001). On the positive side, stacking is no longer apparent in basketball, and real progress has been made in some other sports. Stacking is by no means exclusively a U.S. phenomenon: cross-cultural research shows that English-speaking Canadian hockey players, African and West Indian soccer players in Britain, and aborigines in Australian rugby are all underrepresented in central positions in their sports (Maguire, 1988; Lavoie, 1989; Hallinan, 1991).

Stacking apparently occurs because some white coaches and owners do not believe that minorities have the mental abilities necessary for central positions (Loy & McElvogue, 1970). This prejudiced attitude relegates minorities to physically demanding positions that generally result in shorter careers (Eitzen & Sage, 2003). In addition, research strongly suggests that marginal white players are more likely to be successful in college and professional sports than marginal minorities (Kooistra et al., 1993).

Stacking also contributes indirectly to the underrepresentation of African Americans and other people of color in coaching and administrative positions, because most successful candidates for these jobs played central positions when they were athletes. In 2001, just 10 percent of NFL head coaches, 20 percent of major league baseball head coaches, 34 percent of NBA head coaches, 22 percent of Division 1-A college basketball head coaches, and 5 percent of big-time college football head coaches were African Americans. There was one Latino head coach in

As traditional gender roles have weakened, female athletes have started participating in sports like football and boxing from which they were historically excluded. In this 2001 match, Laila Ali, on the right, defeated Jacqui Frasier. Both are the daughters of former heavyweight champions.

major league baseball, but none in major league football or basketball, and not one big-time professional sports team was owned by an African American or a Latino (Lapchick, 2002). In December of 2002, Robert Johnson, the founder of BET, bought the new NBA franchise in Charlotte, NC, becoming the first African American owner of a big-time sports team. In addition, despite obvious but occasional exceptions like Michael Jordan and Tiger Woods, most minority athletes have only limited opportunities to earn money through endorsements.

Because of these hard realities, many prominent black Americans have strongly urged African American youth to think carefully before setting their sights on a career in professional sports (Asch, 1977; Hoberman, 1997). Despite the presence of many successful minority athletes as role models, the hard fact is that there simply are not very many opportunities at the top. The odds of a high-school football player making it to the NFL are 1,222 to 1; in men's basketball the figure jumps to 2,681 to 1 (Coakley, 2001). There are 12 times as many African American lawyers and doctors as there are black major league athletes (Coakley, 2001).

Sexism in Sport

Like racial and ethnic minorities, women have also made impressive gains in sport in recent decades. Nevertheless, they too often experience less than fully equal treatment (Hargreaves, 1994; Nelson, 1994; Malec, 1997).

Women rarely participated in organized sports in the United States until the later 19th century. At this time, substantial numbers became involved in croquet, roller skating, golf, bowling, and bicycling (Vertinsky, 1994). Also during these years, many women's colleges began programs in swimming, basketball, and field hockey. (The *Then and Now* box on the facing page discusses the evolution of women's basketball). Unfortunately, most of these pioneering efforts had ended by the 1920s, done in by college administrators and female physical education teachers who thought athletic competition was incompatible

INTERNET CONNECTIONS

Take a look at Gender Equity in Sports:
http://bailiwick.lib.uiowa.edu/ge/

The contents will provide you with a detailed history of women's quest for equality in sports, including a graphic look at Title IX legislation and its impact on the issues involved. After you have examined this Website, answer the following questions: Whether you are male or female, do you think the changes that have taken place in women's sports over the past several decades have made a difference in terms of women's overall quest for social equality? Why or why not? To what extent is there equity in sports at your institution?

THEN AND NOW

Women's Basketball: Before and After Title IX

Between the 1920s and the 1970s, competitive team sport in the United States was essentially an all-male domain. Women were not totally banned, but rather were limited to those sports considered "appropriate" for them. At private clubs, middle- and upper-class women engaged in such "feminine" recreational activities as tennis and golf, croquet and archery, swimming, horseback riding, and ice skating. In the 1920s, women's fencing, track and field, and a few gymnastic events were added to the Olympics. Individual athletes such as Sonja Henie (ice skating), Helen Wills (tennis), Gertrude Ederle (swimming), and Babe Didrikson Zaharias (golf) became national heroines.

However, women's athletics were not only separate from men's sports in high schools and colleges, they were also clearly inferior to them. While boys prepared for varsity competition, with the ultimate goal of winning championships for their school, girls were confined to calisthenics and to girls' games—basketball, volleyball, field hockey, track and field—played by girls' rules.

The history of women's basketball nicely illustrates the changing gender gap in sports. After the sport was invented in 1891, it quickly became popular among college women, who loved the freedom of movement and vigorous competition. Ironically, however, female physical educators led the drive to portray basketball as a threat to women. Serious competition, they argued, could foster such unfeminine qualities as roughness, determination, tenacity, and goal orientation, qualities that would make young women unattractive to the opposite sex. These women feared that sports might interfere with girls' future happiness as homemakers. Senda Berenson, director of physical education at Smith College, argued that women must be protected from the "evils" of male sports (Rader, 1990).

In the 1890s, Berenson developed a modified set of rules to make women's basketball "less stressful." There were six rather than five players on a side. The court was divided into three backcourt and three frontcourt sectors. Players were prohibited from moving out of their sector, dribbling, snatching the ball from an opponent's hands, or even talking during play. These rules resulted in a "stand-and-pass" game as boring to players as to spectators. Girls continued to play basketball by "boys' rules" at many high schools and colleges well into the 1920s. But opposition to competitive team sports for women was growing.

In 1923, the Women's Division of the National Amateur Athletic Foundation (NAAF) adopted a platform opposing varsity competition. Representing their school, college, or university in public athletic competitions was seen as a male prerogative. The only appropriate role for women at coed schools was a supportive one, on the cheerleading squad. Women athletes, the NAAF declared, must be "protected from exploitation for the enjoyment of spectators, the athletic reputation, or the commercial advantage of any school or organization. . . ." Women's colleges were viewed as extensions of the family where young women received additional training in the social graces. Intercollegiate games would require students to leave their protective campuses and perform before audiences of both sexes, risking their modesty and reputations. In keeping with the feminine role, women's athletics should be noncompetitive and inclusive: "a sport for every girl, and every girl in a game" (Rader, 1990:232).

The NAAF endorsed four alternatives to interscholastic and intercollegiate competition. One was *intramural competition* among students at the same school or college (with no outside spectators). In *telegraphic meets,* colleges didn't play face-to-face but rather, the results of intramural competitions were telegraphed to "competing" schools. On *play days,* women from several schools got together, but competition was minimized by the random assignment of girls from different schools to one-day-only teams. The primary emphasis was on social interaction, not competition. On *sports days,* teams from different schools or colleges competed, but the focus was on recreation. Which teams won or lost was not even reported, and schools whose teams played too aggressively or too well risked not being invited back. In general, girls' games offered limited opportunities for participants to develop their athletic potential to the fullest and generated little enthusiasm among female students.

In the 1970s, as part of a rising tide of feminism, players and coaches across the country began rebelling against such restrictions. In basketball, women's high school and college teams threw out "girls' rules" and switched to a five-player, full-court game. Title IX gave this grassroots movement legal backing. But change has been slow and uneven. In the 1980s, women tennis and track stars began to attract national attention. But not until the mid- to late 1990s were women's team sports granted full professional status, with the creation and subsequent substantial success of the Women's National Basketball Association (WNBA).

1. What are the messages about the meaning of being female that were communicated by girls' rules basketball?

2. Are there continuing inequalities between men's and women's sports? If so, why have they persisted?

Source: Rader, 1990.

with traditional gender-role expectations. These opponents of female participation argued, incorrectly, that vigorous athletic activity led to problems in childbearing, damaged the uterus and breasts, developed unsightly muscles, and caused nervous breakdowns (Sargent, 1912).

Between the 1920s and the early 1970s, opportunities for women in athletics, especially at the high-school and college levels, were very limited. But all this began to change when the Educational Amendments Act of 1972 was passed, over the strong opposition of the NCAA. **Title IX** of the act mandates that

> no person in the United States shall, on the basis of sex, be excluded from participation in, be denied the benefits of, or be subjected to discrimination under any education program or activity receiving federal financial assistance.

Title IX requires that schools provide substantially equal athletic opportunities to both genders. While some of the details of what the Act mandates are still being clarified in the courts, Title IX has dramatically altered women's sports. In 1971, 3,667,000 high-school boys participated in organized sports programs compared with just 294,000 girls. Today the figures are 3.921 million for boys and 2.784 million for girls; 41 percent of high-school athletes are female (Eitzen & Sage, 2003:319).

Changes have also occurred at the college level. Before Title IX, about 15 percent of college athletes were female, and female sports in coeducational colleges rarely received more than 2 or 3 percent of the total athletic budget. By the late 1990s, women made up 40 percent of varsity athletes and received 41 percent of all scholarship aid (NCAA, 1999). The continuing disparity results primarily from the emphasis large schools place on the revenue-producing sports of football and men's basketball.

Women have become much more visible in the professional ranks as well with the increasing popularity of the WNBA and of such outstanding competitors as tennis superstars Venus and Serena Williams.

In addition, female participation in nonschool-based sports has increased greatly over the past 25 years. Today, over a million girls are playing in youth soccer leagues. For years, Little League baseball firmly resisted gender integration, but as many as 200,000 girls now play on Little League teams (www.littleleague.org).

Athletic prowess in women has historically been considered unfeminine. Opponents of gender equity maintained that athletics and femininity were incompatible, and women who excelled at sports ran the risk of being labeled lesbians (Blinde & Taub, 1992; Griffin, 1998). These stereotypes were applied to all female athletes, but especially to those who played traditionally male sports like baseball and basketball. Women who swam, played tennis or golf, or figure-skated faced considerably less hostility (Kane & Lenskyj, 1998).

Early research suggested that sexist stereotypes created significant gender-role problems for many female athletes, but newer studies demonstrate that the problem is becoming less serious (Blinde & Taub, 1993; Crane, 2001). However, a relatively recent study of women on the LPGA tour found that some still felt a distinct tension between their identities as women and as golfers (Crosset, 1995), and many female athletes continue to make it a point to wear makeup and jewelry during games and to tie their long hair back with pink ribbons, which symbolic interactionists interpret as efforts to reaffirm their feminine identity (Crane, 2001).

It would seem logical that recent sharp increases in female participation in competitive sports would have led to equal opportunities for women as coaches and administrators, but this isn't necessarily the case. In the early days of Title IX, women's intercollegiate athletics were under the control of an essentially all-female organization called the Association for Intercollegiate Athletics for Women (AIAW). However, the NCAA moved into women's sports in 1981, and within a year the AIAW collapsed. Since then, women's athletics have come to closely resemble the highly competitive male model. More significantly, as women's sports have become better funded, the percentage of female coaches has declined and men have moved into many of the most desirable positions (Acosta & Carpenter, 2000).

In the early 1970s, virtually all collegiate women's teams were coached by women; by 2000, the figure had fallen to just 45.6 percent, the lowest in history (Coakley, 2001). Female coaches still typically earn just over half of the salaries of their male counterparts. In 1972, over 90 percent of Division 1 women's sports programs were administered by women; by 2002, only 8.4 percent still were. Women currently make up just 4 of the 18 members of the NCAA Division 1 Board of Directors.

Overall, it is clear that attitudes and norms about race and gender constantly intrude into sport. And this intrusion is insidious. It actually works against what sport is designed to do: to allow any athlete to achieve to the height of his or her ability. Continued racism and sexism in sports demonstrates that the playing field is not yet fully level.

SOCIETY CONNECTIONS

Censorship and the Electronic Media

Despite First Amendment guarantees of freedom of speech, the United States has a long tradition of censoring unpopular ideas and graphic content in the mass media (Garry, 1993; Fraleigh & Truman, 1997). While the courts have generally been reluctant, especially in recent decades, to significantly restrict the written word, freedom of speech has been far more problematic in the movies and other popular arts (Sanders, 1994). In 1915, the Supreme Court ruled that film was a business, not an art form, and accordingly was not constitutionally protected speech. This judgment was not reversed until 1952 (Heins, 1993).

Advocates of censorship generally focus on graphic sexual content and, to a lesser extent, on violence. They use the hypodermic model of media influence, arguing that media sexuality and violence directly encourage such behavior and desensitize children to antisocial acts (Callahan & Appleyard, 1997). Their opponents do not necessarily deny such effects, although they tend to minimize their seriousness, but they believe that restricting freedom of speech poses a more serious problem (Maines, 1993; Zuckerman, 1995).

In practice, the government has rarely acted directly as a censor, because the motion picture, television, and popular music industries voluntarily developed their own rating systems. In 1922, a group of Hollywood producers and directors first published a code of standards for what could and could not be shown on screen (Plagenz, 1997). But in the later 1950s, the industry began to relax its puritanical standards, and films became markedly more explicit. This immediately led to renewed demands for outright censorship. Hollywood responded in 1968 by establishing the G-PG-R-X rating system. In 1984, the PG-13 rating was introduced after criticism of violent content in *Indiana Jones and the Temple of Doom*. In 1990, the NC-17 designation was developed to allow audiences to differentiate between serious films with strong erotic or violent content and outright pornography (Heins, 1993).

Similar voluntary rating systems have been introduced in both popular music and television. In 1985, the music industry started applying a "parental advisory" sticker to potentially offensive releases, mostly rap and heavy metal (Minnow & LeMay, 1995), and in 1997, television introduced a detailed rating system.

Voluntarily imposed ratings have been very popular with parents and appear to be firmly established. Critics, however, point out that these schemes amount to a kind of pre-censorship, because most theaters will not book NC-17 films, some music stores hesitate to stock CDs with parental advisory labels, and networks resist airing television programs with MA (mature) ratings. Under these circumstances, artists and writers—creators of popular culture—feel strong commercial pressure to avoid controversial sexual material and violence. Furthermore, content warnings may actually be counterproductive, attracting some adolescents precisely because they identify certain discs as "forbidden fruit."

Among the latest developments in the censorship wars are technologies such as the *v-chip*, a device that allows parents to block the reception of television programs they don't want their children to watch. In 1996, Congress mandated that all new television sets include v-chip technology. Some applaud this legislation as a victory in the battle against televised violence, but others see it as a high-tech variation of existing rating systems and another step toward restricting freedom of speech through pre-censorship (Zoglin, 1996; Thierer & Chapman, 1997). In any event, very few parents appear to be making much use of the v-chip (Price, 1998).

Efforts to control potentially offensive material on the Internet have also run into difficulties. The 1996 Communications Decency Act, the Child On-Line Protection Act of 1998, and the Children's Internet Protection Act of 2000 have all been successfully challenged, in whole or in part, as overly restrictive of free speech rights (Sobel, 1999). Technologies similar to the v-chip are available for PCs, but again it is not clear how widely or effectively they are being used.

SUMMARY

1. Once largely informal, recreational activities have become increasingly institutionalized over the past two centuries.

2. The emerging institutions of sport and the mass media are important forms of modern popular culture.

3. Sport occupies an intermediate position between play and spectacle. It is enormously popular in the United States and may be analyzed as a microcosm of society.

4. Sport serves various functions, including providing entertainment, contributing to socialization, promoting individual and cultural identity, and encouraging military preparedness by keeping youth physically fit.

5. Conflict theorists maintain that sport exploits and dehumanizes athletes, overemphasizes winning, and promotes excessive commercialism and nationalism.

6. Applied to sport, symbolic interactionism draws attention to issues such as the development of gender roles and the use of Native American team names and mascots.

7. People in different classes participate in and watch different sports. Research suggests that sport participation is often loosely linked with upward social mobility.

8. Religions often use sport to attract support. Conversely, sport can be seen as a functional equivalent of religion with its own sacred rituals, heroes, and shrines.

9. According to the Postman thesis, the nature of a society's media has a strong impact on its conception of childhood.

10. Early studies of the media often employed a hypodermic model, which incorrectly suggested that the media's effects on their audiences are direct rather than mediated.

11. The social functions of the media include providing entertainment, facilitating social interaction, socialization, and promoting social control.

12. Conflict theorists believe that the media primarily defend the interests of the rich and powerful.

13. Symbolic interactionists and postmodern theorists focus on how media definitions of social reality affect the ways in which people understand the world in which they live.

14. The media and sport enjoy an unequal symbiotic relationship in which sport depends more on the media than the media do on sport.

15. Sport frequently promotes violent behavior. It also can encourage such forms of deviance as the use of illicit performance-enhancing drugs.

16. African Americans and other people of color have made considerable progress in gaining equal treatment in sports, although subtle forms of discrimination such as stacking still exist.

17. Opportunities in sport for women have expanded greatly as gender stereotypes have begun to fade.

18. The government rarely censors the media in the United States because the popular culture industries have developed voluntary rating systems.

KEY TERMS

conspicuous consumption 542
halo effect 541
hypodermic model 547

Lombardi ethic 541
popular culture 538
spectacle 538

sport 538
stacking 553
Title IX 556

CRITICAL THINKING QUESTIONS

1. Sport and the media have both been strongly criticized by conflict theorists, who claim that they negatively affect society. On the other hand, functionalists believe popular culture contributes positively to social life. Select a particular form of popular culture, indicate whether you feel its influence on society is basically positive or negative, and support your position.

2. On the whole, do you think that sport and the media mainly reflect the society in which they develop, or do they significantly shape society? Defend your position.

3. Are current rating systems for films, television programs, and popular music useful? Should government actively censor the media?

INVESTIGATE WITH CONTENT SELECT

 Begin your research using Content-Select for this chapter by following the directions found on page 27 of this text to visit Prentice Hall's Research Navigator Website. Enter these search terms into the search field:

Socialization
Title IX
Popular Music

EXERCISE 4. RELIGIOUS DIFFERENCES

Americans often differ in core religious beliefs. Catholics regard the Pope to be religiously infallible, but Protestants don't. Catholics and Protestants believe Christ is God, but Jews don't. Catholics, Protestants and Jews believe in one God, but atheists don't.

Beliefs aside, there are important sociological differences among America's religions. You can explore these at the Companion Website for this text at http://www.prenhall.com/lindsey. Click on the cover of this book, and select the appropriate iNTERSECTIONS exercise from the drop-down menu at the top. (Make sure Relig is the Row Variable.)

Here each respondent's religion is categorized in the most common way: Protestant, Catholic, Jewish, or none. Sixty-four percent of GSS respondents are Protestant, 25 percent are Catholic, only 2 percent are Jews, and 9 percent say they have no religion. (Other religions are represented among the respondents, but for simplicity we are ignoring those with very small numbers.)

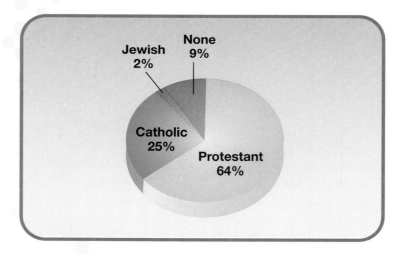

Do you think all these religions have a similar racial composition? That is, do Catholicism and Judaism have as high a proportion of black members as the Protestant denominations do? To what extent are blacks represented among those who say they have no religion at all?

You can use CHIP to find these answers, but there is a good reason to use it slightly differently than in prior exercises. Instead of calculating percentages *down the columns*, as you have done previously, it is convenient here to calculate percentages *across the rows*. You do this by setting CHIP for "% Across" at the upper left of your screen.

Select Race as your Column Variable. Now the screen shows you what percentage of each religion is white, and what percentage is black. (Since we are counting only two races, these necessarily add to 100 percent.) What percentage of Protestants are black? What percentage of Catholics? What percentage of Jews are black? What percentage of those with no religion are black? What do you conclude about racial differences among the religions?

(Notice that if we had calculated percentages down the columns, as usually done, we would not be able to say much about the characteristics of Jews because there are so few of them. Try it. By calculating percentages across the rows, we more easily compare the different religions.)

Are there educational differences among the religions? You can see by selecting Degree as the Column Variable. (Don't forget, % Across.) Which religion has adherents with the highest educational levels? Which one has the lowest educational levels? How do you account for these differences? What effect, if any, do you think educational differences might have on the different practices of these religions?

Do you think the religions are different in terms of perceived social class of members? Take a look.

Another background variable that may be important is place of residence, here categorized as either an urban setting (a city or suburbs) or a rural setting (country or small town). Are there any surprises in comparing religions on place of residence?

Write a capsule description of the sociological characteristics of each religion. Interpret why they differ. Do you think the sociological differences among religions relate in any way to their differing beliefs?

21
FORMAL ORGANIZATIONS
AND THE SOCIOLOGY OF WORK

Voices from the Workplace

Studs Terkel is a journalist who has spent his life interviewing ordinary people, usually about sociologically oriented issues. In one of his best-known books, *Working*, Terkel presents a variety of firsthand observations about the world of work. Here are excerpts from three of his interviews:

Phil Stallings, spot welder on the Ford Assembly line:
I stand in one spot, about [a] two or three foot area, all night. The only time a person stops is when the line stops. We do about 32 jobs per car, per unit. Forty-eight units an hour, 8 hours a day. Thirty-two times 48 times 8. Figure it out. That's how many times I push that button. . . . It doesn't stop. It just goes and goes and goes. I bet there's men who have lived and died out there, never seen the end of that line. (Terkel, 1985:221–222)

Sharon Atkins, receptionist for a large business:
You're just there to filter people and filter telephone calls. You're there just to handle equipment. You're treated like a piece of equipment, like the telephone. You come in at nine, you open the door, you look at the piece of machinery, you plug in the headpiece. That's how my day begins. You tremble when you hear the first ring. After that, it's sort of downhill. (Terkel, 1985:57–58)

Ray Wax, stockbroker:
It's up at 6:30. I read *The New York Times* and *The Wall Street Journal* before eight. I read the Dow Jones ticker tape between 8 and 10. At 3:30, when the market closes, I work until 4:30 or 5. I put in a great deal of technical work. I listen to news reports avidly. I try to determine what's happening. I'm totally immersed in what I'm doing. (Terkel, 1985:441)

The Dilbert Principle

Sociologists sometimes investigate social issues by studying popular culture—films, television programs, music, even comic strips. The strip that best captures the feel of the workplace is undoubtedly "Dilbert" (Scott Adams, 1996; Levy, 1996). Created by Scott Adams, a former middle manager at Pacific Bell, "Dilbert" is currently distributed to about 2000 newspapers in 57 countries, "Dilbert" books have topped the bestseller lists, and there was even a short-lived "Dilbert" television program.

The comic strip is a nightmarish parody of the bureaucratic work environment. Dilbert and his fellow employees toil away at meaningless tasks, isolated from each other by the walls of their tiny cubicles, supervised by a totally incompetent boss, and required to attend endless meetings that serve no identifiable purpose. Their ability to accomplish anything at work is constantly subverted by clueless management consultants, inane mission statements, absurd management fads, and the ever-present threat of downsizing. The underlying premise of this insane universe is the Dilbert Principle: ". . . the most ineffective workers are systematically moved to the place where they can do the least damage: management" (Adams, 1996:14).

This chapter examines two interrelated topics that help explain the work experiences of Phil Stallings, Sharon Atkins, Ray Wax, and Dilbert. First, we consider formal organizations, which have come to dominate not only work but also many other spheres of public life, including education, medicine, politics, sports, and religion. Then we look at the workplace with a particular emphasis on how bureaucratic formal organizations have transformed the human experience of work in industrial and postindustrial societies.

Source: DILBERT reprinted by permission of United Features Syndicate, Inc.

FORMAL ORGANIZATIONS AND BUREAUCRACY

A **formal organization** is a special type of secondary group (see Chapter 4) designed to allow a relatively large number of people to accomplish complex goals (Haas & Drabek, 1973; Hall, 1996). Formal organizations are characterized by clearly stated operating principles, special mechanisms to coordinate the activities of their members, clear lines of authority and communication, identifiable leaders, and unambiguous boundaries. Examples of formal organizations abound in today's world: your college or university, the federal government, the New York City Fire Department, Microsoft, Enron.

The study of formal organizations is important because there are so many of them and because they have become very large—the federal government directly employs over 5 million people. Indeed, we live in an age of formal organizations (Perrow, 1991; Volti, 1995). They shape how we think and how we act toward each other in an increasingly wide variety of contexts (Ritzer, 1996). If we wish to influence others, we do so more and more by joining formal organizations.

Types of Formal Organizations

There are three general approaches that formal organizations may use to encourage their members to conform to their role expectations. They may force obedience, they may reward it, or they may promote conformity by engaging their members' moral commitment (Etzioni, 1975). In real life the three strategies are often mixed.

A *coercive organization*—a prison, for example—secures obedience through force and the threat of punishment. Most total institutions (see Chapter 5), such as mental hospitals, are largely coercive. When

there is a military draft, the army is, at least from the point of view of some draftees, a coercive organization. But force is a relatively ineffective strategy because a great deal of time and energy must be devoted to exerting social control over unwilling participants.

Businesses and other *utilitarian organizations* reward their employees with money and other valued goods and privileges. This is generally a less costly way to obtain compliance. Today's military relies heavily on this approach. It offers new recruits incentives such as job training and money for a college education. Utilitarian organizations are more efficient than coercive ones, but the minute the money runs out, compliance becomes problematic.

A third strategy maximizes involvement with very limited social control costs. *Voluntary associations* use *normative power*—that is, they secure almost limitless obedience by pursuing goals to which their members are personally committed. Examples include the Methodist Church, the United Auto Workers, the Republican Party, the Sierra Club, and self-help groups like Alcoholics Anonymous (Wuthnow, 1994). In the wake of September 11th, the military has shifted substantially toward this strategy in its recruitment efforts by emphasizing patriotism and the need to defend the United States from terrorism.

The United States has long been characterized by a very high level of membership in voluntary associations. There are at least 200,000 such groups in the United States today (Krysan & D'Antonio, 1992). A sizable majority of citizens participate in at least one voluntary association, and about 25 percent belong to three or more (Curtis et al., 1992). In part, this extensive associational involvement reflects the long-term historical decline in the size and strength of the family in modern urban societies (see Chapter 15). Many former functions of extended families—such as providing sociability, mutual aid, and some forms of

Careers in the 21st Century

As the 21st century dawns, the job prospects for college graduates look bright. Many students enjoy the luxury of choosing among several good job offers months before commencement day. But tomorrow's career paths may be quite different from those experienced by previous generations.

Between the 1960s and the early 1990s, the route to success was relatively straightforward. Ambitious men—and increasingly, women—took positions as executive trainees at major corporations, worked hard, made the right connections, gradually moved into middle or upper management, and, ideally, retired with comfortable pensions. No longer. In 1997 alone, U.S. corporations laid off 103,000 employees. Jobs in sales and services multiplied, while positions in management declined. Most new jobs are with small companies (499 employees or less), not large corporations.

What can new graduates expect? Here is how some members of the class of 1997 started out (Meredith, 1997). William D. Lucy (University of Missouri, marketing major) turned down two other offers to accept a job at Enterprise Rent-a-Car, where his duties include working behind the counter, picking up customers at their homes and offices, and even washing cars—hardly tasks that require a college degree. Why did he choose Enterprise? Because of the company's entrepreneurial spirit. The chief executive describes Enterprise as "a confederation of small businesses" (Meredith, 1997, p. 10). All new hires start at the bottom for salaries of $22,000 to $30,000. If they demonstrate responsibility and initiative, they can expect promotions within their first year or two, with raises tied to their branch's performance.

Rachel D. Gunderson (University of Wisconsin, journalism major) chose a job as a merchandise analyst at the Target discount-store chain. Two months into the job, she is in charge of potting soil.

More importantly, she is learning how to analyze flow charts, place electronic orders, and keep Target's 750 stores supplied with 20 different types of dirt. Whatever the product, successful trainees can expect to become full-fledged buyers, at salaries ranging from $40,000 to $70,000, in four to five years.

Malane Rogers (University of Arkansas, industrial engineering major) works for Andersen Consulting, a giant temporary firm offering much higher starting salaries ($31,000 to $45,000) and more challenging work than the old secretarial/clerical "temp" agencies. Ms Rogers' current assignment is to find data on Texas Instruments' huge mainframe computers and produce easy-to-read reports for company executives. Many Fortune 500 corporations depend on Andersen to fill the gaps created when they lay off full-time employees.

More than likely, today's college graduates will change jobs at least once during their 20s, joining the ranks of what *Newsweek* magazine called the "New Nomads" (McGinn & McCormick, 1999). Company loyalty is no longer a prerequisite for promotions and raises; on the contrary, mass layoffs in the 1990s showed that "steady jobs" have become the exception, not the rule. New jobs (such as webmaster, wireless engineer, and desktop publisher) appear almost every year, and employers are competing for workers with technological, sales, and human or public relations experience. Today's workers have more choices, and hence more independence, than past generations enjoyed. Increasingly, U.S. workers are using their current jobs to develop expertise they can transfer from one company or industry to another, in some cases job-hopping around the world. In one survey, more than one in four workers had been at their current job less than 12 months.

The number of self-employed free agents, working as everything from personal trainer to urban planner, has also

grown—in part because it costs a company less to hire outside contractors for specific projects than to take on full-time employees and in part because workers prefer the freedom and flexibility of being their own bosses. Even within companies, employees are redesigning their jobs and launching their own ventures under the corporate umbrella. For example, after working at several different jobs, Neil Teplica settled down in real estate and became one of his company's most valued employees. At age 35, Teplica requested (and was granted) flex time, began traveling to remote places, and started an offbeat travel Website called "What's Going On." The following year, he and his flex-time partner began negotiating a deal with America OnLine (Marin & Gegax, 1997:74).

One possible scenario is that 21st century workers will spend their 20s as "nomads," become dedicated company men and women in their 30s, and will choose self-employment in their 40s and 50s, when most people's skills peak. This new flexibility may exact a cost, however. In addition to becoming an expert in a particular area, tomorrow's worker will also need to develop skills in advertising (to sell him- or herself to different employers), finance (to arrange start-up costs for a new venture and manage his or her own retirement plan), and technology (to keep up-to-date). Self-confidence, self-reliance, and a high tolerance for ambiguity and risk will be important.

1. On the whole, do you regard the changes discussed in this article as positive or negative? Explain your view.

2. Do you think the changing character of the U.S. workplace will make it easier or harder for people to combine work with family involvement?

Sources: Marin & Gegax, 1997; Meredith, 1997; McGinn & McCormick, 1999.

advanced socialization—are today increasingly sought in voluntary associations.

CLASS, RACE, GENDER, AND VOLUNTARY ASSOCIATIONS What sort of people are most likely to participate in voluntary associations? The clearest finding involves class: People from higher socioeconomic backgrounds are considerably more likely to hold multiple organizational memberships (Gilbert & Kahl, 1993). Such individuals have both the money and the time to be joiners. In turn, belonging to clubs and other such groups constitutes an important element of their cultural capital. Working-class people frequently are involved in unions, churches, and sports-related organizations, but their overall level of participation tends to be lower.

Research generally suggests that white people are somewhat more likely to become organizationally involved than African Americans and Latinos, but this is primarily because members of minority groups continue to rank somewhat lower than whites on the average with regard to class position (Guterbock & Fries, 1997).

Men and women participate in voluntary associations in similar numbers (Guterbock & Fries, 1997). Predominantly female associations have been extremely important in U.S. history—consider, for example, the settlement house and suffrage movements. Unfortunately, the contributions of these associations have commonly been devalued due to institutionalized sexism.

Bureaucracy

Most contemporary formal organizations take the form of **bureaucracies,** elaborately structured secondary groups designed to allow relatively large numbers of people to accomplish routine tasks as efficiently as possible. This emphasis on efficiency runs counter to popular understandings of bureaucracy, but if this form of organization was not reasonably efficient, it would not have come to dominate the modern world as it has (Evans & Rauch, 1999).

Bureaucracies are not new; as early as 4000 B.C.E., governments in China, Egypt, and Mesopotamia were organized along bureaucratic lines (Wallace, 1983). However, before the industrial revolution, few organizations could have been described as true bureaucracies, whereas over the past two centuries bureaucratic structures have expanded tremendously and outcompeted all other types of organizations (Volti, 1995).

Max Weber studied bureaucratic organization as part of his effort to understand the origins of modern society (Weber, 1947) (see Chapter 24). His analysis of bureaucracy takes the form of an **ideal type,** a description that emphasizes and even exaggerates a phe-

The logic of bureaucracy dictates that authority should be structured in a hierarchical fashion with a small number of people, such as this business executive, at the top and holding most of the power.

nomenon's most distinctive or characteristic qualities. Ideal type models are meant to identify the core or essence of a phenomenon; they are not necessarily entirely accurate descriptions of empirical reality (Blau & Meyer, 1987; Drysdale, 1996). Thus, the following six points drawn from Weber describe what a bureaucracy is supposed to be like, although real-life organizations may be more or less bureaucratic, depending on how closely they resemble the model.

- *An extensive division of labor.* Each participant in the organization is expected to accomplish a relatively narrow, specialized set of tasks; these bureaucratic roles work together in order to effectively promote the achievement of the organization's goals. For example, each employee of a university has a different specialized task to perform, from the academic dean, to the chairperson of the sociology department, to the reference librarian, to a worker in the snack bar.

- *Explicit written rules and regulations.* If there is ever any question about an individual's role or responsibilities, all he or she has to do is look it up. Faculty, staff, and students are all given handbooks that explain the rules by which their university operates.

- *Written records.* A written record not only makes it possible to prove that the rules have been followed, but also provides a precedent in case a similar issue arises in the future. For example, if a student is caught drinking in a dry dorm, it will be much easier for the campus authorities to decide how to handle the case if written records have been maintained documenting what was done the last time something like this happened.

- *A hierarchy of authority.* Bureaucratic statuses are ranked, and everyone in the organization has both a boss and subordinates, except for those at the very top (the chair of the board of trustees) and at the very bottom (a newly-hired member of the custodial staff). Power is vested in the bureaucratic role itself (Weber called it an *office*), not in the person currently playing the role.
- *Hiring and promotion on the basis of objective qualifications.* Like all bureaucracies, universities are expected to be meritocracies, hiring and promoting solely on the basis of specialized skills and knowledge. For example, a university hires faculty members only if they have the appropriate degrees and a solid record of teaching and research.
- *Impartial, universalistic treatment.* Bias and favoritism are to be avoided. Every student, administrator, and faculty member is to be treated like everyone else occupying a similar position. The desire not to violate this principle explains why many organizations have anti-nepotism rules, which prohibit hiring close relatives of current employees. It also explains why some professors may refuse to allow their children to enroll in their classes.

The final two principles of Weber's ideal type model are sometimes violated in the real world. This does not mean the model is inaccurate, but rather that these real-life organizations are less than fully bureaucratic. It also means that they are more likely to fail over the long run as they compete with organizations that reflect the model more precisely and thus are run more efficiently.

This reminds us once again of the crucial point that all of the ideal type characteristics of bureaucracy ultimately serve a single purpose: to make the organization as efficient—or, in Weber's terms, as rational—as possible. By **rationality,** Weber means consciously using the most effective means to pursue a chosen end. He believed the modern world was undergoing a continual process of **rationalization,** in which efficiency was becoming more and more characteristic of all spheres of life. Thus, for example, a relentlessly rational bureaucracy like Blockbuster is driving out less efficient video stores that hire friends of the owners despite that they are not very good workers or that stock mostly films the owners like but which are not all that popular with the general public.

In the first half of the twentieth century, most U.S. grocery stores were small, locally-owned operations offering only a limited variety of goods. Stores like this were unable to compete with modern, bureaucratically structured chain supermarkets featuring lower prices, modern technology, and a much wider selection of items for sale.

Weber was not optimistic about the long-term consequences of rationalization. Highly rationalized social systems can be oppressive and dehumanizing. Weber believed that we were at risk of being trapped in a restrictive "iron cage" of bureaucratic rationality. As he put it, "It is horrible to think that the world would one day be filled with nothing but these little cogs, little men clinging to little jobs and striving for better ones" (Bendix, 1962).

Highly rationalized social systems stamp out the personal, traditional, emotional, whimsical aspects of life; in Weber's terms, they "disenchant" the world. But, from within the iron cage, it is hard to develop a convincing argument that we should spend more time smelling the roses and less time fixated on the bottom line. The problems created by excessive rationality are discussed further in Chapter 24.

INFORMAL LIFE WITHIN THE BUREAUCRACY The oppressive quality of bureaucratic rationality helps explain why all organizations are characterized by an *informal structure* as well as a formal one. Informal relationships inevitably grow up between the particular people who occupy bureaucratic statuses (Perrow, 1986). Weber's abstract model does not take into account "bureaucracy's other face" (Page, 1946), but he was certainly aware of its existence (Blau & Meyer, 1987; Adams & Sydie, 2001).

A number of symbolic interactionist studies of bureaucratic functioning have demonstrated the importance of informal structure. Whatever organizations we research, we invariably discover that informal norms emerge among the participants. These norms complement, modify, and in some cases oppose the organization's official guidelines (Vallas, 1999). In other words, a bureaucracy's formal structure matters, but so do the people who staff it.

Sometimes the informal structure promotes the accomplishment of the organization's goals. If the formal guidelines are too rigid or do not fit the present circumstances, workers may develop new rules that cut through the red tape (Scott, 1981; Pandey & Kingsley, 2000). Informal communication networks—grapevines—disseminate information through the organization more rapidly and broadly than do routine channels. And bonding through informal interaction with coworkers improves worker morale, which can in turn increase productivity (Barnard, 1938; Perrow, 1986).

On the other hand, informal norms may arise that hinder an organization's ability to achieve its goals. This often occurs among lower-ranking participants in large, rigid industrial bureaucracies. For example, in a classic early study in which researchers investigated a Western Electric plant near Chicago, they found that the workers informally rejected the production quotas set by management, replaced them with their own lower quotas, and sarcastically labeled those who strove to meet management's norms as "speed kings" or "rate busters." People who reported slacking fellow workers to the bosses were called "squealers" and were ostracized (Roethlisberger & Dickson, 1939).

From a functionalist perspective, such informal norms reduce the organization's productivity. The conflict perspective, however, sees informal structure as a way workers attempt to protect themselves from victimization by their employers (Burawoy, 1980).

The point is that in order to understand a bureaucracy, we must consider both its formal and informal structure. The actual character of an organization is always a sort of *negotiated order:* The formal structure is modified through compromises with the preferences of the people staffing it (Strauss et al., 1964).

DYSFUNCTIONS OF BUREAUCRACY Bureaucracies accomplish certain kinds of tasks extremely well, especially when the job is fairly simple and routine or when it is only rarely necessary to deviate from standard procedures. But the fact that bureaucracies are highly rational and efficient does not make them equally suitable for all purposes, nor does it mean that they do not generate certain problems. In fact, bureaucracies are prone to a number of major dysfunctions unless precautions are taken against them.

1. *Communication Problems.* Communication generally flows readily down the bureaucratic hierarchy, but underlings may hesitate to report a problem to their superiors, especially if it makes them look bad or will require them to do extra work. As a result, unless special steps (like suggestion boxes) are taken to encourage lower-level participants to communicate freely, decisions may be made on the basis of faulty information with negative consequences for bureaucratic functioning (Blau & Meyer, 1987).

2. *Trained Incapacity.* The elaborate division of labor in a bureaucracy can lead to a kind of tunnel vision that keeps individuals from responding effectively to new situations. When a new problem arises, bureaucrats sometimes keep their heads down and avoid making adaptive decisions. "It's not my responsibility," they cry. Thorstein Veblen (1933) referred to this problem as **trained incapacity.**

Robert Merton (1968) put the problem slightly differently: In some cases, people who work in large formal organizations develop a general mind-set, called the *bureaucratic personality*, that makes them rigid and inflexible. This image of the blinkered bureaucrat has been popular for decades. Most recent research, however, tends to refute Merton's claim. Although bureaucrats may well display trained incapacity *in their official roles*, as individuals they have often been found to be creative, flexible and adaptive, and inclined to tolerate nonconformity (Kohn, 1978; Foster, 1990).

3. *Bureaucratic Ritualism.* In a closely related dysfunction, bureaucrats can become so committed to obeying the official guidelines that the rules, in effect, become the organization's ends, even when such behavior ultimately blocks attainment of the group's real goals. This is the familiar problem of "red tape" or **bureaucratic ritualism** (Merton, 1968; Coleman, 1990; Kiser & Schneider, 1994; Pandey & Kingsley, 2000). If someone well up in the hierarchy regularly reviews the relevance of the rules and determines if they are being applied appropriately, bureaucratic ritualism can be substantially reduced.

4. *Goal Displacement.* Another way bureaucracies can lose sight of their original goals is through **goal displacement:** Under some circumstances, an organization may devote most of its attention to survival rather than to achieving its ends. As Weber (1978) noted, bureaucracies are very hard to destroy.

Goal displacement is likely to occur when the public strongly opposes a bureaucracy. For example, small

These people are waiting in line for their unemployment checks. The impersonal formality of large bureaucracies reduces bias but often makes clients feel stifled by the red tape of bureaucratic ritualism.

socialist parties in the United States have been forced to focus on survival to the exclusion of other activities in these conservative times. Goal displacement can also occur when an organization succeeds in achieving its main objective. When this happens, it usually selects a new goal, a process called *goal succession.* The classic example is the March of Dimes, which was established to raise money for polio research. But when the Salk and Sabin vaccines were developed and polio was essentially eradicated in the late 1950s, the organization did not simply go out of business (Sills, 1957). Too many people derived their livelihood, status, and identity from their membership in it (see Selznick, 1957), so a new goal was chosen—the elimination of birth defects—an objective that is, not coincidentally, unlikely to be achieved in the near future.

5. *Parkinson's Law.* This dysfunction and the next one, like the Dilbert Principle, were originally proposed in jest, but in fact they accurately reflect some underlying realities of organizational life. **Parkinson's Law** states that work in a bureaucracy expands to fill the time available for its completion (Parkinson, 1962). Because employees know that they must look fully engaged in their work in order to keep their jobs, they create busy work and may even hire assistants—who must in turn be supervised—to complete the busy work. The result is an overgrown, bloated bureaucracy that could accomplish its goals with far fewer employees.

6. *The Peter Principle.* Bureaucrats who perform well in entry-level jobs are normally rewarded by being promoted up the hierarchy, often into administrative positions (Peter & Hull, 1969). Thus, teachers become principals and floor nurses become head nurses. If they continue to do well in their new jobs, they are promoted again. But the skills that ensure success at one level do not necessarily guarantee good performance in higher-level jobs. Sooner or later most people find themselves in positions in which they do not succeed. This is the **Peter Principle**—that bureaucrats will be promoted until they reach their "level of incompetence."

Bureaucracies hesitate to fire or demote dedicated, long-term employees, so the workers tend to stay at this level, creating a logjam of deadwood toward the top of the hierarchy. Meanwhile, their work is being done by subordinates who have not yet reached their own level of incompetence or who lack the formal credentials for advancement. One solution to the Peter Principle is to create well-paid and prestigious upper-level positions (like "master teachers") that require the same skills that workers have demonstrated in lower-level roles.

7. *Oligarchy.* Finally, there is substantial evidence that even if their members are personally committed to running the organization democratically, bureaucracies frequently succumb to what political sociologist Robert Michels (1876–1936) called the **iron law of oligarchy:** They fall under the control of an oligarchy, a small number of top leaders (Michels, 1962; Tolson, 1995). In fact, Michels went so far as to say that "who says organization says oligarchy."

Why does this occur? It is inefficient for organizations to spread power among too many people, especially if decisions must be made quickly, so a group of leaders always emerges. Even if these people try to avoid becoming an elite, through their leadership experience they inevitably acquire skills and knowledge not available to the rank and file.

Furthermore, most members are too busy to get involved in the daily life of the organization, so they willingly leave most of the decisions to the emerging leadership. Eventually these leaders start benefiting from their position of power, and they become a largely unaccountable oligarchy (Tolson, 1995).

Michels thought that the rise of a leadership elite was inevitable, and considerable research shows that, indeed, it is very common (Lipset et al., 1956; Fox & Arquitt, 1985; Cnaan, 1991). However, the histories of some modern groups, especially those associated with the liberation movements that began in the 1960s and 1970s, demonstrate that oligarchy can be avoided, or at least minimized. Leadership positions must be rotated regularly and power deliberately dispersed across the bureaucracy (Olsen, 1978; Staggenborg, 1988; Fisher, 1994; Jarley et al., 2000). One downside is that because all members must be given the opportunity to voice their opinions, highly democratic organizations often experience difficulty making decisions quickly.

Refining Weber's Model

As the preceding discussion makes clear, bureaucracies have their problems. Ever since the onset of the industrial era, people have tried to modify Weber's model in order to respond to its limitations. We will review five such efforts in the chronological order in which they arose.

SCIENTIFIC MANAGEMENT Scientific management was an early effort to improve bureaucratic functioning on the factory floor by accentuating some of the defining characteristics of Weber's model. Initially developed by Frederick Winslow Taylor (1856–1915), and hence sometimes called *Taylorism*, scientific management relied heavily on time-and-motion studies, which broke down the physical process of working on the assembly line into its most minute details and then restructured the process in order to maximize efficiency (Miller & Form, 1964).

Taylorism essentially viewed the industrial worker as little more than a machine. Employees, it was assumed, could not think for themselves; they needed to be told exactly how to do their jobs. Work was thus *deskilled*. In addition, scientific management assumed that laborers were motivated strictly by economics, so they had to be closely supervised and paid on a piecework basis, earning a set sum for each item they turned out. Taylorism took no notice at all of the informal relationships that developed between workers.

Scientific management did increase productivity, and it made it easier to replace workers—outcomes that pleased management. But it also rendered employees powerless and widened the gap between labor and management (Zuboff, 1988; Westrum, 1991). Most workers hated Taylorism (Braverman, 1974; Ritzer, 1996). A new management strategy that was more in touch with workers' human needs emerged early in the 20th century (Perrow, 1986).

THE HUMAN RELATIONS APPROACH By the 1920s, industrial sociologists were becoming aware of the importance of the informal norms that develop on the factory floor (Mayo, 1933). They began to advocate a new approach to management designed to promote positive human relations between workers. This perspective was grounded in the assumption that if the human needs of bureaucratic employees were met, morale would increase, workers would be more likely to accept the company's goals as their own, and productivity would go up (Argyris, 1960; Auster, 1996). Thus, the human relations approach was characterized, first, by marginally closer and more supportive relationships between bosses and workers and, second, by deliberate efforts to promote primary interaction and teamwork among workers through mechanisms such as company sports leagues.

This philosophy seemed to represent a considerable advance over scientific management; at least workers were being treated like people, not machines. But conflict theorists were quick to point out that the human relations approach could be interpreted as little more than manipulative window dressing. Workers were still largely powerless in their relationship with the bosses; the new style partially obscured—but did not change—this reality (Burris, 1989). Like scientific management, the human relations approach is a low-trust system. Not until the later 1960s did a high-trust system emerge that actually empowered the workers.

COLLECTIVES The collective is not a modification of Weber's model so much as a repudiation of it. Instead of an elaborate division of labor, collective workers are nonspecialized. Instead of a top-down hierarchy, collectives feature participatory democracy; they may have spokespersons, but there are no bosses. Human relations within the collective are, ideally, warm and personal. There are few written rules. Objective merit is not completely ignored, but it is only one of several factors taken into account in personnel decisions (Rothschild & Whitt, 1986).

Collective work organizations have existed in the United States since the early 19th century, especially in the form of communes. But the model gained popularity in the 1960s when thousands of "alternative institutions" were established—food co-ops, free medical and legal clinics, alternative schools—some of which endure to this day.

Collective organizations sacrifice the efficiency and profitability of the traditional bureaucracy in order to escape the dehumanization of the "iron cage." They are often very satisfying places to work, although the amount of time necessary to reach fully

Employee picnics are an important component of the human relations approach to bureaucratic management. Company-sponsored social events bring workers together and strengthen their interpersonal bonds. However, critics point out that the human relations school fails to empower workers in their ongoing struggle with management over salaries and working conditions.

democratic decisions can be frustrating. But collectives tend to be small, with an average of about six workers, and generally cannot compete effectively with bureaucracies. Accordingly, the collective was never considered as a serious model for major U.S. formal organizations. However, some of its qualities are incorporated in two refinements of bureaucracy—the Japanese model and the "humanized" model—that have become popular over the past several decades. These two models assume that workers, who are typically much better educated today than they were in the days of Taylor, are capable of making good decisions and are happier and more productive when they are allowed to do so.

THE JAPANESE MODEL Japan's dramatic rise as a world economic leader in the 1970s led many U.S. organizational theorists to consider adopting some of the distinctive features of the Japanese bureaucracies of that era (Cole, 1989; Lincoln & Kalleberg, 1990; Florida & Kenney, 1991). In particular, five aspects of Japanese corporate life attracted attention (Vogel, 1979; Ouchi, 1982; Lindsey, 1998):

Collective Hiring and Promotion In the classic model, Japanese firms hired a group of management trainees and promoted them on the basis of seniority; individual merit, except in extreme cases, only became relevant later in one's career. This practice promoted a team orientation.

Holistic Training Instead of being narrowly specialized, Japanese managers were moved from department to department during their careers. In this way, they developed a general understanding of how the organization as a whole functioned.

Decentralized Decision Making Although much less democratic than the collective model, Japanese firms encouraged input from all their workers. This was meant to increase morale and commitment to the organization.

Lifetime Employment Japanese managers rarely looked to advance their careers by moving from one company to another, as is common in the United States. Promotion was generally from within. Downsizing—at least until recently—was rare: Top executives sometimes took pay cuts rather than fire their employees.

Total Involvement In order to build employee loyalty, Japanese firms were paternalistically involved in their workers' lives. Businesses sponsored collective recreational activities and encouraged on-the-job rituals such as mass calisthenics, the singing of company songs, and the wearing of company uniforms. Workers and managers were encouraged to think of each other as part of a huge extended family. Naturally, this tended to minimize "we/they" thinking and support for unions.

Could the United States and other Western nations adopt this model of bureaucracy? Probably not completely (Florida & Kenney, 1991; Tsutsui, 1998). The United States is a much more individualistic society than Japan; many elements of the Japanese model seem overly constraining to us. Company songs and volleyball teams have little appeal. Management and union leaders are often unwilling to give up even a little of their power (Grenier, 1988), and many workers think being involved in decision making may have no effect other than increasing their workload.

U.S. enthusiasm for the Japanese model has also waned as the health of the Japanese economy has begun to falter (Besser, 1993). Complaints have been raised by workers that despite the façade of democracy, upper management still makes all the major decisions. Some executives feel that collective promotion by seniority rather than individual promotion by merit is wasteful. With labor costs rising and productivity falling below the U.S. rate, some Japanese managers are questioning the basic model. Layoffs are up, fewer workers are being offered lifetime tenure, and merit pay is becoming more common (Hamada, 1992; Clark & Ogawa, 1997; Nathan, 1999).

THE FLEXIBLE AND HUMANE BUREAUCRACY

Over the past several decades, many observers have concluded that the traditional model of bureaucracy, originally designed to organize minimally motivated and often ill-educated workers so as to produce highly standardized material goods, is increasingly inappropriate for the modern workplace. Today most employees are well-trained and highly skilled workers who deal with people rather than things and do work that requires constant case-by-case adjustment. In other words, a model of formal organization that worked well for the Model T assembly line is inappropriate for a computer research-and-development company in California's Silicon Valley (Vaill, 1989; Reich, 1991; Peters, 1992). Something new is needed.

There are many different approaches to the problem. Some talk about humanizing bureaucracy (Kanter, 1977, 1983), self-managed work teams (Yeatts, 1991), "ad-hocracies" (Bennis & Slater, 1968), flexible organizations, or the horizontal model (Byrne, 1993). Most of these images of 21st century organizations share certain common themes:

Temporary Work Teams Workers do not stay permanently in a single organizational structure. Instead, a diverse group of specialists is assigned to work together for a while in order to complete a certain task. Then the team is dissolved and its members are reassigned to other groups working on other projects. Within the team, the interaction is intense, often more closely resembling that in a primary group than that in a secondary one (Yeatts, 1991).

Collective Responsibility Although the performance of individuals is assessed, the primary emphasis is placed on the effectiveness of the team.

Minimal Hierarchy Highly skilled workers neither need to be nor enjoy being ordered around—one of the core themes of "Dilbert." A humanized bureaucracy emphasizes colleagueship and resembles a network more than a pyramid. Decision making within the work team is, to a considerable extent, democratic.

Fewer Rules Because it is assumed that workers are able to cope with many situations on their own, there is less need for detailed guidelines.

Social Inclusiveness The U.S. labor force is becoming increasingly diverse. Modern organizations go out of their way to encourage full participation by women and minorities. Ability is valued over ascription.

More Opportunities for Advancement Humanized organizations try to develop the abilities of all of their members. Dead-end jobs are minimized, and training programs to enhance workers' skills are emphasized.

All these factors build loyalty to the work team and, by extension, to the employer. Absenteeism declines. Research shows that humanized and flexible organizations are, as a rule, happier, more productive, and more profitable (Peters & Waterman, 1982; Kanter, 1983; Shonk, 1992; Drucker, 1993). Unfortunately, businesses in the United States often hesitate

Modern models of the workplace stress the importance of constructing small, temporary, cohesive teams of employees who bring a variety of different skills to bear on the project at hand.

to accept new organizational models, especially when they substantially empower workers (Baron et al., 1988; Cole, 1989). So not only has adoption of the new model been relatively slow, but employees have also sometimes discovered that work relations in flexible organizations are less egalitarian than they had initially expected.

THE CHANGING CHARACTER OF WORK

We turn next to the sociology of work. We begin by introducing some key terminology and discussing several important changes that have taken place in the workplace in recent decades.

Sectors of the Economy and Labor Markets

Sociologists identify three distinct sectors of the economy of modern societies and two different labor markets.

THE THREE SECTORS OF THE ECONOMY Work may be divided into three broad categories or sectors. The *primary sector* includes jobs in which material goods are obtained directly from nature—for example, farming, mining, and fishing. Manufacturing industries make up the *secondary sector*, and services constitute the *tertiary sector*. The category of service jobs is extremely broad, including such diverse occupations as teachers, physicians, fast-food workers, typists, ministers, housekeepers, police officers, and child-care workers.

The federal government has identified over 820 distinct occupations and over 20,000 occupational specialties within these general categories (U.S. Department of Labor, Bureau of Labor Statistics, 2001). The distribution of people in these various jobs has changed greatly over the past century.

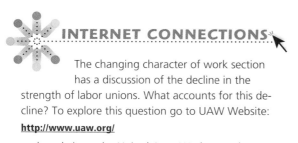

INTERNET CONNECTIONS

The changing character of work section has a discussion of the decline in the strength of labor unions. What accounts for this decline? To explore this question go to UAW Website:

http://www.uaw.org/

and read about the United Auto Workers and some labor issues of concern. Do you think unions serve a useful purpose or not in today's workplace? Why or why not?

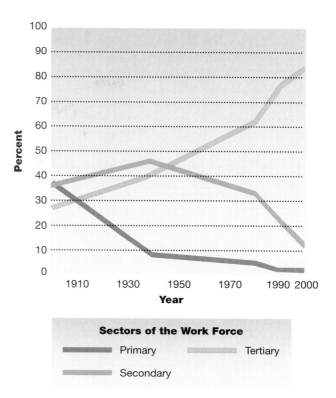

FIGURE 21.1 **Three Sectors of the American Work Force, 1900–2000.**

Source: Statistical Abstract, various years and 2001 Statistical Abstract—Table 593.

As Figure 21.1 demonstrates, the primary sector has declined sharply (Hodson & Sullivan, 2002). In the early 19th century, about 80 percent of all workers toiled in primary sector jobs, mainly as farmers. At that time, the typical farmer could feed only about five people. In 1900, about half the labor force was still in the primary sector. Today that figure has declined to less than 3 percent. This change is the result of two principal factors: growing opportunities in other sectors and technological changes that enable each farmer to feed 70 or 80 people. Today the family farm is vanishing rapidly and everywhere being replaced by corporate agribusiness.

Secondary sector manufacturing jobs peaked around midcentury at about 40 percent of the labor force. They have been declining ever since, as the United States moves from an industrial to a postindustrial society (see Chapter 4). Today the secondary sector makes up 13.5 percent of all jobs, a figure that is projected to drop as low as 10 percent by 2020 (Rifkin, 1995).

The tertiary sector has expanded rapidly during the 20th century, accounting for about 30 percent of all jobs in 1900, about half in 1955, and 84 percent today. Over 90 percent of all new jobs are located in this sector (Crispell, 1990; Plunkert, 1990).

THE TWO LABOR MARKETS Regardless of the sector in which a job is located, it may be further classified as part of either the primary or the secondary labor market. **Primary labor market** jobs are, simply put, good jobs. They offer at least a living wage, often provide interesting work experiences, may lead to better positions in the future, and provide fringe benefits such as health insurance, paid vacations, and retirement plans (Bailey & Waldinger, 1991). Most primary labor market jobs are white-collar service jobs or unionized, highly skilled blue-collar positions. They are disproportionately held by white males (Browne, 1999). About one-third of the service jobs currently being created in the United States are in the primary labor market.

On the other hand, jobs in the **secondary labor market** are jobs that do not offer the advantages of primary labor market jobs. Examples include seasonal farm work, unskilled industrial labor, and service jobs such as janitorial work and positions in the fast-food business. They are primarily filled by women, immigrants, and minorities (Browne, 1999). These are the kinds of jobs you are in college to avoid. Fully two-thirds of all new service jobs are in the secondary labor market. These positions are sometimes derisively referred to as "McJobs" because employment at fast-food franchises like McDonald's is one of the most rapidly expanding and representative of all secondary labor market jobs.

Change in the Primary Labor Market: Professionalization

One of the most important developments in the primary labor market in recent decades has been a sharp increase in the number of professional jobs (Brint, 1994). In everyday usage, a professional is simply someone who is paid for his or her work—for example, a professional (as opposed to an amateur) athlete. But sociologists use the term differently, defining a **profession** as a prestigious white-collar occupation that displays the following characteristics (Hughes, 1965; Friedson, 1986):

- A rigorous education covering both theory and practice. Thus, aspiring doctors must learn anatomy and biochemistry as well as the practical skills needed to heal patients. In addition, professionals are expected to keep up to date with the literature in their field.

- A professional association that controls entry into and expulsion from the field. The American Medical Association and the American Bar Association are examples of such groups. Professional associations defend the claim that only one's fellow professionals have enough knowledge to make decisions concerning an individual's right to engage in a given occupation. In other words, a profession follows a *norm of autonomy*. The professional association also usually accredits educational programs in its field and publishes a code of ethics.

- A *norm of authority*, which states that professionals have the right, at least up to a point, to tell their clients what services they need (Hodson & Sullivan, 2002). Customers at a grocery store buy whatever they want; a doctor's patients expect, at least up to a point, to be told what needs to be done to keep them healthy.

- A *norm of altruism*, which states that professionals are at least partly motivated by the desire to do good rather than being exclusively driven by financial considerations.

The law, medicine, and the ministry were among the first occupations to professionalize. Like all professionals, lawyers are trained in the theory as well as practice of their craft, are governed by a powerful professional association, enjoy considerable authority over their clients, and are expected to obey the norm of altruism.

In recent decades, as clients have become increasingly empowered, many people have begun to challenge the autonomy and authority of professionals and to doubt their altruistic motivation (Brint, 1994). But the traditional professions, including medicine, law, academics, and the ministry, have been reasonably successful in defending their status.

Meanwhile, people in a number of other occupations, seeking to increase their prestige and autonomy, have undertaken a process of **professionalization,** which mainly involves increasing the amount of education needed to enter the field and establishing a professional association (Abbott, 1988; Halpern, 1992). Dentists and certified public accountants have largely completed this process, while social workers, computer scientists, teachers, and nurses are in the midst of it.

Two factors help explain the rather slow progress of professionalization in teaching, social work, and nursing. First, most people in these fields are female, and sexist attitudes make it relatively difficult for women to validate their claim to professional status (Williams, 1992). Second, these workers are increasingly found in bureaucracies where they must acknowledge the authority of nonprofessionals such as hospital administrators and school boards who are above them in the organizational hierarchy—obviously a direct challenge to the norm of professional autonomy (Leicht & Fennell, 1997).

Under these circumstances, some occupations are actually undergoing *deprofessionalization*, a process whereby their work is being partially deskilled. Pharmacists, who used to counsel clients and prepare medicines, now do little more in some cases than count pills (Ritzer & Walczak, 1988; Hodson & Sullivan, 2002).

Even some higher professionals have discovered that work in a bureaucracy can be constraining (Bok, 1993). For instance, physicians who work for HMOs find that organizational rules often limit their ability to do everything for their patients that their professional socialization tells them ought to be done. The movement of more and more professionals into bureaucracies threatens to reduce the prestige of many fields, including both medicine and the law.

The Secondary Labor Market

Real median wages—that is, wages adjusted for inflation—have been declining in the United States for several decades for all except the most affluent workers (Borjas, 1995). The loss has been most severe for workers lacking college degrees (Mischel & Burtless, 1995). Millions of employees in the United States are working longer hours today just to avoid falling farther behind (Rifkin, 1995).

Among the hardest hit are people who work for minimum wage, about 6 percent of the total labor force. One-third of minimum wage earners work full-time, and 63 percent of these full-time workers are female. Because the minimum wage is not indexed to the inflation rate and because the government has tended to resist raising it, the real value of the minimum wage has been eroding for decades. The 1968 minimum wage of $1.60 would have been worth $7.92 in 2000 dollars, but in 2000 the actual minimum wage was only $5.15 (2001 Statistical Abstract, Table 624). In the 1960s, a full-time minimum wage worker earned 105 percent of a poverty line income for a family of four; by the early 1990s, that figure had dropped below 80 percent (Quigley, 1995; Greenstein, 1996).

Two factors are especially important in explaining this wage stagnation: the globalization of the economy and the decline of the union movement (Mishel, 1995).

GLOBALIZATION The most obvious effect of globalization has been the loss of jobs in the United States

Over the past several decades, many thousands of American-owned factories have been relocated to nations in the developing world, such as Mexico, where wages are low, unions are weak or nonexistent, and environmental regulations are rarely enforced.

when they are exported to nations where wages are far lower than they are here, primarily in Latin America and Asia. Most of these displaced workers end up taking service jobs in the secondary labor market with lower pay and fewer benefits (Kletzer, 1991). Globalization also helps explain why those workers who do retain their jobs find their real earnings slipping: In a global economy, Americans compete against laborers in places like Indonesia, where factory wages may be as low as $1.35 a day. Naturally, this means that U.S. wages tend to decline (Barnet & Cavanaugh, 1994; Yates, 1994).

THE DECLINING STRENGTH OF UNIONS Well into the 20th century, the union movement met heavy and often violent opposition from both capitalists and government. Thousands of men and women were beaten, imprisoned, and even killed for demanding an 8-hour workday or minimal workplace safety standards (Dulles & Dubofsky, 1984). But by the mid-1930s unions had finally secured the right to bargain collectively for their members (McCammon, 1993). Over the next several decades, they achieved not only an 8-hour workday but also health insurance, pension plans, sick leave, unemployment benefits, and paid vacations (Shostak, 1990).

At the end of World War II, about one-third of all nonfarm workers were unionized, with the largest

Although the union movement has been gradually losing members as the number of jobs in the "smokestack" industries has declined over the past three decades, many sociologists believe that unionization remains workers' most effective means of protecting their hard-earned wages and benefits.

representation in heavy "smokestack" industries in the North and Midwest. In absolute numbers, unions peaked at about 25 million members in the early 1970s. Research consistently shows that union members earn more than nonmembers (Wiatrowski, 1994) and that they are more productive as well (Galenson, 1996; Gunderson & Ponak, 2000). Furthermore, when unions are strong, there is a spillover effect: Businesses pay their nonunion workers well in hopes of keeping them from organizing (Amott, 1993). Unions do have their problems, including a history of hostility to women, minorities, and immigrants (Mort, 2000)—but they have clearly bettered the lives of most U.S. workers.

Since the 1970s, however, the union movement has declined and power has shifted dramatically back to management (Harrison, 1994). Figure 21.2 illustrates historic trends in union membership. Today slightly over 16 million people are union members, and less than 14 percent of the nonfarm labor force is organized. Unions are seeing some of their hard-won victories slipping away, as benefits and wages are routinely reduced (Hathaway, 1993). Strikes have become far less common since the government has given its support to the permanent hiring of nonunion replacement workers (Galenson, 1996). The union movement is much stronger in Europe. In 1995, 91 percent of Swedish workers, 80 percent of those in Denmark, and 44 percent of Italian workers were union members, but unions are gradually losing power abroad as well as in the United States (Human Development Report, 1998).

There are several reasons for this downward trend in the United States. First, many highly unionized industrial jobs have disappeared with the shift to a service economy and the relocation of millions of jobs abroad. Also, anti-union conservatives have controlled either the executive or the legislative branches of the federal government (or both) since 1980. Finally, the union movement has been damaged in recent years by a series of well-publicized scandals involving corruption and infiltration by organized crime figures.

Can unions regain enough power to stop or even reverse the erosion of pay and benefits? Will workers' anger over shrinking real wages overcome the unions' negative image? Perhaps—but nothing seems likely to reverse the globalization of jobs or the decline of the manufacturing sector. Many unions are now trying to organize the public sector—40 percent of government workers are now unionized—and to increase the number of women and lower-skill service workers in their ranks (Shostak, 1999). In another line of attack, unions are expanding internationally in order to increase the wages of foreign workers, and thus, indirectly, to do the same for workers in the United States (Cavanagh & Broad, 1996). However, these are difficult goals, and the short-run outlook for unions is clouded.

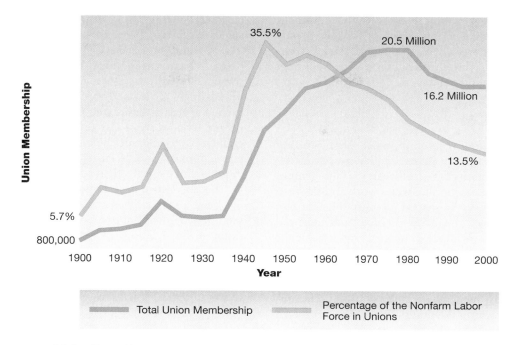

FIGURE 21.2 Union Membership Trends, 1900–2000.

Sources: Larry J. Griffin, Philip J. O'Connell, and Holly J. McCammon, 1989, "National Variation in the Context of Struggle." *Canadian Review of Sociology and Anthropology* 26, 1 (February): pp. 37–68. Reprinted by permission of Larry J. Griffin. 2001 U.S. Statistical Abstract, Table 637.

Contingency Work

Another important trend in modern societies is the growth of the **contingency workforce,** workers who are not permanent, full-time employees of a single firm (Peters, 1992; Castro, 1993). This type of employment is expanding rapidly: The contingency workforce grew 250 percent between 1985 and 1995, years when the overall number of employees increased by less than 20 percent. Contingency workers have historically been primarily low-skill workers, but in recent years large numbers of highly skilled knowledge workers have also taken these jobs. Roughly 30 percent of all workers are now in the contingency workforce, and further increases appear inevitable (Moore, 1994). In fact, within a decade or two a majority of all employees are expected to fall into one of the following three categories (Morrow, 1993; Larson, 1996):

- *Temporary workers* generally are employed by employee-leasing firms like Manpower, Incorporated (Castro, 1993; Henson, 1996). Most "temps" work at low-skill service jobs.
- *Part-time workers* are also increasing rapidly (Howell, 1994; Tilly, 1996). For example, 80 percent of K-Mart's 250,000 employees work less than 30 hours per week. About 75 percent of part-timers are female, and up to 90 percent of part-time workers say that they would prefer to work full time (Collins, 1994).

- *Independent contractors* are hired in a process called outsourcing or subcontracting by firms that previously would have given the work to regular employees. These workers are also called consultants and freelancers (Lozano, 1989; Larson, 1996; Greenhouse, 1998). Unlike part-timers, they are full-time workers; unlike temps, they tend to be highly skilled. White-collar unions view outsourcing as a major threat, especially when "downsized" former employees are hired back as independent contractors at lower salaries and with no fringe benefits. Downsizing is discussed further later in this chapter.

Contingency work does provide certain advantages, especially to women and students who cannot or prefer not to take conventional full-time jobs because of household or academic responsibilities. But the primary beneficiary is the corporation. It obtains a docile, nonunionized labor force at low wages without having to provide health insurance, vacations, or other fringe benefits (Henson, 1996).

Independent contractors are sometimes paid well enough to purchase their own health insurance and set up their own pensions, but this is not true for most part-timers or temps. This explains why 82 percent of all independent contractors like their present job arrangement but this is true of only 39 percent of other types of contingency workers (U.S. Department of Labor, 1995). Contingency employment also weakens employees' ability to protest job discrimination or dangerous working conditions. More generally, contingency work virtually eliminates job security and weakens the already fragile social contract between workers and employers.

Telecommuting

Before the industrial revolution, most manufacturing took place in the home in a system called cottage industry. The introduction of the factory in the 18th century led to a radical separation between work and home, a change that definitively shaped people's lives for two centuries. However, the invention of fax machines and the Internet has now made it increasingly possible for people to work at home in what Alvin Toffler (1980) calls the electronic cottage and others refer to as **telecommuting** (Barker & Christensen, 1998). Currently, about 10 percent of the labor force telecommutes at least some of the time, a figure that is expected to rise substantially in the near future (Nie, 1999).

Many home workers are self-employed, but others work for large firms. For example, over 10 percent of AT&T's workforce telecommutes (Boroughs, 1995). The production of this text was greatly facilitated by telecommuting: It was written by two sociologists, one working at a college in Kentucky and the other writing at her home in St. Louis. Our developmental editor works out of her home in Texas, and the project is coordinated by editors located at Prentice Hall's main office in New Jersey.

Telecommuting has many advantages (Volti, 1995). It allows workers more autonomy than they would have in a conventional work setting and eliminates wasted time driving to and from work every day. It lets people work full time yet also be constantly available for their children (Carey & Jerding, 1999). It allows workers who live in remote areas to hold jobs that previously were available only to city dwellers. And it has given an increased range of options to the physically disabled (Nelson, 1995). The primary drawback of the electronic cottage is isolation: Many telecommuters miss the human contact with coworkers that is part of the conventional workplace.

SOCIOLOGICAL THEORY AND THE EXPERIENCE OF WORK

Many people think of work as nothing more than a way to obtain a paycheck, but it's really much more important than that. We typically spend more time working than engaged in any other activity. People who work together—construction workers and police officers, for example—often form tightly bonded occupational subcultures with very distinct norms and values (Riemer, 1979; Pavalko, 1988).

In addition, work is a critical element in shaping people's identities in modern societies; when we meet someone, we almost always inquire, "What do you do for a living?" (Friedland & Robertson, 1990). Work is usually a master status (see Chapter 4), which is why people who work in less prestigious jobs sometimes euphemize or upgrade their occupational titles: "Sanitary engineer" and "security specialist" convey much more positive images than sewer worker and bouncer!

Because work is so important in people's lives, it has been a major focus of sociological theory. In this section, we introduce two classic theoretical contributions to the sociology of work, one dealing with the origins of the work ethic and the other exploring why workers in bureaucracies sometimes lack strong motivation to work. We also briefly discuss a related topic, contemporary empirical research into job satisfaction.

The Protestant Ethic

In 1905 Max Weber published one of the most important sociological studies ever written, an investigation into the origins of what is commonly called the work ethic. This book, *The Protestant Ethic and the Spirit of Capitalism*, sparked one of the most intense debates in the history of ideas.

Weber's inquiry was part of his ongoing effort to show that ideas can be important causes of social change. This position contrasts with Marx's contention that new structural arrangements—especially altered economic relationships between members of society—provide the best explanation for change.

More specifically, Weber was interested in the birth of a type of capitalism that arose in Europe during the Protestant Reformation, which he believed to be significantly different from earlier varieties of capitalism that had existed for millennia. *Rational capitalism*, as one might expect, is capitalism that reflects the spirit of rationalization. That is, the relentless and unending accumulation of money—using the most efficient means possible—is viewed as an end in itself rather than as simply a means of obtaining valued goods and services.

Weber noted that capitalism of this sort had emerged primarily in the Protestant areas of northern Europe, and that Protestants seemed to be more actively involved in capitalism than were their Catholic neighbors. Marx would have said that Protestantism, an idea, grew in response to capitalism, a new structural factor. But Weber found evidence that certain aspects of Protestantism predated and thus led to rational capitalism.

In the 16th century, both Protestantism and Catholicism formally endorsed the notion that the pursuit of profit—while not entirely immoral—was at best ethically questionable. However, a series of religious

SOCIOLOGY OF EVERYDAY LIFE

The Rewards of "Dirty Work": Garbage Collectors

"Dirty work" is stigmatized in all societies. As sociologist Everett Hughes once pointed out, in order for some members of society to be clean and pure, someone else must take care of unclean, often taboo work, such as handling dead bodies and filth. In India and Japan, such jobs were (and to some extent still are) relegated to the Dalits (or Untouchables) and the Eta, respectively. Both groups were regarded as ritually impure. Our society does not have formal taboos against dirty work, but some jobs are rated near the bottom of the scale of occupational prestige and are viewed as not quite respectable, certainly not something to brag about. Garbage collection is a good example.

Why would anyone choose to become a garbage collector? Stewart Perry (1978) asked this question of sanitation workers for the Sunset Scavenger Business in San Francisco. For a job that requires little training or education, the pay is relatively good. But pay was not what drew men to the job.

One attraction of becoming a garbage collector was variety. The job involves many different activities, including driving the truck, hauling cans, operating the blade, solving problems with customers, and so on. Collecting garbage also means being outdoors and moving around. Several of the men Perry met had worked at higher paying, higher prestige office jobs for a while, but they chose to return to sanitation routes. "Staying in one place all day? Naw!" (Perry, p. 80). On another level, variety meant the unexpected: Every day brought something different. They talked about witnessing a robbery, calling in a fire alarm and getting residents out of the building before the fire truck ar-

rived, and about the time that the FBI requested that they save all the rubbish from a house under surveillance.

The garbage itself was full of surprises. Almost every day the men found something of interest, whether a good book, a child's toy, or a fixable radio. Almost inevitably, garbage men became collectors. As one informant suggested, no matter what you want, eventually you'll find it. His own collection included a brass rail from a bar and a rubber life raft; in the course of his research, Perry acquired a rare 17th-century book of sermons and a sheepskin rug.

Garbage men became intimately familiar with the neighborhoods in which they worked. Watching children grow up, couples marry or separate, or one house or block deteriorating while another was being renovated, had the appeal of an ongoing story, not unlike a soap opera on TV. They witnessed not just public performances, but also what Erving Goffman called the "backstage" of life. The respectable facades in affluent neighborhoods cannot hide the alcoholism a garbage man detects from cans full of empty liquor bottles or the sexual longings symbolized by bundles of pornographic magazines.

A second attraction of garbage collection was a sense of camaraderie among workers. The friendships people make on the job are a major source of satisfaction in any occupation. Many Sunset workers came from the same (Italian) ethnic background and in some cases from the same neighborhood. Often their fathers, uncles, and other relatives, as well as old family friends, had also worked for the company. All of the men hoped that their own sons would go to college and make something better of themselves. But at

least 30 were following in their father's footsteps—indeed, working for no pay until they had proved themselves and were offered a job. These intergenerational family ties and friendships made the company a familiar and welcome place—and a stronghold of tradition for members of ethnic communities that were beginning to break apart.

Third, the garbage collectors liked working at their own pace, scheduling their own breaks, deciding when to do their paperwork—in short, being their own bosses. Freedom from constant supervision did not mean that they did as little work at the slowest rate possible. To the contrary, they worked as fast as they could manage.

Equally important—and in this Sunset may be unusual—the men owned shares in the business. Being a shareholder meant, first, having a permanent job. If company profits declined, workers would have to accept lower wages, but they could not be laid off. Shareholder dividends, distributed around Christmas, were welcome but usually modest (about $600). Most important was pride of ownership and the feeling that they were more than just workers.

Collecting garbage may be "dirty work" in many peoples' eyes, but these men were proud of what they did for a living.

1. What are some of the qualities that can make a job "dirty" in some people's eyes? What does this tell us about this society's values?

2. Can you think of some other jobs that most people regard as "dirty work"? Do some of them, like scavenger, have hidden appeals?

Sources: Hughes, 1962; Perry, 1978.

As one might expect from his authorship of such aphorisms as "A penny saved is a penny earned," or "Up, sluggard, and waste not life; in the grave will be sleeping enough," Benjamin Franklin was a strong proponent of a secularized version of the Protestant work ethic.

developments at the beginning of the Reformation lent covert support to the emerging entrepreneurial spirit.

First of all, Martin Luther, the architect of the Reformation, taught that God gave each person a particular role or *calling* on Earth. Whether you were a minister, a mother, a blacksmith, or a business owner, God expected you to work hard at your calling; this was a way to glorify Him.

Luther also introduced the notion that people have a direct and unmediated relationship with God. This meant that salvation could not be guaranteed by the church; whether you went to heaven was entirely up to you and God.

In the next generation, John Calvin (1509–1564) took Luther's ideas a crucial step further with the idea of *predestination*—the idea that God decided before a person was born whether that individual would be saved. Nothing we can do on Earth can change our predestined fate—or even let us know whether we are saved.

Given these beliefs, all we can do is work hard at our calling and live a modest life, shunning, as Calvin urged, worldly pleasures. But, in practice, the uncertainty of not knowing one's fate or even being able to influence it was unbearable. Gradually, people became convinced that surely God would cause the elect to succeed in their callings as a sign of divine favor. Naturally,

those who thought this way worked very hard to convince themselves and others that they were indeed saved.

Because they were such hard workers, Calvinist business owners tended to become wealthy. Moreover, they reinvested much of their profit back into their businesses—after giving a share to the church—so that they became more and more prosperous. Note that by this logic, you could never be too rich because you could never be entirely sure that you were among the elect. Any slowdown in the accumulation of profit cast your future after death into doubt. So rational capitalism, unlike earlier forms, implied an entirely unlimited quest for economic success.

Over the centuries, this motivational pattern became disconnected from its religious justification; what remained was intense socialization to achieve economic success. In the 19th century, Calvinistic Protestants still enjoyed an economic edge. But today many Catholics and others have clearly accepted a secularized version of the work ethic and are as highly motivated as—or more so than—their Protestant neighbors.

Are Americans still committed to the Protestant ethic? Certainly Ray Wax, the stockbroker we met at the beginning of this chapter, seems highly motivated. However, some observers suspect that the work ethic may be weakening in the contemporary United States and that it is being gradually replaced by a more hedonistic philosophy that stresses personal growth and fulfillment over economic success (Schor, 1991; Applebaum, 1998). On the other hand, substantial research suggests the presence of a strong work ethic in Japan and parts of Southeast Asia, which bodes well for those nations' continued economic growth (Levy, 1992). Interestingly, the origins of the Japanese work ethic have been traced to non-Christian religious developments in the 18th and 19th centuries (Bellah, 1957).

Alienation and Job Satisfaction

Conflict theorist Karl Marx, who originated the concept, considered alienation to be a structural phenomenon, much more than simply disliking your job (Ollman, 1971; McClellan, 1977). In Marx's view, **alienation** occurs whenever people are controlled by social institutions that seem to be beyond their ability to influence. It may arise in many settings. Governments, workplaces, schools, and religions are all ultimately human creations, Marx argued, but they often grow so large and their power over us becomes so coercive that we forget that we created them and that we can, at least collectively and in theory, change them (Seeman, 1972).

Specifically regarding work, Marx stressed that under certain structural conditions, workers feel alienated or estranged from the productive process, from the products of their labor, from their fellow workers, and ultimately from themselves. Alienated workers feel *powerless* on the job, and they may consider their work *meaningless* because they do not see how their efforts contribute to the final outcome or product (Blauner, 1964). The "Dilbert" strip on page 564 provides an outstanding illustration of the powerlessness felt by alienated workers.

Marx believed alienation resulted from capitalism (Young, 1975), and some observers suggest that it is widespread in the U.S. workplace (Terkel, 1985; Erickson & Vallas, 1990; Geyer & Heinz, 1992). However, the high levels of alienation that were present in the former Soviet Union strongly suggest that the principal cause of alienation is bureaucracy, not capitalism.

The assembly line is arguably the ultimate expression of Weber's rational bureaucracy (Thompson, 1983). As the account by Phil Stallings at the beginning of this chapter notes, assembly line workers must keep pace with the line, which dictates even minor details of the work process. In Weber's words, the worker is reduced to ". . . a small cog in a ceaselessly moving mechanism that prescribes to him [*sic*] an endlessly fixed routine . . ." (Weber, 1978:988). Not only are the employees utterly lacking in autonomy, but their work is also largely meaningless because they do such a small part of the whole task that they do not see their place in the larger scheme of things (Schooler & Naoi, 1988). Because their jobs have been deskilled, they take little if any pride in what they do (Braverman, 1974; Feldberg & Glenn, 1982). They are also isolated from their coworkers by noise and by having to stay at their work station whenever the line is running.

Marx believed that a need for self-expression through work was an inherent part of human nature, so an alienated person could not be a fully authentic human being. Alienation has been found to be related to problems such as alcoholism, drug abuse, mental and physical illness, family violence, and political extremism. But today many people seem to deliberately seek out alienating work situations that ask little of them except mindless obedience. These workers seem content to endure five days of tedium so that they can come to life on the weekend. Critics of Marx say that the existence of these people refutes his basic assumption concerning human nature. His defenders respond that bureaucratic capitalism, a fundamentally flawed system, creates warped and flawed individuals.

Can any of the approaches to modifying bureaucracy discussed earlier in this chapter reduce alienation? Taylorism clearly intensifies the problem by reducing worker autonomy to a minimum. To the extent that the human relations approach is superficial window dressing, it has a similar effect. However, the other three models, and especially collectives and humanized systems, hold some promise as antidotes to alienation. Each substantially empowers the worker, calls for a less rigid division of labor, and genuinely encourages the development of primary relationships within the workplace. If these models are adopted in the emerging postindustrial service economy, work alienation may well decline.

JOB SATISFACTION Few modern researchers make use of Marx's structural concept of alienation; they tend instead to study the loosely similar social-psychological condition termed *job satisfaction*. In contrast to the findings of studies of alienation discussed previously, sociologists using survey research techniques generally find a fairly high self-reported level of satisfaction among workers. According to the 1998 General Social Survey, whose respondents are selected randomly from all adults, 48.4 percent of all Americans report that they are "very satisfied" with their jobs, and another 35 percent are "moderately satisfied." Only 16.5 percent are unsatisfied (Stark, 2002).

Workers at McDonald's and other fast food franchises rarely if ever have to exercise initiative or make decisions; everything is spelled out for them in the company's rulebook. This low level of autonomy helps explain why jobs like these are often highly alienating.

GLOBAL CONNECTIONS

Sweatshop Barbie

"I am an old woman even before my twentieth birthday."

These words were spoken by Primitwa, a young girl who is one of 4,500 employees of the Dynamics company, located on the outskirts of Bangkok, Thailand. She labors 12 hours a day, six days a week, with no vacations, no sick leave, no benefits, and no job security. In return she earns between $6 and $7 per day.

You don't know Primitwa, but you are no doubt familiar with the product she makes at Dynamics: Barbie™ dolls. Barbies are manufactured for subpoverty wages by young women and girls in a number of factories located in Thailand, Indonesia, and China.

One of the consequences of globalization has been the creation of many millions of jobs like Primitwa's, mostly in Southeast Asia and Latin America. Firms like Dynamics are owned by, or subcontract with, multinational corporations located in the United States and the other developed countries. The multinationals benefit by taking advantage of the very low wages for which women will work in

the developing world, having few if any other options.

Actually, Primitwa may be relatively lucky: Many of the girls she grew up with in a village in poverty-stricken northern Thailand were sold by their parents as sex slaves, often when they were as young as 11 or 12, usually for a couple hundred dollars. Instead, Primitwa was sent to work in the nation's capital and required to send some of her meager earnings home to help support her relatives.

Low pay is only one of the problems these girls and women experience; even more serious are the health hazards. Over 75 percent of Dynamics' workers experience breathing problems as a result of dust in the air from the fabrics used to make Barbie's clothes or from lead and other poisonous chemicals used in manufacturing the dolls. Others experience nausea and dizziness, difficulty sleeping, irregular periods, and hair and memory loss. At least four have died recently.

Of course, the workers would not suffer from so much illness if they wore protective masks. Masks are available, but, like uniforms and their scissors, they must

be purchased from the factory and, like most of her coworkers, Primitwa can't afford to buy them.

Thai government officials do not step in and require improvements because they are well aware that if they attempt to establish even modest workplace standards, employers will simply relocate to another poor nation with even slacker regulations. Some U.S. firms do make efforts to minimize the most appalling abuses, but it's easy to get around them: At Dynamics, workers are routinely fired after 118 days on the job because the firm's U.S. mother company requires that some benefits be given to workers after they have been employed for 120 days. Of course, they are immediately rehired—for another 118 days.

1. What can people in the United States do to protest this kind of exploitation?

2. Are abuses like those recounted here an inevitable consequence of capitalism, as Marx would have argued, or are they aberrations that will be eliminated in time?

Source: Foek, 1997.

Roughly 68 percent of all adults say that they would continue working if they won the lottery (Stark, 2002), and between 80 and 90 percent of all white-collar professionals—but only about a quarter of blue-collar workers—would choose the same job if they could relive their lives (Tausky, 1984). Figures 21.3 and 21.4 illustrate the effects of age, educational level, income, and gender on job satisfaction.

These findings can be interpreted in two quite distinct ways. Perhaps most people really are, for the most part, happy with their work, or maybe few of us are willing to admit to dissatisfaction because, given widespread classism (see Chapter 10), being in a bad job can only mean that an individual is personally inadequate. It is quite possible that workers who are structurally alienated could nevertheless report a fairly high level of job satisfaction.

In general, older workers say they are more content with their jobs than younger ones; this may be be-

cause older people typically have better jobs, or it may suggest that people lower their expectations after working for a few years. White-collar workers are more satisfied than blue-collar workers, and union members are particularly dissatisfied, probably because unions raise people's expectations by convincing them that they can substantially improve their working conditions (Schwochau, 1987; Hodson & Sullivan, 2002).

Women and minorities are particularly likely to work in alienating settings (Loscocco & Spitze, 1990). Sharon Atkins' job as a receptionist, discussed at the beginning of this chapter, provides a good example. However, despite being in objectively less desirable jobs, on the average, women express about the same level of job satisfaction as men—clearly a result of internalized lower expectations (Weaver & Matthews, 1990; Tolbert & Moen, 1998). This observation suggests that we need to consider the important issue of how women experience the modern workplace.

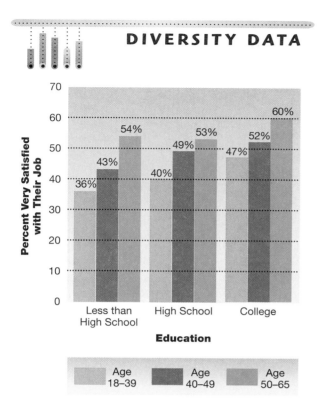

DIVERSITY DATA

FIGURE 21.3 **How Do Age and Education Affect Job Satisfaction?** Job satisfaction among full-time workers rises steadily with age and with level of educational attainment. Are older workers more satisfied because they are in better jobs or because they have learned to reduce their expectations?

Source: NORC. General Social Surveys, 1972–2000. Chicago: National Opinion Research Center, 2000. Reprinted by permission of NORC, Chicago, IL.

LIFE CONNECTIONS

Women in the Workplace

Women have entered the paid labor force in enormous numbers in recent decades (see Chapter 13). In 1960, about 38 percent of all working-age women were in the labor force; today over 60 percent are. Women accounted for fully two-thirds of the increase in the U.S. labor force between 1982 and 1995. Consequently, employers are being forced to rethink the character of the workplace environment.

Historically, most women were hired for gender-typed, "pink-collar" jobs. These jobs were poorly paid, offered little chance of career advancement, and reinforced sexist stereotypes (Lowe, 1987). The traditional secretary, for example, worked under the direct supervision of a man to whom she provided a variety of services, often including tasks like making coffee and picking up dry cleaning, which would never have been expected of a male worker (Millman & Kanter, 1975).

Much of this is changing. Today, women's problems are less likely to result from a company's formal policies than from its informal norms or, as they are sometimes called, its **organizational culture** (Reed & Hughes, 1992; Pheysey, 1993; Trice & Beyer, 1993). Women often find the organizational culture of a firm hostile or at best nonsupportive (Reskin & Padovic, 1994). The traditional corporate organizational culture is distinctly masculine, stressing toughness, competition, and aggression (Hearn et al., 1989). Women are sometimes devalued because they are seen as weak (Baron & Newman, 1990; Mills & Tancred, 1992; Kemp, 1994). Employers may falsely assume that they do not take their jobs as seriously as they take their family lives. Thus, women may be

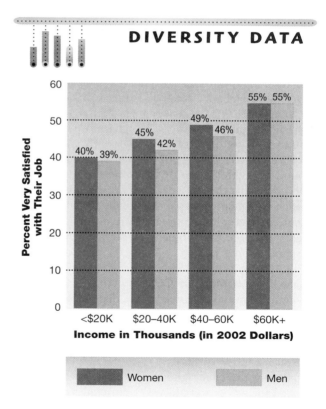

DIVERSITY DATA

FIGURE 21.4 **How Do Income and Gender Affect Job Satisfaction?** Job satisfaction among full-time workers rises steadily as annual income goes up. However, women are more satisfied than men at all income levels except those earning over $60 thousand per year despite the fact that they generally earn less money then men do. How would you explain this seeming incongruity?

Source: NORC. General Social Surveys, 1972–2000. Chicago: National Opinion Research Center, 2000. Reprinted by permission of NORC, Chicago, IL.

hired, but eventually they are still likely to bump up against the "glass ceiling" (see Chapter 12).

Rosabeth Moss Kanter (1977, 1983) has written a classic analysis of the problems that typically face the first few women (or persons of color) who are hired to work in executive positions in the still predominantly male (and white) corporate world. These people are often treated as *tokens* (Epstein, 1970). The first female hired is likely to be seen more as a woman than as a fellow worker. She may feel pressured to adopt one of a small number of rigidly defined office roles, each of which is derived from male stereotypes of women: the mother, the sex object, the mascot, or the stern "iron maiden" (Millman & Kanter, 1975). Because she is so visible, she is likely to be under extreme pressure to do well. She may feel that she must work twice as hard as anyone else (Kanter & Stein, 1979). She is often lonely, excluded from the personal as well as the career advantages of the informal office network (Benokraitis & Feagin, 1986). She may be unable to find a senior executive who will mentor her.

Some observers have suggested that women could soften and humanize the masculine organizational culture (Hennig & Jardin, 1977). Research indicates that as a result of gender-role socialization, most women prefer an interpersonal style that emphasizes collaboration and helping coworkers. Women are more likely than men to ask questions and share information, and they are more responsive to the human needs of those around them (Helgesen, 1990; Tannen, 1994; Morgen, 1994). Perhaps the current increase in the number of women in management will eventually make corporate organizational culture more humane, although it seems equally possible that women will simply learn to play the game by men's rules.

WORKING WOMEN OF COLOR Although virtually all women have experienced some degree of discrimination at work, a look at the experiences of African American women and Latinas reminds us once again of the importance of the combined effects of gender and race (Lindsey, 1997).

Before the civil rights era, women of color who worked for wages were largely restricted to domestic service and to a few menial manual labor positions. Over the last three or four decades substantial numbers of minority women have moved into the clerical and sales fields, but they remain heavily concentrated in lower-paying and less prestigious jobs (Reskin & Padavic, 1994). While a few women of color, such as President Bush's National Security Advisor, Condoleeza Rice, have achieved spectacular success, in general, as Figure 21.5 demonstrates, African American women and Latinas continue to earn less than whites of either gender or minority males.

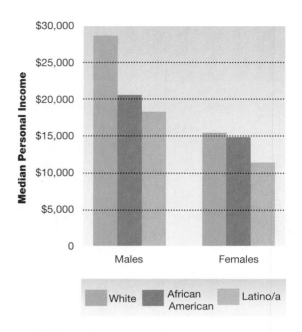

FIGURE 21.5 Median Personal Income by Race and Gender, 1999.

Source: 2001 US Statistical Abstract, Table 675.

SOCIETY CONNECTIONS

The Darker Side of Work

We have already discussed a number of social issues that have arisen in the workplace, including declining real wages, alienation, and the problems faced by working women. In this final section we briefly consider three additional concerns: unemployment, downsizing, and electronic surveillance.

Unemployment

Work provides us with a predictable temporal structure for organizing our daily lives (Fryer & McKenna, 1987). It gives us opportunities to use our innate abilities and learned skills. It provides some of our most valued interactions with other people. Unemployment diminishes self-esteem, isolates fired workers from their former coworkers, and can even threaten an individual's core identity (Kessler et al., 1989). It has been found to be related to a host of pathologies, including domestic abuse, alcoholism, drug use, divorce, and suicide (Hamilton et al., 1990; Catalano et al., 1993; Turner, 1995).

There are several different types of unemployment. Some are short term and thus of less concern to sociologists. These include the *seasonal unemployment* of some farm workers and the *cyclical unemployment* caused by periodic swings of the business cycle.

Structural unemployment, which results from a mismatch between the skills of the workforce and the current needs of the economy, is of greater sociological interest (McEachern, 1994). For example, because DVDs are rapidly replacing VCRs, specialized VCR repair workers may soon experience difficulty finding employment.

The official unemployment rates reported on the nightly news do not accurately portray the size or character of the unemployed population. These figures were developed primarily so that employers can determine how many people are actively looking for work, not how serious the unemployment problem really is. As a result, they exclude several groups of people, including (a) **discouraged workers,** who have given up looking for jobs, (b) part-time workers who would prefer full-time employment, and (c) the **underemployed,** who are working but at jobs that do not make full use of their skills (Carnoy & Levin, 1985; Hodson & Sullivan, 2002).

The official unemployment rate has been relatively low in recent years; however, by the end of 2002 it had risen to 6 percent. If we add in discouraged workers, the figure increases to about 9 percent—or roughly 10 million people. The relatively low rate of unemployment in recent years should not necessarily be interpreted as evidence that most workers feel secure in their current positions. In fact, unemployment rates are often low when jobs are scarce, because people stay where they are. Rates may be higher when there are plenty of jobs, because people may feel more free to quit their current job to look for a better one.

Even when official rates are low, unemployment touches many people. At least two-thirds of all workers will experience involuntary unemployment at some time in their lives (Kates et al., 1990). During a recession year, as much as one-fifth of the labor force may be out of work at least briefly.

Table 21.1 illustrates how official unemployment rates vary by age, gender, education, and race. In general, joblessness is higher among young people, men, and the poorly educated. Young, lower-class high-school dropouts routinely experience unemployment at rates of 25 percent or more (Kasarda, 1990). Minorities, particularly African Americans, have long suffered especially high rates, generally at least twice those of the general population (Seccombe, 1999). In some inner-city neighborhoods, true unemployment rates for teenagers routinely exceed 50 percent.

Downsizing

Traditionally, unemployment has been a more serious problem among blue-collar workers than in the white-collar workforce, but since about 1980, major corporations have been firing or downsizing substantial numbers of executives (Sennett, 1998). Between 1980 and 1995, roughly 24.8 million manual workers and 18.7 million white-collar employees lost their jobs. During this period the Fortune 500 companies alone downsized about 5 million people (Uchitelle & Kleinfeld, 1996).

Most of these highly skilled workers never expected to lose their positions; for this reason, they may actually be more distressed than their blue-collar counterparts. As previously mentioned, losing a job has consequences far beyond going without a paycheck. Consider this comment by a man named Don, who lost an academic position at age 41 and found it extremely difficult to obtain a comparable job:

> I know that it takes a very weak man to lose his way when he has a beautiful wife and four healthy children living under his roof, no debt, over $3,000 left in the bank, and he's not in a war or facing anything even close to real peril, but I was so lost. . . . There were too many people, too many talented and driven people, waiting at every slot for a way in. (Snyder, 1997)

TABLE 21.1

Social Characteristics of Officially Unemployed Workers, 2000

Percent Unemployed

Overall	4.0
Age	
16 to 19	13.1
20 to 24	7.1
25 to 44	3.3
45 to 64	2.5
65 and up	3.1
Sex	
Male	3.9
Female	4.1
Race	
White	3.5
Black	7.6
Hispanic	5.7
Educational Attainment	
Not High School Graduate	7.9
High School Graduate, No College	3.8
College, No Degree	3.0
College Graduate	1.5
Percent of Unemployed without Work for:	
Fewer Than 5 Weeks	45.0
5–10 Weeks	23.0
11–14 Weeks	8.9
15–26 Weeks	11.8
27 Weeks or More	11.4

Source: 2001 Statistical Abstract, Tables 598 and 604.

Most downsized executives and professionals do eventually find work, but usually in less prestigious firms and at a lower salary (Rosen, 1987; Moore, 1990). After receiving 96 rejection letters from colleges and universities, Don worked as a greenskeeper, a construction laborer, a house painter, and a cottage caretaker (Matthews, 1997). Many downsized white-collar workers ultimately join the contingency workforce as consultants and independent contractors (Harrison, 1994).

Electronic Surveillance

Before the industrial revolution, individuals who left home to work were controlled by the direct, face-to-face supervision of their superiors. The expansion of bureaucracy changed the character of social control in the workplace: Supervision became less personal but more intensive (Goldman & Van Houten, 1977; Heydebrand, 1977; Perrow, 1986). It is exactly these qualities that make the assembly line so alienating.

Management's ability to control workers has been further expanded by advances in computer technology (Giddens, 1990). Computerized surveillance allows superiors to monitor phone calls and e-mail and to assess worker productivity on a minute-by-minute basis (Sewell & Wilkinson, 1992; Rule & Brantley, 1992; Gwynne & Dickerson, 1997).

According to sociologist Gary Marx, we are at risk of becoming a "surveillance society." Computerized methods of collecting and storing information and su-

INTERNET CONNECTIONS

The *society connections* feature in this chapter deals in part with **electronic surveillance,** which has become an increasingly controversial issue over the past decade in American society. The American Civil Liberties Union (ACLU) maintains a Website dealing with the issues surrounding electronic surveillance in the workplace: "Privacy in America: Electronic Monitoring":

http://www.aclu.org/library/pbr2.html

Reading the contents of this site will provide you with an excellent overview. After you have evaluated this material, write a brief report on the major issues involved. Do you believe there is sufficient justification for employers to electronically monitor their employees? How will workplace culture change because of electronic monitoring of employees?

pervising work threaten our last vestiges of personal and workplace privacy (Marx, 1985a, 1985b). Marx and others are calling for new legislation to limit the expansion of technological control before we slip into computerized totalitarianism (Marx, 1988; Flaherty, 1989).

SUMMARY

1. Formal organizations have come to dominate many aspects of life in modern societies.
2. There are three basic types of formal organizations: coercive organizations, utilitarian organizations, and voluntary associations.
3. A bureaucracy is a special type of formal organization designed to allow large numbers of people to efficiently accomplish routine tasks. Max Weber developed a well-known six-point ideal type model of bureaucracy.
4. Weber saw modern society as moving toward ever greater levels of bureaucratic rationality and interpreted this trend as a major social problem.
5. Real-life bureaucratic functioning is strongly influenced by the internal structures that develop among bureaucratic employees and is frequently impeded by various bureaucratic dysfunctions.
6. Scientific management and the human relations school were early efforts to respond to the inefficiencies of bureaucracies. More recent reform efforts include the antibureaucratic collective model, the Japanese model, and the emerging "humanized" model.
7. Sociologists have identified three sectors of the economy—primary, secondary, and tertiary—and two labor markets, primary and secondary.

8. In recent decades, the number of jobs that are organized as professions has increased substantially.
9. The real wages of many U.S. workers, especially those in the secondary labor market, have been declining due to globalization and the weakening of the union movement.
10. The contingency workforce—temporary workers, part-time workers, and independent contractors—has been expanding rapidly.
11. Computers and fax machines allow increasing numbers of workers to earn a living without leaving their homes, an innovation known as telecommuting.
12. Max Weber believed that the strong work ethic associated with rational capitalism was an unintended consequence of doctrinal changes introduced during the Protestant reformation.
13. Many U.S. workers experience high levels of alienation, a condition of powerlessness that comes from not being able to control or even influence one's working conditions.
14. Levels of job satisfaction vary sharply among different types of workers.
15. Women have entered the workplace in unprecedented numbers in recent years. While real progress has been made, many female workers continue to confront hostile organizational cultures, tokenism, and dead-end jobs. Women of color are heavily concentrated toward the bottom of the occupational prestige ladder.
16. Structural unemployment is a major problem for both blue-collar workers and downsized executives.
17. Electronic surveillance is becoming increasingly common and increasingly problemsome in the modern workplace.

KEY TERMS

alienation 580
bureaucracy 566
bureaucratic ritualism 568
contingency workforce 577
discouraged workers 585
formal organization 564
goal displacement 568
ideal type 566

iron law of oligarchy 569
organizational culture 583
Parkinson's Law 569
Peter Principle 569
primary labor market 574
profession 574
professionalization 575
rationality 567

rationalization 567
secondary labor market 574
structural unemployment 585
telecommuting 578
trained incapacity 568
underemployed 585

CRITICAL THINKING QUESTIONS

1. Do you think it's possible for workers to find personal fulfillment in a conventional bureaucratic organization? Why or why not?
2. Which of the proposals to modify bureaucratic structure strike you as most promising? Explain your answer.
3. Do you believe that the work ethic—the commitment to hard work as a value—is declining in the United States today? If so, why has this happened, and how might it be strengthened?
4. How has work changed since your parents entered the labor force? What further changes do you expect to see during the next few decades? On the whole, do you think these changes will be positive or negative?

INVESTIGATE WITH CONTENT SELECT

Journal Research Collections from ContentSelect Begin your research using ContentSelect for this chapter by following the directions found on page 27 of this text to visit Prentice Hall's Research Navigator Website. Enter these search terms into the search field:

Bureaucracy
Professionalization
Unemployment

22
POPULATION, URBANIZATION, AND THE ENVIRONMENT

Back to Saigon

Vietnam is a country in transition, but in transition to its own past, to subordination, and to poverty. Ho Chi Minh City, formerly called Saigon, is the center of the transformation. Ho Chi Minh City, for all the hope of economic development, is reverting to its former identity. While not yet as bad as in Bangkok or Jakarta, traffic is a serious problem. Bicycles still dominate, but on Sunday nights a sea of motorbikes converge on the city center. There is no attempt being made to build adequate mass transit and no infrastructure to deal with the increase of private transport. Drainage is poor; garbage collection is unreliable. A declining health system faces more health problems from the sicknesses of overcrowding, respiratory diseases, and lung and eye infections as dust, grit, carbon dioxide, and industrial pollution fill the air. In air-conditioned malls people can forget briefly that they are in Saigon and imagine they are anywhere in the world—anywhere but where they must stay and make their lives. (Adapted from Seabrook, 1996:146, 163–64)

Women as the First Environment

The Akwesasne Mohawk reservation has been singled out as the most polluted among 63 Native communities in Canada's Great Lake Basin. On the U.S. side of the border, things aren't much better. A General Motors plant may be the biggest PCB dump site yet uncovered. PCB is a chemical known to cause brain, liver, and skin disorders in humans. The Mohawk reservation is downstream from the General Motors site, and PCBs have made it a hotbed of contamination. Katsi Cook, a Mohawk woman and midwife, promotes breastfeeding among her people. "Women are the first environment," she explains. "We accumulate toxic chemicals dumped into the waters that

are stored in our body fat and excreted through breastmilk, our sacred link to our babies." Katsi and a group of women banded together to form the Akwesasne Mothers' Milk Project to understand the scope of the challenge they face and to seek scientific help. They are organizers and investigators—not merely research objects—of an ongoing breastmilk study. Their agenda is not only to document the connection between women and the environment, but to clean up the environment. (Adapted from LaDuke, 1998)

One of the principal objectives of sociology is to document the influence of social connectedness on human social behavior. These vignettes demonstrate the profound consequences of interconnectedness and the impossibility of separating humans from any of their environments—social, psychological, and physical. Technology, a unifying theme of this chapter, is both a cause and an effect of trends related to population, urbanization, and environmental change. Perhaps more than any other topics in this book, these represent the interdependent nature of our world. An urban dweller in Vietnam and a Canadian Mohawk woman have much in common. They (and we) are all sheltered in the same global environment.

POPULATION: DEMOGRAPHIC INTERDEPENDENCE

In order to approach the topic of population, we need to understand some basic elements of **demography:** the scientific study of population focusing on its size, distribution, and composition, and how birth, death, and migration rates influence each element. Demography is one-dimensional in time, picturing all countries on a single continuum of change (Kirk, 1986). It provides snapshots of populations as they change from traditional to modern, from developing to developed, from rural to urban. Demography tells us *how* change occurs. Sociology examines the demographic portraits to explain *why*.

Studying Population: Demographic Tools

Studies of population depend on gathering accurate statistics. The statistics frequently used by demographers are gathered from a **census,** in which a population is fully counted and measured according to key demographic characteristics. Birth and death rates are two of the most important statistics provided by census data. Along with census data, a number of organizations continually gather information on a range of variables that are demographically important. For example, the Centers for Disease Control in Atlanta and the World Health Organization in Geneva monitor the when, where, and who of infectious diseases. Demographers assess the overall impact of death rates from diseases on population growth or decline.

Determining the world's population today and tomorrow ultimately depends on knowing three facts: how many people are born (the birthrate), how long they live (the life expectancy rate), and when they will die (the mortality rate). The most common measure of birth is the **crude birthrate,** the annual number of births per 1,000 population. Chapter 19 explained that the infant mortality rate (IMR)—the number of infants who die before they reach their first birthday—is a good measure of the overall health and well-being of a society. The focus in this chapter is on a specific birthrate measure, the **fertility rate,** which is actual reproductive behavior determined by annual number of live births per 1,000 to women of childbearing age. It differs from the *fecundity rate,* the biological potential for bearing children, which appears to be influenced by factors such as health technology, nutrition, and the environment. Demography demonstrates, for example, that what were previously believed to be biological limits of childbearing now have been expanded.

Another useful demographic indicator of population change is the **migration rate,** the movement of people in and out of various areas, specifically tracked according to political boundaries. It is very important when charting the global urbanization that has moved millions of people out of rural areas in the developing world (J. Allen, 2001). Urbanization still occurs in the developed world, primarily as movement of people from central cities into suburbs. Since we cannot migrate from the planet Earth, migration does not affect world population.

Understanding Development: The Demographic Transition

Demographers report that for centuries the typical global population pattern showed high levels of both fertility and mortality, so overall population growth was minimal. About two and a half centuries ago in Europe that pattern began to change. The extraordi-nary rate of growth of the human population in the last half of the 20th century is traced directly to the influences of that period (around 1750). By now, your sociological imagination will allow you to predict that the fundamental influence was the Industrial Revolution. England was the world's first country to experience this revolution and was socially, economically, politically, and demographically transformed in the process. Europe and then North America followed suit, so that by the early 19th century, the Industrial Revolution was in full swing in the Western world. Remember that development is associated with progress, modernization, and an overall improvement in the life chances and lifestyle of all people impacted by it. Industrialization is its most important element.

One model that helps explain the effect of industrialization on population is called the **demographic transition,** a three-stage model that describes the change from high fertility and mortality rates to lower ones (Figure 22.1). In the first stage, the rate of population growth is slow because high fertility rates and high mortality rates offset one another. In the second stage, fertility rates remain high but mortality rates decrease, so there is a rapid growth in population. By the third stage, population falls to replacement levels or even lower, because both fertility and mortality rates decrease. Evidence for the demographic transition worldwide is that the fertility rate is declining in all regions of the world. In the 1950s the average number was five births per woman; today it is less than three. The demographic transition is linked to two other significant results worldwide—a lower IMR and an increase in life expectancy (Chapter 19). These changes occur in the wake of industrialization, which introduces improvements in health, nutrition, education, and sanitation (Jack, 1999; World Bank, 2002). Thus, even with a decline in fertility, population can still increase at an astounding rate.

A good example of the long-range result of the demographic transition is a **population pyramid,** a figure that provides the age and sex structure of a population at a given point in time (see Figure 22.2 on page 592). When the demographic transition occurs, population growth becomes stabilized and the "pyramid" instead resembles a vertical rectangle. Individuals not only survive infancy, the most precarious time of life, but people survive well into old age. As explained in Chapter 14, this pattern of global graying is associated with major social and economic consequences related to health policy, patterns of caregiving, changes in family structure, and labor-force participation. Global graying also suggests that a combination of physical, social, and psychological life-enhancing qualities are now available for a sizable proportion of the world's population. The good news

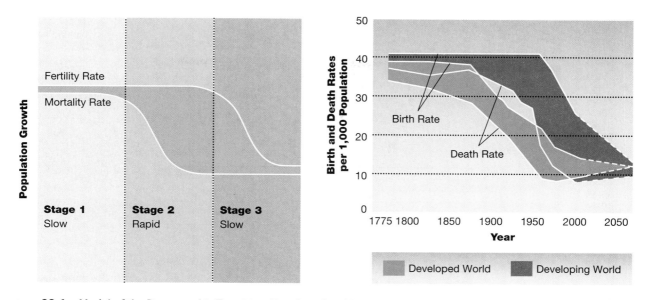

FIGURE 22.1 Model of the Demographic Transition: Developed and Developing World.

Sources: Gray, 1993; *World Development Report*, 1982, 1997.

predicted by the demographic transition is that the Stage 3 world will be healthier and life enhancing.

The bad news is that even with the worldwide decline in fertility, fertility rates in the developing world have not declined fast enough to stem population growth, which may be threatening the very existence of our increasingly fragile planet. The world population doubled in the last 40 years, and estimates suggest that if the population continues to grow at the current rate, it will double again in the *next* 40 years (see Figure 22.3 on page 593). Close to 1 billion people were added to our planet in the 1990s alone, the greatest increase in a single decade. World population growth is equivalent to about three babies born every second (Haub & Cornelius, 2001).

POPULATION GROWTH Demographers project that the percentage of the global population living in the developing world will be close to 90 percent by mid-century, with most of these people living in megacities in Asia and Latin America, such as Mexico City, São Paulo, Calcutta, and Manila. To understand the population surge of the developing world, it is important to distinguish between the *rate* of population growth and actual *number* of people. In many developing countries population growth rates diminished after peaking in 1970 at about 2.5 percent. If the demographic transition continues in the developing world so that fertility rates steadily decline, the effect on the global population would be a growth rate of about 1 percent. However, it is estimated that even this small growth rate will generate about an additional 2 billion people worldwide by 2025. As implied

by a youthful age structure in a population pyramid, the large majority of these will come from developing countries. Half the world is now under age 25, most young people live in the developing world, and there are over a billion young people between 15 and 24. Described as the largest "youthquake" ever, these 1 billion teenagers just entering their reproductive years will be the parents of the next generation. The staggering prediction is that virtually *100 percent* of the projected growth rate of the world's population by 2025 will be in the developing world (Population Reference Bureau, 2001a; United Nations Population Fund, 2002).

Projected rates of population growth are based on demographic modeling in a number of scenarios.

INTERNET CONNECTIONS

After reading the different theories in the textbook go to Zero Population Growth:

http://www.zpg.org/

and under hotlinks click on population factoids. After reading the different factoids listed describe some of the contemporary issues in the relationship between environment and population growth. What are some population issues in the world today? What is being done about the issues?

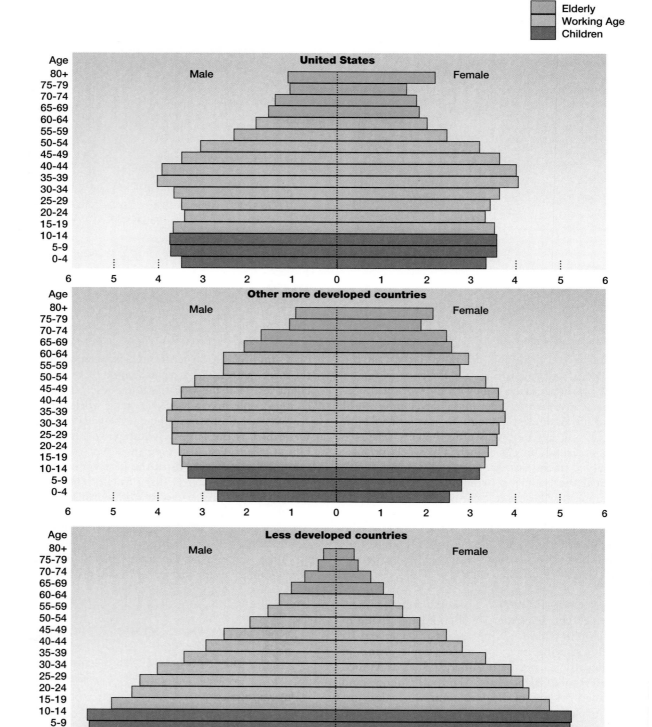

FIGURE 22.2 Population Pyramids of the United States and Other Developed and Less Developed Countries.

Source: McDevitt & Rowe, 2002 (U.S. Bureau of the Census).

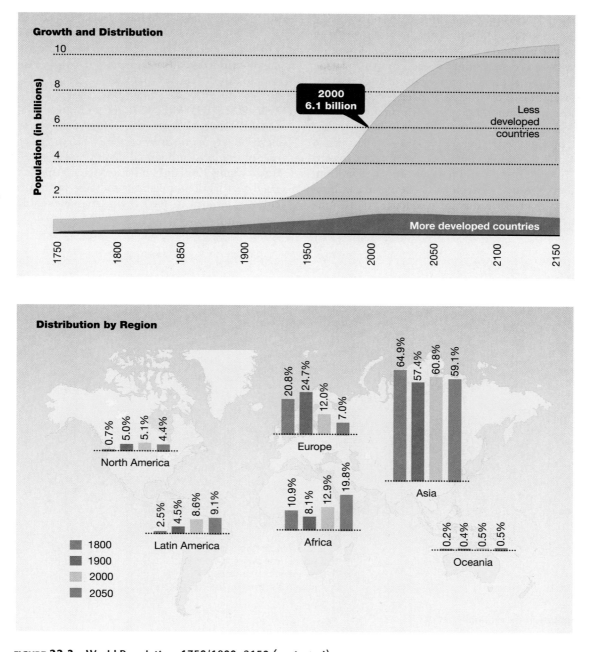

FIGURE 22.3 World Population, 1750/1800–2150 (projected).

Source: Population Reference Bureau, Washington, DC. 2002. http://www.prb.org/Content/NavigationMenu. Reprinted by permission.

Population policies in many countries are guided by the goal of *Zero Population Growth* (ZPG), which suggests that if most young people marry and each married couple has two children, the population will replace itself and the growth rate will remain static. In the developed world, the fertility rate of about 1.6 children per woman is already below replacement level. In the developing world, the fertility rate is just under three children. Some projections estimate that replacement level in the developing world will be reached between 2035 and 2050 (Population Connection, 2002; United Nations Population Fund, 2002). If the demographic transition is accurate, birthrates will inevitably fall. There is widespread agreement that a decline in birthrate is a prerequisite for development and poverty reduction (Bayer, 2000; Thomas et al., 2000). As we will see, however, there is much more disagreement about how a decline in birthrate will or should occur.

Another problem in determining population growth in the developing world is that the demographic transition is modeled on the Western version of the Industrial Revolution; events may not proceed the same way in the developing world. Rapid population growth in the developing world intensifies urban and environmental threats, and it can set back or even defeat development efforts. As a species we are in the midst of a major biophysical transformation of the Earth and are confronting limited planetary resources. In 1700, only five cities had populations of one-half million people. By 1900, the number rose to 43, and 16 of these had populations of over 1 million. Today there are over 400 cities that exceed 1 million people, and many of these are megacities of 10 mil-

lion people plus (Habitat, 2001; United Nations, 2001) (Figure 22.4). According to this argument, the world's resources and ecosystem simply cannot sustain continued growth (Hinrichsen, 1999). How many people can the earth support?

THE MALTHUS PREDICTION Thomas Malthus is considered to be one of the first demographers. In 1798 he wrote *An Essay on the Principles of Population*, one of the most influential demographic studies of all time. Using England and Europe as a model, he argued that while populations increase faster than agriculture's ability to feed them, it is inevitable that a

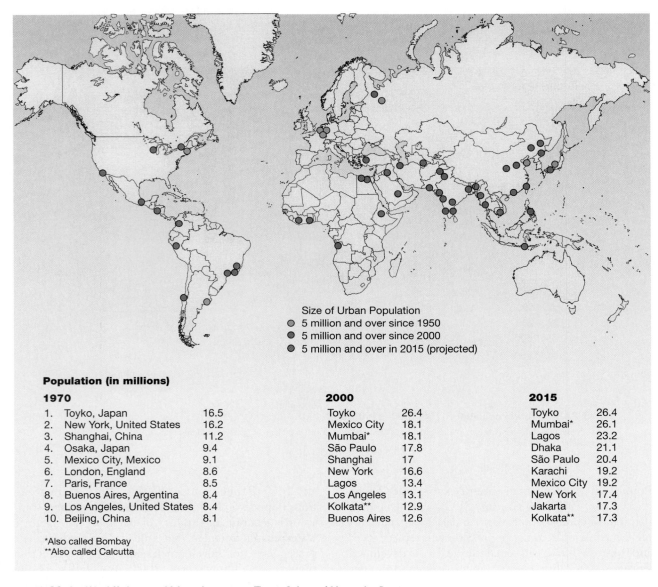

Size of Urban Population
- 5 million and over since 1950
- 5 million and over since 2000
- 5 million and over in 2015 (projected)

Population (in millions)

1970		2000		2015	
1. Toyko, Japan	16.5	Toyko	26.4	Toyko	26.4
2. New York, United States	16.2	Mexico City	18.1	Mumbai*	26.1
3. Shanghai, China	11.2	Mumbai*	18.1	Lagos	23.2
4. Osaka, Japan	9.4	São Paulo	17.8	Dhaka	21.1
5. Mexico City, Mexico	9.1	Shanghai	17	São Paulo	20.4
6. London, England	8.6	New York	16.6	Karachi	19.2
7. Paris, France	8.5	Lagos	13.4	Mexico City	19.2
8. Buenos Aires, Argentina	8.4	Los Angeles	13.1	New York	17.4
9. Los Angeles, United States	8.4	Kolkata**	12.9	Jakarta	17.3
10. Beijing, China	8.1	Buenos Aires	12.6	Kolkata**	17.3

*Also called Bombay
**Also called Calcutta

FIGURE 22.4 World's Largest Urban Areas over Time, Selected Years, by Region and Ten Largest.

Sources: Adapted from United Nations Population Fund, 2001; United Nations Population Division, 2002. Population Reference Bureau, Washington, DC. 2002. http://www.prb.org.

population will outstrip its ability to survive. When labor is sold for the purposes of production, the process includes three steps:

1. A rise in population leads to a rise in food prices through increased demand.
2. A rise in food prices means the same amount of money buys less food. Real wages fall as more labor comes onto the market.
3. As real wages fall, mortality increases through starvation, malnutrition, and disease, (Gray 1993). In the battle of people against food, it is the people who lose.

According to Malthus, the laws of nature dominate human desires. He argued that one such law is the "passion between the sexes," which is so powerful and unalterable that population, unless checked, will double itself every 25 years. The checks he notes are famine and epidemics that will result in human misery and death. Malthus's position appears to be compatible with the argument that the earth cannot sustain itself indefinitely with uncontrolled population growth.

Explaining Population Trends: Sociological Theory

Both Malthus and functionalism suggest that if social disequilibrium is produced due to unchecked population growth, other checks are necessary to return the system to a state of balance or equilibrium. Malthus called them *positive checks*, and included common diseases, epidemics, wars, plague, and famine. "Positive" for Malthus meant necessary or inevitable rather than desirable. In his later writings, Malthus also included "moral restraints," such as delaying marriage and abstaining from "promiscuous intercourse, unnatural passions and violations of the marriage bed," as preventive checks on population. According to Malthus, the culprits responsible for economic crisis leading to social instability and the resulting dismal positive checks include dependent, lower-class people whose unbridled passions lead to uncontrollable population increases. As for preventive checks, Malthus was realistic about his own gender and believed that moral restraints among men were not particularly prevalent (Leisinger & Schmitt, 1994:47).

Émile Durkheim (1893/1964), a founder of functionalism, asserted that society was doomed unless it could adapt to more people competing for fewer resources. Unlike Malthus, Durkheim saw this situation as a way to stimulate development. Population problems would create the incentive to make more productive use of land, which in turn would increase the division of labor. Farmers become specialists in certain crops. They sell their products to other specialists who package, market, and sell to consumers. The complex

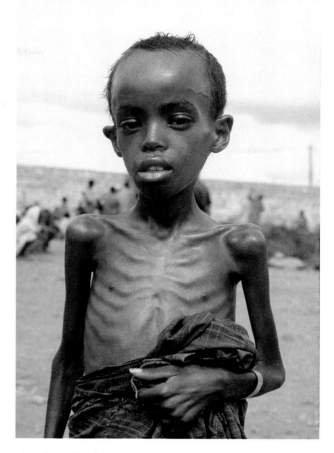

According to Malthus, starvation occurs when a population grows so fast that it outstrips the food supply. However, famine and starvation are more likely caused by factors such as war and the unequal distribution of available food.

division of labor is responsible for the interdependence that makes modern society not only orderly, but possible; the potential liabilities associated with population growth and density become social assets.

Contemporary functionalism looks not to inevitable Malthusian natural laws or evolution to return the social system to equilibrium but rather to creative, flexible human social behavior. Adaptability is the functionalist key that opens the door to understanding how societies cope with population changes. Humans are capable of self-regulation, including altering marriage patterns and birth-control techniques. Before the development of modern contraceptives, breastfeeding—which can reduce the likelihood of frequent pregnancies—was a common birth control technique. Functionalists would support the view that poor people the world over are not helpless captives of sexual passion, incapable of regulating their own fertility, with or without the aid of contraceptives (Eberstadt, 1995:28). In the direst circumstances, humans have resorted to infanticide or gerontocide of the feeble, the infirm, or the nonproductive. In each case, adaptability of human social behavior, whether positive or negative, restores social equilibrium.

Like Durkheim, conflict theorist Karl Marx (1867/1975) believed that population growth can aid social progress. Durkheim and Marx also shared a view that a minimum population density was necessary for the birth of the great cites that would be the homes for social progress (Petersen, 1998). An adequate population base is essential for industrial development and urbanization.

At this point the viewpoints of Marx and Durkheim diverge. For Marx, the offender behind human misery tied to lack of food is capitalism, which dictates how food and all other resources are distributed. Capitalism creates an incentive to maintain workers (proletariat) who will produce more than they will consume. Since capitalism depends on an unequal distribution of resources, the root of the problem is found in this inequality, not in population numbers. The smaller number of wealthy consume at the expense of the greater number of poor. Neither population growth nor the shortage of food creates the food problem; it is created by the shortage of jobs. Capitalism offers little or no incentive to expand jobs to meet all but the minimal needs of workers. Marx believed that population growth can serve economic development, but that it is impossible under capitalism.

The Marxian perspective has been borne out in one very important way: Rich nations and richer people in all nations possess and consume most of the wealth. From colonial times to the present, the economies of the developing world have been oriented to export and not to meeting the needs of the larger population that produce the exported goods. Conflict theory focuses on the continued dependency of the poor nations on the rich nations, even generations after the end of colonialism.

The contemporary variant of this approach is *dependency theory*, which provides an important framework for social change (Chapters 9 and 24). The population of the developing world may be growing faster than the output of goods and services necessary to sustain genuine development (World Bank, 2002). There is clear evidence, however, that it is not population pressure but food maldistribution, poverty, and political policies that are the main causes of hunger in the developing world. Available food cannot be purchased by the urban poor, and government expenditures to ensure their food security are low as budget priorities (Shah, 2000; Garrett, 2001; Pinstrup-Andersen et al., 2001). Almost 80 percent of malnourished children under age 5 live in countries with food surpluses, and many of these countries, such as India, Bangladesh and Kenya, export food (Toler, 2000). Yet

unless the developing world can catch up in industrial and agricultural expansion, *and* unless political priorities change, population increases can only make matters worse.

The "catch-up" process can be described as *cultural lag*. Technological development has favorably impacted death rates, but the process has happened so quickly that fertility rates have not been balanced in correspondence. Cultural lag can also explain why so many developing countries remain snared in the middle of the demographic transition.

Both the functionalist and conflict perspectives provide clues to understanding the relationship between population growth and economic development, especially in terms of adequacy of food supply. But the "people versus food" hypothesis that results in starvation is the direst of all possible outcomes of population pressure. Many other options are available, including migration. For rural people, migration due to famine or war is far less frequent than the economic necessity of moving away from subsistence farming. With the substitution of cash crops and the trend toward agribusiness, the land can no longer support many rural families, a trend that occurred in the 20th century in the United States. For others, migration is voluntary, as they hear the call of the city with its promises of cash wages. Development through industrialization heralds jobs. It also heralds the growth of cities.

URBANIZATION

For the first time in human history, almost half the human population (3 billion) live in cities. In 1900 only 14 percent of the world was urban, and only 12 cities had 1 million or more people. A century later there are over 400 cities with 1 million or more people (Population Reference Bureau, 2001b). For the foreseeable future, most of the world's population growth will be in the cities of the already poverty-ridden areas of Asia, Africa, and Latin America (Lowy, 2002; United Nations Population Division, 2002). Crowded conditions, noise and air pollution, large pockets of poverty, and limited but expensive residential space are the byproducts of urban life throughout the world. These urban byproducts may be negative, but people continue to choose urban life over an imagined rural life offering space, tranquility, and serenity.

The word **urban** simply means a place of settlement, often called a city, that is populated more densely than rural areas. **Urbanization** is the process of city population growth. The greater the number of people living in an area, the more urban it is. Urban, then, is a matter of degree (Leeds, 1994). The prob-

THEN AND NOW

The Birth and Growth of Cities

With a population of about 600, Jericho was one of the first urban settlements. It arose in the Middle East between 8,000 and 10,000 years ago. By today's standards Jericho was minuscule, but because its 600 people lived close to one another and had a reliable source of food that could support those not engaged in agriculture, Jericho qualifies as a city. Most important, the intersection of the lives of city dwellers created a lifestyle distinctly different from their rural counterparts. Free from the demands of producing their own food, the city spawned craftspeople, shopkeepers, and religious and political leaders who provided specialized services. The birth of civilization could occur only through the birth of cities. As sociology explains, when people come together in sustained interaction, their individual lives and their social surroundings are changed forever.

Ongoing urban growth began about 5,500 years ago in areas near the confluence of major rivers and oceans—the Tigris and Euphrates in Mesopotamia, the Nile River of North Africa, the Indus and Yellow Rivers of Asia, and the ports along the West African and Chinese coastlines. The first "modern" cities can be traced here. Cities of 30,000 inhabitants were typical, with Athens peaking at 100,000 and Rome estimated at 1 million by the first century B.C.E. (Before Common Era).

Archeological and historical records of life in these and other cities such as Shanghai and Constantinople (now Istanbul, Turkey) are extensive and provide mixed, often contradictory images. These cities are praised for their sacredness, beauty, or technological achievements, but condemned for their vice, moral decay, and as sites of corruption, crime, and pestilence.

After the sack of Rome in the sixth century C.E., urban life deteriorated throughout Europe. Between 1347 and 1350 bubonic plague reduced Europe's population by about one-third, with most deaths occurring in cities. Larger cities in Asia were also vulnerable to periodic pillaging by warlords, which kept city expansion at a minimum. Until the 17th century in Europe, most cities were market towns with populations of no more than 3,000. When the food surplus and trade that allowed the first cities to develop was augmented by industrialization, our concept of the city and our ideas and ideals about social life were altered irrevocably.

Industrialization spawns specialization, another requirement for urban growth. Urbanization is better understood as a complex interaction of different types of specialized functions, including neighborhoods (localities), technology, and institutions. Urban residents also organize their lives around a host of institutions, which

have evolved to meet specialized needs. A journey to Manhattan on a Saturday evening by a family living 30 miles away in Upper Saddle River, New Jersey, may find them enjoying Moroccan food after watching *Titanic* on Broadway and visiting the Museum of Modern Art. Within a few city blocks of the intersection of Times Square and Broadway in New York City, a dazzling array of entertainment and dining offerings is available to meet every conceivable taste.

Ten thousand years ago Jericho was the world's largest city with 600 people. With population estimates ranging between 24 and 26 million, Tokyo, São Paulo, and Mexico City are competing for that distinction today. Throughout their histories, the residents of these cities have relied on one another in various ways. With a world economy fueling global urbanization, cities will become even more interdependent.

1. Identify the cities in your state, region, or country that have expanded the most. What accounts for that expansion?

2. How is your life organized around neighborhood, technology, and institutions? Which of these three influences your activities the most?

Sources: Fischer, 1984; Leeds, 1994; Griffin, 2000; King, 2000.

---

lem with these simple definitions is that the distinction between rural and urban is reduced to merely a matter of numbers. However, sociology demonstrates how the size of the community in which people reside has a profound impact on their lives.

Global Urbanization

The developed world is about twice as urbanized as the developing world, but by 2030, urbanization in the developing world is expected to increase almost 20 percent compared to less than 5 percent in the developed world. Europe, Australia, Canada, and the United States are between 80 percent and 85 percent urbanized (United Nations Population Division, 2002; World Bank, 2002). Urban growth in these three regions has been from urban to suburban. In the developed world, the retreat from the cities has been led by the affluent. In the developing world, urban growth has been led by the poor, who were once clustered in rural areas. Although in-migration accounts for less overall increase than natural increases in the urban population, the combination of the two factors produces staggering numbers of urbanites (Zhang, 2002). The urban trend is on the fast track in Asia and Africa, and on the fastest track in Latin America, where over three-fourths of the population is already urbanized (United Nations Population Division, 2002). The number of cities in poor countries exceeds that of the industrialized world, and the urban population of the developing world is double that of the developed world. Consider such demographic changes in light of the following facts:

1. By 2015, there will be 27 cities with populations over 10 million, 22 of them in the developing world (Barnett & Luloffs, 2001).
2. In most large cities of the developing world, at least one-quarter of the population lives in absolute poverty, and their numbers are growing (Haddad et al., 1999; Mitlin & Satterthwaite, 2001).
3. Among the world's cities with the fastest growing urban population, the top 20 are in Africa, only 30 percent of which is urban (Gupta & Asher, 1998; City Poverty, 2002).
4. Two-thirds of Asia's population are expected to be living in urban areas by 2020. China has the largest urban population in the world, but India continues to have the largest absolute increase in urban population of any country in the world—and India is still over 70 percent rural (Deedes, 2000; Yeung, 2001; World Bank, 2002)!
5. The two largest cities in the developing world are in Latin America—Mexico City and São Paulo, Brazil. Their populations of 20 million are expected to reach 25 million in the next decade (Hardoy et al., 2001; Gazetteer, 2002; United Nations Population Division, 2002).

The tidal wave of rural migrants is swamping cities throughout Asia, Africa, and South America (World Urban Forum, 2002). Urban migration is partly explained by poor subsistence farmers selling off small parcels of land for low prices to agribusinesses. Cities offer hope to those who are quitting a desperate life on the soil for a marginally less desperate life as squatters in urban slums. In the Malthusian view, cities such as Kolkata, Manila, Mexico City, and Nairobi cannot indefinitely support a burgeoning population of the very poor. The city becomes a "miseropolis" (McGurn, 1997). Disease and famine eventually follow the flood of new migrants into cities, which do not have the resources to accommodate them.

The residents of the world's cities, including those in developing countries, have enjoyed a much higher standard of living than their rural counterparts. Rural poverty accounts for over 60 percent of global poverty, but it reaches 90 percent in Bangladesh and China and between 65 and 90 percent in sub-Saharan Africa (Khan, 2000). Cities of the developing world offer opportunities for jobs and education, better housing, and health care. Traditionally, people living in cities have a quality of life superior to that of their rural counterparts (Stren & Polese, 2000; Population Reference Bureau, 2001c). But will a population explosion of rural migrants and long-term urban poor transform the once prosperous cities into vast wastelands of urban squalor?

Global cities are centers of population growth, political action, and economic activities that are becoming the dominant force in national and world economies (Hill & Kim, 2000; Shin & Timberlake, 2000; Taylor et al., 2001). In most developing countries, one city dominates the national scene and has the highest concentration of its nation's urban population (Beaverstock et al., 2000). In Jakarta, Indonesia (the fourth most populous nation in the world), for example, the number of migrants increased over 100 percent and the total population increased by almost 200 percent in just three decades (Population Reference Bureau, 1999; Hardoy et al., 2001). Because urban regions have large numbers of potential consumers, they can entice foreign investment and generate high levels of growth from within (Sit, 2001). Global cities can serve as engines of economic growth and prosperity for their urban residents.

Urban patterns and processes also vary according to a nation's position in the world economy. Dependency theory suggests that if a nation is strangled by economic reliance on other nations, only a small elite will benefit from global linkages. The economic restructuring that accompanies development brings few benefits to the urban poor (Narayan et al., 2000; Wade, 2001). A variation of this argument—called *urban bias*—is that class conflict is not between foreign or national interests or even between labor and capital, but between urban and rural. The rural sector contains most of the world's poverty, but the urban sector gets most of the world's wealth. As centers of power, cities maintain economic dominance over rural areas. As expressed by a peasant from Kenya,

> I thought I should go to the capital to look for work. Why? Because when money is borrowed from foreign lands, it goes to build Nairobi . . . all our labour goes to fatten Nairobi and the big towns. (Gugler, 1996b:211)

Both dependency theory and urban bias suggest that only a small urban elite benefits from the increased growth and economic dominance of global cities.

In sociological terms, these two views reappear as the basic functionalist and conflict approaches to urban processes, yet these approaches offer important

City planners have addressed the issue of how to guide and manage growth in earnest. Large cities must be flexible and responsive to changes that come with rapid growth. Both functionalism and conflict theory would concede that public and private sectors together must serve the needs of the poor as well as improve urban productivity. City planners strike bargains with private landowners to achieve public objectives. In São Paulo, Brazil, and Mumbai, India, for example, government-sponsored housing for low-income families is allowed to be constructed at greater height and density, thereby allowing private developers to realize greater profits. Private–public partnerships and strong community support are also reaping benefits for road construction, sanitation, and urban renewal in these cities—successes played out in other cities in the regions (Pathak, 1999; Da Silva, 2000; Mohan, 2001; Patel & Mitlin, 2001). Successful programs have been launched in Manila, Bangkok, and Karachi by working with NGOs and bringing in local groups at the very beginning of urban development projects (Hasan, 1999; Hardoy, et al., 2001; Stren, 2001). In order to be successful, strategic planning and construction must go hand in hand with community-based development and participation of residents who will be directly impacted by the projects.

Many cities in the industrialized world have slowed or even reversed economic and environmental decline with long-term infusion of public funds priming the pump for private investment—including Houston, Miami, Memphis, and Toronto in North America; Amsterdam, Copenhagen, and Munich in Europe; and Omuta and Sendai in Japan (Cooper, 1999; Beatley, 200l; *Economist*, 2001b; Gilman, 2001; Kitano, 2001). The gains may be smaller, but similar strategies are meeting with success in neighborhoods of large cities in the developing world, most notably those in East and Southeast Asia (Prospects for Development, 2001). The challenge of the 21st century is to maintain a public–private balance that serves the needs of all of the globe's urban citizens—both rich and poor alike.

Urbanization in the United States

Because urbanization is a matter of degree, the demarcation between urban and rural is a gradual one. Two hundred years ago, 90 percent of the population of the United States lived in rural areas. According to the U.S. Bureau of the Census (2001:Table 30), the United States is about 81 percent urbanized, up by almost 2 percent from just a decade ago. Two predictions about continued urban expansion are implied: (1) It may have reached its environmental limits—limits dictated by water, desert, mountains, or other uninhabitable locations; and/or (2) remaining (arable) land suitable for

Jakarta, Indonesia dominates the entire nation, not only because of its massive population, but because of its vital importance to the nation's economy. Jakarta provides most jobs for the nation as a whole, and urban dwellers get to these jobs by whatever means available.

points of convergence. The reality is that urban growth, fueled by rural in-migration, will continue and that democratic governments cannot forcibly cut it off. If governments seek to minimize migration of rural people to urban areas, they must do so within an acceptable democratic and human rights framework (Habitat, 2001). In China, for example, people can be arrested and imprisoned for migration without official permission. China is currently rethinking its household registration system, which restricts people to live and work in certain areas, since large numbers of rural residents manage to bypass the system and flock to cities to escape both poverty and a taxation system that burdens farmers more than city residents (*Economist*, 2000, 2001a; Jie & Taubmann, 2002; Yan et al., 2002). To date, China is the only country in the developing world to manage urban growth effectively—but China is not democratic.

agriculture will continue to shrink. To survive the Malthusian endpoint, therefore, the United States must be more technologically efficient in food production or must import more food. Regardless of which option occurs, urban expansion at this point means cities literally bumping into one another.

Keeping up with urban growth also means that terminology used to designate it must be continually modified. A **metropolitan area** is a central city and surrounding smaller cities that function as an integrated economy. The **suburbs,** smaller surrounding urban areas outside the political boundaries of the central city, are often municipalities in themselves. A **megalopolis** is a system of several metropolitan areas and their surrounding suburbs that expand until they overlap. Although these terms provide images of urban growth, they are too vague for demographers, politicians concerned about numbers of voters, and city planners interested in providing services. More precise definitions use population numbers. The Census Bureau designates a **Metropolitan Statistical Area (MSA)** as a central city of at least 50,000 people and its adjacent urbanized areas. When the largest MSAs are grouped together, they become a **Con-**solidated **Metropolitan Statistical Area (CMSA)** and form the megalopolis mentioned above. As Table 22.1 indicates, MSAs and CMSAs have multiplied as the United States has urbanized. For sociology, the population numbers are important because they signify that the population of the United States is increasingly becoming interdependent, hence more specialized in function.

Suburbanization

The United States is decentralizing quicker than any other society in history (Siegel, 2000:40). The thousands of people who came to cities to work in the defense industry during World War II remained after the war, spawning the largest population increase in U.S. history. The dream of home ownership was in the reach of thousands of World War II veterans who could use their veteran status to purchase affordable housing. These factors provided the right mix for the most important urban population trend of the 20th century: the suburbanization of the United States. Almost three-fourths of today's urban population is suburbanized (Orfield, 2002).

TABLE 22.1

Largest Consolidated Metropolitan Statistical Areas and Fastest Growing Metropolitan Statistical Areas in the United States

Largest CMSAs in 2000

Rank	CMSA	Approximate Population in Millions
1	New York	21.2
2	Los Angeles	16.3
3	Chicago	9.5
4	Washington	7.6
5	San Francisco	7.0
6	Philadelphia	6.2
7	Boston	5.8
8	Detroit	5.5
9	Dallas	5.2
10	Houston	4.7

Fastest growing MSAs, 1990–2000

Rank	MSA	Percent Increase
1	Las Vegas, Nevada	83.3
2	Naples, Florida	65.3
3	Yuma, Arizona	49.7
4	McAllen-Edinburg-Mission, Texas	48.5
5	Austin-San Marcos, Texas	47.7
6	Fayetteville-Springdale-Rogers, Arkansas	47.5
7	Boise City, Idaho	46.1
8	Phoenix-Mesa, Arizona	45.3
9	Laredo, Texas	44.9
10	Provo-Orem, Utah	39.8

Sources: Perry and Mackun, 2001 (U.S. Census Bureau); U.S. Bureau of the Census, 2002: Table 31.

CLASS AND RACE IN SUBURBIA Like many neighborhoods in central cities, suburbs cater to different segments of the population. Upper- and middle-class residents live in expensive homes with manicured lawns and a minivan in the driveway and commute to white-collar jobs in the city or, increasingly, to outerbelt headquarters. The working classes are located closer to the first outer rims of cities. Although social class homogeneity is still the suburban norm, suburbs today are gradually becoming more diverse in social class for several important reasons. First, poorer residents of central cities often buy their first homes in the cheaper and deteriorating inner suburban ring. Second, public housing, often the site for concentrated areas of suburban poverty, is increasingly being built in suburbs populated by the working- and lower-middle classes. Third, many of the remaining manufacturing plants dot suburban landscapes throughout the United States, within short commuting distance for their working class employees. Finally, inner suburban rings are often the first homes to immigrants who are not affluent, but who are better off financially than inner city residents (Goetz, 2000; Walker & Lewis, 2001; Merola, 2002).

When minority status is factored in, the suburbanization of racial and ethnic groups is beginning to catch up with whites. Racial and ethnic minorities comprise almost one-third of the suburban population in the 102 largest MSAs, up from one-fifth since 1990 (Frey, 2001). Asians are the fastest growing racial group in the suburbs, followed by Latinos and African Americans. In suburban regions, residential location is similar for whites, Asians, and Latinos. Asians and whites live in places of equivalent social standing. Latinos live in poorer suburbs than whites. Suburban African Americans live in poorer areas than other races even after accounting for differences in income, education, and home ownership (Kahn, 2001; Whelan, 2001). Housing markets biased against African Americans help explain the pattern that middle-income blacks are as likely to live in racially segregated suburbs and send their children to racially segregated schools as their less affluent counterparts (Phelan & Schneider, 1996; Orfield & Yun, 1999; Reardon & Yun, 2001). Thus, compared to all other races, African Americans are more likely to be thwarted in housing and educational payoffs for upward social mobility.

The stereotyped image of the cozy suburbs as isolated areas of white affluence removed from the pressure of work and the noise and dirt of the central city is far from reality (Bradley, 2000). Pockets of poverty exist throughout suburbia, some suburbs are uniformly poor, and numbers of suburban homeless are increasing. Suburbia is inhabited by people of all ages and all household types, not just the suburban pioneers of young families with young children. The oldest suburbs closest to the city rim are likely to be both low income and stagnant. Except for decreased population density and a greater number of single-family residences, some of the social problems of the suburbs increasingly resemble those of larger cities (Williams, 2000). However, they remain the most desired residential form in the United States.

SUBURBAN POLITICAL AUTONOMY Although suburbs overall are becoming more heterogeneous in terms of race, ethnicity, and income, the normative suburban resident is middle class, educated, politically savvy, and works hard to ensure that the community is not strangled or transformed by new development (Carlisle, 1999; Ross, 2001). As suburbanites seek more and more control over their lifestyles, the number of separate suburban municipalities has skyrocketed. In the 25 largest MSAs in the United States, there are over 4,600 suburban jurisdictions (Orfield, 2002). Suburbs control a broad range of municipal services, including schools, police and fire protection, trash collection, and recreational facilities. Besides tax increases, the price for control includes a confusing and often conflicting array of services. For example, homes have been allowed to burn to the ground because of lack of agreements about providing water or fire protection for those outside municipal boundaries. In a megalopolis, where suburbs bump into other suburbs, it is nearly impossible to distinguish between them. Suburbanization is responsible for the urbanites' enhanced quality of life, but it has come at the expense of the cities around which suburbs have grown.

Decline or Renaissance of the Central City?

As measured in jobs, housing, and education, the economic and social consequences of population loss in the flight to the suburbs has been profound. Many industries have followed their employees to the suburbs, enticed by favorable taxes and retention of employees who are more satisfied with a suburban work site. The number of central-city jobs lost when manufacturing plants and small businesses close is higher than the service jobs that replace them. Cities then must raise taxes on the remaining businesses to maintain the same level of services. Lowered services and higher taxes decrease satisfaction with the city, causing more businesses to flee. When suburban businesses are spread out in separate townships, MSAs also lose advantages vital to national prosperity and international competition (Gans, 1991; Madden, 2000).

With middle-class suburban flight, inner-city neighborhoods are left with vacant, rapidly deteriorating homes. Strict housing-quality codes for the middle class can initially be used to legally exclude the poor from high growth areas. But when the neighborhood changes, codes are relaxed to keep houses occupied. Low-income people cannot afford to maintain the homes. As its housing deteriorates, reverberations are felt throughout the neighborhood, causing an overall decline of SES and an increased concentration of urban poverty (Small & Newman, 2001).

Property values are directly linked to school quality. Given the job and housing situation, the education consequences of population loss due to suburbanization are predictable. The tax base for public education is eroded, so better teachers cannot be attracted by either higher pay or good working conditions. The remaining middle class often send their children to private schools. Although successful strategies have helped curtail the deterioration of central-city public schools, a solid and predictable tax-paying population is necessary to fuel any central-city revival (see Chapter 16).

ENVIRONMENTAL RACISM AND CLASSISM Urban decline is also associated with environmental inequality. Central-city residents, who are disproportionately likely to be poor and racial minorities, are vulnerable to health risks from pollution, the release of toxic chemicals into sewers and ground water, lead-based paint and asbestos in poorly maintained apartments, and from the overall effects of a degraded urban ecosystem (Brown, 2000; Pulido, 2000; McLaughlin et al., 2001). Relaxed environmental standards to keep industrial plants in the city, the location of hazardous facilities near slum areas, street corners as dumping grounds for waste, and abandoned buildings also contribute to the environmental crisis faced by central-

city residents (Daniels & Friedman, 1999; D. Allen, 2001). The "environmental justice movement" was formed to correct environmental inequity, and to recognize the intersection of civil rights and environmental rights (Bryner, 2002; Getches & Pellow, 2002).

URBAN RENEWAL Three major forms of urban renewal emerged in the 1970s in response to the rapid decline of cities. The first form is **gentrification,** the renovation of specific working-class or poor neighborhoods to attract new, affluent residents. As the most visible form of urban renewal, gentrification upgrades an entire neighborhood, particularly as small businesses, such as dry cleaners, pubs, restaurants, and specialty stores, emerge to cater to newcomers. Most important, gentrification reestablishes a middle-class tax base. The second form of urban renewal is related to the first. People can qualify for low-rate federal loans to upgrade homes and businesses near gentrified neighborhoods. However, one of the requirements is that homeowners correct longstanding housing-code violations or risk being evicted. Poor people who are evicted from their homes usually move into public housing that is more densely concentrated with poverty, poorly maintained, and often crime ridden. Overall, the public housing option has been disastrous for residents. The failure of metropolitan governments to provide adequate and safe housing for their citizens is exemplified in the infamous Pruett-Igoe public housing project in St. Louis (Varady et al., 1998; Kennedy & Leonard, 2000). Rampant with crime and drugs, Pruett-Igoe was literally bombed out of existence.

It is clear that stemming the tide of urban decline rests on two key factors. The first factor is increasing

The idea of environmental racism is evident in areas where sites of hazardous wastes and fumes exist near the homes and schools of people of color. The African American community next to this oil refinery alongside the Mississippi River in Louisiana is known as "cancer alley" because of abnormally high levels of cancer among its residents.

When nationwide chains place new stores in poorer neighborhoods, such as this one in Harlem, they demonstrate their belief in the benefits of gentrification. Such urban renewal efforts profit both the store and the residents of the community in which it is placed.

the availability of affordable housing that deconcentrates poverty and provides access to jobs, public transportation, decent schools, and social services. The second factor is enticing larger businesses to remain or relocate in downtown areas and small businesses and restaurants to open throughout the city, especially in neighborhoods where people from all social classes can interact. Some cities have been successful in offering attractive housing options to young couples and single people who desire the freedom and flexibility of urban living. But once they have children, it is difficult to keep them from fleeing to the suburbs. And contrary to what many people believe, using public funds for big-ticket projects to revitalize downtown—such as stadiums, shopping malls, and casinos—does little to halt urban decline. Tourists come and go, and commuters return to the suburbs after work. Community development programs that connect people from all segments of the city and suburbs in a vital lifeline where they need one another stand a better chance of success (Gratz & Mintz, 1998; Rutheiser, 1999; Cashin, 2000).

If a central city continues to decline, the effect will inevitably be felt in the suburbs. All sociological theories underscore the fact of urban interdependence. The rise of megalopolises indicates that urban–suburban interconnections are so tangled that even affluent suburbs can face economic disaster if the central cities and industries they grew around falter.

Sociological Explanations for Urban Trends

Sociologists can help explain patterns of urbanization. Industrialization helped create not only the discipline of sociology, but also the important early subfield of urban sociology (Chapter 1).

URBAN ECOLOGY At the turn of the century, using Chicago as his laboratory, sociologist Robert Park (1916, 1926) began to explore patterns of urbanization, which led to the development of **urban ecology,** a field focused on the relationships between urban populations and their physical and spatial environments. The ecological approach suggests that population density in urban areas increases competition for scarce land, resulting in the distinctive spatial patterns found in most cities. Park declared that typical patterns of urban growth occurred in all industrial nations (Park et al., 1925). Using Chicago as a prototype, he developed the *concentric zone model* of urban growth. This model described the organization of industrial cities according to manufacturing, occupational, and residential areas that radiated out from a central business district (CBD). Zones were interdependent but distinct by function. The homes of the wealthy would not be located next door to a manufacturing plant. The result was a distribution of population according to land use.

The automobile dramatically changed land use patterns, and there were numerous modifications of the original concentric zone model to explain the changes. The two most notable are the *sector concept* (Hoyt, 1939, 1943) and the *multiple nuclei model* (Harris & Ullman, 1945), both of which are based on the evolution of cities from a central business district (CBD). With Minneapolis and San Francisco as examples, the sector concept suggests that urban growth occurs according to transportation lines. Housing and businesses follow highways and railroads, for instance, and extend in wedges outward from the CBD. With Boston as an example, the multiple nuclei model suggests that many discrete centers (nuclei) develop according to some specialized activity, such as finance or heavy industry.

GLOBAL CONNECTIONS

Neighborhoods of the Globe

People living in cities often conjure up images of rural life as more simple, virtuous, and wholesome than their own. Yet research consistently shows that although people define the "good" life in the countryside, they still prefer to live in cities. There is a strong rural bias, but there is a stronger urban preference. Sociologists suggest that this preference is linked to the fact that cities *can* provide what residents of small towns also have: a sense of community. Communities are made up of residents who share common values, interact on a face-to-face basis, and have a strong sense of identification with their residential neighborhood.

The notion of community-within-city is demonstrated in research in some of the world's most poverty-stricken cities. Squatters in Lima, Peru, refugees in Peshawar, Pakistan, and Cairo's cemetery dwellers live precarious but socially integrated lives. A study of Tondo, one of Manila's poorest districts, for example, suggests that poverty itself increases contact, help, and identification among neighbors, all fostered by a common lifestyle. Social isolation and alienation are not caused by life in these neighborhoods but when communities—as poor as they are—are torn apart, especially through compulsory eviction.

By recognizing that even the poorest cities on the planet have self-contained viable communities, local governments find it easier to mobilize the urban population for development projects. Programs bring together urban planners and residents to build community *empowerment* through high levels of resident participation. An already established sense of community is a catalyst for better development outcomes. Neighborhood councils in Nigeria and Colombia engage residents in self-help strategies to upgrade housing and integrate economic activities to serve community needs. South Africa has embarked on an ambitious program to determine how best to serve tight-knit communities of the old apartheid townships by designing and planning housing and businesses that suit the social and economic needs of their neighborhoods.

In the United States, the idea that neighborhoods with strong, primary ties endure despite urban change took sociological root in the 1960s with an important study of a poor ethnic neighborhood in Boston's West End. This study showed that vital social linkages persisted, even when the community was severely affected by changes that compromised its physical and economic integrity, such as deterioration of schools and churches and loss of small businesses. Residents existed in an "urban village," seeing their neighborhood as a low-rent district—not as a slum. Later research on cities throughout the United States shows that neighborhoods have special meaning to residents, especially when they function as networks of informal social support and as havens from the stress of contemporary life.

Perhaps because social change is happening so fast, and in light of the urban transformation of the developing world, people develop community bonds rather quickly. When faced with a potentially alienating urban environment, city dwellers all over the world—including its poorest parts—mark their neighborhoods with distinctive, self-chosen ways of life. Gone are the older sociological views of the world's urban poor as rampant with social pathologies that paralyze them both socially and economically. Newer research shows that urbanites throughout the globe, whether in Copenhagen, Cairo, or Calcutta, domesticate the urban monolith through community-building.

1. Where would you rather live—in a small town or an urban area? How is this preference affected by where you grew up? By your images of rural and city life?

2. How does your residence, college, neighborhood, town, or city reflect the idea of community?

Sources: Gans, 1962, 1967; Lomnitz, 1988; Chavis & Wandersman, 1990; Mabogunje, 1990; Awotona, 1995; Etzioni, 1995; Laquian, 1996; Sampson & Raudenbush, 1999; Friedmann, 2002.

Subsequent ecological models attempted to keep up with the fast-paced process of urbanization, but fewer and fewer patterns that fit the spatial ideas contained in the models emerged. Also, with its focus on the geography of land-use patterns, urban ecology tended to ignore both the social problems that resulted from these patterns, such as the dramatic shift of the population to the suburbs, and why urban land was developed in ways that did not pay off economically.

SYMBOLS AND URBANIZATION Early research showed that sentiment affects land use. Over a half century ago, Bostonians sought to preserve Beacon Hill, the Boston Common, and colonial cemeteries scattered through the central business district that thwarted business expansion. The value of the land had more to do with sentiment than with economics (Firey, 1945). Boston has retained this characteristic ever since. Central Park in New York City and Forest Park in St. Louis, large green spaces surrounded by million-dollar real estate, are a few of the numerous examples of the sentiment-symbol relationship found in urban areas around the globe (Anderson & Loughlin, 1986; Boyer, 1993; Low, 1999; Beatley, 2000; Lungo, 2000). As symbolic interactionists suggest, urban space can be attached with positive or negative meaning. When city parks are viewed as places for leisure and tranquility and are associated with civic pride, urban residents use them more and will contribute financially to their upkeep. When parks are viewed as places where "disreputable" people congregate, they are associated with fear and crime and are abandoned by urban residents, which in turn leads to their deterioration. The way the parks are socially constructed may create a beneficial or detrimental self-fulfilling prophecy. *Symbolic capital* —a powerful but invisible reality that people invest in their social space—may be as important to urban residents as economic capital (Bourdieu, 1998; Smith, 2001; Rykwert, 2000).

NEW URBAN SOCIOLOGY Because urban ecology could not adequately account for emerging land-use patterns or explain the social problems that emerged with these patterns, other models were needed. The new urban sociology focuses on social inequality and conflict. Cities are analyzed according to politics, ideology, the production of capital, and patterns of consumption, which produce advantages for some groups and disadvantages for others. There is a clear emphasis on the political economy as a driving force of urbanization (Smith, 1995; Byrne, 2001). Whereas earlier sociologists saw urban patterns motivated mostly by individual desires, the newer approach includes the influence of municipal regulations combined with economic incentives. For example, reasons for moving to the suburbs might include fear of crime, affordable housing for residents, and municipal tax incentives for developers and businesses (Gottdiener, 1999). The new urban sociology model has a strong conflict perspective that fits well with the view that cities are shaped by their location in a physical and economic hierarchy, and that a city's wealth and political power can also shape the cities around them (Harvey, 2000).

Symbolic interactionists suggest that people construct a symbolic world that is especially meaningful to them in carrying out their work and living activities, including the "built" environment that surrounds them, such as their cities, suburbs, and neighborhoods. Located within each of these built environments are a variety of subcultures, including those based on ethnicity, religion, race, gender, age, and disability (Gottdiener, 1999). For example, people with disabilities live and work in urban spaces offering accessible transportation and barrier-free residences (Gleeson, 2001; Urban Studies, 2001). Research on poor, African American women living in inner cities

show intensive neighborhood ties because networks of kin and church are also located in their neighborhoods and can be turned to for social, emotional, and financial support. Rather than a place of entrapment, a neighborhood is viewed as place for empowerment. In turn, neighborhoods are vitalized (Gilbert, 1998). Ethnic heritage is celebrated in festivals featuring traditional food, crafts, and dress, inviting other urbanites to join in the celebrations. Such festivals help urban dwellers to adjust to and symbolically construct urban life.

Urbanism as a Way of Life

The impact of urban life on its residents has been an ongoing research focus for sociologists. Much of this work is founded on Louis Wirth's (1938) classic essay,

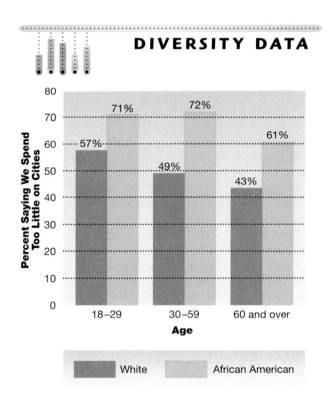

FIGURE 22.5 **Percent Who Say We Spend Too Little on Cities, by Age and Race.** Although well over half of respondents in all age groups say we are spending too little to solve problems of big cities, Africans Americans are on average 20 percent more likely to say this than whites. How can knowledge about the intersection of race and age patterns for people living in big cities explain these findings?

Source: NORC. General Social Surveys, 1972–2000, Chicago: National Opinion Research Center, 2000. Reprinted by permission of NORC, Chicago, IL.

Some urban sociologists suggest that cities may provide sources of entertainment and diversion for their dwellers, but the payment for it is isolation or detachment from others. This view has less support today.

Urbanism as a Way of Life. Wirth popularized a view of city life in which population density and social heterogeneity paved the way for a social structure based on impersonal, transitory, secondary relationships. According to Wirth (1938:55), in the city "our physical contacts are close, but our social contacts are distant."

Anthropologist Robert Redfield's (1941, 1947) work in peasant villages in Mexico support Wirth's images. Redfield described an "ideal" folk society as small, economically self-sufficient, and highly integrated. Continuous face-to-face interaction produces a strong sense of community. In cities, secondary groups replace the primary group ties of rural life.

A functionalist interpretation of both Wirth and Redfield maintains that secondary groups serve city dwellers well. With loss of primary contacts, people must find other outlets to meet social needs, so they come together in formal and voluntary associations. These adaptations to the onslaught of stressful urban living are used as psychological protection. Although these groups meet social needs, the city dweller pays a price. The city is comprised of a mosaic of little "selves," which touch but do not interpenetrate. Thus, the fragmented self is a distinctive feature of urban life (Cohen, 1993). The result is an efficient, rational, and sophisticated city dweller who is also anonymous, isolated, and interpersonally detached from other residents. Urban anomie (normlessness) and alienation are also common. If cities break down interpersonally, they will break down socially.

Wirth's essay is one of the most cited in all of sociology. How has his account stood the empirical test of time? In U.S. cities as well as globally, Wirth was correct in asserting that urbanization has a profound impact on all social life. But how that impact is actualized varies according to several factors. For example, common stressors in the rapidly growing cities of South Asia are noise, air pollution, and crowding, which interact to produce perceptions for some city dwellers that they have less control over their lives. In a study conducted in India and Bangladesh, people who were informed of the effects of air pollution and crowding actually felt worse than those who had not been given any information (Ruback et al., 1997)!

The most important impact on urban residents is economic. Urban decline is linked to a shredding of social ties in those areas hit hardest by job loss. Virtually every central city in the United States continues to experience a steady decrease in manufacturing, leading to unemployment and worsening poverty in the inner city. Referred to as the *spatial mismatch hypothesis*, an already weakened social fabric declines further as people who can afford to do so move out of deteriorating neighborhoods (Wilson, 1987; Small & Newman, 2001). For example, a suburban residence is important in improving job prospects for young African American inner-city men, even if they must still contend with racial discrimination (Stoll, 1999). The people who remain in the core cities are the poorest and the most psychologically vulnerable to the stresses of urban life. However, poverty does not always produce urban social breakdown. The evidence is clear that a sense of community can exist among those who dwell in deteriorated homes, located on littered streets, in crime ridden urban areas. Lurking within urban slums across the globe are vital neighborhoods bound together by a sense of identification, urgency, and social need. These neighborhoods are also connected because they share the same ecological environment.

ENVIRONMENT: ECOLOGICAL INTERDEPENDENCE

The most important question for environmental sociology in the 21st century is whether the activities of the previous centuries have set humanity on a collision course with the environment. Human activity has impacted every part of the planet and every ecosystem—no matter how remote—and poses both great possibility and great danger to our planetary future (United Nations Population Fund, 2002). The two most important direct causes of environmental destruction are population growth and industrial expansion (Dobkowski & Wallimann, 2002). Because both industry and population are concentrated in cities, urbanization is the indirect or mediating cause of environmental decline (Hardoy et al., 2001). Astounding economic growth magnifies already existing problems of the urban environment. The global economy has expanded more in the last 7 years than in the 10,000 years since agriculture began (Brown et al., 2000).

Evidence shows that people are becoming more conscious of the environment and that recycling is now a way of life for many, especially when children are socialized at school and at home in these efforts.

The Role of Technology

The technology that enabled the unprecedented economic growth of the 20th century has had a dramatic effect on our natural resources: Global consumption of wood has doubled, paper use has increased six times, and use of fossil fuels is up nearly fivefold. Grain consumption has tripled, and fish consumption has increased fivefold (see Figure 22.6 on page 120). The resulting environmental stress includes shrinking forests and wetlands, eroding soil and coral reefs, pollution of international waters, collapsing fisheries, vanishing plant and animal species, and rising temperatures (Allen, 1999; Fraser, 2000; Bryner, 2001; Bright & Mattoon, 2001). Half the world's population lives on coastlines, rivers, and estuaries, including rural people who rely on waterways for their livelihoods—fishing, transportation, communication, and irrigation for farmlands. Based on UN population predictions, by 2050 one in five people is likely to live in a country with severe shortages of fresh water serious enough to threaten health and economic well-being (United Nations Population Fund, 2001; World Health Organization, 2001).

The environmental change that has generated the most attention worldwide is the global temperature rise. Referred to as **global warming** or the *greenhouse effect*, temperature increases are linked to the burning of fossil fuels, industrial and agricultural waste, and other emissions such as the fluorocarbons used in refrigeration and air conditioning. These emissions are associated with ozone-layer depletion and the speed-up of global warming (Gelbspan, 1997; Gupta & Asher, 1998). In addition, the effect of rising temperatures on human health is documented in increased rates of skin cancer and the reemergence of diseases such as cholera and viral fevers, traced to changes in land use as a result of urbanization and development (Tickell, 1996). Although some people are skeptical about the impact of global warming, there is mounting evidence that it is the planet's biggest environmental problem (McKibben, 1998; Massey, 2001; Kirkman, 2002).

Global warming's link to other climatic changes is an excellent example of ecological interdependence. Recall the monumental global impact a few years ago of *El Niño*, the nickname for an ocean/atmosphere system normally occurring off the Peruvian Coast about every 5 to 7 years. El Niño changes the temperature of much of the Pacific Ocean, which in turn causes the air above it to be heated or cooled. From 1991 to 2003, the effects of four El Niño events eventually showed up as torrential rain in the Pacific, drought in Africa and Latin America, landslides in California, and deadly tornadoes in Alabama and Florida. Prolonged drought and flooding ravaged crops throughout the developing world, causing food

World Energy Consumption by Region

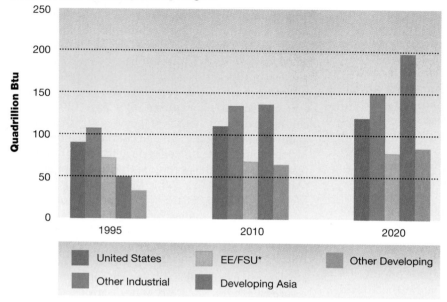

World Oil Consumption and Production by Region

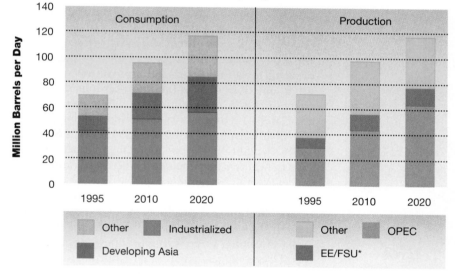

FIGURE 22.6 **Energy Consumption and Projected Demand by Regions of the World.**

Source: Department of Energy, Energy Information Administration, Washington, DC., 2002. http//www.eia.doe.gov.

*Eastern Europe and Former Soviet Union

shortages and malnutrition in some areas and famine and starvation in others. In 1997, thousands of miles of primary rain forests in Indonesia, Malaysia, and New Guinea, already thinned out by massive logging, easily caught fire following prolonged drought. El Niño may have been the final link on a causal chain originating with industrial expansion (Lush, 1998; Roddick, 1999).

However, the demographic transition suggests that industrial expansion is required for development and that the economic benefits to families will reduce fertility rates, decreasing demands on the environment. In the long run, however, industrial growth may be ecologically sound (Duesterberg & London,

2001). The underlying problem is that in the short run industrial expansion has created environmental havoc. And for much of the developing world stuck in Stage 2 of the demographic transition, fertility rates are not declining as fast as mortality rates. The result is massive population increases that further strain the ecosystem.

Research consistently documents that environmental degradation varies according to a country's level of affluence (Keohane, 1996; Meier & Stiglitz, 2000; Barnett, 2001). The developed world has had a great deal of success in cleaning up more localized environmental damages because their economies have

INTERNET CONNECTIONS

After reading about the environment and ecological interdependence in the text go to the World Resources Institute:

http://www.wri.org/wri/

and click on World Resources 2000–2001 looks at "People and Ecosystems: The Fraying Web of Life." Click on the different links to access information on the state of the environment. Write a short report on the status of the environment. What are the sources of the problems discussed on the Website? What can be done about them?

the resources and requisite political momentum to use public monies for environmental purposes. In the United States, there is widespread bipartisan support for increased attention to environmental causes, especially those related to curbing global warming. Spending for environmental improvement and international agreements to deal with global ecological threats are of great concern at the polls (Sodden, 1999; Vig & Craft, 2000).

This concern is justified, since technologically advanced nations consume the majority of the world's resources and contribute more to environmental degradation than the less advanced nations (Asthana & Shukla, 2002). Consider the following data:

- One citizen in the United States consumes about 30 times as much as a citizen in India.
- The richest 20 percent of the population consumes 86 percent of all goods and services produced on the planet and produces over half of all carbon dioxide emissions, while the poorest 20 percent consumes 1.3 percent of goods and services and produces 3 percent of carbon dioxide emissions.
- If everyone on Earth consumed as much as the average North American, it would require four more earths to provide all the material and energy she or he currently uses. (Population Connection, 2002)

Such examples are often drawn upon by leaders in developing nations in the game of ecopolitics.

The Game of Ecopolitics

Countries in the developing world are unquestionably aware of their environmental plight. Industrial pollutants must be cleaned up, toxic waste needs to be

stored safely, and forests need to be preserved rather than plundered—but not at the expense of economic expansion. World leaders take turns dealing the cards in a game of "greenhouse politics," and as conflict theorists suggest, the division between rich and poor countries determines which ones are played. As the gap widens, the reversal of practices and policies threatening to the environment is hindered (Barnett, 2001; Lewis, 2002).

In 1997, 160 nations signed the Kyoto Protocol, which identified what industrialized and developing nations can do to reduce emissions of the gases implicated in global warming. Based on an economic profile, each country is assigned a target reduction (averaging about 5.2 percent from 1990 levels by 2012). Targets for poorer countries are less stringent or nonexistent. Developing nations argue that since wealthier countries account for about 60 percent of

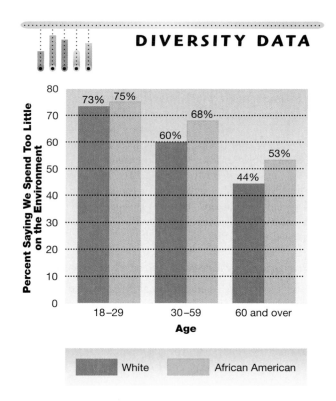

FIGURE 22.7 People Who Say We Spend Too Little on the Environment, by Age and Race. Although half of all respondents say we spend too little on the environment, whites and African Americans under age 30 are significantly more likely to say this. Why do you think that there is a wider age difference rather than a race difference on this issue?

Source: NORC. General Social Surveys, 1972–2000. Chicago: National Opinion Research Center, 2000. Reprinted by permission of NORC, Chicago, IL.

heat-trapping carbon monoxide emissions, they need to shoulder the economic burden in reducing them. Leaders representing the caucus of developing nations in environmental talks say that they cannot afford to devote a large share of precious resources to reduce emissions when there is an ongoing daily struggle to feed and clothe their burgeoning populations. On the other hand, nations of the developed world cite figures indicating that the massive population increases in the developing world will soon be responsible for exceeding the greenhouse gas emissions of the developed world (Blackman, 2002). There is skepticism that future emissions can be reduced at all (Stevens, 1997a, 1997b; Yandle, 1999).

What is unique about this debate is that the developing world can muster support for its side simply through the undeniable fact of ecological interdependence. From a sociological perspective, conflict theory takes center stage in explaining the issue. Many of today's global ecological problems stem from the very nature of modernization and how modernization itself has polarized the world into two classes of nations, one rich and the other poor. Environmental conflict cannot be reduced to climate control or other ecological problems without considering the politics that mediate the process (Roberts, 2001). Recent talks to finally implement the Kyoto Protocol stalled when the United States refused to sign off on the treaty, citing both harm to the U.S. economy and because it excused heavily polluting nations like India and China from any obligations to reduce emissions (Associated Press, 2001; Worldwatch, 2001). However, the United States recognizes that in the game of ecopolitics, wealthy nations can no longer take the autonomous role to which they had become accustomed (Agarwal et al., 2002; Sachs, 2002).

Strategies for Environmental Success

Global efforts are needed to deal effectively with environmental problems. Environmental action plans that bring together a wide array of stakeholders also have a better record of success. The more successful plans account for the realities of the political economy, the environmental movement, and biotechnology.

ECOLOGICAL PARTNERS The rich and poor nations have reached several important compromises that represent at least some cautious optimism concerning the world's ecological problems. Through UN efforts, the Global Environment Facility (GEF) was initiated in 1990. GEF is a pilot program that provides funds to developing countries to work on environmental problems, including global warming, pollution of international waters, and the depletion of the ozone layer (GEF, 1995). GEF's success has been modest, but in its brief history support has been gained from governments, private industry, and NGOs who usually have conflicting priorities. With World Bank funds, GEF has recently been repolished to help developing countries in their continued efforts to address global environmental concerns (Global Environment Team, 1999).

In a program known as the "debt-for-nature" swap, developing countries are rewarded for adopting conservation measures to safeguard their rain forests and biodiversity by writing off a portion of their foreign debts (Jakobeit, 1996:127). The program has been most successful in Costa Rica, a country already committed to conservation, as it is in the throes of deforestation. Yet Costa Rica could fund only a fraction of its conservation program from this source. Other parts of Latin America and Jamaica joined the program but could not gather enough additional funding to make it effective. While hardly a success story at this point, the debt-for-nature swap is a creative approach to conservation in public–private (government-NGO) partnership.

ENVIRONMENTALISM The environmentalism movement is steadily growing, drawing support from diverse groups the world over. Environmental activists are often recruited through *ecotourism*—which allows travelers to experience remote natural or cultural areas without disturbing them. Ecotourism is marketed as an environmentally responsible and educationally beneficial way for travelers to acquire an ecological consciousness. Ecotourism's explosion in popularity, however, is also causing concern that sheer numbers of travelers to remote areas will upset both the ecology and economy of the places that are visited (McLaren, 1997; Zebich-Knos, 2002). It is apparent, however, that ecotourists return home with a greater respect for the environment and are therefore likely to support environmental causes (Honey, 1999).

Some women are drawn into environmentalism through **ecofeminism**, a branch of feminist social theory connecting the degradation and oppression of women with the degradation of the ecosystem. Drawing on earth-based spiritual imagery, ecofeminism suggests that earth's original balance was upset through patriarchal domination of the planet (Griffin, 1995; Warren, 1997). The planet can be healed and ecological harmony restored through political action emphasizing the principle of equality of all species (Bowerbank, 2001). Although feminists, ecologists, and other NGOs may disagree on how to carry out this healing, the principles of ecofeminism offer a good bridge to build consensus and expand the environmentalism movement (Sargisson, 2001; Smith, 2001).

BIOTECHNOLOGY Technology may be able to increase agricultural production without sacrificing profit or the environment (Shah & Strong, 1999). The story of the green revolution illustrates the cost–benefit analysis. In the mid-20th century the "**green revolution**" was the term given to the industrial and technological innovations (biotechnology) used to produce high-yield crops that would solve the world's food supply problem. Biotechnology was developed to selectively breed crops not only to increase yield, but to boost nutritional content. Worldwide grain harvests, for example, achieved outstanding results, but at a grave ecological and social cost (Schnaiberg & Gould, 1994). Costly irrigation systems were needed to provide the abundant water necessary for a successful harvest. In many areas of the world, chemical fertilizers, pesticide, and genetically engineered seed, used haphazardly and without proper checks, transformed renewable soil fertility and plant life into a nonrenewable resource (Shiva, 1992). Newer evidence suggests that biotechnology raises productivity but also produces a number of negative side effects: agrosystems become artificial, unstable, degraded, and nutritionally depleted, and biodiversity is reduced (Henao & Baante, 2001; Snell, 2001). The health consequences of biotechnology for both farmers and consumers are unknown at this point (Keeler, 2001). Biotechnology has allowed the developing world to produce more food per capita than ever in history, but more of its people are malnourished.

Opponents of the biotechnology approach to solving the world's food problems point out that the planet's natural resources are being consumed faster than they are replenished or recycled and that there are biological and physical limits to what nature can provide. Technology is exploiting the earth's natural resources and future generations will be harmed (Gowdy, 2002). Technology has managed to come up with solutions to many human dilemmas, but there is no guarantee that ingenuity will continue to work. What if technology is too little and too late (Getting it Right, 2000; Dilworth, 2002)?

On the positive side, there are hints that a second green revolution is making global headway, with the lessons from the first one to guide it. The action agenda includes using environmentally friendly and appropriate technology to revitalize small farms and keep water and soil healthy (Horne & McDermott, 2001). For urban ecosystems, improvements in recycling, use of organic waste management, and the economical use of water can save resources (Wienberg et al., 2000). The technological optimist believes that the second green revolution will produce technology to meet current needs and can develop equivalent or superior options for future generations. If technology is culturally and ecologically appropriate as well as sustainable, the second green revolution may stand a better chance of success across the globe.

Sustainable Development

The interdependence of population, urbanization, and environmental problems must be taken into account to deal with them effectively. **Sustainable development (SD)** is a process requiring international cooperation that provides humane ways for the human species to live on the planet indefinitely without risking the future of either the planet or its inhabitants. Under the United Nations, two worldwide summits (the Rio Conference on Environment and Development in 1992 and the Johannesburg World Summit on Sustainable Development in 2002) encouraged governments to partner with NGOs and private industry to make a bold commitment to applying SD principles in every area where humans impact on the environment. Ideally, applying SD principles involves slowing population growth, alleviating hunger, and enhancing the growth of environmentally friendly cities throughout the world. This is a tall order. There are forces working both for and against SD. Sociological functionalism focuses on the cooperative efforts that will restrict some uses of our environmental systems in order to protect them. Conflict theory suggests that SD will be limited by powerful economic interests until competing interests muster enough resources to challenge them effectively. Symbolic interactionism focuses on how people envision the process, culturally construct definitions around it, and then operate on those definitions. All three perspectives would accept the ecological principle that human and nonhuman species interact, change, and evolve with their environments. Sociologists suggest that policies to enhance sustainable development in environmentally sound ways are more successful when this ecological principle is not violated (Litfin, 1999; OECD, 2001).

LIFE CONNECTIONS

Autocentric America and Urban Sprawl

The United States is a car-dependent nation. The critical ingredient in the expansion of cities was the automobile and the transportation system designed around it. In addition, the automobile spawned suburbanization. As metropolitan areas continue to expand, suburbs are swallowed up by other suburbs encroaching on their outer rims, forming new megalopolises. The resulting urban sprawl, with single-family residences close to highways, supermarkets, and recreational facilities, requires an "autocentric" existence. Suburbanites drive 31 percent more than their central-city counterparts (Kahn, 2000).

The first suburbs were often referred to as dormitory or bedroom communities, because people slept there but relied on their cars to get to the central city that served most other aspects of their lives, from their jobs to their recreational activities. After World War II, suburbs began to develop their own services to accommodate residents, with less and less reliance on the city. Suburban municipalities incorporated politically and developed their own school districts, hospitals, shopping, and recreational areas. Tax incentives enticed businesses and jobs to the suburbs. One-third of suburban residents live and work there. Some suburbs could now exist independently from the core host cities that spawned them.

Edge Cities

Some suburbs have socially and economically distanced themselves so much from their host city that a "post-suburbia" urban form is developing on the rural fringes of MSAs (Teaford, 1997). This form is the **edge city,** a large suburban community located on the periphery of a metropolitan area that functions independently from the host city. Except for occasional forays into downtown for a sports event, play, or visit to the art museum, edge-city residents rarely venture beyond their highway outerbelts. With fewer people commuting to inner suburbs or central cities, and to protect their separation, many edge cities have defeated proposals to extend mass transit in their areas. Through low taxes, cheap undeveloped land, and quality single family homes at reasonable prices, edge cities have attracted the lion's share of new housing and commercial development over the last 25 years (Williams, 2000). With edge cities attracting businesses in the service industries at faster rates than central cities and older suburbs, demands for semi-skilled labor is increasing. With jobs readily available, new immigrants are likely to make their first home in edge cities and suburbs (Greene, 1997; Micklethwait, 2000; Little & Triest, 2002). Strapped by transportation and long commutes, it is highly unlikely that inner-city residents would seek these jobs. In turn, second-generation immigrants are building small businesses and offering culturally desired services, such as ethnic food and entertainment, to the new arrivals. Such economic linkages may strengthen the edge city but at the expense of the host metropolitan area (McKee & McKee, 2001).

The automobile is the lifeline of the edge city, even more so than the suburbs closer to the central city where better public transportation is available. Zoning regulations further meld edge-city residents to their cars. Unlike in central-city neighborhoods, zoning codes dictate that homes, businesses, and schools be built separately from one another. Residential neighborhoods are less likely than shopping malls and public parks to provide spaces for people to meet and interact (Minerd, 2000). Critics of this approach claim that edge cities have negative social effects that isolate people from one another (Duany et al., 2000). A healthy street life cannot be maintained when people spend more time in their cars than on their front porches.

ESCAPE TO NOWHERE   Escape from the congestion of the central city is an illusion when people recognize they are hemmed in by development. California is the symbol of urban sprawl. It is oriented to an autocentric drive-in culture, and this pattern is repeating itself on the edges of virtually every metropolitan area throughout the United States. Research conducted in Orange County, California, shows that the perceived quality of life and sense of community of suburban residents decreases over time because of urbanization, especially in larger, higher density, and more ethnically diverse suburbs. As Kenneth Jackson (1985:281) explains in his historical analysis of U.S. suburbs:

> No longer forced outside by the heat and humidity, no longer attracted by the corner drugstore, and no longer within walking distance of relatives, suburbanites often choose to remain in the family room. When they do venture out, it is often through a garage into an air-conditioned automobile. Streets are no longer places to promenade, but passageways for high-powered machines.

Suburbs swallow everything in their forward march to rural areas, at the expense of the environment and the central cities they leave behind. Detroit and Washington, D.C., are examples of cities that have become shadows of their former selves in the march to the once greener pastures of suburbia.

ENVIRONMENTAL DISASTER   But the greener pastures of suburbia have been ecologically eroded. Suburbanization is resource-intensive and resource-depleting. Fuel and land consumption as a result of suburban expansion have impacted the surrounding ecosystems in destructive ways. In many cases, over 90 percent of native flora and fauna are eradicated. This eradication is mostly due to one fact: Habitats are paved over. The habitat is fragmented, native populations are isolated, and access to predators and invasive plants is opened (McKinney, 2000). Uncontrolled urban sprawl is wreaking havoc on biodiversity and is threatening many plants and animals throughout the United States (Lassila, 1999). While there is a great deal of conservation effort directed at preserving national parks, wetlands, and undeveloped land far from cities, the environmental consequences of urban sprawl have often been overlooked (Light, 2001).

Smart Growth

Despite the negative consequences of urban sprawl and car-dependency, people in the United States, especially those with young children, desire suburban living. Suburbanites are also keenly aware that unless urban sprawl is controlled, it can dangerously alter the lifestyle they worked so hard to achieve (Mitchell, 2001). People want to restrict suburban development, protect greenspace, and redevelop older suburbs, but not at the expense of their own (O'Meara, 1999a; Pew Center, 2000). The political reality is that while suburbanites want to reign in urban sprawl, they do not want to sacrifice their large homes, and they resist the low-density life advocated by anti-sprawl initiatives (NAHB, 1999).

There are some models that offer a way out of this dilemma. *Smart Growth* is an efficient and environmentally friendly strategy that coordinates land-use planning. It recognizes that new development is needed but that the quality of life of residents should not be comprised as a result. The strategy is based on consensus and inclusion of all people affected by urban sprawl at all stages of any proposed development scheme. Smart Growth strategies have had some successes, generating optimism that urban sprawl can be brought under control to the benefit of all parties. Most important, by redirecting development efforts to older suburbs, the central city also benefits (Myers, 2000; Shaw & Utt, 2000).

Another model also offers optimism. Two decades ago Portland, Oregon, limited urban sprawl by creating an "urban growth boundary" (UGB) over the city's surrounding farmland. UGB zones are regulated as to what can be built and how far development can extend. Developers are required to provide housing for low-income people when homes for the middle class and affluent are built. Older urban zones are reclaimed and revitalized before development is extended outward. Environmental impact studies are required before any development takes place. The UGB model appears to meet the interests of farmers, environmentalists, businesses, and suburban residents. Portland looks inward rather than outward in terms of development (America's Cities, 1998; O'Meara, 1999b). Although Portland's UGB plan predates Smart Growth, its similar strategies of consensus building and redirected development sowed the seeds for success.

Portland is as autocentric as most other U.S. cities, but its efforts to curtail suburban sprawl are impressive. Whether its UGB model can be successful in other cities is uncertain. What is certain, however, is that suburbia and edge cites are still viably connected to their host cities. Unless suburbanization can be curtailed, or at least controlled, it will be to the detriment of both central city and suburbia.

INTERNET CONNECTIONS

A wealth of population data on the United States can be found at U.S. Census Website:

http://www.census.gov/main/www/cen2000.html

On "select a State" select your home state and also select the United States. Describe the demographic characteristics of your state. How do they compare to the rest of the United States?

SOCIETY CONNECTIONS

Population Control

Acceptable methods of environmentally sustainable development may be easier to find than acceptable methods of limiting population growth. Although intensely personal, sexuality and reproduction are highly political. As noted by a participant of a reproductive health conference held in Africa, "government, parents, and religious leaders are all literally in bed with us" (Berer, 1993:1). It is also very clear that the population explosion in the developing world is making poor people poorer, the hungry hungrier, and weakening an already fragile environment. It is vitally important to stabilize population if development goals are to be realized. Slowing the rate of population growth ultimately depends on a decline in fertility, an objective that has generated both support and controversy worldwide (Bayer, 2000).

The Status of Women

The most contentious issue in international debates about population involves the role and status of women. In 1994 the United Nations International Conference on Population and Development convened in Cairo to debate future population policy for the globe. The conference agreed that population management and the provision of humanitarian-based reproductive health-related services should be top government priorities, especially in the context of sustainable development (Cohen & Richards, 1994). Of all factors associated with falling birthrates, the most powerful, direct, and established link is improvement in the lives of women (Presser & Sen, 2000; McGuire, 2001; Sarin, 2001). The fourth UN Conference on Women, held in 1995 in Beijing, again reinforced the idea that women's emancipation is key to solving problems related to population, environment, and economic development (Johnson & Turnbull, 1995). In mid-decade reviews of the two conferences, delegations were able to overcome political, cultural, and religious differences and reach consensus that reproductive health included its impact on the social, mental, and physical well-being of women, especially as related to family planning. The strongest advocates for family planning are women from developing nations (Tsui et al., 1997; Petchesky & Judd, 1998; Ashford & Makinson, 1999).

Family planning is the deceptively simple notion that couples have the right and means to decide how many children they will have. Effective contraception is the number one cause of declining fertility throughout the world. The condom is the most widely used method, followed by birth-control pills. Surgical sterilization of women as a birth control method occurs more often than vasectomies for men. Abstinence is the least used method of contraception. When abortion is a legal option, it is highest in countries where other birth-control options are limited, a trend most likely in the poorer countries of the world. Evidence is consistent suggesting that countries adopting family-planning strategies with safe and effective birth control have lower rates of unwanted pregnancy, abortion, and maternal and infant deaths (AGI, 1998; Kantner & Westley, 1998; Berer, 2000; Sarin, 2002).

Global concern regarding high population growth masks the fact that through effective birth control, countries nearing the end of the demographic transition, such as South Korea, Taiwan, and Thailand, have attained fertility rates near or at replacement level (Greenspan, 1994; Westley, 2002). The percentage of couples in the developing world who use family planning increased from 10 to 50 percent in the last three decades. For the first time in history, most of the world could see an absolute decline in population growth by the middle of the next century *if* family-planning efforts can be maintained (Crossette, 2002; United Nations Population Fund, 2002). However, an unmet need for family planning still exists for the vast majority of the developing world.

The *unmet need hypothesis* suggests that effective birth control, particularly in developing countries, is wanted but either unavailable or culturally unacceptable (Figure 22.8). The critical factor linked to unmet needs is the status of women. Over 100 million married women of childbearing age say they want to postpone or end childbearing but are not currently using

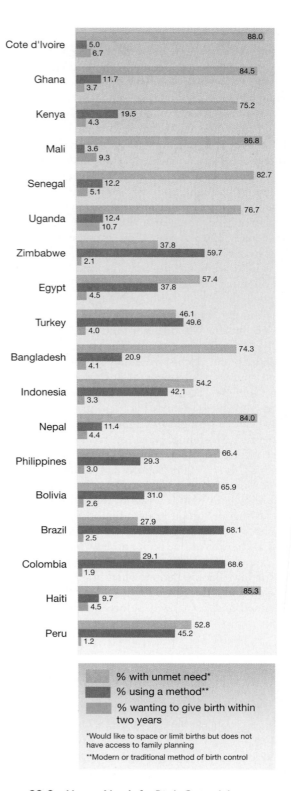

FIGURE 22.8 Unmet Needs for Birth Control Among Women Who Gave Birth the Previous Year, Selected Countries in the Developing World.

Source: Table 1 (adapted) from "Contraceptive Use, Intention to Use, and Unmet Needs During Extended Postpartum Period" by John A. Ross and William L. Winfrey, *International Family Planning Perspectives.* Volume 27, No. 1, March 2001. Copyright © 2001. Reprinted by permission of the Alan Guttmacher Institute.

contraceptives. With declines in infant mortality, couples now desire fewer children, and women desire fewer than men (Rafalimanana & Westoff, 2001; Upadhyay, 2001). Women are bound by laws and customs that restrict education and job opportunities associated with decision making in their families.

SOCIOLOGICAL PERSPECTIVES A combination of conflict theory and symbolic interactionism is useful in explaining these patterns. There are powerful cultural definitions of sexual expression and women's roles in family life. Men and women accept the idea that a woman's foremost role is childbearer, taking precedence over her role as wife. Fertility rates may be lowered when alternative definitions of women's roles are embraced by both genders. Female empowerment also leads to increased autonomy in decision making; research suggests that organization of peer groups, support by NGOs, and mobilization of community resources and public services are the most effective strategies in helping women implement their reproductive preferences (Tsui et al., 1997; Maiga, 2001; Sangani, 2001; Shannon, 2001).

There is strong support for the idea that the focus of population policy should move beyond attaining population goals to guaranteeing full reproductive rights (Johnson & Nurick, 1995; Bayer, 2000; Jacobson, 2001). Such a policy would also work against the abuses of forced pregnancy, a frequent outcome in Latin America and Africa, and forced abortions, a common outcome in China. Population programs that deny condom usage because it is culturally offensive and then offer female sterilization or abortion as

the only options to childbearing risk reproductive health and abridge human rights (Mason, 1994; Kantner & Westley, 1998; Ashford, 2001; Liu, 2001). Policies designed to meet the unmet need for contraception must balance cultural sensitivity with women's rights.

Malthus Revisited

Malthus has haunted us throughout our exploration of population, urbanization, and the environment. How do his predictions stand the test of time?

Over a long period of time, the Industrial Revolution in the West was able to economically absorb a growing population. Population growth was apace with food production and the demand for workers. By comparison, the contemporary developing world is industrializing so rapidly that, as we saw, agricultural production and the environment in which it is produced are at risk. Population growth is no longer viewed as an unequivocal benefit to development because it is no longer favorable to economic production. The inability of the planet to feed itself, Malthus would say, is just around the corner. He would also view the unmet need hypothesis as an indication that people cannot control their sexual passions. In later editions of his essay he did suggest that altering marriage patterns (positive checks) affects the fertility rate. Overall, however, for Malthus population is destined to increase until checked by famine.

What Malthus failed to recognize is the monumental role of social processes in explaining both population growth and food production. Despite

Throughout the world, urban development and city planning projects that have strong community-based participation and government support are successful in stemming problems associated with both unplanned urban growth and urban decline, such as this clean-up project in one of Nairobi, Kenya's largest slums.

unmet needs for contraception, poor couples are not unregulated in their sexual passions. Spacing births by breast feeding may not be the most reliable birth-control mechanism, but it has been used by couples for centuries (UNICEF, 2000). The presumed population pressure played a less important role in the Irish potato famine of the 1800s than Ireland's colonial status, which required the export of potatoes to England. More than 1 million Irish people—about one in every nine—died because when the potato crop failed they could not afford to purchase the other plentiful food available (Japikse, 1994; Thornton, 1998). As in the developing world today, it is poverty and not lack of food that causes malnutrition and starvation.

Malthus also did not predict the green revolution. We have seen that technology linked with social and economic development has transformed the produc-

tive potential of many nations and relaxed some constraints imposed by the physical environment. Farmers in drought areas have evolved sophisticated strategies to cope with environmental risks. In Mali, a land tenure system allows farmers reciprocal access to resources both between and within ecosystems in times of environmental stress when their own systems are not productive enough (Moorehead, 1992). Sociology emphasizes the flexibility of culture and the enormous variability of human inventiveness in the common struggle for the survival of humanity. With the cooperative efforts of nations throughout the world, population growth is expected to stabilize in union with environmentally acceptable approaches to sustainable development.

SUMMARY

1. Demography is the scientific study of the size, distribution, and composition of population over time. To account for population changes, demographers analyze fertility, birth, death, and migration rates, among others.

2. In Europe and North America, the Industrial Revolution caused a profound drop in fertility and mortality rates and a corresponding increase in life expectancy, referred to as the demographic transition.

3. In 1789, Thomas Malthus predicted that population growth would eventually outstrip agricultural production, causing widespread famine and death. Malthus was pessimistic about people's ability to change behavior to deal with food shortages.

4. Émile Durkheim's functionalist approach saw population growth as a stimulus for industrial development. Unlike Malthus, Durkheim believed humans could adapt to increased population.

5. Karl Marx believed capitalism's unequal distribution of resources and food is the cause of human misery. Contemporary conflict theorists emphasize the maldistribution of resources and the economic dependency of poor nations on rich nations.

6. Urbanization is the process of city population growth. About half the world's population lives in

urban areas. The developing world is still mostly rural, but its cities are rapidly growing due to rural migrants.

7. The United States is 80 percent urban. The most important urban population trend in the United States is suburbanization; population loss to suburbs threatens central cities. Urban renewal efforts focus on gentrification for the middle class and making housing affordable for the poor.

8. The earliest sociological explanation for city growth was urban ecology—analysis of the relationship between population and physical space. Urban trends such as decentralization and suburbanization led to the development of the new urban sociology, which focuses on the political economy, and urban symbolism to explain urban patterns.

9. According to Louis Wirth and Robert Redfield, compared to intimate rural communities, cities tend to foster impersonal and distant social relations. Urban life puts people at risk for normlessness and alienation, but many urban neighborhoods maintain a strong sense of community.

10. Though industrialization has economic benefits, it has degraded the environment globally, such as through global warming. Developing countries have limited resources and rapidly growing popu-

lations, and face a trade-off between economic development and environmental protection.

11. The goal of sustainable development is to continue economic development but also protect the environment.

12. Half the U.S. population lives in automobile-dependent suburbs and edge cities that have much autonomy but remain linked to the host city. Urban sprawl threatens suburban lifestyles.

13. Improving the status of women is the single most effective way to slow global population growth.

14. From a sociological viewpoint, Malthus was incorrect because he did not account for the major role of social processes in explaining population growth and food production.

KEY TERMS

census 590
Consolidated Metropolitan Statistical Area (CMSA) 600
crude birthrate 590
demographic transition 590
demography 589
ecofeminism 610
edge cities 612
fertility rate 590

gentrification 602
global cities 598
global warming 607
green revolution 611
megalopolis 600
metropolitan area 600
Metropolitan Statistical Area (MSA) 600
migration rate 590

population pyramid 590
suburbs 600
sustainable development (SD) 611
urban 596
urban ecology 603
urbanization 596

CRITICAL THINKING QUESTIONS

1. Demonstrate how the idea of interdependence shapes population, urbanization, and the environment. What role does technology play in each of these areas?

2. How do functionalism and conflict theory explain the trend that the poor are migrating to the cities of the developing world, but the middle class and affluent are migrating out of cities to the suburbs of the developed world?

3. How can the process of sustainable global development work to the benefit of the poor, who are often displaced by the process?

4. From a symbolic interactionist view, what culturally appropriate methods would you suggest to meet couples' "unmet need" for contraception?

INVESTIGATE WITH CONTENT SELECT

 Begin your research using Content-Select for this chapter by following the directions found on page 27 of this text to visit Prentice Hall's Research Navigator Website. Enter these search terms into the search field:

Population
Census
Urbanization

23
COLLECTIVE BEHAVIOR AND SOCIAL MOVEMENTS

Protesting the World Trade Organization

Tens of thousands of activists took to the streets of Seattle in mid-December 1999 to protest a meeting of the World Trade Organization, an international group they believed to be working on behalf of powerful multinational corporations and against the interests of the majority of the world's people, especially those in the developing world. Graying veterans of the social movements of the 1960s and 1970s were enthralled, convinced that the heady days of their youth had returned. But this was not your father's protest.

For one thing, the Seattle demonstrations were coordinated over the Internet, not by means of blurry flyers run off on mimeograph machines. This meant that participants could be drawn from all over the country or even from other nations, not just from the local area. In addition, the crowds were far more diverse than they had been in the days of the civil rights movement and the Vietnam War protests. Teamsters and steelworkers mingled with environmentalists, feminists, animal rights activists, and anarchists. Tactics ranged from peaceful demonstrations to guerilla warfare. In the end, the protestors succeeded in disrupting the WTO meetings, but at a cost of over $3 million in property damage and over 500 arrests. (Elliott, 1999; Klee, 1999; Morganthau, 2000)

Osama Made Me Wait in Line!

As frequently occurs in disaster situations, numerous rumors arose in the hours immediately following the September 11, 2001, attacks on the World Trade Center and the Pentagon. One of the most popular concerned gasoline prices: People all over the country apparently assumed that any crisis involving the Middle East would interrupt the supply of gas to the United States and that as a result prices would soon soar.

By 4:30 in the afternoon, 20 or more cars were lined up outside most of the filling stations in Owensboro, Kentucky's third largest community. A local man named Darian Boling was quoted as saying, "Gas is going up to three or four dollars a gallon. I just heard it on the radio. Actually, I didn't hear it, but others did." Jennifer McDowell, waiting in the same line as Darian, said that one of her friends had heard that gas in nearby Evansville, Indiana, was already $4 a gallon and that the Alaska pipeline was being closed. One station sold 1,700 gallons in a single hour. No actual shortages ever occurred. (Vied et al., 2001)

COLLECTIVE BEHAVIOR

You may well wonder what a political protest and a rumor have in common. Sociologists would see both as examples of **collective behavior,** relatively spontaneous, short-lived, unconventional, and unorganized activity by large numbers of people that occurs when norms are unclear or rapidly changing.

Most of the patterns of social action we have discussed in this text to this point are relatively highly *institutionalized.* This means that the norms that guide behavior are relatively firmly established in people's minds. Going to school, voting, taking a date to the movies, or working for a large company are routine, stable, highly predictable activities. Everyone knows pretty much what to expect in these types of situations.

But sometimes the norms are less well established and people are largely left to their own devices in deciding how to act. There are no clear scripts to guide us when a fire breaks out in a theater, when terrorists fly airplanes into buildings, or when mobs roam the streets, breaking store windows and looting. Under such circumstances, we must improvise, and the usual result is collective behavior of one type or another (Turner & Killian, 1993; Goode, 1992; Marx & McAdam, 1994; Locher, 2002).

As Figure 23.1 suggests, the various forms of collective behavior may be arranged along a rough

Although the 1992 Los Angeles riots were sparked by anger over a jury's failure to convict white officers accused of beating a black man, looters came from a variety of ethnic and racial backgrounds. Total property losses from the riots exceeded one billion dollars.

continuum from the most to the least institutionalized. The most spontaneous, least structured types—panic and mass hysteria—are located toward the bottom. Mobs, riots, fashions, and fads occupy the middle range, while social and political movements

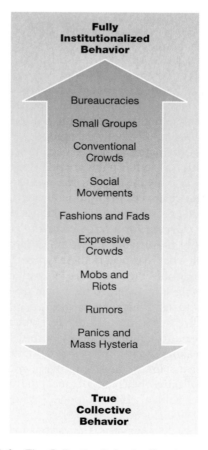

FIGURE 23.1 The Collective Behavior Continuum.

are toward the top because they display some marked similarities with fully institutionalized behavior.

This chapter begins with a look at the simpler, less-structured forms of collective behavior and at the major theories that have been developed to explain them. Then we examine social movements, which have traditionally been analyzed in sociology as a complex and enduring type of collective behavior. We conclude with a look at the training of movement activists and a quick overview of some current trends in social movement development.

Explaining Collective Behavior

Under what circumstances do people riot, spread rumors, or follow fads and crazes? Social scientists have proposed several major theories to explain these sorts of behavior, including contagion theory, value-added theory, and emergent-norm theory (McPhail, 1997).

CONTAGION THEORY Early theories of collective behavior primarily addressed mobs and riots. They emphasized psychological factors, especially the irrationality of the crowd, and suggested that the contagious excitement generated by being caught up in a mob or riot commonly led to a collective or herd mentality. The normal restraints of civilization were swept aside and participants, encouraged by the anonymity of the crowd, acted like unreasoning animals (LeBon, 1960). Feeling invincible, members of a crowd sometimes committed atrocities that appalled them when they returned to their senses.

The metaphor of contagion was obviously chosen to convey the view that collective behavior resembles a kind of mental illness. Another theory, developed

Some members of protest crowds appear far more passionate than others, but most share the same basic point of view. Contagion theory suggests that this unanimity develops out of the crowd experience itself.

more recently by symbolic interactionist Herbert Blumer, takes a somewhat similar view (1969a). Though Blumer recognized that crowd members retained most if not all of their reasoning ability, he was still greatly impressed by the emotional character of collective behavior. His theory emphasized the processes of *milling* and *circular reaction:* Participants were visualized as continually wandering through the crowd (milling) and gradually intensifying their own emotionality by feeding off the nonverbal cues of others (circular reaction).

Today, sociologists consider contagion theory, especially LeBon's formulation, to be seriously biased. Its adherents were primarily upper- and middle-class individuals who felt personally threatened by collective behavior. While crowds can indeed sway the emotions, research suggests that their members are by no means as irrational as contagion theory claims (McPhail, 1991; Locher, 2002).

VALUE-ADDED THEORY In the early 1960s, functionalist Neil Smelser (1962) published a very influential theory of collective behavior. Smelser identified six conditions that must be met before any episode of collective behavior can begin. Each requirement must be in place before the next one can become relevant in the development of a riot, panic, fad, or social movement. We illustrate this theory by using it to analyze the major riot that took place in Los Angeles late in April 1992, following the failure of an all-white jury to convict four white police officers who had been videotaped beating an African American traffic violator named Rodney King (Baldassare, 1994; Cannon, 1997; Bergesen & Herman, 1998).

- First, the society must be *structurally conducive* to collective behavior. That is, it must be organized in a way that allows or permits such activity. The fact that the citizens of South Central Los Angeles enjoyed the constitutional right to assemble and protest was a key factor promoting conduciveness. Their ability to communicate easily with one another because most of them spoke the same language was another important factor facilitating the riot.
- Smelser's second precondition is *structural strain:* The target population becomes discontent because of what are perceived as unjust social conditions. Strain disturbs the smooth, predictable functioning of the social system. The Rodney King incident did not occur in a vacuum; it was merely the most recent expression of anger over the discrimination that people of color have long experienced in this country.
- Third, a *generalized belief* must emerge to explain what is wrong—why people are feeling strain—and what can be done to relieve the pressure. The generalized belief that developed in South Central after the King incident held that police brutality, poverty, and the general lack of opportunities available to members of the community were the inevitable consequences of white racism.
- Next, a *precipitating incident* must occur, some event that sums up the whole situation in microcosm and galvanizes the populace into action. This was accomplished by media reports of the "not guilty" verdict in the trial of the four police officers who had beaten Rodney King.

- Smelser's fifth point, *mobilization for action*, refers to the actual onset of the episode. In this case, people began rioting and looting.
- Finally, the role of agents of *social control* becomes relevant. The response of the police and national guard can cool tensions or, as was the case in South Central, it may further inflame passions and intensify and prolong collective behavior.

Smelser's theory is very useful as a means of thinking about the reasons why an episode of collective behavior does (or does not) occur, and it is clearly more value-neutral than contagion theory. However, conflict theorists have correctly pointed out that value-added theory reflects the questionable functionalist assumption that social systems are normally stable and change only when dysfunctional elements (strains) arise (Lewis, 1989; Locher, 2002).

EMERGENT-NORM THEORY Emergent-norm theory proposes yet another way of explaining crowd functioning, one grounded in the symbolic interactionist perspective (Turner & Killian, 1993). This theory is based on the observation that collective behavior generally arises when expectations regarding how to act are relatively vague. Under these circumstances, crowd members may propose various courses of action, sometimes verbally and sometimes by example. Some of these suggestions will be ignored, while others will be readily accepted, becoming new shared norms (Weller & Quarantelli, 1973). Thus, crowd norms develop or *emerge* from ongoing interaction. Those who do not agree with these norms are free to leave; those who accept them stay, which leads the entire group to display the unity of purpose that contagion theorists find important (McPhail & Wohlstein, 1983).

A good example of emergent-norm theory in action occurred at a protest staged at the British embassy in Dublin, which was observed by one of the authors of this text. At one point, an obviously inebriated participant started to throw stones at the building, but no one copied him, and the speaker urged him to stop, which he did. A few minutes later, another crowd member verbally suggested that the group move to the American embassy to protest U.S. support for the British presence in Northern Ireland. Several other people shouted their support for this plan, and in the end the whole group walked over to the American embassy.

One of the greatest strengths of emergent-norm theory is that it views collective behavior participants as largely rational (Quarantelli & Dynes, 1970; Berk, 1974; Turner, 1996; Aguirre et al., 1998). For example, in the Los Angeles riots, emergent norms encouraged the looters to target stores owned by Korean immigrants, who were widely believed to be exploiting the community, whereas shops owned by blacks were less likely to be attacked.

Forms of Collective Behavior

Sociologists generally refer to the people engaged in collective behavior as a *collectivity* rather than a group in order to emphasize the weakness of the bonds connecting them. Formally speaking, a collectivity is a substantial number of people who interact guided by loosely defined norms. Unlike groups, collectivities generate little solidarity or group loyalty, usually last only a short while, have no clear boundaries, recognize few leaders, and display only a limited division of labor.

There are two distinct types of collectivities. In *localized collectivities*, the participants are in each other's immediate physical presence. In *dispersed collectivities*, the participants are not all in the same place at the same time (Turner & Killian, 1993).

LOCALIZED COLLECTIVITIES The two principal varieties of collective behavior that take place on a face-to-face basis are crowds—including mobs, riots, and demonstrations—and panics.

Crowds Crowds are temporary gatherings of people who influence each other in some way and share a common focus of attention (Snow et al., 1981). Crowd behavior typically displays some of the qualities emphasized by contagion theorists. Because individuals blend into a crowd, they are relatively anonymous. This often increases their willingness to violate conventional norms because they know they probably will not be held accountable for their behavior. The permissive atmosphere of the crowd and the physical presence of large numbers of other people generate a sense of urgency. Faced with a relatively unscripted situation, crowd members tend to become suggestible and emotionally aroused (Turner & Killian, 1993). The dominant emotion in a crowd may be joy, anger, fear, or some combination of the three (Lofland, 1985).

The best known typology of crowd behavior was developed by Herbert Blumer (1969). He identified four basic types of crowds: casual, conventional, expressive, and acting. However, since crowds are inherently volatile, it is important to remember that one type can easily change into another.

The **casual crowd** is the simplest form of collective behavior. It consists of a number of people who gather to watch some event such as a movie star signing autographs, a street performer, or an automobile accident. Casual crowds are little more than aggregates (see Chapter 4), with few emergent norms and little if any structure or leadership (Wright, 1978).

Conventional crowds grow out of relatively structured gatherings such as parades, sports events, and funerals. These activities attract audiences that

Neil Smelser's value-added theory points out that the actions of social control agents have a major effect on whether a riot is quickly extinguished or continues for days.

usually act in line with well-established, institutionalized norms. Occasionally, however, spectators display a certain amount of emotional and nonstandard behavior, under which circumstances they may be seen as engaging in borderline collective behavior.

Most people find the experience of being caught up in a highly emotional crowd simultaneously frightening and exhilarating. On occasion, we deliberately seek out collective behavior experiences because they are an enjoyable way to release our emotions (Rose, 1982). These gatherings may be called **expressive crowds.** Sometimes—as with the crowds of students who gather annually during spring break at resorts like South Padre Island, Texas, or the revelers at Mardi Gras in New Orleans—the dominant emotion is joy. In other cases, the most apparent emotion is grief, as in the outpourings of sorrow that erupted in the crowds that gathered after the death of Princess Diana. In either case, an expressive crowd directs its attention inward, focusing primarily on the feelings of its participants.

When the dominant emotion in a crowd is anger, and its attention is focused outward, we speak of an **acting crowd.** A **mob** is a highly emotional acting crowd that pursues a specific target, attacks it, and then fades away. Mobs frequently arise in revolutionary situations (Tilly, 1992). Think of the anti-tax mobs in Boston during the American Revolution or the previously mentioned anti-British demonstration in Dublin.

Lynch mobs occupy a singular place in U.S. history (Tolnay & Beck, 1998). They are identified with vigilante justice on the frontier and, in particular, with white attacks on African Americans. Between 1880 and 1930, about 5,000 African American men were hung by lynch mobs in the South, in many cases under suspicion—often unfounded—of having expressed sexual interest in white women (Franklin, 1967; Raper, 1970). In the West, Mexican and Asian men were the most likely victims of lynch mobs (Mirande, 1987).

Unlike a mob, a **riot** is an acting crowd that directs its hostility toward a wide and shifting range of targets, moving from one to the next in a relatively unpredictable manner. Also unlike mobs, riots may continue for days, with the participants dispersing and regrouping in response to the actions of the police and national guard (McPhail, 1994). The Los Angeles riots lasted six days.

When people think of riots, they are likely to think first of the United States's long history of race riots. In the 20th century, major racially motivated

The thousands of people who celebrate Mardi Gras each February in the streets of New Orleans make up what Herbert Blumer calls an expressive crowd. Most of them participate simply to enjoy the emotional experience of being part of a large crowd of exuberant revelers.

riots took place in Chicago in 1919, in the Watts district of Los Angeles in 1965, in dozens of cities—most notably Detroit and Newark—in the later 1960s, in Miami in 1980, and in Los Angeles again in 1992. Before the 1960s, U.S. race riots usually took the form of whites attacking black neighborhoods. Recent incidents have been more likely to involve African Americans and other minority groups destroying property, looting, and fighting with the police in their own communities (Spilerman, 1976; Porter & Dunn, 1984; Bergesen & Herman, 1998).

Many people assume that rioters come from the dregs of society, the "criminal class"—a view sometimes called the "riff-raff theory." However, research shows that a surprisingly broad cross section of the community typically participates in large-scale race riots (National Advisory Commission on Civil Disorders, 1968; McPhail, 1991).

Most people are quick to condemn rioters, but some individuals in riot-prone communities take a different stance. They point out that civil disturbances are sometimes the only way to direct the attention of the larger society to the plight of poor minorities. Symbolic interactionists note in particular that what outsiders call "riots" and regard as nothing more than criminal behavior are often defined as "insurrections" or even "rebellions" by those who participate in them (Hackworth, 1992; Jacobs, 1996).

By no means are all riots about race. For example, in 1886 the Chicago police attacked a large crowd of labor sympathizers in what came to be called the Haymarket riot, killing 11 people. Police riots also took place in 1963 in Birmingham, Alabama, when the authorities brutally victimized civil rights demonstrators, and in Chicago in 1968 during the national Democratic Party convention.

Riots are also common in prisons, occurring most recently in 1971 at Attica in New York and in 1980 at the New Mexico State Penitentiary (New York State Special Commission on Attica, 1972; Useem, 1985). Finally, some serious riots occur at sporting events (Roadburg, 1980; Burns, 1998), perhaps most notably at British soccer matches. In the United States, sports riots have frequently occurred after local teams have won professional championships. Examples include outbreaks in Detroit in 1990; in Chicago in 1992; in Montreal, Dallas, and Chicago in 1993; in Denver in 1998 and 1999; and in Los Angeles in 2000 (Locher, 2002:94). Sports riots generally reflect a complex mixture of anger and joy.

A fifth type, the **protest crowd,** has been added to the four originally identified by Blumer (McPhail & Wohlstein, 1983). Protest crowds are deliberately assembled by the leaders of social movements to demonstrate their public support. Examples of protest crowds include the 1963 civil rights rally in Washington, D.C., where over 250,000 people heard Martin Luther King give his immortal "I have a dream" speech; the mammoth demonstrations against the Vietnam War of the late 1960s; the 1995 Million Man March in Washington; the 1999 WTO protests in Seattle, which were discussed at the beginning of this chapter; and the widespread demonstrations early in 2003 opposing military intervention in Iraq.

Panics A **panic** is a type of localized collective behavior in which a large number of people respond to a real or imaginary threat with a desperate, uncoordinated, seemingly irrational flight to secure safety—often placing themselves in more danger than they would have otherwise faced. The classic panic results from someone yelling "fire" in a crowded building; in

INTERNET CONNECTIONS

This chapter opens with a brief discussion of the Los Angeles riots of 1992, which involved the beating of a young African American man named Rodney King. As pointed out in the text, the riots were set off by the failure of an all-white jury in suburban Simi Valley to convict any of the officers involved. Since the Rodney King incident, a great deal of controversy has ensued regarding the conduct of these police officers and whether their actions were in any way justified, and, if not, what triggered the brutality. On the Internet, go to

http://blackhistorypages.com/

There, you will click on **riots** then click **rate it** under each description of different riots. What were the incidents that sparked the riot? What theory in the text best explains why riots occur?

a mad rush to find an exit, smaller and weaker people are trampled underfoot. This kind of panic is quite rare, but often very deadly. Panics occurred in 1903 at the Iroquois Theater in Chicago (602 dead); in 1942 at the Coconut Grove nightclub in Boston (491 dead); in 1980 at the Beverly Hills Supper Club in Southgate, Kentucky (164 dead); and in Mecca, a religious site in Saudi Arabia, in 1990 (1,426 dead).

Panics can occur only under rather special circumstances. Escape must be possible, but not certain; there must be a sense that only some people will be able to get out. If there is no chance to escape—and people know this—there will usually be no panic (Smelser, 1963). In addition, the lines of communication from the front of the crowd—near the exit—to the rear must break down (Brown & Goldin, 1973). Even under these circumstances, panic may not occur (Schultz, 1964). Thus, for example, until very close to the end, many passengers and crew members of the *Titanic* continued to help load people into lifeboats, obeying the "women and children first" norm.

While panics appear mindless, sociologists emphasize that given the amount of information available, rushing toward an exit may well appear to be the most rational course of action at the time (Quarantelli, 1957).

Besides the classic model, there are several other types of panic, but all are variations on the same basic theme (Thompson, 1998). Sometimes people are not trying to escape, but rather to gain entry. This was the case at a 1979 concert by the rock group The Who at Cincinnati's Riverfront Stadium, when 11

people died as the crowd pushed forward in a frantic crush for the best nonreserved seats; at a soccer match in 1989 in Sheffield, England, when 95 people were killed; and at a basketball game in 1991 at the City College of New York when 9 died (see Lewis & Kelsey, 1994).

DISPERSED COLLECTIVITIES In a dispersed collectivity, numerous individuals or small groups who are not in each other's direct physical presence react in an emotional and relatively unconventional way to a common stimulus (Lofland, 1981). In most cases, the media are centrally involved in this process (Goode, 1992). There are five major types of dispersed collective behavior: rumors; mass hysteria; disaster behavior; fashions, fads, and crazes; and public opinion.

Rumors A **rumor** is unverified information passed informally from person to person (Rosnow & Fine, 1976). Rumors arise in ambiguous situations when people desperately want accurate information but none is available (Shibutani, 1966; Berk, 1974; Koenig, 1985). People are particularly likely to believe rumors if they are very anxious and if the bearer is regarded as generally credible. Rumors are hard to stop; people often continue to believe them even after more accurate information has become available (Tannen, 1990).

Sociologists analyze rumors somewhat more positively than most people do. Rather than emphasizing their inaccuracies, they view them as a kind of collective effort to solve problems and interpret reality in order to reduce anxiety (Rosnow, 1991). They frequently help people adapt to social change (Rosnow & Fine, 1976; Kapferer, 1992).

Only occasionally are rumors deliberately manipulative. However, distortions routinely arise as they are passed along. They generally become shorter, and one central theme emerges as the heart of the rumor; social psychologists call these processes *leveling* and *sharpening*. They are also modified or *assimilated* in line with the interests of those who are conveying them (Allport & Postman, 1947).

Rumor is not only a type of collective behavior in itself, it also plays an important role in the genesis and development of mobs, riots, panics, fads, and, as we saw in the account of the post-September 11 rumors concerning gasoline prices, in disaster behavior. Furthermore, modern means of communication, especially the Internet, have substantially increased the speed whereby a rumor may spread.

There are two special types of rumors: gossip and urban legends. **Gossip** consists of rumors about other peoples' personal affairs (Cooley, 1962). It is more likely than other types of rumor to be passed on to bolster the teller's status (Koenig, 1985). Gossip may concern one's friends or the rich and (in)famous.

GLOBAL CONNECTIONS

An Egyptian Urban Legend

The rumor first appeared on the Internet early in 2000. From there it was spread by word of mouth and by means of leaflets distributed in markets, schools, and mosques in the poorer sections of Cairo, Alexandria, and Mansoura. It claimed that if you held a bottle of Coca-Cola up to a mirror, the reversed logo read "La Muhammad La Makka" in Arabic, which translates to "No Mohammad, No Mecca." In addition, Pepsi Cola Egypt's name in English was said to be identical to the acronym for the Jewish slogan, "Pay Every Penny to Save Israel."

The absurdity of the rumors seemed obvious; the Coke logo was designed in 1886 in Atlanta, Georgia, by a man named Frank Robinson who was most certainly not trying to slur Islam. Similarly, there is no evidence whatsoever that Pepsi Cola is a Zionist front group. In May 2000 the issue was taken to Grand Mufti Sheik Nasr Farid Wasel, Egypt's most prominent religious leader, who ruled

that "the trademark does not injure Islam or Muslims directly or indirectly." He also reminded his followers that people who spread false claims would suffer 70 autumns in Hell. Islamic legal scholars at the Ifta'a Institute concurred with Wasel's judgment, yet reports suggested that Coke's sales had dropped 10 to 15 percent. In an effort to counter the rumor, the price of Coke was reduced, and all secular street ads for the product were replaced by posters emblazoned with religious sayings. There is No God But Allah, Mohammad is His Prophet, Drink Coke.

The incident reminded some observers of a similar controversy in the Islamic world 3 years earlier when Nike was forced to recall 38,000 pairs of shoes because Islamist activists had charged that the company's logo was blasphemously close to the Arabic word for Allah.

Like all urban legends, these rumors are best understood as moral lessons. As globalization has proceeded, millions of Muslims have come to fear, in many cases quite correctly, that various aspects

of Western civilization are being forced on them. Recent confrontations between the United States and Iran, Afghanistan, and Iraq have intensified these concerns. Under these circumstances, Coca-Cola became a convenient way of symbolizing the conflict. The underlying message of the rumor is to steer clear of all things Western lest the Islamic world become corrupted.

1. Do you think that the makers of Coke and Pepsi will be able to convince most Muslims that these rumors are false? Explain your position.

2. For some years, conservative Christians have charged that Proctor & Gamble's crescent moon logo symbolized the corporation's support for Satanism. What are the similarities and differences between this urban legend and the one discussed here?

Sources: Ghalwash, 2000; Abdel-Hamid, 2000; Mursi, 2000.

Urban legends are rumors that recount ironic and usually grisly events that supposedly happened to "a friend of a friend" (Brunvand, 1980). For example, there is the tale about a drug-addicted babysitter who stuffed a baby instead of a turkey and cooked it in the microwave. In late 1978, an urban legend claiming that McDonald's was using ground-up worms rather than beef in its hamburgers swept the nation (Rice, 1981; Koenig, 1985). In the urban legend called "Kentucky fried rat," a customer is served a rat that accidentally fell into the fryer at a fast food restaurant.

Most urban legends are modern cautionary tales that play off anxieties about the rapid pace of change in modern society. The basic moral is always the same: The world is a dangerous place and the old ways are the best. If women just stayed home and prepared family dinners, nobody would have to risk eating out at a restaurant or entrusting their children to incompetent sitters.

Sometimes the media pick up urban legends and disseminate them. Examples include the false claims that large numbers of children are abducted by Satanists and sacrificed in rituals (Richardson et al., 1991), and that deranged people are putting razor blades in the apples they pass out at Halloween. When rumors like these are reported in the media, they can spark episodes of mass hysteria.

Mass Hysteria **Mass hysteria** is similar to panic in that it is an intense, fearful, and seemingly irrational reaction to a perceived but often misunderstood or imaginary threat. However, it is longer lasting than panic and takes place in at least partially dispersed collectivities. One of the best-known cases of mass hysteria was the terror felt by many thousands of people across the country in response to Orson Welles's Mercury Theater radio broadcast of *The War of the Worlds* on Halloween eve, 1938 (Cantril,

1940). Two other examples of this relatively rare type of collective behavior follow:

- In 1954 in Seattle, hundreds of motorists became concerned over tiny pits that seemed to be appearing on the windshields of their cars. No empirical cause was ever identified; some people attributed the damage to atomic bomb tests. In reality, people were merely noticing the minor damage that occurs to all cars from small airborne particles of gravel. They had suddenly started looking *at* their windshields, not *through* them (Medalia & Larson, 1958).

- In November 1998, large numbers of students and teachers at Warren County High School in McMinnville, Tennessee, started experiencing the symptoms of serious illness: headache, dizziness, nausea, and difficulty breathing. One hundred seventy were admitted to the emergency room. The school was closed down for two weeks while the air and water underwent rigorous testing. No physical cause of the illness was ever found. (Athans, 2000).

What is going on here? Sometimes people who are under intense strain that they can neither control nor reduce find a collective outlet for their tensions in an outbreak of mass hysteria. In the Seattle incident, the principal source of strain was fear of the Cold War and nuclear weapons; in McMinnville the underlying cause was less clear. In any event, while the hysteria does not address the real sources of people's fears, it does help to relieve their tension.

Disaster Behavior When hurricanes, earthquakes, tidal waves, or other natural or humanly created disasters strike communities, most everyday institutionalized behavior patterns are no longer effective or even possible. Accordingly, people must improvise, developing new norms in order to cope with the devastation.

When the scope of the disaster is overwhelming, the result may be widespread demoralization and anomie (Erickson, 1976). But contrary to the conventional wisdom, the usual reaction is much more adaptive. New patterns of organization and community leadership emerge rapidly, often so quickly that much of the aid that pours in from the outside is unneeded (Quarantelli, 1978), as was the case in the 2001 terrorist attack against the World Trade Center.

Fashion, Fads, and Crazes **Fashion** refers to periodic changes in the popularity of styles of hair, clothes, automobiles, architecture, music, sports, language, and even pets. Fashions change relatively gradually and show considerable historical continuity (Lofland, 1985). Fashion is a relatively institutionalized form of collective behavior, heavily influenced by manufacturers in search of profits (Klapp, 1972).

This type of collective behavior is largely limited to modern societies where change is valued, people are sufficiently affluent to follow the latest trends, and the mass media disseminate information about which styles are currently popular (Lofland, 1973). Keeping up with fashion is an important way in which people in modern

This crowd fleeing the collapse of the south tower of the World Trade Center is a good example of the sort of uncoordinated collective behavior that frequently occurs immediately after a major disaster.

After the initial panic has passed, behavior in disaster situations quickly becomes routine and institutionalized. Here rescue workers comb through the debris of the World Trade Center four days after the terrorist attack.

societies can establish a claim to a distinctive—but not too distinctive—personal identity (Simmel, 1971).

The wealthy are usually the trendsetters. Over time, modified versions of fashions embraced by the elite trickle down to the masses—at which point, of course, the upper classes have inevitably moved on to a different style (Davis, 1992). Occasionally, however, styles move up rather than down the class ladder, as when middle- and upper-class youth began wearing proletarian fashions like blue jeans and work shirts in the 1960s. Such a show of pseudo-egalitarianism seems especially appropriate in a society like that of the United States that preaches the value of equality but does not actually allow as much upward mobility as many people would like to believe.

Fads are shorter lived than fashions, adopted briefly and enthusiastically and then quickly abandoned (Johnson, 1985; Locher, 2002). They usually have a playful quality. Fads tend to appeal especially to the young and clearly are used to validate personal status with one's peers (Turner & Killian, 1993). They are

extensively publicized by the media and spread through friendship networks (Aguirre et al., 1988). Fads are usually regarded with amusement or disdain by outsiders. Unlike fashions, they have little historical continuity and have few if any lasting consequences.

There are four distinct types of fads (Lofland, 1993):

- *Object fads*—hula hoops, Rubik cubes, Cabbage Patch dolls, pogs, tamagotchis, Beanie Babies, Air Jordans, Pokemon cards, furbys.
- *Idea fads*—astrology, UFOs, feng shui, the occult.
- *Activity fads*—body piercing, bungee jumping, streaking, tattooing, moshing, disco dancing.
- *Personality fads*—Elvis, Davy Crockett, Princess Di, Michael Jordan, Britney Spears.

A **craze** is a relatively long-lasting fad with significant economic or cultural implications (Lofland, 1981). The classic example is "tulipmania," an extreme passion for tulips that swept over Holland in 1634, appreciably distorting the Dutch economic structure. More recent examples include Beatlemania, *Star Trek*, video games, downloading from Napster, and the exercise and fitness craze.

Adolescents are often attracted to clothing and hairstyle fads. They provide a convenient way of proclaiming a distinct identity that a person shares with a few friends but that differentiates that person sharply from everyone else. In the early 1980s, punk styles were popular; today, body piercing plays a similar role.

Publics The **public** is the least coordinated type of dispersed collective behavior. A public is a large number of people, not necessarily in direct contact with each other, who are interested in a particular controversial issue (Lang & Lang, 1961; Turner & Killian, 1993). Thus, every major area of popular concern—welfare, abortion, national defense, affirmative action, education—creates a separate and distinct public.

In everyday usage, the phrase *public opinion* usually refers to a sort of "snapshot" based on survey research of the opinions of a large number of people at a given point in time. In contrast, collective behavior researchers conceptualize a public as an enduring collectivity of people who maintain interest in a particular issue over an extended period of time.

When a public becomes organized enough to actively convey its point of view to decision makers, then it has become either an interest group or a social movement (Greenberg & Page, 1996).

SOCIAL MOVEMENTS

Social movements are everywhere in modern societies. Among the most visible today in the United States are environmentalism, the pro-choice and pro-life movements, feminism, the movement for the rights of the disabled, movements for and against tougher gun control, the white supremacist movement, the animal rights movement, the gay liberation movement, and the numerous movements focused on the identity and rights of racial and ethnic minority groups.

A **social movement** is a relatively large and organized group of people working for or opposing social change and using at least some unconventional or uninstitutionalized methods (Wilson, 1973; Marx & McAdam, 1994). The wealthy and powerful can generally use their positions and influential personal networks to bring about the changes they favor. But the vast majority of the population, lacking access to established channels of power, find social movements to be the most practical way to promote change (Piven & Cloward, 1977; Adams, 1991; Tarrow, 1994).

Until about 30 years ago, social movements were almost always analyzed as a type of collective behavior, perhaps because the fervor of some participants impressed many early sociologists as threatening and somewhat irrational. There are, however, some major differences between collective behavior and social movements.

Compared to the elementary forms of collective behavior, social movements are longer lasting, better organized, more goal oriented, and have far more significant effects on the society in which they arise. These characteristics have led modern scholars to question whether social movements should be lumped together in the same conceptual category as riots, rumor, and fads (McAdam et al., 1988; Locher, 2002).

Most social movements include a number of distinct formal organizations, referred to as *social movement organizations (SMOs)*—each of which works in its own way in support of the basic goals of the entire movement (Goode, 1992). Thus, for example, SMOs within the general environmental movement include the Audubon Society, the Sierra Club, Earth First!, and Greenpeace. Typically, SMOs specialize; some concentrate on direct political action while others try to influence legislation; each may appeal to a different element of the larger population (Maheu, 1995). Though SMOs sometimes compete with one another, they usually complement one another's activities (Cable & Cable, 1995).

The overall level of social movement activity in a society fluctuates. Sometimes there are many movements competing for attention while at other times relatively few are active (Zald, 1992; Tilly, 1993). These cycles have been referred to as *waves of protest* (Tarrow, 1994). The 1930s and the period between 1960 and 1975 were both characterized by a dramatic profusion of social movement activity. As anyone who lived through these years can testify, there was an almost palpable sense of change in the air (Zald & McCarthy, 1987; Koopmans, 1993).

Waves of protest sometimes arise from major social dislocations caused by factors such as wars, economic recessions, technological innovations, or unusual demographic events such as the baby boom. The activism of the 1960s and early 1970s was also aided by the affluence of the era, which allowed young social movement supporters to work for change rather than worry about making a living.

The various movements that arise during an era of protest also tend to reinforce one another. Supporters of the civil rights, feminist, student, antiwar, and environmental movements learned from one another's mistakes and were buoyed by one another's successes, a phenomenon called *social movement spillover* (Meyer & Whittier, 1994).

Sociologists study the development of social movements at three levels. They ask why individual people join movements—the microlevel of analysis; how organizational factors influence movement development—the intermediate level; and how larger social and political factors affect movement growth—the macrolevel.

Why Do People Join Social Movements?

Turner and Killian (1987) suggest that there are five general kinds of people who participate in social movements:

- *The ego-involved*—individuals who are deeply and personally committed to the goals of the movement.
- *The concerned*—those who support the goals of the movement but do not make it the center of their lives.
- *The insecure*—participants who enjoy being involved with the movement principally because it provides them with friends, entertainment, and a sense of purpose.
- *Spectators*—people who do not particularly support the movement but watch its demonstrations because they are curious about them.
- *Exploiters*—individuals who are using the movement's activities for their own private purposes, such as vendors hawking cold drinks at a mass meeting.

Theoretical explanations for movement participation focus primarily on the ego-involved, the concerned, and the insecure. Like contagion theory, early microlevel explanations of social movement membership saw participants as less than fully rational. However, more modern approaches disagree, generally interpreting joining a movement as the most effective way that relatively powerless people can promote collective goals. In this section, we review four major theories of movement participation, beginning with the oldest.

MASS-SOCIETY THEORY Strongly influenced by their abhorrence of the atrocities committed in Europe by supporters of the Nazi movement, theorists in the mass-society school largely discounted the reasons that supporters themselves gave for joining movements—which tend to emphasize the importance of the changes they are trying to bring about. Instead, they focused on members' personal inadequacies (Hoffer, 1951; Kornhauser, 1959; Feuer,

INTERNET CONNECTIONS

Amnesty International is an organization devoted to human rights causes around the globe. To explore what the organization is about and how they go about bringing political change go to:

http://www.amnesty.org/

After browsing the Website answer the following questions. Do you agree with the political causes of Amnesty International? What are some reasons why you agree or disagree with the goals of Amnesty International?

1969). Participants were depicted as frustrated, socially isolated individuals in modern mass societies who felt insignificant and powerless. They joined movements in order to lose themselves in ill-considered ventures to remake the world.

Subsequent research has seriously challenged the basic assumptions of the mass-society approach. Most activists—in the civil rights movement (Morris, 1984; McAdam, 1988), in other 1960s movements, or even Nazis (Lipset, 1963; Oberschall, 1973)—are not isolates; they are normally well integrated into functioning social networks (McAdam & Paulsen, 1994).

RELATIVE DEPRIVATION THEORY Theorists next focused on the discontent that activists themselves claimed to be their primary reason for joining social movements. Attention was directed to the notion of **relative deprivation,** a conscious feeling of a negative discrepancy between legitimate expectations and perceived actualities (Morrison, 1971; Wilson, 1973). Relative deprivation theory argues that people compare their situation with the situations of members of relevant reference groups and conclude that change is necessary (Gurr, 1970).

This theory helps explain the somewhat surprising fact that movements tend to arise not when conditions are at their worst but rather when things seem to be getting better. During times of absolute deprivation, most people simply concentrate on survival; when life starts improving and expectations rise, they are more likely to develop a sense of relative deprivation and join social movements. This school of thought is also compatible with research that shows most movement supporters come from the middle ranks of society, not from the most downtrodden groups (McAdam, 1988; Fendrich & Lovoy, 1988).

Denton Morrison (1971) suggests that there are two basic types of relative deprivation—aspirational and decremental (see Figure 23.2). In *aspirational relative deprivation*, something happens to raise people's hopes, but then they do not see any real improvement in their lives. This type of relative deprivation is commonly associated with the birth of left-wing or liberal movements; for example, the hopes raised within the African American community in 1954 by the *Brown vs. Board of Education* school desegregation ruling were frustrated by white Southern resistance in the following years, producing aspirational relative deprivation and eventually leading to the civil rights movement of the 1960s.

On the other hand, *decremental relative deprivation* occurs when a group of people would be content with a continuation of the status quo, but believe that in fact conditions are worsening. Movements arising out of this type of relative deprivation tend to be right-wing or conservative; for example, the modern right to life movement arose when the 1974 *Roe vs. Wade*

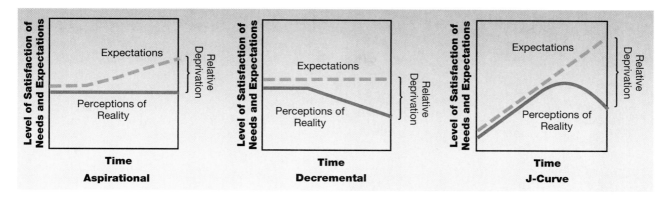

FIGURE 23.2 Three Types of Relative Deprivation

ruling made it clear that U.S. society was becoming more supportive of abortion rights.

Political scientist James Davies (1962) has proposed a third type, which he calls *J-curve relative deprivation* (see Figure 23.2). For quite some time, social conditions appear to be improving in line with people's rising expectations; but then, although their hopes continue to escalate, people see their lives suddenly becoming worse. Davies suggests that J-curve relative deprivation preceded several major revolutions, including the French Revolution of 1789 and the 1917 Bolshevik Revolution in Russia.

Relative deprivation theory is an advance over mass-society theory in that it takes activists' discontent seriously. However, critics point out that there is always a certain amount of relative deprivation present in society, yet movements do not always arise. Thus, deprivation alone cannot fully explain movement growth (Wilson & Orum, 1976; Gurney & Tierney, 1982; Johnson & Klandermans, 1995).

Furthermore, the concept of relative deprivation has been attacked as circular. Theorists argue that movements arise because of relative deprivation, but all too often the only way they can demonstrate the existence of that deprivation is by pointing to the emergence of social movements (Jenkins & Perrow, 1977).

RECRUITMENT THROUGH NETWORKS Beginning in the 1980s, some social movement theorists began to emphasize the importance of preexisting networks in the recruitment of members (Marwell et al., 1988; Cable, 1992). This "micro-mobilization" perspective effectively turns mass society theory on its head by stressing that activists maintain extensive relationships with like-minded others.

In support of this view, research has repeatedly shown that people often join social movements because their friends or relatives are members (Snow et al., 1980); sometimes entire families have a tradition of activism. Furthermore, the most successful movements are often those whose members maintain

a dense network of interpersonal connections, a network that helps the movement obtain the various resources it needs (Opp & Gern, 1993; Marx & McAdam, 1994). Relative deprivation and ideological commitment are certainly important, but they often arise or at least reach their peak only after members have been recruited into a movement by their friends and been socialized to accept the movement's worldview (McAdam et al., 1988; Hirsh, 1990).

FRAME ALIGNMENT The newest theoretical perspective to address the issue of why people join movements takes a symbolic interactionist approach. The frame-alignment approach emphasizes the process by which movements shape or "frame" the definition of the situation in order to attempt to recruit new members. (Snow et al., 1986; Snow & Benford, 1988). The "collective action frame" that a movement constructs has three elements: an "injustice component" designed essentially to promote relative deprivation; an "agency component," meant to convince potential recruits that the movement really can make a difference; and an "identity component," which enhances commitment by building a strong collective identity with the movement and its goals (Gamson, 1992).

The collective-action frame must be reasonably congruent with the interests, understandings, and values held by the target population. It must extend the perspectives of prospective members by increasing their outrage and building their commitment to the movement (W. Gamson, 1991; Jasper & Poulsen, 1995). The process of frame alignment is essentially similar to the establishment of what Marx called class consciousness (see Chapter 10).

Resource-Mobilization Theory

Resource-mobilization theory has been the dominant school of thought regarding social-movement development for most of the past three decades (Klandermans, 1994). Resource-mobilization theorists are not

Contemporary social movement activists are well aware that access to the mass media is a critical organizational resource. Many demonstrations are held primarily so that they will be reported on the evening news.

so much concerned with why individuals join movements as they are with analyzing SMOs as formal organizations (see Chapter 21) and isolating the structural factors that explain which movements succeed and which fail (Oberschall, 1973; McCarthy & Zald, 1977; Jenkins, 1983; Oberschall, 1993).

This school argues that movement outcomes are principally determined not by ideas, but by how effectively SMOs acquire and use key resources (Walsh, 1981; Gamson, 1990). Far from seeing movements as irrational, resource-mobilization theorists interpret them as frequently embodying high levels of what Weber termed *bureaucratic rationality* (see Chapter 21) (Jenkins & Perrow, 1977; Tilly, 1978; Opp, 1989).

Some SMO resources are quite concrete: money, fax machines, telephones, computers. Others are more abstract but no less important; chief among these is effective leadership. In the earliest phases of social-movement development, leadership is often based on charisma. But once a coherent organizational structure emerges, administrators generally become more important than agitators or prophets (Wilson, 1973). During periods of intense movement activity, leaders may switch from one movement to another—for example, from the civil rights movement to the antiwar and feminist causes—bringing their organizational skills with them.

Supporters are another crucial movement resource (Freeman, 1979). Recruited mostly from the personal networks of current members, followers not only serve as demonstrators but also provide crucial financial and other material assistance.

Sometimes SMO supporters are drawn from population elements that hope to benefit directly from the success of the movement. Others are "conscience constituents," such as whites who supported the civil rights struggle or men who endorse feminism (McCarthy & Zald, 1973). Outsiders often provide the largest share of movement financing (Oberschall, 1973; McCarthy & Zald, 1977).

Access to the mass media is a particularly crucial organizational resource (Molotch, 1979; Zald, 1992). In fact, social movements and the media have a symbiotic relationship: Movement activities are often compelling news items, and media coverage is an important means of recruiting and consciousness-raising for activist groups (Gamson & Wolfsfeld, 1993).

However, the relationship between movements and the mass media is always edgy. By definition, movements promote a definition of reality that is somewhat different from the one that most people accept, whereas the media normally attempt to position themselves to attract the largest possible audience. As a result, activists constantly criticize the media for sensationalized coverage and for missing what they consider the real issues (Gitlin, 1980).

The principal criticism of resource-mobilization theory is that, not unlike the mass-society approach, the approach tends to ignore the grievances that spur relative deprivation and the ideas that the movement promotes (Klandermans, 1984; Zygmunt, 1986; Buechler, 1993; Scott, 1995) except to the extent that they help recruit new members (Benford, 1993).

The Political-Process Approach

The political-process approach is a relatively recent, historically based type of social-movement theory. It focuses on the changing relationship over time between movements and the macrolevel political and economic systems of the societies in which they emerge (Tilly, 1978; McAdam, 1982; Quadagno, 1992; Tarrow, 1994). This highly sophisticated school of thought examines systemic factors that either encourage or discourage movement activism and success. It also assesses the impact of movements on the larger society. Two of the principal findings of this school are that movements emerge more readily in democratic societies and that weak governments are especially vulnerable to pressure from activists (Jenkins & Perrow, 1977).

Except for the largely discredited mass-society approach, each of the micro, organizational, and macro theories helps us understand the dynamics of movement development. None is adequate by itself, but taken as a whole this body of sociological theorizing answers most of the important questions about social movements (Kowalewski & Porter, 1992; Marx & McAdam, 1994).

SOCIAL MOVEMENT TYPES AND CAREERS

Among the many issues that interest sociologists of social movements, two have attracted particular attention. First, can we reduce the bewildering variety of social movements into a small number of distinct types? And, second, is there a sequence of stages (often called a career) through which most movements pass?

Varieties of Social Movements

Social movements may be classified on the basis of several different criteria:

- Some aim for relatively modest changes, while others advocate broad, sweeping transformations (Turner & Killian, 1993).

INTERNET CONNECTIONS

There have been a number of reform movements in the United States. One is the women's suffrage movement. To find more information about the movement go to:

http://www.rochester.edu/SBA/history.html

After you have looked at the information on the site write a description of the various groups and issues involved in the movement. How has it changed over time?

- Some advocate changes that are progressive or generally in line with the direction in which society is moving, while others work to reverse current trends (Turner & Killian, 1993; Garner, 1996).
- Some seek immediate change, while others are content to work for more gradual improvement (Blumer, 1974).
- Some target individuals for change, while others focus on larger systems or whole societies (Aberle, 1966).

The first two issues are especially important. We use them as the basis for our discussion of three very broad types of social movements: reformist, revolutionary, and reactionary.

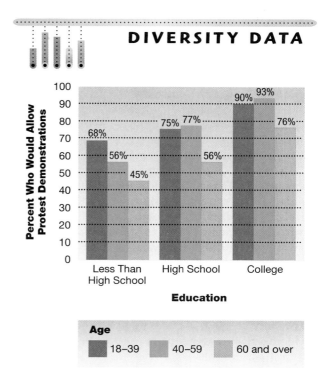

DIVERSITY DATA

FIGURE 23.3   How Do Age and Education Affect Approval of Anti-Government Demonstrations? Regardless of age, people with higher levels of education are more likely to accept the legitimacy of public protest. However, individuals between 40 and 59 with at least a high school education are actually more supportive of protest than those in their twenties and thirties. This is the generation that was in school during the great wave of movement activism of the 1960s and 1970s. How might the attitudes of this age group affect social movements today?

Source: NORC. General Social Surveys, 1972–2000. Chicago: National Opinion Research Center, 2000. Reprinted by permission of NORC, Chicago, IL.

REFORMIST MOVEMENTS Reformist movements aim for relatively small-scale or limited progressive change. They do not try to substantially alter society's basic political, economic, or stratification systems, or to reverse the general direction in which society is currently moving. Examples include the civil rights movement, the 19th century movement for female suffrage, most environmental groups, the movement protesting the war in Vietnam, and the pro-choice movement.

In other words, reformist movements work within the system. While they may use moderately unconventional tactics like sit-ins and mass demonstrations, they almost always avoid violence. They at least grudgingly accept the current political and legal institutions and accordingly devote most of their energies to trying to change laws and governmental policies (Greenberg, 1994). Reformist movements are common in democratic societies where citizens have the right to work peacefully for change.

Those who oppose the goals of reformist movements usually try to depict them as more extreme than they really are. For example, most SMOs in the contemporary gay rights movement advocate relatively modest reforms, such as including sexual preference in antidiscrimination statutes and increasing funding for AIDS research. But opponents of gay rights commonly paint these groups in sinister terms, arguing that the gay movement is a serious threat to "family values" and "Christian morality." Sometimes opponents of a movement are aided in their efforts by the existence of small, highly visible extremist groups within broadly reformist movements. For example, anti-environmentalists frequently point to actions of small radical groups, such as pouring drums of toxic waste over the desks of the executives of polluting corporations, as evidence that the whole movement is extreme.

REVOLUTIONARY MOVEMENTS Some social movements seek broad and sweeping progressive changes, including major alterations in society's economic and political institutions and system of stratification (Hopper, 1950). These movements typically arise when efforts to bring about reform have failed or proven inadequate, or in authoritarian societies where virtually any attempt to implement social change is considered subversive by the government. By definition, these movements work outside of the established institutional structure.

Such groups are commonly called **revolutionary movements,** although this term is somewhat deceptive. Sometimes efforts to topple one group of political leaders and replace them with other individuals, but not alter the basic structure of society, are termed *revolutions.* But such events are not really revolutions in the sense we are using this word. Such uprisings—for example, the American revolution of 1776—may be termed *political revolutions,* reserving the term *social revolution* for more sweeping changes such as occurred in the French Revolution of 1789, the Iranian Revolution of 1979, and the Russian Revolutions of 1917 and 1989 (Skocpol, 1979). Other examples of revolutionary movements include the Black Panther Party of the late 1960s and the international communist movement.

Revolutionary movements frequently embrace extreme and violent tactics; terrorism (discussed at greater length in Chapter 18) has been employed, often quite effectively, by groups such as the Irish Republican Army, Peru's Shining Path, and Osama bin Laden's Al Qaeda. On the other hand, dramatic social change was brought about by revolutionary movements in Russia and South Africa with a minimum of bloodshed during the last two decades.

Sometimes people seek fundamental change not by challenging the existing system directly, but by withdrawing from it and creating their own alternate societies. Such efforts are called *utopian movements* (Alexander & Gill, 1984; Berger, 1988). Utopians usually form communes such as the 19th century Oneida Colony or the Shaker settlements. Others retain some connections with the larger society but also create their own institutions. Examples include the free schools and people's medical clinics that counterculture members founded in the 1970s (Rothschild-Whitt, 1979) and that still exist in some parts of the country (Garner, 1996). Utopian movements that feature an ideology that is religious rather than secular have a much stronger record of survival. Sacred belief systems seem to be more effective in sustaining commitment in the face of a hostile or at least indifferent society (Kanter, 1973).

REACTIONARY MOVEMENTS Some social movements seek to reverse the general direction of social change and return to an earlier and, in their view, better time. Though their conception of the way things used to be is often distorted or wholly mythic, it nevertheless serves to rally the support of people who are uncomfortable with the present and fear the future. These groups, whether seeking large-scale or modest change, are called **reactionary movements.** Examples include the Ku Klux Klan, the militia movement, the Christian Right, the anti-feminist Eagle Forum, and the pro-life movement.

Reactionary movements often arise when the actual or impending success of a progressive movement alarms people with a vested interest in the status quo. Such groups are termed **countermovements** (Mottl, 1980; Lo, 1982; Lyman, 1995). For example, the early successes of the civil rights movement revived the Klan and led to the creation of White Citizens' Councils all across the Deep South (Dobratz & Shanks-Meile, 1997).

Neo-Nazis are among the most extreme of all contemporary reactionary movements. This protest march by the Aryan Nation in Coeur D'Aline, Idaho, attracted a small number of supporters and a large crowd of counterdemonstrators.

DIVERSITY DATA

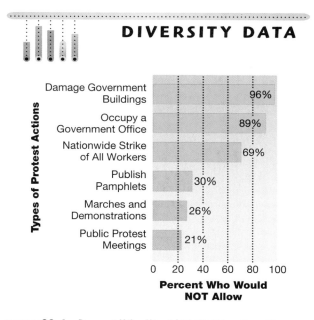

FIGURE 23.4 **Percent Who Would NOT Allow Specific Protest Actions Against Government** Large majorities of Americans reject violent or disruptive protest tactics. However, between one-fifth and one-third of the general public also would not allow dissenters to express their anti-government feelings in writing or at public meetings despite the fact that such activities are clearly protected by the First Amendment. What are the potential consequences of the fact that so many people are prepared to deny others their right to freedom of speech?

Source: NORC. General Social Surveys, 1972–2000. Chicago: National Opinion Research Center, 2000. Reprinted by permission of NORC, Chicago, IL.

Many sociologists expect to see reactionary movements gain strength around the world as the ongoing globalization of the economy forces more and more traditional people into increasingly direct contact with modern societies. Consider the growing popularity of Islamist "fundamentalist" movements throughout much of the Muslim world. This may be only the first of many waves of opposition to the broad social and cultural trends that are currently transforming lives and nations on a global scale.

Social Movement Careers

A number of scholars have proposed models of the developmental stages through which social movements pass (Zald & Ash, 1966; Blumer, 1969a; Mauss, 1975; Spector & Kitsuse, 1977; Tilly, 1978). Although these models somewhat oversimplify reality, they are nevertheless useful in thinking about how movements often change as they age. Each uses somewhat different terminology, but most identify four general career phases: incipience, coalescence, bureaucratization, and decline.

INCIPIENCE In its earliest phase, a social movement is not an organized group but rather a general mood of discontent or relative deprivation among some segments of society. Incipient movements often arise during the societal disruption caused by events such as war, economic crisis, migration, major technological change, or similar upheavals.

During this stage one or more individuals appear who give voice and definition to the widespread but poorly understood sense of unease felt by significant

THEN AND NOW

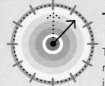

The Pro-Life Movement Under Fire

The anti-abortion or right-to-life movement is a classic example of a countermovement, one that seeks to reverse current patterns of social change. The history of this group also provides some insights into the life cycle of social movements.

The 1960s were an era of social upheaval in the United States. Throughout this period, the number of women (especially married women and mothers) entering the workforce grew steadily. To many Americans, "women's liberation" symbolized everything that had gone wrong in the 1960s. Feminists, they argued, threatened to undermine the traditional religious and family values that had made the United States strong. The Supreme Court decision in *Roe v. Wade* (1974), which held that a woman has the right to decide whether to terminate a pregnancy during the first six months, marked a turning point. Hailed as a victory by supporters of women's rights, the ruling galvanized the opposition.

In the 1970s and the 1980s, abortion became a symbolic marker between Americans who were alarmed by social change, sought to maintain traditional gender roles, and viewed motherhood as a sacred calling, and those who welcomed change, sought gender equality, and viewed motherhood as only one of many roles a woman might (or might not) choose. The right-to-life movement united groups that had traditionally been suspicious of one another—urban Catholics and rural Southern Protestants, as well as white (and some black) working-class Americans. The movement also played a key role in the emergence of the "New Right." To a large degree, a candidate's stand on abortion became a political litmus test. The pro-life movement gained numbers and influence, culminat-

ing in the election of conservative abortion foe Republican Ronald Reagan as president in 1980.

Through the 1970s and 1980s, the anti-abortion movement pursued its goal—the repeal of *Roe v. Wade*—primarily through conventional politics and peaceful protest. Gradually, the Supreme Court, Congress, and state legislatures placed more and more restrictions on abortion, including mandatory waiting periods of several hours or days, the requirement that teenagers obtain parental consent, and a ban on so-called "partial birth" abortions.

In the late 1980s, the pro-life movement became more confrontational and militant. This often occurs when a movement has achieved some, but only partial, success. Out of frustration, some SMOs begin to employ unconventional tactics. Much as the nonviolent civil rights movement gave rise to the militant Black Panthers, the pro-life movement spawned "Operation Rescue." Members of this group began by staging prayer vigils outside women's health clinics but soon escalated to establishing blockades around clinics, using posters portraying aborted near-term fetuses to frighten clinic workers and patients, picketing the homes of physicians who performed abortions, mailing gruesome films to patients, telephoning threats to abortion providers, and the like. These tactics were quite effective. Many doctors stopped performing abortions, and in rural and conservative areas, a woman who is legally entitled to an abortion may have great difficulty obtaining one. But another effect was to mobilize the pro-choice movement to stage counterdemonstrations, arrange clinic escorts, and lobby Congress to pass laws against blockading clinics.

Beginning with the murder of Dr. David Gunn in March 1993, some hard-

core anti-abortion activists turned to violence. There have been murders (several of doctors) and numerous sniper attacks, physical assaults, and stalkings. Dozens of clinics have been bombed, set on fire, or vandalized. Hundreds of phoned and faxed threats have been reported. In some communities, activists have circulated "WANTED" posters with the photographs, names, and addresses of abortionists. Lists of abortion providers are posted on Websites like the "Nuremberg Files"; the name of Dr. Barnett Slepian was crossed off one such list the night he was murdered outside his home by a sniper. Some groups, such as Pro-Life Virginia and the American Coalition of Life Activists, openly promote violence and charge the government with repression of their right to free speech.

The majority of those who oppose abortion are appalled by these violent tactics, with the result that the pro-life movement has become increasingly fragmented. If terrorism is the "weapon of the weak," these violent assaults may suggest that the anti-abortion movement has lost momentum and support. Nevertheless, extremist rhetoric does create an atmosphere of permissiveness in which individuals may take justice into their own hands.

1. How would the various theories of movement development analyze the pro-life crusade? In particular, consider the relative deprivation, frame-alignment, resource-mobilization, and value-added perspectives.

2. In what ways has the violent fringe of the pro-life movement harmed the larger movement? In what ways has it helped?

3. Is there any way in which the two sides of the abortion debate can find common ground?

Sources: Chafe, 1991; Blanchard, 1994; Rubin, 1995; Gegax & Clemetson, 1998.

numbers of people. They are agitators and prophets, initially operating without any substantial organizational base.

In the words of C. Wright Mills (see Chapter 1), these early leaders teach people to reinterpret their "personal troubles" as "public issues." For example, before the birth of the modern feminist movement, Betty Friedan wrote a widely read book called *The Feminine Mystique* (1963) in which she used the phrase "the problem that has no name" to identify the discontent felt in the 1950s by educated women who were expected to happily abandon their career plans in order to be wives and mothers.

COALESCENCE After public consciousness has been raised, the next step is to actually build a movement. The women's rights component of modern feminism was organized largely around preexisting networks of socially and politically active women, many of whom had participated in John Kennedy's

Rachel Carson published Silent Spring *in 1962, almost ten years before the coalescence of the environmental movement. In it she presented the first widely-read account of the problems of pollution and environmental degradation that have now become familiar to virtually everyone.*

1961 Presidential Commission on the Status of Women (Brownmiller, 1999; Rosen, 2000; Treanor, 2002). A formal organization is established, concerns are focused, leaders are selected, and tactics are chosen. Alliances are often built with other like-minded movements. The group begins to pursue its goals actively, in the process attracting attention from the media. While early media coverage is likely to be skeptical and distorted, it does spread public awareness of the new movement, which often attracts supporters and key organizational resources.

BUREAUCRATIZATION If the movement succeeds in attracting followers and appears to be making progress toward achieving its goals, it tends to experience strong pressures to become more highly structured. Its internal division of labor becomes more elaborate, the staff grows, and leaders gradually become administrators. As the movement gains in stature and becomes increasingly respectable, its tactics usually become less confrontational. This causes some of the more extreme and enthusiastic members to criticize it for becoming part of "the establishment." For example, as the National Organization for Women (NOW) began to bureaucratize, some of its early members charged that by designating formal leaders and adopting a bureaucratic structure, it had "sold out" (Staggenborg, 1988; Brownmiller, 1999; Rosen, 2000).

DECLINE Although social movements are much longer lived than the elementary forms of collective behavior, they are ultimately always temporary. Whether they succeed or fail in their efforts to promote or resist change, all eventually end (Miller, 1985; Locher, 2002).

A movement may be considered successful if the major changes it seeks are implemented and/or if its leaders come to be recognized as legitimate spokespersons for their cause (Gamson, 1990; Rochon & Mazmanian, 1993). Under these circumstances, the movement tends to become an interest group—part of the political institution—and by definition no longer a social movement (von Eschen et al., 1976; Piven & Cloward, 1977). Such was the fate of NOW, the NAACP, and the U.S. labor movement.

In some cases, political leaders pursue a policy of *co-optation*, adopting watered-down versions of the changes advocated by a reformist movement and offering movement leaders rewarding positions within the power structure (Meyer, 1993). A few true believers may keep the group alive but, deprived of the issues that originally motivated its members, the co-opted movement becomes impotent.

Other movements experience *goal displacement:* So much attention is devoted to simply keeping the group alive that it largely loses track of the changes it was originally created to advocate (see Chapter 21). This is especially likely to occur when progress has been slow and it has been hard to maintain the participants' enthusiasm (Zald & Ash, 1966; McCarthy & Zald, 1973; Oegema & Klandermans, 1994).

Perhaps the most common single cause of movement decline is *fragmentation* (Frey et al., 1992). Disagreements about goals or strategies can easily split a movement, as can overt or covert power struggles (Ryan, 1989). Fragmentation is especially likely after the loss of a charismatic leader. For example, after the death of Elijah Muhammad, the founder of the Nation of Islam, the group split into two movements, one led by the founder's son, Wallace, and the other by Lewis Farakahn.

Finally, a social movement may decline as a result of *repression* (Opp & Roehl, 1990; Della Porta, 1995). Repression by the authorities is a common fate of revolutionary movements. This was the case with the International Workers of the World, a Marxist labor movement of the 1930s, and the Black Panthers of the late 1960s, many of whose key leaders were killed by the police (Marine, 1969). However, repression is a risky tactic because it can easily create martyrs. It is much safer to *ridicule* a movement into insignificance, a control strategy that is almost impossible to fight effectively. This was the strategy used to discredit and eventually destroy most of the more extreme SMOs in the women's liberation movement.

LIFE CONNECTIONS

Training Social Movement Activists

If you were intent upon constructing a social movement, one of your first concerns would inevitably be with recruiting and training supporters. As resource mobilization theory emphasizes, dedicated members are among the most important resources on which movements depend. Because the struggle to bring about social change is often a long one, it is critical that a core of activists be available to lead the movement and provide continuity as less committed members come and go. For this reason, many movements have gone out of their way to provide some sort of relatively structured training experience for their adherents.

Social movement training programs serve a number of functions. They provide participants with a detailed and coherent exposition of the movement's understanding of the social problem it is attempting to remediate. In theoretical terms, the participants' sense of relative deprivation is heightened, and they are provided with an appropriate conceptual frame. Participants are also taught a variety of specific tactics as well as the broader philosophy (such as nonviolence)

that informs the movement's choice of how to pursue its goals. The trainees also form strong interpersonal bonds with their fellow activists that help them to endure the rejection and abuse that so often accompany movement participation.

Until recently, most social movements provided their own training programs. For example, the Northern student volunteers who participated in the Freedom Summer voter registration and freedom school projects in Mississippi trained in two week-long sessions held in June 1964 on the campus of the Western College for Women in Oxford, Ohio (Belfrage, 1965; McAdam, 1988). These workshops, sponsored by the National Council of Churches, included large morale-building and general orientation meetings, smaller section meetings for activists interested in particular issues, and intensive training for the groups of 5 to 10 people who would actually be working together in Mississippi. The latter workshops included role-playing sessions and lessons in self-defense.

In the decades since the great wave of activism of the 1960s and 1970s, many movements have become more professional, a trend that is discussed in greater depth in the next section of this chapter. One aspect of this professionalization process has been the development of broadly based training programs run by veteran activists and designed to serve the needs of people interested in protesting a variety of different issues.

Perhaps the best-known of the groups providing activist training is the Ruckus Society, founded in 1995 by John Sellers, who was at the time 27-year-old veteran of the environmental group Greenpeace (Crenson, 2000; "Direct Action Figure," 2000; www.ruckus.org). Ruckus is a nonprofit, tax-exempt organization based in Berkeley, California. Its slogan is "Actions speak louder than words." The group has trained many hundreds of activists interested in labor, human rights, and environmental issues in the techniques of nonviolent direct action, especially civil disobedience.

The primary vehicle by which Ruckus trains movement participants is the week long "Action Camp." Held in rural areas around the country, the camps emphasize the history, philosophy, and techniques of nonviolent protest and feature extensive role playing. Specific units of instruction include:

- *Scouting*—Maps and photos, dealing with the authorities, introduction to security, dealing with barriers, evasion.
- *Action Planning and Coordination.*
- *Climbing*—Basic ropework, belaying, rapelling, etc.
- *Electronics*—Radios, scanners, frequency analyzers, computers, and databases.

- *Blockades*—Tree sits, vehicle blockades, water blockades, bridge actions.
- *Media Training*—Crafting leads and soundbites, pitching the story, spin control, and message delivery.
- *Banner Workshop.*
- *Political Theater.* (www.ruckus.org/workshops.html)

Ruckus is distinctive in comparison to earlier training programs in several ways. It is far more sophisticated than the 1960s groups were in its understanding of how to manipulate the media and in its computer savvy. It is oriented toward left-wing activism in general rather than toward any specific issue. And its style is more contemporary; as its founders put it, "There's a different dynamic. It's not the pony-tailed, gray-haired guys who remember the sixties" (Crenson, 2000). "We plot and scheme and conspire to save the planet. We have a blast" ("Direct Action Figure," 2000). Ruckus played a major role in training activists for the Seattle World Trade Organization demonstrations and for street protests at the 2000 Republican and Democratic National Conventions. Its leaders are looking forward to a long and contentious future.

SOCIETY CONNECTIONS

Current Trends in Social Movement Development

Starting in the late 1970s, sociologists began to notice a trend away from social movements that arose spontaneously at the grassroots level and toward the increasing professionalization of movement activity. More recently, a new type of movement has begun to emerge all around the world, less oriented to economics and more concerned with cultural and lifestyle issues.

Professional Social Movements

Most of the major social movements that arose during the great wave of activism of the 1960s and 1970s were amateur efforts, staffed by people whose main qualifications for leadership were speaking ability and ideological fervor. The inexperience of these leaders often severely handicapped the movements' efforts to achieve their goals.

Over time, many of these leaders began to gain expertise in organizational management. Frequently, as a result of social-movement spillover, individuals moved from one group to another, gaining valuable experience. The result was the emergence of what have been called *professional social movements* (McCarthy & Zald, 1973, 1977). Today, groups as diverse as the Sierra Club, NOW, and the NAACP are managed by full-time professionals who are highly skilled in fund raising, obtaining positive publicity from the media, and organizing well-structured and carefully controlled public demonstrations.

In some ways, professionalization is positive. Professional movements present an image of respectability, which helps them solicit funds from foundations, the government, and well-heeled supporters (McCrea & Markle, 1989). Leadership by careerists also provides long-term organizational continuity, which often improves the movement's effectiveness. Movement coalitions can be formed more easily when leaders know one other and share a common understanding of their role (Staggenborg, 1988).

And yet something has been lost when movements are headed by people whose desire to run a well-organized campaign may seem stronger than their passion for the cause. Professional managers, with at least one eye firmly fixed on the financial bottom line, may push a movement away from even moderately radical goals or tactics in order to avoid alienating wealthy potential donors. In professional movements, most members do little more than pay dues, read newsletters, and show up for the occasional rally (Kleidman, 1994). But where is the passion? How can professional movements maintain the "white-hot" commitment that seems so essential? At a minimum, social movements need to nurture a few small, relatively radical SMOs. Not only are such groups a critical source of enthusiasm and new ideas, but they also allow more conventional SMOs to present their goals as reasonable and moderate compared to the programs advocated by their "loony" compatriots.

New Social Movements

Partly in response to the professionalization trend, a new type of grassroots movement has begun to appear, called—logically enough—**new social movements** (Melucci, 1980, 1989; Touraine, 1981; McAdam et al., 1988; Larana et al., 1994; Kriesi et al., 1995; Scott, 1995). Most are concerned with issues such as protecting the environment, opposing nuclear power, changing the social definitions of gays and women, and securing animal rights. These are the chief characteristics of the new social movements:

- They are ideologically inclusive, resisting the impulse to carve out narrow areas of concern. Movements like ecological feminism, the struggle against environmental racism, or women's peace groups stress the interconnections among various seemingly distinct causes (Merchant, 1983; Epstein, 1991; Bullard & Wright, 1992; Mies & Shiva, 1993). Many activists therefore participate in several new social movements at the same time.
- Unlike earlier progressive movements, which frequently accepted the Marxist view that capitalism

was the primary impediment to the changes they were seeking, most new social movements do not consider the overthrow of capitalism to be their primary goal. In fact, these movements are more likely to consider the government irrelevant to their concerns than they are to identify it as either an enemy or a potential ally.

- While most individual new social movement groups are small and localized, they are linked together in global networks. This is especially appropriate because many of the causes in which these movements are interested—above all, that of the environment—clearly transcend national boundaries.
- New social movements are nonbureaucratic and highly participatory. In many cases, they are as much about providing a fulfilling and liberating lifestyle as they are concerned with actually promoting social change (Gamson & Wolfsfeld, 1993). Like the 1970s feminist movement, they deliberately bridge the gap between the personal and the political. Their members join, in large part, to obtain a sense of autonomy and self-determination.

- New social movements are strongly oriented toward emotionality and tend to be suspicious of authority, science, and rationality, orientations that they share with the New Age counterculture (Scott, 1990; Garner, 1996). They often deliberately seek confrontation, sometimes simply for the sake of confrontation.
- Like many other recent social movements, the new social movements attract mostly middle-class members—usually well-educated professionals and other knowledge workers.

In a sense, these two trends—the professionalization of much movement activity and the emergence of the deliberately nonprofessional new social movements—represent two sides of the same coin. Both may be seen as attempts to promote a new wave of social change by redefining the nature of the social movement. Will a contemporary rebirth of large-scale activism be spurred by professional movements, new social movements, or some synthesis of the two? We will know soon enough.

SUMMARY

1. Collective behavior arises in situations in which institutionalized norms appear inadequate because they are unclear or rapidly changing. It tends to be relatively short-lived, spontaneous, and unorganized.

2. Contagion theory emphasizes the emotional dimensions of collective behavior.

3. Neil Smelser's value-added theory identifies six factors that must be present if collective behavior is to occur: structural conduciveness, structural strain, a generalized belief, a precipitating incident, mobilization for action, and social control.

4. Emergent-norm theory suggests that definitions of appropriate behavior gradually develop out of ongoing crowd interaction.

5. Crowds and panics are the major types of localized collectivities. There are five varieties of crowds: casual, conventional, expressive, acting, and protest.

6. The major forms of dispersed collectivities include rumors; mass hysteria; disaster behavior; fashion, fads, and crazes; and publics.

7. Social movements are collective efforts to promote or resist change that use at least some relatively uninstitutionalized methods.

8. The formal organizations that promote the goals of social movements are known as SMOs.

9. The level of movement activity in a society fluctuates over time.

10. There are five general types of movement participants: the ego-involved, the concerned, the insecure, spectators, and exploiters.

11. Mass-society theory, now generally discredited, suggests people join social movements to compensate for their own personal inadequacies.

12. Relative-deprivation theory explains movement membership as a consequence of people feeling a negative discrepancy between their present situa-

tion and the circumstances to which they feel they are entitled. There are three principal types of relative deprivation: aspirational, decremental, and J-curve.

13. Modern explanations of movement membership focus on recruitment through interpersonal networks and on the process of frame alignment.

14. Resource-mobilization theory analyzes the origin and development of social movements in terms of their ability to obtain and make effective use of such resources as leadership, supporters, and access to the mass media.

15. Political process theory is a macrolevel approach that studies the relationship between social-movement development and the political and economic structure of the society where the movement arises.

16. Reformist social movements work for relatively small-scale changes, whereas revolutionary movements seek to change a society's fundamental economic, political, and stratification systems. Reactionary social movements try to reverse the direction in which change is currently moving.

17. Many social movements pass through a four-stage career or life-cycle pattern of incipience, coalescence, bureaucratization, and decline.

18. Social movements commonly sponsor structured training programs for their members.

19. Movements are becoming increasingly professionalized. But sociologists have also noticed the emergence of a new type of movement that is ideologically inclusive, global in scope, highly participatory, and emotional.

KEY TERMS

acting crowd 623
casual crowd 622
collective behavior 619
conventional crowd 622
countermovement 634
craze 628
crowd 622
expressive crowd 623
fads 628

fashion 627
gossip 625
mass hysteria 626
mob 623
new social movement 639
panic 624
protest crowd 624
public 629
reactionary movement 634

reformist movement 634
relative deprivation 630
revolutionary movement 634
riot 623
rumor 625
social movement 629
urban legend 626

CRITICAL THINKING QUESTIONS

1. In explaining participation in collective behavior and social movements, some theories emphasize the members' personal qualities, whereas others stress such external factors as the availability of resources and problems in the larger society. Which approach do you find more useful? Why do you think different people might prefer one type of theory over the other?

2. Are minority riots better understood as political protests or as deviant behavior? Why?

3. Is the dividing line between reformist and revolutionary movements clear cut? How would you classify such modern movements as feminism, environmentalism, gun control, and gay rights? Can the members of your class reach a consensus regarding these movements?

4. Why do you think there is less social movement activity today than there was in the late 1960s? Do you think there will be a new wave of movement activity in the early 21st century? Why or why not?

INVESTIGATE WITH CONTENT SELECT

Journal Research
Collections from
ContentSelect
Begin your research using ContentSelect for this chapter by following the directions found on page 27 of this text to visit Prentice Hall's Research Navigator Website. Enter these search terms into the search field:

Panic
Rumor
Urban Legend

24
SOCIAL CHANGE, GLOBALIZATION, AND DEVELOPMENT

Economies of Exclusion

We have glimpses of a new world economic order. The best glimpses may not be found in the high rises in Tokyo or Manhattan, nor in the stark desolation of Mogadishu and Kinshasa. A better glimpse of the future can be found in Bangkok, Tijuana, Rio de Janeiro, and Nairobi, where economic miracles and social nightmares coexist daily—all these hot, noisy, hazy mixtures of hope and despair. They provide the products and services for a growing, global middle class and open the door for the otherwise excluded to join them. Without fundamental changes, however, it will be a rapidly revolving door, offering an invitation, a quick glimpse of air conditioned affluence, and then a swift return to the street. (Adapted from Sernau, 1997:49)

The Sociology of Cell Phones

Like many other technological innovations, cell phones are having a substantial impact on contemporary social life. They allow us to stay more closely in touch with friends and family regardless of where we are, and they greatly speed up the flow of information; on the other hand, they have further accelerated the often dizzying pace of modern life, and they probably have increased the number of traffic accidents because they often distract drivers from focusing fully on the road.

Sociologists are especially interested in how new technologies spread out among various segments of the population as they become increasingly popular. Recent research provides some interesting information about this issue. Once primarily a male preserve, cell phones are now used roughly equally by both genders. Similarly, the age range of people most likely to own them has expanded from 35–50 to 18–64, although the elderly remain markedly less

likely to adopt this new technology. Cell phone use rises with education and income, as one might expect, but Asians, African Americans, and Latinos are all more likely than whites to own some sort of mobile communications device. These findings suggest that there may be less of a "digital divide" between the races with regard to cell phones than there is with more costly technological innovations such as personal computers. (Katz & Aspden, 1998)

As was emphasized in Chapter 1, social change has been a central concern of sociology since its emergence as a distinct discipline. In this final chapter, we review and expand upon change-related themes that are discussed throughout the text. The most important of these themes relate to **globalization**—the vision of the world as a single social space where diverse societies borrow, learn, and compete against one another—and **development**—programs designed to upgrade the standard of living of the world's poor in ways that allow them to sustain themselves.

We begin with an overview of the major concepts and perspectives that sociologists use to analyze change and with a discussion of the sources of social change. Next, the chapter reviews the theories of change developed by Durkheim, Marx, and Weber, and show how each has been modified to interpret ongoing social change in the contemporary developed world. The chapter concludes with a focus on critical issues confronting developing nations in our increasingly globalized world.

WHAT IS SOCIAL CHANGE?

Social change is a very broad concept, referring to alterations over time in social structure, culture, and behavior patterns (Moore, 1967). Social change is continual and universal. It occurs at all levels of social

THEN AND NOW

Sixty Years of Social Change

Consider some of the changes that have taken place in the United States in the six decades since the end of World War II:

- In 1945, the South was still segregated by law: African Americans were required to attend separate (and inferior) schools, drink from "colored" water fountains, and sit in the back of the bus. Interracial dating was strictly taboo. Throughout the country, legally enforceable restrictive covenants ensured that homes in desirable neighborhoods would not be resold to blacks, Latinos, Asians, Jews, and sometimes even to Catholics. Most women were housewives; efforts by women to enter prestigious, traditionally male professions were strongly resisted; and the demand for equal pay for equal work was widely regarded as radical.

- The divorce rate was less than half of what it is now, and divorcing couples faced significant legal barriers as well as strong social disapproval. Sex was not discussed in polite company, and homosexuality was such a taboo subject that a schoolteacher who even mentioned it could expect to be fired. Many young people remained virgins throughout their adolescence.

- The majority of the public trusted the government. Nobody except a few scientists worried about the environment. The Berlin Wall was brand new, and the collapse of communism was unimaginable. Official crime rates were a quarter to a third of what they are now, and only a small group of people at the bottom of the social ladder used illicit drugs. Few college students knew anyone who had ever used marijuana, much less harder drugs.

- Television was in its infancy. There were no microwave ovens, no stereos,

no DVDs, no rock 'n' roll, no rap. Most movies were filmed in black and white. There were no interstate highways, no indoor shopping malls, no HMOs, and very few fast-food franchises. Pizza was just being introduced. Cars had no seatbelts and no air bags. Trips to the moon, industrial robots, computers, and fax machines were found only in the pages of science-fiction novels.

And now, the obvious question: How will society change in the next sixty years? It's impossible to predict exactly what will happen in the future, but we can be confident that many aspects of life today will appear just as old-fashioned in 2065 as the United States in 1945 seems to us now.

1. What aspects of social life do you expect *not* to undergo substantial change prior to the middle of the 21st century? Explain your choices.

---

life, from whole societies to microlevel social interactions. Sometimes it is predictable; often it is not. It may be gradual or abrupt, but the unmistakable global trend is toward an ever more rapid pace of change.

Change takes place in both social structure and culture, and each influences the other. Cultural change may involve *discoveries*—uncovering aspects of reality that were previously unknown, such as the existence of dinosaurs—or *inventions*—recombinations of existing material or nonmaterial culture elements in order to create something new, like the automobile, the cell phone, or the idea of a university (see Chapter 3) (White, 1949). Social change can arise within a culture, or it can enter from outside through a process of *diffusion* (Linton, 1936); anthropologists believe that the vast majority of all change in any given society originates somewhere else. However, cultural elements almost never diffuse into a new setting without some modification (Lauer, 1991).

A number of factors determine whether a new idea or technology will be accepted (Etzkowitz, 1992). In general, changes are more likely to be adopted (a)

if they originate from cutting edge sources—from Silicon Valley rather than from Bolivia; (b) if they respond to a strongly felt need among the public—the reason the metric system has not been widely accepted whereas DVDs have been; (c) if they are material rather than nonmaterial, as predicted by culture lag theory (see Chapter 3); and (d) if they are broadly compatible with people's existing values—the reason the highly effective French abortion pill RU-486 was not available in the United States until 2000 and why its use continues to meet strong resistance, especially in regions of the country where the pro-life movement is strong.

The spread of a new idea or invention usually follows a curvilinear pattern. A few pioneers, generally people with strong connections to relatively broad social networks, gradually pick up on the new development. Then, the bulk of the population adopts it, often quite rapidly. This is currently taking place with regard to cell phones, as noted in the chapter-opening vignette. Finally, a relatively small number of stragglers grudgingly jump on the bandwagon (Coleman et al., 1957).

The communications media play an important role in spreading public awareness of innovations because they can accomplish this far more rapidly than is possible through word of mouth. Thus, the printing press, radios, telephones, televisions—and, today, the Internet—have all contributed to the escalating pace of social change (Zaret, 1996).

Resistance to change in developing societies is often strong because of *cultural inertia*, a deep preference for traditional ways of living and thinking (Inglehart & Baker, 2000). Cultural inertia is often based in religious institutions. The medieval Catholic church, for example, vehemently opposed the scientific worldview of Galileo (Manchester, 1993). Since that time, conservative religions have fought hard against such changes as the abolition of slavery, female suffrage, the teaching of evolution, civil rights, the end of apartheid in South Africa, the right to abortion, and the public acceptance of homosexuality.

Opponents of change may be described as **vested interests,** a term coined by Thorstein Veblen (1964) to refer to individuals and groups whose advantages are threatened by impending social change. The Luddites, for example, were textile workers in the early years of the Industrial Revolution who deliberately sabotaged the new machines that threatened their livelihood (Sale, 1996). People today who are uncomfortable with computers are sometimes called neo-Luddites (Bauerlein, 1996).

Other examples of vested interests abound: The American Medical Association resists national health care, the National Rifle Association opposes gun control legislation, the tobacco industry fights restrictions on smoking, and teachers' unions oppose school voucher plans.

SOURCES OF SOCIAL CHANGE

Sociologists have identified numerous sources of social change, including the natural environment, demographic change, new ideas, innovations in technology, the government, competition and war, elite-initiated change, and social movements. Let's look at each of these sources more closely.

The Natural Environment

Human social and cultural patterns are constantly shifting to adapt to changes in the physical environment. Sometimes the changes are sudden, as when earthquakes and floods disrupt everyday social life (Erickson, 1976; 1994). Even more significant are gradual but long-lasting changes in climate, such as the slow expansion of the Sahara Desert, the loss of topsoil on the western plains that resulted in the Dust Bowl of the 1930s, and the worldwide coastal flooding that will occur should global warming partially melt the polar ice caps (Lemonick, 2001).

Demographic Change

Alterations in the size, composition, and distribution of the human population have led to a variety of major social changes. The rapid growth of the world's population that accompanied industrialization had far-reaching effects (see Chapter 22). Conversely, dramatic declines in the population of indigenous peoples such as the Native Americans, mainly due to diseases introduced by Europeans, have had catastrophic effects on their ability to maintain their cultures (Oswalt & Neely, 1999).

Vested interests oppose social changes because they fear their consequences. Here Phillip Morris CEO William Campbell testifies before a congressional hearing in an unsuccessful effort to prevent further governmental regulation of the tobacco industry.

Changes in the composition of the population are also important. When the enormous Baby Boom generation reached young adulthood in the 1960s, the crime rate soared (see Chapter 9). Today, their children, the "Baby Boom Echo," are crowding the schools (Crispell, 1995). Early in the 21st century, graying Boomers may well force changes in Social Security and in the health care delivery system, as discussed in Chapters 14 and 19 respectively (Griswold, 1994; Roush, 1996).

Immigration and high minority birth rates are also having profound effects on society. Soon, people of color will collectively constitute a numerical majority of the population, ushering in an era that many sociologists believe will mandate a deeper commitment to multiculturalism (see Chapter 12).

New Ideas

New ways of thought change how people see the world, and they call for structural and cultural adjustments (Kuhn, 1970). The development of the scientific method (Chapter 2), of revolutionary Marxism (Chapter 10), of the Protestant work ethic (Chapter 21), and of rational bureaucracy (also Chapter 21) are good examples.

New Technologies

Technologies are tools and the skills needed to manufacture and use them. They are the artificial means by which humans extend their ability to manipulate the environment (Teich, 1993; Volti, 1995; MacKenzie & Wajcman, 1999). Technological change is especially significant because, like population (see Chapter 22), it has the potential to increase geometrically. Each major new development further expands the culture base, providing more elements that can be re-combined to yield ever more rapid change in the future (Freeman, 1974).

Consider the humble microwave oven. It has led to many unexpected, or latent, social changes. Microwaves reduce the amount of time it takes to cook meals, thus freeing more women to enter the workforce. They make it easier to prepare single-portion meals, which makes it simpler to live alone, which in turn makes divorce marginally less unattractive. Microwaves also allow family members to eat whenever it is convenient, which has weakened the tradition of family meals and, arguably, somewhat weakened the family (Ritzer, 2000). We could make similar observations about virtually any major new technology, including the electric light bulb, the automobile, television, cellular phones, computers, new reproductive technologies, and genetic engineering (Peterson, 1994; Fukuyama, 1999).

At the same time, however, we must avoid *technological determinism*, the view that technology is the only important source of social change. New technologies are important, but each society decides how (and if) it will use them (Lauer, 1991).

Government

The rise of modern nation-states with strong governments has contributed directly to social change. Strong, centralized political leadership can mobilize large-scale efforts to alter the character of a society. In the United States, for example, the government has significantly contributed to major changes in civil rights and environmentalism. Furthermore, patriotism helps people to accept the dislocations that often accompany large-scale change, convincing them that their suffering is necessary "for the good of the nation" (Greenfield, 1992).

Technological developments are an important source of social change. The shift from conventional mail to e-mail has greatly increased the ease and speed of communication. Sociologists are currently exploring additional consequences of the computer revolution.

Competition and War

High levels of competition—whether to develop a new technology or to succeed in business—often inspire innovation. Good examples include the invention of the automobile, the airplane, and the computer, as well as the effort to unravel the mysteries of the DNA molecule. In each case, several individuals or teams were competing with one another to perfect the new technology, and in each case the rivalry clearly speeded up the process.

War can also serve as a spur to significant innovations, from new medicines, including sulfa and penicillin, to nuclear power and space travel (Nisbet, 1988; Chirot, 1994).

Institutionalized Social Change

In the past, most social change just happened, but in the modern era more and more of it is deliberately planned. Sometimes, as previously noted, this planning is done by government. But today, especially in the developed world, virtually every major organization—from universities to corporations—has created specialized research and development branches to plan for the future. In other words, we have institutionalized social change.

Social Movements

While institutional elites plan for change from above, as we saw in Chapter 23, the less powerful are simultaneously organizing social movements and pushing for change from below. Sometimes, as in the case of the civil rights movement, these popular efforts gain the grudging support of government. At other times, as with the anti-war and pro-life movements, they work against the government. And sometimes they aim for revolutionary change in the government itself, as did the movements that led to both of the Russian revolutions in the twentieth century (Skocpol, 1979).

THEORETICAL PERSPECTIVES ON SOCIAL CHANGE

Four general theoretical perspectives on social change—cyclical, evolutionary, functional, and conflict—have emerged from the writings of sociologists and other scholars. These four theories attempt to describe the broad patterns by which all societies develop; they exist on the borderline between social science and philosophy.

Cyclical Theory

Before the industrial era, most people thought about societal change by means of an analogy with the seasons or with the human life cycle. This interpretation denies that social change is directional; instead, societies rise and fall in a series of trendless cycles (Moore, 1974). The most important causes of social change are believed by cyclic theorists to be *immanent*, or located within each society, just as the genetic "blueprint" for a mature oak tree lies deep within every acorn (Hughes, 1962).

Historians have long been especially attracted to the cyclic view, as in Oswald Spengler's *The Decline and Fall of the West* (1928), which drew striking parallels between the late Roman Empire and early 20th-century Europe. The English historian Arnold Toynbee (1889–1975) also believed that civilizations rose and fell, but he was less pessimistic than Spengler (Toynbee, 1946). Toynbee maintained that societies must meet an endless series of external and internal challenges. If these challenges are either too easily overcome or too severe, the society will collapse. But as long as "creative elites" can respond effectively to the challenges, their society will endure.

Paul Kennedy, a contemporary historian, also views the course of social change as broadly cyclical. He argues that great civilizations decline when they devote so many resources to the military that their domestic economies weaken. This, he believes, is a problem that the United States may currently be facing (Kennedy, 1988).

The best-known sociologist whose work reflects a cyclical view is probably Pitirim Sorokin (1889–1968). Sorokin wrote that societies alternate between *sensate eras*, in which ultimate truth is believed to be discoverable through scientific research, and *ideational periods*, during which people seek truth through the transcendent (Sorokin, 1941). Every aspect of culture—from government to family to art—reflects the underlying character of the era, either sensate or ideational. Sorokin posited that after centuries, the possibilities of one cultural pattern become exhausted and society inevitably shifts either to the other type or, occasionally, to a short-lived *idealistic era*, in which both possibilities are blended smoothly together. He thought that contemporary civilization was in an "overripe" sensate phase, almost ready to shift to another pattern, probably ideational, with faith replacing reason and science.

CRITIQUE Cyclical theory is appealing because some things really do appear to change in cycles, from hemlines to the stock market (Caplow, 1991). But in other cases, especially where the adoption of new technologies such as television or computers is involved, there does appear to be a direction to change. Furthermore, cyclic theory is more descriptive than analytic; it really doesn't tell us *why* societies change. It may be that cyclic theory was more applicable in the past than it is in the rapidly changing modern era (Wilkinson, 1987).

Evolutionary Theory

In contrast to the cyclical approach, evolutionary theory maintains that social change is indeed moving in a direction. Specifically, the general trend of history is toward greater complexity and increased institutional differentiation—that is, in the direction of ever more specialized institutional arrangements (Dietz et al., 1990; Adams & Sydie, 2001). Thus, for example, education began as one of the family's many functions, but later it shifted to a separate institutional setting—initially the one-room, all-grade schoolhouse but now the large, immensely complex, highly specialized, modern multiversity.

Evolutionary thought shares one key assumption with cyclic theory: Both see change as largely immanent. For evolutionists, all societies have a natural internal dynamic that impels them to become ever more adaptive in order to successfully compete with other societies for survival. Thus, classic evolutionary theorists maintained that change is normally progress.

It should be evident that this approach is grounded in Charles Darwin's theory of biological evolution. Darwin had an immense influence on 19th-century social thought, especially that of the English sociologist Herbert Spencer (Spencer, 1860; Adams & Sydie, 2001). Spencer and his followers thought that all societies would ultimately follow the same evolutionary path—or set sequence of stages—and would all end up looking very much like 19th-century Europe (Inkeles, 1998). This approach to change is called **unilinear** (one line) **evolutionary theory.**

Auguste Comte, the "father of sociology," also accepted unilinear evolutionary theory. He saw all societies progressing from a theological stage to a metaphysical stage and, ultimately, to a positive or scientific stage (Comte, 1858). As we discussed in Chapter 4, Émile Durkheim (1933) wrote about the historical transition from societies bonded by *mechanical solidarity* to societies held together by *organic solidarity*, and Ferdinand Tönnies (1963) proposed that societies evolve from *Gemeinschaft* to *Gesellschaft*.

CRITIQUE Unilinear evolutionary theory, especially in its earlier versions, was severely criticized for at least three reasons. First, it simply does not fit the facts: Not all traditional societies are organized in the same way, and when they do change, they do not all pass through the same stages.

Second, the underlying evolutionary assumption that all change is ultimately progress is obviously based on a value judgment, one that became increasingly difficult to maintain in the face of the world wars and societal upheavals that characterized the 20th century (Smart, 1990; Harper, 1993).

Finally, unilinear evolutionary theory was all too easily used to defend colonialism. If every culture is eventually going to be like the "advanced" European societies, then it seemed only natural and right that people in "backward" parts of the world should be brought under Europeans' "benevolent" political and economic control. Kipling called this "improvement" of colonized peoples "the white man's burden." And

The increasing size and complexity of the modern city is a good example of the sort of social change that is easily analyzed using evolutionary theory.

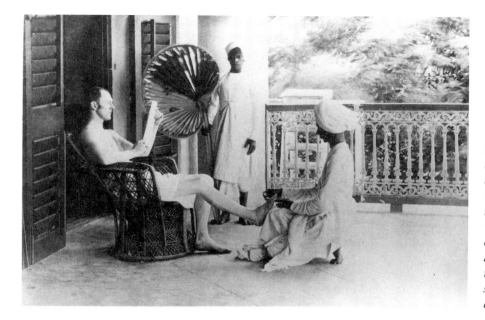

Unilinear evolutionary theory was extremely popular during the colonial era of the later nineteenth century. This perspective supported the view that European societies were more "advanced" than those of India and other countries in Asia and Africa, and implied that it was only proper that Europeans should dominate these societies both politically and economically.

if, in the process, Europeans became wealthy using the labor power and natural resources of their colonies, what could be wrong with that? This logic helps explain the great popularity of evolutionary theory in the 19th century. Recognition of the harm that resulted from colonial exploitation later contributed to widespread scholarly rejection of unilinear thought (Nisbet, 1969). However, many people in the developed world continue to view the poorer cultures as backward and inferior, reflecting the core assumptions of classic evolutionism.

Some sociologists, most notably Neil Smelser (1973) and Gerhard and Jean Lenski (Nolan & Lenski, 1999) (see Chapter 4), have modified evolutionary thinking. They have retained the idea that as societies grow, they tend to become more complex, institutionally differentiated, and adaptive, but they reject the notion that change is necessarily progress and recognize that societies may change at different paces and in quite different ways (Sahlins & Service, 1960). This approach, which remains quite popular today, is called **multilinear evolutionary theory.** However, some critics point out that a few societies have become less rather than more complex and differentiated (Alexander & Colomy, 1990).

Functionalist Theory

As we saw in Chapter 1, classic functionalist theory argues that stability, not change, is the natural order of things. As formulated by Talcott Parsons (1951), functionalism assumes that the origins of change always lie outside a social system and that most, if not all, social change can be understood as an effort to re-

store the equilibrium that has been disrupted by external forces. For example, the feminist movement has contributed directly to massive increases in the number of mothers who work outside of the home over the past three decades. This change has thrown the social system out of balance because there were initially few child-care options available to these working mothers. In response, there has been a substantial (though still inadequate) growth of the daycare industry, which has begun to restore equilibrium to the system. As this example suggests, functionalists tend to see most change as slow and adaptive. If the pressure for social change is too great, the system simply collapses.

CRITIQUE Classic functionalism has been severely faulted for its implicit assumption that change is abnormal, which does not fit most people's experience, especially today. Furthermore, many critics believe that it cannot adequately explain abrupt or revolutionary change (Giddens, 1987).

In response, Parsons's later work acknowledged several inherent causes of change, including imperfect integration between the parts of a social system—for example, the current mismatch between the number of people who are graduating from college in the United States and the (smaller) number of available jobs that actually require college skills. Parsons also blended the key assumption of evolutionary theory into his reworked functionalism, arguing that the tendency of all social systems to become more complex and differentiated means that the equilibrium point does not remain static over time; it is a *moving equilibrium* (Parsons, 1966).

Conflict Theory

Conflict theory refutes the functionalist claim that social change is secondary or abnormal. Quite the opposite: Since society is based on the struggle of various competing interest groups for scarce goods and services, social life is constantly changing as one party and then another achieves dominance (Wuthnow, 1989a). The source of change may be either external or immanent, although classic Marxist thought stresses the latter, referring to internal pressures for change as *contradictions*. For example, as technology expands, capitalists must increase the level of education received by their workers so that they can keep up to date, yet the more education they receive, the more likely they are to achieve class consciousness and rise in revolution.

CRITIQUE Conflict theory accounts for the universality of social change and is well prepared to explain revolutionary and discontinuous change. On the other hand, it fails to acknowledge that change sometimes proceeds gradually and without much apparent conflict.

THE GREAT TRANSFORMATION

The term **modernization** refers to the sum total of the structural and cultural changes that accompanied the industrial revolution. More specifically, the shift to inanimate sources of energy in Europe and North America led to the following major social transformations (Smelser, 1973; Chase-Dunn & Hall, 1997; Fukuyama, 1999):

- The growth of a large middle class and some reduction in the misery of the poor (see Chapters 10 and 11).
- A movement away from the importance of ascribed status and toward greater emphasis on equal rights, leading to considerably reduced discrimination against ethnic and racial minorities, women, and other disadvantaged groups (see Chapters 12–14).
- An unparalleled shift in the role of women across the globe, especially in their massive move into the labor force (see Chapter 13).
- The emergence and general acceptance of new family and household forms, especially single-parent families and couples living together without marriage (see Chapter 15).
- A massive increase in global literacy (see Chapter 16).
- The decreased global significance of the role of religion in major social institutions, especially the political economy (see Chapters 17, 18, and 24).

- A great increase in the size and power of the government (see Chapter 18).
- A shift from acute to chronic diseases as the major killers of people across the globe (see Chapter 19).
- An unprecedented increase in the human population resulting from sharp declines in mortality linked to advances in sanitation, health, and medicine (see Chapters 19 and 22).
- The spread of rational bureaucracy into almost all aspects of social life (see Chapter 21).

These social changes have in turn altered individual behavior patterns, creating a personal orientation termed **modernity**. Modern people, unlike those living in traditional, preindustrial societies, are more open to new experiences; tend to reject traditional patterns of authority, valuing science and rationality in their stead; are much more future-oriented and less fatalistic; strongly desire upward social mobility; and accept a much more diverse set of beliefs (Inkeles, 1973; Berger, 1977).

Today, at the same time that the developing nations are modernizing, the developed societies are moving out of the industrial era and into a new phase. In **postindustrial society,** manufacturing is largely replaced by knowledge-based service industries. Workers devote most of their time to producing information rather than material objects (Bell, 1976; Hage & Powers, 1992; Esping-Andersen, 1999). The computer replaces the steam engine and the assembly line. This transition is occurring even more rapidly than the shift from farming to manufacturing did, and there is every reason to believe that it will cause—as did the industrial revolution before it—a host of social problems.

The difficulty of moving into the postindustrial era has stimulated the rise of a school of thought called **postmodernism.** Postmodernist thinkers reject many of the basic ideas of modernity. Specifically, they deny the idea that science and rationality are viable means of discovering truth. They also reject the notion that current patterns of social change represent any kind of progress (Jameson, 1991; Best & Kellner, 1991; Ritzer, 1997). In its most extreme form, postmodernism denies that there is any objective meaning in written communications beyond that which the observer reads into them. At this point in its development, postmodernism has probably produced more questions than answers, but its popularity hints at the intellectual turmoil caused by the transition to postindustrial society.

An important part of the sociologist's task in the 21st century is to study the social problems that arise in the developed world as a result of the transition into postindustrial society. However, this does not mean that the problems that led to the birth of the discipline in the early industrial era—such as poverty, discrimination, alienation, and anomie—are no longer relevant. They continue to confront us today, although in somewhat different forms.

SOCIAL CHANGE IN THE DEVELOPED WORLD

Each of the three 19th-century theorists who are generally regarded as sociology's most important founders—Émile Durkheim, Karl Marx, and Max Weber—analyzed modernization and interpreted different aspects of this process as problematic.

Durkheim observed that as industrialization proceeded, people played increasingly differentiated roles in the expanding economy. In the past, when almost everyone farmed, people all accepted pretty much the

Modern conflict theorists have substantially broadened Marx's notion of class conflict. They recognize that many different groups of people—for example, the gay activists staging this demonstration—are continually struggling with other groups for power, prestige, and material advantage.

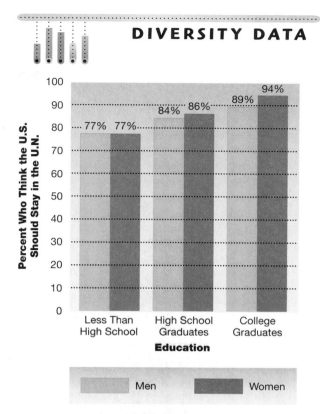

DIVERSITY DATA

Percent Who Think the U.S. Should Stay in the U.N.

- Less Than High School: Men 77%, Women 77%
- High School Graduates: Men 84%, Women 86%
- College Graduates: Men 89%, Women 94%

Men / Women

FIGURE 24.1 How Do Education and Gender Affect Support for U.S. Participation in the United Nations? Most Americans believe that we should stay in the U.N., with somewhat greater support for this position among the better educated. Gender has little influence on opinions except among the college educated, where women are somewhat more supportive of the U.N. than are men. How would you explain these findings?

Source: NORC. General Social Surveys, 1972–2000. Chicago: National Opinion Research Center, 2000. Reprinted by permission of NORC, Chicago, IL.

same values, or, in Durkheim's terms, they shared a *collective consciousness.* This collective consciousness both produced and reflected the mechanical solidarity that in turn provided moral guidance and held society together. Today, however, people frequently hold very different values. While economic interdependence provides a certain amount of unity (organic solidarity), the weakening of the collective consciousness leads, in Durkheim's view, to widespread uncertainty about how to think and behave, a condition he called *anomie.* Anomie leads in turn to a host of social problems, including crime, drug abuse, broken families, and suicide (see Chapter 8).

For Marx, the growth of industrial society sharpened and clarified class conflict, ultimately leaving only two major classes struggling with each other, the

GLOBAL CONNECTIONS

Social Change: Islamization as Countermodernization

• Boutiques in Iran display sleeveless black dresses and white miniskirts even though wearing such garments in public is outlawed. A voice on a loudspeaker reminds women to keep their veils properly in place. Outside a crowded pizza parlor in wealthy north Teheran, young women in full Islamic dress name their favorite bands: Metallica, Pink Floyd, and Guns 'N' Roses. They get videos of these groups from illicit satellite dishes hidden under mattresses or concealed by clothes hung permanently out to dry.

• In Kabul, Afghanistan's capital city, women feel the breeze running though their hair and the sun on their faces as they venture out of their homes for the first time in modest clothing but not in the fully enveloped *burqa*. Only a short time ago, being outside without a burqa put them at risk of death by stoning or a firing squad.

Modernization spawned by global social change is swift, massive, and overwhelming in its effects, especially for those in the developing world. Modernization offers an array of tantalizing products, services, and opportunities for a different lifestyle, but at perhaps a steep

price: the inevitable erosion of tradition. When modernization collides with tradition, support to revitalize, rediscover, and readapt cultural traditions increases. The scramble to stop the erosion of cultural traditions often occurs under an anti-Western banner—the artifacts of Western culture that have been spread to every corner of the world are rejected. Efforts by fundamentalists to create, or recreate, religious states are typical expressions of this rejection.

Countermodernization, or antimodernization, is a social movement that either resists modernization or promotes ways to neutralize its effects. Throughout much of the Muslim world, countermodernization takes the form of *Islamization,* a religious fundamentalist movement seeking a return to an idealized version of Islam as a remedy against corrupt Western values. With Islamization, religion and state are inseparable, and all laws governing public and private life have a religious basis. Islamization is replayed in South Asia (Pakistan and Bangladesh), in the Middle East (Saudi Arabia and Iraq), and in North Africa (Egypt and Sudan). Until the Taliban takeover of Afghanistan in 1996, its most virulent expression worldwide was the Iranian revolution that propelled Khomeini to power after the overthrow of the Shah of Iran in 1979. As elsewhere in the Muslim world, in both

Afghanistan and Iran, Islamic authorities or "mullahs" have long played an influential role in virtually all aspects of social life.

Islamization in Iran and Afghanistan targets women as being corrupted by the West. Islamic identity would be restored to women and to society when they returned to their primary domestic roles. Islam is invoked to deny reproductive choice, educational opportunity, and paid employment. In both countries women have been executed for adultery and prostitution, often defined as simply being seen with a non-kin male, or beaten, many to the point of death, for clothing that reveals too much of a woman's body. Islamization under the Taliban banned employment and schools for girls, and hospitals serving women closed, lest women come into contact with men to whom they are not related. With a better infrastructure, Islamization in Iran was (and is) not as extreme in its treatment of women. Women receive medical care in facilities designed for them, and girls are in gender-segregated schools. However, women in Iran remain under the strict control of their fathers or husbands, are restricted from a variety of paid employment, and must answer to Islamic authorities for violations of traditional gender roles, most related to marriage, family, and motherhood.

bourgeoisie and the proletariat. Over time, he believed, the proletariat would be ground further and further down until eventually its members achieved class consciousness and revolted. The primary problem of the industrial era, in Marx's opinion, was *class oppression* (see Chapter 10).

Weber saw industrial society as both cause and consequence of a process of *rationalization*, the systematic examination of all aspects of social life in order to identify the most technically efficient means of accomplishing chosen ends. The problem was that this relentless rationalization process seemed to have

become an "iron cage" that sacrificed everything spontaneous and humanistic to bottom-line efficiency (see Chapter 22).

Updating Durkheim

Undeniably, anomie continues to plague modern society. Social conservatives decry the weakening of time-honored values like patriotism, family, and Christianity. Though we were probably never as strongly committed to these ideals as traditionalists would like to believe, it is very clear that as we have

Islamization round the globe increases the likelihood that women will be discouraged or even outlawed from non-domestic roles. Even after the Taliban were dislodged from power in Afghanistan, women in many regions still don the completely enveloping burqa that conceals their bodies and identities when they venture outside their homes.

can never be sustained. Iran is quietly making overtures to investors and Western leaders that should help re-open its doors to the world. As the opening in this box suggests, despite the government's best efforts to maintain the fervor of Islamization, a liberalizing current is now coursing through Iranian life. Although the swift demise of the Taliban in Afghanistan occurred because of the repercussions of the terrorist attacks, it is still clear that their extreme version of Islamic countermodernization—also condemned by Muslims throughout the world—would have eventually sealed their fate and dislodged them from power.

1. Based on your knowledge of social change and globalization, predict what path Islamization will take in the next two decades in the Middle East and South Asia. How will Islamic nations deal with the influence of Western values on their societies?

2. What are the U.S. equivalents to countermodernization movements or trends? How has the U.S. government and other social institutions responded to these trends?

When social change conflicted with cultural traditions in Iran and Afghanistan, countermodernization was favored to deal with the conflict. In discussing Islamization in Iran and the form it took under the Taliban in Afghanistan in the last two editions of this text, we predicted that when a large part of the population is kept out of the labor force and human rights are violated, the world would respond first with condemnation and then with sanctions, with economic crisis close behind. Both Khomeini and the Taliban are gone, but Islamization continues on a different, less extreme course. Excessive countermodernization

Sources: Usman, 1985; Ask & Tjomsland, 1998; Rasekh, 1998; Afkhami, 2001, Maley, 2001; Rashid, 2001; Lindsey, 1990, 1995, 2002.

become a more diverse people, fewer shared values hold us together than did so in the past.

Durkheim was correct in observing that organic solidarity provides a measure of functional integration, but life in modern society lacks the passionate unity that comes from a strong core of shared sacred values. Traditional life stifles individualism, but many people feel that we have lost our sense of moral community, and that this is too great a price to pay for the freedom and privacy of the modern city (Selznick, 1992).

In a widely read essay entitled "Bowling Alone," Robert Putnam identified the problem as a decline in **social capital,** by which he meant the ". . . features of social organization such as networks, norms, and social trust that facilitate coordination and cooperation for mutual benefit" (Putnam, 1995:67). He sees signs of this decline everywhere, from plummeting levels of trust in government and low voter turnout to reduced membership in unions, PTAs, churches, and other voluntary associations. This is of particular concern because affluence and education, which usually accompany civic involvement, have been rising at the same time that participation has declined.

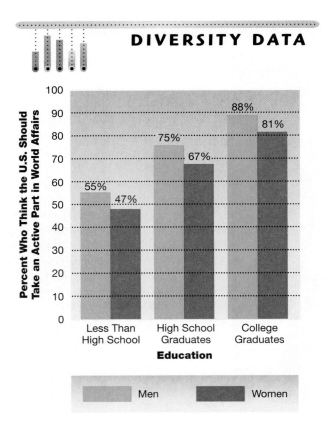

DIVERSITY DATA

FIGURE 24.2 How Do Education and Gender Affect Attitudes Concerning Whether the United States Should Take an Active Part in World Affairs? As educational attainment rises, both men and women become less isolationist; however, at each educational level, men are more supportive of international involvement than women. How might gender role socialization affect people's views on this issue?

Source: NORC. General Social Surveys, 1972–2000. Chicago: National Opinion Research Center, 2000. Reprinted by permission of NORC, Chicago, IL.

Perhaps, however, the picture isn't as grim as Putnam suggests. A survey conducted for the AARP showed fairly high levels of civic involvement despite rampant cynicism about politics, especially at the national level (Guterbock & Fries, 1997). The average citizen was found to have 4.2 memberships in voluntary associations; only one in seven had none. The study found by far the highest levels of anomie and the lowest civic involvement among adults aged 25 and younger. Whether this will change once this generation settles down remains to be seen.

Is it possible for a modern society to reverse the trend toward individualism? Can we rebuild moral community? Are there any overarching values uniting nearly all Americans? Was the wave of patriotism that swept across the United States after the September 11 terrorist attacks a temporary phenomenon, or

did it suggest the beginnings of a rebirth of substantial value consensus?

Perhaps the best we can hope for is what Durkheim envisioned: the restoration of some measure of moral unity to groups of relatively similar people, while the society as a whole remains morally fragmented but held together functionally through organic solidarity. If there are few shared values among all Americans, maybe there are some common values among environmentalists or Latinos or *Star Wars* fans. Sociologists have speculated that the Internet may help to unify people who do not live near one another but who share common interests (Griswold, 1994; Hornsby, 1998).

In one effort to rebuild moral community, sociologist Amitai Etzioni (1988, 1993) helped establish the *communitarian movement.* Communitarians recognize that we cannot simply return to the *Gemeinschaft* of preindustrial days, but they are actively engaged in searching for ways to reduce the anomic disconnectedness of modern life. In particular, they argue that we must balance our demand for individual rights with a stronger commitment to our collective responsibilities. This is yet another example of the activist tradition that has been part of sociology since the days of Comte and Marx.

Updating Marx

A number of major historical changes have compelled 20th-century sociologists to substantially rethink Marx's work. Marx did not foresee (a) that the bourgeoisie would globalize the capitalist system, thereby further maximizing their profit by exploiting the labor and natural resources of the developing world; (b) that the process of collective bargaining would improve the proletariat's living conditions enough to greatly retard the development of class consciousness among them; or (c) that a huge new middle class of

INTERNET CONNECTIONS

Go to the World Bank Website:

http://www.worldbank.org/

Read the articles on development. Also, click on development topics, select a topic, and read about it. Afterward, answer the following questions. What factors are important in bringing about economic change and development? What are some impediments to change?

salaried white-collar workers would arise who are structurally proletariat but who have accepted the worldview of the bourgeoisie (Vago, 1998).

Probably the most useful updating of the conflict tradition comes from the work of Ralf Dahrendorf, a German sociologist who has taught in the United States and is now at Oxford University in England (and is a member of the British House of Lords) (Dahrendorf, 1959, 1973). Dahrendorf writes that although class conflict was the most visible form of intergroup struggle in Marx's day, in the modern world many other groups of people—including racial and ethnic minorities, women, consumers, gays, the elderly, children, college students, the obese, and the physically disabled—recognize their oppression and are now struggling to obtain prestige, material advantages, and power.

Dahrendorf's key insight is that Marxist class conflict is simply one example of a much more general type of conflict over what he terms *authority relations*. He argues as follows:

1. In any social system with a formally legitimated system of authority, there will always be two fundamentally opposed groups of people: those who have the authority to give orders, to reward conformity to these orders, and to punish disobedience; and those who must follow these orders lest they be punished. Conflict is always dichotomous, whether it involves classes or any other type of group.
2. The true interest of the dominant group is always to preserve the present situation, and the true interest of subordinate groups is always to change the status quo.

Much of Dahrendorf's work explores the conditions under which subordinate groups—those that lack authority—come to recognize their true interests. He also investigates the factors that shape the intensity, violence, and consequences of the ensuing conflict. But it is his concept of authority relations that is crucial because it demonstrates that the core of Marx's theory is not outdated. In fact, modified Marxist theory contributes tremendously to understanding the dynamics of all sorts of intergroup conflicts in today's highly diverse society.

Dahrendorf's analysis is, in a sense, pessimistic, because, unlike Marx, he does not foresee any end to social conflict. There will always be groups of people who have authority and others who do not. Few people like to take orders. But conflict is not necessarily negative; it can produce badly needed change, as the struggles of the civil rights and feminist movements show. Dahrendorf's vision of the future is not tranquil, but it does envision a society where oppressed people will continue to fight, often successfully, to improve their lives.

Updating Weber

Max Weber doubted that society could escape the iron cage of rationalization, and the history of the 20th century suggests that his skepticism was well grounded. It is true that assembly-line workers are increasingly robots rather than human beings, and there is a trend, especially in the knowledge-oriented sectors of the emerging postindustrial economy, toward the flexible bureaucracies that were discussed in Chapter 21. Nevertheless, bureaucratic rationality continues to define more and more sectors of modern life.

George Ritzer convincingly argues that modern societies are in the grip of an even more relentless rationalization process than Weber observed (Ritzer, 2000). Ritzer calls this trend **McDonaldization,** "the process by which the principles of the fast-food restaurant are coming to dominate more and more sectors of American society as well as of the rest of the world" (Ritzer, 2000:1). Whether we look at banks, schools, recreation, the health care system, the media, or even funerals, four basic principles of McDonaldization seem to be ever present.

First, McDonaldization mandates *efficiency*. In fast-food restaurants, the process of preparing food and moving the clientele along is as streamlined as possible: The menu is simplified, and customers are put to work filling their own soda cups and busing their own tables, all in the name of greater efficiency. To take just one of many possible parallel examples, in the modern university the registration process is highly formalized, and multiple-choice tests are increasingly computer generated and computer graded, all in the name of greater efficiency.

McDonaldization also maximizes *calculability*. Every component of each menu item is precisely measured, and great emphasis is put on how quickly food is delivered to the customers. Similarly, quantity is stressed over quality: It's a Big Mac, not a Delicious Mac. In higher education, students often choose schools based on their numerical rankings, and schools accept students largely on the basis of their class rank and test scores. Students evaluate their teachers on quantitative scales, and faculty seeking tenure must publish a large number of research articles.

Third, McDonaldization emphasizes *predictability*. Every Big Mac is exactly like every other Big Mac. No surprises. Regarding the university, each semester is organized in a highly predictable fashion with the same progression of registration, midterms, and final examinations.

Finally, McDonaldization maximizes *institutional control over workers and customers*. As anyone who has ever worked at a fast-food restaurant knows, almost every aspect of the job is guided by nonhuman technology, from fryers that cook potatoes automatically to computerized cash registers. Human choice is minimized. Consumers are subtly encouraged to eat their food and clear out. In the university, a relatively rigid curriculum, detailed syllabi, and fixed time periods all help control the educational process.

Ritzer does not deny that people like many aspects of McDonaldization. It does produce high profits, and it fits well in a culture that values efficiency, but it also has an irrational side. To Ritzer, ". . . rational systems are unreasonable systems that deny the humanity, the human reason, of the people who work within them or are served by them. In other words, rational systems are dehumanizing" (2000:123–124). In the fast-food restaurant, workers can use only a few of their skills, and customers are reduced to managed automatons. Relationships between customers and workers are dehumanized because they are reduced to prepackaged impersonal scripts—"Would you like fries with that?"

Can McDonaldization be reversed? Like Weber before him, Ritzer is doubtful. He encourages people to create less rationalized niches in order to live a less dehumanized life, but the plain fact is that most people today like McDonaldized efficiency, calculability, and predictability, and perhaps even control.

SOCIAL CHANGE IN THE DEVELOPING WORLD

Social change, globalization, and development go hand in hand. This section of the chapter focuses on **developing nations,** the United Nations designation

for those less developed countries (LDCs) with poverty-level incomes per capita. They are characterized by agriculturally based economies, high levels of illiteracy, joblessness, overpopulation, and reliance on raw materials for export. Most of these nations are in Africa, Asia, Latin America, the Caribbean, and the South Pacific. Even among these nations, some are more developed than others. Since there is no simple way to classify the world in discrete categories of "development," it is best to view the regions and nations of the world according to indicators that make some richer or poorer than others. We will see how these indicators are based on a nation's *political economy* (Chapter 18) and largely determine how it fares in the process of globalization.

Development, Capitalism, and Democracy

Aid to other nations for both political and humanitarian purposes has been an ingredient of United States foreign policy almost from its founding. After World War II, the United States ushered in a strategy linking foreign aid with development. Newly independent countries (NICs), such as Nigeria, Kenya, and India, had weak economies. To obtain badly needed capital and economic assistance, they could turn to the rich world of North America and Europe or to the newly formed Communist bloc. Many NICs preferred the former option, in part because communist nations were struggling with development issues of their own and offered more in military aid but less in

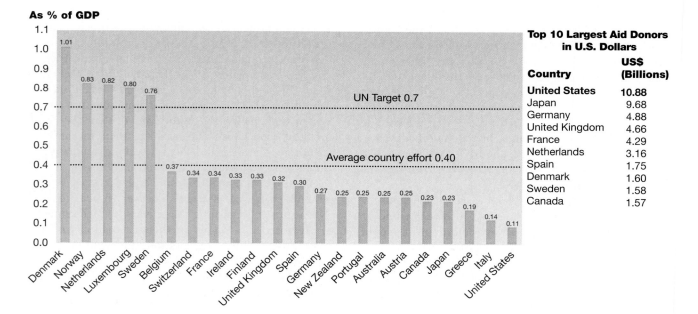

FIGURE 24.3 **Official Development Assistance (ODA) from OECD Countries, 2001.**

Source: Adapted from Organisation for Economic Co-operation and Development, 2002 "A Mixed Picture of Official Development Assistance in 2001." http://www.oecd.org/dac/stats.

development assistance (Arnold, 1988). Although the United States provides less of its Gross National Product to foreign aid than almost any other developed country (see Figure 24.3), developing nations depend on U.S. aid to bolster their infrastructures through agriculture, housing, health, and education programs. In simple humanitarian terms, development assistance allows millions of people worldwide to survive.

Foreign aid also helped assure that the NICs remained sympathetic to Western political and economic aims. Even following the disintegration of the Soviet system, the political goal behind foreign aid persists: Development assistance is designed to diffuse democracy and capitalism to the developing world.

The United States Agency for International Development (USAID) is the major foreign economic assistance program of the U.S. government; it promotes long-term and equitable economic growth in developing nations. USAID encourages economic reforms through programs offering the most economic growth with the least amount of government intervention and control. Since USAID also believes that people should not suffer from actions that will eventually improve their lives, it puts a high priority on cushioning the effects of reform on the poor (USAID, 2002). However, as a key agency of U.S. foreign policy, this priority poses a dilemma: USAID's humanitarian goal of reducing poverty often works against its political goal of spreading capitalism and democracy.

With the end of the Cold War, liberal democracy made great strides globally and ushered in the belief that economic and political liberalism go hand in hand (Fukuyama, 1992). Rapid economic growth across the globe during the next two decades strengthened the assertion that democracy, capitalism, and development thrive on one another (see Chapter 18). This assertion highlights both the economic failures of the Communist bloc and research documenting that democratic participation infuses development, enhances social equity, and favorably impacts economic and individual well-being (Eisler et al., 1995; Gills, 2000; Bauer, 2002). Democracies have the strongest economic performance, even when controlling for initial economic conditions and economic shocks like war and natural disaster (Brenner, 2002; Nagel, 2002). LDCs with the lowest level of political rights have the slowest gains in overall human development and respect for human rights (Cingranelli & Richards, 1999). The argument that highly authoritarian governments can reverse economic chaos in LDCs is not convincing (Nagel, 2001; Boaz, 2002).

When the government of an LDC is accountable to its citizens and committed to implementing social change through policies encouraging high levels of citizen participation, economic development and socioeconomic equality are enhanced (Wickrama &

Mulford, 1996). A good example is Kerala, a state in democratic India with a long tradition of participatory democracy, relatively equitable distribution of income, lower fertility rate, and a history of providing more public funding for primary and secondary education, worker training, and industrial expansion than do other Indian states. Kerala's investment in its people is associated with its strong record of economic development (Repetto, 1995; Heller, 1997; Ramanathaiyer & MacPherson, 2000).

CRITIQUE. Two major criticisms are leveled at the democracy-capitalism-development link. First, critics charge that the link ignores the fact that capitalism is becoming more diverse and is better seen as a family of subsystems rather than as one system. In the emerging democracies of Russia and Central and Eastern Europe, capitalism exists in an incredibly complex universe of market economies (Anders, 2002; Marangos, 2002). These economies may be called capitalistic because they are fast becoming privatized and market-driven. At the same time, they retain major elements of the earlier Soviet model of worker ownership and collective styles of management (Logue & Bell, 2000; Kotz, 2001).

Governments of these new market economies actively seek foreign investment wherever they can get it, whether from private investors, multinational corporations, authoritarian regimes such as Saudi Arabia, or democratic ones such as Germany and Canada (Garibaldi et al., 2001; Schiller et al., 2000; Head & Ries, 2002). Overall, capitalism takes a different form in LDCs than in the developed world because most developing world countries adapt their styles of capitalism to collectivistic values. Western capitalism is more consistent with cultural values related to individualism. Indeed, the cultural value of individualism translates to the "market individualism" on which capitalism was founded (Moore, 1997; Brown & Lauder, 2001).

Many LDCs adopt *state capitalism*—a model where government projects are financed with public funds, but the projects function under market conditions. Like other forms of capitalism, this form is also extremely varied (Howard & King, 2001; Liodakis, 2001). Some countries, such as South Korea, Taiwan, Hungary, and Poland, have achieved strong economic growth under fairly rigid, state-controlled economic policies, while other countries, such as Tanzania and Peru, have suffered under state capitalism. Singapore, Mexico, Brazil, Oman, and Bahrain have experienced rapid growth despite one-party or military rule (Huang & Marshall, 1997; O'Reilly, 1999; Greskovits & Bohle, 2001).

Capitalism thrives today in some developing nations characterized by high degrees of political repression, such as Saudi Arabia, the Gulf States, and

Aid as a Percent of GDP, 1980–2006

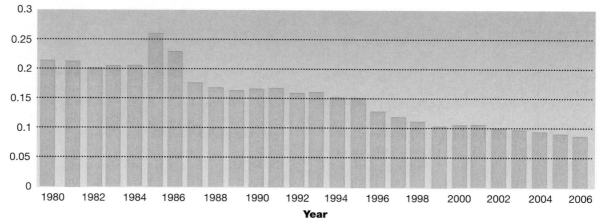

Who Receives ODA/OA (US$ million)

Top Ten Recipients of Gross ODA

1. Russia (OA)	1,154
2. Israel (OA)	967
3. Egypt	799
4. Ukraine (OA)	282
5. Indonesia	194
6. Jordan	179
7. Colombia	169
8. Bosnia and Herzegovina	152
9. India	148
10. Peru	136

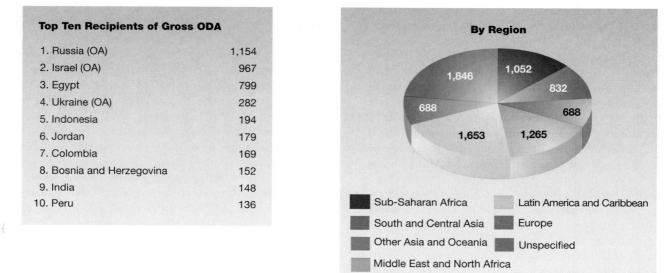

By Region

- Sub-Saharan Africa
- South and Central Asia
- Other Asia and Oceania
- Middle East and North Africa
- Latin America and Caribbean
- Europe
- Unspecified

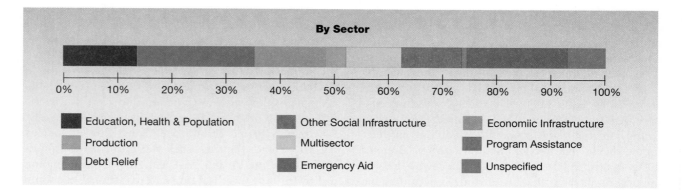

By Sector

- Education, Health & Population
- Production
- Debt Relief
- Other Social Infrastructure
- Multisector
- Emergency Aid
- Economiic Infrastructure
- Program Assistance
- Unspecified

FIGURE 24.4   **United States Spending on Official Development Assistance (ODA).**

*Official Development Assistance or Official Aid

Sources: Center on Budget and Policy Priorities, Office of Management and Budget, 2002. *Figures for 2002–2006 estimated from budget proposal; Organisation for Economic Co-operation and Development, 2002. "Aid and Debt Statistics: Donor Aid Charts." http:www.oecd/org/dac/stats.

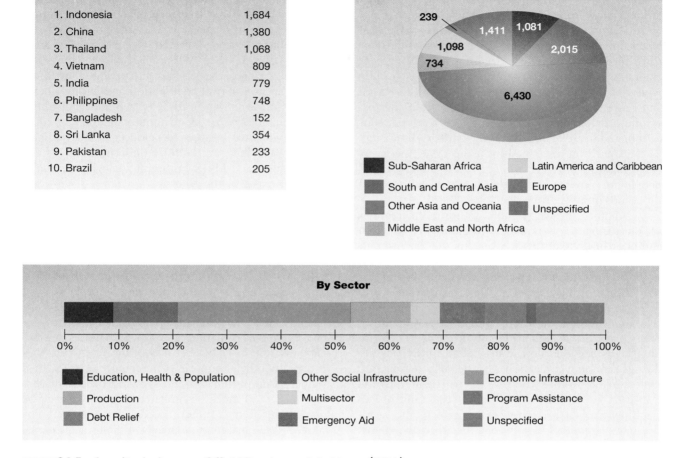

Who Receives ODA (US$ million)

Top Ten Recipients of Gross ODA

1. Indonesia	1,684
2. China	1,380
3. Thailand	1,068
4. Vietnam	809
5. India	779
6. Philippines	748
7. Bangladesh	152
8. Sri Lanka	354
9. Pakistan	233
10. Brazil	205

By Region

239, 1,411, 1,081, 1,098, 2,015, 734, 6,430

- Sub-Saharan Africa
- South and Central Asia
- Other Asia and Oceania
- Middle East and North Africa
- Latin America and Caribbean
- Europe
- Unspecified

By Sector

0% 10% 20% 30% 40% 50% 60% 70% 80% 90% 100%

- Education, Health & Population
- Production
- Debt Relief
- Other Social Infrastructure
- Multisector
- Emergency Aid
- Economic Infrastructure
- Program Assistance
- Unspecified

FIGURE 24.5 Spending by Japan on Official Development Assistance (ODA) (US$ million).

Source: Organisation for Economic Co-operation and Development, 2002. "Aid and Debt Statistics: Donor Aid Charts." http:www.oecd/org/dac/stats.

China. A good example of this connection is found in China's Special Economic Zones (SEZ) where capitalism has exploded. Although the government restricts migration and carefully monitors who is to be employed in these zones, they are designated as places where a market system can operate relatively unencumbered. The Chinese use SEZs to entice foreign investors, offering incentives such as cheap labor for investors to build and operate the factories. However, China carefully oversees the entire investment process, ensures that Chinese managers are installed in the businesses, and monitors how globalization will be acted out when it takes place on their turf (Zhang & Kristensen, 2001; Yan, 2002).

The second criticism of the democracy-capitalism-development link is that poverty initially increases when a nation makes the transition to a market economy. The World Bank provides loans for development projects, and the International Monetary Fund (IMF) promotes international trade and monitors the currencies of the globe. The IMF gives the "seal of approval" to the World Bank for its loans to LDCs. These two agencies have become the custodians of much of the world's economic investment. Backed by the IMF, the World Bank will provide loans for economic development if an LDC agrees to **structural adjustment (SA)**—conditions requiring economies be restructured to permit liberalization of their markets by eliminating barriers to trade and investment. They must offer market-driven approaches free of government regulation. A new generation of super-rich has emerged with such approaches, but the gap between rich and poor has widened and pushed many people in LDCs into poverty (Haseler, 2000; Khor, 2001).

To meet SA conditions, many nations in sub-Saharan Africa and Latin America were forced to cut in half already limited funding for programs in education, health, subsidies to farmers, and worker training. Not only did these cuts stall gains in public health and literacy, wages to poor people declined and many farmers were forced off their lands (Saul & Leys, 1999; Toussaint, 1999; Orjiako, 2001). IMF loan rescheduling in Mexico required that subsidies for basic foods be eliminated, resulting in a 50 percent cut in minimum wages and an increase in absolute poverty for 10 million people (Kelly, 1999). In Russia and Eastern Europe, the cushion the former socialist system provided in the way of subsidies for food, education, and health care have been virtually eliminated. In the transition to capitalism in the 1990s the Russian economy collapsed, forcing many "middle-class" people into poverty and further impoverishing tens of thousands more (D'Intino & Sinisi, 2001).

Calls for a return to more authoritarian regimes are increasing in some LDCs. The chasm between rich and poor in Russia is made worse by the rise of organized crime and stolen assets by corrupt officials. With a central government unwilling or unable to monitor the effects of privatization, Russia's entrance into democracy is filled with despair rather than hope (Holmstrom & Smith, 2000; Merkl, 2000). Capitalism offers growth but insecurity; socialism offers security but stagnation (Gordon, 2001). The initial poverty during economic transition may become permanent. Unless market reform can ease the pain caused by the transition to capitalism and LDCs can catch up to wealthier nations through economic growth, the "security but stagnation" belief reemerges to work against both democracy and development (Braguinsky & Yavlinsky, 2000; Haynes & Husan, 2000).

The Global Economy

International economic interdependence has existed in some form for centuries. The current model is based on the concept of a **global economy**, the multitude of commodity exchanges uniting consumers and producers across the globe. *Global* is a more inclusive concept than *international* because there is a tighter bond between consumers and producers as well as between regions, cities, and even neighborhoods (McMichael, 1996). The theories of global stratification introduced in Chapter 10 are concerned with the emergence of the global economy.

The global economy in the 21st century is different from earlier models in several important ways. The global marketplace is no longer dominated by one or two nations, so economic power is more widely distributed. There has also been a massive increase in international trade, and both production and sales have been internationalized (Kim, 1999). The extent to which financial markets have internationalized is demonstrated by the swift repercussions of

stock market crashes in Asia, Europe, Latin America, and United States in 1987, 1997, and 2000. For example, the devaluation of the Thai baht in 1997 rapidly resulted in a currency crisis throughout Asia (Kobayashi, 1999). Asia's LDC economies, which depend heavily on Japanese trade, investment, and imports, continue to be buffeted by Japan's rocky stock market (Lim, 2001). Multinational corporations, and their migrating managers and fluctuating labor force, require more political cooperation and cultural flexibility to meet market needs. For better or worse, the global economy virtually guarantees greater economic interdependence between developed and developing nations (Daniels et al., 2002; Sullivan, 2002). Economic gains and losses in one nation will eventually be experienced by the others.

In addition, the global economy in the 21st century will be boosted by multinational corporations—powerful economic players that came of age after the Cold War and that now influence the destinies of million of people. **Multinational corporations (MNCs)**, also called *transnational corporations*, are large private businesses operating in several countries. Some MNCs are so large and extended and exert such enormous economic impact that they may be outside the control of any single government (Haley, 2001). MNC's may escape taxation in LDCs because of the ease of moving capital to other countries where they operate. In a global economy that is rapidly growing, market-driven, and more and more laissez-faire, democracy may be compromised if corporate needs win out over employee needs as well as the needs of the broader population in nation where MNCs do business (Kingston, 2000; Melman, 2001; Tabb, 2002).

QUALITY OF LIFE AND POVERTY The data are somewhat confusing when trying to sort out the overall effect of the global economy on the well-being of people in the developing world. Important quality of life indicators such as access to education and improvements in health have improved in most LDCs (Chapters 19 and 20). Employment opportunities for workers in LDCs have also increased, especially in the clothing and small electronics industries. Jobs are moving from the developed to the developing world at a dramatic rate and provide a livelihood for masses of rural migrants to urban areas. On the other hand, the emergence of the global economy is correlated with the increase in poverty worldwide. The global economy is not growing fast enough to absorb the one-fourth of the world's population already living in absolute poverty.

THE INFORMAL SECTOR The vast majority of those who do live in absolute poverty eke out an unstable and marginal existence; most of them earn less than one dollar a day. They labor long and hard but either they do not receive pay or the pay they do receive is undocumented in a nation's Gross Domestic Product or other traditional economic indicators (OECD, 2002). Often referred to as the "underground economy," these people in the **informal sector** include subsistence farmers, street vendors, and the mass of urban laborers who work in home-based and small-scale production. Other informal sector jobs are prostitution, child care, and domestic work performed by women. Because of lack of training and education, they cannot fit the employment needs of the global economy's formal sector. Informal sector labor is usually based on casual arrangements, kinship, and personal relationships rather than on contracts or formal guarantees (International Labour Organization, 2000, 2002). They lose out on any social protections a job "contract" offers, such as health insurance, sick pay, retirement benefits, and collective bargaining (Unni & Rani, 2001).

Although informal sector work is not counted in official economic figures, the work itself makes an enormous contribution to the economies of the LDCs. More than half of the developing world's labor force is self-employed, and most of these people work in the informal sector. Informal sector employment in sub-Saharan Africa is almost 75 percent and in Asia it is 63 percent (Charmes, 2000). On the consumer side, the informal sector fills a "poverty niche" not provided by the formal sector for the world's poor. Money may be exchanged for goods or services, but often barter between workers and consumers provides the exchange basis. The informal sector makes it possible to understand the overlooked but vital economic forces that contribute to the survival of the poor.

Since the global economy is boosted by structural adjustment policies that look toward long-term growth, it may take another generation to determine their success in spurring development. We already know that many countries are mired in the "catch-up process" that has served to make matters worse for the poor in LDCs, especially those in the informal sector. Thus, for now it is difficult to determine the extent to which the global economy has impacted quality of life in rural or urban areas in LDCs and whether the poor have been largely helped or harmed. However, when considering overall regions of the world, it appears that Asia is faring much better than Africa.

THE PACIFIC CENTURY With Asia's increasingly powerful role in the global economy, the new millennium has been hailed as the "Pacific Century" (Foot & Walter, 1999). Japan and China take the commanding roles. Japan's spectacular economic growth has fueled the economies of their neighbors and trans-Pacific trade overall (Kingston, 2001; Nakagane, 2002). Almost three-fourths of Japan's foreign aid stays in Asia (see Figure 24.5 on page 658). Even with Japan's stock market woes, its economy is con-

With massive foreign investment, cheap labor, giant manufacturing plants and the 1997 return of Hong Kong, which also houses the world's largest container port (only a small part of it shown here), China is fueling Asia's rapidly expanding role in the lucrative global economy. One result is that the 21st century has been hailed as the "Pacific Century."

sidered rich and strong enough to weather various economic crises internally and maintain economic dominance in the region (Kanaya & Woo, 2001; Pilat, 2002). China's commanding role is tied to the acquisition of rich Hong Kong, massive economic growth in Shanghai, the positive effect of globalization of its economy, and the most sweeping economic liberalization policies in Chinese history, all of which helped gain China's entrance into the World Trade Organization (Guo, 2001; Bhattasali & Kawai, 2002). China is fast becoming the largest and most lucrative market in the world. Overseas Chinese also contribute to China's economy, as investors, as managers of MNCs, and in economic assistance to relatives on the Mainland. If China can deal with other development issues it faces, such as the grinding poverty, illiteracy, and gender inequity facing its rural people and the religious and cultural turmoil impacting its ethnic minorities, China is likely to overtake Japan as the dominant force in Asia's political economy before mid-century (Lindsey, 1999; Brown, 2000; Mok et al., 2002).

Life chances have also improved throughout most of Asia. In closing the global human development gap, the most successful countries are in East Asia, with Taiwan, South Korea, Hong Kong, and Singapore

SOCIOLOGY OF EVERYDAY LIFE

Refugees: Past, Present, and Uncertain Future

There is no greater sorrow on earth than the loss of one's native land.
—Euripides, 431 BC

On December 10, 1948, the United Nations proclaimed the Universal Declaration of Human Rights (see Table 24.1 on page 666) that established the principle of asylum for refugees. The Declaration was prompted by the Holocaust of World War II, which propelled thousands of Jews into refugee status. In 1950 the United Nations High Commissioner for Refugees (UNHCR) was established on a three-year mandate to aid the remaining victims of World War II and then go out of business. Not only did the first European crises not go away, but over a half century of war, famine, and natural disaster has exploded into today's global refugee emergency: 1 in every 300 people in the world is a refugee. With the help of NGOs, U.N.-sponsored refugee camps dot the globe and attest to UNHCR's expanded mission. Consider the following facts demonstrating the profound importance of that mission:

- After helping resettle more than 1 million World War II refugees, UNHCR aided a huge refugee population fleeing into Austria from the Hungarian uprising in 1956.
- By 1969 Africa became the epicenter for refugees, and by the 1980s half

the world's refugees were in Africa. In 1974, thousands of Burundi refugees fled to Tanzania from war. Half a million Eritreans escaped to Sudan during the 30-year war following Ethiopia's annexation of Eritrea in 1962. Ethiopians themselves became internal refugees by famine coming in the wake of war. Since then, millions of Africans have been uprooted from their homelands. In 1994, as many as 1 million were massacred in Rwanda's genocide, and thousands of refugees died later from cholera in huge camps set up in neighboring countries. Refugees from Liberia and Sierra Leone displaced by ongoing civil war and famine have flooded U.N. camps in West Africa.

- In the 1980s civil war racked El Salvador and Nicaragua, and swept through Central America. UNHCR, USAID, and other agencies offered support. Many refugees were granted asylum in the United States.
- Hundreds of thousands fled Viet Nam and Cambodia in the early 1980s. Asylum was offered by Britain, Germany, and the United States to those targeted by the communists because they aided the United States during the Viet Nam War.
- In the late 1970s and throughout the 1980s over a million Afghans fled into Pakistan and Iran with the Soviet invasion. When the Soviets left, many who returned home were forced to flee

again when civil war erupted and human rights abuses in Taliban-controlled regions became widespread. At its peak in 1990, the Afghan refugee population reached 6 million, making it the world's largest humanitarian crisis.

- The refugee crisis came full circle when UNHCR again aided refugees in Europe. The Balkan/Kosovo crisis and civil war in former Yugoslavia produced millions of new refugees from all nationalities, ethnic groups, and religions.
- Throughout its history, UNHCR has been plagued with safety issues in refugee camps. Rape of refugee women, theft of supplies, and forced recruitment of men and boys are always threats.

In 2002 the total number of "official" refugees worldwide approached 20 million. But this number reaches 50 million when counting uprooted people who remain in their own countries or those who wander between safe havens and remain uncounted. It also does not include almost 4 million displaced Palestinians who are covered under the U.N. Relief and Works Agency. Thirty countries host between 50,000 and 100,000 refugees, and three countries—Iran, Pakistan and Germany—host between 1 and 2 million. The good news is that millions of refugees have returned home. These include 1.3 million Rwandans, 1.8 million

---

leading the pack. Life expectancy is higher and infant mortality is lower in these countries than in the United States. And with such robust economies, these countries are no longer considered part of the "developing world." Southeast Asia's LDCs, such as Thailand, Malaysia, and Indonesia, have rapidly improved their standard of living and are becoming the world's most important manufacturing centers (Grayson & Smith, 2001; Hewison, 2001; Embong, 2002). Vietnam is focusing on international engagement, encouraging foreign investment, and retreating from a cen-

trally planned economy, all of which are helping its economy to rebound (Pierre, 2000; Beresford, 2001). South Asia is still lagging behind its neighbors, but India has reduced the proportion of people in poverty by 25 percent in two decades, and its electronic industries are booming. Pakistan is making rapid gains in literacy, and Nepal, one of Asia's poorest countries, has almost doubled its human development rating since 1975 (World Bank, 2002). The terrorist attacks have drawn the world's attention to Central Asia, and that attention has sparked a great deal of economic

Country of Origin	Host Country	Total
Afghanistan	Pakistan / Iran	3,809,600
Burundi	Tanzania	554,000
Iraq	Iran	530,100
Sudan	Uganda / Ethiopia / D.R. Congo / Kenya / C.A.R.	489,500
Angola	Zambia / D.R. Congo / Namibia	470,600
Somalia	Kenya / Yemen / Ethiopia / USA / United Kingdom	439,900
Bosnia-Herzegovina	Yugoslavia / USA / Sweden / Denmark / Netherlands	426,000
Democratic Rep. Congo	Tanzania / Congo / Zambia / Rwanda / Burundi	392,100
Vietnam	China / USA	353,200

Origins of Major Refugee Populations
Source: UNHCR, 2002.

civilians throughout the Balkans, 2 million Kurds returning to Iraq after the Gulf War, and thousands of young Eritreans who had never set foot in their homeland. UNHCR announced that refugee status will end for the 207,000 East Timorese who returned home without incident after the 1999 war of independence. To date Afghanistan has the largest number of returnees—almost 2 million. Afghanistan's new government wants to stage a carefully structured "repatriation" process; if the almost 4 million Afghans eagerly waiting to return do so too quickly, it could swamp the nation's infrastructure and threaten its fragile recovery.

What does the future hold for the enormous number of uprooted people worldwide? Money donated to NGOs working with refugees is at an all-time high, but economic downturns and the fear of terrorism and war ever present on the horizon have prompted many countries to make asylum more difficult. Hosting refugees does not guarantee that they will be given asylum in the host country. The United States has resettled more refugees than any other country—close to 70,000 in 2001—but cannot accommodate all asylum seekers. An average of thirty-five civil wars raged globally in the last five years, and UNHCR reports that citizens in "safe" countries are afraid of being engulfed by refugees. UNHCR and the NGOs who work in refugee assistance must convince the world that international cooperation is vital and that refugee resettlement and asylum is in everyone's best interest.

Forced displacement is both a cause and effect of political instability. The refugee crisis is in essence a crisis related to global interdependence. Both functionalist and conflict theorists agree that it cannot be solved by nations acting alone. Political unrest and ethnic conflict will escalate in the developed world if it fails to realistically deal with the refugee issue. The challenge of the new millennium will be to ensure the security of all people. Unless people feel secure in their own homes, the security of nations all over the world will be threatened.

1. Demonstrate how the refugee crisis is related to global interdependence.

2. What solutions to the refugee crisis would be offered by conflict theorists and functionalists?

Sources: Wilkinson, 2000; Kanhema & Rappeport, 2001; del Mundo, 2002; UNHCR, 2002; World of Refugee Women, 2002.

infusion into the region. The jury is still out on North Korea, which remains mired in famine after decades of economic chaos and political isolation. Amid allegations of North Korea's nuclear buildup, cautious but optimistic dialogues with South Korea and its Asian neighbors have been jeopardized (Jeffries, 2001; BBC, 2002). When dialogue is re-opened, North Korea's entrance as a novice partner in the global economy is likely to be encouraged. Overall, Asia's LDCs should be in a better position to decrease their dependency relationship to the developed world.

THE AFRICAN CONTRAST Africa contrasts sharply with the economic progress of Asia. The bottom twenty-five countries in the World Bank's Human Development Index are all in Africa, and twenty-three of these are sub-Saharan nations (World Bank, 2002). Some of these countries have actually deteriorated on quality of life measures (Chapter 19) and many others remain wedged in ethnic conflict, political instability, and ongoing civil wars that have generated periodic famine and created a permanent refugee population. Ongoing crises require donors to use limited resources for short-term relief, which puts long-term development measures on hold.

However, there is some cautious optimism expressed with international trade agreements designed to enhance Africa's role in the global economy. These agreements are based on structural adjustment, foreign investment, and intense, overseas marketing of high-quality African products, including clothing, handicrafts, coffee, and tea (Mshomba, 2000; Gibbon, 2002). Sub-Saharan nations with higher levels of economic growth, including South Africa, Botswana, and Zambia, are also likely to have multiparty systems and high levels of local governance, and to be free of military rule (Bartlett, 2001; Marais, 2001; Hope, 2002).

Predictions for Africa's future are tied to market-friendly strategies and slower population growth, both of which have been more successful in Asia (Rodnik, 1999; Fosu & Senbet, 2001). How sub-Saharan Africa will fare in riding out the catch-up process of structural adjustment is even more unclear than in Asia. Life chances for millions of people will be decided by these strategies.

Nongovernmental Organizations

Fueled by the global economy, massive social change in the LDCs creates many dilemmas for development planners. Resolving these dilemmas to the benefit of the LDCs is one task of nongovernmental organizations (NGOs). **Nongovernmental organizations** are nonprofit groups primarily concerned with relief, development, and advocacy for the poor. Although most NGOs are privately funded, governments often channel assistance through them. Over half of USAID funds are channeled through hundreds of NGOs instead of governments. These NGOs are engaged in a variety of relief and long-term development assistance projects, such as refugee resettlement, famine relief, literacy, health enhancement, and agricultural improvement (Global Issues, 2002). With the advent of the Internet and email, people in remote regions have been able to organize with others around the world on behalf of the poor and disempowered (Mater, 2001; Welch, 2001). NGOs are often the first advocates for those who initially lack the resources to effectively lobby for themselves. The goal of many NGOs is to provide tools, such as leadership training, to ensure that those who are directly impacted by development have a strong voice in the process. Once grassroots leaders emerge, NGOs continue to offer mentoring and financial support but more as partners and less as supervisors in development programs (Smillie & Hailey, 2001). NGOs began in the 1970s, grew to adolescence in the 1980s, and came of age in the 1990s. It is estimated that over a half million NGOs are active around the globe (Lindenberg & Bryant, 2001; Brown & Kalegaonkar, 2002).

NGOs symbolize globalization. Their rapidly growing numbers and influence in the development arena have captured the attention of world leaders, politicians, and MNCs who seek out NGO expertise when development assistance programs are started or when new companies enter an LDC looking for cheap labor (Larson, 2002; Richardson & Allegrate, 2002). Global economic growth has raised expectations that positive social change is occurring. This growth helped create the urban middle class who have become the leaders in the NGOs of the developing world. As powerful as governments and MNCs are in a global economy oriented to profit, they can no longer ignore NGOs. Profit-making businesses and not-for-profit development programs—whether government controlled or not—can be in peril without NGO partnering. Since aid dollars are scarce, governments must now work with grassroots organizations or risk losing development funds entirely. Some observers believe that the rise of NGOs may be as significant for the 21st century as the rise of nation-states was for the 19th (Lewis & Wallace, 2000; Warkentin, 2001). As sociological conflict theory suggests, NGOs bring resources to the development table to get the most advantages for their constituents. Profit may rule the global economy, but NGOs watch the profit-making process to ensure that the poor can gain some benefit from it.

However, NGOs must accept the underlying reality that governmental agencies like USAID expect to have a substantial voice in how their aid is dispersed. Like many governments that disperse assistance funds, the United States expects aid recipients to work toward a free-market capitalistic economy and a democratic political system, even though these arrangements initially work to the disadvantage of the poor (Boas, 2001). Thus, NGOs have an important role in representing the interests of those who must weather the turmoil connected with the early stages of economic development.

LIFE CONNECTIONS

Microenterprise

Propelled by NGOs advocating for the world's poor, the informal sector of the global economy has been made more visible. Since large-scale development projects have largely ignored the informal sector where most of the poorest of the poor reside, **microenterprise programs** to address their needs have arisen. These programs consist of core segments of income-earning manufacturing or agricultural activities located in or around the household. Microenterprise is linked to the buzzword in the development assistance community, *microcredit*, or microenterprise lending, where groups of four or five borrowers receive small loans at commercial interest rates to start or expand small businesses and open their first savings accounts (Khandker, 1999). Peer lending is the most important feature of microcredit, so a group assumes responsibility for each other's loans: If one fails, they all fail (Conlin, 1999; Anderson et al., 2002).

Microcredit began twenty-five years ago when economic professor Muhammad Yunus founded the Grameen ("village") bank of Bangladesh and extended credit to people too poor to qualify for loans at other banks. The first microcredit lending came from his own pocket. He lent $26 to a group of 42 workers who bought materials for a day's work weaving chairs and making pots. At the end of the first day as independent business owners, they sold their wares, made a profit, and soon repaid the loan. The 62 cents per worker from the $26 loan began the microcredit movement (Micro-loans, 1997). The Grameen program was astonishingly successful. Not only did 97 percent repay their loans at a 20 percent interest rate, but their microenterprises became sustainable and allowed their families to survive.

Women and Microcredit

Microcredit works better for the very poor because the very poor are usually women. Muhammad Yunus noticed very early that women used profits from microenterprise activities to feed their children and build their businesses, whereas men spent profits on electronics and personal goods. A growing body of research suggests that when women have disposable income, it is used in ways to sustain their family's long-term needs, such as nutrition, health care, and education. In addition, data on Grameen Bank borrowers show women's loan repayment rates above 98 percent. Because social and economic benefits are much greater when money is loaned to women, the Grameen Bank decided to concentrate on them. Almost 2.5 million Grameen borrowers in Bangladesh are women, compared to about 125,000 men (*Grameen Dialogue*, 1999; Mahal & Lindgren, 2002). The successes of Grameen in Bangladesh have been replayed with microcredit schemes targeted to women in Peru, Philippines, Bolivia, and other parts of the developing world (Gow, 2000; Navajas et al., 2000; Ypeij, 2000). Microcredit is particularly effective in the developing world, since those countries are likely to have collectivistic cultures. In addition, it capitalizes on gender socialization patterns, which build cooperative networks among women from early in life.

CRITIQUE. Lending money to women through microcredit is not without a downside. Some research indicates that when women are lent money, men often gain control of the funds, making loan repayment difficult. These women do repay their loans but often under intense pressure from their peers and bank workers who may threaten public humiliation for failure to pay. Challenging cultural and religious norms about women's traditional roles may also increase household tension, and in turn domestic violence may escalate (Rahman, 1999). However, other research suggests that microcredit lending does offer women a major step to empowerment, cultural obstacles can be overcome, and women and their families, including the men, benefit as a result (Hays-Mitchell, 1999). As Grameen Bank founder Yunus notes:

> . . . each individual is very important. She alone can influence the lives of others within communities, nations within and beyond her own time. We need to build enabling environments to discover the limits of our potential. (Adapted from *Countdown 2005*, 1997:2)

Microenterprise: A Sociological Perspective

Along with the gender connection, from a sociological perspective the success of microcredit is related to three key factors. First, microcredit accounts for the informal sector in economic activities. Definitions of productive work include unpaid economic activities, most of which are performed by women. Borrowers can offer their weaving, domestic, or agricultural skills as "collateral," which would be dismissed by conventional lenders. Second, microcredit fits a "trickle-up" model of economic development, allowing the poor to participate directly in decisions impacting their lives. Money flows "up" to families and communities from the poor who directly receive it. This approach differs greatly from the traditional "trickle-down" model, which assumes that when development money is provided to manufacturers or other formal-sector institutions, jobs for the poor will be created (Fujita, 2001; Hassan, 2002). Trickle-down models support modernization theory, structural adjustment, the expansion of multinational corporations, and the belief that LDCs will follow the same path of development as in the West. Third, money is channeled through NGOs who work directly with the poor, often as volunteers, rather than through government channels. This minimizes bureaucratic entanglements, saves time, and reduces overhead costs. Overall, a sociological perspective bolsters other research suggesting that microcredit lending is a viable grassroots policy for international development (Snow & Buss, 2001; Woller & Woodworth, 2001).

The Grameen model has been replayed in over forty-five countries. Although microcredit appears to hold more promise for success in the world's poorest countries, such as Bangladesh, its model has been successfully adapted to the developed world, including the United States (Graham & Manning, 2000; Sanders, 2002). The promise microcredit holds for the world's poor was officially recognized with the "Microenterprise for Self-Reliance Act of 2000" (reauthorized in 2002), which pledges $200 million of USAID funding per year specifically for microenterprise assistance projects through 2006. Microcredit is a very small part of the foreign aid package of the United States, but its strategies for successful development projects abroad are being monitored carefully by NGOs and public agencies serving the developed world (Carr & Tong, 2002). Microenterprise demonstrates that globalization flows in many directions and that successful LDCs can offer guidance to its neighbors in the developed world (Snow et al., 2001).

SOCIETY CONNECTIONS

The New Consensus on Human Rights

In 1993 the United Nations convened the World Conference of Human Rights, bringing together 171 nations and scores of NGOs in the largest gathering of its kind in history. *Human rights* are those rights inherent to human beings in any culture (Chapter 3). They include not only civil and political rights, but also economic, social, and cultural rights, all of which should be enjoyed and protected. Even as attendees signed off on the Declaration (see Table 24.1), thorny issues related to development, social change, and cultural interference remained unresolved.

The United Nations has long maintained that economic and social development cannot proceed without the political freedom to participate in the process, including dissent. However, some governments argued that restricting political freedoms is

INTERNET CONNECTIONS

Go to the "Human Rights Watch" site:

http://www.hrw.org/un/

Read the contents of this opening page. Then click on the articles and read the contents. After you have read a few articles answer the following questions: What is your personal stance on human rights issues? Do you think that American society should pay more attention to human rights worldwide? If so, what more should be done to ensure these rights? If not, why not?

TABLE **24.1**

The Universal Declaration of Human Rights

1. All humans are born free and equal in dignity and rights.

2. Everyone is entitled to all rights and freedoms set forth in this Declaration without distinction of any kind, such as race, color, sex, language, religion, political or other opinion, national or social origin.

3. Everyone has a right to life, liberty, and security.

4. No one shall be held in slavery or servitude.

5. No one shall be subject to torture or to cruel, inhuman, or degrading treatment or punishment.

6. All are equal before the law and entitled to equal protection of the law.

7. Everyone has the right to seek and to enjoy in other countries asylum from persecution.

8. Everyone has the right to a nationality.

9. Everyone has the right to freedom of peaceful assembly and association.

10. Everyone has the right to work and to just conditions of work.

11. Everyone has the right to a standard of living adequate for health and well-being.

12. Everyone has the right to education.

13. Everyone has duties to the community in which the full development of one's personality is possible.

Abridged from the Declaration proclaimed by the General Assembly of the United Nations on December 10, 1948.
Source: Reoch, 1994.

---

necessary to jumpstart their economies. Other delegates argued that the very idea of universal human rights conflicts with some of their cultural practices and customs, specifically related to religion and the roles of women (Lerner, 2000). Still others wanted to divorce civil rights, which are easier to agree on, from economic rights. In their eyes, the issue of development should be completely separated from the issue of human rights (Webster & Cingarell, 1998). This is despite the fact that thirty articles in the Declaration specify those socioeconomic rights which are at the core of the globe's development efforts. The split between the developed and developing nations on these was apparent with charges that the Declaration itself was nothing more than "bourgeois rights" or "Western rights" (Reoch, 1994).

LDCs have a strong case that the West imprinted the Declaration in line with its own economic interests. Data on the negative impact of economic programs that help business but hurt the poor because of decreased government help are used to bolster the LDC case. NGOs working directly with LDCs are more supportive of this side of the debate. Some social scientists also support the LDC side, since it is consistent with *cultural relativism* (Chapter 3). Yet when cultural relativism is used as a banner to oppress or deny human rights, scientists, like other citizens around the globe, are much less supportive (Macklin, 1999; Dembour, 2001). On the other hand, developed nations point to data showing that development is more successful in democracies and serves the interests of *most* people across the globe. A favorable economic environment is a necessary condition for social equity. Powerful international financial institutions are more supportive of this side of the argument. Many scientists also support this side, maintaining that science needs a free and open atmosphere to conduct its work, and democracy provides the best option.

Sociology and the Human Rights Debate

The debate about human rights is far from resolved. However, sociological insights that we have encountered throughout the text shed light on the debate and may help with its eventual resolution. First, of all the social institutions, the economy is the major engine for social change, and economic development is a necessary condition for improved social equity. The Declaration supports this principle. Second, new patterns of global cooperation are needed if development is to succeed. Sociological theory helps explain these patterns, and sociological research offers good indicators to measure the progress of development. Third, sociological work on multiculturalism in the global economy bolsters the Declaration's emphasis on the rights of minorities. These rights include developing their own culture, speaking their own language, and practicing their own religion as they see fit. Since minorities may include women, people with disabilities, the aged, gay men and lesbians, among others, the Declaration embraces cultural relativism.

It is the cultural relativism issue that sociologists point to as the most difficult one to resolve. Can ethnic diversity and minority rights be accommodated in nations with governments organized and defined according to ethnicity or religion (Brems, 2001; Henrard, 2002)? As civil wars in Rwanda, Somalia, Cambodia, and Bosnia so vividly demonstrate, such governments all too commonly discriminate against minorities. Genocide is one result. Cultural relativism cannot be defended when any minority is denied access to a livelihood. For example, women, who are also a minority group, have been denied employment, health care, and education in support of an Islamic countermoderniza-

Economic progress in sub-Saharan Africa is stalled when women are kept out of school and cannot earn income because they are expected to marry early and take on all domestic tasks, including food production. However, when microenterprise and other training programs allow women to earn cash, they are likely to spend it on educating both their sons and daughters.

Fundamentalists in religious states who believe that Western influence compromises religious integrity often create gender segregated schools where boys learn to read the holy scriptures, such as this school for Pakistani and Afghan boys near the Afghanistan border in Peshawar. Female illiteracy in religious states is often quite high since girls may be denied any or all but a minimal education, which raises the issue that their human rights are violated.

tion movement. Cultural relativism, which is supposed to be beneficial, is used to the disadvantage of women and other minorities across the globe (Afkhami, 2001; Coomaraswamy, 2001; Merry, 2001).

Human rights are also supported by the democratizing influence of the media. Television has forever etched on the global consciousness the jubilation when the Berlin Wall fell and the tragedy of Tiananmen Square. The emergence of a worldwide electronic network of NGOs, including groups such as Amnesty International and Human Rights Watch, also monitors governments on human rights (Brown, 2001; Winston, 2001). And when considering the consequences of terrorism on innocent people who

occupy the same religious, ethnic, or racial groups as the terrorists, global monitoring of human rights becomes even more important.

Despite ongoing debates, the die appears to be cast in support of human rights. Worldwide consensus on human rights is clearly emerging, Activists, politicians, and ordinary citizens insist that economic development proceed only within a human rights framework (Arts, 2000; Crawford, 2001). And, as sociology tells us over and over again, rapidly increasing global interdependence cannot help but aid progress in translating the concept of universal human rights to reality.

SUMMARY

1. Social change is a feature of all societies. However, its pace has increased dramatically over the past few centuries. Cultural change may take the form of invention, discovery, or diffusion. Resistance to change is motivated by cultural inertia and promoted by the actions of vested interests.

2. Major sources of social change include the natural environment, demographic change, new ideas and technologies, government, competition and war, deliberate planning, and social movements.

3. Cyclical theory sees societies as moving through long-term, directionless phases of growth and decay. Evolutionary theory suggests that societies tend to change in the direction of greater complexity and increased institutional differentiation.

4. Classic functional theory interpreted most social change as an effort to restore systemic equilibrium. Conflict theory sees change as a natural consequence of struggles between competing groups for scarce resources.

5. Over the past two hundred years, large parts of the world have undergone modernization. The fully developed nations are now moving into a postindustrial phase.

6. Sociologists working in the Durkheimian tradition regard the rise of anomie and the consequent weakening of the social bond as a major problem of contemporary developed societies.

7. Post-Marxist conflict theorists like Ralf Dahrendorf have redefined the problem of class struggle in terms of the broader concept of authority relations.

8. George Ritzer, working in the Weberian tradition, sees McDonaldization as an extension of bureaucratic rationality.

9. U.S. foreign aid to the developing world is provided to promote development, reduce poverty, and spread capitalism and democracy,

10. Structural adjustment to developing nations is designed to open markets free of government control, but it also serves to initially increase poverty.

11. Multinational corporations, nongovernmental organizations, and the informal sector of workers whose economic output is not officially counted are all important contributors to the global economy.

12. With Japan and China in the lead, Asia is increasing its power in the global economy. Sub-Saharan Africa lags much further behind in economic growth.

13. Microenterprise and microcredit lending programs allowing the very poor, mostly women, to start small businesses are among the most important development assistance programs. Their successes in the developing nations have been replicated in developed nations.

14. Despite issues about cultural relativism, especially related to religion, an international consensus on basic human rights is emerging.

KEY TERMS

countermodernization 652
developing nations 656
development 643
global economy 660
globalization 643
informal sector 661
McDonaldization 655
microenterprise programs 664

modernity 650
multilinear evolutionary theory 649
multinational corporations (MNCs) 660
nongovernmental organizations (NGOs) 664
postindustrial society 650
postmodernism 650

social capital 653
social change 643
structural adjustment 659
technologies 646
unilinear evolutionary theory 648
vested interests 645

CRITICAL THINKING QUESTIONS

1. Americans have traditionally found evolutionary and functional theories of change more appealing than the cyclical and conflict approaches. What distinctive aspects of U.S. history and culture might help to explain this observation?

2. Which set of problems poses the most serious threat to developed societies: those identified by modern theorists working in the tradition of Durkheim, in the tradition of Marx, or in the tradition of Weber? Explain your reasoning.

3. How can the link between democracy and development be strengthened in LDCs that do not have capitalist systems? What role can NGOs play in this process?

4. How would the various theories of social change explain countermodernization? What predictions would each theory make regarding the likelihood that countermodernization efforts will be successful?

INVESTIGATE WITH CONTENT SELECT

 Begin your research using Content-Select for this chapter by following the directions found on page 27 of this text to visit Prentice Hall's Research Navigator Website. Enter these search terms into the search field:

Nongovernmental Organization
McDonaldization
Postmodernism

iNTERSECTIONS

EXERCISE 5. CHANGING GENDER ROLES

Americans growing up in the 1950s often pictured the ideal family as having a father (the "breadwinner") who left every weekday morning to earn money at work, and a mother (the "homemaker") who cleaned house, cooked, and took care of the children. How many people do you know who still regard these as the preferred gender roles?

GSS respondents were asked to agree or disagree with the statement, "It is much better for everyone involved if the man is the achiever outside the home and the woman takes care of the home and family." Forty-three percent agreed; 57 percent disagreed.

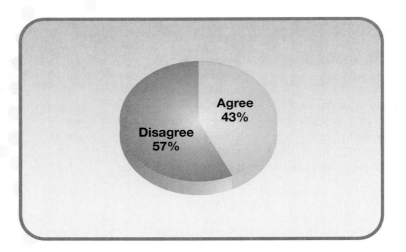

Do you think the people who came of age during the 1950s or earlier (probably including your parents or grandparents) are more likely to value these traditional gender roles than today's younger generation? Make a guess and check it out at the Companion Website™ for this text, http://www.prenhall.com/lindsey. Click on the cover of this book, and select the appropriate INTERSECTIONS exercise from the drop-down menu at the top. (Make sure CHIP is set for % Down, and its Row Variable is Fefam.)

Respondents are sorted into three age categories: young (18 to 35 years old), middle age (36 to 59 years old), and old (60+). See what percentage in each age category agrees with the traditional gender roles. Do you find a "generation gap" or not? If so, does it mostly separate the young from the middle aged, or the middle aged from older respondents?

Perhaps this question reveals some sexism in American society. It's hard to guess if men and women see eye to eye about traditional gender roles. Some men want to keep their wives in the kitchen, tending their babies; but other husbands value the income their wives bring in from outside jobs. Some wives want professional careers, but other women would rather be homemakers than "wage slaves." With CHIP, you can tell from the GSS whether men and women agree or not about traditional gender roles. What is the percentage of men who support the traditional roles? What is the percentage of women? Are these percentages much different?

Do you expect any racial difference in attitudes about traditional gender roles? Using CHIP, see if black and white respondents are similar or different in their views about each spouse's family obligations.

Finally, see if there are differences across social classes. Respondents named their social class as lower class, working class, middle class, or upper class. (You know from Exercise 3 that most people see themselves in the middle or working classes.) Which social class, if any, is most tied to the traditional roles? Do you see any continuous change in attitude as social class goes up (or down)?

Summarize your findings about traditional gender roles. What do you think best explains the generation gap in views? Do you think that as people age, they become more conservative (or wiser, or more stubborn)?

Do the many racial or class segments of American society adhere to traditional gender roles in different ways? Within each of these segments, would you guess that older respondents are more traditional than younger respondents? Can you think of any way to test that possibility using CHIP and the GSS? (Hint: Look at the relationship between Race and Fefam while controlling by Age.)

In a paragraph, summarize your major findings about differing views toward traditional gender roles. Then, in a separate paragraph, theorize why these differing views are present in American society today.

GLOSSARY

absolute poverty Poverty defined as an inability to satisfy basic needs for food, shelter, and clothing.

achieved status Statuses that we acquire over time as a result of our own actions.

acting crowd A type of crowd that directs its members' hostile emotions toward some external target.

activity theory Theory explaining that successful aging is linked to middle-aged norms, so roles should be continued, substituted, and expanded.

acute disease Characterized by sudden onset, rapid peak, and limited duration resulting in either recovery or death.

adaptation The process enabling a culture to maintain equilibrium despite fluctuations in the culture.

adversarial principle A legal tradition whereby guilt or innocence is determined by a contest between the prosecution and the defense.

affirmative action Employment policy that takes either voluntary or involuntary action to increase, maintain, or change the number, rank, or position of certain categories of employees, usually defined by their race or gender.

age grades Sets of behavioral expectations that are linked to chronological and biological age that change as we get older.

ageism Devaluation and negative stereotyping of the elderly.

agents of socialization The people, groups, and social institutions that provide the critical information needed for children to become fully functioning members of society.

age stratification theory Explains how society uses age strata or categories to make distinctions about people.

aggregate A collection of people who are physically at the same place at the same time but do not interact in any meaningful way.

aging-out A process by which crime rates decline sharply once individuals reach their mid-30s.

alienation Marx's term for a situation in which people are controlled by social institutions that seem beyond their ability to influence.

androcentrism Male-centered norms that operate throughout all social institutions and become the standard to which all people adhere.

animism The belief that supernatural beings or spirits inhabit living things and inanimate objects.

anticipatory socialization A process whereby people practice what they want to achieve.

applied sociology The view that sociologists should put their knowledge and skills to work in the real world.

ascribed status Statuses into which we are born and that we cannot change, or that we acquire involuntarily over the life course.

assimilation The process by which minorities shed their differences and blend in with the dominant group.

assortive mating A pattern in which coupling occurs based on similarity rather than chance.

authoritarian leader A leader who makes the major decisions for a group.

authoritarian regime A type of political system that excludes the people from any meaningful participation in decision making.

authority Power that is widely perceived by subordinates as legitimate.

beliefs Ideas and attitudes shared by a culture about what is considered true or false.

bilateral (bilineal) descent Most common in Western societies, a system that uses both mother and father to trace family lines.

birth cohort All the people born at a given point in time who age together and experience events in history as a group.

bisexual The category for people with shifting sexual orientations; they are sexually responsive to either gender.

blended families Also called reconstituted families, families in which children from parents' prior relationships are brought together in a new family.

bourgeoisie Marx's term for the class that owns the means of production.

bureaucracy A formal organization designed to allow large numbers of people to accomplish routine tasks in the most efficient possible way.

bureaucratic ritualism The tendency in bureaucracies to focus more on the rules than on the goal.

busing The transporting of children of different races to schools according to a racial parity formula to achieve school desegregation.

capitalism An economic system based on the private ownership of the means of production.

caste system A system of stratification made up of several sharply distinct ascribed groups or castes. Caste systems allow little or no social mobility.

casual crowd A simple type of crowd lacking significant emergent norms, structure, or leadership.

category Individuals who share a social status but do not interact.

census When a population is fully counted according to key demographic characteristics.

charismatic authority Weber's term for power legitimated by an individual's claim to possess extraordinary or unique personal qualities.

chivalry hypothesis The view that females have been treated less harshly by the criminal justice system in deference to their gender.

chronic disease Characterized by gradual onset, long duration, and little chance for complete recovery, often resulting in death.

church Inclusive religious body that brings together a moral community of believers in formal worship and accommodates itself to the larger secular world.

civil law A tradition of imposing law on a society from above.

civil religion Also called secular religion, a system of values associated with sacred symbols integrated into broader society and shared by members of that society regardless of their own religious affiliations.

class consciousness Marx's term for an awareness of the implications of your class position.

classical liberalism A political philosophy that emphasizes the rights of the individual and suggests that the state should be just powerful enough to protect these rights.

classism An ideology that legitimates economic inequality.

collective behavior Relatively spontaneous, short-lived, unconventional, and unorganized activity by large numbers of people arising in situations where norms are unclear or rapidly changing.

colonialism A system whereby high-income nations take political, economic, and cultural control of less developed societies.

common law A tradition of developing law over time through the accumulation of numerous cases.

commune A collective household where people, who may or may not be related, share roles typically associated with families.

comparable worth The idea that male and female jobs should be assessed according to skill level, effort, and responsibility; used mainly to upgrade women in primarily female jobs.

conservatism A political philosophy that emphasizes order and opposes most social change.

Consolidated Metropolitan Statistical Area (CMSA) When the largest Metropolitan Statistical Areas are grouped together to form one or more megalopolises.

conspicuous consumption Veblen's term for a means of validating social status, especially in the upper class, by wasting money or other resources on nonessentials.

contact hypothesis The theory that certain types of intergroup interaction can reduce prejudice.

content analysis A technique that systematically codes and quantifies the content of documents, such as magazines, newspapers, and archival sources.

contingency work force Workers who are not permanent, full-time employees of a single firm.

continuity theory Suggests that previously developed personality characteristics continue into old age and serve as guidelines for adjusting to aging.

control group The subject group in an experiment that is not exposed to the independent variable.

control variable The variable held constant to help clarify the relationship between the independent and dependent variable.

conventional crowd A type of crowd that develops when an audience expresses some sort of institutionalized emotionality.

corporate crime Criminal acts committed by businesses against employees, customers, or the public.

correlation A condition in which two variables are associated in a patterned way so that a change in one corresponds to a change in another; also called covariation.

counterculture A subculture with values and norms in opposition to the dominant culture.

countermodernization A movement in society that either resists certain aspects of modernization or promotes ways to neutralize their effects.

countermovement A social movement that arises to oppose the goals of another movement.

craze A relatively long-lasting fad with significant economic or cultural implications.

credentialism An emphasis on credentials; qualifications for a job or social status based on the completion of some aspect of formal education.

crime A violation of a formal statute enacted by a legitimate government.

crowd A temporary gathering of people who influence each other in some way and share a focus of attention.

crude birthrate The annual number of births per 1000 population.

cult Most often organized around a charismatic leader who provides the basis for a new, unconventional religion, usually with no clearly defined structure; associated with tension, suspicion, and hostility from the larger society.

cultural capital Bourdieu's term for the subcultural patterns into which members of high-ranking strata are socialized.

cultural imperialism The strong and continuing influence of the former colonial powers over the cultures of societies throughout the developing world.

cultural integration The process in which cultural elements are closely connected and mutually interdependent.

cultural lag The gap between the time an artifact is introduced and the time it is integrated into a culture's value system.

cultural relativism The principle that all cultures have intrinsic worth and each must be evaluated and understood by its own standards.

cultural universals Common features found in all societies.

culture A human society's total way of life; it is learned and shared and includes values, customs, material objects, and symbols.

culture of poverty Subcultural values among the poor, especially the inability to defer gratification, that supposedly make it difficult for them to escape poverty.

culture shock Experiences of alienation, depression, or loneliness when entering a culture vastly different from one's own.

Davis-Moore thesis The view that structured social inequality is functional for society because it ensures that key statuses will be held by highly capable people.

debunking Looking beyond obvious explanations for social behavior and seeking out less obvious and deeper explanations.

decriminalization A policy whereby previously illegal goods or services are legally allowed to adults under certain conditions.

deficiency theory An approach to stratification that explains social inequality as the consequence of individual variations in ability.

degradation ceremony A public ritual whose purpose is to attach a stigma.

deindustrialization The transformation of an economy from a manufacturing to a service base.

democracy A political system in which the people have a significant voice in the government and in which their formal consent is the basis for the legitimacy of the state.

democratic leader A leader who encourages group discussion and input.

demographic transition A three-stage model describing the change from high fertility and mortality to lower ones.

demography Scientific study of population that focuses on size, distribution, and composition and how birth, death, and migration influence each.

denomination Socially accepted and legally recognized religious body that is self-governing, where local congregations have an official relationship with a larger church.

dependent variable The variable presumed to be changed or caused by the independent variable.

deviance Behavior, beliefs, or conditions that are considered by relatively powerful segments of society to be serious violations of important norms.

developing nations The United Nations designation to refer to those less developed countries (LDCs) with poverty-level incomes per capita.

development Programs designed to upgrade the standard of the living of the world's poor in ways that allow them to sustain themselves.

diffusion The borrowing of cultural elements from one society to another.

direct institutional discrimination Openly discriminatory practices by institutions.

discouraged workers Unemployed workers who have stopped looking for a job.

discrimination Treating individuals unequally and unjustly on the basis of their category memberships.

disengagement theory Theory explaining that successful aging is linked to a gradual, beneficial, and mutual role withdrawal between the elderly and society.

dramaturgical approach Analyzing social interaction as if it is a play acted on a stage.

dysfunction Anything that keeps social systems from operating smoothly and efficiently (Merton).

ecclesia When a church is institutionalized as a formal part of a state and claims citizens as members.

ecofeminism A branch of feminist social theory connecting the degradation and oppression of women with the degradation of the ecosystem.

ecological fallacy Uncritically applying group-level findings to particular individuals.

economy The institution that organizes the production, distribution, and consumption of material goods and services.

edge city A large suburban community located on the periphery of a metropolitan area that functions independently from the host city.

egalitarian marriage A form of marriage in which partners share decision making and assign roles based on talent and choice rather than on traditional gender beliefs.

ego Freud's term for the part of the personality that mediates between biological drives and the culture that would deny them.

elite model The view that real political power is concentrated in the hands of a small and cohesive group of top bureaucrats.

empirical evidence Information that can be apprehended directly through observation and sensory experience.

end point fallacy The symbolic interactionist assertion that new labels produce new behavior in an ongoing process.

endogamy A cultural norm in which people marry within certain groups.

epidemiology The study of the causes and distribution of disease, and disability in a given population.

equilibrium The tendency of social systems to resist change.

ethnic group A category of people who are seen by themselves and others as sharing a distinct subculture.

ethnocentrism The tendency to evaluate one's own culture as superior to others.

ethnography A description of the customs, beliefs, and values of a culture by a researcher typically spending a prolonged period living with members of the culture.

ethnomethodology The study of how people socially construct their everyday world and give meaning to their experiences and interactions.

exogamy A cultural norm in which people marry outside a particular group.

experimental group The subject group in an experiment that is exposed to the independent variable.

expressive crowd A type of crowd whose main function is to provide an opportunity for emotional release among its members.

expressive leader A leader who is principally concerned with maintaining group morale.

extended family A family that consists of parents, dependent children, and other relatives, usually of at least three generations, living in the same household.

fads Short-lived but intense periods of enthusiasm for new elements in a culture.

false consciousness Marx's term for anything that retards the growth of class consciousness.

family of orientation The family we grow up in and the vehicle for primary socialization.

family of procreation The family we establish at marriage.

fashion Periodic fluctuations in the popularity of styles of such things as clothes, hair styles, or automobiles.

fee-for-service Health care where the patient pays for each service provided.

feminism An inclusive worldwide movement to end sexism and sexist oppression by empowering women.

feminization of poverty An increase in the percentage of women who are in the poverty population.

fertility rate Actual reproductive behavior determined by annual number of births per 1000 to women of childbearing age. A more sensitive measure than the crude birthrate.

fictive kin People who are not related by blood or marriage but are accepted as family members, a pattern common in African American families.

field research Research design aimed at collecting data directly in natural settings on what people say and do.

folkways Informal norms that suggest customary ways of behaving.

formal organization A large secondary group designed to accomplish specific tasks by means of an elaborate internal division of labor.

formal social control Efforts to discourage deviance made by people whose jobs require them to punish nonconformity and reward obedience.

functional illiteracy The inability to do the reading, writing, or basic math necessary to carry out daily activities.

fundamentalism A movement designed to revitalize faith by returning to the traditional ways the religion was practiced in the past.

Gemeinschaft Tönnies's term for a society based on natural will relationships.

gender Those social, cultural, and psychological characteristics linked to male and female that define people as masculine and feminine.

gendered racism The intensified prejudice and discrimination experienced by women who are also members of subordinate racial or ethinc groups.

gender identity The awareness that the two sexes behave differently and that two gender roles are proper.

gender roles Expected attitudes and behaviors a society associates with each sex.

gender schema theory The theory that suggests that once a child learns cultural definitions of gender, they become the key structures around which all other information is organized.

gender socialization The process by which individuals learn the cultural behavior of feminine or masculine that is associated with the biological sex of female or male.

gender typing Stereotypes based on gender that become a normative expectation when the majority of an occupation is made up of one gender.

general deterrence Punishing an offender in order to keep others from committing crimes.

generalized other The ability to understand broader cultural norms and judge what a typical person might think or do.

genocide The extermination of all or most of the members of a minority group.

gentrification A process of renovating specific working-class or poor neighborhoods to attract new, more affluent residents.

gerontocracy Cultures in which the elderly, primarily the oldest males, hold the most powerful positions.

gerontology The scientific study of aging with an emphasis on the elderly population.

Gesellschaft Tönnies's term for a society constructed primarily on the basis of rational will relationships.

glass ceiling Argument that women fail to rise to senior level positions because they encounter invisible and artificial barriers constructed by male management.

global cities Centers of population growth, political actions, and economic activities that are becoming the dominant force in national and world economies.

global economy The multitude of commodity exchanges that unite consumers and producers around the world.

global stratification The division of the nations of the world into richer and poorer categories.

global warming Also called the greenhouse effect, associated with temperature increases linked to burning fossil fuels and industrial and agricultural waste.

globalization The vision of the world as a single social space where diverse societies borrow, learn, and compete against one another.

goal displacement The tendency for bureaucracies to focus more on organizational survival than on achieving their primary goals.

gossip Rumors about other people's personal affairs.

green revolution The industrial and technological innovations used to produce high yield crops that would help solve the world's food supply problems.

groupthink A tendency for highly cohesive groups to make poor decisions because of conformity pressures.

halo effect The tendency to assume that a single characteristic of an individual may be broadened into a general evaluation of that person; thus an athlete who is good at sports may come to be seen as a generally good person.

Hawthorne effect A phenomenon in which research subjects are influenced by the knowledge that they are in an experiment or study, thus contaminating the results of the study.

health Defined by the World Health Organization, a state of complete physical, mental, and social well-being, not merely the absence of disease or infirmity.

health maintenance organization (HMO) A prepaid health plan where health providers are contracted or salaried employees.

hermaphrodites Children born with both male and female sexual organs or ambiguous genitals.

heterosexual The category for people who have sexual preferences for those of the other gender.

hidden curriculum All the informal, unwritten norms and rules that keep students in line.

holistic health Treating the whole person, with a focus on wellness and prevention.

homogamy The likelihood of becoming attracted to and marrying someone similar to yourself.

homophobia Negative attitudes and overall intolerance against homosexuals and homosexuality.

homosexual The category for people who have sexual preference and erotic attraction for people of their own gender.

horizontal mobility Social mobility that occurs when an individual moves from one status to another, both of which occupy roughly similar levels in a stratification hierarchy.

household A person or group of people occupying a housing unit.

human rights Those rights inherent to human beings, including dignity, personal integrity, inviolability of body and mind, and civil and political rights.

hypodermic model A theory that assumes the media have a simple, one-way, direct effect on their audiences.

hypothesis An expectation or prediction derived from a theory; the probable outcome of the research question.

I Mead's term for that aspect of self that is spontaneous, creative, and impulsive.

id Freud's term for an individual's biological drives and impulses that strive for gratification.

ideal type Weber's term for a description of a phenomenon that emphasizes and even exaggerates its most distinctive and characteristic qualities.

ideology A belief that legitimates patterns of structured social inequality.

immanent change Change whose causes are internal to the society or other social group in question.

impression management Information and cues we provide to others to present ourselves in a favorable light.

incidence The number of new cases of a disease during a specified time period.

income Salaries, rents, interest, and dividends received from stocks and bonds.

independent variable The variable presumed to cause change in the dependent variable.

index crimes Eight street crimes given special attention in the FBI's *Uniform Crime Reports.*

indirect institutional discrimination Policies that appear to be neutral or colorblind but, in practice, discriminate against minority groups.

individual discrimination Intentional discrimination by particular individuals.

informal sector The economic activities of people such as subsistence farmers and urban laborers who work in small-scale home-based production.

informal social control Efforts to discourage deviance made by friends and family.

informed consent A condition in which potential subjects have enough knowledge about the research to determine whether they choose to participate.

in-group A group to which individuals belong and toward which they feel pride and loyalty.

inquisitorial principle A legal tradition whereby guilt or innocence is determined by a judge without an adversarial contest between defense and prosecution.

instrumental leader A leader who is principally concerned with accomplishing a group's task.

intergenerational social mobility Social mobility measured by comparing an individual's class position with that of his or her parents or grandparents.

intragenerational social mobility Social mobility that occurs during an individual's lifetime.

iron law of oligarchy Michels's theory that all organizations eventually fall under the control of a small group of top leaders.

Kuznets curve A graphic representation of the relationship between economic development and economic inequality at the societal level.

labeling theory A perspective that investigates the effects on deviants of being publicly identified as such.

laissez-faire leader A leader who is highly nondirective.

language A shared symbol system of rules and meanings that govern the production and interpretation of speech.

latent functions The unintended and often nonobvious functions of some social phenomenon (Merton).

laws Formal norms codified and enforced by the legal power of the state.

life course The perspective that considers the roles people play over a lifetime and the ages associated with these roles.

Lombardi ethic The view that in competitive situations, winning is the only important value.

looking-glass self Cooley's term for the idea that we use other people as a mirror to gain an image of ourselves.

macrosociology The study of large-scale social phenomena.

magnet schools Selective, high quality innercity schools created in the wake of busing; suburban white students are recruited for these schools.

mainstreaming The integration of special-needs students into the overall classroom or school.

managed care Designed to control health care costs by measures such as requiring authorization for hospitalization and expensive treatment.

manifest functions The obvious and intended functions of some social phenomenon (Merton).

mass hysteria An intense, fearful, and seemingly irrational reaction to a perceived but often misunderstood or imaginary threat that occurs in at least partially dispersed collectivities.

master status A status that is exceptionally powerful in determining an individual's identity.

material culture The tangible and concrete artifacts, physical objects, and items found in a society.

matrilineal descent A system in which the family name is traced through the mother's line and daughters and female kin usually inherit property.

matrilocal residence A pattern in which a couple moves into the wife's house at marriage.

McDonaldization Ritzer's term for the process by which bureaucratic principles come to shape more and more of social life.

me Mead's term for the socialized self; the one that makes us concerned about how others judge us.

means-tested Refers to government programs that are only provided to persons falling below a particular income level.

measurement The process of assigning values, such as numbers to variables.

mechanical solidarity Durkheim's term for internal cohesion that results from people being very much like each other.

Medicaid Joint federal and state welfare program, assisting welfare and low income persons of any age to get medical care.

medicalization A process that legitimizes medical control over parts of a person's life or in society as a whole.

medicalization of deviance Reconceptualizing the character of a deviant from "evil" to "sick."

Medicare Health insurance funded through Social Security for those 65 and over and covering some persons of any age with certain disabilities.

megalopolis A system of several metropolitan areas and their surrounding suburbs that expand until they overlap.

meritocracy A system in which individuals are hired and promoted solely on the basis of their specialized skills and knowledge.

metropolitan area A central city with surrounding smaller cities that function as an integrated economy.

Metropolitan Statistical Area (MSA) A central city of at least 5000 people and its adjacent urbanized areas.

microenterprise programs Small scale income-earning manufacturing or agricultural activities located in or near the household.

microsociology The study of the details of interaction between people, mostly in small-group settings.

migration rate The movement of people in and out of various areas.

minority group A category of people who lack power and experience prejudice and discrimination.

mixed economy An economic system that combines elements of capitalism and socialism; also called a social democracy.

mob An acting crowd that directs its hostility toward a specific target.

modern liberalism A political philosophy that combines a strong welfare state with private property and market economics.

modernity The personal orientations characteristic of people living in a modernized society.

modernization The sum total of the structural and cultural changes which accompanied the industrial revolution.

monogamy Marriage to one spouse at a time.

monopoly A situation in which a single provider dominates a market.

monotheism Belief in one all powerful and all knowing god.

morbidity rate The amount of disease or illness in a population over a given time period.

mores Norms that carry a strong sense of social importance and necessity.

mortality rate The total number of deaths expressed as a percentage of the population in a given time period, usually a year.

multiculturalism The concept that different cultural groups exist side by side within the same culture and the belief that the heritage of each should be understood and respected.

multilinear evolutionary theory A variety of evolutionary thought in which different societies are seen as changing at different paces and in different directions.

multinational corporations (MNCs) Private business enterprises operating in several countries that have a powerful economic impact worldwide. Also called transnational corporations.

national health insurance Health coverage provided as a right of citizenship in a country regardless of ability to pay.

negative sanction A punishment intended to discourage deviance.

neocolonialism A system whereby previously colonial societies continue to be economically and culturally dominated by their former colonial masters or by multinational corporations.

network A broad web of social ties that radiates out from a given individual.

New Christian Right (NCR) A fundamentalist political movement composed of mostly Protestant conservative pressure groups with an agenda for returning morality to U.S. society.

new social movement An ideologically inclusive, globally linked social movement that emphasizes participation, identity, and emotionality.

nongovernmental organizations (NGOs) A wide variety of privately funded nonprofit groups, most of which are concerned with development, economic relief, and advocacy for the poor.

nonmaterial culture The intangible and abstract components of a society, including values, beliefs, and traditions.

nonverbal communication The ways people communicate without words, including body movements, facial expressions, personal space, and touching.

norms Rules of conduct that guide people's behavior in specific situations.

nuclear family A family that consists of wife, husband, and their dependent children who live apart from other relatives in their own residence.

objective approach Operationalizing the variable of class by assigning individuals to class positions on the basis of indicators such as income or occupation.

occupational crime Criminal acts committed by employees against their employers.

operational definition Guideline that specifies how a concept will be empirically measured.

organic solidarity Durkheim's term for internal cohesion that results from economic interdependency.

organizational culture The informal norms found within a formal organization.

organized crime Crime conducted by relatively large-scale and highly structured syndicates that routinely use corruption and violence to maximize their profits.

out-group A group to which individuals do not belong and toward that they feel disdain and possibly hostility.

panic A type of localized collective behavior in which a large number of people respond to a real or imaginary threat with a desperate, uncoordinated, seemingly irrational flight to secure safety.

Parkinson's Law Theory that work in a bureaucracy expands to fill the time available for its completion.

participant observation A fieldwork technique in which the researcher witnesses or engages firsthand in the activities of the group or culture under study.

patriarchal (patriarchy) Male-dominated social structures leading to the oppression of women.

patrilineal descent A system in which the family name is traced through the father's line and sons and male kin usually inherit property.

patrilocal residence A pattern in which a couple moves into the husband's house at marriage.

peer groups Groups made up of people who are the same age and generally share the same interests and positions.

personality The distinctive complex of attitudes, beliefs, behaviors, and values that makes up an individual.

Peter Principle Theory that bureaucrats are promoted until they reach their level of incompetence, where they then stay.

plea bargaining A system by which defendants agree to plead guilty to a lesser charge rather than proceed to a formal trial.

pluralism A situation in which minority and dominant groups retain their cultural identity yet do not experience discrimination and participate in common economic and political institutions. (Ch. 12)

pluralism The view that competition among elites tends to disperse political power broadly among different individuals and groups. (Ch. 18)

political economy A concept that describes how power and authority are structured in modern societies; it acknowledges the extensive interdependency of the economic and political institutions.

polyandry A rare form of plural marriage allowing a woman to marry more than one man at a time, usually brothers.

polygamy Marriage to more than one spouse at a time.

polygyny The most common form of plural marriage, allowing a man to marry more than one woman at a time.

polytheism Belief in many gods; can either be diffuse where all gods are equal or hierarchal where gods are ranked in importance or power.

popular culture Commercialized art and entertainment designed to attract a mass audience.

population The entire group of people who are the focus of a body of research and to whom the results will be generalized.

population pyramid A visual representation of the age and sex structure of a population at a given point in time.

positive sanction A reward intended to encourage conformity.

positivism An approach to understanding human behavior through the scientific method.

postmodernism An intellectual movement that emphasizes that the meaning of writings, art, or other "texts" is largely or entirely read into the "text" by the observer.

postindustrial society A society in which manufacturing is largely replaced by knowledge-based service activities.

power The ability to compel others to act as the powerholder wishes, even if they attempt to resist.

prejudice A negative attitude toward an entire category of people.

prevalence The total number of cases of a disease during a specified time period.

primary aging The physical and biological changes that accompany the aging process.

primary deviance Any deviant act that is not followed by labeling.

primary group Cooley's term for small groups characterized by warm, informal, and long-lasting interaction.

primary labor market Jobs that provide decent wages, interesting work, benefits, and a possibility of career advancement.

primary socialization Occurring mostly during the early years of life, the stage when language is learned and the first sense of self is gained.

profane Durkheim's term for the world of everyday objects; anything that is not sacred.

profession A prestigious white-collar occupation governed by a professional association.

professionalization The process by which occupations become increasingly professional.

proletariat Marx's term for the class that must sell its labor to the bourgeoisie in order to survive.

protest crowd A type of crowd assembled by the leaders of a social movement to demonstrate its popular support.

public A large number of people who are interested in a particular controversial issue.

pure sociology The view that sociologists should limit their activities to researching the facts and developing theories to explain them.

qualitative analysis Nonnumerical analysis of data to discover underlying meanings, explore relationships, and build theory.

quantitative analysis Data that can be readily translated into numbers.

questionnaires Data collection devices that are filled out by the respondent and returned directly or by mail.

race A category of people who are believed to be physically distinct from others.

racism The ideology that maintains one race is inherently superior to another.

random sample Also called a probability sample; one in which the researcher can calculate the likelihood that any subject in the population will be included in the sample.

rational choice theory Assumes that people's decisions are made on the basis of a determination of the costs and benefits of each alternative.

rational-legal authority Power legitimated by legally enacted rules and regulations, especially in a bureaucracy (Weber).

rationality Weber's term for consciously using the most effective means in order to pursue a chosen end.

rationalization The process by which human activities become more and more oriented toward the deliberate selection of the most efficient way to accomplish any particular task (Weber).

reactionary movement A social movement that seeks to reverse the general direction of social life.

reference group People to whom we look in order to evaluate our own behavior.

reformist movement A social movement that aims for relatively small-scale progressive change.

relative deprivation A conscious feeling of a negative discrepancy between legitimate aspirations and perceived actualities.

relative poverty Poverty defined as an inability to afford goods and services that most people take for granted in a given society.

reliability An issue in measurement quality asking whether you would get the same results if you repeated the measurement; consistency of measurement.

religion A unified system of beliefs and practices relative to the sacred.

religious law A legal tradition in which the source of law is believed to be divine.

religious pluralism A system that exists when many religions are tolerated, often in competition with one another for members.

reputational approach Operationalizing the variable of class by asking well-informed members of a community to locate other people's positions in the stratification system.

research design An organized plan for collecting data that is guided by the research question and hypothesis.

resocialization The process people go through to remedy patterns of behavior that society finds destructive or to alter behavior to make it fit with other personal or social goals.

revolutionary movement A social movement that aims for broad and sweeping progressive change.

riot An acting crowd that directs its hostility toward a wide and shifting array of targets.

rites of passage Formal events, such as a retirement dinner, that mark important life transitions.

role Cultural norms that define the behaviors expected of an individual occupying a particular status.

role conflict Difficulty performing one role associated with one status because of incompatibility with another role associated with a different status.

role set All of the roles associated with a single status.

role strain Difficulty performing all the elements of the role set connected to a single social status.

role-taking Imagining what it is like to be in other people's shoes in order to increase empathy and social connectedness.

routinization of charisma The transformation from charismatic to either traditional or rational-legal authority (Weber).

ruling class model The view that political power is concentrated in the hands of big business and the upper class.

rumor Unverified information, passed informally from person to person.

sacred Durkheim's term for things set apart from the everyday world that inspire awe and reverence.

sample A subset or part of a larger population that is being studied.

sanction A penalty for norm violation as well as approval or disapproval for norm adherence.

sandwich generation Care givers to the elderly, primarily women, who are caught between caring for two generations—their children and their elderly parents—at the same time.

Sapir-Whorf hypothesis The idea that language determines thought; also called linguistic relativity.

scapegoat A person who is unfairly blamed for other people's problems.

schema Cognitive structures used to understand the world and process new information.

scientific method A systematic procedure for acquiring knowledge that relies on empirical evidence.

secondary aging Aging due to the lifetime of stresses our bodies are subjected to, which include disease, emotional trauma, and age prejudice.

secondary analysis Research in which data already available and created for other purposes are accessed and reanalyzed.

secondary deviance A period of time following labeling during which deviants reorganize their lives around their stigma.

secondary group A group that is formal, emotionally cool, and often temporary.

secondary labor market Jobs that pay poorly, are boring, and provide few benefits and little opportunity for advancement.

sect A smaller religious body, with exclusive or voluntary membership, which is aloof or hostile to the secular society surrounding it.

secular religion *See* civil religion.

secularization The process in which religion, challenged by science and modernization, loses its influence on society.

segregation The physical and social separation of dominant and minority groups.

self The unique sense of identity that distinguishes each individual from all other individuals.

self-fulfilling prophecy Expectations about others lead them to behave in ways that confirm the expectations.

separatism A policy of voluntary structural and cultural isolation from the dominant group.

serial monogamy A pattern of marriage–divorce–remarriage.

sex Those biological characteristics distinguishing male and female.

sexism The belief that one category, female, is inferior to the other category, male.

sexual dimorphism The separation of the sexes into two distinct groups.

sexual harassment Unwelcome sexual advances, requests for sexual favors, and other verbal or physical conduct of a sexual nature.

sexual orientation A person's preference for sexual partners; generally divided into two broad categories, heterosexuality and homosexuality.

sexual scripts Shared beliefs about what society considers acceptable sexual thoughts, feelings, and behavior for each gender.

sexuality A type of social interaction where we perceive, experience, and express ourselves as sexual beings.

sick role Behaviors that are socially expected of a sick person according to prevailing norms.

significant others People whose approval and affection we desire who are therefore most important to the development of our self-concept.

social capital Features of social organization that facilitate coordination and cooperation for mutual benefit.

social change Alterations over time in social structure, culture, and behavior patterns.

social class A category of people who share a common position in a vertical hierarchy of differential social reward.

social construction of reality Our perception of reality as shaped by the subjective meanings we bring to any experience or social interaction.

social control The measures taken by members of a society that are intended to ensure conformity to norms.

social Darwinism Opposition to aid to the poor on the grounds that such assistance interferes with natural selection.

social group Two or more people who regularly interact and feel some sense of solidarity or common identity.

social institution A predictable, established way to provide for one of society's basic needs.

social interaction How people behave toward one another when they meet.

social marginality The condition of being partially excluded from the mainstream of society.

social mobility A change in an individual's or group's position in a stratification hierarchy.

social movement A relatively large and organized group of people working for or opposing social change and using of at least some unconventional or uninstitutionalized means.

social stratification The division of a large group or society into ranked categories of people.

social structure The relatively stable patterns of social interaction that characterize human social life.

socialism A political philosophy that advocates collective control over the economy in order to reduce inequality and social injustice.

socialization The lifelong process by which we learn our culture, develop our sense of self, and become functioning members of society.

society A sizable number of people who interact, share a culture, and usually live in a single geographic territory.

sociobiology The science that uses evolutionary theory and genetic inheritance to examine the biological roots of social behavior.

socioeconomic status (SES) An objective measure of class position based on income, occupation, and education.

sociology The systematic and scientific study of human social behavior.

specific deterrence Punishing an offender in order to keep that individual from committing further crimes.

spectacle A highly institutionalized form of sport; also known as *corporate sport.*

sport Institutionalized, competitive activities that involve vigorous physical exertion or relatively complex physical skills motivated by both personal enjoyment and external rewards.

spurious relationship An observed relationship that is not a true one because it is caused by another variable.

stacking Disproportionately assigning minorities to noncentral sports positions that are low in leadership responsibility and outcome control.

state The institution that maintains a monopoly over the legitimate use of force within a given territorial area.

state autonomy model The view that political power is concentrated in the hands of top government officials and professional experts.

state socialism A political system in which the state owns the means of production; seen as a transitional stage between capitalism and communism.

status Social positions that people occupy.

status groups Weber's term for strata based on different lifestyles.

status inconsistency A situation in which an individual occupies several ranked statuses, some of which are evaluated more positively than others.

status set All the statuses that a given individual occupies.

stereotype A broad generalization about a category of people that is applied globally.

stigma A powerfully negative public identity.

strata Segments of a large population that receive different amounts of valued resources by virtue of their position in a ranked system of structural inequality.

structural adjustment Conditions requiring that economies be restructured to permit liberalization of markets by eliminating barriers to trade and investment.

structural mobility Social mobility that results principally from changes in the range of occupations that are available in a society.

structural unemployment Unemployment resulting from a mismatch between the skills of the work force and the current needs of the economy.

subculture Segments of a culture that share characteristics that distinguish it from the broader culture.

subjective approach Operationalizing the variable of class by directly asking people to identify their own class position.

suburbs Smaller surrounding urban areas usually outside the political boundary of a central city.

superego Freud's term for all the norms, values, and morals that are learned through socialization; similar to conscience.

survey research Most frequently used research design in sociology typically using questionnaires and interviews for data collection.

sustainable development Humane ways for the human species to live on the Earth indefinitely without compromising the future of either the planet or its inhabitants; involves international cooperation.

symbol Something that stands for or represents something else.

technology Tools and the body of knowledge pertaining to their use that help accomplish social tasks.

telecommuting Working at home by means of technology such as fax machines and the Internet.

terrorism The use or threat of violence as a political strategy.

tertiary deviance Efforts by organized groups of deviants to secure acceptance.

theism Belief in one or more independent supernatural beings (gods) who do not exist on earth and who are more powerful than people.

theology A systematic formulation of religious doctrine.

theoretical perspective A general orientation within sociology that guides research and theory construction.

theory An explanation of the relationship between specific facts.

Thomas Theorem The idea that what people define as real is real in its consequences.

Title IX A 1972 law that requires rough gender equality in the funding of interscholastic and intercollegiate sports.

total institutions Places of residence and work that exert complete control over the people they contain.

totalitarianism A type of authoritarian regime that has unlimited power to intervene in people's everyday lives.

tracking The practice of grouping children according to an assessment of their ability.

traditional authority Weber's term for authority legitimated by long-established cultural patterns.

trained incapacity The bureaucratic tendency to respond to new situations ineffectively.

transgender Describes people who do not conform to culturally defined traditional gender roles associated with their sex.

underemployment Working at a job that does not make full use of your skills and qualifications.

unilinear evolutionary theory A variety of evolutionary thinking that sees all societies as progressing through a set sequence of stages and ultimately closely resembling each other.

unobtrusive measures Methods of data collection in which the researcher does not interact with what or who is being studied.

urban Pertaining to a place of settlement, often called a city, that is populated more densely than rural areas.

urban ecology A field of urban sociology that studies the relationships between urban populations and their physical and spatial environments.

urban legend Rumors that recount ironic and usually grisly events that supposedly happen to "a friend of a friend."

urbanization The process of city population growth.

validity An issue in measurement quality asking whether you are measuring what you think you are measuring.

values Beliefs about ideal goals and behavior that serve as standards for social life.

variable A characteristic or trait that can be measured.

vertical mobility Social mobility up or down a stratification hierarchy.

vested interests Veblen's term for individuals or groups whose advantages are threatened by impending social change.

victim blaming Considering individuals responsible for negative conditions that are in fact primarily the result of larger structural factors beyond their control.

victimless crime Crimes created when the criminal law is used to prohibit the exchange of strongly desired goods and services between willing adults.

victimology A subfield of criminology devoted to the study of the victims of crime.

wealth Net accumulated assets including homes, land, automobiles, jewelry, factories, and stocks and bonds.

white-collar crime Criminal acts committed by high-status people in the course of their occupations.

Zero Population Growth (ZPG) Also called replacement level; occurs when the population growth rate is static, or zero, because each couple has two children to replace them.

REFERENCES

AARP. 2002a. "What is AARP?" AARP Facts. American Association of Retired Persons. Available: http:www.org/what_is.

AARP. 2002b. "Facts about grandparents raising grandchildren." Available: http//:www.aarp.or/confacts/grandparents/grandfacts.

Abadinsky, Howard. 1990. *Organized Crime*, 3rd ed. Chicago: Nelson-Hall.

Abbey, Antonia, Pam Mcausian, & Lisa Thomson Ross. 1998. "Sexual assault perception by college men: The role of alcohol, misperception of sexual intent and sexual beliefs and experiences." *Journal of Social and Clinical Psychology* 17(2): 167–95.

Abbott, Andrew. 1988. *The System of Professions*. Chicago: University of Chicago Press.

Abdel-Hamid, Hoda. 2000. "Cola label tiff." *ABC News.com*. Available: abcnews.go.com/sections/world/DailyNews/egypt000518_coke.html

Abel, Emily K. 2001. "Historical perspectives on caregiving: Documenting women's experiences." In Alexis J. Walker et al. (eds.), *Families in Later Life: Connections and Transitions*. Thousand Oaks, CA: Pine Forge.

Abelson, Philip H. 2001. "Developmental appropriateness review—Years of promise: A comprehensive learning strategy for America's children." In Williamson M. Evers, Lance T. Izumi, & Pamela A. Riley (eds.), *School Reform: The Critical Issues*. Stanford, CA: Hoover Institution: 36–38.

Abercrombie, Nicholas, Stephen Hill, & Bryan S. Turner (eds.), 1990. *Dominant Ideologies*. Cambridge, MA: Unwin Hyman.

Aberle, David F., A. K. Cohen, A. K. David, M. J. Leng, Jr., & F. N. Sutton. 1950. "The functional prerequisites of a society." *Ethics* 60: 100–110.

Aberle, David. 1966. *The Peyote Religion Among the Navajo*. Chicago: Aldine.

Aberle, David. 1982. *The Peyote Religion Among the Navajo*. Chicago: University of Chicago Press.

Abselson, Reed. 1999. "A push from the top shatters a glass ceiling." *New York Times* August 22: 1, 23.

Academy for Educational Development. 2002. "AED focus issue: Basic education." Available: http://www.aed.org/edu.

Acker, Joan. 1999. "Rewriting class, race, and gender: Problems in feminist rethinking." In Myra Marx Feree, Judith Lorber, & Beth B. Hess (eds.), *Revisioning Gender*. Thousand Oaks, CA: Sage: 44–69.

Acosta, R. V., & L. J. Carpenter. 2000. "Women in intercollegiate sport." Unpublished paper, summarized in Coakley (2001).

Adams, Bert N., & R. A. Sydie. 2001. *Sociological Theory*. Thousand Oaks, CA: Pine Forge.

Adams, Kathryn Betts. 2001. "Depressive symptoms, depletion, or developmental change? Multidimensionality in the geriatric depression scale according to contemporary interpretations of the disengagement theory of Aging." *Dissertation Abstracts International Section A: Humanities & Social Sciences*. 61(12-A): 4897.

Adams, Mike S., James D. Johnson, & T. David Evans. 1998. "Racial Differences in Informal Labeling Effects," *Deviant Behavior* 19: 157–171.

Adams, Scott. 1996. *The Dilbert Principle*. New York: HarperCollins.

Adams, Tom. 1991. *Grass Roots: How Ordinary People Are Changing America*. New York: Citadel.

Adams-Price, Carolyn (ed.). 1998. *Creativity and Successful Aging: Theoretical and Empirical Approaches*. New York: Springer.

Aday, David P. Jr. 1989. *Social Control at the Margins: Toward a General Understanding of Deviance*. Belmont, CA: Wadsworth.

Addams, Jane. 1981. *Twenty Years at Hull House*. New York: Signet. Originally published in 1910.

Adherents. 2002. "Largest religious groups in the United States of America." Available: http://www.adherents.com/rel_USA.

Adler, Patricia A., & Peter Adler. 1991. *Backboards & Blackboards: College Athletes & Role Engulfment*. New York: Columbia University Press.

Adler, Shelley E. 2001. "Integrating personal belief systems: Patient-practitioner communication." In Erika Brady (ed.), *Healing Logics: Culture and Medicine in Modern Health Belief Systems*. Logan, UT: Utah State University: 115–28.

Adorno, Theodor W., Else Frenkel-Brunswick, D. J. Levinson, & R. N. Sanford. 1950. *The Authoritarian Personality*. New York: Harper & Row.

ADRDA, 2002. "Statistics about Alzheimer's disease." Available: http://www.alz.org/AboutAD/Statistics.

Afkhami, Mahnaz. 2001. "Gender apartheid, cultural relativism, and women's human rights in Muslim societies." In Marjorie Agosin (ed.), *Women, Gender and Human Rights: A Global Perspective*: 234–45.

Agadjanian, Victor, & Alex Chika Ezeh. 2000. "Polygyny, gender relations and reproduction in Ghana." *Journal of Comparative Family Studies* 31(4): 427–41.

Aganbegyan, A. 1989. *Peristroika*. New York: Scribner.

Agarwal, Anil, Sunita Narain, & Anju Sharma. 2002. "The global commons and environmental justice—Climate change. In John Byrne, Leigh Glover, & Cecilia Martinez (eds.), *Environmental Justice: Discourses in International Political Economy*. New Brunswick, NJ: Transaction: 171–202.

Ageton, Suzanne, & Delbert Elliott. 1973. *The Effect of Legal Processing on Self-Concept*. Boulder, CO: Institute of Behavioral Science.

AGI. 1998. "Support for family planning improves women's lives." *Issues in Brief* 23. Washington, DC: Alan Guttmacher Institute. Available: http://www.agi-usa.org/pubs/ib23.

Agnew, Robert, & David Petersen. 1989. "Leisure and delinquency." *Social Problems*, 36: 322–50.

Aguirre, B. E., Dennis Wenger, & Gabriela Vigo. 1998. "A test of the emergent-norm theory of collective behavior." *Sociological Forum* (13/2): 301–320.

Aguirre, B. E., E. L. Quarantelli, & J. L. Mendoza. 1988. "The collective behavior of fads." *American Sociological Review* 53: 569–84.

AHMA. 2002. "About AHMA." American Holistic Medical Association. Available: http:www.holisitcmedicine.org/contents.

Akard, Patrick. 1992. "Corporate mobilization and political power." *American Sociological Review* 57: 597–615.

Akers, Ronald L. 1992. *Drugs, Alcohol, and Society*. Belmont, CA: Wadsworth.

Akers, Ronald L. 1997. *Criminological Theories*, 2nd ed. Los Angeles: Roxbury.

Akinsanya, Adeoye. 1994. "The World Bank & Expropriation Disputes in Africa." In Volker Bornschier & Peter Lengyel (eds.), *Conflicts & New Departures in World Society*, Vol. 3. New Brunswick, NJ: Transaction: 129–158.

Akiyama, Mitoshi, Seishi Kyoizumi, Yoichiro Kusunoki, Yuko Kirai, Kazumi Tanabi, & John B. Cologne. 1996. "Monitoring exposure to atomic bomb radiation by somatic mutation." Available: http://ehpnet1.niehs.nih.gov/docs/1996/Suppl-3/akitama.

Alba, R. D. 1992. "Ethnicity." In E. F. Borgotta & M. L. Borgotta, (eds.), *Encyclopedia of Sociology*, Vol. 1. New York: Macmillan: 575–584.

Albanese, Jay. 1989. *Organized Crime in America*, 2nd ed. Cincinnati: Anderson.

Albee, Robin. 2000. "A clergywoman of the new generation: Evolving interpretations of gender and faith." *Sociology of Religion* 61(4): 461–6.

Albrecht, Carol M., Mark A. Fossett, Cynthia M. Cready, & K. Jill Kiecolt. 1997. "Mate availability, women's marriage prevalence, and husband's education." *Journal of Family Issues* 18(4): 429–52.

Aldag, R. J., & S. R. Fuller. 1993. "Beyond fiasco: A reappraisal of the groupthink phenomenon and a new model of group decision processes." *Psychological Bulletin* 113: 533–522.

Aldrich, Nelson W. Jr. 1988. *Old Money: The Mythology of America's Upper Class*. New York: Vintage.

Aldridge, Alan. 2000. *Religion in the Contemporary World: A Sociological Introduction*. Cambridge, UK: Polity.

Alexander, Edward. 1994. "Multiculturalists and anti-semitism." *Society* 31: 58–64.

Alexander, Jeffrey C., & Steven J. Sherwood. 2002. "Mythic gestures: Robert N. Bellah and cultural sociology." In Richard Madsen, William M. Sullivan, Ann Swindler, & Steven M. Tipton (eds.), *Meaning and Modernity: Religion, Polity, and Self*. Berkeley: University of California: 1–14

Alexander, Jeffrey, & Paul Colomy. 1990. "Neofunctionalism." In George Ritzer, (ed.), *Frontiers of Social Theory: The New Synthesis*. New York: Columbia University Press: 33–67.

Alexander, Michele G., & Wendy Wood. 2000. "Women, men and positive emotions: A social role interpretation." In Agneta H. Fischer (ed.), *Gender and Emotion: Social Psychological Perspectives*. Cambridge, UK: Cambridge University.

Alexander, Peter, & Roger Gill, eds. 1984. *Utopias*. London: Duckworth.

Alexander, Susan. 1999. "The gender role paradox in youth culture: An analysis of women in music videos." *Michigan Sociological Review* 13: 46–64.

Alexander, Yonah. 1994. *Middle Eastern Terrorism*. New York: Hall.

Algoe, Sara B., Brenda N. Buswell, & John D. DeLamater. 2000. "Gender and job status as contextual cues for the interpretation of facial expression of emotion." *Sex Roles* 42(3–4): 183–208.

Ali, Lorraine. 2002. "Laughter's new profile." *Newsweek* 139: (April 22): 61.

Allen, David W. 2001. "Social class, race, and toxic releases in American counties." *Social Science Journal* 38(1): 13–25.

Allen, Henry Southworth. 1994. *Going too far enough: American culture at century's end*. Washington, DC: Smithsonian Institution.

Allen, Jeremiah. 2001. "The state of the art in modeling migration in the LDCs: A comment on J. K. Bruekner and H. A. Kim." *Journal of Regional Science* 41(3): 531–38.

Allen, Michael P. 1987. *The Founding Fortunes*. New York: Dutton.

Allen, Michael P., & Phillip Broyles. 1991. "Campaign financing reform and the presidential campaign contributions of wealthy capitalist families." *Social Science Quarterly* 72: 738–50.

Allen, Walter R., & Joseph D. Jewell. 1995. "African-American education since *An American Dilemma*." *Daedalus* 174/1: 77–100.

Allen, Walter, Darnell M. Hunt, & Derrick I. M. Gilbert. 1997. "Race-conscious academic policy in higher education." *Educational Policy* (11/4): 443–478.

Allen, William. 1999. "Plants extinction can only lead to ours, scientists say." *St. Louis Post-Dispatch* (August 8): A6.

Allgeier, Elizabeth Rice, & Albert R. Allgeier. 2000. *Sexual Interactions*. Boston: Houghton Mifflin.

Allison, Julie, & Lawrence Wrightman. 1993. *Rape: The Misunderstood Crime*. Newbury Park, CA: Sage.

Allport, Gordon W., & Leo Postman. 1947. *The Psychology of Rumor*. New York: Holt.

Allport, Gordon. 1958. *The Nature of Prejudice*. New York: Doubleday.

Allyn, David. 2000. *Make Love Not War: The Sexual Revolution—An Unfettered History*. Boston: Little, Brown.

Al-Olayan, Fahad S., & Kiran Karande. 2000. "A content analysis of magazine advertisements from the United States and the Arab world." *Journal of Advertising* 29(3): 69–82.

Alper, Bob. 2002. "Bob Alper Media: Dr. Robert A. Alper Rabbi, author, stand-up comic." http://bobalper.com/media

Alter, Jonathan, & Mark Miller. 2000. "A life or death gamble." *Newsweek* (May 29): 22–27.

Alter, Jonathan. 1996. "Washington washes its hands." *Newsweek* (August 12): 42–44.

Alter, Jonathan. 2000. "The death penalty on trial." *Newsweek* (June 12): 24–34.

Alzheimer's Disease. 2002. "Alzheimer's disease, fiscal year 2002: Hearing before a subcommittee of the Committee on Appropriations, United States Senate, 107th Congress, First Session: Special hearing." April 3. Washington, DC: U.S. Government Printing Office.

Amaladoss, Michael. 2001. "Religions for peace: Can the ambiguous phenomenon of religion be a factor in peacemaking?" *America* 185 (Dec 10): 6–8.

Amato, Paul R. 2000. "The consequences of divorce for adults and children." *Journal of Marriage and the Family* 62(4): 1269–87.

Amato, Paul R. 2001. "Children of divorce in the 1990s: An update of the Amato and Keith (1991) meta-analysis." *Journal of Family Psychology* 15(3): 355–70.

Amato, Paul R., & Alan Booth. 1995. "Changes in gender role attitudes and perceived marital quality." *American Sociological Review* 60(1): 58–66.

Amato, Paul R., & Alan Booth. 2000. *A Generation at Risk: Growing Up in an Era of Family Upheaval.* Cambridge, MA: Harvard University.

Amato, Paul R., & Alan Booth. 2001. "The legacy of parents' marital discord: Consequences for children's marital quality." *Journal of Personality and Social Psychology* 81(4): 627–38.

Amato, Paul R., & Juliana M. Sobolewski. 2001. "The effects of divorce and marital discord on adult children's psychological well-being." *American Sociological Review* 66(6): 900–921.

Amba, Joyce C. 2002. "Sexual activity and contraceptive practices among teenagers in the United States, 1988 and 1995." *Vital and Health Statistics.* Series 23(21) (May). Department of Health and Human Services. Centers for Disease Control and National Center for Health Statistics.

America, Richard F. 1995. "Has affirmative action repaid society's debt to African Americans?" *Business and Society Review* (Summer).

America. "Facing 2002." 186(1): 3.

America's Cities. 1998. "America's cities: They can yet be resurrected." *Economist* (January 10): 17–19.

American Academy of Pediatrics. 2001. "Media violence." *Pediatrics* 108(5): 1222–26.

American Council on Education. 2001a. "Educating all of one nation: Affirming diversity in the 21st century: Developing a proactive agenda." 50(20): Special Supplement.

American Council on Education. 2001b. *Annual Status Report on Minorities in Higher Education.* Washington, DC: American Council on Education.

American Council on Education. 2002. "Disparities continue for women and minorities in degree completion, NCES data show." *Facts in Brief* 51(1): (Jan. 14).

American Demographics. 2001. "Assigning guilt." 23(11): 23

American Identity. 2002. "Census finds 'American' identity rising in U.S." *New York Times* (June 9): 19.

American Medical News. 2002. "HMO enrollment shrinks again." News in Brief: May 6. Available: http://www.ama-assn.org/sci-pubsamnewspick_02/bibf0506.

American Psychological Association, 1985. *Developing a National Agenda to Address Women's Health Needs.* Washington, DC: APA.

American Sociological Association. 1997. *Code of Ethics of the American Sociological Association.* Washington, DC: American Sociological Association.

American Sociological Association. 1999. *Careers in Sociology,* 5th ed. Washington, DC: ASA.

Amick, Benjamin C., III, & John N. Lavis. 2000. "Labor markets and health: A framework and set of applications." In Alvin R. Tarlov & Robert F. St. Peter (eds.), *The Society and Population Health Reader. Volume II—A State and Community Perspective.* New York: New Press: 178–210.

Ammerman, Nancy Tatom. 1997. "Organized religion in a voluntaristic society." *Sociology of Religion* 58: 203–15.

Amott, Teresa. 1993. *Caught In the Crisis: Women and the U.S. Economy Today.* New York: Monthly Review Press.

Anastasio, P. A., K. C. Rose, & J. Chapman. 1999. "Can the media create public opinion? A social-identity approach." *Current Directions in Psychological Science* 8(5): 152–55.

Ancheta, Rebecca Wepsic. 2002. "Discourse of rules: Women talk about cosmetic surgery." In Kathryn Strother Ratcliff (ed.), *Women and Health: Power, Technology, and Conflict in a Gendered World.* Boston: Allyn & Bacon: 43–49.

Andaya, Barbara. 2002. "Religious revivalism." Presentation to the Asian Studies Development Program Institute on Southeast Asia, East-West Center, Honolulu, Hawaii July 29.

Anders, Aslund. 2002. *Building Capitalism: The Transformation of the Former Soviet Bloc.* Cambridge, NY: Cambridge University.

Anders, Gary C. 1999. "Indian gaming: Financial and regulatory issues." In Troy R. Johnson (ed.), *Contemporary Native American Political Issues.* Walnut Creek, CA: AltaMira: 163–73.

Andersen, Robin. 2002. "The thrill is gone: Advertising, gender representation and the loss of desire." In Eileen R. Meehan & Ellen Riordan (eds.), *Sex and Money: Feminism and Political Economy in the Media.* Minneapolis: University of Minnesota: 223–39.

Anderson, C. A., & Brad J. Bushman. 2001. "Effects of violent video games on aggressive behavior, aggressive cognition, aggressive affect, physiological arousal, and prosocial behavior: A meta-analytic review of the scientific literature." *Psychological Science* 12(5): 353–959.

Anderson, C. Leigh, Laura Locker, & Rachel Nugent. 2002. "Microcredit, social capital, and common pool resources." *World Development* 30(1): 95–105.

Anderson, Catherine, & Caroline Loughlin. 1986. *Forest Park.* Columbia, MO: Junior League of St. Louis and University of Missouri.

Anderson, Elijah. 1990. *Streetwise: Race, Class and Change in an Urban Community.* Chicago: University of Chicago.

Anderson, Elijah. 1995. "The black male in public." In Spencer E. Cahill (ed.), *Inside Social Life: Readings in Sociological Psychology and Microsociology.* Los Angeles: Roxbury.

Anderson, Irina, & Victoria Swainson. 2001. "Perceived motivations for rape: Gender differences in beliefs about female and male rape." *Current Research in Social Psychology* 6(8).

Anderson, John. 1994. "Held hostage in Hollywood: Female stars buy into bad roles, big time." *St. Louis Post-Dispatch* (December 4): 3C.

Anderson, Kristin. 1999. "Situating gender and emotion: Moderators of emotion talk in friends' conversation." *Dissertation Abstracts International: Section B: The Sciences and Engineering.* 59(11B): 6089. University of California-Santa Cruz.

Anderson, Margaret L., & Patricia H. Collins (eds.). 1998. *Race, Class, and Gender,* 3rd ed. Belmont, CA: Wadsworth.

Anderson, Margaret. 2001. "A nation's downward spiral into cynicism: Revisiting Clarence Thomas and Anita Hill." *SWS Network News* 28(4): 20–21.

Anderson, Robert N. 2001. "Deaths: Leading causes for 1999." *National Vital Statistics Reports* 49(11) October 12.

Andrews, D. A., & J. Stephen Warmith. 1989. "Personality & crime: knowledge & construction in criminology." *Justice Quarterly* 6: 289–310.

Andrews, D. A., & James Bonta. 1994. *The Psychology of Criminal Conduct.* Cincinnati: Anderson.

Andrews, Edmund L. 2002. "Deep shock in Germany, where guns are rare." *New York Times* (April 28):15.

Andrews, Molly. 1999. "The seductiveness of agelessness." *Aging and Society* 19(3): 301–18.

Andryszewski, Tricia. 2000. *Gay Rights.* Brookfield, CT: Twenty-First Century Books.

Andsager, Julie L., & Kimberly Roe. 1999. "Country music video in country's year of the woman." *Journal of Communication* 49(1): 69–82.

Angelides, Steven. 2001. *A History of Bisexuality.* Chicago: University of Chicago.

Angus, David, & Jeffrey Mirel. 1995. "Rhetoric and reality: The high school curriculum." In Diane Ravitch & Maris A. Vinovskis (eds.), *Learning From the Past: What History Teaches Us About School Reform.* Baltimore, MD: Johns Hopkins University: 295–328.

Annin, Peter, & Tom Morganthau. 1997. "The verdict: Death." *Newsweek* (June 23): 40–42.

Ansalone, George. 2000. "Keeping on track: A reassessment of tracking in schools." *Race, Gender and Class in Education* 7(3): 108–32.

Anwar, Zainah. 2001. "What Islam? Whose Islam? Sisters in Malaysian pluralism." In Robert F. Hefner (ed.), *The Politics of Multiculturalism: Pluralism and Citizenship in Malaysia, Singapore, and Indonesia.* Honolulu: University of Hawaii.

Anway, Carol L. 1996. *Daughters of Another Path: Experiences of American Women Choosing Islam.* Lee's Summit, MO: Yawna.

Anzaldua, Gloria E. 1995. "The strength of my rebellion." In Sheila Ruth (ed.), *Issues in Feminism: An Introduction to Women's Studies.* Mountain View, CA: Mayfield.

Apostolidis, P. 2000. *Stations of the Cross: Adomo and Christian Right Radio.* Durham, NC: Duke University.

Applebaum, Herbert. 1998. *The American Work Ethic and the Changing Work Force.* Westport, CT: Greenwood.

Applebome, Peter. 1998. "No room for childhood in a world of little adults." *New York Times* (May 10): 4–1, 4–3.

Appleby, R. Scott, & Martin E. Marty. 2002. "Fundamentalism (think again)." *Foreign Policy* (Jan. 1).

Appleby, R. Scott. 2000. *The Ambivalence of the Sacred: Religion, Violence, and Reconciliation.* Lanham, MD: Rowman & Littlefield.

Appy, Christian, & Alexander Bloom. 2001. "Vietnam mythology and the rise of public cynicism." In Alexander Bloom (ed.), *Long Time Gone: Sixties America Then and Now.* Oxford, NY: Oxford University: 47–74.

Apt, Nana Araba. 1992. "Family support to elderly people in Ghana." In Hal Kendig, Akiko Hashimoto, & Larry C. Coppare (eds.), *Family Support for the Elderly: The International Experience.* New York: Oxford University Press.

Apt, Nana Araba. 2001. "Rapid urbanization and living arrangements of older persons in Africa." In *Living Arrangements of Older Persons: Critical Issues and Policy Responses.* New York: United Nations.

Aptheker, Herbert. 1990. "W. E. B. Du Bois: Struggle, not despair," *Clinical Sociology Review* 8: 58–65.

Archer, Dane, & Rosemary Gartner. 1984. *Violence and Crime in Cross-National Perspective.* New Haven, CT: Yale University Press.

Archer, Melanie, & Judith R. Blau. 1994. "Class formation in 19th century America." *Annual Review of Sociology* 19: 17–41.

Argyris, Chris. 1960. *Understanding Organizational Behavior.* Homewood, IL: Dorsey.

Arian, Asher. 1999 "On demography and politics in the Jewish future." *Society* 36(4): 21–26.

Aries, Philippe. 1962. *Centuries of Childhood.* New York: Random House.

Armas, Generao C. 2001. "Census finds almost 600,000 households nationwide include same-sex couples." Newsday (August 22). Available: http:www .newsday.com/news/local/ny-bc-census-samesex.

Armstrong, Elizabeth. 1995. *Mental Health Issues in Primary Care: A Practical Guide.* London: Macmillan.

Armstrong, Karen. 2000a. *Islam: A Short History.* New York: Modern Library.

Armstrong, Karen. 2000b. *The Battle for God: Fundamentalism in Judaism, Christianity and Islam.* New York: Alfred A. Knopf.

Armstrong, Karen. 2001. "Cries of rage and frustration." *New Statesman* (Sept 24).

Arnaut, Genevieve L. Y., Donald K. Fromme, & Barre M. Stoll. 2000. "A qualitative analysis of stepfamilies: The biological parent." *Journal of Divorce & Remarriage* 33(3–4): 111–28.

Arnold, Guy. 1988. *The Third World Handbook.* London: Cassell Educational.

Aronson, P. 1999. "The balancing act: Young women's expectations and experiences of work and family." *Research in the Sociology of Work* 7: 55–83.

Arrighi, Giovanni. 1994. *The Long 20th Century.* New York: Verso.

Arts, Karin. 2000. *Integrating Human Rights into Development Cooperation: The Case of the Lomé Convention.* The Hague: Kluwer Arts International.

Artz, Nancy, Jeanne Munger, & Warren Purdy. 1999. "Gender issues in advertising language." *Women & Language* 22(2): 20–26.

Arvanites, Thomas. 1992. "Increasing imprisonment: A function of crime or socioeconomic factors?" *American Journal of Criminal Justice* 17: 19–38.

Asch, Arthur. 1977. "Send your children to the libraries," *The New York Times* (February 6): S–2.

Asch, Solomon. 1952. "Effects of group pressure upon the modification and distortion of judgements." In Guy Swanson, Theodore M. Newcomb, & Eugene L. Hartley, (eds.), *Readings In Social Psychology*. New York: Holt, Rinehart & Winston.

Ashford, Lori S. 2001. "New population policies: Advancing women's health and rights." *Population Bulletin* 56(1): 1–44.

Ashford, Lori S., & Carolyn Makinson. 1999. *Reproductive Health in Policy and Practice: Case Studies from Brazil, India, Morocco, and Uganda*. Washington, DC: Population Reference Bureau.

Asimov, Isaac. 1988. *Prelude to Foundation*. New York: Bantam.

Associated Press, 2001. "3 students are accused of plotting school attack." *St. Louis Post-Dispatch* (Nov. 25): A3.

Associated Press. 2001. "165 nations agree to rules for pact cutting back carbon emissions." *St. Louis Post-Dispatch* (November 11): A15.

Association of American Colleges & Universities. 1999. "The chilly climate: Quantifying its impact." *On Campus with Women* 28(4) (Summer): 5.

Asthana, Vandana, & A. C. Shukla. 2002. "Politics of environmental protection: A fiscal analysis." In Stuart S. Nagel (ed.), *Environmental Policy and Developing Nations*. Jefferson, NC: McFarland: 271–87.

Atchley, Robert C. 1999. "Continuity theory, self, and social structure." In Carol D. Ryff & Victor W. Marshall (eds.), *The Self in the Aging Process*. New York: Springer: 94–121.

Atchley, Robert C. 2000. *Social Forces and Aging*. Belmont, CA: Wadsworth.

Athans, Marego. 2000. "Mass hysteria diagnosis unpopular, not uncommon," *Evansville Courier & Press* (May 7): A-12.

Atkins, David C., & Neil S. Jacobson. 2001. "Understanding infidelity: Correlates in a national random sample." *Journal of Family Psychology* 15(4): 735–49.

Atkins, David C., S. Dimidjian, & Neil S. Jacobson. 2001. "Why do people have affairs? Recent research and future directions about attributions for extramarital affairs." In V. Manusov & J. H. Harvey (eds.), *Attribution Communication Behavior and Close Relationships*. Cambridge UK: Cambridge University: 210–36.

Atkinson, Anthony B., Lee Rainwater, & Timothy M. Smeeding. 1995. *Income Distribution in OECD Countries*. Paris: Organization for Economic Cooperation & Development.

Audi, Robert. 2000. *Religious Commitment and Secular Reason*. Cambridge, UK: Cambridge University.

Auerbach, James A., & Richard S. Belous (eds.). 1998. *The Inequality Paradox*. Washington, DC: National Policy Association.

Aufderheide, Patricia (ed.). 1997. *Conglomerates and the Media*. New York: New Press.

Auletta, Ken. 1982. *The Underclass*. New York: Random House.

Auster, Carol J. 1996. *The Sociology of Work: Concepts & Cases*. Thousand Oaks, CA: Pine Forge.

Austin, James, & John Irwin. 1989. *Who Goes to Prison?* San Francisco: National Council on Crime & Delinquency.

AVERT. 2002. "HIV and AIDS in Africa: How many people are infected with HIV/AIDS?". Available: http://www.avert.org/aafrica.

Awotona, Adenrele. 1995. "Focus: Integration and urbanisation of existing townships in South Africa." *Urbanisation*, Newsletter of the Overseas Development Administration 1: 4–5.

Axelrod, Jennifer L., Michael A. Lease, & Charlotte A. Kennedy. 2002. "Children's social constructions of popularity." *Social Development* 11(1): 87–109.

Axtman, Kris. 2002. "Insanity defense fails for Texas mother." *Christian Science Monitor* 94 (March 14): 2.

Ayers, William, Rick Ayers, & Bernadine Dohrn. 2001. "Introduction: Resisting zero tolerance." In William Ayers, Bernadine Dohrn, & Rick Ayers (eds.), *Zero Tolerance: Resisting the Drive for Punishment in Our Schools*. New York: New Press.

Ayres, B. Drummond, Jr. 1996. "U.S. judge blocks voters' initiative on job preference." *The New York Times* (Nov. 28): A1+.

Babbie, Earl. 1994. *What Is Society?* Thousand Oaks, CA: Pine Forge.

Babbie, Earl. 1998. "Must sociological theory and sociological practice be so far apart?" Comment on J. H. Turner. *Sociological Perspectives* 41(2): 259–61.

Babbie, Earl. 2001. *The Practice of Social Research*, 9th ed. Belmont, CA: Wadsworth.

Baca Zinn, Maxine, & Barbara Wells. 2000. "Diversity within Latino families: New lessons for family studies." In David H. Demo, Katherine R. Allen, & Mark A. Fine (eds.), *Handbook of Family Diversity*. New York: Oxford University: 252–73.

Baca Zinn, Maxine. 2000. "Feminism and family studies for a new century." *The Annals of the American Academy of Political and Social Science* 571 (September): 42–56.

Bachman, Ronet. 1992. *Death and Violence on the Reservation*. New York: Auburn House.

Bachrach, Peter, & Morton Baratz. 1970. *Power and Poverty*. New York: Oxford University Press.

Bacon, Elizabeth E. 1980. *Central Asians Under Russian Rule: A Study In Cultural Change*. Ithaca, NY: Cornell University Press.

Badinter, Elisabeth. 1995. *XY: On Masculine Identity*. New York: Columbia University.

Bagguley, Paul, & Kirk Mann. 1992. "Idle thieving bastards? Scholarly representation of the 'underclass.' " *Work, Employment and Society* (6/1): 113–126.

Bagley, Christopher, & Pierre Tremblay. 1998. "On the prevalence of homosexuality and bisexuality, in a random community survey of 750 men aged 18 to 27." *Journal of Homosexuality* 36(2): 1–18.

Bailey, Frankie, & Donna Hale (eds.). 1998. *Popular Culture, Crime and Justice*. Belmont, CA: West/Wadsworth.

Bailey, Thomas, & Roger Waldinger. 1991. "Primary, secondary & enclave labor markets," *American Sociological Review* 56: 432–445.

Bainbridge, William S. 1997a. "Sectarian tension." In Thomas E. Dowdy & Patrick H. MacNamara (eds.), *Religion: North American Style*. New Brunswick, NJ: Rutgers University: 86–103.

Bainbridge, William S. 1997b. *The Sociology of Social Movements*. New York: Routledge.

Bakanic, Von. 1995. "I'm not prejudiced, but...A deeper look at racial attitudes." *Sociological Inquiry* (65/1): 67–86.

Baker, Bruce L., Jeffrey J. Wood, & Philip A. Cowan. 2002. "Behavior problems and peer rejection in preschool boys and girls." *Journal of Genetic Psychology* 163(1): 72–88.

Baker, Robert, & Linda Emanuel. 2000. "The efficacy of professional ethics: The AMA code of ethics in historical and current perspective." *Hastings Center Report* 30(4): S13–S16.

Baker, Wayne E., & Robert R. Faulkner. 1993. "The social organization of conspiracy: Illegal networks in the electrical equipment industry," *American Sociological Review* 58: 837–60.

Baldassare, Mark (ed.). 1994. *The Los Angeles Riots*. Boulder: Westview.

Baldridge, David. 2001. "Indian elders: Family traditions in crisis." *American Behavioral Scientist* 44(9): 1515–527.

Baldwin, Bruce A. 1988. *Beyond the Cornucopia Kids: How to Raise Healthy Achieving Children*. Wilmington, NC: Direction Dynamics.

Baldwin, John D., & Janice I. Baldwin. 1997. "Gender differences in sexual interest." *Archives of Sexual Behavior* 26(2): 181–210.

Bales, Kevin. 1999. *Disposable People: New Slavery In the Global Economy*. Berkeley: University of California.

Bales, Robert F. 1950. *Interaction Process Analysis*. Reading, MA: Addison-Wesley.

Bales, Robert F. 1951. "Channels of communication in small groups." *American Sociological Review* 16: 461–468.

Bales, Robert F. 1953. "The equilibrium problem in small groups." In Talcott Parsons, Robert F. Bales & Edward A. Shils (eds.), *Working Papers in the Theory of Action*. Glencoe: Free Press.

Balkwell, James W. 1990. "Ethnic inequality and the rate of homicide." *Social Forces* 69: 53–70.

Baltes, Paul B. 1997. "Psychological aspects of aging." In David Magnusson (ed.), *The Lifespan Development of Individuals: Behavioral, Neurobiological, and Psychosocial Perspectives: A Synthesis*. New York: Cambridge University: 427–60.

Baltzell, E. Digby. 1990. "Upperclass and elites." *Society* 27 (January/February): 72–75.

Bancroft, Robyne. 2001. "Everything relates, or a holistic approach to Aboriginal indigenous cultural heritage." In Peter Seitel (ed.), *Safeguarding Traditional Cultures: A Global Assessment*. Washington, DC: Smithsonian Institution Center for Folklife and Cultural Heritage: 70–74.

Bandura, Albert, & Richard H. Walters. 1963. *Social Learning and Personality Development*. New York: Holt, Rinehart & Winston.

Bandura, Albert. 1973. *Aggression: A Social Learning Analysis*. Upper Saddle River, NJ: Prentice Hall.

Bane, Mary Jo, & David T. Ellwood. 1994. *Welfare Realities: From Rhetoric to Reform*. Cambridge, MA: Harvard University Press.

Banerjee, Neela. 2001. "Some bullies seek ways to soften up: Toughness has risks for women executives." *New York Times* (August 10): C1, C2.

Banfield, Edward C. 1974. *The Unheavenly City Revisited*. Boston: Little, Brown.

Banks, James A. 2002. *An Introduction to Multicultural Education*. Boston: Allyn & Bacon.

Barber, Benjamin R. 1984. *Strong Democracy: Participatory Politics for a New Age*. Berkeley: University of California.

Barber, Benjamin R. 1995. *Jihad vs. McWorld*. New York: Ballantine.

Barber, Benjamin R. 1997. "Public schooling: Education for democracy." In John L. Goodlad & Timothy J. McKinnon (eds.), *The Public Purpose of Education and Schooling*. San Francisco: Jossey-Bass: 21–32.

Barer, Barbara M. 2002. "Men and women aging differently." In Harold Cox (ed.), *Aging* (Annual Editions). Guilford, CT: McGraw-Hill/Dushkin.

Barich, Rachel, & Denise D. Bielby. 1996. "Rethinking marriage: Change and stability in expectations." *Journal of Family Issues* 17: 139–69.

Barker, Kathleen, & Kathleen Christensen. 1998. *Contingent Work*. Ithaca, NY: Industrial Relations Press.

Barker, P. R., G. Manderscheid, & I. G. Gendershot. 1992. "Serious mental illness and disability in the adult household population in the United States, 1989." In R. W. Manderscheid & M. A. Sonnenschein, (eds.), *Mental Health, United States, 1992*. Washington, DC: Center for Mental Health Services & National Institute of Mental Health.

Barker, Valerie, Kimberly Noels, Julie Duck, Michael Hecht, Richarde Clement, & Howard Giles. 2001. "The English-only movement: A communication analysis of changing perceptions of language vitality." *Journal of Communication* 51(1): 3–37.

Barlett, Donald L., & James B. Steele. 1994. *America: Who Really Pays the Taxes?* New York: Touchstone–Simon & Schuster.

Barlow, Dudley. 2001. "Struggling in the mainstream." *The Education Digest* 66(5): 38–41.

Barnard, Chester. 1938. *The Functions of the Executive*. Cambridge, MA: Harvard University Press.

Barnard, Herbert P. 1998. "The Netherlands: Let's Be Realistic." *The World and I* 13 (October): 66–69.

Barnet, Richard J. 1993. "The end of jobs." *Harpers* 287/1720: 47–52.

Barnet, Richard J., & John Cavanagh. 1994. *Global Dreams: Imperial Institutions and the New World Order*. New York: Simon & Schuster.

Barnett, Camille Cates, & Francine Luloffs. 2001. "Sustainable cities." Center for International Development, Research Triangle Park, North Carolina. Available: http://www.rti.org/cid/scsummary.

Barnett, John. 2001. *The Meaning of Environmental Security: Ecological Politics and Policy in the New Security Era*. London: Zed.

Barnett, Victoria. 2000. "Payback." *Christian Century* (October 25).

Barnighausen, Till, & Rainer Sauerborn. 2002. "One hundred and eighteen years of the German health insurance system: Are there any lessons for middle- and low-income countries?" *Social Science & Medicine* 54(10): 1559–87.

Barnitz, Laura. 2001. "Effectively responding to the commercial exploitation of children: A comprehensive approach to prevention, protection, and reintegration services." *Child Welfare* 80(5): 597–610.

Baron, Dennis. 2002. "Will anyone accept the good news on literacy?" *The Chronicle of Higher Education* 48(2): B10.

Baron, James N., & Andrew E. Newman. 1990. "For what it's worth." *American Sociological Review* 55: 155–75.

Baron, James N., P. D. Jennings, & Frank R. Dobbin. 1988. "Mission control? The development of personnel systems in U.S. industry." *American Journal of Sociology* 53: 497–514.

Barone, Michael. 1998. "How Hispanics are Americanizing." *Wall Street Journal.* (February 6): A22.

Barr, Robert D., & William H. Parrett. 2001. *Hope Fulfilled for At-Risk Youth: K–12 Programs that Work.* Needham Hts., MA: Allyn & Bacon.

Barrett, Anne E. 1999. "Social support and life satisfaction among the never married: Examining the effects of age." *Research on Aging* 21(1): 46–72.

Barrett, David B. 2001. *New Believers: Sects, 'Cults,' and Alternative Religions.* New York: Sterling.

Barrett, David B., George T. Kurian, & Todd M. Johnson (eds.). 2001. *World Christian Encyclopedia: A Comparative Survey of Churches and Religions—AD 30 to 2200.* Oxford, NY: Oxford University.

Barrett, Richard A. 1991. *Culture and Conduct: An Excursion in Anthropology.* Belmont, CA: Wadsworth.

Barrett, Rusty. 2002. "Is queer theory important for sociolinguistic theory?" In Kathryn Campbell-Kibler (ed.), *Language and Sexuality: Contesting Meaning in Theory and Practice.* Stanford, CA: CSLI: 25–44.

Barringer, H. R., R. W. Gardner, & M. J. Levin. 1993. *Asians and Pacific Islanders in the United States.* New York: Russell Sage.

Barry, Kathleen. 1979. *Female Sexual Slavery.* New York: Basic Books.

Barry, Patricia. 2002. "Down-to-the-wire battle over drugs." *AARP Bulletin* (July–August): 3–5.

Bartkowski, John P. 2000. "Breaking walls, raising fences: Masculinity, intimacy and accountability among Promise Keepers." *Sociology of Religion* 61(1): 33–53.

Bartlett, Dave. 2001. "Human rights, democracy & the donors: The first MMD government in Zambia." *Review of African Political Economy* 28(87)March:83–91.

Barton, Edward Read. 2000. "Parallels between mythopoetic men's work/men's peer mutual support groups and selected feminist theories." In Edward Read Barton (ed.). *Mythopoetic Perspectives of Men's Healing Work: An Anthology of Therapists and Others.* Westport, CT: Bergin & Garvey: 3–20.

Bartos, Omar. 1995. "Growth of Russian organized crime poses serious threat." *CJ International* 11: 8–9.

Bartsch, Robert A., Teresa Burnett, R. Diller, & Elizabeth Rankin-Williams. 2000. "Gender representation in television commercials: Updating an update." *Sex Roles* 43(9–10): 735–43.

Basow, Susan A. 1992. *Gender Stereotypes: Traditions and Alternatives.* Belmont, CA: Wadsworth.

Basow, Susan A., & Kelly Johnson. 2000. "Predictors of homophobia in female college students." *Sex Roles* 42(5–6): 391–404.

Baudrillard, Jean. 1988. *America.* London: Verso.

Baudrillard, Jean. 1995. *The Gulf War Did Not Take Place.* Bloomington: University of Indiana Press.

Bauer, Peter. 2002. "Transition in the East: Democracy and the market." In David Boaz (ed.), *Toward Liberty: The Idea that is Changing the World.* Washington, DC: Cato Institute: 192–98.

Bauerlein, Monika. 1996. "The Luddites are back." *Utne Reader* (March–April): 24, 26.

Baum, Dan. 1996. *Smoke and Mirrors: The War on Drugs and the Politics of Failure.* Boston: Little, Brown.

Baum, Don. 2000. "Invisible Nation." *Rolling Stone* (December 7): 44–45, 124.

Bauman, Kurt. 1999. "Shifting family definitions: The effect of cohabitation and other nonfamily household relationships on measures of poverty." *Demography* 36(3): 315–25.

Baumann, Zygmunt. 1991. *Modernity and the Holocaust.* Ithaca, NY: Cornell University Press.

Bayer, Ronald (ed.). 2000. "Health policy and ethics forum: The population debate." *American Journal of Pubic Health* 90(12): 1838–47.

BBC News, 2001. "Chernobyl's cancer world record." Available: http://news.bbc.co.uk/1 /hi/health.

BBC. 2002. "North Korea faces 'looming' food crisis." *BBC News.* (April 10). Available: http://news.bbc.co.uk/1/hi/world/asia-pacific.

Beach, Stephen W. 1977. "Religion and political change in Northern Ireland." *Sociological Analysis* (38/1): 37–48.

Beals, Alan R. 1980. *Gopalpur: A South Indian Village.* New York: Holt, Rinehart and Winston.

Beatley, Timothy. 2000. *Green Urbanism: Learning from European Cities.* Washington, DC: Island Press.

Beaumont, Sherry L., Monica Ruggeri, & Viviane C. B. Vasconcelos. 2001. "Similarities and differences in mother–daughter and mother–son conversation during preadolescence and adolescence." *Journal of Language and Social Psychology* 20(4): 419–44.

Beaverstock, Jonathan V., Richard G. Smith, & Peter J. Taylor. 2000. "World–city network: A new metageography?" *Annals of the Association of American Geographers* 90(1): 123–34.

Beck, Allen J., & Paige M. Harrison. 2001. *Prisoners in 2000.* Washington, DC: Bureau of Justice Statistics.

Becker, Gary S. 1994. "Working women's staunchest allies: Supply and demand." In Susan F. Feiner (ed.), *Race & Gender in the American Economy: Views from Across the Spectrum.* Upper Saddle River, NJ: Prentice Hall.

Becker, Howard S. 1963. *Outsiders.* New York: Free Press.

Becker, Julian. 1977. *Hitler's Children.* Philadelphia: Lippincott.

Becker, Penny Edgell, & Pawan H. Dhingra. 2001. "Religious involvement and volunteering: Implications for civil society." *Sociology of Religion* 62(3): 315–35.

Beeghley, Leonard. 2000. *The Structure of Social Stratification in the United States,* 4th ed. Boston: Allyn & Bacon.

Beeghley, Leonard. 2000. *The Structure of Social Stratification in the United States,* 3rd ed. Needham Heights, MA: Allyn & Bacon.

Beer, Amy. 2002. "Periodical pressures: Magazines for U.S. Latinas." In Eileen R. Meehan & Ellen Riordan (eds.), *Sex & Money: Feminism and Political Economy in the Media.* Minneapolis, MN: University of Minnesota: 164–80.

Beers, David. 1991. "Just Say Whoa!" *Mother Jones* 16 (July/August): 38–43 and 42–56.

Beggs, John J. 1995. "The institutional environment: Implications for race and gender inequality in the U.S. labor market." *American Sociological Review* 60: 612–33.

Begley, Sharon. 2000. "The Stereotype Trap." *Newsweek* (November 6): 66–67

Belfrage, Sally. 1965. *Freedom Summer.* Greenwich, CT: Fawcett.

Belknap, Joanne. 1996. *The Invisible Woman: Gender, Crime and Justice.* Belmont, CA: Wadsworth.

Bell, Daniel. 1953. "Crime as an American way of life." *Antioch Review* 13: 131–54.

Bell, Daniel. 1976. *The Coming of Post-Industrial Society: A Venture in Social Forecasting.* New York: Basic Books.

Bell, Daniel. 1999. *The Coming of Postindustrial Society: A Venture in Social Forecasting.* New York: Basic Books.

Bell, Derrick. 1992. *Race, Racism and American Law.* Boston: Little, Brown.

Bell, J. Bowyer. 1975. *The Secret Army: A History of the IRA: 1916–70.* Cambridge, MA: MIT Press.

Bell, Ronny A., Sara A. Quandt, Thomas A. Arcury, Juliana McDonald, & Mara Z. Vitolins. 2000. "Health behaviors of rural white, African American and Native American elders." *American Journal of Health Behavior* 24(5): 349–60.

Bell, Wendell. 1981. "Neocolonialism." In *Encyclopedia of Sociology.* Guilford, CT: Dushkin: 193.

Bellah, Robert N. 1967. "Civil religion in America." *Daedalus* 96: 1–21.

Bellah, Robert N. 1970. *Beyond Belief.* New York: Harper.

Bellah, Robert, Richard Madsen, William M. Sullivan, Ann Swidler, & Steven M. Tipton. 1985. *Habits of the Heart.* New York: Harper & Row.

Bellah, Robert. 1957. *Tokagawa Religion.* Glencoe, IL: Free Press.

Bellamy, R. V., Jr. 1998. "The evolving television sports marketplace." In Lawrence A. Wenner (ed.), *MediaSport.* New York: Routledge: 173–87.

Belsie, Laurent. 1999. "School busing: An era of decline." *Christian Science Monitor* (Feb. 2) Available: http://www.csmonitor.com/durable/1999/02/02plsl.htm.

Belsky, Jay, & John Kelly. 1995. "His and hers transition." In Mark Robert Rank & Edward L. Kain (eds.), *Diversity and Change in Families: Patterns, Prospects and Policies.* Upper Saddle River, NJ: Prentice Hall.

Belz, H. 1991. *Equality Transformed: A Quarter Century of Affirmative Action.* New Brunswick, NJ: Rutgers University Press.

Bem, Sandra Lipsitz. 1981. "Gender schema theory: A cognitive account of sex-typing." *Psychological Review* 88: 354–64.

Bem, Sandra Lipsitz. 1983. "Gender schema theory and its implications for child development: Raising gender-aschematic children in a gender-schematic society." *Signs* 8: 598–616.

Bem, Sandra Lipsitz. 1996. "Transforming the debate on sexual inequality: From biological difference in institutionalized androcentrism." In Joan C. Chrisler, Carla Golden, & Patricia D. Rozee (eds.). *Lectures on the Psychology of Women.* New York: McGraw-Hill.

Bendix, Richard. 1962. *Max Weber: An Intellectual Portrait.* Garden City, NY: Anchor.

Bendroth, M. L. 1999. "Fundamentalism and the family: Gender, culture, and the American pro-family movement." *Journal of Women's History* 10(4): 35–53.

Bendyna, Mary E., John C. Green, & Mark J. Rozell. 2001. "Uneasy alliance: Conservative Catholics and the Christian Right. *Sociology of Religion* 62(1): 51–64.

Benedict, J. 1998. *Athletes and Acquaintance Rape.* Thousand Oaks, CA: Sage.

Benenson, Joyce F., Catherine Nicholson, and Angela Waite. 2001. "The influence of group size on children's competitive behavior." *Child Development* 72(3): 921–28.

Benford, Robert D. 1993. "Frame disputes within the nuclear disarmament movement." *Social Forces* 71: 677–701.

Bengston, Vern L., & J. F. Robertson (eds.). 1985. *Grandparenthood.* Beverly Hills, CA: Sage.

Bengston, Vern L., Margaret N. Reedy, & Chad Gordon. 1985. "Aging and self conceptions: Personality processes and social contexts." In James E. Birren & K. Warner Schaie (eds.), *Handbook of the Psychology of Aging.* New York: Van Nostrand Reinhold.

Benjamin, Jessica. 1988. *The Bonds of Love: Psychoanalysis, Feminism and the Problem of Domination.* New York: Pantheon.

Benjet, Corina, & Laura Hernandez-Guzman. 2001. "Gender differences in psychological well-being of Mexican early adolescents." *Adolescence* 36 (Spring): 47–65.

Bennett, Pamela, & Xie Yu. 2000. "Explaining the black–white gap in college attendance: Racial differences versus socioeconomic determinants research." Paper presented at the Population Association of America. New York, March.

Bennis, Warren G., & Philip E. Slater. 1968. *The Temporary Society.* New York: Harper & Row.

Benokraitis, Nijole V., & Joe R. Feagin. 1986. *Modern Sexism.* Upper Saddle River, NJ: Prentice Hall.

Bensley, Lillian, & Juliet Van Eenwyk. 2001. "Video games and real-life aggression: Review of the literature." *Journal of Adolescent Health* 29(4): 244–57.

Bentham, Jeremy. 1967. *A Fragment on Government and an Introduction to the Principle of Morals & Legislation.* Oxford, England: Basil Blackwell.

Berberoglu, Berch. 1990. *Political Sociology: A Comparative/Historical Approach.* Dix Hills, NY: General Hall.

Berer, M. 2000. "Making abortion safe: A matter of good public health policy and practice." *Bulletin of the World Health Organization* 78(5): 580.

Berer, Marge. 1993. "Reproductive health: Towards a definition." In *Reproductive Health Policy & Programs: Reflections on the African Experience.* A Conference Report, Harare, July. Washington, DC: Henry J. Kaiser Foundation.

Beresford, Melanie. 2001. "Vietnam: The transition from central planning." In Garry Rodan, Kevin Hewison, & Richard Robison (eds.), *The Political Economy of South-East Asia: Conflicts, Crises and Change.* New York: Oxford University.

Berg, Ivar, & Mayer Zald. 1978. "Business and society." *Annual Review of Sociology* 4: 115–43.

Bergen, Raquel Kennedy, & Kathleen A. Bogle. 2000. "Exploring the connection between pornography and sexual violence." *Violence and Victims* 15(3): 227–34.

Berger, Bennett M. 1988. "Utopia and its environment," *Society* (Jan/Feb): 37–41.

Berger, Brigitte, & Peter L. Berger. 1991. "The family and modern society." In Mark Hutter (ed.), *The Family Experience: A Reader in Cultural Diversity.* New York: Macmillan.

Berger, Candyce S. 2001. "Infant mortality: A reflection of the quality of life." *Health & Social Work* 26(4): 277–82.

Berger, Joseph, Robert Z. Norman, James W. Balkwell, & Roy F. Smith. 1992. "Status inconsistency in task situations: A test of four status processing principles." *American Sociological Review* 57: 843–55.

Berger, Leslie. 2002. "The therapy generation: As pressures rise, campus mental health services struggle to keep up." *New York Times Magazine* (January 13): 31–33, 40, 42–43.

Berger, Peter L. 1963. *Invitation to Sociology: A Humanistic Perspective.* Garden City, NY: Anchor.

Berger, Peter L., & Thomas Luckmann. 1966. *The Social Construction of Reality.* New York: Doubleday.

Berger, Peter. 1967. *The Sacred Canopy: Elements of a Sociological Theory of Religion.* New York: Doubleday.

Berger, Peter. 1977. *Facing up to Modernity: Excursions in Society, Politics and Religion.* New York: Basic Books.

Berger, Peter. 1986. *The Capitalist Revolution: 50 Propositions About Prosperity, Equality and Liberty.* New York: Basic.

Berger, Peter. 1997. *Redeeming Laughter: The Comic Dimension of Human Experience.* New York: Walter de Gruyter.

Berger, Peter. 2001. "Postscript." In Linda Woodhead with Paul Heelas & David Martin (eds.), *Peter Berger and the Study of Religion.* London: Routledge: 189–98.

Bergesen, Albert, & Max Herman. 1998. "Immigration, race & riot: The 1992 Los Angeles uprising." *American Sociological Review* (63/1): 39–54.

Bergmann, Barbara R. 2002. "What is affirmative action?" In Roberta Satow (ed.), *Gender and Social Life.* Needham Hts., MA: Allyn & Bacon.

Berk, Richard A. 1974. *Collective Behavior.* Dubuque, IA: Brown.

Berk, Richard A., & Sarah F. Berk. 1979. *Labor and Leisure at Home: Content and Organization of the Household Day.* Beverly Hills, CA: Sage.

Berkman, Lisa F. 2000. "Social networks and health: The bonds that heal." In Alvin R. Tarlov & Robert F. St. Peter (eds.), *The Society and Population Health Reader. Volume II—A State and Community Perspective.* New York: New Press: 259–77.

Berkman, Lisa F., Thomas Glass, & Ian Brissette. 2000. "From social integration to health: Durkheim in the new millennium." *Social Science & Medicine* 51(6): 843–57.

Berkowitz, Leonard. 1993. *Aggression: Its Causes, Consequences & Control.* New York: McGraw-Hill.

Berlin, Isaiah. 1963. *Karl Marx: His Life & Environment.* New York: Oxford University Press.

Bernstein, Aaron. 2002. "The time bomb in the workplace: Illiteracy." *Business Week* 3771 (Feb. 25): 122.

Bernstein, Richard. 2001. "Dictatorship of virtue: Multiculturalism in elementary and secondary schools." In Williamson M. Evers, Lance T. Izumi, & Pamela A. Riley (eds.), *School Reform: The Critical Issues.* Stanford, CA: Hoover Institution: 48–65.

Berrick, Jill D. 1995. *Faces of Poverty.* New York: Oxford University Press.

Berrios, G. E. 1995. *The History of Mental Symptoms: Descriptive Psychopathology Since the 19th Century.* New York: Cambridge University Press.

Berry, Gordon L. 1998. "Black family life on television and the socialization of the African American child: Images of marginality." *Journal of Comparative Family Studies* 29(2): 233–42.

Berry, Jeffrey. 1997. *The Interest Group Society,* 3rd ed. New York: Longman.

Besser, Terry L. 1993. "A critical approach to the study of Japanese management." *Humanity and Society* (16/2): 176–95.

Best, Steven, & Douglas Kellner. 1991. *Postmodern Theory: Critical Interrogations.* New York: Guilford.

Beteille, Andre. 1996. *Caste, Class & Power: Changing Patterns of Stratification in a Tanjore Village,* 2nd ed. Delhi: Oxford University Press.

Bettivia, Rhiannon. 2001. "Girl culture: We must continue to revisit it." In Angharad N. Valdivia (ed.), *A Latina in the Land of Hollywood and Other Essays on Media Culture.* Tucson, AZ: University of Arizona.

Beyene, Yewoubdar, Gay Becker, & Nury Mayen. 2002. "Perception of aging and sense of well-being among Latino elderly." *Journal of Cross-Cultural Gerontology* 17(2): 155–72.

Beyrer, Chris. 2001. "Shan women and girls in the sex industry in Southeast Asia: Political causes and human rights implications." *Social Science and Medicine* 53(4): 543050.

Bhatia, Sunil. 2002. "Acculturation, dialogical voices and the construction of the diasporic self." *Theory & Psychology* 12(1): 55–77.

Bhattasali, Deepak, & Masashiro Kawai. 2002. "Implications of China's accession into the World Trade Organization." In Hanns Gunther Hilpert & Rene Haak (eds.), *Japan and China: Cooperation, Competition, and Conflict.* New York: Palgrave.

Bianchi, Suzanne M. 1999. "Feminization and juvenilization of poverty: Trends, risks, causes, and consequences." *Annual Review of Sociology* 25: 307–33.

Bianchi, Suzanne M., & Lynne M. Casper. 2001. "American families resilient after 50 years of change." Washington DC: Population Reference Bureau (News Release, January 5).

Biari, Yanjie. 1997. "Bringing strong ties back in: Indirect ties, bridges, and job search in China." *American Sociological Review* 63: 366–385.

Biblarz, Timothy, Vern L. Bengtson & Alexander Bacur. 1996. "Social Mobility Across Generations," *Journal of Marriage and the Family* 58: 188–200.

Biderman, Albert D., & James P. Lynch. 1991. *Understanding Crime Incidence Statistics: Why the UCR Diverges from the NCS.* New York: Springer-Verlag.

Bilukha, Oleg O. 2002. "Internalization of Western standards of appearance, body dissatisfaction and dieting in urban educated Ukrainian females." *European Eating Disorders Review* 10(2).

Binder, Ron. 2001. "Changing a culture: Sexual assault prevention in the fraternity and sorority community." In Allen J. Ottens & Kathy Hoteling (eds.), *Sexual Violence on Campus: Policies, Programs and Perspectives.* New York: Springer: 120–40.

Binstock, Robert H. 2000. "Older people and voter participation: Past and future." *Gerontologist* 40: 18–31.

Birdsall, Nancy. 2000. "Life is unfair: Inequality in the world." In Robert M. Jackson (ed.), *Global Issues 00/01.* Guilford, CT: Dushkin/McGraw-Hill: 19–26.

Bissinger, H. G. 1991. *Friday Night Lights.* New York: Harper & Row.

Black, Jan Knippers. 1991. "Dowry abuse: No happily ever after for Indian brides." *Contemporary Review* 258: 237–39.

Blackman, Allen. 2002. "The economics of technology diffusion: Implications for greenhouse gas mitigation in developing countries." In Stuart S. Nagel (ed.), *Environmental Policy and Developing Nations.* Jefferson, NC: McFarland: 288–306.

Blair, Bruce. 1993. *The Logic of Accidental Nuclear War.* Washington, DC: Brookings Institution.

Blake, Wayne E., & Carol Anderson Darling. 2000. "Quality of life: Perceptions of African Americans." *Journal of Black Studies* 30(3): 411–27.

Blakely, Edward J., & Mary Gail Snyder. 1998. *Fortress America.* Washington, DC: Brookings Institute.

Blanchard, Dallas. 1994. *The Anti-Abortion Movement and the Rise of the Religious Right.* New York: Twayne.

Blankenship, Kim. 1993. "Bringing gender and race in: US employment discrimination policy." *Gender & Society* 7: 204–226.

Blasi, Gary. 1994. "And we are not seen: Ideological and political barriers to understanding homelessness." *American Behavioral Scientist* 37(4): 563–86.

Blau, Peter & Otis Dudley Duncan. 1967. *The American Occupational Structure.* New York: Wiley.

Blau, Peter M., & Marshall W. Meyer. 1987. *Bureaucracy in Modern Society,* 3rd ed. New York: Random House.

Blauner, Bob. 1989. *Black Lives, White Lives: Three Decades of Race Relations in America.* Berkeley: University of California Press.

Blauner, Robert. 1964. *Alienation and Freedom.* Chicago: University of Chicago Press.

Blauner, Robert. 1972. *Racial Oppression in America.* New York: Harper & Row.

Blazak, Randy. 2001. "White boys to terrorist men: Target recruitment of Nazi skinheads." *American Behavioral Scientist* 44(6): 982–1000.

Blinde, E. M., & D. E. Taub. 1993. "Sports participation & women's personal empowerment." *Journal of Sport and Social Issues* (17/1): 47–60.

Blinde, Elaine M., & Diane E. Taub. 1992. "Women athletes as falsely accused deviants: Managing the lesbian stigma." *Sociological Quarterly* (33/Winter): 521–33.

Bloch, Francis, & Harl Ryder. 2000. "Two-sided search: Marriages and matchmakers." *International Economic Review* 41(1): 93–115.

Bloch, Maurice. 1994. "Language, anthropology, and cognitive science." In Robert Borofsky, (ed.), *Assessing Cultural Anthropology.* New York: McGraw-Hill.

Block, Alan A. 1983. *East Side—West Side: Organizing Crime in New York, 1930–1959.* New Brunswick, NJ: Rutgers University Press.

Block, Alan A. 1991. *Perspectives on Organizing Crime.* Amsterdam: Kluwer.

Block, Alan A., & William J. Chambliss. 1981. *Organizing Crime.* New York: Elsevier.

Block, R. 1994. "The tragedy of Rwanda." *New York Review of Books* 41: 3–8.

Bloom, Allen. 1987. *The Closing of the American Mind.* New York: Simon & Schuster.

Bloom, Paul, & Frank C. Keil. 2001. "Thinking through language." *Mind & Language* 16(4): 351–67.

Blumer, Herbert G. 1969a. *Symbolic Interactionism: Perspective and Method.* Upper Saddle River, NJ: Prentice Hall.

Blumer, Herbert. 1969b. "Collective behavior." In Alfred M. Lee, (ed.), *Principles of Sociology,* 3rd ed. New York: Barnes & Noble: 65–121.

Blumer, Herbert. 1974. "Social movements." In R. Serge Denisoff, (ed.), *The Sociology of Dissent.* New York: Harcourt Brace Jovanovich: 74–90.

Blumler, J., & C. Spicer. 1990. "Prospects for creativity in the new television marketplace." *Journal of Communication* 40(4): 78–101.

Blumstein, Alfred. 1993. "Racial Disproportionality of U.S. Prison Populations Revisited." *University of Colorado Law Review* 64/3.

Bly, Robert. 1990. *Iron John: A Book about Men*. Reading, MA: Addison-Wesley.

Boas, Morten. 2001. "Multilateral development banks, environmental impact assessments, and nongovernmental organizations in U.S. foreign policy." In Paul G. Harris (ed.), *The Environment, International Relations, and U.S. Foreign Policy*. Washington, DC: Georgetown University: 178–96.

Boaz, David (ed.). 2002. *Toward Liberty: The Idea that is Changing the World*. Washington, DC: Cato Institute.

Bobo, Lawrence, & Vincent L. Hutchings. 1996. "Perceptions of racial group competition." *American Sociological Review* 61(6): 951–972.

Bobo, Lawrence. 1991. "Social responsibility, individuality and redistributive policies." *Sociological Forum* 6: 71–92.

Bobo, Lawrence. 2001. "Perceptions of racial group competition: Extending Blumer's theory of group position to a multiracial social context." In Michael A. Hogg and Dominic Abrams (eds.), *Intergroup Relations: Essential Readings*. Philadelphia: Psychology Press: 71–90.

Bodley, John H. 2000. *Cultural Anthropology: Tribes, States, and the Global System*. Mountain View, CA: London.

Boesch, C. 1999. *The Chimpanzees of the Tai Forest*. Oxford, UK: Oxford University.

Boesch, Christophe, & Michael Tomasello. 1998. "Chimpanzees and human cultures." *Current Anthropology* 39: 591–614.

Bohlen, C. 1995. "Catholics defying an infallible church." *The New York Times* (November 26): E3.

Bok, Dereck C. 1993. *The Cost of Talent*. New York: Free Press.

Bold, Mary. 2001. "Blended families: Building block 2." Center for Parent Education, University of North Texas. Available: http://www.unt.edu/cpe/module1blk2blend.

Bolego, C., A. Polli, & R. Paoletti. 2002. "Smoking and gender." *Cardiovascular Research* 53(3): 568–76.

Bollen, Kenneth A., & Stephen J. Appold. 1993. "National Industrial Structure & the Global System." *American Sociological Review* 58: 283–301.

Bombeck, Erma. 1987. *The Ties That Bind...and Gag*. New York: Fawcett Crest.

Bonacich, Edna. 1972. "A theory of ethnic antagonism: The split labor market." *American Sociological Review* 37: 547–49.

Bonacich, Edna. 1976. "Advanced capitalism & black/white relations in the U.S." *American Sociological Review* 41: 34–51.

Borchard, Kurt. 2000. "Fear of and sympathy toward homeless men in Las Vegas." *Humanity and Society* 24(1): 3–18.

Bordewich, Fergus M. 1996. *Killing the White Man's Indian*. New York: Anchor/Doubleday.

Borjas, George J. 1995. "The internationalization of the U.S. labor market and the wage structure." *Federal Reserve Bank of NY Economic Review* (1/1): 3–9.

Bornschier, Volker. 1995. *Western Society in Transition*. New Brunswick, NJ: Transaction.

Boroughs, Don L. 1995. "Telecommuting picks up speed." *U.S. News & World Report* (July 17): 42.

Boserup, Ester. 1970. *Women's Role in Economic Development*. London: Elgar.

Boskin, Joseph. 1997. *Rebellious Laughter: Humor in American Culture*. Syracuse, NY: Syracuse University.

Botkin, Darla R., M. O'Neal Weeks, & Jeanette E. Morris. 2000. "Changing marriage role expectations: 1961–1996." *Sex Roles* 42(9–10): 933–42.

Bouffard, Jeffrey, M. Lyn Exum, & Raymond Paternoster. 2000. "Whither the beast? The role of emotions in a rational choice theory of crime." In Sally S. Simpson (ed.), *Of Crime and Criminality*. Thousand Oaks, CA: Pine Forge: 159–178.

Boulding, Elise. 1976. *The Underside of History*. Boulder, CO: Westview.

Bouma, Gary D. 1993. *The Research Process*. Melbourne, AS: Oxford University.

Bourdeau, Pierre, Jean-Claude Chamboredom, & Jean-Claude Passeron. 1991. *The Craft of Sociology*. New York: de Gruyter.

Bourdieu, Pierre. 1984. *Distinction: A Social Critique of the Judgement of Taste*. Cambridge, MA: Harvard University Press.

Bourdieu, Pierre. 1987. *Choses Dites*. Paris: Edition de Minuit.

Bourdieu, Pierre. 1998. *Practical Reason: On the Theory of Action*. Cambridge, UK: Polity.

Boushey, Heather. 2001. "Closing the wage gap." *Charleston Sunday Gazette* (April 8).

Bowen, William G., & Derek K. Bok. 1999. *The Shape of the River: Long-Term Consequences of Considering Race in College and University Admissions*. Princeton, NJ: Princeton University Press.

Bowerbank, Sylvia. 2001. "Of mice and women: Early modern roots of ecological feminism." *Women and Environments International Magazine* 52/53 (Fall): 27–9.

Bowie, Fiona. 2000. *The Anthropology of Religion*. Oxford, UK: Blackwell.

Bowles, Samuel, & Herbert Gintis. 1976. *Schooling in Capitalist America: Educational Reform and the Contradictions of Economic Life*. New York: Basic Books.

Bowles, Samuel. 1977. "Unequal education and the reproduction of the social division of labor." In Jerome Karabel & A. H. Halsey, (eds.), *Power and Ideology in Education*. New York: Oxford University Press: 137–153.

Boyd, R., & P. Richerson. 1996. "Why culture is common but cultural evolution is rare." *Proceedings of the British Academy* 88: 77–93.

Boyer, Ernest L. 1994. "Ready to learn: A mandate for the nation." In Daniel J. Curran & Claire M. Renzetti (eds.), *Contemporary Societies: Problems and Prospects*. Upper Saddle River, NJ: Prentice Hall: 443–51.

Boyer, M. Christine. 1993. "The city of illusion: New York's public places." In Paul L. Knox (ed.), *The Restless Urban Landscape*. Upper Saddle River, NJ: Prentice Hall: 111–26.

Boyer-Pennington, Michelle E., John Pennington, & Camille Spink. 2001. "Student expectations and optimism toward marriage as a function of parental divorce." *Journal of Divorce and Remarriage* 34(3–4): 71–87.

Boyes, William, & Michael Melvin. 1994. *Economics*, 2nd ed. Boston: Houghton Mifflin.

Boykin, A. Wade. 1994. "Harvesting talent and culture: African-American children and educational reform." In Robert J. Rossi (ed.), *Schools and Students at Risk: Context and Framework for Positive Change*. New York: Teacher's College Press, Columbia University: 116–38.

Boyle, Michael H., & Ellen L. Lipman. 2002. "Do places matter? Socioeconomic disadvantage and behavioral problems of children in Canada." *Journal of Consulting & Clinical Psychology* 70(2): 378–89.

Bracey, Gerald Watkins. 2002. *The War Against America's Public Schools: Privatizing Schools, Commercializing Education*. Boston: Allyn & Bacon.

Bradley, Jennifer. 2000. "Private suburbs, public lives." *American Prospect* 11 (May 22): 46–49.

Bradley, Robert H., & Robert F. Corwyn. 2002. "Socioeconomic status and child development." *Annual Review of Psychology* 53: 371–99.

Bradshaw, York, & Michael Wallace. 1996. *Global Inequalities*. Thousand Oaks, CA: Pine Forge.

Bradshaw, York. 1988. "Reassessing economic dependency and uneven development: The Kenyan experience." *American Sociological Review* 53: 693–708.

Braguinsky, Serguey V., & Grigory Yavlinsky. 2000. *Incentives and Institutions: The Transition to a Market Economy*. Princeton, NJ: Princeton University.

Brailsford, Dennis. 1991. *Sport, Time and Society*. New York: Routledge.

Brain, John V. 2000. "About atonement and reparations." *The Sentinel* (November).

Braithwaite, John. 1981. "The myth of social class and criminality, reconsidered." *American Sociological Review*. 46: 36–58.

Braithwaite, John. 1985. "White-collar crime." *Annual Review of Sociology* 11: 1–25.

Bramlett, Matthew D., & William D. Mosher. 2001. "First marriage dissolution, divorce, and remarriage: United States." *Advance Data (CDC)* No. 323, May 31. Centers for Disease Control & National Center for Health Statistics.

Brand, Jeffrey E., Bradley S. Greenberg, & Dana Mastro. 2002. "Minorities and the mass media: Television in the 21st century." In Jennings Bryant & Dolf Zillmann (eds.), *Media Effects: Advance in Theory and Research*. Mahwah, NJ: Lawrence Erlbaum: 333–51.

Brandl, Bonnie. 2000. "Power and control: Understanding domestic abuse in later life." *Generations* 24(2): 39–45.

Braunstein, Peter, & Michael William Doyle (eds.). 2001. *Imagine Nation: The American Counterculture of the 1960s and 1970s*. New York: Routlege.

Braverman, H. 1974. *Labor and Monopoly Capital*. New York: Monthly Review Press.

Breakaway. 1995. "Mass wedding in India aims to evade dowry tradition." *St. Louis Post-Dispatch* (April 9): 12D.

Brecher, Jeremy, & Tim Costello. 1994. *Global Village or Global Pillage? Economic Reconstruction from the Bottom Up*. Boston: South End.

Breen, Michael. 1998. *The Koreans: Who They Are, What They Want, Where Their Future Lies*. New York: St. Martin's.

Brems, Eva. 2001. *Human Rights: Universality and Diversity*. The Hague: Martinus Nijhoff.

Brenner, Barbara A. 2000. "Sister support: Women create a breast cancer movement." In Anne S. Kasper & Susan J. Ferguson (eds.), *Breast Cancer: Society Shapes an Epidemic*. New York: St. Martin's: 325–54.

Brenner, R. 1977. "The Origins of Capitalist Development: A Critique of Neo-Smithian Marxism." *New Left Review* 104: 25–92.

Brenner, Reuven. 2002. "The causes of economic growth." In David Boaz (ed.), *Toward Liberty: The Idea that is Changing the World*. Washington, DC: Cato Institute: 69–80.

Brewer, Dominic J., Eric R. Eide, & Ronald G. Ehrenberg. 1999. "Does it pay to attend an elite private college? Cross-cohort evidence on the effects of college type on earnings." *The Journal of Human Resources* 34(1): 104–23.

Bridges, George F., & Robert D. Crutchfield. 1988. "Law, social standing and imprisonment." *Social Forces* 66: 699–724.

Bridges, J. S. 1989. "Sex differences in occupational values." *Sex Roles* 20: 205–211.

Brigham, Roblyn Anderson. 2001. "From school girls to working women: Transitions to adult roles in the 1970s, 1980s, and 1990s." *Dissertation Abstracts International, A: The Humanities and Social Sciences* 62(5) (November): 1959-A. Brandeis University.

Bright, Chris, & Ashly Mattoon. 2001. "The restoration of a hotspot begins." *Worldwatch* 14: November/December.

Brint, Steven, Mary F. Contreras, & Michael T. Matthews. 2001. "Socialization messages in primary schools: An organizational analysis." *Sociology of Education* 74(3): 157–80.

Brint, Steven. 1994. *In an Age of Experts: The Changing Role of Professionals in Politics and Public Life*. Princeton, NJ: Princeton University Press.

Brinton, Henry R. 1999. "Taking the church to uncharted waters." *Washington Post* (April 4): B1.

Brock, David. 2001. *Blinded by the Right: The Conscience of an Ex-Conservative*. New York: Crown.

Brodeur, Paul. 1985. *Outrageous Misconduct: The Asbestos Industry on Trial*. New York: Pantheon.

Brody, Gene H., Rand Conger, Frederick X. Gibbons, Xiaojia Ge, Velma McBride-Murry, Meg Gerrard, & Ronald L. Simons. 2001. "The influence of neighborhood disadvantage, collective socialization, and parenting on African American children's affiliation with deviant peers." *Child Development* 72(4): 1231–46.

Brohm, Jean-Marie. 1978. *Sport: A Prison of Measured Time*. London: Inks Links.

Bronner, Ethan. 1999. "In a revolution of rules, campuses go full circle." *New York Times* (March 3): A15.

Bronner, Ethan. 1999. "Rethinking America's school of hard knocks." *New York Times* (May 30): 1, 3.

Brooke, James. 1990. "Brazil's new chief gives radical plan to halt inflation." *The New York Times* (March 17): 1, 45.

Brooks, David. 2002. "Love the service here: Proposal to use Americorps volunteers in anti-terrorism effort." *New York Times Magazine* (November 25): 34.

Brooks, Roy L. 1996. *Integration or Separation?* Cambridge, MA: Harvard University Press.

Broughton, David, Jennifer Lee, & Ross Nethery. 2000. "Numbers show sports rank among best for big business." *The Coloradoan* (January 16): D-1.

Brown, Coramae R. 1993. *Unequal Justice: A Question of Color*. Bloomington: University of Indiana Press.

Brown, David A., & Sarah T. Boysen. 2000. "Spontaneous discrimination of natural stimuli by chimpanzees (Pan troglodytes)." *Journal of Comparative Psychology* 114(4): 392–400.

Brown, Dee. 1991. *Wonderous Times on the Frontier*. Little Rock, AR: August House.

Brown, Duane. 2002. "The role of world and cultural values in occupational choice, satisfaction and success: A theoretical statement." *Journal of Counseling & Development* 80(1): 48–56.

Brown, John. 1983. "Neighborhood policing in West Berlin." *Police Studies* (5/4): 29–32.

Brown, L. David, & Archana Kalegaonkar. 2002. "Support organizations and the evolution of the NGO sector." *Nonprofit and Voluntary Sector Quarterly* 31(2): 231–58.

Brown, Lester R., Christopher Flavin, Hilary French, et al. 2000. *State of the World: A Worldwatch Institute Report on Progress toward a Sustainable Society*. New York: Norton.

Brown, Lester, Christopher Flavin, & Hilary French et al. 1999. *State of the World: A Worldwatch Institute Report on Progress toward a Sustainable Society*. New York: W.W. Norton.

Brown, Lester. 1994. *Vital Signs 1994: The Trends That Are Shaping Our Future*. New York: Norton.

Brown, Malcolm J. 2000. "The plight of the rural elderly in South Africa: A case for a community development cadre?" *Community Development Journal* 34(2): 143–50.

Brown, Michael, & Amy Goldin. 1973. *Collective Behavior*. Pacific Palisades, CA: Goodyear.

Brown, Michael. 2000. "The New Age and related forms of contemporary spirituality." In Raymond Scupin (ed.), *Religion and Culture: An Anthropological Focus*. Upper Saddle River, NJ: Prentice Hall: 421–432.

Brown, Phil. 2000. "Environment and health." In Chloe E. Bird, Peter Conrad, & Allen M. Fremont (eds.), *Handbook of Medical Sociology*. Upper Saddle River, NJ: Prentice Hall: 143–58.

Brown, Phillip, & Hugh Lauder. 2001. *Capitalism and Social Progress: The Future of Society in a Global Economy*. Houndmills, UK: Palgrave.

Brown, Rajeswary Ampalavanar. 2000. *Chinese Big Business and the Wealth of Asian Nations*. Houndmills, UK: Palgrave.

Brown, Shirley Vining. 1996. "Responding to the new demographics in higher education." In Laura I. Rendon & Richard O. Hope (eds.), *Educating a New Majority: Transforming America's Educational System for Diversity*. San Francisco: Jossey-Bass: 71–96.

Brown, Susan L., & Alan Booth, 1997. "Cohabitation versus marriage: A comparison of relationship quality." *Journal of Marriage and the Family* 58(3): 668–78.

Brown, Ursula M. 2000. *The Interracial Experience: Growing Up Black/White in the United States*. Westport, CT: Praeger.

Brown, Widney. 2001. "Human Rights Watch: An overview." In Claude E. Welch, Jr. (ed.), *NGOs and Human Rights: Promise and Performance*. Philadelphia: University of Pennsylvania: 72–84

Browne, A., & S. S. Bassuk. 1997. "Intimate violence in the lives of homeless and poorly housed women." *American Journal of Orthopsychiatry* 67: 261–278.

Browne, Beverly A. 1998. "Gender stereotypes in advertising on children's television in the 1990s: A cross-national study." *Journal of Advertising* 27(1): 83–96.

Browne, Irene (ed.). 1999. *Latinas and African American Women at Work*. New York: Russell Sage.

Browne, Judith A. 2001. "The ABCs of school discipline: Lessons from Miami-Dade County." In William Ayers, Bernadine Dohrn, & Rick Ayers (eds.), *Zero Tolerance: Resisting the Drive for Punishment in Our Schools*. New York: New Press: 188–201.

Brownmiller, Susan. 1999. *In Our Time: Memoir of a Revolution*. New York: Dell.

Bruce, Steve. 1996. *Religion in the Modern World: From Cathedrals to Cults*. New York: Oxford University Press.

Bruce, Steve. 1999. *Choice and Religion*. New York: Oxford University.

Bruce, Steve. 2001. "The curious case of the unnecessary recantation: Berger and secularization" In Linda Woodhead, Paul Heelas & David Martin (eds.), *Peter Berger and the Study of Religion*. London: Routledge.

Bruess, Carol J., & Judy C. Pearson. 1996. "Gendered Patterns in Family Communication." In Julia T. Wood, (ed.), *Gendered Relationships*. Mountain View, CA: Mayfield.

Brumann, Christoph. 2002. "Discussion and criticism: On culture and symbols." *Current Anthropology* 43(3).

Brunvand, Jan Harold. 1980. "Urban legends: Folklore for today." *Psychology Today* 14.

Brustad, Robert J. 1996. "Attraction to physical activity in urban schoolchildren: Parental socialization and gender influence." *Research Quarterly for Exercise & Sport* (67): 316–24.

Bryant, Chalandra M., & Rand D. Conger. 1999. "Marital success and domains of social support in long-term relationships: Does the influence of network members ever end?" *Journal of Marriage and the Family* 61(2): 437–50.

Bryant, Chalandra, & Rand D. Conger. 2002. "An intergenerational model of romantic relationship development." In Anita L. Vangelisti, Harry T. Rels, & Mary Anne Fitzpatrick (eds.), *Stability and Change in Personal Relationships*. Cambridge, UK: Cambridge University.

Bryce, Amy. 1999. "Bhopal disaster spurs U.S. industry, legislative action." U.S. Chemical Safety Board. Available: http:www.chemsafety.gov/lib/bhopal01.

Bryjak, George J., & Michael P. Soroka. 1994. *Sociology: Cultural Diversity in a Changing World*, 2nd ed. Boston: Allyn & Bacon.

Bryman, Daniel. 1998. "The logic of ethnic terrorism." *Studies in Conflict & Terrorism* 21: 149–69.

Bryner, Gary C. 2001. *Gaia's Wager: Environmental Movements and the Challenge of Sustainability*. Lanham, MD: Rowman & Littlefield.

Bryner, Gary C. 2002. "Assessing claims of environmental justice: Conceptual frameworks." In Kathryn M. Mutz, Gary C. Bryner, & Douglas S. Kenney (eds.), *Justice and Natural Resources*. Washington, DC: Island Press: 31–55.

Buchmann, Claudia, & Emily Hannum. 2001. "Education and stratification in developing countries: A review of theories and research." *Annual Review of Sociology* 27: 77–102.

Bucholtz, M., A. C. Liang, & L. A. Sutton (eds.). 1999. *Reinventing Identities: The Gendered Self in Discourse*. New York: Oxford University.

Buck, Elizabeth. 1993. *Paradise Remade: The Politics of Culture and History in Hawaii*. Philadelphia: Temple University.

Buck, James. 1998. *Preparing for Terrorism*. Albany, NY: Delmar.

Bucy, E. P., & P. D'Angelo. 1999. "The crisis of political communication." In M. E. Roloff (ed.), *Communication Yearbook 22*. Thousand Oaks, CA: Sage: 301–340.

Buddenbaum, Judith M., & Daniel A. Stout. 1996."Religion and mass media use: A review of the mass communication and sociology literature." In D. A. Stout & J. M. Buddenbaum, (eds.), *Religion and Mass Media: Audience and Adaptations*. Thousand Oaks, CA: Sage: 12–34.

Buechler, Steven M. 1993. "Beyond resource mobilization? Emerging trends in social movement theory." *The Sociological Quarterly* 34: 217–235.

Buhs, Eric S., & Gary W. Ladd. 2001. "Peer rejection as antecedent of young children's school adjustment: An examination of mediating processes." *Developmental Psychology* 37(4): 550–60.

Bullard, Robert B., & Beverly H. Wright. 1992. "The quest for environmental equity." In Riley E. Dunlap & Angela T. Mertig, (eds.), *American Environmentalism*. New York: Taylor & Francis: 39–49.

Bullock, Katherine. 2000. "Challenging media representations of the veil: Contemporary Muslim women's re-veiling movement." *American Journal of Islamic Social Sciences* 17(3): 22–53.

Bullough, Vern, & Bonnie Bullough. 1987. *Women and Prostitution: A Social History*. Buffalo, NY: Prometheus.

Buraway, Michael. 1997. "Review essay: The Soviet descent into capitalism." *American Journal of Sociology* (102/5): 1430–44.

Burawoy, Michael. 1980. *Manufacturing Consent*. Chicago: University of Chicago Press.

Bureau of Justice Statistics. 2000. "Section 2: Public attitudes toward crime and criminal justice-related topics." *Sourcebook of Criminal Justice Statistics*. Washington, DC: U.S. Department of Justice.

Bureau of Justice Statistics. 2001. *Criminal Victimization, 2000*. Washington, DC: U.S. Department of Justice.

Burge, Micah, & David Lester. 2001. "Predicting suicide ideation in high school students." *Psychological Reports* 89(2): 283–84.

Burgoon, J. K., & N. E. Dunbar. 2000. "An interactionist perspective on dominance-submission: Interpersonal dominance as a dynamic, situationally contingent social skill." *Communication Monographs* 67(1): 96–121.

Burka, Madeline. 2002. "The academy for educational development: Providing knowledge to improve lives." *Global HealthLink* July-August: 7, 21.

Burke, Nancy. 1998. *Teachers are Special: A Tribute to Those Who Educate, Encourage and Inspire*. New York: Random House.

Burkett, Elinor. 1997. "God Created Me To Be a Slave." *New York Times Sunday Magazine* (October 12): 56–60.

Burkett, Elinor. 2001. *Another Planet: A Year in the Life of a Suburban High School*. New York: HarperCollins.

Burleson, Brant R., & Wayne H. Denton, 1997. "The relationship between communication skill and marital satisfaction: Some moderating effects." *Journal of Marriage and the Family* 59(4): 884–902.

Burn, Shawn Meghan. 2000. "Heterosexuals' use of 'fag' and 'queer' to deride one another: A contributor to heterosexism and stigma." *Journal of Homosexuality* 40(2): 1–11.

Burnett, Paul C. 2002. "Teacher praise and feedback and student's perceptions of the classroom environment." *Educational Psychology* 22(1): 1–16.

Burns, Marty. 1998. "Celebration riots: Close to home." *Sports Illustrated* (88/24): 28.

Burris, Beverly H. 1989. "Technocratic organization and control." *Organization Studies* (10/1): 1–22.

Burstein, Paul. 1991. "Reverse discrimination cases in the federal courts." *Sociological Quarterly* (32/4): 511–28.

Burstyn, V. 1999. *The Rites of Men: Manhood, Politics, and the Culture of Sport*. Toronto: University of Toronto Press.

Burt, Martha R. 1992. *Over the Edge*. New York: Russell Sage.

Burt, R. S. 1998. "The gender of social capital." *Rationality & Society* 10(1): 5–46.

Burtless, Gary, (ed.). 1990. *A Future of Lousy Jobs? The Changing Structure of U.S. Wages*. Washington, DC: Brookings Institute.

Bury, Michael. 2000. "On chronic disease and disability." In Chloe E. Bird, Peter Conrad, & Allen M. Fremont (eds.), *Handbook of Medical Sociology*. Upper Saddle River, NJ: Prentice Hall: 173–83.

Bushman, Brad J. & C. A. Anderson. 2001. "Media violence and the American public: Scientific facts versus media misinformation." *American Psychologist* 56(June–July): 477–89.

Bushman, Brad J., & L. Rowell Huesmann. 2001. "Effects of televised violence on aggression." In Dorothy G. Singer & Jerome L. Singer (eds.), *Handbook of Children and the Media*. Thousand Oaks, CA: Sage.

Buss, David M., David P. Schmidt, & Todd K. Shackelford. 2001. *Psychology, Evolution & Gender* 3(3): 211–39.

Butler, D., & F. L. Geis. 1990. "Nonverbal affect responses to male & female leaders." *Journal of Personality & Social Psychology* 58: 48–59.

Butsch, Ricard. 1992. "Class and gender in four decades of television comedy." *Critical Studies in Mass Communication* 9: 387–99.

Butsch, Richard. 2000. "Ralph, Fred, Archie, and Homer: Why television keeps recreating the white, male working-class buffoon." In Tracey E. Ore (ed.), *The Social Construction of Difference and Inequality: Race, Class, Gender, and Sexuality*. Mountain View, CA: Mayfield: 361–70.

Byrne, David. 2001. *Understanding the Urban*. Basingstoke, UK: Palgrave.

Byrne, Donn, & Kathryn Kelly. 1981. *An Introduction to Personality*. Upper Saddle River, NJ: Prentice Hall.

Byrne, John A. 1993. "The horizontal corporation." *Business Week* (December 20): 76–81.

Bystrom, Dianne G., Terry A. Robertson, & Mary Christine Banwart. 2000. "Framing the fight: An analysis of media coverage of female and male candidates in primary races for governor and U.S. Senate in 2000." *American Behavioral Scientist* 44(12): 1999–2003.

Çagatay, Nilüfer. 2001. *Trade, Gender and Poverty*. United Nations Development Program. New York: United Nations.

Çagatay, Nilüfer, Caren Grown, & Aida Santiago. 1989. "The Nairobi women's conference: Toward a global feminism." In Laurel Richardson & Verta Taylor (eds.), *Feminist Frontiers II: Rethinking Sex, Gender, and Society*. New York: Random House.

Cable, Sherry, & Charles Cable. 1995. *Environmental Problems, Grassroots Solutions*. New York: St. Martin's Press.

Cable, Sherry. 1992. "Women's social movement involvement." *Sociological Quarterly* (33/1): 35–50.

Society Cage, Mary C. 1993. "Graduation rates of American Indians and blacks improve, lag behind others." *Chronicle of Higher Education* (May 26): A29.

Cahill, Spencer E. (ed.). 1995a. *Inside Social Life: Readings in Sociological Psychology and Microsociology*. Los Angeles: Roxbury.

Cahill, Spencer E., (ed.). 1995b. "Erving Goffman." Chapter 12 in Joel M. Charon, *Symbolic Interaction: An Introduction, An Interpretation, An Integration*. Upper Saddle River, NJ: Prentice Hall: 186–201.

Calafell, Francesca, Audrey Shuster, & William C. Speed. 1999. "Genealogy reconstructions from short tandem repeat genotypes in an Amazonian population." *American Journal of Physical Anthropology* 108(2): 137–46.

Calasanti, Toni M. 2000. "Incorporating diversity." In Elizabeth W. Markson & Lisa Ann Hollis-Sawyer (eds.), *Intersections of Aging: Readings in Social Gerontology*. Los Angeles, CA: Roxbury: 188–202.

Calavita, K., & H. N. Pontell. 1991. "Other people's money revisited: Collective embezzlement in the Savings and Loan and Insurance industries." *Social Problems* 38: 94–112.

Caldwell, John C., I. O. Orubuloye, & Pat Caldwell. 2000. "Female genital mutilation: Conditions of decline." *Population Research and Policy Review* 19(3): 233–54.

Calhoun, C., & H. Hiller. 1988. "Coping with insidious injuries: The case of Johns-Manville Corporation and asbestos exposure." *Social Problems* 35/2: 162–81.

Calhoun-Brown, Allison. 2000. "Upon this rock: The black church, nonviolence, and the civil rights movement." *Political Science & Politics* 33(2): 168–74.

Calkowski, Marcia. 2000. "Buddhism." In Raymond Scupin (ed.), *Religion and Culture: An Anthropological Focus*. Upper Saddle River, NJ: Prentice Hall: 249–74.

Callahan, Daniel. 1994. "From explosion to implosion: Transforming healthcare." In William Kornblum & Carolyn D. Smith (eds.), *The Healing Experience: Readings on the Social Context of Health Care*. Englewood Cliffs, NJ: Prentice Hall: 195–208.

Callahan, Sidney, & Bryan Appleyard. 1997. "Violence in the media should be censored." In Byron L. Stay (ed.), *Censorship*. San Diego: Greenhaven: 154–59.

Cameron, Deborah, 1998. "Gender, language and discourse: A review essay." *Signs* 23: 945–74.

Campo-Flores, Arian. 2001. "A town's two faces." *Newsweek* (June 4): 34–35

Canada, Geoffrey. 1995. *Fist, Stick, Gun: A Personal History of Violence in America*. Boston: Beacon.

Canada, Katherine, & Richard Pringle. 2000. "The role of gender in classroom interactions: A social context approach." In Michael S. Kimmel (ed.), *The Gendered Society Reader*. New York: Oxford University: 229–56.

Candland, Douglas Keith. 1995. *Feral Children and Clever Animals: Reflections on Human Nature*. New York: Oxford University.

Cannold, Leslie. 2000. *The Abortion Myth: Feminism, Morality, and the Hard Choices Women Make*. Hanover, NH: Wesleyan University.

Cannon, Angie. 1999. "DWB: Driving while black." *U.S. News and World Report*. (March 15).

Cannon, Lou. 1997. *Official Negligence*. New York: Times Books.

Cantor, Joanne L., L. Rowell Huesmann, Jo Groebel, Neil M. Malamuth, Emily A. Impett, Edward Donnerstein, Stacy Smith, & Brad J. Bushman. 2001. "Some hazards of television viewing: Fears, aggression and sexual attitudes." In Dorothy G. Singer & Jerome L. Singer (eds.), *Handbook of Children and the Media*. Thousand Oaks, CA: Sage: 207–307.

Cantril, Hadley. 1940. *The Invasion from Mars: A Study in the Psychology of Panic*. Princeton, NJ: Princeton University Press.

Caplan, Nathan, Marcella H. Choy, & John K. Whitmore. 1992. "Indochinese refugee families and academic achievement." *Scientific American* 266: 36–42.

Caplow, Theodore, Louis Hicks, & Ben J. Wattenberg. 2001. *The First Measured Century*. Washington, DC: AEI Press.

Caplow, Theodore. 1991. *American Social Trends*. New York: Harcourt Brace Jovanovich.

Capozza, Dora, & Rupert Brown (eds.). 2000. *Social Identity Processes: Trends in Theory and Research*. London: Sage.

Carder, Paula C. 2002. "Promoting independence: An analysis of assisted living facility marketing materials." *Research on Aging* 24(1): 106–23.

Carey, Anne R., & Elys A. McLean. 1997. "Heard it through the grapevine?" *USA Today* (September 15): B-1.

Carey, Anne R., & Grant Jerding. 1999. "What workers want." *USA Today* (August 17): B-1.

Carli, Linda L. 2001. "Gender and social influence." *Journal of Social Issues* 57(4): 725–41.

Carlisle, John. 1999. "The campaign against urban sprawl: Declaring war on the American Dream." Report No. 239: April. Washington, DC: National Center for Public Policy Research.

Carlson, S., & R. Michalowski. 1997. "Crime, Unemployment, and Social Structures of Accumulation." *Justice Quarterly* 14: 209–239.

Carmichael, Stokeley, & Charles V. Hamilton. 1967. *Black Power: The Politics of Liberation in American Education*. New York: Random House.

Carnoy, Martin, & Henry M. Levin. 1985. *Schooling and Work In the Democratic State*. Stanford, CA: Stanford University Press.

Caro, Francis G. 2001. "Consumer choice in health coverage: A mixed blessing." *Journal of Aging & Social Policy* 12(2): 1–3.

Carp, Frances M. 2000. *Elder Abuse in the Family: An Interdisciplinary Model*. New York: Springer.

Carpenter, Laura. 2002. "Gender and the meaning and experience of virginity loss in the contemporary United States." *Gender & Society* 6(3): 345–65.

Carr, Deborah. 2001. "Widowhood: Research dispels some common myths." Paper presented at the Population Association of America, (March). Available: http:www.umich.edu/~newsinfo/Releases/2001/Mar01.

Carr, James H., & Zhong Yi Tong (ed.). 2002. *Replicating Microfinance in the United States*. Washington, DC: Woodrow Wilson Center.

Carrigan, Marylyn, & Isabelle Szmigin. 2000. "Advertising and older consumers: Image and ageism." *Business Ethics* 9(1): 42–50.

Carrington, Christopher. 1999. *No Place Like Home: Relationships and Family Life among Lesbians and Gay Men*. Chicago: University of Chicago.

Carroll, Jackson W., & Wade Clark Roof, (eds.), 1993. *Beyond Establishment: Protestant Identity in a Post-Protestant Age*. Louisville, KY: Westminster/John Knox Press.

Carson, R., J. Butcher, & J. Coleman. 1988. *Abnormal Psychology and Modern Life*. Glenvie, IL: Scott Foresman.

Carter, David L., & Louis A. Radelet. 1999. *The Police in the Community*, 6th ed. Upper Saddle River, NJ: Prentice Hall.

Casalego, Federico. 1996. "Cyberspace: A New Territory for Interaction in a Magic Time." *Societies* 51 (Feburary): 39–48.

Cashin, Sheryll D. 2000. "Public subsidies and the role of suburbanization in urban economic development: A reply to Timothy Bates." *Economic Development Quarterly* 14(3): 242–47.

Cashmore, E. Ellis. 1996. *Dictionary of Race and Ethnic Relations*, 4th ed. London: Routledge.

Casper, Lynne M., & Philip N. Cohen. 2000. "How does POSSLQ measure up? National estimates of cohabitation." *Demography* 37(2): 237–45.

Casper, Lynne M., & Suzanne M. Bianchi. 2002. *Continuity & Change in the American Family*. Thousand Oaks, CA: Sage.

Caspi, Avshalom, & Brent W. Roberts. 1999. "Personality continuity and change across the life course." In Lawrence A. Pervin & Oliver P. John (eds.), *Handbook of Personality: Theory and Research*. New York: Guilford.

Cassidy, J. 1995. "Who killed the middle class?" *New Yorker* (October 16): 113–124.

Cassidy, M. L., & G. R. Lee. 1989. "The study of polyandry: A critique and synthesis." *Journal of Comparative Family Studies* 20(1): 1–11.

Castells, Manuel. 1996. *The Information Age: Economy, Society and Culture*. London: Blackwell.

Castells, Manuel. 1996. *The Rise of the Network Society*. Cambridge, MA: Blackwell.

Castells, Manuel. 1997. *The Power of Identity*. Malden, MA: Blackwell.

Castle, Nicholas G. 2001. "Relocation of the elderly." *Medical Care Research & Review* 58(3): 291–33.

Castleman, Harry, & Walter Podrazik. 1982. *Watching TV: Four Decades of American Television*. New York: McGraw-Hill.

Castro, Janice. 1993. "Disposable workers," *Time* (131/14): 43–47.

Catalano, Ralph, David Dooley, Georjeanna Wilson, & Richard Hough. 1993. "Job loss and alcohol abuse." *Journal of Health and Social Behavior* 34: 215–25.

Cavalli-Sforza, Luca, Paolo Menozzi, & Alberto Piazza. 1994. *The History and Geography of Human Genes*. Princeton, NJ: Princeton University Press.

Cavanagh, J., & R. Broad. 1996. "Global reach: Workers fight the multinationals," *The Nation* (March 18): 21–24.

Cavender, Gray. 1995. "Alternative theories." In Joseph F. Sheley, (ed.), *Criminology: A Contemporary Handbook*, 2nd ed. Belmont, CA: Wadsworth: 349–71.

Caygill, Lisa, Anne Campbell, & Louisa Shirley. 2002. "Sex-typed preferences in three domains: Do two-year-olds need cognitive variables?" *British Journal of Psychology* 93(2): 203–17.

Center for Medicaid & Medicare Services. 2002. "National health expenditures projections: 2001–2011." Available: http:www.cms.hhs.gov/statistics/nhe/projections-2001/highights.

Center for Policy Alternatives. 2002. "Equal pay." 2002 Policy Summary. Washington, DC: Center for Policy Alternatives. Available: http://www.stateaction.org.

Center on Budget and Policy Priorities. 2001. "Declining share of children lived with single parents in the late 1990s." June 15. Available: http://www.cbpp.org/6-15-01wel2.

Centers for Disease Control. 1997. *Teen Sex Down, New Study Shows.* (January). Washington, DC: Health and Human Services.

Centers for Disease Control. 2002. "HIV/AIDS among U.S. women: Minority and young women continuing risk." Divisions of HIV/AIDS Prevention, CDC. Available: http://cdc.gov/hiv/facts/women.

Centers for Disease Control. 2002. "Obesity trends: Prevalence of obesity among U.S. adults by characteristics." http://www.cdc.gov/nccdphp/dnpa/obesity/trend/prev_char

Cernovich, Stephen A. 1978. "Value orientations and delinquency involvement," *Criminology* 15: 443–458.

Certain, Laura K., & Robert S. Kahn. 2002. "Prevalence, correlates, and trajectory of television viewing among infants and toddlers." *Pediatrics* 109(4): 634–42.

Cerulo, Karen A., Janet M. Ruane, & Mary Chayko. 1992. "Technological ties that bind: Media-generated primary groups." *Communication Research* 19: 109–129.

Chafe, W. H. 1991. *The Paradox of Change: American Women in the Twentieth Century.* New York: Oxford University Press.

Chall, Jeanne S. 2000. *The Academic Achievement Challenge: What Really Works in the Classroom.* New York: Guilford.

Chambliss, William J. 1969. *Crime and The Legal Process.* New York: McGraw-Hill.

Chambliss, William J. 1973. "The Saints and the Roughnecks." *Society* (2/1): 24–31.

Chambliss, William J. 1988. *On the Take: From Petty Crooks to Presidents.* Bloomington: University of Indiana Press.

Chambliss, William J. 1994. "Policing the ghetto underclass: The politics of law and law enforcement." *Social Problems* 41: 177–94.

Chan, C. 1992. "Cultural considerations in counseling Asian American lesbians and gay men." In S. Dworkin & F. Guiterres (ed.), *Counseling Gay Men and Lesbians: Journey to the End of the Rainbow.* Alexandria, VA: American Association of Counseling and Development.

Chan, S. 1991. *Asian-Americans.* Boston: Twayne.

Chang, Grace. 2000. *Disposable Domestics: Immigrant Women Workers in the Global Economy.* Cambridge, MA: South End.

Chaplin, Duncan, & Jane Hannaway. 1998. "African American high scorers project: Technical report." *Volume 2—Schools and Neighborhood Factors and SAT Performance.* Washington, DC: Urban Institute.

Charatan, Fred. 2002. "Mentally ill mother escapes death penalty but faces life imprisonment." *British Medical Journal* 324 (March 23): 694.

Charmes, Jacques. 2000. "Informal sector, poverty and gender: A review of empirical evidence." Background paper for the *World Development Report, 2001.* Versailles-St. Quentin en Yvelines, France: Center of Economics and Ethics for Environment and Development (C3ED).

Charon, Joel M. 1995. *Symbolic Interaction: An Introduction, An Interpretation, An Integration.* Upper Saddle River, NJ: Prentice Hall.

Charon, Mona. 1997. "Women in the military not a good idea." *St. Louis Post Dispatch* : 7B.

Chase, Susan E., & Mary F. Rogers. 2001. *Mothers and Children: Feminist Analyses and Personal Narratives.* New Brunswick, NJ: Rutgers University.

Chase-Dunn, Christopher, & Thomas D. Hall. 1997. *Rise and Demise: Comparing World Systems.* Boulder, CO: Westview.

Chase-Dunn, Christopher. 1990. *Global Formation: Structures of the World Economy.* Cambridge, MA: Basil Blackwell.

Chasin, B. H. 1997. *Inequality and Violence in the United States: Casualties of Capitalism.* New York: Humanities Press.

Chatty, Dawn. 2000. "Women working in Oman: Individual choice and cultural constraints." *International Journal of Middle East Studies* 32(2): 241–54.

Chaucer, L. S. 1998. *Reconcilable Differences: Confronting Beauty, Pornography and the Future of Feminism.* Berkeley, CA: University of California.

Chaves, Mark, & Philip S. Gorski. 2001. "Religious pluralism and religious participation." *Annual Review of Sociology* 27: 261–281.

Chavis, David M., & Abraham Wandersman. 1990. "Sense of community in the urban environment: A catalyst for participation and community development." *American Journal of Community Psychology* 18: 55–81.

Chen, Anne C., & Anju G. Chaudhary. 1991. "Asia and the Pacific." In *Global Journalism: Survey of International Communication,* 2nd ed. New York: Longman.

Chen, Chuansheng, & Haro   r, & Heidi Taam. 1999, *A Different World: Children's Perceptions of Race and Class in Media.* Oakland, CA: Children Now.

Cheng, Simon H., & Wen H. Kuo. 2000. "Family socialization of ethnic identity among Chinese American preadolescents." *Journal of Comparative Family Studies* 31(4): 463–84.

Cherlin, Andrew J. 1992. *Marriage, Divorce, Remarriage.* Cambridge, MA: Harvard University.

Cherlin, Andrew J. 1998. "By the numbers." *New York Times Magazine* (April 5): 39–41.

Cherlin, Andrew J. 1999. "Going to extremes: Family structure, children's well-being, and social science." *Demography* 36(4): 421–8.

Cheshire, Tamara. 2001. "Cultural transmission in urban American Indian families." *American Behavioral Scientist* 44(9): 1528–35.

Chesler, Ellen. 2001. "New options, new politics." *American Prospect* (Fall): A12–A14.

Chesney-Lind, Meda, & Randall G. Shelden. 1998. *Girls, Delinquency, and Juvenile Justice,* 2nd ed. Belmont, CA: Wadsworth.

Cheung, Yuet-Wah & Agnes M. C. Ng. 1988. "Social factors in adolescent deviant behavior in Hong Kong." *International Journal of Comparative and Applied Criminal Justice* (12): 27–44.

Chevannes, M. 2002. "Issues in educating health professionals to meet the diverse needs of patients and other service users from ethnic minority groups." *Journal of Advanced Nursing* 39(3): 290–98.

Child, J. 1994. *Management in China During the Age of Reform.* Cambridge, UK: Cambridge University.

Child, J., & L. Markoczy. 1993. "Host country managerial behavior and learning in Chinese and Hungarian joint ventures." *Journal of Management Studies* 30: 611–31.

Childe, V. Gordon. 1951. *Social Evolution.* Cleveland: World.

Children's Defense Fund. 2001. *The State of America's Children, Yearbook 2001.* Boston: Beacon.

Chilman, Catherine Street. 1995. "Hispanic families in the United States: Research perspectives." In Mark Robert Rank & Edward T. Kain (eds.), *Diversity and Change in Families: Patterns, Prospects, and Policies.* Upper Saddle River, NJ: Prentice Hall.

Chin, Ko-Lin. 1990. *Chinese Subculture and Criminality: Nontraditional Crime Groups in America.* Westport, CT: Greenwood.

Chino, A., & D. Funabiki. 1984. "A Cross-validation on sex differences in the expression of depression." *Sex Roles* 11: 175–187.

Chira, Susan. 1998. *A Mother's Place: Taking the Debate about Working Mothers Beyond Guilt and Blame.* New York: HarperCollins.

Chirocos, Ted, Sarah Escholtz, & Marc Gretz. 1997. "Crime, news, and fear of crime." *Social Problems* (44): 342–57.

Chirot, Daniel. 1994. *How Societies Change.* Thousand Oaks, CA: Pine Forge.

Choi, Namkee G. 2001. "Relationship between life satisfaction and postretirement employment among older women." *International Journal of Aging & Human Development* 52(1): 45–70.

Chollar, Susan. 1995. "Happy families: Who says they all have to be alike?" In Kathleen R. Gilbert (ed.), *Marriage and the Family 95/96* (Annual Editions). Guilford, CT: Dushkin/Brown & Benchmark.

Christian Century. 2000. "Ugandan death toll surpasses Jonestown's." (April 12).

Christiano, Kevin J. 2000. "Religion and the family in modern American culture." In Sharon K. Houseknecht & Jerry G. Pankhurst (eds.), *Family, Religion and Social Change in Diverse Societies.* New York: Oxford University: 43–78.

Christie, Kathy. 2001. "The lagging literacy." *Phi Delta Kappan* 62(10): 729–31.

Christie, Sandra, & Linda L. Lindsey, 1997. "Gender and the workplace." Chapter 9 in Linda Lindsey, *Gender Roles: A Sociological Perspective.* Upper Saddle River, NJ: Prentice Hall.

Chrohn, J. 1995. *Mixed Matches: How to Create Successful Interracial, Interethnic and Interfaith Marriages.* New York: Fawcett Columbine.

Church, George J. 1996. "Ripping up welfare." *Time* (148/8): 18–22.

Churchill, Ward. 1994. *Indians Are Us?* Monroe, ME: Common Courage Press.

Cicerello, Antoinette, & Eugene P. Sheehan. 1995. "Personal advertisements: A content analysis." *Journal of Social Behavior and Personality* 10: 751–56.

Cingranelli, David L., & David L. Richards, 1999. "The respect for human rights at the end of the Cold War." *Journal of Peace Research* 36(5): 511–34.

City Poverty. 2002. "Global urban poverty and international development and cooperation." Available: http://www.citypoverty.net/background.

Clark, Charles S. 1993. "Cults in America." *CQ Researcher* 3(May 7): 385–408.

Clark, David. 2002. "Between hope and acceptance: The medicalisation of dying." *British Medical Journal* 324(7342): 905–907.

Clark, Robert L., & Naohiro Ogawa. 1997. "Transition from career jobs to retirement in Japan." *Industrial Relations* (36/2): 255–270.

Clarke, Victoria. 2001. "What about the children? Arguments against lesbian and gay parenting." *Women's Studies International Forum* 24(5): 555–70.

Clason, Marmy. 2000. "The social construction of sexual harassment." *Women & Language* 23(2): 56.

Claussen, Dane S. (ed.). 1999. *Standing on the Promises: The Promise Keepers and the Revival of Manhood.* Cleveland, OH: Pilgrim Press.

Claussen, Dane S. 2000. " 'So far, news coverage of Promise Keepers has been more like advertising': The strange case of Christian men and the print mass media." In Dane S. Claussen (ed.), *The Promise Keepers: Essays on Masculinity and Christianity.* Jefferson, NC: McFarland: 281–307.

Clawson, Don, Alan Neustadt, & Denise Scott. 1992. *Money Talks: Corporate PACs & Political Influence.* New York: Basic Books.

Cleaver, Joan. 1999. "Surfing for seniors: Where to find them, how to reach them in cyberspace." *Marketing News* 33 (July 19): 1.

Clements, M. 1998. *The Impoverished Woman: Single Women Reinventing Single Life.* New York: W.W. Norton.

Clemetson, Lynette, & Keith Naughton. 2001. "Patriotism vs. Ethnic Pride: An American Dilemma." *Newsweek* (September 24): 69.

Clemetson, Lynette. 2000. "Color my world." *Newsweek* (May 8): 70–74.

Clendinen, Dudley, & Adam Nagourney. 1999. *Out for Good: The Struggle to Build a Gay Rights Movement in America.* New York: Simon & Schuster.

Clinard, Marshall B. 1990. *Corporate Corruption: The Abuse of Power.* New York: Praeger.

Clinard, Marshall B., & P. C. Yeager. 1980. *Corporate Crime.* New York: Free Press.

Clinard, Marshall B., & Richard Quinney. 1973. *Criminal Behavior Systems: A Typology.* New York: Holt Rinehart and Winston.

Clory, M. Nathaniel, Sr. 2001. "A personal reflection on television's messages and images, and a challenge to future practitioners." In Elizabeth L. Toth (ed.), *The Gender Challenge to Media: Diverse Voices from the Field.* Cresskill, NJ: Hampton: 219–39.

Clum, John M. 2002. *He's All Man: Learning Masculinity, Gayness and Love from American Movies.* New York: Palgrave.

CMMR. 2002. "Featured analysis: The aftermath/CMMR archives on Proposition 227." *Language Policy and Language Rights.* Center for Multilingual, Multicultural Research, University of Southern California.

Cnaan, Ram A. 1991. "Neighborhood-representing organizations: How democratic are they?" *Social Science Review* (December): 614–34.

CNN. 2000. "Same-sex marriage laws across the United States." May 25. Available: http://www.cnn.com/2000/LAW/05/25/same.sex.marriages.

CNN. 2002. "Pope responds to sex abuse cases." March 22. Available: http://www.cnn.com/2002/WORLD/europe/03/21/vatican.sex.abuse.

CNN. 2002. "Study: 1950s nuclear fallout worse than thought." Available: http://www.cnn.com/2002/US03/01/nuclear.fallout.

Coakley, Jay, & Peter Donnelly (eds.). 1999. *Inside Sports.* London: Routledge.

Coakley, Jay. 2001. *Sport in Society: Issues and Controversies,* 7th ed. New York: McGraw-Hill.

Coast, Ernestina. 2002. "Masai socioeconomic conditions: A cross-border comparison." *Human Ecology: An Interdisciplinary Journal* 30(1): 79–107

Coates, Jennifer. 1988. "Gossip revisited: Language in all-female groups." In Jennifer Coates & Deborah Cameron (eds.), *Women in Their Speech Communities: New Perspectives on Language and Sex.* Harlow, Essex, UK: Longman.

Cobb, Ron. 1997. "The king and I." *St. Louis Post-Dispatch* (June 1): 8T.

Cockerham, William C. 1995b. *The Global Society.* New York: McGraw-Hill.

Cockerham, William. 2001. *Medical Sociology* (8th edition). Upper Saddle River, NJ: Prentice Hall.

Coder, John, Lee Rainwater, & Timothy Smeeding. 1989. "Inequality among children and elderly in ten modern nations." *American Economic Review* 79/2: 320–324.

Cohen, Albert. 1965. "The sociology of the deviant act: Anomie theory & beyond." *American Sociological Review* 30: 5–14.

Cohen, Anthony. 1993. "The future of the self." In Anthony Cohen & Katsuyoshi Fukui (eds.), *Humanising the City? Social Contexts of Urban Life at the Turn of the Millennium.* Edinburgh, UK: Edinburgh University: 201–21.

Cohen, Steven M. 2000. "Relationship to Israel." North American Jewish Data Bank. *Data Bank News* (Special Issue, Fall): 7.

Cohen, Susan A., & Cory L. Richards. 1994. "The Cairo consensus: Development and women." *International Family Planning Perspectives.* 20(4): 150–55.

Cohen, Susan, & Mary Fainsod Katzenstein. 1991. "The war over the family is not over the family." In Mark Hutter (ed.), *The Family Experience: A Reader in Cultural Diversity.* New York: Macmillan.

Cohen-Almagor, Raphael. 2002. "Why the Netherlands?" *Journal of Law, Medicine & Ethics* 30(1): 95–104.

Cohler, Bertram J., & Galatzer-Levy, Robert M. 2000. *The Course of Gay and Lesbian Lives: Social and Psychological Perspectives.* Chicago: University of Chicago.

Cohn, D'Vera. 2001. "Census finds record gains in South's black population." *Evansville Courier & Press* (May 6): A4.

Colapinto, John. 2000. *As Nature Made Him: The Boy Who Was Raised as a Girl.* New York: HarperCollins.

Cole, David. 1994. "Five myths about immigration." *The Nation* 259 (October 17): 410–12.

Cole, David. 1999. *No Equal Justice: Race and Class in the American Criminal Justice System.* New York: New Press.

Cole, Elizabeth R., Alyssa N. Zucker, & Lauren E. Duncan. 2001. "Changing society, changing women." In Rhoda K. Unger (ed.), *Handbook of the Psychology of Women and Gender.* New York: Wiley: 410–23.

Cole, Robert A. 2000. "Promising to be a man: Promise Keepers and the organizational constitution of masculinity." In Dane S. Claussen (ed.), *The Promise Keepers: Essays on Masculinity and Christianity.* Jefferson, NC: McFarland: 113–32.

Cole, Robert E. 1989. *Strategies for Learning.* Berkeley, CA: University of California Press.

Coleman, J. 1998. *The Criminal Elite: Understanding White-Collar Crime.* New York: St. Martin's Press.

Coleman, James S. 1990. "Rational organization," *Rationality and Society* 2: 94–105.

Coleman, James S. et al. 1966. *Equality of Educational Opportunity.* Washington, DC: US. Government Printing Office.

Coleman, James S., Elihu Katz, & Herbert Menzel. 1957. "The diffusion of innovation among physicians." *Sociometry* 20: 253–69.

Coleman, James W. & Donald R. Cressey. 1999. *Social Problems,* 7th ed. New York: Longman.

Coleman, John A. 1970. "Civil religion." *Sociological Analysis* 31(2): 76.

Coleman, John A. 2002. "Selling God in America: American commercial culture as a climate of hospitality to religion." In Richard. Madsen, William M. Sullivan, Ann Swidler, & Steven M. Tipton (eds.), *Meaning and Modernity: Religion, Polity, and Self.* Berkeley: University of California: 136–49.

Coleman, John, & Debi Rocker. 1998. *Teenage Sexuality: Health, Risk and Education.* Amsterdam: Harwood.

Coleman, Marilyn., Lawrence H. Ganong, & Mark A. Fine. 2000. "Reinvestigating remarriage: Another decade of progress." *Journal of Marriage and the Family* 62(4): 1288–1307.

College Board. 2001. "2001 College-bound seniors are the largest, most diverse group in history." *College Board News* (August 28). Available: http://www.college-board.com/press/senior01.

Collins, Patricia H. 1990. *Black Feminist Thought: Knowledge, Consciousness and the Politics of Empowerment.* Cambridge, MA: Unwin & Hyman.

Collins, Patricia Hill. 1996. "Toward a new vision: Race, class and gender as categories of analysis and connection." In Karen E. Rosenblum & Toni-Michelle Travies (eds.), *The Meaning of Difference: American Constructions of Race, Sex and Gender, Social Class and Sexual Orientation.* New York: McGraw-Hill.

Collins, Randall, & Michael Makowsky. 1998. *The Discovery of Society,* 6th ed. New York: McGraw-Hill.

Collins, Randall, & Scott Coltrane. 2001. *Sociology of Marriage and the Family: Gender, Love, and Property.* Chicago: Nelson-Hall.

Collins, Randall. 1975. *Conflict Sociology: Toward an Explanatory Science.* New York: Academic Press.

Collins, Randall. 1989. "Sociology: Proscience or antiscience." *American Sociological Review* 54: 124–139.

Collins, Sara. 1994. "The new migrant workers." *U.S. News & World Report* 117 (July 4): 553–55.

Coltrane, Scott, & Melinda Messineo. 2000. "The perpetuation of subtle prejudice: Race and gender imagery in 1990s television advertising." *Sex Roles* 42(5–6): 363–89.

Coltrane, Scott. 1996. *Family Man: Fatherhood, Housework, and Gender Equity.* New York: Oxford University.

Coltrane, Scott. 1997. "Scientific heal-truths and postmodern parody in the family values debate." *Contemporary Sociology* 26(1): 7–10.

Coltrane, Scott. 1998. *Gender and Families.* Thousand Oaks, CA: Pine Forge.

Combs, Cindy C. 2000. *Terrorism in the 21st Century,* 2nd ed. Upper Saddle River, NJ: Prentice Hall.

ComedyLab. 2002. " List of short books" and "State slogans." News/politics jokes. Jokes.com. Available: http://www.thecomedylab.com.

Comte, Auguste. 1858. *The Positive Philosophy.* New York: Calvin Blanchard.

Condravy, Jace, Esther Skirboll, & Rhoda Taylor. 1998. "Faculty perceptions of classroom gender dynamics." *Women and Language* 21(1): 18–27.

Conley, Dalton. 2000. *Honkey.* Berkeley: University of California.

Conlin, Michael. 1999. "Peer group micro-lending programs in Canada and the United States." *Journal of Development Economics* 60(1): 249–69.

Connell, Joan. 1998. "Searching for God in cyberspace." Available: http://www.goethe.de/br/sap/macumba/conellsho.

Conner, Karen Ann. 2000. *Continuing to Care: Older Americans and their Families.* New York: Falmer.

Conrad, John P. 1983. "Deterrence, the death penalty, and the data." In Ernest van den Haag & John P. Conrad, (eds.), *The Death Penalty: A Debate.* New York: Plenum.

Conrad, Peter, & Joseph W. Schneider. 1980. *Deviance and Medicalization: From Badness to Sickness.* St. Louis: Mosby.

Conrad, Peter. 1993. "Rationing health care: A sociological reflection." *Research in the Sociology of Health Care* 10: 3–22.

Conroy, Carol A. 1998. "Influence of gender and program of enrollment on adolescents' and teens' occupational and educational aspirations." *Journal of Vocational and Technical Education* 14(2): 18–28.

Constable, Nicole. 1997. *Maid to Order in Hong Kong: Stories of Filipina Workers.* Ithaca: Cornell University.

Constantine, Madonna G., & Sha'kema M. Blackmon. 2002. "Black adolescents' racial socialization experiences: Their relations to home, school, and peer self-esteem." *Journal of Black Studies* 32(3): 322–35.

Constantine-Simms, Delroy. 2001. *The Greatest Taboo: Homosexuality in Black Communities.* Los Angeles: Alyson.

Conway, M. M. 1991. *Political Participation in the United States,* 2nd ed. Washington, DC: Congressional Quarterly.

Cook, Judith A., & Eric R. Wright. 1995. "Medical sociology and the study of severe mental illness: Reflections on past accomplishments and directions for future research." *Journal of Health and Social Behavior* (Extra Issue). 1995: 95–114.

Cooley, Charles Horton. 1902/1983. *Human Nature and the Social Order.* New Brunswick, NJ: Transaction.

Cooley, Charles Horton. 1909. *Social Organization.* New York: Scribner's.

Cooley, Charles Horton. 1962. *Social Organization.* New York: Schocken. Originally published in 1909.

Coomaraswamy, Radhika. 2001. "Different but free: Cultural relativism and women's rights as human rights." In Courtney W. Howland (ed.), *Religious Fundamentalisms and Human Rights of Women.* New York: Palgrave.

Cooney, Teresa M., & Kathleen Dunne. 2001. "Intimate relationships in later life: Current realities, future prospects." *Journal of Family Issues* 22(7): 838–58.

Coontz, Stephanie. 1992. *The Way We Never Were: American Families and the Nostalgia Trap.* New York: Basic Books.

Cooper, H. A. A. 1978. "Terrorism: The problem of the problem definition." *Chitty's Law Journal* 26: 105–108.

Cooper, Matthew. 1999. "Spatial discourses and social boundaries: Re-imagining the Toronto waterfront." In Setha M. Low (ed.), *Theorizing the City: The New Urban Anthropology Reader.* New Brunswick, NJ: Rutgers University.

Corell, Shelley J. 2001. "Gender and the career choice process: The role of biased self-assessments." *American Journal of Sociology* 106(6): 691–730.

Corless, Roger. 2002. "Buddhism: China." In John Bowker (ed.), *The Cambridge Illustrated History of Religions.* Cambridge, UK: Cambridge University: 94–97.

Cornish, Derek, & Ronald Clarke, (eds.). 1986. *The Reasoning Criminal: Rational Choice Perspectives On Offending.* New York: Springer Verlag.

Cornwell, Gretchen T., David J. Eggebeen, & Laurie L. Meschke. 1996. "The changing family context of early adolescence." *Journal of Early Adolescence* 16(2): 141–56.

Corr, Charles A., & Donna M. Corr. 2000. "Anticipatory mourning and coping with dying: Similarities, differences, and suggested guidelines for helpers." In Therese A. Rondo (ed.), 2000. *Clinical Dimensions of Anticipatory Mourning: Theory and Practice in Working with the Dying, their Loved Ones and their Caregivers.* Champaign, IL: Research Press: 223–51.

Corr, Charles A., & Kenneth J. Dokka. 2001. "Master concepts in the field of death dying and bereavement: Coping versus adaptive strategies." *Omega* 43(3): 183–99.

Cose, Elis. 2000. "Our new look: The colors of race." *Newsweek.* (January 1): 28–30.

Coser, Lewis. 1956. *The Functions of Social Conflict.* New York: Free Press.

Coser, Rose L. 1991. *In Defense of Modernity: Role Complexity & Internal Autonomy.* Stanford, CA: Stanford University Press.

Cosgrove, Lisa. 2000. "Crying out loud: Understanding women's emotional distress as both lived experience and social construction." *Feminism & Psychology* 10(2): 247–68.

Costello, Cynthia B., & Anne J. Stone. 2002. *The American Woman: 2001–2002: Getting to the Top.* New York: Women's Research & Education Institute.

Coupland, Douglas. 1991. *Generation X.* New York: St, Martin's.

Cowan, Gloria. 2000a. "Beliefs about causes of four types of rape." *Sex Roles* 42(9–10): 807–823.

Cowan, Gloria. 2000b. "Women's hostility toward women and rape and sexual harassment myths." *Violence Against Women* 6(3): 238–46.

Cox, Harold G. 2000. *Later Life: The Realities of Aging.* Upper Saddle River, NJ: Prentice-Hall.

Cox, Harvey. 2002. "Mammon and the culture of the market: A socio-theological critique." In Richard Madsen, William M. Sullivan, Ann Swidler, & Steven M. Tipton (eds.), *Meaning and Modernity: Religion, Polity, and Self.* Berkeley: University of California: 124–35.

Cox, James L. 1996. "The classification of 'primal religions' as a non-empirical Christian theological construct." *Studies in World Christianity* 2(1): 55–76.

Cox, Oliver. 1948. *Caste, Class and Race.* Detroit: Wayne State University Press.

CPS, 2001. "Highlights of women's earnings in 2000." *Current Population Survey,* August. Washington, DC: U.S. Census Bureau/Bureau of Labor Statistics.

Crandall, C. S. 1995. "Do parents discriminate against their heavyweight daughters?" *Personality & Social Psychology Bulletin* 21: 724–735.

Crandall, Christian S. 2002. "Social norms and the expression and suppression of prejudice: The struggle for internalization." *Journal of Personality and Social Psychology* 82(3): 359–78.

Crane, Vikki. 2001. "We can be athletic and feminine, but do we want to?" *Quest* (53/1): 115–16.

Crank, John. 1997. *Understanding Police Culture.* Cincinnati: Anderson.

Crawford, Gordon. 2001. *Foreign Aid and Political Reform: A Comparative Analysis of Democracy Assistance and Political Conditionality.* Houndmills, UK: Palgrave.

Crawford, James. 1997. "The Official English policy." Issues in U.S. Language Policy. Available: http://ourworld.compuserve.com/homepages/JWCRAWFORD /question.

Crawford, James. 2000. *At War with Diversity: U.S. Language Policy in an Age of Anxiety.* Clavedon, UK: Multilingual Matters.

Crawford, James. 2002. Language policy web site and emporium. Available: http://ourworld.compuserve.com/homepages/JWCRAWFORD/home.

Crawford, Mary. 1995. *Talking Difference: On Gender and Language.* Thousand Oaks, CA: Sage.

Crawford, Mary. 2001. "Gender and language." In Rhoda K. Unger (ed.), *Handbook of the Psychology of Women and Gender.* New York: John Wiley & Sons.

Cready, Cynthia M., & Mark A. Fossett. 1997. "Mate availability and African American family structure in the U.S. nonmetropolitan South." *Journal of Marriage and the Family* 59(1): 192–203.

Crenson, Matt. 2000. "Social activism class in session." *Owensboro (Ky) Messenger-Inquirer* (April 9): 5.

Crispell, Diane. 1990. "Workers in 2000." *American Demographics* (March): 36–40.

Crispell, Diane. 1995. "Generations to 2025." *American Demographics* 17 (January): 4ff.

Cristofalo, Vincent, Maria Tresini, Marykay Francis, & Craig Volker 1999. "Biological theories of senescence." In Vern Bengston & K. Warner Schaie (eds.), *Handbook of Theories of Aging.* New York: Springer.

Critchlow, Donald T., & Ellis W. Hawley, (eds.). 1989. *Poverty and Public Policy in Modern America.* Chicago: Dorsey.

Cronin, E. David, 1969. *Black Moses: The Story of Marcus Garvey.* Madison: University of Wisconsin Press.

Crosbie, Paul V., (ed.). 1975. *Interaction in Small Groups.* New York: Macmillan.

Crosby, Alfred W. 1986. *Biological Imperialism: The Biological Expansion of Europe, 900–1900.* Cambridge, UK: Cambridge University.

Crosby, Faye J., & Cheryl VanDeVeer, (eds.). 2001. *Sex, Race and Merit: Debating Affirmative Action in Education and Employment.* Ann Arbor: University of Michigan Press.

Crosette, Barbara. 2002. "Population estimates fall as poor women assert control." *New York Times* (March 10).

Crosset, Todd W. 1995. *Outsiders in the Clubhouse: The World of Women's Professional Golf.* Albany, NY: State University of New York Press.

Crosset, Todd W., Jeffrey R. Benedict, & Mark A. McDonald. 1995. "Male student-athletes reported for assault." *Journal of Sport & Social Issues* 19: 126–140.

Crossette, B. 1997. "What Modern Slavery Is and Isn't." *New York Times* (July 27).

Crossette, Barbara. 1998. "Women see key gains since talks in Beijing." *New York Times International* (March 8): Y11.

Croteau, David, & William Hoynes. 1997. *Media/Society.* Thousand Oaks, CA: Sage.

Crowder, Kyle D., & Stewart E. Tolnay. 2000. "A new marriage squeeze for black women: The role of racial intermarriage by black men." *Journal of Marriage and the Family* 62: 792–807.

Crystal, David. 2000. *Language Death.* Cambridge, UK: Cambridge University.

Csordas, Thomas J., & Arthur Kleinman. 1996. "The therapeutic process." In C. F. Sargent & T. M Johnson (eds.), *Medical Anthropology: Contemporary Theory and Method.* Westport, CT: Praeger.

Cumming, Elaine, & William E. Henry. 1961. *Growing Old: The Process of Disengagement.* New York: Basic Books.

Cunnen, Jacquelyn, & Cathryn Claussen. 1999. "Gender portrayals in sports-prod-
uct point-of-purchase advertising." *Women in Sport and Physical Activity Journal* 8(2): (September 30): 73.

Cunningham, Graham. 1999. *Religion and Magic.* Edinburgh, UK: Edinburgh University.

Cunningham, Mick. 2001. "Parental influences on the gendered division of household labor." *American Sociological Review* 66(2): 184–203.

Curran, Daniel J., & Claire M. Renzetti. 2001. *Theories of Crime,* 2nd ed. Needham Heights, MA: Allyn & Bacon.

Curran, Laura, & Laura S. Abrams. 2000. "Making men into dads: Fatherhood, the state, and welfare reform. *Gender and Society* 14(5): 662–78.

Currie, Elliott. 1998. *Crime and Punishment in America.* New York: Metropolitan.

Curry, G. David & Scott H. Decker. 1998. *Confronting Gangs: Crime & Community.* Los Angeles: Roxbury: 65–67.

Curry, George E., (ed.). 1996. *The Affirmative Action Debate.* Reading, MA: Addison-Wesley.

Curry, Tim. 1993. "A little pain never hurt anyone." *Symbolic Interaction* (16/3): 273–90.

Curtis, J. E., E. G. Grabb, & D. Baer. 1992. "Voluntary association membership in 15 countries." *American Sociological Review* 57: 139–52.

Cushman, L., A. Davidson, & D. Kalmuss. 1996. "Marital relationship change in the transition to parenthood: A reexamination as interpreted through transition theory." *Journal of Family Nursing* 45: 415–26.

Cuzzort, R. P., & Edith W. King. 2002. *Social Thought into the 21st Century,* 6th ed. Fort Worth, TX: Harcourt.

D'Antonio, William V., James D. Davidson, Dean R. Hoge, & Ruth A. Wallace. 1989. *American Catholic Laity in a Changing Church.* Kansas City: Sheed & Ward.

D'Apolito, Rosemary. 2000. "The activist role of the black church: A theoretical analysis and an empirical investigation of one contemporary activist black church." *Journal of Black Studies* 31(1): 96–123.

D'Intino, Robert S., & John A. Sinisi. 2001. "Rethinking the transition to capitalism: Taking the assumption of self-interested behavior seriously." *Pennsylvania Economic Review* 10(1): 88–96.

D'Souza, Dinesh. 1999. "The billionaire next door." *Forbes* (164/9): 50–62.

Da Silva, Ana Amelia. 2000. "Sao Paulo and the challenges for social sustainability: The case of an urban housing policy." In Mario Polese & Richard Stren (eds.), *The Social Sustainability of Cities: Diversity and the Management of Change.* Toronto: University of Toronto: 202–27.

Dahl, Robert. 1958. "A critique of the ruling elite model." *American Political Science Review* 52: 463–69.

Dahl, Robert. 1961. *Who Governs?* New Haven, CT: Yale University Press.

Dahl, Robert. 1968. *Pluralist Democracy in the United States.* Chicago: Rand McNally.

Dahl, Robert. 1982. *Dilemmas of Pluralist Democracy.* New Haven, CT: Yale University Press.

Dahrendorf, Ralf. 1959. *Class & Class Conflict in Industrial Society.* Stanford, CA: Stanford University Press.

Dalaker, Jospeh. 1999. *Poverty in the United States, 1998.* Washington, DC: GPO.

Dalton, Clare, & Elizabeth M. Schneider. 2000. *Battered Women and the Law.* New York: Foundation Press.

Dalton, George. 1967. *Tribal and Peasant Economies.* Garden City, NY: Natural History Press.

Dandaneau, Steven P. 2001. *Taking It Big: Developing Sociological Consciousness in Postmodern Times.* Thousand Oaks, CA: Pine Forge.

Daniel, Jessica Henderson. 1999. "Adolescent girls of color: Declaring their place and 'voice.' " In Norine G. Johnson, Michael C. Roberts, & Judith Worrell (eds.), *Beyond Appearance: A New Look at Adolescent Girls.* Washington, DC: American Psychological Association.

Daniels, Cynthia. 1993. "There's no place like home." In Alison M. Jaggar & Paula S. Rothenberg (eds.), *Feminist Frameworks: Alternative Theoretical Accounts of the Relations Between Women and Men.* New York: McGraw-Hill.

Daniels, John D., Lee H. Radebaugh, & Daniel P. Sullivan. 2002. *Globalization and Business.* Upper Saddle River, NJ: Prentice Hall.

Dannefer, Dale, & Russell K. Schutt. 1982. "Race and juvenile processing in court and police agencies." *American Journal of Sociology* 87: 1113–132.

Dansky, B. S., & D. G. Kilpatrick. 1997. "Effects of sexual harassment." In W. O'Donahue (ed.), *Sexual Harassment: Theory, Research and Treatment.* New York: Allyn & Bacon: 152–74.

Danziger, Sheldon, & Peter Gottschalk (eds.). 1995. *Uneven Tides: Rising Inequality in America.* New York: Russell Sage.

Darby, C. 2002. "Patient/parent assessment of the quality of care." *Ambulatory Pediatrics* 2(4): 345–48.

Darby, John. 1995. *Northern Ireland: Managing Difference.* London: Minority Rights Group International.

Darling-Hammond, Linda. 1997. "Education, equity and the right to learn." In John L. Goodlad & Timothy J. McMannon (eds.), *The Public Purpose of Education and Schooling.* San Francisco: Jossey-Bass: 41–54.

Darnton, Nina. 1985. "Woman and stress on the job and at home." *New York Times* (August 8): C-1.

Dart, John. 2001. "Bin Laden's strategy: War and the religious imagination." *Christian Century* (Nov. 7).

Daswani, 1999. "Second wives club." *South China Morning Post Magazine,* November 28: 7–14

Davidson, Kate. 2001. "Later life widowhood, selfishness and new partnership choices: A gendered perspective." *Ageing & Society* 21(3): 297–317.

Davidson, O. G. 1993. *Under Fire: The NRA and the Battle For Gun Control.* New York: Henry Holt.

Davies, James C. 1962. "Toward a theory of revolution." *American Sociological Review* 27/1: 5–19.

Davies, Lorraine, William R. Avison, & Donna D. McAlpine. 1997. "Significant life experiences and depression among single and married mothers." *Journal of Marriage and the Family* 59(2): 294–308.

Davies, Lorraine. 1995. "A closer look at gender and distress among the never-married." *Women and Health* 23: 13–30.

Davis, James F. 1978. *Minority-Dominant Relations: A Sociological Analysis.* Arlington Heights, IL: AHM.

Davis, Kingsley, & Wilbert E. Moore. 1945. "Some principles of stratification." *American Sociological Review* 10: 242–49.

Davis, Kingsley. 1947. "Final note on a case of extreme isolation." *American Journal of Sociology* 52: 432–37.

Davis, Nancy J. & Robert V. Robinson. 1998. "Do Wives Matter? Class Identities of Wives and Husbands in the United States, 1974–1994," *Social Forces* 76: 1063–1086.

Davis, Nancy J. 1992. "Teaching About inequality: Student resistance, paralysis, and rage." *Teaching Sociology* 20 (July): 232–238.

Davis, Theodore J. 1995. "The Occupational Mobility of Black Males Revisited," *Social Science Journal* 32: 121–136.

Davis-Friedmann, Deborah. 1991. *Long Lives: Chinese Elderly and the Communist Revolution.* Stanford, CA: Stanford University Press.

Dawsey, James M. 2001. "Liberation theology and economic development." *American Journal of Economics and Sociology* 60(5): 203–12.

Dawson, Lorne L. 1998. "Anti-modernism, modernism and post-modernism: Struggling with the cultural significance of new religious movements." *Sociology of Religion* 59(2): 131–56.

Day, Katherine. 2001. "The renaissance of community economic development among African-American churches in the 1990s." In Richard Fenn (ed.), *The Blackwell Companion to the Sociology of Religion.* Oxford, UK: Blackwell: 321–35.

de Bendern, Paul. 2000. "Arctic ozone loss seen increasing cancer in Europe." Planet Earth, January 22. Available: http://www.space.com/scienceastronomy/planetearth/europe_ozone.

de Haan, Jurriaan. 2002. "The ethics of euthanasia: Advocates perspectives." *Bioethics* 16(2): 154–72.

de Klerk, Vivian. 1990. "Slang? A male domain?" *Sex Roles* 22(9–10): 589–606.

De Lehr, Esther Contreras. 1992. "Aging and family support in Mexico." In Hal Kendig, Akido Hasimoto, & Larry C. Coppard (eds.), *Family Support for the Elderly: The International Experience.* New York: Oxford University Press.

Dearing, Eric, Kathleen McCartney, & Beck A. Taylor. 2001. "Change in family income-to-needs matters more for children with less." *Child Development* 72(6): 1779–93.

Debehnke, D., & M. C. Decker. 2002. "The effects of a physician-nurse patient care team on patient satisfaction in an academic ED." *American Journal of Emergency Medicine* 20(4): 267–70.

Decker, Scott H., & Carol W. Kohlfield. 1990. "Certainty, Severity, and the Probability of Crime." *Policy Studies Journal* 19: 2–21.

DeCurtis, Anthony. 2000. "Eminem's hate rhymes." *Rolling Stone* 846 (August 3): 17–18, 21.

Dedman, Bill. 1999. "DNA tests are freeing scores of prison inmates." *New York Times* (April 19): A12.

Deedes, William. 2000. "Is rural Asia dying?" *Asian Affairs* 31(pt. 3): 259–62.

Deegan, Mary Jo. 1988. "W. E. B. DuBois & the women of Hull House, 1895–1899." *American Sociologist* (Winter): 301–311.

Deegan, Mary Jo. 1991. *Women In Sociology: A Bio-Bibliographical Sourcebook.* New York: Greenwood.

DeGenova, Mary Kay. 1997. *Families in Cultural Context: Strengths and Challenges in Diversity.* Mountain View, CA: Mayfield.

Degher, Douglas, & Gerald Hughes. 1991. "The identity change process: A field study of obesity." *Deviant Behavior* 12: 385–402.

del Mundo, Fernando, 2002. "Rush hour: Afghanistan." *Refugees* 2(127): 22–27.

Delaney, Kevin K. 1992. *Strategic Bankruptcy.* Berkeley: University of California Press.

Delattre, Edwin J. 1990. "New faces of organized crime." *American Enterprise* 1: 38–45.

DeLew, Nancy. 2000. "Medicare: 35 years of service." *Health Care Financing Review* 22(1): 75–103.

Delgado, Richard, (ed.). 1995. *Critical Race Theory: The Cutting Edge.* Philadelphia: Temple University Press.

Della Piana, L. 1995. "Categories count." *Poverty and Race* 4: 11–12.

Della Porta, Donatella. 1995. *Social Movements, Political Violence and the State.* New York: Cambridge University Press.

Dellinger, Kirsten, & Christine L. Williams. 1997. "Makeup at work: Negotiating appearance rules." *Gender & Society* 11(2): 151–77.

DeLuca, Tom. 1998. "Joe the Bookie and the class voting gap," *American Demographics* (20/11): 26–29.

Dembour, Marie-Benedicte. 2001. "Following the movement of a pendulum: Between universalism and relativism." In Jane K. Cowan, Marie-Benedicte Dembour, & Richard A, Wilson (eds.), *Culture and Rights: Anthropological Perspectives.* Cambridge, UK: Cambridge University:56–79.

Demerath, Nicholas J., & Rhys H. Williams. 1990. "Religion and power in the American experience." In T. Robbins & D. Anthony (eds.), *In Gods We Trust: New Patterns of Religious Pluralism in America.* New Brunswick, NJ: Transaction: 427–48.

Demmert, William G., Jr. 1996. "Indian nations at risk: An educational strategy for action." In Laura I. Rendon & Richard O. Hope (eds.), *Educating a New Majority: Transforming America's Educational System for Diversity.* San Francisco: Jossey-Bass: 2311–64.

Dennerstein, L., E. Dudley, & J. Guthrie. 2002. "Empty nest or revolving door? A prospective of women's quality of life in midlife during the phase of children leaving and reentering home." *Psychological Medicine* 32: 545–50.

Dentan, R. K. 1968. *The Semai: A Nonviolent People of Malaya.* New York: Holt, Rinehart & Winston.

Denton, Robert E., & Gary C. Woodward. 1992. *Political Communication.* Westport, CT: Praeger.

Denzin, Norman. 1992. *Symbolic Interactionism and Cultural Studies: The Politics of Interpretation.* Cambridge, MA: Blackwell.

Denzin, Norman. 1993. "Sexuality and gender: An interactionist/poststructural reading." In Paula England (ed.), *Theory on Gender/Feminism on Theory.* New York: Aldine DeGruyter.

DeParle, J. 1998. "In booming economy, poor still struggle to pay the rent." *New York Times* (June 16).

DeParle, Jason. 1992. "Why marginal changes don't rescue the welfare system." *The New York Times* (March 1): E3.

DePaulo, B. M., C. S. LeMay, & J. Epstein. 1991. "Effects of importance of success on effectiveness in deceiving." *Personality and Social Psychology Bulletin* 1: 14–24.

Derickson, Alan. 2002. "Health for three-thirds of the nation: Public health advocacy of universal access to health care in the United States." *American Journal of Public Health* 92(2): 189–90.

Dershowitz, Alan B. 1997. *The Vanishing American Jew: In Search of Jewish Identity for the Next Century.* Boston: Little, Brown.

Dervarics, Charles. 1998. "Is welfare reform reforming welfare?" *Population Today* (26/10): 1–2.

DeSpelder, Lynne, & Albert Lee Strickland. 1996. *The Last Dance: Encountering Death and Dying.* Mountain View, CA: Mayfield.

DeVault, Marjorie L. 1999. *Liberating Method: Feminism and Social Research.* Philadelphia: Temple University.

DeVenzio, Dick. 1986. *Rip-Off U.* Charlotte, NC: Fool Court.

Devereux, Paul G., & Gerald P. Ginsburg. 2001. "Sociality effects on the production of laughter." *Journal of General Psychology (Special Issue: Humor and Laughter)* 128(2): 227–40.

Devine, Francis E. 1982. "Cesare Beccaria and the theoretical foundations of modern penal jurisprudence." *New England Journal on Prison Law* 7: 8–21.

DeWalt, Kathleen Musante, & Billie R. DeWalt. 2002. *Participant Observations: A Guide for Fieldworkers.* Walnut Creek, CA: AltaMira.

DeWan, George. 2002. "Plagiarism: Stealing writer's words." *Newsday.* Available: http://www.newsday.com/news/education/sbp/ny-sbp0507.

Diamond, Milton, & H. K. Sigmundson. 1997. "Management of intersexuality: Guidelines for dealing with people with ambiguous genitalia." *Archives of Pediatric and Adolescent Medicine* 151: 1046–50.

Diaz, Rafael M., George Ayala, & Edward Bein. 2001. "The impact of homophobia, poverty, and racism on the mental health of gay and bisexual Latino men: Findings from three U.S. cities." *American Journal of Public Health* 91(6): 927–32.

Diehl, Manfred. 1999. "Self-development in adulthood and aging: The role of critical life events." In Carol D. Ryff & Victor W. Marshall (eds.), *The Self in the Aging Process.* New York: Springer: 150–86.

Dietz, L. 1998. "An examination of violence and gender role portrayals in video games: Implications for gender socialization and aggressive behavior." *Sex Roles* 38: 425–42.

Dietz, Thomas, Tom R. Burns, & Frederick Buttel. 1990. "Evolutionary thinking in sociology: An examination of current thinking." *Sociological Forum* 5.

Dietz, Tracy L. 1995. "Patterns of intergenerational assistance within the Mexican American family: Is the family taking care of the older generation's needs?" *Journal of Family Issues* 16(3): 344–56.

Dill, Bonnie Thornton, 1994. "Fictive kin, paper sons, and compadrazgo: Women of color and the struggle for family survival." In Maxine Baca Zinn & Bonnie Thornton Dill (eds.), *Women of Color in U.S. Society.* Philadelphia: Temple University.

Dill, Bonnie Thorton. 1999. "Fictive kin, paper sons, and compadrazgo: Women of color and the struggle for family survival." In Stephanie Coontz (ed.), *American Families: A Multicultural Reader.* New York: Routledge: 2–29.

Dilworth, Craig. 2002. "Population, technology and development: The vicious-circle principle and the theory of human development." In Michael. N. Dobkowski & Isidor Wallimann (eds.), *On the Edge of Scarcity: Environment, Resources, Population, Sustainability, and Conflict.* Syracuse, NY: Syracuse University: 77–92.

"Direct Action Figure," 2000. *Mother Jones* (September/October): 23.

Dittman, Ralf W. 1998. "Ambiguous genitalia, gender-identity problems, and sex reassignment." *Journal of Sex & Marital Therapy* 24(4): 255–71.

Diver-Stamnes, Ann C. 1995. *Lives in the Balance: Youth, Poverty, and Education in Watts.* Albany, NY: State University of New York Press.

Divorce, 2002. "World divorce statistics." *Divorce Magazine.* Available: http://www.divorcemag.com/statistics/statsWorld.

Doane, Ashley W. Jr. 1993. "Bringing the majority back in." Presented at the annual meeting of the Society for the Study of Social Problems.

Dobash, R. Emerson, Margo Wilson, & Martin Daly. 2000. "The myth of sexual symmetry in marital violence." In Michael S. Kimmel (ed.), *The Gendered Society Reader.* New York: Oxford University: 375–91.

Dobkowski, Michael N., & Isidor Wallimann. 2002. Introduction: On the edge of scarcity." In M. N. Dobkowski & I. Wallimann (eds.), *On the Edge of Scarcity: Environment, Resources, Population, Sustainability, and Conflict.* Syracuse, NY: Syracuse University.

Dobratz, Betty, & Stephanie Shanks-Meile. 1997. *White Power, White Pride!.* New York: Twayne.

Doezema, Jo. 1998. "Forced to choose: Beyond the voluntary v. forced prostitution dichotomy." In Kamala Kempadoo & Jo Doezema (eds.), *Global Sex Workers: Rights, Resistance, and Redefinition.* New York: Routledge: 34–50.

Dohrenwend, Bruce P., & Barbara Snell Dohrenwend. 1974. "Social and cultural influences on psychopathology." *Annual review of Psychology* 25: 417–52.

Doka, Kenneth A., & Terry Martin. 2001. "Take it like a man: Masculine response to loss." In Dale A. Lund (ed.), *Men Coping with Grief.* Amityville, NY: Baywood.

Dolbeare, Cushing. 1995. *Out of Reach: Why Everyday People Can't Find Affordable Housing.* Washington, DC: Low Income Housing Information Service.

Dollard, John, Neal E. Miller, Leonard W. Doob, O. H. Mowrer, & Robert R. Sears. 1939. *Frustration and Aggression.* New Haven, CT: Yale University Press.

Dombrowski, Daniel A., & Robert Deltete. 2000. *A Brief, Liberal, Catholic Defense of Abortion.* Urbana: University of Illinois.

Domhoff, G. William. 1974. *The Bohemian Grove & Other Retreats: A Study in Ruling-Class Cohesiveness.* New York: Harper & Row.

Domhoff, G. William. 1979. *The Powers That Be.* New York: Random House.

Domhoff, G. William. 1996. *State Autonomy or Class Dominance?* New York: Aldine DeGruyter.

Domhoff, G. William. 1998. *Who Rules America? Power & Politics in the Year 2000,* 3rd ed. Mountain View, CA: Mayfield.

Donahue, Steve. 1999. "English enters mix to reach Latino viewers." *Electronic Media* (July 26): 13, 18.

Donath, J. S. 1997. "Identity Deception in the Virtual Community." In

Donnelly, Peter, & Kevin Young. 1988. "The construction and confirmation of identity in sport subcultures." In *Sociology of Sport Journal* (5/3): 223–40.

Donnelly, Peter. 2000. "Interpretive approaches to the sociology of sport." In Jay Coakley & E. Dunning (eds.), *Handbook of Sports Studies.* London: Sage: 77–91.

Donziger, Steven R., (ed.) 1996. *The Real War on Crime: The Report of the National Criminal Justice Commission.* New York: Harper Perennial.

Doob, Christopher B. 1999. *Racism: An American Cauldron,* 3rd ed. New York: Longman.

Dorrien, Gary. 2001. "Berger: Theology and sociology." In Linda Woodhead with Paul Heelas & David Martin (eds.), *Peter Berger and the Study of Religion.* London: Routledge: 26–39.

Douglas, Marie C. 1993. "The Mutter-Kind-Heim at Frankfurt am Main." *International Journal of Comparative & Applied Criminal Justice* (17/1): 181–87.

Douglas, William, & Beth M. Olson. 1995. "Beyond family structure: The family in domestic comedy." *Journal of Broadcasting & Electronic Media* 39: 236–61.

Downes, David. 1992. "The case for going Dutch: The lessons of post-war penal policy." *The Political Quarterly* (63/1): 12–24.

Downie, Mark. 1977. "Pinto madness." *Mother Jones* 2.

Doyle, Rodger Pirnie. 1997. "Female illiteracy worldwide." *Scientific American* 276: 20.

Dreger, Alice Domurt. 1998. *Hermaphrodites and the Medical Invention of Sex.* Cambridge, MA: Harvard University.

Dreman, Solly. 1997. *The Family on the Threshold of the 21st Century: Trends and Implications.* Mahwah, NJ: Lawrence Erlbaum.

Drescher, Jack, & William Alanson White. 2002. "Sexual conversion ('reparative') therapies: History and update." In Billy E. Jones & Marjorie J. Hill (eds.), *Mental Health Issues in Lesbian, Gay, Bisexual and Transgender Communities. Review of Psychiatry.* Volume 21. No. 4. Washington, DC: American Psychiatric Publishing.

Dresser, N. 1994. "Even smiling can have a serious side." *Los Angeles Times* (May 9): 1,5.

Drucker, Peter F. 1993. *Post-Capitalist Society.* New York: HarperCollins.

Drucker, Peter. 1969. *The Age of Discontinuity.* New York: Harper & Row.

Drysdale, John. 1996. "How are social scientific concepts formed?" *Sociological Theory* 14: 71–88.

Du Bois, W. E. B. 1899. *The Philadelphia Negro: A Social Study.* Philadelphia: University of Pennsylvania Press.

Du Bois, W. E. B. 1903. *The Souls of Black Folk.* New York: Dover.

Du Bois, W. E. B. 1968. *The Autobiography of W. E. B. Du Bois.* New York: International.

Duany, Andres, Elizabeth Plater-Zyberk, & Jeff Speck. 2000. *Suburban Nation: The Rise of Sprawl and the Decline of the American Dream.* New York: North Point.

Dubey, Meenal. 2001. "Dowry victim couldn't take it any more." *Hindustan Times.* November 20. Available: http://www.hindustantimes.com.

DuBois, W. E. B. 1899. *The Philadelphia Negro: A Social Study:* Philadelphia: University of Pennsylvania Press.

DuBois, W. E. B. 1903. *The Souls of Black Folk.* New York: Dover.

DuBois, W. E. B. 1968. *The Autobiography of W. E. B. DuBois.* New York: International.

Dudley, William, (ed.). 1998. *Native Americans: Opposing Viewpoints.* San Diego: Greenhaven.

Duesterberg, Thomas J., & Herbert I. London. 2001. "The great transition and the long-term perspective." In T. J. Duesterberg & H. I. London (eds.), *Riding the Next Wave: Why this Century will be a Golden Age for Workers, the Environment, and Developing Countries.* Washington, DC: Brookings Institution.

Duke, J. T. 1976. *Conflict & Power in Social Life.* Provo, UT: Brigham Young University Press.

Dulles, Foster R., & Melvyn Dubofsky. 1984. *Labor in America,* 4th ed. Arlington Heights, IL: Harlan Davidson.

Dumais, Susan A. 2002. "Cultural capital, gender and school success: The role of habitus." *Sociology of Education* 75(1): 44–68.

Duncan Greg J., W. Jean Yeung, Jeanne Brooks-Gunn, & Judith R. Smith. 1998. "How much does childhood poverty affect the life chances of children?" *American Sociological Review* (63/3): 406–423.

Duncan, Greg J., Timothy Smeeding, & Willard Rogers. 1992. "The incredible shrinking middle class." *American Demographics* 14/4: 34–39.

Duneier, Mitchell. 1999. *Sidewalk.* New York: Farrar, Straus, and Giroux.

Dunham, Jack (ed.). 2001. *Stress in the Workplace: Past, Present, and Future.* London: Whurr.

Dunning, E. 1999. *Sport Matters.* London: Routledge.

duPreez, Peter. 1994. *Genocide: The Psychology of Mass Murder.* New York: Marion Boyers.

Durkheim, Emile. 1893/1964. *The Division of Labor in Society.* New York: Free Press.

Durkheim, Emile. 1897/1964. *Suicide.* Glencoe, IL: Free Press.

Durkheim, Emile. 1898/1956. *Education and Sociology* (Sherwood D. Fox, trans.). Glencoe, IL: Free Press. 1964. *The Division of Labor in Society* (George Simpson, trans.), New York: Free Press.

Durkheim, Emile. 1912/1954. *The Elementary Forms of Religious Life.* Glencoe, IL: Free Press.

Durkheim, Emile. 1933. *The Division of Labor in Society.* New York: Free Press. Originally published in 1893.

Durkheim, Emile. 1966. *Suicide.* New York: Free Press.

Dutch Legalize Euthanasia. 2002. "Dutch legalize euthanasia, the first such national law." *New York Times* 151 (April 1): A5.

Dworkin, Ronald W. 2001. "The medicalization of unhappiness." *Public Interest* 144(Summer): 85–99.

Dworkin, Shari L., & Michael A. Messner. 1999. "Just do…what? Sports, bodies, gender." In Myra M. Ferree, Judith Lorber, and Beth B. Hess (eds.), *Revisioning Gender.* Thousand Oaks, CA: Sage: 341–61.

Dye, Thomas. 1995. *Who's Running America? The Clinton Years,* 6th ed. Upper Saddle River, NJ: Prentice-Hall.

Dziech, Billie Wright, & Michael W. Hawkins. 2000. "Male students: The invisible casualties." In Edmund Wall (ed.), *Sexual Harassment, Confrontation and Decisions.* Amherst, NY: Prometheus: 48–62.

Eagly, A. H., & B. T. Johnson. 1990. "Gender & leadership style." *Psychological Bulletin* 108: 233–256.

Eagly, A. H., & S. J. Karau. 1991. "Gender & the emergence of leaders." *Journal of Personality & Social Psychology* 60: 687–710.

Eagly, A. H., R. D. Ashmore, M. G. Makhijani, & L. C. Longo. 1991. "What is beautiful is good, but…: A meta-analytic review of research on the physical attractiveness stereotype." *Psychological Bulletin* 110: 109–28.

Eagly, Alice H. 1992. "Uneven progress: Social psychology and the study of attitudes." *Journal of Personality and Social Psychology* (63): 693–710.

Eagly, Alice H., & Wendy Wood. 1999. "The origins of sex differences in human behavior: Evolved dispositions versus social roles." *American Psychologist* 54(6): 408–423.

"East Timor Gains Independence." 2002. *USA Today* (May 19).

Easterbrook, Gregg. 1999. "Watch and learn: Yes, the media do make us more violent." *The New Republic* (May 17): 22–25.

Easterly, William. 2001. "Can institutions resolve ethnic conflict?" *Economic Development and Social Change* 49(4): 687–706.

Eaton, Susan E. 2001. *The Other Boston Busing Story: What's Won and Lost Across the Boundary Line.* New Haven: Yale University.

Eberstadt, Nicholas. 1995. "What is population policy?" *Society* 32(4): 26–29.

Eck, Diana L. 2001. *A New Religious America: How a Christian Country Has Now Become the World's Most Religiously Diverse Nation.* San Francisco: HarperCollins.

Eckerman, Liz. 2000. "Gendering indicators of health and well-being: Is quality of life neutral?" *Social Indicators Research* 52(1): 29–54.

Economist. 2000. "Germany's age-old problem." 3555(8174): 54.

Economist. 2000. "Misery behind migration: Jiashan, China." *Economist* 357 (Nov. 18): 52–54.

Economist. 2001a. "Off to the city." *Economist* 360 (Sept. 1): 36.

Economist. 2001b. "The blob that ate East Texas." *Economist* 359 (June 23): 30–32.

Edelstein, Linda N. 1999. *The Art of Midlife: Courage and Creative Living for Women.* Westport, CT: Bergin & Garvey.

Eder, Donna, & David A. Kinney. 1995. "The effect of middle school extracurricular activities on adolescent's popularity and peer status." *Youth and Society* 26(3): 298–324.

Edin, Kathryn. 2000a. "What do low-income single mothers say about marriage?" *Social Problems* 47(1): 112–33.

Edin, Kathryn. 2000b. "Few good men: Why poor mothers don't marry or remarry." *American Prospect* 11(4): 26–31.

Edmonds, P. 1993. "After war: Parade to shelters." *USA Today* (June 1): A-4.

Edmondson, Brad. 1997. "The wired bunch." *American Demographics* (49/6): 10–15.

Education Reforms and Students a Risk. 1996. Available: http://www.ed.gov/pubs// AtRiskSER.

Edwards, Harry. 1973. *Sociology of Sport.* Homewood, IL: Dorsey.

Edwards, Richard. 1985. *Contested Terrain: The Transformation of the Workplace in the 20th Century.* New York: Basic.

Edwards, Tamala. 2000. "Flying solo." *Time* (August 28): 47–53.

Egan, Jennifer. 1999. "Why a priest?" *The New York Times Magazine* (April 4): 28–33.

Egan, Susan K., & David G. Perry. 2001. "Gender identity: A multidimensional analysis for psychological adjustment." *Developmental Psychology* 37(4): 451–63.

Egolf, Brenda, Judith Lasker, Stewart Wolf, & Louise Potvin. 1993. "The Roseto Effect." *American Journal of Public Health* 82: 1089–1092.

Ehrenreich, Barbara. 1998. "The silenced majority: Why the working person has disappeared from American media and culture." In Margaret L. Anderson & Patricia Hill Collins (eds.), *Race, Class and Gender: An Anthology.* Belmont, CA: Wadsworth: 147–49.

Ehrle, Glenda M. 2001. "Grandchildren as moderator variables in the family: Social, physiological, and intellectual development of grandparents who are raising them." In Elena I. Grigorenko & Robert J. Sternberg (eds.), *Family Environment and Intellectual Functioning: A Life-Span Perspective.* Mahwah, NJ: Lawrence Erlbaum.

Ehrlich, Howard J. 1973. *The Social Psychology of Prejudice.* New York: Wiley Interscience.

Einhorn, Bruce et al. 2000. "China's tangled web: Will Beijing ruin the net by trying to control it?" *Business Week International* (July 17): 28.

Einstadter, Werner, & Stuart Henry. 1995. *Criminological Theory: An Analysis of Its Underlying Assumptions.* Fort Worth, TX: Harcourt Brace.

Eisen, Arnold M. 1997. *Taking Hold of Torah: Jewish Commitment and Community in America.* Bloomington: Indiana University.

Eisenberg, David M., Roger B. Davis, Susan L. Ettner, Scott Appel, Sonja Wilkey, Maria Von Rompay, & Ronald Kessler. 1998. "Trends in alternative medicine use in the United States, 1990–1997: Results of a follow-up national survey." *Journal of the American Medical Association* 280: 1569–75.

Eisenberg, N. 2002. "Prosocial behavior, empathy and sympathy." In Marc H. Bornstein, Lucy Davidson, Corey L. M. Keyes, & Kristin Moore (eds.). *Positive Development across the Life Course.* Mahwah, NJ: Lawrence Erlbaum.

Eisenstadt, S. N. 1973. *Tradition, Change and Modernity.* New York: Wiley.

Eisenstein, Zillah R. 1994. *The Color of Gender: Reimaging Democracy.* Berkeley: University of California.

Eisler, Diane, & David Loye. 1990. *The Partnership Way.* New York: Harper-SanFrancisco.

Eisler, Diane, David Loye, & Kari Norgaard. 1995. *Women, Men, and the Global Quality of Life. A Report of the Gender Equity and Quality of Life Project of the Center for Partnership Studies.* Pacific Grove, CA: Center for Partnership Studies.

Eitzen, D. Stanley, & George H. Sage. 2003. *Sociology of North American Sport,* 7th ed. New York: McGraw-Hill.

Eitzen, D. Stanley, & M. Baca Zinn. 1992. *Social Problems,* 5th ed. Boston: Allyn & Bacon.

Eitzen, D. Stanley. 1990. "The dark side of competition in American society." *Vital Speeches* (56/1): 185–86.

Eitzen, D. Stanley. 1996. "Classism in sport." *Journal of Sport and Social Issues* (20/February): 113–16.

Eitzen, D. Stanley. 1999. *Fair and Foul: Beyond the Myths and Paradoxes of Sport.* Lanham, MD: Rowman & Littlefield.

Ekerdt, David J. 1998. "The busy ethic: Moral continuity between work and retirement." In Harold G. Cox (ed.). *Aging: Annual Editions, 98/99.* Guilford, CT: Dushkin/McGraw-Hill: 128–133.

Ekman, Paul & M. O'Sullivan. 1991. "Facial expression: Methods, means and moods." In Robert S. Feldman & B. Rime (eds.), *Fundamentals of Nonverbal Behavior.* Cambridge, UK: Cambridge University.

Ekman, Paul, Wallace V. Friesen & M. O'Sullivan. 1988. "Smiles when lying." *Journal of Personality and Social Psychology* 54: 414–20.

el Saadawi, Nawal. 1980. *The Hidden Faces of Eve: Women in the Arab World.* London: Zed.

Elazar, Daniel J. 2000. "Organizations and philanthropy." North American Jewish Data Bank. *Data Bank News* (Special Issue, Fall): 5–7.

Elber, Lynn. 2002. "African-Americans 'ghettoized' in sitcoms, UCLA study finds." *Evansville Courier-Press* (June 5).

Elizabeth, Vivienne. 2000. "Cohabitation, marriage, and the unruly consequences of difference." *Gender & Society.* 14(1) 87–110.

Ellen, Ingrid Gould, Tod Mijanovich, & Keri-Nicole Dillman. 2001. "Neighborhood effects on health: Exploring the links and assessing the evidence." *Journal of Urban Affairs* 23(3/4): 391–408.

Elliot, Leland & Cynthia Brantley. 1997. *Sex on Campus: The Naked Truth about the Real Lives of College Students.* New York: Random House.

Elliott, Marta, & Lauren J. Krivo. 1991. "Structural determinants of homelessness in the United States." *Social Problems* 38: 113–131.

Elliott, Michael. 1993. "Global Mafia." *Newsweek* (December 13): 22–29.

Elliott, Michael. 1999. "The new radicals." *Newsweek* (December 13).

Ellis, Alan L., & Robert W. Mitchell. 2000. "Sexual orientation." In Lenore T. Szuchman & Frank Muscarella (eds.), *Psychological Perspectives on Human Sexuality.* New York: John Wiley.

Ellis, Lee, & Anthony Walsh. 2000. *Criminology: A Global Perspective.* Boston: Allyn & Bacon.

Ellis, Lee, & Harry Hoffman, (eds.). 1990. *Crime in Biological, Social and Moral Contexts.* New York: Praeger.

Ellison, Christopher G., & David A. Gay. 1989. "Black political participation revisited." *Social Science Quarterly* 70: 101–119.

Elliston, Deborah. 1999. "Negotiating transnational sexual economies: Female and same-sex sexuality in 'Tahiti and Her Islands.' " In Evelyn Blackwood & Saskia Wieringa (eds.), *Female Desires: Same-Sex Relations and Transgender Practices across Cultures.* New York: Columbia University.

Ellyson, S. L., J. F. Dovidio, & C. E. Brown. 1992. "The look of power: Gender differences and similarities." In Cecilia Ridgeway (ed.), *Gender, Interaction and Inequality.* New York: Springer-Verlag: 50–80.

Ember, Carol R., & Melvin Ember. 2001. *Cross-Cultural Research Methods.* Walnut Creek, CA: AltaMira.

Embong, Abdul Rahman. 2002. *State-led Modernization and the New Middle Class in Malaysia.* New York: Palgrave.

Emimbeyer, Mustafa, & Jeff Goodwin. 1994. "Network analysis, culture, & the problem of agency." *American Journal of Sociology* 99: 1411–1454.

Engles, Friedrich. 1942 (original 1884). *The Origin of the Family, Private Property, and the State.* New York: International.

Enoch, M, David Ball, & N. Hadrian. 2001. *Uncommon Psychiatric Symptoms.* New York: Arnold.

Entessar, Nader. 1988. "Criminal law and the legal system in revolutionary Iran." *Boston College Third World Journal,* 8(1): 91–102.

Entine, John. 2000. *Taboo.* New York: Public Affairs Press.

Environment News Service. 2001. "Environment: Counting Chernobyl's cancer costs." Lycos, October 23. Available: http://ens.lycos.com/ens/oct2001.

Epstein, Barbara. 1991. *Political Protest and Cultural Revolution.* Berkeley, CA: University of California Press.

Epstein, Cynthia F. 1970. *Women's Place: Options and Limits on Professional Careers.* Berkeley: University of California Press.

Erera, Pauline I., & Karen I. Fredriksen. 1999. "Lesbian stepfamilies: A unique family structure." *Families in Society* 80(3): 263–70.

Erickson, Kai T. 1962. "Notes on the sociology of deviance." *Social Problems* 9: 307–14.

Erickson, Kai T. 1966. *Wayward Puritans: A Study in the Sociology of Deviance.* New York: Wiley.

Erickson, Kai, & Steven B. Vallas, (eds.). 1990. *The Nature of Work: Sociological Perspectives.* New Haven, CT: Yale University Press.

Eriksen, Thomas Hylland. 2001. *Small Places, Large Issues: An Introduction to Social and Cultural Anthropology.* London: Pluto.

Erikson, Erik. 1963. *Childhood and Society.* New York: Norton.

Eschholz, Sarah, & Jana Bufkin. 2001. "Crime in the movies: Investigating the efficacy of measures of both sex and gender for predicting victimization and offending in film." *Sociological Forum* 16(4): 655–76.

Eshleman, J. Ross. 2000. *The Family: An Introduction.* 9th ed. Boston: Allyn & Bacon.

Eskridge, William N., & Nan D. Hunter. 2001. *Sexuality, Gender and the Law.* New York: Foundation Press.

Esping-Andersen, G. 1999. *Social Foundations of Postindustrial Economics.* New York: Oxford University Press.

Esping-Anderson, Gosta. 1990. *The Three Worlds of Welfare Capitalism.* Cambridge, MA: Polity.

Esposito, John L. 2002. *Unholy War: Terror in the Name of Islam.* Oxford, NY: Oxford University.

Esposito, John L., & John O. Voll. 2001. *Makers of Contemporary Islam.* Oxford, NY: Oxford University.

Esposito, John L., Darrell J. Fasching, & Todd Lewis. 2001. "Islam: The many faces of the Muslim experience." In *World Religions Today.* Oxford, NY: Oxford University: 181–229.

Estrada, Kelly, & Peter L. McLaren. 1993. "A dialogue on multiculturalism and democratic culture." *Educational Researcher* 22(3): 27–33.

Etzioni, Amitai. 1964. *Modern Organizations.* Upper Saddle River, NJ: Prentice Hall.

Etzioni, Amitai. 1975. *A Comparative Analysis of Complex Organization,* revised ed. New York: Free Press.

Etzioni, Amitai. 1988. *The Moral Dimension.* New York: Free Press.

Etzioni, Amitai. 1993. *The Spirit of Community.* New York: Crown.

Etzioni, Amitai. 1995. "The attack on community: The grooved debate." *Society* 32(5): 12–17.

Etzioni-Halevy (ed.). 1997. *Classes and Elites in Democracy and Democratization.* New York: Garland.

Etzkowitz, Henry. 1992. "Inventions." In Edgar Borgatta & Marie L. Borgatta, (eds.), *Encyclopedia of Sociology.* New York: Macmillan: 1001–5.

Evans, Lorraine, & Kimberley Davies. 2000. "No sissy boys here: A content analysis of the representation of masculinity in elementary school reading textbooks." *Sex Roles* 42(3–4): 255–70.

Evans, Peter, & James E. Rauch. 1999. "Bureaucracy and growth," *American Sociological Review* (64): 748–765.

Evans, Peter. 1979. *Dependent Development: The Alliance of Multinational, State and Local Capital in Brazil.* Princeton, NJ: Princeton University Press.

Evans-Pritchard, E. E. 1940. *The Nuer.* New York: Oxford University Press.

Everington, Caroline, Brenda Stevens, & Victoria Renner Winters. 1999. "Teachers' attitudes, felt competence, and need of support for implementation of inclusive educational programs." *Psychological Reports* 85(1): 331–38.

Eyada, Moustafa H. 2001. "Female genital mutilation: A descriptive study." *Journal of Sex & Marital Therapy* 27(5): 453–58.

Ezekiel, Raphael S. 1995. *The Racist Mind: Portraits of American Neo-Nazis and Klansmen.* New York: Viking.

Ezorsky, G. 1991. *Affirmative Action.* Ithaca, NY: Cornell University Press.

Fabjancic, Nina. 1999. "Media representations of women in politics." *Teorija in Praksa* 36(1): (January–February): 74–86.

Fagot, Beverly I. 1994. "Peer relations and the development of competence in boys and girls." In Campbell Leaper (ed.), *Childhood Gender Segregation: Causes and Consequences.* San Francisco: Jossey-Bass.

Fagot, Beverly I., & Leslie Leve. 1998. "Gender identity and play." In Doris Pronin Fromberg & Doris Bergen (eds.), *Play from Birth to Twelve and Beyond: Contexts, Perspectives, and Meanings.* New York: Garland.

Fairchild, Erika. 1993. *Comparative Criminal Justice Systems.* Belmont, CA: Wadsworth.

Fallows, James. 1994. *Looking at the Sun: The Rise of the New East Asian Economic & Political System.* New York: Pantheon.

Faludi, Susan. 2000. *Stiffed: The Betrayal of the American Man.* San Francisco: HarperCollins.

Fan, Cindy, & Youqin Huang. 1998. "Waves of rural brides: Female marriage migration in China." *Annals of the Association of American Geographers* 88(2): 227–51.

Fan, Pi-Ling, & Margaret Mooney Marini. 2000. "Influences on gender-role attitudes during the transition to adulthood." *Social Science Research* 29(2): 258–83.

Fang, Yuan, Wang Chuanbin, & Song Yuhua. 1992. "Support of the elderly in China." In Hal Kendig, Akiko Hashimoto, & Larry C. Coppard (eds.), *Family Support for the Elderly: The International Experience.* New York: Oxford University Press.

Faris, Robert E. & H. W. Dunham. 1939. *Mental Disorders in Urban Areas.* Chicago: University of Chicago Press.

Faris, Robert E. L. 1979. *Chicago Sociology: 1920–1932.* Chicago: University of Chicago Press.

Farkas, George, Christy Lleras, & Steve Maczuga. 2002. "Does oppositional culture exist in minority and poverty peer groups?" *American Sociological Review* 67(1): 148–55.

Farley, John E. 1998. *Sociology,* 4th ed. Upper Saddle River, NJ: Prentice Hall.

Farley, Reynolds. 1996. *The New American Reality.* New York: Russell Sage Foundation.

Farone, Stephen et al. 1993. "Intellectual performance and school failure in children with attention deficit hyperactivity disorder and in their siblings." *Journal of Abnormal Psychology* 102: 616–23.

Fay, B. 1987. *Critical Social Science: Liberation & Its Limits.* Ithaca, NY: Cornell University Press.

Feagin, Joe R. & Herman Vera. 1995. *White Racism: The Basics.* New York: Routledge.

Feagin, Joe R. 1999. "The continuing significance of race." In Norman R. Yetman (ed.), *The Dynamics of Race and Ethnicity in American Life,* 6th ed. Boston: Allyn & Bacon: 384–399.

Feagin, Joe R., & Clairece B. Feagin. 1999. *Racial and Ethnic Relations,* 6th ed. Upper Saddle River, NJ: Prentice-Hall.

Federal Bureau of Investigation. 2001. *Crime in the United States, 2000.* Washington, DC: U.S. Department of Justice.

Federal Reserve Bank of New York. 2002. U.S. Economy and Financial Markets. "Health service indicators: Medical care, expenditures, inflation and employment." Available: http://www.ny.frb.org/rmaghome/dirchrts/sec10.

Feener, Michael. 2002. "Islam." Presentation to the Asian Studies Development Program Institute on Southeast Asia, East-West Center, Honolulu, Hawaii July 25.

Feinberg, Leslie. 2001. "Trans health crisis: For us it's life or death." *American Journal of Public Health* 91(6): 897–900.

Feingold, A. 1992. "Good-looking people are not what we think." *Psychological Bulletin* 11: 304–41.

Feinman, Clarice. 1994. *Women in the Criminal Justice System.* Westport, CT: Praeger.

Feldberg, Roslyn, & Evelyn N. Glenn. 1982. "Technology and work degradation." In Joan Rothschild, (ed.), *Women, Technology and Innovation.* New York: Pergamon.

Fendrich, James M., & Kenneth L. Lovoy. 1988. "Back to the future." *American Sociological Review* 53: 780–84.

Ferguson, Dianne L., Audrey Desjarlais, & Gwen Meyer. 2000. *Improving Education: The Promise of Inclusive Learning.* Education Development Center. Newton, MA: National Institute for Urban School Improvement.

Fernandez, Roberto N., & Nancy Weinberg. 1997. "Sifting and sorting: Personal contacts and hiring in a retail bank." *American Sociological Review* 62(6): 883–902.

Fernandez-Kelly, Maria Patricia. 2001. "Maquiladoras: The view from the inside." In Gwen Kirk & Margo Okazawa-Rey (eds.), *Women's Lives: Multicultural Perspectives.* Mountain View, CA: Mayfield: 279–87.

Ferraro, Kenneth F. 1995. *Fear of Crime: Interpreting Victimization Risk.* Albany: SUNY Press.

Ferraro, Kenneth F. 2001. "Aging and role transitions." In Robert H. Binstock & Linda K. George (eds.), *Handbook of Aging and the Social Sciences.* San Diego, CA: Academic Press.

Festinger, Leon, Henry W. Riecken, & Stanley Schacter. 1956. *When Prophecy Fails.* Minneapolis: University of Minnesota.

Fetto, John. 1999. "Down for the count." *American Demographics* (21/11): 46–47.

Fetto, John. 2000. "Be mine." *American Demographics* 22(2): 11–12.

Feuer, Lewis. 1969. *The Conflict of Generations.* New York: Basic.

Fidler, Jon. 1999. "Kibbutz: What, why, when, where?". *Focus on Israel* (October). Available: http://www.mfa.gov.il/mfa/go.asp.

Fidler, Roger. 1997. *Mediamorphosis: Understanding New Media.* Thousand Oaks, CA: Sage.

Fiedler, Fred E. 1967. *A Theory of Leadership Effectiveness.* New York: McGraw-Hill.

Fiedler, Fred E. 1981. "Leadership effectiveness." *American Behavioral Scientist* 24: 619–632.

Fields, Jason, & Lynne M. Casper. 2001. "America's families and living arrangements." *Current Population Reports* (June). U.S. Census Bureau.

Fijnaut, Cyrille. 1990. "Organized crime: A comparison between the USA and Western Europe." *British Journal of Criminology* 30: 321–40.

Filmer, D., & L. Pritchett. 1999. "The effect of household wealth on educational attainment: Evidence from 35 countries." *Population Development Review* 25: 85–120.

Fine, Michelle, & Kersha Smith. 2001. "Zero tolerance: Reflections on a failed policy that won't die." In William Ayers, Bernadine Dohrn, & Rick Ayers (eds.), *Zero Tolerance: Resisting the Drive for Punishment in Our Schools.* New York: New Press: 256–64.

Fineman, Howard, & Michael Isikoff. 2002. "Lights Out: Enron's Failed Power Play." *Newsweek* 89/3 (January 21): 15–18.

Fingerhut, Lois H. 1993. "Firearm mortality among children, youth and young adults 1–34 years of age, trends and current status: United States, 1985–1990." *Advance Data* 231 (March 23): 1–20.

Finke, Roger. 2001. "The new holy clubs: Testing church-to-sect propositions." *Sociology of Religion* 62(2): 175–89.

Finkelhor, David, et al. 1990. "Sexual abuse in a national survey of adult men and women." *Child Abuse and Neglect* 14(1): 19–28.

Finkenauer, Catrin, Wim Meeus, Annerieke Oosterwegel, Rutger C. M. E. Engels. 2002. In Thomas M. Brinthaupt & Richard P. Lipka (eds.), *Understanding Early Adolescent Self and Identity: Applications and Interventions.* Albany, NY: State University of New York.

Finley, Colleen, & Eric Corty. 1995. "Rape on campus: The prevalence of sexual assault while enrolled in college." *Journal of College Student Development* 34: 113–17.

Finley, M., & M. Schinder. 1999. "Punitive Juvenile Justice Policies and Their Impact on Minority Youth." *Federal Probation* (December).

Finn, Patrick J. 1999. *Literacy with an Attitude: Educating Working-Class Children in Their Own Self-Interest.* Albany: State University of New York.

Firebaugh, Glenn, & Frank D. Beck. 1994. "Does economic growth benefit the masses? Growth, dependence and welfare in the third world." *American Sociological Review* (59/5): 631–53.

Firebaugh, Glenn. 1992. "Growth effects of foreign & domestic investments." *American Journal of Sociology* (98/1): 105–30.

Firey, Walter. 1945. "Sentiment and symbolism as ecological variables." *American Sociological Review* 10: 140–48.

First Book. 2001. "Magnitude: Facts on illiteracy." Available: http://www.firstbook.org/about/factsonilliteracy.

Fiscella, Kevin. 1999. "Is lower income associated with greater biopsychosocial morbidity? Implications for physicians working with underserved patients." *Journal of Family Practice* 48(5): 372–89.

Fischer, Claude S. 1982. *To Dwell Among Friends: Personal Networks in Town & City.* Chicago: University of Chicago Press.

Fischer, Claude S. 1984. *The Urban Experience.* San Diego: Harcourt Brace Jovanovich.

Fischer, Claude S., Michael Hout, Martin S. Jankowski, Samuel R. Lucas, Ann Swidler, & Kim Voss. 1996. *Inequality by Design: Cracking the Bell Curve Myth.* Princeton, NJ: Princeton University Press.

Fischer, David H. 1989. *Albion's Seed: Four British Folkways in America.* New York: Oxford University Press.

Fischer, Irmgard. 1994. "'Go and suffer oppression' said God's messenger to Hagar." In Elisabeth Schussler Fiorenza & M. Shawn Copeland, (eds.), *Violence Against Women.* London: Stichtin Concillium/SCM Press.

Fischman, Josh. 2001. "Do men experience menopause?" *U.S. News & World Report* 141(July 30) 47.

Fishbein, D. H. (ed.). 2000. *The Science, Treatment and Prevention of Antisocial Behaviors: Applications to the Criminal Justice System.* Kingston, NJ: Civic Research Institute.

Fishbein, Harold D. 1996. *Peer Prejudice and Discrimination.* Boulder, CO: Westview.

Fishel, Elizabeth. 2000. *Reunion: The Girls We Used to Be, the Women We Became.* New York: Random House.

Fisher, Douglas B., Nancy Frey, & Caren Sax. 1999. *Inclusive Elementary Schools: Recipes for Success.* Colorado Springs, CO: PEAK Parent Center.

Fisher, Elizabeth. 1979. *Woman's Creation: Sexual Evolution & the Shaping of Society.* New York: Anchor.

Fisher, Julie. 1994. "Is the iron law of oligarchy rusting away in the Third World?" *World Development* (22/2): 55ff.

Flaherty, David. 1989. *Protecting Privacy in Surveillance Societies.* Chapel Hill, NC: University of North Carolina Press.

Flaherty, Mary. 1999. "The influence of a language gender system of perception." *Tohoku Psychologica Folia* 58: 1–10.

Flaherty, Mary. 2001. "How a language gender system creeps into perception." *Journal of Cross-Cultural Psychology* 32(1): 18–31.

Flannagan, Dorothy, Lynne Baker-Ward, & Loranel Graham. 1995. "Talk about preschool: Patterns of topic discussion and elaboration related to gender and ethnicity." *Sex Roles* 32(1–2): 1–15.

Fletcher, Anne C., Deborah Newsome, Paniela Nockerson, & Ronda Bazley. 2001. "Social network closure and child adjustment." *Merrill-Palmer Quarterly* 47(4): 500–531.

Fletcher, Michael A. 2002. "Diversity's future? Socioeconomic criteria, not race, used to desegregate San Francisco schools." *Washington Post* (March 18): A01.

Flood, Gavin. 2002. "Indian religions and the Hindu tradition." In John Bowker (ed.), *The Cambridge Illustrated History of Religions.* Cambridge, UK: Cambridge University: 24–53.

Florida, Richard, & Martin Kenney. 1991. "Transplanted organizations." *American Sociological Review* 56: 381–98.

Flowers, R. Barri. 1998. *The Prostitution of Women and Girls.* Jefferson, NC: McFarland.

Flowers, R. Barri. 2001. "The sex industry's worldwide exploitation of children." *Annals of the American Academy of Political and Social Science* 575 (May): 147–57.

Floyd, Frank J., & Terry S. Stein. 2002. "Sexual orientation identity formation among gay, lesbian and bisexual youths: Multiple patterns of milestones." *Journal of Research on Adolescence* 12(2): 167–91.

Foek, Anton. 1997. "Sweatshop Barbie: Exploitation of third world labor," *The Humanist* (Jan/Feb): 9–13.

Foley, Douglas E. 2001. "The great American football ritual." In James M. Henslin (ed.), *Down to Earth Sociology: Introductory Readings,* 10th ed. New York: Free Press: 454–67.

Foley, Sallie, & Dennis P. Sugrue. 2002. *Sex Matters for Women: A Complete Guide for Taking Care of Your Sexual Self.* New York: Guilford.

Folts, W. Edward, & Kenneth B. Muir. 2002. "Housing for older adults: New lessons from the past." *Research on Aging* 24(1): 10–28.

Fong, Timothy P. 2002. *The Contemporary Asian American Experience: Beyond the Model Minority.* Upper Saddle River, NJ: Prentice Hall.

Fontanarosa, Phil B. (ed.). 2000. *Alternative Medicine: An Objective Assessment.* Chicago: American Medical Association.

Foot, Rosemary, & Andrew Walter. 1999. "Whatever happened to the Pacific Century?" *Review of International Studies* 25: 245–69.

Forer, L. G. 1984. *Money & Justice.* New York: Norton.

Form, William. 1996. *Segmented Labor, Fractured Politics.* New York: Plenum.

Forrest, James A., & Robert S. Feldman. 2000. "Detecting deception and judge's involvement: Lower task involvement leads to better lie detection." *Personality and Social Psychology Bulletin* 26(1): 118–25.

Fortier, Jana. 2001. "Sharing, hoarding, and theft: Exchange and resistance in forager-farmer relations." *Ethnology* 40(3): 193–211.

Foster, Johanna. 1999. "An invitation to dialogue: Clarifying the position of feminist gender theory in relation to sexual difference theory." *Gender & Society* 13(4): 431–56.

Foster, John L. 1990. "Bureaucratic rigidity revisited." *Social Science Quarterly* 71: 223–38.

Foster, Michele. 2001. "Education and socialization: A review of the literature." In William H. Watkins, James H. Lewis, & Victoria Chou, (eds.), *Race and Education: The Roles of History and Society in Educating African American Students.* Boston: Allyn & Bacon: 200–224.

Fosu, Augustin K. 1997. "Occupational Gains of Black Women Since the 1964 Civil Rights Act," *American Economic Review* 87: 311–15.

Fosu, Augustin Kwasi, & Lemma Senbet. 2001. "Financial and currency crises: An overview." *Journal of African Economies* 10(1): Suppl. 1: 1–15.

Foucault, Michael. 1990. The uses of pleasure, Volume II of Robert Hurley (trans.), *The History of Sexuality.* New York: Vintage.

Fouts, Roger S. 1994. "Transmission of a human gestural language in a chimpanzee mother-infant relationship." In R. A. Gardner et al. (eds.), *The Ethological Roots of Culture.* Boston: Dordrecht: 257–70.

Fox, Elaine, & George R. Arquitt. 1985. "The VFW and the 'Iron Law of Oligarchy.'" In James M. Henslin, (ed.), *Down to Earth Sociology,* 4th ed. New York: Free Press: 147–55.

Fox, James Alan, & Marianne W. Zawitz. 2001. "Homicide trends in the United States." Bureau of Justice Statistics, U.S. Department of Justice. Available: http://www.ojp.usdoj.gov/bjs/homicide/homtrnd.

Fraleigh, Douglas M., & Joseph S. Truman. 1997. *Freedom of Speech in the Marketplace of Ideas.* New York: St. Martin's.

Frammolino, Ralph. 2001. "Title I's $118 billion fails to close gap." In Williamson M. Evers, Lance T. Izumi, & Pamela A. Riley (eds.), *School Reform: The Critical Issues.* Stanford, CA: Hoover Institution: 390–97.

France, David. 2000. "Slavery's New Face," *Newsweek* (December 18): 61–65.

Franco, Nathalie, & Mary J. Levitt. 1998. "The social ecology of middle childhood: Family support, friendship quality and self-esteem." *Family Relations: Interdisciplinary Journal of Applied Family Studies* 47(4): 315–21.

Frank, Jacquelyn Beth. 2002. *The Paradox of Aging in Place in Assisted Living.* Westport, CT: Bergin & Garvey.

Frank, Nancy, & Michael Lynch. 1992. *Corporate Crime, Corporate Violence.* Albany, NY: Harrow & Heston.

Frankish, C. James, Brenda Kwan, Pamela A. Higgins, Joan Wharf, & Craig Larsen. 2002. "Challenges of citizen participation in regional health authorities." *Social Science & Medicine* 54(10): 1471–80.

Franklin, Clyde W. 1994. "Men's studies, the men's movement, and the study of black masculinities: Further demystification of masculinities in America." In Richard G. Majors & Jacob U. Gordon (eds.), *The American Black Male: His Present Status and His Future.* Chicago: Nelson-Hall.

Franklin, John Hope. 1967. *From Slavery to Freedom: A History of Negro Americans,* 3rd ed. New York: Vintage.

Franklin, V. P. 2000. "'A way out of no way': The Bible and Catholic evangelization among African Americans in the United States." In Vincent L. Wimbush & Rosamond C. Rodman (eds.), *African Americans and the Bible.* New York: Continuum: 650–60.

Fraser, Barbara J. 2000. "Lust for life: To bioprospectors, nature is as good as gold." *Sierra* 85 (May/June): 20–21.

Fraser, Steven (ed.). 1995. *The Bell Curve Wars.* New York: Basic.

Frayser, Suzanne G. 1999. "Human sexuality: The whole is more than the sum of its parts." In David N. Suggs & Andrew W. Miracle (eds.), *Culture, Biology and Sexuality.* Athens, GA: University of Georgia.

Frayser, Suzanne G. 2002. "Discovering the value of cross-cultural research on human sexuality." In Michael W. Wiederman & Bernard E. Whitley (eds.), *Handbook for Conducting Research on Human Sexuality.* Mahwah, NJ: Lawrence Erlbaum: 425–43.

Frayser, Suzanne G., & Thomas J. Whitby. 1995. *Studies in Human Sexuality.* Englewood, CO: Libraries Unlimited.

Frederickson, George M. 1981. *White Supremacy: A Comparative Study in American and South African History.* New York: Oxford University Press.

Fredricks, Jennifer L., and Jacquelynne S. Eccles. 2002. "Children's competence and value beliefs from childhood through adolescence: Growth trajectories in two male-sex-typed domains." *Developmental Psychology* 38(4): 519–33.

Free, Marvin D. 1996. *African Americans and the Criminal Justice System.* New York: Garland.

Free, Marvin D., Jr. 1994. "Religiosity, religious conservatism, bonds to school and juvenile delinquency among three categories of drug users." *Deviant Behavior* 15: 151–170.

Freedman, Marc. 2001. "Structural lead: Building new institutions for an aging America." In Nancy Morrow-Howell, James Hinterlong, & Michael Sherraden (eds.), *Productive Aging: Concepts and Challenges.* Baltimore, MD: Johns Hopkins University: 245–59.

Freedman, Samuel G. 2000. *Jew vs. Jew: The Struggle for the Soul of American Jewry.* New York: Simon & Schuster.

Freedom House. 1999. *Freedom in the World, 1998–1999.* New York: Freedom House.

Freeman, David M. 1974. *Technology and Society.* Chicago: Rand McNally.

Freeman, Jo. 1979. "The origins of the women's liberation movement." *American Journal of Sociology* 78: 792–811.

Freeman, Richard B. 1999. *The New Inequality.* Boston: Beacon.

Freeman, Richard B. 2000. "The feminization of work in the U.S.A.: A new era for (man)kind?" In Siv S. Gustafsson & Daniele E. Meulders (eds.), *Gender and the Labour Market: Econometric Evidence of Obstacles to Achieving Gender Equality.* Basingstoke, Hampshire, UK: Macmillan.

Freimuth, Vicki S., Sandra Crouse Quinn, Stephen B. Thomas, Galen Cole, Eric Zook, & Ted Duncan. 2001. "African Americans' view on research and the Tuskegee syphilis study." *Social Science and Medicine* 52(5): 797–808.

Freire, Paulo & Donaldo Macedo. 1995. "A dialogue: culture, language, and race." *Harvard Educational Review* 65(3): 377–402.

Freire, Paulo. 1970. *Pedagogy of the Oppressed.* New York: Seabury.

Freud, Sigmund. 1961. *Civilization and Its Discontents.* New York: W. W. Norton.

Freud, Sigmund. 1962. *Three Contributions to the Theory of Sex.* New York: E. P. Dutton.

Freud, Sigmund. 1963. "Introductory lectures on psychoanalysis." In J. Strachley (ed. and trans.), *The Standard Edition of the Complete Psychological Works of Sigmund Freud.* London: Hogarth.

Freund, Peter E. S., & Meredith B. McGuire. 1991. *Health, Illness and the Social Body: A Critical Sociology.* Upper Saddle River, NJ: Prentice Hall.

Frey, R. Scott, Thomas Dietz, & Linda Kalof. 1992. "Characteristics of successful American protest groups." *American Journal of Sociology* 98: 368–87.

Frey, William H. 2001. "Melting the suburbs: A Census 2000 study of suburban diversity." June 1–17. Brookings Institution Center on Urban and Metropolitan Policy. Washington, DC.

Frey, William H., & Jonathan Tilove. 1995. "Immigrants in, native whites out." *New York Times Magazine* (August 20): 44–45.

Friedan, Betty. 1963. *The Feminine Mystique.* New York: W. W. Norton.

Friedell Morris. 2001. "Incipient dementia: A victim's perspective." In Elizabeth W. Markson & Lisa Ann Hollis-Sawyer (eds.), *Intersections of Aging; Readings in Social Gerontology.* Los Angeles: Roxbury: 381–85.

Friedland, Roger, & A. F. Robertson, (eds.). 1990. *Beyond the Marketplace.* New York: Aldine de Gruyter.

Friedland, Roger. 2001. "Religious nationalism and the problem of collective representation." *Annual Review of Sociology* 27: 125–52.

Friedman, Lawrence M. & Robert V. Percival. 1981. *The Roots of Justice.* Chapel Hill: University of No. Carolina Press.

Friedman, Milton. 2001. "Public schools: Make them private." In Williamson M. Evers, Lance T. Izumi, & Pamela A. Riley (eds.), *School Reform: The Critical Issues.* Stanford, CA: Hoover Institution: 339–45.

Friedman, Richard C., & Jennifer I. Downey. 2002. *Sexual Orientation and Psychoanalysis: Social Science and Clinical Practice.* New York: Columbia University.

Friedman, Thomas L. 1999. *The Lexus and the Olive Tree.* New York: Farrar, Straus & Giroux.

Friedmann, John. 2002. *The Prospect of Cities.* Minneapolis: University of Minnesota.

Friedrich, Carl J., & Zbigniew K. Brzezinski. 1965. *Totalitarian Dictatorship and Autocracy,* 2nd ed. Cambridge, MA: Harvard University Press.

Friedrichs, David. 1996. *Trusted Criminals.* Belmont, CA: Wadsworth.

Friedson, Eliot. 1986. *Professional Powers.* Chicago: University of Chicago Press.

Frontline. 2001. "Hunting bin Laden" and "Al-Qaeda." Available: http:www.pbs.org/wgbh/pages/frontline/shows/binladen.

Frug, Mary Jo. 1998. *Women and the Law.* New York: Foundation Press.

Fryer, David, & Stephen McKenna. 1987. "The laying off of hands—unemployment and the experience of time." In Stephen Fineman, (ed.), *Unemployment: Personal & Social Consequences.* London: Tavistock.

Fu, Xuanning, & Tim B. Heaton. 2000. "Status exchange in intermarriage among Hawaiians, Japanese, Filipinos and Caucasians in Hawaii: 1983–1994." *Journal of Comparative Family Studies* 31(1): 45–61.

Fujita, Koichi. 2001. "Credit flowing from the poor to the rich—The financial market and the role of the Grameen Bank in rural Bangladesh: Reply." *Developing Economies* 39(4): 436–39.

Fukuyama, Francis. 1992. *The End of History and the Last Man.* New York: Penguin.

Fukuyama, Francis. 1999. *The Great Disruption: Human Nature and the Reconstitution of Social Order.* New York: Free Press.

Fuligni, Andrew J., Jacquelynne S. Eccles, Bonnie L. Barber, & Peggy Clements. 2001. "Early adolescent peer orientation and adjustment during high school." *Development Psychology* 37(1): 28–36.

Fuligni, Andrew J., Tiffany Yip, & Vivian Tseng. 2002. "The impact of family obligation on the daily activities and psychological well-being of Chinese American adolescents." *Child Development* 73(1): 302–314.

Fuligni, Andrew J., Vivian Tseng, & May Lam. 1999. "Attitudes toward family obligations among adolescents with Asian, Latin American, and European backgrounds." *Child Development* 70(4): 1030–44.

Fuller, C. J. (ed.). 1996. *Caste Today.* New Delhi: Oxford University Press.

Fuller, K. 2002. "Eradicating essentialism from cultural competency education." *Academic Medicine* 77(3): 198–201.

Furr, Susan R., John S. Westefeld, Gaye N. McConnell, J. Marshall Jenkins. 2001. "Suicide and depression among college students: A decade later." *Professional Psychology: Research and Practice* 32(1): 97–100.

Furstenberg, Frank R., & Kathleen E. Kiernan. 2001. "Delayed parental divorce: How much do children benefit?" *Journal of Marriage and the Family* 63(2): 446–57.

Fussell, Paul. 1992. *Class: A Guide Through the American Status System.* New York: Touchstone.

Gabbidon, Shaun L. 2001. "African American male college students after the Million Man March: An exploratory study." *Journal of African American Men:* 15–26.

Gabor, Andrea. 1995. "Crashing the 'old boy' party." *New York Times* (January 8): Sect. 3, p. 1, 6.

Gabriel, Trip. 1996. "Computers help unite campuses, but also drive some students apart." *New York Times* (November 11).

Gadsden, Vivian L. 2001. "Comment: Cultural discontinuity, race, gender, and the school experiences of children." In William H. Watkins, James H. Lewis, & Victoria Chou, (eds.), *Race and Education: The Roles of History and Society in Educating African American Students.* Boston: Allyn & Bacon: 159–72.

Gagnon, John H. 1990. The explicit and implicit of the scripting perspective in sex research." *Annual Review of Sex Research* 1: 1–43.

Gaines, Donna. 1991. *Teenage Wasteland: Suburbia's Dead End Kids.* New York: Pantheon.

Galenson, Walter. 1996. *The American Labor Movement, 1955–1995.* Westport, CT: Greenwood.

Gallagher, Eugene B. 1995. "Culture and technology in health care as exemplified in Gulf Arab medicine." In Eugene B. Gallagher & Janardan Subedi (eds.), *Global Perspectives on Health Care.* Englewood Cliffs, NJ: Prentice Hall: 83–93.

Gallup, George H., Jr., & Timothy K. Jones. 2000. *The Next American Spirituality: Finding God in the Twenty-First Century.* Colorado Springs, CO: Cook Communications Ministries.

Gallup, George, & Jim Castelli. 1989. *The American Catholic People: Their Beliefs, Practices, and Values.* Garden City, NY: Doubleday.

Gamson, William A. 1990. *The Strategy of Social Protest,* 2nd ed. Belmont, CA: Wadsworth.

Gamson, William A. 1991. "Commitment and agency in social movements." *Sociological Forum* 6: 27–50.

Gamson, William A. 1992. *Talking Politics.* Cambridge, England: Cambridge University Press.

Gamson, William A., & Gadi Wolfsfeld. 1993. "Movements and media as interacting systems." *The Annals* 528: 114–25.

Ganong, Lawrence H., & Marilyn Coleman. 1999. *Changing Families, Changing Responsibilities: Family Obligations Following Divorce and Remarriage.* Mahwah, NJ: Lawrence Erlbaum.

Gans, Herbert J. 1962. *The Urban Villagers.* New York: Free Press.

Gans, Herbert J. 1967. *The Levittowners.* New York: Random House.

Gans, Herbert J. 1991. *People, Plans, and Policies: Essays on Poverty, Racism, and other National Urban Problems.* New York: Columbia University Press.

Gans, Herbert. 1979. "Symbolic ethnicity: The future of ethnic groups and cultures in America." *Ethnic and Racial Studies* 2: 1–20.

Gans, Peter. 1996. "The so-called underclass and the future of antipoverty policy." In M. Brinton Lykes, et al. (eds.), *Myths About the Powerless.* Philadelphia: Temple University Press: 87–101.

Ganz, P. A. 2002. "What outcomes matter to patients: A physician-researcher point of view." *Medical Care* 40(6), Suppl. III: 11–9.

Garbarino, Merwyn S., & Robert F. Sasso. 1994. *Native American Heritage,* 3rd ed. Prospect Heights, IL: Waveland.

Gardiner, James C., Dennis P. Tansley, & Dewey J. Ertz. 2002. "Native Americans: Future directions." In F. Richard Ferraro (ed.), *Minority and Cross-Cultural Aspects of Neuropsychological Assessment.* Bristol, PA: Swets & Zeitlinger.

Gardner, Katy. 1999. "Location and relocation: Home, 'the field,' and anthropological ethics (Sylhet, Bangladesh)." In C. W. Watson (ed.), *Being There: Fieldwork in Anthropology.* London: Pluto Press: 49–73.

Gardner, Marilyn. 1995. "Of super dads, and absent ones." In Kathleen R. Gilbert (ed.), *Marriage and the Family 95/96* (Annual Editions). Guilford, CT: Dushkin/Brown & Benchmark.

Garfinkel, Harold. 1956. "Conditions of successful degradation ceremonies." *American Journal of Sociology* (61/2): 420–24.

Garfinkel, Harold. 1967. *Studies in Ethnomethology.* Englewood Cliffs, NJ: Prentice Hall.

Garfinkel, Harold. 2001. "A condition of and experiments with 'trust' as a condition of concerted stable actions." In Jodi O'Brien & Peter Kollack (eds.), *The Production of Reality: Essays and Readings on Social Interaction.* Thousand Oaks, CA: Pine Forge: 381–92.

Garibaldi, Pietro et al. 2001. "What moves capital to transition economies?" *IMF Staff Papers* 48(Special Issue): 109–45.

Garner, Roberta Ash. 1996. *Contemporary Movements & Ideologies.* New York: McGraw-Hill.

Garrett, Anne G. 2001. *Keeping American Schools Safe: A Handbook.* Jefferson, NC: McFarland.

Garrett, James L. 2001. "Achieving urban food and nutrition security in the developing world." In Per Pinstrup-Andersen & Rajul Pandya-Lorch (eds.), *The Unfinished Agenda: Perspectives on Overcoming Hunger, Poverty, and Environmental Degradation.* Washington, DC: International Food Policy and Research Institute.

Garrity, J. 1989. "A clash of cultures on the Hopi reservation." *Sports Illustrated* (71/21): 10–17.

Garry, Patrick. 1993. *An American Paradox: Censorship in a Nation of Free Speech.* Westport, CT: Praeger.

Garvin, Glenn. 2001. "Loco completamente loco: The many failures of bilingual education." In Williamson M. Evers, Lance T. Izumi, & Pamela A. Riley (eds.), *School Reform: The Critical Issues.* Stanford, CA: Hoover Instituion: Malden, MA: Blackwell: 217–39.

Gatchel, Robert J., Andrew Baum, & David S. Krantz. 1989. *An Introduction to Health Psychology.* New York: Random House.

Gates, Henry L., Jr. 1992. "Integrating the American mind." In Henry L. Gates (ed.), *Loose Cannons: Notes on the Culture Wars.* New York: Oxford: 105–120.

Gavron, Daniel. 2000. *The Kibbutz: Awakening from Utopia.* Lanham, MD: Rowman & Littlefield.

Gaw, A. C. 1993. *Culture, Ethnicity and Mental Illness.* Washington, DC: Psychiatric Press.

Gazetteer, 2001. "Metropolitan areas with more than one million inhabitants–Population for 2002." The World Gazetteer. Available: http://www.world-gazetteer.com/st/statn.

Geerkin, Michael, & Walter Gove. 1983. *At Home and at Work: The Family's Allocation of Labor.* Beverly Hills, CA: Sage.

GEF. 1995. Global Environmental Facility. *Bulletin and Quarterly Operational Summary.* No. 14.

Gegax, T. Trent, & Lynette Clemetson. 1998. The abortion wars come home." *Newsweek* (November 9): 34–35.

Gehring, John. 2001. "Colleges: Minorities and college." *Education Week* 21(5): 10.

Geis, Florence L. 1993. "Self-fulfilling prophecies: A social psychological view of gender." In Anne E. Beall & Robert J. Sternberg (eds.), *The Psychology of Gender.* New York: Guilford.

Gelbspan, Ross. 1997. *The Heat is On.* Reading, MA: Addison-Wesley.

Gelles, Richard J., & Murray A. Straus. 1987. "Is violence toward children increasing? A comparison of 1975–1985 national survey rates. *Journal of Interpersonal Violence* 2: 212–22.

Gelles, Richard J., & Murray A. Straus. 1995. "Profiling violent families." In Mark Robert Rank & Edward L. Kain (eds.), *Diversity and Change in Families: Patterns, Prospects, and Policies.* Englewood Cliffs, NJ: Prentice Hall.

George, John, & Laird M. Wilcox. 1996. *American Extremists.* Amherst, NY: Prometheus.

Gerbner, George, L. Gross, M. Morgan, & Nancy Signorelli. 1994. "Growing up with television: The cultivation perspective." In J. Bryant & D. Zillmann (eds.), *Media Effects.* Hillsdale, NJ: Lawrence Erlbaum.

Gerlach, Michael. 1992. *Alliance Capitalism.* Berkeley: University of California Press.

Gerson, Kathleen. 2002. "Moral dilemmas, moral strategies, and the transformation of gender: Lessons from two generations of work and family change." *Gender & Society* 16(1): 8–28.

Gerstel, N., & McGonagle K. 1999. "Job leaves and the limits of the Family and Medical Leave Act." *Work & Occupations* 26: 510–34.

Gerth, Hans H., & C. Wright Mills, (eds.). 1958. *From Max Weber: Essays In Sociology.* New York: Galaxy.

Gesalman, Anne Belli, & Lynette Clemetson. 2002. "A crazy system." *Newsweek* 139 (March 25): 30.

Getches, David H., & David N. Pellow. 2002. "Beyond traditional environmental justice." In Kathryn M. Mutz, Gary C. Bryner, & Douglas S. Kenney (eds.), *Justice and Natural Resources.* Washington, DC: Island Press: 3–29.

Getting it Right. 2000. "Getting it right: How to ensure a better future? Prepare for victory today." *Sierra* (January/February): 40–47, 117.

Gevitz, Norman. 1998. "Osteopathic medicine: From deviance to difference." In Norman Gevitz (ed.), *Other Healers: Unorthodox Medicine in America.* Baltimore, MD: Johns Hopkins University.

Geyer, Felix, & Walter R. Heinz, (eds.) 1992. *Alienation, Society and the Individual.* New Brunswick, NJ: Transaction.

Geyman, John P. 2002. *Health Care in America: Can Our Ailing System be Healed?* Boston: Butterworth-Heinemann.

Ghalwash, Mae. 2000. "Rumors sweep Egypt that Coke logo is blasphemous." *Owensboro (Ky) Messenger-Inquirer* (June 22): 2A.

Ghose, Malini. 2001 "Women and empowerment through literacy." In David R. Olson & Nancy Torrance (eds.), *The Making of Literate Societies.* 296–316.

Giacalone, Robert A., & Jon W. Beard. 1994. "Impression management, diversity, and international management." *American Behavioral Scientist* 37(5): 621–36.

Giago, Tom. 1998. "Indian-named mascots: An assault on self-esteem." In Susan Lobo and Steve Talbot, (eds.), *Native American Voices: A Reader.* New York: Longman: 204–6.

Giannetti, Charlene C., & Margaret Sagarese. 2001. "Does your child click with a clique? Help your child uncover the truth about cliques and belonging." *Our Children* 26(6) (March): 9–10.

Gibbon, Peter. 2002. "Present-day capitalism , the new international trade regime and Africa." *Review of African Political Economy* 29(91): 95–112.

Gibbons, Don. 1994. *Talking About Crime and Criminals: Problems and Issues in Theory Development in Criminology.* Englewood Cliffs, NJ: Prentice Hall.

Gibbs, Jack P. 1975. *Crime, Punishment and Deterrence.* New York: Elsevier.

Gibbs, Jack P. 1987. "An incorrigible positivist." *Criminology* 12: 2–3.

Gibbs, Jack P. 1989. *Control: Sociology's Central Notion.* Urbana: University of Illinois Press.

Giddens, Anthony. 1987. *Social Theory and Modern Sociology.* Stanford, CA: Stanford University Press.

Giddens, Anthony. 1990. *The Consequences of Modernity.* Cambridge, England: Polity Press.

Gigliotti, Richard J., & Heather K. Huff. 1995. "Role related conflicts, strains and stresses of older-adult college students." *Sociological Focus* (28/3): 329–342.

Gilbert, Dennis, & Joseph A. Kahl. 1993. *The American Class Structure: A New Synthesis,* 4th ed. Belmont, CA: Wadsworth.

Gilbert, Melissa R. 1998. "Race, space and power: The survival strategies of working poor women." *Annals of the Association of American Geographers* 88(4): 595–621.

Gill, Stephen, & David Law. 1988. *Global Political Economy: Perspectives, Problems & Policies.* Baltimore: Johns Hopkins University Press.

Gille, Zsuzsa. 2001. "Critical ethnography in the time of globalization: Toward a new concept of site." *Cultural Studies/Critical Methodologies* 1(3) (August 1): 319–34.

Gilligan, Carol A. 1982. *In a Different Voice.* Cambridge, MA: Harvard University.

Gills, Barry K. 2000. "The crisis of postwar East Asian capitalism: American power, democracy and the vicissitudes of globalization." *Review of International Studies* 26(3): 381–403.

Gilman, Theodore J. 2001. *No Miracles Here: Fighting Urban Decline in Japan and the United States.* Albany, NY: State University of Albany.

Gitlin, Todd. 1980. *The Whole World Is Watching.* Berkeley, CA: University of California Press.

Gitlin, Todd. 1983. *Inside Prime Time.* New York: Basic.

Gittings, John. 2000. "China to outlaw 'second wives.'" *The Guardian*, October 27. Available: http://www.guardian.co.uk.

Giuliano, Traci A., Kathryn E. Popp, & Jennifer L. Knight. 2000. "Football versus Barbies: Childhood play activities as predictors of sport participation by women." *Sex Roles* 42(3–4): 159–81.

Glaser, Nathan. 1976. *Affirmative Discrimination.* New York: Basic.

Glasgow, D. 1981. *The Black Underclass.* New York: Vintage.

Glassman, James K. 2001. "Class acts: How charter schools are revamping public education in Arizona—and beyond." In Williamson M. Evers, Lance T. Izumi, & Pamela A. Riley (eds.), *School Reform: The Critical Issues.* Stanford, CA: Hoover Institution: 362–73.

Glazer, Nathan. 1997. *We Are All Multiculturalists Now.* Cambridge, MA: Harvard.

Glazer, Sarah. 2000. "Postmodern nursing." *Public Interest* 140(Summer): 3–16.

Glazier, Jack. 2000. "Judaism." In Raymond Scupin (ed.), *Religion and Culture: An Anthropological Focus.* Upper Saddle River, NJ: Prentice Hall: 322–40.

Gleeson, Brendan. 2001. "Disability and the open city." *Urban Studies* 38(2): 251–65.

Glenn, Evelyn N., & Roslyn L. Feldberg. 1995. "Clerical work: The female occupation." In Jo Freeman (ed.), *Women: A Feminist Perspective.* Mountain View, CA: Mayfield: 262–86.

Glenn, Evelyn Nakano, & Stacey G. H. Yap. 2000. "Chinese-American families." In Timothy P. Fong & Larry H. Shingawa (eds.), *Asian Americans: Experiences and Perspectives.* Upper Saddle River, NJ: Prentice Hall: 277–92.

Glenn, Norval D. 1997. "A reconsideration of the effect of no-fault divorce on divorce rates." *Journal of Marriage and the Family* 59(4): 1023–30.

Glick, J. E., F. D. Bean, & V. W. Van Hook. 1997. "Immigration and changing patterns of extended family household structure in the United States." *Journal of Marriage and the Family* 59: 177–91.

Global Issues. 2002. "Non-governmental organizations on development issues." Available: http://www.globalissues.org/TradeRelated/Poverty/NGOs.

Glock, Charles Y., & Rodney Stark. 1965. *Religion and Society in Tension.* Chicago: Rand McNally.

Glouchevitch, Philip. 1992. *Juggernaut: The German Way of Business.* New York: Simon & Schuster.

Glover, Rebecca J. 1994. "Using moral and epistemological reasoning as predictors of prejudice." *Journal of Social Psychology* 134: 633–640.

Glover, Rebecca. 2000. "Developmental tasks of adulthood: Implications for counseling community college students." *Community College Journal of Research and Practice* 24(6): 505–514.

Gmelch, George. 1978. "Baseball magic." *Human Nature* (1/8): 35.

Gnida, John J. 1995. "Teaching 'nature versus nurture': The case of African-American athletic success." *Teaching Sociology* (23/4): 389–95.

Goad, Tom W. 2002. *Information Literacy and Workplace Performance.* Westport, CT: Quorum.

Goering, Paula, Donald Wasylenki, & Janet Durbin. 2000. "Canada's mental health system." *International Journal of Law & Psychiatry* 23(3–4): 345–59.

Goetz, Edward G. 2000. "The politics of poverty deconcentration and housing demolition." *Journal of Urban Affairs* 22(2): 157–73.

Goffman, Erving. 1959a. *The Presentation of Self in Everyday Life.* Garden City, NY: Doubleday (Anchor).

Goffman, Erving. 1959b. "The moral career of the mental patient." *Psychiatry* (22): 125–31.

Goffman, Erving. 1961a. *Asylums: Essays on the Social Situation of Mental Patients and Other Inmates.* Garden City, NY: Anchor Books.

Goffman, Erving. 1961b. *Encounters.* Indianapolis: Bobbs-Merrill.

Goffman, Erving. 1963a. *Behavior in Public Places.* New York: Free Press.

Goffman, Erving. 1963b. *Stigma: Notes on the Management of Spoiled Identity.* Upper Saddle River, NJ: Prentice Hall.

Goffman, Erving. 1967. *Interaction Ritual.* Garden City, NY: Doubleday.

Goffman, Erving. 1974. *Frame Analysis.* New York: Harper & Row.

Goldberg, Carey. 1998. "Little Drop in College Binge Drinking." *New York Times* (August 11): A14.

Golden, S. 1992. *The Women Outside.* Berkeley: University of California Press.

Goldman, H. H., R. G. Frank & T. G. McGuire. 1994. "Mental Health Care," in E. Ginzberg, ed., *Critical Issues In US Health Care Reform.* Boulder, CO: Westview.

Goldman, P., & D. R. Van Houten. 1977. "Managerial strategies and the worker: A marxist analysis of bureaucracy." *Sociological Quarterly* 18: 108–25.

Goldsborough, Reid. 2000. "Bridging the digital divide." *Tech Directions* 59(10): 13.

Goldstein, Joshua R. 1999. "Kinship networks that cross racial lines: The exception or the rule?" *Demography* 36(3): 399–407.

Gonzalez, Norma. 1995. "Processual approaches to multicultural education." *Journal of Applied Behavioral Science* 31(2): 233–44.

Goodall, Jane. 1986. *The Chimpanzees of Gombe: Patterns of Behavior.* Cambridge, MA: Harvard University.

Goodburn, Elizabeth, & Oona Campbell. 2001. "Reducing maternal mortality in the developing world: Sector-wide approaches may be key." *British Medical Journal* 322(7291): 91720.

Goode, Erich. 1989. *Drugs in American Society.* NY: McGraw-Hill.

Goode, Erich. 1992. *Collective Behavior.* Fort Worth, TX: Harcourt Brace Jovanovich.

Goode, Erich. 1997. *Between Politics and Reason: The Drug Legalization Debate.* New York: St. Martin's Press.

Goode, Erich. 1997. *Deviant Behavior,* 5th ed. Upper Saddle River, NJ: Prentice Hall.

Goodgame, Dan. 1993. "Welfare for the well-off." *Time* 141 (February 22): 36–38.

Goodstein, Laurie. 1998. "Religious right, frustrated, trying new tactic on G.O.P." *The New York Times* (March 23): A1, A12.

Goodwin, Beverly J. 1996. "The impact of popular culture on images of African American women." In Joan C. Chrisler, Carla Golden, & Patricia D. Rozee (eds.), *Lectures on the Psychology of Women.* New York: McGraw-Hill.

Gould, Susan Dorr, & Glenn Klipp. 2002. "Managed care members talk about trust." *Social Science & Medicine* 54(6): 879–88.

Gordon, David. 1973. "Capitalism, class and crime in America." *Crime & Delinquency* 19: 163–86.

Gordon, Milton M. 1964. *Assimilation in American Life.* New York: Oxford University Press.

Gordon, Milton M. 1978. *Human Nature, Class and Ethnicity.* New York: Oxford University Press.

Gordon, Myron J. 2001. "Growth and security under welfare-corporate capitalism and market socialism." *Brazilian Journal of Political Economy/Revista de Economia Politica* 21(3): 65–80.

Gordon, R. 1998. "The limits of limits on divorce." *Yale Law Review* 107(5): 1435–65.

Gorey, K. M., & D. R. Leslie. 1997. "The prevalence of child sexual abuse: Integrative review for potential response and measurement biases." *Child Abuse and Neglect* 21: 391–98.

Gorin, Stephen B. 2001. "Medicare and prescription drugs: Prospects for reform." *Health & Social Work* 26(2): 115–18.

Gortmaker, S. L., A. Must, J. M. Perrin, A. M. Sobel, & W. H. Dietz. 1993. "Social and economic consequences of overweight in adolescence and young adulthood," *New England Journal of Medicine* 329: 1008–1012.

Gottdiener, Mark. 1999. *The New Urban Sociology.* New York: McGraw-Hill.

Gottfredson, Don M. 1995. "Prison Is Not Enough," *Corrections Today* 57 (August): 16–20.

Gottfredson, Michael, & Don Gottfredson. 1988. *Decision Making in Criminal Justice: Toward the Rational Exercise of Discretion,* 2nd. ed. New York: Plenum.

Gottfredson, Michael, & Travis Hirschi. 1990. *A General Theory of Crime.* Stanford, CA: Stanford University Press.

Gottschalk, Peter. 1997. "Inequality, income growth, and mobility: The basic facts." *Journal of Economic Perspectives* 11 (Spring): 21–40.

Gourevitch, Phillip. 1995. "After the genocide." *New Yorker* (Dec 18): 78–94.

Gourevitch, Phillip. 1998. *We Wish to Inform You that Tomorrow We Will Be Killed with Our Families: Stories from Rwanda.* New York: Farrar, Straus & Giroux.

Gove, Walter R. & Jeanette Tudor. 1973. "Adult sex roles and mental illness," *American Journal of Sociology* 78: 812–835.

Gove, Walter R., Carolyn Briggs Style, & Michael Highes. 1990. "The effect of marriage on the well-being of adults." *Journal of Family Issues* 11: 4–35.

Gow, Kathryn N. 2000. "Banking on women: Achieving healthy economies through microfinance." *WE International* 48/49: 11–13.

Gowdy, John M. 2002. "Biophysical limits to the human expropriation of nature." In Michael. N. Dobkowski & Isidor Wallimann (eds.), *On the Edge of Scarcity: Environment, Resources, Population, Sustainability, and Conflict.* Syracuse, NY: Syracuse University: 34–46.

Grady, Denise. 1998. "To aid doctors, A.M.A. Journal devotes entire issue to alternative medicine." *New York Times* November 11: A23.

Graff, Harvey J. 1995. *Conflicting Paths: Growing Up in America.* Cambridge, MA: Harvard University.

Graff, Harvey J. 1995. *The Labyrinths of Literacy: Reflections on Literacy Past and Present.* Pittsburgh, PA: University of Pittsburgh.

Graff, Harvey J., Stan Jones, & Brian V. Street. 1997. "Working papers on literacy No. 1:1–28." Centre for Literacy, Montreal, Canada.

Graham, Patricia Albjerg. 1995. "Assimilation, adjustment, and access: An antiquarian view of American education." In Diane Ravitch & Maris A. Vinovskis (eds.), *Learning from the Past: What History Teaches Us about School Reform.* Baltimore, MD: Johns Hopkins University: 4–24.

Graham, Patricia E., & Linda M. Manning. 2000. "Women's poverty and entrepreneurship: Replicating microloan programs in the developed world." *Journal of Economics* 26(2): 23–33.

Grajeda, Tony. 2002. "The 'feminization' of rock." In Roger Beebe, Denise Fulbrook, & Ben Saunders (eds.), *Rock over the Edge: Transformations in Popular Music Culture.* Durham, NC: Duke University: 233–54.

Grameen Dialogue. 1999. Dhaka. No. 37 (January).

Gramsci, A. 1971. *Selections From Prison Notebooks.* London: Routledge & Kegan Paul.

Gramsci, Antonio. 1959. *The Modern Prince and Other Writings.* New York: International Publishers.

Granovetter, Mark. 1973. "The strength of weak ties." *American Journal of Sociology* 78: 1360–1380.

Granovetter, Mark. 1995. *Getting a Job: A Study of Contacts and Careers*, 2nd ed. Chicago: University of Chicago Press.

Grant, Linda, & Reuben A. Buford May. 1999. "The promises and perils of ethnography in the new millennium: Lessons from teaching." *Journal of Contemporary Ethnography* 28(5): 549–60.

Grant, Linda. 1993. *Sexing the Millennium: A Political History of the Sexual Revolution*. London: Harper Collins.

Grasmick, Harold, Charles Tittle, Robert Bursik, & Bruce Arneklev. 1993. "Testing the core empirical indications of Gottfredson and Hirschi's general theory of crime." *Journal of Research in Crime and Delinquency* (30): 5–29.

Gratz, Roberta Brandes, & Norman Mintz. 1998. *Cities Back from the Edge: New Life for Downtown*. New York: John Wiley.

Graves, Sherryl Browne. 1999. "Television and prejudice reduction." *Journal of Social Issues* 55(4): 707–727.

Gray, Alastair. 1993. *World Health and Disease*. Buckingham, UK: Open University Press.

Gray, Denis D. 1996. "Crying 'timber' in the rainforest." *Japan Times* (August 25): 9, 11.

Gray, John. 1986. *Liberalism: Concepts in Social Thought*. Minneapolis: University of Minnesota Press.

Gray, Wayne, & John Scholz. 1993. "Does regulatory enforcement work?" *Law & Society Review* 27: 1771–191.

Grayson, James Huntley. 2002. "Korean religion." In John Bowker (ed.), *Cambridge Illustrated History of Religions*. Cambridge, UK: Cambridge University: 144–49.

Greeley, Andrew M. 1997. "Coleman revisited: Religious structures as a source of social capital." *American Behavioral Scientist* 40: 587–94.

Green, Paul. 2001. "Demographic shifts and educational challenges in the 21st century." *School Business Affairs* 67(4): 25–31,51.

Greenberg, Anna. 2001. "What young voters want: Help with college and a reason to believe in government." *The Nation* 274(5) (February 11): 14–15.

Greenberg, Anna. 2001. "Will choice be aborted?" *American Prospect* (Fall): A25–A28.

Greenberg, David F., & Ronald C. Kessler. 1982. "The effects of arrests on crime: A multivariate panel analysis." *Social Forces* 60: 771–90.

Greenberg, David, (ed.). 1981. *Crime and Capitalism*. Palo Alto, CA: Mayfield.

Greenberg, Edward S., & Benjamin I. Page. 1996. *The Struggle for Democracy*, 2nd ed. New York: Addison-Wesley.

Greenberg, Elizabeth, Reynaldo F. Marcias, David Rhodes, & Tsze Chan. 2001. *English Literacy and Language Minorities in the United States*. (August). U.S. Department of Education. Washington, DC: National Center for Education Statistics.

Greenberg, Jack. 1994. *Crusaders in the Courts*. New York: Basic.

Greenberg, Sarah. 2001. "Spousal caregiving: In sickness and in health." *Journal of Gerontological SocialWork* 35(4): 69–82.

Greene, Jamie Candelaria. 2001. "Misperspectives on literacy: A critique of an Anglocentric bias in histories of American history." In Ellen Cushman, Eugene R. Kintgen, Barry M. Kroll, & Mike Rose (eds.), *Literacy: A Critical Sourcebook*. Boston: Bedford/St. Martin's: 234–43.

Greene, Richard P. 1997. "Chicago's new immigrants, indigenous poor and edge cities." *Annals of the American Academy of Political and Social Science* 551 (May): 178–90.

Greenfield, Liah. 1992. *Nationalism: Five Roads to Modernity*. Cambridge, MA: Harvard University Press.

Greengross, Sally. 2002. "Aging well." In Harold Cox (ed.), *Aging* (Annual Editions). Guilford, CT: McGraw-Hill/Dushkin: 42–43.

Greenhouse, Linda. 1995. "Justices, 5 to 4, cast doubts on U.S. programs that give preferences based on race." *The New York Times* (June 13): A1+.

Greenhouse, Steven. 1998. "Equal Work, Less-Equal Perks," *New York Times* (March 30): C-1.

Greenspan, Allison. 1994. "After the demographic transition: Policy responses to low fertility in four Asian countries." *Asia-Pacific Population and Policy*. East-West Center Program on Population 30 (September).

Greenstein, R. 1996. *Raising Families with a Full-Time Worker Out of Poverty*. Washington: Center on Budget and Policy Priorities.

Greenstone, David. 1968. *Labor in American Politics*. Chicago: University of Chicago Press.

Greider, William. 1997. *One World Ready or Not: The Manic Logic of Global Capitalism*. New York: Simon & Schuster.

Greif, Geoffrey L. 1995. "Single fathers with custody following separation and divorce." *Marriage and Family Review* 20(1–2): 213–32.

Grembowski, David E., Karen S. Cook, Donald L. Patrick, & Amy Elizabeth Roussel. 2002. "Managed care and the U.S. health care system: A social exchange perspective." *Social Science & Medicine* 54(8): 1167–80.

Grenier, Guillermo. 1988. *Inhuman Relations: Quality Circles and Anti-Unionism In American Industry*. Philadelphia: Temple University Press.

Greskovits, Bela, & Dorothee Bohle, 2001. "Development paths on Europe's periphery: Hungary's and Poland's return to Europe compared." *Polish Sociological Review* 1(133): 3–27.

Grieco, Elizabeth M., & Rachel C. Cassidy. 2001. "Overview of race and Hispanic origin." *Census 2000 Brief*, March. U.S. Census Bureau.

Griffin, Keith. 2000. "Culture and economic growth: The state and globalization." In Jan Nederveen Pieterse (ed.), *Global Futures: Shaping Globalization*. London: Zed: 203–223.

Griffin, Pat. 1998. *Strong Women, Deep Closets: Lesbians and Homophobia in Sport*. Champaign, IL: Human Kinetics.

Griffin, S. 1995. *The Eros of Everyday Life*. New York: Doubleday.

Griffiths, M. 1998. "Violent video games and aggression: A review of the literature." *Aggression and Violent Behavior* 4: 203–212.

Grills, Scott. 1998. "An invitation to the field: Fieldwork and pragmatists' lessons." In Scott Grills (ed.), *Doing Ethnographic Research: Fieldwork Settings*. Thousand Oaks, CA: Sage: 3–18.

Grimes, Michael D. 1991. *Class in 20th Century American Sociology*. New York: Praeger.

Grissner, David, & Ann Flannigan. 2002. *Tracking the Improvement in State Achievement Using NAEP Data*. Santa Monica, CA: RAND.

Griswold, Wendy. 1994. *Cultures and Societies in a Changing World*. Thousand Oaks, CA: Pine Forge.

Grogan, Sarah, & Helen Richards. 2002. "Body image: Focus groups with boys and men." *Men & Masculinities* 4(3): 219–32.

Grubb, W. Norton. 1995. "The old problem of 'new students': Purpose, content, and pedagogy." In Erwin Flaxman & Harry Passow (eds.), "Changing Populations Changing Schools." *Ninety-Fourth Yearbook of the National Society for the Study of Education, Part II*. Chicago: NSSE: 4–29.

Grundy, Emily. 2001. "Living arrangements and the health of older persons in developed countries." In *Living Arrangements of Older Persons: Critical Issues and Policy Responses*. New York: United Nations.

Grusky, David, & Robert M. Hauser. 1984. "Comparative social mobility revisited: Models of convergence and divergence in 16 countries." *American Sociological Review* 49: 19–38.

Gugler, Josef. 1996a. "Regional trajectories in the urban transformation: Convergences and divergences." In Josef Gugler (ed.), *The Urban Transformation of the Developing World*. Oxford, UK: Oxford University: 1–14.

Gugler, Josef. 1996b. "Urbanization in Africa south of the Sahara: New identities in conflict." In Josef Gugler (ed.), *The Urban Transformation of the Developing World*. Oxford, UK: Oxford University: 211–51.

Guilbert, Douglas E., Nicholas A. Vacc, & Kay Pasley. 2000. "The relationship of gender role beliefs, negativity, distancing, and marital instability." *Journal of Counseling and Therapy for Couples and Families*. 8(2): 124–32.

Guinn, Bobby, & Vern Vincent. 2002. "Determinants of coping responses among Mexican American adolescents." *Journal of School Health* 72(4): 152–6.

Gullo, Karen. 2001. "Prison Population Increases But at Slower Rate." *Evansville Courier & Press* (March 26): A5.

Gumbiner, Jann. 1998. "Professors as models and mentors: Does gender matter?" *Psychological Reports* 82(1): 94.

Gump, Linda S., Samuel Roll, & Richard C. Baker. 2000. "The moral justification scale: Reliability and validity of a new measure of care and justice orientations." *Adolescence* 35(137): 67–76.

Gunderson, Morley, & Allen Ponak. 2000. *Union-Management Relations in Canada*, 4th ed. Reading, MA: Addison-Wesley.

Gunther, A. C. 1998. "The pervasive press inference: Effects of mass media on perceived public opinion." *Communication Research* 25(5): 486–504.

Guo, Shuqing. 2001. "The impact of globalization on China's economy." In Shahid Yusuf, Simon Evenett, & Weiping Wu (eds.), *Facets of Globalization: International and Local Dimensions of Development*. Washington, DC: World Bank: 93–104.

Gupta, Avijit, & Mukul G. Asher. 1998. *Environment and the Developing World: Principles, Policies and Management*. Chinchester, UK: John Wiley.

Gurley, John G. 1984. "Marx's contributions and their relevance today." *American Economic Review* 74: 110–15.

Gurney, Joan M., & Kathleen T. Tierney. 1982. "Relative deprivation and social movements." *Sociological Quarterly* 23: 33–47.

Gurr, Ted R. 1970. *Why Men Rebel*. Princeton, NJ: Princeton University Press.

Guterbock, Thomas M., & John C. Fries. 1997. *Maintaining America's Social Fabric*. Washington, DC: AARP.

Gutman, Gloria M., Annette Stark, Alan Donald, & B. Lynn Beattie. 2001. "Contributions of self-reported health ratings to predicting frailty, institutionalization, and death over a 5-year period." *International Psychogeriatrics* 13(Suppl 1): 223–31.

Gutmann, Stephanie. 2002. "The abyss yawns." *New York Times Magazine* (January 14): 32.

Gutner, Toddi. 2002. "A balancing act for Gen X women." *Business Week* (January 21): 83.

Guttmann, Allen. 1978. *From Ritual to Record*. New York: Columbia University Press.

Haas, J. E., & T. E. Drabek. 1973. *Complex Organizations: A Sociological Perspective*. New York: Macmillan.

Haas, Jack, & William Shaffir. 1993. "The cloak of competence." In James M. Henslin (ed.), *Down to Earth Sociology: Introductory Readings*. New York: The Free Press.

Habermas, Jurgen. 1976. *Legitimation Crisis*. London: Heinemann.

Habermas, Jurgen. 1990. *Moral Consciousness and Communicative Action*. Cambridge, MA: MIT Press.

Habitat. 2001. *The State of the World's Cities*. Nairobi, Kenya: United Nations Center for Human Settlements.

Hacker, Andrew. 1992. *Two Nations: Black and White, Separate, Hostile, Unequal*. New York: Ballantine.

Hacker, Andrew. 1997. *Money*. New York: Scribner.

Hacker, Frederick J. 1978. *Criminals, Crusaders and Crazies: Terror and Terrorism in Our Time*. Santa Monica, CA: Rand.

Hacker, Holly K. 2000. "Gaps between race and achievement pose thorny problems for educators." *St. Louis Post-Dispatch* (June 4): B1,B5.

Hackstaff, Karla B. 1999. *Marriage in a Culture of Divorce*. Philadelphia: Temple University.

Hackworth, David. 1992. "This was no riot, it was a revolt." *Newsweek* (119/21): 22.

Haddad, Lawrence, Marie T. Ruel, & James L. Garrett. 1999. "Are urban poverty and undernutrition growing? Some newly assembled evidence." *World Development* 27(11): 1891–904.

Haddad, Yvonne, & John L. Esposito (eds.). 1998. *Muslims on the Americanization Path?* Atlanta: Scholars Press.

Hadden, Jeffrey K. 1993. "The rise and fall of American televangelism." *Annals of the American Academy of Political and Social Science* 527(May): 113–14.

Haeberle, Steven H. 1999. "Gay and lesbian rights: Emerging trends in public opinion and voting behavior." In Ellen D. B. Riggle & Barry L. Tadlock (eds.), *Gays and Lesbians in the Democratic Process.* New York: Columbia University: 146–69.

Hafner, Katie. 1994. "Making Sense of the Internet." *Newsweek* (October 24): 46–48.

Hagan, Jacqueline M. 1998. "Social networks, gender, and immigrant incorporation." *American Sociological Review* 63(1): 55–67.

Hagan, John, A. R. Gillis, & John Simpson. 1985. "The class structure of gender and delinquency: Toward a power-control theory of common delinquent behavior." *American Journal of Sociology* 90 (May): 1151–178.

Hagan, John. 1994. *Crime and Disrepute.* Thousand Oaks, CA: Sage.

Hage, Jerald, & Charles H. Powers. 1992. *Post-Industrial Lives: Roles and Relationships in the 21st Century.* Newbury Park, CA: Sage.

Hagedorn, Jessica. 2000, "Asia women: No joy, no luck." In Timothy P. Fong & Larry H. Shinagawa (eds.), *Asian Americans: Experiences and Perspectives.* Upper Saddle River, NJ: Prentice Hall: 264–69.

Hague, Gill, & Ellen Malos. 1999. "Homeless children and domestic violence." In Stuart Cumella (ed.), *Homeless Children: Problems and Needs.* London: Jessica Kingsley.

Hale, Janice E. 2001. *Learning while Black: Creating Educational Excellence for African American Children.* Baltimore, MD: Johns Hopkins University.

Haley, Usha C. V. 2001. *Multinational Corporations in Political Environments: Ethics, Values, and Strategies.* River Edge, NJ: World Scientific.

Hall, Carla S. 2001. "Competing interests among children and the elderly: Testing the generational equity perspective cross-nationally." *Dissertation Abstracts International, A: The Humanities and Social Sciences* 62(4) (October) 1586-A.

Hall, Christine C., & Matthew J. Crum. 1994. "Women and 'bodyisms' in television beer commercials." *Sex Roles* 31(5–6): 329–37.

Hall, Edward T. 1959. *The Silent Language.* Greenwich, CT: Fawcett.

Hall, Edward T. 1966. *The Hidden Dimension.* Garden City, NY: Doubleday.

Hall, John R., with Philip D. Schuyler & Sylvaine Trinh. 2000. *Apocalypse Observed: Religious Movements and Violence in North America, Europe and Japan.* London: Routledge.

Hall, Judith A., & Gregory B. Friedman. 1999. "Status, gender and nonverbal behavior: A study of structured interactions between employees of a company." *Personality and Social Psychology Bulletin* 25(9): 1082–91.

Hall, Richard H. 1996. *Organizations: Structures, Processes and Outcomes,* 6th ed. Upper Saddle River, NJ: Prentice Hall.

Hall, Stephen S. 1999. "The troubled lives of boys: The bully in the mirror." *New York Times Magazine* (August 22): 30–35, 58.

Hallinan, Christopher. 1991. "Aborigines and positional segregation in the Australian Rugby League." *International Review for the Sociology of Sport* 26: 69–81.

Halloran, Fumiko Mori. 1994. "Flunking the grade: Americans seek educational diversity and get ignorance." *Japan Update* (January): 10–11.

Halpern, Diane F. 2000. *Sex Differences in Cognitive Ability.* Mahwah, NJ: Lawrence Erlbaum.

Halpern, Sydney A. 1992. "Dynamics of professional control, internal coalitions and crossprofessional boundaries." *American Journal of Sociology* 97: 994–1021.

Halstead, Mark J. 2001. "Living in different worlds: Gender differences in the developing sexual values and attitudes of primary school children." *Sex Education* 1(1): 59–76.

Hamada, T. 1992. "Under the silk banner." In T. S. Lebra, (ed.), *Japanese Social Organization.* Honolulu: University of Honolulu Press.

Hamilton, Malcolm. 2001. *The Sociology of Religion: Theoretical and Comparative Perspectives.* London: Routledge.

Hamilton, V. Lee, Clifford L. Broman, William S. Hoffman, & Deborah S. Renner. 1990. "Hard times & vulnerable people." *Journal of Health and Social Behavior* 31: 123–40.

Hamm, Jill V., & Hardin L. K. 2001. "African American and white adolescents' strategies for managing cultural diversity in predominantly white high schools." *Journal of Youth and Adolescence* 30(3): 281–303.

Hammer, Joshua. 1994. "Death Watch." *Newsweek* (August 8): 14–17.

Hammer, Joshua. 1998. "Shunned at Berkeley." *Newsweek* (October): 70–71.

Hanania, Ray. 2002. "Humor is what we need at this time of tragedy." Available: http://www.hanania.com/humor/humor.

Handel, Warren H. 1993. *Contemporary Sociological Theory.* Englewood Cliffs, NJ: Prentice Hall.

Handler, Lisa Frances. 2001. "Show me your company and I'll show you who you are: Women's friendships, gender construction and the limits of resistance." *Dissertation Abstracts International, A: The Humanities and Social Sciences* 62(1) (July): 337-A.

Handlin, Oscar. 1992. "The newcomers." In Paula Rotherberg, (ed.), *Race, Class & Gender in the United States.* New York: St. Martin's.

Handwerker, W. Penn. 2001. *Quick Ethnography.* Walnut Creek, CA: AltaMira.

Handy, Robert T. 1991. *Undermined Establishment: Church-State Relations in America, 1880–1920.* Princeton: Princeton University Press.

Haney, Lynne. 1996. "Homeboys, babies, men in suits." *American Sociological Review* 61: 759–778.

Hannah, Annette, & Tamar Murachver. 1999. "Gender and conversational style as predictors of conversational behavior." *Journal of Language and Social Psychology* 18(2): 153–74.

Hanson, F. Allan. 2000. "How tests create what they are intended to measure." In

Ann Filer (ed.), *Assessment: Social Practice and Social Product.* London: RoutledgeFalmer: 67–81.

Harding, Susan Friend. 2001. *The Book of Jerry Falwell: Fundamentalist Language and Politics.* Princeton University.

Hardoy, Jorge E., Diana Mitlin, & David Satterthwaite. 2001. *Environmental Problems in an Urbanizing World.* London: Earthscan.

Hare, A. P., H. H. Blumberg, M. F. Davis, & V. Kent. 1994. *Small Group Research: A Handbook.* Norwood, NJ: Ablex.

Hare-Mustin, Rachel T. 1992. "China's marriage law: A model for family responsibilities and relationships." *Family Process* 21: 477–81.

Hargreaves, J. 1994. *Sporting Females: Critical Issues in the History and Sociology of Women's Sports.* London: Routledge.

Hargrove, Thomas. 2001. "Welfare reform plan reveals small group of unemployable." *Evansville Courier & Press* (May 22): A7.

Harjo, Suzan Shown. 1993. "The American Indian experience." In Harriette Pipes McAdoo (ed.), *Family Ethnicity: Strength in Diversity.* Newbury Park, CA: Sage.

Harkey, J. D., L. Miles & W. A. Rushing. 1976. "The relationship between social class and functional status," *Journal of Health and Social Beha*Harlow, Harry, & Margaret Kuenne Harlow. 1970. "The young monkeys." In P. Kramer (ed.), *Readings in Developmental Psychology Today.* Del Mar, CA: CRM Books.

Harper, C. L. 1993. *Exploring Social Change,* 2nd ed. Upper Saddle River, NJ: Prentice Hall.

Harrington, Michael. 1977. *The Vast Majority: A Journey to the World's Poor.* New York: Simon & Schuster.

Harris, Chauncy D., & Edward L. Ullman. 1945. "The nature of cities." *Annals of the American Academy of Political and Social Science* 242: 7–17.

Harris, Helen. 1995. "Rethinking Polynesian heterosexual relationships." In William Jankowiak (ed.), *Romantic Passion.* New York: Columbia University Press: 96–127.

Harris, Ian, Joes B. Torres, & Dale Allender. 1994. "The responses of African American men to dominant norms of masculinity within the United States." *Sex Roles* 31(11–12): 703–19.

Harris, Kathleen M. 1993. "Work and welfare among single mothers in poverty." *American Journal of Sociology* 99/2: 317–352.

Harris, Marvin. 1977. *Cannibals & Kings: The Origins of Cultures.* New York: Random House.

Harris, Marvin. 1979. *Cultural Materialism: The Struggle for a Science of Culture.* New York: Random House.

Harris, Marvin. 1981. *America Now: The Anthropology of a Changing Culture.* New York: Simon & Schuster.

Harris, Marvin. 1994. "Cultural materialism is alive and well and won't go away until something better comes along." In Robert Borofsky, (ed.), *Assessing Cultural Anthropology.* New York: McGraw-Hill.

Harris, Nigel. 1987. *The End of the Third World: Newly Industrializing Countries and the Decline of an Ideology.* Harmondsworth, England: Penguin.

Harrison, B. 1994. *Lean and Mean: The Changing Landscape of Corporate Power in the Age of Flexibility.* New York: Basic Books.

Harrison, Kristen. 2001. "Ourselves, our bodies: Thin-ideal media, self-discrepancies, and eating disorder symptomatology in adolescents." *Journal of Social and Clinical Psychology* 20(3) 289–323.

Harrison, Lawrence E. 1992. *Who Prospers? How Cultural Values Shape Economic and Political Success.* New York: Basic.

Harrison, Lawrence E., & Samuel P. Huntington (eds.). 2000. *Culture Matters: How Values Shape Human Progress.* New York: Basic Books.

Harrison, Paul. 1993. *Inside the Third World: The Anatomy of Poverty,* 3rd ed. London: Penguin.

Hart, Bethne, Peter Sainsbury, & Stephanie Short. 1998. "Whose dying? A sociological critique of the "good death." *Mortality* 3(1): 65–77.

Hart, Elizabeth et al. 1994. "Developmental change in attention-deficit hyperactivity disorder in boys." *Journal of Consulting & Clinical Psychology* 62: 472–91.

Hart, Paul. 1991. "Groupthink, risk-taking & recklessness." *Politics & the Individual* (1/1): 67–90.

Harter, Lynn M., Ronald J. Stephens, & Phyllis M. Rapp. 2000. "President Clinton's apology for the Tuskegee syphilis experiment: A narrative of remembrance, redefinition, and reconciliation." *Howard Journal of Communications* 11(1): 19–34.

Hartley, Eugene. 1946. *Problems in Prejudice.* New York: King's Crown Press.

Hartley, Heather. 2002. "The system of alignments challenging physician professional dominance: An elaborated theory of countervailing powers." *Sociology of Health and Illness* 24(2): 178–207.

Harvey, David L. 1993. *Potter Addition: Poverty, Family, and Kinship in a Heartland Community.* New York: Aldine de Gruyter.

Harvey, David. 2000. *Spaces of Hope.* Berkeley, CA: University of California.

Harvey, Elizabeth. 1999. "Short-term and long-term effects of early parental employment on children of the National Longitudinal Survey of Youth." *Developmental Psychology* 35(2): 445–59.

Hasan, Arif. 1999. *Understanding Karachi.* Karachi, Pakistan: City Press.

Haseler, Stephen. 2000. *The Super-rich: The Unjust New World of Global Capitalism.* New York: St. Martin's.

Hasell, Mary Joyce, & John Scanzoni. 2000. "Cohousing in HUD housing: Problems and prospects." *Journal of Architectural and Planning Research* 17(2): 133–45.

Hassan, M. Kabir. 2002. "The microfinance revolution and the Grameen Bank experience in Bangladesh." *Financial Markets, Institutions, and Instruments* 11(3): 205–65.

Hathaway, Dale A. 1993. *Can Workers Have a Voice? The Politics of Deindustrialization in Pittsburgh.* University Park, PA: Penn State University Press.

Haub, Carl, & Diana Cornelius. 2001. *The 2001 World Population Data Sheet.* Washington, DC: Population Reference Bureau.

Hauerwas, Stanley. 2002. "On being a Christian and an American." In Richard Madsen, William M. Sullivan, Ann Swidler, & Steven M. Tipton (eds.), *Meaning and Modernity: Religion, Polity, and Self*. Berkeley CA: University of California: 224–35.

Haviland, William A. 1999. *Cultural Anthropology*, 9th ed. Orlando, FL: Haviland.

Hawkins, Billy. 2000. "Reading a Promise Keepers' event: The intersection of race and religion." In Dane S. Claussen (ed.), *The Promise Keepers: Essays on Masculinity and Christianity*. Jefferson, NC: McFarland: 182–93.

Hawkins, K., & J. M. Thomas, (eds.). 1984. *Enforcing Regulation*. Boston: Kluwer-Nijhoff.

Hawley, Amos. 1950. *Human Ecology: A Theory of Community Structure*. New York: Ronald Press.

Hawn, Carleen. 2001. "New hope for Generation X: Career paths after September 11." *Forbes* 168 (November 26): 152.

Hayes, Bernadette C., & Audrey Vandenheuvel. 1994. "Attitudes toward mandatory retirement: An international comparison." *International Journal of Aging and Human Development*. 39(3): 209–31.

Haynes, Gladys Verneal Oosting. 2001. "Playmate selections of preschool children." *Dissertation Abstracts International Section A: Humanities & Social Sciences* 62(3-A) (September): 907.

Haynes, Michael, & Rumy Husan. 2000. "National equality and the catch-up period: Some 'growth alone' scenarios." *Journal of Economic Issues* 34(3): 693–705.

Hays-Mitchell, M. 1999. "From survivor to entrepreneur: Gendered dimensions of microenterprise development in Peru." *Environment and Planning A* 31(2): 251–71.

Hayward, Mark D., & Melonie Heron. 1999. "Racial inequality in active life among adult Americans." *Demography* 36: 77–91.

Hazelett, S., C. Powell, & V. Androulakakis. 2002. "Patients' behavior at the time of injury: Effect on nurses' perception of pain level and subsequent treatment." *Pain Management Nursing* 3(1): 28–35.

Head, Keith, & John Ries. 2002. "Canadian business in East Asia." In A. E. Safarian, & Wendy Dobson (eds.), *East Asia in Transition: Economic and Security Challenges*. HSBC Bank Canada Papers. Toronto: University of Toronto.

Healey, Kevin. 2000. "The irresolvable tension: Agape and masculinity in the Promise Keepers movement." In Dane S. Claussen (ed.), *The Promise Keepers: Essays on Masculinity and Christianity*. Jefferson, NC: McFarland: 215–25.

Healey, Tim, & Karen Ross. 2002. "Growing old invisibly: Older viewers talk television." *Media Culture & Society* 24(1): 105–20.

Health Canada. 2001. *Canada Health Act Annual Report, 2000–2001*. Ottawa, CAN: Minster of Public Works and Government Services.

Hearn, Jeff, Deborah L. Sheppard, Petra T. Sherriff & Gibson Burrell, eds. 1989. *The Sexuality of Organizations*. Newbury Park, CA: Sage.

Heckathorn, Douglas D. 1990. "Collective sanctions and compliance norms: A formal theory of group-mediated social control." *American Sociological Review* 55: 366–84.

Heelas, Paul. 2000. "Expressive spirituality and humanistic expressivism." In S. Sutcliffe & M. Bowman (eds.), *Beyond the New Age*. Edinburgh, UK: Edinburgh University.

Hegarty, Peter. 2002. "'It's not a choice, it's the way we're built': Symbolic beliefs about sexual orientation in the U.S. and Britain." *Journal of Community & Applied Social Psychology* 23(3): 153–66.

Heidensohn, Frances. 1991. "Women and crime in Europe." In Frances Heidensohn and M. Farrell, (eds.), *Crime In Europe*. London: Routledge: 55–83.

Heilman, Samuel. 1999. "Separated but not divorced." *Society* 36(4): 8–14.

Heimer, Karen. 1997. "Socioeconomic status, subcultural definitions & violent delinquency." *Social Forces* 75: 799–833.

Heins, Marjorie. 1993. *Sex, Sin, and Blasphemy: A Guide to America's Censorship Wars*. New York: New Press.

Helgesen, Sally. 1990. *The Female Advantage: Women's Ways of Leadership*. New York: Doubleday.

Heller, Patrick. 1997. "Social capital as a product of class mobilization and state intervention: Industrial workers in Kerala, India." In Peter Evans (ed.), *State-Society Synergy: Government and Social Capital in Development*. Berkeley, CA: International and Area Studies.

Hellinger, Marlis, & Hadumod Bussman. 2002. "The linguistic presentation of women and men." In M. Hellinger & H. Bussman (eds.), *Gender Across Languages: The Linguistic Representations of Women and Men. Vol. 2: Impact Studies in Language and Society*. Amsterdam: John Benjamins.

Helweg, Robert, Lisbeth Anderson, & Gerald Tindal. 2001. "Influence of elementary student gender on teachers' perceptions of mathematics achievement." *Journal of Educational Research* 95(2): 93–102.

Henao, Julio, & Carlos Baanante. 2001. "Nutrient depletion in the agricultural soils of Africa." In Per Pinstrup-Andersen & Rajul Pandya-Lorch (eds.), *The Unfinished Agenda: Perspectives on Overcoming Hunger, Poverty, and Environmental Degradation*. Washington, DC: International Food Policy and Research Institute.

Henderson, Carter. 1998. "Today's affluent oldsters: Marketers see gold in gray." *The Futurist* (November): 19–23.

Henderson, Dianne L. 2001. "Prevalence of gender DIF in mixed format high school exist examination." Paper presented at the American Educational Research Association, April, Seattle.

Hendin, Herbert. 1995. *Suicide in America*. New York: W. W. Norton.

Hendin, Herbert. 2002. "The Dutch experience." *Issues in Law & Medicine* 17(3): 223–46.

Henley, B. 1977. *Body Politics*. Upper Saddle River, NJ: Prentice Hall.

Hennig, Margaret, & Anne Jardin. 1977. *The Managerial Woman*. Garden City, NY: Doubleday.

Henrard, Kristin. 2002. *Minority Protection in Post-Aparthied South Africa: Human Rights, Minority Rights, and Self-Dertermination*. Westport, CT: Praeger.

Henry, David B. 2000. "Peer groups, families, and school failure among urban children: Elements of risk and successful interventions." *Preventing School Failure* 44(3): 97–104.

Henson, Kevin. 1996. *The Temp*. Philadelphia: Temple University Press.

Herbert, Wray. 1999. "Taking it step by step." *U.S. News & World Report* 127(21): 67.

Herideen, Penelope E. 1998. *Policy, Pedagogy and Social Inequality: Community College Student Realities in Post-Industrial America*. Westport, CT: Bergin & Garvey.

Herman, Edward S., & Noam Chomsky. 1988. *Manufacturing Consent: The Political Economy of the Mass Media*. New York: Pantheon.

Herman, Judith Lewis. 2000. *Father–Daughter Incest*. Cambridge, MA: Harvard University.

Herman, Louis M., Elia Y. K. Herman, Marina Ivancic, Adam A. Pack, & David S. Matus. 2001. "The bottlenosed dolphin's (Tursiops truncatus) understanding of gestures as symbolic representations of its body parts." *Animal Learning and Behavior* 29(3): 250–64.

Hermans, Hubert J. M., & Piotr K. Oles. 1999. "Midlife crisis in men: Affective organization and personal meanings." *Human Relations* 52(11): 1403–26.

Herrnstein, Richard J., & Charles Murray. 1994. *The Bell Curve: Intelligence and Class Structure in American Life*. New York: Free Press.

Hesse-Biber, Sharlene Janice. 2000. *Working Women in America: Split Dreams*. New York: Oxford University.

Hetherington, E. Mavis, & John Kelly. 2002. *For Better or for Worse: Divorce Reconsidered*. New York: W.W. Norton.

Hewison, Kevin. 2001. "Thailand's capitalism: Development through boom or bust." In Garry Rodan, Kevin Hewison, & Richard Robison (eds.), *The Political Economy of South-East Asia: Conflicts, Crises and Change*. New York: Oxford University.

Heyck, Denis L. 1994. *Barrios and Borderlands: Cultures of Latinos and Latinas in the United States*. New York: Routledge.

Heydebrand, W. 1977. "Organizational contradictions in public bureaucracies: Toward a Marxian theory of organizations." *Sociological Quarterly* 18: 83–107.

HHS News. 2002. "HHS expands health plan options in Medicare+Choice: New demonstration program to feature PPO option in 23 states." August 27. U.S. Department of Health and Human Services. Available: http://www.hhs.gov/news/press/2002pres/20020827.

Hickey, Eric W. 2002. *Serial Murderers and Their Victims*, 3rd ed. Belmont, CA: Wadsworth.

Hickey, Mary C. 1999. "Not your grandfather's retirement." *Business Week* (July 19): 138.

Hicks, Alexander, & Joya Mishra. 1993. "Political resources and the growth of welfare in affluent democracies, 1960–1982." *American Journal of Sociology* 99: 668–710.

Hicks, Jennifer. 2002. "The economics of race and gender." (February 6.) Women's Village. Available: http://www.imdiversity.com/villages/women.

Hiedemann, B., O. Suhomlinova, & A. M. O'Rand. 1998. "Economic independence, economic status, and empty nest in midlife marital disruption." *Journal of Marriage and the Family* 60: 219–31.

Higginbotham, Elizabeth. 2000. "Women and employment: Obstacles and prospects." Women's History Month Presentation at Maryville University of St. Louis, March 16.

Higginbotham, Elizabeth. 2002. "Black professional women: Job ceilings and employment sectors." In Roberta Satow (ed.), *Gender and Social Life*. Needham Hts., MA: Allyn & Bacon.

Higgs, Robert J. 1995. *God in the Stadium*. Lexington: University Press of Kentucky.

Higley, John, & Richard Gunther (eds.). 1992. *Elites and Democratic Consolidation in Latin America and Southern Europe*. New York: Cambridge University Press.

Hill, Hal. 1994. "ASEAN Economic Development: An Analytical Survey—The State of the Field," *Journal of Asian Studies* 53: 832–866.

Hill, Richard Child, & June Woo Kim. 2000. "Global cities and development states: New York, Tokyo and Seoul." *Urban Studies* 37(12): 2167–95.

Hill, Shirley A. 1999. *African American Children: Socialization and Development in Families*. Thousand Oaks, CA: Sage.

Hill, Shirley A. 2001. Class, race and gender dimensions of child rearing in African American families." *Journal of Black Studies* 31(4): 494–508.

Hillman, Jennifer L. 2000. *Clinical Perspectives on Elderly Sexuality*. New York: Academic/Plenum.

Hills, S. L. 1987. *Corporate Violence: Injury and Death for Profit*. Totowa, NJ: Rowman & Littlefield.

Hilton, Jeanne M., Stephan Desrochers, & Esther L. Devall. 2001. "Comparison of role demands, relationships, and child functioning in single-mother, single-father, and intact families." *Journal of Divorce and Remarriage* 35(1–2): 29–56.

Hingorani, Monica. 2001. "The right to life: The story of Ramin Khaleghi." *Race & Class* 43(2): 128–31.

Hinrichsen, Don. 1999. "6,000,000,000 consumption machines." *International Wildlife* (September/October).

Hirschi, Travis, & Michael Gottfredson. 1983. "Age and the explanation of crime." *American Journal of Sociology*, 89: 552–84.

Hirschi, Travis. 1969. *Causes of Delinquency*. Berkeley: University of California Press.

Hirschman, Charles. 1983. "America's melting pot reconsidered." *Annual Review of Sociology* 9: 397–423.

Hirsh, Eric L. 1990. "Sacrifice for the cause." *American Sociological Review* 55: 243–54.

Hitchcock, Amanda. 2001. "Rising number of dowry deaths in India." July 4. World Socialist Web Site. Available: http://www.wsws.org/articles.

Hoare, Carol Hren. 2002. *Erikson on Development in Adulthood: New Insights from the Unpublished Papers*. Oxford, NY: Oxford University.

Hoberman, John. 1997. *Darwin's Athletes*. Boston: Houghton Mifflin.

Hochschild, Arlie Russell. 2002. "Coming of age, seeking an identity." *New York Times* (March 8): E1, E10.

Hochschild, Arlie. 1989. *The Second Shift: Working Parents and the Revolution at Home.* New York: Viking.

Hockstader, Lee, 1995. "For women, new Russia is far from liberating." *Washington Post* (September 1): A25, A31.

Hodgson, Dorothy L. 1999. "Once intrepid warriors: Modernity and the production of Masai masculinity." Ethnology 38(2): 121–51.

Hodson, Randy, & Teresa A. Sullivan. 2002. *The Social Organization of Work*, 3rd. ed. Belmont, CA: Wadsworth.

Hoebel, E. Adamson. 1978. *The Cheyennes.* Fort Worth, TX: Holt Rinehart Winston.

Hoecker-Drysdale, Susan. 1992. *Harriet Martineau: First Woman Sociologist.* New York: Berg.

Hoffer, Eric. 1951. *The True Believer.* New York: Harper & Row.

Hoffman, Bruce. 1999. *Inside Terrorism.* New York: Columbia University Press.

Hoffman, Earl Dirk, Jr., Barbara S. Klees, & Catherine Curtis. 2000. "Overview of the Medicare and Medicaid programs." *Health Care Financing Review* 22(1): 175–93.

Hoffman, Lois W., & Deborah D. Kloska. 1995. "Parents' gender-based attitudes toward marital roles and child rearing: Development and validation of new measures." *Sex Roles* 32: 273–95.

Hoffmann, Melissa L., & Kimberly K. Powlishta. 2001. "Gender segregation in childhood: A test of the interaction style theory." *Journal of Genetic Psychology* 162(3): 298–313.

Hoffnung, Michelle. 1995. "Motherhood: Contemporary conflict for women." In Jo Freeman (ed.) *Women: A Feminist Perspective.* Mountain View, CA: Mayfield: 162–181.

Hoh, Erling. 1999. "Waning Moon." *Far Eastern Economic Review* 162(17): 54–6.

Holgraves, Thomas M. 2002. *Language as Social Action: Social Psychology and Language Use.* Mahwah, NJ: Lawrence Erlbaum.

Holland, Dorothy, & Margaret A. Eisenhart. 1990. *Educated in Romance: Women, Achievement and College Culture.* Chicago: University of Chicago.

Holland, Jesse J. 2002. "FBI Figures Show Crime On the Rise," *Washington Post* (June 24): A-1.

Hollis, Daniel W. 1998. "Cultural origins of New Age cults." *Journal of Interdisciplinary Studies* 10: 31–47.

Holmes, Julia A. 1999. "The least restrictive environment: Is inclusion the best for all special needs students?" Paper presented at the Mid-South Educational Research Association, Point Clear, Alabama, November.

Holmes, Steven A. 1998. "Economy lifts incomes of single black women who head households." *New York Times* (August 18): A10.

Holmstrom, Nancy, & Richard Smith. 2000. "The necessity of gangster capitalism: Primitive accumulation in Russia and China." *Monthly Review* 51(9): 1–15.

Homans, George C. 1950. *The Human Group.* New York: Harcourt Brace.

Homans, George C. 1951. *The Western Electric Researches.* Indianapolis, IN: Bobbs-Merrill.

Home, Jim, & Maura McDermott. 2001. *The Next Green Revolution: Essential Steps to a Healthy, Sustainable Agriculture.* Binghamton, NY: Haworth.

Hondagneu-Sotelo, Pierrette. 1994. "Regulating the unregulated? Domestic workers' social networks." *Social Problems* 41: 50–64.

Honey, Martha. 1999. *Ecotourism and Sustainable Development: Who Controls Paradise?* Washington, DC: Island Press.

Hong, Nansook. 1998. *In the Shadow of the Moon: My Life in the Reverend Sun Myong Moon's Family.* Boston: Little, Brown.

Hook, Donald. 1989. *Death in the Balance.* Lexington, MA: Heath.

Hope, Kempe Ronald. 2001. *From Crisis to Renewal: Development Policy and Management in Africa.* Leiden: Brill.

Hopper, D. Ian. 2000. "Welfare Rolls Keep Shrinking," *Evansville Courier-Press* (August 23).

Hopper, Rex D. 1950. "The revolutionary process: A frame of reference for the study of revolutionary movements." *Social Forces* 25: 270–79.

Hornby, Garry, & Roger Kidd. 2001. "Transfer from special to mainstream: Ten years later." *British Journal of Special Education* 28(1): 10–17.

Horne, Christine. 2001. "The enforcement of norms: Group cohesion and metanorms." *Social Psychology Quarterly* 64(3): 253–66.

Hornsby, Anne M. 1998. "Surfing the net for community." In Peter Kvisto (ed.), *Illuminating Social Life.* Thousand Oaks, CA. Pine Forge: 63–106.

Horowitz, Stephan M., Molly T. Laflin, & T. Weis. 2001. "Differences between sexual orientation and groups and social background, quality of life, and health behaviors." *Journal of Sex Research* 38(3): 205–218.

Horst, Marilyn L. 1995. "Model for management of services to low income pediatric asthma patients." *Social Work in Health Care* 21(1): 129–36.

Hoschschild, Jennifer. 1995. *Facing Up to the American Dream: Race, Class and the Soul of the Nation.* Princeton, NJ: Princeton University Press.

Hosenball, Mark. 1999. "It is not the act of a few bad apples." *Newsweek* (May 17).

Hostetler, John A. 1980. *Amish Society*, 3rd ed. Baltimore: Johns Hopkins University Press.

Hostetler, John A., & Gertrude E. Huntington. 1971. *Children in Amish Society.* New York: Holt, Rinehart & Winston.

Houghton, John. 1997. *Global Warming: The Complete Briefing*, 2nd ed. New York: Cambridge University Press.

Houseknecht, Sharon K., & Jaya Sastry. 1996. "Family 'decline' and child well-being: A comparative assessment." *Journal of Marriage and the Family* 58(3): 726–39.

Hout, Michael, Clem Brooks, & Jeff Manza. 1995. "The Democratic class struggle in the United States, 1948–1992." *American Sociological Review* 60: 805–828.

Howard, Judith A. 2000. "The social psychology of identities." *Annual Review of Sociology* 26: 367–93.

Howard, M. C., & J. E. King. 2001. " 'State capitalism' in the Soviet Union." *History of Economics Review* No. 34 (Summer): 110–26.

Howell, David. 1994. "The skills myth." *The American Prospect* 18: 81–90.

Howes, C. 1988. "Peer interaction of young children." *Monographs of the Society for Research in Child Development.* 53: 1 (Serial No. 217).

Hoxie, Frederick E., & Peter Iverson, (eds.). 1998. *Indians in American History: An Introduction*, 2nd ed. Wheeling, IL: Harlan Davidson.

Hoyt, Homer. 1939. *The Structure and Growth of American Neighborhoods in Residential Cities.* Washington, DC: Federal Housing Authority.

Hoyt, Homer. 1943. "The structure and growth of American cities in the post-war era." *American Journal of Sociology* 48: 475–92.

Hrdy, Sarah Blaffer. 1999. *The Woman that Never Evolved.* Cambridge, MA: Harvard University Press.

Hsieh, Chin-Chi, & M. D. Pugh. 1993. "Poverty, income inequality, and violent crime." *Criminal Justice Review* 18: 182–199.

Huang, Chien Ju, & Harvey Marshall. 1997. "The effects of state strength on economic growth in the Third World: A critical perspective on World-System Theory." In Joseph E. Behar & Alfred G. Cuzan, (eds.), *At the Crossroads of Development: Transnational Challenges to Developed and Developing Societies.* Leiden, Netherlands: E. J. Brill: 19–37.

Hubbard, S. 1998. *Faith in Sports.* New York: Doubleday.

Huber, Christian. 1994. "Needle Park: What Can We Learn From the Zurich Experiment?" *Addiction* (89/5): 413–417.

Huber, Joan, & William H. Form. 1973. *Income & Ideology.* New York: Free Press.

Huber, Joan. 1995. "Centennial essay: Institutional perspectives on sociology." *American Journal of Sociology* 101: 194–216.

Huber, Karl D., Joseph G. Rosengeld, & Catherine A. Fiorello. 2001. "The differential impact of inclusion and inclusive practices on high, average, and low achieving general education students." *Psychology in the Schools* 38(6): 497–504.

HUD. 1999. *Homelessness and the People They Serve.* Housing and Urban Development. Washington, DC.

Hudson, Winthrop S. 1973. *Religion in America.* New York: Charles Scribner's Sons.

Huesmann, L. Rowell, (ed.). 1994. *Aggressive Behavior: Current Perspectives.* New York: Plenum.

Hughes, Everett C. 1965. "Professions." In Kenneth S. Lynn (ed.), *The Professions in America.* Boston: Houghton-Mifflin: 1–14.

Hughes, Everett. 1962. "Good people and dirty work." *Social Problems* 10: 3–11.

Hughes, Everett. 1945. "Dilemmas and contradictions of status." *American Journal of Sociology* 50: 353–359.

Hughes, Robert, 2002. "Divorce: Quick answers." Outreach & Extension: University of Missouri and Lincoln University. Available: http//:www.missourifamilies.org.

Huizenga, Rob. 1994. *You're OK, It's Just a Bruise.* New York: St. Martin's Press.

Huizinga, David, & Delbert S. Elliott. 1987. "Juvenile offenders: Prevalence, offender incidence and arrest rates by race." *Crime & Delinquency* 33(2): 206–23.

Human Rights Watch. 2000. "Punishment and Prejudice: Racial Disparities in the War on Drugs." New York: HRW.

Humphreys, Laud. 1970. *Tearoom Trade: Impersonal Sex in Public Places.* Chicago: Aldine.

Hungerford, T. L. 2001. "The economic consequences of widowhood on elderly women in the United States and Germany." *Gerontologist* 41(1): 103–11.

Hunt, Larry L. 2001. "Religion, gender and the Hispanic experience in the United States: Catholic/Protestant differences in religious involvement, social status and gender-role attitudes." *Review of Religious Research* 43(2): 139–60.

Hunt, Larry L., & Matthew O. Hunt. 2001. "Race, religion, and religious involvement: A comparative study of whites and African Americans." *Social Forces* 80(2): 605–31.

Hunt, M. 1974. *Sexual Behavior in the 1970s.* Chicago: Playboy.

Hunt, Stephen J. 2002. *Religion in Western Society.* London: Palgrave.

Hunt, Stephen J., Malcolm Hamilton, & Tony Walter (eds.). 1998. *Charismatic Christianity: Sociological Perspectives.* New York: St. Martin's.

Hunter, Andrea G., & James Earl Davis. 1994. "Hidden voices of black men: The meaning, structure and complexity of manhood." *Journal of Black Studies* 25(1): 20–40.

Hunter, Herbert, (ed.). 2000. *The Sociology of Oliver C. Cox.* Stamford, CT: JAI Press.

Hurst, Charles E. 1992. *Social Inequality: Forms, Causes and Consequences.* Boston: Allyn & Bacon.

Hussong, Andrea M. 2000a. "Perceived peer context and adolescent adjustment." *Journal of Research on Adolescence* 10(4): 391–15.

Hussong, Andrea M. 2000b. "The settings of adolescent alcohol and drug use." *Journal of Youth and Adolescence* 29(1): 107–119.

Huston, Michelle, & Pepper Schwartz. 1996. "Gendered dynamics in the romantic relationships of lesbians and gay men." In Julie T. Wood (ed.), *Gendered Relationships.* Mountain View, CA: Mayfield.

Hyde, Janet Shibley. 1996. *Half the Human Experience: The Psychology of Women.* Lexington, MA: D. C. Heath.

Hyman, Herbert H. 1942. "The psychology of status." *Archives of Psychology* 38.

Hyun, Eunsook. 2001. "The cultural complexity that affects young children's contemporary growth, change and learning." Paper presented at the American Educational Research Association, Seattle, April.

Iannaccone, Laurence R. 1997. "Rational choice: Framework for the scientific study of religion." In Lawrence A. Young (ed.), *Rational Choice Theory and Religion: Summary and Assessment.* New York: Routledge: 25–45.

Ibarra, Herminia. 1995. "Race, opportunity, and diversity of social circles in managerial networks." *Academy of Management Journal* 38(3): 673–703.

IGC. 2000. "Loss to Arctic ozone layer worsens." *Econonet Headlines*, Institute for Global Communications (April 5). Available: http://www.igc.org/igc/en/hl.

Inciardi, James A. 1992. *The War on Drugs II*. Mountain View, CA: Mayfield.

Inciardi, James, (ed.). 1980. *Radical Criminology: The Coming Crisis*. Beverly Hills: Sage.

Indian Health Service. 1999. "Trends in Indian health." Washington, DC: U.S. Department of Health and Human Services.

Inglehart, Ronald &, Wayne E. Baker. 2000. "Modernization, culture change, and the persistence of traditional values." *American Sociological Review* 65: 19–51.

Inglehart, Ronald. 1996. *Modernization and Postmodernization: Cultural, Economic, and Political Change in Forty-three Societies*. Princeton, NJ: Princeton University Press.

Ingram, Paul. 2002. "Buddhism: Japan." In John Bowker (ed.), *The Cambridge Illustrated History of Religions*. Cambridge, UK: Cambridge University: 98–105.

Inkeles, Alex. 1973. "Making man modern." In Amitai Etzioni & Eva Etzioni-Halvey, (eds.), *Social Change—Sources, Patterns and Consequences*. New York: Basic Books: 342–61.

Inkeles, Alex. 1983. *Exploring Individual Modernity*. New York: Columbia University Press.

Inkeles, Alex. 1998. *One World Emerging?* Boulder, CO: Westview.

Inman, Chris. 1996. "Friendships among men: Closeness in the doing." In Julia T. Wood, (ed.), *Gendered Relationships*. Mountain View, CA: Mayfield.

Institutionalizing Gender Equality. 2000. *Institutionalizing Gender Equality: Commitment, Policy and Practice: A Global Source Book. 2000*. Oxford, UK: OXFAM.

International Labour Organization. 2000. "Skills development for the informal economy: Who are they?" Available: http://www.ilo.org/public/english/employment/skills/informal/who.

International Labour Organization. 2002. KILM 7. "Informal sector employment."

Intons-Peterson, Margaret Jean. 1988. *Children's Concepts of Gender*. Norwood, NJ: Ablex.

Irvine, Leslie. 1998. "Organizational ethics and fieldwork realities." In Scott Grills (ed.), *Doing Ethnographic Research: Fieldwork Settings*. Thousand Oaks, CA: Sage: 167–83.

Irwin, John, & James Austin. 1994. *It Is About Time: America's Imprisonment Binge*. Belmont, CA: Wadsworth.

Irwin, Sarah. 1999. "Later life, inequality, and sociological theory." *Aging and Society* 19(6): 691–715.

Isbister, John. 1998. *Promises Not Kept: The Betrayal of Social Change in the Third World*. West Hartford, CT: Kumarian.

Ishii, Tooru. 2001. "A boundary of common sense." *Japanese Journal of Social Psychology* 16(3): 133–46.

Ishii-Kuntz, M. 1997. "Intergenerational relationships among Chinese, Japanese, and Korean Americans. *Family Relations* 46: 23–32.

Issues. 2002. "George W. Bush on health care." Issues 2002: Every Political Leader on Every Issue. Available: http://www.issues2000.prg/Celeb/George_W_Bush_Health_Care.

Itzin, Catherine. 2001. "Incest, pedophilia, pornography and prostitution: Making familial males more visible as the abusers." *Child Abuse Review* 10(1): 35–45.

Iverson, Peter. 1998. *"We are still here": American Indians in the 20th century*. Wheeling, IL: Harlan Davidson.

Jabusch, Willard E. 2000. "The myth of cohabitation: Research by L. Waite." *America* 183(10): 14–16.

Jack, William. *Principles of Health Economics for Developing Countries*. 1999. World Bank Institute Development Studies Series. Washington, DC: World Bank.

Jackman, Mary R., & Robert W. Jackman. 1983. *Class Awareness in the United States*. Berkeley: University of California.

Jackson, Cynthia L. 2001. *African American Education: A Reference Handbook*. Santa Barbara, CA: ABC-CLIO.

Jackson, Deborah D., & Elizabeth E. Chapleski. 2000. "Not traditional, not assimilated: Elderly American Indians and the notion of 'cohort'." *Journal of Cross-Cultural Gerontology* 15(3): 229–59.

Jackson, Jesse. 1996. *Legal Lynching: Racism, Injustice and the Death Penalty*. New York: Marlowe & Company.

Jackson, Kenneth T. 1985. *Crabgrass Frontier: The Suburbanization of the United States*. New York: Oxford University Press.

Jackson, Linda A., Ruth E. Fluery, & Donna M. Lewandowski. 1996. "Feminism: Definitions, support and correlates of support among male and female college students." *Sex Roles* 34: 687–93.

Jackson, Pamela B., Peggy A. Thoits & Howard F. Taylor. 1995. "Composition of the workplace and psychological well-being." *Social Forces* 74: 543–557.

Jackson, Shirley A. 1998. " 'Something about the word': African American women and feminism.." In Kathleen M. Blee (ed.), *No Middle Ground: Women and Radical Protest*. New York: New York University.

Jacobs, Andrew W. 2000. "Violent cast of high school hazing mirrors society, experts say." *New York Times* (March5): 27–28.

Jacobs, Charles, & Mohamad Athie. 1994. "Bought and sold." *The New York Times* (July 13): A–11.

Jacobs, D. 1989. "Inequality and economic crime." *Sociology and Social Research*, (66/1): 12–28.

Jacobs, James B. 1989. *Drunk Driving*. Chicago: University of Chicago Press.

Jacobs, Jane. 1970. *The Economy of Cities*. New York: Vintage.

Jacobs, Ronald N. 1996. "Civil society and crisis: Culture, discourse & the Rodney King beating." *American Journal of Sociology*.

Jacobs, Sue-Ellen, Wesley Thomas, & Sabine Long. 1997. *Two-Spirit People*. Urbana and Champaign, IL: University of Illinois.

Jacobson, David. 1995. "Incomplete institution or culture shock: Institutional and processual models of stepfamily instability." *Journal of Divorce and Remarriage* 24(1–2): 3–18.

Jacobson, Doranne, & Susan S. Wadley. 1995. *Women in India: Two Perspectives*. New Delhi, India: Manohar.

Jacobson, Jodi. 2001. "Transforming family planning programs: A framework for advancing the reproductive rights agenda." Paper presented at the Global Health Council annual conference. Washington, DC: May 29–June 1.

Jacobson, Matthew F. 1998. *Whiteness of a Different Color*. Cambridge, MA: Harvard.

Jacoby, Susan. 2000. "Money: America's love–hate relationship with the almighty dollar." *Modern Maturity* (July–August): 36–40.

Jacquard, Roland. 2001. "The guidebook of Jihad." *Time* (Oct. 29): 58.

Jacquet, Susan E., & Catherine A. Surra. 2001. "Parental divorce and premarital couples: Commitment and other relationship characteristics." *Journal of Marriage and the Family* 63(3): 627–38.

Jaffee, David. 1998. *Levels of Socio-Economic Development Theory*. West Hartford, CT: Praeger.

Jaffee, Sara, & Janet Shibley Hyde. 2000. "Gender differences in moral analysis: A meta-analysis." *Psychological Bulletin* 126(5): 703–726.

Jain, A., & J. Belsky. 1997. "Fathering and acculturation: Immigrant Indian families with young children." *Journal of Marriage and the Family* 59: 873–83.

Jakobeit, Cord. 1996. "Nonstate actors leading the way: Debt-for-nature swaps." In Robert O. Keohane & Mary A. Levy (eds.), *Institutions for Environmental Aid: Pitfalls and Promise*. Cambridge, MA: Massachusetts Institute of Technology Press: 127–66.

Jameson, Frederic. 1991. *Postmodernism, or the Cultural Logic of Late Capitalism*. Durham, NC: Duke University Press.

Jamieson, Amie, Andrea Curry, & Gladys Martinez. 2001. "School enrollment in the United States: Social and economic characteristics, October 1999." *Current Population Reports* (March). U.S. Census Bureau.

Jandt, Fred E. 2001. *Intercultural Communication: An Introduction*. Thousand Oaks, CA: Sage.

Janis, Irving. 1972. *Victims of Groupthink*. Boston: Houghton-Mifflin.

Janofsky, M. 1998. "Shortage of housing for poor grows in U.S." *New York Times* (April 28).

Janus, Chris G. 1996. "Slavery Abolished? Only Officially," *Christian Science Monitor* (May 17): 18.

Janus, Samuel, & Cynthia Janus. 1993. *The Janus Report on Sexual Behavior*. New York: Wiley.

Japikse, Catharina. 1994. "The Irish potato famine." *EPA Journal* 20(3/4): 44.

Jarly, Paul, Jack Fiorito, & John T. Delaney. 2000. "National union governance," *Journal of Labor Research* (21/2): 227–246.

Jasper, James M., & Jane D. Poulsen. 1995. "Recruiting strangers and friends." *Social Problems* 42/4: 493–512.

Jasso, Guillermino. 1999. "How Much Injustice Is There in the World? *American Sociological Review* 64: 133–168.

Jeffries, Ian. 2001. *Economies in Transition: A Guide to China, Cuba. Mongolia, North Korea and Vietnam at the Turn of the Twenty-First Century*. London: Routledge.

Jelen, Ted G. 1999. "On the hegemony of liberal individualism: A reply to Williams." *Sociology of Religion* 60(1): 35–40.

Jencks, C. 1994. *The Homeless*. Cambridge, MA: Harvard University Press.

Jencks, Christopher, & Paul E. Peterson. (eds.). 1991. *The Urban Underclass*. Washington, DC: Brookings Institute.

Jenkins, Brian M. 2001. "The organization men: Anatomy of a terrorist attack." In James F. Hoge & Gideon Rose (eds.), *How Did it Happen? Terrorism and the New War*. New York: Public Affairs: 1–14.

Jenkins, Brian, & Yonah Alexander (eds.). 1987. *The Terrorism Reader*. New York: Meridian.

Jenkins, J. Craig 1983. "Resource mobilization theory and the study of social movements." *Annual Review of Sociology*: 527–53.

Jenkins, J. Craig, & Barbara Brents. 1989. "Social protest, hegemonic competition and social reform: The political origins of the American welfare state." *American Sociological Review*, 54: 891–909.

Jenkins, J. Craig, & Charles Perrow. 1977. "Insurgency of the powerless." *American Sociological Review* 42/2: 249–68.

Jenkins, J. Craig. 1985. *The Politics of Insurgency*. New York: Columbia University Press.

Jenkins, R. 1994a. "Rethinking ethnicity: Identity categorization and power." *Ethnic & Racial Studies* 17: 197–223.

Jenness, V. 1993. *Making it Work: The Prostitute Rights Movement in Perspective*. New York: Aldine de Gruyter.

Jenness, Valerie. 1990. "From sex as sin to sex as work: COYOTE and the reorganization of prostitution as a social problem." *Social Problems* 37: 103–20.

Jensen, Arthur R. 1969. "How much can we boost IQ and scholastic achievement?" *Harvard Educational Review* 39: 1–123.

Jensvold, Mary Lee A., & R. Allen Gardner. 2000. "Interactive use of sign language by cross-fostered chimpanzees (Pan troglodytes)." *Journal of Comparative Psychology* 114(4): 335–46.

Jiang, Lin. 1995. "Changing kinship structure and its implications for old-age support in urban and rural China." *Population Studies* 49(1): 127–45.

Jie, Fan, & Wolfgang Taubmann. 2002. "Migrant enclaves in large Chinese cities." In John R. Logan (ed.), *The New Chinese City: Globalization and Market Reform*. Oxford, UK: Blackwell: 183–97.

Jimenez-Vasquez, R. 1995. "Hispanics: Cubans." *Encyclopedia of Social Work*. Washington, DC: National Association of Social Work.

Joe, Jennie R., & Dorothy Lonewolf Miller. 1994. "Cultural survival and contemporary American Indian women in the city." In Maxine Baca Zinn & Bonnie Thornton Dill (eds.), *Women's History.* New York: Routledge.

Johannesburg Summit. 2002. "With a sense of urgency, Johannesburg Summit sets an action agenda." September 4. United Nations World Summit on Sustainable Development. Available: http://johannesburgsummit.org.

Johansen, Bruce E. 1997. "Race, ethnicity and the media." In Alan Wells & Ernest A. Hakanen, (eds.), *Mass Media and Society.* Greenwich, CT: Ablex: 513–25.

John, D., & B. A. Shelton. 1997. "The production of gender among black and white women and men: The case of household labor." *Sex Roles* 36: 171–93.

John, R. 2000. "Chronic health problems of American Indian elders: Individual, cultural, and social influence." *Gerontologist* 40(1): 43.

Johnson, Colleen L. 1999. "Fictive kin among oldest African Americans in the San Francisco Bay area." *Journal of Gerontology, Series B: Psychological Sciences and Social Sciences* 54B(6): S368–S375.

Johnson, Colleen L. 2000. "Adaptation of oldest old black Americans." In Elizabeth W. Markson & Lisa Ann Hollis-Sawyer (eds.), *Intersections of Aging: Readings in Social Gerontology.* Los Angeles, CA: 133–41.

Johnson, Hank, & Bert Klandermans, (eds.), 1995. *Social Movements and Culture.* Minneapolis: University of Minnesota Press.

Johnson, Ida M., & Robert T. Sigler. 2000. "Forced sexual intercourse among intimates." *Journal of Family Violence* 15(1): 95–108.

Johnson, J. Alleyne. 1995. "Life after death: Pedagogy in an urban classroom." *Harvard Educational Review* 65(2): 213–30.

Johnson, Jeanette H., & Wendy Turnbull. 1995. "The women's conference: Where aspirations and realities met." *International Family Planning Perspectives* 21(4): 155–59.

Johnson, Jeffrey, P. Cohen, E. M. Smailes, S. Kasen, and J. S. Brook. 2002. "Television viewing and aggressive behavior during adolescence and adulthood." *Science Magazine* (March 28): 2468–71.

Johnson, L., P. O'Malley, & J. Bachman. 1997. *National Survey Results on Drug Use from the Monitoring the Future Study, 1976–1996.* Washington, DC: GPO.

Johnson, Miriam. 1997. "Review of six prominent sociology of the family textbooks in teaching, research and reference section." *Contemporary Sociology* 26(3): 395–99.

Johnson, Nan E., & Jacob J. Climo. 2000. "Aging and eldercare in more developed countries: The United States, South Korea and Puerto Rico." *Journal of Family Issues* 21(5): 531–40.

Johnson, Richard A. 1985. *American Fads.* New York: Beech Tree.

Johnson, Robert. 1990. *Death Work: A Study of the Modern Execution Process.* Pacific Grove, CA: Brooks/Cole.

Johnson, Stephen D. 2000. "Who supports the Promise Keepers?" *Sociology of Religion* 61(1): 93–104.

Johnson, Tim. 1995. "The dealer's edge." *Native Americas* (12/1–2).

Johnson, Victoria, & Robert Nurick. 1995. "Behind the headlines: The ethics of the population and environment debate." *International Affairs* 71: 547–65.

Johnstone, Penelope. 2002. "Islam." In John Bowker (ed.), *The Cambridge Illustrated History of Religions.* Cambridge, UK: Cambridge University: 270–303.

Johnstone, Ronald L. 1992. *Religion in Society: A Sociology of Religion.* Upper Saddle River, NJ: Prentice Hall.

Johnstone, Ronald L. 1997. *Religion in Society,* 5th ed. Englewood Cliffs, NJ: Prentice Hall.

Jones, James H. 1993. *Bad Blood: The Tuskegee Syphilis Experiment.* New York: Free Press.

Jones, James M. 1997. *Prejudice and Racism,* 2nd ed. New York: McGraw-Hill.

Jones, Melkinda. 2002. *Social Psychology of Prejudice.* Upper Saddle River, NJ: Prentice Hall.

Jones, Michael Owen, Patrick A. Polk, & Ysamur Flores-Pena. 2001. "Invisible hospitals: Botanicas in ethnic health care." In Erika Brady (ed.), *Healing Logics: Culture and Medicine in Modern Health Belief Systems.* Logan, UT: Utah State University: 39–87.

Jones, Rodney & Mark McDonough. 1998. *Tracking Nuclear Proliferation.* Washington, DC: Carnegie Endowment for International Peace.

Jones, Vinetta C., & Rochelle Clemson. 1996. "Promoting effective teaching for diversity." In Laura I. Rendon & Richard O. Hope (eds.), *Educating a New Majority: Transforming America's Educational System for Diversity.* San Francisco: Jossey-Bass: 159–67.

Jordan, Ellen, & Angela Cowan. 1995. "Warrior narratives in the kindergarten classroom: Renegotiating the social contract?" *Gender & Society* 9(6): 727–43.

Jordan, Grant. 1990. "The pluralism of pluralism: An anti-theory." *Political Studies* 38: 286–301.

Josephson, Jyl J. 1997. *Gender, Families and State: Child Support Policies in the United States.* New York: Rowman & Littlefield.

Josephson, Matthew. 1934. *The Robber Barons.* New York: Harcourt Brace.

Juergensmeyer, Mark. 2000. *Terror in the Mind of God.* Berkeley: University of California.

Jung, Ingrid, & Adama Ouane. 2001. "Literacy and social development: Policy and implementation." In David R. Olson & Nancy Torrance (eds.), *The Making of Literate Societies.* Malden, MA: Blackwell: 310–36.

Kacapyr, Elia. 1996. "Are you middle class?" *American Demographics* (October): 30–35.

Kaestle, Carl F. 1995. "Literate America: High-level adult literacy as a national goal." In Diane Ravitch & Maris A. Vinovskis (eds.), *Learning from the Past: What History Teaches Us About School Reform.* Baltimore, MD: Johns Hopkins University: pp. 330–54.

Kahlenberg, Richard D. 2001a. "Learning from James Coleman." *Public Interest* 144: 54–72.

Kahlenberg, Richard D. 2001b. *All Together Now: Creating Middle Class Schools through Public Choice.* Washington, DC: Brookings Institution.

Kahn, Matthew. 2000. "The environmental impact of suburbanization." *Journal of Policy Analysis and Management.* 19(4): 569–86.

Kahn, Matthew. 2001. "Does urban sprawl reduce the black/white housing consumption gap?" *Housing Policy Debate* 12(1): 77–87.

Kaiser Family Foundation. 2001a. "The insured: A primer." Pub. #2228: March.

Kaiser Family Foundation. 2001b. "The insured and their access to health care." Kaiser Commission on Medicaid and the Uninsured. January.

Kaiser Family Foundation. 2002b. "The global HIV/AIDS epidemic." HIV/AIDS Policy Fact Sheet: July. Washington, DC: Kaiser Family Foundation.

Kaiser Family Foundation. 2002c. *Trends and Indicators in the Changing Health Care Marketplace, 2002:Chartbook.* Washington, DC: Kaiser Family Foundation.

Kalick, S. Michael. 1988. "Physical attractiveness as a status cue." *Journal of Experimental Social Psychology* 24: 469–489.

Kalish, Susan. 1995. "Interracial births increase as U.S. ponders racial definitions." *Population Today* (23/4): 1–2.

Kalmijn, Matthijs, & Henk Flap. 2001. "Assortive meeting and mating: Unintended consequences of organized settings for partner choices." *Social Forces* 79(4): 1289–312.

Kalmijn, Matthijs. 1998. "Intermarriage and homogamy: Causes, patterns, trends." *Annual Review of Sociology* 24(1): 395–421.

Kalof, Linda 1999. "The effects of gender and music video imagery on sexual attitudes." *Journal of Social Psychology* 139(3): 378–85.

Kalof, Linda, Kimberly K. Eby, Jennifer L. Matheson, & Rob J. Ktoska. 2001. "The influence of race and gender on student self-reports of sexual harassment by college professors." *Gender & Society* 15(2): 282–302.

Kalof, Linda. 1993. "Dilemmas of femininity: Gender and the social construction of sexual imagery." *Sociological Quarterly* 34(4): 639–51.

Kameda, T., & S. Sugimori. 1999. "Psychological Entrapment in Group Decision Making." *Journal of Personality & Social Psychology* 65: 282–292.

Kamen, Paula. 2000. *Her Way: Young Women Remake the Sexual Revolution.* New York: New York University.

Kaminer, Wendy. 2000. "Gay rites." *American Prospect* 11(8) (Feb. 28): 6–7

Kammen, Michael. 1998. "The study of popular culture has acquired legitimacy, but still lacks cohesion." *The Chronicle of Higher Education* (July 3): B4–B5.

Kanahele, Pualini Kanaka'ole. 2001. "The role of education: Acculturation back to the future." In Peter Seitel (ed.), *Safeguarding Traditional Cultures: A Global Assessment.* Washington, DC: Smithsonian Institution Center for Folklife and Cultural Heritage: 67–69.

Kanaya, Akihiro, & David Woo. 2001. *The Japanese Banking Crisis of the 1990s: Sources and Lessons.* Princeton, NJ: International Economic Section, Princeton University.

Kandal, Terry R. 1988. *The Woman in Classical Sociological Theory.* Miami: Florida International University Press.

Kandel, Denise, & Mark Davies. 1991. "Friendship networks, intimacy and illicit drug use in young adults." *Criminology* (29): 441–67.

Kane, Emily W. 2000. "Racial and ethnic variations in gender-related attitudes." *Annual Review of Sociology* 26(1): 419–39.

Kane, Mary Jo, & Helen J. Lenskyj. 1998. "Media treatment of female athletes." In Lawrence A. Wenner (ed.), *MediaSport.* New York: Routledge.

Kane, Robert L., & Rosalie A. Kane. 1994. "Satisfaction guaranteed." In William Fornblum & Carolyn D. Smith (eds.), *The Leading Experience: Readings on the Social Context of Health Care.* Upper Saddle River, NJ: Prentice Hall: 171–76.

Kang, Mee-Eun. 1997. "The portrayal of women's images in magazine advertisements: Goffman's gender analysis revisited." *Sex Roles* 37(11–12): 979–96.

Kanhema, Newton, & Wendy Rappeport. 2001. "At last: One of the world's largest and oldest refugee communities begins to go home." *Refugees,* 26–29.

Kanne, Bernice. 1995. "Guy stuff: A new man is regular Joe." *St. Louis Post-Dispatch* (October 29): 7E.

Kanter, Rosabeth M. 1977. *Men and Women of the Corporation.* New York: Basic Books.

Kanter, Rosabeth Moss, & Barry A. Stein. 1979. "The gender pioneers: Women in an industrial sales force." In Rosabeth Moss Kanter, & Barry A. Stein, (eds.), *Life in Organizations.* New York: Basic Books: 134–60.

Kanter, Rosabeth Moss. 1973. *Communes: Creating and Managing the Collective Life.* New York: Harper & Row.

Kanter, Rosabeth Moss. 1983. *The Change Masters.* New York: Simon & Schuster.

Kantner, Andrew, & Sidney B. Westley. 1998. "Family planning for new mothers in the Philippines." *Asia-Pacific Population and Policy* 47 (October). East-West Center, Honolulu.

Kantor, Martin. 1998. *Homophobia.* Westport, CT: Praeger.

Kantrowitz, Barbara, & Keith Naughton. 2001. "Generation 9–11." *Newsweek* 128 (November 12): 46–56.

Kantrowitz, Barbara, Pat Wingert, Margaret Nelson, Julie Halpert, John Lauerman, Tara Weingarten, Anne Belli Gesalman, & Beth Dickey. 2001. "The parent trap" (cover story). *Newsweek* 137(5): 49–52.

Kantrowitz, Barbara. 1994. "In search of the sacred." *Newsweek* (November 28): 53–55.

Kapferer, Jean-Noel. 1992. "How rumors are born." *Society* 29: 53–60.

Kaplan, Richard L. 1999. "Top ten myths about Social Security." In Lawrence A. Frolik (ed.), *Aging and the Law: An Interdisciplinary Reader.* Philadelphia: Temple University: 132–45.

Kaplan, S. J., D. Pelcovitz, & V. Labruna. 1999. "Child and adolescent abuse and neglect research: A review of the past 10 years. Part I: Physical and emotional abuse and neglect." *Journal of the American Academy of Child and Adolescent Psychiatry* 38: 1214–22.

Kappler, Victor E., Mark Blumberg, & Gary W. Potter. 1996. *The Mythology of Crime & Criminal Justice.* Prospect Heights, IL: Waveland.

Karmen, Andrew. 2000. *Crime Victims*, 4th ed. Belmont, CA: Wadsworth.

Kates, Nick K., Barrie S. Grieff, & Duane Q. Hagen. 1990. *The Psychosocial Impact of Job Loss*. Washington: American Psychiatric Press.

Katovich, Michael A., & Marya S. Makowski. 1999. "Music periods in the rock and post rock eras: The rise of female performers on a provocative stage." *Studies in Symbolic Interaction* 23: 141–66.

Katz, J. N. 1995. *The Invention of Heterosexuality*. New York: Dutton.

Katz, James E., & Philip Aspden. 1998. "Theories, data, and the potential impacts of mobile communications." *Technological Forecasting and Social Change* 57: 133–156.

Katz, Michael B. 1995. *Improving Poor People*. Princeton, NJ: Princeton University Press.

Kaufman, Gayle. 1999. "The portrayal of men's family roles in television commercials." *Sex Roles* 41(5–6): 439–58.

Kaufman, P., X. Chen, & S. P. Choy et al. 2000. *Indicators of School Crime and Safety, 2000*. National Center for Education Statistics and Office of Justice Programs, Washington, DC: U.S. Department of Education and U.S. Department of Justice.

Kaus, Mickey. 1997. "The GOP's welfare gut check." *Newsweek* (June 30): 38.

Kawachi, Ichiro, & Bruce P. Kennedy. 2002. *The Health of Nations: Why Inequality Is Harmful to Your Health*. New York: New Press.

Kawachi, Ichiro, Bruce P. Kennedy, & Richard C. Wilkinson (eds.). 1999. *The Society and Population Health Reader: Income Inequality and Health*. New York: New Press.

Kawachi, Ichiro. 2000. "Social cohesion and health." In Alvin R. Tarlov & Robert F. St. Peter (eds.), *The Society and Population Health Reader. Volume II—A State and Community Perspective*. New York: New Press: 57–74.

Kay, Paul, Brent Berlin, Luisa Maffi, & William Merrifield. 1997. "Color naming across languages." In C. L. Hardin & Luisa Maffi (eds.), *Color Categories in Thought and Language and Cambridge*, NY: Cambridge University: 21–56.

Keating, Elizabeth. 2001. "Space." In Alessandro Duranti (ed.), *Key Terms in Language and Culture*. Malden, MA: Blackwell.

Keeler, Barbara. 2001. "A nation of lab rats." *Sierra* (July/August): 45.

Keillor, Garrison. 1994. "It's good old monogamy that's really sexy." *Time* (October 17): 71.

Keister, Lisa A. 2000. *Wealth in America: Trends in Wealth Inequality*. New York: Cambridge University Press.

Keith, Jennie, Christine L. Fry, Anthony P. Glascock, Charlotte Ikels, Jeanette Dickerson-Putman, Henry C. Harpending, & Patricia Draper. 1994. *The Aging Experience: Diversity and Commonality Across Cultures*. Thousand Oaks, CA: Sage.

Keith, Jennie. 1992. "Care-taking in cultural context: Anthropological queries." In Hal Kendig, Akiko Hashimoto, & Larry C. Coppard (eds.), *Family Support for the Elderly: The International Experience*. New York: Oxford University Press.

Keizai Koho Center. 1999. *Japan 1999: An International Comparison*. Tokyo: Keizai Koho Center (Japan Institute for Social and Economic Affairs).

Kelder, Richard. 1996. "Rethinking literacy studies from the past to the present." Paper presented at the World Conference on Literacy, Philadelphia, March.

Kelle, Helga. 2000. "Gender and territoriality in games played by nine- to twelve-year old schoolchildren." *Journal of Contemporary Ethnography* 29(2): 164–97.

Keller, Helen. 1917. *The Story of My Life*. Garden City, NY: Doubleday.

Keller, James R. 2001. *Queer (Un)friendly Film and Television*. Jefferson, NC: McFarland.

Keller, Robert, & Edward Sbarbaro. 1994. *Prisons in Crisis*. Albany, NY: Harrow & Heston.

Keller, Sarah. 1996. "Traditional beliefs part of people's lives." *Network* 17(1). Family Health International. Available: http://www.fhi.org/en/fp/fppubs/network/v17–1.

Kelley, Jonathan & M. D. R. Evans. 1995. "Class and class conflict in six western nations." *American Sociological Review* 60: 157–78.

Kelley, Jonathan, & M. D. R. Evans. 1993. "The legitimization of inequality: Occupational earnings in nine nations." *American Journal of Sociology* 99.

Kelling, George L., & Catherine M. Coles. 1996. *Fixing Broken Windows: Restoring Order and Reducing Crime in Our Communities*. New York: Free Press.

Kelly, E. L. 1999. "Theorizing corporate family policies: How advocates built 'the business case' for 'family-friendly' programs." *Research in the Sociology of Work* 7: 169–202.

Kelly, James R. 1999. "Sociology and public theology: A case study of pro-choice/pro-life common ground." *Sociology of Religion* 60(2): 99–124.

Kelly, Joan B. 2000. "Children's adjustment in conflicted marriage and divorce: A decade review of research." *Journal of the American Academy of Child and Adolescent Psychiatry* 39(8): 963–73.

Kelly, Rita Mae. 1997. "Sex-role spillover: Personal, familial, and organizational roles." In *Workplace/Women's Place: An Anthology*. Los Angeles: Roxbury: 150–60.

Kelly, Thomas J. 1999. *The Effects of Economic Adjustment in Mexico*. Aldershot, Hants, UK: Ashgate.

Keltkangas-Jaervinen, Liisa, Laura Pakaslahti, & Anu Karjalainen. 2002. "Relationships between adolescent prosocial problem-solving strategies, prosocial behaviour, and social acceptance." *International Journal of Behavioral Development* 26(2): 137–44.

Kemp, Alice Abel. 1995. "Poverty and welfare for women." In Jo Freeman (ed.), *Women: A Feminist Perspective*. Mountain View, CA: Mayfield.

Kempf, Kimberly L. (ed.), 1990. *Measurement Issues in Criminology*. New York: Springer-Verlag.

Kenmochi, Takashi. 1992. "Defusing the examination war: How can companies and parents relieve pressure on students?" *Japan Update* (December): 12–15.

Kennedy, Leslie W., & Vincent F. Sacco. 1998. *Crime Victims In Context*. Los Angeles: Roxbury.

Kennedy, Maureen, & Paul Leonard. 2001. "Dealing with neighborhood change: A primer on gentrification and policy choices." Washington, DC: Brookings Institution. Available: http://www.policylink.org/pdfs/brookingsgentrification.

Kennedy, Mike. 1999. "A century of progress." *American School and University* 72(4): 10–12, 14, 16, 20.

Kennedy, Paul M. 1988. *The Rise & Fall Of the Great Powers*. New York: Random House.

Kennedy, Paul. 1997. "Preparing for the 21st century: Winners and losers." In Robert M. Jackson (ed.), *Global Issues 97/98*. Guilford, CT: Dushkin/McGraw-Hill: 8–24.

Kennelly, Ivy, Judith Lorber, & Sabine N. Metz. 2001. "What is gender?" *American Sociological Review* 66(4): 598–605.

Kennelly, Ivy. 2001. "On morals, manners, and gender inequality." *Qualitative Sociology* 24(1): 135–40.

Kenway, Jane, & Elizabeth Bullen. 2001. *Consuming Children: Education, Entertainment, and Advertising*. Buckingham, UK: Open University.

Keohane, Robert O. 1996. "Analyzing the effectiveness of international environmental institutions." In Robert O. Keohane & Marc A. Levy (eds.), *Institutions for Environmental Aid: Pitfalls and Promises*. Cambridge, MA: Massachusetts Institute of Technology: 3–27.

Kerbo, Harold R. 2000. *Social Stratification and Inequality*, 4th ed. Boston: McGraw Hill.

Kerbo, Harold R. G., John A. McKinstry. 1998. *Modern Japan*. New York: McGraw-Hill.

Kerr, Mary Margaret, & C. Michael Nelson. 2002. *Strategies for Addressing Behavior Problems in the Classroom*. Upper Saddle River, NJ: Merrill/Prentice Hall.

Kesner, John E., & Patrick C. McKenry. 2001. Single parenthood and social competence in children of color." *Families in Society* 82(2): 136–44.

Kessler, Ronald C., J. Blake Turner, & James S. House. 1989. "Unemployment, reemployment and emotional functions in a community sample." *American Sociological Review* 54: 648–57.

Kessler, Ronald C., Roger B. Davis, David F. Foster, Maria I. Van Rompay, Ellen E. Walters, Sonja A. Wilkey, Ted J. Kaptchuk, & David M. Eisenberg. 2001. "Long-term trends in the use of complementary and alternative medical therapies in the United States." *Annals of Internal Medicine* 135(August 21): 262–68.

Kettl, Donald F. 1991. "The savings and loan bailout: The mismatch between the headlines and the issues." *PS* 24/3: 441–47.

Khan, Mahmood Hasan. 2000. "Rural poverty in developing countries." *Finance & Development* 37(4): 26–29.

Khandker, Shahidur R. 1998. *Fighting Poverty with Microcredit: Experience in Bangladesh*. New York: Oxford University.

Khashan, Hilal, & Lina Kreidie. 2001. "The social and economic correlates of Islamic religiosity." *World Affairs* 164(2): 83–96.

Khatami, Siamak. 1997. "Between class and nation: Ideology and radical Basque ethnonationalism." *Studies in Conflict & Terrorism* 20: 395–417.

Khor, Kok Peng. 2001. *Rethinking Globalization: Critical Issues and Policy Choices*. London: Zed.

Kim, Hak-Min. 1999. *Globalization of International Financial Markets: Causes and Consequences*. Aldershot, Hants, UK: Ashgate.

Kim, Jungmeen E., & Phyllis Moen. 2002. "Retirement transitions, gender and psychological well-being: A life-course ecological model." *Journal of Gerontology* 57B(3): 212–22.

Kim, Walter, & Wendy Cole. 2000. "Twice as nice: Expensive second weddings." *Time* 155(25): 53–54.

Kimble, Charles E., & J. I. Musgrove. 1988. "Dominance in arguing in mixed-sex dyads: Visual dominance patterns, talking time and speech loudness." *Journal of Research in Personality* 22: 1–16.

Kincheloe, Joe L. 1999. "How do we tell the workers? The socioeconomic foundations of work and vocational education." U.S.: Colorado. ERIC.

Kinder, Marsha. 1999. "Kids' media culture: An introduction." In Marsha Kinder (ed.). *Kids' Media Culture*. Durham, NC: Duke University.

King, A. 1995. "Outline of a practical theory of football violence." *Sociology* (29): 635–51.

King, Anthony D. 2000. "Cities: Contradictory utopias." In Jan Nederveen Pieterse (ed.), *Global Futures: Shaping Globalization*. London: Zed: 224–241.

King, Kathleen S., & Mary Ann Johnson. 2002. "Biological, psychological, and social issues facing older adults in residential care." In Robert D. Hill & Brian L. Thorn (eds.), *Geriatric Residential Care*. Mahwah, NJ: Lawrence Erlbaum: 39–55.

Kingston, Eric R., & John B. Williamson. 2001. "Economic status of the elderly." In Robert H. Binstock & Linda K. George (eds.), *Handbook of Aging and the Social Sciences*. San Diego, CA: Academic Press.

Kingston, Jeff. 2001. *Japan in Transformation, 1952–2000*. Harlow, UK: Longman.

Kingston, Shane. 1995. "Terrorism, the media, and the Northern Ireland conflict." *Studies in Conflict & Terrorism* 18: 207–215.

Kingston, William. 2000. "A spectre is haunting the world: The spectre of global capitalism." *Journal of Evolutionary Economics* 10(1–2): 83–108.

Kinney, Terry A., Brian A. Smith, & Bonny Donzella. 2001. "The influence of sex, gender, self-discrepancies, and self-awareness on anger and verbal aggressiveness among U.S. college students." *Journal of Social Psychology* 141(2): 245–76.

Kinsella, Kevin, & Victoria A. Velkoff. 2001. "An aging world: 2001." *International Population Reports* (November). U.S. Census Bureau. Washington, DC: U.S. Department of Commerce.

Kinsella, Kevin. 2000. "Demographic dimensions of global aging." *Journal of Family Issues* 21(5): 541–58.

Kinsey Institute. 1999. "Prevalence of homosexuality: Brief summary of U.S. studies." (Compiled June 1999). Available: http://www.kinseyinstitue.org/resources/bib-homoprev.

Kinsey, Alfred E., Wardell B. Pomeroy, & Clyde E. Martin, & H. Gephard. 1953. *Sexual Behavior of the Human Female*. Philadelphia: Saunders.

Kinsey, Alfred E., Wardell B. Pomeroy, & Clyde E. Martin. 1948. *Sexual Behavior in the Human Male*. Philadelphia: Saunders.

Kinsman, Gary. 1992. "Men loving men: The challenge of gay liberation." In Michael S. Kimmel & Michael A. Messner (eds.), *Men's Lives*. New York: Macmillan.

Kiple, Kenneth F., & Kriemhild Connee Omelas (eds.). 2000. *The Cambridge World History of Food*. Cambridge, UK: Cambridge University.

Kirk, Dudley. 1986. "Foreword." In W. Penn Handwerker (ed.), *Culture and Reproduction: An Anthropological Critique of Demographic Transition Theory*. Boulder, CO: Westview.

Kirkman, Robert. 2002. *Skeptical Environmentalism: The Limits of Philosophy and Science*. Bloomington: Indiana University.

Kirkpatrick Johnson, Monica. 2001. "Job values in the young adult transition: Change and stability with age." *Social Psychology Quarterly* 64(4): 297–317.

Kirsch, Irwin S., Ann Jungeblut, Lynn Jenkins, & Andrew Kolstad. 2001. "Adult literacy in America." In Ellen Cushman, Eugene R. Kintgen, Barry M. Kroll, & Mike Rose (eds.), *Literacy: A Critical Sourcebook*. Boston: Bedford/St. Martin's: 644–59.

Kirschner, Stuart M., & Gary J. Galperin. 2002. "The defense of extreme emotional disturbance in New York County: Pleas and outcomes." *Behavioral Sciences & the Law* 20(1–2): 47–50.

Kiser, Edgar, & Joachim Schneider. 1994. "Bureaucracy and Efficiency." *American Sociological Review* (59/2): 187–204.

Kitano, H. 1980. *Race Relations*. Upper Saddle River, NJ: Prentice-Hall.

Kitano, Harry H. L., & Roger Daniels. 1995. *Asian Americans: Emerging Minorities*. Englewood Cliffs, NJ: Prentice Hall.

Kitano, Naohiro. 2001. "Analysis of spatial organization and transportation demand in an expanding urban area: Sendai, Japan, 1972–92." In Shahid Yusuf, Simon Evenett, & Weiping Wu (eds.), *Facets of Globalization: International and Local Dimensions of Development*. Washington, DC: World Bank: 260–78.

Kite, Mary E., & Bernard Whitley. 1996. "Sex differences in attitudes toward homosexual persons, behaviors, and civil rights: A meta-analysis." *Personality and Social Psychology Bulletin* 22: 336–53.

Kitsuse, John I. 1980. "Coming out all over: Deviants and the politics of social problems." *Social Problems* (28/1): 1–13.

Kivisto, Peter. 1994. "The rise or fall of the Christian right: Conflicting reports from the frontlines." *Sociology of Religion* 55(3): 223–37.

Kiyosaki, Robert. 2002. *Rich Dads Retire Young, Retire Rich: How to Get Rich and Stay Rich Forever*. New York: Warner Business.

Klagsbrun, Francis. 1995. "Marriages that last." In Mark Robert Rank & Edward L. Kain (eds.), *Diversity and Change in Families: Patterns, Prospects, and Policies*. Upper Saddle River, NJ: Prentice Hall.

Klandermans, Bert. 1984. "Mobilization & participation." *American Sociological Review* 49: 583–600.

Klandermans, Bert. 1994. "Targeting the critical mass." *Social Psychological Quarterly* 57: 360–67.

Klapp, Orris E. 1972. *Currents of Unrest*. New York: Holt.

Klee, Kenneth. 1999. "The siege of Seattle," *Newsweek* (December 13).

Kleidman, Robert. 1994. "Volunteer activism & professionalism in social movement organizations." *Social Problems* 41: 257–76.

Kleiman, Angela B. 1998. "Schooling, literacy and social change: Elements for a critical approach to the study of literacy." In Marta Kohl de Oliveira and Jaan Valsiner (eds.), *Literacy in Human Development*. Stamford, CT: Ablex: 183–225.

Klein, Dorie. 1995. "The etiology of female crime: A review of the literature." In Barbara R. Price & Natalie J. Sokoloff, (eds.), *The Criminal Justice System and Women*, 2nd ed. New York: McGraw-Hill: 30–46.

Klein, Hugh, Kenneth S. Shiffman, & Denise A. Welka. 2000. "Gender-related content of animated cartoons, 1930 to the present." *Advances in Gender Research* 4: 291–317.

Klein, Lloyd. 1996. "Close encounters of the media kind: Class conflict on daytime talk shows." Paper presented at the annual meeting of the American Sociological Association, San Francisco, August.

Klein, Stephen P., Susan Turner, & Joan Petersilia. 1988. *Racial Equity in Sentencing*. Santa Monica: Rand.

Kleinke, C. L. 1986. "Gaze and eye contact: A research review." *Psychological Bulletin* 16: 740–45.

Kleinman, Arthur. 1988. *The Illness Narratives: Suffering, Healing and the Human Condition*. New York: Basic Books.

Kleinman, Sherryl, & Martha A. Copp. 1993. *Emotions and Fieldwork*. Qualitative Research Methods Series 28. Newbury Park, CA: Sage.

Kleinplatz, Peggy J. 2000. "On the outside looking in: In search of women's sexual experience." *Women & Therapy* 24(1–2): 123–32.

Klenke, Karin. 1996. *Women & Leadership*. New York: Springer.

Klentrou, Panagiota, Anthony F. Bogaert, & Chris Friesen. 2002. "Age of puberty and sexual orientation in a national probability sample." *Archives of Sexual Behavior* 31(1): 73–81.

Kleyman, Paul. 2000. " 'Geezer' bashing continues to slant Social Security coverage." American Society on Aging. Available: http:www.asaaging.org/at/at-216/mcgeezer.

Klinghoffer, David. 1998. *Lord Will Gather Me In: My Journey to Jewish Orthodoxy*. New York: Free Press.

Kloehn, Steve. 1997. "Most alternative sects are safe, experts say." *Chicago Tribune* (March 28): 1: 7.

Klofas, J., & S. Stojkovic (eds.). 1995. *Crime and Justice in the Year 2010*. Belmont, CA: Wadsworth.

Kluegel, James R. 1990. "Trends in whites' explanations of the black-white gap in socioeconomic status, 1977–1989." *American Sociological Review* 55: 512–25.

Kluegel, James R., & Elliot R. Smith. 1986. *Beliefs About Inequality: Americans' Views of What Is and What Ought to Be*. Hawthorne, NY: Aldine de Gruyter.

Klugman, Karen. 1999. "A bad hair day for G.I. Joe." In Beverly Lyon Clark & Margaret R. Higonnet (eds.), *Girls, Boys, Books, Toys: Gender in Children's Literature and Culture*. Baltimore: Johns Hopkins University: 169–82.

Kluwer, Esther S., Jose A. M. Heesink, & Evert Van De Vliert. 1997. *Journal of Marriage and the Family* 59(3): 635–53.

Knight, Jennifer L., & Traci A. Giuliano. 2001. "He's a Laker, she's a 'looker': The consequences of gender-stereotypical portrayals of male and female athletes by the print media." *Sex Roles* 45(3–4): 217–29.

Knox, George W. 2001. The Satan's Disciples: A gang profile. *Journal of Gang Research* 8(4): 57–76.

Knudson-Martin, Carmen, & Anne Rankin Mahoney. 1998. "Language and processes in the construction of equality in new marriages." *Family Relations* 47(1): 81–91.

Kobayashi, Hideo. 1999. "The strategy of Japanese multinationals in the Asia-Pacific region at the turn of the century." *Economies et Societes* 33 (11–12): 289–310.

Koch, Jeffrey W. 1999. "Candidate gender and assessments of Senate candidates." *Social Science Quarterly* 80(1): 84–96.

Kochen, M., (ed.). 1989. *The Small World*. Norwood, NJ: Ablex.

Koegel, Paul M., Audrey Burnam, & Jim Baumohl. 1996. "The Causes of Homelessness." In Jim Baumohl, (ed.), *Homelessness in America*. Phoenix: Oryx Press: 24–33.

Koenig, Fredrick. 1985. *Rumor in the Marketplace*. Dover, Delaware: Auburn House.

Kohlberg, Lawrence. 1966. "A cognitive-developmental analysis of children's sex-role concepts and attitudes." In Eleanor E. Maccoby (ed.), *The Development of Sex Differences*. Stanford, CA: Stanford University.

Kohlberg, Lawrence. 1969. "Stage and sequence: The cognitive developmental approach to socialization. " In David A. Goslin (ed.), *Handbook of Socialization Theory and Research*. Chicago: Rand McNally.

Kohlberg, Lawrence. 1969. *Stages in the Development of Moral Thought and Action*. New York: Holt Rinehart & Winston.

Kohlberg, Lawrence. 1981. *The Psychology of Moral Development: The Nature and Validity of Moral Stages*. New York: Harper & Row.

Kohn, Alfie. 1986. *No Contest: The Case Against Competition*. Boston: Houghton Mifflin.

Kohn, Alfie. 1994. "Sports create unhealthy competition." In William Dudley (ed.), *Sports in America: Opposing Viewpoints*. San Diego: Greenhaven: 17–20.

Kohn, Melvin L. 1977. *Class and Conformity: A Study in Values*, 2nd ed. Homewood, IL: Dorsey.

Kohn, Melvin. 1978. "The benefits of bureaucracy." *Human Nature* (August): 60–66.

Kohut, Andrew, & Melissa Rogers. 2002. "Americans struggle with religion's role at home and abroad March 20." The Pew Research Center for the People and the Press. Available: http:www//pewforum.org/publications.

Kolata, Gina. 2002. "Research suggests more health care may not be better." *New York Times* (July 21): 1, 20.

Kollock, P., & M. Smith (eds.). 1997. *Communities in Cyberspace*. Berkeley: University of California Press.

Komai, Hiroshi. 2001. *Foreign Migrants in Contemporary Japan*. Melbourne, AS: Trans-Pacific Press.

Komarow, Steven. 2002. "Afghan women face rough road ahead." *USA Today* (March).

Kono, Clifford, Donald Palmer, Roger Friedland, & Matthew Zafonte. 1998. "Lost in space: The geography of interlocking corporate directorates." *American Journal of Sociology* (103/4): 863–911.

Kooistra, Paul, John S. Mahoney, & Lisha Bridges. 1993. "The unequal opportunity for equal ability hypothesis: Racism in the NFL?" *Sociology of Sport Journal* 10: 241–55.

Koopmans, Ruud. 1993. "The dynamics of protest waves." *American Sociological Review* 58: 637–58.

Korey, William. 1998. *NGOs and the Universal Declaration of Human Rights*. New York: St. Martin's.

Kornhauser, William. 1959. *The Politics of Mass Society*. New York: Free Press.

Kosmin, Barry, & Egon Mayer. 2001a. "American Religious Identity Survey *(ARIS).*" The Graduate Center, City University of New York. Available: http://www.gc.cuny.edu/studies/aris.

Kosmin, Barry, & Egon Mayer. 2001b. "Profile of the U.S. Muslim population." *ARIS Report No. 2* (October). American Religious Identity Survey. The Graduate Center, City University of New York.

Koszczuk, Jackie. 1999. "Gender equity in sports: Will Hastert go the mat?" *CQ Weekly* 57(13): 745–6.

Kotkin, Joel. 1993. *Tribes: How Race, Religion & Identity Determine Success in the New Global Economy*. New York: Random House.

Kotler, Jennifer A., Aletha C. Huston, & John C. Wright. 2001. "Television use in families with children." In Jennings Bryant & J. Alison Bryant (eds.), *Television and the American Family*. Mahwah, NJ: Lawrence Erlbaum: 33–48.

Kottak, Conrad Phillip. 1987. *Cultural Anthropology*. New York: Random House.

Kotz, David M. 2001. "Is Russia becoming capitalistic?" *Science and Society* 65(2): 157–81.

Kouba, Leonard & Judith Muasher. 1985. "Female circumcision in Africa: An overview." *African Studies Review* 28(1): 95–110.

Kourvetaris, George. 1997. *Political Sociology: Structure and Function*. Boston: Allyn & Bacon.

Kowalewski, David, & Karen L. Porter. 1992. "Ecoprotest: Alienation, deprivation or resources." *Social Science Quarterly* 73/3: 523–34.

Kozol, Jonathan. 1991. *Savage Inequalities: Children in America's Schools*. New York: Crown.

Krashen, Stephen. 2001. "Bilingual education works." *Rethinking Schools: An Urban Education Journal*. 15.(2). Available: http:www.rethinkingschools.org/Archives/15.

Kratcoski, Peter C., & Lucille D. Kratcoski. 1996. *Juvenile Delinquency*, 4th ed. Upper Saddle River, NJ: Prentice Hall.

Kraut, Robert Vicki: Lundmark, Michael Patterson, Sara Kiesler, Trides Mukopadhyay & William Scherlis. 1998. "Internet Paradox." *American Psychologist* 55: 1017–1031.

Kraybill, Donald B. 1989. *The Riddle of Amish Culture*. Baltimore, MD: Johns Hopkins University Press.

Krisberg, Barry et al. 1987. "The incarceration of minority youth." *Crime and Delinquency* 33(2): 173–205.

Kritsof, Nicholas D. 1997. "Where children rule." *New York Times Magazine* (August 17): 40–44.

Kroger, Jane. 1996. *Identity in Adolescence: The Balance Between Self and Other*. London: Routledge.

Kroska, Amy. 2000. "Time for theoretical bargaining: Reexamining theories of household labor." Paper presented at the American Sociological Association. Washington, DC (August).

Krovetz, Martin L. 1999. *Fostering Resiliency: Expecting All Students to Use their Minds and Hearts Well*. Thousand Oaks, CA: Corwin.

Krueger, Bill. 2001. "How aging is covered in the print media." *Generations* 25(3): 10–12.

Krysan, Maria, & William V. D'Antonio. 1992. "Voluntary associations." In Edgar F. Borgatta, & Marie L. Borgatta, (eds.), *Encyclopedia of Sociology*. New York: Macmillan: 2231–34.

Kubler-Ross, Elisabeth. 1969. *On Death and Dying*. New York: Macmillan.

Kuczynski, Alex. 2001. "The new feminine mystique: Variety of brash magazines upset the old stereotypes." *New York Times* (September 7): C1, C8.

Kuhlmann, Annette. 1996. "Indian country in the 1990s: Changing roles of American Indian women." Paper presented at the Midwest Sociological Society, Chicago, April.

Kuhn, Thomas. 1970. *The Structure of Scientific Revolutions*, 2nd ed. Chicago: University of Chicago Press.

Kuisel, Richard. 1993. *Seducing the French: The Dilemma of Americanization*. Berkeley: University of California.

Kulick, Don. 2000. "Gay and lesbian language." *Annual Review of Anthropology* 29: 243–85.

Kulick, Don. 2002. "Queer linguistics?" In Kathryn Campbell-Kibler (ed.), *Language and Sexuality: Contesting Meaning in Theory and Practice*. Stanford, CA: CSLI: 65–68.

Kumar, Krishnan. 1995. *From Post-Industrial to Post-Modern Society: New Theories of the Contemporary World*. Oxford, UK: Blackwell.

Kumar, Vinod. 1998. "Perspectives on activity and aging in the developing world." *Journal of Aging & Physical Activity* 6(3): 205–206.

Kurdek, Lawrence A. 1998. "Relationship outcomes and their predictors: Longitudinal evidence from heterosexual married, gay, gay cohabiting, and lesbian cohabiting couples." *Journal of Marriage and the Family* 60: 553–68.

Kurdek, Lawrence A., & Chad Kennedy. 2001. "Differences between couples who end their marriage by fault or no-fault legal procedures." *Journal of Family Psychology* 15(2): 241–53.

Kurian, Priya A. 2000. *Engendering the Environment: Gender in the World Bank's Environmental Policies*. Aldershot Burlington, VT: Ashgate.

Kurtz, Demie. 1995. *For Richer, For Poorer: Mothers Confront Divorce*. New York: Routledge.

Kurtz, S. M. 2002. "Doctor-patient communication: Principles and practices." *Canadian Journal of Neurological Sciences* 29(June): Suppl 2: S23–29.

Kutner, B., C. Wilkins & P. Yarrow. 1952. "Verbal attitudes and overt behavior involving racial prejudice." *Journal of Abnormal and Social Psychology* 47: 649–52.

Kuttner, Robert. 2001. "Body politics." *American Prospect* (Fall): A1.

Kuypers, J. A., & Vern L. Bengston. 1973. "Competence and social breakdown: A social psychological view of aging." *Human Development* 16(2): 37–49.

Kuznets, Simon. 1955. "Economic growth and income inequality." *The American Economic Review* 45: 1–28.

La Dou, Joseph. 1991. "Deadly migration: Hazardous industries' flight to the Third World." *Technology Review* 94/5: 46–53.

LaCelle-Peterson, Mark. 2000. "Choosing not to know: How assessment policies and practices obscure the education of language minority students." In Ann Filer (ed.), *Assessment: Social Practice and Social Product*. London: RoutledgeFalmer: 27–42.

Lacourse, Eric, Michael Claes, & Martine Villeneuve. 2001. "Heavy metal music and adolescent suicide risk." *Journal of Youth and Adolescence* 30(3): 321–32.

Ladd, Everett C., & Karlyn H. Bowman. 1998. *Attitudes Toward Economic Inequality*. Washington, DC: AEI Press.

Ladd,. Tony, & James A. Mathisen. 1999. *Muscular Christianity*. Grand Rapids, MI: Baker.

LaDuke, Winona. 1998. "Breastmilk, PCBs and motherhood." In Gwyn & Margo Okazawa-Rey (eds.), *Women's Lives: Multicultural Perspectives*. Mountain View, CA: Mayfield: 415–17.

LaFrance, Marianne. 2001. "Gender and social interaction." In Rhoda K. Unger (ed.), *Handbook of the Psychology of Women and Gender*. New York: John Wiley & Sons: 245–55.

Lake, Celinda C., & Vincent J. Breglio. 1992. "Different voices, different views: The politics of gender." In Paula Ries & Anne J. Stone (eds.), *The American Woman, 1992–93: A Status Report*. New York: W. W. Norton.

Lakoff, Robin. 1975. *Language and Women's Place*. New York: Colophon.

Lakoff, Robin. 1991. "You are what you say." In Evelyn Ashton-Jones & Gary A. Olson, (eds.), *The Gender Reader*. Boston: Allyn & Bacon.

Lakshmanan, Indira A. R. 2002. "Afghans calling 4.4m to classes." *Boston Globe* (March 23). Available: http://www.boston.com/dailyglobe2/082/nation/Afghans.

Lame Deer, John, & Richard Erdoes. 1972. *Lame Deer, Seeker of Visions*. New York: Simon & Schuster.

Lamont, Michelle, & Marcel Fournier. 1992. *Cultivating Differences: Symbolic Boundaries & the Making of Inequality*. Chicago: University of Chicago Press.

Lamont, Michelle. 1997. "Money, morals, and manners." In David M. Newman (ed.), *Sociology: Exploring the Architecture of Daily Life—Readings*. Thousand Oaks, CA: Pine Forge: 224–240.

Lancaster, William. 1997. *The Rwala Bedouin Today*. Prospect Heights, IL: Waveland.

Lancet. 2002. "A step forward for humanity?" 359(9310): 903.

Land, Kenneth C., Patricia L. McCall, & Lawrence E. Cohen. 1990. "Structural covariates of homicide rates: Are there any invariances across time and social space?" *American Journal of Sociology*, 95: 922–63.

Landén, M., O. Bodlund, L. Ekselius, G. Hambert, & B. Lundstrom. 2001. *Lakartidningen* 98 (July 25): 3322–26.

Landry, Bart. 1988. *The New Black Middle Class*. Berkeley: University of California Press.

Landry, Bart. 2000. *Black Working Wives: Pioneers of the American Family Revolution*. Berkeley: University of California.

Lane, David. 1985. *State and Politics in the USSR*. Oxford, UK: Blackwell.

Lane, Frederick S. 2001. *Obscene Profits: The Entrepreneurs of Pornography in the Cyber Age*. New York: Routlege.

Lane, Jan-Erik, & Svante O. Ersson. 1991. *Politics and Society In Western Europe*, 2nd ed. Newbury Park, CA: Sage.

Lane, Robert E. 2001. "Self-reliance and empathy: The enemies of poverty—and of the poor." *Political Psychology* 22(3): 473–92.

Lang, Eric. 1992. "Role conflict." In Edgar F. Borgatta & Marie L. Borgatta, eds., *Encyclopedia of Sociology*. New York: Macmillan: 1676–1679.

Lang, Kurt, & Gladys E. Lang. 1961. *Collective Dynamics*. New York: Thomas Y. Crowell.

Langan, Patrick A. 1991. "America's soaring prison population." *Science* (251): 1568–573.

Langlois, J. H., & L. Musselman. 1995. "Myths and mysteries of beauty." In D. R. Calhoun (ed.), *1996 Yearbook of Science and the Future*. Chicago: Encyclopedia Britannica.

Langston, D. 1992. "Tired of playing monopoly?" In M. L. Anderson, & P. H. Collins, (eds.), *Race, Class and Gender: An Anthology*. Belmont, CA: Wadsworth.

Langton, Phyllis A. 1994. "Obstetricians resistance to independent private practice by nurse-midwives in Washington, D.C. hospitals." *Women and Health* 22(1): 27–48.

Lannoy, Richard. 1975. *The Speaking Tree: A Study of Indian Culture and Society*. New York: Oxford University Press.

Lansford, Jennifer E., & Jeffrey G. Parker. 1999. "Children's interaction in triads: Behavioral profiles and effects of gender and patterns of friendships among members." *Developmental Psychology* 35(1): 8093.

Lantz, Paula M., John W. Lynch, James S. House, James M. Lepkowski, Richard P. Mero, Mark A. Musick, & David R. Williams. 2001. "Socioeconomic disparities in health change in a longitudinal study of U.S. adults: The role of health risk behaviors." *Social Science and Medicine* 53(1): 29–40.

Laosa, Luis M. 2001. "The new segregation." *ETS Policy Notes* 10(1)

Lapchick, Richard E. 2002. "2001 Racial and Gender Report Card." Boston: Center for the Study of Sport in Society. Available: www.sportinsociety.org.

Lapham, Lewis H. 1988. *Money & Class in America: Notes and Observations on our Civil Religion*. New York: Weidenfield and Nicolson.

LaPierre, Richard. 1934. "Attitudes versus actions." *Social Forces* 13: 230–37.

Laqueur, Walter. 1999. *The New Terrorism*. New York: Oxford University Press.

Laqueur, Walter. 2001. "Left, right and beyond: The changing face of terror." In James F. Hoge & Gideon Rose (eds.), *How Did it Happen? Terrorism and the New War*. New York: Public Affairs: 71–82.

Laquian, Aprodicio A. 1996. "The multi-ethnic and multicultural city: An Asian perspective." *International Social Science Journal* 48: 43–54.

Larana, E., H. Johnson, & J. R. Gusfield, (eds.) 1994. *New Social Movements: From Ideology to Identity*. Philadelphia: Temple University Press.

Larese, Steve. 2001. "Contemporary Indian economies in New Mexico." In Albert L. Hurtado & Peter Iverson (eds.), *Major Problems in American Indian History*, 2nd ed. Boston: Houghton Mifflin: 499–503.

Larmer, Brook. 1992. "Dead end kids." *Newsweek* (May 25): 38–40.

LaRose, H., J. Tracy & S. J. McKelvie. 1993. "Effects of gender on the physical attractiveness stereotype." *Journal of Psychology* 127: 677–80.

Larsen, Ralph S. 2002. "Business in partnership with the nonprofit sector." In C. Everett Koop, Clarence E. Pearson, & M. Roy Schwartz (eds.), *Critical Issues in Global Health*. San Francisco, CA: Jossey-Bass: 414–22.

Larson, C. J. 1995. "Theory & applied sociology." *Journal of Applied Sociology* 12(9): 13–29.

Larson, Gerald James. 1994. "Hinduism in India and in America." In Jacob Neusner (ed.), *World Religions in America: An Introduction*. Louisville, KY: Westminster/John Knox: 177–202.

Larson, Jan. 1996. "Temps are here to stay." *American Demographics* 18 (February): 26–31.

Lasch, Christopher. 1979. *Haven in a Heartless World*. New York: Basic Books.

Laslett, Barbara. 1990. "Unfeeling knowledge: Emotion & objectivity in the history of sociology." *Sociological Forum* 5: 413–434.

Lassila, Kathrin Day. 1999. "The new suburbanites." *Amicus Journal* 21(2): 16–21.

Latham, Michael C. 1997. *Human Nutrition in the Developing World*. United Nations: Food and Agriculture Organization.

Latham, Rob. 2002. *Consuming Youth: Vampires, Cyborgs and the Culture of Consumption*. Chicago: University of Chicago.

"Latinos failing to share in nation's economic boom." 2000. *Evansville Courier & Press* (March 26): A10.

Lauer, Robert H. 1991. *Perspectives on Social Change*, 4th ed. Boston: Allyn & Bacon.

Lauer, Robert H., & Jeanette C. Lauer. 1991. *Marriage and Family: The Quest for Intimacy*. Dubuque, IA: William C. Brown.

Lauer, Robert H., Jeanette C. Lauer, & Sarah T. Kerr. 1990. "The long-term marriage: Perceptions of stability and satisfaction." *International Journal of Aging and Human Development* 31(3): 189–95.

Laumann, Edward O., & Jenna Mahay. 2002. "The social organization of women's sexuality." In Gina M. Wingood & Ralph J. DiClemente (eds.), *Handbook of Women's Sexual and Reproductive Health: Issues in Women's Health*. New York: Kluwer Academic/Plenum: 43–70.

Laumann, Edward O., John H. Gagnon, Robert T. Michael, & Stuart, Michaels. 1994. *The Social Organization of Sexuality: Sexual Practices in the United States*. Chicago: University of Chicago.

Laumann, Edward, & David Knoke. 1987. *The Organizational State*. Madison: University of Wisconsin Press.

Lauzen, Martha M. 1999. "Stuck in primetime: A television study of gender." Los Angeles: Women in Film. Available: www.wif.org/features).

Lavoie, Marc. 1989. "Stacking, performance differentials and salary discrimination in professional ice hockey." *Sociology of Sport Journal* 6: 17–35.

Lawrence, Charles R., & Mari J. Matsuda. 1997. *We Won't Go Back*. New York: Houghton Mifflin.

Laws, Judith Long, & Pepper Schwartz. 1981. *Sexual Scripts: The Social Construction of Female Sexuality*. Washington, DC: University Press.

Lawson, Erma Jean, & Aaron Thompson. 1999. *Black Men and Divorce*. Thousand Oaks, CA: Sage.

Lazarsfeld, P. F., & J. G. Reitz. 1989. "History of applied sociology." *Sociological Practice* 7: 42–52.

Le Naour, Jean-Yves. 2001. "Laughter and tears in the Great War: The need for laughter/the guilt of humor." *Journal of European Studies* 31(3/4): 265–75.

Leaper, Campbell. 2002. "Parenting girls and boys." *In Handbook of Parenting, Volume I: Children and Parenting*. Mahwah, NJ: Lawrence Erlbaum: 189–225.

Lease, A. Michele, & Jennifer L. Axelrod. 2001. "Position of peer group's perceived organizational structure: Relation to social status and friendship." *Journal of Early Adolescence* 21(4): 377–40.

LeBon, Gustave. 1960. *The Crowd: A Study of the Popular Mind*. New York: Viking. Originally published in 1896.

Lee, Barrett A. 1992. "Homelessness." In Edgar F. Borgatta & Marie L. Borgatta (eds.), *Encyclopedia of Sociology*, Vol. 2. New York: Macmillan: 843–847.

Lee, Deborah. 2000. "Hegemonic masculinity and male feminisation: The sexual harassment of men at work."

Lee, Martin A., & Norman Solomon. 1990. *Unreliable Sources: A Guide to Detecting Bias in News Media*. New York: Lyle Stuart.

Lee, Richard M., & Tina Hsin-tine Liu. 2001. "Coping with intergenerational family conflict: Comparison of Asian Americans, Hispanic and European American college students." *Journal of Counseling Psychology* 48(4): 410–19.

Lee, Richard. 2002. *The Dobe/'hoansi*. Belmont, CA: Wadsworth/Thompson.

Lee, S. M. 1993. "Racial classifications in the U.S. census, 1890–1990." *Ethnic and Racial Studies* 16: 75–94.

Lee, Sharon M. 1998. "Asian Americans: Diverse and growing." *Population Bulletin* 53(2).

Lee, Shu-ching, 1953. "China's traditional family: Its characteristics and disintegration." *American Sociological Review* 18: 272–80.

Lee, Stacey J. 1996. *Unraveling the "Model Minority" Stereotype: Listening to Asian American Youth*. New York: Teacher's College Press.

Lee, Valerie E. 2001. *Restructuring High Schools for Equity and Excellence: What Works*. New York: Teacher's College Press.

Lee-Treweek, Geraldine, & Stephanie Linkogle (eds.). 2000. *Danger in the Field: Risk and Ethics in Social Research*. London: Routledge.

Lefcourt, Herbert M. 2000. *Humor: The Psychology of Living Bouyantly*. New York: Kluwer Academic/Plenum.

Lefcourt, Herbert M. 2002. "Humor." In C. R. Snyder & Shane J. Lopez (eds.), *Handbook of Positive Psychology*. London: Oxford University.

Leiblum, Sandra R. 2002. "Reconsidering gender differences in sexual desire: An update." *Journal of Sexual & Relationship Therapy* 17(1): 57–68.

Leibovici, Leonard, & Michael Lievre. 2002. "Medicalisation: Peering from inside medicine." *British Medical Journal* 324(April 13): 866.

Leicht, Kevin T., & Mary L. Fennell. 1997. "The changing organizational context of professional work." In John Hagan (ed.) *Annual Review of Sociology—1997*. Palo Alto, CA: Annual Reviews: 215–231.

Leisinger, Klaus, & Karin Schmitt. 1994. *All Our People: Population Policy with a Human Face*. Washington, DC: Island Press.

Lemann, Nicholas. 1991. *The Promised Land: The Great Black Migration and How It Changed America*. New York: Vintage.

Lemert, Charles. 1997. *Postmodernism Is Not What You Think*. Malden, MA: Blackwell.

Lemert, Charles. 2002. *Social Things*, 2nd ed. Lanham, MD: Rowman & Littlefield.

Lemert, Edwin M. 1951. *Social Pathology*. New York: McGraw-Hill.

Lemonick, Michael D. 2001. "Feeling the heat: Life in the greenhouse." *Time* (April 9): 22–29.

Lengermann, Patricia M., & Jill Niebrugge-Brantley. 1998. *The Women Founders: Sociology & Social Theory, 1830–1930*. New York: McGraw-Hill.

Lengermann, Patricia M., & Jill Niebrugge-Brantley. 2000. "Contemporary feminist theory." In George Ritzer, *Modern Sociological Theory*. New York: McGraw-Hill: 307–355.

Lenski, Gerhard. 1954. "Status crystallization: A nonvertical dimension of social status." *American Sociological Review* 19: 405–13.

Lenski, Gerhard. 1956. "Social participation and status crystallization." *American Sociological Review* 21: 458–64.

Lenski, Gerhard. 1966. *Power and Privilege: A Theory of Social Stratification*. New York: McGraw-Hill.

Leon, Sy. 1996. *None of the Above*. San Francisco: Fox & Wilkes.

Leonard, Wilbert M., II. 1998. *A Sociological Perspective of Sport*, 5th ed. Boston: Allyn & Bacon.

Lepel, Karen. 2001. "Race, Hispanic ethnicity, and the future of the college business major in the United States." *Journal of Education for Business* 76(4): 209–15.

Lerman, H. 1996. *Pigeonholing Women's Misery*. New York: Basic.

Lerner, Max, ed. 1948. *The Portable Veblen*. New York: Penguin.

Lerner, Nathan. 2000. *Religion, Beliefs, and International Human Rights*. Maryknoll, NY: Orbis.

LeRoy, Lauren. 2002. "Health foundations respond to the uninsured." In Peter Edelman, Dallas L. Salisbury, & Pamela J. Larson (eds.), *The Future of Social Insurance: Incremental Action or Fundamental Reform?* Washington, DC: National Academy of Social Insurance: 265–71.

Leslie, Connie. 1995. "You can't high-jump if the bar is set too low." *Newsweek* (November 6): 82–83.

Lester, David, & Melissa Whipple. 1996. "Music preference, depression, suicidal preoccupation, and personality: Comment on Stack and Gundlach's papers." *Suicide and Life-Threatening Behavior* 26: 68–70.

Lester, David. (1999/2000). "The social causes of suicide: A look at Durkeim's *Le Suicide* one hundred years later." *Omega: Journal of Death & Dying* 40(2): 307–221.

Lester, David. 1997. *Suicide in American Indians*. New York: Nova.

Lester, David. 2000. "Suicide in emigrants from the Indian subcontinent." *Transcultural Psychiatry* 37(2): 243–54.

Lever, Janet, & S. Wheeler. 1993. "Mass media and the experience of sport," *Communication Research* (20/1): 125–43.

Lever, Janet. 1978. "Sex differences in the complexity of children's play and games." *American Sociological Review* 43(4): 471–83.

Lever, Janet. 1983. *Soccer Madness*. Chicago: University of Chicago Press.

Levine J. M., & R. L. Moreland. 1998. "Small groups." In D. T. Gilbert at al. (eds.), *Handbook of Social Psychology*. New York: Random House: 415–469.

Levine, A., & J. Cureton (eds.). 1998. *When Hope and Fear Collide: A Portrait of Today's College Student*. San Francisco: Jossey-Bass.

Levine, Martin P. 1998. *Gay Macho: The Life and Death of the Homosexual Clone*. New York: New York University.

Levine, Robert S., James E. Foster, Robert E. Fullilove, Mindy L. Fullilove, Nathaniel C. Briggs, Pamela C. Hull, Baqar A. Husaini, & Charles H. Hennekens. 2001. "Black-white inequalities in mortality and life expectancy, 1933–1999: Implications for Healthy People 2010." *Public Health Reports* 116(5): 474–83.

Levinson, Daniel. 1978. *The Seasons of a Man's Life*. New York: Knopf.

Levinson, Daniel. 1986. "A conception of adult development." *American Psychologist* 41: 3–13.

Levinson, David. 1989. *Family Violence in Cross-Cultural Perspective*. Newbury Park, CA: Sage.

Levinson, S. C. 1996. "Language and space." *Annual Review of Anthropology* 25: 463–71.

Levinson, S. C. 1997. "From outer to inner space: Linguistic categories and non-linguistic thinking." In J. Nuyts & E. Pederson (eds.), *The Relationship between Linguistic and Conceptual Representation*. Cambridge, UK: Cambridge University: 13–45.

Levstik, Linda S. 2001. "Daily acts of ordinary courage: Gender-equitable practice in the social studies classroom." In Patricia O'Reilly & Elizabeth M. Penn (eds.), *Educating Young Adolescent Girls*. Mahwah, NJ: Lawrence Erlbaum: 189–211.

Levy, Becca R., & R. Banaji Mahzarin. 2002. "Implicit ageism." In Todd D. Nelson (ed.), *Ageism: Stereotyping and Prejudice Against Older Persons*. Cambridge, MA: MIT Press.

Levy, Frank. 1988. *Dollars & Dreams: The Changing American Income Distribution*. New York: W. W. Norton.

Levy, Marion J. Jr. 1992. "Confucianism and modernization." *Society* (24/4): 15–18.

Levy, Steven. 1996. "Working in Dilbert's world." *Newsweek* (August 12): 52–57.

Lewelling, Vickie W. 1997. "Official English and English plus: An update." *ERIC Digest*. (May): EDO-FL-97-07.

Lewis, Chris H. 2002. "Global industrial civilization: The necessary collapse." In Michael N. Dobkowski & Isidor Wallimann (eds.), *On the Edge of Scarcity: Environment, Resources, Population, Sustainability, and Conflict*. Syracuse, NY: Syracuse University: 16–29.

Lewis, David L. 1993. *The Biography of a Race: 1868–1919*, New York: Holt.

Lewis, David, & Tina Wallace (eds.). 2000. *New Roles and Relevance: Development NGOs and the Challenge of Change*. Bloomfield, CT: Kumarian.

Lewis, J. D., & R. Smith. 1980. *American Sociology and Pragmatism*. Chicago: University of Chicago Press.

Lewis, Jerry M. 1989. "A value-added analysis of the Heysel Stadium soccer riot." *Current Psychology* (8/1): 15–29.

Lewis, Jerry M., & Michael Kelsey. 1994. "The crowd crush at Hillsborough." In Russell Dynes & Kathleen Tierney (eds.), *Disasters, Collective Behavior & Social Organization*. Newark: University of Delaware.

Lewis, M. 1978. *The Culture of Inequality*. New York: New American Library.

Lewis, Mark. 2001. "Publishing: The Ambrose saga." *Forbes* (February 27). Available: http://www.forbes.com/2002/01/10.

Lewis, Mark. S. 1996. "Supply and demand for teachers of color." *ERIC Digest*. Washington, DC: ERIC Clearinghouse on Teaching and Teacher Education.

Lewis, Oscar. 1966. "The culture of poverty." *Scientific American 115* (October): 19–25.

Lewis, Pierce, Casey McCracken, & Roger Hunt. 1994. "Politics: Who cares?" *American Demographics* (16/10): 20–26.

Li, Shu-Chen. 2002. "Age is not necessarily aging: Another step towards understanding the 'clocks' that time aging." *Gerontology* 48(1): 5–12.

Liang, Clara. 2001. "Red light green light: Has China achieved its goals through the 2000 Internet revolution?". Available: http://law.vanderbilt.edu/journal/Vol345/Liang.

Liazos, Alexander. 1972. "The poverty of the sociology of deviance: Nuts, sluts and perverts." *Social Problems* (20/1): 103–20.

Liben, Lynn S., Holleen R. Krogh, & Rebecca S. Bigler. 2001. "Pink and blue collar jobs: Children's judgments of job status and job aspirations in relation to sex of worker." *Journal of Experimental Child Psychology* 79(4): 346–63.

Lichtenberger, B., & G. Naulleau. 1993. "Cultural conflicts and synergies in the management of French-German joint ventures." In P. S. Kirkbride (ed.), *Human Resource Management in Europe: Perspectives for the Nineties.* London: Routledge.

Lichtenstein, Bronwen. 2000. "Secret encounters: Black men, bisexuality, and AIDS in Alabama." *Medical Anthropology Quarterly* 14(3): 374–93.

Lichter, Daniel T., & David J. Eggebeen. 1993. "Rich kids, poor kids: Changing income inequality among American children." *Social Forces* 73: 761–780.

Lichter, Daniel T., & Nancy C. Landale. 1995. "Parental work, family structure, and poverty among Latino children." *Journal of Marriage and the Family* 57: 346–54.

Lichter, S. R., L. S. Lichter, & S. Rothman. 1994. *Prime Time: How TV Portrays American Culture.* Washington, DC: Regency.

Lichter, S. Robert, & Daniel R. Amundson. 1997. "Distorted reality: Hispanic characters in TV entertainment." In Clara Rodriquez E. *Latin Looks.* Boulder, CO: Westview Press: 57–72.

Lichter, S. Robert, & Daniel R. Amundson. 2000. "Distorted reality: Hispanic characters in tv entertainment." In Clara Rodriguez (ed.), *Latin Looks,* Boulder, CO: Westview: 57–92.

Lieberson, Stanley. 1992. "Einstein, Renoir, & Greely: Some thoughts about evidence in sociology." *American Sociological Review* 57: 1–15.

Liebow, Elliot. 1967. *Tally's Corner: A Study of Negro Streetcorner Men.* Boston: Little, Brown.

Liebow, Elliott. 1995. *Tell Them Who I Am: The Lives of Homeless Women.* New York: Penguin.

Lienemann, Wolfgang. 1998. "Churches and homosexuality: An overview of recent official church statements on sexual orientation." *Ecumenical Review.* January.

"Life after welfare is not exactly a bed of roses," 1999. *Evansville Courier-Press* (from the Associate Press) (May 12).

Liff, Sonia, & Kate Ward. 2001. "Distorted views through the glass ceiling: The construction of women's understandings of promotion and senior management positions." *Gender, Work & Organization* 8(1): 19–36.

Light, Andrews. 2001. "The urban blind spot in environmental ethics." *Environmental Politics* 10(1): 7–35.

Light, Donald W. 2000. "The medical profession and organizational change: From professional dominance to countervailing power." Chloe E. Bird, Peter Conrad, & Allen M. Fremont (eds.), *Handbook of Medical Sociology.* Upper Saddle River, NJ: Prentice Hall: 201–15.

Light, Donald W., & David Hughes. 2001. "Introduction: A sociological perspective on rationing: Power, rhetoric and situated practice." *Sociology of Health and Illness* 23(5): 551–69.

Light, Ivan H., & Edna Bonacich. 1988. *Immigrant Entrepreneurs: Koreans in Los Angeles, 1965–1982.* Berkeley: University of California Press.

Ligos, Melinda. 2001. "Escape route from sexist attitudes on Wall Street." *New York Times* (May 30): C10.

Lim, Hua Sing. 2001. *Japan's Role in Asia.* Singapore: Times Academic Press.

Lin, Nan, & Wen Xie. 1988. "Occupational prestige in urban China." *American Journal of Sociology* 93/4: 793–832.

Lincoln, James R., & Arne L. Kalleberg. 1990. *Culture Control and Commitment.* Cambridge, MA: Cambridge University Press.

Lind, Michael. 1995. *The Next American Nation.* New York: Free Press.

Lindblom, Charles. 1977. *Politics and Markets.* New York: Basic.

Lindenberg, Marc, & Coralie Bryant. 2001. *Going Global: Transforming Relief and Development NGOs.* Bloomfield, CT: Kumarian.

Lindgren, Sue A. 1995. *Justice Expenditures and Employment.* Washington, DC: Bureau of Justice Statistics.

Lindlof, T. 1995. *Qualitative Communications Research Methods.* Thousand Oaks, CA: Sage.

Lindner, Eileen W. 2002. *Yearbook of American & Canadian Churches.* New York: National Council of Churches.

Lindsey, Linda L. 1990. "The health status of Afghan refugees: Focus on women." *Women in Development Forum.* Women in Development Publication Series (August), Michigan State University.

Lindsey, Linda L. 1992. "Gender and the workplace: Some lessons from Japan." Paper presented at the Midwest Sociological Society, Kansas City.

Lindsey, Linda L. 1996a. "Full-time homemaker as unpaid laborer." In Paula J. Dubeck & Kathryn Borman (eds.), *Women and Work: A Handbook.* New York: Garland.

Lindsey, Linda L. 1996b. "Women and agriculture in the developing world." In Paula J. Dubeck & Kathryn Borman (eds.), *Women and Work: A Handbook.* New York: Garland: 435–37.

Lindsey, Linda L. 1997. *Gender Roles: A Sociological Perspective,* 3rd ed. Upper Saddle River, NJ: Prentice Hall.

Lindsey, Linda L. 1998. "Gender issues in Japanese style management: Implications for American corporations." Paper presented at the Asian Studies Development Program National Conference. Baltimore. (March).

Lindsey, Linda L. 1999. "Chinese minority women and empowerment." Paper presented at the Midwest Sociological Society, Minneapolis. (April).

Lindsey, Linda L. 1999. "The politics of cultural identity and minority women in China." Paper presented at the Mid-Atlantic Region for Asian Studies, Gettysburg, PA.

Lindsey, Linda L. 2000. "Living arrangements for the elderly: Alternatives to institutionalization." In Jeffrey C. Delafuente & Ronald B. Steward (eds.), *Therapeutics in the Elderly.* Cincinnati: Harvey Whitney Books.

Lindsey, Linda L. 2002. "Gender segregation in the global context: Focus on Afghanistan." Paper presented at the Midwest Sociological Society, Milwaukee, April.

Lindsey, Linda L. 2002. "Globalization and human rights: Focus on Afghan women." In *September 11 and Beyond.* Upper Saddle River, NJ: Prentice Hall: 62–67.

Link, B. G., F. T. Cullen, J. Frank, & J. F. Wozniak. 1987. "The social rejection of former mental patients." *American Journal of Sociology* (54/3).

Link, B. G., E. Susser, A. Stueve, J. Phelan, R. E. Moore, & E. Struening. 1994. "Lifetime and five-year prevalence of homelessness in the United States." *American Journal of Public Health:* 1907–1912.

Link, Bruce G., & Jo C. Phelan. 2001. "Conceptualizing stigma." *Annual Review of Sociology* 27: 363–385.

Linton, Ralph. 1936. *The Study of Man.* New York: Appleton-Century- Crofts.

Linz, Juan J. 1964. "An authoritarian regime: Spain." In Erik Allardt & Yrjo Littunen (eds.), *Ideologies and Party Systems.* Helsinki: Academic Bookstore.

Linz, Juan, & Alfred Stepan, (eds.). 1996. *Problems of Democratic Transition and Consolidation.* Baltimore, MD: Johns Hopkins University Press.

Liodakis, George. 2001. "The political economy of the transition and the transformation crisis in Eastern Europe." *East-West Journal of Economics and Business* 4(2): 45–64.

Lipke, David. 2000. "The state of matrimony." *American Demographics* 22(11): 14, 16.

Lipman, Steve. 2002. "Comic coexistence: Arab and Jewish comedians in Long Island show lend some laughs to difficult times." *The Jewish Week* (April 26).

Lipovetsky, Gilles. 1994. *The Empire of Fashion.* Princeton, NJ: Princeton University Press.

Lippa, Richard A., & Francisco D. Tan. 2001. "Does culture moderate the relationship between sexual orientation and gender-related personality traits?" *Cross-cultural Research: The Journal of Comparative Social Science* 35(1): 65–87.

Lippy, Charles H. 1999. "Pluralism and American religious life in the later twentieth century." In Peter W. Williams (ed.), *Perspectives on American Religion and Culture.* Malden, MA: Blackwell: 48–60.

Lips, Hilary M. 2001. *Sex & Gender: An Introduction.* Mountain View, CA: Mayfield.

Lipset, S. M. 1963. *Political Man: The Social Bases of Politics.* Garden City, New York: Anchor.

Lipset, S. M., Martin Trow, & James S. Coleman. 1956. *Union Democracy.* New York: Free Press.

Lipset, S. M. 1960. *Political Man: The Social Bases of Politics.* Garden City, NY: Doubleday.

Lipset, Seymour M. 1959. "Democracy and working-class authoritarianism." *American Sociological Review* 24: 482–502.

Lipset, Seymour M. 1982. "Social mobility in industrial societies." *Public Opinion* 5 (June/July): 41–44.

Lipset, Seymour Martin, & Reinhard Bendix. 1959. *Social Mobility in Industrial Society.* Berkeley: University of California Press.

Lipset, Seymour Martin, & William Schneider. 1983. *The Confidence Gap.* New York: Free Press.

Lipset, Seymour Martin. 1996. *American Exceptionalism: A Double-Edged Sword.* New York: W. W. Norton.

Lipton, Jack P., & Alan M. Hershaft. 1984. "Girl, woman, guy, man: The effects of sexist labeling." *Sex Roles* 10(3–4): 183–94.

Litfin, Karen T. 1999. "Constructing environmental security and ecological interdependence." *Global Governance* 5(3): 359–67.

Little, Craig B. 1995. *Deviance and Control.* Itasca, IL: Peacock.

Little, Jane Sneddon, & Robert K. Triest. 2002. "The impact of demographic change on U.S. labor markets." *New England Economic Review.* 1:47–67.

Liu, Yongfeng. 2001. "Improving adolescent reproductive health in China." Paper presented at the Global Health Council annual conference. Washington, DC: May 29–June 1.

Lively, Kit, Yi Shun Lai, Lisa Levinson, & Dylan Rivera. 1995. "Academics assess effect of new ban on racial preferences." *Chronicle of Higher Education* (August 1): A1.

Lloyd, Dorothy M. 1999. "Preparing exemplary teachers for the twenty-first century: Challenges and opportunities as we use what we know." In Kenneth A. Sirotnik & Roger Soder (eds.), *The Beat of a Different Drummer: Essays on Educational Renewal in Honor of John I. Goodlad.* New York: Peter Lang: 45–58.

Lloyd, Kim M., & Scott J. South. 1996. "Contextual influences on young men's transition to first marriage." *Social Forces* 74: 1097–119.

Lloyd-Sherlock, Peter. 2000. "Old age and poverty in developing countries: New policy challenges." *World Development* 28(12): 2157–68.

Lo, Clarence Y. H. 1982. "Countermovements & conservative movements in the contemporary US." *Annual Review of Sociology* 8: 107–34.

Locher, David A. 2002. *Collective Behavior.* Upper Saddle River, NJ: Prentice Hall.

Lockey, A. S., & R. D. Hardern. 2001. "Decision making by emergency physicians when assessing cardiac arrest patients on arrival at hospital." *Resuscitation* 50(1): 51–6.

Lockhart, Charles. 2001. *Protecting the Elderly: How Culture Shapes Social Policy.* University Park, PA: Pennsylvania State University.

Lockhart, William H. 2000. " 'We are one in life,' but not of one gender ideology: Unity, ambiguity and the Promise Keepers." *Sociology of Religion* 61(1): 73–92.

Lockheed, Marlaine E., & A. M. Verspoor et al. 1991. *Improving Primary Education in Developing Countries.* New York: Oxford University.

Lofland, John F. 1981. "Collective behavior: The elementary forms." In N. Rosenberg & R. H. Turner, (eds.), *Social Psychology: Sociological Perspectives.* New York: Basic.

Lofland, John. 1985. *Protest.* New Brunswick, NJ: Transaction.

Lofland, Lyn. 1973. *A World of Strangers.* New York: Basic.

Loftus, Jeni. 2001. "America's liberalization in attitudes toward homosexuality." *American Sociological Review* 66(5): 762–82.

Logue, John, & Daniel Bell. 2000. "Who will inherit the 'worker's paradise'? Worker ownership and enterprise efficiency in Russian privatization." In M. Donald Hancock & John Logue (eds.), *Transitions to Capitalism and Democracy in Russia and Central Europe: Achievements, Problems, Prospects.* Westport, CT: Praeger: 29–66.

Lombroso-Ferreo, G. 1972. *Lombroso's Criminal Man.* Montclair, NJ: Patterson Smith.

Lomnitz, Larissa. 1988. "The social and economic organization of a Mexican shanty town." In Josef Gugler (ed.), *The Urbanization of the Third World.* Oxford, UK: Oxford University: 242–63.

Long, Rachel. 2001. "When is ALF more than just an ALF?" *Contemporary Longterm Care* 24(3): 18–22.

Lonsway, Kimberly A. 1998. *First Year Campus Acquaintance Rape Education (FYCARE): Evaluating the Impact on Knowledge, Ideology, and Behavior.* Chicago: American Bar Foundation.

Lopez, Luis Enrique. 2001. "Literacy and intercultural bilingual education in the Andes." In David R. Olson & Nancy Torrance (eds.), *The Making of Literate Societies.* Malden, MA: Blackwell: 201–24.

Lorber, Judith. 1994. *Paradoxes of Gender.* New Haven, CT: Yale University Press.

Lorenz, Konrad. 1963. *On Aggression.* New York: Harcourt Brace & World.

Loscocco, Karyn A., & Glenna Spitze. 1990. "Working conditions, social support and the well-being of female and male factory workers." *Journal of Health & Social Behavior* 31: 313–27.

Lott, Bernice, & Diane Maluso. 1993. "The social learning of gender." In Anne E. Beall & Robert J. Sternberg (eds.), *The Psychology of Gender.* New York: Guilford.

Louie, Miriam Ching Yoon, & Nguyen Louie. 1998. "The conversation begins." In Gwyn Kirk & Margo Okazawa-Rey (eds.), *Women's Lives: Multicultural Perspectives.* Mountain View, CA: Mayfield: 145–51.

Louie, Miriam Ching. 2000. "Breaking the cycle: Women workers confront corporate greed globally." In Renae Bredin & Analouise Keating (eds.), *Perspectives: Gender Studies.* Madison, WI: Courseware: 199–211.

Loutfi, Martha Fetherolf (ed.). 2001. *Women, Gender, and Work: What is Equality and How Do We Get There?* Geneva: International Labour Office.

Loveless, Tom. 1999a. *The Tracking Wars: State Reform Meets School Policy.* Washington, DC: Brookings Institution.

Loveless, Tom. 1999b. "Will tracking reform promote social equity?" *Educational Leadership* 56(7): 28–32.

Low, Bobbi S. 2000. *Why Sex Matters: A Darwinian Look at Human Behavior.* Princeton, NJ: Princeton University.

Low, Setha. 1999. "Spatializing culture: The social production and social construction of public space in Costa Rica." In Setha Low (ed.), *Theorizing the City: The New Urban Anthropology Reader.* New Brunswick, NJ: Rutgers University: 111–137.

Lowe, Graham S. 1987. *Women in the Administrative Revolution: The Feminization of Clerical Work.* Toronto: University of Toronto Press.

Lowery, E. H. 1993. *Freedom and Community.* Albany: State University of New York.

Lowes, Mark D. 1999. *Inside the Sports Pages.* Toronto: University of Toronto Press.

Lowy, Joan. 2002. "World news: World city dwellers to outnumber rural." *Pittsburgh Post-Gazette* (April 8): 2.

Loy, John W. Jr. 1972. "Social origins and occupational mobility patterns of a selected sample of American athletes." *International Review of Sport Sociology* 7: 5–12.

Loy, John W., & D. Booth. 2000. "Functionalism, sport, and society." In Jay Coakley & E. Dunning (eds.), *Handbook of Sports Studies.* London: Sage: 9–27.

Loy, John W., & Joseph F. McElvogue. 1970. "Racial segregation in American sport." *International Review of Sport Sociology* (5): 5–24.

Lozano, Beverly. 1989. *The Invisible Work Force.* New York: Free Press.

Lubeck, Sally, Patricia Jessup, Mary deVries, & Jackie Post. 2001. "The role of culture in program improvement." *Early Childhood Research Quarterly* 16: 499–523.

Lucal, Betsy. 1994. "Class stratification in introductory textbooks: Relational or distributional models?" *Teaching Sociology* 22: 139–150.

Lucas, Samuel Roundfield. 1999. *Tracking Inequality: Stratification and Mobility in American High Schools.* New York: Teacher's College Press.

Lucas, Scott E. 1994. *Steroids.* Hillside, NJ: Enslow.

Lucy, John A. 1997. "Linguistic relativity." *Annual Review of Anthropology* 26: 291–312.

Lueptow, Lloyd B., Lori Garovich-Szabo, & Margaret B. Lueptow. 2001. "Social change and the persistence of sex-typing." *Social Forces* 80(1).

Luker, Kristin. 1978. *Taking Chances: Abortion and the Decision Not to Contracept.* Berkeley and Los Angeles: University of California.

Lukes, Steven. 1974. *Power.* London: Macmillan.

Lundskow, George N. 2002. *Awakening to an Uncertain Future: A Case Study of the Promise Keepers.* New York: Peter Lang.

Lungo, Mario. 2000. "Downtown San Salvador: Housing public spaces and economic transformation." In Mario Polese & Richard Stren (eds.), *The Social Sustainability of Cities: Diversity and the Management of Change.* Toronto: University of Toronto: 228–49.

Luo, Jar-Der. 1997. "The significance of networks in the initiation of small businesses in Taiwan." *Sociological Focus* 12(2): 297–317.

Lurie, Alison. 1981. *The Language of Clothes.* New York: Vintage.

Lush, Tamara. 1998. "El Nino winter has misery to spare." *USA Today* (February 24): 3A.

Luther, William M. 2001. *The Marketing Plan: How to Prepare and Implement It.* New York: AMACOM.

Lyman, Stanford M., ed. 1995. *Social Movements: Critiques, Concepts, Case Studies.* NY: New York University Press.

Lynch, Edward A. 1998. "Reform and religion in Latin America." *Orbis* 42(2): 263–81.

Lynch, John W., George A. Kaplan & Sarah J. Shema. 1997. "Cumulative Impact of Sustained Economic Hardship on Physical, Cognitive, Psychological, and Social Functioning," *New England Journal of Medicine* (337/26): 1889–1895.

Lynch, John W., George A. Kaplan, Elsie R. Pamuk, Richard D. Cohen, Katherine E. Heck, Jennifer L. Balfour, & Irene H. Yen. 1999. In Ichiro Kawachi, Bruce P. Kennedy, & Richard G. Wilkinson (eds.), *The Society and Population Health Reader, Volume I—Income Inequality and Wealth.* New York: New Press: 9–81.

Lynch, Lisa M. 2000. "Trends in and consequences of investments in children." In Sheldon H. Danziger & Jane Waldfogel (eds.), *Securing the Future: Investing in Children from Birth to College.* New York: Russell Sage.

Lynch, Merrill. 1994. "Rediscovering Criminology: Lessons From the Marxist Tradition." In Donald McQuarie & Patrick McGuire (eds.), *Marxist Sociology: Surveys of Contemporary Theory & Research.* New York: General Hall.

Lynch, Michael, & W. Byron Groves. 1989. *A Primer in Radical Criminology,* 2nd ed. Albany, NY: Harrow & Heston.

Lynch, Michael. 1994. "Rediscovering criminology: Lessons from the Marxist tradition." In Donald McQuarie & Patrick McGuire (eds.), *Marxist Sociology: Surveys of Contemporary Theory and Research.* New York: General Hall.

Lyon, David. 2000. *Jesus in Disneyland: Religion in Postmodern Times.* Cambridge, UK: Polity.

Lyotard, Jean F. 1993. *The Post-Modern Explained.* Minneapolis: University of Minnesota Press.

Lyson, T. A., & G. D. Squires. 1993. "The 'lost generation' of sociologists." *ASA Footnotes* 21: 4–5.

Mabogunje, Akin L. 1990. "The organization of urban communities in Nigeria." *International Social Science Journal* 42(3): 355–66.

Mabry, Marcus. 1999. "The Price Tag on Freedom," *Newsweek* (June 3): 50–51.

Macaulay, Marcia. 2001. "Tough talk: Indirectness and gender in requests for information." *Journal of Pragmatics* 33(2): 293–316.

Maccoby, Eleanor E. 1998. *The Two Sexes: Growing Up Apart, Coming Together.* Cambridge, MA: Belknap/Harvard University.

Maccoby, Eleanor E. 2000. "Perspectives on gender development." *International Journal of Behavioral Development* 24(4): 398–406.

MacCoun, Robert J., & Peter Reuter. 1999. "Does Europe Do It Better?" *The Nation* (September 20): 28–30.

Machacek, John. 2002. "Prescription drugs hot issue again in 2002 election." *TimesRecorder* (July 5). Available: http:www.zanesvilletimesrecorder.com/news/stories/20020705.

Mack, Raymond W., & Calvin P. Bradford. 1979. *Transforming America: Patterns of Social Change,* 2nd ed. New York: Random House.

MacKay, Judith. 2001. "Global sex: Sexuality and sexual practices around the world." *Sexual & Relational Therapy* 16(1).

MacKenzie, Donald A., & Judy Wajcman (eds). 1999. *The Social Shaping of Technology,* 2nd ed. Bristol, PA: Taylor & Francis.

Mackey, Ricard A., & Bernard A. O'Brien. 1999. "Adaptation in lasting marriages." *Families in Society* 80(6): 587–96.

MacKinnon, Catharine A. 2000a. "The social causes of sexual harassment." In Edmund Wall (ed.), *Sexual Harassment, Confrontation and Decisions.* Amherst, NY: Prometheus: 141–56.

MacKinnon, Catharine A. 2000b. "Sexual harassment as sex discrimination." In Edmund Wall (ed.), *Sexual Harassment, Confrontation and Decisions.* Amherst, NY: Prometheus: 157–66.

MacKinnon, Catherine A. 2001. *Sex Equality.* New York: Foundation Press.

MacKinnon, Catherine. 1983. "Feminism, Marxism, method, and the state: An agenda for theory." *Signs* 7: 635–658.

MacKinnon, Catherine. 1989. *Toward a Feminist Theory of the State.* Cambridge, MA: Harvard University.

MacKinnon, Neil J., & Tom Langford. 1994. "The meaning of occupational scores." *The Sociological Quarterly* 35/2: 215–245.

MacKinnon-Lewis, Carol, James M. Frabutt, & Angela M. Walker. 2002. "Racial socialization messages and the quality of mother/child interactions in African American families." *Journal of Early Adolescence* 22(2): 200–217.

Macklin, Ruth. 1999. *Against Relativism: Cultural Diversity and the Search for Ethical Universals in Medicine.* New York: Oxford University.

MacLeod, Jay. 1987. *Ain't No Makin' It.* Boulder, CO: Westview.

MacLeod, Roderick D., & Mary Potter. 2001. "On reflection: Doctors learning to care for people who are dying." *Social Science & Medicine* 52(11): 1719–27.

MacRae, C. Neil, Charles Stangor, & Miles Hewstone. 1999. 1996. *Stereotypes & Stereotyping.* New York: Guilford.

Madden, Janice Fanning. 2000. "Jobs, cities, and suburbs in the global economy." *Annals of the American Academy of Political and Social Science* 572 (Nov.): 78–89.

Madsen, Richard, William M. Sullivan, Ann Swidler, & Steven M. Sherwood. 2002. "Introduction." In R. Madsen, W. M. Sullivan, A. Swidler, & S. M. Tipton (eds.), *Meaning and Modernity: Religion, Polity, and Self.* Berkeley: University of California.

Madsen, Richard. 2002. "Comparative cosmopolis: Discovering different paths to moral integration in the modern ecumene." In R. Madsen, W. M. Sullivan, A. Swidler, & S. M. Tipton (eds.), *Meaning and Modernity: Religion, Polity, and Self.* Berkeley: University of Califonia: 105–123.

Magana, Sandra M. 1999. "Puerto Rican families caring for an adult with mental retardation: Role of familism." *American Journal on Mental Retardation* 104(5): 466–82.

Magonet, Jonathan. 2002. "Judaism." In John Bowker (ed.), *The Cambridge Illustrated History of Religions.* Cambridge, UK: Cambridge University: 180–213.

Maguire, Joe A. 1988. "Race & position assignment in English soccer." *Sociology of Sport Journal* 5: 257–69.

Maguire, Kathleen, & Ann L. Pastore, eds. 2001. *Sourcebook of Criminal Justice Statistics.* Available: www.albany.edu/sourcebook.

Maguire, P. 1984. "Women in development: An alternative analysis." Boston: Center for International Education, University of Massachusetts.

Mahal, Montarin, & Elaine Lindgren. 2002. "Microfinance and women's empowerment in rural Bangladesh." Paper presented at the Midwest Sociological Society, Milwaukee.

Maheu, Louis, (ed.), 1995. *Social Movements & Social Classes.* Newbury Park, CA: Sage.

Mahmoody, Betty. 1991. *Not Without My Daughter.* New York: St. Martin's.

Mahoney, Annette, Nalini Tarakeshwar, Aaron B. Swank, & Kenneth I. Pargament. 2001. "Religion in the home in the 1980s and 1990s: A meta-analytic review and conceptual analysis of links between religion, marriage, and parenting." *Journal of Family Psychology* 15(4): 559–96.

Mahony, Diana L., & Louis G. Lipman. 2001. "Theme issue on humor and laughter: Guest editor's introduction." *Journal of General Psychology* 128(2): 117.

Maiese, D. R. 2001. "Healthy people 2010—leading health indicators for women." *Women's Health Issues* 12(4): 155–64.

Maiga, Modibo. 2001. "Groupe pivot: Capacity building successes and lessons learned." Paper presented at the Global Health Council annual conference. Washington, DC: May 29–June 1.

Maines, Patrick D. 1993. "Whatever happened to free speech?" *American Journalism Review* (November).

Malcomson, Scott L. 2000. *The American Misadventure of Race.* New York: Farrar, Straus & Giroux.

Malec, Michael A. 1997. "Gender equity in athletics." In Gregg L. Carter (ed.), *Perspectives on Current Social Problems.* Boston: Allyn & Bacon: 209–218.

Maley, William (ed.). 2001. *Fundamentalism Reborn? Afghanistan and the Taliban.* New York: New York University.

Malsen, Geoff. 2000. "Australia's Aborigines struggle to keep gains and exhibit their value." *Times Higher Education Supplement* 1520 (January 1): 10–11.

Manchester, William. 1993. *A World Lit Only by Fire.* Boston: Little, Brown.

Mandel, Michael, & Paul Magnusson. 1993. "The economics of crime." *Business Week* (December 13): 72–85.

Mann, Judy. 2000. "We need the abortion pill now." *Washington Post* (June 23): C9.

Manning, Wendy D., & Nancy S. Landale, 1996. "Racial and ethnic differences in premarital childbearing." *Journal of Marriage and the Family* 58(1): 63–77.

Mantsios, Gregory. 2001. "Media magic: Making class invisible." In Paula S. Rothenberg (ed.), *Race, Class and Gender in the United States.* New York: Worth: 563–71.

Mantsios, G. 1995. "Media magic: Making class invisible." In Paula S. Rothenberg, (ed.), *Race, Class and Gender in the United States.* New York: St. Martin's.

Marais, Hein. 2001. *South Africa: Limits to Change: The Political Economy of Transition.* Cape Town, South Africa: University of Cape Town.

Maran, Meredith. 2000. *Class Dismissed: A Year in the Life of an American High School, A Glimpse into the Heart of a Nation.* New York: St. Martin's.

Marangos, John. 2002. "A political economy approach to the neoclassical model of transition." *American Journal of Economics and Sociology* 61(1): 259–76.

Maras, Pam, & Rupert Brown. 2000. "Effects of different forms of school contact on children's attitudes toward disabled and nondisabled peers." *The British Journal of Educational Psychology* 70: 337–51.

Marcus, Robert E., & Phyllis D. Betzer. 1996. "Attachment and antisocial behavior in early adolescence." *Journal of Early Adolescence* 16(2): 229–48.

Marger, Martin N. 1993. "The mass media as a power institution." in Marvin E. Olsen & Martin N. Marger (eds.), *Power in Modern Societies.* Boulder, CO: Westview: 238–249.

Marger, Martin N. 2000. *Racial and Ethnic Relations,* 5th ed. Belmont, CA: Wadsworth.

Marger, Martin N. 2002. *Social Inequality: Patterns and Processes,* 2nd ed. Boston: McGraw-Hill.

Marger, Martin. 1998. *Social Inequality: Patterns and Processes.* Mountain View, CA: Mayfield.

Margolin, Leslie. 1992. "Deviance on record." *Social Problems* 39: 58–70.

Marin, Rick, & T. Trent Gegax. 1997. "'Sell in,' bliss out." *Newsweek* (December 8): 72–74.

Marine, Gene. 1969. *The Black Panthers.* New York: Signet.

Mark, N. 1998. "Beyond individual differences: Social differentiation from first principles." *American Sociological Review* 63: 309–330.

Markert, John. 2001. "Sing a song of drug use-abuse: Four decades of drug lyrics in popular music." *Sociological Inquiry* 71(2): 194–220.

Marks, Guy. 1999. "The winds of change." *Geographical Magazine* 71(10): 20–5.

Marks, James. 2002. "Charting new directions in health promotion policy." February 15. Centers for Disease Control. Available: http://www.ncsl.org/programs/health/marks.

Marks, Jonathan. 1994. "Black, white, other." *Natural History* 8: 32–35.

Marks, Nadine. 1996. "Socioeconomic status, gender, and health at midlife." *Research in the Sociology of Health Care* 13(a): 135–52.

Marks, Stephen R. 1994. "Intimacy in the public realm: The case of co-workers." *Social Forces* 72: 843–858.

Markson, Elizabeth W., & Carol A. Taylor. 2000. "The mirror has two faces." *Aging & Society* 20(2): 137–60.

Marquardt, Michael J., & Lisa Horvath. 2001. *Global Teams: How Top Multinationals Span Boundaries and Cultures with High-Speed Teamwork.* Palo Alto, CA: Davies-Black.

Marriot, M. 1998. "Internet unleashing a dialogue on race," *New York Times* (March 8).

Marsden, George M. 1991. *Understanding Fundamentalism and Evangelicalism.* Grand Rapids, MI: William B. Eerdmans.

Marsden, Peter V. 1992. "Social network theory." In Edgar F. Borgatta & Marie L. Borgatta, (eds.), *Encyclopedia of Sociology,* vol 4. New York: Macmillan: 1887–1894.

Marshall, Barbara L. 2000. *Configuring Gender: Explorations in Gender and Politics.* Peterborough, Ontario, CN: Broadview.

Marshall, Donald S. 1971. "Too much sex in Mangaia." *Psychology Today* (4/9): 43 ff.

Martin, Carol Lynn, & Lisa M. Dinella. 2002. "Children's gender cognitions, the social environment, and sex differences in cognitive domains." In Ann McGillicuddy-De Lisi & Richard De Lisi (eds.), *Biology, Society and Behavior: The Development of Sex Differences in Cognition: Advances in Applied Developmental Psychology, Volume 21.* Westport, CT: Ablex: 207–39.

Martin, Carol Lynn. 2000. "Cognitive theories of gender development." In Thomas Eckes & Hanns M. Trautner (eds.), *The Developmental Social Psychology of Gender.* Mahwah, NJ: Lawrence Erlbaum.

Martin, James. 2001. "Television after September 11." *America* 185 (December 10): 20–21.

Martin, Patricia Yancey, & Robert H. Hummer. 2001. "Fraternities and rape on campus." In Laurel Richardson, Verta Taylor, & Nancy Whittier (eds.), *Feminist Frontiers 5.* Boston: McGraw-Hill: 444–53.

Martin, Susan Erlich. 1995. "Sexual harassment: The link joining gender stratification, sexuality and women's economic status." In Jo Freeman (ed.), *Women: A Feminist Perspective.* Mountain View, CA: Mayfield.

Martin, Teresa, & Larry Bumpass. 1989. "Recent trends in marital disruption." *Demography* 26: 37–51.

Martin, William G., & Mark Beittel. 1998. "Toward a global sociology? Evaluating current conceptions, methods, and practices." *Sociological Quarterly* 39: 139–61.

Martinez, Gaspar. 2001. *Confronting the Mastery of God: Political, Liberation, and Public Theologies.* New York: Continuum.

Martinson, Robert. 1974. "What works? Questions and answers about prison reform." *Public Interest* 35: 22–54.

Marty, Martin E. 1959. *The New Shape of American Religion.* New York: Harper & Row.

Marty, Martin E. 1974. "Two kinds of civil religion." In Russell E. Richey & Donald G. Jones, (eds.), *Civil Religion in America.* New York: Harper & Row: 139–57.

Marwell, Gerald, Pamela Oliver, & Ralph Prahl. 1988. "Social networks & collective action." *American Journal of Sociology* 94: 502–34.

Marwick, Charles. 2002. "U.S. report calls for tighter controls on complementary medicine." *British Medical Journal* 324(April 13): 870.

Marx, Anthony W. 1998. *Making Race and Nation: A Comparison of South Africa, the United States, and Brazil.* Cambridge: Cambridge University.

Marx, Gary T., & Douglas McAdam. 1994. *Collective Behavior and Social Movements.* Upper Saddle River, NJ: Prentice Hall.

Marx, Gary. 1985a. "The surveillance society." *The Futurist* 19 (June): 21–26.

Marx, Gary. 1985b. "I'll be watching you: Reflections on the new surveillance." *Dissent* 32 (Winter): 26–34.

Marx, Gary. 1988. *Undercover: Police Surveillance in America.* Berkeley: University of California Press.

Marx, Karl. 1848/1964. *Karl Marx: Early Writings.* (T. B. Bottomore, ed.). New York: McGraw-Hill.

Marx, Karl. 1867/1975. *Capital: A Critique of Political Economy.* New York: International.

Masini, Blasé Edward. 1998. "Socialization and selection processes of adolescent peer groups." *Dissertation Abstracts International: Section B: The Sciences & Engineering* 59(6-B) (December): 3096. Loyola University.

Masland, T. 1994. "Will it be peace or punishment?" *Newsweek* (August 1): 3.

Mason, Andrew, Sang-Hypo Lee, & Gerard Russo. 2002 "As Asia's population ages, worries grow about the future." *Asia Pacific Issues* 58 (January). Honolulu, HI: East-West Center.

Mason, Gail. 2002. *The Spectacle of Violence: Homophobia, Gender and Knowledge.* London: Routledge.

Mason, Karen Openheim. 1994. "Do population programs violate women's human rights?" *AsiaPacific Issues* No. 15: August.

Mason, Mary Ann, Arlene Skolnick, & Stephen D. Sugarman (eds.). 1998. *All Our Families: New Policies for a New Century.* New York: Oxford University.

Masoro, Edward J. 1999. *Challenges of Biological Aging.* New York: Springer.

Massey, D. S. & N. A. Denton. 1993. *American Apartheid: Segregation and the Making of the Underclass.* Cambridge, MA: Harvard University Press.

Massey, Rachel. 2001. "Global warming: An opportunity for world response." *Humanist* 61(2): 5–7.

Masters, William H., & Virginia Johnson. 1966. *Human Sexual Response.* Boston: Little, Brown.

Masters, William H., & Virginia Johnson. 1970. *Human Sexual Inadequacy.* Boston: Little, Brown.

Mastrofski, Stephen D., & R. Richard Ritti. 1996. "Police training and the effects of organization on drunk driving enforcement." *Justice Quarterly* 13: 291–320.

Mater, Marie A. 2001. "A structural transformation for a global public sphere? The use of new technologies by nongovernmental organizations and the United Nations." In Robert Asen & Daniel C. Brouwer (eds.), *Counterpublics and the State*. Albany: State University of New York.

Mathews, T. J., Fay Menacker, & Marian F. MacDorman. 2002. "Infant mortality statistics from the 2000 period linked birth/infant death data set." *National Vital Statistics Reports* 50(12): August 28.

Mathews, T. J., Marian F. MacDorman, & Fay Menacker. 2002. "Infant mortality statistics from the 1999 period linked birth/infant death data set." *National Vital Statistics Reports* 50(4) January 30.

Mathews, T. J., S. J. Ventura, S. C. Curtin, & J. A. Martin. 1998. *Births of Hispanics: 1989–1995*. Washington, DC: National Center for Health Statistics.

Mathewson, Clayton Dane. 2001. "A theoretical study of masculine archetypes: Embraced and rejected in children's cinema." *Dissertation Abstracts International, A: The Humanities and Social Sciences* 62(5) (November): 1962-A.

Mathiesen, James A. 1990. "Reviving 'muscular christianity': Gil Dodds & the institutionalization of sports evangelism." *Sociological Focus*: 23: 233–49.

Maton, Kenneth I., & Elizabeth A. Wells. 1995. "Religion as a community resource for well-being: Prevention, healing, and empowerment pathways." *Journal of Social Issues* 51: 177–93.

Matsueda, Ross L. 1992. "Reflected appraisals, parental labeling and delinquency," *American Journal of Sociology* 97: 1577–1611.

Matsumoto, David. 2000. *Culture and Psychology: People Around the World*. Belmont, CA: Wadsworth.

Matthews, Anne. 1997. "Without a parachute." *New York Times Book Reviews* (May 18).

Mattis, Mary C. 2001. "Advancing women in business organizations: Key leadership roles and behaviors of senior leaders and middle managers." *Journal of Management Development* 20(4): 371–88.

Matza, David. 1969. *Becoming Deviant*. Upper Saddle River, NJ: Prentice Hall, 1969.

Maudlin, Karen L. 2001. "Succeeding at second marriages." *Marriage Partnership* 18(3): 52–56.

Mauer, Marc. 1999. "Lock 'Em Up and Throw Away the Key." In Kenneth C. Haas & Geoffrey P. Alpert (eds.), *The Dilemmas of Corrections*, 4th ed. Prospect Heights, IL: Waveland: 30–43.

Maushart, Susan. 1999. *The Mask of Motherhood.: How Becoming a Mother Changes Everything and Why We Pretend it Doesn't*. New York: New Press (W.W. Norton).

Mauss, Armand L. 1975. *Social Problems as Social Movements*. Philadelphia: Lippincott.

Mayer, Ann Elizabeth. 1999. "Islamic law and human rights: Conundrums and equivocations." In Carrie Gustafson & Peter Juviler (eds.), *Religion and Human Rights: Competing Claims?* Armonk, NY: M. E. Sharpe: 177–98.

Mayer, Egon, & Barry A. Kosmin. 2001. *American Jewish Identity Survey*. The Graduate Center, City University of New York.

Mayer, Susan. 1997. *What Money Can't Buy*. Cambridge, MA: Harvard University Press.

Mayo, Elton. 1933. *The Human Problems of an Industrial Civilization*. New York: Macmillan.

Mazur, Allan. 1993. "Signs of status in bridal portraits." *Sociological Forum* 8: 273–84.

McAdam, Doug, & Ronnelle Paulsen. 1994. "Specifying the relationship between social ties and activism." *American Journal of Sociology* 99: 640–67.

McAdam, Doug, John D. McCarthy, & Mayer N. Zald. 1988. "Social movements." In Neil J. Smelser (ed.), *Handbook of Sociology*. Newbury Park, CA: Sage: 695–737.

McAdam, Doug. 1982. *Political Process and the Development of Black Insurgency*. Chicago: University of Chicago Press.

McAdam, Doug. 1988. *Freedom Summer*. New York: Oxford University Press.

McAdams, Deborah D. 1999. "Men central to comedy: The Man Show." *Broadcasting & Cable 129* (August 8): 27.

McAdams, Richard P. 1993. *Lessons from Abroad: How Other Countries Educate Their Children*. Lancaster, PA: Technomic.

McCaig, Linda F., & Ly Nghi. 2002. "National hospital ambulatory medical care survey, 2000: Emergency department summary." *Advance Data* No. 326(April 22). Vital and Health Statistics, Centers for Disease Control.

McCall, Leslie. 2000. "Gender and the new inequality: Explaining the college/non-college wage gap." *American Sociological Review* 65(2): 234–55.

McCammon, Holly J. 1993. "From Repressive Intervention to Integrative Prevention: The US State's Legal Management of Labor Militance, 1881–1978," *Social Forces* 71: 569–601.

McCarthy, Barry. 2001. "Male sexuality after fifty." *Journal of Family Psychotherapy*. 12(1): 29–37.

McCarthy, John D., & Mayer N. Zald. 1973. *The Trend of Social Movements in America*. Morristown, NJ: General Learning Press.

McCarthy, John D., & Mayer N. Zald. 1977. "Resource mobilization & social movements: A partial theory." *American Journal of Sociology* 82: 1212–41.

McCarthy, Michael. 2002. "U.S. panel calls for more support of alternative medicine." *Lancet* 359(April 6): 1213.

McCauley, C. 1989. "The nature of social influence in groupthink: Compliance & internalization." *Journal of Personality & Social Psychology* 57: 250–260.

McClaren, Angus. 1999. *Twentieth-Century Sexuality: A History*. Oxford, UK: Blackwell.

McClure, E. B. 2000. "A meta-analytic review of sex differences in facial expression processing and their development in infants, children, and adolescents." *Psychological Bulletin* 126(3): 424–53.

McCord, John, & Richard E. Tremblay (eds.). 1992. *Preventing Antisocial Behavior: Interventions from Birth Through Adolescence*. New York: Guilford.

McCorkle, Richard. 1993. "Research note: Punish and rehabilitate?" *Crime & Delinquency* 39: 240–252.

McCormick, John, & Claudia Kalb. 1998. "Dying for a Drink." *Newsweek* (June 15): 30–34.

McCormick, John. 1998. "The wrongly condemned." *Newsweek* (November 9): 64.

McCormick, John. 1999. "Coming two days shy of martyrdom." *Newsweek* (February 15): 35.

McCrea, Frances B., & Gerald E. Markle. 1989. *Minutes to Midnight: Nuclear Weapons Protest in America*. Newbury Park, CA: Sage.

McCulloch, Merlien. 1994. "The politics of Indian gaming." *Publius* (24/3): 99–112.

McDannell, Colleen. 1995. *Material Christianity: Religion and Popular Culture in America*. New Haven, CT: Yale University Press.

McDevitt, Thomas M., & Patricia M. Rowe. 2001. "The United States in international context." *Census 2000 Brief*. February. Washington, DC: U.S. Census Bureau.

McDonald, J. Fred. 1994. *One Nation Under Television*. Chicago: Nelson-Hall.

McEachern, William. 1994. *Economics: A Contemporary Introduction*. Cincinnati: South-Western.

McFague, Sallie. 1993. *The Body of God: An Ecological Spirituality*. Minneapolis: Fortress.

McGinn, Daniel, & John McCormick. 1999. "Your next job." *Newsweek* (February 1): 43–45.

McGinn, Susan Killenberg. 2002. "Friend or foe? Aggressiveness in primates rare; most social behavior affiliated." *Record* 26(23) (March): 1,6. Washington University in St. Louis.

McGrath, Breeda. 1999. "National policy on inclusion of students with special education needs in Italy, Ireland and the United States." ERIC No. ED436875.

McGreal, Chris. 2002. "Mandela breaks his taboo." *The Guardian* (August 26): Guardian International.

McGrew, W. C. 1998. "Culture in nonhuman primates?" *Annual Review of Anthropology* 27: 301–28.

McGuigan, William M., & Clara C. Pratt. 2001. "The predictive impact of domestic violence on three types of child mistreatment." *Child Abuse & Neglect*. 25(7): 869–93.

McGuire, Peggy. 2001. "Gender mainstreaming is necessary for effective health targets." Paper presented at the Global Health Council annual conference. Washington, DC: May 29–June 1.

McGurn, William. 1997. "City limits." *Far Eastern Economic Review* 160: 34–37.

McKee, David L., & Yosra A. McKee. 2001. "Edge cities and the viability of metropolitan economies: Contributions to flexibility and external linkages by new urban service environments." *American Journal of Economics and Sociology* 60(1): 171–84.

McKeever, Matthew, & Nicholas H. Wolfinger. 2001. "Reexamining the economic costs of marital disruption for women." *Social Science Quarterly* 82(1): 202–17.

McKelvey, Charles. 1994. *The African-American Movement*. Dix Hills, NJ: General Hall.

McKelvey, Mary W., & Patrick C. McKenry. 2000. "The psychological well-being of black and white mothers following marital dissolution." *Psychology of Women's Quarterly* 24(1): 4–14.

McKenzie, James F., Robert R. Pinger, & Jerome E. Kotecki. 2002. *An Introduction to Community Health*. Sudbury, MA: Jones and Bartlett.

McKibben, Bill. 1998. "A special moment in history." *Atlantic Monthly* (May): 55–76.

McKinlay, John. B. 1999. "The end of the golden age of doctoring." *New England Research Institutes Network* (Summer): 1, 3.

McKinney, Michael L. 2000. "There goes the neighborhood." *Forum for Applied Research and Public Policy* 15(3): 23–7.

McKormick, John, & Evan Thomas. 1997. One family's journey from welfare to work." *Newsweek* (May 26): 28–32.

McLaren, Deborah. 1997. *Rethinking Tourism and Ecotravel: The Paving of Paradise and What You Can Do to Stop It*. Bloomfield, CT: Kumarian.

McLaughlin, Diane K., C. Shannon Stokes, & Atsuko Nonoyama. 2001. "Residence and income inequality: Effects on mortality among U.S. countries." *Rural Sociology* 66(4): 579–98.

McLellan, David (ed.). 1977. *Karl Marx: Selected Writings*. New York: Oxford University Press.

McLeod, Douglas M., Benjamin H. Detenber, & William P. Eveland, Jr. 2001. "Behind the third-person effect: Differentiating perceptual processes for self and other." *Journal of Communication* 51(4): 678–95.

McLeod, Douglas M., William P. Eveland, Jr., & Amy L. Nathanson. 1997. "Support for censorship of violent and misogynic rap lyrics: An analysis of the third-person effect." *Communication Research* 24: 153–74.

McLloyd, Vonnie C., Ana Mari Cauce, & David Takeuchi. 2000. "Marital processes and parental socialization in families of color: A decade review of research." *Journal of Marriage and the Family* 62(4): 1070–93.

McLoughlin, Merrill. 1988. "Men versus women: The new debate over sex differences." *U.S. News and World Report* (August 8): 48,51–56.

McLuhan, Marshall. 1964. *Understanding Media*. New York: McGraw Hill.

McManus, Patricia A., & Thomas A. DiPrete. 2001. "Losers and winners: The financial consequences of separation and divorce for men." *American Sociological Review* 66(2): 246–68.

McMichael, Philip. 1996. *Development and Social Change: A Global Perspective*. Thousand Oaks, CA: Pine Forge.

McNamee, Stephen J., & Robert K. Miller, Jr. 1998. "Inheritance & Stratification," in Robert K. Miller, Jr., & Stephen J. McNamee (eds.), *Inheritance & Wealth in America*. New York: Plenum.

McPhail, Clark, & Ronald T. Wohlstein. 1983. "Individual & collective behaviors within gatherings, demonstrations & riots." *Annual Review of Sociology* 9: 579–600.

McPhail, Clark. 1991. *The Myth of the Madding Crowd*. New York: deGruyter.

McPhail, Clark. 1994. "The dark side of purpose: Individual and collective violence in riots." *Sociological Quarterly* (35/1): 1–32.

McPhail, Clark. 1997. "Stereotypes of crowds and collective behavior." *Studies in Symbolic Interactionism* (3): 35–58.

Mead, George Herbert. 1934. *Mind, Self, and Society.* Chicago: University of Chicago.

Mead, Margaret. 1935. *Sex and Temperament in Three Primitive Societies.* New York: William Morrow.

Mead, Margaret. 1942. *And Keep Your Powder Dry: An Anthropologist Looks at America.* New York: Morrow.

Mead, N., P. Bower, & M. Hann. 2002. "The impact of general practitioners' patient-centeredness on patients' post-consultation satisfaction and enablement." *Social Science & Medicine* 55(2): 283–99.

Mears, Daniel P., & Christopher G. Ellison. 2000. "Who buys New Age material? Exploring sociodemographic, religious, network and contextual correlates of New Age consumption." *Sociology of Religion* 61(3): 289–313.

Meat Shortage. 2002. Available: http://www.asianjoke.com/korean/meat_shortage.

Mecca, Susan J., & Linda J. Rubin. 1999. "Definitional research on African American students and sexual harassment." *Psychology of Women Quarterly* 23(4): 813–17.

Mechanic, David. 1989. *Mental Health and Social Policy.* Englewood Cliffs, NJ: Prentice-Hall.

Mechanic, David. 2002. "Socio-cultural implications of changing organizational technologies in the provision of care." *Social Science & Medicine* 54(3): 459–67.

Meckler, Laura. 2001. "Welfare caseloads rising again in some states." *Owensboro (Ky) Messenger-Inquirer* (April 4): 3-A.

Medalia, Nehum Z., & Otto N. Larson. 1958. "Diffusion and belief in a collective delusion." *American Sociological Review* 23: 221–32.

Media Awareness. 2000. "The media and masculinity." Oakland, CA: Children Now. Media Awareness Network. Available: http:www.media-awareness.ca/eng/issues/stats.

Mediascope. 2000. "Violence, women and the media." Issue Brief Series. Studio City, CA: Mediascope Press.

Medicare. 2002. "Medicare premium amounts for 2002." Medicare: The official U.S. government site for people with Medicare. Available: http://www.medicare.gov/Basics/Amounts2002.

Meeks, Loretta F., Wendell A. Meeks, & Claudia A. Warren. 2000. "Racial desegregation: Magnet schools, vouchers, privatization, and home schooling." *Education and Urban Society* 33(1): 88–101.

Meeus, Wim, Rutger C. M. E. Engels, & Maja Dekovic. 2002. "Parenting practices, social skills and peer relationships in adolescence." *Social Behavior & Personality* 30(1): 3–18.

Mehan, H. Mercer, & R. Rueda. 1997. "Special education." In *Encyclopedia of Education and Sociology.* New York: Garland.

Meier, Gerald, & Joseph E. Stiglitz (eds.). 2000. *Frontiers of Development: The Future in Perspective.* New York: Oxford University.

Meiss, Alan. 2001. "50 ways to annoy Osama bin Laden." Jokes.com. Available: http://thecomedylab.com/results/detail.

Meldrum, Helen, & Mary L. Hardy. 2001. *Provider-Patient Relationships.* Boston: Butterworth-Heinemann.

Melendez, Michele M. 2002. "Mocking our enemies is an American tradition." *St. Louis Post-Dispatch* (June 12): E1, E2.

Melman, Seymour. 2001. *After Capitalism: From Managerialism to Workplace Democracy.* New York: Alfred A. Knopf.

Melton, Willie, & Linda L. Lindsey. 1987. "Instrumental and expressive values in mate selection among college students revisited: Feminism, love and economic necessity." Paper presented at the Midwest Sociological Society, Chicago, April.

Melucci, Alberto. 1980. "The new social movements: A theoretical approach." *Social Science Information* 19/2: 199–226.

Melucci, Alberto. 1989. *Nomads of the Present: Social Movements and Individual Needs in Contemporary Society.* London: Hutchinson Radius.

Mena, Jennifer, 2000. "Men's groups delve into the concept of 'machismo.'" *St. Louis Post-Dispatch* (December 31): EV8.

Menard, Scott. 1995. "A developmental test of Mertonian anomie theory." *Journal of Research in Crime & Delinquency* 32: 136–74.

Mendenhall, Mark E., & Carolyn Wiley. 1994. "Strangers in a strange land: The relationship between expatriate adjustment and impression management." *American Behavioral Scientist* 37(5): 605–20.

Mennino, Sue Falter, & April Brayfield. 2002. "Job–family trade-offs: The multidimensional effects of gender." *Work & Occupations* 29(2): 226–56.

Mental Health Weekly 2002. "Yates case could spur changes in Texas insanity defense." 12 (April 1): 3–5.

Merchant, Carolyn. 1983. *The Death of Nature: Women, Ecology and the Scientific Revolution.* New York: Harper & Row.

Meredith, Robyn. 1997. "For this we sent you to college?" *The New York Times* (June 8): F1, 11–12.

Merkl, Peter H. 2000. "The Russian prospect: Hope and despair." In M. Donald Hancock & John Logue (eds.), *Transitions to Capitalism and Democracy in Russia and Central Europe: Achievements, Problems, Prospects.* Westport, CT: Praeger: 95–116.

Mernissi, Fatima. 1987. *Beyond the Veil: Male-Female Dynamics in Modern Muslim Society.* Bloomington, IN: Indiana University Press.

Merola, Stacey S. 2001. "The ideal suburb turns 50." American Sociological Association, *Footnotes* (February): 8.

Merrick, Elizabeth. 1999. "Like chewing gravel: On the experience of analyzing qualitative research findings and using a feminist epistemology." *Psychology of Women Quarterly* 23(1): 47–57.

Merry, Sally Engle. 2001. "Changing rights, changing culture." In Jane K. Cowan,

Marie-Benedicte Dembour, & Richard A, Wilson (eds.), *Culture and Rights: Anthropological Perspectives.* Cambridge, UK: Cambridge University: 31–55.

Merton, Robert K. 1938. "Social structure and anomie." *American Sociological Review* (3): 672–82.

Merton, Robert K. 1948. "Discrimination & the American creed." In Robert MacIver (ed.), *Discrimination and National Welfare.* New York: Institute for Religious & Social Studies.

Merton, Robert K. 1967. "Manifest & latent functions." In *On Theoretical Sociology.* New York: Free Press: 73–137.

Merton, Robert K. 1968. *Social Theory & Social Structure,* 2nd ed. New York: Free Press.

Merton, Robert K., & Alice S. Kitt. 1950. "Contributions to the theory of reference group behavior." In Robert K. Merton & Paul L. Lazarsfeld, (eds.), *Continuities in Social Research.* New York: Free Press: 40–105.

Messenger, John. 1971. *Inis Beag.* Prospect Heights, IL: Waveland.

Messeri, Peter, Merril Silverstein, & Eugene Litwak. 1993. "Choosing optimal support groups." *Journal of Health & Social Behavior* 34: 122–137.

Messner, Michael. 1990. "Boyhood, organized sports & the construction of masculinities." *Journal of Contemporary Ethnography* (18/4): 416–44.

Messner, Steven, & Richard Rosenfeld. 1994. *Crime and the American Dream.* Belmont, CA: Wadsworth.

Methvin, Eugene H. 1997. "Mugged by reality." *Policy Review* (July/August).

Metz, Isabel, & Phyllis Tharenou. 2001. "Women's career advancement: The relative contribution of human and social capital." *Group & Organization Management* 26(3): 312–42.

Meyer, David S. 1993. "Institutionalizing dissent." *Sociological Forum* 8: 157–80.

Meyer, David S., & Nancy Whittier. 1994. "Social movement spillover." *Social Problems* 41: 277–98.

Meyer, Madonna Harrington. 1996. "Family status and poverty among older women: The gendered distribution of retirement income in the United States." In Jill Quadagno & Debra Street (eds.), *Aging in the Twenty-First Century.* New York: St. Martin's: 464–79.

Meyers, Linda I. 2000. "Gay or straight? Why do we really want to know?" *Journal of Gay & Lesbian Psychotherapy* 4(2): 47–59.

Meyerson, D. E., & J. K. Fletcher. 2000. "A modest manifesto for shattering the glass ceiling." *Harvard Business Review:* 127–36.

Meyrowitz, Joshua. 1984. "The adultlike child & the childlike adult: Socialization in an electronic age." *Daedalus* 113: 19–48.

Mezey, Susan Gluck. 1998. "Law and equality." In Sheila Ruth (ed.). *Issues in Feminism: An Introduction to Women's Studies.* Mountain View, CA: Mayfield: 406–17.

Michael, Robert T. 1995. "Measuring poverty: A new approach." *Focus* 12/1: 2–13.

Michael, Robert T., John H. Gagnon, Edward O. Laumann, & Gina Kolata. 1994. *Sex in America: A Definitive Study.* Boston: Little, Brown.

Michaels, Marguerite. 1993. "Rio's dead end kids." *Time* (August 9): 35, 37.

Michels, Robert. 1962. *Political Parties.* New York: Dover.

Micklewait, John. 2000. "The next America: U.S. business is waking up to the new Americans." *Economist* 354 (March 11): 15–16.

Micro-Loans. 1997. "Micro-loans for the very poor." *New York Times* (February 16).

Middleton, DeWight R. 2002. *Exotics and Erotics: Human Cultural and Sexual Diversity.* Prospect Heights, IL: Waveland.

Miech, R. A., A. Caspi, T. E. Moffitt, B. R. Entner Wright, & P. A. Silva. 1999. "Low Socioeconomic Status & Mental Disorders; A Longitudinal Study of Selection & Causation During Young Adulthood." *American Journal of Sociology* 104.

Mies, Maria, & Vendana Shiva. 1993. *Ecofeminism.* Highlands, NJ: Zed.

Miethe, Terance, & Charles A. Moore. 1986. "Racial differences in criminal processing." *Sociological Quarterly* 27: 217–237.

Milburn, Michael A., Roxanne Mather, & Sheree D. Conrad. 2000. "The effects of viewing R-rated movie scenes that objectify women on perceptions of date rape." *Sex Roles* 43(9–10): 645–54.

Miles, Robert. 1989. *Racism.* London: Tavistock/Routledge.

Milgram, Stanley. 1963. "Behavioral study of obedience." *Journal of Abnormal and Social Psychology* 67: 371–78.

Milgram, Stanley. 1967. "The small world problem." *Psychology Today* 1: 61–67.

Milgram, Stanley. 1974. *Obedience to Authority.* New York: Harper and Row.

Miliband, Ralph. 1977. *Marxism and Politics.* New York: Oxford University Press.

Miller, A. 2000. "The construction of a Black fundamentalist worldview: The role of Bible schools." In Vincent L. Wimbush & Rosamond C. Rodman (eds.), *African Americans and the Bible: Sacred Texts and Textures.* New York: Continuum.

Miller, D. C., & W. H. Form. 1964. *Industrial Sociology,* 2nd ed. New York: Harper.

Miller, David L. 1985. *Introduction to Collective Behavior.* Belmont, CA: Wadsworth.

Miller, David. 1991. "A vision of market socialism." *Dissent* 38: 406–414.

Miller, Donald E. 1997. *Reinventing American Protestantism: Christianity in the New Millennium.* Berkeley, CA: University of California Press.

Miller, Geralyn. 2001. "Newspaper coverage and gender: An analysis of the 1996 Illinois state legislative House district races." *Women & Politics* 22(3): 83–100.

Miller, Richard A. 1999. "Biology of aging and longevity." In William R. Hazzard et al., (eds.), *Principles of Geriatric Medicine and Gerontology.* New York: McGraw-Hill, Health Professions Division: 3–20.

Miller, Walter. 1958. "Lower-class culture as a generating milieu of gang delinquency." *Journal of Social Issues* (14): 5–19.

Millett, Kate. 1995. "Sexual politics." In Stevi Jackson et al. (eds.), *Women's Studies Essential Readings.* New York: New York University.

Millman, Marcia, & Rosabeth Moss Kanter. 1975. *Another Voice.* New York: Doubleday.

Mills, Albert J., & Peta Tancred (eds.). 1992. *Gendering Organizational Analysis.* Newbury Park, CA: Sage.

Mills, C. Wright. 1956. *The Power Elite.* New York: Oxford University Press.

Mills, C. Wright. 1959. *The Sociological Imagination.* New York: Oxford University Press.

Mills, Robert J. 2001. "Health insurance coverage: 2000." *Current Population Reports* (September). U.S. Bureau of the Census: Department of Commerce.

Milly, Deborah J. 2000. "The rights of foreign migrant workers in Asia." In Michael Jacobsen & Ole Bruun (eds.), *Human Rights and Asian Values: Contesting National Identities and Cultural Representations in Asia.* Richmond, Surrey, UK: Curzon: 301–21.

Milner, Murray Jr. 1994. *Status & Sacredness.* New York: Oxford University Press.

Milovanovic, Dragan. 1996. "Postmodern criminology: Mapping the terrain." *Justice Quarterly* 13: 567–610.

Milton S. Eisenhower Foundation. 1993. *Investing in Children and Youth: Reconstructing Our Cities.* Washington, DC: Milton S. Eisenhower Foundation.

Minai, Naila. 1991. "Women in early Islam." In Carol J. Verburg (ed.), *Ourselves Among Others: Cross-Cultural Readings for Writers.* Boston: Bedford Books.

Mineau, Geraldine P., Ken R. Smith, & Lee L. Bean. 2002. "Historical trends of survival among widows and widowers." *Social Science & Medicine* 54(2): 245–54.

Miner, Horace. 1956. "Body ritual among the Nacirema." *American Anthropologist* 58(3): 503–507.

Minerd, Jeff. 2000. "Impacts of sprawl." *Futurist* 34(4): 10–11.

Mingione, Enzo, & Enrico Pugliese. 1994. "Rural subsistence, migration, urbanization and the new global food regime." In Bonanno, Alessandro, et al. (eds.), *From Columbus to ConAgra: The Globalization of Agriculture and Food.* Lawrence, KS: University Press of Kansas: 52–68.

Minino, Arialdi, & Betty L. Smith. 2001. "Deaths: Preliminary data for 2000." *National Vital Statistics Reports* 49(12): October 9.

Minnow, Newton N., & Craig L. LeMay. 1995. *Abandoned in the Wasteland: Children, Television & the First Amendment.* New York: Hill & Wang.

Mio, Jeffrey Scott, & Gene I. Awakuni. 2000. *Resistance to Multiculturalism: Issues and Interventions.* Philadelphia: Brunner/Mazel.

Miracle, Tina S., Andrew W. Miracle, & Roy F. Baumeister. 2003. *Human Sexuality: Meeting Your Basic Needs.* Upper Saddle River, NJ: Prentice Hall.

Mirande, Alfredo. 1987. *Gringo Justice.* South Bend, IN: University of Notre Dame Press.

Mirande, Alfredo. 1997. *Hombres y Machos: Masculinity and Latino Culture.* Boulder, CO: Westview.

Miringoff, Marc, & Marque-Luisa Miringoff. 1999. *The Social Health of the Nation: How America is Really Doing.* New York: Oxford University.

Mirowsky, John, & Catherine E. Ross. 1999. "Economic hardship declines with age: Reply to Hardy and Hazelrigg." *American Sociological Review* 64(4): 577–84.

Mirowsky, John. 1995. "Age and the sense of control." *Social Psychological Quarterly* 58(1): 31–43.

Mirrors: America as a Foreign Culture, 2nd ed. Belmont, CA: West/Wadsworth: 43–43.

Mirsky, Steve. 2002. "Divining comedy: Can researchers dissect humor without killing the patient?" *Scientific American* 286 (March): 103.

Mischel, Lawrence, & Gary Burtless. 1995. *Recent Wage Trends: The Implications for Low-Wage Workers.* Washington, DC: Economic Policy Institute.

Mischel, Lawrence, Jared Bernstein & John Schmitt. 1999. *The State of Working America.* Ithaca, NY: Cornell University Press.

Mischel, W. A. 1966. "A social learning view of sex differences in behavior." In Eleanor E. Maccoby (ed.), *The Development of Sex Differences.* Stanford, CA: Stanford University.

Mishel, Lawrence. 1995. "Rising tides, sinking wages." *The American Prospect* 23 (Fall): 60–64.

Misztal, Barbara A. 1993. "Understanding political change in eastern Europe: A sociological perspective." *Society* (27/3): 451–71.

Misztal, Bronislaw, & J. Craig Jenkins. 1995. "Starting from scratch is not always the same: The politics of protest and the post-communist transitions in Poland and Hungary." In J. Craig Jenkins & Bert Klandermans (eds.), *The Politics of Social Movements.* Minneapolis: University of Minnesota Press: 324–64.

Mitchell, J. M., & B. J. Kemp. 2000. "Quality of life in assisted living: A multidimensional analysis." *Journal of Gerontology* 55B: 117–27.

Mitchell, John G. 2001. The American dream: Urban sprawl. *National Geographic Magazine* Interactive Edition http:www.nationalgeographic.com/ngm/0107 (July).

Mitchell, Katie. 2002. "Women's morality: A test of Gilligan's theory." *Journal of Social Distress & the Homeless* 11(1): 81–110.

Mitchie, Gregory. 2001. "Ground zero." In William Ayers, Bernadine Dohrn, & Rick Ayers (eds.), *Zero Tolerance: Resisting the Drive for Punishment in our Schools.* New York: New Press: 3–14.

Mitlin, Diana, & David Satterthwaite. 2001. "Urban poverty: Some thoughts about its scale and nature and about responses to it." In Shahid Yusuf, Simon Evenett, & Weiping Wu (eds.), *Facets of Globalization: International and Local Dimensions of Development.* Washington, DC: World Bank: 93–220.

Miwa, Yoshiro. 1996. *Firms and Industrial Organization in Japan.* New York: New York University.

Miyazawa, Setsuo. 1992. *Policing in Japan.* Albany: SUNY Press.

Mladenka, Kenneth R. 1991. "Public employee unions, reformism, and black employment in 1200 American Cities." *Urban Affairs Quarterly* 26: 532–548.

MMWR. 2002. "Infant mortality and low birth weight among black and white infants—United States, 1980–2000. *Morbidity & Mortality Weekly Report* (July 6): 12.

MMWR. 2002a. "Women and smoking: A report of the surgeon general." *Morbidity and Mortality Weekly Report* 51(August 30): No. RR-12.

MMWR. 2002b. "Recent trends in mortality rates for four major cancers, by sex and race/ethnicity—United States, 1990–1998.⁶ *Morbidity and Mortality Weekly Report* 51(3): January 25: 49–53.

Moe, Terry M. 2001. *Schools, Vouchers and the American Public.* Washington, DC: Brookings Institution.

Moen, Matthew C. 1994. "From revolution to evolution: The changing nature of the Christian right." *Sociology of Religion* 3: 345–57.

Moen, Phyllis, Julie Robison, & Donna Dempster-McClain. 1995. "Caregiving and women's well-being: A life course approach." *Journal of Health and Social Behavior* 36(3): 259–73.

Möen, Phyllis, Julie Robison, & Vivian Fields. 2000. "Women's work and caregiving roles: A life course approach." In Eleanor Palo Stoller & Rose Campbell Gibson (eds.), *World of Difference: Inequality in the Aging Experience.* Thousand Oaks, CA: Pine Forge.

Moffatt, Michael. 1989. *Coming of Age in New Jersey: College and American Culture.* New Brunswick, NJ: Rutgers University.

Moghadam, Valentine M. 1999. "Gender and the global economy." In Myra Marx Feree, Judith Lorber, & Beth B. Hess (eds.), *Revisioning Gender.* Thousand Oaks, CA: Sage: 128–60.

Mohan, Rakesh. 2001. "Financing of sub-national public investment in India." In Shahid Yusuf, Simon Evenett, & Weiping Wu (eds.), *Facets of Globalization: International and Local Dimensions of Development.* Washington, DC: World Bank: 238–57.

Mohanty, Chandra Talpade. 1999. "Women workers and capitalist scripts: Ideologies of domination, common interests, and the politics of solidarity." In Sharlene Hesse-Biber, Christina Gilmartin, & Robin Lydenberg (eds.), *Feminist Approaches to Theory and Methodology.* New York: Oxford University: 362–88.

Mok, Ka-Ho, Lina Wong, & Grace Lee. 2002. "The challenges of global capitalism: Unemployment and state workers' reactions and responses in post-reform China." *International Journal of Human Resource Management* 13(3): 399–415.

Mokdad, A. H., M. Serdula, W. Dietz, et al. 2000. "The continuing obesity epidemic in the United States." *Journal of the American Medical Association* 284: 1650–51.

Mokhiber, Russell. 1988. *Corporate Crime and Violence.* San Francisco: Sierra Club.

Molina, Olga. 2000a. "African American women's unique divorce experiences." *Journal of Divorce and Remarriage* 32(3/4): 93–99.

Molina, Olga. 2000b. "Divorce and domestic violence among African American women." *Journal of Divorce and Remarriage* 34(1/2): 131–41.

Molotch, Harvey. 1979. "Media and movements." In Meyer N. Zald & John D. McCarthy (eds.), *The Dynamics of Social Movements.* Cambridge, MA: Winthrop.

Mondimore, Francis Mark. 1996. *A Natural History of Homosexuality.* Baltimore: Johns Hopkins University.

Money, John, & Anke A. Ehrhardt. 1972. *Man and Woman, Boy and Girl.* Baltimore, MD: Johns Hopkins University.

Money, John, & P. Tucker. 1975. *Sexual Signatures.* Boston: Little, Brown.

Monroe, R. R. 1978. *Brain Dysfunction in Aggressive Criminals.* Lexington, MA: D. C. Heath.

Monsour, Michael. 2002. *Women and Men as Friends: Relationships across the Life Span in the 21st Century.* Mahwah, NJ: Lawrence Erlbaum.

Montagu, M. F. Ashley. 1964. *The Concept of Race.* New York: Free Press.

Montero-Sieburth, Martha, & Michael Christian Batt. 2001. "An overview of the educational models used to explain the academic achievement of Latino students: Implications for research and policies into the new millennium." In Robert E. Slavin & Margarita Calderson (eds.), *Effective Programs for Latino Students.* Mahwah, NJ: Lawrence Erlbaum: 331–68.

Montgomery, James D. 1992. "Job search and network composition." *American Sociological Review* 57: 586–596.

Montgomery, Lori. 1996. "Study backs crime prevention efforts." *Owensboro (KY) Messenger-Inquirer* (June 20).

Moon, Katharine H. S. 2002. "Migrant workers' movements in Japan and South Korea." In Craig N. Murphy (ed.), *Egalitarian Politics in the Age of Globalization.* Basingstoke, Hampshire, UK: Palgrave.

Moore, Alinde J., & Dorothy C. Stratton. 2002. *Resilient Widowers: Older Men Speak for Themselves.* New York: Springer.

Moore, Dorothy P. 1990. "An examination of present research on the female entrepreneur: Suggested research strategies for the 1990's." *Journal of Business Ethics* 9: 275–81.

Moore, Elizabeth, & Michael Mills. 1990. "The neglected victims and unexamined costs of white-collar crime." *Crime and Delinquency* 36/3: 408–18.

Moore, Gwen. 1991. "Structural determinants of men's and women's personal networks." *American Sociological Review* (55/5): 726–735.

Moore, Jim. 2001. "Affordable assisted living." *Contemporary Longterm Care* 24(1): 27.

Moore, Mick. 1997. "Societies, polities and capitalists in developing countries: A literature review." *Journal of Development Studies* 33: 287–363.

Moore, Nelwyn B., J. Kenneth Davidson, & J. Kenneth Davidson, Sr. 2000. *Journal of Sex & Marital Therapy* 26(3).

Moore, Joan. 1994. "Permanently temporary: The new employment relationship in US society." In D. J. Curran, & C. M. Renzetti (eds.), *Contemporary Societies.* Upper Saddle River, NJ: Prentice Hall: 37–48.

Moore, Wilbert E. 1967. *Order & Change: Essays in Comparative Sociology.* New York: Wiley.

Moore, Wilbert E. 1974. *Social Change,* 2nd ed. Upper Saddle River, NJ: Prentice-Hall.

Moore, Wilbert E. 1979. *World Modernization: The Limits of Convergence.* New York: Elsevier.

Moorehead, Richard. 1992. "Land tenure and environmental conflict: The case of the Inland Niger Delta, Mali." In Jyrki Käkönen (ed.), *Perspectives on Environmental Conflict and International Relations* London: Pinter: 96–115.

Morgan, Leslie A. 2000. "The continuing gender gap in later life economic security." *Journal of Aging & Social Policy* 11(2–3): 157–65.

Morganthau, Tom, & Ginny Carroll. 1996. "The backlash wars." *Newsweek* (April 1): 54–55.

Morganthau, Tom. 1988. "The housing crunch." *Newsweek* 111 (January 4): 18–20.

Morganthau, Tom. 1995. "The lull before the storm." *Newsweek* (December 4): 40–42.

Morgenthau, Tom. 2000. "Getting ready for 'Seattle II.'" *Newsweek* (April 24): 40.

Morris, Aldon D. 1984. *The Origins of the Civil Rights Movement.* New York: Free Press.

Morrison, Denton E. 1971. "Some notes toward theory on relative deprivation, social movements and social change." *American Behavioral Scientist* 14/5: 675–90.

Morrison, Donna Ruane, & Mary Jo Coiro. 1999. "Parental conflict and marital disruption: Do children benefit when high-conflict marriages are dissolved?" *Journal of Marriage and the Family* 61(3): 626–37.

Morrison, Joan, & Robert K. Morrison. 2001. *From Camelot to Kent State: The Sixties Experience in the Words of Those Who Lived It.* Oxford, NY: Oxford University.

Morrison, Nancy C., & Jeanine Clavenna-Valleroy. 1998. "Perceptions of maternal support as related to self-concept and self-report of depression in sexually abused female adolescents." *Journal of Child Sexual Abuse* 7(1): 23–40.

Morrow, Lance. 1993. "The temping of America." *Time* 131/19: 40–41.

Morrow-Howell, Nancy, James Hinterlong, Michael Sherraden, & Philip Rozario. 2001. "Advancing research on productivity in later life." In N. Morrow-Howell, J. Hinterlong, & M. Sherraden (eds), *Productive Aging: Concepts and Challenges.* Baltimore: Johns Hopkins University: 285–311.

Morry, Marian M., & Erica Winkler. 2001. "Student acceptance and expectation of sexual assault." *Canadian Journal of Behavioural Science* 33(3): 188–92.

Mort, Jo-Ann, & Gary Brenner. 2000. "Kibbutzim: Will they survive the new Israel?" *Dissent* 47(3): 64–70.

Mort, Jo-Ann. 2000. *Not Your Father's Union Movement.* New York: Verso.

Morton, Joel. 2000. "Silencing the men's movement: Gender, ideology and popular discourse." In Edward Read Barton (ed.), *Mythopoetic Perspectives of Men's Healing Work: An Anthology of Therapists and Others.* Westport, CT: Bergin & Garvey: 87–99.

Morton, Lois Wright. 2001. *Health Care Restructuring: Market Theory vs. Civil Society.* Westport, CT: Auburn House.

Mottl, Tahi L. 1980. "The analysis of countermovements." *Social Problems* 27: 620–35.

Moy, James. 2000. "The death of Asia on the American field of representation." In Timothy P. Fong & Larry H. Shinagawa (eds.), *Asian Americans: Experiences and Perspectives.* Upper Saddle River, NJ: Prentice Hall: 258–63.

Mshomba, Richard E. 2000. *Africa in the Global Economy.* Boulder, CO: Reinner.

Mucha, Janusz L. 1998. "An outsider's view of American culture." In Philip R. DeVita & James D. Armstrong (eds.), *Distant*

Mufwene, Salikoko S. 1998. "Forms of address: How their social functions may vary." In Philip R. DeVita & James D. Armstrong (eds.), *Distant Mirrors: America as a Foreign Culture.* Belmont, CA: West/Wadsworth: 55–59.

Mulcahy, Aogan. 1995. "'Headhunter' or real cop? Identity in the world of internal affairs officers." *Journal of Contemporary Ethnography* 24: 99–130.

Mumford, Emily. 1983. *Medical Sociology: Patients, Providers and Policies.* New York: Random House.

Mundell, E. J. 2002. "Majority of HIV patients using alternative meds." Medline Plus Health Information: August 23. Available: http:www.nlm.nih.gov/medlineplus/news/fullstory 9082.

Munroe, Robert L. 1999. "A behavioral orientation." *Ethos* 27(1): 104–14.

Munshi, Shoma (ed.). 2001. *Images of the Modern Woman in Asia: Global Media, Local Meanings.* Richmond, UK: Curzon.

Murdock, George Peter. 1945. "The common denominator of cultures." In Ralph Linton (ed.), *The Science of Man in World Crisis.* New York: Columbia University.

Murnen, Sarah K. 2000. "Gender and the use of sexually degrading language." *Psychology of Women Quarterly* 24(4): 319–27.

Murphy, David. 2001. "Losing battle: Self-immolation of apparent members of banned Falun Gong movement provides Beijing with ammunition." *Far Eastern Economic Review* 164 (Feb. 15): 24–5.

Murphy, Robert F. 1994. "The dialectics of deeds and words." In Robert Borofsky (ed.), *Assessing Cultural Anthropology.* New York: McGraw-Hill.

Murray, Alison. 2001. *Pink Fits: Sex, Subcultures and Discourses in the Asia-Pacific.* Victoria, AUS: Monash Asia Institute.

Murray, Carolyn Bennett, & Jelani Mandara. 2002. "Racial identity development in African American children: Cognitive and experiential antecedents." In Harriette Pipes McAdoo (ed.), *Black Children: Social, Educational, and Parental Environments.* Thousand Oaks, CA: Sage: 73–96.

Murray, Stephen O. 2000. *Homosexualities.* Chicago: University of Chicago.

Mursi, Muhammad. 2000. "Soft drink bottlers turn to religion." *Middle East Times.* Available: www.metimes.com/2K/issue2000–25/bus/soft_drink_bottlers.html.

Musto, David F. 1987. *The American Disease: Origins of Narcotic Control,* expanded edition. New York: Oxford University Press.

Mutchler, Jan E., & Jacqueline L. Angel. 2000. "Policy development and the older Latino population in the 21st Century." *Journal of Aging & Social Policy* 11(2–3): 177–88.

Mutchler, Matt G. 2000. "Seeking sexual lives: Gay youth and masculinity tension." In Peter Nardi (ed.), *Gay Masculinities.* Thousand Oaks: Sage.

Myers, Phyllis. 2000. *Green Ballot Measures: Election Day 1999: A Catalyst for Local*

Action to Shape Growth. Washington, DC: Brookings Center on Urban and Metropolitan Policy.

Myers, Robert J. 2000. "Why Medicare Part A and Part B, as well as Medicaid?" *Health Care Financing Review* 22(1): 53–4.

Myers, Scott M., & Alan Booth. 1996. "Men's retirement and marital quality." *Journal of Family Issues* 17(3): 336–51.

Myers, Scott. 1999. "Residential mobility as a way of life: Evidence of intergenerational similarities." *Journal of Marriage and the Family* 61(4): 871–80.

Myles, John, & Adnan Turgeon. 1994. "Comparative studies in class structure." *Annual Review of Sociology* 20: 103–124.

Myrdal, Gunnar. 1962. *Challenge to Affluence.* New York: Pantheon.

Nabi, Robin L., & Jennifer L. Horner. 2001. "Victims with voices: How abused women conceptualize the problem of spousal abuse and implications for intervention and prevention." *Journal of Family Violence* 16(3): 237–53.

Nadelman, Ethan. 1995. "Switzerland's Heroin Experiment." *National Review* (47/13): 46–47.

Nader, Ralph, & Mark Green. 1972. "Crime in the suites." *New Republic* (April 29): 17–19.

Naffine, Ngaire. 1996. *Feminism and Criminology.* Philadelphia: Temple University Press.

Nagel, Joane. 1996. *American Indian Ethnic Renewal: Red Power and the Resurgence of Identity and Culture.* New York: Oxford University Press.

Nagel, Joane. 1997. *American Indian Ethnic Renewal.* New York: Oxford University Press.

Nagel, Joann. 1994. "Constructing ethnicity." *Social Problems* 41: 152–76.

Nagel, Stuart (ed.). 2001. *Handbook of Win-Win Economics.* Huntington, NY: Nova Science.

Nagel, Stuart (ed.). 2002. *Diverse Perspectives on Peace, Prosperity and Democracy.* Huntington, NY: Nova Science.

Nagin, Daniel S., & Raymond Paternoster. 1991. "The Preventive Effects of the Perceived Risk of Arrest." *Criminology* 29: 561–85.

Nagin, Daniel, & Raymond Paternoster. 1993. "Enduring individual differences and rational choice theories of crime." *Law and Society Review* 27: 467–89.

NAHB. 1999. *NAHB Smart Growth Report.* Washington, DC: National Association of Home Builders. Available: http://www.nahb.com.

Najafizadeh, Mehrangiz, & Lewis A. Mennerick. 1992. "Sociology of education or sociology of ethnocentrism? The portrayal of education in U.S. introductory sociology textbooks." *Teaching Sociology* 20/3: 215–21.

Nakagane, Katsuji. 2002. "Japanese direct investment in China: Its effect on China's economic development." In Hanns Gunther Hilpert & Rene Haak (eds.), *Japan and China: Cooperation, Competition, and Conflict.* New York: Palgrave.

Nakao, Keiko & Judith Treas. 1994. "Updating Occupational Prestige and Socioeconomic Scores," in Peter V. Marsden, ed., *Sociological Methodology.* Washington, DC: American Sociological Association: 1–72.

Nakosteen, R. A., & M. A. Zimmer. 1997. "Men, money and marriage: Are high earners more prone than low earners to marry?" *Social Science Quarterly* 78: 66–82.

Nanda, Serena. 1997. "The hijras of India." In Martin B. Duberman (ed.), *A Queer World: The Center for Lesbian and Gay Studies Reader.* New York: Center for Lesbian and Gay Studies, City University.

Napora, Joe. 2001. "Orality and literacy, intimacy and alienation: The eternal, internal, contradictions of teaching composition." *Changing English: Studies in Reading and Culture* 9(1): 67–76.

Narayan, Deepa, Raj Patel, Kai Schafft, Anne Rademacher, & Sarah Koch-Schulte. 2000. *Voices of the Poor: Can Anyone Hear Us?* Published for the World Bank. New York: Oxford University.

Nardi, Peter M. 2000. "Changing gay and lesbian images in the media." In Tracey E. Ore (ed.), *The Social Construction of Difference: Race, Class, Gender, and Sexuality.* Mountain View, CA: Mayfield: 384–96.

Natadecha-Sponsel, Poranee. 1998. "The young, the rich, and the famous: Individualism as an American cultural value." In Philip R. DeVita & James D. Armstrong (eds.), *Distant Mirrors: America as a Foreign Culture.* Belmont, CA: West/Wadsworth: 68–73.

Natale, Jo Anna. 1998. "Education in black and white: How kids learn racism—And how schools can help unlearn it." *American School Board Journal* 185(2): 18–23.

Nathan, John. 1999. *Sony: The Private Life.* New York: Houghton-Mifflin.

Nathanson, Amy L. 2001. "Mediation of children's television viewing: Working toward conceptual clarity and common understanding." In William B. Gudykunst (ed.), *Communication Yearbook 25.* Mahwah, NJ: Lawrence Erlbaum: 115–51.

National Advisory Commission on Civil Disorders. 1968. *Report of the National Advisory Commission on Civil Disorders.* New York: Bantam.

National Cancer Institute. 1997. "Estimated exposures in thyroid doses received by the American people from Iodine-131 in fallout following Nevada atmospheric nuclear bomb tests." Bethesda, MD: National Cancer Institute. Available: http://rex.nci.gov/massmedia/Fallout.

National Center for Children in Poverty. *Child Poverty Fact Sheet* (July). Washington, DC.

National Center for Education Statistics. 2000. *Digest of Education Statistics.* Office of Educational Research and Improvement. Washington, DC: U.S. Department of Education.

National Center for Education Statistics. 2001a. *Indicators of School Crime and Safety.* Office of Educational Research and Improvement. Washington, DC: U.S. Department of Education

National Center for Education Statistics. 2001b. "Projections of Education Statistics to 2011." Available: http://www.nces.ed.gov/pubs2001/proj01/tables.

National Center for Health Statistics. 2001. Centers for Disease Control. Available: http://www.cdc.gov/nchs/products/pubs/pubd/hestats/healinsur.

National Coalition for the Homeless (NCH) & National Law Center on Homelessness and Poverty (NLCHP). 2002. *Illegal to be Homeless: The Criminalization of Homelessness in the United States.* Washington, DC: Authors.

National Commission on Excellence in Education. 1983. *A Nation at Risk: The Imperative for Educational Reform.* Washington, DC: National Commission on Excellence in Education.

National Criminal Justice Association. 1996. *The Real War on Crime.* New York: Harper.

National Institutes of Health. 2002. "Electroacupuncture trial is NCCAM's first intramural study." National Center for Complementary and Alternative Medicine (NCCAM): June 12. Available: http://www.nih.gov/news/pr/jun2002.nccam-12.

National Law Center on Homelessness and Poverty (NLCHP). 2002. "Homelessness and poverty in America." Available: http://www.nlchp.org.

National Opinion Research Center. 1994. *General Social Surveys, 1972–1994: Cumulative Codebook.* Chicago: NORC.

National Research Council. 2000. *From Neurons to Neighborhoods: The Science of Early Childhood Development.* Washington, DC: National Academy Press.

National Strategy for Suicide Prevention. 2001. "At a glance–Suicide among the elderly." U.S. Department of Health and Human Services. Available: http:www.mentalhealth.org/suicideprevention/elderly.

Navalas, Setgio et al. 2000. "Microcredit and the poorest of the poor: Theory and evidence from Bolivia." *World Development* 28(2): 333–46.

Navarro, Vicente. 1986. *Crisis, Health and Medicine: A Social Critique.* New York: Tavistock.

NCAA. 1999. *1997–1998 NCAA Gender-Equity Study.* Indianapolis: NCAA.

NCQA. 2001. "Managed care and the U.S. health industry." National Committee for Quality Assurance. Available: http://www.ncqa.org/some/2001.

Nee, Victor, Jimy M. Sanders, & Scott Sernau. 1994. "Job transitions in an immigrant metropolis." *American Sociological Review* 59: 849–72.

Neighbors, Catherine J. 2001. "The construct of sexual orientation in ordinary language." *Dissertation Abstracts International: Section B: The Sciences and Engineering* 61(9-B): 4997.

Nelson, Jack. 1995. "The Internet, the virtual community, and those with disabilities." *Disability Studies Quarterly* 15: 15–20.

Nelson, Mariah B. 1994. *The Stronger Women Get, The More Men Love Football: Sexism & the American Culture of Sports.* New York: Harcourt Brace.

Nemeth, Mary. 1998. "Amazing greys." In Harold Cox (ed.). *Annual Aging: Annual Editions, 98/99.* Guilford, CT: Dushkin/McGraw-Hill: 90–97.

Nettles, Michael T., & Catherine M. Millett. 2000. *Student Access in Community Colleges—New Expeditions: Charting the Second Century of Community Colleges.* Issues Paper No. 1. Washington, DC: American Association of Community Colleges

Neugarten, Bernice L., & Karol K. Weinstein. 1964. "The changing American grandparents." *Journal of Marriage and the Family* 26: 199–204.

Neugarten, Bernice L., Robert J. Havinghurst, & Sheldon S. Tobin. 1968. "Personality patterns and aging." In Bernice L. Neugarten (ed.), *Middle Age and Aging.* Chicago: University of Chicago Press: 173–77.

New York State Special Commission on Attica. 1972. *Attica: The Official Report On the New York State Special Commission on Attica.* New York: Bantam.

Newberger, Eli H. 1999. *The Men They Will Become: The Nature and Nurture of Male Character.* Reading, MA: Perseus.

Newcomb, Horace (ed.). 2000. *Television: The Critical View,* 6th ed. New York: Oxford University Press.

Newdorf, David. 1991. "Bailout agencies like to do it in secret." *Washington Journalism Review* 13/4: 15–16.

Newfield, Jack, & Paul Dubrul. 1979. "The political economy of organized crime." In Jerome H. Skolnick, and Elliott Currie (eds.). *Crisis in American Institutions,* 4th ed. Boston: Little Brown: 414–27.

Newman, Barbara M., & Philip R. Newman. 2001. "Group identity and alienation: Giving the we its due." *Journal of Youth and Adolescence* 30(5): 515–38.

Newman, Katherine S. 2001. "Local caring: Social capital and social responsibility in New York's minority neighborhoods." In Alice S. Rossi (ed.), *Caring and Doing for Others in the Domains of Family, Work and Community.* Chicago: University of Chicago: 157–77.

Newman, Katherine. 1999. *Falling From Grace.* Berkeley: University of California.

Newman, William M. 1973. *American Pluralism: A Study of Minority Groups and Social Theory.* New York: Harper & Row.

Newton, Michael. 2002. *Savage Girls and Wild Boys.* London: Faber.

Nezlek, John B., & Peter Derks. 2001. "Use of humor as a coping mechanism, psychological adjustment and social interaction." *Humor: International Journal of Humor Research.* 14(4): 395–413.

Ni, Hanyu, & Robin Cohen. 2002. "Trends in health insurance coverage by race/ethnicity among persons under 65 years of age: United States, 1997–2001."

Nichols, Roger L. (ed.). 1992. *The American Indian: Past and Present,* 4th ed. New York: McGraw-Hill.

Nicholson, James A. 1998. "What research says about ability grouping and academic achievement." EDRS. Accession No.: ED426129. ERIC.

Nie, Norman H. 1999. "Tracking our techno-future." *American Demographics* (July): 50–52.

Niebuhr, Gustav. 1999. "Alternative religions as a growth industry: How the Internet and airplanes spread a faith." *New York Times* (December 25): C1–C3.

Niebuhr, Richard. 1999. "Alternative religions as a growing industry." *New York Times* (December 25): C1.

Nielsen, Francois. 1994. "Income Inequality and Industrial Development: Dualism Revisited." *American Sociological Review* 59: 654–677.

Niemi, Nancy Susan. 2001. "Silencing the noise of students' gender identity construction in middle school discourse." *Dissertation Abstracts International, A: The Humanities and Social Sciences* 62(2) (August), 524-A. University of Rochester.

Nisbet, Robert A. 1969. *Social Change & History.* New York: Oxford University Press.

Nisbet, Robert A. 1988. *The Present Age.* New York: Harper & Row.

Nisbet, Robert A., & Robert G. Perrin. 1977. *The Social Bond,* 2nd ed. New York: Knopf.

Nixon, Howard L., II. 1993. "Accepting the risks of pain and injury in sport." *Sociology of Sport Journal* (10/June): 183–96.

Noel, D. L. 1991. "A theory of the origin of ethnic stratification." In N. R. Yetman (ed.), *Majority & Minority.* Boston: Allyn & Bacon: 113–125.

Noguera, Paul. 2001. "Finding safety where we least expect it: The role of social capital in preventing school violence." In William Ayers, Bernadine Dohrn, & Rick Ayers (eds.), *Zero Tolerance: Resisting the Drive for Punishment in our Schools.* New York: New Press: 202–18.

Nolan, Patrick, & Gerhard E. Lenski. 1999. *Human Societies: An Introduction to Macrosociology,* 8th ed. New York: McGraw-Hill.

Noley, G. 1990. "The foster child of American education." In G. E. Thomas (ed.), *Race Relations in the 1980s & 1990s.* New York: Hemisphere: 239–48.

NOMAS. 2000. "A brief history of NOMAS and the M&Ms." Available: http:www.nomas.org/history.

Noonan, John T. 1998. *The Luster of our Country: The American Experience of Religious Freedom.* Berkeley: University of California.

NORC. 1996. *General Social Survey, 1996.* Chicago: NORC.

NORC. 1999. *General Social Surveys, 1976–1998.* Chicago: National Opinion Research Center.

NORC. 2000. *General Social Survey, 1972–2000: Cumulative Codebook.* Chicago: National Opinion Research Center.

Nordlinger, Eric A. 1981. *On the Autonomy of the Democratic State.* Cambridge, MA: Harvard University Press.

Nordmann, Nancy. "The marginalisation of students with learning disabilities as a function of school philosophy and practice." *Journal of Moral Education* 30(3): 273–86.

Norman, Michael. 1998. "Getting serious about adultery." *New York Times* (July 4): A15, A17.

Normandeau, Andre. 1993. "Community policing in Canada: A review of some recent studies." *American Journal of Police* (12/1): 57–73.

Norris, Mary E. 1992. "The impact of development on women: A specific-factors analysis." *Journal of Development Economics* 38(1): 183–201.

Norris, Pippa. 1997. *Women, Media and Politics.* New York: Oxford University Press.

Norton, Mary Beth, & Ruth M. Alexander (eds.). "Remember the ladies letters." (by Abigail Adams). In *Major Problems in American Women's History.* Lexington, MA: D. C. Heath.

NOW, 1998. *Issue Report: Same-Sex Marriage.* National Organization of Women. Available: http://www.now.org/issues/lgbi/marr-rep.

Nunez, Ralph, & Cybelle Fox. 1999. "A snapshot of family homelessness across America." *Political Science Quarterly* 114(2): 289–308.

Nurse, Andrea. 1999. *Muslin Palestine: The Ideology of Hamas.* London: Harwood.

Nussbaum, Karen. 2002. Working Women. Washington, DC: AFL-CIO. Available: http:www.aflcio.org/women.

O'Ballance, Edgar. 1979. *The Language of Violence: The Blood Politics of Terrorism.* San Rafael, CA: Presidio.

O'Brien, Jodi, & Peter Kollock. 2001. "Meaning is negotiated through interaction." In J. O'Brien and P. Kollack (eds.), *The Production of Reality: Essays and Readings on Social Interaction.* Thousand Oaks, CA: Pine Forge: 189–205.

O'Connell, Martin T. 1997. "Children with single parents: How they fare." CENBR/97-1:September. Washington, DC: U.S. Census Bureau.

O'Connor, Bonnie B., & David J. Huford, 2001. "Understanding folk medicine." In Erika Brady (ed.), *Healing Logics: Culture and Medicine in Modern Health Belief Systems.* Logan, UT: Utah State University: 13–38.

O'Dea, Thomas. 1966. *The Sociology of Religion.* Upper Saddle River, NJ: Prentice Hall.

O'Donnell, Guillermo A. 1979. *Modernization and Bureaucratic-Authoritarianism.* Berkeley: Institute for International Studies, University of California.

O'Hanlon, Michael. 2000. "A view from afar: Memories of New Guinea highland warfare." In Paul Dresch, Wendy James, & David Parkin (eds.), *Anthropologists in a Wider World: Essays on Field Research.* New York: Berghahn.

O'Hare, William P. 1992. "America's minorities: The demographics of diversity." *Population Bulletin* 47(4). Washington, DC: Population Reference Bureau.

O'Kane, James M. 1992. *The Crooked Ladder: Gangsters, Ethnicity and the American Dream.* New Brunswick, NJ: Transaction.

O'Leary, Eleanor, & Inge M. Nieuwstraten. 2001. "Emerging psychological issues in talking about death and dying: A discourse analytic study." *International Journal for the Advancement of Counseling* 23(3): 179–99.

O'Malley, Padraig. 1990. *Northern Ireland: Questions of Nuance.* Belfast: Blackstaff Press.

O'Meara, Molly. 1999a. "U.S. voters tell suburbia to slow down." *Worldwatch* 12(4): 9.

O'Meara, Molly. 1999b. "How mid-sized cities can avoid strangulation." *Public Management* 81(5): 8–15.

O'Reilly, Marc J. 1999. "Oil monarchies without oil: Omani and Bahraini security in a post-oil era." *Middle East Policy* 6(3): 78–92.

O'Reilly, Patricia. 2001. "Learning to be a girl." In Patricia O'Reilly & Elizabeth M. Penn (eds.), *Educating Young Adolescent Girls.* Mahwah, NJ: Lawrence Erlbaum: 11–27.

O'Toole, Kimberly Hamilton. 2001. "A sociocultural analysis of the gender and racial representations in films offering a vision of the future of humanity." *Dissertation Abstracts International, A: The Humanities and Social Sciences* 62 (August): 781-A.

Oakes, Jeannie, & Martin Lipton. 1996. "Developing alternatives to tracking and grading." In Laura I. Rendon & Richard O. Hope (eds.), *Educating a New Majority: Transforming America's Educational System for Diversity.* San Francisco: Jossey-Bass: 168–200.

Oakes, Jeannie, & Martin Lipton. 1999. *Teaching to Change the World.* Boston: McGraw-Hill.

Oakes, Jeannie, Karen Hunter Quartz, Steve Ryan, & Martin Lipton. 2000. *Becoming Good American Schools: The Struggle for Civic Virtue in Education Reform.* San Francisco: Jossey-Bass.

Oberlander, Jonathan, & Theodore R. Marmor. 2001. "The path to universal health care." In Robert L. Borsage & Roger Hickey (eds.), *The Next Agenda: Blueprint for a New Progressive Movement.* Boulder, CO: Westview.

Oberschall, Anthony. 1973. *Social Conflict and Social Movements.* Englewood Cliffs, NJ: Prentice Hall.

Oberschall, Anthony. 1993. *Social Movements: Ideologies, Interests and Identities.* New Brunswick, NJ: Transaction.

OECD Health Data. 2002. "Frequently asked data." Organization for Economic Cooperation and Development. Table 2: Infant mortality-Deaths per 1000 live births and Table 9: Total Expenditures on health, per capita US$. Available: http://www.oecd.org/EN/document.

OECD, 2001. *Policies to Enhance Sustainable Development.* Paris: Organisation for Economic Cooperation and Development.

OECD. 2000. Reforms for an Aging Society. Paris: Organisation for Economic Co-operation and Development.

OECD. 2002. *Measuring the Non-Observed Economy: A Handbook.* Paris: Organisation for Economic Co-operation and Development.

Oegema, Dirk, & Bert Klandermans. 1994. "Why social movement sympathizers don't participate." *American Sociological Review* 59: 703–22.

Office of Child Support Enforcement. 2000. "Getting to know the future customers of the office of child support." U.S. Department of Health and Human Services. Available: http://www.acf.dhhs.gov/programs/cse/pubs/reports/projections.

Ogburn, William F. 1938. "The changing family." *Family* 19: 139–43.

Ojeda, Amparo B. 1998. "Growing up American: Doing the right Thing." In Philip R. DeVita & James D. Armstrong, (eds.), *Distant Mirrors: America as a Foreign Culture.* Belmont, CA: West/Wadsworth: 50–54.

Oliver, Melvin L., & Thomas M. Shapiro. 1995. *Black Wealth/White Wealth: A New Perspective on Racial Inequality.* New York: Routledge.

Ollman, Bertell. 1971. *Alienation.* Cambridge, England: Cambridge University Press.

Olmstead, Michael S., & A. Paul Hare. 1978. *The Small Group,* 2nd ed. New York: Random House.

Olmstead, R. E., S. M. Guy, P. M. O'Malley, & P. M. Bentler. 1991. "Longitudinal assessment of the relationship between self-esteem, fatalism, loneliness, and substance abuse." *Journal of Social Behavior and Personality* 6: 749–70.

Olsen, Gregg M. 1996. "Re-modeling Sweden." *Social Problems* (43/1): 1–20.

Olsen, Mancur E. 1978. *The Process of Social Organization: Power in Social Systems,* 2nd ed. New York: Holt, Rinehart & Winston.

Olson, David V. A. 1999. "Religious pluralism and U.S. church membership: A reassessment." *Sociology of Religion* 60(2): 149–73.

Olson, Karen L., Janice M. Morse, & Jane E. Smith. 2000/2001. "Linking trajectories of illness and dying." Omega 42(4): 293–308.

Olson, Laura Katz. 1999. "Women and old-age income security in the United States." In *Aging in a Gendered World: Women's Issues and Identities.* Santo Domingo, Dominican Republic: International Research and Training Institute for the Advancement of Women.

Olzak, Susan, & Joann Nagel (eds.). 1986. *Competitive Ethnic Relations.* San Diego: Academic Press.

Olzak, Susan, Suzanne Shanahan, & Elizabeth West. 1994. "School desegregation, interracial exposure, and antibusing activity in contemporary urban America." *American Journal of Sociology* 100(1): 196–241.

Omi, Michael, & Howard Winant. 1994. *Racial Formation in the United States,* 2nd ed. New York: Routledge.

Omoto, Allen M. 1999. "Lesbian, gay, and bisexual issues in public policy: Some of the relevance and realities of psychological science." In Janis S. Bohan, Glenda M. Russell et al. (eds.), Sexual Violence on Campus: Policies, Programs and Perspectives. New York: New York University.

"Once-Safe Japan Plagued by Vicious Crime." 2000. *Evansville Courier & Press* (February 13): A10.

Onyekwuluje, Anne. B. 1999. "Multiculturalism, diversity and the impact parents and schools have on societal race relations." *School Community Journal* 8(2): 55–71.

Opp, Karl-Dieter, & Christine Gern. 1993. "Dissident groups, personal networks and spontaneous cooperation." *American Sociological Review* 58: 659–80.

Opp, Karl-Dieter, & Wolfgang Roehl. 1990. "Repression, micromobilization and political protest." *Social Forces* 69: 521–47.

Opp, Karl-Dieter. 1989. *The Rationality of Political Protest.* Boulder, CO: Westview.

Orenstein, Peggy. 1997. "Shortchanging girls: Gender socialization in schools." In Dana Dunn (ed.), *Workplace/Women's Place: An Anthology.* Los Angeles: Roxbury: 43–52.

Orenstein, Peggy. 2001. "Unbalanced equations: Girls, math, and the confidence gap." In Roberta Satow (ed.), *Gender and Social Life.* Needham Hts, MA: Allyn & Bacon.

Orfield, Gary, & John T. Yun. 1999. "Resegregation in American Schools." The Civil Rights Project Available: http://www.law.harvard.edu/civilrights/publications/resegregation/99.

Orfield, Gary. 2001a. "Introduction." In Gary Orfield (ed.), *Diversity Challenged: Evidence on the Impact of Affirmative Action.* Cambridge, MA: Harvard Education Publishing Group: 1–30.

Orfield, Gary. 2001b. *Schools More Segregated: Consequences of a Decade of Resegregation.* Cambridge, MA: Harvard Civil Rights Project.

Orfield, Myron. 2002. *American Metropolitics: The New Suburban Reality.* Washington, DC: Brookings Institution.

Orjiako, Humphrey. 2001. *Killing Sub-Saharan Africa with Aid.* Huntington, NY: Nova Science.

Orshansky, Mollie. 1969. "How poverty is measured." *Monthly Labor Review* 92/2: 37–41.

Orum, Anthony M. 2001. *Introduction to Political Sociology,* 4th ed. Upper Saddle River, NJ: Prentice Hall.

Osborne, David. 2001. "Healthy competition." In Williamson M. Evers, Lance T. Izumi, & Pamela A. Riley (eds.), *School Reform: The Critical Issues.* Stanford, CA: Hoover Institution: 273–80.

Osborne, Jason W. 2000. "Testing stereotype threat: Does anxiety explain race and sex difference in achievement?" *Contemporary Educational Psychology* 26(3): 291–310.

OSHA. 2002. "Workplace violence." Occupational Safety & Health Administration, U.S. Department of Labor. Available: http://www.osha-slc.gov/oshinfo/priorities/violence.

Ossowski, Stanislaw. 1983. "Marx's concept of class." In T. Bottomore & P. Goode (eds.), *Readings in Marxist Sociology.* New York: Oxford University Press: 99–102.

Oswalt, Wendell H., & Sharlotte Neely. 1999. *This Land Was Theirs,* 6th ed. Mountain View, CA: Mayfield.

Ottens, Allen J. 2001. "The scope of sexual violence on campus." In Allen J. Ottens & Kathy Hotelling (eds.), *Sexual Violence on Campus: Policies, Programs and Perspectives.* New York: Springer: 1–29.

Overholser, Geneva. 2001. "Labor Day is hardly reason to celebrate for the common worker." *Evansville Courier & Press* (September 3): A-7.

Overman, Steven J. 1997. *The Influence of the Protestant Ethic on Sport and Recreation.* Brookfield, VT: Avebury.

Owens, Timothy J. (ed.). 2000. *Self and Identity in the Life Course in Cross-Cultural Perspective.* Stamford, CT: JAI.

Owomero, Basil. 1988. "Crime in Tanzania: Contradictions of a socialist experiment," *International Journal of Comparative and Applied Criminal Justice* 12: 177–89.

Oyler, Dianne W. 2002. "Re-inventing oral tradition: The modern epic of Souleymane Kante." *Research in African Literatures* 33(1): 75–94.

Pablo, Marcia. 2001. "Preservation as perpetuation." *American Indian Quarterly* 25(1): 20.

Pacey, Susan. 1999. "Torture, transformation or treatment? Ethics and physical interventions to the sexual self." *Sexual & Marital Therapy* 14(3): 255–75.

Pacheco, Arturo. 1999. "Moving toward democracy: Lessons learned." In Kenneth A. Sirotnik & Roger Soder (eds.), *The Beat of a Different Drummer: Essays on Educational Renewal in Honor of John I. Goodlad.* New York: Peter Lang: 231–43.

Paci, E., G. Miccinesi, F. Toscani, M. Tamburini, et al. 2001. "Quality of life Assessment and outcome of palliative care." *Journal of Pain Symptom Management* 21: 179–88.

Page, Charles H. 1946. "Bureaucracy's other face," *Social Forces* 25 (October): 89–94.

Page, Joseph A. 1995. *The Brazilians.* Reading, MA: Addison-Wesley.

Page, Stephen, (ed.). 2001. *CEIC Review* 10: 1–6. National Research Center on Education in the Inner Cities.

Palmer, Carleton, & Mark Hazelrigg. 2000. "The guilty but mentally ill verdict: A review and conceptual analysis of intent and impact." *Journal of the American Academy of Psychiatry & the Law* 28(1): 47–54.

Palmer, Janet Patricia. 2001. "Animating cultural politics: Disney, race, and social movements in the 1990s." *Dissertation Abstracts International: Section A: The Humanities and Social Sciences* 61(10) (April): 4188–89.

Palmer, Parker J. 1998. *The Courage to Teach: Exploring the Inner Landscape of a Teacher's Life.* San Francisco: Jossey-Bass.

Paludi, Michele A. 1996. *Sexual Harassment on College Campuses: Abusing the Ivory Power.* Albany, NY: State University of New York.

Pandey, Sanjay K., & Gordon A. Kingsley. 2000. "Examining red tape in public and private organizations." *Journal of Public Administration Research & Theory* (10/4): 779–799.

Pandya, Sheel M. 2001. "Nursing homes." Independent Living Long-Term Care Team. AARP Research Center. Available: http://research.aarp.org/health/fs10r_nursing.

Parade Magazine. 1991. "Sexual harassment: Gender gap on Capitol Hill." November 17: 10.

Parenti, Michael. 1986. *Inventing Reality: The Politics of the Mass Media.* New York: St. Martin's Press.

Parenti, Michael. 1992. *Make-Believe Media: The Politics of Entertainment.* New York: St. Martin's.

Parenti, Michael. 1995. *Democracy for the Few,* 6th ed. New York: St. Martin's Press.

Parenti, Michael. 2002. *Democracy for the Few.* New York: St. Martin's.

Park, Robert Ezra, Ernest Burgess, & Roderick McKenzie (eds.). 1925. *The City.* Chicago: University of Chicago Press.

Park, Robert Ezra. 1916. "The city: Suggestions for the investigation of human behavior in an urban environment."*American Journal of Sociology* 20: 577–612.

Park, Robert Ezra. 1926. "Succession, an ecological concept." *American Sociological Review* 1: 171–79.

Parker, Robert N. 1995. "Violent crime." In Joseph F. Sheley (ed.). *Criminology: A Contemporary Handbook,* 2nd ed. Belmont, CA: Wadsworth: 169–85.

Parkinson, C. N. 1962. *Parkinson's Law,* 2nd ed. Boston: Houghton Mifflin.

Parks, Malcolm R. 1996. "Making friends in cyberspace." *Journal of Communication* 46: 80–96.

Parlee, Mary Brown. 1989. "Conversational politics." In Laurel Richardson & Verta

Taylor (eds.), *Feminist Frontiers II: Rethinking Sex, Gender and Society*. New York: Random House.

Parrillo, Vincent N. 2000. *Strangers to These Shores*, 6th ed. Boston: Allyn & Bacon.

Parris, Tom. 2000. "Contemplating religion and environment on the Net." *Environment* (July).

Parsons, Talcott, & Robert F. Bales. 1955. *Family, Socialization and Interaction Process*. Glencoe, IL: Free Press.

Parsons, Talcott. 1951. *The Social System*. Glencoe, IL: Free Press.

Parsons, Talcott. 1964. "Definitions of health and illness in light of American values and social structure." In Talcott Parsons (ed.), *Social Structure and Personality*. New York: The Free Press.

Parsons, Talcott. 1966. *Societies: Evolutionary & Comparative Perspectives*. Upper Saddle River, NJ: Prentice Hall.

Pasley, Kay, & Carmelle Minton. 2001. "Generative fathering: After divorce and remarriage: Beyond the 'disappearing dad.'" In Theodore F. Cohn (ed.), *Men and Masculinity: A Text Reader*. Belmont, CA: Wadsworth: 239–48.

Passas, N., & R. Agnew. 1997. *The Future of Anomie Theory*. Boston: Northeastern University Press.

Passell, Peter. 1996. "Asia's Path to More Equality & More Money For All." *New York Times* (August 25): E5.

Pastalan, L. A. 1982. "Research in environment and aging: An alternative to theory." In M. Powell Lawton, P. G. Windley, & T. O. Byerts (eds.), *Aging and the Environment: Theoretical Approaches*. New York: Springer.

Pasternak, Burton, Carol R. Ember, & Melvin Ember. 1997. *Sex, Gender and Kinship: A Cross-Cultural Perspective*. Upper Saddle River, NJ: Prentice Hall.

Patel, Sheela, & Diana Mitlin. 2001. "The work of SPARC and its partners Mahila Milan and the National Slum Dwellers Federation in India." IIED paper on Poverty Reduction in Urban Areas.

Pathak, Bindeshwar. 1999. "Sanitation is the key to healthy cities: A profile of Sulabh International." *Environment and Urbanization* 11(1): 221–29.

Patrick, Helen, Allison M. Ryan, Corinne Alfeld-Liro, Jennifer A. Fredricks, Ludmilla Z. Hruda, & Jacquelynne S. Eccles. 1999. "Adolescents' commitment to developing talent: The role of peers in continuing motivation for sports and the arts." *Journal of Youth and Adolescence* 28(6): 741–63.

Patterson, James T. 1994. *America's Struggle with Poverty, 1990–1994*. Cambridge, MA: Harvard University Press.

Patterson, Orlando. 1982. *Slavery & Social Death: A Comparative Study*. Cambridge, MA: Harvard University Press.

Pavri, Shireen, & Richard L. Luftig. 2000. "The social face of inclusive education: Are students with learning disabilities really included in the classroom?" *Preventing School Failure* 45(1): 8–14.

Payne, Kaye E. 2001. *Different but Equal: Communication between the Sexes*. Westport, CT: Praeger/Greenwood.

Pearce, Frank, & Steve Tombs. 1997. "Hazards, law & class: Contextualizing the regulation of corporate crime." *Social and Legal Studies* 6: 79: 107.

Pearson, Alyn. 2000. "Rape culture: Media and message." *Off Our Backs* 30 (Aug/Sept): 13–14.

Pearson, Ethel Specter. 1999. *The Sexual Century*. New Haven, CT: Yale University.

Peatrik, Anne-Marie. 1995. "The rule and the number: East African generational and age-set systems." *L'Homme 35*, 4 (April–June): 13–49.

Pedraza, Sylvia, & Ruben Rumbaut, (eds.). 1996. *Origins and Destinies: Immigration, Race and Ethnicity in America*. Belmont, CA: Wadsworth.

Peerandina, Saleem. 1998. "Giving, withholding, and meeting midway: A poet's ethnography." In Philip R. DeVita & James D. Armstrong (eds.), *Distant Mirrors: America as a Foreign Culture*. Belmont, CA: West/Wadsworth: 17–28.

Pepinsky, Harold E., & Richard Quinney (eds.). 1993. *Criminology as Peacemaking*. Bloomington, IN: Indiana University Press.

Per Pinstrup-Andersen, Rajul Pandya-Lorch, & Mark W. Rosegrant. 2001. "Global food security: A review of the challenges. In Per Pinstrup-Andersen & Rajul Pandya-Lorch (eds.), *The Unfinished Agenda: Perspectives on Overcoming Hunger, Poverty, and Environmental Degradation*. Washington, DC: International Food Policy and Research Institute.

Perdue, William D. 1993. *Systemic Crisis*. Fort Worth, TX: Harcourt.

Perl, P., & David V. A. Olson. 2000. "Religious market share and intensity of church involvement in five denominations." *Journal for the Scientific Study of Religion* 38: 12–31.

Perl, Richard F. 1998. *Terrorism, the Media, and the 21st Century*. Washington, DC: Congressional Research Service.

Perrine, Daniel M. 1994. "The view from platform zero: How Holland handles its drug problem." *America* 171: (October 15) 9–12.

Perrow, Charles. 1991. "A society of organizations." *Theory and Society* (20/6): 725–62.

Perry, Alex. 2001. "Crossing the line." *Time* (May 7): 18–21.

Perry, Joellen. 2000. "Retirees stay wired to kids—and to one another." *U.S. News & World Report 128* (June): 80.

Perry, Stewart A. 1978. *San Francisco Scavengers: Dirty Work & the Pride of Ownership*. Berkeley: U of California Press.

Perske, Robert. 2001. "A joint statement: Stop the execution of persons with mental retardation." *Mental Retardation* 39(4): 327–28.

Peschek, Joseph. 1987. *Policy-Planning Organizations*. Philadelphia: Temple University Press.

Petchesky, Rosalind P., & Karen Judd (eds.). 1998. *Negotiating Reproductive Rights: Women's Perspectives Across Countries and Culture*. New York: St. Martin's.

Peter, Lawrence J., & Raymond Hull. 1969. *The Peter Principle*. New York: Morrow.

Peters, Joan. K. 1998. *Loving Our Children without Sacrificing Our Selves*. Reading, MA: Addison-Wesley.

Peters, Julie Stone. 1999. "Reply: Reconceptualizing the relationship between religion, women, culture, and human rights." In Carrie Gustafson & Peter Juviler (eds.), *Religion and Human Rights: Competing Claims?* Armonk, NY: M. E. Sharpe: 140–44.

Peters, Thomas J., & Robert H. Waterman, Jr. 1982. *In Search of Excellence*. New York: Warner.

Peters, Tom J. 1992. *Liberation Management*. New York: Knopf.

Petersen, William. 1998. *Malthus: Founder of Modern Demography*. New Brunswick, NJ: Transaction.

Peterson del Mar, David. 1996. *What Trouble I Have Seen: A History of Violence Against Wives*. Cambridge, MA: Harvard University.

Peterson, John L. 1994. *The Road to 2015: Profiles of the Future*. Corte Madera, CA: Waite Group.

Peterson, Richard R. 1996. "A re-evaluation of the economic consequences of divorce." *American Sociological Review* 61(3)(June): 528–536.

Pew Center. 2000. "Straight talk from Americans: 2000." A national survey for the Pew Center for Civic Journalism conducted by Princeton Survey Research Associates. Washington, DC.

Phelan, J., B. G. Link, R. E. Moore, & A. Stueve. 1997. "The stigma of homelessness." *Social Psychology Quarterly* 60: 323–337.

Phelan, Jo, Bruce G. Link, Robert E. Moore, & Ann Seuve. 1997. "The Stigma of Homelessness," *Social Psychology Quarterly* 60: 323–337.

Phelan, Thomas J., & Mark Schneider. 1996. "Race, ethnicity and class in American suburbs." *Urban Affairs Review* 31: 659–80.

Pheysey, Diana. 1993. *Organizational Cultures: Types and Transformations*. London: Routledge.

Philaretou, Andreas G., & Katherine R. Allen. 2001. "Reconstructing masculinity and sexuality." *Journal of Men's Studies* 9(3): 301–321.

Phillips, David P. 1980. "The deterrent effect of capital punishment: New evidence on an old controversy." *American Journal of Sociology* 86: 139–48.

Phillips, G. M., & J. T. Wood (eds.). 1984. *Emergent Issues in Human Decision Making*. Carbondale: Southern Illinois University Press.

Phillips, Jacqueline S., & Navaz Peshotan Bhavnagri. 2002. "The Masai's education and empowerment." *Childhood Education* 78(3): 140–46.

Phillips, Kevin. 1991. *The Politics of Rich and Poor*. New York: Simon & Schuster.

Phillips, Kevin. 1994. *Arrogant Capital*. Boston: Little, Brown.

Phillips, L. E. 1999. "Love, American style." *American Demographics* 21: 56–57.

Phillips, Susan. 1999. *Wallbangin': Graffiti and Gangs in L.A.* Chicago: University of Chicago.

Phinney, Jean S., & Karmela Liebkind. 2001. "Ethnic identity, immigration and well-being: An international perspective." *Journal of Social Issues* 57(3): 493–510.

Piaget, Jean, & Barbel Inhelder. 1969. *The Psychology of the Child*. New York: Basic Books.

Piaget, Jean. 1950. *The Psychology of Intelligence*. Boston: Routledge & Kegan Paul.

Pienta, Amy Mehraban, Mark D. Hayward, & Kristi Rahrig Jenkins. 2000. "Health consequences of marriage for the retirement years." *Journal of Family Issues* 21(5): 559–86.

Pierce, Dean. 2001. "Language, science and queer people: Social and cultural change strategies." In Mary E. Swigonski & Robin S. Mama (eds.), *From Hate Crimes to Human Rights: A Tribute to Matthew Shepard*. New York: Haworth.

Pierre, Andrew J. 2000. "Vietnam's contradictions." *Foreign Affairs* 79(6): 69–86.

Pilat, Dirk. 2002. "The long-term performance of the Japanese economy." In Angus Maddison, S. Prasada Rao, & William F. Shepherd (eds.), *The Asian Economies in the Twentieth Century*. Cheltenham, UK: Elgar.

Pillemer, Karl, Phyllis Moen, Elaine Wethington, & Nina Glasgow. 2000. *Social Integration in the Second Half of Life*. Baltimore, MD: Johns Hopkins University.

Pimentel, Ellen Efron. 2000. "Just how do I love thee?: Marital relations in urban China." *Journal of Marriage and the Family* 62(1): 32–47.

Pinar, William. 2001. *The Gender of Racial Politics and Violence in America: Lynching, Prison Rape, & the Crisis of Masculinity*. New York: P. Lang.

Pinderhughes, Dianne M. 1987. *Race and Ethnicity in Chicago Politics: A Reexamination of Pluralist Theory*. Chicago: University of Chicago.

Pinkney, Alphonso. 2000. *Black Americans*, 5th ed. Upper Saddle River, NJ: Prentice-Hall.

Pinto, Mary Beth. 2000. "On the nature and properties of appeals used in direct-to-consumer advertising of prescription drugs." *Psychological Reports* 86(2): 597–607.

Pirenne, Henri. 1937. *Economic & Social History of Medieval Europe*. New York: Harcourt, Brace & World.

Piven, Frances Fox, & Richard A. Cloward. 1977. *Poor People's Movements: Why They Succeed, How They Fail*. New York: Random House.

Piven, Frances, & Richard Cloward. 1978. *Why Americans Don't Vote*. New York: Pantheon.

Plagenz, George R. 1997. "Censorship of the entertainment media may be necessary." In Byron L. Stay (ed.), *Censorship*. San Diego: Greenhaven: 148–150.

Plessy v. Ferguson. 2001. "Plessy v. Ferguson, 1896." In Paula S. Rothenberg (ed.), *Race, Class and Gender in the United States*. New York: Worth: 480–482.

Plummer, David C. 2001. "The quest for modern manhood: Masculine stereotypes, peer culture and the social significance of homophobia." *Journal of Adolescence* 24(1): 15–23.

Plummer, David. 1999. *One of the Boys: Masculinity, Homophobia, and Modern Manhood*. Binghamton, NY: Harrington Park.

Plunkert, Lois M. 1990. "The 1980s: A decade of job growth and industry shifts." *Monthly Labor Review* (September): 3–15.

Podolny, Joel M., & James N. Baron. 1997. "Resources and relationships: Social networks and mobility in the workplace." *American Sociological Review* 62(5): 673–693.

Poggie, John J. Jr., & Richard B. Pollnac. 1988. "Danger and rituals of avoidance among New England fisherman." *MAST: Maritime Anthropological Studies* 1: 67–88.

Pohl, Rudiger. 1996. "The transition from communism to capitalism in East Germany." *Society* (33/4): 62–65.

Poire, B. A., J. K. Burgoon, & R. Parrott. 1992. "Status and privacy restoring communication in the workplace." *Journal of Applied Communication Research* 4: 419–36.

Pokras, Olivia, & Violet Woo. 1999. "Health profile of racial and ethnic minorities in the United States." *Ethnicity & Health* 4(3): 117–20.

Polakow, Valerie. 1993. *Lives on the Edge: Single Mothers and Their Children in the Other America.* Chicago: University of Chicago Press.

Political Humor, 2002. "Osama bin Laden late-night jokes." Available: http://politicalhumor.about.com/library/blbinladenjokes.

Politics, 2002. Available: http://www.bigpuns.com/puns/politics.

Pollack, Andrew. 1996. "A cyberspace front in a multicultural war." *New York Times* (August 7): D1, 4.

Pollock, Joycelyn M. 1999. *Criminal Women.* Cincinnati: Anderson.

Pomfret, John. 2002. "In China, the rich seek to become the 'big rich.' " *Washington Post Foreign Service* (March 17): A01.

Pontell, Henry A. 1984. *A Capacity to Punish.* Bloomington, IN: Indiana University Press.

Popenoe, David. 1993. "American family decline, 1960–1990: A review and appraisal." *Journal of Marriage and the Family* 55: 527–42.

Popenoe, David. 2000. "Modern marriage: Revising the cultural script." In Michael S. Kimmel (ed.), *The Gendered Society Reader.* New York: Oxford University: 151–66.

Poplin, Dennis. 1979. *Communities,* 2nd ed. New York: Macmillan.

Poppema, Suzzanne. 1999. "The future of Roe v. Wade: Medical." In Patricia Ojea & Barbara Quigley (eds.), *Women's Studies: Annual Editions, 99–00.* Guilford, CT: Dushkin/McGraw-Hill: 117–18.

Poppen, Paul J. 1995. "Gender and patterns of sexual risk taking in college students." *Sex Roles* 32(7–8): 545–55.

Population Connection. 2002. "Population and environment." Washington, DC. Available: http://www.populationconnection.org/Reports.

Population Reference Bureau, 2001b. "What percent of the world's people live in urban settings?". June. Available: http://www.prb.org/template.cfm?Secton=QuickFacts.

Population Reference Bureau. 1999. "Mid-1999 world projections by country." Washington, DC: Population Reference Bureau.

Population Reference Bureau. 2001a. *The World's Youth 2000.* Washington, DC.

Population Reference Bureau. 2001c. "Judging a country by its cities." March. Available: http://www.prb.org/template.cfm?Secton=QuickFacts.

Population Reference Bureau. 2002. *Ameristat (2000 Census, Marriage/Family; Race/Ethnicty).* Available: http://www.ameristat.org.

Porter, Alan L., & William H. Read (eds.). 1999. *The Information Revolution: Current and Future Consequences.* Greenwich, CT: Ablex.

Porter, B., & M. Dunn. 1984. *The Miami Riot of 1970: Crossing the Bounds.* Lexington, MA: Lexington.

Porter, Eduardo. 2000. "Why the Latino market is so hard to count." *Wall Street Journal* (Eastern Ed.) (October 13); B1, B4.

Portes, Alejandro, & Ruben G. Rumbaut. 1990. *Immigrant America.* Berkeley: University of California Press.

Posavac, Heidi D., Steven S. Posavac, & Richard G. Weigle. 2001. "Reducing the impact of media images on women at risk for body image disturbance: Three targeted interventions." *Journal of Social and Clinical Psychology* 20(3): 324–40.

Posen, Barry. 1991. *Inadvertent Escalation.* Ithaca, NY: Cornell University Press.

Postman, Neil. 1985. *Amusing Ourselves to Death.* New York: Viking.

Powell, A. G. 1996. *Lessons from Privilege: The American Prep School Tradition.* Cambridge, MA: Harvard University.

Powell, Francis D., & Albert F Wessen (eds.). 1999. *Health Care Systems in Transition: An International Perspective.* Thousand Oaks, CA: Sage.

Power, Carla. 1999. "Europeans Just Say 'Maybe.'" *Newsweek* (November 1): 53–54

Powers Bill. 2001. "Quiet! Dad is dusting his G.I. Joes." *New York Times* 151(5) (December 30): Section 9, p. 1

Powers, Susan. 1992. "Sexual harassment: Civil rights act increases liability." *HR Focus* 2: 12.

Prah, Kwesi. 2001. "Language, literacy the production and reproduction of knowledge, and the challenge of African development." In David R. Olson & Nancy Torrance (eds.), *The Making of Literate Societies.* Malden, MA: Blackwell: 23–141.

Prebish, Charles S. (ed.). 1993. *Religion and Sport: The Meeting of Sacred and Profane.* Westport, CT: Greenwood.

Presser, Harriet, & Gita Sen. 2000. *Women's Empowerment and Demographic Processes: Moving Beyond Cairo.* New York: Oxford University.

Prettyman, Sadra Spikard. 1998. "Discourses on adolescence, gender, and schooling: An overview." *Educational Studies: A Journal In the Foundations of Education* 29: 4: 329–40.

Price, Monroe E. (ed.). 1998. *The V-Chip Debate.* Mahwah, NJ: Lawrence Erlbaum.

Pride, Richard A., & Harry Vaughn May, Jr. 1999. "Neighborhood schools Again? Race, educational interest, and traditional values." *Urban Education* 34(3): 389–410.

PRNewswire. 2002. "Future of Israel." (March 23). Pub: Gale Group.

Prospects for Development, 2001. "Global Economic Prospects and the Developing Countries, 2001." Washington, DC: World Bank. Available: http://www.worldbank.org/prospects/gep2001.

Puddington, Arch. 1994. "Black anti-semitism and how it grows." *Commentary* (April).

Puddington, Arch. 1995. "What to do about affirmative action." *Commentary* (June).

Pulido, Laura. 2000. "Rethinking environmental racism: White privilege and urban development in southern California." *Annals of the Association of American Geographers* 90(1): 12–40.

Pulkkinen, Lea, & Avashalom Caspi (eds.). 2002. *Paths to Successful Development: Personality in the Life Course.* Cambridge, NY: Cambridge University.

Purvis, Andrew. 1996. "A contagion of genocide." *Time* (July 8): 38–39.

Putnam, Robert D. 1995. "Bowling alone: America's declining social capital." *Journal of Democracy* (6/1): 65–78.

Quadagno, Jill, & Jennifer Reid. 1999. "The political economy perspective in aging." In Vern L. Bengtson & Klaus Warner Schaie (eds.), *Handbook of Theories of Aging."* New York: Springer: 344–58.

Quadagno, Jill. 1992. "Social movements and state transformation." *American Sociological Review* 57: 616–34.

Quadagno, Jill. 1999. *Aging and the Life Course: An Introduction to Social Gerontology.* Boston: McGraw-Hill College.

Quadagno, Jill. 2002. *Aging and the Life Course: An Introduction to Social Gerontology.* Boston: McGraw-Hill.

Quaiser-Pohl, Claudia, & Wolfgang Lehmann. 2002. "Girls' spatial abilities: Charting the contributions of experiences and attitudes in different academic groups." *British Journal of Educational Psychology* 72(2): 245–60.

Qualter, Terence. 1985. *Opinion Control in the Democracies.* New York: St. Martin's.

Quarantelli, Enrico L. (ed.). 1978. *Disasters: Theory & Research.* Beverly Hills, CA: Sage.

Quarantelli, Enrico L. 1957. "The behavior of panic participants." *Sociology & Social Research* 41: 187–94.

Quarantelli, Enrico L., & Russell R. Dynes. 1970. "Property norms & looting." *Phylon* 31: 168–82.

Quartaroli, Tina Anne. 2001. "From the Summer of Love to the Golden Years: A feminist approach to political generations, social networks and women's elder-years living choices." *Dissertation Abstracts International, A: The Humanities and Social Sciences* 62(3) (September). 1230-A.

Quicke, Andrew, & Karen Robinson 2000. "Keeping the promise of a moral majority: A historical/critical comparison of the Promise Keepers and the Christian Coalition, 1989–98." In Dane S. Claussen (ed.), *The Promise Keepers: Essays on Masculinity and Christianity.* Jefferson, NC: McFarland: 7–19.

Quigley, William. 1995. "The minimum wage and the working poor." *America* (June 3): 6–7.

Quinn, Catherine Anne. 2002. "Dementia: A cause of complicated grieving." In Gerry R. Cox, Robert A. Bendiksen, & Robert G. Stevenson (eds.), *Complicated Grieving and Bereavement: Understanding and Treating People Experiencing Loss.* Amityville, NY: Baywood.

Quinn, R. P., B. A. Gutek, & J. T. Walsh. 1980. "Telephone interviewing: A reappraisal and a field experiment." *Basic and Applied Social Psychology* 1: 127–53.

Quinney, Richard. 1970. *The Social Reality of Crime.* Boston: Little, Brown.

Quinney, Richard. 1971. *Criminology.* Boston: Little Brown.

Quinney, Richard. 1972. "The ideology of law." *Issues in Criminology* (7/1).

Quinney, Richard. 1977. *Class, State and Crime.* New York: David McKay.

Rachlin, Katherine. 2002. "Transgender individuals' experiences of psychotherapy." *International Journal of Transgenderism* 6(1): (January–March).

Radelet, Michael L., & Hugo A. Bedau. 1992. *In Spite of Innocence: Erroneous Convictions in Capital Cases.* Boston: Northeastern University Press.

Rader, Benjamin G. 1990. *American Sports,* 2nd ed. Upper Saddle River, NJ: Prentice-Hall.

Rafalimanana, Hantamalala, & Charles F. Westoff. 2001. "Gap between preferred and actual birth intervals in Sub-Saharan Africa: Implications for fertility and child health." *DHS Analytical Studies* No. 2: March. Calverton, MD: ORC Macro.

Rahman, Aminur. 1999. "Micro-credit initiatives for equitable and sustainable development: Who pays?" *World Development* 27(1): 67–82.

Rahman, Anika, & Nahid Toubia. 2000. *Female Genital Mutilation: A Guide to Laws and Policies Worldwide.* New York: St. Martin's.

Rai, Shirin. 2002. *Gender and the Political Economy of Development: From Nationalism to Globalization.* Cambridge, UK: Polity.

Ramanathaiyer, Sundar, & Stewart MacPherson. 2000. *Social Development in Kerala: Illusion or Reality?* Aldershot, Hants, UK: Ashgate.

Ramdas, Lalita. 2001. "Women and literacy: A quest for justice." In Ellen Cushman, Eugene R. Kintgen, Barry M. Kroll, & Mike Rose (eds.), *Literacy: A Critical Sourcebook.* Boston: Bedford/St. Martin's: 629–43.

Ramos, Francisco Martins. 1998. "My American glasses." In Philip R. DeVita & James D. Armstrong (eds.), *Distant Mirrors: America as a Foreign Culture.* Belmont, CA: West/Wadsworth: 9–160.

Rank, Mark R. 1989. "Fertility among women on welfare." *American Sociological Review* 54: 296–304.

Rank, Mark R. 2000. "Poverty and economic hardship in families." In David H. Demo, Katherine Allen, & Mark A. Fine (eds.), *Handbook of Family Diversity.* New York: Oxford University.

Rankin, Bruce H., & James M. Quane. 2002. "Social contexts and urban adolescent outcomes: The interrelated effects of neighborhoods, families, and peers on African-American youth." *Social Problems* 49(1): 79–100.

Ranson, Gillian, & William Joseph Reeves. 1996. "Gender earnings, and proportions of women: Lessons from a high-tech occupation." *Gender & Society* 10(2): 168–84.

Raper, Arthur F. 1970. *The Tragedy of Lynching.* New York: Dover.

Rapport, Nigel, & Joanna Overing. 2000. *Social and Cultural Anthropology: The Key Concepts.* London: Routledge.

Rashid, Ahmed. 2001. *Taliban: Militant Islam, Oil and Fundamentalism in Central Asia.* New Haven, CT: Yale University.

Rastogi, Mudita, & Karen S. Wampler. 1999. "Adult daughters' perceptions of the mother–daughter relationship: A cross-cultural comparison." *Family Relations* 48(3): 327–36.

Rathaus, S. A., J. S. Nevid, & J. Fichner-Rathaus. 1997. *Human Sexuality in a World of Diversity*, 3rd ed. Boston: Allyn & Bacon.

Rathus, Spencer A., Jeffrey S. Nevid, & Lois Fichner-Rathus. 1997. *Human Sexuality in a World of Diversity*. Boston: Allyn & Bacon.

Ravin, James G., & Christie A. Kenyon. 1998. "Artistic vision in old age: Claude Monet and Edgar Degas." In Carolyn Adams-Price (ed.), *Creativity and Successful Aging: Theoretical and Empirical Approaches*. New York: Springer: 251–68.

Ravitch, Diane. 2000. *Left Back: A Century of Failed School Reform*. New York: Simon & Schuster.

Ravitch, Diane. 2001. "Student performance: The national agenda in education." In Kurt Finsterbusch (ed.), *Social Problems 01/02*. Guilford, CT: McGraw-Hill/Dushkin: 141–45.

Ray, J. J. 1991. "Authoritarianism is a dodo." *European Sociological Review* 7(1): 73–75.

Ray, Melvin, & William Downs. 1986. "An empirical test of labeling theory using longitudinal data," *Journal of Research in Crime and Delinquency* (23): 169–94.

Reaching Teens of Color. 2000. "Marketers need to take into account what influences African-American and Latino teens." *Restaurant Hospitality* 74(5): 20.

Reardon, Sean F., & John T. Yun. 2001. "Suburban racial change and suburban school segregation." *Sociology of Education* 74(2): 79–101.

Rebhun, Uzi. 1999. "Jewish identification in intermarriage: Does a spouse's religion (Catholic vs. Protestant) matter?" *Sociology of Religion* 60(1): 71–88.

Reckless, Walter. 1969. *The Crime Problem*. New York: Appleton-Century-Crofts.

Redfield, Robert. 1941. *The Folk Culture of Yucatan*. Chicago: University of Chicago Press.

Redfield, Robert. 1947. The folk society. *American Journal of Sociology* 52: 293–308.

Reed, Americus II. 2002. "Social identity as a useful perspective for self-concept-based consumer research." *Psychology & Marketing* 19(3): 235–66.

Reed, Michael, & Michael Hughes (eds.). 1992. *Rethinking Organization: New Directions in Organization Theory and Analysis*. Newbury Park, CA: Sage.

Reed, Ralph. 1996. *Active Faith: How Christians are Changing the Soul of American Politics*. New York: Free Press.

Rees, C. R., & A. W. Miracle. 2000. "Sport and education." In Jay Coakley & E. Dunning (eds.), *Handbook of Sports Studies*. London: Sage: 277–90.

Reeve, Simon. 1999. *The New Jackals: Ramzi Yousef, Osama bin Laden, and the Future of Terrorism*. Boston: Northeastern University Press.

Reeves, Joy B., & Ray L. Darville. 1994. "Social contact patterns and satisfaction with retirement of women in dual-career/earner families." *International Journal of Aging and Human Development* 39(2): 163–75.

Reeves, Marth E. 2000. *Suppressed, Forced Out and Fired: How Successful Women Lose their Jobs*. Westport, CT: Quorum.

Regan, P. C., & E. Berscheid. 1997. "Gender differences in characteristics desired in a potential sexual and marriage partner." *Journal of Psychology and Human Sexuality* 9: 25–37.

Regev, Martha J. 1995. "Producing artistic value: The case of rock music." *Sociological Quarterly* 35(1): 85–102.

Regier, D. 1991. *Psychiatric Disorders in America: The Epidemiological Catchment Areas Study*. New York: Free Press.

Regnerus, Mark D., Christian Smith, & David Sikkink. 1998. "Who gives to the poor? The influence of religious tradition and political location on the personal generosity of Americans toward the poor." *Journal for the Scientific Study of Religion* 37: 481–93.

Reich, Robert B. 1991. *The Work of Nations: Preparing Ourselves for Twenty-First Century Capitalism*. New York: Knopf.

Reichel, Phillip L. 1994. *Comparative Criminal Justice Systems: A Topical Approach*. Upper Saddle River, NJ: Prentice Hall.

Reid, Karla Scoon. 2001. "Charlotte schools desegregated, court rules." *Education Week* 21 (Oct. 3): 3.

Reid, S. T. 1991. *Crime and Criminology*. Fort Worth, TX: Holt, Rinehart & Winston.

Reiman, Jeffrey. 1995. *The Rich Get Richer and the Poor Get Prison*, 4th ed. Boston: Allyn & Bacon.

Reinarman, Craig & Harry G. Levine. 1989. "The crack attack." in J. Best, ed., *Images of Issues: Typifying Contemporary Social Problems*. New York: Aldine deGruyter: 115–38.

Reitzes, Donald C., Elizabeth J. Mutran, & Maria E. Fernandez. 1996. "Does retirement hurt well-being? Factors influencing self-esteem and depression among retirees and workers." *The Gerontologist* (October): 649–56.

Religion. 2002. Available: http://www.bigpuns.com/puns/religion.

Religious Movements. 2000. "The Unification Church." Available: http://religiousmovements.lib.edu/nrms/unification2.

Rendon, Laura I., & Richard O. Hope. 1996. "An educational system in crisis." In Laura I. Rendon & Richard O. Hope (eds.), *Educating a New Majority: Transforming America's Educational System for Diversity*. San Francisco: Josey-Bass: 1–32.

Reoch, Richard. 1994. "Human rights: The new consensus." In *Human Rights: The New Consensus*. London: Regency Press in association with the United Nations High Commissioner for Refugees.

Repetto, Robert. 1995. *The "Second India" Revisited*. Washington, DC: World Resources Institute.

Research Dialogues. 1999. "Women and retirement." Issue No. 61 (October). TIAA-CREF Institute.

Reskin, Barbara F. 1998. *The Realities of Affirmative Action in Employment*. Washington, DC: American Sociological Association.

Reskin, Barbara F. 2000. "Bringing the men back in: Sex differentiation and the devaluation of women's work." In Michael S. Kimmel (ed.), *The Gendered Society Reader*. New York: Oxford University: 257–70.

Reskin, Barbara, & Irene Padovic. 1994. *Women and Men at Work*. Thousand Oaks, CA: Pine Forge.

Reverby, Susan M. (ed.). 2000. *Tuskegee's Truths: Rethinking the Tuskegee Syphilis Study*. Chapel Hill, NC: University of North Carolina.

"Reverse discrimination of whites is rare, labor study reports." 1995. *The New York Times* (March 31): A23.Reynolds, J. Lynn, & Rodney A. Reynolds. 2000. "Ecumenical Promise Keepers: Oxymoron or fidelity?" In Dane S. Claussen (ed.), *The Promise Keepers: Essays on Masculinity and Christianity*. Jefferson, NC: McFarland: 175–81.

Reynolds, John R., & Jennifer Pemberton. 2001. "Rising college expectations among youth in the United States: A comparison of the 1979 and 1997 NLSY." *The Journal of Human Resources* 36(4): 703–26.

Reynolds, Larry T. 1992. "A retrospective on 'race': The career of a concept." *Sociological Focus* 25(1): 1–14.

Reynolds, Paul Davidson. 1982. *Ethics and Social Science Research*. Upper Saddle River, NJ: Prentice Hall.

Rhinegold, H. 1994. *The Virtual Community*. New York: Harper.

Rhoads, Steven E. 1993. *Incomparable Worth: Pay Equity Meets the Market*. New York: Cambridge University.

Rhode, Deborah L. 1993. "Gender equality and employment policy." In Sherri Matteo (ed.), *American Women in the Nineties: Today's Critical Issues*. Boston: Northeastern University.

Rhode, Deborah L. 2001. *Balanced Lives: Changing the Culture of Legal Practice*. Chicago: Commission of Women in the Profession, American Bar Association.

Riccio, R. 1992. "Street Crime Strategies: The Changing Schemata of Streetwalkers." *Environment & Behavior* 24: 555–570.

Rice, Berkely. 1981. "Gourmet worms: Antidote to a rumor." *Psychology Today* 15 (August): 20–21.

Rice, Patricia. 2002. "Sexual abuse by priests." *St. Louis Post-Dispatch* (April 28): B1,B4.

Rice, Susan. 2001. "Sexuality and intimacy for aging women." In J. Dianne Garner & Susan O. Mercer (eds.), *Women as they Age*. New York: Haworth.

Rich, Spencer. 1993. "Organ transplants: Rationing by wallet? Uninsured are unlikely recipients, raising questions of fairness." In The Washington Post Writers Group (eds.), *Society in Crisis: The Washington Post Social Problems Companion*. Boston: Allyn & Bacon: 228–31.

Richard, Amy D. 2000. *International Trafficking in Women to the United States*. Washington, DC: Center for the Study of Intelligence.

Richard, Emmanuelle. 1998. "Cuba's new information war: Keeping the Internet revolution under control." *Online Journalism Review* (May 6). Available: http://ojr.usc.edu/content/story.cfm?request=238.

Richardson, James T., Joel Best, & David G. Bromley. 1991. "Satanism as a social problem." In James T. Richardson, Joel Best, & David G. Bromley (eds.), *The Satanism Scare*. New York: Aldine deGruyter: 3–17.

Richardson, William C., & John P. Allegrante. 2002. In C. Everett Koop, Clarence E. Pearson, & M. Roy Schwartz (eds.), *Critical Issues in global Health*. San Francisco, CA: Jossey-Bass 375–83.

Richter, P., & L. Francis. 1998. *Gone but not Forgotten*. London: Darton, Longman & Todd.

Ridgeway, Cecelia L., Elizabeth H. Boyle, Kathy J. Kuipers, & Dawn T. Robinson. 1998. "How Do Status Beliefs Develop?" *American Sociological Review* 63: 331–350.

Ridgeway, Cecelia. 1991. "The social construction of status value." *Social Forces* 70/24: 367–386.

Ridgeway, Cecelia L. 2000. "Gender, status and leadership." *Journal of Social Issues* 57(4): 637–55.

Ridgeway, Cecilia L., & Lynn Smith-Lovin. 1999. "The gender system and interaction." *Annual Review of Sociology* 25: 191–216.

Rieff, David. 1995. *Slaughterhouse: Bosnia and the Failure of the West*. New York: Touchstone.

Riemer, Jeffrey W. 1979. *Hard Hats: The Work World of Construction Workers*. Beverly Hills, CA: Sage.

Rifkin, Jeremy. 1995. *The End of Work*. New York: Putnam.

Rigauer, B. 2000. "Marxist theories." In Jay Coakley & E. Dunning (eds.), *Handbook of Sports Studies*. London: Sage: 28–47.

Riger, Stephanie. 2000. *Transforming Psychology: Gender in Theory and Practice*. New York: Oxford University.

Riggle, Ellen D. B., & Barry L. Tadlock. 1999. "Gays and lesbians in the democratic process" Past, present and future." In Ellen Riggle and Barry Tadlock (eds.). *Gays and Lesbians in the Democratic Process*. New York: Columbia University: 1–21.

Riley, Matilda White, Anne Foner, & Joan Waring. 1988. "Sociology of age." In Neil Smelser (ed.), *Handbook of Sociology*. Beverly Hills, CA: Sage.

Riley, Matilda White. 1987. "On the significance of age in sociology." *American Sociological Review* 52: 1–14.

Riley, Pamela J., & Gary Kiger. 1999. "Moral discourse on domestic labor: Gender, power and identity in families." *Social Science Journal* 36(3): 541–48.

Riordan, Catherine A., Tamara Gross, & Cathlin C. Maloney. 1994. "Self-monitoring, gender, and the personal consequences of impression management." *American Behavioral Scientist* 37(5): 715–25.

Riordan, Ellen. 2002. "Intersections and new directions: On feminism and political economy." In Eileen R. Meehan & Ellen Riordan (eds.), *Sex and Money: Feminism and Political Economy in the Media*. Minneapolis: University of Minnesota: 3–15.

Rishe, Patrick James. 1999. "Gender gaps and the presence and profitability of college football." *Social Science Quarterly* 80(4): 702–17.

Risman, Barbara J., & Danette Johnson-Summerfield, 2001. "Doing it fairly: A study of postgender marriages." In Theodore F. Cohen (ed.), *Men and Masculinity: A Text Reader*. Belmont, CA: Wadsworth.

Risman, Barbara, & Pepper Schwartz. 2002. "After the sexual revolution: Gender politics in teen dating." *Contexts* 1(1) (Spring): 16–24.

Ritzer, George A., & David Walcazk. 1988. "Rationalization and the deprofessionalization of physicians," *Social Forces* 67/1: 1–22.

Ritzer, George. 1994. *Sociological Beginnings*. New York: McGraw-Hill.

Ritzer, George. 1996. *The McDonaldization of Society*, revised ed. Thousand Oaks, CA: Pine Forge.

Ritzer, George. 1997. *Postmodern Social Theory*. New York: McGraw-Hill.

Ritzer, George. 2000. "The sociology of consumption: A sub-field in search of discovery." *Footnotes* (February).

Ritzer, George. 2000. *The McDonaldization of Society*, New Century Edition. Thousand Oaks, CA: Pine Forge.

Ritzman, Rosemary L., & Donald Tomaskovic-Devey. 1992. "Life chances and support for equality and equity as normative and counternormative distribution rules." *Social Forces* 70: 745–763.

Roadburg, Allan. 1980. "Factors precipitating fan violence." *British Journal of Sociology* 31: 265–76.

Roane, Kit R. 2002. "The long arm of abuse: Problem priests cross not just states but oceans as well." *U.S. News & World Report* (May 6): 26–29.

Robarchek, C. A., & R. K. Dentan. 1979. "Conflict, emotion, and abreaction: Resolution and conflict among the Semai Senoi." *Ethos* 7: 104–23.

Robben, Antonius C. G. M. 1995. "Politics of truth and emotion among victims and perpetrators of violence." In Carolyn Nordstrom & Antonius C. G. M. Robben (eds.), *Fieldwork Under Fire: Contemporary Studies of Violence and Survival*. Berkeley, CA: University of California.

Robbins, Kevin. 1999. "Two school shootings have chilling similarities." *St. Louis Post-Dispatch.* (April 15): A1, A8.

Robbins, Richard H. 2002. *Global Problems and the Culture of Capitalism*. Boston: Allyn & Bacon.

Robbins, Steven. 2001. "NGOs, 'bushmen,' and double vision: The khomani San land claim and the cultural politics of 'community' and 'development' in the Kalahari." *Journal of Southern African Studies* 27(4): 83353.

Roberts, Christy D., Laura M. Stough, & Linda H. Parrish. 2002. "The role of genetic counseling in the elective termination of pregnancies involving fetuses with disabilities." *Journal of Special Education* 36(1): 48–55.

Roberts, George W. 1994. "Brother to brother: African American modes of relating among men." *Journal of Black Studies* 24(4): 379–90.

Roberts, J. Timmons. 2001. "Global inequality and climate change." *Society & Natural Resources* 14 (6): 501–9.

Roberts, Robert E. L., & Vern L. Bengston. 1996. "Affective ties to parents in early adulthood and self-esteem across twenty years." *Social Psychology Quarterly* 59(1): 96–106.

Roberts, Steven V. 1995. "Open arms for online democracy." *US News & World Report* (118/2): 10.

Robertson, Roland. 1988. "The sociological significance of culture: Some general considerations." *Theory, Culture and Society* 5 (February): 3–23.

Robins, Richard W., & Brent W. Roberts. 2001. "A longitudinal study of personality change in young adulthood." *Journal of Personality* 69(4): 617–40.

Robinson, B. A. 2001. "Religions of the world: Numbers of adherents; rates of growth." Available: http://www.religioustolerance.org/worldrel.

Robinson, Holly. 2000. "The Brady Bunch, 2000." *Parents* 75(11): 147–54.

Roccas, Sonia, & Marilynn Brewer. 2001. Social identity complexity." *Personality & Social Psychology Review* 6(2): 88–106.

Rochon, Thomas R., & Daniel A. Mazmanian. 1993. "Social movements & the policy process." *The Annals* 528: 75–88.

Rock, J. 1985. "Symbolic interactionism." In A. Kuper & J. Kuper (eds.), *The Social Science Encyclopedia*. London: Routledge & Kegan Paul.

Roddick, Jacqueline. 1999. "El Nino, El Viejo and the global shaping of Latin America: Surviving the UNCED coups." *Third World Quarterly* 20(4): 771–800.

Rodgers, Joseph Lee, Paul A. Nakonezny, & Robert D. Shull. 1999. "Did no-fault divorce legislation matter? Definitely yes and sometimes no: Reply to N. D. Glenn." *Journal of Marriage and the Family* 61(3): 803–809.

Rodnik, Dani. 1999. "The new global economy and developing countries: Making openness work." Policy Essay No. 24. Washington, DC: Overseas Development Council.

Rodriguez, Eric M., & Suzanne C. Ouellette. 2000. "Religion and masculinity in the everyday lives of gay men." In Peter Nardi (ed.), *Gay Masculinities*. Thousand Oaks: Sage.

Roeckelein, Jon E. 2002. *The Psychology of Humor: A Reference Guide and Annotated Bibliography*. Westport, CT: Greenwood.

Roen, Katrina. 2002. "'Either/or' and 'both/neither': Discursive tensions in transgender studies." *Signs* 27(2): 501–22.

Rogers, Mary F. 1999. *Barbie Culture*. London: Sage.

Rogers, Stacy J., & Danelle D. DeBoer. 2001. "Changes in wives' income: Effects on marital satisfaction, psychological well-being, and the risk of divorce." *Journal of Marriage and the Family* 63(2): 458–72.

Rogers, Stacy J., & L. White. 1998. "Satisfaction with parenting: The role of marital happiness, family structure and parent's gender." *Journal of Marriage and the Family* 60: 293–308.

Rogers, Stacy J., & Paul R. Amato. 2000. "Have changes in gender relations affected marital quality?" *Social Forces* 79(2): 731–53.

Romero, Mary, Pierrette Hondagneu-Sotelo, & Vilma Ortiz, (eds.). 1997. *Challenging Fronteras: Structuring Latina and Latino Lives in the U.S.* New York: Routledge.

Rong, Xue L., & Linda Grant. 1992. "Ethnicity, generation and school attainment of Asians, Hispanics and non-Hispanic whites." *Sociological Quarterly* 33: 625–36.

Roof, Judith. 1997. "The girl I never wanted to be: Identity, identification, and narrative." In Martin B. Duberman (ed.), *A Queer World: The Center for Lesbian and Gay Studies Reader*. New York: Center for Lesbian and Gay Studies, City University.

Roof, Wade C. 1979. "Socioeconomic differentials among white socioreligious groups in the United States," *Social Forces* 58: 280–289.

Roof, Wade Clark. 1999. *Spiritual Marketplace: Baby Boomers and the Remaking of American Religion*. Princeton, NJ: Princeton University.

Root, Maria. P. P. 2001. *Love's Revolution: Interracial Marriage*. Philadelphia: Temple University.

Ropers, Richard H. 1991. *Persistent Poverty: The American Dream Turned Nightmare*. New York: Plenum.

Roscoe, Will. 1998. *Changing Ones: Third and Fourth Genders in Native North America*. New York: St. Martin's.

Rose, Arnold. 1951. *The Roots of Racism*. Paris: UNESCO.

Rose, Arnold. 1968. *The Power Structure*. New York: Oxford University Press.

Rose, Jerry D. 1982. *Outbreaks: The Sociology of Collective Behavior*. New York: Free Press.

Rose, Peter I. 1990. *They and We: Racial and Ethnic Relations in the United States*. 4th ed. New York: McGraw-Hill.

Rosecrance, John. 1988. *Gambling Without Guilt*. Pacific Grove, CA: Brooks/Cole.

Rosen, Ellen I. 1987. *Bitter Choices: Blue Collar Women in and out of Work*. Chicago: University of Chicago Press.

Rosen, Ruth. 2000. *The World Split Open*. New York: Penguin.

Rosen, Ruth. 2000. *The World Split Open: How the Modern Women's Movement Changed America*. New York: Penguin

Rosenbaum, Sara, Alexandra Stewart, & Joel Teitelbaum. 2001. "Testimony before the Special Committee on Aging, United States Senate regarding long-term care after Olmstead: Developing the building blocks for change." September 24. Washington, DC: George Washington University Medical Center & School of Public Health and Health Services.

Rosenberger, Leif. 1996. *America's Drug War Debacle*. London: Avebury Press.

Rosenblatt , Paul C., Terri A. Karis, & Richard D. Powell. 1995. *Multiracial Couples*. Thousand Oaks, CA: Sage

Rosener, Judy B. 1995. *America's Competitive Secret: Utilizing Women as a Management Strategy*. New York: Oxford University Press.

Rosenfeld, Sarah. 1997. "Labeling Mental Illness: The Effects of Received Services and Perceived Stigma on Life Satisfaction." *American Sociological Review* 62(4): 660–672.

Rosenhan, David L. 1973. "On being sane in insane places," *Science* 179: 250–258.

Rosenstone, Steven J., & John M. Hansen. 1993. *Mobilization, Participation & Democracy in America*. New York: Macmillan.

Rosenthal, Jack. 1997. "The age boom." *The New York Times Magazine* (March 9): 39–43.

Rosenthal, Jack. 2001. "The age boom." In Elizabeth W. Markson & Lisa Ann Hollis-Sawyer (eds.),*Intersections of Aging: Readings in Social Gerontology*. Los Angeles: Roxbury: 60–64.

Rosenthal, Robert, & Lenore Jacobson. 1968. *Pygmalion in the Classroom: Teacher Expectations and Pupils' Intellectual Development*. New York: Holt, Rinehart and Winston.

Rosenthal, Robert. 1995. "Critiquing Pygmalion: A 25-year perspective." *Current Directions in Psychological Science* 4: 171–72.

Rosier, Katherine Brown. 2000. *Mothering Inner-City Children*. New Brunswick, NJ: Rutgers University.

Rosnow, Ralph L. 1991. "Inside rumor: A personal journey." *American Psychologist* 46: 484–96.

Rosnow, Ralph L., & Gary A. Fine. 1976. *Rumor and Gossip: The Social Psychology of Hearsay*. New York: Elsevier.

Rosoff, S., H. Pontell, & R. Tillman. 1998. *Profit Without Honor: White-Collar Crime and the Looting of America*. Upper Saddle River, NJ: Prentice Hall.

Ross, Benjamin. 2001. "Suburbs, status and sprawl." *Dissent* 48(1): 50–5.

Rossi, Alice S. 2001. "The impact of family problems on social responsibility." In Alice S. Rossi (ed.), *Caring and Doing For Others: Social Responsibility in the Domains of Family, Work and Community*. Chicago: University of Chicago: 321–47.

Rossi, Peter H., James D. Wright, Gene A Fisher, & Georgianna Willis. 1987. "The urban homeless: Estimating composition and size." *Science* 235 (March 13): 1136–1140.

Rossides, Daniel W. 1990. *Comparative Societies: Social Types and Their Interrelationships*. Upper Saddle River, NJ: Prentice Hall.

Rostow, Walt W. 1978. *The World Economy: History and Prospect*. Austin: University of Texas Press.

Rostow, Walt W. 1990. *The Stages of Economic Growth: A Non-Communist Manifesto*, 3rd ed. New York: Cambridge University Press.

Roszak, Theodore. 1969. *The Making of a Counter-Culture: Reflections on the Technocratic Society and Its Youthful Opposition*. New York: Doubleday.

Roth, Gunther. 1968. "Personal rulership, patrimonialism and empire-building." *World Politics.* 20: 124–206.

Rothblum, E. D. 1982. "Women's socialization and the prevalence of depression: The feminine mistake." *Woman & Therapy* 1: 5–13.

Rothenberg, Paula S. (ed.). 1998. *Race, Class, and Gender in the United States*, 4th ed. New York: St. Martin's Press.

Rothman, Barbara Katz, & Mary Beth Caschetta. 1995. "Treating health: Women and medicine." In Jo Freeman (ed.), *Women: A Feminist Perspective*. Mountain View, CA: Mayfield: 65–78.

Rothman, Stanley, & Amy E. Black. 1998. "Who rules now? American elites in the 1990s." *Society* (35/6): 17–20.

Rothschild, Joyce, & J. Allen Whitt. 1986. *The Cooperative Workplace*. Cambridge, England: Cambridge University Press.

Rothschild-Whitt, Joyce. 1979. "The collectivist organization." *American Sociological Review* 44: 509–27.

Rouse, Linda P. 2002. *Marital and Sexual Lifestyles in the United States: Attitudes, Behaviors and Relationships in Social Context*. Binghamton, NY: Haworth Clinical Practice Press.

Rouse, Linda P. 2002. *Marital and Sexual Lifestyles in the United States: Attitudes, Behaviors and Relationships in Social Context*. Binghamton, NY: Haworth.

Roush, Wade. 1996. "Demography: Live long & prosper." *Science* 273: 42.

Royal Dutch Society, 1994. *Administration and Compounding of Euthanasic Agents*. Royal Dutch Society for the Advancement of Pharmacy. The Hague: Netherlands.

RSJ. 2000. "A matter of survival: Bilingual education." (July 15). Reconciliation and Social Justice Library, Commonwealth of Australia. Available: http://www.austlii.edu.au/au/rsjproject/rsjlibrary/parliamentary/languahe/50.

Ruane, Joseph, & Jennifer Todd. 1996. *The Dynamics of Conflict in Northern Ireland*. Cambridge, England: Cambridge University Press.

Ruback, R. Barry, Janek Pandey, & Hamida Akhtar Begum. 1997. "Urban stressors in South Asia: Impact on male and female pedestrians in Delhi and Dhaka." *Journal of Cross-Cultural Psychology* 28: 23–43.

Rubin, Beth A. 1986. "Class struggle American style: Unions, strikes & wages." *American Sociological Review* 51/5: 618–31.

Rubin, Lillian B. 1976. *Worlds of Pain: Life in the Working-Class Family*. New York: Basic.

Rubin, Lillian. 1994. *Families on the Fault Line*. New York: HarperCollins.

Rubin, Rita, with Susan Headden. 1995. Physicians under fire." *U.S. News & World Report* (January 16).

Ruder, Suzy. 1998. "We teach all." *Educational Leadership* 58(1): 49–51.

Rudkin, Laura, & Kyroakos S. Markides. 2001. "Measuring the socioeconomic status of elderly people in health studies with special focus on the minority elderly." *Journal of Mental Health & Aging* 7(1): 53–66.

Rueschemeyer, Dietrich, & Theda Skocpol. 1996. *States, Social Knowledge, and the Origins of Modern Social Policies*. Princeton, NJ: Princeton University Press.

Rueschemeyer, Dietrich, Evelyne H. Stephens, & John D. Stephens. 1992. *Capitalist Development and Democracy*. Chicago: University of Chicago Press.

Ruggles, Patricia. 1989. "Short and long-term poverty in the United States." Washington, DC: Urban Institute.

Ruiz-Beltran, Martin, & Jimmy K. Kamau. 2001. "The socio-economic and cultural impediments to well-being along the U.S.-Mexico border." *Journal of Community Health* 26(2): 123–32.

Rule, James, & Peter Brantley. 1992. "Computerized surveillance in the workplace: Forms & delusions." *Sociological Forum* (7/3): 405–23.

Rumm, Peter D., Peter Cummings, & Margot R. Krauss. 2000. "Identified spouse abuse as a risk factor for child abuse." *Child Abuse & Neglect* 24(11): 1375–81.

Rummel, Rudolph. 1995. *Democide*. New Brunswick, NJ: Transaction.

Runciman, W. G. 1990. "How many classes are there in contemporary British society?" *Sociology* 24: 377–96.

Rupp, Leila J. 1999. *A Desired Past: A Short History of Same-Sex Love in America*. Chicago: University of Chicago.

Ruppe, David. 2001. "Nursing home abuse." ABC News, July 30. http:www.abcnews.go.com/sections/us/DailyNews/nursinhomes_elderlyabuse.

Ruscher, Janet B. 2001. *Prejudiced Communication: A Social Psychological Perspective*. New York: Guilford.

Rusk, David. 1999. Inside *Game/Outside Game: Urban Policies for the Twenty-first Century*. Washington, DC: Brookings Institution.

Russell, Cheryl. 1995. "Overworked? Overwhelmed?" *American Demographics* 17/3: 8.

Russell, Cheryl. 1998. "The haves and the want-nots." *American Demographics* 20(4): 10–12.

Russell, Diana E. H. 1998. *Dangerous Relationships: Pornography, Misogyny and Rape*. London: Sage.

Russo, Nancy Felipe, & Jody D. Horn. 1995. "Unwanted pregnancy and its resolution: Options, implications." In Jo Freeman (ed.), *Women: A Feminist Perspective*. Mountain View, CA: Mayfield: 47–64.

Ruth, Sheila. 1998. *Issues in Feminism: An Introduction to Women's Studies*, 2nd ed. Mountain View, CA: Mayfield.

Rutheiser, Charles. 1999. "Making place in the nonplace urban realm: Notes on the revitalization of downtown Atlanta." In Setha Low (ed.), *Theorizing the City: The New Urban Anthropology Reader*. New Brunswick, NJ: Rutgers University: 317–41.

Ryan, Allison M. 2001. "The peer group as a context for the development of young adolescent motivation and achievement." *Child Development* 72(4): 1135–50.

Ryan, Barbara. 1989. "Ideological purity & feminism." *Gender & Society* 3: 239–57.

Ryan, John, & William M. Wentworth. 1999. *Media and Society*. Needham Heights, MA: Allyn & Bacon.

Ryan, P., & G. Rush (eds.). 1997. *Understanding Organized Crime in Global Perspective*. Thousand Oaks, CA: Sage.

Ryan, Scott. D. 2000. "Examining social workers' placement recommendations of children with gay and lesbian adoptive parents." *Families in Society* 81(5): 517–28.

Ryan, Susan. 1999. "Unleashing the savage within." *American Enterprise* 10(4) (July/August): 17.

Ryan, William. 1971. *Blaming the Victim*. New York: Pantheon.

Rydell, C. Peter, & Susan S. Everingham. 1994. *Controlling Cocaine: Supply and Demand*. Santa Monica, CA: RAND.

Rykwert, Joseph. 2000. *The Seduction of Place: The City in the Twenty-First Century*. New York: Pantheon.

Sabo, Don, M. J. Melnick, & B. E. Vanfossen. 1993. "High school athletic participation & postsecondary educational and occupational mobility." *Sociology Of Sport Journal* (10/1): 44–56.

Sabo, Don. 1995. "Pigskin, patriarchy and pain." In Paula S. Rothenberg (ed.), *Race, Class, and Gender in the United States: An Integrated Study*, 3rd ed. New York: St. Martin's: 227–30.

Sachs, Wolfgang. 2002. "Ecology, justice, and the end of development." In John Byrne, Leigh Glover, & Cecilia Martinez (eds.), *Environmental Justice: Discourses in International Political Economy*. New Brunswick, NJ: Transaction: 19–38.

Sack, Allen L. 1991. "The underground economy of college football." *Sociology of Sport Journal* (8/March): 1–15.

Sack, Allen L., & E. J. Staurowsky. 1998. *College Athletes for Hire*. Westport, CT: Praeger.

Sadker, Myra, & David Sadker. 1990. "Confronting sexism in the college classroom." In Susan L. Gabriel & Isaiah Smithson (eds.), *Gender in the Classroom: Power and Pedagogy*. Urbana, IL: University of Illinois.

Sadler, William A. 2000. *The Third Age: Six Principles of Growth and Renewal after Forty*. Cambridge, MA: Perseus.

Sage, George H. 1998. *Power and Ideology in American Sport: A Critical Perspective*, 2nd ed. Champaign, IL: Human Kinetics.

Sahlins, Marshall D. 1960. "The origin of society." *Scientific American* (September): 76–87.

Sahlins, Marshall D. 1972. *Stone Age Economics*. Chicago: Aldine.

Sahlins, Marshall D., & Elman R. Service. 1960. *Evolution and Culture*. Ann Arbor: University of Michigan Press.

Sahlins, Marshall, 1976. *Culture and Practical Reason*. Chicago: University of Chicago.

Sahlins, Marshall. 1999. "What is anthropological enlightenment? Some lessons of the twentieth century." *Annual Review of Anthropology* 28: 1–21.

Saitoti, Tepilit Ole. 1994. "The initiation of a Maasai warrior." In Elvio Angeloni (ed.), *Anthropology 93/94*. Guilford, CT: Dushkin.

Sakalli, Nuray. 2002. "Application of the attribution-value model of prejudice to homosexuality." *Journal of Social Psychology* 142(2): 264–71.

Sakolovsky, Jay. 2000. "Images of aging." In Elizabeth W. Markson & Lisa Ann Hollis-Sawyer (eds.), *Intersections of Aging: Readings in Social Gerontology*. Los Angeles: Roxbury: 6–11.

Salamon, Julie. 2002. "Children's TV catches up with how kids watch." *New York Times* (June 9)Section 2: 1,27.

Sale, Kirkpatrick. 1996. *Rebels Against the Future*. Reading, MA: Addison-Wesley.

Sales, Bruce D., & Susan Folkman (eds.). 2000. *Ethics in Research with Human Participants*. Washington, DC: American Psychological Association.

Salkind, Neil J. 2000. *Exploring Research*, 4th ed. Upper Saddle River, NJ: Prentice Hall.

Saltzberg, Elayne, & Joan C. Chrisler. 1995. "Beauty is the beast: The psychological effects of the pursuit of the perfect female body." In Jo Freeman (ed.), *Women: A Feminist Perspective*. Mountain View, CA: Mayfield: 306–15.

SAMHSA. 2002. "Alcohol use among girls." Substance Abuse and Mental Health Services Administration, U.S. Department of Health and Human Services. Available: http://www.health.org/govpubs/rpo993.

Sampson, Robert J. 1987. "Urban black violence: The effect of male joblessness and family disruption." *American Journal of Sociology* 93: 348–82.

Sampson, Robert, & Stephen W. Raudenbush. 1999. "Systematic social observation of public spaces: A new look at disorder in urban neighborhoods." *American Journal of Sociology* 105(3): 603–51.

Samuel, Terrence. 1999. "Poor fathers have been slipping out of their children's lives: The welfare revolution may bring them back." *St. Louis Post-Dispatch*. (March 28): A4.

Samuels, David. 1999. "The making of a fugitive." (Anti-abortion odyssey). *New York Times* (March 21): 47–53, 62.

Samuelson, Paul A., & William D. Nordhaus. 1989. *Economics*, 13th ed. New York: McGraw-Hill.

Sanbonmatsu, Kira. 2002. "Gender stereotypes and vote choice." *American Journal of Political Science* 46(1): 20–34.

Sanday, Peggy Reeves. 2000. "The socio-cultural context of rape: A cross-cultural study." In Michael S. Kimmel (ed.), *The Gendered Society Reader*. New York: Oxford University: 55–72.

Sanders, Barry. 1994. *A Is for Ox: Violence, Electronic Media, and the Silencing of the Written Word*. New York: Pantheon.

Sanders, Cynthia K. 2002. "The impact of microenterprise assistance programs: A comparative study of program participants, nonparticipants, and other low-wage workers." *Social Service Review* 76(2): 321–40.

Sanders, Thomas G. 1987. "Brazilian street children." *USFI Reports* numbers 17–18.

Sangani, Misti. 2001. "Learning from women's NGOs for better health." Paper presented at the Global Health Council annual conference. Washington, DC: May 29–June 1.

Sanz, Timothy L. 1992. "Nuclear terrorism: Selected research materials." *Low Intensity Conflict & Law Enforcement* 1.

Sapir, Edward. 1949. *Language: An Introduction to the Study of Speech*. New York: Harcourt, Brace & World.

Sargent, Dudley A. 1912. "Are athletics making girls masculine?" *Ladies Home Journal* 29: 72.

Sargisson, Lucy. 2001. "What's wrong with ecofeminism?" *Environmental Politics* 10(1): 52–64.

Sarin, Radhika. 2002. "Population, women, environment: Connecting the dots." *Reporter* (Spring/Summer): 6–9.

Sarlo, Chris. 2000. "Single-parent families: Then and now—What are the consequences for the children?". *Fraser Forum* (July). Available: http://www.theinvoledfather.com.

Sasaki, Hiroki, Todd S. Elwyn, & Michael D. Fetters. 2002. "Responsibility and cancer disclosure in Japan." *Social Science & Medicine* 54(2): 281–93.

Sasaki, Naoto. 1990. *Management and Industrial Structure in Japan.* Oxford, UK: Pergamon.

Sass, Justine, & Lori Ashford. 2002. *2002 Women of Our World.* Washington, DC: Population Reference Bureau. Available: http:www.prb.org.

Sassler, Sharon, & Robert Schoen. 1999. "The effect of attitudes and economic activity on marriage." *Journal of Marriage and the Family* 61: 147–59.

Sauerwein, Kristina. 1996. "Survey of students: Sexual harassment an issue for many." *St. Louis Post-Dispatch Metro Post.* (January 17): 2W.

Saul, John S., & Colin Leys. 1999. "Sub-Saharan Africa in global capitalism." *Monthly Review* 51(3): 13–30.

Savage-Rumbaugh, Stewart G. Shanker, & Talbot J. Taylor. 1998. *Apes, Language and the Human Mind.* Oxford, UK: Oxford University.

Savant, Marilyn Vos. 1999. "Ask Marilyn." *Parade Magazine* (February 12): 8.

Savelsberg, Joachim J. 1994. "Knowledge, domination and criminal punishment." *American Journal of Sociology* 99: 911–43.

Savishinsky, Joel S. 2000. *Breaking the Watch: The Meanings of Retirement in America.* Ithaca, NY: Cornell University.

Savoie, Ghislain. 1999. "The comparative advantages of bilingualism on the job market: Survey of studies." *New Canadian Perspectives: Official Languages and the Economy.* Department of Canadian Heritage. Available: http:www.pch.gc.ca/offlangoff/perspectives/english/econo.

Sawhill, Isabel. 2001. "From welfare to work." *Brookings Review* (Summer): 4–7.

SBA. 2001. "Women in business, 2001." (October). Washington, DC: U.S. Small Business Administration Office of Advocacy.

Schaefer, Richard T. 2000. *Racial and Ethnic Groups,* 8th ed. Upper Saddle River, NJ: Prentice-Hall.

Schaffert, Richard W. 1992. *Media Coverage and Political Terrorists.* New York: Harcourt Brace.

Schaie, K. Warner (ed.). 1990. "Intellectual development in adulthood." In James E. Birren, & K. Warner Schaie (eds.), *Handbook of the Psychology of Aging.* San Diego: Academic Press.

Scharlach, Andrew W., & Karen I. Fredrikson. 1994. "Elder care versus adult care: Does care recipient age make a difference?" *Research on Aging* 16(1): 43–68.

Scharrer, Erica. 2001. "From wise to foolish: The portrayal of the sitcom father, 1950s–1990s." *Journal of Broadcasting and Electronic Media* 45(1): 23–40.

Scharrer, Erica. 2001. "Men, muscles, and machismo: The relationship between television exposure and aggression and hostility in the presence of hypermasculinity." *Media Psychology* 3(2): 159–88.

Schatzman, Leonard, & Anselm Strauss. 1972. "Social class and modes of communication." In Saul D. Feldman & Gerald W. Thiebar (eds.), *Life Styles: Diversity in American Society.* Boston: Little, Brown: 48–60.

Scheel, Karen R., & John S. Westefield. 1999. "Heavy metal music and adolescent suicidality: An empirical investigation." *Adolescence* 34(134): 253–73.

Scheff, Thomas J. 1963. "The role of the mentally ill and the dynamics of mental disorder." *Sociometry* 26: 436–453.

Scheff, Thomas J. 1984. *Being Mentally Ill: A Sociological Theory,* 2nd ed. New York: Aldine.

Schellenberg, Kathryn (ed.). 1996. *Computers and Society,* 6th ed. Guilford, CT: Dushkin.

Schiamberg, Lawrence B., & Daphna Gans. 2000. "Elder abuse by adult children: An applied ecological framework for understanding contextual risk." *International Journal of Aging & Human Development* 50(4): 329–59.

Schifter, Jacobo, & Johnny Madrigal. 2000. *The Sexual Construction of Latino Youth: Implications for the Spread of HIV/AIDS.* New York: Haworth.

Schilder, Arn J., Cornelis Kennedy, Irene L. Goldstone, Russel D. Ogden, Robert S. Hogg, & Michael V. O'Shaugnessy. 2001. "'Being dealt with as whole person': Care seeking and adherence—the benefits of culturally competent care." *Social Science & Medicine* 52(11): 1643–59.

Schiller, Brent, M. Donald Hancock, & John Logue. 2000. "The international context of economic and political transitions." In M. Donald Hancock & John Logue (eds.), *Transitions to Capitalism and Democracy in Russia and Central Europe: Achievements, Problems, Prospects.* Westport, CT: Praeger: 315–26.

Schiller, Herbert. 1992. *Mass Communication and the American Empire,* 2nd ed. Boulder, CO: Westview.

Schiller, Nina Glick, Stephen Crystal, & Denver Lewellen. 1994. "Risky business: The cultural construction of AIDS risk groups." *Social Science and Medicine* 38(10): 1337–46.

Schippers, Mimi. 2002. *Rockin' Out of the Box: Gender Maneuvering in Alternative Hard Rock.* New Brunswick, NJ: Rutgers University.

Schiraldi, Vincent, & Jason Ziedenberg. 2001. "How distorted coverage of juvenile crime affects public policy." In William Ayers, Bernadine Dohrn, & Rick Ayers (eds.), *Zero Tolerance: Resisting the Drive for Punishment in Our Schools.* New York: New Press: 114–125.

Schnaiberg, Allan, & Kenneth Alan Gould. 1994. *Environment and Society: The Enduring Conflict.* New York: St. Martin's.

Schneider, K., S. Swan, & L. F. Fitzgerald. 1997. "Job-related psychological effects of sexual harassment in the workplace: Empirical studies from two organizations." *Journal of Applied Psychology* 82: 401–15.

Schneider, Linda, & Arnold Silverman. 2000. *Global Sociology: Introducing Five Contemporary Societies.* New York: McGraw-Hill.

Schodolski, Vincent J., & Charles M. Madigan. 1997. "The deadly riddle of Heaven's Gate: How they perished." *Chicago Tribune* (March 28): 1–1, 1–6.

Schofield, Janet Ward. 2001. "Maximizing the benefits of school diversity: Lessons from school desegregation research." In Gary Orfield (ed.), *Diversity Challenged: Evi-*

dence on the Impact of Affirmative Action. Cambridge, MA: Harvard Education Publishing Group: 99–109.

Schonenbaum, Stephen E. (ed.). 1998. *Does Capital Punishment Deter Crime?* San Diego: Greenhaven.

Schooler, Carmi, & Atushi Naoi. 1988. "The psychological effects of traditional and economically peripheral job settings in Japan." *American Journal of Sociology* 94: 335–55.

Schor, Juliet B. 1991. *The Overworked American: The Unexpected Decline of Leisure.* New York: Basic.

Schrag, Peter. 1996. "Backing off Bakke: The new assault on affirmative action." *The Nation* 262 (April 22): 11–14.

Schulhofer, Stephen J. 1992. "Plea Bargaining As Disaster." *Yale Law Journal* 101: 1987.

Schulte, Bernd, 1998. "Social assistance in the member states of the European Union: Common features and continuing differences." In Theodore R. Marmor & Philip R. DeJong (eds.), *Aging, Social Security and Affordability.* Aldershot, Hants, UK: Ashgate: 3–27.

Schultz, Duane P. 1964. *Panic Behavior.* New York: Random House.

Schultze, Quentin J. 1996. "Evangelicals' uneasy alliance with the media." In Daniel A. Stout & Judith M. Buddenbaum (eds.), *Religion and Mass Media: Audiences and Adaptations.* Thousand Oaks, CA: Sage: 61–73.

Schulz, Jim. 2001. *The Economics of Aging.* Westport, CT: Auburn House.

Schumpeter, Joseph. 1942. *Capitalism, Socialism and Democracy.* New York: Harper.

Schur, Edwin M. 1979. *Interpreting Deviance: A Sociological Introduction.* New York: Harper and Row.

Schur, Edwin M. 1984. *Labeling Women Deviant: Gender, Stigma & Social Control.* New York: Random House.

Schur, Edwin. 1971. *Labeling Deviant Behavior.* New York: Harper & Row.

Schur, Edwin. 1973. *Radical Non-Intervention.* Upper Saddle River, NJ: Prentice-Hall.

Schur, Edwin. 1980. *The Politics of Deviance.* Upper Saddle River, NJ: Prentice-Hall.

Schuster, John W., Mary Louise Hemmeter, & Melinda Jones Ault. 2001. "Instruction of students with moderate and severe disabilities in elementary classrooms." *Early Childhood Research Quarterly* 16(3): 329–41.

Schwartz, Barry. 1975. *Queuing and Waiting: Studies in the Social Organization of Access and Delay.* Chicago: University of Chicago Press.

Schwartz, John E., & Thomas J. Volgy. 1993. "Above the poverty line—but poor." *The Nation* (February 15): 191–192.

Schwartz, Norbert. 1998. "Warmer and more social: Recent developments in cognitive social psychology." *Annual Review of Sociology* 24: 239–64.

Schwartz, Pepper, & Virginia Rutter. 1998. *The Gender of Sexuality.* Thousand Oaks, CA: Pine Forge.

Schwartz, Pepper. 1994. *Peer Marriage: How Love Between Equals Really Works.* New York: Free Press.

Schwartz, R. D., & J. H. Skolnick. 1962. "Two studies of legal stigma." *Social Problems* (10): 133–38.

Schwartz, Sidney. 2000. *Finding a Spiritual Home: How a New Generation of Jews Can Transform the American Synagogue.* New York: Jossey-Bass.

Schweitzer, Marjorie M. 1983. "The elders: Cultural dimensions of aging in two American Indian communities." In Jay Sololovsky (ed.), *Growing Old in Different Societies: Cross-Cultural Perspectives.* Belmont, CA: Wadsworth.

Schwochau, Susan. 1987. "Union effects on job attitudes." *Industrial and Labor Relations Review* 40: 209–24.

Scott, Alan. 1990. *Ideology and the New Social Movements.* London: Routledge.

Scott, Catherine V. 1995. *Gender and Development: Rethinking Modernization and Dependency Theory.* Boulder, CO: Lynne Rienner.

Scott, Christopher F., & Susan Sprecher. 2000. "Sexuality in marriage, dating and other relationships: A decade review." *Journal of Marriage & the Family* 62(4): 999–1017.

Scott, W. Richard, Martin Ruef, Peter J. Mendel, & Carol A. Caronna. 2000. *Institutional Change and Healthcare Organizations: From Professional Dominance to Managed Care.* Chicago: University of Chicago.

Scott, W. Richard. 1981. *Organizations: Rational, Natural and Open Systems.* Upper Saddle River, NJ: Prentice Hall.

Scupin, Raymond. 1998. *Cultural Anthropology: A Global Perspective.* Upper Saddle River, NJ: Prentice Hall.

Scupin, Raymond. 2000. "Islam." In R. Scupin (ed.), *Religion and Culture: An Anthropological Focus.* Upper Saddle River, NJ: Prentice Hall: 395–420.

Se'ver, Aysan. 1999. "Sexual harassment: Where we were, where we are and prospects for the new millennium: Introduction to the special issue." *The Canadian Review of Sociology and Anthropology* 36(4): 469–97.

Seabrook, Jeremy. 1996. *In the Cities of the South: Scenes from a Developing World.* London: Verso.

Seaford, Helen. 2001. "Children and childhood: Perceptions and realities." *Political Quarterly* 72(4): 454–65.

Seale, Patrick. 1992. *Abu Nidal: A Gun For Hire.* New York: Random House.

Seccombe, Karen. 1999. *So You Think I Drive a Cadillac?* Needham Heights, MA: Allyn & Bacon.

Seeman, Melvin, Teresa Seeman, & Marnie Sayles. 1985. "Social networks & health status." *Social Psychology Quarterly* (48/3): 237–248.

Seeman, Melvin. 1972. "The signals of '68: Alienation in pre-crisis France." *American Sociological Review* (37/3): 385–402.

Seitel, Peter (ed). 2001. *Safeguarding Traditional Cultures: A Global Assessment.* Washington, DC: Smithsonian Institution Center for Folklife and Cultural Heritage.

Sekhon, Joti. 2000. *Modern India.* New York: McGraw-Hill.

Seliger, Martin. 1976. *Ideology and Politics*. London: George Allen & Unwin.

Sell, R. L., J. A. Wells, & D. Wypij. 1995. "The prevalence of homosexual behavior and attraction in the United States, the United Kingdom and France: Results of national populaton-based samples. *Archives of Sexual Behavior*: 235–48.

Selnow, Gary W. 1985. "Sex differences in uses and perceptions of profanity." *Sex Roles* 12(3–4): 303–12.

Selznick, Philip. 1957. *Leadership in Organizations*. Evanston, IL: Row, Peterson.

Selznick, Philip. 1992. *The Moral Commonwealth*. Berkeley: University of California Press.

Sennett, Richard, & Jonathan Cobb. 1973. *The Hidden Injuries of Class*. New York: Vintage.

Sennett, Richard. 1998. *The Corrosion of Character: The Personal Consequences of Work in the New Capitalism*. New York: Norton.

Serbin, Lisa A., Diane Poulin-Dubois, Karen A. Colburne, Maya G. Sen, & Julie A. Eichstedt. 2001. "Gender stereotyping in infancy: Visual preferences for and knowledge of stereotyped toys in the second year." *International Journal of Behavioral Development* 25(1).

Serbin, Lisa A., Kimberly K. Powlishta, & Judith Gulko. 1993. "The development of sex typing in middle childhood." *Monographs of the Society for Research in Child Development* 58(2), Serial No. 232: 1–74.

Sernau, Scott. 1997. "Economies of exclusion: Economic change and the global underclass." In Joseph E. Behar & Alfred G. Cuzan, (eds.), *At the Crossroads of Development: Transnational Challenges to Developed and Developing Societies*. Leiden, Netherlands: E. J. Brill: 38–51.

Sernau, Scott. 2001. *Worlds Apart: Social Inequalities in a New Century*. Thousand Oaks, CA: Pine Forge.

Service, Elman R. 1966. *The Hunters*. Upper Saddle River, NJ: Prentice Hall.

Sewell, Graham, & Barry Wilkinson. 1992. "Someone to watch over me." *Sociology* 26: 271–89.

Seymour, J. E. 2001. *Critical Moments: Death and Dying in Intensive Care*. Buckingham, UK: Open University.

Shah, Anup. 2001. "Causes of poverty—Hunger and poverty." Available: http:www.globalissues.org/TradeRelated/Poverty/Hunger.

Shah, Mahendra, & Maurice Strong. 1999. *Food in the 21st Century: From Science to Sustainable Agriculture*. Consultative Group on International Agricultural Research (CGIAR). Washington, DC: World Bank.

Shakur, Sanyika. 1993. *Monster: The Autobiography of an L.A. Gang Member*. New York: Penguin.

Shamir, Shlomo. 2002. "Reform movement adds feminine touch to Torah interpretation." *Ha'aretz* May 18. Available: http://www.haaretzdaily.com/hasen/pages/ShArt.

Shanklin, R. 1993. *Anthropology and Race*. Belmont, CA: Wadsworth.

Shannon, Sarah. 2001. "Working with women to share knowledge." Paper presented at the Global Health Council annual conference. Washington, DC: May 29–June 1.

Shannon, Thomas R. 1989. *World System Perspective*. Boulder, CO: Westview.

Shapiro, Isaac, & Robert Greenstein. 1991. *Selective Prosperity*. Washington, DC: Center on Budget and Policy Priorities.

Shapiro, Isaac. 2001. "As a share of the economy and the budget, U.S. development and humanitarian aid would drop to post-WWII lows in 2002." June 18. Washington, DC: Center on Budget and Policy Priorities. Available: http://www.cbpp.org.

Sharma, Ursula M. 1996. "Using alternative therapies: Marginal medicine and central concerns." In Basiro Davey, Alastair Gray, & Clive Seale (eds.), *Health and Disease: A Reader*. Buckingham, UK: Open University: 38–44.

Sharp, Edlaine B., & Mark Joslyn. 2001. "Individual and contextual effects on attributions about pornography." *Journal of Politics* 63(2): 501–519.

Sharpe, Sue. 2001. "Going for it: Young women face the future." *Feminism & Psychology* 11(2): 177–81.

Shaughnessy, Michael F., Fred Cordova, Fida Mohammed, & Meehee Kang. 1998. "Multiculturalism: Toward the new millennium." *School Field* 9(3–4): 45–59.

Shaw, Jane S., & Ronald D. Utt (eds.). 2000. *A Guide to Smart Growth: Shattering Myths, Providing Solutions*. Washington, DC: Heritage Foundation.

Shaw, Simon W. W. 2002. "Land tenure policies, Masai traditions, and wildlife conversation in Kenya." *Society & Natural Resources* 15 (January): 79–88.

Sheehy, Gail. 1976. *Passages: Predictable Crises of Adult Life*. New York: Dutton.

Sheehy, Gail. 1995. *New Passages: Mapping Your Life Across Time*. New York: Random House.

Sheinberg, Marcia, & Peter Fraenkel. 2000. *The Relational Trauma of Incest: A Family-Base Approach to Treatment*. New York: Guilford.

Sheler, Jeffery L. 2002. "Faith in America." *U.S. News & World Report* (May 6): 40–49.

Shellenberger, Sue. 2002. "Trends point to future of more-focused work, parenting and learning." *Wall Street Journal* (January 9): B1.

Shelton, Beth Anne, & Juanita Firestone. 1989. "Household labor time and the gender gap in earnings." *Gender & Society* 3(1): 105–12.

Shen, Ce, & John B. Williamson. 1997. "Child Mortality, Women's Status, Economic Dependency & State Strength: A Cross-National Study of Less Developed Countries," *Social Forces* 76: 667–694.

Sherkat, Darren E. 1998. "Counterculture or continuity: Competing influences on baby boomers' religious orientations and participation." *Social Forces* 76(3): 1087–114.

Sherkat, Darren E. 2001. "Tracking the restructuring of American religion: Religious affiliation and patterns of religious mobility, 1973–1998." *Social Forces* 79(4): 1459–73.

Sherkat, Darren E., & Christopher G. Ellison. 1999. "Recent developments and current controversies in the sociology of religion." *Annual Review of Sociology* 25: 363–94.

Sherman, Lawrence W., & Douglas A. Smith. 1992. "Crime, punishment and stake in conformity." *American Sociological Review* 57/5: 680–690.

Sherman, Lawrence W., & Richard A. Berk. 1984. "The specific deterrent effects of arrest for domestic violence." *American Sociological Review* 49: 261–72.

Shi, Leiyu, & Barbara Starfield. 2001. "The effect of the primary care physician supply and income inequality on mortality among blacks and whites in U.S. metropolitan areas." *American Journal of Public Health* 91(8): 1246–50.

Shibutani, Tamotsu. 1966. *Improvised News: A Study of Rumor*. Indianapolis: Bobbs-Merrill.

Shils, Edward. 1962. *Political Development in New States*. The Hague: Mouton.

Shin, Kyoung-Ho, & Michael Timberlake. 2000. "World cities in Asia: Cliques, centrality, and connectedness." *Urban Studies* 37(12): 2257–85.

Shinberg, Diane S. 2001. "Sex and sickness: Gender and socioeconomic inequalities in adult health." *Dissertation Abstracts International, A: The Humanities and Social Sciences* 62(4), October: 1591-A.

Shinn, Marybeth, & Beth C. Weitzman. 1997. "Homeless Families are Different," in J. Baumohl (ed.), *Homelessness in America*. Phoenix: Oryx Press: 109–122.

Shiva, Vandana. 1992. "Resources." In Wolfgang Sachs (ed.), *The Development Dictionary: A Guide to Knowledge as Power*. London: Zed: 206–218.

Shonk, James H. 1992. *Team-Based Organization*. Homewood, IL: Irwin.

Shook, Nancy J., Deborah A. Gerrity, Joan Jurich, & Allen E. Segrist. 2000. "Courtship violence among college students: A comparison of verbally and physically abusive couples." *Journal of Family Violence* 15(1): 1–22.

Shorris, Earl. 1992. *Latinos: A Biography of the People*. New York: Norton.

Short, James. 1960. "Differential association as a hypothesis." *Social Problems* (8): 14–24.

Shostak, Arthur B. 1999. *CyberUnion: Empowering Labor Through Computer Technology*. Armonk, NY: M. E. Sharpe.

Shostak, Arthur. 1990. *Robust Unionism*. Ithaca, NY: Industrial and Labor Relations Press.

Shostak, Marjorie. 1994. "Memories of a !Kung girlhood." In Elvio Angeloni (ed.), *Anthropology 93/94*. Guilford, CT: Dushkin.

Shropshire, K. 1996. *In Black and White: Race and Sports in America*. New York: NYU Press.

Shrum, L. J. 2002. "Media consumption and perceptions of social reality: Effects and underlying processes." In Jennings Bryant & Dolf Zillmann (eds.), *Media Effects: Advance in Theory and Research*. Mahwah, NJ: Lawrence Erlbaum.

Shuiteman, Jayne. 2001. "Feminist approaches to addressing violence against women." In Allen J. Ottens & Kathy Hotelling (eds.), *Sexual Violence on Campus: Policies, Programs, and Perspectives*. New York: Springer: 76–97.

Shupe, Anson. 1998. "Frame alignment and strategic evolution in social movements: The case of Sun Myung's Unification Church." In Anson Shupe & Bronislaw Misztal (eds.), *Religion, Mobilization and Social Action*. Westport, CT: Praeger: 197–215.

Shweder, Richard A. 2000. "What about female genital mutilation? And why understanding culture matters in the first place." *Daedalus* 129(Fall): 209–232.

Sidel, Ruth. 1996. *Keeping Women and Children Last*. New York: Penguin.

Sidel, Ruth. 1999. "Family policy in Sweden: Lessons for the United States." In R. Heiner (ed.), *Social Problems and Social Solutions: A Cross-Cultural Perspective*. Needham Hts., MA: Allyn & Bacon.

Siegel, Fred. 2000. "America's startling new urban geography." *American Enterprise* 11(5): 40–42.

Siegel, Larry J. 2000. *Criminology*, 7th ed. Belmont, CA: Wadsworth.

Siegel, Larry. 1995. *Criminology*, 5th ed. Minneapolis: West.

Siegrist, Johannes. 2001. "A theory of occupational stress." In Jack Dunham (ed.), *Stress in the Workplace: Past, Present, and Future*. London: Whurr: 52–66.

Sigelman, L. 1998. "Hail to the Redskins? Public reactions to a racially insensitive team name." *Sociology of Sport Journal* (14/4): 315–25.

Sigelman, Lee, & Paul J. Wahlbeck. 1999. "Gender proportionality in intercollegiate athletics: The mathematics of the Title IX compliance." *Social Science Quarterly* 80(3): 518–36.

Sigelman, Lee, & Susan Welch. 1993. "The contact hypothesis revisited." *Social Forces* 71: 781–95.

Sigelman, Lee, Timothy Bledsoe, Susan Welch, & Michael W. Combs. 1996. "Making contact? Black-white social interaction in an urban setting." *American Journal of Sociology* 5: 1302–1332.

SIGI. 2001. "Statistics." Sisterhood is Global Institute. Available: http:www.sigi.org.Resources/stats.

Signorelli, Nancy, & Michael Morgan. 1990. *Cultivation Analysis*. Newbury Park, CA: Sage.

Signorelli, Nancy. 1989. "Television and conceptions about sex roles." *Sex Roles* (21/5–6): 341–60.

Signorielli, Nancy. 2001. "Aging on television: The picture in the nineties." *Generations* 25(3): 34–38.

Silbiger, Shannon, & Claire Brooks. 2002. "Generation disconNext." *Brandweek* 43(11): March 11, 22–23.

Sills, David L. 1957. *The Volunteers*. Glencoe, IL: Free Press.

Silvas, Sharon, Barbara Jenkins, & Polly Grant. 1993. "The overvoice: Images of women in the media." In Jodi Wentzel et al., (eds.), *Women's Studies Thinking Women*. Dubuque, IA: Kendall/Hunt.

Silverstein, M. 1998. "Contemporary transformations of local linguistic communities." *Annual Review of Anthropology* 27: 401–26.

Silverstein, M. 2001. "The limits of awareness." In Allessandro Duranti (ed.), *Linguistic Anthropology: A Reader*. Oxford, UK: Blackwell.

Simmel, Georg. 1950. *The Sociology of Georg Simmel*, ed. and trans. by Kurt H. Wolff. Glencoe, IL: Free Press.

Simmel, Georg. 1971. "Fashion." In Donald N. Levine (ed.), *Georg Simmel: On Individuality & Social Forms*. Chicago: University of Chicago Press. Originally published in 1904.

Simmons, Melanie. 1999. "Theorizing prostitution: The question of agency." In *Sex Work and Sex Workers* (Sexuality & Culture, Volume 2). New Brunswick, NJ: Transaction.

Simmons, Tavia, & Grace O'Neill. 2001. "Households and families: 2000." *Census 2000 Brief*. U.S. Census Bureau.

Simon, A. 1998. "The relationship between stereotypes of and attitudes toward lesbians and gays." In G. M. Herek (ed.), *Stigma and Sexual Orientation: Understanding Prejudice Against Lesbians, Gay Men, and Bisexuals*. Thousand Oaks, CA: Sage: 62–81.

Simon, D. R., & D. Stanley Eitzen. 1986. *Elite Deviance*. Boston: Allyn & Bacon.

Simon, Robin W. 1995. "Gender, multiple roles, role meaning and mental health," *Journal of Health and Social Behavior* (36/2): 182–194.

Simon, Robin W., & Kristen Marcussen. 1999. "Marital transitions, marital beliefs, and mental health." *Journal of Health and Social Behavior* 40: 111–25.

Simons, Ronald L., & Phyllis A. Gray. 1989. "Perceived blocked opportunity as an explanation of delinquency among lower-class black males." *Journal of Research in Crime and Delinquency* (26): 90–101.

Simonton, Dean K. 1990. "Creativity in later years: Optimistic prospects for achievement." *The Gerontologist* 30(5): 626–31.

Simonton, Dean Keith. 2002. *Great Psychologists and Their Times: Scientific Insights into Psychology's History*. Washington, DC: American Psychological Association.

Simpson, George E., & Milton J. Yinger. 1985. *Racial and Cultural Minorities*, 5th. ed. New York: Plenum.

Simpson, Kevin. 2001. "Sporting dreams die on the 'Rez.'" In D. Stanley Eitzen (ed.), *Sport in Contemporary Society*, 6th ed. New York: Worth: 267–74.

Simpson, Miles. 1998. "Suicide and religion: Did Durkheim commit the ecological fallacy. Or did Van Poppel and Day?" *American Sociological Review* 63(6): 895–96.

Simpson, Richard L. 1956. "A modification of the functional theory of social stratification." *Social Forces* 35: 132–37.

Singer, M. I., D. B. Miller, S. Guo, D. J. Flannery, T. Frierson, & K. Slovak. 1999. "Contributors to violent behavior among elementary school and middle school children." *Pediatrics* 104(4 Pt. 1): 878–84.

Sinnott, Jan D., & Kim Shifren. 2001. "Gender and aging: Gender differences and gender roles." In James E. Birren (ed.), *Handbook of the Psychology of Aging*. San Diego, CA: Academic Press.

Sipes, Richard G. 1996. "Sports as a control for aggression." In D. Stanley Eitzen (ed.), *Sports in Contemporary Society*, 6th ed. New York: St. Martin's: 154–60.

Sirius, R. U. 1998. "Viewpoint: The new counterculture." *Time* 152 (Nov. 9).

Sit, Victor F. S. 2001. "Globalization, foreign direct investment, and urbanization in developing countries." In Shahid Yusuf, Simon Evenett, & Weiping Wu (eds.), *Facets of Globalization: International and Local Dimensions of Development*. Washington, DC: World Bank: 11–45.

Sizer, Theodore, & Nancy Sizer. 1999. *The Students are Watching*. Boston: Beacon.

Sizer, Theodore. 1999. "Back to a Place Called School." In Kenneth A. Sirotnik & Roger Soder (eds.), *The Beat of a Different Drummer: Essays on Educational Renewal in Honor of John I. Goodlad*. New York: Peter Lang: 103–18.

Sjoberg, Gideon, & Roger Nett. 1997. *A Methodology for Social Research*. Prospect Heights, IL: Waveland.

Skiba, Russell. 2001. "When is disproportionality discrimination? The overrepresentation of black students in school suspension." In William Ayers, Bernadine Dohrn, & Rick Ayers (eds.), *Zero Tolerance: Resisting the Drive for Punishment in our Schools*. New York: New Press: 176–187.

Sklar, Holly. 1999. "U.S. Boom Just Letting Workers Keep Pace with Costs," *Owensboro (KY) Messenger-Inquirer* (Oct 10).

Sklar, Leslie. 1995. *Sociology of the Global System*, 2nd. ed. Baltimore: Johns Hopkins University Press.

Skocpol, Theda. 1979. *States and Social Revolutions: A Comparative Analysis of France, Russia and China*. New York: Cambridge University Press.

Skocpol, Theda. 1985. "Bringing the state back in: Strategies of analysis in current research." In Peter Evans, Dietrich Rueschemeyer, & Theda Skocpol, (eds.) *Bringing the State Back In*. New York: Cambridge University Press: 3–37.

Skolnick, Jerome H. 1994. *Justice Without Trial: Law Enforcement in a Democratic Society*, 3rd ed. New York: Macmillan.

Slann, Martin. 1993. "The state as terrorist." In Bernard Schechterman & Martin Slann (eds.), *Annual Editions: Violence and Terrorism*, 3rd ed. Guilford, CT: Dushkin: 68–71.

Slavin, Robert E., & Olatokunbo Fashola. 1998. *Show Me the Evidence! Proven and Promising Programs for America's Schools*. Thousand Oaks, CA: Corwin.

Slayden, David, & Rita K. Whillock (eds.). 1999. *Soundbite Culture*. Thousand Oaks, CA: Sage.

Sleeter, Christine E., & Peter McLaren (eds.). 1995. *Multicultural Education, Critical Pedagogy, and the Politics of Difference*. Albany, NY: State University of New York Press.

Sloan, Ethyl. 1985. *Biology of Women*. New York: John Creiley.

Sluzki, Carlos E. 2001. "Drug-company influence on medical education in the U.S.A." *American Journal of Orthopsychiatry* 71(2): 148–49.

Smailes, Elizabeth M., Stephanie Kasen, Judith S. Brook, Jeffrey G. Johnson, & Patricia Cohen. 2002. "Television viewing and aggressive behavior during adolescence and adulthood. *Science* 295(5564): 2468–71.

Smaje, Chris. 2000. "Race, ethnicity and health." In Chloe E. Bird, Peter Conrad, & Allen M. Fremont (eds.), *Handbook of Medical Sociology* (5th edition). Upper Saddle River, NJ: Prentice Hall: 114–28.

Small, Margaret, & Kellie Dressler Tetrick. 2001. "School violence: An overview." *Juvenile Justice* 8(1): (June).

Small, Mario Luis, & Katherine Newman. 2001. "Urban poverty after the truly disadvantaged: The Rediscovery of the family, the neighborhood, and culture." *Annual Review of Sociology* 27: 23–45

Smart, Barry. 1990. "On the disorder of things." *Sociology* (24/3): 397–416.

Smedley, Audrey. 1999. *Race in North America*. Boulder, CO: Westview.

Smeeding, Timothy M. 1998. "U.S. income inequality in a cross-national perspective." In James A Auerbach & Richard S. Belous (eds.), *The Inequality Paradox*. Washington, DC: National Policy Association: 194–217.

Smelser, Neil J. 1973. "Toward a theory of modernization." In Amitai Etzioni & Eva Etzioni-Halvey (eds.), *Social Change—Sources, Patterns and Consequences*. New York: Basic: 268–84.

Smelser, Neil J. 1988. "Social structure." In Neil J. Smelser (ed.), *Handbook of Sociology*. Newbury Park, CA: Sage: 103–129.

Smelser, Neil. 1963. *Theory of Collective Behavior*. Glencoe, IL: Free Press.

Smillie, Ian, & John Hailey. 2001. *Managing for Change: Leadership, Strategy, and Management in Asian NGOs*. London: Earthscan.

Smith, C. E. 1991. *Courts and the Poor*. Chicago: Norton

Smith, D. Clayton. 2001. "Environmentalism, feminism and gender." *Sociological Inquiry* 71(3): 314–34.

Smith, Dan. 1997. *The State of War and Peace Atlas*. Baltimore, MD: Penguin.

Smith, David A. 1995. "The new urban sociology meets the old: Rereading some classical human ecology." *Urban Affairs Review* 30(3): 432–57.

Smith, Dorothy. 1992. *The Everyday World as Problematic*. Boston: Northeastern University Press.

Smith, Douglas A., & Patrick R. Gartin. 1989. "Specifying specific deterrence: The influence of arrest on future criminal activity." *American Sociological Review* 54: 94–105.

Smith, Douglas, Christy Visher, & G. Roger Jajoura. 1991. "Dimensions of delinquency." *Journal of Research in Crime and Delinquency* (28): 6–32.

Smith, Earl, & Wilbert M. Leonard, II. 1997. "25 years of stacking research in major league baseball." *Sociological Focus* (30/4): 321–31.

Smith, Herman W. 1991. *Strategies of Social Research*. Orlando, FL: Holt, Rinehart and Winston.

Smith, Jane E., V. Ann Waldorf, & David L. Trembath. 1990. "Single white male looking for thin, very attractive..." *Sex Roles* 23(11–12): 675–85.

Smith, Jane I. 1999. *Islam in America*. New York: Columbia University.

Smith, Ken R. 1996. "Risk of mortality following widowhood: Age and sex differences by mode of death." *Social Biology* 43(1–2).

Smith, Marsha, & Leah Moreau. 1998. "What is love anyway? Cross-cultural and gender differences defining romantic love among Chinese and American students." Paper presented at the Midwest Sociological Society. Kansas City, MO, April.

Smith, Mick. 2001. *An Ethics of Place: Radical Ecology, Postmodernity, and Social Theory*. Albany: State University of New York.

Smith, Peter K., & Linda M. Drew. 2002. "Grandparenthood." In Marc H. Bornstein (ed.), *Handbook of Parenting: Volume 3, Being and Becoming a Parent*: Mahwah, NJ: Lawrence Erlbaum: 141–72.

Smith, Stacy L., & Barbara J. Wilson. 2002. "Children's consumption of and fear reactions to television news." *Media Psychology* 4(1): 1–26.

Smith, Stacy L., Barbara J. Wilson, & Carolyn M. Colvin. 2002. "Engaging in violence on American television: A comparison of child, teen, and adult perpetrators." *Journal of Communication* 52(1): 36–60.

Smith, Stephen, William McIntosh, & Doxis Bazzini. 1999. "Are the beautiful good in Hollywood? An investigation of the beauty-and-goodness stereotype on film." *Basic and Applied Social Psychology* 21(1): 69–80.

Smith, Vern E. 2001. "Debating the wages of slavery." *Newsweek* (August 27): 20–24.

Smith, Vern E., & Daniel Pedersen. 1997. South toward home." *Newsweek* (July 14): 36–38.

Smith, William L. 1999. *Families and Communes*. Newbury Park, CA: Sage.

Smith, Wilma F. 1999. "Serving as moral stewards of the school." In Wilma F. Smith & Gary D. Fenstermacher (eds.), *Leadership for Educational Renewal: Developing a Cadre of Leaders*. San Francisco: Jossey-Bass: 155–185.

Smith, Yolanda L. S., L. Cohen, & Peggy T. Cohen-Kettenis. 2002. "Postoperative psychological functioning of adolescent transsexuals: A Rorschach study." *Archives of Sexual Behavior* 31(3): 255–61.

Smith, Yolanda L. S., Stephanie H. M. von Goozen, & Peggy T. Cohen-Kettenis. 2001. "Adolescents with gender-identity disorder who were accepted or rejected for sex reassignment surgery: A prospective follow-up study." *Journal of the American Academy of Child & Adolescent Psychiatry* 40(4): 472–81.

Smock, Pamela J., Wendy D. Manning, & Sanjiv Gupta. 1999. "The effect of marriage and divorce on women's economic well-being." *American Sociological Review* 64(6): 794–812.

Smock, Pamela. J. 2000. "Cohabitation in the United States: An appraisal of research themes, findings and interpretations." *Annual Review of Sociology* 26: 1–20.

Smolowe, J. 1993. "Giving the cold shoulder." *Time* (December 6).

Smolowe, J. 1995. "One drug, two sentences." *Time*, (June 19): 45.

Snell, Marilyn Berlin. 2001, "Against the grain: Why poor nations would lose in a biotech war on hunger." *Sierra* (July/August): 30–33.

Snell, T. L. 1996. *Capital Punishment*. 1995. Washington, DC: U.S. Department of Justice, Office of Justice Programs.

Sness, Tracy L. 2001. *Capital Punishment, 2000*. Washington, DC: Bureau of Justice Statistics.

Snodgrass, S. E. 1992. "Further effects of role versus gender on interpersonal sensitivity." *Journal of Personality and Social Psychology* 62: 154–58.

Snow, David A., & Robert D. Benford. 1988. "Ideology, frame resonance and participant mobilization." *International Social Movement Research* 1: 197–217.

Snow, David A., E. Burke Rochford, Jr., Steven K. Worden, & Robert D. Benford. 1986. "Frame alignment processes, micromobilization and movement participation," *American Sociological Review* 51: 464–81.

Snow, David A., Louis A. Zurcher Jr., & Robert Peters. 1981. "Victory celebrations as theater." *Symbolic Interaction* 4/1.

Snow, David A., Louis A. Zurcher, Jr., & Sheldon Ekland-Olson. 1980. "Social networks and social movements." *American Sociological Review* 80: 787–801.

Snow, David, & Leon Anderson. 1993. *Down on Their Luck*. Berkeley: University of California Press.

Snow, Douglas, & Terry F. Buss. 2001. "Development and the role of microcredit." *Policy Studies Journal* 29(2): 296–307.

Snow, Douglas, Terry F. Buss, & Colette Dumas. 2001. "Sustaining microcredit programs: Lessons learned over two decades of practice." In Mark R. Daniels (ed.), *Creating Sustainable Community Programs: Examples of Collaborative Public Administration*. Westport, CTL Praeger: 95–113.

Snyder, Don J. 1997. *The Cliff Walk*. Boston: Little, Brown.

Snyder, H. 2002. *Juvenile Arrests, 2000*. Washington, DC: Office of Juvenile Justice & Delinquency Prevention.

Snyder, Howard N. 1999. "Juvenile arrests, 1998." *Juvenile Justice Bulletin*. December. Office of Justice Programs. U.S. Department of Justice.

Snyder, Mark. 1997. "When belief creates reality: The self-fulfilling impact of first impressions on social interaction prophecy." In Jodi O'Brien & Peter Kollock (eds.), *The Production of Reality: Essays and Readings on Social Interaction*. Thousand Oaks, CA: Pine Forge, pp. 438–42.

So, Alvin Y. 1990. *Social Change and Development: Modernization, Dependency and World System Theories*. Newbury Park, CA: Sage.

So, Alvin Y. 2001. "Social relations between Pearl River Delta and Hong Kong." Presentation to the Pearl River Delta seminar, Asian Studies Development Program. Robert Black College, University of Hong Kong, May 29.

Soares, Luiz. 1996. "Introduction." In *UNESCO Conference on Multiculturalism, Globalization and Identity*. Rio de Janeiro.

Sobel, David (ed.). 1999. *Filters and Freedom: Free Speech Perspectives on Internet Content Controls*. Washington, DC: Electronic Privacy Information Center.

Social Security Administration. 2001. "Facts and figures about Social Security." Washington, DC: Social Security Administration.

Sodden, Dennis (ed.). 1999. *The Environmental Presidency*. Albany: State University of New York.

Sokolovsky, Jay. 2000. "Images of aging." In Elizabeth W. Markson & Lisa Ann Hollis-Sawyer (eds.), *Intersections of Aging: Reading in Social Gerontology*. Los Angeles, CA: Roxbury: 6–11.

Solomon, Richard, & Cynthia Pierce Liefeld. 1998. "Effectiveness of a family support center approach to adolescent mothers: Repeat pregnancy and school drop-out rates." *Family Relations* 47(2): 139–44.

Solon, Gary. 1992. "Intergenerational income mobility in the United States." *American Economic Review* (June).

Sontag, Deborah. 2002. "Who was responsible for Elizabeth Shin?" 2002. *New York Times Magazine*: 56–61, 94, 139.

Sorensen, Elaine. 1994. *Comparable Worth: Is It a Worthy Policy?* Princeton, NJ: Princeton University Press.

Sorenson, E., & C. Zieman. 2000. "Child support offers some protection against poverty." Washington, DC: Urban Institute. http://www.newfederalism.org

Sorenson, Georg. 1998. *Democracy and Democratization*, 2nd ed. Boulder, CO: Westview.

Sorokin, Pitirim A. 1941. *Social and Cultural Dynamics*. New York: American.

Sorokin, Pitirim A. 1959. (Original edition, 1927.) *Social and Cultural Mobility*. New York: Free Press.

Sosis, Richard. 2000. "Religion and intergroup cooperation: Preliminary results of a comparative analysis of utopian communities." *Cross-Cultural Research* 34(1): 70–87.

Southern Poverty Law Center. 1998. "The year in hate." *Intelligence Report* (Winter).

Southern Poverty Law Center. 2002. "Intelligence Report." Available: http://www.splcenter.org/intelligenceproject/ip-mainptm.

Sowell, Thomas. 1972. *Black Education: Myths and Tragedies*. New York: McKay.

Sowell, Thomas. 1981. *Ethnic America*. New York: Basic Books.

Spalter-Roth, Roberta, & Heidi Hartmann. 1999. "Small happiness: The feminist struggle to integrate social research with social action." In Sharlene Hesse-Biber, Christina Gilmartin, & Robin Lydenberg (eds.), *Feminist Approaches to Theory and Methodology*. New York: Oxford University: 333–47.

Spalter-Roth, Roberta, & Sunhwa Lee. 2000. "Profile of ASA Membership." *Footnotes* (March).

Sparks, Allister. 1990. *The Mind of South Africa*. New York: Knopf.

Sparks, Richard. 1980. "A critique of Marxist criminology." In Norval Morris & Michael Tonry (eds.), *Crime and Justice*, Vol. 2. Chicago: University of Chicago Press: 159–208.

Sparks, Richard. 1992. *Television and the Drama of Crime: Moral Tales and the Place of Crime in Public Life*. Buckingham, UK: Open University Press.

Special Protection Measures. 1995. "On preservation of indigenous languages." *Australia's First Report under Article 441a on the United Nations Convention on the Rights of the Child*. Report No. 1799 (December). Commonwealth of Australia. Available: http://law.gov.au.publications/croc/crochdi.

Spector, Malcolm, & John Kitsuse. 1977. *Constructing Social Problems*. Menlo Park, CA: Cummings.

Spektor, Alex. 2002. "September 11, 2001 victims." Available: http://www.september11victims.com/september11victims/STATISTIC.

Spencer, Herbert. 1860. *The Social Organism*. London: Greenwood.

Spender, Dale. 1989. *The Writing or the Sex: Or Why You Don't Have to Read Women's Writing to Know It's No Good*. New York: Teacher's College Press.

Spengler, Oswald. 1928. *The Decline and Fall of the West*. New York: Alfred A. Knopf.

Spickard, Paul R. 1991. *Mixed Blood: Intermarriage and Ethnic Identity In Twentieth-Century America*. Madison: University of Wisconsin Press.

Spilerman, S. 1976. "Structural characteristics of cities and the severity of racial disorders." *American Sociological Review* 41: 771–93.

Spindel, Carol. 2000. *Dancing at Halftime*. New York: NYU Press.

Spitze, Glenna. 1986. "The division of task responsibility in U.S. households: Longitudinal adjustments to change." *Social Forces* 64 (March): 689–701.

Spitzer, Brenda L., Katherine A. Henderson, & Marilyn T. Zaivian. 1999. "Gender differences in population versus media body sizes: A comparison over four decades." *Sex Roles* 40(7–8): 545–65.

Spraggins, Renee E. 2001. "U.S. Census Bureau releases profile of nation's women." Available: http:www.census.gov/Press-Release/www2001.

Spring, Joel. 1998. *Education and the Rise of the Global Economy*. Mahwah, NJ: Lawrence Erlbaum.

Sreberny, Annabelle, & Liesbet van Zoonen (eds.). 2000. *Gender Politics and Communication*. Cresskill, NJ: Hampton.

Srole, Leo, Thomas S. Langer, Stanley T. Michael, Marvin K. Opler & Thomas A. C. Rennie. 1962. *Mental Health in the Metropolis: The Midtown Manhattan Study*. New York: McGraw-Hill.

SSBR, 2000. Social Statistics Briefing Room: Education. Available: http://www.whitehous.gov/fsbr.education.

Stacey, Judith. 1996. *In the Name of the Family: Rethinking Family Values in the Postmodern Age*. Boston: Beacon Press.

Stack, Carol B. 1975. *All Our Kin: Strategies for Survival in a Black Community*. New York: Harper & Row.

Stack, Carol. 1996. *Call to Home: African-American Reclaim the Rural South*. New York: Basic Books.

Stack, S. 1990. "Execution publicity and homicide in South Carolina: A research note." *Sociological Quarterly* (31/4): 559–611.

Stack, Steven. 1998. "Heavy metal, religiosity, and suicide acceptability." *Suicide and Life Threatening Behavior* 28(4): 388–94.

Stack, Steven. 2000. "Blues fans and suicide acceptability." *Death Studies* 24(3): 223–31.

Stackhouse, Max L., with Peter J. Paris. 2000. *God and Globalization, Volume I: Religion and the Powers of the Common Life*. Harrisburg, PA: Trinity.

Staggenborg, Suzanne. 1988. "The consequences of professionalization and formalization in the pro-choice movement." *American Sociological Review* 53: 586–606.

Stampp, Kenneth M. 1956. *The Peculiar Institution*. New York: Random House.

Stanley, Alessandra. 1997. "Democracy in Russia: Women's lib is just cosmetic." *New York Times* (May 11): 3.

Stanley, Alessandra. 2002. "Why the Cardinals kept mum." *The New York Times* (April 28): 3.

Stanley, David. 2000. *Moon Handbooks: Tahiti*. Emeryville, CA: Avalon.

Stanovnik, Tine, Nada Stropnik, & Christopher Prinz (eds.). 2000, *Economic Well-Being of the Elderly: A Comparison across Five European Countries*. Aldershot, UK: Ashgate.

Staples, Brent. 1997. "Just walk on by: A black man ponders his power to alter public space." In Estelle Disch (ed.). *Reconstructing Gender: A Multicultural Anthology*. Mountain View, CA: Mayfield: 165–68.

Staples, Robert. 1997. "An overview of race and marital status." In Harriette Pipes McAdoo (ed.), *Black Families*. Thousand Oaks, CA: Sage: 269–72.

Stark, Rodney, & Laurence R. Iannaccone. 1994. "A supply-side reinterpretation of the 'secularization' of Europe." *Journal for the Scientific Study of Religion* 33(1): 230–52.

Stark, Rodney, & William S. Bainbridge. 1985. *The Future of Religion: Secularization, Revival and Cult Formation*. Berkeley & Los Angeles: University of California Press.

Stark, Rodney. 1996a. "Why religious movements succeed or fail: A revised general model." *Journal of Contemporary Religion* 11: 133–46.

Stark, Rodney. 1996a. *Sociology*, 6th ed. Belmont, CA: Wadsworth: 255–56.

Stark, Rodney. 1996b. *The Rise of Christianity: A Sociologist Reconsiders History*. Princeton, NJ: Princeton University Press.

Stark, Rodney. 1999. "Secularization: R.I.P." *Sociology of Religion* 60(3): 249–73.

Stark, Rodney. 2001. *One True God*. Princeton, NJ: Princeton University.

Stark, Rodney. 2002. *Doing Sociology: A Global Perspective*, 4th ed. Belmont, CA: Wadsworth.

Starr, Paul. 1982. *The Social Transformation of American Medicine*. New York: Basic Books.

Stasio, Marilyn. 2001. "It's not just a 'women's issue' anymore." *Parade Magazine*. St. Louis Post-Dispatch (January 21): 14, 16.

Staton, Ann Q. 1990. *Communication and Student Socialization*. Norwood, NJ: Ablex.

Staudt, Kathleen. 1998. *Policy, Politics & Gender: Women Gaining Ground*. West Hartford, CT: Kumarian.

Stave, Sondra Astor. 1995. *Achieving Racial Balance: Case Studies of Contemporary School Desegregation*. Westport, CT: Greenwood.

Steele, Shelby. 1990. "A negative vote on affirmative action." *The New York Times Magazine* (May 13): 46–49+.

Steensland, Brian, Jerry Z. Park, Mark D. Regnerus, Lynn D. Robinson, W. Bradford Wilcox, & Robert D. Woodberry. 2000. "The measurement of American religion: Toward improving the state of the art." *Social Forces* 79(1): 291–318.

Steffensmeier, Darrell, & Cathy Streifel. 1991. "Age, gender and crime across three historical periods: 1935, 1960 and 1985." *Social Forces* (69/3): 869–94.

Steffensmeier, Darrell, & M. D. Harer. 1991. "Did crime rise or fall during the Reagan presidency? *Journal of Crime and Delinquency*. 28: 330–59.

Steffensmeier, Darrell, & Stephen Demuth. 2000. "Ethnicity and sentencing outcomes in U.S. federal court: Who is punished more harshly?" *American Sociological Review* (65): 705–729.

Steil, Janice M. 1995. "Supermoms and second shifts: Marital inequality in the 1990s." In Jo Freeman (ed.), *Women: A Feminist Perspective*. Mountain View, CA: Mayfield: 149–161.

Steil, Janice, & Beth Turetsky. 1987. "Is equal better? The relationship between marital equality and psychological symptomology." In S. Oskamp (ed.), *Family Processes and Problems: Social Psychological Aspects*. Beverly Hills, CA: Sage.

Stein, Nan, N. Marshall, & L. Troop. 1999. *Secrets in Public: Sexual Harassment in Our Schools*. Wellesley, MA: Wellesley College Center for Research on Women.

Steinberg, Shirley R., & Joe L. Kincheloe (eds.). 1998. *Kinderculture: The Corporate Construction of Childhood (The Edge: Critical Studies in Educational Theory)*. Scranton, NY: HarperCollins

Steinberg, Steven Jay. 1999. "Gender rules: Boys and puberty vs. schools and public policy." *Ph.D. Dissertation*, University of California, Los Angeles.

Steinem, Gloria. 1995. "Sex, lies and advertising." In Jo Freeman (ed.), *Women: A Feminist Perspective*. Mountain View, CA: Mayfield.

Steinmetz, Suzanne K. 1988. *Duty Bound: Elder Abuse and Family Care*. Newbury Park, CA: Sage Publications.

Stencel, Mark. 1999. "20 years later: A nuclear nightmare in Pennsylvania." *Washington Post*: March 27. Available: http://www.washingtonpost.co/wp-srv/national/longterm/tmi/tmi.

Stetson, Dorothy McBride. 1997. *Women's Rights in the U.S.A.: Policy Debates and Gender Roles*. Pacific Grove, CA: Brooks/Cole.

Stevens, Carol. 1999. "How women get bad medicine." In Amy Kesselman, Linda McNair, & Nancy Schniedewind (eds.), *Women: Images and Realities*. Mountain View, CA: Mayfield: 267–72.

Stevens, Evelyn P. 2000. "Marianismo: The other face of machismo in Latin America." In Anne Minas (ed.), *Gender Basics*. Belmont, CA: Wadsworth: 456–63.

Stevens, William. 1997a. "Battle stage is set: Clinton proposal on global warming defines issues for rich and poor alike." *New York Times* (October 23).

Stevens, William. 1997b. "Greenhouse gas issue: Haggling over fairness." *The New York Times* (November 30).

Stevenson, Harold W. 1992. "Learning from Asian Schools." *Scientific American* (December): 70–76.

Stevenson, Robert G. 2002. "Helping peers to support themselves: The role of peer support in times of crisis." In Robert G. Stevenson (ed.), *What Will We Do? Preparing a School Community to Cope with Crises*. Amityville, NY: Baywood: 193–200.

Stewart, Karen. 1998. "Women in business: The experiences of women in the U.S. workforce." In Donna Musialowski Ashcraft (ed.), *Women's Work: A Survey of Scholarship by and about Women*. New York: Haworth.

Stewart, L. P., A. D. Stewart, S. A. Friedley, & P. J. Cooper. 1990. *Communication Between the Sexes: Sex Differences and Sex Role Stereotypes*. Scottsdale, AZ: Gorsuch Scarisbrick.

Stiers, Gretchen A. 2000. *From this Day Forward: Commitment, Marriage, and Family in Lesbian and Gay Relationships*. New York: St. Martin's.

Stiff, J. B., & G. R. Miller, C. Sleight, P. I. Mongeau, R. Gardelck, & R. Rogan. 1989. "Explanations for visual cue primacy in judgments of honesty and deceit." *Journal of Personality and Social Psychology* 156: 555–64.

Stille, Alexander. 2001. "Grounded by an income gap." *New York Times* (December 15): A15, A17.

Stinchcombe, Arthur. 1968. *Constructing Social Theories*. Chicago: University of Chicago Press.

Stogdill, R. M. 1974. *Handbook of Leadership*. New York: Free Press.

Stohs, Joanne Hoven. 2000. "Multicultural women's experience of household labor, conflicts, and equity." *Sex Roles* 42(5–6): 339–61.

Stoll, Michael A. 1999. "Spatial mismatch, discrimination, and male youth employment in the Washington, DC area: Implications for residential mobility." *Journal of Policy Analysis and Management* 18(1): 77–98.

Stott, C., & S. Reicher. 1998. "How conflict escalates." *Sociology* (32): 353–77.

Strange, Mary Zeiss. 2002. "Female priests provide answer." *USA Today* (April 4): 13A

Straubhaar, Joseph, & Robert LaRose. 2002. *Media Now*. Belmont, CA: Wadsworth.

Strauss, Anselm, Leonard Schatzman, Rue Bucher, Danuta Ehrlich, & Melvin Sabslim. 1964. *Psychiatric Ideologies and Institutions*. New York: Free Press.

Strauss, Anselm. 1977. *Negotiations: Varieties, Contexts, Processes & Social Order*. San Francisco: Jossey-Bass.

Strauss, Valerie. 2000. "Equal opportunity learning." *Washington Post* Feb. 22:A09.

Streib, Gordon F. 2002. "An introduction to retirement communities." *Research on Aging* 24(1): 3–9.

Streitmatter, Rodger. 2001. *Voices of Revolution: The Dissident Press in America*. New York: Columbia University.

Stren, Richard, & Mario Polese. 2000. "Understanding the new sociocultural dynamics of cities: Comparative urban policy in a global context." In Mario Polese & Richard Stren (eds.), *The Social Sustainability of Cities: Diversity and the Management of Change*. Toronto: University of Toronto: 3–37.

Stren, Richard. 2001. "Urban governance and politics in a global context: The growing importance of localities." In Shahid Yusuf, Simon Evenett, & Weiping Wu (eds.), *Facets of Globalization: International and Local Dimensions of Development*. Washington, DC: World Bank: 147–170.

Strikwerda, Robert A., & Larry May. 1992. "Male friendship and intimacy." In Larry May & Robert Stikwerda (eds.), *Rethinking Masculinity: Philosophical Explorations in Light of Feminism*. Lanham, MD: Rowman and Littlefield.

Stromquist, Nelly P. 1998. "The institutionalization of gender and its impact on educational policy." *Comparative Education* 34(1): 85–100.

Stroup, Atlee L., & Gene E. Pollock. 1999. "Economic well-being among white elderly divorced." *Journal of Divorce & Remarriage* 31(3–4): 53–68.

Strouse, Darcy L. 1999. "Adolescent crowd orientations: A social and temporal analysis." In Jeffrey A. McLellan & Mary Jo V. Pugh (eds.), *The Roles of Peer Groups in Adolescent Social Identity: Exploring the Stability and Change*. San Francisco: Jossey-Bass.

Stryker, Robin. 2001. "The disparate impact and the quota debates: Law, labor market sociology, and equal employment practices." *Sociological Quarterly* 42(1): 13–46.

Stryker, Sheldon. 1990. "Symbolic interactionism: Themes & variations." In M. Rosenberg & R. H. Turner (eds.), *Social Psychology: Sociological Perspectives*. New Brunswick, NJ: Transaction.

Sturm, Roland, Carole Roan Gresenz, & Mackenbach, G. 2002. "Relations of income inequality and family income to chronic medical conditions and mental health disorders: National survey in U.S.A." *British Medical Journal* 324(January 5): 20–23.

Suarez-Orozco, Carola, & Marcelo M. Suarez-Orozco. 2001. *Children of Immigration*. Cambridge, MA: Harvard University.

Subramanian, S. 1997. "Economic considerations in mate selection criteria." Paper presented at the American Psychological Association, Chicago.

Sue, Derald Wing, & David Sue. 1999. *Counseling the Culturally Different: Theory and Practice*. New York: John Wiley.

Suggs, Welch. 2000. "Graduation rates for athletes hold steady." *Chronicle of Higher Education* (December 1): A-47–A49.

Sullivan, Jeremiah J. 2002. *The Future of Corporate Globalization: From Extended Order to the Global Village*. Westport, CT: Quorum.

Sullivan, Thomas J. 1992. *Applied Sociology: Research & Critical Thinking*. New York: Macmillan.

Sultan, Aisha. 2001. "Gas scare at Granite City High shakes officials, spurs more security." *St. Louis Post-Dispatch* (Feb. 4): C1, C7.

Sumner, W. G. 1883. *What Social Classes Owe to Each Other*. New York: Harper & Brothers.

Sumner, William Graham. 1960. *Folkways*. New York: New American Library. Originally published in 1906.

Sun, L. H. 1990. "China seeks ways to protect elderly: Support agreements replacing traditional respect for the elderly." *Washington Post* (October 23): A1, A18.

Sun, Yongmin. 2001. "Family environment and adolescents' well-being before and after parents' marital disruption: A longitudinal analysis." *Journal of Marriage and the Family* 63(3): 697–713.

Sung, Betty Lee. 1994. "Bicultural conflict." In Elvio Angeloni (ed.), *Anthropology 93/94*. Guilford, CT: Dushkin.

Sung, Kyu-taik. 2000. "Respect for elders: Myths and realities in East Asia." *Journal of Aging and Identity* 5(4): 197–205.

Suppe, Frederick (ed.). 1974. *The Structure of Scientific Theories*. Urbana: University of Illinois Press.

Surette, Ray, 1998. *Media, Crime, and Criminal Justice*, 2nd ed. Belmont, CA: West/Wadsworth.

Suro, Roberto. 1999. *Watching America's Door: The Immigration Backlash and the New Policy Debate*. Washington, DC: Century Foundation.

Sutherland, Edwin H. 1940. "White-collar criminality." *American Sociological Review* (5): 1–12.

Sutherland, Edwin. 1949. *White-Collar Crime*. New York: Dryden.

Sutton, Mark Q. 2000. *An Introduction to Native North America*. Needham Heights, MA: Allyn & Bacon.

Swaddling, Judith. 1999. *The Ancient Olympic Games*, 2nd ed. Austin: University of Texas.

Swatos, William H. 1998. "Globalization and religious fundamentalism. In Peter Kivisto (ed.), *Illuminating Social Life: Classical and Contemporary Theory Revisited*. Thousand Oaks, CA: Pine Forge: 285–308.

Sweeney, M. M. 1998. "Remarriage of women and men after divorce: The role of socioeconomic prospects." *Journal of Family Issues* 18: 479–502.

Swidler, Leonard, & Paul Mojzes. 2000. *The Study of Religion in an Age of Global Dialogue*. Philadelphia: Temple University.

Swift, Richard. 1991. "Among the believers." *Utne Reader* 45 (May/June): 99–104.

Sygnatur, E., & G. Toscano. 2000. "Work related homicides: The facts" *Compensation and Working Conditions* (Spring).

Syme, S. Leonard & Lisa F. Berkman. 1994. "Social class: Susceptibility and illness." In Peter Conrad & Rochelle Kern (eds.), *Sociology of Health and Illness: Critical Perspectives*. New York: St. Martin's: 28–34.

Syme, S. Leonard, & Irene H. Yen. 2000. "Social epidemiology and medical sociology: Different approaches to the same problem." In Chloe E. Bird, Peter Conrad, & Allen M. Fremont (eds.), *Handbook of Medical Sociology*. Upper Saddle River, NJ: Prentice Hall: 365–76.

Syme, S. Leonard, & Lisa F. Berkman. 1997. "Social class, susceptibility and sickness." In Peter Conrad (ed.), *The Sociology of Health and Illness*, 5th ed. New York: St. Martin's: 29–35.

Szasz, Thomas S. 1961. *The Myth of Mental Illness*. New York: Harper & Row.

Szasz, Thomas. 2000. "Mental disorders are not diseases." *USA Today Magazine* 128 (January): 30–31.

Tabb, William K. 2002. *Unequal Partners: A Primer on Globalization*. New York: New Press.

Tabbarah, Melissa, Merril Silverstein, & Teresa Seeman. 2000. "A health and demographic profile of noninstitutionalized older Americans residing in environments with home modifications." *Journal of Aging & Health* 12(2): 204–28.

Tabor, James D., & Eugene V. Gallagher. 1995. *Why Waco? Cults and the Battle for Religious Freedom in America*. Berkeley, CA: University of California.

Tagney, June Price, & Ronda L. Dearing. 2002. "Gender differences in morality." In Robert F. Bornstein & Joseph M. Masling (eds.), *The Psychodynamics of Gender and*

Gender Roles: Empirical Studies in Psychoanalytic Theories, Volume 10. Washington, DC: American Psychological Association.

Taipei Times. 2001. "Japanese cram schools start to fail." December 26. Available: http://www.taipeitimes.com/news/2001/12/26.

Tajfel, Henri. 1982. "Social psychology of intergroup relations." In *Annual Review of Psychology.* Palo Alto, CA: Annual Reviews: 1–39.

Takaki, Ronald. 1993. *A Different Mirror: A History of Multicultural America.* Boston: Little, Brown.

Takezawa, Yasuko I. 1995. *Breaking the Silence: Redress and Japanese American Ethnicity.* Ithaca, NY: Cornell University Press.

Talbani, Aziz, and Parveen Hasanali. 2000. "Adolescent females between tradition and modernity: Gender role socialization in South Asian immigrant culture." *Journal of Adolescence* 23(5): 615–27.

Talbot, Margaret. 1999. "The little white bombshell." *New York Times Magazine* (June 11): 39–43, 61–63.

Tamborini, Ron, Dana E. Mastro, Rebecca M. Chory-Assad, & Ren He Huang. 2000. "The color of crime and the court: A content analysis of minority representation on television." *Journalism & Mass Communication Quarterly* 77(3): 639–53.

Tannen, Deborah. 1994. *Gender and Discourse.* New York: Oxford University.

Tannen, Deborah. 1994. *Talking From 9 to 5.* New York: William Morrow.

Tannen, Deborah. 2001. *You Just Don't Understand: Men and Women in Conversation.* New York: Quill.

Tao, Xuelian et al. 2002. "Herbal extract may help rheumatoid arthritis." Medline Plus Health Information: August 7. Available: http://www.nlm.nih.gov/medlineplus/news/fullstory 8832.

Tardif, Twila, Erika Hoff, & Brett Laursen. 2002. "Socioeconomic status and parenting." In March H. Bornstein (ed.), *Handbook of Parenting: Volume 2: Biology and Ecology of Parenting.* Mahwah, NJ: Lawrence Erlbaum.

Tarrow, Sidney G. 1994. *Power In Movement: Social Movements, Collective Action and Politics.* New York: Cambridge University Press.

Taubman, Peter Maas. 2001. "The callings of sexual identities." In Glenn M. Hudak & Paul Kihn (eds.), *Labeling: Pedagogy and Politics.* New York: Routledge.

Tausky, Curt. 1984. *Work and Society.* Itasca, IL: Peacock.

Tavris, Carol. 1996. "The mismeasure of woman." In Karen E. Rosenblum & Carol Travis (eds.), *The Meaning of Difference: American Constructions of Race, Sex, Gender, Social Class, and Sexual Orientation.* New York: McGraw-Hill.

Taylor, Charles. 1995. *Multiculturalism and the Politics of Recognition.* Princeton, NJ: Princeton University Press.

Taylor, Eric R. 1998. *Lethal Mists.* Commack, NY: Nova.

Taylor, Howard F. 1992. "The structure of a national black leadership network: Preliminary findings." Unpublished manuscript, cited in Margaret L. Anderson, & Howard F. Taylor. 2002. *Sociology: Understanding a Diverse Society,* 2nd ed. Belmont, CA: Wadsworth.

Taylor, Maxwell, & Helen Ryan. 1988. "Fanaticism, political suicide, and terrorism." *Terrorism* 11: 91–111.

Taylor, Peter J., Michael Hoyler, & David R. F. Walker. 2001. "A new mapping of the world for the new millennium." *Geographical Journal* 167(pt.3): 213–22.

Teaford, Jon C. 1997. *Post-Suburbia: Government and Politics in the Edge Cities.* Baltimore, MD: Johns Hopkins University.

Technical Note. 2000. "Technical note on same-sex unmarried partner data from the 1990 and 2000 censuses." Census 2000/ U.S. Census Bureau. Available: http://www.census.gov/population/www/cen2000/samesex.

Teich, Albert H. (ed.). 1993. *Technology and the Future,* 6th ed. New York: St. Martin's Press.

Teicher, Stacy A. 2002, "Stages of American identity." *Christian Science Monitor* 94(99): 15.

Telzrow, Cathy F. 1999. "IDEA Amendments of 1997: Promise or pitfall for special education reform." *Journal of School Psychology* 37(1): 7–28.

Temple, Johnny. 1999. "Noise from the underground." *Nation* (October 18).

Tenenbaum, Harriet R., & Campbell Leaper. 2002. "Are parents' gender schemas related to their children's gender-related cognitions? A meta-analysis." *Developmental Psychology* 38: 615–30.

Tennenbaum, David. 1977. "Research studies of personality & criminality." *Journal of Criminal Justice* 5: 1–19.

Terkel, Studs. 1985. *Working.* New York: Penguin.

Terrill, Richard J. 1999. *World Criminal Justice Systems,* 4th ed. Cincinnati: Anderson.

Terrion, Jenepher Lennox, & Blake E. Ashforth. 2002 "From 'I' to 'we': The role of putdown humor and identity in the development of a temporary group." *Human Relations* 55(1): 55–88.

Tessler, Richard C. & Deborah L. Dennis. 1992. "Mental illness among homeless adults," *Research in Community and Mental Health* 7: 3–53.

Texdorf, Christiane, Martin H. Schmidt, Guenter Esser, Martin Gerhold, & Manfred Laucht. 2002. "Early mother–infant interaction as a precursor to childhood social withdrawal." *Child Psychiatry & Human Development* 32(4): 277–93.

"The Boss's Pay." 2001. *Wall Street Journal* (April 6): R9.

"The Forbes 400." 1999. *Forbes* (164/9): 414–418.

"The Secret of Japan's Safe Streets." 1994. *The Economist* 331 (April 16): 38–40.

Theberge, Nancy. 1997. "It's part of the game: Physicality and the production of gender in women's ice hockey." *Gender & Society* (11/February): 69–87.

Theorell, Tores. 2001. "Stress and health from a work perspective." In Jack Dunham (ed.), *Stress in the Workplace: Past, Present, and Future.* London: Whurr: 34–51.

Thierer, Adam, & Stephen Chapman. 1997. "The V-chip will result in censorship." In Byron L. Stay (ed.), *Censorship.* San Diego: Greenhaven: 171–75.

Thoits, Peggy A. 1986. "Multiple identities: Examining gender and marital status differences in distress." *American Sociological Review* 51: 259–72.

Thom, Mary. 2000. "Promises to keep." *Now It's a Global Movement: Ford Foundation Report.* (Special Issue on Women) (Winter): 30–33.

Thomas, Melvin E., & Linda A. Treiber. 2000. "Race, gender, and status: A content analysis of print advertisements in four popular magazines." *Sociological Spectrum* 20(3): 357–71.

Thomas, Scott. 1999. "Religion and international society." In Jeff Haynes (ed.), *Religion, Globalization and Political Culture in the Third World.* London: McMillan 28–44.

Thomas, Stephen B. 2001. "The color line: Race matters in the elimination of health disparities." *American Journal of Public Health* 91(7): 1046–48.

Thomas, Vinod, Mansoor Dailami, Ashok Dhareshwar, Daniel Kaufman, Nalin Kishor, Ramon E. Lopez, & Yan Wang. 2000. *The Quality of Growth.* New York: World Bank and Oxford University.

Thomas, W. I. 1923. *The Unadjusted Girl.* New York: Harper & Row.

Thomas, W. I., & D. S. Thomas. 1928. *The Child in America.* New York: Knopf.

Thomas-Lester, Avis. 1995. "Domestic violence." *Washington Post* (January 17): C5.

Thompson, Hunter S. 1966. *Hell's Angels.* New York: Ballantine.

Thompson, Kenneth. 1998. *Moral Panics.* London: Routledge.

Thompson, William E. 1983. "Hanging tongues: A sociological encounter with the assembly line." *Qualitative Sociology* 6: 215–37.

Thomson, Michael. 1998. *Reproducing Narrative: Gender, Reproduction and Law.* Aldershot, UK: Ashgate.

Thomson, Rob, Tamar Murachver, & James Green. 2001. "Where is the gender in gendered language?" *Psychological Science* 12(2): (March).

Thorne, Barrie. 1997. "Girls and boys together…but mostly apart: Gender arrangements in elementary schools." In Laurel Richardson, Verta Taylor, & Nancy Whittier (eds.), *Feminist Frontiers IV.* New York: McGraw-Hill: 176–87.

Thornton, Mark. 1998. "What caused the Irish potato famine?" *Free Market* 16(4).

Thurlow, Crispin. 2001. "Naming the 'outside within': Homophobic pejoratives and the verbal abuse of lesbian, gay and bisexual high-school students." *Journal of Adolescence* 24(1): 25–38.

Thurow, Lester C. 1999. *Building Wealth.* New York: Harper/Collins.

Tickamyer, Ann R., & Teresa A. Wood. 1998. "Identifying participation in the informal economy using survey research methods." *Rural Sociology* 63(2): 323–29.

Tickell, Crispin. 1996. "Rising temperatures place cities at risk." *Forum for Applied Research and Public Policy* 11: 134–36.

Tilly, Charles. 1978. *From Mobilization to Revolution.* Reading, MA: Addison-Wesley.

Tilly, Charles. 1992. *Coercion, Capital and European States, AD 990–1992.* Cambridge, MA: Basil Blackwell.

Tilly, Charles. 1993. *European Revolutions, 1492–1992.* Oxford, England: Blackwell.

Tilly, Chris. 1996. *Half a Job.* Philadelphia: Temple University Press.

Title IX at 30. 2002. "Title IX at 30: Report card reveals there is still room for improvement." Available: http://womenssportsfoundation.org/cgi-bin/iowa/issues/disc/article.

Titma, Mikk, & Nancy Tuma. 2001. *Modern Russia.* New York: McGraw Hill.

Tittle, Charles R., & Robert F. Meier. 1990. "Specifying the SES/delinquency relationship." *Criminology* 28: 271–99.

Tittle, Charles R., W. J. Villemez, & D. A. Smith. 1978. "The myth of social class and criminality: An empirical assessment of the empirical evidence." *American Sociological Review* 43: 643–56.

Tittle, Charles. 1975. "Labeling and crime: An empirical evaluation." In Walter Gove (ed.), *The Labeling of Deviance.* New York: John Wiley: 79–100.

Tjosvold, D., I. R. Andrews, & J. T. Struthers. 1992. "Leadership influence." *Journal of Social Psychology* 132: 39–50.

Toby, Jackson. 1979. "The new criminology is the old sentimentality." *Criminology* (16): 513–26.

Toffler, Alvin. 1980. *The Third Wave.* New York: Bantam.

Tolbert, Pamela S., & Phyllis Moen. 1998. "Men's and women's definitions of 'good' jobs." *Work & Occupations* 25: 168–194.

Toler, Deborah. 2000. "Biotechnology not the answer to global hunger." *Knight Ridder/Tribune* (July 25).

Tolman, Deborah L. 2001. "Echoes of sexual objectification: Listening for one girl's erotic voice." In Deborah L. Tolman & Mary Brydon-Miller (eds.), *From Subjects to Subjectivities: A Handbook of Interpretive and Participatory Methods.* New York: New York University: 130–44.

Tolnay, Stewart, & E. M. Beck. 1998. *A Festival of Violence: An Analysis of Southern Lynchings, 1882–1930.* Urbana: University of Illinois Press.

Tolson, Jay. 1995. "The trouble with elites," *The Wilson Quarterly* (19/1): 6–8.

Tomasello, Michael, & J. Call. 1997. *Primate Cognition.* Oxford, UK: Oxford University.

Tomasello, Michael. 1999. "The human adaptation for culture." *Annual Review of Anthropology* 28: ii–xxiii.

Tomasello, Michael. 2002. "Some facts about primate (including human) communication and social learning." In Angelo Cangelosi & Domenico Parisi (eds.), *Simulating the Evolution of Language.* New York: Springer-Verlag: 327–40.

Toner, Robin, & Sheryl Gay Stolberg. 2002. "Decade after health care crisis soaring costs bring new strains." *New York Times* (August 11): 1,18–19.

Tönnies, Ferdinand. 1963. *Community and Society.* New York: Harper & Row. Originally published in 1887.

Tonry, Michael. 1995. *Malign Neglect: Race, Crime and Punishment in America.* New York: Oxford.

"Top players produce up to $1 million in revenue for their universities." 1994. *Chronicle of Higher Education* (April 13): A33–34.

Topping, Donald M. 1992. "Literacy and cultural erosion in the Pacific Islands." In

Fraida Dubin & Natalie A. Kuhlman (eds.), *Cross-Cultural Literacy: Global Perspectives on Reading and Writing.* Upper Saddle River, NJ: Regents/Prentice Hall.

Tordoff, William. 1992. "The impact of ideology on development," *Journal of International Development* 4/1: 41–53.

Toro-Morn, Maura I. 1995. "Gender, class, family, and migration: Puerto Rican women in Chicago." *Gender & Society* 9(6): 712–26.

Torres, Carlos Alberto, & Theodore R. Mitchell. 1998. "Introduction." In C. A. Torres and T. R. Mitchell (eds.), *Sociology of Education: Emerging Perspectives.* Albany: State University of New York: 1–18.

Torry, S. 1997. "ABA leader criticizes admissions policies." *Washington Post* (August 5): A7.

Touraine, Alain. 1981. *The Voice & the Eye.* Cambridge, England: Cambridge University Press.

Toussaint, Eric. 1999. *Your Money or Your Life! The Tyranny of Global Finance.* London: Pluto Press.

Toynbee, Arnold J. 1946. *A Study of History.* New York: Oxford University Press.

Traphagan, John W. 2000. *Taming Oblivion: Aging Bodies and the Fear of Senility in Japan.* Albany, NY: State University of New York.

Travers, Jeffrey, & Stanley Milgram. 1969. "An experimental study of the small world problem." *Sociometry* 32: 425–443.

Travis, Cheryl Brown, & Jill D. Compton. 2001. "Feminism and health in the decade of behavior." *Psychology of Women Quarterly* 25(4): 312–23.

Treanor, Nick (ed.). 2002. *The Feminist Movement.* San Diego: Greenhaven.

Treas, J., & D. Giesen. 2000. "Sexual infidelity among married and co-habiting Americans." *Journal of Marriage and the Family* 62: 48–60.

Trebach, Arnold. 1989. "Why not decriminalize?" *New Perspectives Quarterly* (6/2): 40–45.

Triandis, Harry C., & Eunkook M. Suh. 2002. "Cultural influences on personality." $$$Tschudin *Annual Review of Psychology* 53: 133–60.

Trible, Phyllis. 1984. *The Texts of Terror.* Philadelphia: Fortress.

Trice, Harrison M., & Janice M. Beyer. 1993. *The Cultures of Work Organizations.* Upper Saddle River, NJ: Prentice Hall.

Triebel, Armin. 2001. "The roles of literacy practices in the activities and institutions of developed and developing countries." In David R. Olson & Nancy Torrance (eds.), *The Making of Literate Societies.* Malden, MA: Blackwell: 19–53.

Trinh, Sylvaine, & John R. Hall. 2000. "The violent path of Aum Shinrikyo." In John R. Hall with Philip D. Schuyler & Sylvaine Trinh, *Apocalypse Observed: Religious Movements and Violence in North America, Europe and Japan.* London: Routledge.

Trudel, Gilles. 2002. "Sexuality and marital life: Results of a survey." *Journal of Sex & Marital Therapy* 28(3): 229–49.

Trujillo, C. (ed.). 1991. *Chicana Lesbians: The Girls Our Mothers Warned Us About.* Berkeley, CA: Third Woman Press.

Trujillo, Octaviana V. 1998. "The Yaqui of Guadalupe, Arizona: A century of cultural survival through trilingualism." *American Indian Culture and Research Journal* 22(4): 67–88.

Trusty, Jerry, Kok-mun Ng, & Maximino Plata. 2000. "Interaction effects of gender, SES, and race-ethnicity on postsecondary educational choices of U.S. students." *Career Development Quarterly* 49(1): 45–59.

Tschudin, Alain, Josep Call, & R. I. M. Dunbar. 2001, "Comprehension of signs of dolphins (Tursiops truncatus)." *Journal of Comparative Psychology* 115(1): 100–105.

Tsui, Amy, Judith Wasserheit, & John Haaga (eds.). 1997. *Reproductive Health in Developing Countries.* Washington, DC: National Academy.

Tsutsui, William M. 1998. *Manufacturing Ideology: Scientific Management in 20th Century Japan.* Princeton, NJ: Princeton University Press.

Tu, Ha T., & James D. Reschovsky. 2002. "Assessments of medical care by enrollees in for-profit and nonprofit health maintenance organizations." *New England Journal of Medicine* 346(17): April 25: 1288–93.

Tumin, Melvin M. 1953. "Some principles of stratification: A critical analysis." *American Sociological Review* 18: 387–393.

Tumin, Melvin M. 1963. "On inequality." *American Sociological Review* 28: 19–26.

Tumin, Melvin M. 1985. *Social Stratification: The Forms and Functions of Inequality,* 2nd ed. Upper Saddle River, NJ: Prentice Hall.

Tumin, Melvin. 1964. "The functionalist approach to social problems." *Social Problems* 12: 379–388.

Tunnell, Kenneth D. 1992. *Choosing Crime: The Criminal Calculus of Property Offenders.* Chicago: Nelson-Hall.

Turestsky, V. 1999. "Child support trends." Center for Law and Social Policy. http://www.clasp.org/pubs/childassurance

Turk, Austin. 1977. "Class, conflict and criminology." *Sociological Focus* 10: 209–20.

Turkle, Sherry. 1995. *Life on the Screen: Identity in the Age of the Internet.* New York: Simon & Schuster.

Turnbull, William, & Jeremy I. M. Carpendale. 2001. "Talk and the development of social understanding." *Early Education & Development* 12(3): 455–77.

Turner, Bryan S. 1991. *Religion and Social Theory.* London: Sage.

Turner, C. F., & E. Martin (eds.). 1984. *Surveying Subjective Phenomena* (Vol. 1). New York: Russell Sage Foundation.

Turner, J. Blake. 1995. "Economic context and the health effects of unemployment." *Journal of health and Social Behavior* 36(3): 213–301.

Turner, Jonathan H., & A. Maryanski. 1979. *Functionalism.* Menlo Park, CA: Benjamin/Cummings.

Turner, Jonathan H., Leonard Beeghley, & Charles H. Powers. 2002. *The Emergence of Sociological Theory,* 5th ed. Belmont, CA: Wadsworth.

Turner, Margery A., & Felicity Skidmore, (eds.). 1999. *Mortgage Lending Discrimination: A Review of Existing Evidence.* Washington, DC: Urban Institute.

Turner, R. J., & D. Lloyd. 1995. "Lifetime traumas and mental health: The significance of cumulative adversity." *Journal of Health and Social Behavior* 36: 360–76.

Turner, R. Jay & Franco Marino. 1994. "Social support and social structure: A descriptive epidemiology," *Journal of Health and Social Behavior* (35/3): 193–212.

Turner, R. Jay & M. O. Wagonfeld. 1967. "Occupational mobility and schizophrenia," *American Sociological Review* 32: 104–113.

Turner, Ralph H., & Lewis M. Killian. 1993. *Collective Behavior,* 4th ed. Upper Saddle River, NJ: Prentice Hall.

Turner, Ralph. 1962. "Role taking: Process versus conformity." In Arnold Rose (ed.), *Human Behavior & Social Processes.* Boston: Houghton Mifflin.

Turner, Ralph. 1996. "The moral issue in collective behavior and collective action." *Mobilization* (1/1): 1–15.

Turner, Stephen P., & Jonathan H. Turner. 1990. *The Impossible Science: An Institutional Analysis of American Sociology.* Newbury Park, CA: Sage.

Turner, Terence, & Carole Nagengast (eds.). 1997. "Universal human rights versus cultural integrity." *Journal of Anthropological Research (Special Issue)* 53: 269–381.

Turner, Terence. 1993. "The role of indigenous peoples in the environmental crisis: The example of the Kayapo of the Brazilian Amazon." *Perspectives in Biology and Medicine,* 36(3): 526–45.

Tuttle, Russell H. 2001. On culture and traditional chimpanzees." *Current Anthropology* 42(3): 407–408.

Twenge, Jean M. 2002. "Birth cohort, social change and personality: The interplay of dysphoria and individualism in the 20th century." In Daniel Cervone & Walter Mischel (eds.), *Advances in Personality Science.* New York: Guilford.

Tygiel, Jules. 1983. *Baseball's Great Experiment: Jackie Robinson and His Legacy.* New York: Oxford University Press.

Tyler, Stephen A. 1986. *India: An Anthropological Perspective.* Prospect Heights, IL: Waveland.

Tylor, Edward Burnett. 1871. *Primitive Culture: Researches into the Development of Mythology, Philosophy, Religion, Language, Art and Custom.* London: John Murray.

Tyre, Peg. 2002. "What's Behind the Numbers?" *Newsweek* (January 14): 11.

U.S. Bureau of Justice Statistics, 2000. *Sourcebook of Criminal Justice Statistics, 1999.* Washington, DC: Department of Justice.

U.S. Bureau of the Census. 1998. *Statistical Abstract of the United States.* Washington, DC: U.S. Department of Commerce.

U.S. Bureau of the Census. 1999. *Statistical Abstract of the United States.* Washington, DC: U.S. Department of Commerce.

U.S. Bureau of the Census. 2001. *Statistical Abstract of the United States* Washington, D.C: U.S. Department of Commerce.

U.S. Bureau of the Census. 2002. *Statistical Abstract of the United States.* Washington, DC: U.S. Department of Commerce.

U.S. Commission on Human Rights. 2000. "Indian tribes: A continuing quest for human survival." In Anne Minas (ed.), *Gender Basics: Feminist Perspectives on Women and Men.* Belmont, CA: Wadsworth: 50–54.

U.S. Conference of Mayors. 1996. *A Status Report on Hunger and Homelessness in America's Cities: 1996.* Washington, DC: Author.

U.S. Department of Education. 2000a. *Twenty-Second Annual Report to Congress on the Implementation of the Individuals with Disabilities Education Act.* Available: http://www.ed.gov/offices/OSERS/OSEP/Products/OSEP2000AnlRpt.

U.S. Department of Education. 2000b. *2000 Annual Report on School Safety.* Washington, DC: U.S. Department of Education and U.S. Department of Justice.

U.S. Department of Education. 2000c. *1999–2000 National Postsecondary Student Aid Study.* Washington, DC: National Center on Education Statistics. Available: http://nces.ed.gov/surveys/npsas.

U.S. Department of Education. 2000d. *Pursuing Excellence: Comparisons of International Eighth-Grade Mathematics and Science Achievement from a U.S. Perspective.* National Center for Statistics. Washington, DC: U.S. Government Printing Office.

U.S. Department of Health and Human Services. 2000. http: \\www.os.dhhs. gov\news\press

U.S. Department of Health and Human Services. 2002. *2002 Head Start Data Sheet.* Administration for Children and Families. Available: http://www2.acf.dhhs.gov/programs/hsb/research/02.

U.S. Department of Justice. 2000. Bureau of Justice Statistics. "Crime characteristics." Available: http://www.ojp.usdoj.gov/bjs/cvict c.

U.S. Department of Justice. 2001. *Indicators of School Crime and Safety, 2001.* Bureau of Justice Statistics and National Center for Education Statistics. Washington, DC: U.S. Government Printing Office.

U.S. Department of Labor. 1991. *Futureworks.* Washington, DC: U.S. Government Printing Office.

U.S. Department of Labor. 2001. Bureau of Labor Statistics (www.bls.gov/Soc).

U.S. Department of State. 2001. *Patterns of Global Terrorism, 2000.* Washington, DC: U.S. Department of State.

U.S. Politics. 2002. "Morphing Osama bin Laden." U.S. Politics: Current Events. Available: http://www.uspolitics.about.com/library/blosama.

U.S. Public Health Service. 1985. *Women's Health: Report of the Public Health Service Task Force on Women's Health Issues, Vol. 1.* 100(1): 73–106. Hyattsville, MD: National Center for Health Statistics.

UAW. 2002. "Women's earnings in 2000." *Jobs, Pay and the Economy.* Available: http://www.uaw.org/publications/jobs_pay.

Uchitelle, L., & N. R. Kleinfeld. 1996. "On the battlefields of business, millions of casualties." *New York Times* (March 3): 1ff.

Udry, Richard J. 2000. "Biological limits of gender construction." *American Sociological Review* 65(3): 443–57.

Uhlenberg, Peter. 1988. "Aging and the social significance of cohorts." In James E. Birren & Vern L. Bengston (eds.), *Emergent Theories of Aging.* New York: Springer.

Umberson, Debra, Kristi Williams, & Susan Sharo. 2000. "Medical sociology and health psychology." In Chloe E. Bird, Peter Conrad, & Allen M. Fremont (eds.), *Handbook of Medical Sociology.* Upper Saddle River, NJ: Prentice Hall: 353–64

Umberson, Debra, Kristin Anderson, Jennifer Glick, & Adam Shapiro. "Domestic violence, personal control, and gender." *Journal of Marriage and the Family* 60(2): 442–52.

UNAIDS. 2002. "Report on the global HIV/AIDS epidemic 2002." *UNAIDS at Barcelona: The Barcelona Report.* Available: http:www.unaids.org/epidemic update/report july02.

UNESCO. 1999. *Manual of Functional Literacy for Indigenous Peoples.* Paris: United Nations Educational, Scientific and Cultural Organization. Available: http://www.unescobk.org/education/appeal/publicat.

UNESCO. 2001. Institute for Statistics. Available: http://www.uis.unesco.org/statis.

UNESCO. 2002. *United Nations Millennium Goals: Data and Trends, 2002.* New York: United Nations Economic and Social Council.

UNHCR. 1998. *The State of the World's Refugees.* Geneva: United Nations High Commissioner for Refugees.

UNHCR. 2002. "Refugees by numbers, 2002." Geneva: United High Commissioner for Refugees.

UNICEF, 2000. *State of the World's Children 2000.* New York: United Nations Children's Fund

UNICEF. 2002. *The State of the World's Children, 2002.* United Nation's Children's Fund. London: Oxford University.

UNICEF. 2002a. "A world without polio." Introduction: June 21. Available: http://www.unicef.org/polio.

UNICEF. 2002b. "Maternal mortality." *The State of the World's Children.* United Nations Children's Fund. London: Oxford University.

Uniform Crime Reports. 1993. *Crime in the United States.* Washington, DC: U.S. Government Printing Office.

Uniform Crime Reports. 1997. *Crime in the United States* (Annual). Federal Bureau of Investigation. Washington, DC: U.S. Government Printing Office.

United Nations Development Program, 2000b. Millennium Development Goals. "Building partnerships to achieve development goals." Available: http://www.undp.org/mdg.

United Nations Development Program. 2000 *Human Development Report 2000: Human Development and Human Rights.* New York: United Nations.

United Nations Development Program. 2000a. "Appendix 1: Millennium Summit development goals." Available: http://www.opt-init.org/framework/pages/appendix1.

United Nations Development Program. 2001. *Human Development Report, 2000.* New York: Oxford University.

United Nations Development Program. 2001. *Human Development Report: 2001: Making New Technologies Work for Human Development.* New York: Oxford University.

United Nations Development Programme. 1999. *Human Development Report: 1999.* New York: Oxford University Press.

United Nations Development Programme. 2000. *Human Development Report 2000.* New York: Oxford University Press.

United Nations Economic and Social Council. 2002. *United Nations Development Goals: Data and Trends, 2002.* Inter-agency expert group on MDG. Statistics Division. New York: United Nations Economic and Social Council. *World Development Indicators.* 2002. Washington, DC: World Bank.

United Nations Population Division. 2002. "World urbanization prospects: The 2001 revision—Data tables and highlights." March 20. Population Division, Department of Economic and Social Affairs.

United Nations Population Fund. 2002. *The State of the World Population 2001.* New York: United Nations

United Nations Population Fund. 2002. *The State of the World Population 2001.* New York: United Nations.

United Nations, 2001. *Compendium of Human Settlement Statistics.* New York: United Nations Department of International Economic and Social Affairs.

United Nations. 1998. *Demographic Yearbook.* Department of Economic and Social Development. New York: United Nations.

United Nations. 1999. *Human Development Report: Globalization with a Human Face.* New York: Oxford University Press.

United Nations. 2001. "Panel 5: Paternity leave, baths, and evil spirits." The States of the World's Children. Available: http://www.unicef.org/sowc01/panels/panel5.

United States Department of Health & Human Services. 2000. *TANF Program: Third Annual Report to Congress.* Washington, DC: GPO.

Unni, Jeemol, & Uma Rani. 2001. "Social protection for informal workers." *Indian Journal of Labour Economics* 44(4): 559–75.

Unsworth, Gabrielle, & Tony Ward. 2001 "Video games and aggressive behavior." *Australian Psychologist* 36(3): 184–92.

Upadhyay, Ushma. 2001. "Informed choice in family planning: Helping people decide." *Population Reports* 24(1): Spring, Series J, No. 50.

Urban Studies. 2001. "Special issue: The barrier-free city." *Urban Studies* 38(2): 231–76.

Urla, Jacqueline, & Alan C. Swedlund. 2000. "The anthropometry of Barbie: Unsettling ideals of the feminine body in popular culture." In Londa Schiebinger (ed.), *Feminism and the Body.* Oxford, UK: Oxford University.

USAID. 2002. "This is USAID." Available: http://www.usaid.gov/about/.

Useem, Bert. 1985. "Disorganization and the New Mexico prison riot." *American Sociological Review* 50: 677–88.

Useem, Michael. 1984. *The Inner Circle.* New York: Oxford University Press.

Usman, Sushil. 1985. "Countermodernization in the Third World countries: Theo-

retical issues and policy implications." Paper presented at the meeting of the North Central Sociological Association, Louisville, April.

Vacon, R. 1990. "Rethinking the war on drugs." *Hartford Courant* (May 27): 1.

Vago, Steven. 1998. *Social Change,* 4th ed. Upper Saddle River, NJ: Prentice Hall.

Vaill, Peter. 1989. *Managing as a Performing Art.* San Francisco: Jossey-Bass.

Valdivia, Angharad N. 2000. *A Latina in the Land of Hollywood and Other Essays on Media Culture.* Tucson, AZ: University of Arizona.

Vallas, Steven P. 1999. "Rethinking post-Fordism: The meaning of workplace flexibility," *Sociological Theory* (17/March): 68–101.

Vallone, Lynne. 1999. "Girls and dolls: Feminism and female youth culture." In Beverly Lyon Clark & Margaret R. Higonnet (eds.), *Girls, Boys, Books, Toys: Gender in Children's Literature and Culture.* Baltimore: Johns Hopkins.

van den Berge, Pierre L. 1973. *Age and Sex In Human Societies.* Belmont, CA: Wadsworth.

Van Den Hoonaard, 2001. "Is research-ethics review a moral panic?" *Canadian Review of Sociology and Anthropology* 38(1): 19–36.

Van Wie, Victoria E., & Alan M. Gross. 2001. "The role of women's explanations for refusal on men's ability to discriminate unwanted sexual behavior in a date rape scenario." *Journal of Family Violence* 16(4): 331–44.

Van Wie, Victoria E., & Gross, Alan M. 2001. "The role of woman's explanations for refusal on men's ability to discriminate unwanted sexual behavior in a date rape scenario." *Journal of Family Violence* 16(4): 331–44.

Vannoy, Dana, Natalia Rimashevskaya, Lisa Cubbins, Marina Malysheva, Elena Meshterkina, & Marina Pisklakova. 1999. *Marriages in Russia: Couples During the Economic Transition.* Westport, CT: Greenwood.

Varady, David P., Wolfgang F. E. Prieser, & Francis P. Russell. 1998. *New Directions in Public Housing.* New Brunswick, NJ: W. E. Upjohn Center for Urban Policy Research.

Vayda, Andrew P. 1994. "Actions, variations, and change: The emerging anti-essentialist view in anthropology." In Robert Borofsky (ed.), *Assessing Cultural Anthropology.* New York: McGraw-Hill.

Veblen, Thorstein. 1933. *The Engineers and the Price System.* New York: Viking.

Veblen, Thorstein. 1934. *The Theory of the Leisure Class.* New York: Modern Library.

Veblen, Thorstein. 1964. *The Vested Interests & the Common Man.* New York: Augustus M. Kelley. Originally published in 1919.

Veiga, John F. "Jack," Luis L. Martins, & Kimberly A. Eddleston. 2002. "Moderators of the relationship between work–family conflict and career satisfaction." *Academy of Management Journal* 45(2): 399–409.

Veneziano, Carol, & Louis Veneziano. 1992. "The relationship between deterrence & moral reasoning." *Criminal Justice Review* 17: 209–16.

Ventura, Stephanie J., & Christine A. Bachrach. 2000. "Nonmarital childbearing in the United States, 1940–99." *National Vital Statistics Reports* 48(16): October 18 (Centers for Disease Control and Prevention).

Vertinsky, Patricia. 1994. "Women, sport, and exercise in the 19th century." In D. Margaret Costa & Sharon R. Guthrie (eds.), *Women & Sport: Interdisciplinary Perspectives.* Champaign, IL: Human Kinetics: 63–82.

Verweij, J., P. Ester, & R. Nauta. 1997. "Secularization as an economic and cultural phenomenon: A cross-national analysis." *Journal for the Scientific Study of Religion* 36: 309–24.

Vied, Steve, Lydia Carrico, & James Mayse. 2001. "Panicked drivers jam local gas stations." *Owensboro (Ky) Messenger-Inquirer* (September 12): 3-C.

Vierck, Elizabeth. 2002. *Growing Old in America.* Detroit, MI: Gale.

Vig, Norman, & Michael Kraft (eds.). 2000. *Environmental Policy: New Directions for the Twenty-First Century.* Washington DC: Congressional Quarterly.

Villani S. 2001. "Impact of media on children and adolescents: A 10-year review of the research." *American Academy of Child and Adolescent Psychiatry* 40(4): 392–401.

Vincent, Charles, & Adrian Furnham. 2001. "Why do patients turn to complementary medicine? An empirical study." In Duana A Matcha (ed.), *Readings in Medical Sociology.* Boston: Allyn & Bacon: 309–18

Vivienne, Elizabeth. 2000. "Cohabitation, marriage, and the unruly consequences of difference." *Gender & Society* 14(1): 87–110.

Vogel, David L., Carolyn M. Tucker, Stephen R. Wester, & Martin Heesacker. 1999. "The impact of sex and situational cues on the endorsement of traditional gender-role attitudes and behaviors in dating couples." *Journal of Social & Personal Relationships* 16(4): 459–73.

Vogel, Ezra F. 1979. *Japan as Number One: Lessons for America.* New York: Harper & Row.

Vogel, Ezra F. 1991. *The Four Little Dragons: The Spread of Industrialization In East Asia.* Cambridge, MA: Harvard University Press.

Volti, Rudi. 1988. *Society and Technology Change.* New York: St. Martin's Press.

Volti, Rudi. 1995. *Society and Technological Change,* 3rd ed. New York: St. Martin's Press.

von Eschen, Donald, Jerome Kirk, & Maurice Pinard. 1976. "The disintegration of the Negro non-violent movement." In Robert H. Lauer (ed.), *Social Movements & Social Change.* Carbondale, IL: SIUP: 203–36.

Wacker, Grant. 2001. "The Christian Right." National Humanities Center. Research Triangle Park, NC. Available: http://www.nhc.rtp.nc.us:8080/tserve/twenty/tkeyinfo/chr_rght.

Waddock, Sandra A. 1995. *Not by Schools Alone: Sharing Responsibility for America's Educational Reform.* Westport, CT: Praeger.

Wade, Jay C., & Olayiwola Okesola. 2002. "Racial peer group selection in African American high school students." *Journal of Multicultural Counseling & Development* 30(2): 96–109.

Wade, Robert. 2001. "Global inequality: Winners and losers." *Economist* 359 (April 28): 72–4.

Wage Gap, 2001. "The wage gap: Myths and facts." In Paula S. Rothenberg (ed.), *Race, Class, and Gender in the United States.* New York: Worth: 292–304.

Wagley, Charles, & Marvin Harris. 1958. *Minorities in the New World.* New York: Columbia University Press.

Waite, Linda J., Christine Bachrach, Michelle Hindin, Elizabeth Thomson, & Arland Thornton (eds.). 2000. *The Ties that Bind: Perspectives on Marriage and Cohabitation.* New York: Aldine de Druyter.

Waite, Linda L., & Maggie Gallagher. 2000. *The Case for Marriage: Why Married People are Happier, Healthier, and Better Off Financially.* New York: Doubleday.

Waitzkin, Howard. 1989. "Marxist perspectives in social medicine." *Social Science and Medicine* 28(11): 1099–101.

Waldman, Amy. 1999. "From high school to real world: For graduates not going to college, the future is now." *New York Times* (June 27): 42.

Waldman, S., & R. Thomas. 1990. "Bonfire of the S&L's: How did it happen?" *Newsweek,* May 21: 20–25, 27–28.

Waldron, Ingrid, Christopher C. Weiss, & Mary Elizabeth Hughes. 1998. "Interacting effects of multiple roles on women's health." *Journal of Health and Social Behavior* 39: 216–36.

Walker, Alan, & Carol Walker. 1995. "Poverty." In Adam Kuper & Jessica Kuper (eds.), *The Social Science Encyclopedia,* 2nd ed., London: Routledge: 655–657.

Walker, Jack L. 1991. *Mobilizing Interest Groups in America.* Ann Arbor: University of Michigan Press.

Walker, Karen. 1994. "Men, women and friendship: What they say, what they do." *Gender & Society* 8(2): 246–65.

Walker, Nancy A. (ed.) 1998. *Women's Magazines 1940–1960: Gender Roles and the Popular Press.* Boston: Bedford/St. Martin's.

Walker, Richard, & Robert D. Lewis. 2001. "Beyond the crabgrass frontier: Industry and the spread of North American cities, 1850–1950." *Journal of Historical Geography* 27(1): 3–19.

Walker, Samuel. 2001. *Sense and Nonsense About Crime and Drugs,* 5th ed. Belmont, CA: Wadsworth.

Walker, Tim. 2001. "Class assignment: Can socioeconomic diversity restore the promise of school integration?" *Teaching Tolerance* 20 (Fall): 34–40.

Wallace, Ronald L. 1983. *Those Who Have Vanished: An Introduction to Prehistory.* Homewood, IL: Dorsey.

Wallace, Ruth A., & Alison Wolf. 1999. *Contemporary Sociological Theory,* 5th ed. Upper Saddle River, NJ: Prentice Hall.

Wallace, Ruth. 1992. *They Call Her Pastor.* Albany, NY: State University of New York.

Wallace, Ruth. 1993. "The social construction of a new leadership role: Catholic women pastors." *Sociology of Religion* (54(1): 31–42.

Wallerstein, Immanuel. 1974. *Capitalist Agriculture and the Origins of the World Economy in the 16th Century.* New York: Academic Press.

Wallerstein, Immanuel. 1990. *The Modern World System II.* New York: Academic Press.

Wallerstein, Judith S., Julia M. Lewis, & Sandra Blakeslee. 2000. *The Unexpected Legacy of Divorce: A 25 Year Landmark Study.* New York: Hyperion.

Walsh, Edward J. 1981. "Resource mobilization and citizen protest in communities around Three Mile Island." *Social Problems* 29: 1–21.

Walt, Vivienne. 2000. "Basic beliefs." *Now It's a Global Movement: Ford Foundation Report.* (Special Issue on Women) (Winter): 18–21.

Walter, Lynn (ed.). 2001. *Women's Rights: A Global View.* Westport, CT: Greenwood.

Walton, John. 1987. "Theory and research on industrialization." *Annual Review of Sociology* 13: 89–103.

Walzer, 2001. "Thinking about the baby: Gender and the division of infant care." In Theodore F. Cohen (ed.), *Men and Masculinity: A Text Reader.* Belmont, CA: Wadsworth: 192–206.

Wang, Ping. 2002. *Aching for Beauty: Footbinding in China.* New York: Anchor Books.

Wang, Zhe. 2001. "Falun Gong: Not a religion but a heresy." *Beijing Review* 44 (March 1): 19–21.

Ward, Martha C. 1999. *A World Full of Women.* Boston: Allyn & Bacon.

Waring, Marilyn. 1988. *If Women Counted: A New Feminist Economics.* San Francisco: HarperSanFrancisco.

Warkentin, Craig. 2001. *Reshaping World Politics: NGOs, the Internet, and Global Civil Society.* Lanham, MD: Rowman & Littlefield.

Warner, Rebecca L., & Brent S. Steel. 1999. "Child rearing as a mechanism for social change: The relationship of child gender to parents' commitment to child equity." *Gender & Society* 13(4): 503–17.

Warner, W. Lloyd, & Paul S. Hunt. 1941. *The Social Life of a Modern Community.* New Haven, CT: Yale University Press.

Warner, W. Lloyd, Paul S. Hunt, Marsha Meeker, & Kenneth Eels. 1949. *Social Class in America.* New York: Harper.

Warr, Mark. 1995. "America's perceptions of crime and punishment." In Joseph F. Sheley (ed.), *Criminology: A Contemporary Handbook,* 2nd ed. Belmont, CA: Wadsworth: 15–31.

Warren, Karen J. 1997. *Ecofeminism: Women, Culture, Nature.* Bloomington: Indiana University.

Wartzman, Rick. 1999. "A push to probe buying habits in Latino homes." *Wall Street Journal* (Eastern Ed.) (August 5): B1+.

Washington Post. 1998. "Education: Gains and gaps." From *What on Earth: A Weekly Look at Trends, People and Events Around the World.* October 24.

Waskul, Dennis. 1997. "Selfhood in the age of computer-mediated interaction." Paper presented at the annual meeting of the Southwest Social Science Association.

Wasserman, J., R. W. Whitmer, T. L. Bazzarre, S. T. Kennedy, N. Merrick, R. Z. Goetzel, R. L. Dunn, & R. J. Ozminkowski. 2000. "Gender-specific effects of modifiable health risk factors on coronary heart disease and related expenditures." *Journal of Occupational and Environmental Medicine* 42(11): 1060–69.

Wasserman, Stanley, & Katherine Faust. 1994. *Social Network Analysis: Methods & Applications.* New York: Cambridge University Press.

Waters, M. S., W. C. Heath, & J. K. Watson. 1995. "A positive model of the determination of religious affiliation." *Social Science Quarterly* 76: 105–23.

Watson, C. W. 1999. "Introduction: The quality of being there." In C. W. Watson (ed.), *Being There: Fieldwork in Anthropology.* London: Pluto Press: 1–24.

Watson, J. Mark. 1988. "Outlaw motorcyclists." In James M. Henslin (ed.), *Down to Earth Sociology,* 5th ed. New York: Free Press: 203–13.

Watson, Ruby S., & Patricia Buckley Ebrey. 1991. *Marriage and Inequality in Chinese Society.* Berkeley, CA: University of California.

Watson, W. E., L. K. Michaelson, & W. Sharp. 1991. "Member competence, group interaction & group decision making." *Journal of Applied Psychology* 76: 803–809.

Wayne, Leslie. 2000. "On Web, voters re-invent grass-roots activism." *New York Times* (May 21): 30.

Weakliem, David, Julia McQuillan, & Tracy Schauer. 1995. "Toward meritocracy? Changing social-class differences in intellectual ability." *Sociology of Education* 68(4): 271–86.

Weatherall, Ann. 2002. *Gender, Language and Discourse.* London: Routledge.

Weaver, Charles N. & Michael D. Matthews. 1990. "Work Satisfaction of Females With Full-Time Employment & Full-Time Housekeeping: 15 Years Later," *Psychological Reports* 66: 1248–1250.

Weaver, Mary Jo. 1999. "American Catholics in the twentieth century." In Peter W. Williams (ed.), *Perspectives on American Religion and Culture.* Malden, MA: Blackwell: 154–67.

Weaver, Shara J., & Edward S. Herold. 2000. "Casual sex and women: Measurement and motivational issues." *Journal of Psychology and Human Sexuality* 12(3): 23–41.

Webb, Eugene J., Donald T. Campbell, Richard D. Schwartz, & Lee Sechrest. 1966. *Unobtrusive Measures: Nonreactive Research in the Social Sciences.* Chicago: Rand McNally.

Weber, Max. 1905/1954. *The Protestant Ethic and the Spirit of Capitalism.* (Talcott Parsons, trans.). New York: Charles Scribner's Sons.

Weber, Max. 1905/1977. *The Protestant Ethic and the Spirit of Capitalism* (trans. Talcott Parsons). New York: Scribner.

Weber, Max. 1919/1946. *From Max Weber: Essays in Sociology.* (trans. and eds. Hans Gerth & C. Wright Mills). New York: Oxford University Press.

Weber, Max. 1925/1975. *The Theory of Social and Economic Organization.* (trans. A. M. Henderson & Talcott Parsons. New York: Oxford University Press.

Weber, Max. 1947. *From Max Weber.* Hans Gerth & C. Wright Mills, (eds.) New York: Oxford University Press.

Weber, Max. 1978. *Economy and Society.* Berkeley, University of California Press.

Webster, Craig, & David Lewis Cingarelli, 1998. "Human rights and developing countries." (Bibliography). In Stuart S. Nagel (ed.), *Policy Within and Across Devloping Nations.* Aldershot, UK: Ashgate: 159.

Webster, Murray, Jr., & Stuart J. Hysom. 1998. "Creating status characteristics." *American Sociological Review* 63(3): 351–378.

Wechsler, William F. 2001. "Strangling the hydra: Targeting al-Qaeda's finances." In James F. Hoge & Gideon Rose (eds.), *How Did it Happen? Terrorism and the New War.* New York: Public Affairs: 129–44.

Wehrfritz, George, and Hideko Takayama. 2000. "The Japan that can say yes." *Newsweek* (June 5): 34–35.

Weibel-Orlando, Joan. 2001. "Grandparenting styles: Native American perspectives." In Alexis J. Walker (ed.), *Families in Later Life: Connections and Transitions.* Thousand Oaks, CA: Pine Forge.

Weiler, Jeanne Drysdale. 2000. *Codes and Contradictions: Race, Gender Identity, and Schooling.* Albany: State University of New York.

Weinberg, Martin S., Illsa L. Lottes, & Liahna E. Gordon. 1997. "Social class background, sexual attitudes, and sexual behavior in a heterosexual undergraduate sample." *Archives of Sexual Behavior* 26(6): 625–42.

Weiner, Michael, (ed.). 1997. *Japan's Minorities: The Illusion of Homogeneity.* London: Routledge.

Weiner, Myron. 1966. *Modernization: The Dynamics of Growth.* New York: Basic Books.

Weisberger, Adam. 1992. "Marginality and its directions." *Sociological Forum* 7: 425–46.

Weisburd, David, Stanton Wheeler, Elin Waring, & Nancy Bode. 1991. *Crimes of the Middle Class: White-Collar Defendants in the Courts.* New Haven, CT: Yale University Press.

Weisgrau, Maxine K. 2000. "Vedic and Hindu traditions." In R. Scupin (ed.), *Religion and Culture: An Anthropological Focus.* Upper Saddle River, NJ: Prentice Hall: 225–48.

Weiss, Jessica. 2000. *To Have and To Hold: Marriage, the Baby Boom and Social Change.* Chicago: University of Chicago.

Weisz, Arlene N., & Beverly M. Black. 2002. "Gender and moral reasoning: African American youth respond to dating dilemmas." *Journal of Human Behavior and the Social Environment* 5(1): 35–52.

Weitz, Rose. 2001. *The Sociology of Health, Illness, and Health Care: A Critical Approach.* Belmont, CA: Wadsworth.

Welch, Claude E., Jr. 2001. *NGOs and Human Rights: Promise and Performance.* Philadelphia: University of Pennsylvania.

Welch, Michael R., David C. Leege, & James C. Cavendish. 1995. "Attitudes toward abortion among U.S. Catholics: Another case of symbolic politics?" *Social Science Quarterly* 76(1): 142–97.

Welch, Michael. 1997. "Violence against women by professional football players." *Journal of Sports and Social Issues.* (21): 392–411.

Welch, Susan, & Lee Sigelman. 1989. "A black gender gap?" *Social Science Quarterly* 70: 120–133.

Welch, Susan, & Lee Sigelman. 1993. "The politics of Hispanic Americans." *Social Science Quarterly* 74: 76–94.

"Welfare mistrust." 1996. *USA Today*, (July 2).

Welie, Jos V. M. 2002. "Why physicians?" *Hastings Center Report* 32(1): 42–44.

Weller, Jack M., & Enrico L. Quarantelli. 1973. "Neglected characteristics of collective behavior," *American Journal of Sociology* 79/3: 665–85.

Wellford, Charles. 1975. "Labeling theory and criminology: An assessment." *Social Problems* 22: 335–47.

Wellman, B., (ed.). 1999. *Networks in the Global Village*. Boulder, CO: Westview.

Wellman, Barry, Janet Salaff, et al. 1996. "Computer networks as social networks." *Annual Review of Sociology* 22: 213–238.

Wellman, Beverly, Merrijoy Kelner, & Blossom T. Wigdor. 2001. "Older adults' use of medical and alternative care." *Journal of Applied Gerontology* 20(1): 3–23.

Wellman, David. 2000. "From evil to illness: Medicalizing racism." *American Journal of Orthopsychiatry* 70(1): 28–32.

Wells, Amy Stuart, & Jeannie Oakes. 1998. "Tracking, detracking and the politics of educational reform." In Carlos Alberto Torres & Theodore R. Mitchell (eds.), *Sociology of Education: Emerging Perspectives*. Albany: State University of New York: 155–80.

Wells, H. G. 1969. *The Time Machine*. Chicago: Children's Press. Originally published in 1895.

Welsh, Sandy. 1999. "Gender and sexual harassment." *Annual Review of Sociology* 25: 169–90.

Wenger, G. Clare. 1992. "The major English speaking countries." In Richard M. Suzman, David P. Willis, & Kenneth G. Manton (eds.), *The Oldest Old*. New York: Oxford University Press.

Wennemo, Irene. 2001. "The transformation of family life." Seminar: The Nordic Alternative (March 12) Stockholm. Available: http://www.nnn.se/seminar.

Wenner, Lawrence (ed.). 1998. *MediaSport*. New York: Routledge.

Wertheimer, Jack. 1997. *A People Divided: Judaism in Contemporary America*. Hanover, NH: Brandeis University/University Press of New England.

Wertz, Richard W., & Dorothy C. Wertz. 1990. "Notes on the decline of midwives and the rise of medical obstetricians." In Peter Conrad & Rochelle Kern (eds.), *The Sociology of Health and Illness: Critical Perspectives*. New York: St. Martin's.

Weslowski, Wlodzimierz. 1966. "Some notes on the functional theory of stratification." In Reinhard Bendix, and Seymour M. Lipset (eds.), *Class Status and Power: Social Stratification in Comparative Perspective*, 2nd ed. New York: Free Press: 28–38.

Wesolowski, Wlodzimierz. 1990. "Transition from authoritarianism to democracy." *Social Research* (57/2): 435–61.

West, Bonnie. 2000. "Freedom!" *Woman's Day* 63 (September 1): 164.

West, Candace, & Don H. Zimmerman. 1983. "Small insults: A study of interruptions in cross-sex conversations between unacquainted persons." In Barrie Thorne, Cheris Kramarae, & Nancy Henley (eds.), *Language, Gender & Society*. Rowley, MA: Newbury House.

West, Candace, & Sarah Fenstermaker, 1995. "Doing difference." *Gender and Society* 9(1): 8–27.

Westley, Sidney B. 2002. "A snapshot of populations in Asia." *Asia-Pacific Population and Policy* 59(October 2001, published in April 2002). East-West Center, Honolulu.

Westling, D. L., & L. Fox. 2000. *Teaching Students with Severe Disabilities*. Upper Saddle River, NJ: Merrill.

Westmarland, Louise. 2001. "Blowing the whistle on police violence: Gender, ethnography, and ethics." *British Journal of Criminology* 41(3): 523–35.

Westphal, David. 1999. "Uninsured ranks up by One Million," *Evansville Courier & Press* (October 4).

Westrum, Ron. 1991. *Technologies and Societies*. Belmont, CA: Wadsworth.

Whalen, William. 1964. *The Latter-Day Saints In the Modern-Day World*. New York: Day.

Wharton, Amy S. (ed.). 2002. *Working in America*. New York: McGraw-Hill.

Wheeler, Stanton, Kenneth Mann, & Austin Sarat. 1988. *Sitting in Judgement: The Sentencing of White-Collar Criminals*. New Haven, CT: Yale University Press.

Whelan, Carolyn. 1998. "A computer for grandma: Seniors with time and money could be the next big market." *Electronic News* 44 (July 27): 44–5.

Whelan, David. 2001. "Baby boom in the burbs." *American Demographics* (July): 20–21.

Whelan, Robert. 1999. *Wild in the Woods: The Myth of the Noble Eco-Savage*. London: Institute of Economic Affairs.

Whitbourne, Susan Krauss. 1999. "Identity and adaptation to the aging process." In Carol D. Ryff & Victor W. Marshall (eds.), *The Self in the Aging Process*. New York: Springer: 122–49.

White House. 2002. "Strengthening Medicare's coverage options: Affordable health care to improve lives." Available: http://www.whitehouse.gov/infocus/medicare.

White, Jack E. 1997. "I'm just who I am." *Time* (May 5): 32–36.

White, Jacquelyn W., Barrie Bondurant, & Cheryl Brown Travis. 2000. "Social construction of sexuality: Unpacking hidden meanings." In Cheryl Brown Travis & Jacquelyn W. White (eds.)., *Sexuality, Society and Feminism*. Washington, DC: American Psychological Association.

White, Janene. 2001. "Adult women in community colleges." *ERIC Digest*. Los Angeles: ERIC Clearinghouse for Community Colleges, University of California.

White, John. 1990. *Black Leadership in America*, 2nd ed. London: Longman.

White, Jonathan R. 2001. "Political eschatology: A theology of antigovernment extremism." Tallahassee: Florida State University Institute for Intergovernmental Research.

White, Jonathan R. 2002. *Terrorism: An Introduction*, 3rd ed. Belmont, CA: Wadsworth.

White, Leslie A. 1949. *The Science of Culture: A Study of Man and Civilization*. New York: Grove.

White, Ralph K., & Ronald O. Lippitt. 1960. *Autocracy & Democracy*. New York: Harper & Bros.

White, Randy Wayne. 1998. "Hey pal, join the club." *Men's Health* 13(2): 66–68.

White, Richard W. 1992. *Rude Awakening: What the Homeless Crisis Tells Us*. San Francisco: ICS.

Whiteman, David. 1994. "The poor aren't poorer." *US News & World Report* (July 25): 33–38.

Whorf, Benjamin Lee. 1956. *Language, Thought and Reality: Selected Writings of Benjamin Lee Whorf* (J. B. Carroll, ed.). New York: Wiley.

Whyte, William Foote. 1943/1981. *Street Corner Society: Social Structure of an Italian Slum*. Chicago: University of Chicago.

Wiatrowski, William J. 1994. "Employee benefits for union and nonunion workers." *Monthly Labor Review* 117: 34–38.

Wickrama, K. A. S., & Charles L. Mulford. 1996. "Political democracy, economic development, disarticulation and social well-being in developing countries." *Sociological Quarterly* 37(3): 375–90.

Wickrama, K. A. S., Frederick O. Lorenz, & Rand D. Conger. 1997. "Marital quality and physical illness: A latent growth curve analysis." *Journal of Marriage and the Family* 59(1): 143–55.

Wiederman, Michael W. 2001. "Gender differences in sexuality: Perceptions, myths and realities." *Family Journal of Counseling and Therapy for Couples and Families* 9(4): 468–71.

Wienberg, Adam S., David N. Pellow, & Allan Schnailberg. 2000. *Urban Recycling and the Search for Sustainable Community Development*. Princeton, NJ: Princeton University.

Wiesner, Diane. 1992. *Your World, Our Health: The Impact of Environmental Degradation on Human Wellbeing*. Dorset, UK: Prism Press.

Wiesner-Hanks, Merry E. 2001. *Gender in History*. Malden, MA: Blackwell.

Wigle, Stanley E., & Donald F. DeMoulin. 1999. "Inclusion in a classroom setting and self-concept." *Journal of At-Risk Issues* 5(2): 27–32.

Wilcox, Clyde, Lara Hewitt, & Dee Alsop. 1996. "The gender gap in attitudes toward the Gulf War." *Journal of Peace Research* 33: 67–82.

Wilkins, Roger. 1995. "The case for affirmative action: Racism has its privileges." *The Nation* (March 27).

Wilkinson, David. 1987. "Central civilization." *Comparative Civilization Review* 17: 31–59.

Wilkinson, Heather (ed.). 2002.*The Perspectives of People with Dementia: Research Methods and Motivations*. London: Jessica Kingsley Publications.

Wilkinson, Ray. 2000. "Refugees: Cover story." *Refugees* 3(120): 3–21.

Williams, Andrea S., & James D. Davidson. 1997. "Catholic conceptions of faith: A generational analysis." In Thomas E. Dowdy & Patrick H. McNamara (eds.), *Religion: North American Style*. New Brunswick, NJ: Rutgers University Press: 124–36.

Williams, Christine L. 1992. "The glass escalator: Hidden advantages for men in the 'female' professions." *Social Problems* (39/3): 253–268.

Williams, Christine L., Patti A. Giuffre, & Kirsten Dellinger. 1999. "Sexuality in the workplace: Organizational control, sexual harassment, and the pursuit of pleasure." *Annual Review of Sociology* 25: 73–93.

Williams, David R., & Colwick M. Wilson. 2001. "Race, ethnicity, and aging." In Robert H. Binstock (ed.), *Handbook of Aging and the Social Sciences*. San Diego, CA: Academic Press: 160–78.

Williams, David R., David T. Takeuchi, & Russell K. Adair. 1992. "Socioeconomic Status & Psychiatric Disorder Among Blacks & Whites." *Journal of Health & Social Behavior* 33: 140–157.

Williams, Donald C. 2000. *Urban Sprawl: A Reference Handbook*. Santa Barbara, CA: ABC-CLIO.

Williams, Joan. 2001. *Unbending Gender: Why Family and Work Conflict and What to Do About it*. New York: Oxford University.

Williams, Joe. 2001. "Freeze frames on fathers." *St. Louis Post-Dispatch* (June 17): F3:

Williams, Lee M., & Michael Lawler. 2001. "Religious heterogamy and religiosity: A comparison of interchurch and same-church individuals." *Journal for the Scientific Study of Religion* 40: 465–78.

Williams, R., & Y. Youssef. 1975. "Division of labor in college football along racial lines." *International Journal of Sports Psychology* 6: 3–13.

Williams, Rhys H. 1999. "Visions of the good society and the religious roots of American political culture." *Sociology of Religion* 60(1): 1–34.

Williams, Rhys H. 2000. "Introduction-Promise Keepers: A comment on religion and social movements." *Sociology of Religion* 61(1): 1–10.

Williams, Robin M., Jr. 1951. *American Society: A Sociological Interpretation*. New York: Alfred Knopf.

Willing, Richard. 2002. "Research downplays risk of cousin marriages." *USA Today*. April 4:3A

Wills, T. A., & M. Filer. 2001. "Social networks and social support." In Andrew Baum, Tracey A. Revenson, & Jerome E. Singer (eds.), *Handbook of Health Psychology*. Mahwah, NJ: Lawrence Erlbaum.

Wilmoth, Janet M. 2001. "Living arrangements among older immigrants in the United States." *Gerontologist* 41(2): 228–38.

Wilson, Anna V. (ed.), 1993. *Homicide: The Victim/Offender Connection*. Cincinnati: Anderson.

Wilson, Barbara J., Stacy L. Smith, W. James Potter, Dale Kunkel, Daniel Linz, Carolyn M. Colvin, and Edward Donnerstein. 2002. "Violence in children's programming: Assessing the risks." *Journal of Communication* 52(1): 5–35.

Wilson, Edward O. 1975. *Sociobiology: The New Synthesis*. Princeton, NJ: Princeton University.

Wilson, Fiona. 2000. "The social construction of sexual harassment and assault on university students." *Journal of Gender Studies* 9(2): 171–87.

Wilson, Francis, & Mamphela Ramphele. 1989. *Uprooting Poverty: The South African Challenge*. New York: Norton.

Wilson, Graham. 1989. *Business and Politics* Chatham, NJ: Chatham House.

Wilson, J. 1994. *Playing by the Rules*. Detroit: Wayne State University Press.

Wilson, James Q. 1983. *Thinking About Crime*, revised edition. New York: Vintage.

Wilson, James Q., & Richard Herrnstein. 1985. *Crime and Human Nature: The Definitive Study of the Causes of Crime*. New York: Simon & Schuster.

Wilson, John. 1973. *Introduction to Social Movements*. New York: Basic.

Wilson, Kenneth L., & Anthony M. Orum. 1976. "Mobilizing people for collective action." *Journal of Political and Military Sociology* 4: 187–202.

Wilson, Steve R., & Eric S. Mankowski. 2000. "Beyond the drum: An exploratory study of group processes in a mythopoetic men's group." In Edward Read Barton (ed.), *Mythopoetic Perspectives of Men's Healing Work: An Anthology of Therapists and Others*. Westport, CT: Bergin & Garvey: 21–45.

Wilson, William H. 1998. "The sociopolitical context of establishing Hawaiian-medium education." *Language, Culture and Curriculum* 11(3): 325–38.

Wilson, William Julius. 1978. *The Declining Significance of Race: Blacks and Changing American Institutions*. Chicago: University of Chicago Press.

Wilson, William Julius. 1987. *The Truly Disadvantaged: The Inner City, the Underclass and Public Policy*. Chicago: University of Chicago Press.

Wilson, William Julius. 1989. "The underclass: Issues, perspectives and public policy." *The Annals* 501: 182–192.

Wilson, William Julius. 1990. "Race-neutral programs and the democratic coalition." *The American Prospect* 1: 75–81.

Wilson, William Julius. 1996. *When Work Disappears*. New York: Random House.

Winkler, Anne E. 1995. "The living arrangements of single mothers with dependent children: An added perspective." *American Journal of Economics and Sociology* 52: 1–18.

Winnick, Louis. 1990. "America's 'model minority.'" *Commentary* 90 (August): 22–29.

Winston, Morton E. 2001. "Assessing the effectiveness of international human rights NGOs: Amnesty International." In Claude E. Welch, Jr. (ed.). *NGOs and Human Rights: Promise and Performance*. Philadelphia: University or Pennsylvania: 25–54.

Wirth, Louis. 1938. "Urbanism as a way of life." *American Journal of Sociology*. 44(1): 1–24.

Wirth, Louis. 1945. "The problem of minority groups." In Ralph Linton (ed.), *The Science of Man In the World Crisis*. New York: Columbia University Press: 347–72.

Witt, Susan D. 2000. "The influence of peers on children's socialization to gender roles." *Early Child Development* 162: 1–7.

Wittfogel, Karl. 1957. *Oriental Despotism: A Comparative Study of Total Power*. New Haven, CT: Yale University Press.

Wogaman, J. Philip. 2000. *Christian Perspectives on Politics*. Louisville, KY: Westminster John Knox.

Wolbrecht, Christina. 2000. *The Politics of Women's Rights: Parties, Positions and Change*. Princeton, NJ: Princeton University.

Wolf, Naomi. 1991. *The Beauty Myth: How Images of Beauty Are Used Against Women*. New York: William Morrow.

Wolf, Rosalie S. 2000. "The nature and scope of elder abuse." *Generations* 24(2): 6–12.

Wolf, Rosalie S. 2001. "Elder abuse." In Sue E. Levkoff, Yeon Kyung Chee, & Shohei Noguchi (eds.), *Aging in Good Health: Multidisciplinary Perspectives*. New York: Springer: 147–60.

Wolff, Edward N. 1995. *Top Heavy: A Study of the Increasing Inequality of Wealth in America*. New York: Twentieth Century Fund Press.

Wolfgang, Marvin E., & Marc Reidel. 1973. "Race, judicial discretion, and the death penalty." *The Annals* 407: 119–133.

Wolfgang, Marvin F., Terence P. Thornberry, & Robert M. Figlio. 1987. *From Boy to Man, From Delinquency to Crime*. Chicago: University of Chicago Press.

Woller, Gary M., & Warner Woodworth. 2001. "Microcredit as grass-roots policy for international development." *Policies Studies Journal* 29(2): 267–82.

Wolpert, Stanley. 1991. *India*. Berkeley: University of California Press.

Womack, Mari. 1992. "Why athletes need ritual: A study of magic among professional athletes." In Shirl J. Hoffman (ed.), *Sport and Religion*. Champaign, IL: Human Kinetics Books.

Women's Sports Foundation. 2002. "Title IX and the Wrestling Coaches Association Lawsuit." (May 30). Available: http://womenssportsfoundation.org/cgi-bin/iowa/issues/rights.

Wong, Loong. 2001. "The Internet and social change in Asia." *Peace Review* 13(3) (September): 381–87.

Woo, Deborah. 1985. "The socioeconomic status of Asian-American women in the labor force." *Sociological Perspectives* 28: 307–28.

Wood, Charles, & Jose de Carvalho. 1988. *The Demography of Inequality in Brazil*. Cambridge, England: Cambridge University Press.

Wood, Daniel B. 1997. "Religion: Buddhist practices make inroads in the U.S." *Christian Science Monitor* 89(237) (Nov. 3): 9.

Wood, Julia T. 1994. *Gendered Lives: Communication, Gender and Culture*. Belmont, CA: Wadsworth.

Wood, Julia T. 2002. "Gender and personal relationships." In Clyde Hendrick & Susan S. Hendrick (eds.), *Close Relationships: A Sourcebook*. Thousand Oaks, CA: Sage.

Wood, Lawrence D. 1996. "Alone among its peers." In Robert Heiner (ed.), *Criminology: A Cross-Cultural Perspective*. St. Paul: West: 197–212.

Woodberry, Robert D., & Christian S. Smith. 1998. "Fundamentalism et al.: Conservative Protestants in America." *Annual Review of Sociology* 24: 25–56.

Woodhead, Linda, & Paul Heelas (eds.). 2000. *Religion in Modern Times*. Oxford, UK: Blackwell.

Woods, Nicola. 1988. "Talking shop: Sex and status as determinants of floor apportionment in a work setting." In J. Coates and D. Cameron (eds.), *Women in their Speech Communities*. London: Longman.

World Bank, 2002. *World Development Report 2002: Institutions for Markets*. New York: Oxford University.

World Bank. 1995. *World Development Report 1995*. London: Oxford University Press.

World Bank. 2000. *Entering the 21st Century: World Development Report 1999/2000*. Washington, DC: World Bank.

World Bank. 2001. "Overview." *Annual Report, 2001*. Available: http://www.worldbank.org/annualreport/2001/overview.

World Bank. 2002. *World Development Indicators, 2002*. Washington, DC: World Bank.

World Education League. 1997. "Who's top?" *The Economist* (March 29): 21–23.

World Factbook. 2001. Washington, DC: Central Intelligence Agency. Available: http://www.cia.gov/pubications/factbook.

World Health Organization. 1995. *The World Health Report 1995: Bridging the Gaps*. Geneva: World Health Organization.

World Health Organization. 1998. *The World Health Report, 1998: Global Health Situation and Trends, 1955–2025*. Geneva: World Health Organization.

World Health Organization. 1999. *World Health Statistics*. Geneva: WHO.

World Health Report. 2001. Mental Health: New Understanding, New Hope. Geneva: World Health Organization.

World of Refugee Women. 2002. Available: http://www.ivillage.co.uk/newspol/camp/refuge/articles.

World Urban Forum. 2002. "UN-Habitat executive director's speech." Nairobi, April 29. Available: http://www.unhabitat.org/uf/ed.

Worldwatch. 2001. "Rejection of Kyoto Protocol based on fallacious reasoning." *Worldwatch* (September/October).

Worrell, Judith. 1996. "Feminist identity in a gendered world." In Joan C. Chrisler, Carla Golden, & Patricia D. Rozee (eds.), *Lectures on the Psychology of Women*. New York: McGraw-Hill.

Worsley, Peter. 1984. *The Three Worlds*. Chicago: University of Chicago Press.

Worsnep, R. 1996. "Helping the homeless." *CQ Researcher* (January 26).

Wresch, William. 1996. *Disconnected: Haves and Have-Nots in the Information Age*. New Brunswick, NJ: Rutgers University Press.

WRI. 2002. "World Resources 2001–2002." Washington, DC: World Resources Institute.

Wright, Eric Olin, & Bill Martin. 1987. "The transformation of the American class structure, 1960–1980." *American Journal of Sociology* 93/1: 1–29.

Wright, Eric Olin. 1985. *Classes*. London: Verso.

Wright, Eric Olin. 1989. *The Debate on Classes*. New York: Verso.

Wright, Eric R. 1995. "Personal networks and anomie." *Sociological Focus* (28/3): 261–282.

Wright, Erik Olin, David Hachen, Cynthia Castello, & Joey Spoogne. 1982. "The American class structure." *American Sociological Review* 47: 709–726.

Wright, Erik Olin. 1979. *Class, Crisis and the State*. London: Verso.

Wright, Erik Olin. 1997. *Class Counts: Comparative Studies in Class Analysis*. Cambridge, UK: Cambridge University Press.

Wright, J. D., P. H. Rossi, & K. Daly. 1983. *Under the Gun: Weapons, Crime and Violence in America*. Chicago: Aldine.

Wright, Lawrence. 1994. "One drop of blood." *New Yorker* (July 25).

Wright, Russell O. 1997. *Life and Death in the United States: Statistics on Life Expectancies, Diseases and Death Rates for the Twentieth Century*. Jefferson, NC: McFarland.

Wright, Sam. 1978. *Crowds and Riots*. Beverly Hills, CA: Sage.

Wrong, Dennis H. 1959. "The functional theory of stratification: Some neglected considerations." *American Sociological Review* 24: 772–82.

Wrong, Dennis H. 1961. "The over-socialized conception of man in modern sociology." *American Sociological Review* 26: 185–193.

Wu, Zheng. 1995. "Premarital cohabitation and postmarital cohabiting union formation." *Journal of Family Issues* 16(2): 212–32.

Wucker, Michele. 2000. "Americans: What we lost, who we are." *Tikkun* 15(1): 17–23.

Wurthnow, Robert. 2000. "The moral minority: Where have all the liberal Protestants gone?" *American Prospect* 11 (May 22): 31–33.

Wuthnow, Robert. 1989. *Communities of Discourse: Ideology and Social Structure in the Reformation*. Cambridge, MA: Harvard University Press.

Wuthnow, Robert. 1993. *Christianity in the Twenty-First Century: Reflections on the Challenges Ahead*. New York: Oxford University Press.

Wuthnow, Robert. 1994. *Sharing the Journey: Support Groups and America's New Quest for Community*. New York: Free Press.

Yan, Xiaopei, Li Jia, Jianping Li, & Jizhuan Weng. 2002. "The development of the Chinese metropolis in the period of transition." In John R. Logan (ed.), *The New Chinese City: Globalization and Market Reform*. Oxford, UK: Blackwell: 37–55.

Yan, Yunxiang. 2002. "Managed globalization: State power and cultural transition in China." In Peter Berger and Samuel P. Huntington (eds.), *Many Globalizations: Cultural Diversity in the Contemporary World*. New York: Oxford University: 19–47.

Yanagishita, Machiko, & Landis MacKellar. 1995. "Homicide in the United States: Who's at risk?" *Population Today*. (23/2): 1–2.

Yandle, Bruce. 1999. "After Kyoto: A global scramble for advantage." *Independent Review* 4(1): 19–39.

Yang, Alan S. 1997. "Attitudes toward homosexuality." *Public Opinion Quarterly* 61: 477–507.

Yang, Fenggang, & Helen Rose Ebaugh. 2001. "Transformations in new immigrant religions and their global implications." *American Sociological Review* 66(2): 269–88.

Yao, Xinzhong. 2002. "Chinese religion." In John Bowker (ed.), *Cambridge Illustrated History of Religions*. Cambridge, UK: Cambridge University: 110–43.

Yates, Michael D. 1994. *Longer Hours, Fewer Jobs*. New York: Monthly Review Press.

Yeatts, Dale E. 1991. "Self-managed work teams: Innovation in progress." *Business & Economic Quarterly* (Fall/Winter): 2–6.

Yellowbird, Michael, & C. Matthew Snipp. 1994. "American Indian families." In Ronald L. Taylor (ed.), *Minority Families in the United States: A Multicultural Perspective*. Upper Saddle River, NJ: Prentice Hall.

Yesalis, C. E., & V. E. Cowart. 1998. *The Steroids Game*. Champaign, IL: Human Kinetics.

Yeung, Yue-man. 2001. "Urban poverty alleviation in the age of globalization in Pacific Asia." In Shahid Yusuf, Simon Evenett, & Weiping Wu (eds.), *Facets of Globalization: International and Local Dimensions of Development*. Washington, DC: World Bank: 221–36.

Yin, Sandra, & Rebecca Gardyn. 2002. "Career matters." *American Demographics* 24(4): 18–19.

Yinger, J. Milton. 1985. "Assimilation in the United States: The Mexican Americans." In W. Connor (ed.), *Mexican Americans in Comparative Perspective*. Washington, DC: Urban Institute Press: 30–55.

Yinger, Milton. 1994. Ethnicity: Source of Strength? Source of Conflict? Albany, NY: State University of New York.

Yip, Andrew K. T. 2002. "Same-sex relationships." In Robin Goodwin (ed.), *Inappropriate Relationships: The Unconventional, the Disapproved, and the Forbidden*. Mahwah, NJ: Lawrence Erlbaum.

Yip, Paul S. F. 2001. "An epidemiological profile of suicides in Beijing, China." *Suicide and Life-Threatening Behavior* 31(1): 62–70.

Yonezawa, Susan, & Jeannie Oakes. 1999. "Making parents partners in the placement process." *Educational Leadership* 56(7): 33–36.

Young, Lawrence A. (ed.). 1997. *Rational Choice Theory and Religion: Summary and Assessment*. New York: Routledge.

Young, Michael, George Denny, Tamara Young, & Raffy Luquis. 2000. "Sexual satisfaction among married women." *American Journal of Health Studies* 16(2): 73–84.

Young, T. R. 1975. "Karl Marx and alienation." *Humboldt Journal of Social Relations* (2/2): 26–33.

Youth Advocate Program International. 2001. *Report on the Commercial Sexual Exploitation of Children in the United States*. November. Washington, DC: Available: http://www.yapi.org.

Ypeij, Johanna Louisa. 2000. *Producing Against Poverty: Female and Male Micro-Enterprenuers in Lima, Peru*. Amsterdam: Amsterdam University.

Zaff, J. F., & E. C. Hair. 2002. "Peer relationships." In Marc H. Bornstein, Lucy Davidson, Corey L. M. Keyes, & Kristin Moore (eds.), *Positive Development across the Life Course*. Mahwah, NJ: Lawrence Erlbaum.

Zald, Mayer N. 1992. "Looking backward to look forward." In Aldon D. Morris & Carol M. Mueller (eds.), *Frontiers in Social Movement Theory*. New Haven, CT: Yale University Press: 326–48.

Zald, Mayer N., & John D. McCarthy (eds.). 1987. *Social Movements in an Organizational Society*. New Brunswick, NJ: Transaction.

Zald, Mayer N., & Roberta Ash. 1966. "Social movement organizations: Growth, decay and change." *Social Forces* 44: 327–41.

Zambrana, Ruth E. 1994. "Puerto Rican families and social well-being." In Maxine Baca Zinn & Bonnie Thornton Dill (eds.), *Women of Color in U.S. Society*. Philadelphia: Temple University.

Zamir, Shamoon. 1995. *Dark Voices: W. E. B. DuBois & American Thought, 1888–1903*. Chicago: University of Chicago Press.

Zaret, David. 1996. "Petitions and the 'Invention' of public opinion in the English revolution." *American Journal of Sociology* 101: 1487–1555.

Zebich-Knos, Michelle. 2002. "Ecotourism, economic development, and the environment in Latin America." In Stuart S. Nagel (ed.), *Environmental Policy and Developing Nations*. Jefferson, NC: McFarland: 245–67.

Zedlewski, Sheila R., & Donald Alderson. 2001. "Do families on welfare in the post-TANF era differ from their pre-TANF counterparts?" Washington, DC: Urban Institute.

Zeichner, Amos, Dominic J. Parrott, & Henry E. Adams. "Homophobia: Personality and attitudinal correlates." 2002. *Personality & Individual Differences* 32(7): 1269–78.

Zellner, W. W. 1995. *Countercultures: A Sociological Analysis*. New York: St. Martin's.

Zellner, William W. 2001. *Extraordinary Groups*, 7th ed. New York: Worth: 1–52.

Zelman, Walter A. 1976. "The sports people play." *Parks & Recreation* 11: 27–38.

Zhang, Jie, & Gustav Christensen. 2001. "The paradox of unequal investment and equal region economic growth in China." *Annals of Regional Science* 35(4): 637–35.

Zhang, Zie. 2002. "Urbanization, population transition, and growth." *Oxford Economic Papers* 54(1): 91–117.

Zhao, Xiong He, & David Lester. 2001. "Elderly suicide in China." *Psychological Reports* 89(3): 675–6.

Zhou, Min. 2000. "Families in the adaptation of the younger generation." In Min Zhou & James V. Gatewood (eds.), *Contemporary Asian America: A Multidisciplinary Reader*. New York: New York University: 315–35.

Zi, Lian. 1995. "Marriages and families." *Fortnightly Review*. Special Issue to the Fourth World U.N. Conference on Women: 86–88.

Zikmund, Barbara Brown, Adair T. Lummis, & Patricia Mei Lin Chang. 1998. *Clergy Women: An Uphill Calling*. Louisville, KY: Westminster John Knox.

Zimbardo, Philip G. 1972. "Pathology of imprisonment." *Society* 9: 4–8.

Zimmer, Michael. 2001. "Explaining marital dissolution: The role of spouses' traits." *Social Science Quarterly* 82(3): 464–77.

Zoglin, Richard. 1996. "Chips ahoy!" *Time* (February 19).

Zorza, Joan. 2001. "Alcohol and sexual violence among college students." In Allen J. Ottens & Kathy Hotelling (eds.), *Sexual Violence on Campus: Policies, Programs and Perspectives*. New York: Springer

Zuboff, Shoshana. 1988. *In the Age of the Smart Machine*. New York: Basic.

Zuckerman, Mortimer B. 1995. "Forest Gump vs. Ice-T," *U.S. News & World Report* (July 24).

Zuker, R. F. 2001. "The sweet sorrow of saying goodbye to the college-bound: Understanding and coping with the empty nest." *Journal of College Admissions* 173: 30–31.

Zweigenhaft, Richard L., & G. William Domhoff. 1991. *Blacks in the White Establishment? A Study of Race and Class in America*. New Haven, CT: Yale University Press.

Zweigenhaft, Richard L., & G. William Domhoff. 1998. *Diversity in the Power Elite*. New Haven, CT: Yale University Press.

Zwerling, L. Steven. 1996. "Expanding external support for at-risk students." In Laura I. Rendon & Richard O. Hope (eds.), *Educating a New Majority: Transforming America's Educational System for Diversity*. San Francisco: Jossey-Bass: pp. 372–389.

Zygmunt, Joseph E. 1986. "Collective behavior as a phase of societal life." *Research in Social Movements, Conflict and Change* 9: 25–46.

PHOTO CREDITS

son, 400; © Steven Rubin/The Image Works, 403; Bob Daemmrich/Stock Boston, 408; Michael Newman/PhotoEdit, 410; Bob Daemmrich/The Image Works, 413; Jack Parsons/Omni-Photo Communications, Inc.—Liaison, 416; © Chuck Savage/Corbis, 417; Laura Dwight/PhotoEdit, 418 (top); Chris Maynard/Getty Images, Inc.—Liaison, 418 (bottom).

Chapter 16 Peter Vander Mark/Stock Boston, 422; Kathy McLaughlin/The Image Works, 424; John Giordano/Saba/Corbis/Saba Press Photos, Inc., 428; Bob Rowan/Progressive Image/Corbis, 431; Elizabeth Crews/The Image Works, 433; Dr. Linda Lindsey, 434; Michael Newman/PhotoEdit, 437 (top); Barbara Stitzer/PhotoEdit, 437 (bottom); Michael Newman/PhotoEdit, 441; Photo by Spencer Platt/Getty Images, Inc.—Liaison, 443.

Chapter 17 Shaun Best/Reuters/TimePix, 452; Annie Griffiths Belt/Corbis, 455; David Turnley/Corbis, 456 (top); ANAX/Imapress/The Image Works, 456 (bottom); Mark C. Burnett/Photo Researchers, Inc., 457; Dave Bartruff/Corbis, 461; Internet/AP/Wide World Photos, 463; Peter Sanders/The Image Works, 467; Sergio Dorantes/Corbis, 469; Brian Vikander/Corbis, 470; AP/Wide World Photos, 472; Bettman/Corbis, 477; Photo by Michael Smith/Newsmakers/Getty Images, Inc.—Liaison, 480.

Chapter 18 Steve Chenn/Corbis, 484; Bob Krist/Corbis, 486; Topham/The Image Works, 487; APTV/AP/Wide World Photos, 489; Photo by Spencer Platt/Getty Images, Inc.—Liaison, 490; David Woo/Getty Images, Inc.—Liaison, 491; Bob Daemmrich/The Image Works, 493; © AFP Photo/Corbis, 494; Allan Tannembaum/The Image Works, 502; AP/Wide World Photos, 503.

Chapter 19 Doug Menuez/Creative Management Partners, 508; Chang Hongen/World Health Organization, 510; Philip James Corwin/Corbis, 512; © Alison Wright/Corbis, 516; AP/Wide World Photos, 519; Robert Harbison, 527; Paul Conklin/PhotoEdit, 528; Corbis Digital Stock, 532.

Chapter 20 Jamie Squire/Allsport Photography (USA), Inc., 536; James Marshall/Corbis, 538; Rick Stewart/Allsort/Getty Images—Allsport Photography, 539; AP/Wide World Photos, 540; Lawrence M. Sawyer, 541; S. Carmona/Corbis, 543; Peter Byron/ Photo

Researchers, Inc., 546 (top); Hulton/Archive by Getty Images, Inc.—Hulton Archive Photos, 546 (bottom); David Young-Wolf/PhotoEdit, 549; Elie Bernager/Getty Images, Inc.—Liaison, 550; Dr. Stephen Beach, 551; © Reuters NewMedia, Inc./Corbis/ Joe Traver, 554.

Chapter 21 Walter Hodges/Getty Images, Inc.—Stone, 562; United Media/United Feature Syndicate, Inc./DILBERT reprinted by permission of United Feature Syndicate, Inc., 564; C. Moore/Corbis, 566; Layne Kennedy/Corbis, 567 (top); Syracuse Newspapers/Stephen Cannerelli/The Image Works, 567 (bottom); Rob Crandall/The Image Works, 569; Michael S. Yamashita/Corbis, 571; Bob Daemmrich/The Image Works, 572; Getty Images, Inc.—Photodisc, 574; Sergio Dorantes/Corbis, 575; AP/Wide World Photos, 576; The Metropolitan Museum of Art, 580; Tony Freeman/PhotoEdit, 581.

Chapter 22 Porterfield/Chickering/Photo Researchers, Inc., 588; Andy Holbrooke/Corbis/Stock Market, 595; Chuck O'Rear/Woodfin Camp & Associates, 599; Mark Ludak/The Image Works, 602; Monika Graff/The Image Works, 603; Leland Bobbe/Getty Images, Inc.—Stone Allstock, 606; David Young-Wolff/PhotoEdit, 607; AP/Wide World Photos, 615.

Chapter 23 Beth A. Keiser/AP/Wide World Photos, 618; Peter Turnley/Corbis, 620; Bettman/Corbis, 621; Richard Baillie/AP/Wide World Photos, 623; AP/Wide World Photos, 624; AP/Wide World Photos, 627; Photo by Preston Keres/US Navy/Getty Images, Inc.—Liaison, 628 (left); Tomi/Getty Images, Inc.—Liaison, 628 (right); Beth A. Keiser/AP/Wide World Photos, 632; © Jeff Greene/Corbis/Sygma, 635; Erich Hartmann/Magnum Photos, Inc., 637.

Chapter 24 AP/Wide World Photos, 642; Mike Theiler/Reuters/Corbis, 645; Henry Diltz/Corbis, 646 (left); Bonnie Kamin/PhotoEdit, 646 (right); Margot Granitsas/The Image Works, 648; Getty Images, Inc.—Liaison, 649; A. Tannembaum—Sygma, 651; AP/Wide World Photos, 653; © Reed Kaestner, 661; Dr. Linda Lindsey, 667 (left); Richard Lord, 667 (right); Dr. Linda Lindsey, 668.

NAME INDEX

SUBJECT INDEX

California v. Cabazon Band of Mission Indians, 499
Canada, health care system, 533–534
Capitalism
  and developing countries, 659–660
  features of, 490
  Marxist view, 262–263, 282
  rational capitalism, 578
  related political systems, 492
  state capitalism, 659
Capital punishment
  execution of innocent, 3–4
  proponent/opponent views, 243–244
Care ethic, 126
Caregivers, of elderly, 386–387
Caste systems, 256, 258
Casual crowds, 622
Category, group membership, 96
Censorship, voluntary systems, 557
Census, 590
Charisma
  charismatic authority, 462, 487–488
  defined, 462
  routinization of, 487–488
Chernobyl, 521–522
Chicago school, history of sociology, 15–16, 603
Child On-Line Protection Act of 1998, 557
Childrearing
  and gender socialization, 344–345
  and social class, 296
Children
  abuse/neglect in family, 417
  in blended families, 411
  child custody and support, 353, 409
  childhood, historical view, 127
  development of. See Socialization
  divorce, effects of, 407, 408
  and family dynamics, 405
  and poverty, 289, 409
  readiness to learn, 449–450
  in single-parent families, 409–410
  street children, 274
  television programs for, 355–356
Children's Internet Protection Act of 2000, 557
Child sexual abuse
  and Catholic priests, 477
  child prostitutes, 191
  family forms of, 417
  functionalist view of, 187
China
  economic growth of, 661
  elderly, treatment of, 373
  second wives phenomenon, 401
Chivalry hypothesis, 240
Christian Coalition, 479
Christianity, origin and beliefs of, 465–467
Chronic disease, 513
Church, as organization, 460–461, 464
Church of Scientology, 464
Church and state separation, 472
Cigarette smoking, stigmatization of, 217–218, 515
Cities
  community-within-city, 604
  and environmental racism, 602
  functionalist view, 606
  global cities, 598
  growth and industrialization, 110–111, 258
  inner-city, 601–602, 606
  largest, global view, 594
  largest, United States, 600
  new urban sociology, 605
  symbols, impact of, 604–605
  urban ecology, 603–604
  urbanism and social structure, 606
  urban renewal, 602–603
Civil law, 232
Civil religion, 460
Civil Rights Act of 1964, Title VII, 165, 351–352
Civil rights movement, 320, 476, 624, 638
Class-conflict thesis, of democratization, 496
Class consciousness, 263
Classism
  defined, 252
  and social stratification, 252–253
Closed-ended questions, 42–43, 45
Coercive organizations, 564
Cognitive dissonance, 51
Cognitive theories, 124–128
  deviance, 205–206
  evaluation of, 126–128
  gender schema theory, 125–126
  moral development, 125
  Piaget's theory, 124–125
Cohabitation
  elderly, 384

and later marriage, 412
Collective behavior
  contagion theory, 620–621
  craze, 628
  crowds, 622–624
  defined, 619
  disaster behavior, 627
  emergent-norm theory, 622
  fads, 628
  fashions, 627–628
  mass hysteria, 626–627
  panics, 624–625
  publics, 629
  rumors, 625–626
  value-added theory, 621–622
Collective conscience, 651
Collectives, 5
Collective work organizations, 570–571
College education. See Higher education
College students
  athletes, 543
  developmental tasks of, 130–131, 134, 138
  diversity of group, 442
  drug and alcohol use, 202
  gender discrimination, 347, 429
  and sexuality, 188–189
Collins, Randall, and conflict theory, 20
Colonialism
  and modernization, 13, 269
  neocolonialism, 270
  and social change, 13, 416
Columbine shooting, 423
Common law, 232
Communal families, 402
Communication
  animal communication, 75
  and bureaucracy, 568
  gender differences, 72–73
  humor, 74–75
  language, 70–75
  nonverbal communication, 72, 153–159
  social class and style of, 297
Communications Decency Act of 1996, 557
Communism, and socialism, 489, 490
Communitarian movement, 654
Communities
  features of, 104–105
  and U.S. society, 11
  virtual communities, 112
Community colleges, 443–444
Community policing, 231
Community-within-city, 604
Comparable worth, 352
Complementary-alternative medicine (CAM), 527
Complete participant, field research, 49
Computer use. See Internet
Comte, Auguste, positivistic approach of, 14, 648
Concrete operational stage, 124
Confidence gap, in U.S. political parties, 501–502
Confidentiality, research subjects, 57
Conflict
  cognitive dissonance, 51
  role conflict, 95
Conflict theory, 20–21
  elements of, 20, 148
  evaluation of, 20–21, 201
  updating Marx's theory, 654–655
Conflict view
  aging, 376
  cultural change, 79–80
  culture, 79
  deviance, 200–201
  education, 426–430, 437
  environmental problems, 610
  family, 399
  family violence, 418
  female empowerment and reproduction, 615
  gender inequality, 337
  health care, 514–515
  health status, 514
  of homelessness, 148
  humor, 74–75
  Internet, 112–113
  marriage gradient, 405
  mass media, 548–549
  nonverbal communication, 158
  population growth, 596
  prejudice and discrimination, 312–313
  religion, 457–458
  sexual harassment, 167
  sexuality, 187–188
  social change, 650
  social interaction, 148
  social stratification, 262–265
  sports, 540–542

workplace violence, 525
Conformity
  control theory, 210
  and deviance, 207
  in groups, 102
  internalization of norms, 198
Confucianism, origin and beliefs of, 469–470
Consensual unions, 415
Conservatism, 489
Conservative Judaism, 478
Consolidated Metropolitan Statistical Area (MSA), 600
Conspicuous consumption, 94, 542
Conspicuous waste, 94
Consumer behavior, survey research, 42–43
Contact hypothesis, 312
Contagion theory, collective behavior, 620–621
Content analysis, 47–48
Contingency workforce, 577–578
Continuity theory, aging, 374
Control group, 38
Control theory, deviance, 210–211, 239
Control variables, 33
Conventional crowds, 622
Cooley, Charles Horton
  on looking-glass self, 120
  and symbolic interactionism, 21
Co-option, 637
Corporate crime, 229–230
Corporations
  management styles, 570–573
  multinational corporations, 660
Correlation, 38
Correlation coefficient, 37
Countercultures, features of, 81–83
Countermodernization, 652–653
Countermovements, 634–635
Court system, 232–233
Craze, 628
Creativity, and aging, 366–367
Credentialism, 425
Crime
  data sources on, 223–224
  defined, 196, 222
  rates, cultural differences, 224–226
  U.S. statistics on, 221, 223–224
  victimology, 241–243, 295
Criminal behavior
  and age, 239
  corporate crime, 229–230
  and deviance, 196
  gender differences, 239–240
  homicide, 226–227
  insanity defense, 141–142
  organized crime, 228–229
  racial/ethnic minorities, 237–239, 322
  rape, 226–227
  and resocialization, 139–142
  and social class, 240–241
  victimless crime, 230
Criminal justice
  adversarial principle, 232
  capital punishment, 243
  dilemma related to, 236
  drug decriminalization, 243–245
  inquisitorial principle, 232
  legal system, 232–233
  natural law approach, 222
  plea bargaining, 233
  police, 231–232
  prisons, 233–236
  religious law, 225, 232
Cross-cultural perspectives. See Cultural differences
Cross-cultural research, guidelines for, 35, 47
Cross-cutting cleavages, 493
Cross-linkage theory, aging, 365–366
Crowds, 622–624
  mobs, 623
  riots, 623–624
  types of, 622–623
Crude birthrate, 590
Cuban Americans, family life, 415
Cults, 462–464
Cultural capital
  defined, 264
  forms of, 266
  and socialization, 135
Cultural change, 76–77
  and adaptation, 78–79
  conflict view, 79–80
  and cultural integration, 76, 77
  and cultural lag, 76–77
  cultural traditions, maintenance of, 86–87
  diffusion, 77

SINGLE PC LICENSE AGREEMENT AND LIMITED WARRANTY

READ THIS LICENSE CAREFULLY BEFORE OPENING THIS PACKAGE. BY OPENING THIS PACKAGE, YOU ARE AGREEING TO THE TERMS AND CONDITIONS OF THIS LICENSE. IF YOU DO NOT AGREE, DO NOT OPEN THE PACKAGE. PROMPTLY RETURN THE UNOPENED PACKAGE AND ALL ACCOMPANYING ITEMS TO THE PLACE YOU OBTAINED THEM [[FOR A FULL REFUND OF ANY SUMS YOU HAVE PAID FOR THE SOFTWARE]]. *THESE TERMS APPLY TO ALL LICENSED SOFTWARE ON THE DISK EXCEPT THAT THE TERMS FOR USE OF ANY SHAREWARE OR FREEWARE ON THE DISKETTES ARE AS SET FORTH IN THE ELECTRONIC LICENSE LOCATED ON THE DISK:*

1. GRANT OF LICENSE and OWNERSHIP: The enclosed computer programs <<and data>> ("Software") are licensed, not sold, to you by Pearson Education, Inc. publishing as Prentice Hall ("We" or the "Company") and in consideration [[of your payment of the license fee, which is part of the price you paid]] [[of your purchase or adoption of the accompanying Company textbooks and/or other materials,]] and your agreement to these terms. We reserve any rights not granted to you. You own only the disk(s) but we and/or our licensors own the Software itself. This license allows you to use and display your copy of the Software on a single computer (i.e., with a single CPU) at a single location for <u>academic</u> use only, so long as you comply with the terms of this Agreement. You may make one copy for back up, or transfer your copy to another CPU, provided that the Software is usable on only one computer.

2. RESTRICTIONS: You may <u>not</u> transfer or distribute the Software or documentation to anyone else. Except for backup, you may not copy the documentation or the Software. You may <u>not</u> network the Software or otherwise use it on more than one computer or computer terminal at the same time. You may <u>not</u> reverse engineer, disassemble, decompile, modify, adapt, translate, or create derivative works based on the Software or the Documentation. You may be held legally responsible for any copying or copyright infringement that is caused by your failure to abide by the terms of these restrictions.

3. TERMINATION: This license is effective until terminated. This license will terminate automatically without notice from the Company if you fail to comply with any provisions or limitations of this license. Upon termination, you shall destroy the Documentation and all copies of the Software. All provisions of this Agreement as to limitation and disclaimer of warranties, limitation of liability, remedies or damages, and our ownership rights shall survive termination.

4. LIMITED WARRANTY AND DISCLAIMER OF WARRANTY: Company warrants that for a period of 60 days from the date you purchase this SOFTWARE (or purchase or adopt the accompanying textbook), the Software, when properly installed and used in accordance with the Documentation, will operate in substantial conformity with the description of the Software set forth in the Documentation, and that for a period of 30 days the disk(s) on which the Software is delivered shall be free from defects in materials and workmanship under normal use. The Company does <u>not</u> warrant that the Software will meet your requirements or that the operation of the Software will be uninterrupted or error-free. Your only remedy and the Company's only obligation under these limited warranties is, at the Company's option, return of the disk for a refund of any amounts paid for it by you or replacement of the disk. THIS LIMITED WARRANTY IS THE ONLY WARRANTY PROVIDED BY THE COMPANY AND ITS LICENSORS, AND THE COMPANY AND ITS LICENSORS DISCLAIM ALL OTHER WARRANTIES, EXPRESS OR IMPLIED, INCLUDING WITHOUT LIMITATION, THE IMPLIED WARRANTIES OF MERCHANTABILITY AND FITNESS FOR A PARTICULAR PURPOSE. THE COMPANY DOES NOT WARRANT, GUARANTEE OR MAKE ANY REPRESENTATION REGARDING THE ACCURACY, RELIABILITY, CURRENTNESS, USE, OR RESULTS OF USE, OF THE SOFTWARE.

5. LIMITATION OF REMEDIES AND DAMAGES: IN NO EVENT, SHALL THE COMPANY OR ITS EMPLOYEES, AGENTS, LICENSORS, OR CONTRACTORS BE LIABLE FOR ANY INCIDENTAL, INDIRECT, SPECIAL, OR CONSEQUENTIAL DAMAGES ARISING OUT OF OR IN CONNECTION WITH THIS LICENSE OR THE SOFTWARE, INCLUDING FOR LOSS OF USE, LOSS OF DATA, LOSS OF INCOME OR PROFIT, OR OTHER LOSSES, SUSTAINED AS A RESULT OF INJURY TO ANY PERSON, OR LOSS OF OR DAMAGE TO PROPERTY, OR CLAIMS OF THIRD PARTIES, EVEN IF THE COMPANY OR AN AUTHORIZED REPRESENTATIVE OF THE COMPANY HAS BEEN ADVISED OF THE POSSIBILITY OF SUCH DAMAGES. IN NO EVENT SHALL THE LIABILITY OF THE COMPANY FOR DAMAGES WITH RESPECT TO THE SOFTWARE EXCEED THE AMOUNTS ACTUALLY PAID BY YOU, IF ANY, FOR THE SOFTWARE OR THE ACCOMPANYING TEXTBOOK. BECAUSE SOME JURISDICTIONS DO NOT ALLOW THE LIMITATION OF LIABILITY IN CERTAIN CIRCUMSTANCES, THE ABOVE LIMITATIONS MAY NOT ALWAYS APPLY TO YOU.

6. GENERAL: THIS AGREEMENT SHALL BE CONSTRUED IN ACCORDANCE WITH THE LAWS OF THE UNITED STATES OF AMERICA AND THE STATE OF NEW YORK, APPLICABLE TO CONTRACTS MADE IN NEW YORK, AND SHALL BENEFIT THE COMPANY, ITS AFFILIATES AND ASSIGNEES. HIS AGREEMENT IS THE COMPLETE AND EXCLUSIVE STATEMENT OF THE AGREEMENT BETWEEN YOU AND THE COMPANY AND SUPERSEDES ALL PROPOSALS OR PRIOR AGREEMENTS, ORAL, OR WRITTEN, AND ANY OTHER COMMUNICATIONS BETWEEN YOU AND THE COMPANY OR ANY REPRESENTATIVE OF THE COMPANY RELATING TO THE SUBJECT MATTER OF THIS AGREEMENT. If you are a U.S. Government user, this Software is licensed with "restricted rights" as set forth in subparagraphs (a)-(d) of the Commercial Computer-Restricted Rights clause at FAR 52.227-19 or in subparagraphs (c)(1)(ii) of the Rights in Technical Data and Computer Software clause at DFARS 252.227-7013, and similar clauses, as applicable.

Should you have any questions concerning this agreement or if you wish to contact the Company for any reason, please contact in writing: Social Sciences Media Editor, Prentice Hall, One Lake Street, Upper Saddle River, NJ 07458.